W9-AAS-616

COLLEGES

WITH PROGRAMS FOR STUDENTS WITH

LEARNING DISABILITIES

OR ATTENTION DEFICIT DISORDERS

SIXTH EDITION

EDITED BY CHARLES T. MANGRUM II, ED.D., AND STEPHEN S. STRICHART, PH.D.

ENDORSED BY COLLEGE PARENTS OF AMERICA

PETERSON'S
THOMSON LEARNING

Australia • Canada • Mexico • Singapore • Spain • United Kingdom • United States

About Peterson's

Founded in 1966, Peterson's, a division of Thomson Learning, is the nation's largest and most respected provider of lifelong learning online resources, software, reference guides, and books. The Education Supersite^{SM} at petersons.com—the Web's most heavily traveled education resource—has searchable databases and interactive tools for contacting U.S.-accredited institutions and programs. CollegeQuest^{SM} (CollegeQuest.com) offers a complete solution for every step of the college decision-making process. GradAdvantage^{TM} (GradAdvantage.org), developed with Educational Testing Service, is the only electronic admissions service capable of sending official graduate test score reports with a candidate's online application. Peterson's serves over 55 million education consumers annually.

Thomson Learning is among the world's leading providers of lifelong learning, serving the needs of individuals, learning institutions, and corporations with products and services for both traditional classrooms and for online learning. For more information about the products and services offered by Thomson Learning, please visit www.thomsonlearning.com. Headquartered in Stamford, Connecticut, with offices worldwide, Thomson Learning is part of The Thomson Corporation (www.thomson.com), a leading e-information and solutions company in the business, professional, and education marketplaces. The Corporation's common shares are listed on the Toronto and London stock exchanges.

Visit Peterson's Education Center on the Internet
(World Wide Web) at www.petersons.com

Copyright © 2000 Peterson's, a division of Thomson Learning. Thomson Learning is a trademark used herein under license.

Previous editions © 1985, 1988, 1992, 1994, 1997

Peterson's makes every reasonable effort to obtain accurate, complete, and timely data from reliable sources. Nevertheless, Peterson's and the third-party data suppliers make no representation or warranty, either expressed or implied, as to the accuracy, timeliness, or completeness of the data or the results to be obtained from using the data, including, but not limited to, its quality, performance, merchantability, or fitness for a particular purpose, non-infringement or otherwise.

Neither Peterson's nor the third-party data suppliers warrant, guarantee, or make any representations that the results from using the data will be successful or will satisfy users' requirements. The entire risk to the results and performance is assumed by the user.

All rights reserved. No part of this work may be reproduced, transcribed, or used in any form or by any means—graphic, electronic, or mechanical, including photocopying, recording, taping, Web distribution, or information storage and retrieval systems—without the prior written permission of the publisher.

For permission to use material from this text or product, contact us by
- Web: www.thomsonrights.com
- Phone: 1-800-730-2214
- Fax: 1-800-730-2215

ISBN 0-7689-0455-2

Printed in the United States of America

10 9 8 7 6 5 4 3 2 1

► CONTENTS ◄

Foreword   v

Preface   vii

Introduction   viii

Types of Assistance Available   1

Selecting a College   4

The Personal Summary Chart   6

Information Resources   7

Quick-Find Chart   9

College Profile Listings   27
    Four-Year Colleges with Comprehensive Programs   27
    Four-Year Colleges with Special Services   77
    Two-Year Colleges with Comprehensive Programs   225
    Two-Year Colleges with Special Services   273

Index   367

About the Authors   373

► FOREWORD ◄

The American Council on Education has sponsored the HEATH Resource Center since 1980, first as a model/demonstration program and, since 1984, as the National Clearinghouse on Postsecondary Education for Individuals with Disabilities, which is funded by the U.S. Department of Education. HEATH collects and disseminates information about education after high school for students with any disability. Opportunities for students with disabilities have grown exponentially in the time since the beginning of the HEATH Resource Center. When I began as Director there were about thirty-five colleges and universities in our Campus Resource File that indicated that they served students with learning disabilities. Many campus disability support staff members, however, were contacting us to find out how they could serve the growing number of students with learning disabilities who were indeed enrolling. Now, nearly twenty years later, our small staff responds to more than 30,000 inquiries annually. These inquiries come to us by telephone, mail, fax, and the Internet. Those asking about resources and other information include students and their parents, grandparents, and significant others, as well as professionals who teach and advise them. We also hear from college administrators, vocational rehabilitation officials, journalists, librarians, and federal, state, and local education officials.

More than half the questions to the HEATH staff concern students with learning disabilities. In the last several years we have had numerous questions about students with attention deficit disorders. The questions are similar: *Where can I study? What accommodations can I expect, and what do I do to receive them? How can I get assistance to pay for the education?* and recently, *I want to go to law school (or other professional or graduate school),* followed by the same questions as above.

The HEATH Resource Center publishes a number of resource papers on many topics, and we have several papers that assist readers to learn how to respond to these questions. We do not list any colleges but rather teach how to structure the search for a postsecondary institution. We do, however, consistently recommend *Peterson's Colleges with Programs for Students with Learning Disabilities or Attention Deficit Disorders* as a comprehensive listing of colleges to explore. The publication of this sixth edition of *Peterson's Colleges with Programs for Students with Learning Disabilities or Attention Deficit Disorders,* which now contains information about services to students with attention deficit disorders and contains more than 750 colleges and universities that serve students with learning disabilities or attention deficit disorders, is tangible testimony to the changes that have occurred over the last two decades.

For more than seventeen years as Director of the HEATH Resource Center, I have both witnessed and proactively encouraged these changes. When HEATH began, our task was to provide technical assistance to colleges and universities about how to make their campuses and programs accessible to students with disabilities. Few in higher education at that time had heard of learning disabilities. There was little information about how to provide support services to such students or where researchers could turn to observe successful college programs. The first HEATH paper on the topic of students with learning disabilities in postsecondary education in 1981 listed and described nine programs. It was from this core of programs that many colleges and universities based their initial provision of services for students with learning disabilities. Since that time, HEATH's mission has expanded to assist postsecondary educational entities of all varieties to be accessible and to provide information to students with disabilities, their families, and those who work with them to achieve the goal of pursuing education after high school.

Over this period of time, there has been a significant increase in the number and percentage of college students with disabilities. In 1978, the first year disability-related data on college students were reported in *American Freshman: National Norms,* 2.6 percent of full-time, first-time freshmen indicated that they had a disability. In the most recent data, *College Freshmen with Disabilities: A Triennial Statistical Profile,* published by HEATH/ American Council on Education in 1995, 9.2 percent of college freshmen reported a disability. Of these, one third of them (more than 45,000) report having a learning disability, which is the fastest-growing disability category.

While data have not yet been collected about college students with attention deficit disorders, professionals writing in the *Journal of Postsecondary Education and Disability* estimate that between 1 and 3 percent of college students have attention deficit disorders. They also report that many support services emerging on campuses for this population are an extension or adaptation of programs originally developed for students with learning disabilities. The literature, once unavailable, on the topic of accommodations and preferred policies for college students with attention deficit disorders is now growing. Publication of the sixth edition of this Peterson's guide recognizes the phenomenon of increasing numbers of students with attention deficit disorders who are seeking college enrollment.

A combination of factors has led to the increase in the number of college learning disability services and programs as well as a dramatic increase in the number of students seeking such programs. In the mid-1970s two significant pieces of legislation became law: the Education of the Handicapped Act (now called the Individuals with Disabilities Education Act—IDEA) and the Rehabilitation Act of 1973, followed by the 1977 regulations implementing Section 504 of that act. Together they reflected Americans' concern about including people with disabilities in regular education (and other federally funded activities) and led to the changes necessary in those programs so that these people, including those with learning disabilities, could participate.

These concerns were further validated with the enactment of the Americans with Disabilities Act (ADA) of 1990. ADA has also had the effect of raising the awareness of educational institutions about their responsibilities to people with disabilities, and that has renewed access activity on many campuses. In addition, at both the secondary and postsecondary levels, educators have increased efforts to teach students with disabilities—including those with learning disabilities—self-advocacy skills, which have heightened their self-determination. Such skills have emboldened students to come forward and request disability-specific accommodations, which may account for the increasing number of students who self-identify. On the other hand, self-advocacy groups, together with ADA, have also resulted in increased litigation about academic accommodations and documentation of disabilities, especially for people with learning disabilities and attention deficit disorders. The resolution of such litigation will continue to shape the nature of *required* modifications and may change the types of special services for which a college or university can charge a fee over and above tuition.

Another factor that must not be overlooked is the significant role that federal funding of demonstration projects in postsecondary education has played in spreading the word about what both campus administrators and students with learning disabilities need to know to succeed. Much of the expanded variety of postsecondary programs for students with learning disabilities can be attributed to the federal initiatives to create model programs to demonstrate support services and related activities in community colleges, four-year colleges, and universities, as well as programs to facilitate the transition from high school to college for students with learning disabilities. During the 1980s, approximately seventy-five demonstration postsecondary programs for students with learning disabilities were federally supported for two- and three-year periods. Many of these were later incorporated into the regular college programming and are included in this guide.

As students have become better prepared, as their aspirations are raised by supportive parents and teachers, and as colleges and universities come to understand the strengths and potential that such students add to campus life, the number of programs for students with learning disabilities has multiplied.

In the past, those of us concerned with information about postsecondary education and disability have hesitated to recommend or endorse directories, guides, or listings of accessible places, for usually such lists imply that only schools on the list serve people with disabilities. I have come to believe, however, that the past several editions of *Peterson's Colleges with Programs for Students with Learning Disabilities or Attention Deficit Disorders* has consistently offered such a wealth of information about so many institutions that we regularly recommend this guide to most inquirers as an excellent reference tool and starting place for those in the process of investigating college choices. In addition to the descriptions of the schools, Peterson's guide provides a great deal of information to enhance one's search. The editors, Stephen Strichart and Charles Mangrum, have prepared useful, *on-target* background material, essays, and specific steps to take to assist readers to select their personal best schools. There is, of course, no substitute for actually visiting a campus firsthand and talking with the disability support services directors as well as other students with disabilities. *Peterson's Colleges with Programs for Students with Learning Disabilities or Attention Deficit Disorders* is an excellent resource to use as one begins the investigation.

Rhona C. Hartman, Director
HEATH Resource Center
National Clearinghouse on Postsecondary Education for
Individuals with Disabilities
American Council on Education
Washington, D.C.

► PREFACE ◄

When we both began our work with students with learning disabilities (LD), there were few colleges providing programs or even services for such students. Those that existed were difficult to find; the few published guides and lists that identified such schools were not very accurate. We had to rely primarily on word of mouth from other professors and parents of students who had LD. As our work continued, we became increasingly aware of the number of colleges and universities adding programs and services for students with LD. But still there was no single, reliable source listing such schools.

In our efforts to update our own lists, we visited and made phone calls to the schools we had heard were making accommodations for students with LD. We asked them about their programs and services, about the numbers of students with LD enrolled or taking classes with them. And we read everything we could find about expanding college opportunities for students with LD.

We published what we had learned in our first book, *College and the Learning Disabled Student* (Grune and Stratton, 1984, 1988). The information in that book was used by many colleges establishing new programs and expanding existing ones for students with LD.

We then began working with the editors at Peterson's on the ambitious task of collecting data on all the colleges and universities in the United States that were responding to the special needs of students with LD. The result was the first edition of this book, published in 1985. Expanded, updated editions published in 1988, 1992, 1994, and 1997 included two-year colleges as well as four-year colleges and universities, information about colleges and universities in Canada, and information about students with attention deficit disorders (ADD) as well as students with learning disabilities.

Now, we are pleased to see the publication of this, the sixth edition of *Peterson's Colleges with Programs for Students with Learning Disabilities or Attention Deficit Disorders*. Section 504 of the Rehabilitation Act of 1973 and the Americans with Disabilities Act (ADA) of 1990 require that all colleges and universities receiving federal funds take action to meet the needs of students with disabilities. The colleges and universities included in this guide go far beyond compliance with these laws. They reach out to students with LD and ADD with an array of resources and a strong commitment to do everything necessary to ensure that these students succeed.

A Word of Caution

As confident as we are with the care and effort that has gone into preparing this new edition, we still want to offer these words of caution: No guide can provide all the information that one needs to make a well-informed college choice. The decision about where to go to college—where to spend one's time, effort, and money—is a very important one, and this book can only be the beginning of that selection process. Studying school catalogs and visiting campuses (or, at the least, speaking by phone to the LD contact people listed at the end of each profile in this guide) will ensure that you have the most accurate and up-to-date college information on which to base your decision.

Charles T. Mangrum II and
Stephen S. Strichart

► INTRODUCTION ◄

Since the publication of the first edition of this guide in 1985, more and more students diagnosed with learning disabilities (LD) and attention deficit disorders (ADD) are going to college, succeeding there, and graduating. They are going to all types of colleges and universities, participating in the mainstream of college life, including advancement to graduate and professional programs. With appropriate knowledge about college programs for students with LD or ADD, the right preparation, and proper guidance, such students can choose a suitable college, major in any area of study, and graduate successfully.

To prepare this guide, we mailed questionnaires to all accredited two-year and four-year colleges and universities in the United States, U.S. territories, and Canada that grant associate or bachelor's degrees (more than 3,377) to identify those with programs or services for students with LD or ADD. The detailed questionnaires were completed by the responsible professionals at the colleges. These professionals were asked to describe special provisions for students with LD or ADD at their institutions. The results are shared in this guide.

HOW TO USE THIS GUIDE

Types of Assistance Available
Here you will find basic information about how colleges and universities throughout the country are responding to the specific needs of students with LD or ADD through their comprehensive programs or special services. This section contains definitions of the criteria we use to qualify for inclusion the 777 programs we have selected to be profiled in this book and explanations of the major components of a higher education learning disabilities or attention deficit disorders program.

Selecting a College
This section provides you with step-by-step guidelines for narrowing your college selections, finding out more about these schools, applying to your top choices, and preparing for a campus visit.

Making the Most of Your College Visit offers advice about when to visit a school and who to speak with while you're there. It includes one list of questions to ask the admission officer and another to ask of students with LD or ADD on campus. The Personal Summary Chart helps you to organize and compare features of different colleges that you are considering.

The two sample letters here may be helpful to you when writing for more information about a school and then requesting an appointment for a campus visit.

The Personal Summary Chart is organized to serve as a useful worksheet for you to fill out as you consider the college profiles. It will provide a structured format to compare the relative ways that different schools may meet your needs.

Information Resources
This is a listing of organizations that can be contacted to provide more information related to higher education for individuals with LD or ADD.

Quick-Find Chart
Organized geographically, this chart provides essential information elements about every college profiled in the guide. You can use it as a quick way to narrow your search. It also functions as a geographic index to the colleges.

College Profile Listings
Here is detailed information about learning disabilities and attention deficit disorders programs and services at specific colleges. The profiles are organized into two primary divisions: four-year colleges, followed by two-year colleges. These two primary divisions are further subdivided into Colleges with Comprehensive Programs—programs specially designed for students with LD or ADD, and Colleges with Special Services—programs that may not be complete but do provide a considerable number of special services to students with LD or ADD. Advice is provided in the *Selecting a College* chapter on page 6 about how to decide which category of programs or services you may desire. The four sections of individual college profiles are presented in this order: Four-Year Colleges with Comprehensive Programs; Four-Year Colleges with Special Services; Two-Year Colleges with Comprehensive Programs; Two-Year Colleges with Special Services.

► TYPES OF ASSISTANCE AVAILABLE ◄

Colleges provide many kinds of assistance to help students with LD or ADD succeed. The descriptions in the College Profile Listings section of this guide identify the assistance provided by each college. In this section of the guide, the kinds of assistance provided to students with LD are explained in detail. Most colleges that offer assistance to students with LD also offer the assistance to students with ADD.

WHAT ARE THE DIFFERENCES BETWEEN COLLEGES WITH COMPREHENSIVE PROGRAMS AND THOSE WITH SPECIAL SERVICES?

This guide distinguishes between colleges that offer comprehensive programs designed specifically for students with LD/ADD and colleges that make a number of special services available but do not offer comprehensive programs.

The typical components of a comprehensive program are diagnostic testing, tutoring, remediation, advisement, special courses, counseling, and a range of auxiliary aids and services. The keys to such a program are that its components are provided in a manner specifically designed to meet the needs of students with LD/ADD and that it is staffed with personnel with appropriate training and experience.

Colleges without comprehensive programs may offer many of the same services as those offered by comprehensive programs, but there are two important differences. First, these colleges generally do not offer quite as wide a range of services as do programs. Second, colleges offering services do not typically have staff members who have significant training or experience working specifically with college students with LD/ADD. Nevertheless, these services can often be very helpful and may be all the assistance some students with LD/ADD need to succeed in college.

Generally, students whose learning disabilities were diagnosed early and who spent much of their school career in special programs or classes might need a comprehensive program, while students who were successful in regular high school classes with some outside assistance might find special services sufficient. Students and their families should examine colleges' offerings and then compare them to the student's needs to find the best fit.

Diagnostic Testing

Diagnostic tests are given to assess cognitive abilities, academic skills, language abilities, perceptual-motor skills, social development, emotional development, and study habits. Information from diagnostic tests is used to prescribe services for the student. This information is used to develop an educational plan, which specifies the assistance that will be provided to a student with LD/ADD.

Remediation

College students with LD/ADD often need remediation to improve their basic skills and assistance in developing compensatory strategies that will minimize the impact of their LD/ADD upon their achievement in college courses. A student's need for remediation depends upon two factors: the severity of the academic and learning deficits and the level of proficiency in the academic skills needed for success in the student's program of studies. Remediation is typically provided in individual or small-group sessions by trained professionals.

Tutoring

Tutoring is designed to help students understand and master the content of their courses. The major objective is to help students pass their courses. Because they see immediate results, students frequently report that tutoring is the most helpful form of assistance. It is most often provided in English, mathematics, physical sciences, and social sciences. It is usually given individually or in small groups by professional tutors who are experts in their subject areas. Sometimes students without LD/ADD who excel in a subject are used as peer tutors.

Special Courses

Frequently, special courses are offered for students with LD/ADD. These courses provide the prerequisite skills and social and emotional awareness necessary to succeed in college. They may be credit or noncredit courses and may or may not count in a student's overall grade point average. Examples of special courses are:

- Developmental reading
- Fundamentals of oral communication
- Study skills
- Note-taking techniques
- Writing research papers
- Memory improvement
- College survival
- Social relationships
- Career planning
- Learning strategies
- Computer skills
- Self-advocacy
- Stress management
- Test taking
- Time management

Auxiliary Aids and Services

Colleges provide a number of auxiliary aids and services to help students with LD/ADD succeed.

Tape Recorders and Taped Textbooks

Students with LD/ADD often have difficulty taking notes from class lectures. The tape recorder becomes a valuable auxiliary aid for them. They are able to tape-record a lecture at the same time they take notes. Later, they can replay the tapes to check their notes for completeness and accuracy. Variable speech-control tape recorders allow students to play back taped material at slower or faster rates than the rate at which the material was originally recorded. The use of a tape recorder reduces the heavy demands upon their auditory memory, language processing, and writing skills. Because of the value of tape recorders, professors are encouraged to allow students with LD/ADD to use them in their classes.

Taped textbooks are used by students with LD/ADD who have difficulty reading college-level materials. College personnel help such students obtain taped textbooks from Recording for the Blind & Dyslexic. The role of staff members is primarily a facilitative one. They familiarize students with the services of Recording for the Blind & Dyslexic and help them complete the necessary application forms. They also help students determine the textbooks needed for future courses to enable the students to submit applications for taped textbooks in sufficient time to receive books prior to the beginning of a new term.

Technological Aids

The expansion of technological aids has produced many benefits for students with LD/ADD. Technological aids that are frequently available to these students are:

- Scientific calculators
- Personal computers
- Personal spelling devices
- Scan and read programs
- Screen-enlarging programs
- Screen readers
- Speech recognition programs
- Personal organizers

Note-takers

Typically, note-takers are students without LD/ADD who are in the same classes as the students who do have LD/ADD. They have been identified as good note-takers who are reliable, are competent in the subject, and have legible handwriting. A duplicate set of notes is given to the student with LD/ADD. Usually the note-taker does not know the identity of the student receiving the notes.

Alternative Examination Arrangements

Alternative arrangements are provided for students who have difficulty taking examinations in the usual manner. Often, students with LD/ADD have difficulty completing a test within a specified time limit, accurately reading test questions, and writing answers. Arrangements are made with professors to allow students to take course examinations with one of a number of alternatives:

- Extended time limits
- Questions dictated onto an audiotape
- Questions read by a proctor
- Responses dictated to a proctor
- Responses dictated onto audiotapes
- Responses typed on a word processor rather than handwritten
- Questions presented in a different format, e.g., multiple choice in place of essay
- Take-home examinations or projects in place of written examinations

Advocacy

College staff members often serve as advocates for students with LD/ADD. They work with professors to ensure that students are given every reasonable opportunity to succeed in their courses. The goal is to have students become their own advocates. Ideally, the activities and roles performed by staff members are phased out as students develop increasing independence. Some of the advocacy activities performed include:

- Requesting lists of required textbooks for taping
- Obtaining permission for students with LD/ADD to tape-record lectures
- Obtaining permission to use a non–class member as a note-taker
- Requesting opportunities for students to take examinations in alternative ways
- Arranging for incomplete grades when students need more time to complete a course
- Arranging for withdrawal from a course without a grade penalty when extra time is not the answer
- Helping professors understand the needs of students with LD/ADD

ADD Services

In addition to the services described for students with LD/ADD, some services are uniquely designed for students with ADD. Students with ADD may be provided with distraction-free study or examination environments, medication management, a personal coach or mentor, or a support group.

Advisement

College students with LD/ADD need careful and ongoing academic advisement for these reasons:

- They frequently enroll in courses that are too difficult for them
- They tend to enroll in the wrong courses
- They often misperceive the progress they are making in courses
- They rarely seek out services they need to overcome academic and social difficulties
- They frequently are overwhelmed by the registration process

- They tend to accept poor advice from well-intentioned peers

It is important for advisers to ensure that such students do not end up with overly difficult course loads, courses out of sequence, or a poorly planned schedule. It is essential that advisers be familiar with the assistance available to students with LD/ADD and the characteristics and needs of these students.

Counseling

To meet social needs, counseling is often necessary. It offers students with LD/ADD a sounding board for their feelings and provides an opportunity for them to develop self-understanding and more effective peer relationships. Counseling available may include group counseling, individual counseling, and career counseling. The major goals are to help college students with LD/ADD reduce anxiety, increase self-confidence and socialization, learn life skills, understand their disability, become better organized, and achieve a sense of normalcy. At many colleges, students with LD/ADD have begun their own support groups.

► SELECTING A COLLEGE ◄

Using the Guide

1. Decide how much assistance you need to succeed in college:
   a. Should you attend a college that offers **Special Services** to its students with LD/ADD? Colleges with special services provide one or more of the following: tutoring, alternative test arrangements, notetakers, taped textbooks, basic skills remediation, diagnostic testing, priority registration, and advocates.
   b. Or, should you attend a college that offers a **Comprehensive Program** especially designed for its students with LD/ADD? Colleges offering comprehensive programs provide the services listed in (a.) above as part of a comprehensive program uniquely designed for students. Most often, special admission procedures must be followed by students with LD/ADD who wish to gain admission to colleges with these programs.
2. Decide whether you want to attend a two-year college or four-year college.
3. Decide in which U.S. states or Canadian provinces you wish to attend college.
4. Use the **Quick-Find Chart** (pages 9–26) to identify the colleges that meet the criteria you selected in steps 1 to 3.
5. For each college identified in step 4, enter the name of the college on the **Personal Summary Chart** on page 6.
6. For each of these colleges, read the complete entry in the **College Profile Listings** section of the guide to obtain the information needed to complete the checklist.
7. From the completed Personal Summary Chart, select those colleges that seem most appropriate. Colleges with the most "yes" responses are most likely to meet your specific needs.
8. Use the sample letter on page 5 to request additional information and application forms.
9. Complete and submit application forms for up to six colleges.
10. Visit the colleges to which you have been accepted. Use the sample letter on page 5 to arrange these visits.
11. When visiting campuses, be sure to take copies of the "General Questions" and "Questions to Ask of Students with LD or ADD" with you.
12. Make your final decision and enroll.

Making the Most of Your College Visit

Reading the profiles in this guide and studying the school catalogs you receive will give you general descriptions about facilities, programs, services, and the like. It won't, however, give you the real feel for a school the way a campus visit will. Walking around campus, visiting the facilities, and getting impressions of the students and faculty will give you a much better sense of what it would be like to go to school there. It will also give you an excellent opportunity to get more detailed and up-to-date information about the things that interest you most at the college.

When to Visit, Who and What to See

If at all possible, see the school or schools in which you're most interested before you apply. This may not be possible when your top choices are far away. Then you may have to visit them after you've been accepted or rely on school brochures and phone calls to get as much information as you can. Plan a visit while classes are in session. Call ahead of time to make an appointment with the admission office and to request a tour of the school. Also ask if the office can arrange for you to meet with some students, including some with LD or ADD. Allow yourself time to walk around campus on your own and, if possible, to drive around the area to see nearby towns and surrounding neighborhoods.

Ask Questions

Write a list of questions about the college to take with you on your campus visit. Use the following questions as a guide for writing your own:
1. Is the campus attractive?
2. Are the residence halls appealing?
3. Do I have a choice of meal plans?
4. Is there a good library?
5. What is the surrounding community like?
6. Can I keep a car on campus?
7. Is travel between college and home easy?
8. Are there good recreational facilities?
9. Is there a comprehensive student health center?
10. Overall, is this a place where I would like to spend my college days? Would I feel comfortable here?

Also, write a list of questions to ask of students with LD or ADD on campus. Use the following questions as a guide for writing your own:
1. Do the staff members understand your needs?
2. Do the staff members provide you with the help you need to succeed in college?
3. Are special materials or equipment you need available?
4. Do your professors understand your needs and try to help you?
5. Is there a staff member you can go to when things are really going poorly?

Student's street address
City, State Zip
Date

Name of College Contact
Name of College or University
Address
City, State Zip

Dear (Dr., Mr., or Ms.) (last name of contact):

I am a student with a learning disability (attention deficit disorder) and am completing my (junior or senior) year at (name of high school). I expect to graduate in (date) and then go on to college.

Please send me information about the assistance you offer to students with learning disabilities. Also send admission forms, a catalog, and any other specific information that you believe will be helpful to me.

Thank you for your assistance.

Sincerely,

Name of student

**Sample Letter
Requesting
Information**

**Sample Letter
Requesting
a Campus Visit**

Student's street address
City, State Zip
Date

Name of College Contact
Name of College or University
Address
City, State Zip

Dear (Dr., Mr., or Ms.) (last name of contact):

I am a student with a learning disability (attention deficit disorder) who has been accepted to your college (university). To help me make a final decision about attending, I wish to visit your campus. During this visit I hope to talk to you regarding the assistance available to students with learning disabilities (attention deficit disorder). I also hope to see the campus and meet some of the students with learning disabilities (attention deficit disorder) who attend your college (university). If possible, would you please arrange a visit for me on any of the following dates: (list two or three available dates)?

I look forward to hearing from you and visiting your campus.

Sincerely,

Name of student

► THE PERSONAL SUMMARY CHART ◄

Directions: Write the names of the colleges that you identified in step 4 at the top of each column. For each question of interest to you, write Yes or No based on the information provided in the college profile.

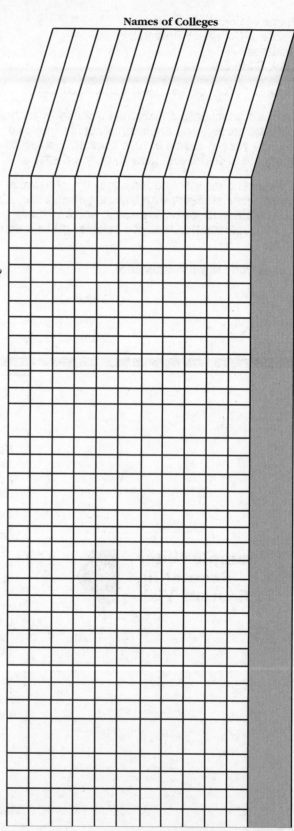

Names of Colleges

1. Is there an official written policy regarding:
   –Substitutions and waivers of admissions requirements?
   –Substitutions and waivers of graduation requirements?
   –Substitutions and waivers of degree requirements?
   –Grade forgiveness?
   –Taking fewer than 12 credits and still maintaining full-time status?
2. Is there a special fee for services?
3. Is there a special summer program for new students?
4. Is there a special orientation for new students?
5. Is diagnostic testing available?
6. Is basic skills remediation available?
7. Is subject-area tutoring available?
8. Are special courses available?
9. Are the following auxiliary aids available?
   –Calculators
   –Personal computers
   –Personal spelling/word-use assistants (e.g., Franklin Speller)
   –Scan and read programs (e.g., Kurzweil)
   –Screen-enlarging programs
   –Screen readers
   –Speech recognition programs (e.g., Dragon)
   –Tape recorders
   –Taped textbooks
   –Other _____
10. Are the following auxiliary services available?
    –Advocates
    –Alternative test arrangements
    –Note-takers
    –Priority registration
    –Readers
    –Scribes
11. Are the following counseling services available?
    –Career
    –Individual
    –Small group/discussion groups
    –Support group
12. Is there a student organization?

Peterson's Colleges for Students with Learning Disabilities or Attention Deficit Disorders

► INFORMATION RESOURCES ◄

Association on Higher Education and Disability (AHEAD)
P.O. Box 21192
Columbus, OH 43221-0192
614-488-4972
Fax: 614-488-1174
E-mail: ahead@postbox.acs.ohio-state.edu
http://www.ahead.org/

Attention Deficit Information Network, Inc. (AD-IN)
475 Hillside Avenue
Needham, MA 02194
781-455-9895
Fax: 781-444-5466
E-mail: adin@gis.net
http://www.addinfonetwork.com

Children and Adults with Attention Deficit Disorders (CHADD)
499 Northwest 70th Avenue
Plantation, FL 33317
800-233-4050
Fax: 954-587-4599
E-mail: national@chadd.org
http://www.chadd.org/

Council for Exceptional Children (CEC)
Division for Learning Disabilities (DLD)
1920 Association Drive
Reston, VA 22091-1589
703-620-3660
888-232-7733
Fax: 703-264-9494
E-mail: servive@cec.sped.org
http://www.cec.sped.org/

Council for Learning Disabilities (CLD)
P.O. Box 40303
Overland Park, KS 66204
913-492-8755
Fax: 913-492-2546
http://www1.winthrop.edu/cld/

HEATH Resource Center
National Clearinghouse on Postsecondary Education for Individuals with Disabilities
American Council on Education
One Dupont Circle, NW, Suite 800
Washington, DC 20036-1110
800-544-3284
Fax: 202-833-4760
E-mail: heath@ace.nche.edu
http://www.heath-resource-center.org

International Dyslexia Association
The Chester Building,
8600 LaSalle Road
Suite 382

Baltimore, MD 21286-2044
410-296-0232
800-222-3123
Fax: 410-321-5069
E-mail: info@interdys.org
http://www.interdys.org/

Learning Disabilities Association of America, Inc. (LDA)
4156 Library Road
Pittsburgh, PA 15234-1349
412-341-1515
Fax: 412-344-0224
E-mail: ldanatl@usaor.net
http://www.ldanatl.org/

Learning Disabilities Association of Canada (LDAC)
323 Chapel Street
Ottawa, Ontario K1N 7Z2
613-238-5721
Fax: 613-235-5391
E-mail: ldactaac@fox.nstn.ca
http://educ.queensu.ca/~lda/

Learning Disabilities Center
331 Milledge Hall
University of Georgia
Athens, GA 30602-5875
706 542-4589
Fax: 706 542-4532
http://www.coe.uga.edu/ldcenter/

Learning Disabilities Network
72 Sharp Street
Suite A-2
Hingham, MA 02043
617-340-5605
Fax: 617-340-5603

National Attention Deficit Disorder Association (NADDA)
9930 Johnnycake Ridge Road
Suite 3E
Mentor, OH 44060
440-350-9595
800-487-2282 (to request information packet)
Fax: 440-350-0223
E-mail: natladda@aol.com
http://www.add.org

National Center for Law and Learning Disabilities (NCLLD)
P.O. Box 368
Cabin John, MD 20818
301-469-8308
Fax: 301-469-9466

National Center for Learning Disabilities (NCLD)
381 Park Avenue, South
Suite 1401
New York, NY 10016

212-545-7510
888-575-7373
Fax: 212-545-9665
http://www.ncld.org/

National Information Center for Children and Youth with Disabilities (NICHCY)
P.O. Box 1492
Washington, DC 20013-1492
800-695-0285
Fax: 202-884-8441
E-mail: nichcy@aed.org
http://www.nichcy.org

Information about nonstandard testing arrangements for the ACT may be obtained from:
National Extended Program
ACT Registration
Extended Time National (81)
1021 William Street
P.O. Box 4068
Iowa City, IA 52243-4068
319-337-1851
Fax: 319-339-3032
http://www.act.org/aap/disab

Special Testing Program
ACT Special Testing (61)

2255 North Dubuque Road
P.O. Box 4028
Iowa City, IA 52243-4028
319-337-1332
Fax: 319-337-1285
http://www.act.org/aap/disab

Information about nonstandard testing arrangements for the SAT may be obtained from:
SAT Services for Students with Disabilities
P.O. Box 6226
Princeton, NJ 08541-6226
609-771-7137
Fax: 609-771-7944
E-mail: sat.ssd@ets.org
http://www.collegeboard.org

Information about obtaining recorded textbooks may be obtained from:
Recording for the Blind & Dyslexic
20 Roszel Road
Princeton, NJ 08540
609-452-0606
800-221-4792
E-mail: custserv@rfbd.org
http://www.rfbd.org/

► QUICK-FIND CHART ◄

	Comp. Program	Special Services	Two-Year	Four-Year	No Special Fee Charged	Page
ALABAMA						
Auburn University		✓		✓	✓	83
Auburn University Montgomery		✓		✓	✓	84
Calhoun Community College		✓	✓		✓	284
George C. Wallace Community College		✓	✓		✓	301
Troy State University Montgomery		✓		✓	✓	182
The University of Alabama		✓		✓	✓	185
The University of Alabama in Huntsville		✓		✓	✓	185
University of North Alabama		✓		✓	✓	200
Wallace State Community College		✓	✓		✓	364
ALASKA						
Alaska Pacific University		✓		✓	✓	79
Sheldon Jackson College		✓		✓	✓	165
University of Alaska Anchorage, Kenai Peninsula College		✓	✓		✓	361
University of Alaska Fairbanks		✓		✓	✓	186
ARIZONA						
Arizona State University		✓		✓	✓	82
Cochise College (Douglas)		✓	✓		✓	290
Northern Arizona University	✓			✓	✓	56
Northland Pioneer College		✓	✓		✓	333
Phoenix College	✓		✓		✓	259
Pima Community College	✓		✓		✓	260
The University of Arizona	✓			✓		64
ARKANSAS						
Arkansas State University	✓			✓	✓	31
South Arkansas Community College		✓	✓		✓	349
University of Arkansas at Little Rock		✓		✓	✓	186
University of Arkansas Community College at Batesville		✓	✓		✓	361
University of the Ozarks	✓			✓		70
Westark College		✓	✓		✓	364
CALIFORNIA						
Academy of Art College	✓			✓	✓	29
Antelope Valley College	✓		✓		✓	228
Biola University		✓		✓	✓	86
Cabrillo College	✓		✓		✓	228
California Polytechnic State University, San Luis Obispo		✓		✓	✓	90

	Comp. Program	Special Services	Two-Year	Four-Year	No Special Fee Charged	Page
California State University, Bakersfield		✓		✓	✓	90
California State University, Dominguez Hills		✓		✓	✓	91
California State University, Fresno		✓		✓	✓	91
California State University, Fullerton		✓		✓	✓	91
California State University, Hayward	✓			✓	✓	34
California State University, Long Beach		✓		✓	✓	92
California State University, Northridge	✓			✓	✓	35
California State University, Sacramento	✓			✓	✓	35
California State University, San Marcos		✓		✓	✓	92
California State University, Stanislaus		✓		✓	✓	93
Cerro Coso Community College	✓		✓		✓	230
College of San Mateo	✓		✓		✓	231
College of the Canyons	✓		✓		✓	231
College of the Desert	✓		✓		✓	232
College of the Siskiyous	✓		✓		✓	232
Crafton Hills College	✓		✓		✓	234
Cuesta College	✓		✓		✓	235
De Anza College	✓		✓		✓	236
Diablo Valley College	✓		✓		✓	237
East Los Angeles College		✓	✓		✓	297
Foothill College	✓		✓		✓	241
Gavilan College	✓		✓		✓	241
Glendale Community College	✓		✓		✓	242
Humboldt State University		✓		✓	✓	120
Imperial Valley College	✓		✓		✓	245
Lake Tahoe Community College		✓	✓		✓	315
Los Angeles Valley College		✓	✓		✓	318
Marymount College, Palos Verdes, California		✓	✓		✓	320
Mendocino College	✓		✓		✓	250
Menlo College		✓		✓	✓	133
Merritt College	✓		✓		✓	251
Mills College	✓			✓	✓	53
MiraCosta College	✓		✓		✓	252
Modesto Junior College	✓		✓		✓	253
Moorpark College	✓		✓		✓	254
Napa Valley College	✓		✓		✓	255
Newschool of Architecture		✓		✓	✓	141
Pacific Union College	✓			✓	✓	56
Palo Verde College		✓	✓		✓	337
Pepperdine University		✓		✓	✓	153
Reedley College	✓		✓		✓	261
Riverside Community College	✓		✓		✓	261
Saint Mary's College of California		✓		✓	✓	162
San Bernardino Valley College	✓		✓		✓	262
San Diego City College	✓		✓		✓	263
San Diego Mesa College		✓	✓		✓	347
San Diego Miramar College	✓		✓		✓	263
San Francisco State University	✓			✓	✓	59
San Jose State University	✓			✓	✓	60
Santa Ana College	✓		✓		✓	264

	Comp. Program	Special Services	Two-Year	Four-Year	No Special Fee Charged	Page
Santa Barbara City College	✓		✓		✓	264
Santa Clara University		✓		✓	✓	163
Sonoma State University		✓		✓	✓	167
Southwestern College		✓	✓		✓	351
Taft College	✓		✓		✓	266
United States International University		✓		✓	✓	183
University of California, Berkeley		✓		✓	✓	187
University of California, Los Angeles		✓		✓	✓	187
University of California, San Diego	✓			✓	✓	65
University of California, Santa Barbara	✓			✓	✓	65
University of Redlands		✓		✓	✓	203
University of Southern California		✓		✓	✓	205
Vanguard University of Southern California		✓		✓	✓	216
Ventura College	✓		✓		✓	267
Vista Community College		✓	✓		✓	364
West Hills Community College	✓		✓		✓	270
West Valley College	✓		✓		✓	270
Whittier College		✓		✓	✓	223
COLORADO						
Arapahoe Community College		✓	✓		✓	277
Colorado Christian University		✓		✓	✓	103
Colorado Northwestern Community College		✓	✓		✓	291
Colorado State University		✓		✓	✓	103
Community College of Aurora		✓	✓		✓	293
Johnson & Wales University		✓	✓		✓	309
Metropolitan State College of Denver		✓		✓	✓	133
Pikes Peak Community College		✓	✓		✓	341
University of Colorado at Boulder	✓			✓	✓	65
University of Colorado at Colorado Springs		✓		✓	✓	188
University of Colorado at Denver		✓		✓	✓	188
University of Denver	✓			✓		66
CONNECTICUT						
Briarwood College		✓	✓		✓	282
Connecticut College		✓		✓	✓	106
Eastern Connecticut State University		✓		✓	✓	110
Housatonic Community College		✓	✓		✓	305
Mitchell College	✓		✓			253
Naugatuck Valley Community College		✓	✓		✓	329
Norwalk Community College		✓	✓		✓	335
Sacred Heart University		✓		✓		159
Three Rivers Community College		✓	✓		✓	359
University of Connecticut	✓			✓	✓	66
University of Hartford		✓		✓	✓	189
University of New Haven		✓		✓	✓	199
DISTRICT OF COLUMBIA						
American University	✓			✓		30
The Catholic University of America		✓		✓	✓	96
The George Washington University		✓		✓	✓	116

	Comp. Program	Special Services	Two-Year	Four-Year	No Special Fee Charged	Page
Trinity College		✓		✓	✓	182
University of the District of Columbia		✓		✓	✓	208
FLORIDA						
Barry University	✓			✓		32
Brevard Community College		✓	✓		✓	281
Broward Community College		✓	✓		✓	283
Daytona Beach Community College		✓	✓		✓	295
Florida Agricultural and Mechanical University	✓			✓	✓	42
Florida Atlantic University		✓		✓	✓	113
Florida Community College at Jacksonville		✓	✓		✓	299
Florida Gulf Coast University		✓		✓	✓	113
Florida International University		✓		✓	✓	114
Hillsborough Community College	✓		✓		✓	243
Johnson & Wales University	✓			✓	✓	45
Lake City Community College	✓		✓		✓	246
Lynn University	✓			✓		49
Manatee Community College		✓	✓			320
Okaloosa-Walton Community College		✓	✓		✓	335
Pensacola Junior College		✓	✓		✓	340
Saint Leo University		✓		✓	✓	161
Santa Fe Community College		✓	✓		✓	347
Seminole Community College		✓	✓		✓	348
Southeastern College of the Assemblies of God		✓		✓	✓	168
Tallahassee Community College		✓	✓		✓	357
University of Miami		✓		✓	✓	195
University of West Florida		✓		✓	✓	211
Valencia Community College		✓	✓		✓	362
GEORGIA						
Abraham Baldwin Agricultural College		✓	✓		✓	275
Albany State University		✓		✓	✓	80
Andrew College	✓		✓			227
Bainbridge College		✓	✓		✓	279
Brenau University	✓			✓		34
Brewton-Parker College		✓		✓	✓	88
Clayton College & State University		✓		✓	✓	99
Columbus State University		✓		✓	✓	105
Emory University		✓		✓	✓	112
Fort Valley State University		✓		✓	✓	115
Georgia College and State University		✓		✓	✓	116
Georgia State University	✓			✓		43
Life University		✓		✓	✓	128
Macon State College		✓		✓	✓	130
North Georgia College & State University		✓		✓	✓	146
Reinhardt College	✓			✓		57
Savannah State University	✓			✓	✓	60
Southern Polytechnic State University		✓		✓	✓	170
State University of West Georgia		✓		✓		176
Toccoa Falls College		✓		✓	✓	181
Valdosta State University		✓		✓	✓	215

	Comp. Program	Special Services	Two-Year	Four-Year	No Special Fee Charged	Page
HAWAII						
Hawaii Community College		✓	✓		✓	303
Leeward Community College	✓		✓		✓	247
University of Hawaii at Hilo		✓		✓	✓	189
IDAHO						
Idaho State University		✓		✓	✓	121
North Idaho College	✓		✓		✓	257
Ricks College		✓	✓		✓	344
University of Idaho		✓		✓	✓	190
ILLINOIS						
Barat College	✓			✓		32
City Colleges of Chicago, Harold Washington College		✓	✓		✓	289
City Colleges of Chicago, Richard J. Daley College		✓	✓		✓	289
College of Lake County		✓	✓		✓	291
Columbia College Chicago		✓		✓	✓	104
DePaul University	✓			✓		39
Illinois Central College		✓	✓		✓	306
Illinois State University		✓		✓	✓	121
International Academy of Merchandising & Design, Ltd.		✓		✓	✓	123
Joliet Junior College		✓	✓		✓	311
Lake Land College		✓	✓		✓	314
Lincoln Land Community College		✓	✓		✓	317
McHenry County College		✓	✓		✓	321
Millikin University		✓		✓	✓	135
Moraine Valley Community College		✓	✓		✓	327
North Central College		✓		✓	✓	144
Northeastern Illinois University		✓		✓	✓	144
Parkland College		✓	✓		✓	337
Robert Morris College		✓		✓	✓	157
Roosevelt University	✓			✓		58
Sauk Valley Community College		✓	✓		✓	348
School of the Art Institute of Chicago		✓		✓	✓	164
Southern Illinois University Carbondale	✓			✓		62
University of Illinois at Urbana-Champaign		✓		✓	✓	191
Western Illinois University		✓		✓	✓	220
William Rainey Harper College	✓		✓			272
INDIANA						
Anderson University	✓			✓	✓	30
Holy Cross College	✓		✓			244
Indiana University Southeast		✓		✓	✓	122
Indiana Wesleyan University		✓		✓	✓	122
Ivy Tech State College-Central Indiana		✓	✓		✓	306
Ivy Tech State College-Columbus		✓	✓		✓	307
Ivy Tech State College-Northeast		✓	✓		✓	307
Ivy Tech State College-Southcentral		✓	✓		✓	308
Ivy Tech State College-Southwest		✓	✓		✓	308
Ivy Tech State College-Wabash Valley		✓	✓		✓	308

	Comp. Program	Special Services	Two-Year	Four-Year	No Special Fee Charged	Page
Purdue University North Central		✓		✓	✓	154
Taylor University		✓		✓	✓	178
University of Indianapolis	✓			✓		67
University of Notre Dame		✓		✓	✓	201
University of Southern Indiana		✓		✓	✓	206
Valparaiso University		✓		✓	✓	215
Vincennes University	✓		✓			268
IOWA						
Central College		✓		✓	✓	96
Coe College		✓		✓	✓	100
Dordt College		✓		✓	✓	109
Ellsworth Community College	✓		✓			239
Hawkeye Community College		✓	✓		✓	303
Iowa Western Community College	✓	✓	✓		✓	245
Kirkwood Community College		✓	✓		✓	313
Loras College	✓			✓		48
Luther College		✓		✓	✓	129
Marshalltown Community College	✓		✓			249
Mount Mercy College		✓		✓	✓	139
Northeast Iowa Community College, Calmar Campus		✓	✓		✓	332
Northeast Iowa Community College, Peosta Campus		✓	✓		✓	332
St. Ambrose University		✓		✓	✓	160
University of Northern Iowa		✓		✓	✓	201
Waldorf College	✓		✓			268
KANSAS						
Barton County Community College		✓	✓		✓	279
Butler County Community College		✓	✓		✓	284
Cloud County Community College		✓	✓		✓	290
Johnson County Community College		✓	✓		✓	310
Kansas State University		✓		✓	✓	125
Labette Community College		✓	✓		✓	313
KENTUCKY						
Ashland Community College		✓	✓		✓	278
Bellarmine College		✓		✓	✓	86
Madisonville Community College		✓	✓		✓	319
Murray State University	✓			✓	✓	54
Thomas More College		✓		✓	✓	180
University of Louisville		✓		✓	✓	192
LOUISIANA						
Louisiana College	✓			✓		48
Louisiana State University at Eunice	✓		✓		✓	248
Louisiana Technical College-Slidell Campus		✓	✓			319
Loyola University New Orleans		✓		✓	✓	129
Nicholls State University	✓			✓		55
Northwestern State University of Louisiana		✓		✓	✓	147
Southeastern Louisiana University		✓		✓	✓	168
Tulane University		✓		✓	✓	183

	Comp. Program	Special Services	Two-Year	Four-Year	No Special Fee Charged	Page
University of Louisiana at Lafayette		✓		✓	✓	191
University of Louisiana at Monroe		✓		✓	✓	192
University of New Orleans		✓		✓	✓	200
MAINE						
Bates College		✓		✓	✓	85
Southern Maine Technical College		✓	✓		✓	350
University of Maine at Machias		✓		✓	✓	192
York County Technical College		✓	✓		✓	366
MARYLAND						
Anne Arundel Community College		✓	✓		✓	277
Chesapeake College		✓	✓		✓	288
College of Notre Dame of Maryland		✓		✓	✓	101
The Community College of Baltimore County-Catonsville Campus		✓	✓		✓	293
The Community College of Baltimore County-Essex Campus		✓	✓		✓	294
Frederick Community College		✓	✓		✓	300
Hood College		✓		✓	✓	119
Howard Community College	✓		✓		✓	244
Montgomery College-Rockville Campus	✓		✓		✓	254
Prince George's Community College		✓	✓		✓	343
Towson University		✓		✓	✓	181
University of Maryland, Baltimore County		✓		✓	✓	193
University of Maryland, College Park		✓		✓	✓	193
University of Maryland Eastern Shore		✓		✓	✓	194
MASSACHUSETTS						
American International College	✓			✓		29
Atlantic Union College	✓			✓		31
Babson College		✓		✓	✓	84
Boston University	✓			✓		34
Bristol Community College		✓	✓		✓	282
Bunker Hill Community College		✓	✓		✓	283
Cape Cod Community College	✓		✓		✓	229
Curry College	✓			✓		38
Fitchburg State College	✓			✓	✓	41
Hampshire College		✓		✓	✓	118
Holyoke Community College		✓	✓		✓	305
Massachusetts College of Liberal Arts		✓		✓	✓	132
Mount Ida College		✓		✓		139
Mount Wachusett Community College		✓	✓		✓	328
Northeastern University	✓			✓		55
Salem State College	✓			✓	✓	59
Springfield College		✓		✓	✓	171
Springfield Technical Community College		✓	✓		✓	354
Suffolk University		✓		✓	✓	177
Tufts University		✓		✓	✓	183
University of Massachusetts Amherst	✓			✓	✓	68
University of Massachusetts Dartmouth		✓		✓	✓	194
Western New England College		✓		✓		220

	Comp. Program	Special Services	Two-Year	Four-Year	No Special Fee Charged	Page
Wheelock College		✓		✓	✓	222
MICHIGAN						
Adrian College		✓		✓	✓	79
Alma College		✓		✓	✓	81
Aquinas College		✓		✓	✓	82
Calvin College		✓		✓	✓	93
Center for Creative Studies—College of Art and Design		✓		✓	✓	96
Charles Stewart Mott Community College		✓	✓		✓	287
Delta College		✓	✓		✓	296
Eastern Michigan University		✓		✓	✓	111
Finlandia University	✓			✓	✓	41
Glen Oaks Community College		✓	✓		✓	301
Kalamazoo Valley Community College		✓	✓		✓	311
Madonna University		✓		✓	✓	130
Montcalm Community College		✓	✓		✓	325
Muskegon Community College		✓	✓		✓	328
Northwestern Michigan College		✓	✓		✓	334
Northwood University		✓		✓	✓	147
Oakland Community College		✓	✓		✓	335
Saginaw Valley State University		✓		✓	✓	160
St. Clair County Community College		✓	✓		✓	345
Schoolcraft College	✓		✓		✓	264
Southwestern Michigan College		✓	✓		✓	352
University of Michigan-Dearborn		✓		✓	✓	195
University of Michigan-Flint		✓		✓	✓	196
Washtenaw Community College	✓		✓		✓	269
Wayne State University		✓		✓	✓	219
MINNESOTA						
Alexandria Technical College		✓	✓		✓	276
Augsburg College	✓			✓	✓	32
The College of St. Scholastica		✓		✓	✓	102
Fond du Lac Tribal and Community College	✓		✓		✓	240
Gustavus Adolphus College		✓		✓	✓	117
Hamline University		✓		✓	✓	118
Hennepin Technical College		✓	✓		✓	304
Lake Superior College	✓		✓		✓	247
Macalester College	✓			✓	✓	49
Minnesota State University, Mankato		✓		✓	✓	136
Minnesota State University Moorhead		✓		✓	✓	136
Minnesota West Community and Technical College-Granite Falls Campus		✓	✓		✓	323
Minnesota West Community and Technical College-Worthington Campus		✓	✓		✓	323
Normandale Community College	✓		✓		✓	256
Northwestern College		✓		✓	✓	146
Rainy River Community College		✓	✓		✓	343
Saint Mary's University of Minnesota		✓		✓	✓	163
St. Paul Technical College		✓	✓		✓	346
University of Minnesota, Crookston		✓		✓	✓	196

	Comp. Program	Special Services	Two-Year	Four-Year	No Special Fee Charged	Page
University of Minnesota, Morris		✓		✓	✓	196
MISSISSIPPI						
Copiah-Lincoln Community College	✓		✓		✓	233
Mississippi Gulf Coast Community College		✓	✓		✓	324
Mississippi State University		✓		✓	✓	136
Northwest Mississippi Community College		✓	✓		✓	334
University of Southern Mississippi		✓		✓	✓	206
MISSOURI						
Central Missouri State University		✓		✓	✓	97
Fontbonne College		✓		✓	✓	114
Longview Community College		✓	✓			318
Missouri Southern State College		✓		✓	✓	137
St. Louis Community College at Meramec		✓	✓		✓	346
Saint Louis University	✓			✓	✓	58
Southwest Missouri State University-West Plains		✓	✓		✓	352
University of Missouri-Columbia	✓			✓	✓	68
University of Missouri-Kansas City		✓		✓	✓	197
Washington University in St. Louis		✓		✓	✓	218
Westminster College	✓			✓		74
MONTANA						
Dawson Community College		✓	✓		✓	295
Flathead Valley Community College	✓		✓		✓	240
Montana State University College of Technology-Great Falls		✓	✓		✓	325
Montana Tech of The University of Montana		✓		✓	✓	138
The University of Montana-Missoula		✓		✓	✓	197
NEBRASKA						
Central Community College-Hastings Campus		✓	✓		✓	286
Central Community College-Platte Campus		✓	✓		✓	286
Creighton University		✓		✓	✓	107
Midland Lutheran College		✓		✓	✓	134
Northeast Community College		✓	✓		✓	331
Union College	✓			✓		64
University of Nebraska-Lincoln		✓		✓	✓	198
NEVADA						
Sierra Nevada College		✓		✓	✓	166
Truckee Meadows Community College	✓		✓		✓	267
NEW HAMPSHIRE						
Colby-Sawyer College		✓		✓	✓	100
Daniel Webster College		✓		✓	✓	108
New Hampshire Community Technical College, Nashua/Claremont		✓	✓		✓	329
New Hampshire Technical Institute		✓	✓		✓	330
Rivier College		✓		✓	✓	157
University of New Hampshire		✓		✓	✓	198
University of New Hampshire at Manchester		✓		✓	✓	198
NEW JERSEY						

	Comp. Program	Special Services	Two-Year	Four-Year	No Special Fee Charged	Page
Atlantic Cape Community College		✓	✓		✓	278
Caldwell College		✓		✓	✓	89
Camden County College	✓		✓		✓	229
Centenary College	✓			✓		36
The College of New Jersey		✓		✓	✓	101
County College of Morris	✓		✓		✓	233
Cumberland County College	✓		✓		✓	235
Georgian Court College		✓		✓		116
Gloucester County College		✓	✓		✓	302
Kean University		✓		✓	✓	125
Mercer County Community College		✓	✓		✓	321
Middlesex County College	✓		✓		✓	251
Monmouth University		✓		✓	✓	138
New Jersey Institute of Technology		✓		✓	✓	140
Ocean County College	✓		✓		✓	258
Passaic County Community College		✓	✓		✓	338
The Richard Stockton College of New Jersey		✓		✓	✓	156
Rider University		✓		✓	✓	157
NEW MEXICO						
Albuquerque Technical Vocational Institute		✓	✓		✓	276
Dona Ana Branch Community College	✓		✓		✓	238
Eastern New Mexico University		✓		✓	✓	111
Eastern New Mexico University-Roswell	✓		✓		✓	238
Luna Vocational Technical Institute	✓		✓		✓	249
New Mexico Institute of Mining and Technology		✓		✓	✓	141
University of New Mexico		✓		✓	✓	199
NEW YORK						
Adelphi University	✓			✓		29
Adirondack Community College	✓		✓		✓	227
Alfred University		✓		✓	✓	80
Broome Community College		✓	✓		✓	282
Canisius College		✓		✓	✓	93
City College of the City University of New York		✓		✓	✓	98
Clinton Community College		✓	✓		✓	289
College of Aeronautics		✓		✓	✓	101
The College of Saint Rose		✓		✓	✓	102
College of Staten Island of the City University of New York		✓		✓	✓	103
Columbia College		✓		✓	✓	104
Concordia College	✓			✓		37
Cornell University		✓		✓	✓	106
Corning Community College		✓	✓		✓	294
The Culinary Institute of America		✓		✓	✓	107
Dowling College	✓			✓		39
Eugenio Maria de Hostos Community College of the City University of New York		✓	✓		✓	298
Fashion Institute of Technology	✓			✓	✓	40
Finger Lakes Community College		✓	✓		✓	299
Fiorello H. LaGuardia Community College of the City University of New York	✓		✓		✓	239

	Comp. Program	Special Services	Two-Year	Four-Year	No Special Fee Charged	Page
Fulton-Montgomery Community College	✓		✓		✓	241
Hamilton College		✓		✓	✓	118
Herkimer County Community College		✓	✓		✓	304
Hofstra University	✓			✓		44
Houghton College		✓		✓	✓	119
Hunter College of the City University of New York		✓		✓	✓	120
Iona College	✓			✓		44
Ithaca College	✓			✓	✓	44
Jamestown Community College		✓	✓		✓	309
Long Island University, C.W. Post Campus	✓			✓		47
Manhattanville College	✓			✓		49
Marist College	✓			✓		50
Marymount Manhattan College	✓			✓		51
Mercy College	✓			✓		51
Mohawk Valley Community College		✓	✓		✓	325
Molloy College		✓		✓	✓	137
Nassau Community College		✓	✓		✓	328
Nazareth College of Rochester		✓		✓	✓	140
New York City Technical College of the City University of New York		✓	✓		✓	330
New York University		✓		✓	✓	142
Queensborough Community College of the City University of New York	✓		✓		✓	260
Queens College of the City University of New York		✓		✓	✓	155
Rensselaer Polytechnic Institute		✓		✓	✓	155
Rochester Institute of Technology		✓		✓	✓	158
Rockland Community College	✓		✓		✓	262
The Sage Colleges		✓		✓		159
St. Bonaventure University		✓		✓	✓	161
St. Lawrence University		✓		✓	✓	161
Siena College		✓		✓	✓	166
State University of New York at Albany		✓		✓	✓	171
State University of New York at Binghamton		✓		✓	✓	172
State University of New York at Oswego		✓		✓	✓	172
State University of New York at Stony Brook		✓		✓	✓	173
State University of New York College at Brockport		✓		✓	✓	173
State University of New York College at Buffalo		✓		✓	✓	173
State University of New York College at Fredonia		✓		✓	✓	174
State University of New York College at Geneseo		✓		✓	✓	174
State University of New York College at Oneonta		✓		✓	✓	174
State University of New York College at Potsdam		✓		✓	✓	175
State University of New York College of Agriculture and Technology at Morrisville		✓	✓		✓	355
State University of New York College of Environmental Science and Forestry		✓		✓		175
State University of New York College of Technology at Alfred		✓	✓		✓	355
State University of New York College of Technology at Canton		✓		✓	✓	176
State University of New York College of Technology at Delhi		✓	✓		✓	356
State University of New York Institute of Technology at Utica/Rome		✓		✓	✓	176

	Comp. Program	Special Services	Two-Year	Four-Year	No Special Fee Charged	Page
Sullivan County Community College	✓		✓		✓	265
Trocaire College		✓	✓		✓	359
University of Rochester		✓		✓	✓	204
Utica College of Syracuse University	✓			✓	✓	73
Vassar College		✓		✓	✓	216
NORTH CAROLINA						
Brevard College		✓		✓	✓	87
Catawba College		✓		✓	✓	95
Catawba Valley Community College		✓	✓		✓	285
Central Piedmont Community College	✓		✓		✓	230
Craven Community College		✓	✓		✓	295
Gardner-Webb University		✓		✓	✓	115
Guilford Technical Community College		✓	✓		✓	302
Johnson C. Smith University		✓		✓	✓	124
Lenoir-Rhyne College		✓		✓	✓	128
Louisburg College	✓		✓			248
Mayland Community College		✓	✓		✓	320
McDowell Technical Community College	✓		✓		✓	250
Meredith College	✓			✓	✓	52
Montgomery Community College		✓	✓		✓	326
North Carolina State University		✓		✓	✓	143
North Carolina Wesleyan College		✓		✓	✓	143
Peace College		✓		✓	✓	152
Piedmont Baptist College	✓			✓	✓	57
Pitt Community College		✓	✓		✓	342
Randolph Community College	✓		✓		✓	261
Robeson Community College		✓	✓		✓	345
Rockingham Community College		✓	✓		✓	345
St. Andrews Presbyterian College		✓		✓	✓	160
Southeastern Community College		✓	✓		✓	350
The University of North Carolina at Chapel Hill	✓			✓	✓	69
The University of North Carolina at Greensboro		✓		✓	✓	200
The University of North Carolina at Wilmington	✓			✓	✓	69
Western Carolina University		✓		✓	✓	219
Wilkes Community College	✓		✓		✓	271
Wingate University		✓		✓	✓	223
NORTH DAKOTA						
Dickinson State University		✓		✓	✓	109
Lake Region State College		✓	✓		✓	315
Minot State University-Bottineau Campus		✓	✓		✓	324
North Dakota State College of Science		✓	✓		✓	331
University of Mary		✓		✓	✓	193
OHIO						
Antioch College		✓		✓	✓	81
Bluffton College		✓		✓	✓	87
Bowling Green State University		✓		✓	✓	87
Central Ohio Technical College		✓	✓		✓	287
Central State University		✓		✓	✓	97

	Comp. Program	Special Services	Two-Year	Four-Year	No Special Fee Charged	Page
Cleveland Institute of Art		✓		✓	✓	100
College of Mount St. Joseph	✓			✓		37
Columbus State Community College		✓	✓		✓	292
Cuyahoga Community College, Eastern Campus	✓		✓		✓	236
Denison University		✓		✓	✓	108
Hocking College		✓	✓		✓	305
Kent State University		✓		✓	✓	126
Kent State University, Ashtabula Campus		✓	✓		✓	312
Kent State University, Trumbull Campus		✓	✓		✓	312
Lakeland Community College		✓	✓		✓	314
Lima Technical College		✓	✓		✓	316
Mercy College of Northwest Ohio		✓	✓		✓	322
Mount Vernon Nazarene College		✓		✓	✓	140
Muskingum College	✓			✓		55
Notre Dame College of Ohio		✓		✓	✓	148
The Ohio State University		✓		✓	✓	148
The Ohio State University at Lima		✓		✓	✓	149
The Ohio State University at Marion		✓		✓	✓	149
The Ohio State University-Newark Campus		✓		✓	✓	149
Shawnee State University		✓		✓	✓	165
Sinclair Community College		✓	✓		✓	349
Stark State College of Technology		✓	✓		✓	354
Terra State Community College		✓	✓		✓	357
University of Dayton		✓		✓	✓	188
Ursuline College	✓			✓		73
Wright State University	✓			✓	✓	76
Xavier University		✓		✓	✓	223
OKLAHOMA						
Northeastern State University		✓		✓	✓	145
Oklahoma City University		✓		✓	✓	150
Oklahoma Panhandle State University		✓		✓	✓	151
Oklahoma State University, Okmulgee		✓	✓		✓	336
Oral Roberts University		✓		✓	✓	151
St. Gregory's University	✓			✓		58
Southeastern Oklahoma State University		✓		✓	✓	169
University of Tulsa		✓		✓	✓	209
OREGON						
Chemeketa Community College		✓	✓		✓	288
Linfield College	✓			✓	✓	47
Linn-Benton Community College		✓	✓		✓	317
Portland Community College		✓	✓		✓	342
Southwestern Oregon Community College		✓	✓		✓	352
Umpqua Community College		✓	✓		✓	360
University of Oregon		✓		✓	✓	202
Western Baptist College		✓		✓	✓	219
PENNSYLVANIA						
Academy of Medical Arts and Business		✓	✓		✓	275
The Art Institute of Pittsburgh		✓	✓		✓	277

	Comp. Program	Special Services	Two-Year	Four-Year	No Special Fee Charged	Page
Bryn Mawr College		✓		✓	✓	89
Carnegie Mellon University		✓		✓	✓	95
College Misericordia	✓			✓	✓	36
Community College of Allegheny County	✓		✓		✓	233
Delaware County Community College	✓		✓		✓	237
Dickinson College		✓		✓	✓	109
Drexel University		✓		✓	✓	110
East Stroudsburg University of Pennsylvania		✓		✓	✓	112
Edinboro University of Pennsylvania	✓			✓		40
Gannon University	✓			✓		42
Harcum College	✓		✓			242
Harrisburg Area Community College		✓	✓		✓	303
Hiram G. Andrews Center	✓		✓		✓	243
Indiana University of Pennsylvania		✓		✓	✓	122
Johnson Technical Institute		✓	✓		✓	310
King's College	✓			✓		45
Lebanon Valley College		✓		✓	✓	127
Marywood University		✓		✓	✓	131
Mercyhurst College	✓			✓		52
Messiah College		✓		✓	✓	133
Millersville University of Pennsylvania		✓		✓	✓	135
Moravian College		✓		✓	✓	138
Northampton County Area Community College	✓		✓		✓	256
Pennsylvania State University Abington College		✓		✓	✓	152
Pennsylvania State University Delaware County Campus of the Commonwealth College	✓		✓		✓	259
Pennsylvania State University Harrisburg Campus of the Capital College		✓		✓	✓	153
Pennsylvania State University Hazleton Campus of the Commonwealth College		✓	✓		✓	339
Pennsylvania State University New Kensington Campus of the Commonwealth College		✓	✓		✓	339
Pennsylvania State University University Park Campus		✓		✓	✓	153
Pennsylvania State University York Campus of the Commonwealth College		✓	✓		✓	340
Shippensburg University of Pennsylvania		✓		✓	✓	166
Temple University		✓		✓	✓	178
Thiel College		✓		✓	✓	180
University of Pittsburgh		✓		✓	✓	202
University of Pittsburgh at Bradford		✓		✓	✓	202
The University of Scranton		✓		✓	✓	204
Villanova University		✓		✓	✓	217
Westmoreland County Community College		✓	✓		✓	366
Widener University	✓			✓	✓	75
RHODE ISLAND						
Brown University		✓		✓	✓	89
Community College of Rhode Island		✓	✓		✓	294
Johnson & Wales University		✓		✓	✓	123
Providence College		✓		✓	✓	154
Rhode Island College		✓		✓	✓	156
Roger Williams University		✓		✓	✓	158

	Comp. Program	Special Services	Two-Year	Four-Year	No Special Fee Charged	Page
University of Rhode Island		✓		✓	✓	204
SOUTH CAROLINA						
Clemson University		✓		✓	✓	99
Johnson & Wales University		✓		✓	✓	124
Limestone College	✓			✓		46
Midlands Technical College		✓	✓		✓	322
South Carolina State University		✓		✓	✓	167
Trident Technical College		✓	✓		✓	359
University of South Carolina		✓		✓	✓	205
University of South Carolina Spartanburg		✓		✓	✓	205
Voorhees College		✓		✓	✓	218
SOUTH DAKOTA						
Northern State University		✓		✓	✓	145
South Dakota School of Mines and Technology		✓		✓	✓	168
Western Dakota Technical Institute	✓		✓		✓	269
TENNESSEE						
Chattanooga State Technical Community College		✓	✓		✓	287
Dyersburg State Community College		✓	✓		✓	296
East Tennessee State University	✓			✓	✓	40
Lee University	✓			✓	✓	46
Middle Tennessee State University	✓			✓	✓	53
Motlow State Community College		✓	✓		✓	327
Nashville State Technical Institute	✓		✓		✓	255
Pellissippi State Technical Community College		✓	✓		✓	338
Roane State Community College		✓	✓		✓	344
Shelby State Community College	✓		✓		✓	265
State Technical Institute at Memphis		✓	✓		✓	355
Tennessee State University	✓			✓	✓	63
The University of Tennessee at Martin	✓			✓	✓	70
The University of Tennessee Knoxville		✓		✓	✓	207
Vanderbilt University		✓		✓	✓	215
TEXAS						
Abilene Christian University		✓		✓	✓	79
Amarillo College		✓	✓		✓	276
Baylor University		✓		✓	✓	85
Blinn College		✓	✓		✓	281
Cedar Valley College	✓		✓		✓	229
Collin County Community College District		✓	✓		✓	291
Concordia University at Austin		✓		✓	✓	106
El Centro College		✓	✓		✓	298
Galveston College		✓	✓		✓	301
Kilgore College		✓	✓		✓	312
Lee College		✓	✓		✓	316
Lon Morris College	✓		✓		✓	248
Midwestern State University		✓		✓	✓	134
Montgomery College		✓	✓		✓	326
North Central Texas College		✓	✓		✓	331
North Lake College	✓		✓		✓	257

	Comp. Program	Special Services	Two-Year	Four-Year	No Special Fee Charged	Page
San Jacinto College-South Campus		✓	✓		✓	347
Schreiner College	✓			✓		61
Southern Methodist University		✓		✓	✓	169
South Plains College		✓	✓		✓	351
Southwest Texas State University	✓			✓	✓	62
Tarleton State University		✓		✓	✓	177
Tarrant County College District		✓	✓		✓	357
Texas A&M University		✓		✓	✓	178
Texas A&M University-Commerce		✓		✓	✓	179
Texas A&M University-Kingsville		✓		✓	✓	179
Texas State Technical College		✓	✓		✓	358
Texas State Technical College-Waco/Marshall Campus		✓	✓		✓	358
Texas Tech University	✓			✓		63
Tyler Junior College		✓	✓		✓	360
University of Houston	✓			✓	✓	67
University of Houston-Clear Lake		✓		✓	✓	190
The University of Texas at Austin		✓		✓	✓	207
The University of Texas at El Paso		✓		✓	✓	208
The University of Texas at San Antonio		✓		✓	✓	208
University of the Incarnate Word		✓		✓	✓	209
UTAH						
Brigham Young University		✓		✓	✓	88
Southern Utah University		✓		✓	✓	170
University of Utah		✓		✓	✓	210
Utah State University		✓		✓	✓	214
VERMONT						
Champlain College		✓		✓	✓	98
Green Mountain College		✓		✓	✓	117
Johnson State College		✓		✓	✓	125
Southern Vermont College		✓		✓	✓	170
University of Vermont	✓			✓	✓	71
Vermont Technical College		✓	✓		✓	362
VIRGINIA						
Averett College		✓		✓	✓	84
Community Hospital of Roanoke Valley-College of Health Sciences		✓		✓	✓	105
Eastern Mennonite University		✓		✓	✓	111
Hampton University		✓		✓	✓	119
John Tyler Community College		✓	✓		✓	311
Liberty University	✓			✓	✓	46
Longwood College		✓		✓	✓	128
New River Community College	✓		✓		✓	256
Norfolk State University		✓		✓	✓	143
Old Dominion University		✓		✓	✓	151
Patrick Henry Community College		✓	✓		✓	338
Randolph-Macon Woman's College		✓		✓	✓	155
Tidewater Community College	✓		✓		✓	266
Virginia Commonwealth University		✓		✓	✓	217

	Comp. Program	Special Services	Two-Year	Four-Year	No Special Fee Charged	Page
Virginia Highlands Community College		✓	✓		✓	363
Virginia Intermont College		✓		✓		217
Virginia Wesleyan College	✓			✓	✓	74
Virginia Western Community College		✓	✓		✓	363
WASHINGTON						
Big Bend Community College		✓	✓		✓	280
Central Washington University		✓		✓	✓	98
Columbia Basin College		✓	✓		✓	292
Edmonds Community College		✓	✓		✓	297
Everett Community College		✓	✓		✓	299
Lake Washington Technical College		✓	✓		✓	316
Olympic College		✓	✓		✓	336
Pierce College		✓	✓		✓	341
Renton Technical College		✓	✓		✓	343
Seattle Pacific University		✓		✓	✓	164
Spokane Community College		✓	✓		✓	353
Tacoma Community College		✓	✓		✓	356
Washington State University		✓		✓	✓	218
Western Washington University		✓		✓	✓	221
Whitman College		✓		✓	✓	222
WEST VIRGINIA						
Bethany College	✓			✓		33
Davis & Elkins College	✓			✓		38
Fairmont State College		✓		✓	✓	113
Glenville State College	✓			✓	✓	43
Marshall University	✓			✓		50
Southern West Virginia Community and Technical College		✓	✓		✓	350
West Virginia State College		✓		✓	✓	221
West Virginia University at Parkersburg	✓		✓		✓	271
West Virginia Wesleyan College		✓		✓	✓	222
WISCONSIN						
Alverno College		✓		✓	✓	81
Blackhawk Technical College		✓	✓		✓	280
Cardinal Stritch University		✓		✓	✓	94
Fox Valley Technical College		✓	✓		✓	300
Lakeshore Technical College	✓		✓		✓	246
Lawrence University		✓		✓	✓	127
Maranatha Baptist Bible College		✓		✓		130
Marian College of Fond du Lac		✓		✓	✓	131
Milwaukee Area Technical College	✓		✓		✓	252
Milwaukee Institute of Art and Design		✓		✓	✓	135
Northeast Wisconsin Technical College		✓	✓		✓	333
Northland College		✓		✓	✓	146
St. Norbert College		✓		✓	✓	163
Southwest Wisconsin Technical College		✓	✓		✓	353
University of Wisconsin-Eau Claire		✓		✓	✓	211
University of Wisconsin-La Crosse		✓		✓	✓	212
University of Wisconsin-Madison		✓		✓	✓	212

	Comp. Program	Special Services	Two-Year	Four-Year	No Special Fee Charged	Page
University of Wisconsin-Oshkosh	✓			✓	✓	72
University of Wisconsin-Parkside		✓		✓	✓	213
University of Wisconsin-Platteville		✓		✓	✓	213
University of Wisconsin-River Falls		✓		✓	✓	213
University of Wisconsin-Sheboygan		✓	✓		✓	362
University of Wisconsin-Superior		✓		✓	✓	214
University of Wisconsin-Whitewater	✓			✓		72
Waukesha County Technical College	✓		✓		✓	269
Western Wisconsin Technical College		✓	✓		✓	365
WYOMING						
Casper College		✓	✓		✓	285
Northwest College	✓		✓		✓	258
Western Wyoming Community College		✓	✓		✓	365
ALBERTA						
Athabasca University		✓		✓		83
University of Calgary		✓		✓	✓	186
BRITISH COLUMBIA						
Okanagan University College		✓		✓	✓	150
Simon Fraser University	✓			✓	✓	61
University College of the Cariboo		✓		✓	✓	184
University College of the Fraser Valley		✓		✓	✓	184
NEW BRUNSWICK						
Mount Allison University	✓			✓	✓	54
NOVA SCOTIA						
Dalhousie University		✓		✓	✓	108
Saint Mary's University		✓		✓	✓	162
ONTARIO						
Carleton University		✓		✓		94
Laurentian University		✓		✓	✓	126
McMaster University		✓		✓	✓	132
Nipissing University		✓		✓	✓	142
Trent University		✓		✓	✓	181
University of Guelph		✓		✓	✓	189
University of Ottawa	✓			✓	✓	69
University of Waterloo		✓		✓	✓	210
The University of Western Ontario		✓		✓	✓	211
University of Windsor	✓			✓	✓	71
Wilfrid Laurier University	✓			✓	✓	75
SASKATCHEWAN						
University of Regina		✓		✓	✓	203

► FOUR-YEAR COLLEGES ◄

WITH COMPREHENSIVE PROGRAMS

ACADEMY OF ART COLLEGE
San Francisco, California

Students with LD Served by Program	147	ADD/ADHD Services	✓
Staff	3 full-time, 12 part-time	Summer Preparation Program	n/a
LD Program or Service Fee	n/a	Alternative Test Arrangements	✓
LD Program Began	1998	LD Student Organization	n/a

Academy Resource Center began offering services in 1998. The program serves approximately 147 undergraduate students. Faculty consists of 3 full-time and 12 part-time staff members. Services are provided by LD specialists, professional tutors, and ESL instructors.

Policies LD services are also available to graduate students.

Special preparation or orientation Optional orientation held individually by special arrangement.

Diagnostic testing Available for study skills, learning strategies, reading, and learning styles.

Basic skills remediation Available in study skills, computer skills, reading, time management, learning strategies, written language, math, and spoken language. Offered one-on-one by LD specialists, professional tutors, and ESL teachers.

Subject-area tutoring Available in most subjects. Offered one-on-one and in small groups by LD specialists and ESL trained teachers.

Counseling and advisement Academic counseling is available.

Auxiliary aids and services *Aids:* tape recorders, taped textbooks. *Services and accommodations:* advocates, alternative test arrangements, and note-takers.

ADD/ADHD Students with ADD/ADHD are eligible for the same services available to students with LD, as well as distraction-free study areas, distraction-free testing environments and personal coach or mentors.

Application *Recommended:* high school transcript, psychoeducational report (3 years old or less), and documentation of high school services (e.g., Individualized Education Program [IEP] or 504 plan). Upon application, documentation of need for special services should be sent only to your LD program or unit. Upon acceptance, documentation of need for special services should be sent only to your LD program or unit. *Application deadline (institutional):* rolling/continuous for fall and rolling/continuous for spring. *Application deadline (LD program):* rolling/continuous for fall and rolling/continuous for spring.

LD program contact Natasha Haugnes, Director of Academy Resource Center, 180 New Montgomery, San Francisco, CA 94105. *Phone:* 415-263-8895. *E-mail:* nhaugnes@academyart.edu.

Application contact Academy of Art College, 79 New Montgomery Street, San Francisco, CA 94105-3410. *Web address:* http://www.academyart.edu/.

ADELPHI UNIVERSITY
Garden City, New York

Students with LD Served by Program	125	ADD/ADHD Services	✓
Staff	17 full-time	Summer Preparation Program	✓
LD Program or Service Fee	✓	Alternative Test Arrangements	✓
LD Program Began	1979	LD Student Organization	n/a

Learning Disabilities Program began offering services in 1979. The program serves approximately 125 undergraduate students. Faculty consists of 17 full-time staff members. Services are provided by academic advisers, counselors, remediation/learning specialists, special education teachers, LD specialists, and professional tutors.

Policies 12 credit hours per semester are required to maintain full-time status and to be eligible for financial aid. LD services are also available to graduate students.

Fees *LD Program or Service Fee:* $4000 per year.

Special preparation or orientation Required summer program offered prior to entering college. Required orientation held during summer prior to enrollment.

Diagnostic testing Available for handwriting, reading, written language, and math.

Basic skills remediation Available in study skills, time management, social skills, learning strategies, and written language. Offered one-on-one by special education teachers, LD specialists, and professional tutors.

Special courses Available in study skills, time management, learning strategies, and written composition skills. All courses are offered for credit; all enter into overall grade point average.

Counseling and advisement Career counseling, individual counseling, small-group counseling, and support groups are available. Academic advisement by a staff member affiliated with the program is available.

Auxiliary aids and services *Aids:* calculators, personal computers, personal spelling/word-use assistants (e.g., Franklin Speller), tape recorders, taped textbooks. *Services and accommodations:* priority registration, alternative test arrangements, readers, note-takers, and scribes.

ADD/ADHD Students with ADD/ADHD are eligible for the same services available to students with LD, as well as distraction-free testing environments.

Application *Required:* high school transcript, ACT or SAT I (extended-time or untimed test accepted), interview, personal statement, letter(s) of recommendation, psychoeducational report (3 years old or less), and documentation of high school services (e.g., Individualized Education Program [IEP] or 504 plan). *Recommended:* participation in extracurricular activities. Upon application, documentation of need for special services should be sent only to your LD program or unit. Upon acceptance, documentation of need for special services should be sent only to your LD program or unit. *Application deadline (institutional):* rolling/continuous for fall and rolling/continuous for spring. *Application deadline (LD program):* rolling/continuous for fall and rolling/continuous for spring.

LD program contact Susan Spencer, Assistant Dean/Director, Learning Disabilities Program, Garden City, NY 11530. *Phone:* 516-877-4710. *Fax:* 516-877-4711. *E-mail:* ldprogram@adelphi.edu.

Application contact Adelphi University, South Avenue, Garden City, NY 11530. *E-mail:* admissions@adelphi.edu. *Web address:* http://www.adelphi.edu/.

AMERICAN INTERNATIONAL COLLEGE
Springfield, Massachusetts

Students with LD Served by Program	100	ADD/ADHD Services	✓
Staff	12 full-time, 3 part-time	Summer Preparation Program	n/a
LD Program or Service Fee	varies	Alternative Test Arrangements	✓
LD Program Began	1977	LD Student Organization	n/a

Supportive Learning Services began offering services in 1977. The program serves approximately 100 undergraduate students. Faculty consists of 12 full-time and 3 part-time staff members. Services are provided by professional tutors.

American International College (continued)

Policies 12 credits per term are required to maintain full-time status and to be eligible for financial aid. LD services are also available to graduate students.

Fees *LD Program or Service Fee:* ranges from $1000 to $3200 per year.

Subject-area tutoring Available in some subjects. Offered one-on-one by professional tutors.

Auxiliary aids and services *Aids:* scan and read programs (e.g., Kurzweil), taped textbooks. *Services and accommodations:* alternative test arrangements, readers, and scribes.

ADD/ADHD Students with ADD/ADHD are eligible for the same services available to students with LD, as well as distraction-free testing environments.

Application *Required:* high school transcript, ACT or SAT I (extended-time or untimed test accepted), interview, letter(s) of recommendation, psychoeducational report (3 years old or less), and documentation of high school services (e.g., Individualized Education Program [IEP] or 504 plan). *Recommended:* participation in extracurricular activities and personal statement. Upon application, documentation of need for special services should be sent only to your LD program or unit. Upon acceptance, documentation of need for special services should be sent only to your LD program or unit. *Application deadline (institutional):* rolling/continuous for fall and rolling/continuous for spring. *Application deadline (LD program):* rolling/continuous for fall and rolling/continuous for spring.

LD program contact Prof. Mary M. Saltus, Coordinator of Supportive Learning Services, Box 50, Springfield, MA 01109. *Phone:* 413-747-6426. *Fax:* 413-787-1803. *E-mail:* aicsls@javanet. com.

Application contact American International College, 1000 State Street, Springfield, MA 01109-3189. *E-mail:* inquiry@www.aic. edu. *Web address:* http://www.aic.edu/.

AMERICAN UNIVERSITY
Washington, District of Columbia

Students with LD Served by Program	200	ADD/ADHD Services	✓
Staff	n/a	Summer Preparation Program	n/a
LD Program or Service Fee	n/a	Alternative Test Arrangements	✓
LD Program Began	1979	LD Student Organization	n/a

Learning Services Program began offering services in 1979. The program serves approximately 200 undergraduate students. Services are provided by academic advisers, counselors, LD specialists, and trained peer tutors.

Policies Students with LD may take up to 17 credit hours per semester; 12 credit hours per semester are required to maintain full-time status and to be eligible for financial aid. LD services are also available to graduate students.

Special preparation or orientation Held after classes begin.

Basic skills remediation Available in study skills, reading, time management, learning strategies, and written language. Offered one-on-one by graduate assistants/students and LD specialists.

Subject-area tutoring Available in most subjects. Offered one-on-one and in small groups by trained peer tutors.

Special courses Available in learning strategies and written composition skills. Some courses are offered for credit; some enter into overall grade point average.

Counseling and advisement Career counseling, individual counseling, small-group counseling, and support groups are available. Academic advisement by a staff member affiliated with the program is available.

Auxiliary aids and services *Aids:* scan and read programs (e.g., Kurzweil), screen-enlarging programs. *Services and accommodations:* advocates, priority registration, alternative test arrangements, readers, note-takers, and scribes.

ADD/ADHD Students with ADD/ADHD are eligible for the same services available to students with LD, as well as distraction-free study areas, distraction-free testing environments, medication management, personal coach or mentors, and support groups for ADD/ADHD.

Application *Required:* high school transcript, participation in extracurricular activities, ACT or SAT I (extended-time or untimed test accepted), personal statement, letter(s) of recommendation, separate application to your LD program or unit, and psychoeducational report (3 years old or less). *Recommended:* interview. Upon application, documentation of need for special services should be sent only to your LD program or unit. Upon acceptance, documentation of need for special services should be sent only to your LD program or unit. *Application deadline (institutional):* 2/1 for fall. *Application deadline (LD program):* 2/1 for fall.

LD program contact Helen Steinberg, Coordinator, Learning Services Program, Mary Graydon Center 201, 4400 Massachusetts Avenue, NW, Washington, DC 20016-8027. *Phone:* 202-885-3360. *Fax:* 202-885-1042. *E-mail:* hsteinb@american.edu.

Application contact American University, 4400 Massachusetts Avenue, NW, Washington, DC 20016-8001. *E-mail:* afa@american. edu. *Web address:* http://www.american.edu/.

ANDERSON UNIVERSITY
Anderson, Indiana

Students with LD Served by Program	60	ADD/ADHD Services	✓
Staff	1 full-time, 1 part-time	Summer Preparation Program	n/a
LD Program or Service Fee	n/a	Alternative Test Arrangements	✓
LD Program Began	1987	LD Student Organization	n/a

Disabled Student Services began offering services in 1987. The program serves approximately 60 undergraduate students. Faculty consists of 1 full-time and 1 part-time staff member. Services are provided by special education teachers and LD specialists.

Policies Students with LD may take up to 16 credit hours per semester; 12 credit hours per semester are required to maintain full-time status and to be eligible for financial aid. LD services are also available to graduate students.

Subject-area tutoring Available in all subjects. Offered one-on-one and in small groups by trained peer tutors and LD specialists.

Special courses Available in study skills. All courses are offered for credit; none enter into overall grade point average.

Auxiliary aids and services *Aids:* calculators, personal computers, screen-enlarging programs, tape recorders, taped textbooks if recommended in testing. *Services and accommodations:* alternative test arrangements, readers, scribes, and notetakers if determined in testing report.

ADD/ADHD Students with ADD/ADHD are eligible for the same services available to students with LD

Application *Required:* high school transcript, ACT or SAT I (extended-time or untimed test accepted), interview, letter(s) of recommendation, psychoeducational report (3 years old or less), and documentation of high school services (e.g., Individualized Education Program [IEP] or 504 plan). Upon application, documentation of need for special services should be sent to both admissions and your LD program or unit. Upon acceptance, documentation of need for special services should be sent to both admissions and your LD program or unit. *Application*

deadline (institutional): rolling/continuous for fall and rolling/continuous for spring. *Application deadline (LD program):* rolling/continuous for fall and rolling/continuous for spring.
LD program contact Rinda Vogelgesang, Director, Disabled Student Services, 1100 East 5th Street, Kissinger Learning Center, Anderson, IN 46012. *Phone:* 765-641-4226. *Fax:* 765-641-3851. *E-mail:* rsvogel@anderson.edu.
Application contact Anderson University, 1100 East Fifth Street, Anderson, IN 46012-3495. *E-mail:* info@anderson.edu. *Web address:* http://www.anderson.edu/.

ARKANSAS STATE UNIVERSITY
Jonesboro, State University, Arkansas

Students with LD Served by Program	150	ADD/ADHD Services	✓
Staff	1 full-time, 3 part-time	Summer Preparation Program	n/a
LD Program or Service Fee	n/a	Alternative Test Arrangements	✓
LD Program Began	n/a	LD Student Organization	✓

Disability Services serves approximately 150 undergraduate students. Faculty consists of 1 full-time and 3 part-time staff members. Services are provided by graduate assistants/students, LD specialists, and professional tutors.
Policies The college has written policies regarding course substitutions. Students with LD may take up to 18 credit hours per semester; 12 credit hours per semester are required to maintain full-time status; 6 credit hours per semester are required to be eligible for financial aid. LD services are also available to graduate students.
Basic skills remediation Available in study skills, time management, social skills, and learning strategies. Offered in small groups by LD specialists.
Special courses Available in study skills. No courses are offered for credit; none enter into overall grade point average.
Counseling and advisement Individual counseling is available.
Auxiliary aids and services *Aids:* calculators, personal computers, personal spelling/word-use assistants (e.g., Franklin Speller), scan and read programs (e.g., Kurzweil), screen-enlarging programs, screen readers, tape recorders, taped textbooks. *Services and accommodations:* advocates, priority registration, alternative test arrangements, readers, note-takers, and scribes.
Student organization There is a student organization for students with LD.
ADD/ADHD Students with ADD/ADHD are eligible for the same services available to students with LD, as well as distraction-free testing environments.
Application *Required:* ACT (extended-time or untimed test accepted), separate application to your LD program or unit, and psychoeducational report (3 years old or less). *Recommended:* documentation of high school services (e.g., Individualized Education Program [IEP] or 504 plan). Upon application, documentation of need for special services should be sent only to your LD program or unit. Upon acceptance, documentation of need for special services should be sent only to your LD program or unit. *Application deadline (institutional):* rolling/continuous for fall and rolling/continuous for spring. *Application deadline (LD program):* rolling/continuous for fall and rolling/continuous for spring.
LD program contact Dr. Philip Hestand, Learning Disability Specialist, PO Box 0360, State University, AR 72467-0360. *Phone:* 870-972-3964. *Fax:* 870-910-8048. *E-mail:* phestand@chickasaw.astate.edu.

Application contact Arkansas State University, P.O. Box 1630, State University, AR 72467. *E-mail:* admissions@chickasaw.astate.edu. *Web address:* http://www.astate.edu/.

ATLANTIC UNION COLLEGE
South Lancaster, Massachusetts

Students with LD Served by Program	35	ADD/ADHD Services	✓
Staff	1 full-time, 3 part-time	Summer Preparation Program	✓
LD Program or Service Fee	n/a	Alternative Test Arrangements	✓
LD Program Began	1994	LD Student Organization	n/a

The Center for Academic Success began offering services in 1994. The program serves approximately 35 undergraduate students. Faculty consists of 1 full-time and 3 part-time staff members. Services are provided by academic advisers, counselors, remediation/learning specialists, diagnostic specialists, special education teachers, LD specialists, and professional tutors.
Policies The college has written policies regarding course substitutions. Students with LD may take up to 12 credit hours per semester; 12 credit hours per semester are required to maintain full-time status and to be eligible for financial aid. LD services are also available to graduate students.
Special preparation or orientation Optional summer program offered prior to entering college. Optional orientation held during summer prior to enrollment and individually by special arrangement.
Diagnostic testing Available for auditory processing, spoken language, learning strategies, reading, written language, learning styles, and visual processing.
Basic skills remediation Available in auditory processing, study skills, reading, time management, handwriting, visual processing, learning strategies, spelling, written language, math, and spoken language. Offered one-on-one and in class-size groups by special education teachers, LD specialists, and professional tutors.
Subject-area tutoring Available in all subjects. Offered one-on-one and in small groups by professional tutors, trained peer tutors, and LD specialists.
Special courses Available in study skills, college survival skills, test taking, reading, time management, learning strategies, vocabulary development, and written composition skills. All courses are offered for credit; all enter into overall grade point average.
Counseling and advisement Career counseling, individual counseling, small-group counseling, and support groups are available. Academic advisement by a staff member affiliated with the program is available.
Auxiliary aids and services *Aids:* personal computers, tape recorders, taped textbooks. *Services and accommodations:* advocates, priority registration, alternative test arrangements, and note-takers.
ADD/ADHD Students with ADD/ADHD are eligible for the same services available to students with LD, as well as support groups for ADD/ADHD.
Application *Required:* letter(s) of recommendation and high school transcript or GED (250 or above). *Recommended:* participation in extracurricular activities and ACT or SAT I (extended-time or untimed test accepted). Upon application, documentation of need for special services should be sent only to your LD program or unit. Upon acceptance, documentation of need for special services should be sent to both admissions and your LD program or unit. *Application deadline (institutional):* rolling/

Atlantic Union College (continued)

continuous for fall and rolling/continuous for spring. *Application deadline (LD program):* rolling/continuous for fall and rolling/continuous for spring.

LD program contact Elizabeth Anderson, Director, Center for Academic Success, PO Box 1000, South Lancaster, MA 01561-1000. *Phone:* 978-368-2416. *Fax:* 978-368-2015. *E-mail:* eanderson@atlanticuc.edu.

Application contact Atlantic Union College, PO Box 1000, South Lancaster, MA 01561-1000. *E-mail:* enroll@math.atlanticuc.edu. *Web address:* http://www.atlanticuc.edu/.

AUGSBURG COLLEGE
Minneapolis, Minnesota

Students with LD Served by Program	95	ADD/ADHD Services	✓
Staff	6 full-time	Summer Preparation Program	n/a
LD Program or Service Fee	n/a	Alternative Test Arrangements	✓
LD Program Began	1982	LD Student Organization	n/a

Center for Learning and Adaptive Student Services (CLASS) began offering services in 1982. The program serves approximately 95 undergraduate students. Faculty consists of 6 full-time staff members. Services are provided by counselors, special education teachers, and LD specialists.

Policies Students with LD may take up to 18 semester credit hours per term; 12 semester credit hours per term are required to maintain full-time status; 8 semester credit hours per term are required to be eligible for financial aid. LD services are also available to graduate students.

Special preparation or orientation Required orientation held before registration, before classes begin, after classes begin, and during summer prior to enrollment.

Basic skills remediation Available in study skills, computer skills, reading, time management, learning strategies, spelling, written language, math, and spoken language. Offered one-on-one by special education teachers and LD specialists.

Auxiliary aids and services *Aids:* personal computers, personal spelling/word-use assistants (e.g., Franklin Speller), scan and read programs (e.g., Kurzweil), screen-enlarging programs, screen readers, speech recognition programs (e.g., Dragon), tape recorders, taped textbooks. *Services and accommodations:* alternative test arrangements, readers, note-takers, and scribes.

ADD/ADHD Students with ADD/ADHD are eligible for the same services available to students with LD

Application *Required:* high school transcript, ACT or SAT I (extended-time or untimed test accepted), interview, personal statement, letter(s) of recommendation, separate application to your LD program or unit, and psychoeducational report (3 years old or less). *Recommended:* documentation of high school services (e.g., Individualized Education Program [IEP] or 504 plan). Upon application, documentation of need for special services should be sent only to your LD program or unit. Upon acceptance, documentation of need for special services should be sent only to your LD program or unit. *Application deadline (institutional):* rolling/continuous for fall and rolling/continuous for spring. *Application deadline (LD program):* rolling/continuous for fall and rolling/continuous for spring.

LD program contact Dr. Robert F. Doljanac, Director, CB #57, 2211 Riverside Avenue, Minneapolis, MN 55454. *Phone:* 612-330-1648. *Fax:* 612-330-1137. *E-mail:* doljanac@augsburg.edu.

Application contact Augsburg College, 2211 Riverside Avenue, Minneapolis, MN 55454-1351. *E-mail:* admissions@augsburg.edu. *Web address:* http://www.augsburg.edu/.

BARAT COLLEGE
Lake Forest, Illinois

Students with LD Served by Program	50	ADD/ADHD Services	✓
Staff	2 full-time, 3 part-time	Summer Preparation Program	n/a
LD Program or Service Fee	varies	Alternative Test Arrangements	✓
LD Program Began	1980	LD Student Organization	n/a

Learning Opportunities Program (LOP) began offering services in 1980. The program serves approximately 50 undergraduate students. Faculty consists of 2 full-time and 3 part-time staff members. Services are provided by LD specialists.

Policies Students with LD may take up to 18 semester hours per semester; 12 semester hours per semester are required to maintain full-time status; 6 semester hours per semester are required to be eligible for financial aid.

Fees *LD Program or Service Fee:* ranges from $1350 to $3600 per year. *Diagnostic Testing Fee:* $750.

Special preparation or orientation Optional orientation held before classes begin.

Diagnostic testing Available for auditory processing, spelling, handwriting, spoken language, study skills, reading, written language, visual processing, math, and reasoning, problem solving.

Basic skills remediation Available in auditory processing, study skills, computer skills, reading, time management, handwriting, visual processing, learning strategies, spelling, written language, math, and spoken language. Offered one-on-one by LD specialists.

Subject-area tutoring Available in all subjects. Offered one-on-one by graduate assistants/students and LD specialists.

Counseling and advisement Individual counseling and support groups are available.

Auxiliary aids and services *Aids:* screen readers, tape recorders, taped textbooks. *Services and accommodations:* alternative test arrangements and note-takers.

ADD/ADHD Students with ADD/ADHD are eligible for the same services available to students with LD, as well as distraction-free testing environments.

Application *Required:* high school transcript, ACT or SAT I (extended-time or untimed test accepted), interview, personal statement, letter(s) of recommendation, separate application to your LD program or unit, and psychoeducational report (4 years old or less). Upon application, documentation of need for special services should be sent only to your LD program or unit. Upon acceptance, documentation of need for special services should be sent only to your LD program or unit. *Application deadline (institutional):* rolling/continuous for fall and rolling/continuous for spring.

LD program contact Donna Witikka, Administrative Assistant, 700 East Westleigh Road, Lake Forest, IL 60045. *Phone:* 847-604-6321. *Fax:* 847-604-6377. *E-mail:* dwitikka@barat.edu.

Application contact Barat College, 700 East Westleigh Road, Lake Forest, IL 60045-3297. *Web address:* http://www.barat.edu/.

BARRY UNIVERSITY
Miami Shores, Florida

Students with LD Served by Program	45	ADD/ADHD Services	✓
Staff	3 full-time, 15 part-time	Summer Preparation Program	n/a
LD Program or Service Fee	✓	Alternative Test Arrangements	✓
LD Program Began	1994	LD Student Organization	n/a

Center for Advanced Learning (CAL) began offering services in 1994. The program serves approximately 45 undergraduate students. Faculty consists of 3 full-time and 15 part-time staff members. Services are provided by academic advisers, remediation/learning specialists, counselors, diagnostic specialists, special education teachers, LD specialists, and professional tutors.

Policies 12 credit hours per semester are required to maintain full-time status and to be eligible for financial aid. LD services are also available to graduate students.

Fees *LD Program or Service Fee:* $1750 per year.

Special preparation or orientation Optional orientation held before registration and before classes begin.

Diagnostic testing Available for spelling, intelligence, study skills, learning strategies, reading, written language, learning styles, and math.

Basic skills remediation Available in study skills, computer skills, reading, time management, learning strategies, spelling, written language, and math. Offered one-on-one, in small groups, and class-size groups by computer-based instruction, regular education teachers, special education teachers, LD specialists, and professional tutors.

Subject-area tutoring Available in all subjects. Offered one-on-one, in small groups, and class-size groups by computer-based instruction, professional tutors, and LD specialists.

Special courses Available in college survival skills, reading, and written composition skills. All courses are offered for credit; none enter into overall grade point average.

Counseling and advisement Career counseling, individual counseling, and small-group counseling are available. Academic advisement by a staff member affiliated with the program is available.

Auxiliary aids and services *Aids:* scan and read programs (e.g., Kurzweil), screen readers, speech recognition programs (e.g., Dragon), tape recorders. *Services and accommodations:* advocates, priority registration, and alternative test arrangements.

ADD/ADHD Students with ADD/ADHD are eligible for the same services available to students with LD, as well as personal coach or mentors.

Application *Required:* high school transcript, ACT or SAT I (extended-time or untimed test accepted), interview, personal statement, letter(s) of recommendation, separate application to your LD program or unit, and psychoeducational report (3 years old or less). *Recommended:* documentation of high school services (e.g., Individualized Education Program [IEP] or 504 plan). Upon application, documentation of need for special services should be sent only to your LD program or unit. Upon acceptance, documentation of need for special services should be sent only to your LD program or unit. *Application deadline (institutional):* rolling/continuous for fall and rolling/continuous for spring. *Application deadline (LD program):* rolling/continuous for fall and rolling/continuous for spring.

LD program contact Vivian Castro, Coordinator, CAL Program, 11300 Northeast 2nd Avenue, Miami Shores, FL 33161. *Phone:* 305-899-3461. *Fax:* 305-899-3778. *E-mail:* vcastro@mail.barry.edu.

Application contact Dave Fletcher, Director of Admissions, Barry University, 11300 Northeast Second Avenue, Miami Shores, FL 33161-6695. *Phone:* 308-699-3146. *Web address:* http://www.barry.edu/.

BETHANY COLLEGE
Bethany, West Virginia

Students with LD Served by Program	40	ADD/ADHD Services	✓
Staff	2 full-time	Summer Preparation Program	✓
LD Program or Service Fee	varies	Alternative Test Arrangements	✓
LD Program Began	1987	LD Student Organization	n/a

Special Advising began offering services in 1987. The program serves approximately 40 undergraduate students. Faculty consists of 2 full-time staff members. Services are provided by LD specialists.

Policies The college has written policies regarding course substitutions and substitution and waivers of requirements for admission and graduation. Students with LD may take up to 18 credit hours per semester; 12 credit hours per semester are required to maintain full-time status and to be eligible for financial aid.

Fees *LD Program or Service Fee:* ranges from $500 to $2500 per year.

Special preparation or orientation Required summer program offered prior to entering college. Required orientation held during summer prior to enrollment and individually by special arrangement.

Basic skills remediation Available in study skills, computer skills, reading, time management, social skills, learning strategies, written language, and math. Offered one-on-one and in class-size groups by computer-based instruction, regular education teachers, and LD specialists.

Subject-area tutoring Available in all subjects. Offered one-on-one and in small groups by computer-based instruction, trained peer tutors, and LD specialists.

Special courses Available in college survival skills, test taking, reading, time management, learning strategies, math, and written composition skills. All courses are offered for credit; none enter into overall grade point average.

Counseling and advisement Career counseling, individual counseling, small-group counseling, and support groups are available.

Auxiliary aids and services *Aids:* calculators, personal computers, personal spelling/word-use assistants (e.g., Franklin Speller), tape recorders, taped textbooks, spellcheck and grammar check computers. *Services and accommodations:* advocates, alternative test arrangements, readers, and note-takers.

ADD/ADHD Students with ADD/ADHD are eligible for the same services available to students with LD, as well as distraction-free study areas, distraction-free testing environments, medication management, personal coach or mentors, and support groups for ADD/ADHD.

Application *Required:* high school transcript, ACT or SAT I (extended-time or untimed test accepted), interview, personal statement, letter(s) of recommendation, separate application to your LD program or unit, psychoeducational report (3 years old or less), and 2.0 GPA. *Recommended:* participation in extracurricular activities and documentation of high school services (e.g., Individualized Education Program [IEP] or 504 plan). Upon application, documentation of need for special services should be sent only to admissions. Upon acceptance, documentation of need for special services should be sent only to your LD program or unit. *Application deadline (institutional):* rolling/continuous for fall and rolling/continuous for spring. *Application deadline (LD program):* rolling/continuous for fall and rolling/continuous for spring.

LD program contact Kathy Tagg, Director of Academic Services and Special Advising, 6 Old Main, Bethany, WV 26032. *Phone:* 304-829-7225. *Fax:* 304-829-7108. *E-mail:* k.tagg@mail.bethanywv.edu.

Bethany College (continued)

Application contact Bethany College, Bethany, WV 26032. *E-mail:* g.forney@mail.bethany.wvnet.edu. *Web address:* http://www.bethanywv.edu/.

BOSTON UNIVERSITY
Boston, Massachusetts

Students with LD Served by Program	550	ADD/ADHD Services	✓
Staff	2 full-time, 10 part-time	Summer Preparation Program	✓
LD Program or Service Fee	✓	Alternative Test Arrangements	n/a
LD Program Began	1978	LD Student Organization	n/a

Learning Disability Support Service (LDSS) began offering services in 1978. The program serves approximately 550 undergraduate students. Faculty consists of 2 full-time and 10 part-time staff members. Services are provided by remediation/learning specialists, diagnostic specialists, LD specialists, professional tutors, and clinical neuropsychologist, LD coordinator.
Policies LD services are also available to graduate students.
Fees *LD Program or Service Fee:* $3200 per year.
Special preparation or orientation Optional summer program offered prior to entering college.
ADD/ADHD Students with ADD/ADHD are eligible for the same services available to students with LD
LD program contact Dr. Lorraine E. Wolf, Clinical Director, Office of Disability Services, 19 Deerfield Street, Boston, MA 02215. *Phone:* 617-353-3658. *Fax:* 617-353-9646. *E-mail:* lwolf@bu.edu.
Application contact Boston University, 121 Bay State Road, Boston, MA 02215. *E-mail:* admissions@bu.edu. *Web address:* http://www.bu.edu/.

BRENAU UNIVERSITY
Gainesville, Georgia

Students with LD Served by Program	46	ADD/ADHD Services	✓
Staff	2 full-time, 1 part-time	Summer Preparation Program	✓
LD Program or Service Fee	varies	Alternative Test Arrangements	✓
LD Program Began	1984	LD Student Organization	✓

Brenau University Learning Center began offering services in 1984. The program serves approximately 46 undergraduate students. Faculty consists of 2 full-time staff members and 1 part-time staff member. Services are provided by academic advisers, remediation/learning specialists, counselors, LD specialists, and professional tutors.
Policies Students with LD may take up to 17 credits per semester; 12 credits per semester are required to maintain full-time status and to be eligible for financial aid. LD services are also available to graduate students.
Fees *LD Program or Service Fee:* ranges from $900 to $6000 per year.
Special preparation or orientation Optional summer program offered prior to entering college. Required orientation held during registration, before classes begin, and during summer prior to enrollment.
Basic skills remediation Available in auditory processing, study skills, computer skills, reading, time management, social skills, visual processing, learning strategies, spelling, written language, math, and spoken language. Offered one-on-one by LD specialists.
Subject-area tutoring Available in all subjects. Offered one-on-one by professional tutors and LD specialists.

Special courses Available in learning strategies. All courses are offered for credit; all enter into overall grade point average.
Counseling and advisement Academic advisement by a staff member affiliated with the program is available.
Auxiliary aids and services *Aids:* calculators, personal computers, personal spelling/word-use assistants (e.g., Franklin Speller), scan and read programs (e.g., Kurzweil), screen-enlarging programs, screen readers, tape recorders, taped textbooks. *Services and accommodations:* advocates, priority registration, alternative test arrangements, and readers.
Student organization There is a student organization for students with LD.
ADD/ADHD Students with ADD/ADHD are eligible for the same services available to students with LD, as well as distraction-free study areas, distraction-free testing environments, personal coach or mentors, and support groups for ADD/ADHD.
Application *Required:* high school transcript, ACT or SAT I (extended-time or untimed test accepted), interview, letter(s) of recommendation, and psychoeducational report (3 years old or less). *Recommended:* participation in extracurricular activities, personal statement, and documentation of high school services (e.g., Individualized Education Program [IEP] or 504 plan). Upon application, documentation of need for special services should be sent only to admissions. Upon acceptance, documentation of need for special services should be sent to both admissions and your LD program or unit. *Application deadline (institutional):* rolling/continuous for fall and rolling/continuous for spring. *Application deadline (LD program):* rolling/continuous for fall and rolling/continuous for spring.
LD program contact Dr. Vincent Yamilkoski, Professor of Education/Director of Learning Disabilities, 1 Centennial Circle, Gainesville, GA 30501. *Phone:* 770-534-6134. *Fax:* 770-534-6221. *E-mail:* vyamilkoski@lib.brenau.edu.
Application contact Brenau University, One Centennial Circle, Gainesville, GA 30501-3697. *E-mail:* upchurch@lib.brenau.edu. *Web address:* http://www.brenau.edu/.

CALIFORNIA STATE UNIVERSITY, HAYWARD
Hayward, California

Students with LD Served by Program	100	ADD/ADHD Services	✓
Staff	1 full-time, 1 part-time	Summer Preparation Program	n/a
LD Program or Service Fee	n/a	Alternative Test Arrangements	✓
LD Program Began	n/a	LD Student Organization	n/a

Student Disability Resource Center serves approximately 100 undergraduate students. Faculty consists of 1 full-time and 1 part-time staff member. Services are provided by counselors and LD specialists.
Policies The college has written policies regarding course substitutions and substitution and waivers of requirements for admission and graduation. Students with LD may take up to 18 units per quarter; 12 units per quarter are required to maintain full-time status; 6 units per quarter are required to be eligible for financial aid. LD services are also available to graduate students.
Subject-area tutoring Available in some subjects. Offered one-on-one through the Trio program.
Counseling and advisement Individual counseling and support groups are available.
Auxiliary aids and services *Aids:* calculators, personal computers, personal spelling/word-use assistants (e.g., Franklin Speller), scan and read programs (e.g., Kurzweil), screen-enlarging programs, screen readers, speech recognition pro-

grams (e.g., Dragon), tape recorders, taped textbooks. *Services and accommodations:* priority registration, alternative test arrangements, readers, note-takers, and scribes.
ADD/ADHD Students with ADD/ADHD are eligible for the same services available to students with LD, as well as distraction-free testing environments.
Application *Required:* high school transcript, ACT or SAT I (extended-time tests accepted), personal statement, separate application to your LD program or unit, and psychoeducational report. *Recommended:* interview and letter(s) of recommendation. Upon application, documentation of need for special services should be sent only to your LD program or unit. Upon acceptance, documentation of need for special services should be sent only to your LD program or unit. *Application deadline (institutional):* rolling/continuous for fall and rolling/continuous for spring. *Application deadline (LD program):* rolling/continuous for fall and rolling/continuous for spring.
LD program contact Russell Wong, Learning Resources Counselor, 25800 Carlos Bee Boulevard, Hayward, CA 94542. *Phone:* 520-885-3868. *Fax:* 510-885-7400. *E-mail:* rwong@csuhayward. edu.
Application contact Susan Lakis, Associate Director of Admissions, California State University, Hayward, 25800 Carlos Bee Boulevard, Hayward, CA 94542-3000. *Phone:* 510-885-3248. *E-mail:* adminfo@csuhayward.edu. *Web address:* http://www. csuhayward.edu/.

CALIFORNIA STATE UNIVERSITY, NORTHRIDGE
Northridge, California

Students with LD Served by Program	378	ADD/ADHD Services	✓
Staff	1 full-time, 2 part-time	Summer Preparation Program	✓
LD Program or Service Fee	n/a	Alternative Test Arrangements	✓
LD Program Began	1986	LD Student Organization	n/a

Students with Disabilities Resources began offering services in 1986. The program serves approximately 378 undergraduate students. Faculty consists of 1 full-time and 2 part-time staff members. Services are provided by LD specialists.
Policies The college has written policies regarding course substitutions. Students with LD may take up to 18 semester hours per semester; 12 semester hours per semester are required to maintain full-time status. LD services are also available to graduate students.
Special preparation or orientation Optional summer program offered prior to entering college. Optional orientation held before classes begin and during summer prior to enrollment.
Diagnostic testing Available for auditory processing, motor skills, spelling, neuropsychological, spoken language, intelligence, reading, written language, visual processing, and math.
Basic skills remediation Available in study skills, computer skills, time management, and learning strategies. Offered one-on-one by trained peer tutors.
Subject-area tutoring Available in some subjects. Offered one-on-one by graduate assistants/students and trained peer tutors.
Counseling and advisement Individual counseling and support groups are available.
Auxiliary aids and services *Aids:* personal computers, scan and read programs (e.g., Kurzweil), screen-enlarging programs, screen readers, speech recognition programs (e.g., Dragon), taped textbooks. *Services and accommodations:* priority registration, alternative test arrangements, readers, note-takers, and scribes.

ADD/ADHD Students with ADD/ADHD are eligible for the same services available to students with LD, as well as distraction-free study areas and distraction-free testing environments.
Application *Required:* high school transcript and ACT or SAT I (extended-time or untimed test accepted). *Recommended:* interview, personal statement, letter(s) of recommendation, and psychoeducational report (3 years old or less). Upon acceptance, documentation of need for special services should be sent only to your LD program or unit.
LD program contact Dr. Lee Axelrod, Learning Disability Specialist, 18111 Nordhoff Street, Northridge, CA 91330-8264. *Phone:* 818-677-2684. *Fax:* 818-677-4932. *E-mail:* lee.axelrod@csun. edu.
Application contact Mary Baxton, Associate Director of Admissions and Records, California State University, Northridge, 18111 Nordhoff Street, Northridge, CA 91330. *Phone:* 818-677-3777. *E-mail:* outreach.recruitment@csun.edu. *Web address:* http:// www.csun.edu/.

CALIFORNIA STATE UNIVERSITY, SACRAMENTO
Sacramento, California

Students with LD Served by Program	330	ADD/ADHD Services	✓
Staff	10 full-time, 12 part-time	Summer Preparation Program	n/a
LD Program or Service Fee	n/a	Alternative Test Arrangements	✓
LD Program Began	1980	LD Student Organization	✓

Services to Students with Disabilities began offering services in 1980. The program serves approximately 330 undergraduate students. Faculty consists of 10 full-time and 12 part-time staff members. Services are provided by counselors, graduate assistants/students, LD specialists, trained peer tutors, and Support Services Coordinator.
Policies The college has written policies regarding course substitutions. LD services are also available to graduate students.
Special preparation or orientation Required orientation held before registration, during registration, before classes begin, after classes begin, during summer prior to enrollment, and individually by special arrangement.
Diagnostic testing Available for auditory processing, motor skills, spelling, handwriting, neuropsychological, spoken language, intelligence, personality, study skills, learning strategies, written language, learning styles, social skills, visual processing, and math.
Basic skills remediation Available in auditory processing, study skills, reading, time management, social skills, visual processing, learning strategies, written language, and math. Offered one-on-one, in small groups, and class-size groups by LD specialists.
Subject-area tutoring Available in most subjects. Offered one-on-one by graduate assistants/students and trained peer tutors.
Special courses Available in career planning, oral communication skills, study skills, college survival skills, practical computer skills, test taking, health and nutrition, reading, time management, learning strategies, self-advocacy, vocabulary development, math, stress management, and written composition skills. Most courses are offered for credit; most enter into overall grade point average.
Counseling and advisement Career counseling, individual counseling, small-group counseling, and support groups are available.

California State University, Sacramento (continued)

Auxiliary aids and services *Aids:* personal computers, scan and read programs (e.g., Kurzweil), tape recorders. *Services and accommodations:* advocates, priority registration, alternative test arrangements, readers, note-takers, scribes, and tutors.

Student organization There is a student organization for students with LD.

ADD/ADHD Students with ADD/ADHD are eligible for the same services available to students with LD, as well as distraction-free testing environments, medication management and support groups for ADD/ADHD.

Application *Required:* high school transcript, SAT I (extended-time test accepted), personal statement, psychoeducational report (5 years old or less), and documentation of high school services (e.g., Individualized Education Program [IEP] or 504 plan). *Recommended:* participation in extracurricular activities, ACT (extended-time test accepted), interview, letter(s) of recommendation, and separate application to your LD program or unit. Upon application, documentation of need for special services should be sent only to admissions. Upon acceptance, documentation of need for special services should be sent to both admissions and your LD program or unit. *Application deadline (institutional):* 9/3 for fall. *Application deadline (LD program):* rolling/continuous for fall and rolling/continuous for spring.

LD program contact Kathleen A. Crown, Learning Disabilities Specialist, 6000 J Street, Sacramento, CA 95819. *Phone:* 916-278-6955. *Fax:* 916-248-7825. *E-mail:* cronink@csus.edu.

Application contact Doris Tormes, Director of University Outreach Services, California State University, Sacramento, 6000 J Street, Sacramento, CA 95819-6048. *Phone:* 916-278-7362. *E-mail:* glasmirel@csus.edu. *Web address:* http://www.csus.edu/.

CENTENARY COLLEGE

Hackettstown, New Jersey

Students with LD Served by Program	55	ADD/ADHD Services	✓
Staff	2 full-time, 3 part-time	Summer Preparation Program	✓
LD Program or Service Fee	✓	Alternative Test Arrangements	✓
LD Program Began	1990	LD Student Organization	n/a

Office of Disability Services—Project ABLE—Intensive Support Program began offering services in 1990. The program serves approximately 55 undergraduate students. Faculty consists of 2 full-time and 3 part-time staff members. Services are provided by academic advisers, remediation/learning specialists, counselors, LD specialists, trained peer tutors, and professional tutors.

Policies Students with LD may take up to 15 credit hours per semester; 12 credit hours per semester are required to maintain full-time status and to be eligible for financial aid.

Fees *LD Program or Service Fee:* $1850 per year.

Special preparation or orientation Summer program offered prior to entering college. Optional orientation held before classes begin, during summer prior to enrollment, and individually by special arrangement.

Basic skills remediation Available in study skills, reading, time management, social skills, learning strategies, spelling, written language, and math. Offered one-on-one and in small groups by computer-based instruction, regular education teachers, special education teachers, LD specialists, and professional tutors.

Subject-area tutoring Available in some subjects. Offered one-on-one by computer-based instruction, professional tutors, graduate assistants/students, trained peer tutors, and LD specialists.

Special courses Available in reading, math, and written composition skills. Most courses are offered for credit; most enter into overall grade point average.

Counseling and advisement Career counseling, individual counseling, and small-group counseling are available. Academic advisement by a staff member affiliated with the program is available.

Auxiliary aids and services *Aids:* calculators, personal computers, scan and read programs (e.g., Kurzweil), tape recorders, taped textbooks. advocates, priority registration, alternative test arrangements, readers, and note-takers.

ADD/ADHD Students with ADD/ADHD are eligible for the same services available to students with LD, as well as distraction-free study areas, distraction-free testing environments, medication management and personal coach or mentors.

Application *Required:* high school transcript, ACT or SAT I (extended-time or untimed test accepted), psychoeducational report (3 years old or less), and documentation of high school services (e.g., Individualized Education Program [IEP] or 504 plan). *Recommended:* participation in extracurricular activities, interview, personal statement, and letter(s) of recommendation. Upon application, documentation of need for special services should be sent only to admissions. Upon acceptance, documentation of need for special services should be sent only to your LD program or unit. *Application deadline (institutional):* rolling/continuous for fall and rolling/continuous for spring. *Application deadline (LD program):* 5/15 for fall and 12/15 for spring.

LD program contact Jeffrey R. Zimdahl, Director of Disability Services, 400 Jefferson Street, Hackettstown, NJ 07840. *Phone:* 908-852-1400 Ext. 2251. *Fax:* 908-813-1984. *E-mail:* zimdahlj@centenarycollege.edu.

Application contact Centenary College, 400 Jefferson Street, Hackettstown, NJ 07840-2100. *Web address:* http://www.centenarycollege.edu/.

COLLEGE MISERICORDIA

Dallas, Pennsylvania

Students with LD Served by Program	75	ADD/ADHD Services	n/a
Staff	4 full-time	Summer Preparation Program	n/a
LD Program or Service Fee	n/a	Alternative Test Arrangements	✓
LD Program Began	1979	LD Student Organization	n/a

Alternative Learner's Project (ALP) began offering services in 1979. The program serves approximately 75 undergraduate students. Faculty consists of 4 full-time staff members. Services are provided by counselors and LD specialists.

Policies Students with LD may take up to 15 credits per semester; 12 credits per semester are required to maintain full-time status and to be eligible for financial aid.

Special preparation or orientation Required orientation held before classes begin and during orientation weekend.

Basic skills remediation Available in study skills, time management, and learning strategies. Offered one-on-one by LD specialists.

Subject-area tutoring Available in all subjects. Offered one-on-one and in small groups by professional tutors, trained peer tutors, and LD specialists.

Special courses Available in career planning, study skills, test taking, time management, and learning strategies. No courses are offered for credit; none enter into overall grade point average.

Counseling and advisement Career counseling and individual counseling are available.

Auxiliary aids and services *Aids:* calculators, tape recorders, taped textbooks. *Services and accommodations:* alternative test arrangements and note-takers.

Application *Required:* high school transcript, ACT or SAT I (extended-time or untimed test accepted), interview, personal statement, letter(s) of recommendation, psychoeducational report, and documentation of high school services (e.g., Individualized Education Program [IEP] or 504 plan). Upon application, documentation of need for special services should be sent only to admissions. Upon acceptance, documentation of need for special services should be sent only to admissions. *Application deadline (institutional):* rolling/continuous for fall and rolling/continuous for spring. *Application deadline (LD program):* rolling/continuous for fall and rolling/continuous for spring.

LD program contact Dr. Joseph Rogan, Director/Professor, 301 Lake Street, Dallas, PA 18612. *Phone:* 570-674-6347. *Fax:* 570-675-2441. *E-mail:* jrogan@miseri.edu.

Application contact College Misericordia, 301 Lake Street, Dallas, PA 18612-1098. *Web address:* http://www.miseri.edu/.

COLLEGE OF MOUNT ST. JOSEPH
Cincinnati, Ohio

Students with LD Served by Program	85	ADD/ADHD Services	✓
Staff	2 full-time, 14 part-time	Summer Preparation Program	n/a
LD Program or Service Fee	varies	Alternative Test Arrangements	✓
LD Program Began	1982	LD Student Organization	n/a

Project EXCEL began offering services in 1982. The program serves approximately 85 undergraduate students. Faculty consists of 2 full-time and 14 part-time staff members. Services are provided by LD specialists and professional tutors.

Policies The college has written policies regarding substitution and waivers of requirements for admission. Students with LD may take up to 18 credit hours per semester; 12 credit hours per semester are required to maintain full-time status and to be eligible for financial aid. LD services are also available to graduate students.

Fees *LD Program or Service Fee:* ranges from $1500 to $3000 per year.

Basic skills remediation Available in study skills, time management, written language, and math. Offered one-on-one.

Subject-area tutoring Available in all subjects. Offered one-on-one and in small groups by professional tutors.

Special courses Available in learning strategies. All courses are offered for credit; all enter into overall grade point average.

Counseling and advisement Career counseling is available.

Auxiliary aids and services *Aids:* personal computers, screen-enlarging programs, speech recognition programs (e.g., Dragon), tape recorders, taped textbooks. *Services and accommodations:* advocates, alternative test arrangements, readers, note-takers, and scribes.

ADD/ADHD Students with ADD/ADHD are eligible for the same services available to students with LD, as well as distraction-free testing environments.

Application *Required:* high school transcript, ACT or SAT I (extended-time or untimed test accepted), interview, letter(s) of recommendation, separate application to your LD program or unit, and psychoeducational report (3 years old or less). *Recommended:* documentation of high school services (e.g., Individualized Education Program [IEP] or 504 plan). Upon application, documentation of need for special services should be sent only to your LD program or unit. Upon acceptance, documentation of need for special services should be sent only to your LD program or unit. *Application deadline (institutional):* rolling/

continuous for fall and rolling/continuous for spring. *Application deadline (LD program):* rolling/continuous for fall and rolling/continuous for spring.

LD program contact Jane Pohlman, Director, 5701 Delhi Road, Cincinnati, OH 45233. *Phone:* 513-244-4623. *Fax:* 513-244-4222. *E-mail:* jane_pohlman@mail.msj.edu.

Application contact College of Mount St. Joseph, 5701 Delhi Road, Cincinnati, OH 45233-1670. *E-mail:* edward_eckel@mail.msj.edu. *Web address:* http://www.msj.edu/.

CONCORDIA COLLEGE
Bronxville, New York

Students with LD Served by Program	25	ADD/ADHD Services	✓
Staff	3 part-time	Summer Preparation Program	n/a
LD Program or Service Fee	varies	Alternative Test Arrangements	✓
LD Program Began	1993	LD Student Organization	n/a

The Concordia Connection Program began offering services in 1993. The program serves approximately 25 undergraduate students. Faculty consists of 3 part-time staff members. Services are provided by counselors, LD specialists, trained peer tutors, and school psychologist.

Policies Students with LD may take up to 21 credits per semester; 12 credits per semester are required to maintain full-time status and to be eligible for financial aid.

Fees *LD Program or Service Fee:* ranges from $1500 to $3000 per year.

Special preparation or orientation Required orientation held before classes begin and during summer prior to enrollment.

Diagnostic testing Available for spelling, spoken language, intelligence, personality, study skills, learning strategies, reading, written language, learning styles, visual processing, and math.

Subject-area tutoring Available in most subjects. Offered one-on-one and in small groups by computer-based instruction, trained peer tutors, and LD specialists.

Special courses Available in college survival skills, test taking, time management, learning strategies, and self-advocacy.

Counseling and advisement Career counseling, individual counseling, and small-group counseling are available.

Auxiliary aids and services *Aids:* calculators, personal spelling/word-use assistants (e.g., Franklin Speller), speech recognition programs (e.g., Dragon), tape recorders. *Services and accommodations:* priority registration, alternative test arrangements, readers, note-takers, and scribes.

ADD/ADHD Students with ADD/ADHD are eligible for the same services available to students with LD, as well as distraction-free study areas and distraction-free testing environments.

Application *Required:* high school transcript, ACT or SAT I (extended-time or untimed test accepted), personal statement, letter(s) of recommendation, psychoeducational report (2 years old or less), and documentation of high school services (e.g., Individualized Education Program [IEP] or 504 plan). *Recommended:* participation in extracurricular activities and interview. Upon application, documentation of need for special services should be sent only to admissions. Upon acceptance, documentation of need for special services should be sent only to admissions. *Application deadline (institutional):* 3/15 for fall and 12/15 for spring. *Application deadline (LD program):* 3/15 for fall and 12/15 for spring.

LD program contact Dr. George Groth, Director, Connection Program, 171 White Plains Road, Bronxville, NY 10708. *Phone:* 914-337-9300 Ext. 2361. *Fax:* 914-268-0399. *E-mail:* ghg@concordia-ny.edu.

Concordia College (continued)

Application contact Concordia College, 171 White Plains Road, Bronxville, NY 10708-1998. *E-mail:* admission@concordia-ny.edu. *Web address:* http://www.concordia-ny.edu/.

CURRY COLLEGE
Milton, Massachusetts

Students with LD Served by Program	350	ADD/ADHD Services	✓
Staff	17 full-time, 14 part-time	Summer Preparation Program	✓
LD Program or Service Fee	✓	Alternative Test Arrangements	✓
LD Program Began	1970	LD Student Organization	n/a

Program for Advancement of Learning (PAL) began offering services in 1970. The program serves approximately 350 undergraduate students. Faculty consists of 17 full-time and 14 part-time staff members. Services are provided by LD specialists.

Policies Students with LD may take up to 18 credit hours per semester; 12 credit hours per semester are required to maintain full-time status; 6 credit hours per semester are required to be eligible for financial aid. LD services are also available to graduate students.

Fees *LD Program or Service Fee:* $3575 per year. *Diagnostic Testing Fee:* ranges from $500 to $900.

Special preparation or orientation Optional summer program offered prior to entering college. Optional orientation held during registration, during summer prior to enrollment, and individually by special arrangement.

Diagnostic testing Available for auditory processing, spelling, spoken language, intelligence, study skills, learning strategies, reading, written language, learning styles, visual processing, and math.

Basic skills remediation Available in auditory processing, study skills, computer skills, reading, time management, handwriting, social skills, visual processing, learning strategies, spelling, written language, math, and spoken language. Offered one-on-one and in small groups by LD specialists and professional mentors.

Subject-area tutoring Available in all subjects. Offered one-on-one, in small groups, and class-size groups by computer-based instruction, professional tutors, trained peer tutors, LD specialists, and coordinated by the Essential Skills Center.

Special courses Available in study skills, college survival skills, test taking, reading, time management, learning strategies, vocabulary development, and written composition skills. All courses are offered for credit; all enter into overall grade point average.

Counseling and advisement Career counseling, individual counseling, small-group counseling, and support groups are available.

Auxiliary aids and services *Aids:* calculators, personal computers, personal spelling/word-use assistants (e.g., Franklin Speller), scan and read programs (e.g., Kurzweil), screen readers, speech recognition programs (e.g., Dragon), tape recorders, taped textbooks, portable keyboards. *Services and accommodations:* advocates and alternative test arrangements.

ADD/ADHD Students with ADD/ADHD are eligible for the same services available to students with LD, as well as distraction-free study areas, distraction-free testing environments and ADD consultant available for individualized counseling.

Application *Required:* high school transcript, personal statement, letter(s) of recommendation, psychoeducational report (2 years old or less), and WAIS-R or WAIS-III and narrative report, achievement testing for levels in subject areas (i.e. math). *Recommended:* participation in extracurricular activities, ACT or SAT I (extended-time or untimed test accepted), interview, and documentation of high school services (e.g., Individualized Education Program [IEP] or 504 plan). Upon application, documentation of need for special services should be sent only to your LD program or unit. *Application deadline (institutional):* 4/1 for fall and 12/1 for spring. *Application deadline (LD program):* 3/1 for fall and 12/1 for spring.

LD program contact Sue Pratt, Coordinator of PAL, 1071 Blue Hill Avenue, Milton, MA 02186. *Phone:* 617-333-2250. *Fax:* 617-333-2018. *E-mail:* spratt@curry.edu.

Application contact Curry College, 1071 Blue Hill Avenue, Milton, MA 02186-9984. *E-mail:* curryadm@curry.edu. *Web address:* http://www.curry.edu:8080/.

DAVIS & ELKINS COLLEGE
Elkins, West Virginia

Students with LD Served by Program	45	ADD/ADHD Services	✓
Staff	3 full-time	Summer Preparation Program	n/a
LD Program or Service Fee	✓	Alternative Test Arrangements	✓
LD Program Began	1987	LD Student Organization	n/a

Learning Disabilities Program began offering services in 1987. The program serves approximately 45 undergraduate students. Faculty consists of 3 full-time staff members. Services are provided by academic advisers, regular education teachers, remediation/learning specialists, diagnostic specialists, special education teachers, LD specialists, and trained peer tutors.

Policies Students with LD may take up to 18 credit hours per semester; 12 credit hours per semester are required to maintain full-time status and to be eligible for financial aid.

Fees *LD Program or Service Fee:* $2500 per year.

Special preparation or orientation Optional orientation held during registration and before classes begin.

Basic skills remediation Available in auditory processing, study skills, computer skills, reading, time management, handwriting, visual processing, learning strategies, spelling, written language, math, and spoken language. Offered one-on-one by LD specialists.

Subject-area tutoring Available in most subjects. Offered one-on-one and in small groups by graduate assistants/students, trained peer tutors, and LD specialists.

Counseling and advisement Academic advisement by a staff member affiliated with the program is available.

Auxiliary aids and services *Aids:* calculators, personal computers, personal spelling/word-use assistants (e.g., Franklin Speller), scan and read programs (e.g., Kurzweil), screen-enlarging programs, screen readers, tape recorders, taped textbooks. *Services and accommodations:* alternative test arrangements, readers, note-takers, scribes, and pre-advising for registration.

ADD/ADHD Students with ADD/ADHD are eligible for the same services available to students with LD, as well as distraction-free study areas, distraction-free testing environments and personal coach or mentors.

Application *Required:* high school transcript, ACT or SAT I (extended-time or untimed test accepted), personal statement, letter(s) of recommendation, separate application to your LD program or unit, psychoeducational report (3 years old or less), and documentation of high school services (e.g., Individualized Education Program [IEP] or 504 plan). *Recommended:* participation in extracurricular activities and interview. Upon application, documentation of need for special services should be sent only to your LD program or unit. Upon acceptance, documentation of need for special services should be sent only to your LD program or unit. *Application deadline (institutional):* rolling/

continuous for fall and rolling/continuous for spring. *Application deadline (LD program):* rolling/continuous for fall and rolling/continuous for spring.

LD program contact Judith Sabol McCauley, Director, 100 Campus Drive, Elkins, WV 26241. *Phone:* 304-637-1229. *Fax:* 304-637-1413. *E-mail:* mccaulj@dne.wvnet.edu.

Application contact Davis & Elkins College, 100 Campus Drive, Elkins, WV 26241-3996. *E-mail:* admiss@dne.wvnet.edu. *Web address:* http://www.dne.edu/.

DEPAUL UNIVERSITY
Chicago, Illinois

Students with LD Served by Program	70	ADD/ADHD Services	✓
Staff	1 full-time, 5 part-time	Summer Preparation Program	n/a
LD Program or Service Fee	varies	Alternative Test Arrangements	✓
LD Program Began	1984	LD Student Organization	n/a

Productive Learning Strategies (PLUS) Program began offering services in 1984. The program serves approximately 70 undergraduate students. Faculty consists of 1 full-time and 5 part-time staff members. Services are provided by diagnostic specialists, graduate assistants/students, and LD specialists.

Policies Students with LD may take up to 18 credit hours per quarter; 12 credit hours per quarter are required to maintain full-time status; 12 credit hours per quarter are required to be eligible for financial aid.

Fees *LD Program or Service Fee:* ranges from $900 to $1500 per year. *Diagnostic Testing Fee:* ranges from $250 to $500.

Diagnostic testing Available for auditory processing, motor skills, spelling, handwriting, spoken language, intelligence, study skills, reading, written language, learning styles, visual processing, and math.

Basic skills remediation Available in study skills, computer skills, reading, time management, learning strategies, and written language. Offered one-on-one by LD specialists.

Auxiliary aids and services *Aids:* tape recorders. *Services and accommodations:* advocates, priority registration, alternative test arrangements, readers, and scribes.

ADD/ADHD Students with ADD/ADHD are eligible for the same services available to students with LD, as well as distraction-free testing environments.

Application *Required:* high school transcript, ACT or SAT I (extended-time or untimed test accepted), personal statement, letter(s) of recommendation, separate application to your LD program or unit, and psychoeducational report (3 years old or less). *Recommended:* participation in extracurricular activities, ACT (extended-time or untimed test accepted), SAT I (extended-time or untimed test accepted), interview, and documentation of high school services (e.g., Individualized Education Program [IEP] or 504 plan). Upon application, documentation of need for special services should be sent only to your LD program or unit. Upon acceptance, documentation of need for special services should be sent only to your LD program or unit. *Application deadline (institutional):* rolling/continuous for fall and rolling/continuous for spring. *Application deadline (LD program):* rolling/continuous for fall and 8/15 for spring.

LD program contact Karen L. Wold, Director, PLUS Program, 2320 North Kenmore, #220, Chicago, IL 60614. *Phone:* 773-325-4239. *Fax:* 773-325-4673. *E-mail:* kwold@wppost.depaul.edu.

Application contact Ray Kennelley, Dean of Admission, DePaul University, 1 East Jackson Boulevard, Chicago, IL 60604-2287. *Phone:* 312-362-8300. *E-mail:* admitdpu@wppost.depaul.edu. *Web address:* http://www.depaul.edu/.

DOWLING COLLEGE
Oakdale, New York

Students with LD Served by Program	23	ADD/ADHD Services	✓
Staff	2 full-time, 25 part-time	Summer Preparation Program	n/a
LD Program or Service Fee	✓	Alternative Test Arrangements	✓
LD Program Began	1987	LD Student Organization	n/a

The Program for College Students with Learning Disabilities began offering services in 1987. The program serves approximately 23 undergraduate students. Faculty consists of 2 full-time and 25 part-time staff members. Services are provided by academic advisers, counselors, special education teachers, graduate assistants/students, teacher trainees, LD specialists, and professional tutors.

Policies The college has written policies regarding course substitutions. 12 credit hours per semester are required to maintain full-time status and to be eligible for financial aid. LD services are also available to graduate students.

Fees *LD Program or Service Fee:* $1500 per year.

Special preparation or orientation Required orientation held after classes begin.

Diagnostic testing Available for spelling, spoken language, reading, and written language.

Special courses Available in writing workshop. No courses are offered for credit; none enter into overall grade point average.

Counseling and advisement Academic advisement by a staff member affiliated with the program is available.

Auxiliary aids and services *Aids:* screen-enlarging programs, screen readers. *Services and accommodations:* advocates, priority registration, alternative test arrangements, readers, note-takers, and scribes.

ADD/ADHD Students with ADD/ADHD are eligible for the same services available to students with LD

Application *Required:* high school transcript, SAT I (extended-time or untimed test accepted), interview, letter(s) of recommendation, separate application to your LD program or unit, psychoeducational report (3 years old or less), and documentation of high school services (e.g., Individualized Education Program [IEP] or 504 plan). Upon application, documentation of need for special services should be sent only to your LD program or unit. Upon acceptance, documentation of need for special services should be sent only to your LD program or unit. *Application deadline (institutional):* rolling/continuous for fall and rolling/continuous for spring. *Application deadline (LD program):* rolling/continuous for fall and rolling/continuous for spring.

LD program contact Dr. Dorothy A. Stracher, Director, Education Program, Idle Hour Boulevard, Oakdale, NY 11769. *Phone:* 631-244-3306. *Fax:* 631-244-5036. *E-mail:* strached@dowling.edu.

Application contact Dowling College, Idle Hour Boulevard, Oakdale, NY 11769-1999. *E-mail:* rowek@dowling.edu. *Web address:* http://www.dowling.edu/.

EAST TENNESSEE STATE UNIVERSITY

Johnson City, Tennessee

Students with LD Served by Program	120	ADD/ADHD Services	✓
Staff	3 full-time, 3 part-time	Summer Preparation Program	n/a
LD Program or Service Fee	n/a	Alternative Test Arrangements	✓
LD Program Began	1996	LD Student Organization	n/a

Disability Services and LEAPO Program began offering services in 1996. The program serves approximately 120 undergraduate students. Faculty consists of 3 full-time and 3 part-time staff members. Services are provided by academic advisers, counselors, graduate assistants/students, LD specialists, and trained peer tutors.

Policies The college has written policies regarding course substitutions and substitution and waivers of requirements for admission. Students with LD may take up to 21 credit hours per term; 12 credit hours per term are required to maintain full-time status and to be eligible for financial aid. LD services are also available to graduate students.

Basic skills remediation Available in study skills, computer skills, reading, social skills, learning strategies, and written language. Offered one-on-one by computer-based instruction and graduate assistants/students.

Subject-area tutoring Available in all subjects. Offered one-on-one and in small groups by graduate assistants/students and trained peer tutors.

Counseling and advisement Career counseling, individual counseling, and support groups are available. Academic advisement by a staff member affiliated with the program is available.

Auxiliary aids and services *Aids:* calculators, personal computers, personal spelling/word-use assistants (e.g., Franklin Speller), scan and read programs (e.g., Kurzweil), screen-enlarging programs, screen readers, tape recorders, taped textbooks. *Services and accommodations:* priority registration, alternative test arrangements, readers, note-takers, and scribes.

ADD/ADHD Students with ADD/ADHD are eligible for the same services available to students with LD, as well as distraction-free study areas, distraction-free testing environments and support groups for ADD/ADHD.

Application *Required:* high school transcript and ACT or SAT I (extended-time tests accepted). Upon application, documentation of need for special services should be sent only to your LD program or unit. Upon acceptance, documentation of need for special services should be sent only to your LD program or unit. *Application deadline (institutional):* rolling/continuous for fall and rolling/continuous for spring. *Application deadline (LD program):* rolling/continuous for fall and rolling/continuous for spring.

LD program contact Heidi Bimrose, Director, Disability Services, Box 70605, Johnson City, TN 37614. *Phone:* 423-439-8346. *Fax:* 423-439-8489. *E-mail:* bimrose@etsu.edu.

Application contact Mike Pitts, Director of Admissions, East Tennessee State University, PO Box 70731, ETSU, Johnson City, TN 37614-0734. *Phone:* 423-439-6861. *E-mail:* pitts@etsuvax.etsu-tn.edu. *Web address:* http://www.etsu.edu/.

EDINBORO UNIVERSITY OF PENNSYLVANIA

Edinboro, Pennsylvania

Students with LD Served by Program	235	ADD/ADHD Services	✓
Staff	2 full-time, 1 part-time	Summer Preparation Program	n/a
LD Program or Service Fee	n/a	Alternative Test Arrangements	✓
LD Program Began	1988	LD Student Organization	✓

Office for Students with Disabilities (OSD) began offering services in 1988. The program serves approximately 235 undergraduate students. Faculty consists of 2 full-time staff members and 1 part-time staff member. Services are provided by special education teachers and school psychologist.

Policies The college has written policies regarding course substitutions. Students with LD may take up to 18 credit hours per semester; 12 credit hours per semester are required to maintain full-time status and to be eligible for financial aid. LD services are also available to graduate students.

Counseling and advisement Individual counseling is available.

Auxiliary aids and services *Aids:* personal computers, screen-enlarging programs, screen readers, speech recognition programs (e.g., Dragon), tape recorders, taped textbooks. *Services and accommodations:* advocates, priority registration, alternative test arrangements, readers, note-takers, and scribes.

Student organization There is a student organization for students with LD.

ADD/ADHD Students with ADD/ADHD are eligible for the same services available to students with LD, as well as distraction-free testing environments.

Application *Required:* psychoeducational report (3 years old or less). *Recommended:* documentation of high school services (e.g., Individualized Education Program [IEP] or 504 plan). Upon application, documentation of need for special services should be sent only to your LD program or unit. Upon acceptance, documentation of need for special services should be sent only to your LD program or unit. *Application deadline (institutional):* rolling/continuous for fall and rolling/continuous for spring. *Application deadline (LD program):* rolling/continuous for fall and rolling/continuous for spring.

LD program contact Kathleen K. Strosser, Assistant to the Director, Office for Students with Disabilities, Shafer Hall, Edinboro, PA 16444-0001. *Phone:* 814-732-2462. *Fax:* 814-732-2866. *E-mail:* strosser@edinboro.edu.

Application contact Edinboro University of Pennsylvania, Edinboro, PA 16444. *Web address:* http://www.edinboro.edu/.

FASHION INSTITUTE OF TECHNOLOGY

New York, New York

Students with LD Served by Program	100	ADD/ADHD Services	✓
Staff	2 full-time, 3 part-time	Summer Preparation Program	n/a
LD Program or Service Fee	n/a	Alternative Test Arrangements	✓
LD Program Began	1987	LD Student Organization	n/a

Program of Services for Students with Special Needs began offering services in 1987. The program serves approximately 100 undergraduate students. Faculty consists of 2 full-time and 3 part-time staff members. Services are provided by academic advisers, counselors, LD specialists, trained peer tutors, and professional tutors.

Policies Students with LD may take up to 18 credit hours per semester; 12 credit hours per semester are required to maintain full-time status and to be eligible for financial aid. LD services are also available to graduate students.
individually by special arrangement.

Basic skills remediation Available in study skills, computer skills, reading, time management, learning strategies, written language, math, and spoken language. Offered one-on-one and in small groups by professional tutors.

Subject-area tutoring Available in all subjects. Offered one-on-one and in small groups by professional tutors and trained peer tutors.

Counseling and advisement Career counseling, individual counseling, and support groups are available. Academic advisement by a staff member affiliated with the program is available.

Auxiliary aids and services *Aids:* scan and read programs (e.g., Kurzweil), screen-enlarging programs, tape recorders, taped textbooks. *Services and accommodations:* advocates, alternative test arrangements, readers, note-takers, and scribes.

ADD/ADHD Students with ADD/ADHD are eligible for the same services available to students with LD, as well as distraction-free testing environments and one-on-one tutorial support.

Application *Required:* high school transcript. *Recommended:* ACT or SAT I (extended-time or untimed test accepted), interview, personal statement, letter(s) of recommendation, psycho-educational report (5 years old or less), documentation of high school services (e.g., Individualized Education Program [IEP] or 504 plan), and contact with ID Coordinator to discuss program services and accommodations needed. Upon application, documentation of need for special services should be sent to both admissions and your LD program or unit. Upon acceptance, documentation of need for special services should be sent to both admissions and your LD program or unit. *Application deadline (institutional):* 1/1 for fall and 10/1 for spring. *Application deadline (LD program):* rolling/continuous for fall and rolling/continuous for spring.

LD program contact Gail Ballard, Program Coordinator, Seventh Avenue at 27th Street, Room B-602, New York, NY 10001-5992. *Phone:* 212-217-7522. *Fax:* 212-217-7192.

Application contact Fashion Institute of Technology, Seventh Avenue at 27th Street, New York, NY 10001-5992. *E-mail:* fitinfo@sfitva.cc.fitsuny.edu. *Web address:* http://www.fitnyc.suny.edu/.

FINLANDIA UNIVERSITY
Hancock, Michigan

Students with LD Served by Program	30	ADD/ADHD Services	✓
Staff	1 full-time	Summer Preparation Program	n/a
LD Program or Service Fee	n/a	Alternative Test Arrangements	✓
LD Program Began	1990	LD Student Organization	n/a

Program for Students With Learning Disabilities began offering services in 1990. The program serves approximately 30 undergraduate students. Faculty consists of 1 full-time staff member. Services are provided by LD specialists.

Policies Students with LD may take up to 18 credit hours per semester; 12 credit hours per semester are required to maintain full-time status; 6 credit hours per semester are required to be eligible for financial aid.

Special preparation or orientation Required orientation held during summer prior to enrollment.

Subject-area tutoring Available in most subjects. Offered one-on-one and in small groups by professional tutors and trained peer tutors.

Auxiliary aids and services *Aids:* scan and read programs (e.g., Kurzweil), taped textbooks. *Services and accommodations:* advocates, alternative test arrangements, readers, note-takers, and scribes.

ADD/ADHD Students with ADD/ADHD are eligible for the same services available to students with LD, as well as distraction-free testing environments.

Application *Required:* high school transcript and documentation of high school services (e.g., Individualized Education Program [IEP] or 504 plan). *Recommended:* interview and psycho-educational report (3 years old or less). Upon application, documentation of need for special services should be sent only to your LD program or unit. Upon acceptance, documentation of need for special services should be sent only to your LD program or unit. *Application deadline (institutional):* rolling/continuous for fall and rolling/continuous for spring. *Application deadline (LD program):* rolling/continuous for fall and rolling/continuous for spring.

LD program contact Carol Bates, Associate Professor/Director, 601 Quincy Street, Hancock, MI 49930. *Phone:* 906-487-7258. *Fax:* 906-487-7567. *E-mail:* cabates@bresnanlink.net.

Application contact Ben Larson, Director of Admissions, Finlandia University, 601 Quincy Street, Hancock, MI 49930-1882. *Phone:* 906-487-7311 Ext. 311. *Web address:* http://www.suomi.edu/.

FITCHBURG STATE COLLEGE
Fitchburg, Massachusetts

Students with LD Served by Program	120	ADD/ADHD Services	✓
Staff	3 full-time, 1 part-time	Summer Preparation Program	n/a
LD Program or Service Fee	n/a	Alternative Test Arrangements	✓
LD Program Began	1992	LD Student Organization	✓

Disability Services began offering services in 1992. The program serves approximately 120 undergraduate students. Faculty consists of 3 full-time staff members and 1 part-time staff member. Services are provided by diagnostic specialists, graduate assistants/students, and trained peer tutors.

Policies The college has written policies regarding substitution and waivers of requirements for admission. LD services are also available to graduate students.

Special preparation or orientation Optional orientation held before classes begin and individually by special arrangement.

Diagnostic testing Available for auditory processing, spelling, handwriting, intelligence, learning strategies, reading, written language, learning styles, visual processing, and math.

Subject-area tutoring Available in all subjects. Offered one-on-one and in small groups by graduate assistants/students and trained peer tutors.

Special courses Available in career planning and practical computer skills. No courses are offered for credit; none enter into overall grade point average.

Counseling and advisement Career counseling and support groups are available.

Auxiliary aids and services *Aids:* calculators, personal computers, personal spelling/word-use assistants (e.g., Franklin Speller), scan and read programs (e.g., Kurzweil), screen-enlarging programs, screen readers, speech recognition programs (e.g., Dragon), tape recorders. *Services and accommodations:* advocates, priority registration, alternative test arrangements, readers, note-takers, and scribes.

Student organization There is a student organization for students with LD.

Fitchburg State College (continued)

ADD/ADHD Students with ADD/ADHD are eligible for the same services available to students with LD, as well as distraction-free study areas, distraction-free testing environments, personal coach or mentors, and support groups for ADD/ADHD.

Application *Required:* high school transcript, personal statement, and letter(s) of recommendation. *Recommended:* participation in extracurricular activities, interview, psychoeducational report (3 years old or less), and documentation of high school services (e.g., Individualized Education Program [IEP] or 504 plan). Upon application, documentation of need for special services should be sent only to admissions. Upon acceptance, documentation of need for special services should be sent only to your LD program or unit. *Application deadline (institutional):* rolling/continuous for fall and rolling/continuous for spring. *Application deadline (LD program):* rolling/continuous for fall and rolling/continuous for spring.

LD program contact Joni Perkins, Secretary, 160 Pearl Street, Fitchburg, MA 01420. *Phone:* 978-665-4020. *Fax:* 978-665-3021. *E-mail:* jperkins@fsc.edu.

Application contact Fitchburg State College, 160 Pearl Street, Fitchburg, MA 01420-2697. *E-mail:* admissions@fsc.edu. *Web address:* http://www.fsc.edu/.

FLORIDA AGRICULTURAL AND MECHANICAL UNIVERSITY
Tallahassee, Florida

Students with LD Served by Program	150	ADD/ADHD Services	✓
Staff	5 full-time, 5 part-time	Summer Preparation Program	✓
LD Program or Service Fee	n/a	Alternative Test Arrangements	✓
LD Program Began	1985	LD Student Organization	✓

Learning Development and Evaluation Center began offering services in 1985. The program serves approximately 150 undergraduate students. Faculty consists of 5 full-time and 5 part-time staff members. Services are provided by counselors, remediation/learning specialists, diagnostic specialists, and professional tutors.

Policies The college has written policies regarding course substitutions, grade forgiveness, and substitution and waivers of requirements for admission and graduation. Students with LD may take up to 12 semester hours per term; 9 semester hours per term are required to maintain full-time status; 12 semester hours per term are required to be eligible for financial aid. LD services are also available to graduate students.

Special preparation or orientation Required summer program offered prior to entering college. Required orientation held before registration.

Diagnostic testing Available for spelling, handwriting, neuropsychological, spoken language, intelligence, personality, study skills, reading, written language, social skills, math, and perceptual skills.

Basic skills remediation Available in study skills, computer skills, reading, time management, handwriting, social skills, learning strategies, spelling, written language, math, and spoken language. Offered by regular education teachers, graduate assistants/students, and LD specialists.

Subject-area tutoring Available in most subjects. Offered one-on-one and in small groups by trained peer tutors and teachers, clubs.

Special courses Available in study skills, college survival skills, practical computer skills, reading, time management, learning strategies, vocabulary development, stress management, and written composition skills. Most courses are offered for credit; most enter into overall grade point average.

Counseling and advisement Career counseling, individual counseling, and small-group counseling are available.

Auxiliary aids and services *Aids:* calculators, personal computers, tape recorders, taped textbooks, typewriters, word processors with spell-check. *Services and accommodations:* advocates, alternative test arrangements, and assistance with notetaking.

Student organization There is a student organization for students with LD.

ADD/ADHD Students with ADD/ADHD are eligible for the same services available to students with LD

Application *Required:* high school transcript, ACT or SAT I (extended-time or untimed test accepted), interview, letter(s) of recommendation, psychoeducational report (3 years old or less), and documentation of disability. *Recommended:* participation in extracurricular activities. *Application deadline (institutional):* 5/30 for fall and 11/10 for spring. *Application deadline (LD program):* 5/30 for fall and 11/10 for spring.

LD program contact Dr. William Hudson, Instructional Specialist, Learning Development and Evaluation Center, Tallahassee, FL 32307. *Phone:* 904-599-3180. *Fax:* 904-651-2513.

Application contact Barbara R. Cox, Director of Admissions, Florida Agricultural and Mechanical University, Office of the University Registrar, Tallahassee, FL 32307. *Phone:* 850-599-3796. *E-mail:* bcox@ns1.famu.edu. *Web address:* http://www.famu.edu/.

GANNON UNIVERSITY
Erie, Pennsylvania

Students with LD Served by Program	60	ADD/ADHD Services	✓
Staff	3 full-time, 3 part-time	Summer Preparation Program	n/a
LD Program or Service Fee	✓	Alternative Test Arrangements	✓
LD Program Began	1986	LD Student Organization	n/a

Program for Students with Learning Disabilities (PSLD) began offering services in 1986. The program serves approximately 60 undergraduate students. Faculty consists of 3 full-time and 3 part-time staff members. Services are provided by remediation/learning specialists, counselors, regular education teachers, special education teachers, LD specialists, and professional tutors.

Policies Students with LD may take up to 18 credit hours per semester; 12 credit hours per semester are required to maintain full-time status and to be eligible for financial aid. LD services are also available to graduate students.

Fees *LD Program or Service Fee:* $600 per year.

Special preparation or orientation Held before classes begin, during summer prior to enrollment, and individually by special arrangement.

Subject-area tutoring Available in most subjects. Offered one-on-one by professional tutors and LD specialists.

Special courses Available in study skills, college survival skills, test taking, time management, learning strategies, self-advocacy, and stress management. All courses are offered for credit; all enter into overall grade point average.

Counseling and advisement Career counseling, individual counseling, and small-group counseling are available.

Auxiliary aids and services *Aids:* calculators, personal computers, personal spelling/word-use assistants (e.g., Franklin Speller), scan and read programs (e.g., Kurzweil), tape recorders, taped textbooks. *Services and accommodations:* advocates, priority registration, alternative test arrangements, readers, and scribes.

ADD/ADHD Students with ADD/ADHD are eligible for the same services available to students with LD, as well as distraction-free study areas, distraction-free testing environments and personal coach or mentors.

Application *Required:* high school transcript, ACT or SAT I (extended-time or untimed test accepted), interview, letter(s) of recommendation, separate application to your LD program or unit, and psychoeducational report (5 years old or less). *Recommended:* participation in extracurricular activities, personal statement, documentation of high school services (e.g., Individualized Education Program [IEP] or 504 plan), and personal visit. Upon application, documentation of need for special services should be sent only to admissions. Upon acceptance, documentation of need for special services should be sent only to your LD program or unit. *Application deadline (institutional):* rolling/continuous for fall and rolling/continuous for spring. *Application deadline (LD program):* rolling/continuous for fall and rolling/continuous for spring.

LD program contact Joyce Lowrey, SSJ, Director, Program for Students with Learning Disabilities, University Square, Erie, PA 16541. *Phone:* 814-871-5326. *Fax:* 814-871-5657. *E-mail:* lawrey@gannon.edu.

Application contact Gannon University, University Square, Erie, PA 16541-0001. *E-mail:* admissions@cluster.gannon.edu. *Web address:* http://www.gannon.edu/.

GEORGIA STATE UNIVERSITY
Atlanta, Georgia

Students with LD Served by Program	125	ADD/ADHD Services	✓
Staff	4 full-time, 8 part-time	Summer Preparation Program	n/a
LD Program or Service Fee	n/a	Alternative Test Arrangements	✓
LD Program Began	1970	LD Student Organization	n/a

Office of Disability Services began offering services in 1970. The program serves approximately 125 undergraduate students. Faculty consists of 4 full-time and 8 part-time staff members. Services are provided by counselors, diagnostic specialists, graduate assistants/students, LD specialists, and professional tutors.

Policies The college has written policies regarding course substitutions and substitution and waivers of requirements for admission. Students with LD may take up to 18 credit hours per semester; 12 credit hours per semester are required to maintain full-time status; 6 credit hours per semester are required to be eligible for financial aid. LD services are also available to graduate students.

Fees *Diagnostic Testing Fee:* $300.

Diagnostic testing Available for auditory processing, motor skills, spelling, neuropsychological, spoken language, intelligence, personality, reading, written language, visual processing, and math.

Basic skills remediation Available in study skills, reading, time management, learning strategies, written language, and math. Offered one-on-one and in class-size groups by graduate assistants/students, LD specialists, and professional tutors.

Subject-area tutoring Available in some subjects. Offered one-on-one by professional tutors and graduate assistants/students.

Counseling and advisement Individual counseling and support groups are available.

Auxiliary aids and services *Aids:* scan and read programs (e.g., Kurzweil), screen-enlarging programs, screen readers, speech recognition programs (e.g., Dragon), taped textbooks. *Services and accommodations:* priority registration, alternative test arrangements, readers, note-takers, and scribes.

ADD/ADHD Students with ADD/ADHD are eligible for the same services available to students with LD, as well as distraction-free testing environments, personal coach or mentors, and support groups for ADD/ADHD.

Application *Required:* high school transcript and ACT or SAT I (extended-time or untimed test accepted). Upon application, documentation of need for special services should be sent only to your LD program or unit. Upon acceptance, documentation of need for special services should be sent only to your LD program or unit. *Application deadline (institutional):* 3/1 for fall and 9/1 for spring. *Application deadline (LD program):* rolling/continuous for fall and rolling/continuous for spring.

LD program contact Louise Bedrossian-Cebula, Cognitive Disabilities Specialist/Instructional Services Coordinator, Office of Disability Services, University Plaza, Atlanta, GA 30303. *Phone:* 404-463-9044. *Fax:* 404-463-9049. *E-mail:* disleb@langate.gsu.edu.

Application contact Georgia State University, University Plaza, Atlanta, GA 30303-3083. *Web address:* http://www.gsu.edu/.

GLENVILLE STATE COLLEGE
Glenville, West Virginia

Students with LD Served by Program	45	ADD/ADHD Services	✓
Staff	2 full-time	Summer Preparation Program	n/a
LD Program or Service Fee	n/a	Alternative Test Arrangements	✓
LD Program Began	n/a	LD Student Organization	n/a

Student Disability Services serves approximately 45 undergraduate students. Faculty consists of 2 full-time staff members. Services are provided by academic advisers, regular education teachers, special education teachers, and trained peer tutors.

Policies Students with LD may take up to 18 credit hours per semester; 12 credit hours per semester are required to maintain full-time status and to be eligible for financial aid.

Special preparation or orientation Optional orientation held individually by special arrangement.

Basic skills remediation Available in study skills, reading, learning strategies, spelling, and math. Offered in class-size groups by regular education teachers and trained peer tutors.

Subject-area tutoring Available in most subjects. Offered one-on-one by trained peer tutors.

Counseling and advisement Career counseling is available. Academic advisement by a staff member affiliated with the program is available.

Auxiliary aids and services *Aids:* calculators, personal computers, personal spelling/word-use assistants (e.g., Franklin Speller), screen-enlarging programs, speech recognition programs (e.g., Dragon), tape recorders, taped textbooks. *Services and accommodations:* alternative test arrangements, readers, and note-takers.

ADD/ADHD Students with ADD/ADHD are eligible for the same services available to students with LD, as well as distraction-free testing environments.

Application *Required:* high school transcript, ACT (extended-time test accepted), and SAT I (extended-time test accepted). Upon application, documentation of need for special services should be sent only to your LD program or unit. Upon acceptance, documentation of need for special services should be

Glenville State College (continued)

sent only to your LD program or unit. *Application deadline (institutional):* rolling/continuous for fall and rolling/continuous for spring.

LD program contact Daniel A. Reed, Coordinator of Student Disability Services, 200 High Street, Glenville, WV 26351. *Phone:* 304-462-4118. *Fax:* 304-462-7495. *E-mail:* sds@glenville.edu.

Application contact Brenda McCartney, Records Assistant, Glenville State College, 200 High Street, Glenville, WV 26351-1200. *Phone:* 304-462-4117. *E-mail:* cottrill@glenville.wvnet.edu. *Web address:* http://www.glenville.wvnet.edu/.

HOFSTRA UNIVERSITY
Hempstead, New York

Students with LD Served by Program	250	ADD/ADHD Services	✓
Staff	4 full-time, 2 part-time	Summer Preparation Program	n/a
LD Program or Service Fee	✓	Alternative Test Arrangements	✓
LD Program Began	1979	LD Student Organization	n/a

Program of Academic Learning Skills (PALS) began offering services in 1979. The program serves approximately 250 undergraduate students. Faculty consists of 4 full-time and 2 part-time staff members. Services are provided by remediation/learning specialists, diagnostic specialists, special education teachers, and LD specialists.

Fees *LD Program or Service Fee:* $5400 per year.

Special preparation or orientation Optional orientation held before registration and during summer prior to enrollment.

Basic skills remediation Available in auditory processing, motor skills, study skills, computer skills, reading, time management, handwriting, social skills, visual processing, learning strategies, spelling, written language, math, and spoken language. Offered one-on-one by LD specialists.

Counseling and advisement Career counseling, individual counseling, small-group counseling, and support groups are available.

Auxiliary aids and services *Aids:* calculators, personal computers, personal spelling/word-use assistants (e.g., Franklin Speller), scan and read programs (e.g., Kurzweil), screen readers, speech recognition programs (e.g., Dragon), tape recorders, taped textbooks. *Services and accommodations:* advocates, alternative test arrangements, readers, note-takers, and scribes.

ADD/ADHD Students with ADD/ADHD are eligible for the same services available to students with LD, as well as distraction-free testing environments.

Application *Required:* high school transcript, ACT or SAT I (extended-time or untimed test accepted), interview, psychoeducational report (1 year old or less), and documentation of high school services (e.g., Individualized Education Program [IEP] or 504 plan). *Recommended:* personal statement and letter(s) of recommendation. Upon application, documentation of need for special services should be sent only to admissions. Upon acceptance, documentation of need for special services should be sent only to your LD program or unit. *Application deadline (LD program):* rolling/continuous for fall and rolling/continuous for spring.

LD program contact Dr. Ignacio L. Gotz, Director, 130 Hofstra University, Hempstead, NY 11549. *Phone:* 516-463-5841. *Fax:* 516-463-4832. *E-mail:* nucizg@hofstra.edu.

Application contact Hofstra University, 100 Hofstra University, Hempstead, NY 11549. *E-mail:* hofstra@hofstra.edu. *Web address:* http://www.hofstra.edu/.

IONA COLLEGE
New Rochelle, New York

Students with LD Served by Program	75	ADD/ADHD Services	✓
Staff	2 full-time, 10 part-time	Summer Preparation Program	✓
LD Program or Service Fee	n/a	Alternative Test Arrangements	n/a
LD Program Began	1981	LD Student Organization	n/a

College Assistance Program began offering services in 1981. The program serves approximately 75 undergraduate students. Faculty consists of 2 full-time and 10 part-time staff members. Services are provided by remediation/learning specialists, counselors, special education teachers, and LD specialists.

Special preparation or orientation Required summer program offered prior to entering college. Required orientation held during summer prior to enrollment.

Counseling and advisement Individual counseling and support groups are available.

Auxiliary aids and services *Aids:* calculators, speech recognition programs (e.g., Dragon), tape recorders, taped textbooks. *Services and accommodations:* readers, note-takers, and scribes.

ADD/ADHD Students with ADD/ADHD are eligible for the same services available to students with LD, as well as distraction-free testing environments and personal coach or mentors.

Application *Required:* high school transcript, ACT or SAT I (extended-time tests accepted), interview, personal statement, letter(s) of recommendation, psychoeducational report (3 years old or less), and documentation of high school services (e.g., Individualized Education Program [IEP] or 504 plan). *Recommended:* standardized achievement tests. Upon application, documentation of need for special services should be sent only to your LD program or unit. Upon acceptance, documentation of need for special services should be sent only to your LD program or unit. *Application deadline (institutional):* rolling/continuous for fall and rolling/continuous for spring. *Application deadline (LD program):* rolling/continuous for fall and rolling/continuous for spring.

LD program contact Madeline Packerman, Director, 715 North Avenue, New Rochelle, NY 10801. *Phone:* 914-633-2582. *Fax:* 914-633-2174. *E-mail:* mpackerman@iona.edu.

Application contact Iona College, 715 North Avenue, New Rochelle, NY 10801-1890. *Web address:* http://www.iona.edu/.

ITHACA COLLEGE
Ithaca, New York

Students with LD Served by Program	500	ADD/ADHD Services	✓
Staff	1 full-time, 1 part-time	Summer Preparation Program	n/a
LD Program or Service Fee	n/a	Alternative Test Arrangements	✓
LD Program Began	1994	LD Student Organization	n/a

Academic Support Services for Students With Disabilities (ASSSD) began offering services in 1994. The program serves approximately 500 undergraduate students. Faculty consists of 1 full-time and 1 part-time staff member. Services are provided by counselors, special education teachers, graduate assistants/students, and professional tutors.

Policies Students with LD may take up to 21 credit hours per semester; 12 credit hours per semester are required to maintain full-time status and to be eligible for financial aid. LD services are also available to graduate students.

Special preparation or orientation Optional orientation held during summer prior to enrollment and individually by special arrangement.

Subject-area tutoring Available in all subjects. Offered one-on-one by graduate assistants/students.

Counseling and advisement Career counseling and individual counseling are available.

Auxiliary aids and services *Aids:* tape recorders, taped textbooks, enlarged materials. *Services and accommodations:* alternative test arrangements, readers, note-takers, and scribes.

ADD/ADHD Students with ADD/ADHD are eligible for the same services available to students with LD, as well as distraction-free testing environments, medication management and personal coach or mentors.

Application *Required:* high school transcript, ACT or SAT I (extended-time or untimed test accepted), interview, personal statement, and letter(s) of recommendation. Upon acceptance, documentation of need for special services should be sent only to your LD program or unit. *Application deadline (institutional):* rolling/continuous for fall and rolling/continuous for spring.

LD program contact Leslie Schettino, Director, 220 Williams Hall, Ithaca, NY 14850. *Phone:* 607-274-1257. *Fax:* 607-274-3957. *E-mail:* lschettino@ithaca.edu.

Application contact Ithaca College, 100 Job Hall, Ithaca, NY 14850-7020. *E-mail:* admission@ithaca.edu. *Web address:* http://www.ithaca.edu/.

JOHNSON & WALES UNIVERSITY
North Miami, Florida

Students with LD Served by Program	100	ADD/ADHD Services	✓
Staff	1 full-time	Summer Preparation Program	n/a
LD Program or Service Fee	n/a	Alternative Test Arrangements	✓
LD Program Began	n/a	LD Student Organization	n/a

Student Success serves approximately 100 undergraduate students. Faculty consists of 1 full-time staff member. Services are provided by counselors, trained peer tutors, and professional tutors.

Policies The college has written policies regarding course substitutions. 12 quarter credit hours per term are required to maintain full-time status; 6 quarter credit hours per term are required to be eligible for financial aid.

Subject-area tutoring Available in most subjects. Offered one-on-one and in small groups by computer-based instruction, professional tutors, and trained peer tutors.

Counseling and advisement Career counseling, individual counseling, and small-group counseling are available.

Auxiliary aids and services *Aids:* calculators, personal computers, personal spelling/word-use assistants (e.g., Franklin Speller), screen-enlarging programs, tape recorders. *Services and accommodations:* priority registration, alternative test arrangements, and copy of instructor notes.

ADD/ADHD Students with ADD/ADHD are eligible for the same services available to students with LD, as well as distraction-free testing environments.

Application *Required:* high school transcript and personal statement. *Recommended:* letter(s) of recommendation. Upon application, documentation of need for special services should be sent only to your LD program or unit. Upon acceptance, documentation of need for special services should be sent only to your LD program or unit.

LD program contact Office of Student Success, 1701 Northeast 127th Street, North Miami, FL 33181. *Phone:* 800-232-2433.

Application contact Johnson & Wales University, 1701 Northeast 127th Street, North Miami, FL 33181. *E-mail:* admissions@jwu.edu. *Web address:* http://www.jwu.edu/.

KING'S COLLEGE
Wilkes-Barre, Pennsylvania

Students with LD Served by Program	50	ADD/ADHD Services	✓
Staff	2 full-time, 1 part-time	Summer Preparation Program	✓
LD Program or Service Fee	✓	Alternative Test Arrangements	✓
LD Program Began	1992	LD Student Organization	✓

Academic Skills Center, First Year Academic Studies Program began offering services in 1992. The program serves approximately 50 undergraduate students. Faculty consists of 2 full-time staff members and 1 part-time staff member. Services are provided by LD specialists and trained peer tutors.

Policies Students with LD may take up to 15 credit hours per semester; 12 credit hours per semester are required to maintain full-time status; 12 credit hours per semester are required to be eligible for financial aid.

Fees *LD Program or Service Fee:* $2000 per year.

Special preparation or orientation Optional summer program offered prior to entering college. Required orientation held during summer prior to enrollment.

Basic skills remediation Available in study skills, reading, time management, learning strategies, and written language. Offered one-on-one by LD specialists.

Subject-area tutoring Available in most subjects. Offered one-on-one and in small groups by trained peer tutors and LD specialists.

Auxiliary aids and services *Aids:* calculators, personal computers, tape recorders, taped textbooks. *Services and accommodations:* advocates, priority registration, alternative test arrangements, readers, note-takers, and scribes.

Student organization There is a student organization for students with LD.

ADD/ADHD Students with ADD/ADHD are eligible for the same services available to students with LD, as well as distraction-free study areas, distraction-free testing environments and personal coach or mentors.

Application *Required:* high school transcript, SAT I (extended-time or untimed test accepted), interview, personal statement, letter(s) of recommendation, separate application to your LD program or unit, psychoeducational report, and documentation of high school services (e.g., Individualized Education Program [IEP] or 504 plan). *Recommended:* participation in extracurricular activities. Upon application, documentation of need for special services should be sent to both admissions and your LD program or unit. Upon acceptance, documentation of need for special services should be sent only to your LD program or unit. *Application deadline (institutional):* rolling/continuous for fall and rolling/continuous for spring. *Application deadline (LD program):* 4/1 for fall.

LD program contact Jacintha Burke, Director, Academic Skills Center, 133 North River Street, Wilkes-Barre, PA 18711. *Phone:* 570-208-5800. *Fax:* 570-825-9049. *E-mail:* jaburke@kings.edu.

Application contact King's College, 133 North River Street, Wilkes-Barre, PA 18711-0801. *E-mail:* admssns@rs01.kings.edu. *Web address:* http://www.kings.edu/.

LEE UNIVERSITY
Cleveland, Tennessee

Students with LD Served by Program	200	ADD/ADHD Services	✓
Staff	1 full-time, 5 part-time	Summer Preparation Program	n/a
LD Program or Service Fee	n/a	Alternative Test Arrangements	✓
LD Program Began	1990	LD Student Organization	n/a

Academic Support Program began offering services in 1990. The program serves approximately 200 undergraduate students. Faculty consists of 1 full-time and 5 part-time staff members. Services are provided by academic advisers, counselors, graduate assistants/students, teacher trainees, and trained peer tutors.

Policies The college has written policies regarding course substitutions, grade forgiveness, and substitution and waivers of requirements for admission and graduation. Students with LD may take up to 14 credit hours per semester; 12 credit hours per semester are required to maintain full-time status; 12 credit hours per semester are required to be eligible for financial aid. LD services are also available to graduate students.

Special preparation or orientation Optional orientation held individually by special arrangement.

Basic skills remediation Available in computer skills, reading, time management, written language, and math. Offered one-on-one and in class-size groups by computer-based instruction, regular education teachers, graduate assistants/students, and trained peer tutors.

Subject-area tutoring Available in most subjects. Offered one-on-one and in small groups by graduate assistants/students and trained peer tutors.

Special courses Available in study skills, reading, learning strategies, math, and written composition skills. Most courses are offered for credit; most enter into overall grade point average.

Counseling and advisement Individual counseling is available. Academic advisement by a staff member affiliated with the program is available.

Auxiliary aids and services *Aids:* personal computers, tape recorders, taped textbooks. *Services and accommodations:* alternative test arrangements, readers, note-takers, and scribes.

ADD/ADHD Students with ADD/ADHD are eligible for the same services available to students with LD, as well as distraction-free study areas, distraction-free testing environments and personal coach or mentors.

Application *Required:* high school transcript, ACT (extended-time or untimed test accepted), SAT I (extended-time or untimed test accepted), personal statement, letter(s) of recommendation, psychoeducational report (3 years old or less), and documentation of high school services (e.g., Individualized Education Program [IEP] or 504 plan). Upon application, documentation of need for special services should be sent to both admissions and your LD program or unit. Upon acceptance, documentation of need for special services should be sent to both admissions and your LD program or unit. *Application deadline (institutional):* rolling/continuous for fall and rolling/continuous for spring. *Application deadline (LD program):* rolling/continuous for fall and rolling/continuous for spring.

LD program contact Susan Sasse, Director, PO Box 3450, Cleveland, TN 37320-3450. *Phone:* 423-614-8181. *Fax:* 423-614-8172. *E-mail:* ssasse@leeuniversity.edu.

Application contact Admissions Coordinator, Lee University, PO Box 3450, Cleveland, TN 37320-3450. *Phone:* 423-614-8500. *Web address:* http://www.leeuniversity.edu/.

LIBERTY UNIVERSITY
Lynchburg, Virginia

Students with LD Served by Program	80	ADD/ADHD Services	✓
Staff	3 full-time	Summer Preparation Program	n/a
LD Program or Service Fee	n/a	Alternative Test Arrangements	✓
LD Program Began	1986	LD Student Organization	n/a

Office of Academic Disability Support began offering services in 1986. The program serves approximately 80 undergraduate students. Faculty consists of 3 full-time staff members. Services are provided by academic advisers and LD specialists.

Policies Students with LD may take up to 18 credit hours per semester; 12 credit hours per semester are required to maintain full-time status and to be eligible for financial aid.

Counseling and advisement Academic advisement by a staff member affiliated with the program is available.

Auxiliary aids and services *Services and accommodations:* advocates, priority registration, and alternative test arrangements.

ADD/ADHD Students with ADD/ADHD are eligible for the same services available to students with LD, as well as distraction-free testing environments.

Application *Required:* high school transcript, ACT or SAT I (extended-time tests accepted), personal statement, letter(s) of recommendation, psychoeducational report (5 years old or less), and documentation of high school services (e.g., Individualized Education Program [IEP] or 504 plan). Upon application, documentation of need for special services should be sent only to admissions. Upon acceptance, documentation of need for special services should be sent only to your LD program or unit. *Application deadline (institutional):* 6/30 for fall and 11/30 for spring (rolling/continuous). *Application deadline (LD program):* rolling/continuous for fall and rolling/continuous for spring.

LD program contact William Denton McHaney, Director, 1971 University Boulevard, Lynchburg, VA 24502-2269. *Phone:* 804-582-2159. *Fax:* 804-582-2468. *E-mail:* wdmchane@liberty.edu.

Application contact Mark Camper, Director of Admissions, Liberty University, 1971 University Boulevard, Lynchburg, VA 24502. *Phone:* 804-582-2778. *Web address:* http://www.liberty.edu/.

LIMESTONE COLLEGE
Gaffney, South Carolina

Students with LD Served by Program	18	ADD/ADHD Services	✓
Staff	1 part-time	Summer Preparation Program	n/a
LD Program or Service Fee	varies	Alternative Test Arrangements	✓
LD Program Began	1991	LD Student Organization	n/a

Program for Alternative Learning Styles (PALS) began offering services in 1991. The program serves approximately 18 undergraduate students. Faculty consists of 1 part-time staff member. Services are provided by academic advisers and trained peer tutors.

Policies Students with LD may take up to 15 credit hours per semester.

Fees *LD Program or Service Fee:* ranges from $1500 to $3000 per year.

Subject-area tutoring Available in most subjects. Offered in small groups by trained peer tutors.

Special courses Available in study skills, college survival skills, and learning strategies. All courses are offered for credit; all enter into overall grade point average.

Counseling and advisement Academic advisement by a staff member affiliated with the program is available.

Auxiliary aids and services *Aids:* tape recorders, taped textbooks. *Services and accommodations:* advocates and alternative test arrangements.

ADD/ADHD Students with ADD/ADHD are eligible for the same services available to students with LD

Application *Required:* high school transcript, ACT or SAT I (untimed tests accepted), interview, separate application to your LD program or unit, and psychoeducational report (3 years old or less). *Recommended:* participation in extracurricular activities, personal statement, letter(s) of recommendation, and documentation of high school services (e.g., Individualized Education Program [IEP] or 504 plan). Upon application, documentation of need for special services should be sent only to your LD program or unit. Upon acceptance, documentation of need for special services should be sent only to your LD program or unit. *Application deadline (institutional):* rolling/continuous for fall and rolling/continuous for spring. *Application deadline (LD program):* rolling/continuous for fall and rolling/continuous for spring.

LD program contact Dr. Joe Pitts, Director, 1115 College Drive, Gaffney, SC 29340. *Phone:* 864-488-4534. *Fax:* 864-487-8706. *E-mail:* jpitts@saint.limestone.edu.

Application contact Terry Capps, Administrative Assistant-Admissions, Limestone College, 1115 College Drive, Gaffney, SC 29340-3798. *Phone:* 864-489-7151 Ext. 554. *Web address:* http://www.limestone.edu.

LINFIELD COLLEGE
McMinnville, Oregon

Students with LD Served by Program	60	ADD/ADHD Services	✓
Staff	1 full-time	Summer Preparation Program	n/a
LD Program or Service Fee	n/a	Alternative Test Arrangements	✓
LD Program Began	1989	LD Student Organization	n/a

Learning Support Services began offering services in 1989. The program serves approximately 60 undergraduate students. Faculty consists of 1 full-time staff member. Services are provided by remediation/learning specialists, LD specialists, and trained peer tutors.

Policies The college has written policies regarding course substitutions, grade forgiveness, and substitution and waivers of requirements for admission and graduation. Students with LD may take up to 18 credit hours per semester; 9 credit hours per semester are required to maintain full-time status; 12 credit hours per semester are required to be eligible for financial aid.

Basic skills remediation Available in study skills, computer skills, reading, time management, social skills, learning strategies, written language, and math. Offered by LD specialists.

Subject-area tutoring Available in most subjects. Offered one-on-one and in small groups by computer-based instruction, trained peer tutors, and LD specialists.

Counseling and advisement Career counseling, individual counseling, small-group counseling, and support groups are available.

Auxiliary aids and services *Aids:* calculators, scan and read programs (e.g., Kurzweil), speech recognition programs (e.g., Dragon), tape recorders. *Services and accommodations:* advocates, priority registration, alternative test arrangements, readers, note-takers, and scribes.

ADD/ADHD Students with ADD/ADHD are eligible for the same services available to students with LD, as well as distraction-free study areas, distraction-free testing environments, medication management and personal coach or mentors.

Application *Required:* high school transcript, personal statement, letter(s) of recommendation, and psychoeducational report (5 years old or less). *Recommended:* participation in extracurricular activities, ACT or SAT I (extended-time or untimed test accepted), and interview. Upon application, documentation of need for special services should be sent to both admissions and your LD program or unit. Upon acceptance, documentation of need for special services should be sent only to your LD program or unit. *Application deadline (institutional):* 4/1 for fall and 12/15 for spring. *Application deadline (LD program):* 4/1 for fall and 12/15 for spring.

LD program contact Dr. Judith L. Haynes, Director, 900 Southeast Baker Street, McMinnville, OR 97128. *Phone:* 503-434-2444. *Fax:* 503-434-2647. *E-mail:* jhaynes@linfield.edu.

Application contact Linfield College, 900 SE Baker Street, McMinnville, OR 97128-6894. *E-mail:* admissions@linfield.edu. *Web address:* http://www.linfield.edu/.

LONG ISLAND UNIVERSITY, C.W. POST CAMPUS
Brookville, New York

Students with LD Served by Program	130	ADD/ADHD Services	✓
Staff	3 full-time, 20 part-time	Summer Preparation Program	n/a
LD Program or Service Fee	✓	Alternative Test Arrangements	✓
LD Program Began	1985	LD Student Organization	n/a

Academic Resource Center began offering services in 1985. The program serves approximately 130 undergraduate students. Faculty consists of 3 full-time and 20 part-time staff members. Services are provided by academic advisers, counselors, graduate assistants/students, LD specialists, trained peer tutors, and professional tutors.

Policies The college has written policies regarding course substitutions and substitution and waivers of requirements for admission.

Fees *LD Program or Service Fee:* $2800 per year.

Special preparation or orientation Required orientation held before classes begin.

Basic skills remediation Available in auditory processing, study skills, computer skills, reading, time management, social skills, visual processing, learning strategies, and written language. Offered one-on-one by graduate assistants/students, LD specialists, professional tutors, and trained peer tutors.

Subject-area tutoring Available in all subjects. Offered one-on-one by professional tutors, graduate assistants/students, trained peer tutors, and LD specialists.

Counseling and advisement Career counseling, individual counseling, and support groups are available. Academic advisement by a staff member affiliated with the program is available.

Auxiliary aids and services *Aids:* calculators, personal computers, personal spelling/word-use assistants (e.g., Franklin Speller), scan and read programs (e.g., Kurzweil), screen readers, tape recorders, taped textbooks. *Services and accommodations:* advocates, alternative test arrangements, readers, note-takers, scribes, and use of PCs to take exams, peer mentoring program for freshman.

ADD/ADHD Students with ADD/ADHD are eligible for the same services available to students with LD, as well as distraction-free study areas and distraction-free testing environments.

Long Island University, C.W. Post Campus (continued)

Application *Required:* high school transcript, ACT or SAT I (extended-time or untimed test accepted), interview, personal statement, letter(s) of recommendation, separate application to your LD program or unit, psychoeducational report (3 years old or less), and documentation of high school services (e.g., Individualized Education Program [IEP] or 504 plan). *Recommended:* participation in extracurricular activities. Upon application, documentation of need for special services should be sent only to your LD program or unit. Upon acceptance, documentation of need for special services should be sent only to your LD program or unit. *Application deadline (institutional):* rolling/continuous for fall and rolling/continuous for spring. *Application deadline (LD program):* rolling/continuous for fall and rolling/continuous for spring.

LD program contact Carol Rundlett, Director, Academic Resource Center, 720 Northern Boulevard, Brookville, NY 11548. *Phone:* 516-299-2937. *Fax:* 516-299-2126. *E-mail:* crundlet@liu.edu.

Application contact Jeffrey Lang, Associate Director of Admissions, Long Island University, C.W. Post Campus, 720 Northern Boulevard, Brookville, NY 11548-1300. *Phone:* 516-299-2900. *E-mail:* admissions@collegehall.liunet.edu. *Web address:* http://www.cwpost.liunet.edu/cwis/cwp/post.html.

LORAS COLLEGE
Dubuque, Iowa

Students with LD Served by Program	75	ADD/ADHD Services	✓
Staff	2 full-time	Summer Preparation Program	n/a
LD Program or Service Fee	varies	Alternative Test Arrangements	✓
LD Program Began	1986	LD Student Organization	n/a

Learning Disabilities Program began offering services in 1986. The program serves approximately 75 undergraduate students. Faculty consists of 2 full-time staff members. Services are provided by remediation/learning specialists, LD specialists, and trained peer tutors.

Policies 12 credit hours per semester are required to maintain full-time status and to be eligible for financial aid. LD services are also available to graduate students.

Fees *LD Program or Service Fee:* ranges from $2305 to $2850 per year. *Diagnostic Testing Fee:* $600.

Special preparation or orientation Required orientation held during registration and after classes begin.

Diagnostic testing Available for spelling, intelligence, personality, reading, written language, social skills, and math.

Basic skills remediation Available in study skills, reading, learning strategies, and written language. Offered one-on-one and in class-size groups by regular education teachers and LD specialists.

Subject-area tutoring Available in most subjects. Offered one-on-one and in small groups by trained peer tutors and LD specialists.

Special courses Available in learning strategies. All courses are offered for credit; all enter into overall grade point average.

Auxiliary aids and services *Aids:* scan and read programs (e.g., Kurzweil), tape recorders, taped textbooks. *Services and accommodations:* priority registration, alternative test arrangements, and note-takers.

ADD/ADHD Students with ADD/ADHD are eligible for the same services available to students with LD, as well as distraction-free testing environments.

Application *Required:* high school transcript, ACT or SAT I (extended-time or untimed test accepted), interview, personal statement, letter(s) of recommendation, and psychoeducational report (3 years old or less). Upon application, documentation of need for special services should be sent only to your LD program or unit. Upon acceptance, documentation of need for special services should be sent only to your LD program or unit. *Application deadline (institutional):* rolling/continuous for fall and rolling/continuous for spring. *Application deadline (LD program):* 10/1 for fall.

LD program contact Rochelle Fury, Secretary, 1450 Alta Vista Street, Mailbox #31, Dubuque, IA 52004-0178. *Phone:* 319-588-7134. *Fax:* 319-588-4959. *E-mail:* rfury@loras.edu.

Application contact Loras College, 1450 Alta Vista, Dubuque, IA 52004-0178. *E-mail:* adms@lora.edu. *Web address:* http://www.loras.edu/.

LOUISIANA COLLEGE
Pineville, Louisiana

Students with LD Served by Program	20	ADD/ADHD Services	✓
Staff	1 full-time, 2 part-time	Summer Preparation Program	n/a
LD Program or Service Fee	varies	Alternative Test Arrangements	✓
LD Program Began	1992	LD Student Organization	n/a

Program to Assist Student Success (PASS) began offering services in 1992. The program serves approximately 20 undergraduate students. Faculty consists of 1 full-time and 2 part-time staff members. Services are provided by academic advisers, remediation/learning specialists, regular education teachers, diagnostic specialists, special education teachers, LD specialists, and trained peer tutors.

Policies Students with LD may take up to 18 credit hours per semester; 12 credit hours per semester are required to maintain full-time status.

Fees *LD Program or Service Fee:* ranges from $500 to $1700 per year.

Special preparation or orientation Optional orientation held individually by special arrangement.

Basic skills remediation Available in study skills, reading, time management, social skills, and math. Offered one-on-one by computer-based instruction, regular education teachers, special education teachers, LD specialists, and trained peer tutors.

Subject-area tutoring Available in all subjects. Offered one-on-one by trained peer tutors, LD specialists, and certified teachers.

Counseling and advisement Academic advisement by a staff member affiliated with the program is available.

Auxiliary aids and services *Aids:* calculators, screen-enlarging programs, speech recognition programs (e.g., Dragon), tape recorders, taped textbooks. *Services and accommodations:* alternative test arrangements, readers, note-takers, and scribes.

ADD/ADHD Students with ADD/ADHD are eligible for the same services available to students with LD, as well as distraction-free study areas and distraction-free testing environments.

Application *Required:* high school transcript, ACT or SAT I (extended-time or untimed test accepted), interview, personal statement, letter(s) of recommendation, and separate application to your LD program or unit. *Recommended:* psychoeducational report and documentation of high school services (e.g., Individualized Education Program [IEP] or 504 plan). Upon application, documentation of need for special services should be sent to both admissions and your LD program or unit. Upon acceptance, documentation of need for special services should be sent to both admissions and your LD program or unit. *Appli-*

cation deadline (institutional): rolling/continuous for fall and rolling/continuous for spring. *Application deadline (LD program):* rolling/continuous for fall and rolling/continuous for spring.
LD program contact Betty P. Matthews, Director, 140 College Drive, PO Box 545, Pineville, LA 71360. *Phone:* 318-487-7629. *E-mail:* pass@lacollege.edu.
Application contact Louisiana College, Box 560, Pineville, LA 71359-0001. *E-mail:* admissions@andria.lacollege.edu. *Web address:* http://www.lacollege.edu/.

LYNN UNIVERSITY
Boca Raton, Florida

Students with LD Served by Program	200	ADD/ADHD Services	n/a
Staff	6 full-time, 12 part-time	Summer Preparation Program	✓
LD Program or Service Fee	✓	Alternative Test Arrangements	✓
LD Program Began	1991	LD Student Organization	n/a

The Advancement Program (TAP) began offering services in 1991. The program serves approximately 200 undergraduate students. Faculty consists of 6 full-time and 12 part-time staff members. Services are provided by academic advisers, counselors, LD specialists, and professional tutors.
Policies LD services are also available to graduate students.
Fees *LD Program or Service Fee:* $8150 per year.
Special preparation or orientation Required summer program offered prior to entering college. Optional orientation held during registration.
Subject-area tutoring Available in all subjects. Offered one-on-one and in small groups by professional tutors and LD specialists.
Special courses Available in psychology, biology, English, sociology. All courses are offered for credit; all enter into overall grade point average.
Counseling and advisement Career counseling and individual counseling are available. Academic advisement by a staff member affiliated with the program is available.
Auxiliary aids and services *Aids:* personal computers, screen-enlarging programs. *Services and accommodations:* advocates, alternative test arrangements, and readers.
Application *Required:* high school transcript, ACT or SAT I (extended-time or untimed test accepted), letter(s) of recommendation, and psychoeducational report (3 years old or less). *Recommended:* participation in extracurricular activities, interview, and personal statement. Upon application, documentation of need for special services should be sent only to admissions. *Application deadline (institutional):* rolling/continuous for fall and rolling/continuous for spring. *Application deadline (LD program):* rolling/continuous for fall and rolling/continuous for spring.
LD program contact Melanie Glines, Admission Counselor, 3601 North Military Trail, Boca Raton, FL 33431. *Phone:* 800-544-8035. *Fax:* 561-241-3552. *E-mail:* melglines@lynn.edu.
Application contact Lynn University, 3601 North Military Trail, Boca Raton, FL 33431-5598. *E-mail:* admission@lynn.edu. *Web address:* http://www.lynn.edu/.

MACALESTER COLLEGE
St. Paul, Minnesota

Students with LD Served by Program	200	ADD/ADHD Services	✓
Staff	3 full-time	Summer Preparation Program	n/a
LD Program or Service Fee	n/a	Alternative Test Arrangements	✓
LD Program Began	1995	LD Student Organization	✓

Disability Services began offering services in 1995. The program serves approximately 200 undergraduate students. Faculty consists of 3 full-time staff members. Services are provided by academic advisers, counselors, graduate assistants/students, and trained peer tutors.
Policies The college has written policies regarding course substitutions.
Basic skills remediation Available in auditory processing, study skills, computer skills, time management, handwriting, visual processing, learning strategies, and written language. Offered one-on-one by computer-based instruction, graduate assistants/students, and trained peer tutors.
Subject-area tutoring Available in some subjects. Offered one-on-one and in small groups by computer-based instruction, graduate assistants/students, and trained peer tutors.
Counseling and advisement Career counseling and individual counseling are available. Academic advisement by a staff member affiliated with the program is available.
Auxiliary aids and services *Aids:* calculators, scan and read programs (e.g., Kurzweil), screen-enlarging programs, screen readers, speech recognition programs (e.g., Dragon), tape recorders. *Services and accommodations:* alternative test arrangements, readers, note-takers, and scribes.
Student organization There is a student organization for students with LD.
ADD/ADHD Students with ADD/ADHD are eligible for the same services available to students with LD, as well as distraction-free testing environments.
Application *Required:* high school transcript, participation in extracurricular activities, ACT or SAT I (extended-time or untimed test accepted), interview, personal statement, and letter(s) of recommendation. Upon application, documentation of need for special services should be sent only to admissions. Upon acceptance, documentation of need for special services should be sent only to your LD program or unit. *Application deadline (institutional):* rolling/continuous for fall.
LD program contact Bob Brandt, Director of Health Services, 1600 Grand Avenue, St. Paul, MN 55105. *Phone:* 651-696-6534. *Fax:* 651-696-6687.
Application contact Macalester College, 1600 Grand Avenue, St. Paul, MN 55105-1899. *E-mail:* admissions@macalstr.edu. *Web address:* http://www.macalester.edu/.

MANHATTANVILLE COLLEGE
Purchase, New York

Students with LD Served by Program	52	ADD/ADHD Services	✓
Staff	4 full-time, 7 part-time	Summer Preparation Program	n/a
LD Program or Service Fee	✓	Alternative Test Arrangements	✓
LD Program Began	1991	LD Student Organization	n/a

HELP Program (Higher Education Learning Program) began offering services in 1991. The program serves approximately 52 undergraduate students. Faculty consists of 4 full-time and 7 part-time staff members. Services are provided by LD specialists.

Manhattanville College (continued)

Fees *LD Program or Service Fee:* $3120 per year.

Special preparation or orientation Optional orientation held before classes begin.

Basic skills remediation Available in study skills, computer skills, reading, time management, social skills, learning strategies, and written language. Offered one-on-one by computer-based instruction, special education teachers, and LD specialists.

Special courses Available in written composition skills. All courses are offered for credit; all enter into overall grade point average.

Counseling and advisement Career counseling, individual counseling, and small-group counseling are available.

Auxiliary aids and services *Aids:* calculators, personal computers, scan and read programs (e.g., Kurzweil), screen readers, speech recognition programs (e.g., Dragon). *Services and accommodations:* alternative test arrangements and note-takers.

ADD/ADHD Students with ADD/ADHD are eligible for the same services available to students with LD, as well as distraction-free testing environments.

Application *Required:* high school transcript, ACT or SAT I (extended-time tests accepted), and letter(s) of recommendation. *Recommended:* participation in extracurricular activities, personal statement, psychoeducational report, and documentation of high school services (e.g., Individualized Education Program [IEP] or 504 plan). Upon acceptance, documentation of need for special services should be sent to both admissions and your LD program or unit. *Application deadline (institutional):* 3/1 for fall and 1/1 for spring. *Application deadline (LD program):* rolling/continuous for fall and rolling/continuous for spring.

LD program contact Myra Gentile, Assistant Director, 2900 Purchase Street, Purchase, NY 10577. *Phone:* 914-323-5313.

Application contact Manhattanville College, 2900 Purchase Street, Purchase, NY 10577-2132. *E-mail:* admission@mville. edu. *Web address:* http://www.manhattanville.edu/.

MARIST COLLEGE
Poughkeepsie, New York

Students with LD Served by Program	80	ADD/ADHD Services	✓
Staff	3 full-time, 3 part-time	Summer Preparation Program	n/a
LD Program or Service Fee	✓	Alternative Test Arrangements	✓
LD Program Began	1982	LD Student Organization	n/a

Learning Disabilities Support Program began offering services in 1982. The program serves approximately 80 undergraduate students. Faculty consists of 3 full-time and 3 part-time staff members. Services are provided by LD specialists.

Policies Students with LD may take up to 12 credit hours per semester; 12 credit hours per semester are required to maintain full-time status. LD services are also available to graduate students.

Fees *LD Program or Service Fee:* $2800 per year.

Subject-area tutoring Available in most subjects. Offered one-on-one and in small groups by trained peer tutors.

Counseling and advisement Individual counseling is available.

Auxiliary aids and services *Aids:* calculators, personal computers, personal spelling/word-use assistants (e.g., Franklin Speller), scan and read programs (e.g., Kurzweil), tape recorders, taped textbooks. *Services and accommodations:* priority registration, alternative test arrangements, readers, note-takers, and scribes.

ADD/ADHD Students with ADD/ADHD are eligible for the same services available to students with LD, as well as distraction-free testing environments.

Application *Required:* high school transcript, ACT or SAT I (extended-time tests accepted), interview, personal statement, letter(s) of recommendation, separate application to your LD program or unit, psychoeducational report (3 years old or less), documentation of high school services (e.g., Individualized Education Program [IEP] or 504 plan), and Test of academic achievement. Upon application, documentation of need for special services should be sent only to your LD program or unit. Upon acceptance, documentation of need for special services should be sent only to your LD program or unit. *Application deadline (institutional):* rolling/continuous for fall and rolling/continuous for spring. *Application deadline (LD program):* rolling/continuous for fall and rolling/continuous for spring.

LD program contact Program Secretary, 290 North Road, Poughkeepsie, NY 12601. *Phone:* 914-575-3274. *Fax:* 914-575-3011.

Application contact Jay Murray, Associate Director of Admissions, Marist College, 290 North Road, Poughkeepsie, NY 12601-1387. *Phone:* 914-575-3226 Ext. 2441. *E-mail:* admissions@marist. edu. *Web address:* http://www.marist.edu/.

MARSHALL UNIVERSITY
Huntington, West Virginia

Students with LD Served by Program	200	ADD/ADHD Services	✓
Staff	7 full-time, 53 part-time	Summer Preparation Program	✓
LD Program or Service Fee	varies	Alternative Test Arrangements	✓
LD Program Began	1981	LD Student Organization	n/a

Higher Education for Learning Problems (HELP) Program began offering services in 1981. The program serves approximately 200 undergraduate students. Faculty consists of 7 full-time and 53 part-time staff members. Services are provided by academic advisers, regular education teachers, remediation/learning specialists, diagnostic specialists, special education teachers, graduate assistants/students, LD specialists, and professional tutors.

Policies The college has written policies regarding course substitutions and substitution and waivers of requirements for admission. Students with LD may take up to 18 credit hours per semester; 12 credit hours per semester are required to maintain full-time status and to be eligible for financial aid. LD services are also available to graduate students.

Fees *LD Program or Service Fee:* ranges from $250 to $3000 per year. *Diagnostic Testing Fee:* ranges from $500 to $650.

Special preparation or orientation Required summer program offered prior to entering college. Required orientation held before registration, during registration, before classes begin, and during summer prior to enrollment.

Diagnostic testing Available for auditory processing, motor skills, spelling, handwriting, neuropsychological, spoken language, intelligence, study skills, learning strategies, reading, written language, learning styles, visual processing, and math.

Basic skills remediation Available in auditory processing, motor skills, study skills, computer skills, reading, time management, handwriting, social skills, visual processing, learning strategies, spelling, written language, math, and spoken language. Offered one-on-one by graduate assistants/students, LD specialists, and trained peer tutors.

Subject-area tutoring Available in all subjects. Offered one-on-one by professional tutors and graduate assistants/students.

Special courses Available in study skills, college survival skills, practical computer skills, and time management. No courses are offered for credit; none enter into overall grade point average.

Counseling and advisement Academic advisement by a staff member affiliated with the program is available.

Auxiliary aids and services *Aids:* calculators, personal computers, personal spelling/word-use assistants (e.g., Franklin Speller), scan and read programs (e.g., Kurzweil), screen readers, tape recorders, taped textbooks. *Services and accommodations:* advocates, priority registration, alternative test arrangements, readers, and scribes.

ADD/ADHD Students with ADD/ADHD are eligible for the same services available to students with LD, as well as distraction-free study areas, distraction-free testing environments and personal coach or mentors.

Application *Required:* high school transcript, ACT or SAT I (extended-time or untimed test accepted), interview, personal statement, letter(s) of recommendation, separate application to your LD program or unit, and psychoeducational report (3 years old or less). *Recommended:* participation in extracurricular activities and documentation of high school services (e.g., Individualized Education Program [IEP] or 504 plan). Upon application, documentation of need for special services should be sent to both admissions and your LD program or unit. *Application deadline (institutional):* rolling/continuous for fall and rolling/continuous for spring. *Application deadline (LD program):* 12/31 for fall and 12/31 for spring.

LD program contact Lynne Weston, Assistant Director, Myers Hall, 520 18th Street, Huntington, WV 25755. *Phone:* 304-696-6316. *Fax:* 304-696-3231. *E-mail:* weston@marshall.edu.

Application contact Marshall University, 400 Hal Greer Boulevard, Huntington, WV 25755-2020. *E-mail:* admissions@marshall.edu. *Web address:* http://www.marshall.edu/.

MARYMOUNT MANHATTAN COLLEGE
New York, New York

Students with LD Served by Program	26	ADD/ADHD Services	✓
Staff	1 full-time, 2 part-time	Summer Preparation Program	n/a
LD Program or Service Fee	✓	Alternative Test Arrangements	✓
LD Program Began	1990	LD Student Organization	n/a

Program for Academic Access began offering services in 1990. The program serves approximately 26 undergraduate students. Faculty consists of 1 full-time and 2 part-time staff members. Services are provided by diagnostic specialists and LD specialists.

Policies Students with LD may take up to 18 credit hours per semester; 3 credit hours per semester are required to maintain full-time status; 12 credit hours per semester are required to be eligible for financial aid.

Fees *LD Program or Service Fee:* $3000 per year.

Special preparation or orientation Required orientation held before classes begin and individually by special arrangement.

Diagnostic testing Available for spelling, study skills, learning strategies, reading, written language, and math.

Basic skills remediation Available in study skills, reading, time management, social skills, learning strategies, spelling, and written language. Offered one-on-one by LD specialists.

Subject-area tutoring Available in most subjects. Offered one-on-one by LD specialists.

Counseling and advisement Individual counseling is available.

Auxiliary aids and services *Aids:* personal computers, speech recognition programs (e.g., Dragon). *Services and accommodations:* advocates, priority registration, alternative test arrangements, and note-takers.

ADD/ADHD Students with ADD/ADHD are eligible for the same services available to students with LD, as well as distraction-free study areas, distraction-free testing environments and personal coach or mentors.

Application *Required:* high school transcript, interview, personal statement, letter(s) of recommendation, separate application to your LD program or unit, and psychoeducational report (1 year old or less). *Recommended:* participation in extracurricular activities and ACT or SAT I (extended-time tests accepted). Upon application, documentation of need for special services should be sent only to admissions. *Application deadline (institutional):* rolling/continuous for fall and rolling/continuous for spring. *Application deadline (LD program):* rolling/continuous for fall and rolling/continuous for spring.

LD program contact Dr. Jacquelyn N. Bonomo, Assistant Director, Program for Academic Access, Speech Pathology Department, 221 East 71st Street, New York, NY 10021. *Phone:* 212-774-0724. *Fax:* 212-517-0541. *E-mail:* jbonomo@mmm.edu.

Application contact Marymount Manhattan College, 221 East 71st Street, New York, NY 10021. *E-mail:* admissions@marymou.edu. *Web address:* http://www.marymount.mmm.edu/.

MERCY COLLEGE
Dobbs Ferry, New York

Students with LD Served by Program	60	ADD/ADHD Services	✓
Staff	1 full-time, 12 part-time	Summer Preparation Program	✓
LD Program or Service Fee	✓	Alternative Test Arrangements	✓
LD Program Began	1988	LD Student Organization	n/a

Striving Towards Abilities Realized (STAR) Program began offering services in 1988. The program serves approximately 60 undergraduate students. Faculty consists of 1 full-time and 12 part-time staff members. Services are provided by academic advisers, counselors, remediation/learning specialists, special education teachers, LD specialists, and professional tutors.

Policies The college has written policies regarding course substitutions and substitution and waivers of requirements for admission. Students with LD may take up to 15 credit hours per semester; 12 credit hours per semester are required to maintain full-time status and to be eligible for financial aid.

Fees *LD Program or Service Fee:* $2675 per year.

Special preparation or orientation Required summer program offered prior to entering college. Required orientation held during summer prior to enrollment.

Basic skills remediation Available in study skills, computer skills, reading, time management, handwriting, social skills, spelling, and written language. Offered in small groups by LD specialists and professional tutors.

Subject-area tutoring Available in all subjects. Offered one-on-one by professional tutors and LD specialists.

Counseling and advisement Career counseling and individual counseling are available. Academic advisement by a staff member affiliated with the program is available.

Auxiliary aids and services *Aids:* calculators, personal spelling/word-use assistants (e.g., Franklin Speller), scan and read programs (e.g., Kurzweil), screen-enlarging programs, tape recorders, taped textbooks. *Services and accommodations:* advocates, alternative test arrangements, readers, note-takers, and scribes.

ADD/ADHD Students with ADD/ADHD are eligible for the same services available to students with LD, as well as distraction-free study areas and distraction-free testing environments.

Application *Required:* high school transcript, participation in extracurricular activities, interview, personal statement, letter(s) of recommendation, separate application to your LD program or

Mercy College (continued)

unit, psychoeducational report (3 years old or less), and documentation of high school services (e.g., Individualized Education Program [IEP] or 504 plan). Upon application, documentation of need for special services should be sent only to your LD program or unit. Upon acceptance, documentation of need for special services should be sent only to your LD program or unit. *Application deadline (institutional):* rolling/continuous for fall and rolling/continuous for spring. *Application deadline (LD program):* rolling/continuous for fall and rolling/continuous for spring.

LD program contact Terry Rich, Director of STAR Program, 555 Broadway, Dobbs Ferry, NY 10522. *Phone:* 914-674-7218. *Fax:* 914-674-7410.

Application contact Mercy College, 555 Broadway, Dobbs Ferry, NY 10522-1189. *E-mail:* admissions@merlin.mercynet. edu. *Web address:* http://www.mercynet.edu/.

MERCYHURST COLLEGE
Erie, Pennsylvania

Students with LD Served by Program	100	ADD/ADHD Services	✓
Staff	1 full-time, 2 part-time	Summer Preparation Program	✓
LD Program or Service Fee	✓	Alternative Test Arrangements	✓
LD Program Began	1986	LD Student Organization	n/a

Program for Students with Learning Disabilities began offering services in 1986. The program serves approximately 100 undergraduate students. Faculty consists of 1 full-time and 2 part-time staff members. Services are provided by graduate assistants/students and LD specialists.

Fees *LD Program or Service Fee:* $1000 per year.

Special preparation or orientation Optional summer program offered prior to entering college. Required orientation held before classes begin.

Basic skills remediation Available in reading, written language, and math. Offered in class-size groups by regular education teachers.

Subject-area tutoring Available in all subjects. Offered one-on-one and in small groups by graduate assistants/students, trained peer tutors, and LD specialists.

Special courses Available in study skills, college survival skills, practical computer skills, test taking, reading, time management, vocabulary development, math, and written composition skills. Some courses are offered for credit; some enter into overall grade point average.

Counseling and advisement Individual counseling is available.

Auxiliary aids and services *Aids:* calculators, personal computers, personal spelling/word-use assistants (e.g., Franklin Speller), scan and read programs (e.g., Kurzweil), screen-enlarging programs, tape recorders, taped textbooks. *Services and accommodations:* priority registration, alternative test arrangements, readers, note-takers, scribes, and tutors.

ADD/ADHD Students with ADD/ADHD are eligible for the same services available to students with LD, as well as distraction-free study areas, distraction-free testing environments and personal coach or mentors.

Application *Required:* high school transcript, ACT or SAT I (extended-time or untimed test accepted), interview, personal statement, letter(s) of recommendation, and psychoeducational report (3 years old or less). *Recommended:* documentation of high school services (e.g., Individualized Education Program [IEP] or 504 plan). Upon application, documentation of need for special services should be sent only to your LD program or unit. Upon acceptance, documentation of need for special services

should be sent only to your LD program or unit. *Application deadline (institutional):* rolling/continuous for fall. *Application deadline (LD program):* rolling/continuous for fall.

LD program contact Dianne Rogers, Director, Learning Differences Program, 501 East 38th Street, Erie, PA 16546-0001. *Phone:* 814-824-2450. *Fax:* 814-824-2438. *E-mail:* drogers@mercyhurst. edu.

Application contact Jim Breckenridge, Director of Undergraduate Admissions, Mercyhurst College, 501 East 38th Street, Erie, PA 16546. *Phone:* 814-824-2573. *E-mail:* admug@paradise.mercy. edu. *Web address:* http://www.mercyhurst.edu/.

MEREDITH COLLEGE
Raleigh, North Carolina

Students with LD Served by Program	141	ADD/ADHD Services	✓
Staff	1 full-time, 2 part-time	Summer Preparation Program	✓
LD Program or Service Fee	n/a	Alternative Test Arrangements	✓
LD Program Began	n/a	LD Student Organization	✓

Counseling Center serves approximately 141 undergraduate students. Faculty consists of 1 full-time and 2 part-time staff members. Services are provided by academic advisers, counselors, regular education teachers, diagnostic specialists, and trained peer tutors.

Policies The college has written policies regarding course substitutions. Students with LD may take up to 18 credit hours per semester; 12 credit hours per semester are required to maintain full-time status; 6 credit hours per semester are required to be eligible for financial aid. LD services are also available to graduate students.

Special preparation or orientation Optional summer program offered prior to entering college. Optional orientation held before registration, during registration, before classes begin, after classes begin, during summer prior to enrollment, and individually by special arrangement.

Basic skills remediation Available in study skills, reading, time management, learning strategies, written language, and math. Offered in small groups and class-size groups by computer-based instruction, regular education teachers, trained peer tutors, and academic advisors.

Subject-area tutoring Available in most subjects. Offered one-on-one, in small groups, and class-size groups by computer-based instruction, graduate assistants/students, and trained peer tutors.

Special courses Available in career planning, study skills, college survival skills, test taking, reading, time management, learning strategies, self-advocacy, math, stress management, written composition skills, and foreign language preparation. Some courses are offered for credit; some enter into overall grade point average.

Counseling and advisement Career counseling, individual counseling, small-group counseling, and support groups are available. Academic advisement by a staff member affiliated with the program is available.

Auxiliary aids and services *Aids:* screen-enlarging programs, screen readers, speech recognition programs (e.g., Dragon), taped textbooks. *Services and accommodations:* advocates, priority registration, alternative test arrangements, readers, note-takers, and scribes.

Student organization There is a student organization for students with LD.

ADD/ADHD Students with ADD/ADHD are eligible for the same services available to students with LD, as well as distraction-free study areas, distraction-free testing environments, personal coach or mentors, and support groups for ADD/ADHD.

Application *Required:* high school transcript, ACT or SAT I (extended-time or untimed test accepted), personal statement, and letter(s) of recommendation. *Recommended:* participation in extracurricular activities and interview. Upon application, documentation of need for special services should be sent only to your LD program or unit. Upon acceptance, documentation of need for special services should be sent only to your LD program or unit. *Application deadline (LD program):* rolling/continuous for fall and rolling/continuous for spring.

LD program contact Lori Ann Stretch, Assistant Counseling Director/Coordinator of Disability Services, 3800 Hillsborough Street, Raleigh, NC 27607. *Phone:* 919-760-8427. *Fax:* 919-760-2383. *E-mail:* stretchl@meredith.edu.

Application contact Meredith College, 3800 Hillsborough Street, Raleigh, NC 27607-5298. *E-mail:* admissions@meredith.edu. *Web address:* http://www.meredith.edu/.

MIDDLE TENNESSEE STATE UNIVERSITY
Murfreesboro, Tennessee

Students with LD Served by Program	150	ADD/ADHD Services	✓
Staff	1 full-time	Summer Preparation Program	n/a
LD Program or Service Fee	n/a	Alternative Test Arrangements	✓
LD Program Began	1997	LD Student Organization	n/a

Disabled Student Services, Learning Disabilities Program began offering services in 1997. The program serves approximately 150 undergraduate students. Faculty consists of 1 full-time staff member. Services are provided by LD specialists.

Policies Students with LD may take up to 18 hours per semester; 12 hours per semester are required to maintain full-time status and to be eligible for financial aid. LD services are also available to graduate students.

Special preparation or orientation Optional orientation held after classes begin and individually by special arrangement.

Basic skills remediation Available in study skills, computer skills, and time management. Offered one-on-one by LD specialists.

Subject-area tutoring Available in some subjects. Offered one-on-one and in small groups by computer-based instruction and graduate assistants/students.

Counseling and advisement Career counseling and individual counseling are available.

Auxiliary aids and services *Aids:* calculators, personal spelling/word-use assistants (e.g., Franklin Speller), scan and read programs (e.g., Kurzweil), screen-enlarging programs, screen readers, speech recognition programs (e.g., Dragon), tape recorders, taped textbooks. *Services and accommodations:* priority registration, alternative test arrangements, readers, note-takers, and scribes.

ADD/ADHD Students with ADD/ADHD are eligible for the same services available to students with LD, as well as distraction-free study areas and distraction-free testing environments.

Application *Required:* high school transcript, ACT or SAT I (extended-time or untimed test accepted), and psychoeducational report. Upon application, documentation of need for special services should be sent only to your LD program or unit. Upon acceptance, documentation of need for special services should be sent only to your LD program or unit. *Application deadline (institutional):* 8/21 for fall and 1/8 for spring. *Application deadline (LD program):* rolling/continuous for fall and rolling/continuous for spring.

LD program contact Melissa Smith, Assistant Director, Disabled Student Services, PO Box 7, Murfreesboro, TN 37132. *Phone:* 615-904-8246. *Fax:* 615-898-4893. *E-mail:* masmith@mtsu.edu.

Application contact Middle Tennessee State University, Murfreesboro, TN 37132. *E-mail:* admissions@mtsu.edu. *Web address:* http://www.mtsu.edu/.

MILLS COLLEGE
Oakland, California

Students with LD Served by Program	85	ADD/ADHD Services	✓
Staff	1 full-time	Summer Preparation Program	n/a
LD Program or Service Fee	n/a	Alternative Test Arrangements	✓
LD Program Began	1992	LD Student Organization	✓

Disabled Students' Services (DSS) began offering services in 1992. The program serves approximately 85 undergraduate students. Faculty consists of 1 full-time staff member. Services are provided by LD specialists.

Policies Students with LD may take up to 16 credit hours per semester; 9 credit hours per semester are required to maintain full-time status and to be eligible for financial aid. LD services are also available to graduate students.

Special preparation or orientation Required orientation held before registration, during registration, before classes begin, after classes begin, during summer prior to enrollment, and individually by special arrangement.

Diagnostic testing Available for auditory processing, motor skills, spelling, handwriting, neuropsychological, spoken language, learning strategies, reading, written language, learning styles, visual processing, math, and Woodcock-Johnson-Revised.

Subject-area tutoring Available in some subjects. Offered one-on-one and in small groups by trained peer tutors.

Counseling and advisement Career counseling, individual counseling, and support groups are available.

Auxiliary aids and services *Aids:* calculators, personal spelling/word-use assistants (e.g., Franklin Speller), scan and read programs (e.g., Kurzweil), screen-enlarging programs, tape recorders, two computers with specialized software. *Services and accommodations:* alternative test arrangements, readers, note-takers, and scribes.

Student organization There is a student organization for students with LD.

ADD/ADHD Students with ADD/ADHD are eligible for the same services available to students with LD, as well as distraction-free testing environments.

Application *Required:* high school transcript, ACT or SAT I (extended-time or untimed test accepted), personal statement, and letter(s) of recommendation. *Recommended:* participation in extracurricular activities and interview. Upon application, documentation of need for special services should be sent only to your LD program or unit. Upon acceptance, documentation of need for special services should be sent only to your LD program or unit. *Application deadline (institutional):* rolling/continuous for fall and rolling/continuous for spring. *Application deadline (LD program):* rolling/continuous for fall and rolling/continuous for spring.

LD program contact Ruth Masayko, Director/Learning Disabilities Specialist, 5000 MacArthur Boulevard, Oakland, CA 94613. *Phone:* 510-430-2264. *Fax:* 510-430-3235. *E-mail:* ruthm@mills.edu.

Mills College (continued)

Application contact Mills College, 5000 MacArthur Boulevard, Oakland, CA 94613-1000. *E-mail:* admission@mills.edu. *Web address:* http://www.mills.edu/.

MOUNT ALLISON UNIVERSITY
Sackville, New Brunswick

Students with LD Served by Program	60	ADD/ADHD Services	n/a
Staff	2 full-time, 1 part-time	Summer Preparation Program	n/a
LD Program or Service Fee	n/a	Alternative Test Arrangements	✓
LD Program Began	1988	LD Student Organization	✓

The Meighen Centre began offering services in 1988. The program serves approximately 60 undergraduate students. Faculty consists of 2 full-time staff members and 1 part-time staff member. Services are provided by academic advisers, counselors, remediation/learning specialists, diagnostic specialists, and LD specialists.

Policies The college has written policies regarding substitution and waivers of requirements for admission. Students with LD may take up to 15 credit hours per term; 9 credit hours per term are required to maintain full-time status and to be eligible for financial aid.

Special preparation or orientation Optional orientation held after classes begin and individually by special arrangement.

Diagnostic testing Available for auditory processing, spelling, neuropsychological, spoken language, intelligence, reading, written language, visual processing, math, and memory.

Special courses Available in test taking, time management, learning strategies, self-advocacy, and written composition skills. No courses are offered for credit; none enter into overall grade point average.

Counseling and advisement Academic advisement by a staff member affiliated with the program is available.

Auxiliary aids and services *Aids:* calculators, personal computers, personal spelling/word-use assistants (e.g., Franklin Speller), tape recorders, taped textbooks. *Services and accommodations:* advocates, alternative test arrangements, readers, and scribes.

Student organization There is a student organization for students with LD.

Application *Required:* high school transcript, letter(s) of recommendation, separate application to your LD program or unit, psychoeducational report (2 years old or less), and writing sample (unedited). *Recommended:* participation in extracurricular activities, interview, and documentation of high school services (e.g., Individualized Education Program [IEP] or 504 plan). Upon application, documentation of need for special services should be sent only to admissions. Upon acceptance, documentation of need for special services should be sent only to your LD program or unit. *Application deadline (institutional):* rolling/continuous for fall. *Application deadline (LD program):* 4/1 for fall.

LD program contact Jane Drover, Coordinator/Learning Specialist, The Meighen Centre, 144 Main Street, Sackville, NB E4L 1A7. *Phone:* 506-364-2527. *Fax:* 506-364-2625. *E-mail:* jdrover@mta.ca.

Application contact Kristine George, Admissions Counselor, Mount Allison University, Student Administrative Services, Sackville, NB E0A 3C0. *Phone:* 506-364-2269. *E-mail:* swallace@mta.ca. *Web address:* http://www.mta.ca.

MURRAY STATE UNIVERSITY
Murray, Kentucky

Students with LD Served by Program	360	ADD/ADHD Services	✓
Staff	3 full-time	Summer Preparation Program	n/a
LD Program or Service Fee	n/a	Alternative Test Arrangements	✓
LD Program Began	1989	LD Student Organization	✓

Services for Students with Learning Disabilities began offering services in 1989. The program serves approximately 360 undergraduate students. Faculty consists of 3 full-time staff members. Services are provided by counselors, diagnostic specialists, graduate assistants/students, LD specialists, and trained peer tutors.

Policies 12 credit hours per semester are required to maintain full-time status; 24 credit hours per year are required to be eligible for financial aid. LD services are also available to graduate students.

Special preparation or orientation Optional orientation held before registration, after classes begin, during summer prior to enrollment, and individually by special arrangement.

Subject-area tutoring Available in most subjects. Offered one-on-one and in small groups by graduate assistants/students and trained peer tutors.

Special courses Available in college survival skills. All courses are offered for credit; none enter into overall grade point average.

Auxiliary aids and services *Aids:* personal computers, personal spelling/word-use assistants (e.g., Franklin Speller), screen-enlarging programs, screen readers, tape recorders, taped textbooks. *Services and accommodations:* advocates, alternative test arrangements, readers, note-takers, and scribes.

Student organization There is a student organization for students with LD.

ADD/ADHD Students with ADD/ADHD are eligible for the same services available to students with LD, as well as distraction-free study areas, distraction-free testing environments, personal coach or mentors, and support groups for ADD/ADHD.

Application *Required:* high school transcript, ACT (extended-time or untimed test accepted), separate application to your LD program or unit, and psychoeducational report (3 years old or less). *Recommended:* documentation of high school services (e.g., Individualized Education Program [IEP] or 504 plan). Upon application, documentation of need for special services should be sent only to your LD program or unit. Upon acceptance, documentation of need for special services should be sent only to your LD program or unit. *Application deadline (institutional):* rolling/continuous for fall and rolling/continuous for spring. *Application deadline (LD program):* 3/30 for fall and 10/30 for spring.

LD program contact Cindy Clemson, Coordinator, Services for Students with Learning Disabilities, Lowry Center, Murray, KY 42071. *Phone:* 270-762-2018. *Fax:* 270-762-4339. *E-mail:* cindy.clemson@murraystate.edu.

Application contact Stacy Bell, Admission Clerk, Murray State University, PO Box 9, Murray, KY 42071-0009. *Phone:* 270-762-3035. *E-mail:* pbryan@msumusik.mursuky.edu. *Web address:* http://www.murraystate.edu/.

MUSKINGUM COLLEGE
New Concord, Ohio

Students with LD Served by Program	140	ADD/ADHD Services	✓
Staff	23 full-time, 12 part-time	Summer Preparation Program	✓
LD Program or Service Fee	✓	Alternative Test Arrangements	✓
LD Program Began	1983	LD Student Organization	✓

Plus Program began offering services in 1983. The program serves approximately 140 undergraduate students. Faculty consists of 23 full-time and 12 part-time staff members. Services are provided by professional tutors.

Policies Students with LD may take up to 20 credit hours per semester; 10 credit hours per semester are required to maintain full-time status and to be eligible for financial aid. LD services are also available to graduate students.

Fees *LD Program or Service Fee:* $3000 per year.

Special preparation or orientation Optional summer program offered prior to entering college.

Diagnostic testing Available for learning strategies.

Subject-area tutoring Available in some subjects. Offered one-on-one and in small groups by professional tutors and trained peer tutors.

Counseling and advisement Individual counseling is available.

Auxiliary aids and services *Aids:* calculators, personal computers, personal spelling/word-use assistants (e.g., Franklin Speller), scan and read programs (e.g., Kurzweil), screen-enlarging programs, screen readers, speech recognition programs (e.g., Dragon), tape recorders, taped textbooks. *Services and accommodations:* advocates, priority registration, alternative test arrangements, readers, note-takers, and scribes.

Student organization There is a student organization for students with LD.

ADD/ADHD Students with ADD/ADHD are eligible for the same services available to students with LD, as well as distraction-free study areas, distraction-free testing environments and support groups for ADD/ADHD.

Application *Required:* high school transcript, ACT or SAT I (extended-time or untimed test accepted), interview, and psychoeducational report (3 years old or less). *Recommended:* participation in extracurricular activities, ACT (extended-time or untimed test accepted), personal statement, letter(s) of recommendation, and documentation of high school services (e.g., Individualized Education Program [IEP] or 504 plan). Upon application, documentation of need for special services should be sent only to your LD program or unit. Upon acceptance, documentation of need for special services should be sent only to your LD program or unit. *Application deadline (institutional):* rolling/continuous for fall and rolling/continuous for spring. *Application deadline (LD program):* rolling/continuous for fall and rolling/continuous for spring.

LD program contact Michelle Butler, Secretary, Center for Advancement of Learning, New Concord, OH 43762. *Phone:* 740-826-8280. *Fax:* 740-826-8404. *E-mail:* butler@muskingum.edu.

Application contact Muskingum College, 163 Stormont Street, New Concord, OH 43762. *E-mail:* adminfo@muskingum.edu. *Web address:* http://www.muskingum.edu/.

NICHOLLS STATE UNIVERSITY
Thibodaux, Louisiana

Students with LD Served by Program	200	ADD/ADHD Services	✓
Staff	1 full-time	Summer Preparation Program	n/a
LD Program or Service Fee	varies	Alternative Test Arrangements	✓
LD Program Began	1995	LD Student Organization	✓

Disabled Student Services began offering services in 1995. The program serves approximately 200 undergraduate students. Faculty consists of 1 full-time staff member. Services are provided by academic advisers, regular education teachers, counselors, remediation/learning specialists, diagnostic specialists, special education teachers, graduate assistants/students, teacher trainees, LD specialists, trained peer tutors, and professional tutors.

Policies The college has written policies regarding substitution and waivers of requirements for admission and graduation. Students with LD may take up to 21 credit hours per semester; 12 credit hours per semester are required to maintain full-time status and to be eligible for financial aid. LD services are also available to graduate students.

Fees *LD Program or Service Fee:* ranges from $0 to $300 per year. *Diagnostic Testing Fee:* ranges from $200 to $500.

Basic skills remediation Offered one-on-one.

Subject-area tutoring Available in most subjects. Offered in small groups by trained peer tutors.

Counseling and advisement Career counseling and individual counseling are available. Academic advisement by a staff member affiliated with the program is available.

Auxiliary aids and services *Aids:* screen-enlarging programs, tape recorders, taped textbooks. *Services and accommodations:* priority registration, alternative test arrangements, and note-takers.

Student organization There is a student organization for students with LD.

ADD/ADHD Students with ADD/ADHD are eligible for the same services available to students with LD

Application *Required:* high school transcript, ACT (extended-time or untimed test accepted), and Documentation if requesting accommodations. Upon application, documentation of need for special services should be sent only to your LD program or unit. Upon acceptance, documentation of need for special services should be sent only to your LD program or unit. *Application deadline (institutional):* rolling/continuous for fall and rolling/continuous for spring. *Application deadline (LD program):* rolling/continuous for fall and rolling/continuous for spring.

LD program contact Carol Ronka, Director, Center for the Study of Dyslexia, Polk Hall, Thibodaux, LA 70310. *Phone:* 504-448-4214.

Application contact Nicholls State University, PO Box 2009-NSU, Thibodaux, LA 70310. *E-mail:* nicholls@nich-nsunet.nich.edu. *Web address:* http://www.nich.edu/.

NORTHEASTERN UNIVERSITY
Boston, Massachusetts

Students with LD Served by Program	250	ADD/ADHD Services	✓
Staff	n/a	Summer Preparation Program	n/a
LD Program or Service Fee	n/a	Alternative Test Arrangements	✓
LD Program Began	1986	LD Student Organization	n/a

Northeastern University (continued)

The college began offering services in 1986. The program serves approximately 250 undergraduate students. Services are provided by counselors and graduate assistants/students.

Policies LD services are also available to graduate students.

Counseling and advisement Individual counseling is available.

Auxiliary aids and services *Aids:* personal computers, personal spelling/word-use assistants (e.g., Franklin Speller), scan and read programs (e.g., Kurzweil), screen readers, tape recorders. *Services and accommodations:* advocates, alternative test arrangements, note-takers, and scribes.

ADD/ADHD Students with ADD/ADHD are eligible for the same services available to students with LD, as well as distraction-free study areas and distraction-free testing environments.

Application *Required:* diagnostic tests. *Recommended:* interview. Upon application, documentation of need for special services should be sent to both admissions and your LD program or unit. Upon acceptance, documentation of need for special services should be sent only to your LD program or unit. *Application deadline (institutional):* rolling/continuous for fall and rolling/continuous for spring.

LD program contact Debbi Auerbach, Service Coordinator, Disability Resource Center, Boston, MA 02115. *Phone:* 617-373-2675. *Fax:* 617-373-7800.

Application contact Northeastern University, 360 Huntington Avenue, Boston, MA 02115-5096. *E-mail:* admissions@neu.edu. *Web address:* http://www.neu.edu/.

NORTHERN ARIZONA UNIVERSITY
Flagstaff, Arizona

Students with LD Served by Program	140	ADD/ADHD Services	✓
Staff	n/a	Summer Preparation Program	n/a
LD Program or Service Fee	n/a	Alternative Test Arrangements	✓
LD Program Began	1981	LD Student Organization	✓

Disability Support Services began offering services in 1981. The program serves approximately 140 undergraduate students. Services are provided by academic advisers, counselors, graduate assistants/students, LD specialists, trained peer tutors, and Assistive technology specialist.

Policies The college has written policies regarding course substitutions, grade forgiveness, and substitution and waivers of requirements for admission. Students with LD may take up to 24 credit hours per semester; 12 credit hours per semester are required to maintain full-time status and to be eligible for financial aid. LD services are also available to graduate students.

Special preparation or orientation Optional orientation held before classes begin and individually by special arrangement.

Subject-area tutoring Available in most subjects. Offered one-on-one by computer-based instruction, graduate assistants/students, trained peer tutors, and LD specialists.

Special courses Available in practical computer skills, test taking, math, and written composition skills.

Counseling and advisement Career counseling, individual counseling, small-group counseling, and support groups are available. Academic advisement by a staff member affiliated with the program is available.

Auxiliary aids and services *Aids:* personal computers, personal spelling/word-use assistants (e.g., Franklin Speller), scan and read programs (e.g., Kurzweil), screen-enlarging programs, screen readers, speech recognition programs (e.g., Dragon), taped textbooks. *Services and accommodations:* advocates, priority registration, alternative test arrangements, readers, note-takers, and scribes.

Student organization There is a student organization for students with LD.

ADD/ADHD Students with ADD/ADHD are eligible for the same services available to students with LD, as well as distraction-free study areas, distraction-free testing environments and medication management.

Application *Required:* high school transcript and ACT or SAT I (extended-time or untimed test accepted). *Recommended:* separate application to your LD program or unit, psychoeducational report (3 years old or less), and Request to Self-identify form. Upon application, documentation of need for special services should be sent only to your LD program or unit. Upon acceptance, documentation of need for special services should be sent only to your LD program or unit. *Application deadline (institutional):* 3/1 for fall and 12/1 for spring. *Application deadline (LD program):* rolling/continuous for fall and rolling/continuous for spring.

LD program contact Michelle Thomas, Learning Disabilities Specialist, Box 5633, Flagstaff, AZ 86011. *Phone:* 520-523-8773. *Fax:* 520-523-8747. *E-mail:* michelle.thomas@nau.edu.

Application contact Northern Arizona University, PO Box 4084, Flagstaff, AZ 86011. *E-mail:* ugrad@nau.edu. *Web address:* http://www.nau.edu/.

PACIFIC UNION COLLEGE
Angwin, California

Students with LD Served by Program	120	ADD/ADHD Services	✓
Staff	2 full-time	Summer Preparation Program	n/a
LD Program or Service Fee	n/a	Alternative Test Arrangements	✓
LD Program Began	1994	LD Student Organization	n/a

Learning disAbilities Program began offering services in 1994. The program serves approximately 120 undergraduate students. Faculty consists of 2 full-time staff members. Services are provided by regular education teachers, counselors, diagnostic specialists, and trained peer tutors.

Policies The college has written policies regarding course substitutions and substitution and waivers of requirements for admission and graduation. LD services are also available to graduate students.

Fees *Diagnostic Testing Fee:* $200.

Special preparation or orientation Optional orientation held before registration and individually by special arrangement.

Diagnostic testing Available for motor skills, spelling, intelligence, personality, written language, and math.

Subject-area tutoring Available in most subjects. Offered one-on-one by trained peer tutors.

Special courses Available in college survival skills. All courses are offered for credit; all enter into overall grade point average.

Counseling and advisement Career counseling, individual counseling, support groups, and time management study skills counseling are available.

Auxiliary aids and services *Aids:* screen readers, speech recognition programs (e.g., Dragon), tape recorders, taped textbooks, 4-track recorder. *Services and accommodations:* advocates, priority registration, alternative test arrangements, readers, note-takers, and scribes.

ADD/ADHD Students with ADD/ADHD are eligible for the same services available to students with LD, as well as distraction-free study areas, distraction-free testing environments, medication management, personal coach or mentors, and support groups for ADD/ADHD.

Application *Required:* high school transcript, ACT or SAT I (extended-time or untimed test accepted), and letter(s) of recommendation. *Recommended:* interview, separate application to your LD program or unit, psychoeducational report, and documentation of high school services (e.g., Individualized Education Program [IEP] or 504 plan). Upon application, documentation of need for special services should be sent to both admissions and your LD program or unit. Upon acceptance, documentation of need for special services should be sent only to your LD program or unit. *Application deadline (institutional):* rolling/continuous for fall and rolling/continuous for spring. *Application deadline (LD program):* rolling/continuous for fall and rolling/continuous for spring.

LD program contact Nancy Jacobo, Director, 1 Angwin Avenue, Angwin, CA 94508. *Phone:* 707-965-7364. *Fax:* 707-965-6797. *E-mail:* njacobo@puc.edu.

Application contact Al Trace, Director of Enrollment Services, Pacific Union College, One Angwin Avenue, Angwin, CA 94508-9707. *Phone:* 800-862-7080. *Web address:* http://www.puc.edu/.

PIEDMONT BAPTIST COLLEGE
Winston-Salem, North Carolina

Students with LD Served by Program	10	ADD/ADHD Services	✓
Staff	1 full-time, 4 part-time	Summer Preparation Program	n/a
LD Program or Service Fee	n/a	Alternative Test Arrangements	✓
LD Program Began	1992	LD Student Organization	n/a

Academic Assistance Program (AAP) began offering services in 1992. The program serves approximately 10 undergraduate students. Faculty consists of 1 full-time and 4 part-time staff members. Services are provided by academic advisers, remediation/learning specialists, regular education teachers, special education teachers, graduate assistants/students, LD specialists, and trained peer tutors.

Policies The college has written policies regarding course substitutions and substitution and waivers of requirements for admission and graduation. LD services are also available to graduate students.

Diagnostic testing Available for reading and learning styles.

Basic skills remediation Available in study skills, reading, time management, learning strategies, written language, and math. Offered one-on-one and in small groups by computer-based instruction, regular education teachers, and trained peer tutors.

Subject-area tutoring Available in most subjects. Offered one-on-one and in small groups by computer-based instruction and trained peer tutors.

Special courses Available in study skills, college survival skills, test taking, reading, time management, learning strategies, vocabulary development, math, and written composition skills. All courses are offered for credit; all enter into overall grade point average.

Counseling and advisement Individual counseling and small-group counseling are available. Academic advisement by a staff member affiliated with the program is available.

Auxiliary aids and services *Aids:* calculators, personal computers, personal spelling/word-use assistants (e.g., Franklin Speller), scan and read programs (e.g., Kurzweil), tape recorders. *Services and accommodations:* advocates and alternative test arrangements.

ADD/ADHD Students with ADD/ADHD are eligible for the same services available to students with LD, as well as distraction-free study areas and distraction-free testing environments.

Application *Required:* high school transcript, ACT or SAT I (extended-time or untimed test accepted), interview, personal statement, and letter(s) of recommendation. *Recommended:* psychoeducational report and documentation of high school services (e.g., Individualized Education Program [IEP] or 504 plan). Upon application, documentation of need for special services should be sent to both admissions and your LD program or unit. Upon acceptance, documentation of need for special services should be sent to both admissions and your LD program or unit.

LD program contact Linda Whiteheart, Instructor/Director, 716 Franklin Street, Winston-Salem, NC 27101. *Phone:* 336-725-8344 Ext. 2218. *E-mail:* whiteli@pbc.edu.

Application contact Piedmont Baptist College, 716 Franklin Street, Winston-Salem, NC 27101-5197. *Web address:* http://www.pbc.edu/.

REINHARDT COLLEGE
Waleska, Georgia

Students with LD Served by Program	55	ADD/ADHD Services	✓
Staff	4 full-time	Summer Preparation Program	n/a
LD Program or Service Fee	varies	Alternative Test Arrangements	✓
LD Program Began	1982	LD Student Organization	n/a

Academic Support Office began offering services in 1982. The program serves approximately 55 undergraduate students. Faculty consists of 4 full-time staff members. Services are provided by counselors, regular education teachers, special education teachers, and LD specialists.

Policies Students with LD may take up to 18 credit hours per semester; 12 credit hours per semester are required to maintain full-time status and to be eligible for financial aid.

Special preparation or orientation Required orientation held before classes begin and individually by special arrangement.

Subject-area tutoring Available in some subjects. Offered in small groups by LD specialists and Faculty.

Counseling and advisement Individual counseling and support groups are available.

Auxiliary aids and services *Aids:* calculators, personal computers, scan and read programs (e.g., Kurzweil), screen-enlarging programs, screen readers, speech recognition programs (e.g., Dragon), tape recorders, taped textbooks. *Services and accommodations:* priority registration, alternative test arrangements, and note-takers.

ADD/ADHD Students with ADD/ADHD are eligible for the same services available to students with LD

Application *Required:* high school transcript, ACT or SAT I (extended-time or untimed test accepted), interview, personal statement, letter(s) of recommendation, separate application to your LD program or unit, psychoeducational report (3 years old or less), and documentation of high school services (e.g., Individualized Education Program [IEP] or 504 plan). *Recommended:* participation in extracurricular activities. Upon application, documentation of need for special services should be sent only to admissions. Upon acceptance, documentation of need for special services should be sent only to your LD program or unit. *Application deadline (institutional):* rolling/continuous for fall and rolling/continuous for spring. *Application deadline (LD program):* rolling/continuous for fall and rolling/continuous for spring.

LD program contact Sylvia Robertson, Director, Academic Support Office, 7300 Reinhardt College Circle, Waleska, GA 30183. *Phone:* 770-720-5567. *Fax:* 770-720-5602. *E-mail:* srr@mail.reinhardt.edu.

Reinhardt College (continued)

Application contact Reinhardt College, 7300 Reinhardt College Circle, Waleska, GA 30183-0128. *E-mail:* admissions@mail.reinhardt.edu. *Web address:* http://www.reinhardt.edu/.

ROOSEVELT UNIVERSITY
Chicago, Illinois

Students with LD Served by Program	50	ADD/ADHD Services	✓
Staff	3 part-time	Summer Preparation Program	n/a
LD Program or Service Fee	✓	Alternative Test Arrangements	✓
LD Program Began	1981	LD Student Organization	n/a

Learning and Support Services Program began offering services in 1981. The program serves approximately 50 undergraduate students. Faculty consists of 3 part-time staff members. Services are provided by LD specialists.

Policies 6 credit hours per semester are required to be eligible for financial aid. LD services are also available to graduate students.

Fees *LD Program or Service Fee:* $1000 per year.

Basic skills remediation Available in auditory processing, study skills, computer skills, reading, time management, social skills, visual processing, learning strategies, spelling, written language, math, and spoken language. Offered one-on-one by LD specialists.

Subject-area tutoring Available in some subjects. Offered one-on-one by LD specialists.

Special courses Available in career planning, study skills, test taking, time management, stress management, and written composition skills. No courses are offered for credit; none enter into overall grade point average.

Counseling and advisement Career counseling, individual counseling, small-group counseling, and support groups are available.

Auxiliary aids and services *Aids:* calculators, personal computers, personal spelling/word-use assistants (e.g., Franklin Speller), scan and read programs (e.g., Kurzweil), screen-enlarging programs, screen readers, speech recognition programs (e.g., Dragon), tape recorders, taped textbooks. *Services and accommodations:* priority registration, alternative test arrangements, readers, note-takers, and scribes.

ADD/ADHD Students with ADD/ADHD are eligible for the same services available to students with LD, as well as distraction-free study areas and distraction-free testing environments.

Application *Required:* high school transcript, ACT (extended-time test accepted), interview, personal statement, separate application to your LD program or unit, and psychoeducational report. *Recommended:* letter(s) of recommendation. Upon application, documentation of need for special services should be sent only to your LD program or unit. Upon acceptance, documentation of need for special services should be sent only to your LD program or unit. *Application deadline (institutional):* rolling/continuous for fall and rolling/continuous for spring. *Application deadline (LD program):* rolling/continuous for fall and rolling/continuous for spring.

LD program contact Nancy Litke, Director of Learning and Support Services, Room 310 HCC, 430 South Michigan Avenue, Chicago, IL 60605. *Phone:* 312-341-3810. *Fax:* 312-341-3735.

Application contact Darren Change, Assistant Director of Admission, Roosevelt University, Office of Admissions, Chicago, IL 60605-1394. *Phone:* 312-341-2440 Ext. 3412. *E-mail:* dessimm@admvsbk.roosevelt.edu. *Web address:* http://www.roosevelt.edu/.

ST. GREGORY'S UNIVERSITY
Shawnee, Oklahoma

Students with LD Served by Program	25	ADD/ADHD Services	✓
Staff	2 full-time, 40 part-time	Summer Preparation Program	n/a
LD Program or Service Fee	✓	Alternative Test Arrangements	✓
LD Program Began	1997	LD Student Organization	n/a

Partners in Learning began offering services in 1997. The program serves approximately 25 undergraduate students. Faculty consists of 2 full-time and 40 part-time staff members. Services are provided by academic advisers, remediation/learning specialists, counselors, and trained peer tutors.

Policies Students with LD may take up to 18 credit hours per semester; 9 credit hours per semester are required to maintain full-time status; 12 credit hours per semester are required to be eligible for financial aid.

Fees *LD Program or Service Fee:* $5000 per year.

Basic skills remediation Available in reading, spelling, and math. Offered one-on-one, in small groups, and class-size groups by regular education teachers.

Subject-area tutoring Available in all subjects. Offered one-on-one by computer-based instruction and trained peer tutors.

Counseling and advisement Academic advisement by a staff member affiliated with the program is available.

Auxiliary aids and services *Aids:* scan and read programs (e.g., Kurzweil), tape recorders, taped textbooks. *Services and accommodations:* advocates, alternative test arrangements, note-takers, scribes, and typing services.

ADD/ADHD Students with ADD/ADHD are eligible for the same services available to students with LD, as well as distraction-free study areas, distraction-free testing environments and personal coach or mentors.

Application *Required:* high school transcript, ACT or SAT I (extended-time tests accepted), interview, personal statement, separate application to your LD program or unit, psychoeducational report (3 years old or less), and documentation of high school services (e.g., Individualized Education Program [IEP] or 504 plan). *Recommended:* participation in extracurricular activities and letter(s) of recommendation. Upon application, documentation of need for special services should be sent only to your LD program or unit. Upon acceptance, documentation of need for special services should be sent only to your LD program or unit. *Application deadline (institutional):* rolling/continuous for fall and rolling/continuous for spring. *Application deadline (LD program):* rolling/continuous for fall and rolling/continuous for spring.

LD program contact Gay Faulk, Director, Partners in Learning, 1900 West MacArthur Drive, Shawnee, OK 74804. *Phone:* 405-878-5398. *Fax:* 405-878-5198. *E-mail:* sgfaulk@sgc.edu.

Application contact St. Gregory's University, 1900 West MacArthur Drive, Shawnee, OK 74804-2499. *Web address:* http://www.sgc.edu/.

SAINT LOUIS UNIVERSITY
St. Louis, Missouri

Students with LD Served by Program	120	ADD/ADHD Services	✓
Staff	1 full-time, 2 part-time	Summer Preparation Program	✓
LD Program or Service Fee	n/a	Alternative Test Arrangements	✓
LD Program Began	1985	LD Student Organization	n/a

Office of Disabilities Services began offering services in 1985. The program serves approximately 120 undergraduate students. Faculty consists of 1 full-time and 2 part-time staff members. Services are provided by academic advisers, counselors, remediation/learning specialists, diagnostic specialists, graduate assistants/students, and trained peer tutors.

Policies LD services are also available to graduate students.

Fees *Diagnostic Testing Fee:* ranges from $80 to $375.

Special preparation or orientation Optional summer program offered prior to entering college.

Diagnostic testing Available for spelling, neuropsychological, intelligence, personality, reading, written language, and math.

Counseling and advisement Academic advisement by a staff member affiliated with the program is available.

Auxiliary aids and services *Aids:* calculators, personal computers, personal spelling/word-use assistants (e.g., Franklin Speller), scan and read programs (e.g., Kurzweil), screen-enlarging programs, screen readers, tape recorders, taped textbooks. *Services and accommodations:* priority registration, alternative test arrangements, readers, note-takers, and scribes.

ADD/ADHD Students with ADD/ADHD are eligible for the same services available to students with LD, as well as distraction-free testing environments.

Application *Required:* high school transcript, ACT or SAT I (extended-time or untimed test accepted), interview, personal statement, letter(s) of recommendation, psychoeducational report (5 years old or less), and documentation of high school services (e.g., Individualized Education Program [IEP] or 504 plan). *Recommended:* participation in extracurricular activities. Upon application, documentation of need for special services should be sent only to your LD program or unit. Upon acceptance, documentation of need for special services should be sent to both admissions and your LD program or unit. *Application deadline (institutional):* rolling/continuous for fall and rolling/continuous for spring.

LD program contact Dr. Charles H. Murphy, Disabilities Counselor, 221 North Grand, Tegeler Hall, Room 300E, St. Louis, MO 63103. *Phone:* 314-977-2965. *Fax:* 314-977-3315. *E-mail:* murphy2@slu.edu.

Application contact Patsy Brooks, Credential Evaluator for Undergraduate Admissions, Saint Louis University, 221 North Grand Boulevard, St. Louis, MO 63103-2097. *Phone:* 314-977-2500. *E-mail:* admitme@sluvca.slu.edu.. *Web address:* http://www.slu.edu/.

SALEM STATE COLLEGE
Salem, Massachusetts

Students with LD Served by Program	250	ADD/ADHD Services	✓
Staff	2 full-time, 5 part-time	Summer Preparation Program	n/a
LD Program or Service Fee	n/a	Alternative Test Arrangements	✓
LD Program Began	1996	LD Student Organization	✓

Office for Students with Disabilities began offering services in 1996. The program serves approximately 250 undergraduate students. Faculty consists of 2 full-time and 5 part-time staff members. Services are provided by graduate assistants/students, teacher trainees, LD specialists, and trained peer tutors.

Policies The college has written policies regarding course substitutions and substitution and waivers of requirements for admission and graduation. LD services are also available to graduate students.

Special preparation or orientation Held before registration.

Diagnostic testing Available for study skills, learning strategies, reading, learning styles, and visual processing.

Basic skills remediation Available in study skills, time management, and learning strategies. Offered one-on-one and in small groups by LD specialists, trained peer tutors, and student peer/mentors.

Subject-area tutoring Available in some subjects. Offered one-on-one and in small groups by computer-based instruction, trained peer tutors, and LD specialists.

Counseling and advisement Career counseling, individual counseling, and support groups are available.

Auxiliary aids and services *Aids:* scan and read programs (e.g., Kurzweil), screen-enlarging programs, screen readers, speech recognition programs (e.g., Dragon), tape recorders, taped textbooks, computer lab. *Services and accommodations:* advocates, priority registration, alternative test arrangements, readers, note-takers, scribes, and assistive technology.

Student organization There is a student organization for students with LD.

ADD/ADHD Students with ADD/ADHD are eligible for the same services available to students with LD, as well as distraction-free study areas, distraction-free testing environments, personal coach or mentors and peer mentor.

Application *Required:* high school transcript, personal statement, letter(s) of recommendation, psychoeducational report (3 years old or less), and documentation of high school services (e.g., Individualized Education Program [IEP] or 504 plan). *Recommended:* participation in extracurricular activities, ACT or SAT I (extended-time or untimed test accepted), interview, and statement to Admissions office requesting to be considered an exception if SAT's not submitted. Upon application, documentation of need for special services should be sent only to admissions. Upon acceptance, documentation of need for special services should be sent to both admissions and your LD program or unit. *Application deadline (institutional):* rolling/continuous for fall and rolling/continuous for spring. *Application deadline (LD program):* rolling/continuous for fall and rolling/continuous for spring.

LD program contact Eileen Berger, Director, Office for Students with Disabilities, 352 Lafayette Street, Salem, MA 01970-5353. *Phone:* 978-542-6217. *Fax:* 978-542-6753. *E-mail:* osd@salem.mass.edu.

Application contact Salem State College, 352 Lafayette Street, Salem, MA 01970-5353. *Web address:* http://www.salem.mass.edu/.

SAN FRANCISCO STATE UNIVERSITY
San Francisco, California

Students with LD Served by Program	375	ADD/ADHD Services	✓
Staff	2 part-time	Summer Preparation Program	n/a
LD Program or Service Fee	n/a	Alternative Test Arrangements	✓
LD Program Began	n/a	LD Student Organization	n/a

Learning Disability Services serves approximately 375 undergraduate students. Faculty consists of 2 part-time staff members. Services are provided by counselors, LD specialists, and trained peer tutors.

Policies The college has written policies regarding course substitutions and substitution and waivers of requirements for admission. Students with LD may take up to 19 credit hours per semester; 12 credit hours per semester are required to maintain full-time status and to be eligible for financial aid. LD services are also available to graduate students.

Subject-area tutoring Available in some subjects. Offered one-on-one and in small groups by trained peer tutors.

San Francisco State University (continued)

Special courses Available in oral communication skills, college survival skills, time management, learning strategies, self-advocacy, and stress management. All courses are offered for credit; all enter into overall grade point average.

Auxiliary aids and services *Aids:* calculators, personal computers, personal spelling/word-use assistants (e.g., Franklin Speller), scan and read programs (e.g., Kurzweil), screen-enlarging programs, screen readers, speech recognition programs (e.g., Dragon), tape recorders, taped textbooks. *Services and accommodations:* advocates, priority registration, alternative test arrangements, readers, note-takers, and scribes.

ADD/ADHD Students with ADD/ADHD are eligible for the same services available to students with LD, as well as distraction-free testing environments.

Application *Required:* high school transcript, ACT or SAT I (extended-time or untimed test accepted), personal statement, separate application to your LD program or unit, psychoeducational report (3 years old or less), and documentation of high school services (e.g., Individualized Education Program [IEP] or 504 plan). *Recommended:* participation in extracurricular activities and letter(s) of recommendation. Upon application, documentation of need for special services should be sent only to your LD program or unit. Upon acceptance, documentation of need for special services should be sent only to your LD program or unit. *Application deadline (institutional):* rolling/continuous for fall and rolling/continuous for spring. *Application deadline (LD program):* rolling/continuous for fall and rolling/continuous for spring.

LD program contact Deidre Defreese, Associate Director, Disability Resource Center, 1600 Holloway Avenue, TI-2, San Francisco, CA 94132. *Phone:* 415-338-2472. *Fax:* 415-338-1041. *E-mail:* defreese@sfsu.edu.

Application contact Patricia Wade, Admissions Officer, San Francisco State University, 1600 Holloway Avenue, San Francisco, CA 94132-1722. *Phone:* 415-338-2037. *E-mail:* ugadmit@apollo.sfsu.edu. *Web address:* http://www.sfsu.edu/.

SAN JOSE STATE UNIVERSITY

San Jose, California

Students with LD Served by Program	650	ADD/ADHD Services	✓
Staff	n/a	Summer Preparation Program	n/a
LD Program or Service Fee	n/a	Alternative Test Arrangements	✓
LD Program Began	n/a	LD Student Organization	n/a

Disability Resource Center (DRC) serves approximately 650 undergraduate students. Services are provided by academic advisers, counselors, diagnostic specialists, LD specialists, and trained peer tutors.

Policies The college has written policies regarding course substitutions, grade forgiveness, and substitution and waivers of requirements for admission and graduation. LD services are also available to graduate students.

Diagnostic testing Available for auditory processing, spelling, neuropsychological, spoken language, intelligence, reading, written language, and visual processing.

Basic skills remediation Available in auditory processing, computer skills, reading, time management, visual processing, learning strategies, written language, and spoken language. Offered one-on-one by computer-based instruction and LD specialists.

Subject-area tutoring Available in some subjects. Offered in small groups by computer-based instruction and LD specialists.

Counseling and advisement Career counseling, individual counseling, and small-group counseling are available. Academic advisement by a staff member affiliated with the program is available.

Auxiliary aids and services *Aids:* personal computers, personal spelling/word-use assistants (e.g., Franklin Speller), scan and read programs (e.g., Kurzweil), screen-enlarging programs, screen readers, speech recognition programs (e.g., Dragon), tape recorders, digital textbooks. *Services and accommodations:* advocates, priority registration, alternative test arrangements, readers, note-takers, and scribes.

ADD/ADHD Students with ADD/ADHD are eligible for the same services available to students with LD, as well as distraction-free testing environments.

Application *Required:* high school transcript, ACT or SAT I (extended-time tests accepted), separate application to your LD program or unit, and psychoeducational report (3 years old or less). *Recommended:* participation in extracurricular activities, personal statement, letter(s) of recommendation, and documentation of high school services (e.g., Individualized Education Program [IEP] or 504 plan). Upon application, documentation of need for special services should be sent only to your LD program or unit.

LD program contact Learning Disabilities Coordinator, 1 Washington Square, San Jose, CA 95192-0168. *Phone:* 408-924-6000. *Fax:* 408-924-5999.

Application contact John Bradbury, Interim Director of Admissions, San Jose State University, One Washington Square, San Jose, CA 95192-0009. *Phone:* 408-924-2000. *Web address:* http://www.sjsu.edu/.

SAVANNAH STATE UNIVERSITY

Savannah, Georgia

Students with LD Served by Program	12	ADD/ADHD Services	✓
Staff	3 full-time	Summer Preparation Program	n/a
LD Program or Service Fee	n/a	Alternative Test Arrangements	✓
LD Program Began	n/a	LD Student Organization	n/a

Comprehensive Counseling Center, Office of Student with Disabilities serves approximately 12 undergraduate students. Faculty consists of 3 full-time staff members. Services are provided by counselors and student affairs advisor.

Policies The college has written policies regarding course substitutions and substitution and waivers of requirements for admission and graduation. LD services are also available to graduate students.

Fees *Diagnostic Testing Fee:* $300.

Special preparation or orientation Optional orientation held during summer prior to enrollment and individually by special arrangement.

Diagnostic testing Available for auditory processing, motor skills, spelling, handwriting, neuropsychological, spoken language, intelligence, personality, learning strategies, reading, written language, learning styles, social skills, visual processing, and math.

Basic skills remediation Available in motor skills, study skills, computer skills, reading, time management, social skills, learning strategies, spelling, written language, and math. Offered one-on-one by computer-based instruction and trained peer tutors.

Subject-area tutoring Available in all subjects. Offered one-on-one by trained peer tutors.

Special courses Available in career planning, oral communication skills, study skills, college survival skills, practical computer skills, test taking, health and nutrition, reading, time management, learning strategies, vocabulary development, math, stress management, and written composition skills. Most courses are offered for credit; most enter into overall grade point average.

Counseling and advisement Career counseling, individual counseling, small-group counseling, support groups, and academic counseling are available.

Auxiliary aids and services *Aids:* calculators, personal computers, personal spelling/word-use assistants (e.g., Franklin Speller), scan and read programs (e.g., Kurzweil), tape recorders, taped textbooks. *Services and accommodations:* advocates, priority registration, alternative test arrangements, readers, and note-takers.

ADD/ADHD Students with ADD/ADHD are eligible for the same services available to students with LD, as well as distraction-free study areas, distraction-free testing environments, medication management and personal coach or mentors.

Application *Required:* high school transcript, participation in extracurricular activities, ACT or SAT I (extended-time or untimed test accepted), interview, personal statement, letter(s) of recommendation, separate application to your LD program or unit, psychoeducational report (3 years old or less), and documentation of high school services (e.g., Individualized Education Program [IEP] or 504 plan). Upon application, documentation of need for special services should be sent only to your LD program or unit. Upon acceptance, documentation of need for special services should be sent only to your LD program or unit. *Application deadline (institutional):* rolling/continuous for fall and rolling/continuous for spring. *Application deadline (LD program):* rolling/continuous for fall and rolling/continuous for spring.

LD program contact Ayo Akorede, Student Affairs Advisor/Service Provider, PO Box 20376, Savannah, GA 31404. *Phone:* 912-356-2202. *Fax:* 912-691-5556. *E-mail:* akoredea@savstate.edu.

Application contact Savannah State University, PO Box 20209, Savannah, GA 31404. *Web address:* http://www.savstate.edu/.

SCHREINER COLLEGE
Kerrville, Texas

Students with LD Served by Program	85	ADD/ADHD Services	✓
Staff	4 full-time, 35 part-time	Summer Preparation Program	n/a
LD Program or Service Fee	✓	Alternative Test Arrangements	✓
LD Program Began	1979	LD Student Organization	n/a

Learning Support Services began offering services in 1979. The program serves approximately 85 undergraduate students. Faculty consists of 4 full-time and 35 part-time staff members. Services are provided by academic advisers, LD specialists, and professional tutors.

Policies The college has written policies regarding course substitutions and substitution and waivers of requirements for admission and graduation. Students with LD may take up to 15 credit hours per semester; 12 credit hours per semester are required to maintain full-time status; 6 credit hours per semester are required to be eligible for financial aid.

Fees *LD Program or Service Fee:* $4260 per year.

Special preparation or orientation Required orientation held before classes begin, after classes begin, and during summer prior to enrollment.

Subject-area tutoring Available in all subjects. Offered one-on-one and in small groups by professional tutors.

Special courses Available in freshman seminar. All courses are offered for credit; all enter into overall grade point average.

Counseling and advisement Academic advisement by a staff member affiliated with the program is available.

Auxiliary aids and services *Aids:* personal computers, taped textbooks. *Services and accommodations:* advocates, alternative test arrangements, readers, note-takers, and scribes.

ADD/ADHD Students with ADD/ADHD are eligible for the same services available to students with LD, as well as distraction-free testing environments.

Application *Required:* high school transcript, interview, personal statement, psychoeducational report (1 year old or less), and WAIS III and individually administered achievement test, statement of disability. *Recommended:* participation in extracurricular activities, ACT or SAT I (extended-time or untimed test accepted), letter(s) of recommendation, and documentation of high school services (e.g., Individualized Education Program [IEP] or 504 plan). Upon application, documentation of need for special services should be sent only to your LD program or unit. Upon acceptance, documentation of need for special services should be sent to both admissions and your LD program or unit. *Application deadline (institutional):* 3/31 for fall and 11/15 for spring. *Application deadline (LD program):* 3/31 for fall and 11/15 for spring.

LD program contact Charles Tait, Admissions Counselor, 2100 Memorial Boulevard, Kerrville, TX 78028. *Phone:* 800-343-4919. *Fax:* 830-792-7226. *E-mail:* ctait@schreiner.edu.

Application contact Schreiner College, 2100 Memorial Boulevard, Kerrville, TX 78028-5697. *Web address:* http://www.schreiner.edu/.

SIMON FRASER UNIVERSITY
Burnaby, British Columbia

Students with LD Served by Program	50	ADD/ADHD Services	✓
Staff	2 full-time, 1 part-time	Summer Preparation Program	n/a
LD Program or Service Fee	n/a	Alternative Test Arrangements	✓
LD Program Began	1999	LD Student Organization	n/a

Centre for Students with Disabilities began offering services in 1999. The program serves approximately 50 undergraduate students. Faculty consists of 2 full-time staff members and 1 part-time staff member. Services are provided by academic advisers, counselors, diagnostic specialists, LD specialists, and trained peer tutors.

Policies The college has written policies regarding substitution and waivers of requirements for admission. Students with LD may take up to 15 credit hours per semester; 6 credit hours per semester are required to maintain full-time status; 9 credit hours per semester are required to be eligible for financial aid. LD services are also available to graduate students.

Special preparation or orientation Optional orientation held after classes begin.

Basic skills remediation Available in study skills, reading, time management, learning strategies, spelling, written language, and math. Offered one-on-one and in small groups by LD specialists.

Subject-area tutoring Available in some subjects. Offered one-on-one by LD specialists.

Special courses Available in study skills, test taking, reading, time management, learning strategies, vocabulary development, math, stress management, and written composition skills. No courses are offered for credit; none enter into overall grade point average.

Simon Fraser University (continued)

Counseling and advisement Individual counseling is available. Academic advisement by a staff member affiliated with the program is available.

Auxiliary aids and services *Aids:* personal computers, personal spelling/word-use assistants (e.g., Franklin Speller), scan and read programs (e.g., Kurzweil), screen-enlarging programs, screen readers, speech recognition programs (e.g., Dragon), tape recorders, taped textbooks. *Services and accommodations:* advocates, priority registration, alternative test arrangements, readers, note-takers, and scribes.

ADD/ADHD Students with ADD/ADHD are eligible for the same services available to students with LD, as well as distraction-free study areas, distraction-free testing environments and personal coach or mentors.

Application *Required:* high school transcript, separate application to your LD program or unit, psychoeducational report (3 years old or less), and documentation of high school services (e.g., Individualized Education Program [IEP] or 504 plan). *Recommended:* participation in extracurricular activities, personal statement, and letter(s) of recommendation. Upon application, documentation of need for special services should be sent to both admissions and your LD program or unit. Upon acceptance, documentation of need for special services should be sent only to your LD program or unit. *Application deadline (institutional):* rolling/continuous for fall and rolling/continuous for spring. *Application deadline (LD program):* rolling/continuous for fall and rolling/continuous for spring.

LD program contact Lorraine Mwenifumbo, Learning Disability Specialist and Policy Coordinator, 8888 University Drive, Burnaby, BC V5A 1S6. *Phone:* 604-291-5381. *Fax:* 604-291-4384. *E-mail:* lmwenifu@sfu.ca.

Application contact Simon Fraser University, 8888 University Drive, Burnaby, BC V5A 1S6. *E-mail:* undergraduate-admissions@sfu.ca. *Web address:* http://www.sfu.ca/.

SOUTHERN ILLINOIS UNIVERSITY CARBONDALE
Carbondale, Illinois

Students with LD Served by Program	150	ADD/ADHD Services	✓
Staff	5 full-time	Summer Preparation Program	n/a
LD Program or Service Fee	✓	Alternative Test Arrangements	✓
LD Program Began	1978	LD Student Organization	n/a

The Achieve Program began offering services in 1978. The program serves approximately 150 undergraduate students. Faculty consists of 5 full-time staff members. Services are provided by remediation/learning specialists, diagnostic specialists, graduate assistants/students, LD specialists, trained peer tutors, and professional tutors.

Policies The college has written policies regarding course substitutions. 12 credit hours per term are required to maintain full-time status and to be eligible for financial aid. LD services are also available to graduate students.

Fees *LD Program or Service Fee:* $4400 per year. *Diagnostic Testing Fee:* $1000.

Special preparation or orientation Required orientation held before classes begin.

Diagnostic testing Available for auditory processing, spelling, handwriting, spoken language, intelligence, study skills, learning strategies, reading, written language, learning styles, visual processing, and math.

Basic skills remediation Available in auditory processing, study skills, computer skills, reading, time management, social skills, visual processing, learning strategies, spelling, written language, and math. Offered one-on-one by graduate assistants/students and LD specialists.

Subject-area tutoring Available in all subjects. Offered one-on-one by graduate assistants/students, trained peer tutors, and LD specialists.

Counseling and advisement Career counseling and individual counseling are available.

Auxiliary aids and services *Aids:* calculators, personal spelling/word-use assistants (e.g., Franklin Speller), tape recorders, taped textbooks. *Services and accommodations:* advocates, alternative test arrangements, readers, note-takers, and scribes.

ADD/ADHD Students with ADD/ADHD are eligible for the same services available to students with LD, as well as distraction-free study areas, distraction-free testing environments and medication management.

Application *Required:* high school transcript, ACT (untimed test accepted), separate application to your LD program or unit, and psychoeducational report. Upon application, documentation of need for special services should be sent only to your LD program or unit. Upon acceptance, documentation of need for special services should be sent only to your LD program or unit. *Application deadline (institutional):* rolling/continuous for fall and rolling/continuous for spring. *Application deadline (LD program):* rolling/continuous for fall and rolling/continuous for spring.

LD program contact Roger Pugh, Developmental Skills Training Specialist, Mailcode 6832, Carbondale, IL 62901. *Phone:* 618-453-2369. *Fax:* 618-453-3711. *E-mail:* rpugh@siu.edu.

Application contact Southern Illinois University Carbondale, Carbondale, IL 62901-6806. *E-mail:* admrec@siu.edu. *Web address:* http://www.siu.edu/siuc/.

SOUTHWEST TEXAS STATE UNIVERSITY
San Marcos, Texas

Students with LD Served by Program	234	ADD/ADHD Services	✓
Staff	7 full-time	Summer Preparation Program	n/a
LD Program or Service Fee	n/a	Alternative Test Arrangements	✓
LD Program Began	1980	LD Student Organization	n/a

Office of Disability Services began offering services in 1980. The program serves approximately 234 undergraduate students. Faculty consists of 7 full-time staff members. Services are provided by counselors, diagnostic specialists, and graduate assistants/students.

Policies The college has written policies regarding substitution and waivers of requirements for admission and graduation. Students with LD may take up to 18 semester hours per term; 12 semester hours per term are required to maintain full-time status and to be eligible for financial aid. LD services are also available to graduate students.

Basic skills remediation Available in learning strategies, spelling, written language, and math. Offered one-on-one, in small groups, and class-size groups by regular education teachers.

Subject-area tutoring Available in most subjects. Offered one-on-one and in small groups by trained peer tutors.

Special courses Available in study skills, college survival skills, and learning strategies. No courses are offered for credit; none enter into overall grade point average.

Counseling and advisement Career counseling, individual counseling, and small-group counseling are available.

Auxiliary aids and services *Aids:* calculators, personal computers, tape recorders, taped textbooks. *Services and accommodations:* advocates, priority registration, alternative test arrangements, and note-takers.

ADD/ADHD Students with ADD/ADHD are eligible for the same services available to students with LD, as well as distraction-free testing environments.

Application *Required:* high school transcript and ACT or SAT I (untimed tests accepted). *Recommended:* letter(s) of recommendation. *Application deadline (institutional):* 7/1 for fall and 12/1 for spring.

LD program contact Richard Poe, Learning Disabilities Specialist, 601 University Drive, San Marcos, TX 78666. *Phone:* 512-245-3451. *Fax:* 512-245-3452. *E-mail:* rp16@swt.edu.

Application contact Southwest Texas State University, Admissions and Visitors Center, San Marcos, TX 78666. *E-mail:* admissions@swt.edu. *Web address:* http://www.swt.edu/.

TENNESSEE STATE UNIVERSITY
Nashville, Tennessee

Students with LD Served by Program	52	ADD/ADHD Services	✓
Staff	1 full-time	Summer Preparation Program	n/a
LD Program or Service Fee	n/a	Alternative Test Arrangements	✓
LD Program Began	1995	LD Student Organization	n/a

Office of Disabled Student Services began offering services in 1995. The program serves approximately 52 undergraduate students. Faculty consists of 1 full-time staff member. Services are provided by graduate assistants/students and LD specialists.

Policies 12 credit hours per semester are required to maintain full-time status; 9 credit hours per semester are required to be eligible for financial aid. LD services are also available to graduate students.

Special preparation or orientation Required orientation held individually by special arrangement.

Basic skills remediation Available in study skills, time management, and learning strategies. Offered one-on-one by graduate assistants/students and LD specialists.

Subject-area tutoring Available in most subjects. Offered one-on-one by graduate assistants/students.

Counseling and advisement Individual counseling is available.

Auxiliary aids and services *Aids:* calculators, personal computers, personal spelling/word-use assistants (e.g., Franklin Speller), scan and read programs (e.g., Kurzweil), screen-enlarging programs, screen readers, speech recognition programs (e.g., Dragon), tape recorders, taped textbooks. *Services and accommodations:* alternative test arrangements and note-takers.

ADD/ADHD Students with ADD/ADHD are eligible for the same services available to students with LD, as well as distraction-free testing environments.

Application *Required:* high school transcript and ACT or SAT I (extended-time tests accepted). Upon application, documentation of need for special services should be sent only to your LD program or unit. Upon acceptance, documentation of need for special services should be sent only to your LD program or unit.

LD program contact James D. Steely, Director, 3500 John Merritt Boulevard, Nashville, TN 37209. *Phone:* 615-963-7400. *Fax:* 615-963-2176. *E-mail:* jsteely@tnstate.edu.

Application contact Vernella Smith, Admissions Coordinator, Tennessee State University, 3500 John A Merritt Boulevard, Nashville, TN 37209-1561. *Phone:* 615-963-5104. *E-mail:* jcade@picard.tnstate.edu. *Web address:* http://www.tnstate.edu/.

TEXAS TECH UNIVERSITY
Lubbock, Texas

Students with LD Served by Program	425	ADD/ADHD Services	✓
Staff	7 full-time	Summer Preparation Program	n/a
LD Program or Service Fee	✓	Alternative Test Arrangements	✓
LD Program Began	1979	LD Student Organization	✓

AccessTECH and TECHniques Center began offering services in 1979. The program serves approximately 425 undergraduate students. Faculty consists of 7 full-time staff members. Services are provided by academic advisers, counselors, diagnostic specialists, graduate assistants/students, and trained peer tutors.

Policies The college has written policies regarding course substitutions. Students with LD may take up to 18 credits per semester; 12 credits per semester are required to maintain full-time status and to be eligible for financial aid. LD services are also available to graduate students.

Fees *LD Program or Service Fee:* $2000 per year.

Special preparation or orientation Optional orientation held before registration, before classes begin, after classes begin, and during summer prior to enrollment.

Basic skills remediation Available in study skills, computer skills, time management, social skills, learning strategies, written language, math, and Note taking, stress management, test taking, career developing, self-advocacy. Offered one-on-one and in small groups by computer-based instruction, graduate assistants/students, trained peer tutors, and Full-time counselors.

Subject-area tutoring Available in all subjects. Offered one-on-one and in small groups by graduate assistants/students and trained peer tutors.

Special courses Available in career planning, study skills, college survival skills, test taking, time management, learning strategies, and self-advocacy. No courses are offered for credit; none enter into overall grade point average.

Counseling and advisement Career counseling, individual counseling, small-group counseling, and support groups are available. Academic advisement by a staff member affiliated with the program is available.

Auxiliary aids and services *Aids:* calculators, personal spelling/word-use assistants (e.g., Franklin Speller), tape recorders, taped textbooks. *Services and accommodations:* priority registration, alternative test arrangements, readers, note-takers, and scribes.

Student organization There is a student organization for students with LD.

ADD/ADHD Students with ADD/ADHD are eligible for the same services available to students with LD, as well as distraction-free study areas and distraction-free testing environments.

Application *Required:* high school transcript, ACT or SAT I (extended-time tests accepted), personal statement, letter(s) of recommendation, separate application to your LD program or unit, psychoeducational report (3 years old or less), and documentation of high school services (e.g., Individualized Education Program [IEP] or 504 plan). Upon application, documentation of need for special services should be sent only to your LD program or unit. Upon acceptance, documentation of need for special services should be sent only to your LD program or unit. *Application deadline (institutional):* rolling/continuous for fall and rolling/continuous for spring. *Application deadline (LD program):* rolling/continuous for fall and rolling/continuous for spring.

LD program contact Leann DiAndreath-Elkins, Counseling Supervisor, Box 42182, 143 Wiggins Hall, Lubbock, TX 79409-1822. *Phone:* 806-742-1822. *Fax:* 806-742-0295. *E-mail:* leann.elkins@ttu.edu.

Texas Tech University (continued)

Application contact Texas Tech University, Box 45005, Lubbock, TX 79409-5005. *E-mail:* a5adms@ttuvm1.ttu.edu. *Web address:* http://www.texastech.edu/.

UNION COLLEGE
Lincoln, Nebraska

Students with LD Served by Program	80	ADD/ADHD Services	✓
Staff	2 full-time, 3 part-time	Summer Preparation Program	n/a
LD Program or Service Fee	n/a	Alternative Test Arrangements	✓
LD Program Began	1985	LD Student Organization	✓

Teaching Learning Center (TLC) began offering services in 1985. The program serves approximately 80 undergraduate students. Faculty consists of 2 full-time and 3 part-time staff members. Services are provided by special education teachers and LD specialists.

Fees *Diagnostic Testing Fee:* $250.

Special preparation or orientation Required orientation held after classes begin.

Diagnostic testing Available for neuropsychological and intelligence.

Basic skills remediation Available in study skills, time management, learning strategies, spelling, and written language. Offered one-on-one and in class-size groups by regular education teachers and LD specialists.

Subject-area tutoring Available in all subjects. Offered one-on-one and in small groups by trained peer tutors and LD specialists.

Auxiliary aids and services *Aids:* speech recognition programs (e.g., Dragon), tape recorders, taped textbooks. *Services and accommodations:* alternative test arrangements, readers, note-takers, and scribes.

Student organization There is a student organization for students with LD.

ADD/ADHD Students with ADD/ADHD are eligible for the same services available to students with LD, as well as distraction-free study areas, distraction-free testing environments and personal coach or mentors.

Application *Required:* high school transcript, ACT (extended-time or untimed test accepted), personal statement, letter(s) of recommendation, separate application to your LD program or unit, and psychoeducational report (3 years old or less). *Recommended:* participation in extracurricular activities, interview, and documentation of high school services (e.g., Individualized Education Program [IEP] or 504 plan). Upon application, documentation of need for special services should be sent only to your LD program or unit. Upon acceptance, documentation of need for special services should be sent only to your LD program or unit. *Application deadline (institutional):* rolling/continuous for fall and rolling/continuous for spring. *Application deadline (LD program):* rolling/continuous for fall and rolling/continuous for spring.

LD program contact Jennifer Forbes, Director, 3800 South 48th Street, Lincoln, NE 68516. *Phone:* 402-486-2506. *E-mail:* jeforbes@ucollege.edu.

Application contact Huda McClelland, Director of Admissions, Union College, 3800 South 48th Street, Lincoln, NE 68506-4300. *Phone:* 402-486-2504. *E-mail:* ucenrol@ucollege.edu. *Web address:* http://www.ucollege.edu/.

THE UNIVERSITY OF ARIZONA
Tucson, Arizona

Students with LD Served by Program	500	ADD/ADHD Services	✓
Staff	21 full-time, 130 part-time	Summer Preparation Program	n/a
LD Program or Service Fee	✓	Alternative Test Arrangements	✓
LD Program Began	1980	LD Student Organization	n/a

Strategic Alternative Learning Techniques began offering services in 1980. The program serves approximately 500 undergraduate students. Faculty consists of 21 full-time and 130 part-time staff members. Services are provided by LD specialists and trained peer tutors.

Policies The college has written policies regarding course substitutions and substitution and waivers of requirements for admission. Students with LD may take up to 18 credit hours per semester; 12 credit hours per semester are required to maintain full-time status and to be eligible for financial aid.

Fees *LD Program or Service Fee:* $3300 per year.

Special preparation or orientation Required orientation held before registration, before classes begin, and during summer prior to enrollment.

Subject-area tutoring Available in most subjects. Offered one-on-one by graduate assistants/students.

Special courses Available in study skills, test taking, time management, learning strategies, and self-advocacy. All courses are offered for credit; all enter into overall grade point average.

Counseling and advisement Career counseling, individual counseling, and support groups are available.

Auxiliary aids and services *Aids:* personal computers, personal spelling/word-use assistants (e.g., Franklin Speller), scan and read programs (e.g., Kurzweil), screen readers, speech recognition programs (e.g., Dragon), tape recorders, taped textbooks. *Services and accommodations:* advocates, priority registration, alternative test arrangements, readers, note-takers, and scribes.

ADD/ADHD Students with ADD/ADHD are eligible for the same services available to students with LD, as well as distraction-free testing environments and support groups for ADD/ADHD.

Application *Required:* high school transcript, ACT or SAT I, personal statement, letter(s) of recommendation, separate application to your LD program or unit, and psychoeducational report (3 years old or less). Upon application, documentation of need for special services should be sent to both admissions and your LD program or unit. Upon acceptance, documentation of need for special services should be sent only to your LD program or unit. *Application deadline (institutional):* rolling/continuous for fall and rolling/continuous for spring. *Application deadline (LD program):* rolling/continuous for fall and rolling/continuous for spring.

LD program contact Shirley Ramsey, Assistant Director, Admissions and Outreach, Room 101, Old Main Building, Tucson, AZ 85721. *Phone:* 520-621-3652. *Fax:* 520-626-3260. *E-mail:* ramsey@u.arizona.edu.

Application contact The University of Arizona, Tucson, AZ 85721. *E-mail:* appinfo@arizona.edu. *Web address:* http://www.arizona.edu/.

UNIVERSITY OF CALIFORNIA, SAN DIEGO

La Jolla, California

Students with LD Served by Program	100	ADD/ADHD Services	✓
Staff	4 full-time, 11 part-time	Summer Preparation Program	n/a
LD Program or Service Fee	n/a	Alternative Test Arrangements	✓
LD Program Began	1990	LD Student Organization	✓

Office for Students with Disabilities (OSD) began offering services in 1990. The program serves approximately 100 undergraduate students. Faculty consists of 4 full-time and 11 part-time staff members. Services are provided by LD specialists.

Policies Students with LD may take up to 16 credit hours per quarter; 12 credit hours per quarter are required to maintain full-time status and to be eligible for financial aid. LD services are also available to graduate students.

Special preparation or orientation Optional orientation held individually by special arrangement.

Special courses Available in study skills, time management, learning strategies, self-advocacy, and stress management. No courses are offered for credit; none enter into overall grade point average.

Counseling and advisement Individual counseling, small-group counseling, and support groups are available.

Auxiliary aids and services *Aids:* calculators, personal computers, personal spelling/word-use assistants (e.g., Franklin Speller), screen-enlarging programs, speech recognition programs (e.g., Dragon), tape recorders, taped textbooks. *Services and accommodations:* advocates, priority registration, alternative test arrangements, readers, and note-takers.

Student organization There is a student organization for students with LD.

ADD/ADHD Students with ADD/ADHD are eligible for the same services available to students with LD, as well as distraction-free testing environments, personal coach or mentors, and support groups for ADD/ADHD.

Application *Required:* high school transcript and ACT or SAT I (extended-time or untimed test accepted). *Recommended:* participation in extracurricular activities and personal statement. Upon application, documentation of need for special services should be sent to both admissions and your LD program or unit. Upon acceptance, documentation of need for special services should be sent to both admissions and your LD program or unit. *Application deadline (institutional):* 11/30 for fall.

LD program contact Naomi E. Levoy, Outreach Assistant, 9500 Gilman Drive, La Jolla, CA 92093-0019. *Phone:* 858-534-4382. *Fax:* 858-534-4650. *E-mail:* nlevoy@ucsd.edu.

Application contact Tim Johnston, Associate Director of Admissions and Outreach, University of California, San Diego, 9500 Gilman Drive, La Jolla, CA 92093-5003. *Phone:* 858-534-4831. *E-mail:* admissionsinfo@ucsd.edu. *Web address:* http://www.ucsd.edu/.

UNIVERSITY OF CALIFORNIA, SANTA BARBARA

Santa Barbara, California

Students with LD Served by Program	250	ADD/ADHD Services	✓
Staff	6 full-time	Summer Preparation Program	n/a
LD Program or Service Fee	n/a	Alternative Test Arrangements	✓
LD Program Began	1985	LD Student Organization	✓

Disabled Students Program began offering services in 1985. The program serves approximately 250 undergraduate students. Faculty consists of 6 full-time staff members. Services are provided by regular education teachers and LD specialists.

Policies Students with LD may take up to 21 units per quarter; 12 units per quarter are required to maintain full-time status and to be eligible for financial aid. LD services are also available to graduate students.

Special preparation or orientation Optional orientation held before classes begin.

Auxiliary aids and services *Aids:* calculators, personal spelling/word-use assistants (e.g., Franklin Speller), scan and read programs (e.g., Kurzweil), screen-enlarging programs, screen readers, speech recognition programs (e.g., Dragon), tape recorders, taped textbooks. *Services and accommodations:* advocates, priority registration, alternative test arrangements, readers, note-takers, scribes, and test proctors.

Student organization There is a student organization for students with LD.

ADD/ADHD Students with ADD/ADHD are eligible for the same services available to students with LD, as well as distraction-free testing environments.

Application *Required:* high school transcript, ACT or SAT I (extended-time tests accepted), personal statement, and SAT II. *Recommended:* participation in extracurricular activities, letter(s) of recommendation, and psychoeducational report (3 years old or less). Upon application, documentation of need for special services should be sent only to admissions. Upon acceptance, documentation of need for special services should be sent only to your LD program or unit. *Application deadline (institutional):* 11/30 for fall. *Application deadline (LD program):* 11/30 for fall.

LD program contact Claudia Nicastro Batty, Disabilities Specialist, Disabled Students Program, Santa Barbara, CA 93106. *Phone:* 805-893-2668. *Fax:* 805-893-7127. *E-mail:* batty-c@sa.ucsb.edu.

Application contact University of California, Santa Barbara, Santa Barbara, CA 93106. *Web address:* http://www.ucsb.edu/.

UNIVERSITY OF COLORADO AT BOULDER

Boulder, Colorado

Students with LD Served by Program	250	ADD/ADHD Services	✓
Staff	3 full-time, 2 part-time	Summer Preparation Program	n/a
LD Program or Service Fee	n/a	Alternative Test Arrangements	✓
LD Program Began	1979	LD Student Organization	n/a

Academic Access and Resources Program began offering services in 1979. The program serves approximately 250 undergraduate students. Faculty consists of 3 full-time and 2 part-time staff members. Services are provided by LD specialists.

University of Colorado at Boulder (continued)

Policies The college has written policies regarding course substitutions. Students with LD may take up to 21 credit hours per semester; 12 credit hours per semester are required to maintain full-time status and to be eligible for financial aid. LD services are also available to graduate students.

Fees *Diagnostic Testing Fee:* $250.

Diagnostic testing Available for auditory processing, motor skills, spelling, reading, written language, visual processing, math, and Comprehensive testing involving cognitive and achievement assessment.

Special courses Available in Modified foreign language courses. All courses are offered for credit; all enter into overall grade point average.

Counseling and advisement Career counseling, individual counseling, and support groups are available.

Auxiliary aids and services *Aids:* scan and read programs (e.g., Kurzweil), screen-enlarging programs, screen readers, speech recognition programs (e.g., Dragon), taped textbooks. *Services and accommodations:* advocates, alternative test arrangements, and note-takers.

ADD/ADHD Students with ADD/ADHD are eligible for the same services available to students with LD, as well as distraction-free testing environments and support groups for ADD/ADHD.

Application *Required:* high school transcript, ACT or SAT I (extended-time or untimed test accepted), and personal statement. *Recommended:* participation in extracurricular activities and letter(s) of recommendation. Upon application, documentation of need for special services should be sent only to your LD program or unit. Upon acceptance, documentation of need for special services should be sent only to your LD program or unit. *Application deadline (institutional):* 2/15 for fall and 10/1 for spring. *Application deadline (LD program):* rolling/continuous for fall and rolling/continuous for spring.

LD program contact Jayne MacArthur, Coordinator, Academic Access and Resources Program, Campus Box 107, Boulder, CO 80309-0107. *Phone:* 303-492-8671. *Fax:* 303-492-5601. *E-mail:* dsinfo@spot.colorado.edu.

Application contact Admission Counselor, University of Colorado at Boulder, Campus Box 30, Boulder, CO 80309-0030. *Phone:* 303-492-6301. *E-mail:* apply@colorado.edu. *Web address:* http://www.colorado.edu/.

UNIVERSITY OF CONNECTICUT
Storrs, Connecticut

Students with LD Served by Program	150	ADD/ADHD Services	n/a
Staff	1 full-time, 5 part-time	Summer Preparation Program	n/a
LD Program or Service Fee	n/a	Alternative Test Arrangements	✓
LD Program Began	1984	LD Student Organization	n/a

University Program for College Students with Learning Disabilities (UPLD) began offering services in 1984. The program serves approximately 150 undergraduate students. Faculty consists of 1 full-time and 5 part-time staff members. Services are provided by graduate assistants/students.

Policies The college has written policies regarding course substitutions. Students with LD may take up to 17 credit hours per semester; 12 credit hours per semester are required to maintain full-time status and to be eligible for financial aid. LD services are also available to graduate students.

Auxiliary aids and services *Aids:* scan and read programs (e.g., Kurzweil), screen-enlarging programs, screen readers, speech recognition programs (e.g., Dragon), tape recorders, taped textbooks. *Services and accommodations:* priority registration, alternative test arrangements, readers, and note-takers.

Application *Required:* high school transcript, ACT or SAT I (extended-time or untimed test accepted), and personal statement. *Recommended:* participation in extracurricular activities and letter(s) of recommendation. Upon acceptance, documentation of need for special services should be sent only to your LD program or unit. *Application deadline (institutional):* 3/1 for fall and 10/15 for spring.

LD program contact Joseph W. Madaus, Director, U-2064, 249 Glenbrook Road, Storrs, CT 06269-2064. *Phone:* 860-486-0178. *Fax:* 860-486-5037. *E-mail:* j.madaus@uconn.edu.

Application contact Brian Usher, Associate Director of Admissions, University of Connecticut, 2131 Hillside Road, U-88, Storrs, CT 06269. *Phone:* 860-486-3137. *E-mail:* beahusky@uconnvm.uconn.edu. *Web address:* http://www.uconn.edu/.

UNIVERSITY OF DENVER
Denver, Colorado

Students with LD Served by Program	220	ADD/ADHD Services	✓
Staff	10 full-time, 4 part-time	Summer Preparation Program	n/a
LD Program or Service Fee	✓	Alternative Test Arrangements	✓
LD Program Began	1982	LD Student Organization	n/a

Learning Effectiveness Program began offering services in 1982. The program serves approximately 220 undergraduate students. Faculty consists of 10 full-time and 4 part-time staff members. Services are provided by academic advisers, counselors, remediation/learning specialists, diagnostic specialists, special education teachers, graduate assistants/students, LD specialists, and professional tutors.

Policies The college has written policies regarding course substitutions and substitution and waivers of requirements for admission and graduation. Students with LD may take up to 18 credit hours per quarter; 12 credit hours per quarter are required to maintain full-time status and to be eligible for financial aid.

Fees *LD Program or Service Fee:* $2550 per year.

Special preparation or orientation Optional orientation held before registration.

Subject-area tutoring Available in all subjects. Offered one-on-one by professional tutors, graduate assistants/students, and LD specialists.

Counseling and advisement Individual counseling is available. Academic advisement by a staff member affiliated with the program is available.

Auxiliary aids and services *Aids:* calculators, personal computers, scan and read programs (e.g., Kurzweil), tape recorders, taped textbooks. *Services and accommodations:* advocates, priority registration, alternative test arrangements, and readers.

ADD/ADHD Students with ADD/ADHD are eligible for the same services available to students with LD, as well as distraction-free testing environments and personal coach or mentors.

Application *Required:* high school transcript, participation in extracurricular activities, ACT or SAT I (extended-time or untimed test accepted), personal statement, letter(s) of recommendation, and psychoeducational report (3 years old or less). *Recommended:* interview, separate application to your LD program or unit, and documentation of high school services (e.g., Individualized Education Program [IEP] or 504 plan). Upon application, documentation of need for special services should be sent only to your LD program or unit. Upon acceptance, documentation of need for special services should be sent only to your LD program or unit. *Application deadline (institutional):* rolling/continuous for fall and rolling/continuous for spring. *Application deadline (LD program):* rolling/continuous for fall and rolling/continuous for spring.

LD program contact Elinor Kaslow, Administrative Assistant, 2050 East Evans Avenue, Denver, CO 80208-2372. *Phone:* 303-871-2372. *Fax:* 303-871-3939. *E-mail:* ekaslow@du.edu.

Application contact Morris Price, Associate Dean of Admission, University of Denver, University Park, Denver, CO 80208. *Phone:* 303-871-3373. *E-mail:* admission@du.edu. *Web address:* http://www.du.edu/.

UNIVERSITY OF HOUSTON
Houston, Texas

Students with LD Served by Program	178	ADD/ADHD Services	✓
Staff	5 full-time, 6 part-time	Summer Preparation Program	n/a
LD Program or Service Fee	n/a	Alternative Test Arrangements	✓
LD Program Began	n/a	LD Student Organization	✓

Center for Students with Disabilities serves approximately 178 undergraduate students. Faculty consists of 5 full-time and 6 part-time staff members. Services are provided by counselors and LD specialists.

Policies Students with LD may take up to 18 credit hours per semester; 12 credit hours per semester are required to maintain full-time status; 6 credit hours per semester are required to be eligible for financial aid. LD services are also available to graduate students.

Fees *Diagnostic Testing Fee:* ranges from $100 to $150. individually by special arrangement.

Diagnostic testing Available for auditory processing, motor skills, spelling, intelligence, personality, reading, written language, social skills, visual processing, and math.

Subject-area tutoring Available in most subjects. Offered one-on-one and in small groups by professional tutors and trained peer tutors.

Special courses Available in career planning, study skills, practical computer skills, test taking, reading, time management, learning strategies, math, stress management, and written composition skills. Some courses are offered for credit; some enter into overall grade point average.

Counseling and advisement Career counseling, individual counseling, and support groups are available.

Auxiliary aids and services *Aids:* personal computers, scan and read programs (e.g., Kurzweil), screen-enlarging programs, tape recorders, taped textbooks. *Services and accommodations:* advocates, priority registration, alternative test arrangements, readers, note-takers, and scribes.

Student organization There is a student organization for students with LD.

ADD/ADHD Students with ADD/ADHD are eligible for the same services available to students with LD, as well as distraction-free testing environments and personal coach or mentors.

Application *Required:* high school transcript, ACT or SAT I (untimed tests accepted), and psychoeducational report (3 years old or less). Upon application, documentation of need for special services should be sent only to your LD program or unit. Upon acceptance, documentation of need for special services should be sent only to your LD program or unit. *Application deadline (institutional):* 7/1 for fall and 12/15 for spring.

LD program contact Barbara H. Poursoltan, Assistant Director, Center for Students with Disabilities, Houston, TX 77204-3243. *Phone:* 713-743-5400. *Fax:* 713-743-5396. *E-mail:* bharmonp@bayou.uh.edu.

Application contact Tyene Houston, Assistant Director of Admissions, University of Houston, 4800 Calhoun, Houston, TX 77204-2161. *Phone:* 713-743-9632. *E-mail:* admissions@uh.edu. *Web address:* http://www.uh.edu/.

UNIVERSITY OF INDIANAPOLIS
Indianapolis, Indiana

Students with LD Served by Program	60	ADD/ADHD Services	✓
Staff	2 full-time, 13 part-time	Summer Preparation Program	✓
LD Program or Service Fee	✓	Alternative Test Arrangements	✓
LD Program Began	1990	LD Student Organization	n/a

Baccalaureate for University of Indianapolis Learning Disabled (BUILD) began offering services in 1990. The program serves approximately 60 undergraduate students. Faculty consists of 2 full-time and 13 part-time staff members. Services are provided by graduate assistants/students, LD specialists, and professional tutors.

Policies The college has written policies regarding course substitutions and substitution and waivers of requirements for admission and graduation. Students with LD may take up to 18 credit hours per semester; 9 credit hours per semester are required to maintain full-time status. LD services are also available to graduate students.

Fees *LD Program or Service Fee:* $3700 per year.

Special preparation or orientation Optional summer program offered prior to entering college. Required orientation held during registration, after classes begin, and individually by special arrangement.

Basic skills remediation Available in study skills, time management, learning strategies, written language, and math. Offered one-on-one by professional tutors.

Subject-area tutoring Available in most subjects. Offered one-on-one and in small groups by professional tutors.

Special courses Available in career planning, study skills, college survival skills, test taking, time management, learning strategies, math, and written composition skills. Most courses are offered for credit; all enter into overall grade point average.

Counseling and advisement Support groups and academic advising are available.

Auxiliary aids and services *Aids:* calculators, scan and read programs (e.g., Kurzweil), screen-enlarging programs, screen readers, speech recognition programs (e.g., Dragon), tape recorders, taped textbooks. *Services and accommodations:* priority registration, alternative test arrangements, readers, scribes, and alternative notetaking services.

ADD/ADHD Students with ADD/ADHD are eligible for the same services available to students with LD, as well as distraction-free study areas and distraction-free testing environments.

Application *Required:* high school transcript, ACT or SAT I (extended-time or untimed test accepted), and separate application to your LD program or unit. *Recommended:* participation in extracurricular activities. Upon application, documentation of need for special services should be sent only to your LD program or unit. Upon acceptance, documentation of need for special services should be sent only to your LD program or unit. *Application deadline (institutional):* rolling/continuous for fall and rolling/continuous for spring. *Application deadline (LD program):* rolling/continuous for fall and rolling/continuous for spring.

University of Indianapolis (continued)

LD program contact Deborah Spinney, Director, 1400 East Hanna Avenue, Indianapolis, IN 46227. *Phone:* 317-788-3536. *Fax:* 317-788-3300. *E-mail:* dspinney@uindy.edu.
Application contact University of Indianapolis, 1400 East Hanna Avenue, Indianapolis, IN 46227-3697. *E-mail:* admissions@gandlf. uindy.edu. *Web address:* http://www.uindy.edu/.

UNIVERSITY OF MASSACHUSETTS AMHERST

Amherst, Massachusetts

Students with LD Served by Program	400	ADD/ADHD Services	✓
Staff	30 part-time	Summer Preparation Program	n/a
LD Program or Service Fee	n/a	Alternative Test Arrangements	✓
LD Program Began	1984	LD Student Organization	n/a

Learning Disabilities Support Services (LDSS) began offering services in 1984. The program serves approximately 400 undergraduate students. Faculty consists of 30 part-time staff members. Services are provided by counselors, diagnostic specialists, graduate assistants/students, and LD specialists.
Policies The college has written policies regarding course substitutions. 12 credits per semester are required to maintain full-time status and to be eligible for financial aid. LD services are also available to graduate students.
Fees *Diagnostic Testing Fee:* ranges from $600 to $800.
Special preparation or orientation Optional orientation held during summer prior to enrollment.
Diagnostic testing Available for auditory processing, motor skills, spelling, handwriting, neuropsychological, spoken language, intelligence, personality, study skills, learning strategies, reading, written language, learning styles, social skills, visual processing, and math.
Subject-area tutoring Available in some subjects. Offered one-on-one by graduate assistants/students.
Counseling and advisement Career counseling and individual counseling are available.
Auxiliary aids and services *Aids:* personal spelling/word-use assistants (e.g., Franklin Speller), scan and read programs (e.g., Kurzweil), screen-enlarging programs, screen readers, speech recognition programs (e.g., Dragon). *Services and accommodations:* advocates, alternative test arrangements, readers, note-takers, and scribes.
ADD/ADHD Students with ADD/ADHD are eligible for the same services available to students with LD
Application *Required:* high school transcript, ACT or SAT I (extended-time or untimed test accepted), and personal statement. *Recommended:* participation in extracurricular activities, letter(s) of recommendation, psychoeducational report (5 years old or less), and documentation of high school services (e.g., Individualized Education Program [IEP] or 504 plan). Upon application, documentation of need for special services should be sent only to admissions. Upon acceptance, documentation of need for special services should be sent only to your LD program or unit. *Application deadline (institutional):* 2/1 for fall and 10/15 for spring.
LD program contact Amanda Zygmont, Office Manager, Learning Disabilites Support Services, 321 Berkshire House, Amherst, MA 01003. *Phone:* 413-545-4602. *Fax:* 413-577-0691. *E-mail:* zygmont@acad.umass.edu.
Application contact University of Massachusetts Amherst, Amherst, MA 01003-0120. *E-mail:* amh.admis@dpc.umassp.edu. *Web address:* http://www.umass.edu/.

UNIVERSITY OF MISSOURI-COLUMBIA
Columbia, Missouri

Students with LD Served by Program	397	ADD/ADHD Services	✓
Staff	5 full-time, 120 part-time	Summer Preparation Program	n/a
LD Program or Service Fee	n/a	Alternative Test Arrangements	✓
LD Program Began	1997	LD Student Organization	n/a

Office of Disability Services began offering services in 1997. The program serves approximately 397 undergraduate students. Faculty consists of 5 full-time and 120 part-time staff members. Services are provided by LD specialists and psychologist.
Policies The college has written policies regarding course substitutions and substitution and waivers of requirements for admission and graduation. Students with LD may take up to 18 credit hours per semester; 9 credit hours per semester are required to maintain full-time status; 12 credit hours per semester are required to be eligible for financial aid. LD services are also available to graduate students.
Special preparation or orientation Optional orientation held individually by special arrangement.
Basic skills remediation Available in study skills, time management, learning strategies, and math. Offered one-on-one and in small groups by professional tutors.
Subject-area tutoring Available in most subjects. Offered one-on-one, in small groups, and class-size groups by professional tutors and graduate assistants/students.
Special courses Available in study skills, college survival skills, test taking, time management, learning strategies, self-advocacy, math, stress management, and written composition skills. Some courses are offered for credit; some enter into overall grade point average.
Counseling and advisement Individual counseling and support groups are available.
Auxiliary aids and services *Aids:* calculators, personal computers, personal spelling/word-use assistants (e.g., Franklin Speller), scan and read programs (e.g., Kurzweil), screen-enlarging programs, screen readers, speech recognition programs (e.g., Dragon), tape recorders, taped textbooks. *Services and accommodations:* advocates, priority registration, alternative test arrangements, readers, note-takers, and scribes.
ADD/ADHD Students with ADD/ADHD are eligible for the same services available to students with LD, as well as distraction-free study areas, distraction-free testing environments, medication management and personal coach or mentors.
Application *Required:* high school transcript and ACT or SAT I (extended-time or untimed test accepted). *Recommended:* personal statement and documentation of high school services (e.g., Individualized Education Program [IEP] or 504 plan). Upon application, documentation of need for special services should be sent only to your LD program or unit. Upon acceptance, documentation of need for special services should be sent only to your LD program or unit.
LD program contact Dr. Sarah Colby Weaver, Director, A38 Brady Commons, Columbia, MO 65201. *Phone:* 573-882-4696. *Fax:* 573-884-9272. *E-mail:* weavers@missouri.edu.
Application contact Georgeanne Porter, Director of Undergraduate Admissions, University of Missouri-Columbia, 305 Jesse Hall, Columbia, MO 65211. *Phone:* 573-882-7786. *Web address:* http://www.missouri.edu/.

THE UNIVERSITY OF NORTH CAROLINA AT CHAPEL HILL

Chapel Hill, North Carolina

Students with LD Served by Program	240	ADD/ADHD Services	✓
Staff	5 full-time, 1 part-time	Summer Preparation Program	n/a
LD Program or Service Fee	n/a	Alternative Test Arrangements	✓
LD Program Began	1988	LD Student Organization	n/a

Learning Disabilities Services began offering services in 1988. The program serves approximately 240 undergraduate students. Faculty consists of 5 full-time staff members and 1 part-time staff member. Services are provided by LD specialists.

Policies The college has written policies regarding course substitutions and grade forgiveness. LD services are also available to graduate students.

Subject-area tutoring Available in some subjects. Offered one-on-one by trained peer tutors.

Auxiliary aids and services *Aids:* tape recorders, taped textbooks. *Services and accommodations:* priority registration, alternative test arrangements, readers, note-takers, and scribes.

ADD/ADHD Students with ADD/ADHD are eligible for the same services available to students with LD, as well as distraction-free study areas, distraction-free testing environments, medication management and personal coach or mentors.

Application *Required:* high school transcript, ACT or SAT I (extended-time or untimed test accepted), and personal statement. Upon application, documentation of need for special services should be sent only to admissions. *Application deadline (institutional):* 1/15 for fall.

LD program contact Dr. Theresa E. L. Maitland, LD/ADHD Specialist, Learning Disabilities Services, 315 Wilson Library/ CB# 3447, Chapel Hill, NC 27599. *Phone:* 919-962-7227. *Fax:* 919-962-3674. *E-mail:* lds@email.unc.edu.

Application contact The University of North Carolina at Chapel Hill, Chapel Hill, NC 27599. *E-mail:* uadm@email.unc.edu. *Web address:* http://www.unc.edu/.

THE UNIVERSITY OF NORTH CAROLINA AT WILMINGTON

Wilmington, North Carolina

Students with LD Served by Program	100	ADD/ADHD Services	✓
Staff	2 full-time	Summer Preparation Program	n/a
LD Program or Service Fee	n/a	Alternative Test Arrangements	✓
LD Program Began	1999	LD Student Organization	n/a

Strategy Enhancement for Achievement (SEA Lab) began offering services in 1999. The program serves approximately 100 undergraduate students. Faculty consists of 2 full-time staff members. Services are provided by counselors, diagnostic specialists, and LD specialists.

Policies 12 credit hours per semester are required to maintain full-time status and to be eligible for financial aid. LD services are also available to graduate students.

Special preparation or orientation Required orientation held before registration, during registration, before classes begin, after classes begin, during summer prior to enrollment, and individually by special arrangement.

Subject-area tutoring Available in most subjects. Offered one-on-one and in small groups by graduate assistants/students, trained peer tutors, and LD specialists.

Special courses Available in study skills, practical computer skills, test taking, reading, time management, learning strategies, and self-advocacy. No courses are offered for credit; none enter into overall grade point average.

Counseling and advisement Career counseling and individual counseling are available.

Auxiliary aids and services *Aids:* calculators, personal spelling/word-use assistants (e.g., Franklin Speller), scan and read programs (e.g., Kurzweil), screen-enlarging programs, screen readers, speech recognition programs (e.g., Dragon), tape recorders. *Services and accommodations:* priority registration, alternative test arrangements, readers, note-takers, and scribes.

ADD/ADHD Students with ADD/ADHD are eligible for the same services available to students with LD, as well as distraction-free testing environments.

Application *Required:* high school transcript, ACT or SAT I (extended-time tests accepted), letter(s) of recommendation, separate application to your LD program or unit, and psychoeducational report (3 years old or less). Upon application, documentation of need for special services should be sent only to your LD program or unit. Upon acceptance, documentation of need for special services should be sent only to your LD program or unit. *Application deadline (institutional):* rolling/continuous for fall and rolling/continuous for spring. *Application deadline (LD program):* rolling/continuous for fall and rolling/continuous for spring.

LD program contact Dr. Margaret Turner, Director, Disability Services, 601 South College Road, Wilmington, NC 28403. *Phone:* 910-962-3746. *Fax:* 910-962-7124.

Application contact The University of North Carolina at Wilmington, 601 South College Road, Wilmington, NC 28403-3201. *E-mail:* admissions@uncwil.edu. *Web address:* http://www. uncwil.edu/.

UNIVERSITY OF OTTAWA

Ottawa, Ontario

Students with LD Served by Program	112	ADD/ADHD Services	✓
Staff	2 full-time	Summer Preparation Program	n/a
LD Program or Service Fee	n/a	Alternative Test Arrangements	n/a
LD Program Began	1989	LD Student Organization	n/a

Learning Assistance Program began offering services in 1989. The program serves approximately 112 undergraduate students. Faculty consists of 2 full-time staff members. Services are provided by diagnostic specialists, LD specialists, trained peer tutors, and consultants, Coordinator of Centre for Special Services.

Policies 12 credits per semester are required to maintain full-time status; 9 credits per semester are required to be eligible for financial aid. LD services are also available to graduate students.

Fees *Diagnostic Testing Fee:* ranges from $800 to $1000.

Diagnostic testing Available for auditory processing, spelling, spoken language, intelligence, study skills, learning strategies, reading, written language, learning styles, visual processing, and cognitive processing.

Basic skills remediation Available in study skills, reading, time management, social skills, learning strategies, spelling, written language, and cognitive processing. Offered one-on-one by LD specialists.

Subject-area tutoring Available in most subjects. Offered one-on-one by graduate assistants/students, trained peer tutors, and LD specialists.

University of Ottawa (continued)

ADD/ADHD Students with ADD/ADHD are eligible for the same services available to students with LD, as well as distraction-free study areas, distraction-free testing environments and personal coach or mentors.

Application *Required:* high school transcript. *Recommended:* psychoeducational report. Upon application, documentation of need for special services should be sent to both admissions and your LD program or unit. Upon acceptance, documentation of need for special services should be sent only to your LD program or unit. *Application deadline (LD program):* rolling/continuous for fall and rolling/continuous for spring.

LD program contact France Corbeil, Consultant, Academic Support Program, 85 University, Room 339, Ottawa, ON K1N 6N5. *Phone:* 613-562-5976. *Fax:* 613-562-5159. *E-mail:* fcorbeil@uottawa.ca.

Application contact University of Ottawa, PO Box 450, Station A, Ottawa, ON K1N 6N5. *E-mail:* liaison@uottawa.ca. *Web address:* http://www.uottawa.ca/.

THE UNIVERSITY OF TENNESSEE AT MARTIN
Martin, Tennessee

Students with LD Served by Program	60	ADD/ADHD Services	✓
Staff	1 full-time, 5 part-time	Summer Preparation Program	✓
LD Program or Service Fee	n/a	Alternative Test Arrangements	✓
LD Program Began	n/a	LD Student Organization	n/a

Program Access for College Enhancement (PACE) serves approximately 60 undergraduate students. Faculty consists of 1 full-time and 5 part-time staff members. Services are provided by academic advisers, graduate assistants/students, LD specialists, and trained peer tutors.

Policies Students with LD may take up to 17 credit hours per semester; 12 credit hours per semester are required to maintain full-time status; 15 hours per semester are required to be eligible for financial aid.

Special preparation or orientation Required summer program offered prior to entering college. Required orientation held during summer prior to enrollment.

Basic skills remediation Available in study skills, computer skills, time management, social skills, and learning strategies. Offered one-on-one and in small groups by computer-based instruction, graduate assistants/students, and trained peer tutors.

Subject-area tutoring Available in all subjects. Offered one-on-one by graduate assistants/students and trained peer tutors.

Counseling and advisement Academic advisement by a staff member affiliated with the program is available.

Auxiliary aids and services *Aids:* calculators, personal computers, personal spelling/word-use assistants (e.g., Franklin Speller), scan and read programs (e.g., Kurzweil), screen readers, speech recognition programs (e.g., Dragon), tape recorders, taped textbooks. *Services and accommodations:* alternative test arrangements and note-takers.

ADD/ADHD Students with ADD/ADHD are eligible for the same services available to students with LD

Application *Required:* high school transcript, ACT (extended-time test accepted), interview, personal statement, separate application to your LD program or unit, psychoeducational report (3 years old or less), and teacher evaluation forms. *Recommended:* documentation of high school services (e.g., Individualized Education Program [IEP] or 504 plan). Upon application, documentation of need for special services should be sent only to your LD program or unit. Upon acceptance, documentation of need

for special services should be sent only to your LD program or unit. *Application deadline (institutional):* rolling/continuous for fall and rolling/continuous for spring. *Application deadline (LD program):* rolling/continuous for fall and rolling/continuous for spring.

LD program contact Michelle Arant, Coordinator, 124 Gooch Hall, Martin, TN 38238. *Phone:* 901-587-7195. *Fax:* 901-587-7956. *E-mail:* marant@utm.edu.

Application contact Judy Rayburn, Director of Admission, The University of Tennessee at Martin, University Street, Martin, TN 38238-1000. *Phone:* 901-587-7032. *E-mail:* admitme@utm.edu. *Web address:* http://www.utm.edu/.

UNIVERSITY OF THE OZARKS
Clarksville, Arkansas

Students with LD Served by Program	88	ADD/ADHD Services	✓
Staff	18 full-time, 2 part-time	Summer Preparation Program	n/a
LD Program or Service Fee	✓	Alternative Test Arrangements	✓
LD Program Began	1971	LD Student Organization	n/a

Jones Learning Center began offering services in 1971. The program serves approximately 88 undergraduate students. Faculty consists of 18 full-time and 2 part-time staff members. Services are provided by diagnostic specialists, LD specialists, trained peer tutors, and master's level program coordinators.

Policies The college has written policies regarding substitution and waivers of requirements for admission. Students with LD may take up to 21 credit hours per semester; 9 credit hours per semester are required to maintain full-time status; 12 credit hours per semester are required to be eligible for financial aid.

Fees *LD Program or Service Fee:* $11350 per year. *Diagnostic Testing Fee:* ranges from $350 to $750.

Special preparation or orientation Required orientation held before registration.

Diagnostic testing Available for auditory processing, motor skills, spelling, spoken language, intelligence, reading, written language, learning styles, visual processing, and math.

Basic skills remediation Available in study skills, computer skills, reading, time management, learning strategies, spelling, written language, and math. Offered in small groups by LD specialists and trained peer tutors.

Subject-area tutoring Available in all subjects. Offered one-on-one and in small groups by professional tutors, trained peer tutors, and LD specialists.

Special courses Available in study skills, college survival skills, test taking, reading, time management, vocabulary development, and written composition skills. All courses are offered for credit; all enter into overall grade point average.

Auxiliary aids and services *Aids:* personal computers, personal spelling/word-use assistants (e.g., Franklin Speller), scan and read programs (e.g., Kurzweil), speech recognition programs (e.g., Dragon), tape recorders, taped textbooks. *Services and accommodations:* advocates, alternative test arrangements, readers, note-takers, and scribes.

ADD/ADHD Students with ADD/ADHD are eligible for the same services available to students with LD, as well as distraction-free study areas, distraction-free testing environments and personal coach or mentors.

Application *Required:* high school transcript, ACT or SAT I (extended-time or untimed test accepted), interview, personal statement, separate application to your LD program or unit, psychoeducational report (3 years old or less), and two-day psychoeducational assessment on campus. *Recommended:* participation in extracurricular activities. Upon application, documentation of need for special services should be sent only to your LD program or unit. Upon acceptance, documentation of need for special services should be sent only to your LD program or unit. *Application deadline (institutional):* rolling/ continuous for fall and rolling/continuous for spring. *Application deadline (LD program):* rolling/continuous for fall and rolling/ continuous for spring.

LD program contact Shannon Rutledge, Secretary, Jones Learning Center, 415 North College Avenue, Clarksville, AR 72830. *Phone:* 501-979-1403. *Fax:* 501-979-1429. *E-mail:* jlc@ozarks. edu.

Application contact University of the Ozarks, 415 North College Avenue, Clarksville, AR 72830-2880. *E-mail:* admiss@ozarks. edu. *Web address:* http://www.ozarks.edu/.

UNIVERSITY OF VERMONT
Burlington, Vermont

Students with LD Served by Program	650	ADD/ADHD Services	✓
Staff	5 full-time, 3 part-time	Summer Preparation Program	n/a
LD Program or Service Fee	n/a	Alternative Test Arrangements	✓
LD Program Began	1978	LD Student Organization	n/a

Specialized Student Services, The Learning Cooperative began offering services in 1978. The program serves approximately 650 undergraduate students. Faculty consists of 5 full-time and 3 part-time staff members. Services are provided by counselors, remediation/learning specialists, diagnostic specialists, special education teachers, and LD specialists.

Policies The college has written policies regarding course substitutions and substitution and waivers of requirements for admission and graduation. LD services are also available to graduate students.

Special preparation or orientation Optional orientation held before classes begin.

Basic skills remediation Available in time management and learning strategies. Offered one-on-one and in small groups by LD specialists and trained peer tutors.

Special courses Available in study skills. All courses are offered for credit; all enter into overall grade point average.

Counseling and advisement Individual counseling and support groups are available.

Auxiliary aids and services *Aids:* scan and read programs (e.g., Kurzweil), screen-enlarging programs, screen readers, taped textbooks. *Services and accommodations:* advocates, priority registration, alternative test arrangements, readers, note-takers, and scribes.

ADD/ADHD Students with ADD/ADHD are eligible for the same services available to students with LD, as well as distraction-free testing environments, personal coach or mentors, and support groups for ADD/ADHD.

Application *Required:* high school transcript, ACT or SAT I (extended-time or untimed test accepted), and personal statement. *Recommended:* participation in extracurricular activities, letter(s) of recommendation, separate application to your LD program or unit, psychoeducational report, and documentation of high school services (e.g., Individualized Education Program [IEP] or 504 plan). Upon application, documentation of need for special services should be sent only to your LD program or unit. Upon acceptance, documentation of need for special services should be sent only to your LD program or unit.

LD program contact Dr. Nancy Oliker, Director, Specialized Student Services, A170 Living/Learning Center, Burlington, VT 05405. *Phone:* 802-656-7753. *Fax:* 802-656-0739.

Application contact Donald M. Honeman, Director of Admissions, University of Vermont, Burlington, VT 05401-3596. *Phone:* 802-656-3370. *E-mail:* admissions@uvm.edu. *Web address:* http://www.uvm.edu/.

UNIVERSITY OF WINDSOR
Windsor, Ontario

Students with LD Served by Program	130	ADD/ADHD Services	✓
Staff	3 full-time	Summer Preparation Program	n/a
LD Program or Service Fee	n/a	Alternative Test Arrangements	✓
LD Program Began	1991	LD Student Organization	✓

Special Needs Programme (Division of Student Affairs) began offering services in 1991. The program serves approximately 130 undergraduate students. Faculty consists of 3 full-time staff members. Services are provided by academic advisers, counselors, remediation/learning specialists, diagnostic specialists, graduate assistants/students, LD specialists, and trained peer tutors.

Policies Students with LD may take up to 15 credit hours per semester; 12 credit hours per semester are required to maintain full-time status; 9 credit hours per semester are required to be eligible for financial aid. LD services are also available to graduate students.

Special preparation or orientation Optional orientation held during registration, before classes begin, and individually by special arrangement.

Diagnostic testing Available for auditory processing, motor skills, spelling, neuropsychological, intelligence, study skills, learning strategies, reading, written language, learning styles, visual processing, and math.

Basic skills remediation Available in motor skills, study skills, computer skills, reading, time management, learning strategies, written language, and math. Offered one-on-one and in small groups by computer-based instruction, LD specialists, trained peer tutors, and education specialist/counselor.

Special courses Available in career planning, study skills, college survival skills, practical computer skills, test taking, reading, time management, learning strategies, vocabulary development, math, and stress management. Some courses are offered for credit; some enter into overall grade point average.

Counseling and advisement Career counseling, individual counseling, small-group counseling, support groups, and financial advising are available. Academic advisement by a staff member affiliated with the program is available.

Auxiliary aids and services *Aids:* calculators, personal computers, scan and read programs (e.g., Kurzweil), screen-enlarging programs, speech recognition programs (e.g., Dragon), tape recorders, taped textbooks. *Services and accommodations:* advocates, priority registration, alternative test arrangements, readers, note-takers, scribes, and oral exams, take-home exams.

Student organization There is a student organization for students with LD.

ADD/ADHD Students with ADD/ADHD are eligible for the same services available to students with LD, as well as distraction-free study areas, distraction-free testing environments, medication management, personal coach or mentors, and support groups for ADD/ADHD.

Application *Required:* high school transcript and psychoeducational report (3 years old or less). *Recommended:* interview, personal statement, letter(s) of recommendation, and documentation of high school services (e.g., Individualized Education Program [IEP] or 504 plan). Upon application, documentation of need for special services should be sent to both admissions and

University of Windsor (continued)

your LD program or unit. Upon acceptance, documentation of need for special services should be sent only to your LD program or unit. *Application deadline (institutional):* 1/5 for fall and 1/11 for spring. *Application deadline (LD program):* rolling/continuous for fall and rolling/continuous for spring.

LD program contact Margaret Crawford, Coordinator, Room 117, Dillon Hall, 401 Sunset Avenue, Windsor, ON N9B 3P4. *Phone:* 519-253-3000 Ext. 3298. *Fax:* 519-973-7095. *E-mail:* crawfm@uwindsor.ca.

Application contact University of Windsor, 401 Sunset Avenue, Windsor, ON N9B 3P4. *E-mail:* liaison@uwindsor.ca. *Web address:* http://www.uwindsor.ca/.

UNIVERSITY OF WISCONSIN-OSHKOSH
Oshkosh, Wisconsin

Students with LD Served by Program	150	ADD/ADHD Services	n/a
Staff	1 full-time, 1 part-time	Summer Preparation Program	✓
LD Program or Service Fee	n/a	Alternative Test Arrangements	✓
LD Program Began	1979	LD Student Organization	✓

Project Success began offering services in 1979. The program serves approximately 150 undergraduate students. Faculty consists of 1 full-time and 1 part-time staff member. Services are provided by remediation/learning specialists, special education teachers, graduate assistants/students, teacher trainees, LD specialists, and trained peer tutors.

Policies The college has written policies regarding substitution and waivers of requirements for admission and graduation. Students with LD may take up to 18 credit hours per semester; 12 credit hours per semester are required to maintain full-time status and to be eligible for financial aid. LD services are also available to graduate students.

Special preparation or orientation Required summer program offered prior to entering college. Held during summer prior to enrollment.

Diagnostic testing Available for auditory processing, spelling, intelligence, reading, written language, and math.

Basic skills remediation Available in study skills, reading, learning strategies, spelling, written language, and math. Offered one-on-one, in small groups, and class-size groups by graduate assistants/students, special education teachers, LD specialists, and trained peer tutors.

Subject-area tutoring Available in most subjects. Offered one-on-one and in small groups by graduate assistants/students, trained peer tutors, and LD specialists.

Special courses Available in career planning, study skills, college survival skills, test taking, reading, time management, learning strategies, self-advocacy, vocabulary development, math, and written composition skills. Some courses are offered for credit; all enter into overall grade point average.

Counseling and advisement Individual counseling is available.

Auxiliary aids and services *Aids:* calculators, personal computers. *Services and accommodations:* advocates and alternative test arrangements.

Student organization There is a student organization for students with LD.

Application *Required:* high school transcript, ACT or SAT I (extended-time or untimed test accepted), and separate application to your LD program or unit. *Recommended:* participation in extracurricular activities, personal statement, and letter(s) of recommendation. *Application deadline (institutional):* 12/1 for fall and 1/1 for spring. *Application deadline (LD program):* 3/15 for fall and 1/1 for spring.

LD program contact William Kitz, Associate Professor, Project Success, 800 Algoma Boulevard, Oshkosh, WI 54901. *Phone:* 920-424-1033. *Fax:* 920-424-0858.

Application contact Richard Hillman, Associate Director of Admissions, University of Wisconsin-Oshkosh, 800 Algoma Boulevard, Oshkosh, WI 54901. *Phone:* 920-424-0202. *E-mail:* oshadmuw@uwosh.edu. *Web address:* http://www.uwosh.edu/.

UNIVERSITY OF WISCONSIN-WHITEWATER
Whitewater, Wisconsin

Students with LD Served by Program	225	ADD/ADHD Services	✓
Staff	2 full-time, 1 part-time	Summer Preparation Program	✓
LD Program or Service Fee	varies	Alternative Test Arrangements	✓
LD Program Began	1977	LD Student Organization	n/a

Project Assistant began offering services in 1977. The program serves approximately 225 undergraduate students. Faculty consists of 2 full-time staff members and 1 part-time staff member. Services are provided by remediation/learning specialists, teacher trainees, LD specialists, and trained peer tutors.

Policies The college has written policies regarding course substitutions, grade forgiveness, and substitution and waivers of requirements for admission and graduation. Students with LD may take up to 18 credit hours per semester; 12 credit hours per semester are required to maintain full-time status and to be eligible for financial aid. LD services are also available to graduate students.

Fees *LD Program or Service Fee:* ranges from $400 to $2700 per year.

Special preparation or orientation Required summer program offered prior to entering college. before registration, during registration, before classes begin, after classes begin, during summer prior to enrollment, and individually by special arrangement.

Diagnostic testing Available for auditory processing, spelling, intelligence, learning strategies, reading, written language, learning styles, visual processing, and math.

Basic skills remediation Available in auditory processing, study skills, computer skills, reading, time management, visual processing, learning strategies, spelling, written language, and math. Offered one-on-one and in small groups by computer-based instruction, LD specialists, teacher trainees, and trained peer tutors.

Subject-area tutoring Available in all subjects. Offered one-on-one and in small groups by trained peer tutors and LD specialists.

Special courses Available in study skills and learning strategies. Some courses are offered for credit; all enter into overall grade point average.

Counseling and advisement Career counseling and individual counseling are available.

Auxiliary aids and services *Aids:* calculators, personal computers, scan and read programs (e.g., Kurzweil), screen readers, taped textbooks. *Services and accommodations:* advocates, alternative test arrangements, readers, note-takers, and scribes.

ADD/ADHD Students with ADD/ADHD are eligible for the same services available to students with LD, as well as distraction-free study areas, distraction-free testing environments and one on one teaching.

Application *Required:* high school transcript, ACT (extended-time or untimed test accepted), personal statement, separate application to your LD program or unit, psychoeducational report (2 years old or less), and documentation of high school services (e.g., Individualized Education Program [IEP] or 504 plan). Upon application, documentation of need for special services should be sent only to your LD program or unit. Upon acceptance, documentation of need for special services should be sent only to your LD program or unit. *Application deadline (institutional):* rolling/continuous for fall and rolling/continuous for spring. *Application deadline (LD program):* rolling/continuous for fall and rolling/continuous for spring.

LD program contact Nancy Amacher, Director, 2021 Roseman Building, Whitewater, WI 53190. *Phone:* 262-472-4788. *Fax:* 262-472-5210. *E-mail:* amachern@mail.uww.edu.

Application contact University of Wisconsin-Whitewater, 800 West Main Street, Whitewater, WI 53190-1790. *E-mail:* uwwadmit@uwwvax.uww.edu. *Web address:* http://www.uww.edu/.

URSULINE COLLEGE
Pepper Pike, Ohio

Students with LD Served by Program	9	ADD/ADHD Services	✓
Staff	2 full-time, 2 part-time	Summer Preparation Program	n/a
LD Program or Service Fee	varies	Alternative Test Arrangements	✓
LD Program Began	1995	LD Student Organization	n/a

Program for Students with Learning Disabilities began offering services in 1995. The program serves approximately 9 undergraduate students. Faculty consists of 2 full-time and 2 part-time staff members. Services are provided by academic advisers, regular education teachers, counselors, remediation/learning specialists, special education teachers, and LD specialists.

Policies The college has written policies regarding course substitutions and substitution and waivers of requirements for admission. Students with LD may take up to 12 credit hours per semester; 12 credit hours per semester are required to maintain full-time status and to be eligible for financial aid. LD services are also available to graduate students.

Fees *LD Program or Service Fee:* ranges from $1200 to $2400 per year.

Special preparation or orientation Held before classes begin.

Basic skills remediation Available in study skills, reading, social skills, learning strategies, written language, and math. Offered one-on-one and in small groups by regular education teachers and LD specialists.

Subject-area tutoring Available in some subjects. Offered one-on-one and in small groups by LD specialists.

Special courses Available in oral communication skills, study skills, test taking, reading, time management, self-advocacy, vocabulary development, math, stress management, and written composition skills. Some courses are offered for credit; some enter into overall grade point average.

Counseling and advisement Career counseling, individual counseling, and support groups are available. Academic advisement by a staff member affiliated with the program is available.

Auxiliary aids and services *Aids:* calculators, personal computers, screen-enlarging programs, speech recognition programs (e.g., Dragon), tape recorders, taped textbooks, reading edge machine. *Services and accommodations:* advocates, priority registration, alternative test arrangements, readers, notetakers, and scribes.

ADD/ADHD Students with ADD/ADHD are eligible for the same services available to students with LD, as well as distraction-free testing environments and support groups for ADD/ADHD.

Application *Required:* high school transcript, ACT or SAT I (extended-time or untimed test accepted), interview, personal statement, letter(s) of recommendation, separate application to your LD program or unit, and psychoeducational report (3 years old or less). *Recommended:* participation in extracurricular activities and documentation of high school services (e.g., Individualized Education Program [IEP] or 504 plan). Upon application, documentation of need for special services should be sent only to your LD program or unit. Upon acceptance, documentation of need for special services should be sent only to your LD program or unit. *Application deadline (institutional):* rolling/continuous for fall and rolling/continuous for spring. *Application deadline (LD program):* rolling/continuous for fall and rolling/continuous for spring.

LD program contact Annette Gromada, Learning Disabilities Specialist, 2500 Lander Road, Pepper Pike, OH 44124-4398. *Phone:* 440-449-2046. *Fax:* 440-646-8318. *E-mail:* agromada@ursuline.edu.

Application contact Ursuline College, 2550 Lander Road, Pepper Pike, OH 44124-4398. *E-mail:* dgiaco@en.com. *Web address:* http://www.ursuline.edu/.

UTICA COLLEGE OF SYRACUSE UNIVERSITY
Utica, New York

Students with LD Served by Program	80	ADD/ADHD Services	✓
Staff	1 full-time, 1 part-time	Summer Preparation Program	n/a
LD Program or Service Fee	n/a	Alternative Test Arrangements	✓
LD Program Began	1981	LD Student Organization	n/a

Learning Services, Academic Support Services began offering services in 1981. The program serves approximately 80 undergraduate students. Faculty consists of 1 full-time and 1 part-time staff member. Services are provided by counselors, diagnostic specialists, special education teachers, and trained peer tutors.

Policies LD services are also available to graduate students.

Fees *Diagnostic Testing Fee:* $100.

Special preparation or orientation Optional orientation held individually by special arrangement.

Diagnostic testing Available for auditory processing, study skills, learning strategies, reading, written language, learning styles, visual processing, and math.

Basic skills remediation Available in auditory processing, study skills, reading, time management, handwriting, learning strategies, spelling, written language, and math. Offered one-on-one by special education teachers.

Subject-area tutoring Available in all subjects. Offered one-on-one by trained peer tutors.

Counseling and advisement Career counseling and individual counseling are available.

Auxiliary aids and services *Aids:* calculators, personal computers, personal spelling/word-use assistants (e.g., Franklin Speller), scan and read programs (e.g., Kurzweil), screen readers, speech recognition programs (e.g., Dragon), tape recorders, taped textbooks. *Services and accommodations:* advocates, priority registration, alternative test arrangements, readers, notetakers, and scribes.

ADD/ADHD Students with ADD/ADHD are eligible for the same services available to students with LD, as well as distraction-free testing environments and personal coach or mentors.

Application *Required:* high school transcript, personal statement, and letter(s) of recommendation. *Recommended:* participation in extracurricular activities, ACT or SAT I (extended-time

Utica College of Syracuse University (continued)

or untimed test accepted), interview, psychoeducational report (3 years old or less), and documentation of high school services (e.g., Individualized Education Program [IEP] or 504 plan). Upon application, documentation of need for special services should be sent only to your LD program or unit. Upon acceptance, documentation of need for special services should be sent only to your LD program or unit. *Application deadline (institutional):* rolling/continuous for fall and rolling/continuous for spring. *Application deadline (LD program):* rolling/continuous for fall and rolling/continuous for spring.

LD program contact Denise Williams, Coordinator of Learning Services, 1600 Burrstone Road, Utica, NY 13502. *Phone:* 315-792-3032. *Fax:* 315-792-3292. *E-mail:* dwilliams@utic.ucsu.edu.

Application contact Utica College of Syracuse University, 1600 Burrstone Road, Utica, NY 13502-4892. *E-mail:* admiss@utica.ucsu.edu. *Web address:* http://www.ucsu.edu/.

VIRGINIA WESLEYAN COLLEGE
Norfolk, Virginia

Students with LD Served by Program	70	ADD/ADHD Services	✓
Staff	1 full-time	Summer Preparation Program	n/a
LD Program or Service Fee	n/a	Alternative Test Arrangements	✓
LD Program Began	1989	LD Student Organization	n/a

Disabilities Services Office began offering services in 1989. The program serves approximately 70 undergraduate students. Faculty consists of 1 full-time staff member. Services are provided by professional tutors and Disabilities Coodinator.
Policies The college has written policies regarding course substitutions and substitution and waivers of requirements for admission. 12 hours per semester are required to maintain full-time status and to be eligible for financial aid.
Special preparation or orientation Required orientation held individually by special arrangement.
Basic skills remediation Available in study skills, time management, written language, and math. Offered one-on-one by professional tutors and trained peer tutors.
Counseling and advisement Academic counseling is available.
Auxiliary aids and services *Aids:* screen-enlarging programs, speech recognition programs (e.g., Dragon), tape recorders. *Services and accommodations:* advocates, priority registration, alternative test arrangements, readers, note-takers, scribes, and academic advising.
ADD/ADHD Students with ADD/ADHD are eligible for the same services available to students with LD, as well as distraction-free study areas, distraction-free testing environments and assistance securing private room.
Application *Required:* high school transcript, SAT I (extended-time test accepted), personal statement, letter(s) of recommendation, and psychoeducational report (4 years old or less). Upon application, documentation of need for special services should be sent only to admissions. Upon acceptance, documentation of need for special services should be sent only to your LD program or unit. *Application deadline (institutional):* rolling/continuous for fall and rolling/continuous for spring. *Application deadline (LD program):* rolling/continuous for fall and rolling/continuous for spring.
LD program contact Fayne Pearson, Disabilities Coordinator, 1584 Wesleyan Drive, Norfolk, VA 23502-3246. *Phone:* 757-455-3246. *E-mail:* fpearson@vwc.edu.
Application contact Virginia Wesleyan College, 1584 Wesleyan Drive, Norfolk, VA 23502-5599. *E-mail:* admissions@vwc.edu. *Web address:* http://www.vwc.edu/.

WESTMINSTER COLLEGE
Fulton, Missouri

Students with LD Served by Program	40	ADD/ADHD Services	n/a
Staff	2 full-time, 1 part-time	Summer Preparation Program	n/a
LD Program or Service Fee	n/a	Alternative Test Arrangements	✓
LD Program Began	1975	LD Student Organization	n/a

Learning Disabilities Program began offering services in 1975. The program serves approximately 40 undergraduate students. Faculty consists of 2 full-time staff members and 1 part-time staff member. Services are provided by remediation/learning specialists and LD specialists.
Policies The college has written policies regarding substitution and waivers of requirements for admission. Students with LD may take up to 18 credit hours per semester; 12 credit hours per semester are required to maintain full-time status. LD services are also available to graduate students.
Special preparation or orientation Held after classes begin.
Basic skills remediation Available in auditory processing, study skills, computer skills, reading, time management, handwriting, visual processing, learning strategies, spelling, written language, math, and spoken language. Offered one-on-one and in class-size groups by LD specialists.
Subject-area tutoring Available in most subjects. Offered one-on-one, in small groups, and class-size groups by professional tutors and LD specialists.
Special courses Available in study skills, learning strategies, and written composition skills. All courses are offered for credit; all enter into overall grade point average.
Counseling and advisement Career counseling and individual counseling are available.
Auxiliary aids and services *Aids:* personal computers, personal spelling/word-use assistants (e.g., Franklin Speller), scan and read programs (e.g., Kurzweil), speech recognition programs (e.g., Dragon), tape recorders, taped textbooks, class notes, personal dictation. *Services and accommodations:* advocates, alternative test arrangements, readers, note-takers, scribes, and academic advising.
Application *Required:* high school transcript, ACT or SAT I (extended-time or untimed test accepted), interview, letter(s) of recommendation, separate application to your LD program or unit, and psychoeducational report (4 years old or less). *Recommended:* participation in extracurricular activities, ACT (extended-time or untimed test accepted), and documentation of high school services (e.g., Individualized Education Program [IEP] or 504 plan). Upon application, documentation of need for special services should be sent only to admissions. Upon acceptance, documentation of need for special services should be sent only to admissions.
LD program contact Hank Ottinger, Director, Learning Disabilities Program, 501 Westminster Avenue, Fulton, MO 65251. *Phone:* 573-592-5304. *Fax:* 573-592-5180. *E-mail:* ottingh@jaynet.wcmo.edu.
Application contact Westminster College, 501 Westminster Avenue, Fulton, MO 65251-1299. *E-mail:* admissions@micro.wcmo.edu. *Web address:* http://www.wcmo.edu/.

WIDENER UNIVERSITY
Chester, Pennsylvania

Students with LD Served by Program	160	ADD/ADHD Services	✓
Staff	2 full-time, 6 part-time	Summer Preparation Program	n/a
LD Program or Service Fee	n/a	Alternative Test Arrangements	✓
LD Program Began	1985	LD Student Organization	n/a

Enable Counseling Service began offering services in 1985. The program serves approximately 160 undergraduate students. Faculty consists of 2 full-time and 6 part-time staff members. Services are provided by remediation/learning specialists, graduate assistants/students, LD specialists, trained peer tutors, and professional tutors.

Policies Students with LD may take up to 18 credit hours per semester; 12 credit hours per semester are required to maintain full-time status and to be eligible for financial aid. LD services are also available to graduate students.

Special preparation or orientation Optional orientation held during registration, before classes begin, after classes begin, during summer prior to enrollment, and individually by special arrangement.

Diagnostic testing Available for auditory processing, motor skills, spelling, handwriting, neuropsychological, spoken language, intelligence, personality, learning strategies, reading, written language, learning styles, visual processing, and math.

Subject-area tutoring Available in all subjects. Offered one-on-one and in small groups by professional tutors, graduate assistants/students, trained peer tutors, and LD specialists.

Counseling and advisement Career counseling, individual counseling, and small-group counseling are available.

Auxiliary aids and services *Aids:* calculators, personal spelling/word-use assistants (e.g., Franklin Speller), scan and read programs (e.g., Kurzweil). *Services and accommodations:* advocates, alternative test arrangements, readers, note-takers, and scribes.

ADD/ADHD Students with ADD/ADHD are eligible for the same services available to students with LD, as well as distraction-free testing environments and personal coach or mentors.

Application *Required:* high school transcript, ACT or SAT I (extended-time or untimed test accepted), personal statement, letter(s) of recommendation, and psychoeducational report (3 years old or less). *Recommended:* participation in extracurricular activities, interview, and documentation of high school services (e.g., Individualized Education Program [IEP] or 504 plan). Upon application, documentation of need for special services should be sent only to admissions. Upon acceptance, documentation of need for special services should be sent only to your LD program or unit. *Application deadline (institutional):* rolling/continuous for fall and rolling/continuous for spring. *Application deadline (LD program):* rolling/continuous for fall and rolling/continuous for spring.

LD program contact Dr. LaVerne R. Ziegenfuss, Assistant Dean of Student Support Services, Lipka Hall, Chester, PA 19013. *Phone:* 610-499-1270. *Fax:* 610-499-1190. *E-mail:* laverne.r.ziegenfuss@widener.edu.

Application contact Widener University, One University Place, Chester, PA 19013-5792. *E-mail:* admissions.office@widener.edu. *Web address:* http://www.widener.edu/.

WILFRID LAURIER UNIVERSITY
Waterloo, Ontario

Students with LD Served by Program	230	ADD/ADHD Services	✓
Staff	3 full-time, 2 part-time	Summer Preparation Program	n/a
LD Program or Service Fee	n/a	Alternative Test Arrangements	✓
LD Program Began	1990	LD Student Organization	n/a

Special Needs Office began offering services in 1990. The program serves approximately 230 undergraduate students. Faculty consists of 3 full-time and 2 part-time staff members. Services are provided by remediation/learning specialists, counselors, regular education teachers, diagnostic specialists, LD specialists, and trained peer tutors.

Policies The college has written policies regarding substitution and waivers of requirements for admission. LD services are also available to graduate students.

Special preparation or orientation Optional orientation held before classes begin, during summer prior to enrollment, and individually by special arrangement.

Diagnostic testing Available for auditory processing, motor skills, spelling, handwriting, spoken language, intelligence, personality, study skills, learning strategies, reading, written language, learning styles, visual processing, and math.

Basic skills remediation Available in study skills, reading, time management, learning strategies, and written language. Offered one-on-one by LD specialists.

Counseling and advisement Career counseling and individual counseling are available.

Auxiliary aids and services *Aids:* calculators, personal computers, screen-enlarging programs, tape recorders, taped textbooks. *Services and accommodations:* advocates, alternative test arrangements, readers, note-takers, and scribes.

ADD/ADHD Students with ADD/ADHD are eligible for the same services available to students with LD, as well as distraction-free study areas, distraction-free testing environments and personal coach or mentors.

Application *Required:* high school transcript. *Recommended:* participation in extracurricular activities, interview, personal statement, letter(s) of recommendation, separate application to your LD program or unit, psychoeducational report (5 years old or less), and documentation of high school services (e.g., Individualized Education Program [IEP] or 504 plan). Upon application, documentation of need for special services should be sent to both admissions and your LD program or unit. Upon acceptance, documentation of need for special services should be sent only to your LD program or unit. *Application deadline (institutional):* 8/13 for fall and 4/9 for spring. *Application deadline (LD program):* rolling/continuous for fall and rolling/continuous for spring.

LD program contact Judy BruynSpecial Needs Office, 75 University Avenue, Waterloo, ON N2L 3C5.

Application contact Wilfrid Laurier University, 75 University Avenue West, Waterloo, ON N2L 3C5. *E-mail:* admissions@mach1.wlu.ca. *Web address:* http://www.wlu.ca/.

WRIGHT STATE UNIVERSITY
Dayton, Ohio

Students with LD Served by Program	250	ADD/ADHD Services	✓
Staff	8 full-time	Summer Preparation Program	n/a
LD Program or Service Fee	n/a	Alternative Test Arrangements	✓
LD Program Began	1975	LD Student Organization	✓

Office of Disability Services began offering services in 1975. The program serves approximately 250 undergraduate students. Faculty consists of 8 full-time staff members. Services are provided by academic advisers, counselors, diagnostic specialists, graduate assistants/students, and trained peer tutors.

Policies The college has written policies regarding course substitutions, grade forgiveness, and substitution and waivers of requirements for admission and graduation. 11 credit hours per quarter are required to maintain full-time status; 12 credit hour per quarter are required to be eligible for financial aid. LD services are also available to graduate students.

Special preparation or orientation Required orientation held before classes begin.

Diagnostic testing Available for auditory processing, neuropsychological, spoken language, intelligence, personality, learning strategies, reading, written language, learning styles, visual processing, and math.

Basic skills remediation Available in reading, time management, learning strategies, written language, and math. Offered in class-size groups by computer-based instruction and regular education teachers.

Subject-area tutoring Available in most subjects. Offered one-on-one by trained peer tutors.

Special courses Available in career planning and college survival skills. All courses are offered for credit; most enter into overall grade point average.

Counseling and advisement Career counseling, individual counseling, and small-group counseling are available. Academic advisement by a staff member affiliated with the program is available.

Auxiliary aids and services *Aids:* calculators, personal computers, scan and read programs (e.g., Kurzweil), screen-enlarging programs, screen readers, speech recognition programs (e.g., Dragon), tape recorders, taped textbooks. *Services and accommodations:* advocates, alternative test arrangements, readers, scribes, and copies of classmates notes.

Student organization There is a student organization for students with LD.

ADD/ADHD Students with ADD/ADHD are eligible for the same services available to students with LD, as well as distraction-free testing environments.

Application *Required:* high school transcript, ACT or SAT I (extended-time tests accepted), interview, personal statement, and separate application to your LD program or unit. *Recommended:* letter(s) of recommendation. Upon application, documentation of need for special services should be sent only to your LD program or unit. Upon acceptance, documentation of need for special services should be sent only to your LD program or unit.

LD program contact Judy Roberts, Assistant Director, E186 Student Union, Dayton, OH 45435. *Phone:* 937-775-5680. *Fax:* 937-775-5795. *E-mail:* judith.roberts@wright.edu.

Application contact Wright State University, 3640 Colonel Glenn Highway, Dayton, OH 45435. *E-mail:* admissions@wright.edu. *Web address:* http://www.wright.edu/.

► FOUR-YEAR COLLEGES ◄

WITH SPECIAL SERVICES

ABILENE CHRISTIAN UNIVERSITY
Abilene, Texas

Students with LD Served by Program	206	ADD/ADHD Services	✓
Staff	4 full-time, 12 part-time	Summer Preparation Program	n/a
LD Program or Service Fee	n/a	Alternative Test Arrangements	✓
LD Program Began	1987	LD Student Organization	n/a

Alpha Academic Services began offering services in 1987. The program serves approximately 206 undergraduate students. Faculty consists of 4 full-time and 12 part-time staff members. Services are provided by counselors, graduate assistants/students, teacher trainees, LD specialists, trained peer tutors, and professional tutors.

Policies Students with LD may take up to 18 credit hours per semester; 12 credit hours per semester are required to maintain full-time status; 12 credit hours per semester are required to be eligible for financial aid. LD services are also available to graduate students.

Special preparation or orientation Optional orientation held individually by special arrangement.

Basic skills remediation Available in study skills, computer skills, reading, time management, learning strategies, spelling, written language, and math. Offered one-on-one and in small groups by graduate assistants/students, professional tutors, and trained peer tutors.

Subject-area tutoring Available in most subjects. Offered one-on-one and in small groups by professional tutors, graduate assistants/students, and trained peer tutors.

Counseling and advisement Career counseling, individual counseling, small-group counseling, and support groups are available.

Auxiliary aids and services *Aids:* calculators, personal computers, scan and read programs (e.g., Kurzweil), speech recognition programs (e.g., Dragon), tape recorders. *Services and accommodations:* advocates, alternative test arrangements, readers, note-takers, and scribes.

ADD/ADHD Students with ADD/ADHD are eligible for the same services available to students with LD, as well as distraction-free study areas, distraction-free testing environments and support groups for ADD/ADHD.

Application *Required:* high school transcript, ACT or SAT I (extended-time or untimed test accepted), interview, personal statement, letter(s) of recommendation, separate application to your LD program or unit, and psychoeducational report (5 years old or less). *Recommended:* participation in extracurricular activities. Upon application, documentation of need for special services should be sent only to your LD program or unit. Upon acceptance, documentation of need for special services should be sent only to your LD program or unit. *Application deadline (LD program):* 8/15 for fall and 12/15 for spring.

LD program contact Ada Dodd, Counselor, ACU Box 29204, Abilene, TX 79699-9204. *Phone:* 915-674-2750. *Fax:* 915-674-6847. *E-mail:* dodda@acu.edu.

Application contact Abilene Christian University, ACU Box 29000, Abilene, TX 79699-9100. *E-mail:* info@admissions.acu.edu. *Web address:* http://www.acu.edu/.

ADRIAN COLLEGE
Adrian, Michigan

Students with LD Served by Program	27	ADD/ADHD Services	✓
Staff	3 full-time, 1 part-time	Summer Preparation Program	n/a
LD Program or Service Fee	n/a	Alternative Test Arrangements	✓
LD Program Began	1989	LD Student Organization	✓

Academic Services began offering services in 1989. The program serves approximately 27 undergraduate students. Faculty consists of 3 full-time staff members and 1 part-time staff member. Services are provided by academic advisers, remediation/learning specialists, and trained peer tutors.

Policies Students with LD may take up to 18 credit hours per semester; 12 credit hours per semester are required to maintain full-time status and to be eligible for financial aid.

Basic skills remediation Available in study skills, reading, learning strategies, written language, and math. Offered one-on-one and in small groups by computer-based instruction, regular education teachers, and LD specialists.

Subject-area tutoring Available in most subjects. Offered one-on-one and in small groups by professional tutors and trained peer tutors.

Special courses Available in college survival skills, reading, math, and written composition skills. Some courses are offered for credit; all enter into overall grade point average.

Counseling and advisement Career counseling, individual counseling, and support groups are available. Academic advisement by a staff member affiliated with the program is available.

Auxiliary aids and services *Aids:* calculators, scan and read programs (e.g., Kurzweil), screen readers, speech recognition programs (e.g., Dragon), tape recorders, taped textbooks. *Services and accommodations:* alternative test arrangements, readers, note-takers, and scribes.

Student organization There is a student organization for students with LD.

ADD/ADHD Students with ADD/ADHD are eligible for the same services available to students with LD, as well as distraction-free study areas and distraction-free testing environments.

Application *Required:* high school transcript and ACT or SAT I (extended-time or untimed test accepted). Upon acceptance, documentation of need for special services should be sent only to your LD program or unit. *Application deadline (institutional):* rolling/continuous for fall and rolling/continuous for spring. *Application deadline (LD program):* rolling/continuous for fall and rolling/continuous for spring.

LD program contact Carol Tapp, Learning Specialist, 110 South Madison Street, Adrian, MI 49221. *Phone:* 517-265-5161 Ext. 4094. *Fax:* 517-264-3181.

Application contact Adrian College, 110 South Madison Street, Adrian, MI 49221-2575. *E-mail:* admission@adrian.adrian.edu. *Web address:* http://www.adrian.edu/.

ALASKA PACIFIC UNIVERSITY
Anchorage, Alaska

Students with LD Served by Program	10	ADD/ADHD Services	✓
Staff	1 full-time	Summer Preparation Program	n/a
LD Program or Service Fee	n/a	Alternative Test Arrangements	✓
LD Program Began	n/a	LD Student Organization	n/a

Alaska Pacific University (continued)

Disabled Student Services serves approximately 10 undergraduate students. Faculty consists of 1 full-time staff member. Services are provided by regular education teachers, trained peer tutors, and Dean of Students.

Policies Students with LD may take up to 18 credit hours per semester; 12 credit hours per semester are required to maintain full-time status; 12 credit hours per semester are required to be eligible for financial aid. LD services are also available to graduate students.

Subject-area tutoring Available in some subjects. Offered one-on-one by graduate assistants/students and trained peer tutors.

Counseling and advisement Career counseling and individual counseling are available.

Auxiliary aids and services *Aids:* tape recorders, taped textbooks. *Services and accommodations:* alternative test arrangements, note-takers, and assistance with admissions.

ADD/ADHD Students with ADD/ADHD are eligible for the same services available to students with LD, as well as distraction-free testing environments and personal coach or mentors.

Application *Required:* high school transcript, SAT I, and personal statement. *Recommended:* documentation of high school services (e.g., Individualized Education Program [IEP] or 504 plan). Upon application, documentation of need for special services should be sent to both admissions and your LD program or unit. Upon acceptance, documentation of need for special services should be sent to both admissions and your LD program or unit. *Application deadline (institutional):* rolling/continuous for fall and rolling/continuous for spring. *Application deadline (LD program):* rolling/continuous for fall and rolling/continuous for spring.

LD program contact Cree Bol, Dean of Students, 4101 University Drive, Anchorage, AK 99508. *Phone:* 907-564-8289. *E-mail:* cree@alaskapacific.edu.

Application contact Alaska Pacific University, 4101 University Drive, Anchorage, AK 99508-4672. *E-mail:* apu@corecom.net. *Web address:* http://www.alaskapacific.edu/.

ALBANY STATE UNIVERSITY
Albany, Georgia

Students with LD Served by Program	35	ADD/ADHD Services	✓
Staff	1 part-time	Summer Preparation Program	n/a
LD Program or Service Fee	n/a	Alternative Test Arrangements	✓
LD Program Began	1980	LD Student Organization	n/a

Disability Student Services Program (DSSP) began offering services in 1980. The program serves approximately 35 undergraduate students. Faculty consists of 1 part-time staff member. Services are provided by academic advisers, counselors, regular education teachers, diagnostic specialists, and LD specialists.

Policies The college has written policies regarding course substitutions, grade forgiveness, and substitution and waivers of requirements for admission and graduation. Students with LD may take up to 19 hours per semester; 12 hours per semester are required to maintain full-time status. LD services are also available to graduate students.

Fees *Diagnostic Testing Fee:* $300.

Diagnostic testing Available for auditory processing, motor skills, spelling, handwriting, neuropsychological, spoken language, intelligence, personality, study skills, learning strategies, reading, written language, learning styles, social skills, visual processing, and math.

Basic skills remediation Available in study skills, reading, time management, learning strategies, written language, and math. Offered in class-size groups by computer-based instruction and regular education teachers.

Subject-area tutoring Available in most subjects. Offered one-on-one by trained peer tutors.

Counseling and advisement Career counseling and individual counseling are available. Academic advisement by a staff member affiliated with the program is available.

Auxiliary aids and services *Aids:* screen-enlarging programs, screen readers, taped textbooks. *Services and accommodations:* advocates, priority registration, alternative test arrangements, readers, and note-takers.

ADD/ADHD Students with ADD/ADHD are eligible for the same services available to students with LD, as well as distraction-free testing environments and medication management.

Application *Required:* high school transcript, ACT or SAT I (extended-time or untimed test accepted), separate application to your LD program or unit, psychoeducational report (3 years old or less), and application fee. *Recommended:* participation in extracurricular activities. Upon application, documentation of need for special services should be sent only to your LD program or unit. Upon acceptance, documentation of need for special services should be sent only to your LD program or unit. *Application deadline (LD program):* rolling/continuous for fall and rolling/continuous for spring.

LD program contact Deborah J. Moore, Assistant Director, Counseling and Testing, 504 College Drive, Albany, GA 31705. *Phone:* 912-430-4667. *Fax:* 912-430-3826. *E-mail:* dmoore@asurams.edu.

Application contact Patricia Price, Assistant Director of Admissions, Albany State University, 504 College Drive, Albany, GA 31705-2717. *Phone:* 912-430-4646. *E-mail:* kcaldwell@rams.alsnet.peachnet.edu. *Web address:* http://www.alsnet.peachnet.edu/.

ALFRED UNIVERSITY
Alfred, New York

Students with LD Served by Program	160	ADD/ADHD Services	✓
Staff	n/a	Summer Preparation Program	n/a
LD Program or Service Fee	n/a	Alternative Test Arrangements	✓
LD Program Began	n/a	LD Student Organization	n/a

Special Academic Services serves approximately 160 undergraduate students. Services are provided by academic consultants.

Subject-area tutoring Available in most subjects. Offered one-on-one and in small groups by trained peer tutors.

Auxiliary aids and services *Aids:* calculators, tape recorders, taped textbooks. *Services and accommodations:* advocates, priority registration, alternative test arrangements, readers, note-takers, and scribes.

ADD/ADHD Students with ADD/ADHD are eligible for the same services available to students with LD, as well as distraction-free testing environments.

Application *Required:* high school transcript, ACT or SAT I, and letter(s) of recommendation. *Recommended:* interview.

LD program contact Dr. Terry Taggart, Director, Special Academic Services, Myers 117, Alfred, NY 14802. *Phone:* 607-871-3379. *Fax:* 607-871-2342.

Application contact Alfred University, Alumni Hall, Alfred, NY 14802-1205. *E-mail:* admssn@bigvax.alfred.edu. *Web address:* http://www.alfred.edu/.

ALMA COLLEGE
Alma, Michigan

Students with LD Served by Program	25	ADD/ADHD Services	✓
Staff	3 full-time, 3 part-time	Summer Preparation Program	✓
LD Program or Service Fee	n/a	Alternative Test Arrangements	✓
LD Program Began	n/a	LD Student Organization	n/a

Center for Student Development serves approximately 25 undergraduate students. Faculty consists of 3 full-time and 3 part-time staff members. Services are provided by academic advisers, counselors, graduate assistants/students, and trained peer tutors.

Special preparation or orientation Optional summer program offered prior to entering college.

Subject-area tutoring Available in most subjects. Offered one-on-one by graduate assistants/students and trained peer tutors.

Special courses Available in career planning, study skills, college survival skills, test taking, reading, time management, learning strategies, and stress management. No courses are offered for credit; none enter into overall grade point average.

Counseling and advisement Career counseling, individual counseling, and support groups are available. Academic advisement by a staff member affiliated with the program is available.

Auxiliary aids and services *Aids:* calculators, personal computers, personal spelling/word-use assistants (e.g., Franklin Speller), scan and read programs (e.g., Kurzweil), screen-enlarging programs, tape recorders, taped textbooks. *Services and accommodations:* advocates, priority registration, alternative test arrangements, and note-takers.

ADD/ADHD Students with ADD/ADHD are eligible for the same services available to students with LD, as well as distraction-free study areas, distraction-free testing environments, medication management and personal coach or mentors.

Application *Required:* high school transcript, ACT or SAT I (extended-time or untimed test accepted), and psychoeducational report (3 years old or less). Upon application, documentation of need for special services should be sent to both admissions and your LD program or unit. Upon acceptance, documentation of need for special services should be sent only to your LD program or unit. *Application deadline (institutional):* rolling/continuous for fall and rolling/continuous for spring.

LD program contact Dr. Robert Perkins, Dean of Student Development, 614 West Superior, Alma, MI 48801. *Phone:* 517-463-7225. *Fax:* 517-463-7353. *E-mail:* perkins@alma.edu.

Application contact Acting Director of Admissions, Alma College, 614 West Superior Street, Alma, MI 48801-1599. *Phone:* 517-463-7139. *E-mail:* admissions@alma.edu. *Web address:* http://www.alma.edu/.

ALVERNO COLLEGE
Milwaukee, Wisconsin

Students with LD Served by Program	85	ADD/ADHD Services	✓
Staff	1 full-time	Summer Preparation Program	n/a
LD Program or Service Fee	n/a	Alternative Test Arrangements	✓
LD Program Began	1986	LD Student Organization	n/a

Instructional Services began offering services in 1986. The program serves approximately 85 undergraduate students. Faculty consists of 1 full-time staff member. Services are provided by regular education teachers, LD specialists, trained peer tutors, and professional tutors.

Policies 12 credit hours per semester are required to maintain full-time status; 6 credit hours per semester are required to be eligible for financial aid. LD services are also available to graduate students.

Special preparation or orientation Required orientation held before classes begin and after classes begin.

Basic skills remediation Available in study skills, computer skills, reading, time management, learning strategies, written language, and math. Offered one-on-one and in small groups by regular education teachers.

Subject-area tutoring Available in some subjects. Offered one-on-one and in small groups by professional tutors and trained peer tutors.

Special courses Available in reading, math, and written composition skills. Some courses are offered for credit.

Counseling and advisement Individual counseling is available.

Auxiliary aids and services *Aids:* calculators, personal computers, personal spelling/word-use assistants (e.g., Franklin Speller), scan and read programs (e.g., Kurzweil), screen-enlarging programs, screen readers, speech recognition programs (e.g., Dragon), tape recorders, taped textbooks. *Services and accommodations:* advocates, priority registration, alternative test arrangements, readers, and note-takers.

ADD/ADHD Students with ADD/ADHD are eligible for the same services available to students with LD, as well as distraction-free testing environments and personal coach or mentors.

Application *Required:* high school transcript, ACT (extended-time or untimed test accepted), personal statement, and psycho-educational report. *Recommended:* letter(s) of recommendation and documentation of high school services (e.g., Individualized Education Program [IEP] or 504 plan). Upon application, documentation of need for special services should be sent only to your LD program or unit. Upon acceptance, documentation of need for special services should be sent only to your LD program or unit. *Application deadline (institutional):* rolling/continuous for fall and rolling/continuous for spring. *Application deadline (LD program):* rolling/continuous for fall and rolling/continuous for spring.

LD program contact Colleen Barnett, Coordinator for Disability Services, PO Box 343922, Milwaukee, WI 53234-3922. *Phone:* 414-382-6026. *Fax:* 414-382-6354. *E-mail:* colleen.barnett@alverno.edu.

Application contact Alverno College, 3400 South 43rd Street, PO Box 343922, Milwaukee, WI 53234-3922. *E-mail:* alvadm5h@exepc.com. *Web address:* http://www.alverno.edu/.

ANTIOCH COLLEGE
Yellow Springs, Ohio

Students with LD Served by Program	90	ADD/ADHD Services	✓
Staff	1 full-time, 8 part-time	Summer Preparation Program	✓
LD Program or Service Fee	n/a	Alternative Test Arrangements	n/a
LD Program Began	1999	LD Student Organization	n/a

Academic Support Center began offering services in 1999. The program serves approximately 90 undergraduate students. Faculty consists of 1 full-time and 8 part-time staff members. Services are provided by academic advisers, remediation/learning specialists, counselors, regular education teachers, teacher trainees, LD specialists, and trained peer tutors.

Policies Students with LD may take up to 22 credit hours per term; 12 credit hours per term are required to maintain full-time status and to be eligible for financial aid.

Antioch College (continued)

Special preparation or orientation Optional summer program offered prior to entering college. Optional orientation held before registration, during registration, before classes begin, after classes begin, during summer prior to enrollment, and individually by special arrangement.

Basic skills remediation Available in study skills, computer skills, reading, time management, social skills, learning strategies, spelling, written language, math, and spoken language. Offered one-on-one and in small groups by LD specialists, trained peer tutors, and instructors.

Subject-area tutoring Available in some subjects. Offered one-on-one by trained peer tutors, LD specialists, and professors.

Special courses Available in study skills, practical computer skills, health and nutrition, time management, learning strategies, math, stress management, and written composition skills. Some courses are offered for credit.

Counseling and advisement Career counseling, individual counseling, and small-group counseling are available. Academic advisement by a staff member affiliated with the program is available.

Auxiliary aids and services *Aids:* screen readers, speech recognition programs (e.g., Dragon), taped textbooks.

ADD/ADHD Students with ADD/ADHD are eligible for the same services available to students with LD, as well as distraction-free study areas and personal coach or mentors.

Application *Required:* high school transcript, personal statement, and letter(s) of recommendation. *Recommended:* participation in extracurricular activities, ACT or SAT I (extended-time or untimed test accepted), interview, psychoeducational report (3 years old or less), and documentation of high school services (e.g., Individualized Education Program [IEP] or 504 plan). Upon application, documentation of need for special services should be sent to both admissions and your LD program or unit. Upon acceptance, documentation of need for special services should be sent only to your LD program or unit. *Application deadline (institutional):* rolling/continuous for fall and rolling/continuous for spring. *Application deadline (LD program):* rolling/continuous for fall and rolling/continuous for spring.

LD program contact Elizabeth England Kennedy, Director of Academic Support Center, 795 Livermore Street, Yellow Springs, OH 45387. *Phone:* 937-767-7331 Ext. 6223. *Fax:* 937-767-6452. *E-mail:* lizek@antioch-college.edu.

Application contact Cathy Paige, Information Manager, Antioch College, 795 Livermore Street, Yellow Springs, OH 45387-1697. *Phone:* 937-767-6400 Ext. 6559. *E-mail:* admissions@college.antioch.edu. *Web address:* http://www.antioch-college.edu/.

AQUINAS COLLEGE
Grand Rapids, Michigan

Students with LD Served by Program	80	ADD/ADHD Services	✓
Staff	4 part-time	Summer Preparation Program	n/a
LD Program or Service Fee	n/a	Alternative Test Arrangements	✓
LD Program Began	1994	LD Student Organization	✓

Academic Achievement Center (AAC) began offering services in 1994. The program serves approximately 80 undergraduate students. Faculty consists of 4 part-time staff members. Services are provided by academic advisers, counselors, LD specialists, trained peer tutors, and professional tutors.

Policies The college has written policies regarding course substitutions and substitution and waivers of requirements for admission and graduation. LD services are also available to graduate students.

Special preparation or orientation Required orientation held individually by special arrangement.

Basic skills remediation Available in study skills, reading, time management, social skills, learning strategies, written language, and math. Offered one-on-one, in small groups, and class-size groups by LD specialists.

Subject-area tutoring Available in most subjects. Offered one-on-one, in small groups, and class-size groups by trained peer tutors.

Special courses Available in reading and written composition skills. All courses are offered for credit; all enter into overall grade point average.

Counseling and advisement Career counseling, individual counseling, small-group counseling, and support groups are available. Academic advisement by a staff member affiliated with the program is available.

Auxiliary aids and services *Aids:* calculators, personal spelling/word-use assistants (e.g., Franklin Speller), screen-enlarging programs, tape recorders, taped textbooks. *Services and accommodations:* advocates, priority registration, alternative test arrangements, readers, note-takers, scribes, and extended time testing.

Student organization There is a student organization for students with LD.

ADD/ADHD Students with ADD/ADHD are eligible for the same services available to students with LD, as well as distraction-free study areas, distraction-free testing environments, medication management, personal coach or mentors, and support groups for ADD/ADHD.

Application *Required:* high school transcript, ACT (extended-time or untimed test accepted), and ACT or SAT I (extended-time or untimed test accepted). *Recommended:* participation in extracurricular activities, SAT I (extended-time or untimed test accepted), interview, personal statement, letter(s) of recommendation, psychoeducational report (3 years old or less), and documentation of high school services (e.g., Individualized Education Program [IEP] or 504 plan). Upon application, documentation of need for special services should be sent only to admissions. Upon acceptance, documentation of need for special services should be sent only to your LD program or unit. *Application deadline (institutional):* rolling/continuous for fall and rolling/continuous for spring.

LD program contact Admissions Office, 1607 Robinson Road SE, Grand Rapids, MI 49506-1799. *Phone:* 616-459-8281 Ext. 5150. *Fax:* 616-732-4431. *E-mail:* admissions@aquinas.edu.

Application contact Mary Kwiatkowski, Staff Assistant/Applications Secretary, Aquinas College, 1607 Robinson Road, SE, Grand Rapids, MI 49506-1799. *Phone:* 616-732-4460 Ext. 5150. *E-mail:* admissions@aquinas.edu. *Web address:* http://www.aquinas.edu/.

ARIZONA STATE UNIVERSITY
Tempe, Arizona

Students with LD Served by Program	322	ADD/ADHD Services	✓
Staff	3 full-time	Summer Preparation Program	n/a
LD Program or Service Fee	n/a	Alternative Test Arrangements	✓
LD Program Began	1982	LD Student Organization	n/a

Disability Resources for Students (DRS) began offering services in 1982. The program serves approximately 322 undergraduate students. Faculty consists of 3 full-time staff members. Services are provided by LD specialists and coordinators.

Policies Students with LD may take up to 18 credit hours per semester; 12 credit hours per semester are required to maintain full-time status. LD services are also available to graduate students.

Special preparation or orientation Required orientation held before classes begin.

Subject-area tutoring Available in some subjects. Offered one-on-one and in small groups by computer-based instruction, graduate assistants/students, and trained peer tutors.

Auxiliary aids and services *Aids:* scan and read programs (e.g., Kurzweil), screen-enlarging programs, screen readers, speech recognition programs (e.g., Dragon), taped textbooks, technology lab with computers and assistive technology. *Services and accommodations:* advocates, priority registration, alternative test arrangements, readers, note-takers, and scribes.

ADD/ADHD Students with ADD/ADHD are eligible for the same services available to students with LD, as well as distraction-reduced testing environment.

Application *Required:* high school transcript and ACT or SAT I (extended-time or untimed test accepted). *Recommended:* personal statement, letter(s) of recommendation, psychoeducational report (3 years old or less), and documentation of high school services (e.g., Individualized Education Program [IEP] or 504 plan). Upon application, documentation of need for special services should be sent only to your LD program or unit. Upon acceptance, documentation of need for special services should be sent only to your LD program or unit. *Application deadline (institutional):* rolling/continuous for fall and rolling/continuous for spring. *Application deadline (LD program):* rolling/continuous for fall and rolling/continuous for spring.

LD program contact Phyllis Jones, Program Coordinator, Disability Resources for Students, Box 873202, Tempe, AZ 85287-3202. *Phone:* 480-965-1234. *Fax:* 480-965-0441. *E-mail:* phyllis.jones@asu.edu.

Application contact Arizona State University, Box 870112, Tempe, AZ 85287-2203. *E-mail:* ugradadm@asuvm.inre.asu.edu. *Web address:* http://www.asu.edu/.

ATHABASCA UNIVERSITY
Athabasca, Alberta

Students with LD Served by Program	50	ADD/ADHD Services	✓
Staff	2 part-time	Summer Preparation Program	n/a
LD Program or Service Fee	varies	Alternative Test Arrangements	✓
LD Program Began	1998	LD Student Organization	n/a

Access to Students with Disabilities began offering services in 1998. The program serves approximately 50 undergraduate students. Faculty consists of 2 part-time staff members. Services are provided by academic advisers, counselors, and ASD Coordinator.

Policies 9 credit hours per semester are required to maintain full-time status; 3 credit hours per semester are required to be eligible for financial aid. LD services are also available to graduate students.

Fees *LD Program or Service Fee:* ranges from $0 to $5000 Canadian dollars per year.

Basic skills remediation Available in training for assistive technological software. Offered one-on-one by regular education teachers, graduate assistants/students, special education teachers, LD specialists, teacher trainees, professional tutors, and trained peer tutors.

Subject-area tutoring Available in most subjects. Offered one-on-one by professional tutors, graduate assistants/students, trained peer tutors, and LD specialists.

Counseling and advisement Career counseling, individual counseling, and academic counseling are available. Academic advisement by a staff member affiliated with the program is available.

Auxiliary aids and services *Aids:* tape recorders, taped textbooks. *Services and accommodations:* advocates, alternative test arrangements, readers, note-takers, and scribes.

ADD/ADHD Students with ADD/ADHD are eligible for the same services available to students with LD, as well as distraction-free testing environments.

Application *Required:* separate application to your LD program or unit. *Recommended:* psychoeducational report (5 years old or less). Upon application, documentation of need for special services should be sent only to your LD program or unit. Upon acceptance, documentation of need for special services should be sent only to your LD program or unit. *Application deadline (institutional):* rolling/continuous for fall and rolling/continuous for spring. *Application deadline (LD program):* rolling/continuous for fall and rolling/continuous for spring.

LD program contact Brenda Moore, Coordinator, Access to Students with Disabilities, Edmonton Learning Centre, Seventh Street Plaza, North Tower, 2nd Floor, 10030-107 Street, Edmonton, AB T5J 3E4. *Phone:* 780-497-3424. *Fax:* 780-497-3411. *E-mail:* brendam@athabascau.ca.

Application contact Margaret Carmichael, Assistant Registrar, Admissions, Athabasca University, 1 University Drive, Athabasca, AB T9S 3A3. *Phone:* 780-675-6377. *E-mail:* reginfo@cs.athabascau.ca. *Web address:* http://www.athabascau.ca/.

AUBURN UNIVERSITY
Auburn, Auburn University, Alabama

Students with LD Served by Program	250	ADD/ADHD Services	✓
Staff	4 full-time, 15 part-time	Summer Preparation Program	n/a
LD Program or Service Fee	n/a	Alternative Test Arrangements	✓
LD Program Began	1990	LD Student Organization	n/a

The Program for Students with Disabilities began offering services in 1990. The program serves approximately 250 undergraduate students. Faculty consists of 4 full-time and 15 part-time staff members. Services are provided by Disability Specialist.

Policies LD services are also available to graduate students.

Auxiliary aids and services *Aids:* scan and read programs (e.g., Kurzweil), screen-enlarging programs, screen readers, speech recognition programs (e.g., Dragon), tape recorders, taped textbooks. *Services and accommodations:* priority registration, alternative test arrangements, readers, note-takers, and scribes.

ADD/ADHD Students with ADD/ADHD are eligible for the same services available to students with LD, as well as distraction-free testing environments.

Application *Required:* high school transcript, ACT or SAT I (extended-time tests accepted), separate application to your LD program or unit, psychoeducational report (3 years old or less), and documentation of high school services (e.g., Individualized Education Program [IEP] or 504 plan). Upon application, documentation of need for special services should be sent only to your LD program or unit. Upon acceptance, documentation of need for special services should be sent only to your LD program or unit.

LD program contact The Program for Students with Disabilities, 1244 Haley Center, Auburn University, AL 36849. *Phone:* 334-844-2096. *Fax:* 334-844-2099.

Application contact Auburn University, 202 Mary Martin Hall, Auburn University, AL 36849-0001. *E-mail:* fletcjt@mail.auburn.edu. *Web address:* http://www.auburn.edu/.

AUBURN UNIVERSITY MONTGOMERY

Montgomery, Alabama

Students with LD Served by Program	70	ADD/ADHD Services	✓
Staff	4 full-time, 4 part-time	Summer Preparation Program	n/a
LD Program or Service Fee	n/a	Alternative Test Arrangements	✓
LD Program Began	1979	LD Student Organization	n/a

Center for Special Services began offering services in 1979. The program serves approximately 70 undergraduate students. Faculty consists of 4 full-time and 4 part-time staff members. Services are provided by Student Services Coordinator, Director, Assistant Director, and student peer counselors.

Policies Students with LD may take up to 21 semester hours per semester; 12 semester hours per semester are required to maintain full-time status and to be eligible for financial aid. LD services are also available to graduate students.

Auxiliary aids and services *Aids:* calculators, personal computers, personal spelling/word-use assistants (e.g., Franklin Speller), scan and read programs (e.g., Kurzweil), screen-enlarging programs, screen readers, speech recognition programs (e.g., Dragon), tape recorders, taped textbooks, vision enhancers, notetaker tablets. *Services and accommodations:* advocates, priority registration, alternative test arrangements, readers, scribes, and interpreters, peer counselors.

ADD/ADHD Students with ADD/ADHD are eligible for the same services available to students with LD, as well as distraction-free study areas and distraction-free testing environments.

Application *Required:* separate application to your LD program or unit and psychoeducational report (3 years old or less). *Recommended:* high school transcript, participation in extracurricular activities, ACT or SAT I (extended-time or untimed test accepted), and documentation of high school services (e.g., Individualized Education Program [IEP] or 504 plan). Upon application, documentation of need for special services should be sent only to your LD program or unit. Upon acceptance, documentation of need for special services should be sent only to your LD program or unit. *Application deadline (institutional):* rolling/continuous for fall and rolling/continuous for spring. *Application deadline (LD program):* rolling/continuous for fall and rolling/continuous for spring.

LD program contact Tamara Massey, Student Services Coordinator, Center for Special Services, PO Box 244023, Montgomery, AL 36124-4023. *Phone:* 334-244-3468. *Fax:* 334-244-3907. *E-mail:* tmassey@mickey.aum.edu.

Application contact Michele Moore, Assistant Director, Admissions, Auburn University Montgomery, PO Box 244023, Montgomery, AL 36124-4023. *Phone:* 334-244-3621. *E-mail:* auminfo@mickey.aum.edu. *Web address:* http://www.aum.edu/.

AVERETT COLLEGE

Danville, Virginia

Students with LD Served by Program	25	ADD/ADHD Services	✓
Staff	2 full-time, 10 part-time	Summer Preparation Program	n/a
LD Program or Service Fee	n/a	Alternative Test Arrangements	✓
LD Program Began	n/a	LD Student Organization	n/a

Support Services for Students with Disabilities serves approximately 25 undergraduate students. Faculty consists of 2 full-time and 10 part-time staff members. Services are provided by academic advisers, counselors, LD specialists, trained peer tutors, professional tutors, and Learning Center Director.

Policies Students with LD may take up to 12 semester hours per semester; 12 semester hours per semester are required to maintain full-time status and to be eligible for financial aid. LD services are also available to graduate students.

Basic skills remediation Available in study skills, computer skills, reading, learning strategies, spelling, written language, and math. Offered one-on-one and in small groups by computer-based instruction, professional tutors, and trained peer tutors.

Subject-area tutoring Available in most subjects. Offered one-on-one and in small groups by computer-based instruction, professional tutors, and trained peer tutors.

Counseling and advisement Career counseling and individual counseling are available. Academic advisement by a staff member affiliated with the program is available.

Auxiliary aids and services *Aids:* personal computers, scan and read programs (e.g., Kurzweil), screen-enlarging programs, screen readers, speech recognition programs (e.g., Dragon), tape recorders, taped textbooks. *Services and accommodations:* alternative test arrangements and note-takers.

ADD/ADHD Students with ADD/ADHD are eligible for the same services available to students with LD, as well as distraction-free testing environments and medication management.

Application *Required:* high school transcript, SAT I (extended-time or untimed test accepted), personal statement, letter(s) of recommendation, and psychoeducational report (3 years old or less). *Recommended:* participation in extracurricular activities, interview, and documentation of high school services (e.g., Individualized Education Program [IEP] or 504 plan). Upon application, documentation of need for special services should be sent only to admissions. Upon acceptance, documentation of need for special services should be sent to both admissions and your LD program or unit. *Application deadline (institutional):* rolling/continuous for fall and rolling/continuous for spring. *Application deadline (LD program):* rolling/continuous for fall and rolling/continuous for spring.

LD program contact Dr. Pamela Riedel, Support Services Coordinator, 428 Frith Hall, Danville, VA 24541. *Phone:* 804-791-5744. *Fax:* 804-791-4392. *E-mail:* priedel@averett.edu.

Application contact Averett College, 420 West Main Street, Danville, VA 24541-3692. *E-mail:* admit@averett.edu. *Web address:* http://www.averett.edu/.

BABSON COLLEGE

Wellesley, Babson Park, Massachusetts

Students with LD Served by Program	110	ADD/ADHD Services	✓
Staff	1 full-time, 1 part-time	Summer Preparation Program	n/a
LD Program or Service Fee	n/a	Alternative Test Arrangements	✓
LD Program Began	1995	LD Student Organization	n/a

Disability Services began offering services in 1995. The program serves approximately 110 undergraduate students. Faculty consists of 1 full-time and 1 part-time staff member. Services are provided by academic advisers.

Policies 12 credits per semester are required to maintain full-time status; 6 credits per semester are required to be eligible for financial aid. LD services are also available to graduate students.

Subject-area tutoring Available in some subjects. Offered one-on-one and in small groups by graduate assistants/students and trained peer tutors.

Special courses Available in career planning, study skills, practical computer skills, test taking, health and nutrition, time management, learning strategies, self-advocacy, stress management, and written composition skills. No courses are offered for credit; none enter into overall grade point average.

Counseling and advisement Career counseling and individual counseling are available. Academic advisement by a staff member affiliated with the program is available.

Auxiliary aids and services *Aids:* calculators, personal computers, personal spelling/word-use assistants (e.g., Franklin Speller), scan and read programs (e.g., Kurzweil), speech recognition programs (e.g., Dragon), tape recorders, taped textbooks. *Services and accommodations:* advocates, alternative test arrangements, readers, note-takers, scribes, and extended time for exams, academic advising.

ADD/ADHD Students with ADD/ADHD are eligible for the same services available to students with LD, as well as distraction-free testing environments, medication management and personal coach or mentors.

Application *Required:* high school transcript, participation in extracurricular activities, ACT or SAT I (extended-time or untimed test accepted), personal statement, and letter(s) of recommendation. *Recommended:* interview and psychoeducational report (3 years old or less). Upon application, documentation of need for special services should be sent only to admissions. Upon acceptance, documentation of need for special services should be sent only to your LD program or unit. *Application deadline (institutional):* 12/1 for fall and 2/1 for spring.

LD program contact Chip Kennedy, Coordinator of Disability Services, Office of Class Deans, Babson Park, MA 02457-0310. *Phone:* 781-239-4075. *Fax:* 781-239-5567. *E-mail:* ckennedy1@ babson.edu.

Application contact Babson College, Office of Undergraduate Admission, Mustard Hall, Babson Park, MA 02157-0310. *E-mail:* ugradadmission@babson.edu. *Web address:* http://www.babson. edu/.

BATES COLLEGE
Lewiston, Maine

Students with LD Served by Program	100	ADD/ADHD Services	✓
Staff	1 full-time, 1 part-time	Summer Preparation Program	n/a
LD Program or Service Fee	n/a	Alternative Test Arrangements	✓
LD Program Began	n/a	LD Student Organization	n/a

Office of the Dean of Students—Special Services for LD Students serves approximately 100 undergraduate students. Faculty consists of 1 full-time and 1 part-time staff member. Services are provided by academic advisers, counselors, diagnostic specialists, LD specialists, trained peer tutors, and deans.

Policies Students with LD may take up to 5 credits per semester; 3 credits per semester are required to maintain full-time status and to be eligible for financial aid.

Fees *Diagnostic Testing Fee:* ranges from $500 to $700.

Diagnostic testing Available for auditory processing, motor skills, spelling, handwriting, neuropsychological, spoken language, intelligence, personality, study skills, learning strategies, reading, written language, learning styles, social skills, visual processing, and math.

Basic skills remediation Available in study skills, time management, and learning strategies. Offered one-on-one by LD specialists.

Subject-area tutoring Available in all subjects. Offered one-on-one by trained peer tutors.

Counseling and advisement Individual counseling and support groups are available. Academic advisement by a staff member affiliated with the program is available.

Auxiliary aids and services *Aids:* personal computers, tape recorders, taped textbooks. *Services and accommodations:* advocates, alternative test arrangements, readers, note-takers, and scribes.

ADD/ADHD Students with ADD/ADHD are eligible for the same services available to students with LD, as well as distraction-free study areas, distraction-free testing environments and medication management.

Application *Required:* high school transcript, participation in extracurricular activities, personal statement, and letter(s) of recommendation. *Recommended:* interview. Upon application, documentation of need for special services should be sent only to admissions. Upon acceptance, documentation of need for special services should be sent only to your LD program or unit. *Application deadline (institutional):* 1/15 for fall and 11/1 for spring.

LD program contact F. Celeste Branham, Dean of Students, 102 Lane Hall, Lewiston, ME 04240. *Phone:* 207-786-6219. *Fax:* 207-786-6219. *E-mail:* cbranham@bates.edu.

Application contact Bates College, 23 Campus Avenue, Lewiston, ME 04240-6028. *E-mail:* admissions@bates.edu. *Web address:* http://www.bates.edu/.

BAYLOR UNIVERSITY
Waco, Texas

Students with LD Served by Program	200	ADD/ADHD Services	✓
Staff	3 full-time	Summer Preparation Program	✓
LD Program or Service Fee	n/a	Alternative Test Arrangements	✓
LD Program Began	1995	LD Student Organization	n/a

Office of Access and Learning Accommodation began offering services in 1995. The program serves approximately 200 undergraduate students. Faculty consists of 3 full-time staff members. Services are provided by academic advisers, counselors, graduate assistants/students, teacher trainees, and trained peer tutors.

Policies 12 hours per semester are required to maintain full-time status and to be eligible for financial aid. LD services are also available to graduate students.

Special preparation or orientation Optional summer program offered prior to entering college. Required orientation held individually by special arrangement.

Subject-area tutoring Available in some subjects. Offered one-on-one and in small groups by graduate assistants/students, trained peer tutors, and LD specialists.

Counseling and advisement Career counseling and individual counseling are available. Academic advisement by a staff member affiliated with the program is available.

Auxiliary aids and services *Aids:* scan and read programs (e.g., Kurzweil), screen-enlarging programs. *Services and accommodations:* advocates, priority registration, alternative test arrangements, readers, note-takers, and scribes.

ADD/ADHD Students with ADD/ADHD are eligible for the same services available to students with LD, as well as distraction-free study areas, distraction-free testing environments, medication management and personal coach or mentors.

Application *Required:* high school transcript, ACT or SAT I (extended-time tests accepted), personal statement, letter(s) of recommendation, separate application to your LD program or unit, and psychoeducational report (2 years old or less). *Recommended:* documentation of high school services (e.g., individu-

Baylor University (continued)

alized education program [iep] or 504 plan). Upon acceptance, documentation of need for special services should be sent only to your LD program or unit. *Application deadline (institutional):* rolling/continuous for fall and rolling/continuous for spring. *Application deadline (LD program):* rolling/continuous for fall and rolling/continuous for spring.

LD program contact Dr. Sheila Graham, Director, Office of Access and Learning Accommodation, PO Box 97204, Waco, TX 76798-7204. *Phone:* 254-710-3605. *Fax:* 254-710-3608. *E-mail:* sheila_graham@baylor.edu.

Application contact Teri Tippit, Director of Recruitment, Baylor University, PO Box 97056, Waco, TX 76798. *Phone:* 254-710-3435. *E-mail:* admissions_office@baylor.edu. *Web address:* http://www.baylor.edu/.

BELLARMINE COLLEGE
Louisville, Kentucky

Students with LD Served by Program	30	ADD/ADHD Services	✓
Staff	1 full-time	Summer Preparation Program	n/a
LD Program or Service Fee	n/a	Alternative Test Arrangements	✓
LD Program Began	1993	LD Student Organization	n/a

Disability Services began offering services in 1993. The program serves approximately 30 undergraduate students. Faculty consists of 1 full-time staff member. Services are provided by academic advisers, counselors, remediation/learning specialists, diagnostic specialists, and trained peer tutors.

Policies The college has written policies regarding course substitutions. Students with LD may take up to 18 credit hours per semester; 12 credit hours per semester are required to maintain full-time status; 6 credit hours per semester are required to be eligible for financial aid. LD services are also available to graduate students.

Diagnostic testing Available for intelligence, personality, reading, math, and clinical interview.

Counseling and advisement Academic advisement by a staff member affiliated with the program is available.

Auxiliary aids and services *Aids:* tape recorders, taped textbooks. *Services and accommodations:* advocates, alternative test arrangements, readers, note-takers, scribes, and classroom/lab modification.

ADD/ADHD Students with ADD/ADHD are eligible for the same services available to students with LD, as well as distraction-free testing environments.

Application *Required:* high school transcript, ACT or SAT I (extended-time or untimed test accepted), letter(s) of recommendation, and class rank, writing sample. *Recommended:* participation in extracurricular activities. Upon application, documentation of need for special services should be sent only to your LD program or unit. Upon acceptance, documentation of need for special services should be sent only to your LD program or unit. *Application deadline (institutional):* rolling/continuous for fall and rolling/continuous for spring. *Application deadline (LD program):* rolling/continuous for fall and rolling/continuous for spring.

LD program contact Dr. Ruth Garvey-Nix, Disability Services Coordinator, 2001 Newburg Road, Louisville, KY 40205. *Phone:* 502-452-8153. *Fax:* 502-452-8050. *E-mail:* rgarveynix@bellarmine.edu.

Application contact Timothy A. Sturgeon, Dean of Admission, Bellarmine College, 2001 Newburg Road, Louisville, KY 40205-0671. *Phone:* 502-452-8131. *Web address:* http://www.bellarmine.edu/.

BIOLA UNIVERSITY
La Mirada, California

Students with LD Served by Program	55	ADD/ADHD Services	✓
Staff	3 part-time	Summer Preparation Program	n/a
LD Program or Service Fee	n/a	Alternative Test Arrangements	✓
LD Program Began	n/a	LD Student Organization	n/a

Office of Disability Services serves approximately 55 undergraduate students. Faculty consists of 3 part-time staff members. Services are provided by academic advisers, counselors, diagnostic specialists, graduate assistants/students, LD specialists, and trained peer tutors.

Policies The college has written policies regarding grade forgiveness. LD services are also available to graduate students.

Basic skills remediation Available in study skills, time management, and learning strategies. Offered one-on-one, in small groups, and class-size groups by regular education teachers and trained peer tutors.

Subject-area tutoring Available in most subjects. Offered one-on-one by trained peer tutors.

Special courses Available in oral communication skills, study skills, college survival skills, practical computer skills, test taking, health and nutrition, reading, time management, learning strategies, math, stress management, and written composition skills. Most courses are offered for credit; all enter into overall grade point average.

Counseling and advisement Academic counseling, psychological counseling is available. Academic advisement by a staff member affiliated with the program is available.

Auxiliary aids and services *Aids:* scan and read programs (e.g., Kurzweil), speech recognition programs (e.g., Dragon), taped textbooks. *Services and accommodations:* advocates, priority registration, alternative test arrangements, readers, note-takers, and scribes.

ADD/ADHD Students with ADD/ADHD are eligible for the same services available to students with LD, as well as distraction-free testing environments and personal coach or mentors.

Application *Required:* high school transcript, ACT or SAT I (extended-time or untimed test accepted), interview, personal statement, and letter(s) of recommendation. *Recommended:* participation in extracurricular activities and separate application to your LD program or unit. Upon application, documentation of need for special services should be sent only to your LD program or unit. Upon acceptance, documentation of need for special services should be sent only to your LD program or unit. *Application deadline (LD program):* rolling/continuous for fall and rolling/continuous for spring.

LD program contact Tim Engle, Coordinator of Disability Services, Office of Disability Services, 13800 Biola Avenue, La Mirada, CA 90639. *Phone:* 562-903-6000 Ext. 5815. *E-mail:* tim_engle@peter.biola.edu.

Application contact Biola University, 13800 Biola Avenue, La Mirada, CA 90639-0001. *E-mail:* admissions@biola.edu. *Web address:* http://www.biola.edu/.

BLUFFTON COLLEGE

Bluffton, Ohio

Students with LD Served by Program	15	ADD/ADHD Services	✓
Staff	1 full-time	Summer Preparation Program	n/a
LD Program or Service Fee	n/a	Alternative Test Arrangements	✓
LD Program Began	1998	LD Student Organization	n/a

Special Student Services began offering services in 1998. The program serves approximately 15 undergraduate students. Faculty consists of 1 full-time staff member. Services are provided by academic advisers, regular education teachers, and diagnostic specialists.

Special preparation or orientation Required orientation held after classes begin and individually by special arrangement.

Diagnostic testing Available for spelling, personality, reading, written language, and math.

Counseling and advisement Individual counseling and small-group counseling are available. Academic advisement by a staff member affiliated with the program is available.

Auxiliary aids and services *Aids:* calculators, personal spelling/word-use assistants (e.g., Franklin Speller), taped textbooks. *Services and accommodations:* advocates, priority registration, alternative test arrangements, readers, note-takers, and scribes.

ADD/ADHD Students with ADD/ADHD are eligible for the same services available to students with LD, as well as personal coach or mentors.

Application *Required:* high school transcript, interview, personal statement, letter(s) of recommendation, and documentation of high school services (e.g., Individualized Education Program [IEP] or 504 plan). *Recommended:* participation in extracurricular activities, ACT or SAT I (extended-time tests accepted), separate application to your LD program or unit, and psychoeducational report (3 years old or less). Upon application, documentation of need for special services should be sent only to admissions. Upon acceptance, documentation of need for special services should be sent only to admissions.

LD program contact Timothy Byers280 West College Avenue, Bluffton, OH 45817. *Phone:* 419-358-3458. *Fax:* 419-358-3323. *E-mail:* byers@bluffton.edu.

Application contact Bluffton College, 280 West College Avenue, Bluffton, OH 45817-1196. *E-mail:* admissions@bluffton.edu. *Web address:* http://www.bluffton.edu/.

BOWLING GREEN STATE UNIVERSITY

Bowling Green, Ohio

Students with LD Served by Program	275	ADD/ADHD Services	✓
Staff	2 full-time	Summer Preparation Program	n/a
LD Program or Service Fee	n/a	Alternative Test Arrangements	✓
LD Program Began	1980	LD Student Organization	n/a

Disability Services for Students began offering services in 1980. The program serves approximately 275 undergraduate students. Faculty consists of 2 full-time staff members. Services are provided by graduate assistants/students.

Policies The college has written policies regarding course substitutions. Students with LD may take up to 18 credit hours per semester; 12 credit hours per semester are required to maintain full-time status and to be eligible for financial aid. LD services are also available to graduate students.

Auxiliary aids and services *Aids:* personal computers, scan and read programs (e.g., Kurzweil), screen-enlarging programs, speech recognition programs (e.g., Dragon), taped textbooks. *Services and accommodations:* priority registration, alternative test arrangements, readers, and note-takers.

ADD/ADHD Students with ADD/ADHD are eligible for the same services available to students with LD, as well as distraction-free testing environments and support groups for ADD/ADHD.

Application Upon acceptance, documentation of need for special services should be sent only to your LD program or unit.

LD program contact Robert D. Cunningham, Director, 413 South Hall, Bowling Green, OH 43403. *Phone:* 419-372-8495. *Fax:* 419-372-8496. *E-mail:* rcunnin@bgnet.bgsu.edu.

Application contact Bowling Green State University, Bowling Green, OH 43403. *E-mail:* admissions@bgnet.bgsu.edu. *Web address:* http://www.bgsu.edu/.

BREVARD COLLEGE

Brevard, North Carolina

Students with LD Served by Program	59	ADD/ADHD Services	✓
Staff	7 part-time	Summer Preparation Program	n/a
LD Program or Service Fee	n/a	Alternative Test Arrangements	✓
LD Program Began	1987	LD Student Organization	n/a

Office for Students with Special Needs and Disabilities began offering services in 1987. The program serves approximately 59 undergraduate students. Faculty consists of 7 part-time staff members. Services are provided by academic advisers, counselors, trained peer tutors, and professional tutors.

Policies The college has written policies regarding course substitutions and grade forgiveness. Students with LD may take up to 20 semester hours per semester; 12 semester hours per semester are required to maintain full-time status and to be eligible for financial aid.

Special preparation or orientation Required orientation held before registration, during registration, before classes begin, after classes begin, and individually by special arrangement.

Diagnostic testing Available for spelling, reading, learning styles, and visual processing.

Basic skills remediation Available in study skills, reading, time management, visual processing, learning strategies, spelling, written language, and math. Offered one-on-one and in class-size groups by regular education teachers, professional tutors, and trained peer tutors.

Subject-area tutoring Available in most subjects. Offered one-on-one by professional tutors, trained peer tutors, and professional instructors.

Special courses Available in career planning, study skills, college survival skills, practical computer skills, test taking, health and nutrition, reading, time management, learning strategies, vocabulary development, math, stress management, and written composition skills. All courses are offered for credit; most enter into overall grade point average.

Counseling and advisement Career counseling, individual counseling, and self-advocacy training, academic counseling are available. Academic advisement by a staff member affiliated with the program is available.

Auxiliary aids and services *Aids:* calculators, personal computers, tape recorders, word processors with spell check. *Services and accommodations:* priority registration, alternative test arrangements, readers, note-takers, scribes, and taping of reading material.

Brevard College (continued)

ADD/ADHD Students with ADD/ADHD are eligible for the same services available to students with LD, as well as distraction-free study areas, distraction-free testing environments and medication management.

Application *Required:* high school transcript and ACT or SAT I (extended-time or untimed test accepted). *Recommended:* participation in extracurricular activities, ACT (extended-time or untimed test accepted), SAT I (extended-time or untimed test accepted), interview, personal statement, letter(s) of recommendation, and psychoeducational report (3 years old or less). Upon application, documentation of need for special services should be sent only to your LD program or unit. Upon acceptance, documentation of need for special services should be sent only to your LD program or unit. *Application deadline (institutional):* rolling/continuous for fall and rolling/continuous for spring. *Application deadline (LD program):* rolling/continuous for fall and rolling/continuous for spring.

LD program contact Susan Kuehn, Director, 400 North Broad Street, Brevard, NC 28712. *Phone:* 828-883-8292 Ext. 2231. *Fax:* 828-884-3790. *E-mail:* skuehn@brevard.edu.

Application contact Brevard College, 400 North Broad Street, Brevard, NC 28712-3306. *E-mail:* admissions@lightnin.brevard.edu. *Web address:* http://www.brevard.edu/.

BREWTON-PARKER COLLEGE
Mt. Vernon, Georgia

Students with LD Served by Program	12	ADD/ADHD Services	✓
Staff	1 full-time	Summer Preparation Program	n/a
LD Program or Service Fee	n/a	Alternative Test Arrangements	✓
LD Program Began	1993	LD Student Organization	n/a

Disability Support Services began offering services in 1993. The program serves approximately 12 undergraduate students. Faculty consists of 1 full-time staff member. Services are provided by counselors and trained peer tutors.

Policies The college has written policies regarding course substitutions, grade forgiveness, and substitution and waivers of requirements for admission and graduation. Students with LD may take up to 16 credit hours per semester; 12 credit hours per semester are required to maintain full-time status and to be eligible for financial aid.

Special preparation or orientation Required orientation held individually by special arrangement.

Basic skills remediation Available in study skills, reading, time management, spelling, written language, and math. Offered in class-size groups by regular education teachers.

Subject-area tutoring Available in some subjects. Offered one-on-one by trained peer tutors.

Counseling and advisement Career counseling and individual counseling are available.

Auxiliary aids and services *Services and accommodations:* priority registration, alternative test arrangements, and note-takers.

ADD/ADHD Students with ADD/ADHD are eligible for the same services available to students with LD, as well as distraction-free study areas and distraction-free testing environments.

Application *Required:* high school transcript, ACT or SAT I (extended-time or untimed test accepted), separate application to your LD program or unit, and psychoeducational report (2 years old or less). Upon application, documentation of need for special services should be sent only to your LD program or unit. Upon acceptance, documentation of need for special services should be sent only to your LD program or unit. *Application*

deadline (institutional): rolling/continuous for fall and rolling/continuous for spring. *Application deadline (LD program):* rolling/continuous for fall and rolling/continuous for spring.

LD program contact Pat Carney Weaver, Coordinator of Disability Support Services, Box 2124, Mt. Vernon, GA 30445. *Phone:* 912-583-3222. *Fax:* 912-583-4498. *E-mail:* pweaver@bpc.edu.

Application contact Brewton-Parker College, Highway 280, Mt. Vernon, GA 30445-0197. *Web address:* http://www.bpc.edu/.

BRIGHAM YOUNG UNIVERSITY
Provo, Utah

Students with LD Served by Program	165	ADD/ADHD Services	✓
Staff	3 full-time, 4 part-time	Summer Preparation Program	n/a
LD Program or Service Fee	n/a	Alternative Test Arrangements	✓
LD Program Began	1995	LD Student Organization	n/a

Services for Students with Disabilities began offering services in 1995. The program serves approximately 165 undergraduate students. Faculty consists of 3 full-time and 4 part-time staff members. Services are provided by counselors, diagnostic specialists, graduate assistants/students, LD specialists, and psychologists.

Policies The college has written policies regarding course substitutions. Students with LD may take up to 19 credit hours per semester; 12 credit hours per semester are required to maintain full-time status and to be eligible for financial aid. LD services are also available to graduate students.

Special preparation or orientation Optional orientation held before classes begin.

Diagnostic testing Available for auditory processing, motor skills, spelling, handwriting, neuropsychological, spoken language, intelligence, personality, learning strategies, reading, written language, learning styles, visual processing, and math.

Counseling and advisement Career counseling and individual counseling are available.

Auxiliary aids and services *Aids:* personal spelling/word-use assistants (e.g., Franklin Speller), scan and read programs (e.g., Kurzweil), screen-enlarging programs, screen readers, speech recognition programs (e.g., Dragon), tape recorders, taped textbooks. *Services and accommodations:* priority registration, alternative test arrangements, readers, note-takers, and scribes.

ADD/ADHD Students with ADD/ADHD are eligible for the same services available to students with LD, as well as distraction-free study areas, distraction-free testing environments and personal coach or mentors.

Application *Required:* high school transcript, ACT (extended-time or untimed test accepted), personal statement, and letter(s) of recommendation. *Recommended:* participation in extracurricular activities. Upon acceptance, documentation of need for special services should be sent only to your LD program or unit. *Application deadline (institutional):* 2/15 for fall and 2/15 for spring.

LD program contact Dr. Mark E. Beecher, Licensed Psychologist/Coordinator, Educational Assessment and Planning, 1520 WSC, PO Box 27920, Provo, UT 84602-7920. *Phone:* 801-378-2767. *Fax:* 801-378-6667. *E-mail:* mark_beecher@byu.edu.

Application contact Brigham Young University, Provo, UT 84602-1001. *E-mail:* admissions@byu.edu. *Web address:* http://www.byu.edu/.

BROWN UNIVERSITY
Providence, Rhode Island

Students with LD Served by Program	175	ADD/ADHD Services	✓
Staff	1 full-time	Summer Preparation Program	n/a
LD Program or Service Fee	n/a	Alternative Test Arrangements	✓
LD Program Began	1984	LD Student Organization	✓

Disability Support Services began offering services in 1984. The program serves approximately 175 undergraduate students. Faculty consists of 1 full-time staff member. Services are provided by LD specialists.

Policies LD services are also available to graduate students.

Special preparation or orientation Held before classes begin and after classes begin.

Special courses Available in career planning, study skills, test taking, reading, time management, learning strategies, self-advocacy, and stress management. No courses are offered for credit.

Counseling and advisement Career counseling, individual counseling, and support groups are available.

Auxiliary aids and services *Aids:* calculators, scan and read programs (e.g., Kurzweil), screen-enlarging programs, screen readers, speech recognition programs (e.g., Dragon), tape recorders, taped textbooks. *Services and accommodations:* advocates, alternative test arrangements, readers, note-takers, and scribes.

Student organization There is a student organization for students with LD.

ADD/ADHD Students with ADD/ADHD are eligible for the same services available to students with LD, as well as distraction-free study areas, distraction-free testing environments and support groups for ADD/ADHD.

Application *Required:* high school transcript, participation in extracurricular activities, ACT or SAT I (extended-time or untimed test accepted), personal statement, and letter(s) of recommendation. *Recommended:* interview. Upon acceptance, documentation of need for special services should be sent only to your LD program or unit. *Application deadline (institutional):* 1/1 for fall and 4/1 for spring.

LD program contact Susan Pliner, Assistant Dean, 26 Benevolents Street, Box P, Providence, RI 02912. *Phone:* 401-863-9588. *Fax:* 401-863-1999. *E-mail:* susan_pliner@brown.edu.

Application contact Brown University, Box 1876, Providence, RI 02912. *E-mail:* admission_undergraduate@brown.edu. *Web address:* http://www.brown.edu/.

BRYN MAWR COLLEGE
Bryn Mawr, Pennsylvania

Students with LD Served by Program	79	ADD/ADHD Services	✓
Staff	1 full-time, 1 part-time	Summer Preparation Program	n/a
LD Program or Service Fee	n/a	Alternative Test Arrangements	✓
LD Program Began	1995	LD Student Organization	n/a

Educational Support Services for Learning began offering services in 1995. The program serves approximately 79 undergraduate students. Faculty consists of 1 full-time and 1 part-time staff member. Services are provided by remediation/learning specialists, counselors, LD specialists, and professional tutors.

Policies The college has written policies regarding course substitutions and grade forgiveness. Students with LD may take up to 5 credits per semester; 3 credits per semester are required to maintain full-time status; 2 credits per semester are required to be eligible for financial aid. LD services are also available to graduate students.

Fees *Diagnostic Testing Fee:* ranges from $150 to $800.

Special preparation or orientation Optional orientation held before classes begin.

Diagnostic testing Available for auditory processing, spelling, handwriting, neuropsychological, spoken language, intelligence, personality, learning strategies, reading, written language, learning styles, and math.

Subject-area tutoring Available in most subjects. Offered one-on-one and in small groups by trained peer tutors and LD specialists.

Auxiliary aids and services *Aids:* screen-enlarging programs. *Services and accommodations:* priority registration, alternative test arrangements, readers, note-takers, and scribes.

ADD/ADHD Students with ADD/ADHD are eligible for the same services available to students with LD, as well as distraction-free study areas, distraction-free testing environments, medication management and personal coach or mentors.

Application *Required:* high school transcript, SAT I (extended-time test accepted), personal statement, and letter(s) of recommendation. *Recommended:* participation in extracurricular activities, ACT, and interview. Upon acceptance, documentation of need for special services should be sent only to your LD program or unit.

LD program contact Lois Mendez-Catlin, Assistant Dean, 101 North Merion Avenue, Bryn Mawr, PA 19010. *Phone:* 610-526-5375. *Fax:* 610-526-7450. *E-mail:* lmendez@brynmawr.edu.

Application contact Bryn Mawr College, 101 North Merion Avenue, Bryn Mawr, PA 19010-2899. *E-mail:* admissions@brynmawr.edu. *Web address:* http://www.brynmawr.edu/.

CALDWELL COLLEGE
Caldwell, New Jersey

Students with LD Served by Program	40	ADD/ADHD Services	✓
Staff	1 full-time	Summer Preparation Program	n/a
LD Program or Service Fee	n/a	Alternative Test Arrangements	✓
LD Program Began	1997	LD Student Organization	n/a

Office of Disability Services began offering services in 1997. The program serves approximately 40 undergraduate students. Faculty consists of 1 full-time staff member. Services are provided by academic advisers, remediation/learning specialists, counselors, regular education teachers, special education teachers, LD specialists, trained peer tutors, and professional tutors.

Policies Students with LD may take up to 12 credit hours per semester; 12 credit hours per semester are required to maintain full-time status and to be eligible for financial aid. LD services are also available to graduate students.

Counseling and advisement Academic advisement by a staff member affiliated with the program is available.

Auxiliary aids and services *Services and accommodations:* advocates, alternative test arrangements, readers, note-takers, and scribes.

ADD/ADHD Students with ADD/ADHD are eligible for the same services available to students with LD, as well as distraction-free study areas, distraction-free testing environments and advocacy.

Application *Required:* high school transcript, ACT or SAT I (extended-time or untimed test accepted), personal statement, and letter(s) of recommendation. *Recommended:* participation in extracurricular activities and interview. Upon acceptance, documentation of need for special services should be sent only to

Caldwell College (continued)

your LD program or unit. *Application deadline (institutional):* rolling/continuous for fall and rolling/continuous for spring. *Application deadline (LD program):* rolling/continuous for fall and rolling/continuous for spring.

LD program contact Joan Serpico, Coordinator of Disability Services, Office of Disability Services, Caldwell, NJ 07006. *Phone:* 973-618-3645. *Fax:* 973-618-3488. *E-mail:* jserpico@caldwell.edu.

Application contact Raymond Sheenan, Executive Director of Admissions, Caldwell College, 9 Ryerson Avenue, Caldwell, NJ 07006-6195. *Phone:* 973-618-3220. *Web address:* http://www.caldwell.edu/.

CALIFORNIA POLYTECHNIC STATE UNIVERSITY, SAN LUIS OBISPO
San Luis Obispo, California

Students with LD Served by Program	400	ADD/ADHD Services	✓
Staff	4 full-time	Summer Preparation Program	n/a
LD Program or Service Fee	n/a	Alternative Test Arrangements	n/a
LD Program Began	n/a	LD Student Organization	✓

Disability Resource Center (DRC) serves approximately 400 undergraduate students. Faculty consists of 4 full-time staff members. Services are provided by academic advisers, diagnostic specialists, LD specialists, and trained peer tutors.

Policies The college has written policies regarding course substitutions and substitution and waivers of requirements for admission and graduation. 12 units per quarter are required to maintain full-time status; 6 units per quarter are required to be eligible for financial aid. LD services are also available to graduate students.

Special preparation or orientation Optional orientation held before registration, during registration, before classes begin, after classes begin, during summer prior to enrollment, and individually by special arrangement.

Diagnostic testing Available for auditory processing, spelling, neuropsychological, spoken language, intelligence, study skills, reading, written language, learning styles, visual processing, and math.

Subject-area tutoring Available in some subjects. Offered one-on-one and in small groups by trained peer tutors.

Counseling and advisement Academic advisement by a staff member affiliated with the program is available.

Auxiliary aids and services *Aids:* calculators, scan and read programs (e.g., Kurzweil), screen-enlarging programs, screen readers, speech recognition programs (e.g., Dragon), tape recorders, taped textbooks. *Services and accommodations:* priority registration, readers, note-takers, and peer advisors, career marketing programs, Disability management advisory.

Student organization There is a student organization for students with LD.

ADD/ADHD Students with ADD/ADHD are eligible for the same services available to students with LD, as well as distraction-free testing environments.

Application *Required:* high school transcript and ACT or SAT I (extended-time or untimed test accepted). *Recommended:* participation in extracurricular activities, interview, personal statement, letter(s) of recommendation, separate application to your LD program or unit, psychoeducational report (5 years old or less), and documentation of high school services (e.g., Individualized Education Program [IEP] or 504 plan). Upon application, documentation of need for special services should be sent only to your LD program or unit. Upon acceptance, documentation

of need for special services should be sent only to your LD program or unit. *Application deadline (institutional):* 11/30 for fall and 8/31 for spring.

LD program contact Ann Fryer, Learning Disabilities Specialist, Disability Resource Center, San Luis Obispo, CA 93407. *Phone:* 805-756-1395. *Fax:* 805-756-5451. *E-mail:* afryer@calpoly.edu.

Application contact California Polytechnic State University, San Luis Obispo, San Luis Obispo, CA 93407. *E-mail:* dp141@oasis.calpoly.edu. *Web address:* http://www.calpoly.edu/.

CALIFORNIA STATE UNIVERSITY, BAKERSFIELD
Bakersfield, California

Students with LD Served by Program	119	ADD/ADHD Services	✓
Staff	3 full-time	Summer Preparation Program	n/a
LD Program or Service Fee	n/a	Alternative Test Arrangements	✓
LD Program Began	1990	LD Student Organization	✓

Services for Students with Disabilities began offering services in 1990. The program serves approximately 119 undergraduate students. Faculty consists of 3 full-time staff members. Services are provided by counselors and LD specialists.

Policies The college has written policies regarding course substitutions, grade forgiveness, and substitution and waivers of requirements for admission and graduation. Students with LD may take up to 21 units per quarter; 12 units per quarter are required to maintain full-time status and to be eligible for financial aid. LD services are also available to graduate students.

Special preparation or orientation Required orientation held individually by special arrangement.

Diagnostic testing Available for LD assessment.

Subject-area tutoring Available in most subjects. Offered one-on-one and in small groups by professional tutors and trained peer tutors.

Special courses Available in learning strategies. All courses are offered for credit; none enter into overall grade point average.

Auxiliary aids and services *Aids:* calculators, scan and read programs (e.g., Kurzweil), screen-enlarging programs, screen readers, speech recognition programs (e.g., Dragon), tape recorders, taped textbooks. *Services and accommodations:* priority registration, alternative test arrangements, readers, note-takers, and scribes.

Student organization There is a student organization for students with LD.

ADD/ADHD Students with ADD/ADHD are eligible for the same services available to students with LD, as well as distraction-free testing environments.

Application *Required:* high school transcript. *Recommended:* participation in extracurricular activities and ACT or SAT I (extended-time tests accepted). Upon application, documentation of need for special services should be sent to both admissions and your LD program or unit. Upon acceptance, documentation of need for special services should be sent to both admissions and your LD program or unit. *Application deadline (institutional):* 11/1 for fall and 8/1 for spring. *Application deadline (LD program):* rolling/continuous for fall and rolling/continuous for spring.

LD program contact Janice Clausen, Director, Services for Students with Disabilities, 9001 Stockdale Highway, Bakersfield, CA 93311-1099. *Phone:* 661-664-3360. *Fax:* 661-664-2171. *E-mail:* jclausen@csub.edu.

Application contact California State University, Bakersfield, 9001 Stockdale Highway, Bakersfield, CA 93311-1099. *Web address:* http://www.csubak.edu/.

CALIFORNIA STATE UNIVERSITY, DOMINGUEZ HILLS

Carson, California

Students with LD Served by Program	200	ADD/ADHD Services	✓
Staff	3 full-time, 1 part-time	Summer Preparation Program	n/a
LD Program or Service Fee	n/a	Alternative Test Arrangements	✓
LD Program Began	1983	LD Student Organization	n/a

Disabled Student Services began offering services in 1983. The program serves approximately 200 undergraduate students. Faculty consists of 3 full-time staff members and 1 part-time staff member. Services are provided by counselors, diagnostic specialists, and LD specialists.

Policies Students with LD may take up to 18 credit hours per semester; 12 credit hours per semester are required to maintain full-time status; 6 credit hours per semester are required to be eligible for financial aid. LD services are also available to graduate students.

Special preparation or orientation Optional orientation held individually by special arrangement.

Diagnostic testing Available for auditory processing, spelling, spoken language, intelligence, learning strategies, reading, written language, learning styles, visual processing, and math.

Auxiliary aids and services *Aids:* calculators, personal computers, personal spelling/word-use assistants (e.g., Franklin Speller), scan and read programs (e.g., Kurzweil), screen-enlarging programs, screen readers, speech recognition programs (e.g., Dragon), tape recorders, taped textbooks. *Services and accommodations:* advocates, priority registration, alternative test arrangements, readers, note-takers, and scribes.

ADD/ADHD Students with ADD/ADHD are eligible for the same services available to students with LD

Application *Required:* high school transcript and ACT or SAT I (extended-time or untimed test accepted). Upon application, documentation of need for special services should be sent only to your LD program or unit. Upon acceptance, documentation of need for special services should be sent only to your LD program or unit. *Application deadline (institutional):* rolling/continuous for fall and rolling/continuous for spring.

LD program contact Patricia Ann Wells, Director, Disable Students Services, 1000 East Victoria Street, Carson, CA 90747. *Phone:* 310-243-3660. *Fax:* 310-516-4247. *E-mail:* pwells@csudh.edu.

Application contact Information Center, California State University, Dominguez Hills, 1000 East Victoria Street, Carson, CA 90747-0001. *Phone:* 310-516-3696. *Web address:* http://www.csudh.edu/.

CALIFORNIA STATE UNIVERSITY, FRESNO

Fresno, California

Students with LD Served by Program	200	ADD/ADHD Services	✓
Staff	n/a	Summer Preparation Program	n/a
LD Program or Service Fee	n/a	Alternative Test Arrangements	✓
LD Program Began	1980	LD Student Organization	✓

Services for Students with Disabilities began offering services in 1980. The program serves approximately 200 undergraduate students. Services are provided by remediation/learning specialists, counselors, diagnostic specialists, and trained peer tutors.

Policies The college has written policies regarding course substitutions. Students with LD may take up to 16 units per semester; 12 units per semester are required to maintain full-time status and to be eligible for financial aid. LD services are also available to graduate students.

Diagnostic testing Available for psycho educational batteries such as WJ-R and WAIS III.

Counseling and advisement Career counseling, individual counseling, and support groups are available.

Auxiliary aids and services *Aids:* calculators, personal computers, personal spelling/word-use assistants (e.g., Franklin Speller), scan and read programs (e.g., Kurzweil), screen-enlarging programs, screen readers, speech recognition programs (e.g., Dragon), tape recorders, taped textbooks. *Services and accommodations:* advocates, priority registration, alternative test arrangements, readers, note-takers, and scribes.

Student organization There is a student organization for students with LD.

ADD/ADHD Students with ADD/ADHD are eligible for the same services available to students with LD

Application *Required:* high school transcript, ACT or SAT I (extended-time tests accepted), psychoeducational report (5 years old or less), and documentation of high school services (e.g., Individualized Education Program [IEP] or 504 plan). Upon application, documentation of need for special services should be sent only to your LD program or unit. Upon acceptance, documentation of need for special services should be sent only to your LD program or unit. *Application deadline (LD program):* rolling/continuous for fall and rolling/continuous for spring.

LD program contact Patricia Blore, Disability Management Specialist, 5200 North Barton, M/S ML 125, Fresno, CA 93740-8014. *Phone:* 559-278-6511. *Fax:* 559-278-4214. *E-mail:* pat_blore@csufresno.edu.

Application contact California State University, Fresno, 5241 North Maple Avenue, Fresno, CA 93740. *E-mail:* donna_mills@csufresno.edu. *Web address:* http://www.csufresno.edu/.

CALIFORNIA STATE UNIVERSITY, FULLERTON

Fullerton, California

Students with LD Served by Program	400	ADD/ADHD Services	✓
Staff	7 full-time, 1 part-time	Summer Preparation Program	n/a
LD Program or Service Fee	n/a	Alternative Test Arrangements	✓
LD Program Began	1981	LD Student Organization	✓

Disabled Student Services began offering services in 1981. The program serves approximately 400 undergraduate students. Faculty consists of 7 full-time staff members and 1 part-time staff member. Services are provided by counselors, diagnostic specialists, and LD specialists.

Policies LD services are also available to graduate students.

Special preparation or orientation Optional orientation held before classes begin and individually by special arrangement.

Diagnostic testing Available for battery to determine presence of LD or ADD.

Counseling and advisement Individual counseling is available.

Auxiliary aids and services *Aids:* scan and read programs (e.g., Kurzweil), screen-enlarging programs, screen readers, speech recognition programs (e.g., Dragon), tape recorders,

California State University, Fullerton (continued)

taped textbooks. *Services and accommodations:* priority registration, alternative test arrangements, readers, note-takers, and scribes.

Student organization There is a student organization for students with LD.

ADD/ADHD Students with ADD/ADHD are eligible for the same services available to students with LD, as well as distraction-free study areas and distraction-free testing environments.

Application *Required:* high school transcript and psychoeducational report (3 years old or less). Upon application, documentation of need for special services should be sent only to your LD program or unit. Upon acceptance, documentation of need for special services should be sent only to your LD program or unit. *Application deadline (institutional):* rolling/continuous for fall and rolling/continuous for spring. *Application deadline (LD program):* rolling/continuous for fall and rolling/continuous for spring.

LD program contact Debra J. Fletcher, Learning Disabilities Specialist, Disabled Student Services, PO Box 6830, Fullerton, CA 92834. *Phone:* 714-278-3117. *Fax:* 714-278-2408.

Application contact Nancy J. Dority, Admissions Director, California State University, Fullerton, PO Box 34080, Fullerton, CA 92834-9480. *Phone:* 714-278-2370. *Web address:* http://www.fullerton.edu/.

CALIFORNIA STATE UNIVERSITY, LONG BEACH
Long Beach, California

Students with LD Served by Program	500	ADD/ADHD Services	✓
Staff	2 full-time, 2 part-time	Summer Preparation Program	n/a
LD Program or Service Fee	n/a	Alternative Test Arrangements	✓
LD Program Began	1979	LD Student Organization	n/a

Stephen Benson Program for Students with Learning Disabilities began offering services in 1979. The program serves approximately 500 undergraduate students. Faculty consists of 2 full-time and 2 part-time staff members. Services are provided by academic advisers, counselors, graduate assistants/students, and LD specialists.

Policies LD services are also available to graduate students.

Special preparation or orientation Optional orientation held after classes begin.

Diagnostic testing Available for auditory processing, spelling, intelligence, reading, written language, visual processing, and math.

Subject-area tutoring Available in most subjects. Offered one-on-one and in small groups by trained peer tutors.

Special courses Available in career planning and learning strategies. All courses are offered for credit; all enter into overall grade point average.

Counseling and advisement Individual counseling is available. Academic advisement by a staff member affiliated with the program is available.

Auxiliary aids and services *Aids:* taped textbooks. *Services and accommodations:* priority registration, alternative test arrangements, readers, and note-takers.

ADD/ADHD Students with ADD/ADHD are eligible for the same services available to students with LD

Application *Required:* high school transcript, ACT or SAT I (extended-time tests accepted), and psychoeducational report (3 years old or less). *Recommended:* personal statement, letter(s) of recommendation, and separate application to your LD program or unit. Upon application, documentation of need for

special services should be sent to both admissions and your LD program or unit. Upon acceptance, documentation of need for special services should be sent only to your LD program or unit.

LD program contact Brian Carey, Assessment Specialist, 1250 Bellflower Boulevard, BH-270, Long Beach, CA 90840-0108. *Phone:* 562-985-4430. *Fax:* 562-985-7183. *E-mail:* bcarey@csulb.edu.

Application contact California State University, Long Beach, 1250 Bellflower Boulevard, Long Beach, CA 90840-0118. *Web address:* http://www.csulb.edu/.

CALIFORNIA STATE UNIVERSITY, SAN MARCOS
San Marcos, California

Students with LD Served by Program	50	ADD/ADHD Services	✓
Staff	4 full-time	Summer Preparation Program	n/a
LD Program or Service Fee	n/a	Alternative Test Arrangements	✓
LD Program Began	1990	LD Student Organization	✓

Disabled Student Services began offering services in 1990. The program serves approximately 50 undergraduate students. Faculty consists of 4 full-time staff members. Services are provided by counselors, LD specialists, trained peer tutors, and psychologist.

Policies The college has written policies regarding course substitutions and substitution and waivers of requirements for admission and graduation. Students with LD may take up to 19 credit hours per semester; 12 credit hours per semester are required to maintain full-time status; 3 credit hours per semester are required to be eligible for financial aid. LD services are also available to graduate students.

Diagnostic testing Available for auditory processing, spelling, intelligence, personality, study skills, learning strategies, reading, written language, learning styles, visual processing, and math.

Subject-area tutoring Available in most subjects. Offered one-on-one by trained peer tutors.

Counseling and advisement Individual counseling and support groups are available.

Auxiliary aids and services *Aids:* calculators, personal computers, personal spelling/word-use assistants (e.g., Franklin Speller), scan and read programs (e.g., Kurzweil), screen-enlarging programs, screen readers, speech recognition programs (e.g., Dragon), tape recorders, taped textbooks. *Services and accommodations:* advocates, priority registration, alternative test arrangements, readers, note-takers, scribes, and supplemental academic advising.

Student organization There is a student organization for students with LD.

ADD/ADHD Students with ADD/ADHD are eligible for the same services available to students with LD, as well as distraction-free testing environments, medication management and ADD evaluation and referral.

Application *Required:* high school transcript, ACT or SAT I (extended-time or untimed test accepted), psychoeducational report (3 years old or less), and application to Disabled Student Services. Upon application, documentation of need for special services should be sent to both admissions and your LD program or unit. Upon acceptance, documentation of need for special services should be sent only to your LD program or unit. *Application deadline (institutional):* rolling/continuous for fall and rolling/continuous for spring. *Application deadline (LD program):* rolling/continuous for fall and rolling/continuous for spring.

LD program contact Dr. Kara Kornher, Psychologist/LD Specialist, Disabled Student Services, San Marcos, CA 92096. *Phone:* 760-750-4905. *Fax:* 760-750-3445. *E-mail:* kkornher@csusm.edu. **Application contact** Terrie Rodriguez, Director of Admissions, California State University, San Marcos, San Marcos, CA 92096-0001. *Phone:* 760-750-4848. *Web address:* http://ww2.csusm. edu/.

CALIFORNIA STATE UNIVERSITY, STANISLAUS
Turlock, California

Students with LD Served by Program	100	ADD/ADHD Services	✓
Staff	1 full-time	Summer Preparation Program	n/a
LD Program or Service Fee	n/a	Alternative Test Arrangements	✓
LD Program Began	1993	LD Student Organization	n/a

Disabled Student Services began offering services in 1993. The program serves approximately 100 undergraduate students. Faculty consists of 1 full-time staff member. Services are provided by remediation/learning specialists, diagnostic specialists, graduate assistants/students, LD specialists, and ADHD Specialist.
Policies The college has written policies regarding course substitutions and substitution and waivers of requirements for admission and graduation. Students with LD may take up to 16 units per semester; 10 units per semester are required to maintain full-time status; 12 units per semester are required to be eligible for financial aid. LD services are also available to graduate students.
Diagnostic testing Available for auditory processing, spelling, intelligence, study skills, learning strategies, reading, written language, learning styles, visual processing, math, and AD/HD testing.
Counseling and advisement Career counseling and individual counseling are available.
Auxiliary aids and services *Aids:* calculators, personal computers, personal spelling/word-use assistants (e.g., Franklin Speller), scan and read programs (e.g., Kurzweil), screen-enlarging programs, speech recognition programs (e.g., Dragon), tape recorders, taped textbooks. *Services and accommodations:* alternative test arrangements, readers, note-takers, and scribes.
ADD/ADHD Students with ADD/ADHD are eligible for the same services available to students with LD, as well as distraction-free testing environments.
Application *Required:* high school transcript, ACT or SAT I (extended-time tests accepted), separate application to your LD program or unit, and psychoeducational report (5 years old or less). *Recommended:* documentation of high school services (e.g., Individualized Education Program [IEP] or 504 plan). Upon application, documentation of need for special services should be sent only to your LD program or unit. Upon acceptance, documentation of need for special services should be sent only to your LD program or unit. *Application deadline (LD program):* rolling/continuous for fall and rolling/continuous for spring.
LD program contact Dr. Anne Reith, LD/ADHD Specialist, Disabled Student Services, SSB-134, Turlock, CA 95382. *Phone:* 209-667-3159. *Fax:* 209-667-3585. *E-mail:* areith@stan.csustan. edu.
Application contact Admissions Office, California State University, Stanislaus, 801 West Monte Vista Avenue, Turlock, CA 95382. *Phone:* 209-667-3070. *E-mail:* outreach@toto.csustan. edu. *Web address:* http://www.csustan.edu/.

CALVIN COLLEGE
Grand Rapids, Michigan

Students with LD Served by Program	80	ADD/ADHD Services	✓
Staff	1 full-time, 1 part-time	Summer Preparation Program	n/a
LD Program or Service Fee	n/a	Alternative Test Arrangements	✓
LD Program Began	1985	LD Student Organization	n/a

Services to Students with Disabilities began offering services in 1985. The program serves approximately 80 undergraduate students. Faculty consists of 1 full-time and 1 part-time staff member. Services are provided by academic advisers, counselors, diagnostic specialists, LD specialists, and trained peer tutors.
Policies Students with LD may take up to 14 credit hours per semester; 12 credit hours per semester are required to maintain full-time status and to be eligible for financial aid. LD services are also available to graduate students.
Special preparation or orientation Optional orientation held during registration.
Diagnostic testing Available for intelligence, study skills, learning strategies, and psycho-educational battery, ADD screening.
Subject-area tutoring Available in some subjects. Offered one-on-one and in small groups by trained peer tutors.
Special courses Available in study skills. No courses are offered for credit; none enter into overall grade point average.
Counseling and advisement Individual counseling and peer coaches are available. Academic advisement by a staff member affiliated with the program is available.
Auxiliary aids and services *Aids:* personal computers, screen-enlarging programs, speech recognition programs (e.g., Dragon), tape recorders, taped textbooks. *Services and accommodations:* priority registration, alternative test arrangements, readers, note-takers, and scribes.
ADD/ADHD Students with ADD/ADHD are eligible for the same services available to students with LD, as well as distraction-free study areas, distraction-free testing environments, personal coach or mentors, and support groups for ADD/ADHD.
Application *Required:* high school transcript, ACT or SAT I (extended-time tests accepted), personal statement, and letter(s) of recommendation. *Recommended:* participation in extracurricular activities. Upon acceptance, documentation of need for special services should be sent only to your LD program or unit. *Application deadline (institutional):* rolling/continuous for fall and rolling/continuous for spring. *Application deadline (LD program):* rolling/continuous for fall and rolling/continuous for spring.
LD program contact Margaret Vriend, Coordinator of Services to Students with Disabilities, 3201 Burton Street, SE, Grand Rapids, MI 49546. *Phone:* 616-957-6077. *Fax:* 616-957-8551. *E-mail:* vriend@calvin.edu.
Application contact Calvin College, 3201 Burton Street, SE, Grand Rapids, MI 49546-4388. *E-mail:* admissions@calvin.edu. *Web address:* http://www.calvin.edu/.

CANISIUS COLLEGE
Buffalo, New York

Students with LD Served by Program	125	ADD/ADHD Services	✓
Staff	3 full-time	Summer Preparation Program	n/a
LD Program or Service Fee	n/a	Alternative Test Arrangements	✓
LD Program Began	n/a	LD Student Organization	✓

Canisius College (continued)

Disability Support Service (DSS) serves approximately 125 undergraduate students. Faculty consists of 3 full-time staff members. Services are provided by academic advisers, regular education teachers, counselors, remediation/learning specialists, graduate assistants/students, trained peer tutors, and professional tutors.

Policies The college has written policies regarding course substitutions and substitution and waivers of requirements for admission and graduation. Students with LD may take up to 15 credit hours per semester; 12 credit hours per semester are required to maintain full-time status and to be eligible for financial aid. LD services are also available to graduate students.

Special preparation or orientation Required orientation held before classes begin, during summer prior to enrollment, and individually by special arrangement.

Diagnostic testing Available for study skills, learning strategies, reading, written language, and math.

Subject-area tutoring Available in some subjects. Offered one-on-one by professional tutors, trained peer tutors, and LD specialists.

Counseling and advisement Career counseling and individual counseling are available. Academic advisement by a staff member affiliated with the program is available.

Auxiliary aids and services *Aids:* calculators, personal computers, tape recorders, taped textbooks. *Services and accommodations:* advocates, priority registration, alternative test arrangements, readers, note-takers, and scribes.

Student organization There is a student organization for students with LD.

ADD/ADHD Students with ADD/ADHD are eligible for the same services available to students with LD, as well as distraction-free testing environments and personal coach or mentors.

Application *Required:* high school transcript, ACT (extended-time test accepted), SAT I (extended-time test accepted), interview, personal statement, separate application to your LD program or unit, psychoeducational report (3 years old or less), and documentation of high school services (e.g., Individualized Education Program [IEP] or 504 plan). *Recommended:* participation in extracurricular activities and letter(s) of recommendation. Upon application, documentation of need for special services should be sent only to your LD program or unit. Upon acceptance, documentation of need for special services should be sent only to your LD program or unit. *Application deadline (institutional):* rolling/continuous for fall and rolling/continuous for spring. *Application deadline (LD program):* rolling/continuous for fall and rolling/continuous for spring.

LD program contact Martha A. Veasey, Director, Disability Support Service, 2001 Main Street, Buffalo, NY 14208-1525. *Phone:* 716-888-3748. *Fax:* 716-888-3747. *E-mail:* veasey@canisius.edu.

Application contact Canisius College, 2001 Main Street, Buffalo, NY 14208-1098. *E-mail:* inquiry@gort.canisius.edu. *Web address:* http://www.canisius.edu/.

CARDINAL STRITCH UNIVERSITY
Milwaukee, Wisconsin

Students with LD Served by Program	30	ADD/ADHD Services	✓
Staff	2 full-time, 3 part-time	Summer Preparation Program	n/a
LD Program or Service Fee	n/a	Alternative Test Arrangements	✓
LD Program Began	1989	LD Student Organization	n/a

Academic Support began offering services in 1989. The program serves approximately 30 undergraduate students. Faculty consists of 2 full-time and 3 part-time staff members. Services are provided by remediation/learning specialists.

Policies 12 credits per semester are required to maintain full-time status and to be eligible for financial aid. LD services are also available to graduate students.

Special preparation or orientation Held individually by special arrangement.

Basic skills remediation Available in study skills, reading, learning strategies, written language, and math. Offered in class-size groups by regular education teachers and professional tutors.

Subject-area tutoring Available in all subjects. Offered one-on-one and in small groups by professional tutors.

Special courses Available in study skills, reading, learning strategies, and math. No courses are offered for credit; none enter into overall grade point average.

Counseling and advisement Career counseling and individual counseling are available.

Auxiliary aids and services *Aids:* calculators, personal computers, screen-enlarging programs, tape recorders, taped textbooks. *Services and accommodations:* priority registration, alternative test arrangements, readers, note-takers, and scribes.

ADD/ADHD Students with ADD/ADHD are eligible for the same services available to students with LD, as well as distraction-free testing environments.

Application *Required:* high school transcript, ACT (extended-time test accepted), interview, personal statement, letter(s) of recommendation, psychoeducational report, and documentation of high school services (e.g., Individualized Education Program [IEP] or 504 plan). Upon application, documentation of need for special services should be sent only to your LD program or unit. Upon acceptance, documentation of need for special services should be sent only to your LD program or unit.

LD program contact Marcia L. Laskey, Director, Academic Support, 6801 North Yates Road, Milwaukee, WI 53217. *Phone:* 414-410-4168. *Fax:* 414-410-4239.

Application contact Cardinal Stritch University, 6801 North Yates Road, Milwaukee, WI 53217-3985. *Web address:* http://www.stritch.edu/.

CARLETON UNIVERSITY
Ottawa, Ontario

Students with LD Served by Program	300	ADD/ADHD Services	✓
Staff	3 full-time, 3 part-time	Summer Preparation Program	n/a
LD Program or Service Fee	varies	Alternative Test Arrangements	✓
LD Program Began	1990	LD Student Organization	✓

Paul Menton Centre began offering services in 1990. The program serves approximately 300 undergraduate students. Faculty consists of 3 full-time and 3 part-time staff members. Services are provided by remediation/learning specialists, counselors, diagnostic specialists, graduate assistants/students, LD specialists, trained peer tutors, and adaptive technology assistant.

Policies LD services are also available to graduate students.

Fees *LD Program or Service Fee:* ranges from $0 to $2000 Canadian dollars per year. *Diagnostic Testing Fee:* $900 Canadian dollars.

Diagnostic testing Available for auditory processing, motor skills, spelling, handwriting, spoken language, intelligence, personality, study skills, learning strategies, reading, written language, learning styles, visual processing, math, and attention, concentration, short term memory, retrieval.

Basic skills remediation Available in study skills, computer skills, reading, time management, learning strategies, spelling, and written language. Offered one-on-one by computer-based instruction, graduate assistants/students, trained peer tutors, and education interns, technology assistant.

Subject-area tutoring Available in some subjects. Offered one-on-one by graduate assistants/students and trained peer tutors.

Counseling and advisement Career counseling is available.

Auxiliary aids and services *Aids:* personal computers, scan and read programs (e.g., Kurzweil), screen-enlarging programs, screen readers, speech recognition programs (e.g., Dragon), tape recorders, taped textbooks, scanner, personal notetaking key board (AlphaSmart), writing organization software. *Services and accommodations:* priority registration, alternative test arrangements, readers, note-takers, scribes, and proofreader, photocopy cards.

Student organization There is a student organization for students with LD.

ADD/ADHD Students with ADD/ADHD are eligible for the same services available to students with LD, as well as distraction-free testing environments, medication management and personal coach or mentors.

Application *Required:* high school transcript. Upon acceptance, documentation of need for special services should be sent only to your LD program or unit.

LD program contact Dr. Nancy McIntyre, Coordinator, Learning Disabilities, Paul Menton Centre, 500 University Centre, 1125 Colonel By Drive, Ottawa, ON K1S 5B6. *Phone:* 613-520-6608. *Fax:* 613-520-3995. *E-mail:* nancy_mcintyre@carleton.ca.

Application contact Jean Mullan, Manager, Undergraduate Recruitment Office, Carleton University, 1125 Colonel By Drive, Ottawa, ON K1S 5B6. *Phone:* 613-520-3663. *E-mail:* liaison@admissions.carleton.ca. *Web address:* http://www.carleton.ca/.

CARNEGIE MELLON UNIVERSITY
Pittsburgh, Pennsylvania

Students with LD Served by Program	130	ADD/ADHD Services	✓
Staff	3 full-time	Summer Preparation Program	n/a
LD Program or Service Fee	n/a	Alternative Test Arrangements	✓
LD Program Began	1989	LD Student Organization	n/a

Equal Opportunity Services (EOS) began offering services in 1989. The program serves approximately 130 undergraduate students. Faculty consists of 3 full-time staff members. Services are provided by academic advisers, counselors, graduate assistants/students, and trained peer tutors.

Policies Students with LD may take up to 38 units per semester; 36 units per semester are required to maintain full-time status; 18 units per semester are required to be eligible for financial aid. LD services are also available to graduate students.

Special preparation or orientation Held individually by special arrangement.

Subject-area tutoring Available in most subjects. Offered one-on-one by graduate assistants/students.

Special courses Available in career planning, oral communication skills, study skills, college survival skills, practical computer skills, test taking, health and nutrition, time management, learning strategies, math, and stress management. No courses are offered for credit; none enter into overall grade point average.

Counseling and advisement Individual counseling is available. Academic advisement by a staff member affiliated with the program is available.

Auxiliary aids and services *Aids:* scan and read programs (e.g., Kurzweil), tape recorders, taped textbooks. *Services and accommodations:* alternative test arrangements, readers, note-takers, and scribes.

ADD/ADHD Students with ADD/ADHD are eligible for the same services available to students with LD, as well as distraction-free testing environments.

Application *Required:* high school transcript, participation in extracurricular activities, ACT or SAT I (extended-time or untimed test accepted), personal statement, and letter(s) of recommendation. *Recommended:* interview. Upon acceptance, documentation of need for special services should be sent only to your LD program or unit. *Application deadline (institutional):* 1/1 for fall and 11/1 for spring.

LD program contact Lisa Zamperini, Disability Services Coordinator, Whitfield Hall, 143 North Craig Street, Pittsburgh, PA 15213. *Phone:* 412-268-2012. *Fax:* 412-268-7472. *E-mail:* ly2t@andrew.cmu.edu.

Application contact Carnegie Mellon University, 5000 Forbes Avenue, Pittsburgh, PA 15213-3891. *E-mail:* undergraduate-admissions+@andrew.cmu.edu. *Web address:* http://www.cmu.edu/.

CATAWBA COLLEGE
Salisbury, North Carolina

Students with LD Served by Program	30	ADD/ADHD Services	✓
Staff	n/a	Summer Preparation Program	n/a
LD Program or Service Fee	n/a	Alternative Test Arrangements	✓
LD Program Began	1995	LD Student Organization	n/a

The Academic Resource Center (ARC) began offering services in 1995. The program serves approximately 30 undergraduate students. Services are provided by LD specialists and trained peer tutors.

Policies The college has written policies regarding course substitutions and substitution and waivers of requirements for admission and graduation. Students with LD may take up to 18 credit hours per semester; 12 credit hours per semester are required to maintain full-time status and to be eligible for financial aid.

Special preparation or orientation Held after classes begin.

Subject-area tutoring Available in all subjects. Offered one-on-one and in small groups by trained peer tutors and LD specialists.

Counseling and advisement Individual counseling is available.

Auxiliary aids and services *Aids:* calculators, personal computers, personal spelling/word-use assistants (e.g., Franklin Speller), taped textbooks. *Services and accommodations:* priority registration, alternative test arrangements, readers, note-takers, and scribes.

ADD/ADHD Students with ADD/ADHD are eligible for the same services available to students with LD, as well as distraction-free testing environments and personal coach or mentors.

Application *Required:* high school transcript, ACT or SAT I (extended-time or untimed test accepted), and personal statement. *Recommended:* participation in extracurricular activities, interview, and letter(s) of recommendation. Upon acceptance, documentation of need for special services should be sent only to your LD program or unit. *Application deadline (institutional):* rolling/continuous for fall and rolling/continuous for spring. *Application deadline (LD program):* rolling/continuous for fall and rolling/continuous for spring.

LD program contact Jan Sabo, Director of The Academic Resource Center, 2300 West Innes Street, Salisbury, NC 28144. *Phone:* 704-637-4259. *Fax:* 704-637-4401. *E-mail:* jlsabo@catawba.edu.

Catawba College (continued)

Application contact Catawba College, 2300 West Innes Street, Salisbury, NC 28144-2488. *E-mail:* cwalters@catawba.edu. *Web address:* http://www.catawba.edu/.

THE CATHOLIC UNIVERSITY OF AMERICA
Washington, District of Columbia

Students with LD Served by Program	150	ADD/ADHD Services	✓
Staff	1 full-time, 14 part-time	Summer Preparation Program	n/a
LD Program or Service Fee	n/a	Alternative Test Arrangements	✓
LD Program Began	1982	LD Student Organization	n/a

Disability Support Services began offering services in 1982. The program serves approximately 150 undergraduate students. Faculty consists of 1 full-time and 14 part-time staff members. Services are provided by academic advisers, remediation/learning specialists, counselors, LD specialists, and trained peer tutors.
Policies The college has written policies regarding course substitutions and substitution and waivers of requirements for admission and graduation. Students with LD may take up to 18 credits per semester; 12 credits per semester are required to maintain full-time status. LD services are also available to graduate students.
Special preparation or orientation Optional orientation held before classes begin, after classes begin, and individually by special arrangement.
Basic skills remediation Available in auditory processing, study skills, reading, time management, learning strategies, spelling, written language, math, and individual counseling. Offered one-on-one, in small groups, and class-size groups by LD specialists and learning counselors.
Subject-area tutoring Available in most subjects. Offered one-on-one and in small groups by trained peer tutors.
Counseling and advisement Individual counseling and support groups are available. Academic advisement by a staff member affiliated with the program is available.
Auxiliary aids and services *Aids:* personal computers, scan and read programs (e.g., Kurzweil), screen-enlarging programs, speech recognition programs (e.g., Dragon), tape recorders, taped textbooks. *Services and accommodations:* advocates, priority registration, alternative test arrangements, readers, note-takers, and scribes.
ADD/ADHD Students with ADD/ADHD are eligible for the same services available to students with LD, as well as distraction-free study areas, distraction-free testing environments, medication management, support groups for ADD/ADHD and singles in dorm.
Application *Required:* high school transcript, ACT or SAT I (extended-time tests accepted), letter(s) of recommendation, and psychoeducational report (3 years old or less). *Recommended:* participation in extracurricular activities, interview, personal statement, separate application to your LD program or unit, and documentation of high school services (e.g., Individualized Education Program [IEP] or 504 plan). Upon application, documentation of need for special services should be sent only to admissions. Upon acceptance, documentation of need for special services should be sent only to your LD program or unit. *Application deadline (institutional):* 2/15 for fall. *Application deadline (LD program):* 2/15 for fall.
LD program contact Bonnie McClellan, Director, Disability Support Services, University Center East—251, Washington, DC 20064. *Phone:* 202-319-5618. *Fax:* 202-319-5126. *E-mail:* mcclellan@cua.edu.

Application contact The Catholic University of America, Cardinal Station Post Office, Washington, DC 20064. *E-mail:* cua-admissions@cua.edu. *Web address:* http://www.cua.edu/.

CENTER FOR CREATIVE STUDIES— COLLEGE OF ART AND DESIGN
Detroit, Michigan

Students with LD Served by Program	50	ADD/ADHD Services	✓
Staff	1 full-time, 15 part-time	Summer Preparation Program	n/a
LD Program or Service Fee	n/a	Alternative Test Arrangements	✓
LD Program Began	1997	LD Student Organization	n/a

Student Success Center began offering services in 1997. The program serves approximately 50 undergraduate students. Faculty consists of 1 full-time and 15 part-time staff members. Services are provided by remediation/learning specialists and trained peer tutors.
Policies Students with LD may take up to 18 credits per semester; 12 credits per semester are required to maintain full-time status; 6 credits per semester are required to be eligible for financial aid. LD services are also available to graduate students.
Basic skills remediation Available in study skills, computer skills, reading, time management, learning strategies, spelling, written language, and basic drawing, studio courses. Offered one-on-one and in small groups by LD specialists and trained peer tutors.
Subject-area tutoring Available in all subjects. Offered one-on-one and in small groups by trained peer tutors and LD specialists.
Auxiliary aids and services *Services and accommodations:* alternative test arrangements.
ADD/ADHD Students with ADD/ADHD are eligible for the same services available to students with LD, as well as distraction-free study areas and distraction-free testing environments.
Application *Required:* high school transcript, ACT or SAT I (extended-time or untimed test accepted), personal statement, and studio portfolio (art). *Recommended:* interview, letter(s) of recommendation, and documentation of high school services (e.g., Individualized Education Program [IEP] or 504 plan). Upon application, documentation of need for special services should be sent only to admissions. Upon acceptance, documentation of need for special services should be sent only to your LD program or unit. *Application deadline (institutional):* rolling/continuous for fall and rolling/continuous for spring. *Application deadline (LD program):* rolling/continuous for fall and rolling/continuous for spring.
LD program contact Sylvia Austermiller, Director, Student Success Center, 201 East Kirby, Detroit, MI 48202. *Phone:* 313-664-7680. *Fax:* 313-872-8377. *E-mail:* sausterm@ccs.cad.edu.
Application contact Center for Creative Studies—College of Art and Design, 201 East Kirby, Detroit, MI 48202-4034. *Web address:* http://www.ccscad.edu/.

CENTRAL COLLEGE
Pella, Iowa

Students with LD Served by Program	20	ADD/ADHD Services	✓
Staff	1 full-time, 2 part-time	Summer Preparation Program	n/a
LD Program or Service Fee	n/a	Alternative Test Arrangements	✓
LD Program Began	n/a	LD Student Organization	n/a

Student Support Services serves approximately 20 undergraduate students. Faculty consists of 1 full-time and 2 part-time staff members. Services are provided by academic advisers, counselors, trained peer tutors, and professional tutors.
Policies The college has written policies regarding course substitutions. Students with LD may take up to 17 credit hours per semester; 12 credit hours per semester are required to maintain full-time status; 12 credit hours per semester are required to be eligible for financial aid.
Basic skills remediation Available in study skills, reading, time management, spelling, and written language. Offered one-on-one, in small groups, and class-size groups by regular education teachers, professional tutors, and trained peer tutors.
Subject-area tutoring Available in most subjects. Offered one-on-one, in small groups, and class-size groups by trained peer tutors.
Counseling and advisement Career counseling and individual counseling are available. Academic advisement by a staff member affiliated with the program is available.
Auxiliary aids and services *Services and accommodations:* advocates, alternative test arrangements, readers, note-takers, and scribes.
ADD/ADHD Students with ADD/ADHD are eligible for the same services available to students with LD, as well as distraction-free study areas and distraction-free testing environments.
Application *Required:* high school transcript, ACT or SAT I (extended-time or untimed test accepted), psychoeducational report (3 years old or less), and documentation of high school services (e.g., Individualized Education Program [IEP] or 504 plan). *Recommended:* participation in extracurricular activities, interview, personal statement, letter(s) of recommendation, and separate application to your LD program or unit. Upon application, documentation of need for special services should be sent only to your LD program or unit. Upon acceptance, documentation of need for special services should be sent only to your LD program or unit. *Application deadline (institutional):* rolling/continuous for fall and rolling/continuous for spring. *Application deadline (LD program):* rolling/continuous for fall and rolling/continuous for spring.
LD program contact Nancy Kroese, Director, Student Support Services, 812 University, Pella, IA 50219. *Phone:* 515-628-5247. *Fax:* 515-628-5338. *E-mail:* kroesen@central.edu.
Application contact Central College, 812 University Street, Pella, IA 50219-1999. *E-mail:* admissions@central.edu. *Web address:* http://www.central.edu/.

CENTRAL MISSOURI STATE UNIVERSITY
Warrensburg, Missouri

Students with LD Served by Program	130	ADD/ADHD Services	✓
Staff	1 full-time, 6 part-time	Summer Preparation Program	n/a
LD Program or Service Fee	n/a	Alternative Test Arrangements	✓
LD Program Began	1990	LD Student Organization	✓

Office of Accessibility Services (OAS) began offering services in 1990. The program serves approximately 130 undergraduate students. Faculty consists of 1 full-time and 6 part-time staff members. Services are provided by graduate assistants/students and LD specialists.
Policies The college has written policies regarding grade forgiveness. Students with LD may take up to 20 credit hours per semester; 12 credit hours per semester are required to main-

tain full-time status; 9 credit hours per semester are required to be eligible for financial aid. LD services are also available to graduate students.
Basic skills remediation Available in study skills, reading, learning strategies, written language, and math. Offered in class-size groups by regular education teachers.
Subject-area tutoring Available in some subjects. Offered in small groups and class-size groups by graduate assistants/students.
Special courses Available in study skills, reading, learning strategies, math, and written composition skills. All courses are offered for credit; all enter into overall grade point average.
Counseling and advisement Individual counseling is available.
Auxiliary aids and services *Aids:* calculators, personal computers, personal spelling/word-use assistants (e.g., Franklin Speller), scan and read programs (e.g., Kurzweil), screen-enlarging programs, screen readers, speech recognition programs (e.g., Dragon), tape recorders, taped textbooks. *Services and accommodations:* advocates, priority registration, alternative test arrangements, readers, note-takers, and scribes.
Student organization There is a student organization for students with LD.
ADD/ADHD Students with ADD/ADHD are eligible for the same services available to students with LD, as well as distraction-free testing environments.
Application *Required:* high school transcript, ACT (extended-time or untimed test accepted), and psychoeducational report. *Recommended:* documentation of high school services (e.g., Individualized Education Program [IEP] or 504 plan). Upon application, documentation of need for special services should be sent only to your LD program or unit. Upon acceptance, documentation of need for special services should be sent only to your LD program or unit. *Application deadline (institutional):* rolling/continuous for fall and rolling/continuous for spring. *Application deadline (LD program):* rolling/continuous for fall and rolling/continuous for spring.
LD program contact Barbara Mayfield, Coordinator, Union 220, Warrensburg, MO 64093. *Phone:* 660-543-4421. *Fax:* 660-543-4724. *E-mail:* mayfield@emsu1.cmsu.edu.
Application contact Central Missouri State University, Warrensburg, MO 64093. *E-mail:* admit@cmsuvmb.cmsu.edu. *Web address:* http://www.cmsu.edu/.

CENTRAL STATE UNIVERSITY
Wilberforce, Ohio

Students with LD Served by Program	20	ADD/ADHD Services	✓
Staff	3 full-time	Summer Preparation Program	n/a
LD Program or Service Fee	n/a	Alternative Test Arrangements	✓
LD Program Began	1999	LD Student Organization	n/a

Office of Disability Services began offering services in 1999. The program serves approximately 20 undergraduate students. Faculty consists of 3 full-time staff members. Services are provided by academic advisers, counselors, and trained peer tutors.
Policies Students with LD may take up to 18 credit hours per quarter; 12 credit hours per quarter are required to maintain full-time status; 6 credit hours per quarter are required to be eligible for financial aid.
Subject-area tutoring Available in most subjects. Offered one-on-one and in small groups by trained peer tutors.
Counseling and advisement Individual counseling is available. Academic advisement by a staff member affiliated with the program is available.

Central State University (continued)

Auxiliary aids and services *Aids:* calculators, speech recognition programs (e.g., Dragon), tape recorders, taped textbooks. *Services and accommodations:* priority registration, alternative test arrangements, readers, note-takers, and scribes.

ADD/ADHD Students with ADD/ADHD are eligible for the same services available to students with LD, as well as distraction-free study areas and distraction-free testing environments.

Application *Required:* high school transcript, ACT or SAT I (extended-time or untimed test accepted), and letter(s) of recommendation. Upon acceptance, documentation of need for special services should be sent only to your LD program or unit.

LD program contact Vonya Thronton, Director, Office of Disability Services, 1400 Brush Row Road, Wilberforce, OH 45384. *Phone:* 937-376-6411. *Fax:* 937-376-6661. *E-mail:* vthornton@csu. ces.edu.

Application contact Central State University, 1400 Brush Row Road, Wilberforce, OH 45384. *Web address:* http://www. centralstate.edu/.

CENTRAL WASHINGTON UNIVERSITY
Ellensburg, Washington

Students with LD Served by Program	250	ADD/ADHD Services	✓
Staff	3 full-time, 25 part-time	Summer Preparation Program	n/a
LD Program or Service Fee	n/a	Alternative Test Arrangements	✓
LD Program Began	1987	LD Student Organization	✓

Disability Support Services began offering services in 1987. The program serves approximately 250 undergraduate students. Faculty consists of 3 full-time and 25 part-time staff members. Services are provided by regular education teachers, graduate assistants/students, and Director, disability accommodation specialist, office manager.

Policies The college has written policies regarding course substitutions. 10 credits per quarter are required to maintain full-time status; 12 credits per quarter are required to be eligible for financial aid. LD services are also available to graduate students.

Special preparation or orientation Required orientation held before registration, during registration, before classes begin, after classes begin, during summer prior to enrollment, and individually by special arrangement.

Special courses Available in academic survival group. No courses are offered for credit; none enter into overall grade point average.

Counseling and advisement Support groups is available.

Auxiliary aids and services *Aids:* personal computers, screen-enlarging programs, screen readers, tape recorders, taped textbooks. *Services and accommodations:* advocates, priority registration, alternative test arrangements, readers, note-takers, and scribes.

Student organization There is a student organization for students with LD.

ADD/ADHD Students with ADD/ADHD are eligible for the same services available to students with LD, as well as distraction-free study areas, distraction-free testing environments and support groups for ADD/ADHD.

Application *Required:* high school transcript and ACT (extended-time or untimed test accepted). Upon application, documentation of need for special services should be sent only to your LD program or unit. Upon acceptance, documentation of need for special services should be sent only to your LD program or unit. *Application deadline (institutional):* rolling/continuous for fall and rolling/continuous for spring. *Application deadline (LD program):* rolling/continuous for fall and rolling/continuous for spring.

LD program contact Nancy Howard, Interim Director, Disability Support Services, 400 East 8th Avenue, Ellensburg, WA 98926-7431. *Phone:* 509-963-2171. *Fax:* 509-963-3235. *E-mail:* wilsonp@ cwu.edu.

Application contact Central Washington University, Mitchell Hall, Ellensburg, WA 98926-7567. *Web address:* http://www.cwu. edu/.

CHAMPLAIN COLLEGE
Burlington, Vermont

Students with LD Served by Program	50	ADD/ADHD Services	✓
Staff	1 part-time	Summer Preparation Program	n/a
LD Program or Service Fee	n/a	Alternative Test Arrangements	✓
LD Program Began	n/a	LD Student Organization	n/a

Support Services for Students with Disabilities serves approximately 50 undergraduate students. Faculty consists of 1 part-time staff member. Services are provided by counselors.

Policies Students with LD may take up to 18 credit hours per semester; 12 credit hours per semester are required to maintain full-time status; 6 credit hours per semester are required to be eligible for financial aid.

Counseling and advisement Individual counseling is available.

Auxiliary aids and services *Aids:* personal computers, screen-enlarging programs, tape recorders, taped textbooks. *Services and accommodations:* alternative test arrangements, readers, and note-takers.

ADD/ADHD Students with ADD/ADHD are eligible for the same services available to students with LD, as well as medication management.

Application *Required:* high school transcript and ACT or SAT I (extended-time or untimed test accepted). *Recommended:* participation in extracurricular activities, interview, personal statement, and letter(s) of recommendation. Upon application, documentation of need for special services should be sent only to your LD program or unit. Upon acceptance, documentation of need for special services should be sent only to your LD program or unit. *Application deadline (institutional):* rolling/continuous for fall and rolling/continuous for spring. *Application deadline (LD program):* rolling/continuous for fall and rolling/continuous for spring.

LD program contact Rebecca Peterson, Coordinator of Support Services for Students with Disabilities, 163 South Willard Street, Burlington, VT 05401. *Phone:* 802-865-6425. *Fax:* 802-860-2764. *E-mail:* peterson@champlain.edu.

Application contact Champlain College, 163 South Willard Street, Burlington, VT 05401. *E-mail:* admission@champlain. edu. *Web address:* http://www.champlain.edu/.

CITY COLLEGE OF THE CITY UNIVERSITY OF NEW YORK
New York, New York

Students with LD Served by Program	25	ADD/ADHD Services	✓
Staff	2 full-time, 6 part-time	Summer Preparation Program	n/a
LD Program or Service Fee	n/a	Alternative Test Arrangements	✓
LD Program Began	1978	LD Student Organization	n/a

Office of Disability and Student Services began offering services in 1978. The program serves approximately 25 undergraduate students. Faculty consists of 2 full-time and 6 part-time staff members. Services are provided by academic advisers, counselors, graduate assistants/students, and assistive technology specialist.

Policies Students with LD may take up to 18 credit hours per semester; 12 credit hours per semester are required to maintain full-time status; 9 credit hours per semester are required to be eligible for financial aid. LD services are also available to graduate students.

Special preparation or orientation Optional orientation held individually by special arrangement.

Special courses Available in study skills, college survival skills, practical computer skills, test taking, time management, self-advocacy, and stress management. No courses are offered for credit; none enter into overall grade point average.

Counseling and advisement Career counseling, individual counseling, and support groups are available. Academic advisement by a staff member affiliated with the program is available.

Auxiliary aids and services *Aids:* calculators, personal computers, personal spelling/word-use assistants (e.g., Franklin Speller), scan and read programs (e.g., Kurzweil), screen-enlarging programs, screen readers, speech recognition programs (e.g., Dragon), tape recorders, taped textbooks. *Services and accommodations:* advocates, priority registration, alternative test arrangements, and note-takers.

ADD/ADHD Students with ADD/ADHD are eligible for the same services available to students with LD, as well as distraction-free study areas and distraction-free testing environments.

Application *Required:* high school transcript, SAT I (extended-time test accepted), interview, and personal statement. Upon application, documentation of need for special services should be sent only to your LD program or unit. Upon acceptance, documentation of need for special services should be sent only to your LD program or unit.

LD program contact Laura Farres, Disabilities Counselor, Office of Disability and Student Services, B-26 Convent Avenue at 138th Street, New York, NY 10031. *Phone:* 212-650-7060. *Fax:* 212-650-5772.

Application contact City College of the City University of New York, Convent Avenue at 138th Street, New York, NY 10031-9198. *E-mail:* adocc@cunyvm.cuny.edu. *Web address:* http://www.ccny.cuny.edu/.

CLAYTON COLLEGE & STATE UNIVERSITY
Morrow, Georgia

Students with LD Served by Program	5	ADD/ADHD Services	✓
Staff	2 full-time	Summer Preparation Program	n/a
LD Program or Service Fee	n/a	Alternative Test Arrangements	✓
LD Program Began	n/a	LD Student Organization	n/a

Disability Services serves approximately 5 undergraduate students. Faculty consists of 2 full-time staff members. Services are provided by academic advisers and counselors.

Counseling and advisement Academic advisement by a staff member affiliated with the program is available.

Auxiliary aids and services *Aids:* screen-enlarging programs, screen readers, speech recognition programs (e.g., Dragon), taped textbooks. *Services and accommodations:* advocates, priority registration, alternative test arrangements, and note-takers.

ADD/ADHD Students with ADD/ADHD are eligible for the same services available to students with LD, as well as distraction-free testing environments.

Application *Required:* high school transcript and ACT or SAT I (extended-time or untimed test accepted). Upon application, documentation of need for special services should be sent only to your LD program or unit. Upon acceptance, documentation of need for special services should be sent only to your LD program or unit. *Application deadline (institutional):* 7/17 for fall and 12/1 for spring.

LD program contact Gina Phillips, Interim Disability Services Coordinator, 5900 North Lee Street, Morrow, GA 30260. *Phone:* 770-961-3515. *E-mail:* ginaphillips@mail.clayton.edu.

Application contact Carol S. Montgomery, Admissions, Clayton College & State University, 5900 North Lee Street, Morrow, GA 30260-0285. *Phone:* 770-961-3500. *E-mail:* csc-info@ce.clayton.peachnet.edu. *Web address:* http://www.clayton.edu/.

CLEMSON UNIVERSITY
Clemson, South Carolina

Students with LD Served by Program	200	ADD/ADHD Services	✓
Staff	2 full-time, 3 part-time	Summer Preparation Program	n/a
LD Program or Service Fee	n/a	Alternative Test Arrangements	✓
LD Program Began	1988	LD Student Organization	n/a

Student Development Services began offering services in 1988. The program serves approximately 200 undergraduate students. Faculty consists of 2 full-time and 3 part-time staff members. Services are provided by counselors and graduate assistants/students.

Policies The college has written policies regarding course substitutions. LD services are also available to graduate students.

Fees *Diagnostic Testing Fee:* ranges from $300 to $500.

Diagnostic testing Available for auditory processing, spelling, intelligence, personality, reading, written language, social skills, visual processing, and math.

Auxiliary aids and services *Aids:* calculators, scan and read programs (e.g., Kurzweil), screen-enlarging programs, screen readers, speech recognition programs (e.g., Dragon), tape recorders, taped textbooks. *Services and accommodations:* advocates, priority registration, alternative test arrangements, readers, note-takers, and scribes.

ADD/ADHD Students with ADD/ADHD are eligible for the same services available to students with LD, as well as distraction-free testing environments, medication management, personal coach or mentors, and support groups for ADD/ADHD.

Application *Required:* high school transcript and ACT or SAT I (extended-time SAT I test accepted). *Recommended:* participation in extracurricular activities, personal statement, and letter(s) of recommendation. Upon application, documentation of need for special services should be sent only to admissions. Upon acceptance, documentation of need for special services should be sent only to your LD program or unit. *Application deadline (institutional):* 5/1 for fall and 12/15 for spring. *Application deadline (LD program):* rolling/continuous for fall and rolling/continuous for spring.

LD program contact Bonnie Martin, Director, Student Disability Services, 707 University Union, Box 344002, Clemson, SC 29634-4002. *Phone:* 864-656-0515. *Fax:* 864-656-0514. *E-mail:* bmartin@clemson.edu.

Application contact Audrey Bodell, Assistant Director of Admissions, Clemson University, 105 Sikes Hall, PO Box 345124, Clemson, SC 29634. *Phone:* 864-656-2287. *Web address:* http://www.clemson.edu/.

CLEVELAND INSTITUTE OF ART

Cleveland, Ohio

Students with LD Served by Program	30	ADD/ADHD Services	✓
Staff	1 full-time	Summer Preparation Program	n/a
LD Program or Service Fee	n/a	Alternative Test Arrangements	✓
LD Program Began	n/a	LD Student Organization	n/a

Academic Services serves approximately 30 undergraduate students. Faculty consists of 1 full-time staff member. Services are provided by academic advisers, regular education teachers, counselors, and trained peer tutors.

Policies Students with LD may take up to 17 credit hours per term; 12 credit hours per term are required to maintain full-time status and to be eligible for financial aid.

Subject-area tutoring Available in some subjects. Offered one-on-one by trained peer tutors and director of tutoring.

Counseling and advisement Individual counseling is available. Academic advisement by a staff member affiliated with the program is available.

Auxiliary aids and services *Aids:* tape recorders, taped textbooks. *Services and accommodations:* advocates, alternative test arrangements, and note-takers.

ADD/ADHD Students with ADD/ADHD are eligible for the same services available to students with LD, as well as distraction-free testing environments.

Application *Required:* high school transcript, ACT or SAT I (extended-time or untimed test accepted), personal statement, and letter(s) of recommendation. *Recommended:* interview. Upon application, documentation of need for special services should be sent only to your LD program or unit. Upon acceptance, documentation of need for special services should be sent to both admissions and your LD program or unit. *Application deadline (institutional):* rolling/continuous for fall and rolling/continuous for spring.

LD program contact Jill Milenski, Associate Director of Academic Services, 1141 East Boulevard, University Circle, Cleveland, OH 44107. *Phone:* 216-421-7462. *Fax:* 216-754-2557. *E-mail:* jmilenski@gate.cia.edu.

Application contact Office of Admissions, Cleveland Institute of Art, 11141 East Boulevard, Cleveland, OH 44106-1700. *Phone:* 216-421-7418. *E-mail:* 74527.17@compuserve.com. *Web address:* http://www.cia.edu/.

COE COLLEGE

Cedar Rapids, Iowa

Students with LD Served by Program	30	ADD/ADHD Services	✓
Staff	3 full-time, 2 part-time	Summer Preparation Program	✓
LD Program or Service Fee	n/a	Alternative Test Arrangements	✓
LD Program Began	1978	LD Student Organization	n/a

Academic Achievement Program began offering services in 1978. The program serves approximately 30 undergraduate students. Faculty consists of 3 full-time and 2 part-time staff members. Services are provided by counselors, remediation/learning specialists, graduate assistants/students, trained peer tutors, and professional tutors.

Special preparation or orientation Optional summer program offered prior to entering college.

Subject-area tutoring Available in most subjects. Offered one-on-one and in small groups by professional tutors and trained peer tutors.

Counseling and advisement Career counseling and individual counseling are available.

Auxiliary aids and services *Services and accommodations:* advocates, alternative test arrangements, and note-takers.

ADD/ADHD Students with ADD/ADHD are eligible for the same services available to students with LD, as well as distraction-free testing environments.

Application *Required:* high school transcript, ACT or SAT I (extended-time or untimed test accepted), personal statement, and letter(s) of recommendation. *Recommended:* participation in extracurricular activities and interview. Upon application, documentation of need for special services should be sent only to your LD program or unit. Upon acceptance, documentation of need for special services should be sent only to your LD program or unit. *Application deadline (institutional):* 3/1 for spring.

LD program contact Lois Kabela-Coates, Director, Academic Achievement Program, 1220 1st Avenue NE, Cedar Rapids, IA 52402. *Phone:* 319-399-8547. *Fax:* 319-399-8503. *E-mail:* lkabela@coe.edu.

Application contact Coe College, 1220 1st Avenue, NE, Cedar Rapids, IA 52402-5070. *E-mail:* admission@coe.edu. *Web address:* http://www.coe.edu/.

COLBY-SAWYER COLLEGE

New London, New Hampshire

Students with LD Served by Program	75	ADD/ADHD Services	✓
Staff	2 full-time, 5 part-time	Summer Preparation Program	n/a
LD Program or Service Fee	n/a	Alternative Test Arrangements	✓
LD Program Began	1987	LD Student Organization	n/a

Academic Development Center began offering services in 1987. The program serves approximately 75 undergraduate students. Faculty consists of 2 full-time and 5 part-time staff members. Services are provided by LD specialists, trained peer tutors, and professional tutors.

Policies Students with LD may take up to 18 credit hours per semester; 12 credit hours per semester are required to maintain full-time status; 6 credit hours per semester are required to be eligible for financial aid.

Basic skills remediation Available in study skills, time management, social skills, learning strategies, written language, and math. Offered one-on-one by LD specialists and professional tutors.

Subject-area tutoring Available in most subjects. Offered one-on-one by professional tutors, trained peer tutors, and LD specialists.

Counseling and advisement Individual counseling is available.

Auxiliary aids and services *Aids:* personal computers, screen readers, speech recognition programs (e.g., Dragon). *Services and accommodations:* advocates, alternative test arrangements, readers, note-takers, and scribes.

ADD/ADHD Students with ADD/ADHD are eligible for the same services available to students with LD, as well as distraction-free testing environments and personal coach or mentors.

Application *Required:* high school transcript, ACT or SAT I (extended-time or untimed test accepted), personal statement, letter(s) of recommendation, and psychoeducational report (3 years old or less). *Recommended:* interview and documentation of high school services (e.g., Individualized Education Program [IEP] or 504 plan). Upon acceptance, documentation of need for special services should be sent only to your LD program or unit. *Application deadline (institutional):* rolling/continuous for fall and rolling/continuous for spring.

LD program contact Dr. Mary Mar, Director of Learning Services, 100 Main Street, New London, NH 03257. *Phone:* 603-526-3711. *Fax:* 603-526-2135. *E-mail:* mmar@colby-sawyer.edu.

Application contact Colby-Sawyer College, 100 Main Street, New London, NH 03257-4648. *E-mail:* csadmiss@colby-sawyer.edu. *Web address:* http://www.colby-sawyer.edu/.

COLLEGE OF AERONAUTICS
Flushing, New York

Students with LD Served by Program	n/a	ADD/ADHD Services	✓
Staff	6 full-time, 8 part-time	Summer Preparation Program	✓
LD Program or Service Fee	n/a	Alternative Test Arrangements	n/a
LD Program Began	n/a	LD Student Organization	n/a

Academic Support Services faculty consists of 6 full-time and 8 part-time staff members. Services are provided by academic advisers, counselors, and trained peer tutors.

Special preparation or orientation Optional summer program offered prior to entering college.

Basic skills remediation Available in reading, written language, and math. Offered one-on-one, in small groups, and class-size groups by regular education teachers.

Subject-area tutoring Available in most subjects. Offered one-on-one and in small groups by trained peer tutors.

Counseling and advisement Career counseling and individual counseling are available. Academic advisement by a staff member affiliated with the program is available.

Auxiliary aids and services *Services and accommodations:* advocates, readers, and note-takers.

ADD/ADHD Students with ADD/ADHD are eligible for the same services available to students with LD

Application *Required:* high school transcript, interview, psychoeducational report, and documentation of high school services (e.g., Individualized Education Program [IEP] or 504 plan). *Recommended:* SAT I. Upon application, documentation of need for special services should be sent to both admissions and your LD program or unit.

LD program contact Sharon McPartland, Coordinator, 8601 23rd Avenue, East Elmhurst, NY 11369. *Phone:* 718-429-6600 Ext. 155. *Fax:* 718-429-0256. *E-mail:* mcpartland@aero.edu.

Application contact Vincent J. Montera, Director of Admissions, College of Aeronautics, 8601 23rd Avenue, Flushing, NY 11369-1037. *Phone:* 718-429-6600 Ext. 188. *E-mail:* pro@aero.edu. *Web address:* http://www.aero.edu/.

THE COLLEGE OF NEW JERSEY
Ewing, New Jersey

Students with LD Served by Program	75	ADD/ADHD Services	✓
Staff	1 full-time, 1 part-time	Summer Preparation Program	n/a
LD Program or Service Fee	n/a	Alternative Test Arrangements	✓
LD Program Began	1988	LD Student Organization	n/a

Office of Differing Abilities Services began offering services in 1988. The program serves approximately 75 undergraduate students. Faculty consists of 1 full-time and 1 part-time staff member. Services are provided by counselors, graduate assistants/students, trained peer tutors, and director.

Policies Students with LD may take up to 18 credit hours per semester; 9 credit hours per semester are required to maintain full-time status; 12 semester hours per semester are required to be eligible for financial aid. LD services are also available to graduate students.

Subject-area tutoring Available in most subjects. Offered one-on-one and in small groups by graduate assistants/students and trained peer tutors.

Counseling and advisement Career counseling, individual counseling, small-group counseling, and support groups are available.

Auxiliary aids and services *Aids:* scan and read programs (e.g., Kurzweil), speech recognition programs (e.g., Dragon), tape recorders, taped textbooks. *Services and accommodations:* advocates, alternative test arrangements, readers, and note-takers.

ADD/ADHD Students with ADD/ADHD are eligible for the same services available to students with LD, as well as distraction-free testing environments.

Application *Required:* high school transcript, ACT (extended-time or untimed test accepted), SAT I (extended-time or untimed test accepted), personal statement, and letter(s) of recommendation. *Recommended:* participation in extracurricular activities. Upon acceptance, documentation of need for special services should be sent only to your LD program or unit. *Application deadline (institutional):* 2/15 for fall and 11/1 for spring. *Application deadline (LD program):* 2/15 for fall and 11/1 for spring.

LD program contact Ann DeGennaro, Director, PO Box 7718, 159 Community Commons, Ewing, NJ 08628-0718. *Phone:* 609-771-2571. *Fax:* 609-637-5131. *E-mail:* degennar@tcnj.edu.

Application contact The College of New Jersey, PO Box 7718, Ewing, NJ 08628. *E-mail:* admiss@vm.tcnj.edu. *Web address:* http://www.tcnj.edu/.

COLLEGE OF NOTRE DAME OF MARYLAND
Baltimore, Maryland

Students with LD Served by Program	20	ADD/ADHD Services	✓
Staff	1 part-time	Summer Preparation Program	n/a
LD Program or Service Fee	n/a	Alternative Test Arrangements	✓
LD Program Began	1994	LD Student Organization	✓

Disability Services began offering services in 1994. The program serves approximately 20 undergraduate students. Faculty consists of 1 part-time staff member. Services are provided by counselors.

Policies Students with LD may take up to 17 credits per semester; 12 credit hours per semester are required to maintain full-time status and to be eligible for financial aid. LD services are also available to graduate students.

Basic skills remediation Available in study skills, time management, and social skills. Offered one-on-one by counselor.

Counseling and advisement Career counseling and individual counseling are available.

Auxiliary aids and services *Aids:* calculators, personal computers, personal spelling/word-use assistants (e.g., Franklin Speller), tape recorders, taped textbooks. *Services and accommodations:* alternative test arrangements, readers, and note-takers.

Student organization There is a student organization for students with LD.

ADD/ADHD Students with ADD/ADHD are eligible for the same services available to students with LD

College of Notre Dame of Maryland (continued)

Application *Required:* high school transcript, ACT or SAT I (extended-time or untimed test accepted), letter(s) of recommendation, and essay. *Recommended:* participation in extracurricular activities, interview, personal statement, psychoeducational report, and documentation of high school services (e.g., Individualized Education Program [IEP] or 504 plan). Upon application, documentation of need for special services should be sent to both admissions and your LD program or unit. Upon acceptance, documentation of need for special services should be sent to both admissions and your LD program or unit. *Application deadline (institutional):* rolling/continuous for fall and rolling/continuous for spring.

LD program contact Dr. Angelita M. Yu, Coordinator of Disability Services, 4701 North Charles Street, Baltimore, MD 21210. *Phone:* 410-532-5379. *Fax:* 410-532-5622. *E-mail:* ayu@ndm.edu.

Application contact College of Notre Dame of Maryland, 4701 North Charles Street, Baltimore, MD 21210-2476. *E-mail:* admiss@ndm.edu. *Web address:* http://www.ndm.edu/.

THE COLLEGE OF SAINT ROSE
Albany, New York

Students with LD Served by Program	50	ADD/ADHD Services	✓
Staff	1 full-time	Summer Preparation Program	n/a
LD Program or Service Fee	n/a	Alternative Test Arrangements	✓
LD Program Began	1985	LD Student Organization	n/a

Services to Students with Disabilities began offering services in 1985. The program serves approximately 50 undergraduate students. Faculty consists of 1 full-time staff member. Services are provided by academic advisers, counselors, and trained peer tutors.

Policies LD services are also available to graduate students.

Special preparation or orientation Optional orientation held before classes begin and individually by special arrangement.

Basic skills remediation Available in reading. Offered one-on-one by computer-based instruction.

Subject-area tutoring Available in most subjects. Offered one-on-one and in small groups by graduate assistants/students and trained peer tutors.

Counseling and advisement Career counseling, individual counseling, small-group counseling, and support groups are available. Academic advisement by a staff member affiliated with the program is available.

Auxiliary aids and services *Aids:* scan and read programs (e.g., Kurzweil), screen-enlarging programs, screen readers, tape recorders, taped textbooks. *Services and accommodations:* alternative test arrangements, readers, note-takers, and scribes.

ADD/ADHD Students with ADD/ADHD are eligible for the same services available to students with LD, as well as distraction-free testing environments.

Application *Required:* high school transcript, participation in extracurricular activities, ACT (extended-time test accepted), SAT I (extended-time test accepted), interview, personal statement, and letter(s) of recommendation. Upon application, documentation of need for special services should be sent only to your LD program or unit. Upon acceptance, documentation of need for special services should be sent only to your LD program or unit. *Application deadline (institutional):* rolling/continuous for fall and rolling/continuous for spring.

LD program contact Mary Van Derzee, Director, Services to Students with Disabilities, 432 Western Avenue, Albany, NY 12203. *Phone:* 518-454-5299. *Fax:* 518-438-3293.

Application contact Mary Elizabeth Amico, Associate Dean of Admissions and Enrollment Services, The College of Saint Rose, 432 Western Avenue, Albany, NY 12203-1419. *Phone:* 518-454-5150. *E-mail:* admit@rosnet.strose.edu. *Web address:* http://www.strose.edu/.

THE COLLEGE OF ST. SCHOLASTICA
Duluth, Minnesota

Students with LD Served by Program	15	ADD/ADHD Services	✓
Staff	1 part-time	Summer Preparation Program	n/a
LD Program or Service Fee	n/a	Alternative Test Arrangements	✓
LD Program Began	1989	LD Student Organization	n/a

Access Center of Academic Support Services began offering services in 1989. The program serves approximately 15 undergraduate students. Faculty consists of 1 part-time staff member. Services are provided by academic advisers.

Policies The college has written policies regarding course substitutions and substitution and waivers of requirements for admission and graduation. Students with LD may take up to 18 credits per semester; 12 credits per semester are required to maintain full-time status and to be eligible for financial aid. LD services are also available to graduate students.

Diagnostic testing Available for intelligence and learning styles.

Basic skills remediation Available in study skills, reading, time management, and learning strategies. Offered one-on-one by trained peer tutors.

Subject-area tutoring Available in some subjects. Offered one-on-one by trained peer tutors.

Counseling and advisement Individual counseling is available. Academic advisement by a staff member affiliated with the program is available.

Auxiliary aids and services *Aids:* scan and read programs (e.g., Kurzweil), screen-enlarging programs, speech recognition programs (e.g., Dragon), taped textbooks. *Services and accommodations:* priority registration, alternative test arrangements, readers, note-takers, and scribes.

ADD/ADHD Students with ADD/ADHD are eligible for the same services available to students with LD, as well as distraction-free testing environments.

Application *Required:* high school transcript and ACT or SAT I (extended-time tests accepted). Upon application, documentation of need for special services should be sent only to your LD program or unit. Upon acceptance, documentation of need for special services should be sent only to your LD program or unit. *Application deadline (institutional):* rolling/continuous for fall and rolling/continuous for spring. *Application deadline (LD program):* rolling/continuous for fall and rolling/continuous for spring.

LD program contact Jay Newcomb, Director of Academic Support Services, 1200 Kenwood Avenue, Duluth, MN 55811. *Phone:* 218-723-6552. *Fax:* 218-723-6482. *E-mail:* njewcomb@css.edu.

Application contact The College of St. Scholastica, 1200 Kenwood Avenue, Duluth, MN 55811-4199. *E-mail:* admissions@css1.css.edu. *Web address:* http://www.css.edu/.

COLLEGE OF STATEN ISLAND OF THE CITY UNIVERSITY OF NEW YORK

Staten Island, New York

Students with LD Served by Program	125	ADD/ADHD Services	✓
Staff	2 full-time, 2 part-time	Summer Preparation Program	✓
LD Program or Service Fee	n/a	Alternative Test Arrangements	✓
LD Program Began	n/a	LD Student Organization	n/a

Office of Disability Services serves approximately 125 undergraduate students. Faculty consists of 2 full-time and 2 part-time staff members. Services are provided by academic advisers and counselors.

Policies The college has written policies regarding course substitutions and substitution and waivers of requirements for admission and graduation. 12 credit hours per semester are required to maintain full-time status; 6 credit hours per semester are required to be eligible for financial aid. LD services are also available to graduate students.

Special preparation or orientation Summer program offered prior to entering college. Optional orientation held after classes begin.

Basic skills remediation Available in study skills, computer skills, reading, learning strategies, spelling, written language, and math. Offered one-on-one by trained peer tutors.

Subject-area tutoring Available in most subjects. Offered one-on-one by trained peer tutors.

Counseling and advisement Individual counseling is available. Academic advisement by a staff member affiliated with the program is available.

Auxiliary aids and services *Aids:* calculators, personal computers, personal spelling/word-use assistants (e.g., Franklin Speller), scan and read programs (e.g., Kurzweil), screen-enlarging programs, screen readers, tape recorders. *Services and accommodations:* advocates, priority registration, alternative test arrangements, readers, and scribes.

ADD/ADHD Students with ADD/ADHD are eligible for the same services available to students with LD, as well as distraction-free study areas and distraction-free testing environments.

Application *Required:* high school transcript, psychoeducational report (5 years old or less), and documentation of high school services (e.g., Individualized Education Program [IEP] or 504 plan). *Recommended:* SAT I (extended-time or untimed test accepted). Upon application, documentation of need for special services should be sent only to your LD program or unit. Upon acceptance, documentation of need for special services should be sent only to your LD program or unit. *Application deadline (institutional):* rolling/continuous for fall and rolling/continuous for spring. *Application deadline (LD program):* rolling/continuous for fall and rolling/continuous for spring.

LD program contact Margaret Venditti, Coordinator for Office of Disability Services, 2800 Victory Boulevard, Staten Island, NY 10314. *Phone:* 718-982-2513. *Fax:* 718-982-2117. *E-mail:* venditti@postbox.csi.cuny.edu.

Application contact Earl Teasley, Director of Admissions and Recruitment, College of Staten Island of the City University of New York, 2800 Victory Boulevard, Staten Island, NY 10314-6600. *Phone:* 718-982-2011. *Web address:* http://www.csi.cuny.edu/.

COLORADO CHRISTIAN UNIVERSITY

Lakewood, Colorado

Students with LD Served by Program	20	ADD/ADHD Services	✓
Staff	2 full-time, 3 part-time	Summer Preparation Program	n/a
LD Program or Service Fee	n/a	Alternative Test Arrangements	n/a
LD Program Began	n/a	LD Student Organization	n/a

Academic Support and Testing Center serves approximately 20 undergraduate students. Faculty consists of 2 full-time and 3 part-time staff members. Services are provided by regular education teachers and trained peer tutors.

Policies 12 credit hours per semester are required to maintain full-time status and to be eligible for financial aid. LD services are also available to graduate students.

Basic skills remediation Available in reading, time management, learning strategies, written language, and math. Offered in class-size groups by regular education teachers.

Subject-area tutoring Available in most subjects. Offered one-on-one and in small groups by trained peer tutors.

ADD/ADHD Students with ADD/ADHD are eligible for the same services available to students with LD, as well as distraction-free testing environments.

Application *Required:* high school transcript, interview, personal statement, letter(s) of recommendation, and psychoeducational report (2 years old or less). *Recommended:* participation in extracurricular activities and ACT (extended-time or untimed test accepted). Upon acceptance, documentation of need for special services should be sent only to your LD program or unit. *Application deadline (institutional):* 3/1 for fall and 12/15 for spring.

LD program contact Joanne Lambert, Testing and Learning Assistance Coordinator, 160 South Garrison Street, Lakewood, CO 80226. *Phone:* 303-963-3266. *Fax:* 303-274-7560. *E-mail:* jlambert@ccu.edu.

Application contact Colorado Christian University, 180 South Garrison Street, Lakewood, CO 80226-7499. *E-mail:* admissions@ccu.edu. *Web address:* http://www.ccu.edu/.

COLORADO STATE UNIVERSITY

Fort Collins, Colorado

Students with LD Served by Program	425	ADD/ADHD Services	✓
Staff	5 full-time, 2 part-time	Summer Preparation Program	n/a
LD Program or Service Fee	n/a	Alternative Test Arrangements	✓
LD Program Began	1983	LD Student Organization	n/a

Resources for Disabled Students began offering services in 1983. The program serves approximately 425 undergraduate students. Faculty consists of 5 full-time and 2 part-time staff members. Services are provided by academic advisers, counselors, diagnostic specialists, and trained peer tutors.

Policies The college has written policies regarding course substitutions. Students with LD may take up to 18 credit hours per semester; 12 credit hours per semester are required to maintain full-time status; 9 credit hours per semester are required to be eligible for financial aid. LD services are also available to graduate students.

Diagnostic testing Available for auditory processing, spelling, neuropsychological, intelligence, personality, study skills, learning strategies, reading, written language, learning styles, social skills, visual processing, and math.

Colorado State University (continued)

Subject-area tutoring Available in most subjects. Offered one-on-one and in small groups by computer-based instruction and trained peer tutors.

Special courses Available in written composition skills. All courses are offered for credit; all enter into overall grade point average.

Counseling and advisement Career counseling, individual counseling, small-group counseling, and support groups are available. Academic advisement by a staff member affiliated with the program is available.

Auxiliary aids and services *Aids:* scan and read programs (e.g., Kurzweil), screen-enlarging programs, screen readers, speech recognition programs (e.g., Dragon), tape recorders, taped textbooks. *Services and accommodations:* advocates, priority registration, alternative test arrangements, readers, note-takers, and scribes.

ADD/ADHD Students with ADD/ADHD are eligible for the same services available to students with LD, as well as distraction-free testing environments.

Application *Required:* high school transcript, ACT or SAT I (extended-time tests accepted), and psychoeducational report. *Recommended:* participation in extracurricular activities, personal statement, and documentation of high school services (e.g., Individualized Education Program [IEP] or 504 plan). Upon acceptance, documentation of need for special services should be sent only to your LD program or unit. *Application deadline (institutional):* 7/1 for fall and 12/1 for spring.

LD program contact Kathleen Ivy, Counselor, 100 General Services, Resources for Disabled Students, Fort Collins, CO 80523. *Phone:* 970-491-6385. *Fax:* 970-491-3457. *E-mail:* kivy@lamar.colostate.edu.

Application contact Colorado State University, Spruce Hall, Fort Collins, CO 80523-0015. *E-mail:* admissions@vines.colostate.edu. *Web address:* http://www.colostate.edu/.

COLUMBIA COLLEGE
New York, New York

Students with LD Served by Program	100	ADD/ADHD Services	✓
Staff	3 full-time, 5 part-time	Summer Preparation Program	n/a
LD Program or Service Fee	n/a	Alternative Test Arrangements	✓
LD Program Began	1990	LD Student Organization	✓

Disability Services began offering services in 1990. The program serves approximately 100 undergraduate students. Faculty consists of 3 full-time and 5 part-time staff members. Services are provided by professional disability services staff.

Policies The college has written policies regarding course substitutions. LD services are also available to graduate students.

Basic skills remediation Available in study skills, reading, time management, visual processing, and learning strategies. Offered one-on-one and in small groups by professional tutors and professional staff.

Subject-area tutoring Available in most subjects. Offered one-on-one and in small groups by professional disability services staff.

Counseling and advisement Career counseling, individual counseling, small-group counseling, and support groups are available.

Auxiliary aids and services *Aids:* calculators, personal spelling/word-use assistants (e.g., Franklin Speller), screen-enlarging programs, tape recorders, taped textbooks. *Services and accommodations:* advocates, priority registration, alternative test arrangements, readers, note-takers, and scribes.

Student organization There is a student organization for students with LD.

ADD/ADHD Students with ADD/ADHD are eligible for the same services available to students with LD, as well as distraction-free study areas, distraction-free testing environments and support groups for ADD/ADHD.

Application *Required:* high school transcript, participation in extracurricular activities, ACT or SAT I (extended-time or untimed test accepted), personal statement, and letter(s) of recommendation. Upon acceptance, documentation of need for special services should be sent only to your LD program or unit. *Application deadline (institutional):* 1/3 for fall.

LD program contact Dr. Lynne M. Bejoian, Director, 2920 Broadway, Lerner Hall Suite 802 MC2605, New York, NY 10027. *Phone:* 212-854-2388. *Fax:* 212-854-3488. *E-mail:* disability@columbia.edu.

Application contact Columbia College, 212 Hamilton Hall, New York, NY 10027. *E-mail:* ugrad-admiss@columbia.edu. *Web address:* http://www.columbia.edu/.

COLUMBIA COLLEGE CHICAGO
Chicago, Illinois

Students with LD Served by Program	75	ADD/ADHD Services	✓
Staff	2 full-time, 2 part-time	Summer Preparation Program	n/a
LD Program or Service Fee	n/a	Alternative Test Arrangements	✓
LD Program Began	n/a	LD Student Organization	n/a

Student Support Services/Conaway Achievement Project serves approximately 75 undergraduate students. Faculty consists of 2 full-time and 2 part-time staff members. Services are provided by counselors, LD specialists, and professional tutors.

Policies 12 credit hours per semester are required to maintain full-time status and to be eligible for financial aid.

Subject-area tutoring Available in some subjects. Offered one-on-one by professional tutors and LD specialists.

Counseling and advisement Career counseling, individual counseling, small-group counseling, and support groups are available.

Auxiliary aids and services *Aids:* calculators, personal spelling/word-use assistants (e.g., Franklin Speller), speech recognition programs (e.g., Dragon), tape recorders. *Services and accommodations:* advocates, priority registration, alternative test arrangements, readers, note-takers, and scribes.

ADD/ADHD Students with ADD/ADHD are eligible for the same services available to students with LD, as well as distraction-free study areas, distraction-free testing environments, personal coach or mentors, and support groups for ADD/ADHD.

Application *Required:* high school transcript and personal statement. *Recommended:* ACT or SAT I. Upon application, documentation of need for special services should be sent only to your LD program or unit. Upon acceptance, documentation of need for special services should be sent only to your LD program or unit. *Application deadline (institutional):* rolling/continuous for fall and rolling/continuous for spring. *Application deadline (LD program):* rolling/continuous for fall and rolling/continuous for spring.

LD program contact Marc K. Malone, Director of Conaway Achievement Project, 600 South Michigan Avenue, Chicago, IL 60605. *Phone:* 312-344-8132. *Fax:* 312-344-8005. *E-mail:* mmalone@popmail.colum.edu.

Application contact Columbia College Chicago, 600 South Michigan Avenue, Chicago, IL 60605-1997. *E-mail:* admissions@mail.colum.edu. *Web address:* http://www.colum.edu/.

COLUMBUS STATE UNIVERSITY

Columbus, Georgia

Students with LD Served by Program	10	ADD/ADHD Services	✓
Staff	1 full-time, 1 part-time	Summer Preparation Program	n/a
LD Program or Service Fee	n/a	Alternative Test Arrangements	✓
LD Program Began	n/a	LD Student Organization	✓

Office of Disability Services serves approximately 10 undergraduate students. Faculty consists of 1 full-time and 1 part-time staff member. Services are provided by academic advisers and graduate assistants/students.

Policies The college has written policies regarding course substitutions, grade forgiveness, and substitution and waivers of requirements for admission and graduation. Students with LD may take up to 15 credit hours per semester; 12 credits per semester are required to maintain full-time status; 6 credits per semester are required to be eligible for financial aid. LD services are also available to graduate students.

Fees *Diagnostic Testing Fee:* $300.

Diagnostic testing Available for auditory processing, motor skills, spelling, intelligence, personality, study skills, learning strategies, reading, written language, learning styles, visual processing, and math.

Basic skills remediation Available in reading, math, and English. Offered in class-size groups by regular education teachers.

Subject-area tutoring Available in most subjects. Offered one-on-one and in small groups by graduate assistants/students.

Special courses Available in career planning, study skills, college survival skills, test taking, time management, and learning strategies. No courses are offered for credit; none enter into overall grade point average.

Counseling and advisement Career counseling, individual counseling, small-group counseling, and support groups are available. Academic advisement by a staff member affiliated with the program is available.

Auxiliary aids and services *Aids:* calculators, personal computers, scan and read programs (e.g., Kurzweil), screen-enlarging programs, screen readers, speech recognition programs (e.g., Dragon), tape recorders, taped textbooks. *Services and accommodations:* priority registration, alternative test arrangements, readers, note-takers, and scribes.

Student organization There is a student organization for students with LD.

ADD/ADHD Students with ADD/ADHD are eligible for the same services available to students with LD, as well as distraction-free study areas and distraction-free testing environments.

Application *Required:* high school transcript, participation in extracurricular activities, ACT or SAT I (extended-time tests accepted), and psychoeducational report (5 years old or less). *Recommended:* documentation of high school services (e.g., Individualized Education Program [IEP] or 504 plan). Upon application, documentation of need for special services should be sent only to your LD program or unit. Upon acceptance, documentation of need for special services should be sent only to your LD program or unit. *Application deadline (institutional):* 8/4 for fall and 12/17 for spring.

LD program contact Aracelis Williams, Coordinator, Office of Disability Services, 4225 University Avenue, Columbus, GA 31907. *Phone:* 706-568-2330. *Fax:* 706-569-3096. *E-mail:* williams_aracelis@colstate.edu.

Application contact Susan Webb, Admission Counselor, Columbus State University, 4225 University Avenue, Columbus, GA 31907-5645. *Phone:* 706-568-2035. *Web address:* http://www.colstate.edu/.

COMMUNITY HOSPITAL OF ROANOKE VALLEY-COLLEGE OF HEALTH SCIENCES

Roanoke, Virginia

Students with LD Served by Program	40	ADD/ADHD Services	✓
Staff	1 full-time, 5 part-time	Summer Preparation Program	n/a
LD Program or Service Fee	n/a	Alternative Test Arrangements	✓
LD Program Began	1988	LD Student Organization	n/a

Disabled Student Services began offering services in 1988. The program serves approximately 40 undergraduate students. Faculty consists of 1 full-time and 5 part-time staff members. Services are provided by academic advisers, remediation/learning specialists, counselors, regular education teachers, graduate assistants/students, trained peer tutors, and professional tutors.

Policies The college has written policies regarding course substitutions, grade forgiveness, and substitution and waivers of requirements for admission and graduation. Students with LD may take up to 21 credit hours per semester; 12 credit hours per semester are required to maintain full-time status; 9 credit hours per semester are required to be eligible for financial aid.

Special preparation or orientation Optional orientation held before registration, during registration, before classes begin, after classes begin, during summer prior to enrollment, and individually by special arrangement.

Diagnostic testing Available for personality, study skills, learning strategies, reading, written language, learning styles, and math.

Basic skills remediation Available in study skills, computer skills, reading, time management, social skills, learning strategies, spelling, written language, and math. Offered one-on-one and in small groups by computer-based instruction, regular education teachers, and LD specialists.

Subject-area tutoring Available in some subjects. Offered one-on-one by computer-based instruction, professional tutors, and trained peer tutors.

Special courses Available in oral communication skills, study skills, college survival skills, test taking, health and nutrition, reading, time management, self-advocacy, stress management, and written composition skills. All courses are offered for credit; all enter into overall grade point average.

Counseling and advisement Career counseling and individual counseling are available. Academic advisement by a staff member affiliated with the program is available.

Auxiliary aids and services *Aids:* calculators, personal computers, scan and read programs (e.g., Kurzweil), speech recognition programs (e.g., Dragon), tape recorders, taped textbooks. *Services and accommodations:* priority registration, alternative test arrangements, readers, and note-takers.

ADD/ADHD Students with ADD/ADHD are eligible for the same services available to students with LD, as well as distraction-free study areas, distraction-free testing environments and personal coach or mentors.

Application *Required:* high school transcript, interview, personal statement, letter(s) of recommendation, and psychoeducational report (3 years old or less). *Recommended:* participation in extracurricular activities and documentation of high school services (e.g., Individualized Education Program [IEP] or 504 plan). Upon application, documentation of need for special services should be sent to both admissions and your LD program or unit. Upon acceptance, documentation of need for special services should be sent only to your LD program or unit. *Application deadline (institutional):* rolling/continuous for fall

Community Hospital of Roanoke Valley-College of Health Sciences (continued)

and rolling/continuous for spring. *Application deadline (LD program):* rolling/continuous for fall and rolling/continuous for spring.

LD program contact Dr. Dave Wiggins, Coordinator of Counseling, PO Box 13186, Roanoke, VA 24031-3186. *Phone:* 540-985-8501. *Fax:* 540-985-9773. *E-mail:* dwiggins@health.chs.edu.

Application contact Heather Todd, Admissions Representative, Community Hospital of Roanoke Valley-College of Health Sciences, PO Box 13186, Roanoke, VA 24031-3186. *Phone:* 540-985-8449. *E-mail:* rrobertson@health.chs.edu. *Web address:* http://www.chs.edu/.

CONCORDIA UNIVERSITY AT AUSTIN
Austin, Texas

Students with LD Served by Program	23	ADD/ADHD Services	✓
Staff	1 full-time	Summer Preparation Program	n/a
LD Program or Service Fee	n/a	Alternative Test Arrangements	✓
LD Program Began	1999	LD Student Organization	n/a

Concordia Student Success Center (CSSC) began offering services in 1999. The program serves approximately 23 undergraduate students. Faculty consists of 1 full-time staff member. Services are provided by academic advisers, remediation/learning specialists, counselors, regular education teachers, LD specialists, and trained peer tutors.

Policies Students with LD may take up to 18 credit hours per long semester; 12 credit hours per long semester are required to maintain full-time status and to be eligible for financial aid.

Special preparation or orientation Optional orientation held during registration, after classes begin, and individually by special arrangement.

Basic skills remediation Available in study skills, time management, learning strategies, written language, and math. Offered one-on-one, in small groups, and class-size groups by trained peer tutors and faculty.

Subject-area tutoring Available in most subjects. Offered one-on-one and in small groups by computer-based instruction, trained peer tutors, LD specialists, and faculty.

Counseling and advisement Career counseling and individual counseling are available. Academic advisement by a staff member affiliated with the program is available.

Auxiliary aids and services *Aids:* personal computers, tape recorders. *Services and accommodations:* alternative test arrangements and note-takers.

ADD/ADHD Students with ADD/ADHD are eligible for the same services available to students with LD, as well as distraction-free study areas, distraction-free testing environments and personal coach or mentors.

Application *Required:* high school transcript, ACT or SAT I (extended-time or untimed test accepted), psychoeducational report (3 years old or less), and documentation of high school services (e.g., Individualized Education Program [IEP] or 504 plan). *Recommended:* participation in extracurricular activities and interview. Upon application, documentation of need for special services should be sent only to your LD program or unit. Upon acceptance, documentation of need for special services should be sent only to your LD program or unit. *Application deadline (institutional):* rolling/continuous for fall and rolling/continuous for spring. *Application deadline (LD program):* rolling/continuous for fall and rolling/continuous for spring.

LD program contact Dr. Beryl A. Dunsmoir, Chair, Behavioral Sciences/Director, Concordia Student Success Center, 3400 IH 35 North, Austin, TX 78705-2799. *Phone:* 512-436-1132. *Fax:* 512-439-8517. *E-mail:* drbad@concordia.edu.

Application contact Concordia University at Austin, 3400 Interstate 35 North, Austin, TX 78705-2799. *E-mail:* ctxadmis@crf.cuis.edu. *Web address:* http://www.concordia.edu/.

CONNECTICUT COLLEGE
New London, Connecticut

Students with LD Served by Program	100	ADD/ADHD Services	✓
Staff	1 full-time, 1 part-time	Summer Preparation Program	n/a
LD Program or Service Fee	n/a	Alternative Test Arrangements	✓
LD Program Began	n/a	LD Student Organization	n/a

Office of Disability Services (ODS) serves approximately 100 undergraduate students. Faculty consists of 1 full-time and 1 part-time staff member. Services are provided by diagnostic specialists, graduate assistants/students, LD specialists, trained peer tutors, and undergraduate aides.

Policies Students with LD may take up to 21 credit hours per semester; 12 credit hours per semester are required to maintain full-time status. LD services are also available to graduate students.

Diagnostic testing Available for auditory processing, spelling, neuropsychological, intelligence, study skills, learning strategies, written language, visual processing, math, and cognitive processing/achievement.

Auxiliary aids and services *Aids:* tape recorders. *Services and accommodations:* advocates, priority registration, alternative test arrangements, readers, note-takers, and scribes.

ADD/ADHD Students with ADD/ADHD are eligible for the same services available to students with LD, as well as distraction-free testing environments, personal coach or mentors, and support groups for ADD/ADHD.

Application *Required:* high school transcript and personal statement. *Recommended:* participation in extracurricular activities, SAT I (extended-time or untimed test accepted), and interview. Upon acceptance, documentation of need for special services should be sent only to your LD program or unit. *Application deadline (institutional):* 1/1 for fall and 11/15 for spring.

LD program contact Dr. Susan L. Duques, Director of Disability Services, Box 5264, 270 Mohegan Avenue, New London, CT 06320-4196. *Phone:* 860-439-5428. *Fax:* 860-439-5430. *E-mail:* slduq@conncoll.edu.

Application contact Connecticut College, 270 Mohegan Avenue, New London, CT 06320-4196. *E-mail:* admit@conncoll.edu. *Web address:* http://www.camel.conncoll.edu/.

CORNELL UNIVERSITY
Ithaca, New York

Students with LD Served by Program	250	ADD/ADHD Services	✓
Staff	2 full-time	Summer Preparation Program	n/a
LD Program or Service Fee	n/a	Alternative Test Arrangements	✓
LD Program Began	1978	LD Student Organization	✓

Student Disability Services began offering services in 1978. The program serves approximately 250 undergraduate students. Faculty consists of 2 full-time staff members. Services are provided by Director and Assistant Director, Student Disability Services.

Policies LD services are also available to graduate students.

Subject-area tutoring Available in all subjects. Offered one-on-one and in small groups by professional tutors and trained peer tutors.

Auxiliary aids and services *Aids:* scan and read programs (e.g., Kurzweil), screen-enlarging programs, screen readers, speech recognition programs (e.g., Dragon), tape recorders, taped textbooks. *Services and accommodations:* priority registration, alternative test arrangements, readers, note-takers, and scribes.

Student organization There is a student organization for students with LD.

ADD/ADHD Students with ADD/ADHD are eligible for the same services available to students with LD, as well as distraction-free testing environments and support groups for ADD/ADHD.

Application *Required:* high school transcript, ACT or SAT I (extended-time or untimed test accepted), interview, personal statement, letter(s) of recommendation, and SAT II. *Recommended:* participation in extracurricular activities. Upon acceptance, documentation of need for special services should be sent only to your LD program or unit. *Application deadline (institutional):* 1/1 for fall and 11/1 for spring.

LD program contact Student Disability Services Office, 424 CCC, Ithaca, NY 14853-2801. *Phone:* 607-254-4545. *Fax:* 607-255-1562. *E-mail:* fjei@cornell.edu.

Application contact Cornell University, 410 Thurston Avenue, Ithaca, NY 14850. *E-mail:* admissions_mailbox@cornell.edu. *Web address:* http://www.cornell.edu/.

CREIGHTON UNIVERSITY
Omaha, Nebraska

Students with LD Served by Program	110	ADD/ADHD Services	✓
Staff	5 full-time, 5 part-time	Summer Preparation Program	n/a
LD Program or Service Fee	n/a	Alternative Test Arrangements	✓
LD Program Began	n/a	LD Student Organization	n/a

Services for Students with Disabilities serves approximately 110 undergraduate students. Faculty consists of 5 full-time and 5 part-time staff members. Services are provided by counselors, diagnostic specialists, trained peer tutors, and professional tutors.

Policies 12 credit hours per semester are required to maintain full-time status; 6 credit hours per semester are required to be eligible for financial aid. LD services are also available to graduate students.

Diagnostic testing Available for auditory processing, motor skills, spelling, handwriting, spoken language, intelligence, personality, study skills, learning strategies, reading, written language, learning styles, visual processing, and math.

Subject-area tutoring Available in most subjects. Offered one-on-one and in small groups by professional tutors and trained peer tutors.

Counseling and advisement Individual counseling is available.

Auxiliary aids and services *Aids:* calculators, personal computers, personal spelling/word-use assistants (e.g., Franklin Speller), scan and read programs (e.g., Kurzweil), screen-enlarging programs, screen readers, tape recorders, taped textbooks. *Services and accommodations:* advocates, priority registration, alternative test arrangements, readers, note-takers, and scribes.

ADD/ADHD Students with ADD/ADHD are eligible for the same services available to students with LD, as well as distraction-free testing environments.

Application *Required:* high school transcript and ACT or SAT I (extended-time tests accepted). *Recommended:* participation in extracurricular activities, personal statement, and letter(s) of

recommendation. Upon application, documentation of need for special services should be sent only to your LD program or unit. Upon acceptance, documentation of need for special services should be sent only to your LD program or unit. *Application deadline (institutional):* rolling/continuous for fall and rolling/continuous for spring. *Application deadline (LD program):* rolling/continuous for fall and rolling/continuous for spring.

LD program contact Wade Pearson, Director, Services for Students with Disabilities, 7800 California Plaza, Omaha, NE 68178. *Phone:* 402-280-2749. *Fax:* 402-280-5579.

Application contact Creighton University, 2500 California Plaza, Omaha, NE 68178-0001. *E-mail:* admissions@creighton.edu. *Web address:* http://www.creighton.edu/.

THE CULINARY INSTITUTE OF AMERICA
Hyde Park, New York

Students with LD Served by Program	150	ADD/ADHD Services	✓
Staff	4 full-time	Summer Preparation Program	n/a
LD Program or Service Fee	n/a	Alternative Test Arrangements	✓
LD Program Began	n/a	LD Student Organization	n/a

The Learning Strategies Center serves approximately 150 undergraduate students. Faculty consists of 4 full-time staff members. Services are provided by remediation/learning specialists, special education teachers, LD specialists, and trained peer tutors.

Policies Students with LD may take up to 16 credit hours per semester; 12 credit hours per semester are required to maintain full-time status and to be eligible for financial aid.

Subject-area tutoring Available in all subjects. Offered one-on-one and in small groups by trained peer tutors and LD specialists.

Special courses Available in study skills. No courses are offered for credit; none enter into overall grade point average.

Counseling and advisement Individual counseling is available.

Auxiliary aids and services *Aids:* scan and read programs (e.g., Kurzweil), speech recognition programs (e.g., Dragon), taped textbooks. *Services and accommodations:* advocates, priority registration, alternative test arrangements, readers, note-takers, scribes, and faculty mentor.

ADD/ADHD Students with ADD/ADHD are eligible for the same services available to students with LD, as well as distraction-free testing environments.

Application *Required:* high school transcript, interview, personal statement, and letter(s) of recommendation. *Recommended:* ACT (extended-time or untimed test accepted) and SAT I (extended-time or untimed test accepted). Upon acceptance, documentation of need for special services should be sent only to your LD program or unit.

LD program contact Jack Rittel, Disability Support Specialist, 433 Albany Post Road, Hyde Park, NY 12538. *Phone:* 914-451-1219. *Fax:* 914-451-1080. *E-mail:* j_rittel@culinary.edu.

Application contact The Culinary Institute of America, 433 Albany Post Road, Hyde Park, NY 12538-1499. *Web address:* http://www.ciachef.edu/.

DALHOUSIE UNIVERSITY
Halifax, Nova Scotia

Students with LD Served by Program	50	ADD/ADHD Services	✓
Staff	1 full-time, 1 part-time	Summer Preparation Program	n/a
LD Program or Service Fee	n/a	Alternative Test Arrangements	✓
LD Program Began	1990	LD Student Organization	✓

Services for Students with Disabilities began offering services in 1990. The program serves approximately 50 undergraduate students. Faculty consists of 1 full-time and 1 part-time staff member. Services are provided by advisor.

Policies LD services are also available to graduate students.

Special preparation or orientation Optional orientation held after classes begin.

Auxiliary aids and services *Aids:* personal computers, scan and read programs (e.g., Kurzweil), screen-enlarging programs, screen readers, speech recognition programs (e.g., Dragon), tape recorders, taped textbooks. *Services and accommodations:* advocates, alternative test arrangements, readers, note-takers, and scribes.

Student organization There is a student organization for students with LD.

ADD/ADHD Students with ADD/ADHD are eligible for the same services available to students with LD, as well as distraction-free study areas and distraction-free testing environments.

Application *Required:* high school transcript. *Recommended:* personal statement. Upon application, documentation of need for special services should be sent only to admissions. Upon acceptance, documentation of need for special services should be sent only to your LD program or unit. *Application deadline (institutional):* 6/1 for fall.

LD program contact Lynn Shokry, Advisor, 6136 University Avenue, Halifax, NS B3H 4J2. *Phone:* 902-494-2836. *Fax:* 902-494-2042. *E-mail:* disabilities@dal.ca.

Application contact Dalhousie University, Halifax, NS B3H-4H6. *E-mail:* admissions@dal.ca. *Web address:* http://www.dal.ca/.

DANIEL WEBSTER COLLEGE
Nashua, New Hampshire

Students with LD Served by Program	10	ADD/ADHD Services	✓
Staff	1 full-time	Summer Preparation Program	n/a
LD Program or Service Fee	n/a	Alternative Test Arrangements	✓
LD Program Began	n/a	LD Student Organization	n/a

Academic Support Services serves approximately 10 undergraduate students. Faculty consists of 1 full-time staff member. Services are provided by academic advisers and Director of Academic Support.

Policies The college has written policies regarding substitution and waivers of requirements for admission. Students with LD may take up to 15 credit hours per semester; 12 credit hours per semester are required to maintain full-time status; 12 credit hours per semester are required to be eligible for financial aid.

Basic skills remediation Available in study skills, reading, time management, learning strategies, and spelling. Offered one-on-one.

Subject-area tutoring Available in most subjects. Offered one-on-one by trained peer tutors and Director of Academic Support.

Counseling and advisement Individual counseling is available. Academic advisement by a staff member affiliated with the program is available.

Auxiliary aids and services *Services and accommodations:* advocates and alternative test arrangements.

ADD/ADHD Students with ADD/ADHD are eligible for the same services available to students with LD, as well as distraction-free study areas, distraction-free testing environments, medication management and personal coach or mentors.

Application *Required:* high school transcript, SAT I, interview, letter(s) of recommendation, separate application to your LD program or unit, and documentation of high school services (e.g., Individualized Education Program [IEP] or 504 plan). *Recommended:* participation in extracurricular activities. Upon application, documentation of need for special services should be sent only to admissions. Upon acceptance, documentation of need for special services should be sent only to your LD program or unit.

LD program contact Kristen Kendrick, Director, Academic Support Services, 20 University Drive, Nashua, NH 03063. *Phone:* 603-577-6612. *Fax:* 603-577-6001. *E-mail:* kendrick@dwc.edu.

Application contact Daniel Webster College, 20 University Drive, Nashua, NH 03063-1300. *E-mail:* admissions@dwc.edu. *Web address:* http://www.dwc.edu/.

DENISON UNIVERSITY
Granville, Ohio

Students with LD Served by Program	120	ADD/ADHD Services	✓
Staff	2 full-time	Summer Preparation Program	n/a
LD Program or Service Fee	n/a	Alternative Test Arrangements	✓
LD Program Began	1987	LD Student Organization	n/a

Academic Support began offering services in 1987. The program serves approximately 120 undergraduate students. Faculty consists of 2 full-time staff members. Services are provided by Associate Dean and Assistant Dean of Academic Support.

Policies Students with LD may take up to 18 credit hours per semester; 12 credit hours per semester are required to maintain full-time status and to be eligible for financial aid.

Special preparation or orientation Optional orientation held before classes begin.

Subject-area tutoring Available in most subjects. Offered one-on-one, in small groups, and class-size groups by trained peer tutors.

Special courses Available in study skills, test taking, time management, and learning strategies. No courses are offered for credit; none enter into overall grade point average.

Counseling and advisement Individual counseling is available.

Auxiliary aids and services *Aids:* scan and read programs (e.g., Kurzweil), taped textbooks. *Services and accommodations:* priority registration, alternative test arrangements, readers, note-takers, and scribes.

ADD/ADHD Students with ADD/ADHD are eligible for the same services available to students with LD, as well as distraction-free testing environments.

Application *Required:* high school transcript, ACT or SAT I (extended-time or untimed test accepted), personal statement, letter(s) of recommendation, and psychoeducational report (3 years old or less). *Recommended:* participation in extracurricular activities and interview. Upon acceptance, documentation of need for special services should be sent only to your LD program or unit. *Application deadline (institutional):* 2/1 for fall and 12/1 for spring. *Application deadline (LD program):* 2/1 for fall and 12/1 for spring.

LD program contact Jennifer Grube Vestal, Associate Dean/Director of Academic Support, 100 South Road, Granville, OH 43023. *Phone:* 740-587-6666. *Fax:* 740-587-6417. *E-mail:* vestal@denison.edu.

Application contact Pennie Miller, Communications Coordinator, Denison University, Box H, Granville, OH 43023. *Phone:* 740-587-6618. *E-mail:* admissions@denison.edu. *Web address:* http://www.denison.edu/.

DICKINSON COLLEGE
Carlisle, Pennsylvania

Students with LD Served by Program	50	ADD/ADHD Services	✓
Staff	1 full-time, 1 part-time	Summer Preparation Program	n/a
LD Program or Service Fee	n/a	Alternative Test Arrangements	✓
LD Program Began	1997	LD Student Organization	n/a

Services for Students with Disabilities began offering services in 1997. The program serves approximately 50 undergraduate students. Faculty consists of 1 full-time and 1 part-time staff member. Services are provided by counselors, LD specialists, and trained peer tutors.
Policies The college has written policies regarding course substitutions. Students with LD may take up to 20 credit hours per semester; 12 credit hours per semester are required to maintain full-time status and to be eligible for financial aid.
Fees *Diagnostic Testing Fee:* ranges from $250 to $600.
Diagnostic testing Available for motor skills, spelling, intelligence, personality, study skills, reading, written language, visual processing, and math.
Subject-area tutoring Available in some subjects. Offered one-on-one by trained peer tutors.
Counseling and advisement Individual counseling is available.
Auxiliary aids and services *Aids:* scan and read programs (e.g., Kurzweil), screen-enlarging programs, tape recorders, taped textbooks. *Services and accommodations:* alternative test arrangements, readers, note-takers, and extended time for exams, testing in a distraction reduced environment.
ADD/ADHD Students with ADD/ADHD are eligible for the same services available to students with LD, as well as distraction-free testing environments, medication management and assistance with time management.
Application *Required:* high school transcript, personal statement, letter(s) of recommendation, psychoeducational report (3 years old or less), and if also ADD see Consortium on ADD/ADHD guidelines and provide appropriate documentation. *Recommended:* participation in extracurricular activities, ACT or SAT I (extended-time or untimed SAT I test accepted), interview, separate application to your LD program or unit, and documentation of high school services (e.g., Individualized Education Program [IEP] or 504 plan). Upon application, documentation of need for special services should be sent only to your LD program or unit. Upon acceptance, documentation of need for special services should be sent to both admissions and your LD program or unit. *Application deadline (institutional):* 2/15 for fall and 12/1 for spring. *Application deadline (LD program):* 2/15 for fall and 12/1 for spring.
LD program contact Keith Jervis, Coordinator, Counseling and Disability Services, PO Box 1773, Carlisle, PA 17013-2896. *Phone:* 717-245-1485. *Fax:* 717-245-1910. *E-mail:* jervis@dickinson.edu.
Application contact Dickinson College, PO Box 1773, Carlisle, PA 17013-2896. *E-mail:* admit@dickinson.edu. *Web address:* http://www.dickinson.edu/.

DICKINSON STATE UNIVERSITY
Dickinson, North Dakota

Students with LD Served by Program	15	ADD/ADHD Services	✓
Staff	1 full-time	Summer Preparation Program	n/a
LD Program or Service Fee	n/a	Alternative Test Arrangements	✓
LD Program Began	n/a	LD Student Organization	n/a

Student Support Services serves approximately 15 undergraduate students. Faculty consists of 1 full-time staff member. Services are provided by trained peer tutors and professional tutors.
Auxiliary aids and services *Aids:* tape recorders, taped textbooks. *Services and accommodations:* priority registration, alternative test arrangements, readers, note-takers, and scribes.
ADD/ADHD Students with ADD/ADHD are eligible for the same services available to students with LD, as well as distraction-free testing environments.
Application *Required:* high school transcript, ACT (extended-time or untimed test accepted), and documentation of high school services (e.g., Individualized Education Program [IEP] or 504 plan). Upon application, documentation of need for special services should be sent only to your LD program or unit. Upon acceptance, documentation of need for special services should be sent only to your LD program or unit. *Application deadline (institutional):* rolling/continuous for fall and rolling/continuous for spring. *Application deadline (LD program):* rolling/continuous for fall and rolling/continuous for spring.
LD program contact Lisa Cantlon, Director of Student Support Services, 291 Campus Drive, Dickinson, ND 58601. *Phone:* 701-483-2029. *Fax:* 701-483-2006. *E-mail:* lcantlon@eagle.dsu.nodak.edu.
Application contact Deb Dazell, Coordinator of Student Recruitment, Dickinson State University, 8th Avenue West and 3rd Street West, Dickinson, ND 58601-4896. *Phone:* 701-483-2175. *E-mail:* dsuhawk@eagle.dsu.nodak.edu. *Web address:* http://www.dsu.nodak.edu/.

DORDT COLLEGE
Sioux Center, Iowa

Students with LD Served by Program	7	ADD/ADHD Services	✓
Staff	1 part-time	Summer Preparation Program	n/a
LD Program or Service Fee	n/a	Alternative Test Arrangements	✓
LD Program Began	1992	LD Student Organization	n/a

Academic Skills Center began offering services in 1992. The program serves approximately 7 undergraduate students. Faculty consists of 1 part-time staff member. Services are provided by special education teachers and trained peer tutors.
Policies Students with LD may take up to 18 credits per semester; 12 credits per semester are required to maintain full-time status and to be eligible for financial aid.
Diagnostic testing Available for spelling, study skills, reading, written language, and math.
Basic skills remediation Available in study skills, reading, time management, learning strategies, spelling, written language, math, and spoken language. Offered one-on-one by computer-based instruction, special education teachers, and trained peer tutors.
Subject-area tutoring Available in most subjects. Offered one-on-one by trained peer tutors.

Dordt College (continued)

Auxiliary aids and services *Aids:* speech recognition programs (e.g., Dragon), tape recorders, taped textbooks. advocates, priority registration, alternative test arrangements, readers, note-takers, and scribes.

ADD/ADHD Students with ADD/ADHD are eligible for the same services available to students with LD, as well as distraction-free testing environments.

Application *Required:* high school transcript, ACT or SAT I (extended-time tests accepted), and personal statement. *Recommended:* letter(s) of recommendation. Upon application, documentation of need for special services should be sent only to your LD program or unit. Upon acceptance, documentation of need for special services should be sent only to your LD program or unit. *Application deadline (institutional):* rolling/continuous for fall and rolling/continuous for spring. *Application deadline (LD program):* rolling/continuous for fall and rolling/continuous for spring.

LD program contact Lavonne Boer, Coordinator of Services for Students with Disabilities, 498 4th Avenue NE, Sioux Center, IA 51250. *Phone:* 712-722-6490. *Fax:* 712-722-4498. *E-mail:* lboer@dordt.edu.

Application contact Dordt College, 498 4th Avenue, NE, Sioux Center, IA 51250-1697. *E-mail:* admissions@dordt.edu. *Web address:* http://www.dordt.edu/.

DREXEL UNIVERSITY
Philadelphia, Pennsylvania

Students with LD Served by Program	93	ADD/ADHD Services	✓
Staff	1 full-time, 1 part-time	Summer Preparation Program	n/a
LD Program or Service Fee	n/a	Alternative Test Arrangements	✓
LD Program Began	1990	LD Student Organization	n/a

Office of Disability Services began offering services in 1990. The program serves approximately 93 undergraduate students. Faculty consists of 1 full-time and 1 part-time staff member. Services are provided by counselors.

Policies Students with LD may take up to 21 credits per term; 12 credits per term are required to maintain full-time status; 6 credits per term are required to be eligible for financial aid. LD services are also available to graduate students.

Basic skills remediation Available in study skills, time management, and learning strategies. Offered one-on-one and in small groups by the Office of Disability Services.

Counseling and advisement Individual counseling is available.

Auxiliary aids and services *Aids:* calculators, personal computers, scan and read programs (e.g., Kurzweil), screen readers, speech recognition programs (e.g., Dragon), tape recorders, taped textbooks. *Services and accommodations:* alternative test arrangements, readers, note-takers, and scribes.

ADD/ADHD Students with ADD/ADHD are eligible for the same services available to students with LD, as well as distraction-free testing environments.

Application *Required:* high school transcript and ACT or SAT I (extended-time tests accepted). *Recommended:* participation in extracurricular activities and letter(s) of recommendation. Upon application, documentation of need for special services should be sent only to your LD program or unit. Upon acceptance, documentation of need for special services should be sent only to your LD program or unit. *Application deadline (institutional):* 3/1 for fall and 3/1 for spring. *Application deadline (LD program):* rolling/continuous for fall and rolling/continuous for spring.

LD program contact Robin A. Stokes, Director, 215 Creese Student Center, 32nd and Chestnut Streets, Philadelphia, PA 19104-2875. *Phone:* 215-895-2506. *Fax:* 215-895-2500. *E-mail:* robinstokes@drexel.edu.

Application contact Drexel University, Room 220, Philadelphia, PA 19104-2875. *E-mail:* undergrad-admissions@post.drexel.edu. *Web address:* http://www.drexel.edu/.

EASTERN CONNECTICUT STATE UNIVERSITY
Willimantic, Connecticut

Students with LD Served by Program	50	ADD/ADHD Services	✓
Staff	1 full-time	Summer Preparation Program	n/a
LD Program or Service Fee	n/a	Alternative Test Arrangements	✓
LD Program Began	1999	LD Student Organization	n/a

Office of Disability Services began offering services in 1999. The program serves approximately 50 undergraduate students. Faculty consists of 1 full-time staff member. Services are provided by special education teachers.

Policies The college has written policies regarding course substitutions and grade forgiveness. Students with LD may take up to 18 credits per semester; 9 credits per semester are required to maintain full-time status; 6 credits per semester are required to be eligible for financial aid. LD services are also available to graduate students.

Counseling and advisement Individual counseling is available.

Auxiliary aids and services *Aids:* calculators, scan and read programs (e.g., Kurzweil), screen-enlarging programs, screen readers, tape recorders, taped textbooks. *Services and accommodations:* priority registration, alternative test arrangements, readers, note-takers, and scribes.

ADD/ADHD Students with ADD/ADHD are eligible for the same services available to students with LD, as well as distraction-free testing environments.

Application *Required:* high school transcript, ACT or SAT I (extended-time or untimed test accepted), letter(s) of recommendation, and psychoeducational report (3 years old or less). *Recommended:* participation in extracurricular activities, interview, personal statement, separate application to your LD program or unit, and documentation of high school services (e.g., Individualized Education Program [IEP] or 504 plan). Upon application, documentation of need for special services should be sent to both admissions and your LD program or unit. Upon acceptance, documentation of need for special services should be sent only to your LD program or unit. *Application deadline (institutional):* rolling/continuous for fall and rolling/continuous for spring. *Application deadline (LD program):* rolling/continuous for fall and rolling/continuous for spring.

LD program contact Dr. Pamela J. Starr, Coordinator, 185 Birch Street, Willimantic, CT 06226. *Phone:* 860-465-5573. *Fax:* 860-465-4560. *E-mail:* starrp@ecsu.ctstateu.edu.

Application contact Eastern Connecticut State University, 83 Windham Street, Willimantic, CT 06226-2295. *E-mail:* admissions@ecsu.ctstateu.edu. *Web address:* http://www.ecsu.ctstateu.edu/.

EASTERN MENNONITE UNIVERSITY
Harrisonburg, Virginia

Students with LD Served by Program	40	ADD/ADHD Services	✓
Staff	3 part-time	Summer Preparation Program	n/a
LD Program or Service Fee	n/a	Alternative Test Arrangements	✓
LD Program Began	1993	LD Student Organization	n/a

Learning Center, Disabilities Support Services began offering services in 1993. The program serves approximately 40 undergraduate students. Faculty consists of 3 part-time staff members. Services are provided by academic advisers, counselors, and trained peer tutors.
Policies Students with LD may take up to 18 credit hours per semester; 12 credit hours per semester are required to maintain full-time status and to be eligible for financial aid. LD services are also available to graduate students.
Subject-area tutoring Available in most subjects. Offered one-on-one and in small groups by trained peer tutors.
Counseling and advisement Individual counseling is available. Academic advisement by a staff member affiliated with the program is available.
Auxiliary aids and services *Aids:* personal computers, screen-enlarging programs, screen readers, tape recorders, taped textbooks. *Services and accommodations:* advocates, alternative test arrangements, and readers.
ADD/ADHD Students with ADD/ADHD are eligible for the same services available to students with LD, as well as distraction-free study areas, distraction-free testing environments and personal coach or mentors.
Application *Required:* high school transcript, ACT or SAT I (extended-time tests accepted), personal statement, letter(s) of recommendation, and psychoeducational report. *Recommended:* participation in extracurricular activities and documentation of high school services (e.g., Individualized Education Program [IEP] or 504 plan). Upon application, documentation of need for special services should be sent only to your LD program or unit. Upon acceptance, documentation of need for special services should be sent only to your LD program or unit. *Application deadline (institutional):* rolling/continuous for fall and rolling/continuous for spring. *Application deadline (LD program):* rolling/continuous for fall and rolling/continuous for spring.
LD program contact Marcia M. Brown, Coordinator, Disabilities Support Services, 1200 Park, Harrisonburg, VA 22802. *Phone:* 540-432-4233. *Fax:* 540-432-4977. *E-mail:* brownmm@emu.edu.
Application contact Eastern Mennonite University, 1200 Park Road, Harrisonburg, VA 22802-2462. *E-mail:* admiss@emu.edu. *Web address:* http://www.emu.edu/.

EASTERN MICHIGAN UNIVERSITY
Ypsilanti, Michigan

Students with LD Served by Program	500	ADD/ADHD Services	✓
Staff	1 full-time, 1 part-time	Summer Preparation Program	n/a
LD Program or Service Fee	n/a	Alternative Test Arrangements	✓
LD Program Began	1990	LD Student Organization	n/a

Access Services Office began offering services in 1990. The program serves approximately 500 undergraduate students. Faculty consists of 1 full-time and 1 part-time staff member. Services are provided by academic advisers, counselors, graduate assistants/students, and trained peer tutors.

Policies Students with LD may take up to 18 credit hours per semester; 12 credit hours per semester are required to maintain full-time status and to be eligible for financial aid. LD services are also available to graduate students.
Basic skills remediation Available in study skills, reading, time management, social skills, learning strategies, written language, and math. Offered one-on-one and in small groups by computer-based instruction, graduate assistants/students, and trained peer tutors.
Subject-area tutoring Offered one-on-one by computer-based instruction, graduate assistants/students, and trained peer tutors.
Counseling and advisement Career counseling, individual counseling, small-group counseling, and support groups are available. Academic advisement by a staff member affiliated with the program is available.
Auxiliary aids and services *Aids:* scan and read programs (e.g., Kurzweil), screen-enlarging programs, screen readers, speech recognition programs (e.g., Dragon), taped textbooks. *Services and accommodations:* advocates, priority registration, alternative test arrangements, readers, note-takers, and scribes.
ADD/ADHD Students with ADD/ADHD are eligible for the same services available to students with LD, as well as distraction-free study areas, distraction-free testing environments and support groups for ADD/ADHD.
Application *Required:* high school transcript and ACT or SAT I (extended-time or untimed test accepted). *Recommended:* personal statement and letter(s) of recommendation. Upon application, documentation of need for special services should be sent only to your LD program or unit. Upon acceptance, documentation of need for special services should be sent only to your LD program or unit. *Application deadline (institutional):* 7/1 for fall and 4/15 for spring.
LD program contact Robert E. Teehan, Student Services Associate, Access Services Office, 203 King Hall, Ypsilanti, MI 48197. *Phone:* 734-487-2470. *Fax:* 734-487-5784. *E-mail:* vet_teehan@online.emich.edu.
Application contact Eastern Michigan University, Ypsilanti, MI 48197. *Web address:* http://www.emich.edu/.

EASTERN NEW MEXICO UNIVERSITY
Portales, New Mexico

Students with LD Served by Program	200	ADD/ADHD Services	✓
Staff	1 full-time, 2 part-time	Summer Preparation Program	n/a
LD Program or Service Fee	n/a	Alternative Test Arrangements	✓
LD Program Began	1980	LD Student Organization	n/a

Services for Students with Disabilities began offering services in 1980. The program serves approximately 200 undergraduate students. Faculty consists of 1 full-time and 2 part-time staff members. Services are provided by remediation/learning specialists.
Policies 12 credit hours per semester are required to maintain full-time status and to be eligible for financial aid. LD services are also available to graduate students.
Subject-area tutoring Available in most subjects. Offered one-on-one by trained peer tutors.
Counseling and advisement Career counseling, support groups, and referral for individual counseling are available.
Auxiliary aids and services *Aids:* calculators, personal spelling/word-use assistants (e.g., Franklin Speller), scan and read programs (e.g., Kurzweil), screen-enlarging programs, screen readers,

Eastern New Mexico University (continued)

speech recognition programs (e.g., Dragon), tape recorders, taped textbooks. *Services and accommodations:* advocates, alternative test arrangements, readers, note-takers, and scribes.

ADD/ADHD Students with ADD/ADHD are eligible for the same services available to students with LD, as well as distraction-free study areas and distraction-free testing environments.

Application *Required:* high school transcript, ACT or SAT I (extended-time or untimed test accepted), letter(s) of recommendation, separate application to your LD program or unit, psychoeducational report (5 years old or less), and documentation of high school services (e.g., Individualized Education Program [IEP] or 504 plan). *Recommended:* interview and personal statement. Upon application, documentation of need for special services should be sent only to your LD program or unit. Upon acceptance, documentation of need for special services should be sent only to your LD program or unit. *Application deadline (institutional):* 1/24 for fall and 8/30 for spring. *Application deadline (LD program):* rolling/continuous for fall and rolling/continuous for spring.

LD program contact Bernita Nutt, Coordinator, Highway 70, Station 34, Portales, NM 88130. *Phone:* 505-562-2280 Ext. 2183. *Fax:* 505-562-2118. *E-mail:* bernita.nutt@enmu.edu.

Application contact Eastern New Mexico University, Station #5 ENMU, Portales, NM 88130. *E-mail:* austinr@email.enmu.edu. *Web address:* http://www.enmu.edu/.

EAST STROUDSBURG UNIVERSITY OF PENNSYLVANIA
East Stroudsburg, Pennsylvania

Students with LD Served by Program	200	ADD/ADHD Services	✓
Staff	1 full-time, 2 part-time	Summer Preparation Program	n/a
LD Program or Service Fee	n/a	Alternative Test Arrangements	n/a
LD Program Began	1987	LD Student Organization	n/a

Disability Services began offering services in 1987. The program serves approximately 200 undergraduate students. Faculty consists of 1 full-time and 2 part-time staff members. Services are provided by LD specialists and assistive technology assistant.

Policies Students with LD may take up to 18 credit hours per semester; 12 credit hours per semester are required to maintain full-time status and to be eligible for financial aid. LD services are also available to graduate students.

Basic skills remediation Available in study skills and time management. Offered one-on-one by LD specialists.

Subject-area tutoring Available in most subjects. Offered one-on-one and in small groups by professional tutors, graduate assistants/students, and trained peer tutors.

Counseling and advisement Career counseling and individual counseling are available.

Auxiliary aids and services *Aids:* calculators, personal spelling/word-use assistants (e.g., Franklin Speller), scan and read programs (e.g., Kurzweil), screen-enlarging programs, speech recognition programs (e.g., Dragon), tape recorders, taped textbooks. *Services and accommodations:* priority registration, readers, note-takers, and scribes.

ADD/ADHD Students with ADD/ADHD are eligible for the same services available to students with LD, as well as distraction-free testing environments and organization and time management instruction and monitoring.

Application *Required:* high school transcript and SAT I (extended-time or untimed test accepted). *Recommended:* participation in extracurricular activities, personal statement, letter(s) of recommendation, psychoeducational report, and documentation of high school services (e.g., Individualized Education Program [IEP] or 504 plan). Upon application, documentation of need for special services should be sent only to your LD program or unit. Upon acceptance, documentation of need for special services should be sent only to your LD program or unit. *Application deadline (institutional):* 3/1 for fall and 12/1 for spring.

LD program contact Dr. Edith Miller, Disability Services Coordinator, 200 Prospect Street, East Stroudsburg, PA 18301. *Phone:* 570-422-3954. *Fax:* 570-422-3898. *E-mail:* emiller@po-box.esu.edu.

Application contact East Stroudsburg University of Pennsylvania, 200 Prospect Street, East Stroudsburg, PA 18301-2999. *E-mail:* atc@po-box.esu.edu. *Web address:* http://www.esu.edu/.

EMORY UNIVERSITY
Atlanta, Georgia

Students with LD Served by Program	200	ADD/ADHD Services	✓
Staff	6 full-time, 1 part-time	Summer Preparation Program	n/a
LD Program or Service Fee	n/a	Alternative Test Arrangements	✓
LD Program Began	1998	LD Student Organization	✓

Office of Disability Services began offering services in 1998. The program serves approximately 200 undergraduate students. Faculty consists of 6 full-time staff members and 1 part-time staff member. Services are provided by counselors, graduate assistants/students, and accommodation specialists.

Policies Students with LD may take up to 18 credit hours per semester; 12 credit hours per semester are required to maintain full-time status; 6 credit hours per semester are required to be eligible for financial aid. LD services are also available to graduate students.

Counseling and advisement Career counseling and individual counseling are available.

Auxiliary aids and services *Aids:* calculators, personal computers, personal spelling/word-use assistants (e.g., Franklin Speller), scan and read programs (e.g., Kurzweil), screen-enlarging programs, screen readers, speech recognition programs (e.g., Dragon), tape recorders, taped textbooks. *Services and accommodations:* advocates, priority registration, alternative test arrangements, readers, note-takers, and scribes.

Student organization There is a student organization for students with LD.

ADD/ADHD Students with ADD/ADHD are eligible for the same services available to students with LD, as well as distraction-free study areas and distraction-free testing environments.

Application *Required:* high school transcript, ACT or SAT I (extended-time or untimed test accepted), personal statement, and letter(s) of recommendation. *Recommended:* participation in extracurricular activities, separate application to your LD program or unit, psychoeducational report, and documentation of high school services (e.g., Individualized Education Program [IEP] or 504 plan). Upon application, documentation of need for special services should be sent only to your LD program or unit. Upon acceptance, documentation of need for special services should be sent only to your LD program or unit. *Application deadline (institutional):* 1/15 for fall and 11/1 for spring. *Application deadline (LD program):* rolling/continuous for fall and rolling/continuous for spring.

LD program contact Gloria W. McCord, Director, Office of Disability Services, 110 Administration Building, Atlanta, GA 30322-0520. *Phone:* 404-727-6016. *Fax:* 404-727-1126. *E-mail:* gmccord@emory.edu.

Application contact Emory University, Boisfeuillet Jones Center-Office of Admissions, Atlanta, GA 30322-1100. *E-mail:* admiss@unix.cc.emory.edu. *Web address:* http://www.emory.edu/.

FAIRMONT STATE COLLEGE
Fairmont, West Virginia

Students with LD Served by Program	80	ADD/ADHD Services	✓
Staff	1 part-time	Summer Preparation Program	n/a
LD Program or Service Fee	n/a	Alternative Test Arrangements	✓
LD Program Began	1993	LD Student Organization	n/a

Student Disabilities Services began offering services in 1993. The program serves approximately 80 undergraduate students. Faculty consists of 1 part-time staff member. Services are provided by academic advisers, regular education teachers, counselors, remediation/learning specialists, and trained peer tutors.
Policies Students with LD may take up to 21 credit hours per semester; 12 credit hours per semester are required to maintain full-time status and to be eligible for financial aid.
Special preparation or orientation Optional orientation held individually by special arrangement.
Diagnostic testing Available for reading, written language, math, and career interest inventory.
Basic skills remediation Available in study skills, reading, time management, learning strategies, written language, and math. Offered in small groups by regular education teachers and professional tutors.
Subject-area tutoring Available in all subjects. Offered one-on-one and in small groups by trained peer tutors.
Special courses Available in college survival skills. No courses are offered for credit; none enter into overall grade point average.
Counseling and advisement Individual counseling is available. Academic advisement by a staff member affiliated with the program is available.
Auxiliary aids and services *Aids:* scan and read programs (e.g., Kurzweil), screen-enlarging programs, screen readers, tape recorders, taped textbooks. *Services and accommodations:* priority registration, alternative test arrangements, readers, note-takers, and scribes.
ADD/ADHD Students with ADD/ADHD are eligible for the same services available to students with LD, as well as distraction-free testing environments.
Application *Required:* high school transcript, ACT or SAT I (extended-time or untimed test accepted), interview, and personal statement. *Recommended:* separate application to your LD program or unit, psychoeducational report (4 years old or less), and documentation of high school services (e.g., Individualized Education Program [IEP] or 504 plan). Upon application, documentation of need for special services should be sent only to your LD program or unit. Upon acceptance, documentation of need for special services should be sent only to your LD program or unit. *Application deadline (LD program):* rolling/continuous for fall and rolling/continuous for spring.
LD program contact Lynn McMullen, Coordinator of Student Disabilities Services, 1201 Locust Avenue, Fairmont, WV 26554. *Phone:* 304-367-4686. *Fax:* 304-366-4870.
Application contact Fairmont State College, 1201 Locust Avenue, Fairmont, WV 26554. *E-mail:* admit@fscvax.fairmont.wvnet.edu. *Web address:* http://www.fscwv.edu/.

FLORIDA ATLANTIC UNIVERSITY
Boca Raton, Florida

Students with LD Served by Program	300	ADD/ADHD Services	✓
Staff	6 full-time, 3 part-time	Summer Preparation Program	n/a
LD Program or Service Fee	n/a	Alternative Test Arrangements	✓
LD Program Began	1981	LD Student Organization	n/a

Office for Students with Disabilities began offering services in 1981. The program serves approximately 300 undergraduate students. Faculty consists of 6 full-time and 3 part-time staff members. Services are provided by academic advisers, counselors, regular education teachers, LD specialists, and trained peer tutors.
Policies The college has written policies regarding course substitutions and grade forgiveness. Students with LD may take up to 12 credit hours per semester; 9 credit hours per semester are required to maintain full-time status and to be eligible for financial aid. LD services are also available to graduate students.
Counseling and advisement Individual counseling is available. Academic advisement by a staff member affiliated with the program is available.
Auxiliary aids and services *Aids:* calculators, personal spelling/word-use assistants (e.g., Franklin Speller), scan and read programs (e.g., Kurzweil), screen-enlarging programs, screen readers, speech recognition programs (e.g., Dragon), tape recorders, taped textbooks. *Services and accommodations:* advocates, alternative test arrangements, readers, note-takers, and scribes.
ADD/ADHD Students with ADD/ADHD are eligible for the same services available to students with LD, as well as distraction-free testing environments.
Application *Required:* high school transcript and ACT or SAT I (extended-time tests accepted). *Recommended:* personal statement and letter(s) of recommendation. Upon application, documentation of need for special services should be sent only to admissions. Upon acceptance, documentation of need for special services should be sent only to your LD program or unit. *Application deadline (institutional):* 6/1 for fall and 10/15 for spring. *Application deadline (LD program):* rolling/continuous for fall and rolling/continuous for spring.
LD program contact Miriam Firpo-Jimenez, Director, 777 Glades Road, LY 175, Boca Raton, FL 33431-0991. *Phone:* 561-297-3880. *Fax:* 561-297-2184. *E-mail:* mfirpo@fau.edu.
Application contact Jared Rosenberg, Coordinator, Freshmen Recruitment, Florida Atlantic University, 777 Glades Road, PO Box 3091, Boca Raton, FL 33431-0991. *Phone:* 561-297-2458. *Web address:* http://www.fau.edu/.

FLORIDA GULF COAST UNIVERSITY
Fort Myers, Florida

Students with LD Served by Program	48	ADD/ADHD Services	✓
Staff	2 full-time, 4 part-time	Summer Preparation Program	n/a
LD Program or Service Fee	n/a	Alternative Test Arrangements	✓
LD Program Began	1997	LD Student Organization	n/a

Office of Multi Access Services (OMAS) began offering services in 1997. The program serves approximately 48 undergraduate students. Faculty consists of 2 full-time and 4 part-time staff members. Services are provided by academic advisers, regular education teachers, graduate assistants/students, trained peer tutors, professional tutors, and Office of Multi Access staff, volunteers.

Florida Gulf Coast University (continued)

Policies The college has written policies regarding course substitutions, grade forgiveness, and substitution and waivers of requirements for admission and graduation. Students with LD may take up to 18 credit hours per semester; 12 credit hours per semester are required to maintain full-time status. LD services are also available to graduate students.

Subject-area tutoring Available in all subjects. Offered in small groups by professional tutors, graduate assistants/students, trained peer tutors, and faculty/staff.

Counseling and advisement Career counseling and individual counseling are available. Academic advisement by a staff member affiliated with the program is available.

Auxiliary aids and services *Aids:* calculators, personal computers, scan and read programs (e.g., Kurzweil), screen-enlarging programs, screen readers, speech recognition programs (e.g., Dragon), tape recorders, taped textbooks, laptop, pocket talker pro, alpha smart keypad. *Services and accommodations:* advocates, priority registration, alternative test arrangements, readers, note-takers, and extension on tests/projects.

ADD/ADHD Students with ADD/ADHD are eligible for the same services available to students with LD, as well as distraction-free study areas and distraction-free testing environments.

Application *Required:* high school transcript, ACT or SAT I (extended-time or untimed test accepted), and psychoeducational report (3 years old or less). *Recommended:* personal statement, letter(s) of recommendation, and documentation of disability. Upon application, documentation of need for special services should be sent only to admissions. Upon acceptance, documentation of need for special services should be sent only to your LD program or unit. *Application deadline (institutional):* 6/1 for fall and 11/1 for spring. *Application deadline (LD program):* 6/1 for fall and 11/2 for spring.

LD program contact Dr. Vincent G. June, Coordinator, 10501 FGCU Boulevard South, Office of Multi Access Services, Fort Meyers, FL 33965-6565. *Phone:* 941-590-7925. *Fax:* 941-590-7975. *E-mail:* vjune@fgcu.edu.

Application contact Michele Yovanovich, Director of Admissions, Florida Gulf Coast University, 10501 FGCU Boulevard South, Fort Myers, FL 33965-6565. *Phone:* 941-590-7878. *Web address:* http://www.fgcu.edu/.

FLORIDA INTERNATIONAL UNIVERSITY
Miami, Florida

Students with LD Served by Program	132	ADD/ADHD Services	✓
Staff	3 full-time	Summer Preparation Program	n/a
LD Program or Service Fee	n/a	Alternative Test Arrangements	✓
LD Program Began	1979	LD Student Organization	✓

Office of Disability Services—ODS began offering services in 1979. The program serves approximately 132 undergraduate students. Faculty consists of 3 full-time staff members. Services are provided by counselors, graduate assistants/students, and LD specialists.

Policies The college has written policies regarding course substitutions, grade forgiveness, and substitution and waivers of requirements for admission and graduation. 12 credit hours per term are required to maintain full-time status and to be eligible for financial aid. LD services are also available to graduate students.

Counseling and advisement Career counseling and individual counseling are available.

Auxiliary aids and services *Aids:* personal computers, scan and read programs (e.g., Kurzweil), screen-enlarging programs, screen readers, speech recognition programs (e.g., Dragon), tape recorders, taped textbooks. *Services and accommodations:* advocates, priority registration, alternative test arrangements, readers, note-takers, and scribes.

Student organization There is a student organization for students with LD.

ADD/ADHD Students with ADD/ADHD are eligible for the same services available to students with LD, as well as distraction-free study areas and distraction-free testing environments.

Application *Required:* high school transcript, ACT or SAT I (extended-time tests accepted), separate application to your LD program or unit, and psychoeducational report. *Recommended:* participation in extracurricular activities, personal statement, and letter(s) of recommendation. Upon application, documentation of need for special services should be sent only to admissions. Upon acceptance, documentation of need for special services should be sent only to your LD program or unit. *Application deadline (institutional):* rolling/continuous for fall and rolling/continuous for spring. *Application deadline (LD program):* rolling/continuous for fall and rolling/continuous for spring.

LD program contact Peter Manheimer, Director, Office of Disability Services, University Park GC 190, Miami, FL 33199. *Phone:* 305-348-3532. *Fax:* 305-348-3850. *E-mail:* manheim@fiu.edu.

Application contact Florida International University, University Park, Miami, FL 33199. *E-mail:* admiss@servms.fiu.edu. *Web address:* http://www.fiu.edu/.

FONTBONNE COLLEGE
St. Louis, Missouri

Students with LD Served by Program	56	ADD/ADHD Services	✓
Staff	1 full-time, 1 part-time	Summer Preparation Program	n/a
LD Program or Service Fee	n/a	Alternative Test Arrangements	✓
LD Program Began	n/a	LD Student Organization	n/a

Kinkel Center for Academic Resources serves approximately 56 undergraduate students. Faculty consists of 1 full-time and 1 part-time staff member. Services are provided by academic advisers, counselors, remediation/learning specialists, trained peer tutors, and professional tutors.

Policies 12 credit hours per semester are required to be eligible for financial aid. LD services are also available to graduate students.

Subject-area tutoring Available in most subjects. Offered one-on-one and in small groups by professional tutors and trained peer tutors.

Counseling and advisement Academic advisement by a staff member affiliated with the program is available.

Auxiliary aids and services *Aids:* calculators, scan and read programs (e.g., Kurzweil), screen-enlarging programs, tape recorders. *Services and accommodations:* alternative test arrangements, readers, note-takers, and scribes.

ADD/ADHD Students with ADD/ADHD are eligible for the same services available to students with LD, as well as distraction-free testing environments.

Application *Required:* high school transcript, ACT or SAT I (extended-time or untimed test accepted), and personal statement. *Recommended:* letter(s) of recommendation. Upon application, documentation of need for special services should be sent only to your LD program or unit. Upon acceptance, documentation of need for special services should be sent only to your LD program or unit. *Application deadline (institutional):* rolling/

continuous for fall and rolling/continuous for spring. *Application deadline (LD program):* rolling/continuous for fall and rolling/continuous for spring.

LD program contact Dr. Jane D. Snyder, Director of Academic Resources, 6800 Wydown Boulevard, St. Louis, MO 63105. *Phone:* 314-889-4571. *Fax:* 314-889-1451. *E-mail:* jsnyder@fontbonne. edu.

Application contact Fontbonne College, 6800 Wydown Boulevard, St. Louis, MO 63105-3098. *E-mail:* pmusen@fontbonne. edu. *Web address:* http://www.fontbonne.edu/.

FORT VALLEY STATE UNIVERSITY
Fort Valley, Georgia

Students with LD Served by Program	20	ADD/ADHD Services	✓
Staff	1 full-time, 1 part-time	Summer Preparation Program	n/a
LD Program or Service Fee	n/a	Alternative Test Arrangements	n/a
LD Program Began	1993	LD Student Organization	n/a

Counseling and Career Development Center began offering services in 1993. The program serves approximately 20 undergraduate students. Faculty consists of 1 full-time and 1 part-time staff member. Services are provided by counselors and graduate assistants/students.

Policies 12 credits per semester are required to maintain full-time status and to be eligible for financial aid. LD services are also available to graduate students.

Fees *Diagnostic Testing Fee:* $300.

Special preparation or orientation Required orientation held before classes begin and during classes.

Diagnostic testing Available for auditory processing, motor skills, spelling, neuropsychological, intelligence, personality, learning strategies, and visual processing.

Basic skills remediation Available in auditory processing, motor skills, computer skills, time management, handwriting, social skills, learning strategies, and math. Offered one-on-one, in small groups, and class-size groups by computer-based instruction, regular education teachers, graduate assistants/students, LD specialists, professional tutors, and trained peer tutors.

Subject-area tutoring Available in most subjects. Offered one-on-one by computer-based instruction, professional tutors, graduate assistants/students, trained peer tutors, and LD specialists.

Counseling and advisement Career counseling, individual counseling, small-group counseling, and support groups are available.

Auxiliary aids and services *Aids:* calculators, personal computers, personal spelling/word-use assistants (e.g., Franklin Speller), screen readers, tape recorders. *Services and accommodations:* advocates, readers, and note-takers.

ADD/ADHD Students with ADD/ADHD are eligible for the same services available to students with LD, as well as personal coach or mentors.

Application *Required:* high school transcript and ACT or SAT I (extended-time tests accepted). *Recommended:* participation in extracurricular activities and letter(s) of recommendation. Upon application, documentation of need for special services should be sent to both admissions and your LD program or unit. Upon acceptance, documentation of need for special services should be sent only to your LD program or unit. *Application deadline (institutional):* 4/23 for fall and 12/6 for spring. *Application deadline (LD program):* rolling/continuous for fall and rolling/continuous for spring.

LD program contact Dr. Myldred P. Hill, Director, Counseling and Career Development Center, Post Office Box 4091, 1005 State University Drive, Fort Valley, GA 31030. *Phone:* 912-825-6202. *Fax:* 912-825-6471. *E-mail:* hill@mail.fvsu.edu.

Application contact Debra McGhee, Admissions Coordinator, Fort Valley State University, 1005 State University Drive, Fort Valley, GA 31030-3298. *Phone:* 912-825-6307. *Web address:* http://www.fvsu.edu/.

GARDNER-WEBB UNIVERSITY
Boiling Springs, North Carolina

Students with LD Served by Program	28	ADD/ADHD Services	✓
Staff	7 full-time	Summer Preparation Program	n/a
LD Program or Service Fee	n/a	Alternative Test Arrangements	✓
LD Program Began	1986	LD Student Organization	n/a

Noel Program for the Disabled began offering services in 1986. The program serves approximately 28 undergraduate students. Faculty consists of 7 full-time staff members. Services are provided by disability specialists.

Policies The college has written policies regarding course substitutions. Students with LD may take up to 18 credit hours per semester; 12 credit hours per semester are required to maintain full-time status and to be eligible for financial aid. LD services are also available to graduate students.

Special preparation or orientation Held before classes begin, after classes begin, and individually by special arrangement.

Basic skills remediation Available in study skills, reading, time management, social skills, learning strategies, written language, and math. Offered in class-size groups by regular education teachers and disability specialists.

Subject-area tutoring Available in all subjects. Offered one-on-one and in small groups by trained peer tutors.

Counseling and advisement Career counseling, individual counseling, and peer mentor are available.

Auxiliary aids and services *Aids:* calculators, personal computers, personal spelling/word-use assistants (e.g., Franklin Speller), scan and read programs (e.g., Kurzweil), screen-enlarging programs, screen readers, speech recognition programs (e.g., Dragon), tape recorders, taped textbooks. *Services and accommodations:* advocates, priority registration, alternative test arrangements, readers, note-takers, and scribes.

ADD/ADHD Students with ADD/ADHD are eligible for the same services available to students with LD, as well as distraction-free testing environments and personal coach or mentors.

Application *Required:* high school transcript, ACT (extended-time or untimed test accepted), SAT I (extended-time or untimed test accepted), and psychoeducational report (4 years old or less). Upon application, documentation of need for special services should be sent only to your LD program or unit. Upon acceptance, documentation of need for special services should be sent only to your LD program or unit. *Application deadline (institutional):* rolling/continuous for fall and rolling/continuous for spring.

LD program contact Sharon Jennings, Director, Box 7274, Boiling Springs, NC 28017. *Phone:* 704-434-4269. *Fax:* 704-406-3524. *E-mail:* sjennings@gardner-webb.edu.

Application contact Gardner-Webb University, PO Box 817, Boiling Springs, NC 28017. *E-mail:* admissions@gardner-webb. edu. *Web address:* http://www.gardner-webb.edu/.

THE GEORGE WASHINGTON UNIVERSITY

Washington, District of Columbia

Students with LD Served by Program	151	ADD/ADHD Services	✓
Staff	2 full-time, 2 part-time	Summer Preparation Program	n/a
LD Program or Service Fee	n/a	Alternative Test Arrangements	✓
LD Program Began	1978	LD Student Organization	n/a

Disability Support Services began offering services in 1978. The program serves approximately 151 undergraduate students. Faculty consists of 2 full-time and 2 part-time staff members. Services are provided by LD specialists.

Policies LD services are also available to graduate students.

Special preparation or orientation Held before classes begin.

Auxiliary aids and services *Aids:* personal computers, scan and read programs (e.g., Kurzweil), screen-enlarging programs, screen readers, speech recognition programs (e.g., Dragon), tape recorders, taped textbooks. *Services and accommodations:* advocates, priority registration, alternative test arrangements, readers, note-takers, and scribes.

ADD/ADHD Students with ADD/ADHD are eligible for the same services available to students with LD, as well as distraction-free study areas, distraction-free testing environments and support groups for ADD/ADHD.

Application *Required:* high school transcript, ACT or SAT I, personal statement, and letter(s) of recommendation. *Recommended:* participation in extracurricular activities, interview, psychoeducational report, and documentation of high school services (e.g., Individualized Education Program [IEP] or 504 plan). Upon application, documentation of need for special services should be sent only to admissions. Upon acceptance, documentation of need for special services should be sent only to your LD program or unit.

LD program contact Christy Willis, Director, Marvin Center, 800 21st Street, NW, Washington, DC 20052. *Phone:* 202-994-8250. *Fax:* 202-994-7610. *E-mail:* cwillis@gwu.edu.

Application contact The George Washington University, Office of Undergraduate Admissions, Washington, DC 20052. *E-mail:* gwadm@gwis2.circ.gwu.edu. *Web address:* http://www.gwu.edu/.

GEORGIA COLLEGE AND STATE UNIVERSITY

Milledgeville, Georgia

Students with LD Served by Program	75	ADD/ADHD Services	✓
Staff	4 part-time	Summer Preparation Program	n/a
LD Program or Service Fee	n/a	Alternative Test Arrangements	✓
LD Program Began	1988	LD Student Organization	n/a

Committee on Learning Accommodation began offering services in 1988. The program serves approximately 75 undergraduate students. Faculty consists of 4 part-time staff members. Services are provided by academic advisers, counselors, and LD specialists.

Policies Students with LD may take up to 18 credit hours per semester; 12 credit hours per semester are required to maintain full-time status and to be eligible for financial aid. LD services are also available to graduate students.

Fees *Diagnostic Testing Fee:* $350.

Diagnostic testing Available for auditory processing, motor skills, spelling, handwriting, neuropsychological, spoken language, intelligence, personality, reading, written language, visual processing, and math.

Counseling and advisement Individual counseling is available. Academic advisement by a staff member affiliated with the program is available.

Auxiliary aids and services *Aids:* taped textbooks. *Services and accommodations:* priority registration and alternative test arrangements.

ADD/ADHD Students with ADD/ADHD are eligible for the same services available to students with LD, as well as distraction-free testing environments.

Application *Required:* high school transcript, ACT or SAT I (extended-time or untimed test accepted), separate application to your LD program or unit, psychoeducational report (3 years old or less), and documentation of high school services (e.g., Individualized Education Program [IEP] or 504 plan). Upon acceptance, documentation of need for special services should be sent only to your LD program or unit. *Application deadline (institutional):* 7/1 for fall and 12/1 for spring.

LD program contact Dr. Craig Smith, Chair, Department of Special Education and Administration, CBX 072, Milledgeville, GA 31061. *Phone:* 912-445-4577. *Fax:* 912-445-6582. *E-mail:* dcsmith@mail.gcsu.edu.

Application contact Maryllis Wolfgang, Director of Admissions, Georgia College and State University, CPO Box 023, Milledgeville, GA 31061. *Phone:* 912-445-6285. *E-mail:* gcsu@mail.gac.peachnet.edu. *Web address:* http://www.gcsu.edu/.

GEORGIAN COURT COLLEGE

Lakewood, New Jersey

Students with LD Served by Program	30	ADD/ADHD Services	✓
Staff	2 full-time, 4 part-time	Summer Preparation Program	n/a
LD Program or Service Fee	✓	Alternative Test Arrangements	✓
LD Program Began	n/a	LD Student Organization	n/a

The Learning Center (TLC) serves approximately 30 undergraduate students. Faculty consists of 2 full-time and 4 part-time staff members. Services are provided by counselors, remediation/learning specialists, special education teachers, and LD specialists.

Policies 12 credit hours per semester are required to maintain full-time status and to be eligible for financial aid.

Fees *LD Program or Service Fee:* $1100 per year. *Diagnostic Testing Fee:* ranges from $250 to $450.

Diagnostic testing Available for neuropsychological, spoken language, social skills, and educational.

Basic skills remediation Available in study skills, reading, time management, learning strategies, and math. Offered in small groups and class-size groups by regular education teachers and special education teachers.

Subject-area tutoring Offered one-on-one and in small groups by professional tutors, trained peer tutors, and LD specialists.

Special courses Available in oral communication skills, study skills, reading, learning strategies, vocabulary development, math, and written composition skills. No courses are offered for credit; none enter into overall grade point average.

Counseling and advisement Career counseling, individual counseling, small-group counseling, and support groups are available.

Auxiliary aids and services *Aids:* calculators, personal computers, tape recorders, taped textbooks, adaptive equipment. *Services and accommodations:* alternative test arrangements, readers, and note-takers.

ADD/ADHD Students with ADD/ADHD are eligible for the same services available to students with LD, as well as distraction-free study areas, distraction-free testing environments and personal coach or mentors.

Application *Required:* high school transcript, ACT or SAT I (extended-time SAT I test accepted), interview, personal statement, and letter(s) of recommendation. *Recommended:* participation in extracurricular activities. Upon application, documentation of need for special services should be sent only to admissions. Upon acceptance, documentation of need for special services should be sent only to your LD program or unit. *Application deadline (institutional):* 8/1 for fall and 1/1 for spring. *Application deadline (LD program):* 8/1 for fall and 1/1 for spring.

LD program contact Patricia Cohen, Director, TLC Program, 900 Lakewood Avenue, Lakewood, NJ 08701-2697. *Phone:* 732-364-2200 Ext. 659. *Fax:* 732-367-3920.

Application contact Georgian Court College, 900 Lakewood Avenue, Lakewood, NJ 08701-2697. *E-mail:* admissions-ugrad@georgian.edu. *Web address:* http://www.georgian.edu/.

GREEN MOUNTAIN COLLEGE
Poultney, Vermont

Students with LD Served by Program	10	ADD/ADHD Services	✓
Staff	3 full-time, 2 part-time	Summer Preparation Program	✓
LD Program or Service Fee	n/a	Alternative Test Arrangements	✓
LD Program Began	n/a	LD Student Organization	n/a

Calhoun Learning Center serves approximately 10 undergraduate students. Faculty consists of 3 full-time and 2 part-time staff members. Services are provided by academic advisers, counselors, remediation/learning specialists, diagnostic specialists, trained peer tutors, and professional tutors.

Policies Students with LD may take up to 18 credit hours per semester; 12 credit hours per semester are required to maintain full-time status and to be eligible for financial aid.

Special preparation or orientation Required summer program offered prior to entering college.

Subject-area tutoring Available in all subjects. Offered one-on-one and in small groups by computer-based instruction, professional tutors, and trained peer tutors.

Counseling and advisement Career counseling, individual counseling, small-group counseling, and support groups are available. Academic advisement by a staff member affiliated with the program is available.

Auxiliary aids and services *Aids:* calculators, personal computers, tape recorders, taped textbooks. *Services and accommodations:* advocates, priority registration, alternative test arrangements, readers, note-takers, and scribes.

ADD/ADHD Students with ADD/ADHD are eligible for the same services available to students with LD, as well as distraction-free study areas, distraction-free testing environments and personal coach or mentors.

Application *Required:* high school transcript, participation in extracurricular activities, ACT or SAT I (extended-time or untimed test accepted), personal statement, letter(s) of recommendation, psychoeducational report (2 years old or less), and documentation of high school services (e.g., Individualized Education Program [IEP] or 504 plan). Upon application, documentation of need for special services should be sent to both admissions and your LD program or unit. Upon acceptance, documentation of need for special services should be sent only to your LD program or unit.

LD program contact Sue Zientara, Director, Calhoun Learning Center, One College Circle, Poultney, VT 05764. *Phone:* 802-287-8232. *Fax:* 802-287-8099. *E-mail:* zientara@greenmtn.edu.

Application contact Green Mountain College, One College Circle, Poultney, VT 05764-1199. *E-mail:* admiss@greenmtn.edu.

GUSTAVUS ADOLPHUS COLLEGE
St. Peter, Minnesota

Students with LD Served by Program	40	ADD/ADHD Services	✓
Staff	1 full-time	Summer Preparation Program	n/a
LD Program or Service Fee	n/a	Alternative Test Arrangements	✓
LD Program Began	n/a	LD Student Organization	n/a

Advising Center serves approximately 40 undergraduate students. Faculty consists of 1 full-time staff member. Services are provided by academic advisers, regular education teachers, counselors, remediation/learning specialists, and LD specialists.

Policies Students with LD may take up to 5 credits per semester; 3 credits per semester are required to maintain full-time status.

Special preparation or orientation Optional orientation held individually by special arrangement.

Basic skills remediation Available in auditory processing, motor skills, study skills, computer skills, reading, time management, handwriting, social skills, visual processing, learning strategies, spelling, written language, math, and spoken language. Offered one-on-one and in small groups by LD specialists.

Subject-area tutoring Available in most subjects. Offered one-on-one, in small groups, and class-size groups by trained peer tutors and LD specialists.

Special courses Available in study skills, college survival skills, test taking, time management, learning strategies, self-advocacy, stress management, and written composition skills. No courses are offered for credit.

Counseling and advisement Career counseling, individual counseling, small-group counseling, and support groups are available. Academic advisement by a staff member affiliated with the program is available.

Auxiliary aids and services *Aids:* screen-enlarging programs, taped textbooks. *Services and accommodations:* advocates, alternative test arrangements, and note-takers.

ADD/ADHD Students with ADD/ADHD are eligible for the same services available to students with LD, as well as distraction-free testing environments.

Application *Required:* high school transcript, ACT or SAT I (extended-time or untimed test accepted), personal statement, and letter(s) of recommendation. *Recommended:* participation in extracurricular activities and interview. Upon application, documentation of need for special services should be sent only to your LD program or unit. Upon acceptance, documentation of need for special services should be sent only to your LD program or unit. *Application deadline (institutional):* 4/15 for fall and 12/15 for spring. *Application deadline (LD program):* 4/15 for fall and 12/15 for spring.

LD program contact Rebecca Cory, Academic Counselor, Advising Center, 800 West College Avenue, St. Peter, MN 56082. *Phone:* 507-933-6124. *E-mail:* rcory@gac.edu.

Application contact Gustavus Adolphus College, 800 West College Avenue, St. Peter, MN 56082-1498. *E-mail:* admission@gac.edu. *Web address:* http://www.gustavus.edu/.

HAMILTON COLLEGE
Clinton, New York

Students with LD Served by Program	40	ADD/ADHD Services	✓
Staff	1 full-time	Summer Preparation Program	n/a
LD Program or Service Fee	n/a	Alternative Test Arrangements	n/a
LD Program Began	n/a	LD Student Organization	n/a

Office of the Dean of Students for Academics serves approximately 40 undergraduate students. Faculty consists of 1 full-time staff member. Services are provided by academic advisers, regular education teachers, counselors, trained peer tutors, and professional tutors.

Policies Students with LD may take up to 12 credit hours per semester; 9 credit hours per semester are required to maintain full-time status and to be eligible for financial aid.

Counseling and advisement Academic advisement by a staff member affiliated with the program is available.

ADD/ADHD Students with ADD/ADHD are eligible for the same services available to students with LD

Application *Required:* high school transcript. *Recommended:* participation in extracurricular activities, ACT or SAT I (extended-time or untimed test accepted), interview, personal statement, and letter(s) of recommendation. Upon application, documentation of need for special services should be sent only to your LD program or unit. Upon acceptance, documentation of need for special services should be sent only to your LD program or unit. *Application deadline (institutional):* 1/15 for fall and 1/15 for spring.

LD program contact Louise Peckingham, Compliance Officer, ADA, 198 College Hill Road, Clinton, NY 13323. *Phone:* 315-859-4305.

Application contact Hamilton College, 198 College Hill Road, Clinton, NY 13323-1296. *E-mail:* admissio@hamilton.edu. *Web address:* http://www.hamilton.edu/.

HAMLINE UNIVERSITY
St. Paul, Minnesota

Students with LD Served by Program	30	ADD/ADHD Services	✓
Staff	2 full-time	Summer Preparation Program	n/a
LD Program or Service Fee	n/a	Alternative Test Arrangements	✓
LD Program Began	1978	LD Student Organization	n/a

Study Resource Center began offering services in 1978. The program serves approximately 30 undergraduate students. Faculty consists of 2 full-time staff members. Services are provided by academic advisers, regular education teachers, graduate assistants/students, teacher trainees, and trained peer tutors.

Policies 12 credit hours per semester are required to maintain full-time status; 6 credit hours per semester are required to be eligible for financial aid. LD services are also available to graduate students.

Special preparation or orientation Optional orientation held individually by special arrangement.

Basic skills remediation Available in study skills, computer skills, time management, learning strategies, and written language. Offered one-on-one by program administrator.

Subject-area tutoring Available in most subjects. Offered one-on-one by trained peer tutors.

Counseling and advisement Academic advisement by a staff member affiliated with the program is available.

Auxiliary aids and services *Aids:* tape recorders, taped textbooks, assistive listening device. *Services and accommodations:* advocates, priority registration, alternative test arrangements, readers, note-takers, and scribes.

ADD/ADHD Students with ADD/ADHD are eligible for the same services available to students with LD, as well as distraction-free study areas, distraction-free testing environments and study skills.

Application *Required:* high school transcript and ACT or SAT I (extended-time or untimed test accepted). *Recommended:* participation in extracurricular activities, personal statement, and letter(s) of recommendation. Upon acceptance, documentation of need for special services should be sent only to your LD program or unit. *Application deadline (institutional):* 8/1 for fall and 1/1 for spring.

LD program contact Barbara Simmons, Assistant Dean for Academic and Student Affairs, Study Resource Center, C-1909, St. Paul, MN 55104-1284. *Phone:* 651-523-2417. *Fax:* 651-523-2809. *E-mail:* bsimmons@gw.hamline.edu.

Application contact Hamline University, 1536 Hewitt Avenue, St. Paul, MN 55104-1284. *E-mail:* admis@seq.hamline.edu. *Web address:* http://www.hamline.edu/.

HAMPSHIRE COLLEGE
Amherst, Massachusetts

Students with LD Served by Program	5	ADD/ADHD Services	✓
Staff	1 part-time	Summer Preparation Program	n/a
LD Program or Service Fee	n/a	Alternative Test Arrangements	✓
LD Program Began	n/a	LD Student Organization	n/a

Learning Disabilities Support Services serves approximately 5 undergraduate students. Faculty consists of 1 part-time staff member. Services are provided by LD specialists.

Special preparation or orientation Optional orientation held before classes begin.

Special courses Available in time management and learning strategies. No courses are offered for credit.

Counseling and advisement Career counseling and individual counseling are available.

Auxiliary aids and services *Aids:* calculators, scan and read programs (e.g., Kurzweil), screen-enlarging programs, screen readers, speech recognition programs (e.g., Dragon), tape recorders, taped textbooks, text help. *Services and accommodations:* priority registration, alternative test arrangements, readers, note-takers, and scribes.

ADD/ADHD Students with ADD/ADHD are eligible for the same services available to students with LD, as well as distraction-free study areas, distraction-free testing environments and medication management.

Application *Required:* high school transcript, participation in extracurricular activities, personal statement, letter(s) of recommendation, and academic writing sample. Upon application, documentation of need for special services should be sent only to admissions. Upon acceptance, documentation of need for special services should be sent only to your LD program or unit. *Application deadline (institutional):* 2/1 for fall and 11/1 for spring.

LD program contact Karyl Lynch, Associate Dean of Advising, Amherst, MA 01002. *Phone:* 413-559-5458. *E-mail:* klynch@hampshire.edu.

Application contact Hampshire College, 893 West Street, Amherst, MA 01002. *E-mail:* admissions@hamp.hampshire.edu. *Web address:* http://www.hampshire.edu/.

HAMPTON UNIVERSITY
Hampton, Virginia

Students with LD Served by Program	45	ADD/ADHD Services	✓
Staff	2 full-time	Summer Preparation Program	n/a
LD Program or Service Fee	n/a	Alternative Test Arrangements	✓
LD Program Began	1993	LD Student Organization	✓

Office of Section 504 Compliance began offering services in 1993. The program serves approximately 45 undergraduate students. Faculty consists of 2 full-time staff members. Services are provided by academic advisers, counselors, and trained peer tutors.

Policies The college has written policies regarding course substitutions, grade forgiveness, and substitution and waivers of requirements for admission and graduation. Students with LD may take up to 18 credit hours per semester; 12 credit hours per semester are required to maintain full-time status and to be eligible for financial aid. LD services are also available to graduate students.

Special preparation or orientation Required orientation held during registration, after classes begin, and individually by special arrangement.

Subject-area tutoring Available in most subjects. Offered one-on-one and in small groups.

Counseling and advisement Career counseling, individual counseling, small-group counseling, and support groups are available. Academic advisement by a staff member affiliated with the program is available.

Auxiliary aids and services *Aids:* personal computers, tape recorders, taped textbooks. *Services and accommodations:* advocates, priority registration, alternative test arrangements, and note-takers.

Student organization There is a student organization for students with LD.

ADD/ADHD Students with ADD/ADHD are eligible for the same services available to students with LD, as well as distraction-free study areas, distraction-free testing environments and support groups for ADD/ADHD.

Application *Required:* high school transcript, ACT (extended-time or untimed test accepted), SAT I (extended-time or untimed test accepted), personal statement, letter(s) of recommendation, separate application to your LD program or unit, and psycho-educational report (3 years old or less). *Recommended:* participation in extracurricular activities and documentation of high school services (e.g., Individualized Education Program [IEP] or 504 plan). Upon application, documentation of need for special services should be sent only to admissions. Upon acceptance, documentation of need for special services should be sent only to your LD program or unit. *Application deadline (institutional):* rolling/continuous for fall and rolling/continuous for spring. *Application deadline (LD program):* rolling/continuous for fall and rolling/continuous for spring.

LD program contact Letizia Gambrell-Boone, Director, Testing Services, 212 Wigwam Building, Hampton, VA 23668. *Phone:* 757-727-5493. *Fax:* 757-727-5544. *E-mail:* letizia.gambrell-boo@hamptonu.edu.

Application contact Leonard M. Jones, Director of Admissions, Hampton University, Hampton, VA 23668. *Phone:* 757-727-5328. *Web address:* http://www.hamptonu.edu/.

HOOD COLLEGE
Frederick, Maryland

Students with LD Served by Program	46	ADD/ADHD Services	✓
Staff	1 part-time	Summer Preparation Program	n/a
LD Program or Service Fee	n/a	Alternative Test Arrangements	✓
LD Program Began	1983	LD Student Organization	✓

Disabilities Services Office began offering services in 1983. The program serves approximately 46 undergraduate students. Faculty consists of 1 part-time staff member. Services are provided by academic advisers, counselors, and trained peer tutors.

Policies The college has written policies regarding course substitutions. Students with LD may take up to 15 credit hours per semester; 12 credit hours per semester are required to maintain full-time status; 6 credit hours per semester are required to be eligible for financial aid. LD services are also available to graduate students.

Counseling and advisement Career counseling and support groups are available. Academic advisement by a staff member affiliated with the program is available.

Auxiliary aids and services *Aids:* calculators, personal computers, scan and read programs (e.g., Kurzweil), screen-enlarging programs, screen readers, speech recognition programs (e.g., Dragon), tape recorders, taped textbooks. *Services and accommodations:* advocates, alternative test arrangements, readers, note-takers, and scribes.

Student organization There is a student organization for students with LD.

ADD/ADHD Students with ADD/ADHD are eligible for the same services available to students with LD, as well as distraction-free study areas, distraction-free testing environments and support groups for ADD/ADHD.

Application *Required:* high school transcript, participation in extracurricular activities, SAT I (extended-time or untimed test accepted), personal statement, and letter(s) of recommendation. *Recommended:* ACT (extended-time or untimed test accepted) and interview. Upon application, documentation of need for special services should be sent only to your LD program or unit. Upon acceptance, documentation of need for special services should be sent only to your LD program or unit. *Application deadline (institutional):* 2/15 for fall and 12/1 for spring.

LD program contact Lynn Schlossberg, Disability Services Coordinator, 401 Rosemont Avenue, Frederick, MD 21701. *Phone:* 301-696-3421. *Fax:* 301-696-3952. *E-mail:* schlossberg@hood.edu.

Application contact Hood College, 401 Rosemont Avenue, Frederick, MD 21701-8575. *E-mail:* admissions@nimue.hood.edu. *Web address:* http://www.hood.edu/.

HOUGHTON COLLEGE
Houghton, New York

Students with LD Served by Program	20	ADD/ADHD Services	✓
Staff	2 part-time	Summer Preparation Program	n/a
LD Program or Service Fee	n/a	Alternative Test Arrangements	✓
LD Program Began	1990	LD Student Organization	n/a

Student Academic Services began offering services in 1990. The program serves approximately 20 undergraduate students. Faculty consists of 2 part-time staff members. Services are provided by counselors and diagnostic specialists.

Houghton College (continued)

Policies The college has written policies regarding course substitutions. Students with LD may take up to 18 semester hours per semester; 12 semester hours per semester are required to maintain full-time status and to be eligible for financial aid.

Special preparation or orientation Optional orientation held individually by special arrangement.

Diagnostic testing Available for spelling, reading, math, and cognitive ability assessment.

Subject-area tutoring Available in some subjects. Offered one-on-one and in small groups by trained peer tutors.

Counseling and advisement Individual counseling and study skills counseling are available.

Auxiliary aids and services *Aids:* tape recorders, taped textbooks. advocates, alternative test arrangements, readers, note-takers, and scribes.

ADD/ADHD Students with ADD/ADHD are eligible for the same services available to students with LD, as well as distraction-free testing environments.

Application *Required:* high school transcript, ACT or SAT I (extended-time tests accepted), personal statement, letter(s) of recommendation, and psychoeducational report (3 years old or less). *Recommended:* participation in extracurricular activities, SAT I (extended-time test accepted), interview, separate application to your LD program or unit, and documentation of high school services (e.g., Individualized Education Program [IEP] or 504 plan). Upon application, documentation of need for special services should be sent only to your LD program or unit. Upon acceptance, documentation of need for special services should be sent only to your LD program or unit. *Application deadline (institutional):* rolling/continuous for fall and rolling/continuous for spring.

LD program contact Dr. Susan Hice, Director, Student Academic Services, 1 Willard Avenue, NAB 115, Houghton, NY 14744. *Phone:* 716-567-9239. *Fax:* 716-567-9570. *E-mail:* shice@houghton.edu.

Application contact Houghton College, PO Box 128, Houghton, NY 14744. *E-mail:* admissions@houghton.edu. *Web address:* http://www.houghton.edu/.

HUMBOLDT STATE UNIVERSITY
Arcata, California

Students with LD Served by Program	300	ADD/ADHD Services	✓
Staff	6 full-time	Summer Preparation Program	n/a
LD Program or Service Fee	n/a	Alternative Test Arrangements	✓
LD Program Began	n/a	LD Student Organization	n/a

Disability Resource Center serves approximately 300 undergraduate students. Faculty consists of 6 full-time staff members. Services are provided by counselors, graduate assistants/students, LD specialists, trained peer tutors, and Director.

Policies The college has written policies regarding course substitutions and substitution and waivers of requirements for admission and graduation. Students with LD may take up to 18 units per semester; 12 units per semester are required to maintain full-time status and to be eligible for financial aid. LD services are also available to graduate students.

Special preparation or orientation Optional orientation held during summer prior to enrollment and by appointment.

Counseling and advisement Career counseling, individual counseling, small-group counseling, and support groups are available.

Auxiliary aids and services *Aids:* scan and read programs (e.g., Kurzweil), screen-enlarging programs, screen readers, speech recognition programs (e.g., Dragon), tape recorders, taped textbooks. *Services and accommodations:* advocates, priority registration, alternative test arrangements, readers, note-takers, and scribes.

ADD/ADHD Students with ADD/ADHD are eligible for the same services available to students with LD

Application *Required:* high school transcript and ACT or SAT I (extended-time or untimed ACT test accepted). Upon application, documentation of need for special services should be sent only to your LD program or unit. Upon acceptance, documentation of need for special services should be sent only to your LD program or unit.

LD program contact Ralph D. McFarland, Director, Disability Resource Center, Arcata, CA 95521-8299. *Phone:* 707-826-4678. *Fax:* 707-826-5397. *E-mail:* rdm7001@axe.humboldt.edu.

Application contact Jeffery Savage, Office of Admissions and School Relations, Humboldt State University, Arcata, CA 95521-8299. *Phone:* 707-826-4402. *E-mail:* hsuinfo@laurel.humboldt.edu. *Web address:* http://www.humboldt.edu/.

HUNTER COLLEGE OF THE CITY UNIVERSITY OF NEW YORK
New York, New York

Students with LD Served by Program	300	ADD/ADHD Services	✓
Staff	4 full-time, 1 part-time	Summer Preparation Program	n/a
LD Program or Service Fee	n/a	Alternative Test Arrangements	✓
LD Program Began	1980	LD Student Organization	n/a

Office for Students with Disabilities began offering services in 1980. The program serves approximately 300 undergraduate students. Faculty consists of 4 full-time staff members and 1 part-time staff member. Services are provided by counselors.

Policies Students with LD may take up to 18 credits per semester; 3 credits per semester are required to maintain full-time status and to be eligible for financial aid. LD services are also available to graduate students.

Special preparation or orientation Optional orientation held before classes begin.

Subject-area tutoring Available in some subjects. Offered one-on-one by students.

Counseling and advisement Career counseling and individual counseling are available.

Auxiliary aids and services *Aids:* scan and read programs (e.g., Kurzweil), screen-enlarging programs, speech recognition programs (e.g., Dragon), tape recorders. *Services and accommodations:* priority registration, alternative test arrangements, and note-takers.

ADD/ADHD Students with ADD/ADHD are eligible for the same services available to students with LD, as well as distraction-free study areas and distraction-free testing environments.

Application *Required:* high school transcript, SAT I (extended-time test accepted), psychoeducational report (3 years old or less), and documentation of high school services (e.g., Individualized Education Program [IEP] or 504 plan). Upon application, documentation of need for special services should be sent only to your LD program or unit. Upon acceptance, documentation of need for special services should be sent only to your LD program or unit. *Application deadline (institutional):* rolling/continuous for fall and rolling/continuous for spring. *Application deadline (LD program):* rolling/continuous for fall and rolling/continuous for spring.

LD program contact Sandra La Porta, Director, 695 Park Avenue, New York City, NY 10021. *Phone:* 212-772-4857.

Application contact Office of Admissions, Hunter College of the City University of New York, 695 Park Avenue, New York, NY 10021-5085. *Phone:* 212-772-4490. *Web address:* http://www. hunter.cuny.edu/.

IDAHO STATE UNIVERSITY
Pocatello, Idaho

Students with LD Served by Program	110	ADD/ADHD Services	✓
Staff	7 full-time, 9 part-time	Summer Preparation Program	n/a
LD Program or Service Fee	n/a	Alternative Test Arrangements	✓
LD Program Began	1992	LD Student Organization	✓

The ADA Disabilities Resource Center began offering services in 1992. The program serves approximately 110 undergraduate students. Faculty consists of 7 full-time and 9 part-time staff members. Services are provided by academic advisers, counselors, diagnostic specialists, and trained peer tutors.

Policies The college has written policies regarding course substitutions. 8 credit hours per semester are required to maintain full-time status; 12 credit hours per semester are required to be eligible for financial aid. LD services are also available to graduate students.

Fees *Diagnostic Testing Fee:* $50.

Diagnostic testing Available for neuropsychological, intelligence, and personality.

Basic skills remediation Available in study skills, computer skills, reading, time management, learning strategies, written language, and math. Offered one-on-one, in small groups, and class-size groups by regular education teachers and trained peer tutors.

Subject-area tutoring Available in some subjects. Offered one-on-one and in small groups by trained peer tutors.

Special courses Available in career planning, study skills, college survival skills, practical computer skills, test taking, health and nutrition, time management, math, stress management, and written composition skills. Most courses are offered for credit; some enter into overall grade point average.

Counseling and advisement Career counseling, individual counseling, small-group counseling, and support groups are available. Academic advisement by a staff member affiliated with the program is available.

Auxiliary aids and services *Aids:* calculators, personal computers, scan and read programs (e.g., Kurzweil), screen-enlarging programs, speech recognition programs (e.g., Dragon), tape recorders, taped textbooks. *Services and accommodations:* advocates, priority registration, alternative test arrangements, readers, note-takers, and scribes.

Student organization There is a student organization for students with LD.

ADD/ADHD Students with ADD/ADHD are eligible for the same services available to students with LD, as well as distraction-free testing environments, medication management and support groups for ADD/ADHD.

Application *Required:* high school transcript, ACT or SAT I (extended-time or untimed test accepted), personal statement, and letter(s) of recommendation. *Recommended:* participation in extracurricular activities, ACT (extended-time or untimed test accepted), SAT I (extended-time or untimed test accepted), and interview. Upon application, documentation of need for special services should be sent only to your LD program or unit. Upon acceptance, documentation of need for special services should be sent only to your LD program or unit. *Application deadline (institutional):* rolling/continuous for fall and rolling/continuous for spring. *Application deadline (LD program):* rolling/continuous for fall and rolling/continuous for spring.

LD program contact Robert A. Campbell, Director, ADA and Disabilities Resource Center, Campus Box 8121, Pocatello, ID 83201. *Phone:* 208-236-3599. *Fax:* 208-236-4617. *E-mail:* camprob1@ isu.edu.

Application contact Guy Hollingsworth, Director of Recruitment, Idaho State University, PO Box 8054, Pocatello, ID 83209. *Phone:* 208-282-3279. *E-mail:* echamike@isu.edu. *Web address:* http://www.isu.edu/.

ILLINOIS STATE UNIVERSITY
Normal, Illinois

Students with LD Served by Program	150	ADD/ADHD Services	✓
Staff	2 full-time	Summer Preparation Program	n/a
LD Program or Service Fee	n/a	Alternative Test Arrangements	✓
LD Program Began	1978	LD Student Organization	✓

Disability Concerns began offering services in 1978. The program serves approximately 150 undergraduate students. Faculty consists of 2 full-time staff members. Services are provided by academic advisers, counselors, and LD specialists.

Policies Students with LD may take up to 18 credit hours per semester; 12 credit hours per semester are required to maintain full-time status and to be eligible for financial aid. LD services are also available to graduate students.

Special preparation or orientation Required orientation held individually by special arrangement and during the intake appointment.

Subject-area tutoring Available in all subjects. Offered one-on-one by trained peer tutors.

Special courses Available in career planning, study skills, time management, and learning strategies. No courses are offered for credit; none enter into overall grade point average.

Counseling and advisement Career counseling, individual counseling, small-group counseling, and support groups are available. Academic advisement by a staff member affiliated with the program is available.

Auxiliary aids and services *Aids:* personal computers, personal spelling/word-use assistants (e.g., Franklin Speller), scan and read programs (e.g., Kurzweil), screen-enlarging programs, screen readers, speech recognition programs (e.g., Dragon), taped textbooks. *Services and accommodations:* advocates, alternative test arrangements, readers, note-takers, and scribes.

Student organization There is a student organization for students with LD.

ADD/ADHD Students with ADD/ADHD are eligible for the same services available to students with LD, as well as distraction-free study areas and distraction-free testing environments.

Application *Required:* high school transcript, ACT or SAT I (extended-time or untimed test accepted), psychoeducational report (3 years old or less), and documentation of high school services (e.g., Individualized Education Program [IEP] or 504 plan). Upon application, documentation of need for special services should be sent only to your LD program or unit. Upon acceptance, documentation of need for special services should be sent only to your LD program or unit. *Application deadline (institutional):* 4/1 for fall and 12/1 for spring. *Application deadline (LD program):* rolling/continuous for fall and rolling/continuous for spring.

LD program contact Ann M. Caldwell, Director, Disability Concerns, Campus Box 1290, Normal, IL 61790-1290. *Phone:* 309-438-5853. *Fax:* 309-438-7713. *E-mail:* ableisu@ilstu.edu.

Illinois State University (continued)

Application contact Illinois State University, Normal, IL 61790-2200. *E-mail:* pawutz@rs6000.cmp.ilstu.edu. *Web address:* http://www.ilstu.edu/.

INDIANA UNIVERSITY OF PENNSYLVANIA

Indiana, Pennsylvania

Students with LD Served by Program	200	ADD/ADHD Services	✓
Staff	1 full-time, 2 part-time	Summer Preparation Program	n/a
LD Program or Service Fee	n/a	Alternative Test Arrangements	✓
LD Program Began	1985	LD Student Organization	✓

Disability Support Services began offering services in 1985. The program serves approximately 200 undergraduate students. Faculty consists of 1 full-time and 2 part-time staff members. Services are provided by academic advisers, graduate assistants/students, trained peer tutors, and peer advisors.

Policies Students with LD may take up to 17 credit hours per semester; 12 credit hours per semester are required to maintain full-time status and to be eligible for financial aid. LD services are also available to graduate students.

Fees *Diagnostic Testing Fee:* $75.

Special preparation or orientation Held before classes begin.

Diagnostic testing Available for neuropsychological, intelligence, reading, written language, and math.

Basic skills remediation Available in study skills and time management. Offered one-on-one and in small groups by graduate assistants/students and faculty.

Special courses Available in career planning. All courses are offered for credit; all enter into overall grade point average.

Counseling and advisement Career counseling and individual counseling are available. Academic advisement by a staff member affiliated with the program is available.

Auxiliary aids and services *Aids:* calculators, personal spelling/word-use assistants (e.g., Franklin Speller), scan and read programs (e.g., Kurzweil), screen-enlarging programs, screen readers, speech recognition programs (e.g., Dragon), tape recorders, taped textbooks. *Services and accommodations:* advocates, priority registration, alternative test arrangements, readers, note-takers, and scribes.

Student organization There is a student organization for students with LD.

ADD/ADHD Students with ADD/ADHD are eligible for the same services available to students with LD, as well as test environment.

Application *Required:* high school transcript, participation in extracurricular activities, SAT I (extended-time or untimed test accepted), personal statement, separate application to your LD program or unit, and psychoeducational report (3 years old or less). Upon application, documentation of need for special services should be sent only to your LD program or unit. Upon acceptance, documentation of need for special services should be sent only to your LD program or unit. *Application deadline (institutional):* rolling/continuous for fall and rolling/continuous for spring. *Application deadline (LD program):* rolling/continuous for fall and rolling/continuous for spring.

LD program contact Dr. Catherine Dugan, Director, Advising and Testing Center, 106 Pratt Hall, Indiana, PA 15705. *Phone:* 724-357-4067. *Fax:* 724-357-4079. *E-mail:* advising-testing@grove.iup.edu.

Application contact Indiana University of Pennsylvania, 216 Pratt Hall, Indiana, PA 15705. *E-mail:* admissions_inquiry@grove.iup.edu. *Web address:* http://www.iup.edu/.

INDIANA UNIVERSITY SOUTHEAST

New Albany, Indiana

Students with LD Served by Program	60	ADD/ADHD Services	✓
Staff	1 full-time	Summer Preparation Program	n/a
LD Program or Service Fee	n/a	Alternative Test Arrangements	✓
LD Program Began	1996	LD Student Organization	✓

Office of Services for Students with Disabilities began offering services in 1996. The program serves approximately 60 undergraduate students. Faculty consists of 1 full-time staff member. Services are provided by academic advisers, regular education teachers, and trained peer tutors.

Policies The college has written policies regarding course substitutions and substitution and waivers of requirements for admission and graduation. 12 credit hours per semester are required to maintain full-time status; 6 credit hours per semester are required to be eligible for financial aid. LD services are also available to graduate students.

Basic skills remediation Available in study skills, learning strategies, written language, and math. Offered in class-size groups by regular education teachers.

Counseling and advisement Career counseling and individual counseling are available. Academic advisement by a staff member affiliated with the program is available.

Auxiliary aids and services *Aids:* personal computers, scan and read programs (e.g., Kurzweil), screen-enlarging programs, screen readers, speech recognition programs (e.g., Dragon). *Services and accommodations:* advocates, priority registration, alternative test arrangements, readers, note-takers, and scribes.

Student organization There is a student organization for students with LD.

ADD/ADHD Students with ADD/ADHD are eligible for the same services available to students with LD, as well as distraction-free testing environments.

Application *Required:* high school transcript and ACT or SAT I (extended-time or untimed test accepted). *Recommended:* participation in extracurricular activities. Upon application, documentation of need for special services should be sent only to your LD program or unit. Upon acceptance, documentation of need for special services should be sent only to your LD program or unit. *Application deadline (institutional):* 8/15 for fall and 1/3 for spring.

LD program contact Jodi James, Coordinator, Library Building Room 022, 4201 Grant Line Road, New Albany, IN 47150. *Phone:* 812-941-2579. *Fax:* 812-941-2589. *E-mail:* jojames@ius.edu.

Application contact Indiana University Southeast, 4201 Grant Line Road, New Albany, IN 47150-6405. *E-mail:* admissions@ius.indiana.edu. *Web address:* http://www.ius.indiana.edu/.

INDIANA WESLEYAN UNIVERSITY

Marion, Indiana

Students with LD Served by Program	60	ADD/ADHD Services	✓
Staff	5 full-time, 2 part-time	Summer Preparation Program	n/a
LD Program or Service Fee	n/a	Alternative Test Arrangements	✓
LD Program Began	1979	LD Student Organization	n/a

Center for Student Support Services began offering services in 1979. The program serves approximately 60 undergraduate students. Faculty consists of 5 full-time and 2 part-time staff members. Services are provided by regular education teachers, counselors, remediation/learning specialists, trained peer tutors, and professional tutors.

Policies Students with LD may take up to 18 credits per semester; 12 credits per semester are required to maintain full-time status; 6 credits per semester are required to be eligible for financial aid.

Special preparation or orientation Optional orientation held individually by special arrangement.

Basic skills remediation Available in study skills, reading, time management, social skills, and written language. Offered one-on-one and in small groups by trained peer tutors.

Subject-area tutoring Available in most subjects. Offered one-on-one and in small groups by professional tutors and trained peer tutors.

Counseling and advisement Career counseling and individual counseling are available.

Auxiliary aids and services *Aids:* calculators, personal computers, scan and read programs (e.g., Kurzweil), screen-enlarging programs, screen readers, speech recognition programs (e.g., Dragon), tape recorders, taped textbooks. *Services and accommodations:* priority registration, alternative test arrangements, readers, note-takers, and scribes.

ADD/ADHD Students with ADD/ADHD are eligible for the same services available to students with LD, as well as distraction-free study areas, distraction-free testing environments, medication management, personal counseling and time management training.

Application *Required:* high school transcript, SAT I (extended-time test accepted), personal statement, and psychoeducational report (3 years old or less). *Recommended:* letter(s) of recommendation and documentation of high school services (e.g., Individualized Education Program [IEP] or 504 plan). Upon application, documentation of need for special services should be sent only to admissions. Upon acceptance, documentation of need for special services should be sent only to your LD program or unit. *Application deadline (institutional):* rolling/continuous for fall and rolling/continuous for spring. *Application deadline (LD program):* rolling/continuous for fall and rolling/continuous for spring.

LD program contact Jerry Harrell, Director, Center for Student Support Services, 1401 South Washington Street, Marion, IN 46953. *Phone:* 765-677-2257. *Fax:* 765-677-2140. *E-mail:* jharrell@indwes.edu.

Application contact Indiana Wesleyan University, 4201 South Washington Street, Marion, IN 46953-4999. *E-mail:* ghollaway@indwes.edu. *Web address:* http://www.indwes.edu/.

INTERNATIONAL ACADEMY OF MERCHANDISING & DESIGN, LTD.
Chicago, Illinois

Students with LD Served by Program	15	ADD/ADHD Services	✓
Staff	1 full-time, 8 part-time	Summer Preparation Program	n/a
LD Program or Service Fee	n/a	Alternative Test Arrangements	✓
LD Program Began	1999	LD Student Organization	n/a

The Learning Center began offering services in 1999. The program serves approximately 15 undergraduate students. Faculty consists of 1 full-time and 8 part-time staff members. Services are provided by counselors, regular education teachers, and trained peer tutors.

Policies Students with LD may take up to 15 credit hours per quarter; 12 credit hours per quarter are required to maintain full-time status and to be eligible for financial aid.

Diagnostic testing Available for reading, written language, and math.

Basic skills remediation Available in study skills, reading, spelling, written language, and math. Offered one-on-one and in small groups by regular education teachers and trained peer tutors.

Subject-area tutoring Available in most subjects. Offered one-on-one and in small groups by trained peer tutors and regular education instructors.

Special courses Available in study skills, time management, and learning strategies. No courses are offered for credit; none enter into overall grade point average.

Counseling and advisement Career counseling and individual counseling are available.

Auxiliary aids and services *Services and accommodations:* alternative test arrangements.

ADD/ADHD Students with ADD/ADHD are eligible for the same services available to students with LD, as well as distraction-free testing environments.

Application *Required:* high school transcript, interview, and psychoeducational report. Upon application, documentation of need for special services should be sent only to your LD program or unit. Upon acceptance, documentation of need for special services should be sent only to your LD program or unit. *Application deadline (institutional):* rolling/continuous for fall and rolling/continuous for spring. *Application deadline (LD program):* rolling/continuous for fall and rolling/continuous for spring.

LD program contact Ann Kellogg, Director of Learning Resources, 1 North State Street, Suite 400, Chicago, IL 60602. *Phone:* 312-980-9200. *Fax:* 312-960-1449. *E-mail:* akellogg@iamd.edu.

Application contact International Academy of Merchandising & Design, Ltd., One North State Street, Suite 400, Chicago, IL 60602-9736. *Web address:* http://www.iamd.edu/.

JOHNSON & WALES UNIVERSITY
Providence, Rhode Island

Students with LD Served by Program	550	ADD/ADHD Services	✓
Staff	3 full-time, 1 part-time	Summer Preparation Program	n/a
LD Program or Service Fee	n/a	Alternative Test Arrangements	✓
LD Program Began	1987	LD Student Organization	✓

Student Success began offering services in 1987. The program serves approximately 550 undergraduate students. Faculty consists of 3 full-time staff members and 1 part-time staff member. Services are provided by academic advisers, counselors, remediation/learning specialists, special education teachers, LD specialists, trained peer tutors, and professional tutors.

Policies The college has written policies regarding course substitutions. Students with LD may take up to 19 quarter credits per term. LD services are also available to graduate students.

Special preparation or orientation Optional orientation held during registration.

Basic skills remediation Available in study skills, reading, time management, social skills, learning strategies, math, and spoken language. Offered one-on-one and in small groups by regular education teachers, LD specialists, and professional tutors.

Subject-area tutoring Available in most subjects. Offered one-on-one and in small groups by professional tutors, graduate assistants/students, trained peer tutors, and LD specialists.

Johnson & Wales University (continued)

Counseling and advisement Career counseling, individual counseling, small-group counseling, and support groups are available. Academic advisement by a staff member affiliated with the program is available.

Auxiliary aids and services *Aids:* taped textbooks. *Services and accommodations:* advocates, priority registration, alternative test arrangements, readers, note-takers, and scribes.

Student organization There is a student organization for students with LD.

ADD/ADHD Students with ADD/ADHD are eligible for the same services available to students with LD, as well as distraction-free testing environments and personal coach or mentors.

Application *Required:* high school transcript. *Recommended:* participation in extracurricular activities and ACT or SAT I. Upon acceptance, documentation of need for special services should be sent only to your LD program or unit. *Application deadline (institutional):* rolling/continuous for fall and rolling/continuous for spring. *Application deadline (LD program):* rolling/continuous for fall and rolling/continuous for spring.

LD program contact Meryl Berstein, Director of Student Success, 8 Abbott Park Place, Providence, RI 02903. *Phone:* 401-598-4589. *Fax:* 401-598-4657. *E-mail:* mberstein@jwu.edu.

Application contact Johnson & Wales University, 8 Abbott Park Place, Providence, RI 02903-3703. *E-mail:* admissions@jwu.edu. *Web address:* http://www.jwu.edu/.

JOHNSON & WALES UNIVERSITY
Charleston, South Carolina

Students with LD Served by Program	70	ADD/ADHD Services	✓
Staff	1 full-time	Summer Preparation Program	n/a
LD Program or Service Fee	n/a	Alternative Test Arrangements	✓
LD Program Began	n/a	LD Student Organization	n/a

Office of Student Success serves approximately 70 undergraduate students. Faculty consists of 1 full-time staff member. Services are provided by academic advisers, counselors, regular education teachers, LD specialists, and trained peer tutors.

Policies Students with LD may take up to 18 credit hours per quarter; 12 credit hours per quarter are required to maintain full-time status; 6 credit hours per quarter are required to be eligible for financial aid.

Special preparation or orientation Optional orientation held during registration.

Diagnostic testing Available for personality, learning strategies, learning styles, and social skills.

Subject-area tutoring Available in most subjects. Offered one-on-one, in small groups, and class-size groups by trained peer tutors, LD specialists, and student success counselors.

Special courses Available in career planning, study skills, test taking, and math. No courses are offered for credit; none enter into overall grade point average.

Counseling and advisement Career counseling, individual counseling, small-group counseling, and support groups are available. Academic advisement by a staff member affiliated with the program is available.

Auxiliary aids and services *Aids:* tape recorders, taped textbooks. *Services and accommodations:* priority registration, alternative test arrangements, readers, and note-takers.

ADD/ADHD Students with ADD/ADHD are eligible for the same services available to students with LD, as well as distraction-free study areas and distraction-free testing environments.

Application *Required:* high school transcript, interview, letter(s) of recommendation, psychoeducational report (3 years old or less), and documentation of high school services (e.g., Individualized Education Program [IEP] or 504 plan). *Recommended:* participation in extracurricular activities and ACT. Upon application, documentation of need for special services should be sent to both admissions and your LD program or unit. Upon acceptance, documentation of need for special services should be sent only to your LD program or unit. *Application deadline (institutional):* rolling/continuous for fall and rolling/continuous for spring. *Application deadline (LD program):* rolling/continuous for fall and rolling/continuous for spring.

LD program contact Tammy Farson, Director of Student Success, 701 East Bay Street, Charleston, SC 29403. *Phone:* 843-727-3028. *Fax:* 843-727-3094. *E-mail:* farson@jwu-sc.edu.

Application contact Johnson & Wales University, PCC Box 1409, 701 East Bay Street, Charleston, SC 29403. *E-mail:* admissions@jwu.edu. *Web address:* http://www.jwu.edu/.

JOHNSON C. SMITH UNIVERSITY
Charlotte, North Carolina

Students with LD Served by Program	16	ADD/ADHD Services	✓
Staff	1 full-time	Summer Preparation Program	n/a
LD Program or Service Fee	n/a	Alternative Test Arrangements	✓
LD Program Began	1991	LD Student Organization	n/a

Disability Services Office began offering services in 1991. The program serves approximately 16 undergraduate students. Faculty consists of 1 full-time staff member. Services are provided by academic advisers, counselors, and graduate assistants/students.

Policies Students with LD may take up to 15 credit hours per semester; 12 credit hours per semester are required to maintain full-time status and to be eligible for financial aid.

Subject-area tutoring Available in all subjects. Offered one-on-one and in small groups by computer-based instruction and graduate assistants/students.

Counseling and advisement Career counseling, individual counseling, and small-group counseling are available. Academic advisement by a staff member affiliated with the program is available.

Auxiliary aids and services *Aids:* calculators, personal computers, speech recognition programs (e.g., Dragon). *Services and accommodations:* advocates, priority registration, alternative test arrangements, readers, note-takers, and scribes.

ADD/ADHD Students with ADD/ADHD are eligible for the same services available to students with LD, as well as distraction-free study areas, distraction-free testing environments and personal coach or mentors.

Application *Required:* high school transcript, ACT or SAT I (extended-time or untimed test accepted), psychoeducational report (3 years old or less), and documentation of high school services (e.g., Individualized Education Program [IEP] or 504 plan). *Recommended:* participation in extracurricular activities, interview, personal statement, and letter(s) of recommendation. Upon application, documentation of need for special services should be sent only to your LD program or unit. Upon acceptance, documentation of need for special services should be sent only to your LD program or unit. *Application deadline (institutional):* rolling/continuous for fall and rolling/continuous for spring. *Application deadline (LD program):* rolling/continuous for fall and rolling/continuous for spring.

LD program contact James Cuthbertson, Coordinator, 100 Beatties Ford Road, Charlotte, NC 28216. *Phone:* 704-378-1282. *Fax:* 704-330-1336. *E-mail:* jcuthbertson@jcsu.edu.
Application contact Johnson C. Smith University, 100 Beatties Ford Road, Charlotte, NC 28216-5398. *Web address:* http://www.jesu.edu/.

JOHNSON STATE COLLEGE
Johnson, Vermont

Students with LD Served by Program	115	ADD/ADHD Services	✓
Staff	1 full-time	Summer Preparation Program	n/a
LD Program or Service Fee	n/a	Alternative Test Arrangements	✓
LD Program Began	n/a	LD Student Organization	✓

Academic Support Services serves approximately 115 undergraduate students. Faculty consists of 1 full-time staff member. Services are provided by academic advisers, counselors, LD specialists, trained peer tutors, and professional tutors.
Policies LD services are also available to graduate students.
Subject-area tutoring Available in most subjects. Offered one-on-one and in small groups by professional tutors and trained peer tutors.
Counseling and advisement Career counseling and individual counseling are available. Academic advisement by a staff member affiliated with the program is available.
Auxiliary aids and services *Aids:* scan and read programs (e.g., Kurzweil), screen-enlarging programs, screen readers, speech recognition programs (e.g., Dragon), tape recorders, taped textbooks. *Services and accommodations:* advocates, alternative test arrangements, readers, and note-takers.
Student organization There is a student organization for students with LD.
ADD/ADHD Students with ADD/ADHD are eligible for the same services available to students with LD, as well as distraction-free testing environments.
Application *Required:* high school transcript, SAT I (extended-time test accepted), interview, letter(s) of recommendation, and psychoeducational report (3 years old or less). *Recommended:* documentation of high school services (e.g., Individualized Education Program [IEP] or 504 plan). Upon application, documentation of need for special services should be sent only to your LD program or unit. Upon acceptance, documentation of need for special services should be sent only to your LD program or unit.
LD program contact Katherine Veilleux, Director of Academic Support Services, Dewey Campus Center, 337 College Hill, Johnson, VT 05656. *Phone:* 802-635-1259. *Fax:* 802-635-1454. *E-mail:* veilleuk@badger.jsc.vsc.edu.
Application contact Gwyneth Harris, Associate Director of Admissions, Johnson State College, RR 2, Box 75, Johnson, VT 05656-9405. *Phone:* 802-635-1219. *E-mail:* jscapply@badger.jsc.vsc.edu. *Web address:* http://www.jsc.vsc.edu/.

KANSAS STATE UNIVERSITY
Manhattan, Kansas

Students with LD Served by Program	300	ADD/ADHD Services	✓
Staff	1 full-time	Summer Preparation Program	n/a
LD Program or Service Fee	n/a	Alternative Test Arrangements	✓
LD Program Began	1980	LD Student Organization	✓

Disabled Student Services began offering services in 1980. The program serves approximately 300 undergraduate students. Faculty consists of 1 full-time staff member. Services are provided by academic advisers, remediation/learning specialists, counselors, graduate assistants/students, LD specialists, trained peer tutors, and professional tutors.
Policies The college has written policies regarding course substitutions. Students with LD may take up to 18 credit hours per semester; 9 credit hours per semester are required to maintain full-time status; 6 credit hours per semester are required to be eligible for financial aid. LD services are also available to graduate students.
Special preparation or orientation Optional orientation held before classes begin.
Special courses Available in study skills. All courses are offered for credit; all enter into overall grade point average.
Counseling and advisement Academic advisement by a staff member affiliated with the program is available.
Auxiliary aids and services *Aids:* calculators, personal computers, personal spelling/word-use assistants (e.g., Franklin Speller), scan and read programs (e.g., Kurzweil), screen-enlarging programs, speech recognition programs (e.g., Dragon), tape recorders, taped textbooks. *Services and accommodations:* priority registration, alternative test arrangements, readers, note-takers, and scribes.
Student organization There is a student organization for students with LD.
ADD/ADHD Students with ADD/ADHD are eligible for the same services available to students with LD, as well as distraction-free testing environments and support groups for ADD/ADHD.
Application *Required:* high school transcript, ACT (extended-time or untimed test accepted), and psychoeducational report (3 years old or less). *Recommended:* documentation of high school services (e.g., Individualized Education Program [IEP] or 504 plan). Upon application, documentation of need for special services should be sent only to your LD program or unit. Upon acceptance, documentation of need for special services should be sent only to your LD program or unit. *Application deadline (institutional):* rolling/continuous for fall. *Application deadline (LD program):* rolling/continuous for fall.
LD program contact Gretchen Holden, Director, Disabled Student Services, 202 Holton Hall, Manhattan, KS 66506. *Phone:* 785-532-6441. *Fax:* 785-532-6457. *E-mail:* dss@ksu.edu.
Application contact Kansas State University, Manhattan, KS 66506. *E-mail:* kstate@ksu.edu. *Web address:* http://www.ksu.edu/.

KEAN UNIVERSITY
Union, New Jersey

Students with LD Served by Program	82	ADD/ADHD Services	✓
Staff	4 part-time	Summer Preparation Program	n/a
LD Program or Service Fee	n/a	Alternative Test Arrangements	✓
LD Program Began	n/a	LD Student Organization	n/a

Project Excel serves approximately 82 undergraduate students. Faculty consists of 4 part-time staff members. Services are provided by academic advisers, counselors, remediation/learning specialists, diagnostic specialists, special education teachers, graduate assistants/students, LD specialists, and trained peer tutors.
Policies Students with LD may take up to 18 credit hours per semester; 12 credit hours per semester are required to maintain full-time status and to be eligible for financial aid. LD services are also available to graduate students.

Kean University (continued)

Fees *Diagnostic Testing Fee:* ranges from $150 to $350.

Special preparation or orientation Required orientation held before classes begin and after classes begin.

Diagnostic testing Available for auditory processing, motor skills, spelling, handwriting, spoken language, intelligence, study skills, learning strategies, reading, written language, learning styles, visual processing, and math.

Basic skills remediation Available in study skills, computer skills, reading, time management, social skills, visual processing, learning strategies, spelling, written language, and math. Offered one-on-one by regular education teachers, special education teachers, LD specialists, and trained peer tutors.

Subject-area tutoring Available in most subjects. Offered one-on-one by professional tutors, graduate assistants/students, and LD specialists.

Counseling and advisement Career counseling and individual counseling are available. Academic advisement by a staff member affiliated with the program is available.

Auxiliary aids and services *Services and accommodations:* advocates, priority registration, alternative test arrangements, and readers.

ADD/ADHD Students with ADD/ADHD are eligible for the same services available to students with LD, as well as distraction-free study areas, distraction-free testing environments and personal coach or mentors.

Application *Required:* high school transcript, ACT or SAT I (extended-time or untimed test accepted), and personal statement. *Recommended:* participation in extracurricular activities, letter(s) of recommendation, separate application to your LD program or unit, and psychoeducational report. Upon application, documentation of need for special services should be sent only to admissions. Upon acceptance, documentation of need for special services should be sent only to your LD program or unit. *Application deadline (institutional):* 5/31 for fall and 11/1 for spring.

LD program contact Dr. Marie Segal, Director, Project Excel, Institute of Child Study, 1000 Morris Avenue, Union, NJ 07083. *Phone:* 908-527-2380. *E-mail:* pexcel@turbo.kean.edu.

Application contact Kean University, 1000 Morris Avenue, Union, NJ 07083. *E-mail:* admitme@turbo.kean.edu. *Web address:* http://www.kean.edu/.

KENT STATE UNIVERSITY
Kent, Ohio

Students with LD Served by Program	250	ADD/ADHD Services	✓
Staff	5 full-time	Summer Preparation Program	n/a
LD Program or Service Fee	n/a	Alternative Test Arrangements	✓
LD Program Began	1964	LD Student Organization	n/a

Student Disability Services began offering services in 1964. The program serves approximately 250 undergraduate students. Faculty consists of 5 full-time staff members. Services are provided by counselors.

Policies Students with LD may take up to 18 credits per semester; 12 credits per semester are required to maintain full-time status; 3 credits per semester are required to be eligible for financial aid. LD services are also available to graduate students.

Special preparation or orientation Optional orientation held before classes begin and after classes begin.

Basic skills remediation Available in study skills, reading, time management, learning strategies, spelling, written language, and math. Offered one-on-one and in small groups by graduate assistants/students, trained peer tutors, and professional learning specialists.

Subject-area tutoring Available in some subjects. Offered one-on-one, in small groups, and class-size groups by graduate assistants/students and trained peer tutors.

Counseling and advisement Support groups is available.

Auxiliary aids and services *Aids:* calculators, personal spelling/word-use assistants (e.g., Franklin Speller), scan and read programs (e.g., Kurzweil), screen-enlarging programs, speech recognition programs (e.g., Dragon), tape recorders, taped textbooks. *Services and accommodations:* priority registration, alternative test arrangements, readers, note-takers, and scribes.

ADD/ADHD Students with ADD/ADHD are eligible for the same services available to students with LD, as well as distraction-free testing environments and support groups for ADD/ADHD.

Application *Required:* high school transcript, ACT or SAT I (extended-time or untimed test accepted), psychoeducational report (5 years old or less), and documentation of high school services (e.g., Individualized Education Program [IEP] or 504 plan). *Recommended:* participation in extracurricular activities. Upon application, documentation of need for special services should be sent only to your LD program or unit. Upon acceptance, documentation of need for special services should be sent only to your LD program or unit. *Application deadline (institutional):* rolling/continuous for fall and rolling/continuous for spring. *Application deadline (LD program):* rolling/continuous for fall and rolling/continuous for spring.

LD program contact Anne L. Jannarone, Director, Student Disability Services, 181 MSC, Kent, OH 44242. *Phone:* 330-672-3391. *Fax:* 330-672-3763. *E-mail:* ajannaro@kent.edu.

Application contact Christopher Buttenschon, Assistant Director of Admissions, Kent State University, 161 Michael Schwartz Center, Kent, OH 44242-0001. *Phone:* 330-672-2444. *E-mail:* kentadm@admissions.kent.edu. *Web address:* http://www.kent.edu/.

LAURENTIAN UNIVERSITY
Sudbury, Ontario

Students with LD Served by Program	85	ADD/ADHD Services	✓
Staff	2 full-time, 1 part-time	Summer Preparation Program	n/a
LD Program or Service Fee	n/a	Alternative Test Arrangements	✓
LD Program Began	1989	LD Student Organization	n/a

Special Needs Office began offering services in 1989. The program serves approximately 85 undergraduate students. Faculty consists of 2 full-time staff members and 1 part-time staff member. Services are provided by academic advisers, counselors, graduate assistants/students, LD specialists, trained peer tutors, and professional tutors.

Policies Students with LD may take up to 15 credits per semester; 12 credits per semester are required to maintain full-time status; 6 credits per semester are required to be eligible for financial aid. LD services are also available to graduate students.

Special preparation or orientation Held during registration, before classes begin, and individually by special arrangement.

Subject-area tutoring Available in all subjects. Offered one-on-one by graduate assistants/students, trained peer tutors, and LD specialists.

Counseling and advisement Career counseling, individual counseling, and academic counseling are available. Academic advisement by a staff member affiliated with the program is available.

Auxiliary aids and services *Aids:* calculators, personal computers, personal spelling/word-use assistants (e.g., Franklin Speller), scan and read programs (e.g., Kurzweil), screen-enlarging programs, screen readers, speech recognition programs (e.g., Dragon), tape recorders, taped textbooks. *Services and accommodations:* advocates, alternative test arrangements, readers, note-takers, scribes, and assistance in academic writing.

ADD/ADHD Students with ADD/ADHD are eligible for the same services available to students with LD, as well as distraction-free study areas and distraction-free testing environments.

Application *Required:* high school transcript and psychoeducational report (3 years old or less). Upon application, documentation of need for special services should be sent only to your LD program or unit. Upon acceptance, documentation of need for special services should be sent only to your LD program or unit. *Application deadline (institutional):* rolling/continuous for fall and rolling/continuous for spring. *Application deadline (LD program):* rolling/continuous for fall and rolling/continuous for spring.

LD program contact Earl Black, Special Needs Coordinator, Ramsey Lake Road, Sudbury, ON P3E 2C6. *E-mail:* eblack@laurentian.ca.

Application contact Laurentian University, Ramsey Lake Road, Sudbury, ON P3E 2C6. *E-mail:* sjunkin@admin.laurentian.ca. *Web address:* http://www.laurentian.ca/.

LAWRENCE UNIVERSITY
Appleton, Wisconsin

Students with LD Served by Program	45	ADD/ADHD Services	✓
Staff	1 full-time	Summer Preparation Program	n/a
LD Program or Service Fee	n/a	Alternative Test Arrangements	✓
LD Program Began	1990	LD Student Organization	✓

Student Academic Services began offering services in 1990. The program serves approximately 45 undergraduate students. Faculty consists of 1 full-time staff member. Services are provided by academic advisers, trained peer tutors, and Assistant Dean, tutoring coordinator.

Basic skills remediation Available in study skills, reading, time management, learning strategies, written language, and math. Offered one-on-one by trained peer tutors.

Subject-area tutoring Available in most subjects. Offered one-on-one by trained peer tutors.

Counseling and advisement Career counseling and individual counseling are available. Academic advisement by a staff member affiliated with the program is available.

Auxiliary aids and services *Services and accommodations:* alternative test arrangements, readers, note-takers, and scribes.

Student organization There is a student organization for students with LD.

ADD/ADHD Students with ADD/ADHD are eligible for the same services available to students with LD, as well as distraction-free study areas, distraction-free testing environments and support groups for ADD/ADHD.

Application *Required:* high school transcript, ACT or SAT I (extended-time or untimed test accepted), interview, personal statement, letter(s) of recommendation, and psychoeducational report (3 years old or less). *Recommended:* participation in extracurricular activities and documentation of high school services (e.g., Individualized Education Program [IEP] or 504 plan).

Upon application, documentation of need for special services should be sent only to your LD program or unit. Upon acceptance, documentation of need for special services should be sent only to your LD program or unit. *Application deadline (institutional):* 1/15 for fall.

LD program contact Geoff Gajewski, Assistant Dean, PO Box 599, Appleton, WI 54912. *Phone:* 920-832-6530. *Fax:* 920-832-6884.

Application contact Lawrence University, PO Box 599, Appleton, WI 54912-0599. *E-mail:* excel@lawrence.edu. *Web address:* http://www.lawrence.edu.

LEBANON VALLEY COLLEGE
Annville, Pennsylvania

Students with LD Served by Program	50	ADD/ADHD Services	✓
Staff	1 part-time	Summer Preparation Program	n/a
LD Program or Service Fee	n/a	Alternative Test Arrangements	✓
LD Program Began	1998	LD Student Organization	n/a

Office of Disability Services (ODS) began offering services in 1998. The program serves approximately 50 undergraduate students. Faculty consists of 1 part-time staff member. Services are provided by LD specialists and trained peer tutors.

Policies The college has written policies regarding course substitutions. Students with LD may take up to 18 credit hours per semester; 12 credit hours per semester are required to maintain full-time status and to be eligible for financial aid. LD services are also available to graduate students.

Special preparation or orientation Optional orientation held after classes begin and individually by special arrangement.

Auxiliary aids and services *Aids:* screen-enlarging programs, screen readers, speech recognition programs (e.g., Dragon), tape recorders, taped textbooks. *Services and accommodations:* priority registration, alternative test arrangements, readers, note-takers, scribes, and intensive assistance, proofreading at the Writing Center.

ADD/ADHD Students with ADD/ADHD are eligible for the same services available to students with LD, as well as distraction-free study areas, distraction-free testing environments and modified coaching: weekly check-in appointments with O.D.S..

Application *Required:* high school transcript, participation in extracurricular activities, SAT I (extended-time or untimed test accepted), and psychoeducational report (3 years old or less). *Recommended:* ACT (extended-time or untimed test accepted), interview, personal statement, letter(s) of recommendation, and documentation of high school services (e.g., Individualized Education Program [IEP] or 504 plan). Upon acceptance, documentation of need for special services should be sent only to your LD program or unit. *Application deadline (institutional):* rolling/continuous for fall and rolling/continuous for spring. *Application deadline (LD program):* rolling/continuous for fall and rolling/continuous for spring.

LD program contact Anne H. Hohenwarter, Coordinator of Disability Services, 101 North College Avenue, Annville, PA 17003-0501. *Phone:* 717-867-6158. *Fax:* 717-867-6979. *E-mail:* hohenwar@lvc.edu.

Application contact Lebanon Valley College, PO Box R, Annville, PA 17003-0501. *E-mail:* admiss@lvc.edu. *Web address:* http://www.lvc.edu/.

LENOIR-RHYNE COLLEGE
Hickory, North Carolina

Students with LD Served by Program	40	ADD/ADHD Services	✓
Staff	1 full-time	Summer Preparation Program	n/a
LD Program or Service Fee	n/a	Alternative Test Arrangements	n/a
LD Program Began	1992	LD Student Organization	n/a

Disability Services Office began offering services in 1992. The program serves approximately 40 undergraduate students. Faculty consists of 1 full-time staff member. Services are provided by graduate assistants/students and disabilities coordinator.

Policies The college has written policies regarding course substitutions. Students with LD may take up to 18 credit hours per semester; 12 credit hours per semester are required to maintain full-time status and to be eligible for financial aid. LD services are also available to graduate students.

Subject-area tutoring Available in some subjects. Offered one-on-one and in small groups by trained peer tutors.

Auxiliary aids and services *Services and accommodations:* readers and note-takers.

ADD/ADHD Students with ADD/ADHD are eligible for the same services available to students with LD, as well as distraction-free study areas and distraction-free testing environments.

Application *Required:* high school transcript, ACT or SAT I (extended-time or untimed test accepted), and psychoeducational report (3 years old or less). *Recommended:* participation in extracurricular activities, interview, letter(s) of recommendation, and documentation of high school services (e.g., Individualized Education Program [IEP] or 504 plan). Upon acceptance, documentation of need for special services should be sent only to your LD program or unit. *Application deadline (institutional):* rolling/continuous for fall and rolling/continuous for spring. *Application deadline (LD program):* rolling/continuous for fall and rolling/continuous for spring.

LD program contact Donavon R. Kirby, Disabilities Coordinator, PO Box 7470, Hickory, NC 28603. *Phone:* 828-328-7296. *Fax:* 828-328-7329. *E-mail:* kirbydr@lrc.edu.

Application contact Lenoir-Rhyne College, 7th Avenue and 8th Street, NE, Hickory, NC 28603. *Web address:* http://www.lrc.edu/.

LIFE UNIVERSITY
Marietta, Georgia

Students with LD Served by Program	10	ADD/ADHD Services	✓
Staff	4 full-time	Summer Preparation Program	n/a
LD Program or Service Fee	n/a	Alternative Test Arrangements	✓
LD Program Began	1994	LD Student Organization	n/a

Academic Assistance Center began offering services in 1994. The program serves approximately 10 undergraduate students. Faculty consists of 4 full-time staff members. Services are provided by academic advisers, regular education teachers, and remediation/learning specialists.

Policies Students with LD may take up to 20 credit hours per quarter; 12 credit hours per quarter are required to maintain full-time status and to be eligible for financial aid. LD services are also available to graduate students.

Counseling and advisement Academic advisement by a staff member affiliated with the program is available.

Auxiliary aids and services *Aids:* scan and read programs (e.g., Kurzweil), screen-enlarging programs, taped textbooks. *Services and accommodations:* advocates, priority registration, alternative test arrangements, and note-takers.

ADD/ADHD Students with ADD/ADHD are eligible for the same services available to students with LD, as well as distraction-free testing environments.

Application *Required:* separate application to your LD program or unit and psychoeducational report (5 years old or less). Upon application, documentation of need for special services should be sent only to your LD program or unit. Upon acceptance, documentation of need for special services should be sent only to your LD program or unit. *Application deadline (institutional):* rolling/continuous for fall and rolling/continuous for spring. *Application deadline (LD program):* rolling/continuous for fall and rolling/continuous for spring.

LD program contact Dr. Ann Drake, Director, 1269 Barclay Circle, Marietta, GA 30075. *Phone:* 770-426-2725. *Fax:* 770-426-2728. *E-mail:* adrake@life.edu.

Application contact Life University, 1269 Barclay Circle, Marietta, GA 30060-2903. *Web address:* http://www.life.edu/.

LONGWOOD COLLEGE
Farmville, Virginia

Students with LD Served by Program	65	ADD/ADHD Services	✓
Staff	1 full-time, 3 part-time	Summer Preparation Program	n/a
LD Program or Service Fee	n/a	Alternative Test Arrangements	✓
LD Program Began	1989	LD Student Organization	n/a

Office of Disability Support Services began offering services in 1989. The program serves approximately 65 undergraduate students. Faculty consists of 1 full-time and 3 part-time staff members. Services are provided by special education teachers, graduate assistants/students, and clerical staff.

Policies Students with LD may take up to 18 credit hours per semester; 12 credit hours per semester are required to maintain full-time status and to be eligible for financial aid.

Special preparation or orientation Optional orientation held individually by special arrangement.

Basic skills remediation Available in study skills, learning strategies, and spelling. Offered one-on-one by computer-based instruction and trained peer tutors.

Subject-area tutoring Available in most subjects. Offered one-on-one, in small groups, and class-size groups by computer-based instruction and trained peer tutors.

Auxiliary aids and services *Aids:* personal computers, scan and read programs (e.g., Kurzweil), screen-enlarging programs, screen readers, tape recorders, taped textbooks. *Services and accommodations:* advocates, priority registration, alternative test arrangements, readers, note-takers, and scribes.

ADD/ADHD Students with ADD/ADHD are eligible for the same services available to students with LD, as well as distraction-free study areas and distraction-free testing environments.

Application *Required:* high school transcript, ACT or SAT I (extended-time or untimed test accepted), personal statement, letter(s) of recommendation, separate application to your LD program or unit, psychoeducational report (3 years old or less), and documentation of high school services (e.g., Individualized Education Program [IEP] or 504 plan). *Recommended:* participation in extracurricular activities, ACT (extended-time or untimed test accepted), SAT I (extended-time or untimed test accepted), and interview. Upon application, documentation of need for special services should be sent only to your LD program or unit. Upon acceptance, documentation of need for special services should be sent only to your LD program or unit.

LD program contact Susan Rood, Director, Disability Support Services/ADA Coordinator, 201 High Street, Farmville, VA 23909-1899. *Phone:* 804-395-2391. *Fax:* 804-395-2252. *E-mail:* srood@longwood.luc.edu.

Application contact Longwood College, 201 High Street, Farmville, VA 23909-1800. *E-mail:* lcadmit@longwood.lwc.edu. *Web address:* http://www.lwc.edu/.

LOYOLA UNIVERSITY NEW ORLEANS
New Orleans, Louisiana

Students with LD Served by Program	105	ADD/ADHD Services	✓
Staff	2 full-time, 1 part-time	Summer Preparation Program	✓
LD Program or Service Fee	n/a	Alternative Test Arrangements	✓
LD Program Began	1988	LD Student Organization	✓

Disability Services began offering services in 1988. The program serves approximately 105 undergraduate students. Faculty consists of 2 full-time staff members and 1 part-time staff member. Services are provided by counselors, remediation/learning specialists, and trained peer tutors.

Policies The college has written policies regarding course substitutions. LD services are also available to graduate students.

Special preparation or orientation Optional summer program offered prior to entering college.

Diagnostic testing Available for auditory processing, spelling, study skills, learning strategies, reading, written language, visual processing, and math.

Basic skills remediation Available in study skills, reading, time management, learning strategies, written language, and math. Offered one-on-one by academic counselors.

Subject-area tutoring Available in most subjects. Offered one-on-one by trained peer tutors and professional staff trained in learning problems.

Counseling and advisement Career counseling, individual counseling, and support groups are available.

Auxiliary aids and services *Aids:* personal computers, screen-enlarging programs, screen readers, speech recognition programs (e.g., Dragon), tape recorders, taped textbooks. *Services and accommodations:* advocates, alternative test arrangements, readers, note-takers, and scribes.

Student organization There is a student organization for students with LD.

ADD/ADHD Students with ADD/ADHD are eligible for the same services available to students with LD, as well as distraction-free study areas, distraction-free testing environments, personal coach or mentors, and support groups for ADD/ADHD.

Application *Required:* high school transcript, ACT or SAT I (extended-time or untimed test accepted), personal statement, and letter(s) of recommendation. *Recommended:* interview. *Application deadline (institutional):* rolling/continuous for fall and rolling/continuous for spring. *Application deadline (LD program):* rolling/continuous for fall and rolling/continuous for spring.

LD program contact Sarah Mead Smith, Director of Disability Services, 6363 St. Charles Avenue, Box 41, New Orleans, LA 70118. *Phone:* 504-865-2990. *Fax:* 504-865-3543. *E-mail:* ssmith@loyno.edu.

Application contact Loyola University New Orleans, 6363 Saint Charles Avenue, New Orleans, LA 70118-6195. *Web address:* http://www.loyno.edu/.

LUTHER COLLEGE
Decorah, Iowa

Students with LD Served by Program	56	ADD/ADHD Services	✓
Staff	2 full-time, 1 part-time	Summer Preparation Program	n/a
LD Program or Service Fee	n/a	Alternative Test Arrangements	✓
LD Program Began	1999	LD Student Organization	n/a

Disability Services began offering services in 1999. The program serves approximately 56 undergraduate students. Faculty consists of 2 full-time staff members and 1 part-time staff member. Services are provided by academic advisers, counselors, and trained peer tutors.

Policies Students with LD may take up to 17 semester hours per semester; 12 semester hours per semester are required to maintain full-time status.

Special preparation or orientation Optional orientation held before classes begin.

Diagnostic testing Available for study skills, learning strategies, reading, and learning styles.

Basic skills remediation Available in study skills, reading, time management, and learning strategies. Offered one-on-one, in small groups, and class-size groups by trained peer tutors.

Subject-area tutoring Available in most subjects. Offered one-on-one, in small groups, and class-size groups by trained peer tutors.

Special courses Available in study skills, college survival skills, test taking, reading, time management, learning strategies, self-advocacy, and stress management. Some courses are offered for credit; all enter into overall grade point average.

Counseling and advisement Career counseling, individual counseling, small-group counseling, and support groups are available. Academic advisement by a staff member affiliated with the program is available.

Auxiliary aids and services *Aids:* calculators, personal computers, scan and read programs (e.g., Kurzweil), speech recognition programs (e.g., Dragon), tape recorders, taped textbooks. *Services and accommodations:* advocates, alternative test arrangements, readers, note-takers, and scribes.

ADD/ADHD Students with ADD/ADHD are eligible for the same services available to students with LD, as well as distraction-free study areas, distraction-free testing environments and personal coach or mentors.

Application *Required:* high school transcript, ACT or SAT I (extended-time or untimed test accepted), letter(s) of recommendation, separate application to your LD program or unit, psychoeducational report (3 years old or less), and documentation of high school services (e.g., Individualized Education Program [IEP] or 504 plan). *Recommended:* participation in extracurricular activities, interview, and personal statement. Upon application, documentation of need for special services should be sent only to your LD program or unit. Upon acceptance, documentation of need for special services should be sent only to your LD program or unit. *Application deadline (institutional):* rolling/continuous for fall and rolling/continuous for spring. *Application deadline (LD program):* rolling/continuous for fall and rolling/continuous for spring.

LD program contact G. Raymundo Rosales, Director, 108 Preus Library, Decorah, IA 52101. *Phone:* 319-387-1270. *E-mail:* equalaccess@luther.edu.

Application contact Luther College, 700 College Drive, Decorah, IA 52101-1045. *E-mail:* admissions@luther.edu. *Web address:* http://www.luther.edu/.

MACON STATE COLLEGE
Macon, Georgia

Students with LD Served by Program	100	ADD/ADHD Services	✓
Staff	2 full-time	Summer Preparation Program	n/a
LD Program or Service Fee	n/a	Alternative Test Arrangements	✓
LD Program Began	1991	LD Student Organization	n/a

Office of Student Services began offering services in 1991. The program serves approximately 100 undergraduate students. Faculty consists of 2 full-time staff members. Services are provided by academic advisers and counselors.

Policies Students with LD may take up to 15 credit hours per semester; 6 credit hours per semester are required to be eligible for financial aid.

Counseling and advisement Career counseling and individual counseling are available. Academic advisement by a staff member affiliated with the program is available.

Auxiliary aids and services *Aids:* scan and read programs (e.g., Kurzweil), screen-enlarging programs, speech recognition programs (e.g., Dragon), tape recorders, taped textbooks. *Services and accommodations:* priority registration, alternative test arrangements, readers, note-takers, and scribes.

ADD/ADHD Students with ADD/ADHD are eligible for the same services available to students with LD, as well as distraction-free testing environments.

Application *Required:* high school transcript, ACT or SAT I (extended-time or untimed test accepted), and psychoeducational report (3 years old or less). *Recommended:* documentation of high school services (e.g., Individualized Education Program [IEP] or 504 plan). Upon application, documentation of need for special services should be sent only to your LD program or unit. Upon acceptance, documentation of need for special services should be sent only to your LD program or unit. *Application deadline (institutional):* rolling/continuous for fall and rolling/continuous for spring. *Application deadline (LD program):* rolling/continuous for fall and rolling/continuous for spring.

LD program contact Ann E. Loyd, Director of Student Services, 100 College Station Drive, Macon, GA 31206. *Phone:* 912-471-2714. *Fax:* 912-471-5730. *E-mail:* aloyd@mail.maconstate.edu.

Application contact Terrell Mitchell, Assistant Director of Admissions, Macon State College, 100 College Station Drive, Macon, GA 31206-5144. *Phone:* 912-471-2800. *E-mail:* mcinfo@cennet.mc.peachnet.edu. *Web address:* http://www.mc.peachnet.edu/.

MADONNA UNIVERSITY
Livonia, Michigan

Students with LD Served by Program	36	ADD/ADHD Services	✓
Staff	4 full-time	Summer Preparation Program	n/a
LD Program or Service Fee	n/a	Alternative Test Arrangements	✓
LD Program Began	1976	LD Student Organization	n/a

Office of Disability Resources began offering services in 1976. The program serves approximately 36 undergraduate students. Faculty consists of 4 full-time staff members. Services are provided by academic advisers, regular education teachers, trained peer tutors, and professional tutors.

Policies Students with LD may take up to 18 semester hours per term; 12 semester hours per term are required to maintain full-time status; 6 semester hours per term are required to be eligible for financial aid. LD services are also available to graduate students.

Special preparation or orientation Optional orientation held individually by special arrangement.

Subject-area tutoring Available in most subjects. Offered one-on-one and in small groups by computer-based instruction, professional tutors, and trained peer tutors.

Counseling and advisement Career counseling, individual counseling, and academic counseling are available. Academic advisement by a staff member affiliated with the program is available.

Auxiliary aids and services *Aids:* scan and read programs (e.g., Kurzweil), screen-enlarging programs, screen readers. *Services and accommodations:* advocates, priority registration, alternative test arrangements, readers, note-takers, and scribes.

ADD/ADHD Students with ADD/ADHD are eligible for the same services available to students with LD, as well as distraction-free testing environments.

Application *Required:* high school transcript, ACT (extended-time or untimed test accepted), interview, personal statement, letter(s) of recommendation, and documentation of disability. *Recommended:* participation in extracurricular activities, SAT I (extended-time or untimed test accepted), and separate application to your LD program or unit. Upon application, documentation of need for special services should be sent only to your LD program or unit. Upon acceptance, documentation of need for special services should be sent only to your LD program or unit. *Application deadline (institutional):* rolling/continuous for fall and rolling/continuous for spring. *Application deadline (LD program):* rolling/continuous for fall and rolling/continuous for spring.

LD program contact Advisor, Office of Disability Resources, 36600 Schoolcraft, Livonia, MI 48150. *Phone:* 734-432-5639. *Fax:* 734-432-5393. *E-mail:* muinfo@smtp.munet.edu.

Application contact Madonna University, 36600 Schoolcraft Road, Livonia, MI 48150-1173. *E-mail:* muinfo@smtp.munet.edu. *Web address:* http://www.munet.edu/.

MARANATHA BAPTIST BIBLE COLLEGE
Watertown, Wisconsin

Students with LD Served by Program	40	ADD/ADHD Services	✓
Staff	1 full-time, 16 part-time	Summer Preparation Program	n/a
LD Program or Service Fee	✓	Alternative Test Arrangements	✓
LD Program Began	1997	LD Student Organization	n/a

Office of Learning Assistance began offering services in 1997. The program serves approximately 40 undergraduate students. Faculty consists of 1 full-time and 16 part-time staff members. Services are provided by counselors, remediation/learning specialists, graduate assistants/students, LD specialists, and trained peer tutors.

Policies Students with LD may take up to 14 credit hours per semester; 12 credit hours per semester are required to maintain full-time status; 6 credit hours per semester are required to be eligible for financial aid.

Fees *LD Program or Service Fee:* $400 per year.

Diagnostic testing Available for spelling, reading, math, and English.

Basic skills remediation Available in study skills, computer skills, reading, time management, learning strategies, written language, and math. Offered one-on-one and in small groups by regular education teachers, graduate assistants/students, LD specialists, and trained peer tutors.

Subject-area tutoring Available in all subjects. Offered one-on-one by trained peer tutors.

Special courses Available in study skills, college survival skills, test taking, reading, time management, learning strategies, math, stress management, and written composition skills. Some courses are offered for credit; some enter into overall grade point average.

Counseling and advisement Individual counseling is available.

Auxiliary aids and services *Aids:* scan and read programs (e.g., Kurzweil), speech recognition programs (e.g., Dragon), tape recorders. *Services and accommodations:* advocates, priority registration, alternative test arrangements, note-takers, scribes, and copies of lecture notes, extra time for projects and papers.

ADD/ADHD Students with ADD/ADHD are eligible for the same services available to students with LD, as well as distraction-free testing environments and personal coach or mentors.

Application *Required:* high school transcript, ACT or SAT I (extended-time or untimed test accepted), personal statement, and letter(s) of recommendation. *Recommended:* interview, psychoeducational report, and documentation of high school services (e.g., Individualized Education Program [IEP] or 504 plan). Upon application, documentation of need for special services should be sent only to admissions. Upon acceptance, documentation of need for special services should be sent only to your LD program or unit. *Application deadline (institutional):* rolling/continuous for fall and rolling/continuous for spring. *Application deadline (LD program):* rolling/continuous for fall and rolling/continuous for spring.

LD program contact Cynthia Midcalf, Director of Learning Assistance, 745 West Main Street, Watertown, WI 53094. *Phone:* 920-206-2341. *Fax:* 920-261-9109. *E-mail:* cmidcalf@mbbc.edu.

Application contact James H. Harrison, Director of Admissions, Maranatha Baptist Bible College, 745 West Main Street, Watertown, WI 53094. *Phone:* 920-206-2327. *E-mail:* admissions@mbbc.edu. *Web address:* http://www.mbbc.edu/.

MARIAN COLLEGE OF FOND DU LAC
Fond du Lac, Wisconsin

Students with LD Served by Program	58	ADD/ADHD Services	✓
Staff	1 full-time	Summer Preparation Program	n/a
LD Program or Service Fee	n/a	Alternative Test Arrangements	✓
LD Program Began	1987	LD Student Organization	n/a

Student Development Center began offering services in 1987. The program serves approximately 58 undergraduate students. Faculty consists of 1 full-time staff member. Services are provided by academic advisers, regular education teachers, counselors, remediation/learning specialists, and trained peer tutors.

Policies Students with LD may take up to 18 credit hours per semester; 12 credit hours per semester are required to maintain full-time status and to be eligible for financial aid. LD services are also available to graduate students.

Basic skills remediation Available in study skills, reading, time management, learning strategies, written language, and math. Offered one-on-one, in small groups, and class-size groups by computer-based instruction, regular education teachers, and trained peer tutors.

Subject-area tutoring Available in most subjects. Offered one-on-one and in small groups by computer-based instruction and trained peer tutors.

Counseling and advisement Academic advisement by a staff member affiliated with the program is available.

Auxiliary aids and services *Aids:* calculators, personal spelling/word-use assistants (e.g., Franklin Speller), tape recorders, taped textbooks. *Services and accommodations:* advocates, alternative test arrangements, readers, note-takers, and scribes.

ADD/ADHD Students with ADD/ADHD are eligible for the same services available to students with LD, as well as distraction-free study areas, distraction-free testing environments and medication management.

Application *Required:* high school transcript, ACT (extended-time or untimed test accepted), and psychoeducational report (3 years old or less). *Recommended:* participation in extracurricular activities, ACT or SAT I (extended-time or untimed test accepted), interview, letter(s) of recommendation, and documentation of high school services (e.g., Individualized Education Program [IEP] or 504 plan). Upon acceptance, documentation of need for special services should be sent to both admissions and your LD program or unit. *Application deadline (institutional):* rolling/continuous for fall and rolling/continuous for spring. *Application deadline (LD program):* rolling/continuous for fall and rolling/continuous for spring.

LD program contact Ellen Mercer, Counselor, 45 South National Avenue, Fond de Lac, WI 54935. *Phone:* 920-923-8097. *E-mail:* emercer@mariancollege.edu.

Application contact Marian College of Fond du Lac, 45 South National Avenue, Fond du Lac, WI 54935-4699. *E-mail:* admit@mariancoll.edu. *Web address:* http://www.mariancollege.edu/.

MARYWOOD UNIVERSITY
Scranton, Pennsylvania

Students with LD Served by Program	28	ADD/ADHD Services	✓
Staff	2 part-time	Summer Preparation Program	n/a
LD Program or Service Fee	n/a	Alternative Test Arrangements	✓
LD Program Began	1992	LD Student Organization	n/a

Office of Special Needs for Students with Disabilities began offering services in 1992. The program serves approximately 28 undergraduate students. Faculty consists of 2 part-time staff members. Services are provided by academic advisers, counselors, remediation/learning specialists, diagnostic specialists, special education teachers, and trained peer tutors.

Policies The college has written policies regarding course substitutions. LD services are also available to graduate students.

Fees *Diagnostic Testing Fee:* ranges from $0 to $35.

Diagnostic testing Available for auditory processing, motor skills, spelling, handwriting, spoken language, intelligence, personality, learning strategies, reading, written language, learning styles, social skills, visual processing, and math.

Basic skills remediation Available in study skills, computer skills, reading, time management, spelling, written language, math, and spoken language. Offered one-on-one, in small groups, and class-size groups by LD specialists and trained peer tutors.

Subject-area tutoring Available in all subjects. Offered one-on-one, in small groups, and class-size groups by trained peer tutors.

Special courses Available in career planning, study skills, college survival skills, practical computer skills, test taking, time management, self-advocacy, stress management, and written composition skills. No courses are offered for credit; none enter into overall grade point average.

Marywood University (continued)

Counseling and advisement Career counseling, individual counseling, small-group counseling, and support groups are available. Academic advisement by a staff member affiliated with the program is available.

Auxiliary aids and services *Aids:* calculators, personal computers, scan and read programs (e.g., Kurzweil), screen-enlarging programs, tape recorders, taped textbooks. *Services and accommodations:* advocates, alternative test arrangements, readers, note-takers, and scribes.

ADD/ADHD Students with ADD/ADHD are eligible for the same services available to students with LD, as well as distraction-free study areas and distraction-free testing environments.

Application *Required:* high school transcript, SAT I (extended-time or untimed test accepted), letter(s) of recommendation, psychoeducational report (4 years old or less), and documentation of high school services (e.g., Individualized Education Program [IEP] or 504 plan). *Recommended:* participation in extra-curricular activities, ACT (extended-time or untimed test accepted), interview, and personal statement. Upon application, documentation of need for special services should be sent to both admissions and your LD program or unit. Upon acceptance, documentation of need for special services should be sent to both admissions and your LD program or unit. *Application deadline (institutional):* rolling/continuous for fall and rolling/continuous for spring. *Application deadline (LD program):* rolling/continuous for fall and rolling/continuous for spring.

LD program contact Sr. M. Eamon O'Neill, Advisor to Students with Disabilities, 2300 Adams Avenue, Scranton, PA 18509. *Phone:* 570-961-4731. *Fax:* 570-961-4744.

Application contact Marywood University, 2300 Adams Avenue, Scranton, PA 18509-1598. *E-mail:* ugadm@ac.marywood.edu. *Web address:* http://www.marywood.edu/.

MASSACHUSETTS COLLEGE OF LIBERAL ARTS
North Adams, Massachusetts

Students with LD Served by Program	50	ADD/ADHD Services	✓
Staff	5 full-time	Summer Preparation Program	✓
LD Program or Service Fee	n/a	Alternative Test Arrangements	✓
LD Program Began	1987	LD Student Organization	n/a

Learning Services Center began offering services in 1987. The program serves approximately 50 undergraduate students. Faculty consists of 5 full-time staff members. Services are provided by regular education teachers, remediation/learning specialists, and trained peer tutors.

Policies The college has written policies regarding substitution and waivers of requirements for admission. Students with LD may take up to 18 credit hours per term; 12 credit hours per term are required to maintain full-time status; 6 credit hours per term are required to be eligible for financial aid.

Special preparation or orientation Optional summer program offered prior to entering college.

Diagnostic testing Available for neuropsychological, intelligence, reading, written language, and math.

Basic skills remediation Available in reading, written language, and math. Offered in small groups and class-size groups by regular education teachers.

Subject-area tutoring Available in most subjects. Offered one-on-one and in small groups by trained peer tutors.

Counseling and advisement Individual counseling is available.

Auxiliary aids and services *Aids:* tape recorders. *Services and accommodations:* priority registration, alternative test arrangements, note-takers, and scribes.

ADD/ADHD Students with ADD/ADHD are eligible for the same services available to students with LD

Application *Required:* high school transcript, personal statement, and letter(s) of recommendation. *Recommended:* SAT I (extended-time or untimed test accepted), psychoeducational report (3 years old or less), and documentation of high school services (e.g., Individualized Education Program [IEP] or 504 plan). Upon application, documentation of need for special services should be sent only to admissions. *Application deadline (institutional):* rolling/continuous for fall and rolling/continuous for spring.

LD program contact Claire Smith, Coordinator of Accommodations for Students with Disabilities, 375 Church Street, North Adams, MA 01247. *Phone:* 413-662-5318. *Fax:* 413-662-5319. *E-mail:* msmith1@mcla.mass.edu.

Application contact Massachusetts College of Liberal Arts, 375 Church Street, North Adams, MA 01247-4100. *E-mail:* admissions@nasc.mass.edu. *Web address:* http://www.mcla.mass.edu/.

MCMASTER UNIVERSITY
Hamilton, Ontario

Students with LD Served by Program	125	ADD/ADHD Services	✓
Staff	4 full-time, 1 part-time	Summer Preparation Program	n/a
LD Program or Service Fee	n/a	Alternative Test Arrangements	✓
LD Program Began	1988	LD Student Organization	n/a

Centre for Student Development began offering services in 1988. The program serves approximately 125 undergraduate students. Faculty consists of 4 full-time staff members and 1 part-time staff member. Services are provided by academic advisers, counselors, LD specialists, and trained peer tutors.

Policies Students with LD may take up to 15 units per term; 12 units per term are required to maintain full-time status; 6 units per term are required to be eligible for financial aid. LD services are also available to graduate students.

Diagnostic testing Available for auditory processing, spelling, intelligence, personality, reading, written language, visual processing, and math.

Counseling and advisement Individual counseling, support groups, and support and study skills are available. Academic advisement by a staff member affiliated with the program is available.

Auxiliary aids and services *Aids:* personal computers, scan and read programs (e.g., Kurzweil), screen-enlarging programs, screen readers, speech recognition programs (e.g., Dragon), tape recorders, taped textbooks. *Services and accommodations:* advocates, alternative test arrangements, readers, note-takers, and scribes.

ADD/ADHD Students with ADD/ADHD are eligible for the same services available to students with LD, as well as distraction-free study areas, distraction-free testing environments, personal coach or mentors, and support groups for ADD/ADHD.

Application *Required:* psychoeducational report (5 years old or less). *Recommended:* Individual Placement Review Committee. Upon acceptance, documentation of need for special services should be sent only to your LD program or unit.

LD program contact Caroline Cayuga, Programme Coordinator/Learning Specialist, Centre for Student Development, Hamilton Hall, Room 409, Hamilton, ON L8S 4K1. *Phone:* 905-525-9140 Ext. 24354. *Fax:* 905-528-3749. *E-mail:* cayugac@mcmaster.ca.

Application contact McMaster University, 1280 Main Street West, Hamilton, ON L8S 4M2. *E-mail:* macadmit@mcmaster.ca. *Web address:* http://www.mcmaster.ca/.

MENLO COLLEGE
Atherton, California

Students with LD Served by Program	50	ADD/ADHD Services	✓
Staff	1 full-time, 2 part-time	Summer Preparation Program	n/a
LD Program or Service Fee	n/a	Alternative Test Arrangements	✓
LD Program Began	n/a	LD Student Organization	n/a

Academic Success Program serves approximately 50 undergraduate students. Faculty consists of 1 full-time and 2 part-time staff members. Services are provided by academic advisers, regular education teachers, counselors, remediation/learning specialists, and trained peer tutors.

Policies Students with LD may take up to 18 credit hours per semester; 12 credit hours per semester are required to maintain full-time status and to be eligible for financial aid.

Special preparation or orientation Optional orientation held individually by special arrangement.

Basic skills remediation Available in study skills, time management, learning strategies, and Task management. Offered one-on-one and in small groups by computer-based instruction and Program Director.

Subject-area tutoring Available in most subjects. Offered one-on-one, in small groups, and class-size groups by trained peer tutors.

Counseling and advisement Individual counseling is available. Academic advisement by a staff member affiliated with the program is available.

Auxiliary aids and services *Aids:* personal computers, taped textbooks. *Services and accommodations:* advocates, alternative test arrangements, and note-takers.

ADD/ADHD Students with ADD/ADHD are eligible for the same services available to students with LD, as well as distraction-free study areas and distraction-free testing environments.

Application *Required:* high school transcript, ACT or SAT I (extended-time or untimed test accepted), personal statement, and letter(s) of recommendation. Upon application, documentation of need for special services should be sent only to your LD program or unit. Upon acceptance, documentation of need for special services should be sent only to your LD program or unit. *Application deadline (institutional):* rolling/continuous for fall and rolling/continuous for spring.

LD program contact Mark Hager, Director, Academic Success Program, 1000 El Camino Real, Atherton, CA 94027. *Phone:* 650-688-3854. *Fax:* 650-462-1932. *E-mail:* mhager@menlo.edu.

Application contact Menlo College, 1000 El Camino Real, Atherton, CA 94027-4301. *E-mail:* admissions@menlo.edu. *Web address:* http://www.menlo.edu/.

MESSIAH COLLEGE
Grantham, Pennsylvania

Students with LD Served by Program	25	ADD/ADHD Services	✓
Staff	2 part-time	Summer Preparation Program	✓
LD Program or Service Fee	n/a	Alternative Test Arrangements	✓
LD Program Began	1996	LD Student Organization	n/a

Disability Services began offering services in 1996. The program serves approximately 25 undergraduate students. Faculty consists of 2 part-time staff members. Services are provided by academic advisers, counselors, and Director.

Policies The college has written policies regarding course substitutions. Students with LD may take up to 16 semester credits per semester; 12 semester credits per semester are required to maintain full-time status and to be eligible for financial aid.

Fees *Diagnostic Testing Fee:* $200.

Special preparation or orientation Required summer program offered prior to entering college. Optional orientation held before classes begin and individually by special arrangement.

Diagnostic testing Available for auditory processing, motor skills, spelling, neuropsychological, intelligence, study skills, learning strategies, reading, written language, learning styles, visual processing, and math.

Subject-area tutoring Available in most subjects. Offered one-on-one by trained peer tutors.

Counseling and advisement Career counseling, individual counseling, small-group counseling, and support groups are available. Academic advisement by a staff member affiliated with the program is available.

Auxiliary aids and services *Aids:* screen-enlarging programs, screen readers, speech recognition programs (e.g., Dragon), tape recorders, taped textbooks. *Services and accommodations:* advocates, priority registration, alternative test arrangements, readers, note-takers, and scribes.

ADD/ADHD Students with ADD/ADHD are eligible for the same services available to students with LD, as well as distraction-free testing environments, medication management and personal coach or mentors.

Application *Required:* ACT or SAT I (extended-time or untimed test accepted), interview, personal statement, and letter(s) of recommendation. *Recommended:* high school transcript and participation in extracurricular activities. Upon application, documentation of need for special services should be sent only to your LD program or unit. Upon acceptance, documentation of need for special services should be sent only to your LD program or unit.

LD program contact Dr. Keith W. Drahn, Director of Disability Services, 1 College Avenue, Grantham, PA 17027. *Phone:* 717-766-2511 Ext. 7258. *Fax:* 717-766-5217. *E-mail:* kdrahn@messiah.edu.

Application contact Messiah College, 1 College Avenue, Grantham, PA 17027. *E-mail:* admiss@messiah.edu. *Web address:* http://www.messiah.edu/.

METROPOLITAN STATE COLLEGE OF DENVER
Denver, Colorado

Students with LD Served by Program	180	ADD/ADHD Services	✓
Staff	3 full-time, 1 part-time	Summer Preparation Program	n/a
LD Program or Service Fee	n/a	Alternative Test Arrangements	✓
LD Program Began	n/a	LD Student Organization	n/a

Disability Services Office serves approximately 180 undergraduate students. Faculty consists of 3 full-time staff members and 1 part-time staff member. Services are provided by counselors and LD specialists.

Policies 12 credit hours per semester are required to maintain full-time status; 6 credit hours per semester are required to be eligible for financial aid. LD services are also available to graduate students.

Metropolitan State College of Denver (continued)

Special preparation or orientation Optional orientation held after classes begin and individually by special arrangement.

Auxiliary aids and services *Aids:* personal spelling/word-use assistants (e.g., Franklin Speller), scan and read programs (e.g., Kurzweil), screen-enlarging programs, screen readers, speech recognition programs (e.g., Dragon), tape recorders, taped textbooks. *Services and accommodations:* advocates, priority registration, alternative test arrangements, readers, note-takers, and scribes.

ADD/ADHD Students with ADD/ADHD are eligible for the same services available to students with LD, as well as distraction-free testing environments and support groups for ADD/ADHD.

Application *Required:* high school transcript and ACT or SAT I (extended-time or untimed test accepted). *Recommended:* participation in extracurricular activities, interview, personal statement, and letter(s) of recommendation. Upon application, documentation of need for special services should be sent only to your LD program or unit. Upon acceptance, documentation of need for special services should be sent only to your LD program or unit. *Application deadline (institutional):* rolling/continuous for fall and rolling/continuous for spring. *Application deadline (LD program):* rolling/continuous for fall and rolling/continuous for spring.

LD program contact Greg Sullivan, Learning Disability Specialist, Auraria Higher Education Center, Disability Services Office, PO Box 173361, Campus Box P, Denver, CO 80217-3361. *Phone:* 303-556-8387. *Fax:* 303-556-2074. *E-mail:* sullivang@ahec.edu.

Application contact Miriam Tapia, Assistant Director, Metropolitan State College of Denver, PO Box 173362, Denver, CO 80217-3362. *Phone:* 303-556-2615. *Web address:* http://www.mscd.edu/.

MIDLAND LUTHERAN COLLEGE
Fremont, Nebraska

Students with LD Served by Program	9	ADD/ADHD Services	✓
Staff	1 full-time, 1 part-time	Summer Preparation Program	n/a
LD Program or Service Fee	n/a	Alternative Test Arrangements	✓
LD Program Began	n/a	LD Student Organization	n/a

Academic Support Services serves approximately 9 undergraduate students. Faculty consists of 1 full-time and 1 part-time staff member. Services are provided by professional staff.

Policies Students with LD may take up to 17 credit hours per semester; 12 credit hours per semester are required to maintain full-time status; 6 credit hours per semester are required to be eligible for financial aid.

Special preparation or orientation Optional orientation held individually by special arrangement.

Auxiliary aids and services *Aids:* tape recorders, taped textbooks. *Services and accommodations:* alternative test arrangements, readers, note-takers, and scribes.

ADD/ADHD Students with ADD/ADHD are eligible for the same services available to students with LD, as well as distraction-free testing environments.

Application *Required:* high school transcript and ACT or SAT I (extended-time or untimed test accepted). *Recommended:* participation in extracurricular activities, interview, personal statement, and letter(s) of recommendation. Upon acceptance, documentation of need for special services should be sent only to admissions. *Application deadline (institutional):* rolling/continuous for fall and rolling/continuous for spring. *Application deadline (LD program):* rolling/continuous for fall and rolling/continuous for spring.

LD program contact Lisa Kramme, Director of Academic Support Services, 900 North Clarkson, Fremont, NE 68025. *Phone:* 402-721-5480 Ext. 6257. *Fax:* 402-727-6223. *E-mail:* kramme@campus.mlc.edu.

Application contact Midland Lutheran College, 900 North Clarkson Street, Fremont, NE 68025-4200. *E-mail:* rkahnk@admin.mlc.edu. *Web address:* http://www.mlc.edu/.

MIDWESTERN STATE UNIVERSITY
Wichita Falls, Texas

Students with LD Served by Program	28	ADD/ADHD Services	✓
Staff	1 full-time, 2 part-time	Summer Preparation Program	n/a
LD Program or Service Fee	n/a	Alternative Test Arrangements	✓
LD Program Began	1990	LD Student Organization	n/a

Office of Disability Services (ODS) began offering services in 1990. The program serves approximately 28 undergraduate students. Faculty consists of 1 full-time and 2 part-time staff members. Services are provided by academic advisers, counselors, graduate assistants/students, and trained peer tutors.

Policies Students with LD may take up to 18 credit hours per semester; 12 credit hours per semester are required to maintain full-time status; 3 credit hours per semester are required to be eligible for financial aid. LD services are also available to graduate students.

Special preparation or orientation Optional orientation held individually by special arrangement.

Subject-area tutoring Available in some subjects. Offered one-on-one and in small groups by computer-based instruction and trained peer tutors.

Special courses Available in college survival skills and learning strategies. All courses are offered for credit; all enter into overall grade point average.

Counseling and advisement Career counseling, individual counseling, small-group counseling, and academic support program are available. Academic advisement by a staff member affiliated with the program is available.

Auxiliary aids and services *Aids:* calculators, personal spelling/word-use assistants (e.g., Franklin Speller), scan and read programs (e.g., Kurzweil), screen-enlarging programs, speech recognition programs (e.g., Dragon), tape recorders, taped textbooks. *Services and accommodations:* advocates, priority registration, alternative test arrangements, readers, note-takers, and scribes.

ADD/ADHD Students with ADD/ADHD are eligible for the same services available to students with LD, as well as distraction-free testing environments.

Application *Required:* high school transcript, ACT or SAT I (extended-time or untimed test accepted), separate application to your LD program or unit, and psychoeducational report (5 years old or less). *Recommended:* participation in extracurricular activities. Upon application, documentation of need for special services should be sent only to your LD program or unit. Upon acceptance, documentation of need for special services should be sent only to your LD program or unit. *Application deadline (institutional):* 8/15 for fall and 1/15 for spring. *Application deadline (LD program):* rolling/continuous for fall and rolling/continuous for spring.

LD program contact Debra J. Higginbotham, Director, 3410 Taft, Wichita Falls, TX 76308. *Phone:* 940-397-4618. *Fax:* 940-397-4934. *E-mail:* fhiggnbd@nexus.mwsu.edu.

Application contact Midwestern State University, 3410 Taft Boulevard, Wichita Falls, TX 76308-2096. *E-mail:* school.relations@nexus.mwsu.edu. *Web address:* http://www.mwsu.edu/.

MILLERSVILLE UNIVERSITY OF PENNSYLVANIA

Millersville, Pennsylvania

Students with LD Served by Program	200	ADD/ADHD Services	✓
Staff	1 full-time	Summer Preparation Program	n/a
LD Program or Service Fee	n/a	Alternative Test Arrangements	✓
LD Program Began	n/a	LD Student Organization	n/a

Learning Disabilities serves approximately 200 undergraduate students. Faculty consists of 1 full-time staff member. Services are provided by academic advisers, counselors, and LD specialists.
Policies LD services are also available to graduate students.
Special preparation or orientation Optional orientation held individually by special arrangement.
Counseling and advisement Career counseling, individual counseling, and academic are available. Academic advisement by a staff member affiliated with the program is available.
Auxiliary aids and services *Aids:* calculators, scan and read programs (e.g., Kurzweil), speech recognition programs (e.g., Dragon), tape recorders, taped textbooks. *Services and accommodations:* advocates, priority registration, alternative test arrangements, readers, note-takers, and scribes.
ADD/ADHD Students with ADD/ADHD are eligible for the same services available to students with LD, as well as distraction-free study areas, distraction-free testing environments and support groups for ADD/ADHD.
Application *Required:* high school transcript, ACT or SAT I (extended-time tests accepted), and psychoeducational report (3 years old or less). Upon acceptance, documentation of need for special services should be sent to both admissions and your LD program or unit. *Application deadline (institutional):* rolling/continuous for fall and rolling/continuous for spring. *Application deadline (LD program):* rolling/continuous for fall and rolling/continuous for spring.
LD program contact Patricia J. Richter, Service Coordinator, Learning Disabilities, 250 Lyle Hall, Millersville, PA 17551-0302. *Phone:* 717-872-3257. *Fax:* 717-871-2493.
Application contact Millersville University of Pennsylvania, PO Box 1002, Millersville, PA 17551-0302. *E-mail:* adm_info@mu3.millersv.edu. *Web address:* http://www.millersv.edu/.

MILLIKIN UNIVERSITY

Decatur, Illinois

Students with LD Served by Program	20	ADD/ADHD Services	✓
Staff	1 full-time	Summer Preparation Program	n/a
LD Program or Service Fee	n/a	Alternative Test Arrangements	✓
LD Program Began	1990	LD Student Organization	n/a

Learning Enhancement Programs Center began offering services in 1990. The program serves approximately 20 undergraduate students. Faculty consists of 1 full-time staff member. Services are provided by Director, Learning Enhancement Programs Center.
Auxiliary aids and services *Services and accommodations:* priority registration, alternative test arrangements, readers, note-takers, and scribes.
ADD/ADHD Students with ADD/ADHD are eligible for the same services available to students with LD, as well as distraction-free study areas, distraction-free testing environments and support groups for ADD/ADHD.

Application *Required:* high school transcript, ACT (extended-time or untimed test accepted), personal statement, letter(s) of recommendation, and psychoeducational report (2 years old or less). *Recommended:* participation in extracurricular activities, SAT I (extended-time or untimed test accepted), and interview. Upon application, documentation of need for special services should be sent only to your LD program or unit. Upon acceptance, documentation of need for special services should be sent only to your LD program or unit. *Application deadline (institutional):* rolling/continuous for fall and rolling/continuous for spring. *Application deadline (LD program):* rolling/continuous for fall and rolling/continuous for spring.
LD program contact Elizabeth M. Abrahamson, Director, Learning Enhancement Programs/ADA/504 Coordinator, 1184 West Main Street, Learning Enhancement Center, Decatur, IL 62522. *Phone:* 217-424-3511. *Fax:* 217-362-6497. *E-mail:* babrahamson@mail.millikin.edu.
Application contact Millikin University, 1184 West Main Street, Decatur, IL 62522. *E-mail:* admis@mail.millikin.edu. *Web address:* http://www.millikin.edu/.

MILWAUKEE INSTITUTE OF ART AND DESIGN

Milwaukee, Wisconsin

Students with LD Served by Program	23	ADD/ADHD Services	✓
Staff	1 full-time, 1 part-time	Summer Preparation Program	n/a
LD Program or Service Fee	n/a	Alternative Test Arrangements	✓
LD Program Began	1998	LD Student Organization	n/a

Learning Resource Center began offering services in 1998. The program serves approximately 23 undergraduate students. Faculty consists of 1 full-time and 1 part-time staff member. Services are provided by remediation/learning specialists, trained peer tutors, and professional tutors.
Policies 12 credit hours per semester are required to maintain full-time status; 6 credit hours per semester are required to be eligible for financial aid.
Basic skills remediation Available in study skills, reading, time management, social skills, learning strategies, spelling, and written language. Offered one-on-one by professional tutors.
Subject-area tutoring Available in most subjects. Offered one-on-one and in small groups by professional tutors.
Counseling and advisement Individual counseling is available.
Auxiliary aids and services *Aids:* tape recorders. *Services and accommodations:* alternative test arrangements, readers, and note-takers.
ADD/ADHD Students with ADD/ADHD are eligible for the same services available to students with LD, as well as distraction-free testing environments and personal coach or mentors.
Application *Required:* high school transcript, interview, and personal statement. *Recommended:* letter(s) of recommendation and separate application to your LD program or unit. Upon application, documentation of need for special services should be sent only to your LD program or unit. Upon acceptance, documentation of need for special services should be sent to both admissions and your LD program or unit. *Application deadline (institutional):* rolling/continuous for fall and rolling/continuous for spring. *Application deadline (LD program):* rolling/continuous for fall and rolling/continuous for spring.
LD program contact Jennifer Crandall, Director of Learning Support, 273 East Erie Street, Milwaukee, WI 53202-6003. *Phone:* 414-276-7889. *Fax:* 414-291-8077. *E-mail:* jcrandal@miad.edu.

Milwaukee Institute of Art and Design (continued)

Application contact Milwaukee Institute of Art and Design, 273 East Erie Street, Milwaukee, WI 53202. *Web address:* http://www.miad.edu/.

MINNESOTA STATE UNIVERSITY, MANKATO

Mankato, Minnesota

Students with LD Served by Program	200	ADD/ADHD Services	✓
Staff	11 part-time	Summer Preparation Program	n/a
LD Program or Service Fee	n/a	Alternative Test Arrangements	✓
LD Program Began	1977	LD Student Organization	✓

Disability Services Office began offering services in 1977. The program serves approximately 200 undergraduate students. Faculty consists of 11 part-time staff members. Services are provided by academic advisers, graduate assistants/students, and trained peer tutors.

Policies LD services are also available to graduate students.

Subject-area tutoring Available in most subjects. Offered one-on-one and in small groups by trained peer tutors.

Counseling and advisement Individual counseling and support groups are available. Academic advisement by a staff member affiliated with the program is available.

Auxiliary aids and services *Aids:* scan and read programs (e.g., Kurzweil), screen-enlarging programs, screen readers, speech recognition programs (e.g., Dragon), tape recorders, taped textbooks. *Services and accommodations:* advocates, priority registration, alternative test arrangements, readers, note-takers, and scribes.

Student organization There is a student organization for students with LD.

ADD/ADHD Students with ADD/ADHD are eligible for the same services available to students with LD, as well as distraction-free testing environments and support groups for ADD/ADHD.

Application *Required:* high school transcript, ACT (extended-time or untimed test accepted), personal statement, letter(s) of recommendation, and psychoeducational report (3 years old or less). *Recommended:* participation in extracurricular activities. Upon application, documentation of need for special services should be sent only to admissions. Upon acceptance, documentation of need for special services should be sent only to your LD program or unit. *Application deadline (institutional):* rolling/continuous for fall and rolling/continuous for spring. *Application deadline (LD program):* rolling/continuous for fall and rolling/continuous for spring.

LD program contact Director, Disability Services Office, 117 Armstrong, Mankato, MN 56001. *Phone:* 507-389-2825. *Fax:* 507-389-1199. *E-mail:* dso@mankato.msus.edu.

Application contact Minnesota State University, Mankato, PO Box 8400, MSU 55, Mankato, MN 56002-8400. *E-mail:* linda_meidl@msl.mankato.msus.edu. *Web address:* http://www.mankato.msus.edu/.

MINNESOTA STATE UNIVERSITY MOORHEAD

Moorhead, Minnesota

Students with LD Served by Program	55	ADD/ADHD Services	✓
Staff	1 full-time, 121 part-time	Summer Preparation Program	n/a
LD Program or Service Fee	n/a	Alternative Test Arrangements	✓
LD Program Began	1990	LD Student Organization	n/a

Disability Services began offering services in 1990. The program serves approximately 55 undergraduate students. Faculty consists of 1 full-time and 121 part-time staff members. Services are provided by academic advisers, regular education teachers, counselors, remediation/learning specialists, graduate assistants/students, and teacher trainees.

Policies Students with LD may take up to 18 credit hours per semester; 12 credit hours per semester are required to maintain full-time status; 6 credit hours per semester are required to be eligible for financial aid. LD services are also available to graduate students.

Counseling and advisement Career counseling and individual counseling are available. Academic advisement by a staff member affiliated with the program is available.

Auxiliary aids and services *Aids:* calculators, personal computers, personal spelling/word-use assistants (e.g., Franklin Speller), scan and read programs (e.g., Kurzweil), screen-enlarging programs, screen readers, speech recognition programs (e.g., Dragon), tape recorders, taped textbooks, adaptive technology lab. *Services and accommodations:* advocates, alternative test arrangements, readers, note-takers, and scribes.

ADD/ADHD Students with ADD/ADHD are eligible for the same services available to students with LD, as well as distraction-free testing environments.

Application *Required:* high school transcript, separate application to your LD program or unit, and psychoeducational report (3 years old or less). *Recommended:* ACT or SAT I (extended-time or untimed test accepted) and documentation of high school services (e.g., Individualized Education Program [IEP] or 504 plan). Upon application, documentation of need for special services should be sent to both admissions and your LD program or unit. Upon acceptance, documentation of need for special services should be sent only to your LD program or unit. *Application deadline (LD program):* rolling/continuous for fall.

LD program contact Greg Toutges, Coordinator, Disability Services, 1104 7th Avenue S, Moorhead, MN 56560. *Phone:* 218-299-5859. *Fax:* 218-287-5050. *E-mail:* toutges@mhd1.moorhead.msus.edu.

Application contact Minnesota State University Moorhead, Owens Hall, Moorhead, MN 56563-0002. *Web address:* http://www.moorhead.msus.edu/.

MISSISSIPPI STATE UNIVERSITY

Mississippi State, Mississippi

Students with LD Served by Program	100	ADD/ADHD Services	✓
Staff	1 full-time, 1 part-time	Summer Preparation Program	n/a
LD Program or Service Fee	n/a	Alternative Test Arrangements	✓
LD Program Began	1989	LD Student Organization	n/a

Student Support Services began offering services in 1989. The program serves approximately 100 undergraduate students. Faculty consists of 1 full-time and 1 part-time staff member. Services are provided by case manager.

Policies The college has written policies regarding course substitutions. Students with LD may take up to 18 credit hours per semester; 12 credit hours per semester are required to maintain full-time status and to be eligible for financial aid. LD services are also available to graduate students.

Auxiliary aids and services *Aids:* calculators, personal computers, personal spelling/word-use assistants (e.g., Franklin Speller), tape recorders, taped textbooks. *Services and accommodations:* advocates, priority registration, alternative test arrangements, readers, note-takers, and scribes.

ADD/ADHD Students with ADD/ADHD are eligible for the same services available to students with LD, as well as extended time/quiet environment for testing.

Application *Required:* high school transcript, ACT (extended-time or untimed test accepted), and psychoeducational report (3 years old or less). *Recommended:* documentation of high school services (e.g., Individualized Education Program [IEP] or 504 plan). Upon application, documentation of need for special services should be sent only to your LD program or unit. Upon acceptance, documentation of need for special services should be sent only to your LD program or unit. *Application deadline (institutional):* rolling/continuous for fall and rolling/continuous for spring. *Application deadline (LD program):* rolling/continuous for fall and rolling/continuous for spring.

LD program contact Debbie Baker, Director, PO Box 806, Mississippi State, MS 39762. *Phone:* 662-325-3335. *Fax:* 662-325-8190. *E-mail:* dbaker@saffairs.msstate.edu.

Application contact Mississippi State University, PO Box 5268, Mississippi State, MS 39762. *E-mail:* admit@admissions.msstate.edu. *Web address:* http://www.msstate.edu/.

MISSOURI SOUTHERN STATE COLLEGE
Joplin, Missouri

Students with LD Served by Program	75	ADD/ADHD Services	✓
Staff	1 full-time, 25 part-time	Summer Preparation Program	n/a
LD Program or Service Fee	n/a	Alternative Test Arrangements	✓
LD Program Began	1985	LD Student Organization	n/a

Services for Students with Disabilities began offering services in 1985. The program serves approximately 75 undergraduate students. Faculty consists of 1 full-time and 25 part-time staff members. Services are provided by remediation/learning specialists, trained peer tutors, and Coordinator of Disability Services.

Policies The college has written policies regarding course substitutions and substitution and waivers of requirements for admission and graduation. Students with LD may take up to 19 credits per semester; 12 credits per semester are required to maintain full-time status.

Basic skills remediation Available in study skills, reading, and time management. Offered in class-size groups by regular education teachers.

Subject-area tutoring Available in some subjects. Offered one-on-one and in small groups by trained peer tutors.

Auxiliary aids and services *Aids:* personal spelling/word-use assistants (e.g., Franklin Speller), scan and read programs (e.g., Kurzweil), screen-enlarging programs, screen readers, speech recognition programs (e.g., Dragon), tape recorders, taped textbooks. *Services and accommodations:* priority registration, alternative test arrangements, readers, note-takers, and scribes.

ADD/ADHD Students with ADD/ADHD are eligible for the same services available to students with LD, as well as distraction-free testing environments.

Application *Required:* high school transcript, ACT (extended-time or untimed test accepted), psychoeducational report (3 years old or less), and documentation of high school services (e.g., Individualized Education Program [IEP] or 504 plan). Upon application, documentation of need for special services should be sent only to your LD program or unit. Upon acceptance, documentation of need for special services should be sent only to your LD program or unit. *Application deadline (institutional):* rolling/continuous for fall and rolling/continuous for spring. *Application deadline (LD program):* rolling/continuous for fall and rolling/continuous for spring.

LD program contact Melissa Locher, Coordinator of Disability Services, 3950 East Newman Road, Joplin, MO 64801. *Phone:* 417-625-9373. *Fax:* 417-659-4456. *E-mail:* locher-m@mail.mssc.edu.

Application contact Missouri Southern State College, 3950 East Newman Road, Joplin, MO 64801-1595. *E-mail:* admis@vm.mssc.edu. *Web address:* http://www.mssc.edu/.

MOLLOY COLLEGE
Rockville Centre, New York

Students with LD Served by Program	30	ADD/ADHD Services	✓
Staff	1 full-time	Summer Preparation Program	✓
LD Program or Service Fee	n/a	Alternative Test Arrangements	✓
LD Program Began	1991	LD Student Organization	n/a

Disability Support Services/Success Through Expanded Education Program (DSS/STEP) began offering services in 1991. The program serves approximately 30 undergraduate students. Faculty consists of 1 full-time staff member. Services are provided by academic advisers, diagnostic specialists, and LD specialists.

Policies Students with LD may take up to 12 credit hours per semester; 12 credit hours per semester are required to maintain full-time status; 3 credit hours per semester are required to be eligible for financial aid. LD services are also available to graduate students.

Special preparation or orientation Optional summer program offered prior to entering college.

Basic skills remediation Available in study skills, reading, time management, social skills, learning strategies, and written language. Offered one-on-one by LD specialists, professional tutors, and trained peer tutors.

Subject-area tutoring Available in all subjects. Offered one-on-one and in small groups by professional tutors and trained peer tutors.

Counseling and advisement Academic advisement by a staff member affiliated with the program is available.

Auxiliary aids and services *Aids:* calculators, personal computers, personal spelling/word-use assistants (e.g., Franklin Speller), scan and read programs (e.g., Kurzweil), tape recorders. *Services and accommodations:* alternative test arrangements, readers, note-takers, and scribes.

ADD/ADHD Students with ADD/ADHD are eligible for the same services available to students with LD, as well as distraction-free study areas and distraction-free testing environments.

Application *Required:* high school transcript, ACT or SAT I (extended-time tests accepted), personal statement, letter(s) of recommendation, psychoeducational report (3 years old or less), and documentation of high school services (e.g., Individualized Education Program [IEP] or 504 plan). *Recommended:* interview and separate application to your LD program or unit. Upon application, documentation of need for special services should be sent only to your LD program or unit. Upon acceptance,

Molloy College (continued)

documentation of need for special services should be sent only to your LD program or unit. *Application deadline (institutional):* rolling/continuous for fall and rolling/continuous for spring. *Application deadline (LD program):* rolling/continuous for fall and rolling/continuous for spring.

LD program contact Sr. Barbara Nirrengarten, Coordinator, 1000 Hempstead Avenue, Rockville Centre, NY 11570. *Phone:* 516-678-5000 Ext. 6381. *Fax:* 516-256-2284. *E-mail:* bnirrengarten@molloy.edu.

Application contact Molloy College, 1000 Hempstead Avenue, Rockville Centre, NY 11571-5002.

MONMOUTH UNIVERSITY
West Long Branch, New Jersey

Students with LD Served by Program	200	ADD/ADHD Services	✓
Staff	4 full-time, 1 part-time	Summer Preparation Program	n/a
LD Program or Service Fee	n/a	Alternative Test Arrangements	✓
LD Program Began	n/a	LD Student Organization	n/a

Department of Disability Services for Students serves approximately 200 undergraduate students. Faculty consists of 4 full-time staff members and 1 part-time staff member. Services are provided by counselors, graduate assistants/students, and LD specialists.

Policies The college has written policies regarding course substitutions. 12 credits per semester are required to maintain full-time status and to be eligible for financial aid. LD services are also available to graduate students.

Special preparation or orientation Held before classes begin and individually by special arrangement.

Special courses Available in career planning, study skills, college survival skills, test taking, time management, learning strategies, self-advocacy, and stress management. All courses are offered for credit; all enter into overall grade point average.

Counseling and advisement Career counseling, individual counseling, and small-group counseling are available.

Auxiliary aids and services *Aids:* calculators, personal computers, personal spelling/word-use assistants (e.g., Franklin Speller), scan and read programs (e.g., Kurzweil), screen-enlarging programs, screen readers, speech recognition programs (e.g., Dragon), tape recorders, taped textbooks. *Services and accommodations:* advocates, priority registration, alternative test arrangements, readers, and note-takers.

ADD/ADHD Students with ADD/ADHD are eligible for the same services available to students with LD, as well as distraction-free study areas, distraction-free testing environments and personal coach or mentors.

Application *Required:* high school transcript and ACT or SAT I (extended-time or untimed test accepted). Upon application, documentation of need for special services should be sent only to your LD program or unit. Upon acceptance, documentation of need for special services should be sent only to your LD program or unit. *Application deadline (institutional):* 4/1 for fall and 1/1 for spring. *Application deadline (LD program):* rolling/continuous for fall and rolling/continuous for spring.

LD program contact David C. Nast, Director, Department of Disability Services for Students, West Long Branch, NJ 07764. *Phone:* 732-571-3460. *Fax:* 732-263-5126. *E-mail:* dnast@monmouth.edu.

Application contact Christine Benol, Associate Director of Undergraduate Admission, Monmouth University, 400 Cedar Avenue, West Long Branch, NJ 07764-1898. *Phone:* 732-571-3456. *E-mail:* barson@mondec.monmouth.edu. *Web address:* http://www.monmouth.edu/.

MONTANA TECH OF THE UNIVERSITY OF MONTANA
Butte, Montana

Students with LD Served by Program	10	ADD/ADHD Services	✓
Staff	3 full-time	Summer Preparation Program	n/a
LD Program or Service Fee	n/a	Alternative Test Arrangements	n/a
LD Program Began	n/a	LD Student Organization	n/a

Student Life Programs—Disability Services serves approximately 10 undergraduate students. Faculty consists of 3 full-time staff members. Services are provided by academic advisers, regular education teachers, counselors, trained peer tutors, and professional tutors.

Policies Students with LD may take up to 18 credit hours per term; 12 credit hours per term are required to maintain full-time status and to be eligible for financial aid. LD services are also available to graduate students.

Counseling and advisement Career counseling and individual counseling are available. Academic advisement by a staff member affiliated with the program is available.

ADD/ADHD Students with ADD/ADHD are eligible for the same services available to students with LD, as well as distraction-free study areas, distraction-free testing environments, medication management and personal coach or mentors.

Application *Required:* high school transcript, ACT or SAT I (extended-time or untimed test accepted), and psychoeducational report (5 years old or less). Upon application, documentation of need for special services should be sent only to admissions. Upon acceptance, documentation of need for special services should be sent only to your LD program or unit. *Application deadline (institutional):* rolling/continuous for fall and rolling/continuous for spring. *Application deadline (LD program):* rolling/continuous for fall and rolling/continuous for spring.

LD program contact Paul Beatty, Dean of Students, 1300 West Park Street, Butte, MT 59701. *Phone:* 406-496-4198. *Fax:* 406-496-4757. *E-mail:* pbeatty@mtech.edu.

Application contact Tony Campeau, Associate Director of Admissions, Montana Tech of The University of Montana, 1300 West Park Street, Butte, MT 59701-8997. *Phone:* 406-496-4178. *E-mail:* admissions@p01.mtech.edu. *Web address:* http://www.mtech.edu/.

MORAVIAN COLLEGE
Bethlehem, Pennsylvania

Students with LD Served by Program	62	ADD/ADHD Services	✓
Staff	1 full-time, 1 part-time	Summer Preparation Program	n/a
LD Program or Service Fee	n/a	Alternative Test Arrangements	✓
LD Program Began	1994	LD Student Organization	n/a

Learning Services began offering services in 1994. The program serves approximately 62 undergraduate students. Faculty consists of 1 full-time and 1 part-time staff member. Services are provided by trained peer tutors and director, assistant director.

Policies The college has written policies regarding course substitutions.

Subject-area tutoring Available in most subjects. Offered one-on-one by trained peer tutors and LD specialists.

Counseling and advisement Career counseling, individual counseling, and small-group counseling are available.

Auxiliary aids and services *Aids:* calculators, personal computers, scan and read programs (e.g., Kurzweil), speech recognition programs (e.g., Dragon), tape recorders, taped textbooks. *Services and accommodations:* alternative test arrangements, readers, note-takers, and scribes.

ADD/ADHD Students with ADD/ADHD are eligible for the same services available to students with LD, as well as distraction-free testing environments and personal coach or mentors.

Application *Required:* high school transcript, ACT or SAT I (extended-time or untimed test accepted), letter(s) of recommendation, and psychoeducational report (3 years old or less). *Recommended:* participation in extracurricular activities, interview, and documentation of high school services (e.g., Individualized Education Program [IEP] or 504 plan). Upon application, documentation of need for special services should be sent only to your LD program or unit. Upon acceptance, documentation of need for special services should be sent to both admissions and your LD program or unit. *Application deadline (institutional):* rolling/continuous for spring.

LD program contact M. Lillian Davenport, Director, Learning Services, 1132 Monocacy Street, Bethlehem, PA 18018. *Phone:* 610-861-1510. *Fax:* 610-861-1577. *E-mail:* memld02@moravian.edu.

Application contact Moravian College, 1200 Main Street, Bethlehem, PA 18018-6650. *E-mail:* admissions@moravian.edu. *Web address:* http://www.moravian.edu/.

MOUNT IDA COLLEGE
Newton Centre, Massachusetts

Students with LD Served by Program	100	ADD/ADHD Services	✓
Staff	1 full-time, 9 part-time	Summer Preparation Program	n/a
LD Program or Service Fee	✓	Alternative Test Arrangements	✓
LD Program Began	1988	LD Student Organization	n/a

Learning Opportunities Program began offering services in 1988. The program serves approximately 100 undergraduate students. Faculty consists of 1 full-time and 9 part-time staff members. Services are provided by LD specialists.

Fees *LD Program or Service Fee:* $2700 per year.

Special preparation or orientation Optional orientation held before registration, before classes begin, during summer prior to enrollment, and individually by special arrangement.

Basic skills remediation Available in study skills, time management, written language, and math. Offered in class-size groups by regular education teachers.

Subject-area tutoring Available in most subjects. Offered one-on-one by professional tutors, trained peer tutors, and LD specialists.

Special courses Available in study skills, college survival skills, test taking, time management, learning strategies, self-advocacy, and stress management. All courses are offered for credit; all enter into overall grade point average.

Auxiliary aids and services *Aids:* calculators, personal computers, personal spelling/word-use assistants (e.g., Franklin Speller), scan and read programs (e.g., Kurzweil), speech recognition programs (e.g., Dragon), tape recorders, taped textbooks. *Services and accommodations:* advocates, priority registration, and alternative test arrangements.

ADD/ADHD Students with ADD/ADHD are eligible for the same services available to students with LD, as well as distraction-free study areas and distraction-free testing environments.

Application *Required:* high school transcript, ACT or SAT I (extended-time or untimed SAT I test accepted), letter(s) of recommendation, separate application to your LD program or unit, and psychoeducational report (3 years old or less). *Recommended:* interview and personal statement. Upon application, documentation of need for special services should be sent only to admissions. Upon acceptance, documentation of need for special services should be sent only to admissions. *Application deadline (institutional):* rolling/continuous for fall and rolling/continuous for spring. *Application deadline (LD program):* rolling/continuous for fall and rolling/continuous for spring.

LD program contact Ashley Delaney, Associate Director of Admissions, Admissions Office, 777 Dedham Street, Newton Centre, MA 02459. *Phone:* 617-928-4535. *Fax:* 617-928-4507. *E-mail:* admissions@mountida.edu.

Application contact Nancy Lemelman, Director of Admissions, Mount Ida College, 777 Dedham Street, Newton Centre, MA 02459-3310. *Phone:* 617-928-4500. *Web address:* http://www.mountida.edu/.

MOUNT MERCY COLLEGE
Cedar Rapids, Iowa

Students with LD Served by Program	55	ADD/ADHD Services	✓
Staff	1 full-time, 1 part-time	Summer Preparation Program	n/a
LD Program or Service Fee	n/a	Alternative Test Arrangements	✓
LD Program Began	1990	LD Student Organization	✓

Academic Achievement began offering services in 1990. The program serves approximately 55 undergraduate students. Faculty consists of 1 full-time and 1 part-time staff member. Services are provided by regular education teachers, counselors, and professional tutors.

Special preparation or orientation Optional orientation held individually by special arrangement.

Diagnostic testing Available for personality, study skills, learning strategies, reading, written language, learning styles, and math.

Basic skills remediation Available in study skills, computer skills, reading, time management, social skills, visual processing, learning strategies, written language, and math. Offered one-on-one, in small groups, and class-size groups by regular education teachers and professional tutors.

Subject-area tutoring Available in some subjects. Offered one-on-one by professional tutors.

Special courses Available in career planning, oral communication skills, study skills, college survival skills, practical computer skills, test taking, reading, time management, learning strategies, self-advocacy, vocabulary development, math, stress management, and written composition skills. Some courses are offered for credit; all enter into overall grade point average.

Counseling and advisement Career counseling, individual counseling, small-group counseling, and support groups are available.

Auxiliary aids and services *Aids:* calculators, tape recorders, taped textbooks. *Services and accommodations:* advocates, alternative test arrangements, readers, note-takers, and scribes.

Student organization There is a student organization for students with LD.

ADD/ADHD Students with ADD/ADHD are eligible for the same services available to students with LD, as well as distraction-free study areas and distraction-free testing environments.

Mount Mercy College (continued)

Application *Required:* high school transcript, ACT (extended-time or untimed test accepted), personal statement, letter(s) of recommendation, and documentation of high school services (e.g., Individualized Education Program [IEP] or 504 plan). *Recommended:* interview and psychoeducational report (5 years old or less). Upon application, documentation of need for special services should be sent to both admissions and your LD program or unit. Upon acceptance, documentation of need for special services should be sent to both admissions and your LD program or unit.

LD program contact Mary Jean Stanton, Director of Academics, 1330 Elmhurst Drive NE, Cedar Rapids, IA 52402. *Phone:* 319-363-8213 Ext. 1204. *Fax:* 319-363-6341. *E-mail:* mstanton@mmc.mtmercy.edu.

Application contact Mount Mercy College, 1330 Elmhurst Drive, NE, Cedar Rapids, IA 52402-4797. *E-mail:* admission@mmc.mtmercy.edu. *Web address:* http://www.mtmercy.edu/.

MOUNT VERNON NAZARENE COLLEGE

Mount Vernon, Ohio

Students with LD Served by Program	30	ADD/ADHD Services	✓
Staff	1 full-time, 1 part-time	Summer Preparation Program	n/a
LD Program or Service Fee	n/a	Alternative Test Arrangements	✓
LD Program Began	1991	LD Student Organization	n/a

Academic Support began offering services in 1991. The program serves approximately 30 undergraduate students. Faculty consists of 1 full-time and 1 part-time staff member. Services are provided by trained peer tutors and Reading Specialists, Director of Academic Support.

Policies Students with LD may take up to 15 credit hours per semester; 9 credit hours per semester are required to maintain full-time status and to be eligible for financial aid.

Subject-area tutoring Available in most subjects. Offered one-on-one by trained peer tutors.

Counseling and advisement Individual counseling is available.

Auxiliary aids and services *Aids:* tape recorders, taped textbooks. *Services and accommodations:* alternative test arrangements, readers, and note-takers.

ADD/ADHD Students with ADD/ADHD are eligible for the same services available to students with LD, as well as distraction-free testing environments.

Application *Required:* high school transcript, ACT (extended-time or untimed test accepted), personal statement, letter(s) of recommendation, and psychoeducational report (3 years old or less). *Recommended:* interview and documentation of high school services (e.g., Individualized Education Program [IEP] or 504 plan). Upon application, documentation of need for special services should be sent only to admissions. Upon acceptance, documentation of need for special services should be sent to both admissions and your LD program or unit. *Application deadline (institutional):* 5/31 for fall and 1/1 for spring. *Application deadline (LD program):* 5/31 for fall and 1/1 for spring.

LD program contact Dr. Carol Matthews, Director of Academic Support, 800 Martinsburg Road, Mount Vernon, OH 43050. *Phone:* 740-397-9000. *Fax:* 740-393-0511. *E-mail:* carol.matthews@munc.edu.

Application contact Mount Vernon Nazarene College, 800 Martinsburg Road, Mount Vernon, OH 43050-9500. *E-mail:* admissions@mvnc.edu. *Web address:* http://www.mvnc.edu/.

NAZARETH COLLEGE OF ROCHESTER

Rochester, New York

Students with LD Served by Program	135	ADD/ADHD Services	✓
Staff	1 part-time	Summer Preparation Program	n/a
LD Program or Service Fee	n/a	Alternative Test Arrangements	✓
LD Program Began	1996	LD Student Organization	n/a

Center for Academic Advisement began offering services in 1996. The program serves approximately 135 undergraduate students. Faculty consists of 1 part-time staff member. Services are provided by graduate assistants/students and Academic Counselor for Students with Disabilities.

Policies The college has written policies regarding course substitutions and substitution and waivers of requirements for admission and graduation. LD services are also available to graduate students.

Counseling and advisement Individual counseling is available.

Auxiliary aids and services *Aids:* calculators, scan and read programs (e.g., Kurzweil), screen-enlarging programs, screen readers, speech recognition programs (e.g., Dragon), tape recorders, taped textbooks. *Services and accommodations:* advocates, priority registration, alternative test arrangements, readers, note-takers, and scribes.

ADD/ADHD Students with ADD/ADHD are eligible for the same services available to students with LD, as well as distraction-free testing environments.

Application *Required:* high school transcript, ACT or SAT I (extended-time or untimed test accepted), personal statement, and letter(s) of recommendation. *Recommended:* participation in extracurricular activities, interview, psychoeducational report (5 years old or less), and documentation of high school services (e.g., Individualized Education Program [IEP] or 504 plan). Upon application, documentation of need for special services should be sent only to your LD program or unit. Upon acceptance, documentation of need for special services should be sent only to your LD program or unit. *Application deadline (institutional):* 3/15 for fall and 12/15 for spring.

LD program contact Annemarie V. House, Academic Counselor for Students with Disabilities, 4245 East Avenue, Rochester, NY 14618-3790. *Phone:* 716-389-2754. *Fax:* 716-586-2452. *E-mail:* avhouse@naz.edu.

Application contact Nazareth College of Rochester, 4245 East Avenue, Rochester, NY 14618-3790. *E-mail:* tkdarin@naz.edu. *Web address:* http://www.naz.edu/.

NEW JERSEY INSTITUTE OF TECHNOLOGY

Newark, New Jersey

Students with LD Served by Program	14	ADD/ADHD Services	✓
Staff	1 part-time	Summer Preparation Program	n/a
LD Program or Service Fee	n/a	Alternative Test Arrangements	✓
LD Program Began	1977	LD Student Organization	n/a

Counseling Center began offering services in 1977. The program serves approximately 14 undergraduate students. Faculty consists of 1 part-time staff member. Services are provided by counselors and peer notetakers, scribes, exam proctors.

Policies Students with LD may take up to 19 credit hours per semester; 12 credit hours per semester are required to maintain full-time status; 1 credit hour per semester is required to be eligible for financial aid. LD services are also available to graduate students.

Basic skills remediation Available in study skills, time management, social skills, and learning strategies. Offered one-on-one by psychologist/staff member.

Counseling and advisement Career counseling, individual counseling, and small-group counseling are available.

Auxiliary aids and services *Aids:* speech recognition programs (e.g., Dragon), tape recorders, taped textbooks. *Services and accommodations:* advocates, alternative test arrangements, readers, note-takers, and scribes.

ADD/ADHD Students with ADD/ADHD are eligible for the same services available to students with LD, as well as distraction-free testing environments and medication management.

Application *Required:* high school transcript and ACT or SAT I (extended-time or untimed test accepted). *Recommended:* participation in extracurricular activities, personal statement, and letter(s) of recommendation. Upon application, documentation of need for special services should be sent only to your LD program or unit. Upon acceptance, documentation of need for special services should be sent only to your LD program or unit. *Application deadline (institutional):* rolling/continuous for fall and rolling/continuous for spring. *Application deadline (LD program):* rolling/continuous for fall and rolling/continuous for spring.

LD program contact Dr. Phyllis Bolling, Associate Director, Counseling Center/Coordinator of Student Disability Services, Counseling Center, 205 Campbell Hall, University Heights, Newark, NJ 07102. *Phone:* 973-596-3420. *Fax:* 973-596-3419. *E-mail:* phyllis.bolling@njit.edu.

Application contact Kathy Kelly, Director of Admissions, New Jersey Institute of Technology, University Heights, Newark, NJ 07102-1982. *Phone:* 973-596-3300. *E-mail:* admissions@njit.edu. *Web address:* http://www.njit.edu/.

NEW MEXICO INSTITUTE OF MINING AND TECHNOLOGY
Socorro, New Mexico

Students with LD Served by Program	60	ADD/ADHD Services	✓
Staff	1 full-time, 1 part-time	Summer Preparation Program	n/a
LD Program or Service Fee	n/a	Alternative Test Arrangements	✓
LD Program Began	1995	LD Student Organization	n/a

Programs for Disabled Students began offering services in 1995. The program serves approximately 60 undergraduate students. Faculty consists of 1 full-time and 1 part-time staff member. Services are provided by counselors.

Policies LD services are also available to graduate students.

Auxiliary aids and services *Aids:* tape recorders, taped textbooks. *Services and accommodations:* alternative test arrangements, readers, note-takers, and scribes.

ADD/ADHD Students with ADD/ADHD are eligible for the same services available to students with LD, as well as distraction-free testing environments, medication management and counselor.

Application *Required:* high school transcript and ACT or SAT I (extended-time tests accepted). Upon application, documentation of need for special services should be sent to both admissions and your LD program or unit. Upon acceptance, documentation of need for special services should be sent to both

admissions and your LD program or unit. *Application deadline (institutional):* 8/1 for fall and 12/15 for spring. *Application deadline (LD program):* 8/1 for fall and 12/15 for spring.

LD program contact Stephany Moore, Grant Writer/Survey Coordinator, 801 Leroy Place, Socorro, NM 87801. *Phone:* 505-835-5292. *Fax:* 505-835-5825. *E-mail:* smoore@admin.nmt.edu.

Application contact New Mexico Institute of Mining and Technology, 801 Leroy Place, Socorro, NM 87801. *E-mail:* admission@admin.nmt.edu. *Web address:* http://www.nmt.edu/.

NEWSCHOOL OF ARCHITECTURE
San Diego, California

Students with LD Served by Program	12	ADD/ADHD Services	✓
Staff	1 part-time	Summer Preparation Program	✓
LD Program or Service Fee	n/a	Alternative Test Arrangements	n/a
LD Program Began	1990	LD Student Organization	n/a

Counseling Department began offering services in 1990. The program serves approximately 12 undergraduate students. Faculty consists of 1 part-time staff member. Services are provided by academic advisers and counselors.

Policies The college has written policies regarding substitution and waivers of requirements for admission. Students with LD may take up to 18 quarter units per quarter; 12 quarter units per quarter are required to maintain full-time status and to be eligible for financial aid. LD services are also available to graduate students.

Special preparation or orientation Optional summer program offered prior to entering college. Held before classes begin. most subjects. Offered one-on-one and in small groups by graduate assistants/students.

Special courses Available in oral communication skills, practical computer skills, math, and written composition skills. All courses are offered for credit; all enter into overall grade point average.

Counseling and advisement Career counseling and individual counseling are available. Academic advisement by a staff member affiliated with the program is available.

Auxiliary aids and services *Aids:* personal computers.

ADD/ADHD Students with ADD/ADHD are eligible for the same services available to students with LD, as well as distraction-free study areas.

Application *Required:* high school transcript and interview. *Recommended:* participation in extracurricular activities, personal statement, and letter(s) of recommendation. Upon application, documentation of need for special services should be sent only to admissions. Upon acceptance, documentation of need for special services should be sent only to admissions. *Application deadline (institutional):* rolling/continuous for fall and rolling/continuous for spring. *Application deadline (LD program):* rolling/continuous for fall and rolling/continuous for spring.

LD program contact Victor Parga, Director of Admissions, 1249 F, San Diego, CA 92101. *Phone:* 619-235-4100. *Fax:* 619-235-4651. *E-mail:* admissions@newschoolarch.edu.

Application contact Newschool of Architecture, 1249 F Street, San Diego, CA 92101-6634. *E-mail:* nsa1249@aol.com. *Web address:* http://www.newschoolarch.edu/.

NEW YORK UNIVERSITY
New York, New York

Students with LD Served by Program	220	ADD/ADHD Services	✓
Staff	1 full-time, 3 part-time	Summer Preparation Program	✓
LD Program or Service Fee	n/a	Alternative Test Arrangements	n/a
LD Program Began	1987	LD Student Organization	n/a

Access to Learning Program began offering services in 1987. The program serves approximately 220 undergraduate students. Faculty consists of 1 full-time and 3 part-time staff members. Services are provided by counselors and LD specialists.

Policies The college has written policies regarding course substitutions. Students with LD may take up to 18 credits per term; 12 credits per term are required to maintain full-time status; 12 credits per term are required to be eligible for financial aid. LD services are also available to graduate students.

Special preparation or orientation Optional summer program offered prior to entering college. Held before classes begin.

Basic skills remediation Available in auditory processing, study skills, reading, time management, visual processing, learning strategies, written language, and spoken language. Offered one-on-one and in small groups by LD specialists.

Counseling and advisement Individual counseling and support groups are available.

Auxiliary aids and services *Aids:* calculators, personal computers, personal spelling/word-use assistants (e.g., Franklin Speller), scan and read programs (e.g., Kurzweil), screen-enlarging programs, screen readers, speech recognition programs (e.g., Dragon), tape recorders, taped textbooks. *Services and accommodations:* advocates, readers, note-takers, and scribes.

ADD/ADHD Students with ADD/ADHD are eligible for the same services available to students with LD, as well as personal coach or mentors.

Application *Required:* high school transcript, participation in extracurricular activities, ACT or SAT I (extended-time or untimed test accepted), personal statement, letter(s) of recommendation, psychoeducational report (3 years old or less), and documentation of high school services (e.g., Individualized Education Program [IEP] or 504 plan). *Recommended:* separate application to your LD program or unit. Upon application, documentation of need for special services should be sent to both admissions and your LD program or unit. Upon acceptance, documentation of need for special services should be sent only to your LD program or unit. *Application deadline (LD program):* rolling/continuous for fall and rolling/continuous for spring.

LD program contact Alexandra Klein, Coordinator, 31 West 4th Street, 4th Floor, New York, NY 10012. *Phone:* 212-998-4980. *Fax:* 212-995-4114. *E-mail:* alexandra.klein@nyu.edu.

Application contact Richard Avitabile, Assistant Vice President for Enrollment Services, New York University, 22 Washington Square North, New York, NY 10012-1019. *Phone:* 212-998-4500. *E-mail:* nyuadmit@uccvm.nyu.edu. *Web address:* http://www.nyu.edu/.

NIPISSING UNIVERSITY
North Bay, Ontario

Students with LD Served by Program	40	ADD/ADHD Services	✓
Staff	5 full-time, 1 part-time	Summer Preparation Program	n/a
LD Program or Service Fee	n/a	Alternative Test Arrangements	✓
LD Program Began	1988	LD Student Organization	n/a

Special Needs Office began offering services in 1988. The program serves approximately 40 undergraduate students. Faculty consists of 5 full-time staff members and 1 part-time staff member. Services are provided by academic advisers, counselors, remediation/learning specialists, diagnostic specialists, LD specialists, trained peer tutors, and professional tutors.

Policies The college has written policies regarding substitution and waivers of requirements for admission. Students with LD may take up to 18 hours per semester; 9 hours per semester are required to maintain full-time status; 3 hours per semester are required to be eligible for financial aid. LD services are also available to graduate students.

Special preparation or orientation Optional orientation held before classes begin and individually by special arrangement.

Diagnostic testing Available for auditory processing, motor skills, spelling, intelligence, personality, study skills, learning strategies, reading, written language, learning styles, visual processing, and math.

Basic skills remediation Available in study skills, computer skills, reading, time management, social skills, learning strategies, spelling, written language, and math. Offered one-on-one and in small groups by computer-based instruction, professional tutors, trained peer tutors, and Academic Skills Program.

Subject-area tutoring Available in most subjects. Offered one-on-one by computer-based instruction, professional tutors, trained peer tutors, and LD specialists.

Counseling and advisement Career counseling and individual counseling are available. Academic advisement by a staff member affiliated with the program is available.

Auxiliary aids and services *Aids:* calculators, personal computers, personal spelling/word-use assistants (e.g., Franklin Speller), scan and read programs (e.g., Kurzweil), screen-enlarging programs, screen readers, speech recognition programs (e.g., Dragon), tape recorders, taped textbooks, organizational software. *Services and accommodations:* advocates, alternative test arrangements, readers, note-takers, and scribes.

ADD/ADHD Students with ADD/ADHD are eligible for the same services available to students with LD, as well as distraction-free testing environments and personal coach or mentors.

Application *Required:* high school transcript, psychoeducational report, and documentation of high school services (e.g., Individualized Education Program [IEP] or 504 plan). *Recommended:* separate application to your LD program or unit. Upon application, documentation of need for special services should be sent to both admissions and your LD program or unit. Upon acceptance, documentation of need for special services should be sent only to your LD program or unit. *Application deadline (institutional):* 9/24 for fall and 5/5 for spring. *Application deadline (LD program):* 9/24 for fall and 5/5 for spring.

LD program contact Bonnie Houston, Special Needs Coordinator, 100 College Drive, Box 5002, North Bay, ON P1B 8L7. *Phone:* 705-474-3461 Ext. 4235. *Fax:* 705-495-2850. *E-mail:* bonnieh@unipissing.ca.

Application contact Andrea Robinson, Associate Registrar, Nipissing University, Box 5002, Station Main, North Bay, ON P1B 8L7. *Phone:* 705-474-3461 Ext. 4516. *Web address:* http://www.unipissing.ca/.

NORFOLK STATE UNIVERSITY
Norfolk, Virginia

Students with LD Served by Program	30	ADD/ADHD Services	✓
Staff	1 full-time, 1 part-time	Summer Preparation Program	✓
LD Program or Service Fee	n/a	Alternative Test Arrangements	✓
LD Program Began	1998	LD Student Organization	n/a

Supporting Students Through Disability Services (SSDS) began offering services in 1998. The program serves approximately 30 undergraduate students. Faculty consists of 1 full-time and 1 part-time staff member. Services are provided by academic advisers, regular education teachers, counselors, remediation/learning specialists, graduate assistants/students, trained peer tutors, and professional tutors.

Policies Students with LD may take up to 12 credits per semester; 12 credits per semester are required to maintain full-time status and to be eligible for financial aid. LD services are also available to graduate students.

Special preparation or orientation Required summer program offered prior to entering college. Optional orientation held before classes begin, during summer prior to enrollment, and individually by special arrangement.

Basic skills remediation Available in study skills, written language, and math. Offered one-on-one by computer-based instruction, regular education teachers, graduate assistants/students, professional tutors, and trained peer tutors.

Subject-area tutoring Available in most subjects. Offered one-on-one by professional tutors, graduate assistants/students, and trained peer tutors.

Special courses Available in career planning, study skills, college survival skills, test taking, time management, self-advocacy, math, and stress management. No courses are offered for credit; none enter into overall grade point average.

Counseling and advisement Career counseling, individual counseling, small-group counseling, and support groups are available. Academic advisement by a staff member affiliated with the program is available.

Auxiliary aids and services *Aids:* calculators, personal computers, personal spelling/word-use assistants (e.g., Franklin Speller), scan and read programs (e.g., Kurzweil), screen-enlarging programs, screen readers, speech recognition programs (e.g., Dragon), tape recorders, taped textbooks. *Services and accommodations:* advocates, priority registration, alternative test arrangements, readers, note-takers, and scribes.

ADD/ADHD Students with ADD/ADHD are eligible for the same services available to students with LD, as well as distraction-free testing environments and support groups for ADD/ADHD.

Application *Required:* psychoeducational report (5 years old or less), documentation of high school services (e.g., Individualized Education Program [IEP] or 504 plan), and Letter from qualified professional insight of disability. Upon application, documentation of need for special services should be sent only to your LD program or unit. Upon acceptance, documentation of need for special services should be sent only to your LD program or unit.

LD program contact Beverly Boone Harris, ADA Coordinator, 700 Park Avenue, Mills E. Godwin Building, Room 309, Norfolk, VA 23464. *Phone:* 757-823-8173. *Fax:* 757-823-2237. *E-mail:* bbharris@nsu.edu.

Application contact Norfolk State University, 2401 Corprew Avenue, Norfolk, VA 23504-3907. *Web address:* http://www.nsu.edu/.

NORTH CAROLINA STATE UNIVERSITY
Raleigh, North Carolina

Students with LD Served by Program	250	ADD/ADHD Services	✓
Staff	2 full-time, 10 part-time	Summer Preparation Program	n/a
LD Program or Service Fee	n/a	Alternative Test Arrangements	✓
LD Program Began	n/a	LD Student Organization	✓

Disability Services for Students serves approximately 250 undergraduate students. Faculty consists of 2 full-time and 10 part-time staff members. Services are provided by services providers.

Policies 12 credit hours per semester are required to maintain full-time status and to be eligible for financial aid. LD services are also available to graduate students.

Subject-area tutoring Available in some subjects. Offered one-on-one by graduate assistants/students and undergraduate students.

Auxiliary aids and services *Aids:* scan and read programs (e.g., Kurzweil), screen-enlarging programs, taped textbooks. *Services and accommodations:* advocates, priority registration, alternative test arrangements, readers, note-takers, and scribes.

Student organization There is a student organization for students with LD.

ADD/ADHD Students with ADD/ADHD are eligible for the same services available to students with LD, as well as distraction-free testing environments.

Application *Required:* high school transcript, ACT or SAT I (extended-time tests accepted), and personal statement. *Recommended:* participation in extracurricular activities. Upon application, documentation of need for special services should be sent only to your LD program or unit. Upon acceptance, documentation of need for special services should be sent only to your LD program or unit. *Application deadline (institutional):* 2/1 for fall and 11/1 for spring. *Application deadline (LD program):* rolling/continuous for fall and rolling/continuous for spring.

LD program contact Dr. Emma Swain, Associate Coordinator, Disability Services for Students, 2815 Cates Avenue, Student Health Center, Suite 1900, Campus Box 7312, Raleigh, NC 27695-7312. *Phone:* 919-515-7653. *Fax:* 919-513-2840. *E-mail:* emma_swain@ncsu.edu.

Application contact North Carolina State University, Box 7103, 112 Peele Hall, Raleigh, NC 27695. *E-mail:* undergrad_admissions@ncsu.edu. *Web address:* http://www.ncsu.edu/.

NORTH CAROLINA WESLEYAN COLLEGE
Rocky Mount, North Carolina

Students with LD Served by Program	40	ADD/ADHD Services	✓
Staff	1 full-time	Summer Preparation Program	n/a
LD Program or Service Fee	n/a	Alternative Test Arrangements	✓
LD Program Began	1994	LD Student Organization	n/a

Disabled Student Services began offering services in 1994. The program serves approximately 40 undergraduate students. Faculty consists of 1 full-time staff member. Services are provided by academic advisers, trained peer tutors, and professional tutors.

North Carolina Wesleyan College (continued)

Policies Students with LD may take up to 18 credit hours per semester; 12 credit hours per semester are required to maintain full-time status and to be eligible for financial aid.

Fees *Diagnostic Testing Fee:* ranges from $500 to $1500.

Special preparation or orientation Required orientation held during summer prior to enrollment.

Diagnostic testing Available for auditory processing, written language, and visual processing.

Subject-area tutoring Available in most subjects. Offered one-on-one and in small groups by professional tutors, trained peer tutors, and disability specialist/coordinator.

Counseling and advisement Career counseling and individual counseling are available. Academic advisement by a staff member affiliated with the program is available.

Auxiliary aids and services *Aids:* calculators, tape recorders, taped textbooks. *Services and accommodations:* alternative test arrangements, readers, note-takers, and scribes.

ADD/ADHD Students with ADD/ADHD are eligible for the same services available to students with LD, as well as distraction-free study areas, distraction-free testing environments, medication management and personal coach or mentors.

Application *Required:* high school transcript, ACT or SAT I (extended-time SAT I test accepted), personal statement, letter(s) of recommendation, psychoeducational report (4 years old or less), and documentation of high school services (e.g., Individualized Education Program [IEP] or 504 plan). *Recommended:* participation in extracurricular activities, interview, and separate application to your LD program or unit. Upon application, documentation of need for special services should be sent to both admissions and your LD program or unit. Upon acceptance, documentation of need for special services should be sent only to your LD program or unit. *Application deadline (institutional):* rolling/continuous for fall and rolling/continuous for spring. *Application deadline (LD program):* rolling/continuous for fall and rolling/continuous for spring.

LD program contact Jennifer Harrison, Coordinator of Disabilities and Pre-Major Advisor, 3400 North Wesleyan Boulevard, Rocky Mount, NC 27804. *Phone:* 252-985-5269. *Fax:* 252-985-5399. *E-mail:* jharrison@ncwc.edu.

Application contact Cecelia Summers, Associate Director of Admissions, North Carolina Wesleyan College, 3400 North Wesleyan Boulevard, Rocky Mount, NC 27804-8677. *Phone:* 800-488-6292 Ext. 5202. *E-mail:* adm@ncwc.edu. *Web address:* http://www.ncwc.edu/.

NORTH CENTRAL COLLEGE
Naperville, Illinois

Students with LD Served by Program	40	ADD/ADHD Services	✓
Staff	1 part-time	Summer Preparation Program	n/a
LD Program or Service Fee	n/a	Alternative Test Arrangements	✓
LD Program Began	1992	LD Student Organization	n/a

LD/ADD Services began offering services in 1992. The program serves approximately 40 undergraduate students. Faculty consists of 1 part-time staff member. Services are provided by academic advisers, counselors, remediation/learning specialists, trained peer tutors, and health services, academic dean, library services, campus security.

Policies Students with LD may take up to 12 credit hours per term; 8 credit hours per term are required to maintain full-time status and to be eligible for financial aid. LD services are also available to graduate students.

Special preparation or orientation Optional orientation held before classes begin.

Subject-area tutoring Available in most subjects. Offered one-on-one and in small groups by trained peer tutors.

Special courses Available in study skills, college survival skills, test taking, time management, and learning strategies. All courses are offered for credit; all enter into overall grade point average.

Counseling and advisement Career counseling and individual counseling are available. Academic advisement by a staff member affiliated with the program is available.

Auxiliary aids and services *Aids:* calculators, personal computers, scan and read programs (e.g., Kurzweil), screen-enlarging programs, tape recorders, taped textbooks. *Services and accommodations:* advocates, alternative test arrangements, readers, and note-takers.

ADD/ADHD Students with ADD/ADHD are eligible for the same services available to students with LD, as well as distraction-free testing environments and personal coach or mentors.

Application *Required:* high school transcript, ACT or SAT I (extended-time or untimed test accepted), interview, letter(s) of recommendation, psychoeducational report (3 years old or less), and documentation of high school services (e.g., Individualized Education Program [IEP] or 504 plan). Upon application, documentation of need for special services should be sent only to admissions. Upon acceptance, documentation of need for special services should be sent to both admissions and your LD program or unit. *Application deadline (institutional):* rolling/continuous for fall and rolling/continuous for spring. *Application deadline (LD program):* rolling/continuous for fall and rolling/continuous for spring.

LD program contact Dee Wiedeman, Coordinator of LD/ADD Services, 30 North Brainard, PO Box 3063, Naperville, IL 60566. *Phone:* 630-637-5264. *Fax:* 630-637-5121. *E-mail:* dmwiedem@noctrl.edu.

Application contact Stephen Potts, Coordinator of Freshman Admission, North Central College, 30 North Brainard St, PO Box 3063, Naperville, IL 60566-7063. *Phone:* 630-637-5815. *E-mail:* ncadm@noctrl.edu. *Web address:* http://www.noctrl.edu/.

NORTHEASTERN ILLINOIS UNIVERSITY
Chicago, Illinois

Students with LD Served by Program	225	ADD/ADHD Services	✓
Staff	2 full-time, 1 part-time	Summer Preparation Program	✓
LD Program or Service Fee	n/a	Alternative Test Arrangements	✓
LD Program Began	1985	LD Student Organization	n/a

Handicap Educational Liaison Program (HELP) began offering services in 1985. The program serves approximately 225 undergraduate students. Faculty consists of 2 full-time staff members and 1 part-time staff member. Services are provided by academic advisers, counselors, remediation/learning specialists, trained peer tutors, and trained student workers.

Policies LD services are also available to graduate students.

Special preparation or orientation Optional summer program offered prior to entering college. Optional orientation held after classes begin and university orientation for all new students.

Subject-area tutoring Available in some subjects. Offered one-on-one by trained peer tutors.

Counseling and advisement Academic advisement by a staff member affiliated with the program is available.

Auxiliary aids and services *Aids:* scan and read programs (e.g., Kurzweil), screen-enlarging programs, screen readers, speech recognition programs (e.g., Dragon), tape recorders. *Services and accommodations:* advocates, priority registration, alternative test arrangements, readers, note-takers, and scribes.
ADD/ADHD Students with ADD/ADHD are eligible for the same services available to students with LD, as well as distraction-free testing environments.
Application *Required:* high school transcript, ACT or SAT I (extended-time or untimed test accepted), separate application to your LD program or unit, psychoeducational report (3 years old or less), and documentation of high school services (e.g., Individualized Education Program [IEP] or 504 plan). Upon acceptance, documentation of need for special services should be sent only to your LD program or unit. *Application deadline (institutional):* 7/1 for fall and 11/1 for spring. *Application deadline (LD program):* 7/1 for fall and 11/1 for spring.
LD program contact Victoria Amey-Flippen, Coordinator/Director, HELP Office—B110, Chicago, IL 60625-4699. *Phone:* 773-583-4050 Ext. 3135. *Fax:* 773-794-6243. *E-mail:* v-amey-flippin@neiu.edu.
Application contact Kay D. Gulli, Administrative Assistant, Northeastern Illinois University, 5500 North St Louis Avenue, Chicago, IL 60625-4699. *Phone:* 773-583-4050 Ext. 3613. *Web address:* http://www.neiu.edu/.

NORTHEASTERN STATE UNIVERSITY
Tahlequah, Oklahoma

Students with LD Served by Program	46	ADD/ADHD Services	✓
Staff	1 full-time, 1 part-time	Summer Preparation Program	n/a
LD Program or Service Fee	n/a	Alternative Test Arrangements	✓
LD Program Began	1990	LD Student Organization	n/a

Office of Student Affairs-Disabled Student Affairs began offering services in 1990. The program serves approximately 46 undergraduate students. Faculty consists of 1 full-time and 1 part-time staff member. Services are provided by counselors, graduate assistants/students, and trained peer tutors.
Policies LD services are also available to graduate students.
Subject-area tutoring Available in most subjects. Offered one-on-one and in small groups by trained peer tutors.
Counseling and advisement Individual counseling and support groups are available.
Auxiliary aids and services *Aids:* screen-enlarging programs, tape recorders, taped textbooks, text magnifiers. *Services and accommodations:* alternative test arrangements, readers, note-takers, scribes, and extended time on quizzes.
ADD/ADHD Students with ADD/ADHD are eligible for the same services available to students with LD, as well as distraction-free study areas, distraction-free testing environments, medication management and support groups for ADD/ADHD.
Application *Required:* high school transcript and ACT. Upon application, documentation of need for special services should be sent to both admissions and your LD program or unit. Upon acceptance, documentation of need for special services should be sent only to your LD program or unit.
LD program contact Jan Smith-Clayton, Assistant to the Dean of Students, 600 North Grand Avenue, Tahlequah, OK 74464. *Phone:* 918-458-2120. *Fax:* 918-458-2340. *E-mail:* smithjan@cherokee.nsuok.edu.
Application contact Northeastern State University, 600 North Grand, Tahlequah, OK 74464-2399. *E-mail:* nowlin@cherokee.nsuok.edu. *Web address:* http://www.nsuok.edu/.

NORTHERN STATE UNIVERSITY
Aberdeen, South Dakota

Students with LD Served by Program	15	ADD/ADHD Services	✓
Staff	1 full-time, 2 part-time	Summer Preparation Program	n/a
LD Program or Service Fee	n/a	Alternative Test Arrangements	✓
LD Program Began	n/a	LD Student Organization	✓

Office of Disability Services serves approximately 15 undergraduate students. Faculty consists of 1 full-time and 2 part-time staff members. Services are provided by graduate assistants/students, trained peer tutors, and professional tutors.
Policies LD services are also available to graduate students.
Subject-area tutoring Available in most subjects. Offered one-on-one and in small groups by computer-based instruction, professional tutors, graduate assistants/students, and trained peer tutors.
Special courses Available in career planning, oral communication skills, study skills, test taking, reading, time management, learning strategies, self-advocacy, vocabulary development, math, stress management, and written composition skills. All courses are offered for credit; all enter into overall grade point average.
Counseling and advisement Career counseling, individual counseling, small-group counseling, and support groups are available.
Auxiliary aids and services *Aids:* calculators, personal computers, personal spelling/word-use assistants (e.g., Franklin Speller), scan and read programs (e.g., Kurzweil), screen-enlarging programs, screen readers, speech recognition programs (e.g., Dragon), tape recorders, taped textbooks. *Services and accommodations:* advocates, priority registration, alternative test arrangements, readers, note-takers, and scribes.
Student organization There is a student organization for students with LD.
ADD/ADHD Students with ADD/ADHD are eligible for the same services available to students with LD, as well as distraction-free study areas, distraction-free testing environments, medication management, personal coach or mentors, and support groups for ADD/ADHD.
Application *Required:* interview, psychoeducational report, and documentation of high school services (e.g., Individualized Education Program [IEP] or 504 plan). *Recommended:* high school transcript. Upon application, documentation of need for special services should be sent only to your LD program or unit. Upon acceptance, documentation of need for special services should be sent only to your LD program or unit. *Application deadline (institutional):* rolling/continuous for fall and rolling/continuous for spring. *Application deadline (LD program):* rolling/continuous for fall and rolling/continuous for spring.
LD program contact Kay Diagle, Director, Disability Services, 1200 South Jay Street, Aberdeen, SD 57401. *Phone:* 605-626-2371. *Fax:* 605-626-3399. *E-mail:* diagle@northern.edu.
Application contact Northern State University, 1200 South Jay Street, Aberdeen, SD 57401-7198. *E-mail:* admissionl@wolf.northern.edu. *Web address:* http://www.northern.edu/.

NORTH GEORGIA COLLEGE & STATE UNIVERSITY
Dahlonega, Georgia

Students with LD Served by Program	35	ADD/ADHD Services	✓
Staff	1 full-time	Summer Preparation Program	n/a
LD Program or Service Fee	n/a	Alternative Test Arrangements	✓
LD Program Began	1991	LD Student Organization	n/a

Division of Learning Support, Student Disability Resources began offering services in 1991. The program serves approximately 35 undergraduate students. Faculty consists of 1 full-time staff member. Services are provided by Coordinator.

Policies The college has written policies regarding course substitutions. Students with LD may take up to 18 credit hours per semester; 12 credit hours per semester are required to maintain full-time status; 6 credit hours per semester are required to be eligible for financial aid. LD services are also available to graduate students.

Fees *Diagnostic Testing Fee:* $300.

Diagnostic testing Available for auditory processing, motor skills, spelling, neuropsychological, spoken language, intelligence, personality, reading, written language, visual processing, and math.

Counseling and advisement Individual counseling is available.

Auxiliary aids and services *Aids:* personal computers, scan and read programs (e.g., Kurzweil), screen-enlarging programs, screen readers, speech recognition programs (e.g., Dragon), tape recorders, taped textbooks. *Services and accommodations:* advocates, priority registration, alternative test arrangements, readers, note-takers, and scribes.

ADD/ADHD Students with ADD/ADHD are eligible for the same services available to students with LD, as well as distraction-free testing environments, personal coach or mentors and individual counseling.

Application *Required:* high school transcript, ACT or SAT I (extended-time tests accepted), interview, and psychoeducational report (5 years old or less). *Recommended:* documentation of high school services (e.g., Individualized Education Program [IEP] or 504 plan). Upon application, documentation of need for special services should be sent only to your LD program or unit. Upon acceptance, documentation of need for special services should be sent only to your LD program or unit. *Application deadline (institutional):* 7/1 for fall and 12/1 for spring. *Application deadline (LD program):* 7/1 for fall and 12/1 for spring.

LD program contact Rodney E. Pennamon, Coordinator, Disability Resources, 221 Barnes Hall, Dahlonega, GA 30597. *Phone:* 706-867-2782. *Fax:* 706-864-1404. *E-mail:* rpennamon@ngc.su.edu.

Application contact Bill Smith, Director of Recruitment, North Georgia College & State University, Admissions Center, Dahlonega, GA 30533. *Phone:* 706-864-1800. *E-mail:* tdavis@nugget.ngc.peachnet.edu. *Web address:* http://www.ngcsu.edu/.

NORTHLAND COLLEGE
Ashland, Wisconsin

Students with LD Served by Program	15	ADD/ADHD Services	✓
Staff	n/a	Summer Preparation Program	n/a
LD Program or Service Fee	n/a	Alternative Test Arrangements	✓
LD Program Began	1980	LD Student Organization	n/a

Academic Support Center began offering services in 1980. The program serves approximately 15 undergraduate students. Services are provided by academic advisers, regular education teachers, counselors, and trained peer tutors.

Policies Students with LD may take up to 17 credits per semester; 12 credits per semester are required to maintain full-time status and to be eligible for financial aid.

Basic skills remediation Available in study skills, reading, time management, learning strategies, written language, and math. Offered one-on-one, in small groups, and class-size groups by special education teachers and trained peer tutors.

Subject-area tutoring Available in most subjects. Offered one-on-one, in small groups, and class-size groups by trained peer tutors.

Counseling and advisement Career counseling, individual counseling, and small-group counseling are available. Academic advisement by a staff member affiliated with the program is available.

Auxiliary aids and services *Services and accommodations:* alternative test arrangements, readers, and note-takers.

ADD/ADHD Students with ADD/ADHD are eligible for the same services available to students with LD, as well as distraction-free testing environments.

Application *Required:* high school transcript, ACT or SAT I (extended-time tests accepted), and personal statement. *Recommended:* participation in extracurricular activities, interview, letter(s) of recommendation, psychoeducational report, and documentation of high school services (e.g., Individualized Education Program [IEP] or 504 plan). Upon application, documentation of need for special services should be sent to both admissions and your LD program or unit. Upon acceptance, documentation of need for special services should be sent to both admissions and your LD program or unit. *Application deadline (institutional):* rolling/continuous for fall and rolling/continuous for spring. *Application deadline (LD program):* rolling/continuous for fall and rolling/continuous for spring.

LD program contact Admission Office, 1411 Ellis Avenue, Ashland, WI 54806. *Phone:* 715-682-1224. *Fax:* 715-682-1258. *E-mail:* admit@northland.edu.

Application contact Northland College, 1411 Ellis Avenue, Ashland, WI 54806-3925. *E-mail:* admit@wakefield.northland.edu. *Web address:* http://www.northland.edu/.

NORTHWESTERN COLLEGE
St. Paul, Minnesota

Students with LD Served by Program	4	ADD/ADHD Services	✓
Staff	1 part-time	Summer Preparation Program	n/a
LD Program or Service Fee	n/a	Alternative Test Arrangements	✓
LD Program Began	1998	LD Student Organization	n/a

Disabilities Office for Support Services (DOSS) began offering services in 1998. The program serves approximately 4 undergraduate students. Faculty consists of 1 part-time staff member. Services are provided by director of disability services.

Policies Students with LD may take up to 18 credit hours per semester; 12 credit hours per semester are required to maintain full-time status and to be eligible for financial aid.

Special preparation or orientation Optional orientation held during registration, before classes begin, and individually by special arrangement.

Auxiliary aids and services *Aids:* calculators, screen-enlarging programs, tape recorders, taped textbooks. *Services and accommodations:* advocates, priority registration, alternative test arrangements, readers, note-takers, and scribes.

ADD/ADHD Students with ADD/ADHD are eligible for the same services available to students with LD, as well as distraction-free study areas, distraction-free testing environments and personal coach or mentors.

Application *Required:* high school transcript, ACT or SAT I (extended-time or untimed test accepted), personal statement, and letter(s) of recommendation. *Recommended:* participation in extracurricular activities, interview, and documentation of high school services (e.g., Individualized Education Program [IEP] or 504 plan). Upon acceptance, documentation of need for special services should be sent only to your LD program or unit. *Application deadline (institutional):* 8/15 for fall and 12/15 for spring. *Application deadline (LD program):* 8/15 for fall and 12/15 for spring.

LD program contact Dr. Yvonne Redmond-Brown, Assistant Professor of Education and Director of Disability Services, 3003 Snelling Avenue North, Saint Paul, MN 55113-1598. *Phone:* 651-631-5221. *Fax:* 651-631-5124. *E-mail:* yrb@nwc.edu.

Application contact Kenneth K. Faffler, Director of Recruitment, Northwestern College, 3003 Snelling Avenue N, St. Paul, MN 55113-1598. *Phone:* 651-631-5209. *E-mail:* admissions@nwc.edu. *Web address:* http://www.nwc.edu/.

NORTHWESTERN STATE UNIVERSITY OF LOUISIANA
Natchitoches, Louisiana

Students with LD Served by Program	130	ADD/ADHD Services	✓
Staff	1 full-time	Summer Preparation Program	n/a
LD Program or Service Fee	n/a	Alternative Test Arrangements	✓
LD Program Began	1992	LD Student Organization	n/a

Office of Disability Services began offering services in 1992. The program serves approximately 130 undergraduate students. Faculty consists of 1 full-time staff member. Services are provided by academic advisers, counselors, and graduate assistants/students.

Policies Students with LD may take up to 21 credit hours per semester; 12 credit hours per semester are required to maintain full-time status and to be eligible for financial aid. LD services are also available to graduate students.

Basic skills remediation Available in study skills, reading, time management, and math. Offered in class-size groups by regular education teachers and graduate assistants/students.

Subject-area tutoring Available in some subjects. Offered one-on-one and in small groups by graduate assistants/students and trained peer tutors.

Counseling and advisement Career counseling, individual counseling, and support groups are available. Academic advisement by a staff member affiliated with the program is available.

Auxiliary aids and services *Aids:* calculators, screen-enlarging programs, speech recognition programs (e.g., Dragon), tape recorders. *Services and accommodations:* alternative test arrangements, readers, note-takers, and scribes.

ADD/ADHD Students with ADD/ADHD are eligible for the same services available to students with LD, as well as distraction-free testing environments.

Application *Required:* high school transcript and ACT or SAT I (extended-time or untimed test accepted). Upon acceptance, documentation of need for special services should be sent only to your LD program or unit. *Application deadline (institutional):* rolling/continuous for fall and rolling/continuous for spring. *Application deadline (LD program):* rolling/continuous for fall and rolling/continuous for spring.

LD program contact Steve Hicks, Coordinator, Disability Services, General College, Kyser Hall, Room 237, Natchitoches, LA 71497. *Phone:* 318-357-6950. *Fax:* 318-357-6475. *E-mail:* hickss@alpha.nsula.edu.

Application contact Northwestern State University of Louisiana, 350 Sam Sibley Drive, Natchitoches, LA 71497. *E-mail:* admissions@alpha.nsula.edu. *Web address:* http://www.NSULA.edu/.

NORTHWOOD UNIVERSITY
Midland, Michigan

Students with LD Served by Program	75	ADD/ADHD Services	✓
Staff	7 full-time	Summer Preparation Program	n/a
LD Program or Service Fee	n/a	Alternative Test Arrangements	✓
LD Program Began	1992	LD Student Organization	n/a

Special Needs Services began offering services in 1992. The program serves approximately 75 undergraduate students. Faculty consists of 7 full-time staff members. Services are provided by academic advisers, counselors, and special education teachers.

Policies LD services are also available to graduate students.

Special preparation or orientation Optional orientation held individually by special arrangement.

Basic skills remediation Available in study skills, reading, time management, and learning strategies. Offered one-on-one by special needs counselor.

Subject-area tutoring Available in some subjects. Offered one-on-one by trained peer tutors.

Special courses Available in study skills. All courses are offered for credit; all enter into overall grade point average.

Counseling and advisement Career counseling and individual counseling are available. Academic advisement by a staff member affiliated with the program is available.

Auxiliary aids and services *Aids:* calculators, tape recorders. *Services and accommodations:* advocates, priority registration, and alternative test arrangements.

ADD/ADHD Students with ADD/ADHD are eligible for the same services available to students with LD, as well as distraction-free study areas and distraction-free testing environments.

Application *Required:* high school transcript, ACT or SAT I (extended-time or untimed test accepted), and personal statement. *Recommended:* participation in extracurricular activities, interview, psychoeducational report (3 years old or less), and documentation of high school services (e.g., Individualized Education Program [IEP] or 504 plan). Upon application, documentation of need for special services should be sent to both admissions and your LD program or unit. Upon acceptance, documentation of need for special services should be sent to both admissions and your LD program or unit.

LD program contact Michael Sullivan, Special Needs Counselor, 4000 Whitting Drive, Midland, MI 48640. *Phone:* 517-837-4465. *Fax:* 517-837-4111.

Application contact Northwood University, 3225 Cook Road, Midland, MI 48640-2398. *E-mail:* admissions@northwood.edu. *Web address:* http://www.northwood.edu/.

NOTRE DAME COLLEGE OF OHIO

South Euclid, Ohio

Students with LD Served by Program	5	ADD/ADHD Services	✓
Staff	1 full-time, 10 part-time	Summer Preparation Program	n/a
LD Program or Service Fee	n/a	Alternative Test Arrangements	n/a
LD Program Began	1989	LD Student Organization	n/a

The Learning Center began offering services in 1989. The program serves approximately 5 undergraduate students. Faculty consists of 1 full-time and 10 part-time staff members. Services are provided by Director of the Learning Center.

Policies LD services are also available to graduate students.

Diagnostic testing Available for study skills, learning strategies, reading, written language, learning styles, and math.

Basic skills remediation Available in study skills, computer skills, reading, time management, learning strategies, spelling, written language, math, and spoken language. Offered one-on-one and in small groups by computer-based instruction and Learning Center Director.

Subject-area tutoring Available in most subjects. Offered one-on-one and in small groups by computer-based instruction and Director of Learning Center.

Special courses Available in college survival skills, practical computer skills, test taking, reading, time management, learning strategies, vocabulary development, stress management, and written composition skills. No courses are offered for credit; none enter into overall grade point average.

Counseling and advisement Career counseling and individual counseling are available.

Auxiliary aids and services *Aids:* personal computers, scan and read programs (e.g., Kurzweil), speech recognition programs (e.g., Dragon). *Services and accommodations:* note-takers.

ADD/ADHD Students with ADD/ADHD are eligible for the same services available to students with LD, as well as distraction-free study areas and distraction-free testing environments.

Application *Required:* high school transcript and ACT or SAT I (extended-time or untimed test accepted). *Recommended:* participation in extracurricular activities, interview, letter(s) of recommendation, and documentation of high school services (e.g., Individualized Education Program [IEP] or 504 plan). Upon application, documentation of need for special services should be sent to both admissions and your LD program or unit. Upon acceptance, documentation of need for special services should be sent to both admissions and your LD program or unit. *Application deadline (institutional):* rolling/continuous for fall and rolling/continuous for spring. *Application deadline (LD program):* rolling/continuous for fall and rolling/continuous for spring.

LD program contact Elizabeth Kadlec, Director of the Learning Center, 4545 College Road, South Euclid, OH 44121. *Phone:* 216-381-1680 Ext. 252. *Fax:* 216-381-3802. *E-mail:* ekadlec@ndc.edu.

Application contact Notre Dame College of Ohio, 4545 College Road, South Euclid, OH 44121-4293. *Web address:* http://www.ndc.edu/.

THE OHIO STATE UNIVERSITY

Columbus, Ohio

Students with LD Served by Program	800	ADD/ADHD Services	✓
Staff	13 full-time, 2 part-time	Summer Preparation Program	n/a
LD Program or Service Fee	n/a	Alternative Test Arrangements	✓
LD Program Began	1980	LD Student Organization	✓

Office of Disability Services began offering services in 1980. The program serves approximately 800 undergraduate students. Faculty consists of 13 full-time and 2 part-time staff members. Services are provided by counselors.

Policies 12 credit hours per quarter are required to maintain full-time status and to be eligible for financial aid. LD services are also available to graduate students.

Fees *Diagnostic Testing Fee:* $225.

Special preparation or orientation Optional orientation held during registration and before classes begin.

Diagnostic testing Available for auditory processing, motor skills, spelling, handwriting, spoken language, intelligence, study skills, learning strategies, reading, written language, visual processing, and math.

Counseling and advisement Career counseling, individual counseling, and support groups are available.

Auxiliary aids and services *Aids:* calculators, personal computers, personal spelling/word-use assistants (e.g., Franklin Speller), scan and read programs (e.g., Kurzweil), screen-enlarging programs, screen readers, speech recognition programs (e.g., Dragon), tape recorders, taped textbooks. *Services and accommodations:* advocates, priority registration, alternative test arrangements, readers, note-takers, and scribes.

Student organization There is a student organization for students with LD.

ADD/ADHD Students with ADD/ADHD are eligible for the same services available to students with LD, as well as distraction-free testing environments and support groups for ADD/ADHD.

Application *Required:* high school transcript, ACT or SAT I (extended-time or untimed test accepted), and psychoeducational report (3 years old or less). *Recommended:* participation in extracurricular activities, personal statement, letter(s) of recommendation, separate application to your LD program or unit, and documentation of high school services (e.g., Individualized Education Program [IEP] or 504 plan). Upon application, documentation of need for special services should be sent only to your LD program or unit. Upon acceptance, documentation of need for special services should be sent only to your LD program or unit. *Application deadline (institutional):* rolling/continuous for spring and 2/15 for fall. *Application deadline (LD program):* rolling/continuous for fall and rolling/continuous for spring.

LD program contact Patty Carlton, Assistant Director, 1760 Neil Avenue, Room 150 Pomerene Hall, Columbus, OH 43210. *Phone:* 614-292-3307. *Fax:* 614-292-4190. *E-mail:* carlton.l@osu.edu.

Application contact Dr. Robin Brown, Director of Undergraduate Admissions, The Ohio State University, 3rd Floor, Lincoln Tower, Columbus, OH 43210. *Phone:* 614-292-3980. *Web address:* http://www.osu.edu/.

THE OHIO STATE UNIVERSITY AT LIMA
Lima, Ohio

Students with LD Served by Program	30	ADD/ADHD Services	✓
Staff	1 part-time	Summer Preparation Program	n/a
LD Program or Service Fee	n/a	Alternative Test Arrangements	✓
LD Program Began	1985	LD Student Organization	n/a

Academic Advising began offering services in 1985. The program serves approximately 30 undergraduate students. Faculty consists of 1 part-time staff member. Services are provided by LD specialists.

Policies 12 credit hours per quarter are required to be eligible for financial aid. LD services are also available to graduate students.

Counseling and advisement Individual counseling and support groups are available.

Auxiliary aids and services *Aids:* taped textbooks. *Services and accommodations:* alternative test arrangements, readers, note-takers, and scribes.

ADD/ADHD Students with ADD/ADHD are eligible for the same services available to students with LD, as well as distraction-free study areas and distraction-free testing environments.

Application *Required:* high school transcript and psychoeducational report (4 years old or less). *Recommended:* separate application to your LD program or unit and documentation of high school services (e.g., Individualized Education Program [IEP] or 504 plan). Upon application, documentation of need for special services should be sent only to your LD program or unit. Upon acceptance, documentation of need for special services should be sent only to your LD program or unit. *Application deadline (institutional):* rolling/continuous for fall and rolling/continuous for spring. *Application deadline (LD program):* rolling/continuous for fall and rolling/continuous for spring.

LD program contact Karen Meyer, Learning Disability Specialist, 4240 Campus Drive, PS 145, Lima, OH 45804. *Phone:* 419-995-8453. *Fax:* 419-995-8483. *E-mail:* meyer.193@osu.edu.

Application contact The Ohio State University at Lima, 4240 Campus Drive, Lima, OH 45804-3576. *Web address:* http://www.ohio-state.edu/.

THE OHIO STATE UNIVERSITY AT MARION
Marion, Ohio

Students with LD Served by Program	20	ADD/ADHD Services	✓
Staff	1 part-time	Summer Preparation Program	n/a
LD Program or Service Fee	n/a	Alternative Test Arrangements	✓
LD Program Began	n/a	LD Student Organization	n/a

Disability Services serves approximately 20 undergraduate students. Faculty consists of 1 part-time staff member. Services are provided by LD specialists, trained peer tutors, and professional tutors.

Policies The college has written policies regarding course substitutions, grade forgiveness, and substitution and waivers of requirements for admission and graduation. LD services are also available to graduate students.

Diagnostic testing Available for auditory processing, spelling, handwriting, spoken language, intelligence, study skills, learning strategies, reading, written language, learning styles, social skills, visual processing, and math.

Basic skills remediation Available in math. Offered in small groups by LD specialists, professional tutors, and trained peer tutors.

Subject-area tutoring Available in most subjects. Offered one-on-one and in small groups by professional tutors, graduate assistants/students, and trained peer tutors.

Counseling and advisement Career counseling and individual counseling are available.

Auxiliary aids and services *Aids:* calculators, personal spelling/word-use assistants (e.g., Franklin Speller), screen-enlarging programs, tape recorders, taped textbooks. *Services and accommodations:* priority registration, alternative test arrangements, readers, and note-takers.

ADD/ADHD Students with ADD/ADHD are eligible for the same services available to students with LD, as well as distraction-free study areas and distraction-free testing environments.

Application *Required:* high school transcript, interview, personal statement, letter(s) of recommendation, psychoeducational report (1 year old or less), and documentation of high school services (e.g., Individualized Education Program [IEP] or 504 plan). *Recommended:* ACT or SAT I (extended-time tests accepted). Upon application, documentation of need for special services should be sent only to your LD program or unit. Upon acceptance, documentation of need for special services should be sent to both admissions and your LD program or unit. *Application deadline (LD program):* rolling/continuous for fall and rolling/continuous for spring.

LD program contact Margaret C. Hazelett, LD Specialist, 1465 Mount Vernon Avenue, Marion, OH 43302. *Phone:* 740-389-OSUM. *E-mail:* hazelett.2@osu.edu.

Application contact The Ohio State University at Marion, 1465 Mount Vernon Avenue, Marion, OH 43302-5695. *Web address:* http://www.ohio-state.edu/.

THE OHIO STATE UNIVERSITY-NEWARK CAMPUS
Newark, Ohio

Students with LD Served by Program	70	ADD/ADHD Services	✓
Staff	4 full-time	Summer Preparation Program	n/a
LD Program or Service Fee	n/a	Alternative Test Arrangements	✓
LD Program Began	1983	LD Student Organization	✓

Office for Disability Services began offering services in 1983. The program serves approximately 70 undergraduate students. Faculty consists of 4 full-time staff members. Services are provided by LD specialists and trained peer tutors.

Policies 12 credit hours per quarter are required to maintain full-time status; 4 credit hours per quarter are required to be eligible for financial aid. LD services are also available to graduate students.

Diagnostic testing Available for auditory processing, neuropsychological, spoken language, study skills, learning strategies, reading, written language, learning styles, and visual processing.

Subject-area tutoring Available in most subjects. Offered one-on-one by trained peer tutors.

Auxiliary aids and services *Aids:* calculators, scan and read programs (e.g., Kurzweil), screen-enlarging programs, screen readers, speech recognition programs (e.g., Dragon), tape record-

The Ohio State University-Newark Campus (continued)

ers, taped textbooks. *Services and accommodations:* priority registration, alternative test arrangements, readers, note-takers, and scribes.

Student organization There is a student organization for students with LD.

ADD/ADHD Students with ADD/ADHD are eligible for the same services available to students with LD, as well as distraction-free study areas and distraction-free testing environments.

Application *Recommended:* high school transcript, psychoeducational report, and documentation of high school services (e.g., Individualized Education Program [IEP] or 504 plan). Upon acceptance, documentation of need for special services should be sent only to your LD program or unit. *Application deadline (institutional):* rolling/continuous for fall and rolling/continuous for spring. *Application deadline (LD program):* rolling/continuous for fall and rolling/continuous for spring.

LD program contact Dr. Phyllis E. Thompson, Program Manager, 1179 University Drive, Newark, OH 43055. *Phone:* 740-366-9246. *Fax:* 740-364-9641. *E-mail:* thompson.33@osu.edu.

Application contact The Ohio State University-Newark Campus, 1179 University Drive, Newark, OH 43055-1797. *Web address:* http://www.ohio-state.edu/.

OKANAGAN UNIVERSITY COLLEGE
Kelowna, British Columbia

Students with LD Served by Program	300	ADD/ADHD Services	✓
Staff	2 full-time, 7 part-time	Summer Preparation Program	n/a
LD Program or Service Fee	n/a	Alternative Test Arrangements	✓
LD Program Began	1989	LD Student Organization	n/a

Disability Services began offering services in 1989. The program serves approximately 300 undergraduate students. Faculty consists of 2 full-time and 7 part-time staff members. Services are provided by academic advisers, regular education teachers, counselors, remediation/learning specialists, diagnostic specialists, LD specialists, trained peer tutors, and professional tutors.

Policies LD services are also available to graduate students.

Basic skills remediation Available in auditory processing, study skills, computer skills, reading, time management, handwriting, visual processing, learning strategies, spelling, written language, math, and spoken language. Offered one-on-one and in small groups by LD specialists, professional tutors, and trained peer tutors.

Subject-area tutoring Available in all subjects. Offered one-on-one and in small groups by professional tutors, trained peer tutors, and LD specialists.

Counseling and advisement Career counseling, individual counseling, small-group counseling, and support groups are available. Academic advisement by a staff member affiliated with the program is available.

Auxiliary aids and services *Aids:* calculators, personal computers, personal spelling/word-use assistants (e.g., Franklin Speller), scan and read programs (e.g., Kurzweil), screen-enlarging programs, screen readers, speech recognition programs (e.g., Dragon), tape recorders, taped textbooks. *Services and accommodations:* alternative test arrangements, readers, note-takers, and scribes.

ADD/ADHD Students with ADD/ADHD are eligible for the same services available to students with LD, as well as distraction-free study areas, distraction-free testing environments and support groups for ADD/ADHD.

Application *Required:* interview and psychoeducational report (5 years old or less). *Recommended:* high school transcript and documentation of high school services (e.g., Individualized Education Program [IEP] or 504 plan). Upon application, documentation of need for special services should be sent only to your LD program or unit. Upon acceptance, documentation of need for special services should be sent only to your LD program or unit. *Application deadline (institutional):* rolling/continuous for fall and rolling/continuous for spring. *Application deadline (LD program):* rolling/continuous for fall and rolling/continuous for spring.

LD program contact Sharon Robbie, Coordinator, Disability Services, 7000 College Way, Vernon, BC V1B 2N5. *Phone:* 250-545-7291. *Fax:* 250-545-3277. *E-mail:* srobbie@okanagan.bc.ca.

Application contact Okanagan University College, 3333 College Way, Kelowna, BC V1V 1V7. *Web address:* http://www.ouc.bc.ca/.

OKLAHOMA CITY UNIVERSITY
Oklahoma City, Oklahoma

Students with LD Served by Program	8	ADD/ADHD Services	✓
Staff	3 part-time	Summer Preparation Program	n/a
LD Program or Service Fee	n/a	Alternative Test Arrangements	✓
LD Program Began	1990	LD Student Organization	n/a

Disability Concerns began offering services in 1990. The program serves approximately 8 undergraduate students. Faculty consists of 3 part-time staff members. Services are provided by academic advisers, regular education teachers, and remediation/learning specialists.

Policies Students with LD may take up to 16 credit hours per semester; 12 credit hours per semester are required to maintain full-time status and to be eligible for financial aid.

Diagnostic testing Available for study skills, learning strategies, reading, learning styles, and visual processing.

Subject-area tutoring Available in most subjects. Offered one-on-one and in small groups by computer-based instruction, professional tutors, trained peer tutors, and LD specialists.

Special courses Available in study skills, test taking, reading, and time management. All courses are offered for credit; all enter into overall grade point average.

Counseling and advisement Career counseling and individual counseling are available. Academic advisement by a staff member affiliated with the program is available.

Auxiliary aids and services *Aids:* screen-enlarging programs, screen readers, tape recorders, taped textbooks. *Services and accommodations:* advocates, alternative test arrangements, and note-takers.

ADD/ADHD Students with ADD/ADHD are eligible for the same services available to students with LD, as well as distraction-free study areas, distraction-free testing environments and medication management.

Application *Required:* high school transcript, ACT or SAT I (extended-time tests accepted), personal statement, letter(s) of recommendation, psychoeducational report (1 year old or less), and documentation of high school services (e.g., Individualized Education Program [IEP] or 504 plan). *Recommended:* participation in extracurricular activities, interview, and separate application to your LD program or unit. Upon application, documentation of need for special services should be sent to both admissions and your LD program or unit. Upon acceptance, documentation of need for special services should be sent to both admissions and your LD program or unit.

LD program contact Dr. William M. Malloy, Vice President for Student Affairs, 2501 North Blackwelder, Oklahoma City, OK 73106. *Phone:* 405-521-5384. *Fax:* 405-557-6043. *E-mail:* bmalloy@okcu.edu.

Application contact Oklahoma City University, 2501 North Blackwelder, Oklahoma City, OK 73106-1402. *E-mail:* uadmissions@frodo.okcu.edu. *Web address:* http://www.okcu.edu/.

OKLAHOMA PANHANDLE STATE UNIVERSITY
Goodwell, Oklahoma

Students with LD Served by Program	16	ADD/ADHD Services	✓
Staff	1 part-time	Summer Preparation Program	n/a
LD Program or Service Fee	n/a	Alternative Test Arrangements	n/a
LD Program Began	1999	LD Student Organization	n/a

Students with Disabilities began offering services in 1999. The program serves approximately 16 undergraduate students. Faculty consists of 1 part-time staff member. Services are provided by academic advisers, regular education teachers, counselors, and professional tutors.

Policies Students with LD may take up to 18 credit hours per semester; 12 credit hours per semester are required to maintain full-time status and to be eligible for financial aid.

Subject-area tutoring Available in most subjects. Offered one-on-one by professional tutors.

Counseling and advisement Career counseling and individual counseling are available. Academic advisement by a staff member affiliated with the program is available.

Auxiliary aids and services *Aids:* calculators, tape recorders, taped textbooks. *Services and accommodations:* advocates.

ADD/ADHD Students with ADD/ADHD are eligible for the same services available to students with LD, as well as personal coach or mentors.

Application *Required:* high school transcript and ACT or SAT I (extended-time tests accepted). Upon application, documentation of need for special services should be sent to both admissions and your LD program or unit. Upon acceptance, documentation of need for special services should be sent only to your LD program or unit. *Application deadline (institutional):* 8/1 for fall and 1/1 for spring. *Application deadline (LD program):* 8/1 for fall and 1/1 for spring.

LD program contact Dr. L. Dirk Hibler, Vice President, Box 430, Goodwell, OK 73939. *Phone:* 580-349-2611. *Fax:* 580-349-3375. *E-mail:* dirk@opsu.edu.

Application contact Melissa Worth, Admissions Counselor, Oklahoma Panhandle State University, PO Box 430, Goodwell, OK 73939-0430. *Phone:* 580-349-2611 Ext. 311. *Web address:* http://www.opsu.edu/.

OLD DOMINION UNIVERSITY
Norfolk, Virginia

Students with LD Served by Program	175	ADD/ADHD Services	✓
Staff	2 full-time, 1 part-time	Summer Preparation Program	n/a
LD Program or Service Fee	n/a	Alternative Test Arrangements	✓
LD Program Began	1987	LD Student Organization	✓

Disability Services began offering services in 1987. The program serves approximately 175 undergraduate students. Faculty consists of 2 full-time staff members and 1 part-time staff member. Services are provided by remediation/learning specialists and graduate assistants/students.

Policies The college has written policies regarding course substitutions and grade forgiveness. Students with LD may take up to 18 credit hours per semester; 12 credit hours per semester are required to maintain full-time status. LD services are also available to graduate students.

Special preparation or orientation Optional orientation held after classes begin.

Basic skills remediation Available in study skills, time management, learning strategies, written language, and math. Offered in class-size groups by regular education teachers.

Special courses Available in college survival skills and Spanish. All courses are offered for credit; all enter into overall grade point average.

Counseling and advisement Support groups is available.

Auxiliary aids and services *Aids:* scan and read programs (e.g., Kurzweil), taped textbooks. *Services and accommodations:* priority registration, alternative test arrangements, and note-takers.

Student organization There is a student organization for students with LD.

ADD/ADHD Students with ADD/ADHD are eligible for the same services available to students with LD, as well as distraction-free testing environments and support groups for ADD/ADHD.

Application *Required:* high school transcript and ACT or SAT I (extended-time or untimed test accepted). *Recommended:* personal statement and letter(s) of recommendation. Upon acceptance, documentation of need for special services should be sent only to your LD program or unit. *Application deadline (institutional):* 2/15 for fall and 10/15 for spring. *Application deadline (LD program):* rolling/continuous for fall and rolling/continuous for spring.

LD program contact Dr. Nancy Olthoff, Director, 2228 Webb Center, Norfolk, VA 23529. *Phone:* 757-683-4655. *Fax:* 757-683-5356. *E-mail:* disabilityservices@odu.edu.

Application contact Old Dominion University, 5215 Hampton Boulevard, Norfolk, VA 23529. *E-mail:* aos@shawnee.oa.odu.edu. *Web address:* http://web.odu.edu/.

ORAL ROBERTS UNIVERSITY
Tulsa, Oklahoma

Students with LD Served by Program	40	ADD/ADHD Services	✓
Staff	1 full-time, 18 part-time	Summer Preparation Program	n/a
LD Program or Service Fee	n/a	Alternative Test Arrangements	✓
LD Program Began	1994	LD Student Organization	n/a

Students Resources began offering services in 1994. The program serves approximately 40 undergraduate students. Faculty consists of 1 full-time and 18 part-time staff members. Services are provided by academic advisers, special education teachers, LD specialists, and trained peer tutors.

Policies Students with LD may take up to 18 credit hours per semester; 12 credit hours per semester are required to maintain full-time status and to be eligible for financial aid. LD services are also available to graduate students.

Special preparation or orientation Required orientation held during registration and individually by special arrangement.

Diagnostic testing Available for reading, written language, and math.

Oral Roberts University (continued)

Basic skills remediation Available in study skills, reading, time management, handwriting, social skills, learning strategies, written language, and math. Offered in class-size groups by regular education teachers.

Subject-area tutoring Available in most subjects. Offered one-on-one and in small groups by trained peer tutors.

Special courses Available in career planning, study skills, college survival skills, test taking, health and nutrition, reading, time management, learning strategies, math, and written composition skills. Most courses are offered for credit; all enter into overall grade point average.

Counseling and advisement Career counseling and individual counseling are available. Academic advisement by a staff member affiliated with the program is available.

Auxiliary aids and services *Aids:* scan and read programs (e.g., Kurzweil), tape recorders, taped textbooks. *Services and accommodations:* advocates, priority registration, alternative test arrangements, readers, note-takers, and scribes.

ADD/ADHD Students with ADD/ADHD are eligible for the same services available to students with LD, as well as distraction-free study areas and distraction-free testing environments.

Application *Required:* high school transcript, ACT or SAT I, personal statement, and letter(s) of recommendation. *Recommended:* participation in extracurricular activities and interview. Upon application, documentation of need for special services should be sent only to your LD program or unit. Upon acceptance, documentation of need for special services should be sent only to your LD program or unit. *Application deadline (institutional):* rolling/continuous for fall and rolling/continuous for spring.

LD program contact Don Roberson, Director of Student Resources, 7777 South Lewis Avenue, Tulsa, OK 74171. *Phone:* 918-495-7018. *Fax:* 918-495-7879. *E-mail:* droberson@oru.edu.

Application contact Oral Roberts University, 7777 South Lewis Avenue, Tulsa, OK 74171-0001. *E-mail:* admissions@oru.edu. *Web address:* http://www.oru.edu/.

PEACE COLLEGE
Raleigh, North Carolina

Students with LD Served by Program	30	ADD/ADHD Services	✓
Staff	1 full-time, 16 part-time	Summer Preparation Program	n/a
LD Program or Service Fee	n/a	Alternative Test Arrangements	✓
LD Program Began	1995	LD Student Organization	n/a

Peace Academic Support Services (PASS) Program began offering services in 1995. The program serves approximately 30 undergraduate students. Faculty consists of 1 full-time and 16 part-time staff members. Services are provided by academic advisers, regular education teachers, counselors, trained peer tutors, and professional tutors.

Policies Students with LD may take up to 18 credit hours per semester; 12 credit hours per semester are required to maintain full-time status and to be eligible for financial aid.

Basic skills remediation Available in study skills, learning strategies, written language, and math. Offered one-on-one and in class-size groups by regular education teachers and professional tutors.

Subject-area tutoring Available in most subjects. Offered one-on-one by professional tutors, graduate assistants/students, trained peer tutors, and director.

Counseling and advisement Academic advisement by a staff member affiliated with the program is available.

Auxiliary aids and services *Services and accommodations:* advocates, alternative test arrangements, note-takers, and tutoring, oral testing.

ADD/ADHD Students with ADD/ADHD are eligible for the same services available to students with LD, as well as distraction-free study areas and distraction-free testing environments.

Application *Required:* high school transcript, ACT or SAT I (extended-time or untimed test accepted), personal statement, letter(s) of recommendation, separate application to your LD program or unit, and psychoeducational report. *Recommended:* participation in extracurricular activities, interview, and documentation of high school services (e.g., Individualized Education Program [IEP] or 504 plan). Upon application, documentation of need for special services should be sent only to admissions. Upon acceptance, documentation of need for special services should be sent only to admissions. *Application deadline (institutional):* 4/1 for fall and 11/1 for spring. *Application deadline (LD program):* rolling/continuous for fall and rolling/continuous for spring.

LD program contact Dr. Ann F. Mann, Director of Academic Support Services, 15 East Peace Street, Raleigh, NC 27604-1194. *Phone:* 919-508-2293. *Fax:* 919-508-2326. *E-mail:* amann@peace.edu.

Application contact Peace College, 15 East Peace Street, Raleigh, NC 27604-1194. *Web address:* http://www.peace.edu/.

PENNSYLVANIA STATE UNIVERSITY ABINGTON COLLEGE
Abington, Pennsylvania

Students with LD Served by Program	30	ADD/ADHD Services	✓
Staff	1 part-time	Summer Preparation Program	n/a
LD Program or Service Fee	n/a	Alternative Test Arrangements	✓
LD Program Began	1984	LD Student Organization	n/a

Learning Center began offering services in 1984. The program serves approximately 30 undergraduate students. Faculty consists of 1 part-time staff member. Services are provided by Disability Contact Liaison.

Policies The college has written policies regarding course substitutions, grade forgiveness, and substitution and waivers of requirements for admission and graduation. Students with LD may take up to 19 credits per semester; 12 credits per semester are required to maintain full-time status.

Auxiliary aids and services *Aids:* personal computers, scan and read programs (e.g., Kurzweil), screen-enlarging programs, screen readers, speech recognition programs (e.g., Dragon), tape recorders, taped textbooks. *Services and accommodations:* priority registration, alternative test arrangements, readers, note-takers, and scribes.

ADD/ADHD Students with ADD/ADHD are eligible for the same services available to students with LD, as well as distraction-free testing environments.

Application *Required:* high school transcript and ACT or SAT I (extended-time or untimed test accepted). *Recommended:* participation in extracurricular activities and personal statement. Upon acceptance, documentation of need for special services should be sent only to your LD program or unit. *Application deadline (institutional):* rolling/continuous for fall and rolling/continuous for spring. *Application deadline (LD program):* rolling/continuous for fall and rolling/continuous for spring.

LD program contact Anne Prior, Disability Contact Liaison/Director, Learning Center, 1600 Woodland Road, 315 Sutherland Building, Abington, PA 19001. *Phone:* 215-881-7537. *Fax:* 215-881-7317. *E-mail:* axp28@psu.edu.

Application contact Pennsylvania State University Abington College, 1600 Woodland Road, Abington, PA 19001-3918. *E-mail:* admissions@psu.edu. *Web address:* http://www.psu.edu/.

PENNSYLVANIA STATE UNIVERSITY HARRISBURG CAMPUS OF THE CAPITAL COLLEGE
Middletown, Pennsylvania

Students with LD Served by Program	35	ADD/ADHD Services	✓
Staff	1 full-time	Summer Preparation Program	n/a
LD Program or Service Fee	n/a	Alternative Test Arrangements	✓
LD Program Began	n/a	LD Student Organization	n/a

Student Assistance Center serves approximately 35 undergraduate students. Faculty consists of 1 full-time staff member. Services are provided by regular education teachers, counselors, trained peer tutors, and professional tutors.
Policies The college has written policies regarding course substitutions, grade forgiveness, and substitution and waivers of requirements for admission and graduation. 12 credits per semester are required to maintain full-time status; 6 credits per semester are required to be eligible for financial aid. LD services are also available to graduate students.
Basic skills remediation Available in study skills, time management, learning strategies, written language, and math. Offered one-on-one by professional tutors and counselors.
Subject-area tutoring Available in most subjects. Offered one-on-one and in small groups by professional tutors and trained peer tutors.
Counseling and advisement Career counseling and individual counseling are available.
Auxiliary aids and services *Aids:* tape recorders, taped textbooks. *Services and accommodations:* advocates, alternative test arrangements, readers, note-takers, and scribes.
ADD/ADHD Students with ADD/ADHD are eligible for the same services available to students with LD, as well as distraction-free testing environments.
Application *Recommended:* interview. Upon acceptance, documentation of need for special services should be sent only to your LD program or unit.
LD program contact Donna Howard, Disability Services Coordinator, 777 West Harrisburg Pike, Middletown, PA 17057. *Phone:* 717-948-6025. *Fax:* 717-948-6261. *E-mail:* djh1@psu.edu.
Application contact Pennsylvania State University Harrisburg Campus of the Capital College, 777 West Harrisburg Pike, Middletown, PA 17057-4898. *E-mail:* admissions@psu.edu. *Web address:* http://www.psu.edu/.

PENNSYLVANIA STATE UNIVERSITY UNIVERSITY PARK CAMPUS
State College, University Park, Pennsylvania

Students with LD Served by Program	350	ADD/ADHD Services	✓
Staff	3 full-time, 1 part-time	Summer Preparation Program	n/a
LD Program or Service Fee	n/a	Alternative Test Arrangements	✓
LD Program Began	1984	LD Student Organization	n/a

Office for Disability Services began offering services in 1984. The program serves approximately 350 undergraduate students. Faculty consists of 3 full-time staff members and 1 part-time staff member. Services are provided by graduate assistants/students, LD specialists, and Director of the Office for Disability Services.
Policies The college has written policies regarding course substitutions, grade forgiveness, and substitution and waivers of requirements for admission and graduation. Students with LD may take up to 19 credits per semester; 12 credits per semester are required to maintain full-time status. LD services are also available to graduate students.
Special preparation or orientation Optional orientation held before classes begin.
Auxiliary aids and services *Aids:* personal computers, scan and read programs (e.g., Kurzweil), screen-enlarging programs, screen readers, speech recognition programs (e.g., Dragon), tape recorders, taped textbooks. *Services and accommodations:* priority registration, alternative test arrangements, readers, note-takers, and scribes.
ADD/ADHD Students with ADD/ADHD are eligible for the same services available to students with LD, as well as distraction-free testing environments.
Application *Required:* high school transcript and ACT or SAT I (extended-time or untimed test accepted). *Recommended:* participation in extracurricular activities and personal statement. Upon acceptance, documentation of need for special services should be sent only to your LD program or unit. *Application deadline (institutional):* rolling/continuous for fall and rolling/continuous for spring. *Application deadline (LD program):* rolling/continuous for fall and rolling/continuous for spring.
LD program contact Marianne Karwacki, Learning Disability Specialist, 105 Boucke Building, University Park, PA 16802. *Phone:* 814-863-2291. *Fax:* 814-863-3217.
Application contact Geoffrey Harford, Director-Admissions Services and Evaluation, Pennsylvania State University University Park Campus, 201 Old Main, University Park, PA 16802-1503. *Phone:* 814-863-0233. *E-mail:* admissions@psu.edu. *Web address:* http://www.psu.edu/.

PEPPERDINE UNIVERSITY
Malibu, California

Students with LD Served by Program	60	ADD/ADHD Services	✓
Staff	1 full-time	Summer Preparation Program	n/a
LD Program or Service Fee	n/a	Alternative Test Arrangements	✓
LD Program Began	1992	LD Student Organization	n/a

Disability Services Office (DSO) began offering services in 1992. The program serves approximately 60 undergraduate students. Faculty consists of 1 full-time staff member. Services are provided by academic advisers, counselors, graduate assistants/students, and LD specialists.
Policies Students with LD may take up to 18 credit hours per semester; 12 credit hours per semester are required to maintain full-time status and to be eligible for financial aid. LD services are also available to graduate students.
Basic skills remediation Available in study skills, computer skills, time management, and learning strategies. Offered one-on-one by LD specialists.
Counseling and advisement Career counseling and individual counseling are available. Academic advisement by a staff member affiliated with the program is available.

Pepperdine University (continued)

Auxiliary aids and services *Aids:* tape recorders, taped textbooks. *Services and accommodations:* advocates, priority registration, alternative test arrangements, note-takers, and ASL interpreters.

ADD/ADHD Students with ADD/ADHD are eligible for the same services available to students with LD, as well as distraction-free study areas and distraction-free testing environments.

Application *Required:* high school transcript, ACT or SAT I (extended-time or untimed test accepted), and letter(s) of recommendation. *Recommended:* participation in extracurricular activities and interview. Upon acceptance, documentation of need for special services should be sent only to your LD program or unit. *Application deadline (institutional):* 1/15 for fall and 10/15 for spring.

LD program contact Trevor Reynolds, Disability Services Coordinator, Disability Services Office, 24255 Pacific Coast Highway, Malibu, CA 90263-4269. *Phone:* 310-456-4269. *Fax:* 310-456-4827. *E-mail:* trevor.reynolds@pepperdine.edu.

Application contact Pepperdine University, 24255 Pacific Coast Highway, Malibu, CA 90263-0002. *E-mail:* admission-seaver@pepperdine.edu. *Web address:* http://www.pepperdine.edu/.

PROVIDENCE COLLEGE
Providence, Rhode Island

Students with LD Served by Program	110	ADD/ADHD Services	✓
Staff	1 full-time, 2 part-time	Summer Preparation Program	n/a
LD Program or Service Fee	n/a	Alternative Test Arrangements	✓
LD Program Began	1985	LD Student Organization	n/a

Office of Academic Services began offering services in 1985. The program serves approximately 110 undergraduate students. Faculty consists of 1 full-time and 2 part-time staff members. Services are provided by LD specialists and trained peer tutors.

Policies The college has written policies regarding course substitutions. LD services are also available to graduate students.

Subject-area tutoring Available in most subjects. Offered one-on-one by trained peer tutors.

Special courses Available in career planning, study skills, college survival skills, practical computer skills, test taking, health and nutrition, reading, time management, learning strategies, self-advocacy, math, stress management, and written composition skills. No courses are offered for credit; none enter into overall grade point average.

Auxiliary aids and services *Aids:* calculators, personal computers, personal spelling/word-use assistants (e.g., Franklin Speller), scan and read programs (e.g., Kurzweil), screen-enlarging programs, screen readers, speech recognition programs (e.g., Dragon), tape recorders, taped textbooks. *Services and accommodations:* priority registration, alternative test arrangements, readers, note-takers, and scribes.

ADD/ADHD Students with ADD/ADHD are eligible for the same services available to students with LD, as well as distraction-free testing environments.

Application *Required:* high school transcript, personal statement, and letter(s) of recommendation. *Recommended:* participation in extracurricular activities, ACT or SAT I (extended-time or untimed test accepted), psychoeducational report (3 years old or less), and documentation of high school services (e.g., Individualized Education Program [IEP] or 504 plan). Upon application, documentation of need for special services should be sent only to admissions. Upon acceptance, documentation of

need for special services should be sent only to your LD program or unit. *Application deadline (institutional):* 11/15 for fall and 1/15 for spring.

LD program contact Rose A. Boyle, Disability Support Services Coordinator, Office of Academic Services, Library 102, Providence, RI 02918. *Phone:* 401-865-2494. *Fax:* 401-865-1219. *E-mail:* rboyle@providence.edu.

Application contact Providence College, River Avenue and Eaton Street, Providence, RI 02918. *E-mail:* pcadmiss@providence.edu. *Web address:* http://www.providence.edu/.

PURDUE UNIVERSITY NORTH CENTRAL
Westville, Indiana

Students with LD Served by Program	28	ADD/ADHD Services	✓
Staff	8 full-time, 25 part-time	Summer Preparation Program	n/a
LD Program or Service Fee	n/a	Alternative Test Arrangements	✓
LD Program Began	1984	LD Student Organization	n/a

Student Support Services began offering services in 1984. The program serves approximately 28 undergraduate students. Faculty consists of 8 full-time and 25 part-time staff members. Services are provided by academic advisers, counselors, and trained peer tutors.

Policies Students with LD may take up to 18 credit hours per semester; 12 credit hours per semester are required to maintain full-time status; 6 credit hours per semester are required to be eligible for financial aid. LD services are also available to graduate students.

Basic skills remediation Available in study skills, reading, written language, and math. Offered in class-size groups by faculty.

Subject-area tutoring Available in some subjects. Offered one-on-one and in small groups by trained peer tutors and academic coordinator.

Counseling and advisement Career counseling, individual counseling, support groups, and academic/personal, social are available. Academic advisement by a staff member affiliated with the program is available.

Auxiliary aids and services *Aids:* calculators, personal computers, scan and read programs (e.g., Kurzweil), screen-enlarging programs, screen readers, speech recognition programs (e.g., Dragon), tape recorders, taped textbooks. *Services and accommodations:* advocates, alternative test arrangements, readers, note-takers, scribes, and notetaker binders.

ADD/ADHD Students with ADD/ADHD are eligible for the same services available to students with LD, as well as distraction-free testing environments.

Application *Required:* high school transcript and ACT or SAT I (extended-time or untimed test accepted). Upon acceptance, documentation of need for special services should be sent only to your LD program or unit. *Application deadline (institutional):* rolling/continuous for fall and rolling/continuous for spring. *Application deadline (LD program):* rolling/continuous for fall and rolling/continuous for spring.

LD program contact Kelly Gossman, Coordinator of Services for Students with Disabilities, 1401 South US 421, Westville, IN 46391-9528. *Phone:* 219-785-5312. *Fax:* 219-785-5544.

Application contact Cathy Buckman, Director of Admissions, Purdue University North Central, 1401 South US Highway 421, Westville, IN 46391-9528. *Phone:* 219-785-5458. *E-mail:* cbuckman@purduenc.edu. *Web address:* http://www.purduenc.edu/.

QUEENS COLLEGE OF THE CITY UNIVERSITY OF NEW YORK

Flushing, New York

Students with LD Served by Program	252	ADD/ADHD Services	✓
Staff	1 full-time	Summer Preparation Program	n/a
LD Program or Service Fee	n/a	Alternative Test Arrangements	✓
LD Program Began	n/a	LD Student Organization	✓

Office of Special Services serves approximately 252 undergraduate students. Faculty consists of 1 full-time staff member. Services are provided by academic advisers, counselors, graduate assistants/students, LD specialists, and trained peer tutors.

Policies The college has written policies regarding course substitutions and substitution and waivers of requirements for admission and graduation. Students with LD may take up to 18 credit hours per semester; 12 credit hours per semester are required to maintain full-time status; 3 credit hours per semester are required to be eligible for financial aid. LD services are also available to graduate students.

Subject-area tutoring Available in all subjects. Offered one-on-one by trained peer tutors.

Special courses Available in math. All courses are offered for credit; all enter into overall grade point average.

Counseling and advisement Career counseling, individual counseling, and support groups are available. Academic advisement by a staff member affiliated with the program is available.

Auxiliary aids and services *Aids:* calculators, personal computers, personal spelling/word-use assistants (e.g., Franklin Speller), scan and read programs (e.g., Kurzweil), screen-enlarging programs, screen readers, speech recognition programs (e.g., Dragon), tape recorders, taped textbooks. *Services and accommodations:* advocates, priority registration, alternative test arrangements, readers, note-takers, and scribes.

Student organization There is a student organization for students with LD.

ADD/ADHD Students with ADD/ADHD are eligible for the same services available to students with LD, as well as personal coach or mentors.

Application *Required:* high school transcript and ACT or SAT I (extended-time or untimed test accepted). Upon acceptance, documentation of need for special services should be sent only to your LD program or unit.

LD program contact Chris Rosa, Director, Special Services, 65-30 Kissena Boulevard, MKH 171, Flushing, NY 11367. *Phone:* 718-997-5870. *Fax:* 718-997-5895. *E-mail:* crosa@qc1.qc.edu.

Application contact Undergraduate Admissions Office, Queens College of the City University of New York, 65-30 Kissena Boulevard, Flushing, NY 11367-1597. *Phone:* 718-997-5600. *E-mail:* admissions@qc.edu. *Web address:* http://www.qc.edu/.

RANDOLPH-MACON WOMAN'S COLLEGE

Lynchburg, Virginia

Students with LD Served by Program	18	ADD/ADHD Services	✓
Staff	1 full-time, 1 part-time	Summer Preparation Program	n/a
LD Program or Service Fee	n/a	Alternative Test Arrangements	✓
LD Program Began	1985	LD Student Organization	n/a

Learning Resources Center (LRC) began offering services in 1985. The program serves approximately 18 undergraduate students. Faculty consists of 1 full-time and 1 part-time staff member.

Policies The college has written policies regarding course substitutions and substitution and waivers of requirements for admission and graduation. Students with LD may take up to 18 credit hours per semester; 12 credit hours per semester are required to maintain full-time status and to be eligible for financial aid.

Subject-area tutoring Available in all subjects. Offered one-on-one by trained peer tutors.

Counseling and advisement Career counseling and individual counseling are available.

Auxiliary aids and services *Aids:* scan and read programs (e.g., Kurzweil), screen-enlarging programs, screen readers. *Services and accommodations:* advocates, priority registration, alternative test arrangements, readers, and note-takers.

ADD/ADHD Students with ADD/ADHD are eligible for the same services available to students with LD, as well as distraction-free study areas, distraction-free testing environments and personal coach or mentors.

Application *Required:* high school transcript, ACT or SAT I (extended-time or untimed test accepted), personal statement, letter(s) of recommendation, psychoeducational report (3 years old or less), documentation of high school services (e.g., Individualized Education Program [IEP] or 504 plan), and written permission/disclosure from student/applicant. *Recommended:* interview. Upon application, documentation of need for special services should be sent to both admissions and your LD program or unit. Upon acceptance, documentation of need for special services should be sent only to your LD program or unit. *Application deadline (institutional):* 3/1 for fall and 12/1 for spring.

LD program contact Margaret Schimmoeller, Assistant Professor/Director of LRC, 2500 Rivermont Avenue, Lynchburg, VA 24503. *Phone:* 804-947-8132. *Fax:* 804-947-8138. *E-mail:* pschimmoeller@rmwc.edu.

Application contact Randolph-Macon Woman's College, 2500 Rivermont Avenue, Lynchburg, VA 24503-1526. *Web address:* http://www.rmwc.edu/.

RENSSELAER POLYTECHNIC INSTITUTE

Troy, New York

Students with LD Served by Program	62	ADD/ADHD Services	✓
Staff	2 part-time	Summer Preparation Program	n/a
LD Program or Service Fee	n/a	Alternative Test Arrangements	✓
LD Program Began	1978	LD Student Organization	n/a

Disabled Student Services began offering services in 1978. The program serves approximately 62 undergraduate students. Faculty consists of 2 part-time staff members. Services are provided by counselors, remediation/learning specialists, and LD specialists.

Policies Students with LD may take up to 21 credit hours per semester. LD services are also available to graduate students.

Special preparation or orientation Optional orientation held during summer prior to enrollment.

Basic skills remediation Available in study skills, reading, time management, learning strategies, and written language. Offered one-on-one and in small groups by LD specialists and trained peer tutors.

Subject-area tutoring Available in most subjects. Offered one-on-one and in small groups by trained peer tutors.

Rensselaer Polytechnic Institute (continued)

Counseling and advisement Career counseling, individual counseling, and peer counselors are available.

Auxiliary aids and services *Aids:* scan and read programs (e.g., Kurzweil), screen-enlarging programs, screen readers, speech recognition programs (e.g., Dragon), tape recorders, taped textbooks. *Services and accommodations:* advocates, priority registration, alternative test arrangements, readers, and note-takers.

ADD/ADHD Students with ADD/ADHD are eligible for the same services available to students with LD, as well as distraction-free testing environments.

Application *Required:* high school transcript, ACT or SAT I (extended-time or untimed test accepted), personal statement, letter(s) of recommendation, and psychoeducational report (3 years old or less). *Recommended:* participation in extracurricular activities and documentation of high school services (e.g., Individualized Education Program [IEP] or 504 plan). Upon acceptance, documentation of need for special services should be sent only to your LD program or unit.

LD program contact Debra Hamilton, Coordinator, Disabled Student Services, Dean of Students Office, 110 8th Street, Troy, NY 12180-3590. *Phone:* 518-276-2746. *Fax:* 518-276-4839.

Application contact Rensselaer Polytechnic Institute, 110 8th Street, Troy, NY 12180-3590. *E-mail:* admissions@rpi.edu. *Web address:* http://www.rpi.edu/.

RHODE ISLAND COLLEGE

Providence, Rhode Island

Students with LD Served by Program	92	ADD/ADHD Services	✓
Staff	1 part-time	Summer Preparation Program	n/a
LD Program or Service Fee	n/a	Alternative Test Arrangements	✓
LD Program Began	1989	LD Student Organization	n/a

Student Life Office Disability Related Services began offering services in 1989. The program serves approximately 92 undergraduate students. Faculty consists of 1 part-time staff member. Services are provided by academic advisers, counselors, remediation/learning specialists, graduate assistants/students, LD specialists, and professional tutors.

Policies The college has written policies regarding course substitutions. Students with LD may take up to 18 credit hours per semester; 12 credit hours per semester are required to maintain full-time status; 6 credit hours per semester are required to be eligible for financial aid. LD services are also available to graduate students.

Special preparation or orientation Optional orientation held before classes begin and during summer prior to enrollment.

Basic skills remediation Available in study skills, reading, time management, learning strategies, written language, and math. Offered one-on-one and in small groups by graduate assistants/students, LD specialists, trained peer tutors, and math learning center, writing center.

Subject-area tutoring Available in some subjects. Offered one-on-one and in small groups by computer-based instruction, graduate assistants/students, trained peer tutors, and LD specialists.

Counseling and advisement Career counseling, individual counseling, small-group counseling, and support groups are available. Academic advisement by a staff member affiliated with the program is available.

Auxiliary aids and services *Aids:* calculators, scan and read programs (e.g., Kurzweil), screen-enlarging programs, speech recognition programs (e.g., Dragon), tape recorders, taped textbooks. *Services and accommodations:* advocates, priority registration, alternative test arrangements, readers, note-takers, and scribes.

ADD/ADHD Students with ADD/ADHD are eligible for the same services available to students with LD, as well as distraction-free study areas, distraction-free testing environments, support groups for ADD/ADHD and assistive technology lab.

Application *Required:* high school transcript, SAT I, and separate application to your LD program or unit.

LD program contact Sara W. Weiss, Peer Advisor for Students with Disabilities, Student Life Office, 600 Mount Pleasant Avenue, Providence, RI 02908. *Phone:* 401-456-8061. *Fax:* 401-456-8379.

Application contact Rhode Island College, 600 Mount Pleasant Avenue, Providence, RI 02908-1924. *Web address:* http://www.ric.edu/.

THE RICHARD STOCKTON COLLEGE OF NEW JERSEY

Pomona, New Jersey

Students with LD Served by Program	150	ADD/ADHD Services	✓
Staff	1 full-time, 2 part-time	Summer Preparation Program	n/a
LD Program or Service Fee	n/a	Alternative Test Arrangements	✓
LD Program Began	1987	LD Student Organization	n/a

Learning Access Program began offering services in 1987. The program serves approximately 150 undergraduate students. Faculty consists of 1 full-time and 2 part-time staff members. Services are provided by academic advisers, counselors, diagnostic specialists, graduate assistants/students, LD specialists, and trained peer tutors.

Policies 12 credit hours per semester are required to maintain full-time status and to be eligible for financial aid. LD services are also available to graduate students.

Diagnostic testing Available for auditory processing, spelling, intelligence, learning strategies, reading, written language, learning styles, visual processing, math, and ADHD.

Subject-area tutoring Available in some subjects. Offered one-on-one and in small groups by graduate assistants/students, trained peer tutors, and skills centers.

Counseling and advisement Career counseling and individual counseling are available. Academic advisement by a staff member affiliated with the program is available.

Auxiliary aids and services *Aids:* speech recognition programs (e.g., Dragon), taped textbooks. *Services and accommodations:* advocates, priority registration, alternative test arrangements, readers, note-takers, and scribes.

ADD/ADHD Students with ADD/ADHD are eligible for the same services available to students with LD, as well as distraction-free testing environments.

Application *Required:* high school transcript and ACT or SAT I (extended-time or untimed test accepted). *Recommended:* interview, personal statement, and letter(s) of recommendation. Upon application, documentation of need for special services should be sent only to your LD program or unit. Upon acceptance, documentation of need for special services should be sent only to your LD program or unit. *Application deadline (institutional):* 5/1 for fall and 12/1 for spring. *Application deadline (LD program):* rolling/continuous for spring and 5/1 for fall.

LD program contact Frances H. Bottone, Learning Disabilities Specialist, PO Box 195, West Quad, Suite 110, Pomona, NJ 08240-0195. *Phone:* 609-652-4988. *Fax:* 609-748-5550. *E-mail:* frances.bottone@stockton.edu.

Application contact The Richard Stockton College of New Jersey, PO Box 195, Jimmie Leeds Road, Pomona, NJ 08240-0195. *E-mail:* admissions@pollux.stockton.edu. *Web address:* http://www.stockton.edu/.

RIDER UNIVERSITY
Lawrenceville, New Jersey

Students with LD Served by Program	110	ADD/ADHD Services	✓
Staff	1 full-time, 1 part-time	Summer Preparation Program	n/a
LD Program or Service Fee	n/a	Alternative Test Arrangements	✓
LD Program Began	1989	LD Student Organization	✓

Learning Disability Services began offering services in 1989. The program serves approximately 110 undergraduate students. Faculty consists of 1 full-time and 1 part-time staff member. Services are provided by graduate assistants/students, LD specialists, trained peer tutors, and professional tutors.
Policies The college has written policies regarding course substitutions and grade forgiveness. Students with LD may take up to 17 credit hours per semester; 12 credit hours per semester are required to maintain full-time status; 6 credit hours per semester are required to be eligible for financial aid. LD services are also available to graduate students.
Basic skills remediation Available in reading, written language, and math. Offered in small groups and class-size groups by computer-based instruction and regular education teachers.
Subject-area tutoring Available in most subjects. Offered one-on-one, in small groups, and class-size groups by computer-based instruction, graduate assistants/students, and trained peer tutors.
Special courses Available in reading. All courses are offered for credit; all enter into overall grade point average.
Auxiliary aids and services *Aids:* calculators, tape recorders, taped textbooks, word processor for use with alternate site tests. *Services and accommodations:* advocates, priority registration, alternative test arrangements, readers, note-takers, and scribes.
Student organization There is a student organization for students with LD.
ADD/ADHD Students with ADD/ADHD are eligible for the same services available to students with LD, as well as distraction-free testing environments.
Application *Required:* high school transcript, ACT or SAT I (extended-time tests accepted), and personal statement. *Recommended:* participation in extracurricular activities, interview, letter(s) of recommendation, psychoeducational report (3 years old or less), and documentation of high school services (e.g., Individualized Education Program [IEP] or 504 plan). Upon application, documentation of need for special services should be sent to both admissions and your LD program or unit. Upon acceptance, documentation of need for special services should be sent only to your LD program or unit. *Application deadline (institutional):* rolling/continuous for fall and rolling/continuous for spring. *Application deadline (LD program):* rolling/continuous for fall and rolling/continuous for spring.
LD program contact Barbara J. Blandford, Director, Learning Disability Services, Academic Annex Room 3, 2083 Lawrenceville Road, Lawrenceville, NJ 08648. *Phone:* 609-896-5000 Ext. 5244. *Fax:* 609-895-5507. *E-mail:* blandfor@rider.edu.
Application contact Rider University, 2083 Lawrenceville Road, Lawrenceville, NJ 08648-3001. *E-mail:* admissions@rider.edu. *Web address:* http://www.rider.edu/.

RIVIER COLLEGE
Nashua, New Hampshire

Students with LD Served by Program	25	ADD/ADHD Services	✓
Staff	2 part-time	Summer Preparation Program	n/a
LD Program or Service Fee	n/a	Alternative Test Arrangements	✓
LD Program Began	1991	LD Student Organization	n/a

Office of Special Needs Services began offering services in 1991. The program serves approximately 25 undergraduate students. Faculty consists of 2 part-time staff members. Services are provided by academic advisers, regular education teachers, counselors, remediation/learning specialists, LD specialists, trained peer tutors, and professional tutors.
Policies 12 credit hours per semester are required to maintain full-time status and to be eligible for financial aid. LD services are also available to graduate students.
Special preparation or orientation Optional orientation held during summer prior to enrollment.
Basic skills remediation Available in study skills, reading, learning strategies, spelling, and written language. Offered one-on-one by LD specialists and professional tutors.
Subject-area tutoring Available in most subjects. Offered one-on-one by trained peer tutors and LD specialists.
Counseling and advisement Career counseling and individual counseling are available. Academic advisement by a staff member affiliated with the program is available.
Auxiliary aids and services *Aids:* personal computers, tape recorders, Alpha Smart. *Services and accommodations:* advocates, priority registration, alternative test arrangements, readers, note-takers, and scribes.
ADD/ADHD Students with ADD/ADHD are eligible for the same services available to students with LD, as well as distraction-free testing environments.
Application *Required:* high school transcript, ACT or SAT I (extended-time or untimed test accepted), personal statement, letter(s) of recommendation, and psychoeducational report (5 years old or less). *Recommended:* participation in extracurricular activities, interview, and documentation of high school services (e.g., Individualized Education Program [IEP] or 504 plan). Upon application, documentation of need for special services should be sent only to your LD program or unit. Upon acceptance, documentation of need for special services should be sent only to your LD program or unit. *Application deadline (institutional):* rolling/continuous for fall and rolling/continuous for spring.
LD program contact Lisa Baroody, Coordinator of Special Needs Services, 420 Main Street, Nashua, NH 03060. *Phone:* 603-897-8497. *Fax:* 603-897-8887. *E-mail:* lbaroody@rivier.edu.
Application contact Rivier College, 420 Main Street, Nashua, NH 03060-5086. *E-mail:* rivadmit@mighty.riv.edu. *Web address:* http://www.rivier.edu/.

ROBERT MORRIS COLLEGE
Chicago, Illinois

Students with LD Served by Program	6	ADD/ADHD Services	✓
Staff	3 full-time, 5 part-time	Summer Preparation Program	n/a
LD Program or Service Fee	n/a	Alternative Test Arrangements	✓
LD Program Began	1980	LD Student Organization	n/a

Robert Morris College (continued)

Dean of Student's Office began offering services in 1980. The program serves approximately 6 undergraduate students. Faculty consists of 3 full-time and 5 part-time staff members. Services are provided by academic advisers, regular education teachers, trained peer tutors, professional tutors, and Resource Center staff, program directors.

Policies Students with LD may take up to 16 credit hours per quarter; 12 credit hours per quarter are required to maintain full-time status; 8 credit hours per quarter are required to be eligible for financial aid.

Subject-area tutoring Available in all subjects. Offered one-on-one and in small groups by computer-based instruction, professional tutors, trained peer tutors, and faculty.

Counseling and advisement Academic advisement by a staff member affiliated with the program is available.

Auxiliary aids and services *Aids:* screen-enlarging programs, screen readers, tape recorders, taped textbooks, audio computer help, test readers. *Services and accommodations:* advocates, alternative test arrangements, readers, note-takers, and scribes.

ADD/ADHD Students with ADD/ADHD are eligible for the same services available to students with LD, as well as distraction-free study areas and distraction-free testing environments.

Application *Required:* high school transcript and interview. *Recommended:* ACT (extended-time or untimed test accepted) and documentation of high school services (e.g., Individualized Education Program [IEP] or 504 plan). Upon application, documentation of need for special services should be sent to both admissions and your LD program or unit. Upon acceptance, documentation of need for special services should be sent to both admissions and your LD program or unit. *Application deadline (institutional):* rolling/continuous for fall and rolling/continuous for spring. *Application deadline (LD program):* rolling/continuous for fall and rolling/continuous for spring.

LD program contact Brittany Mylott, Director, Lopata Resource Center, 401 South State Street, Chicago, IL 60605. *Phone:* 312-935-6892. *Fax:* 312-935-6861. *E-mail:* bmylott@smtp.rmcil.edu.
Application contact Robert Morris College, 180 North LaSalle Street, Chicago, IL 60601-2592. *E-mail:* enroll@rmcil.edu. *Web address:* http://www.rmcil.edu/.

ROCHESTER INSTITUTE OF TECHNOLOGY
Rochester, New York

Students with LD Served by Program	400	ADD/ADHD Services	✓
Staff	3 full-time, 1 part-time	Summer Preparation Program	n/a
LD Program or Service Fee	n/a	Alternative Test Arrangements	✓
LD Program Began	1995	LD Student Organization	n/a

Disability Services Office began offering services in 1995. The program serves approximately 400 undergraduate students. Faculty consists of 3 full-time staff members and 1 part-time staff member. Services are provided by academic advisers, regular education teachers, counselors, remediation/learning specialists, LD specialists, trained peer tutors, and professional tutors.

Policies LD services are also available to graduate students.

Special preparation or orientation Optional orientation held before classes begin, after classes begin, and individually by special arrangement.

Basic skills remediation Available in study skills, time management, learning strategies, and written language. Offered one-on-one and in small groups by regular education teachers, LD specialists, and trained peer tutors.

Subject-area tutoring Available in all subjects. Offered one-on-one by professional tutors and trained peer tutors.

Counseling and advisement Academic advisement by a staff member affiliated with the program is available.

Auxiliary aids and services *Aids:* calculators, personal spelling/word-use assistants (e.g., Franklin Speller), scan and read programs (e.g., Kurzweil), screen-enlarging programs, tape recorders, taped textbooks. *Services and accommodations:* priority registration, alternative test arrangements, readers, note-takers, and scribes.

ADD/ADHD Students with ADD/ADHD are eligible for the same services available to students with LD, as well as distraction-free study areas and distraction-free testing environments.

Application *Required:* high school transcript and ACT or SAT I. *Recommended:* interview and letter(s) of recommendation. Upon application, documentation of need for special services should be sent only to your LD program or unit. Upon acceptance, documentation of need for special services should be sent only to your LD program or unit.

LD program contact Pamela A. Lloyd, Coordinator of Disability Services, 28 Lomb Memorial Drive, Rochester, NY 14623. *Phone:* 716-475-7804. *Fax:* 716-475-2215. *E-mail:* palldc@rit.edu.
Application contact Rochester Institute of Technology, One Lomb Memorial Drive, Rochester, NY 14623-5604. *E-mail:* admissions@rit.edu. *Web address:* http://www.rit.edu/.

ROGER WILLIAMS UNIVERSITY
Bristol, Rhode Island

Students with LD Served by Program	150	ADD/ADHD Services	✓
Staff	1 full-time	Summer Preparation Program	n/a
LD Program or Service Fee	n/a	Alternative Test Arrangements	✓
LD Program Began	1990	LD Student Organization	n/a

Center for Academic Development began offering services in 1990. The program serves approximately 150 undergraduate students. Faculty consists of 1 full-time staff member. Services are provided by LD specialists.

Policies Students with LD may take up to 17 credit hours per semester; 12 credit hours per semester are required to maintain full-time status; 6 credit hours per semester are required to be eligible for financial aid.

Auxiliary aids and services *Services and accommodations:* priority registration, alternative test arrangements, readers, note-takers, scribes, and distraction-free testing area.

ADD/ADHD Students with ADD/ADHD are eligible for the same services available to students with LD, as well as distraction-free testing environments.

Application *Required:* high school transcript, ACT or SAT I (extended-time or untimed test accepted), personal statement, and psychoeducational report (3 years old or less). *Recommended:* participation in extracurricular activities, interview, letter(s) of recommendation, and documentation of high school services (e.g., Individualized Education Program [IEP] or 504 plan). Upon acceptance, documentation of need for special services should be sent only to your LD program or unit. *Application deadline (institutional):* rolling/continuous for fall and rolling/continuous for spring. *Application deadline (LD program):* rolling/continuous for fall and rolling/continuous for spring.

LD program contact Laura B. Choiniere, Learning Specialist, One Old Ferry Road, Bristol, RI 02809. *Phone:* 401-254-3038. *Fax:* 401-254-3302. *E-mail:* lbc@alpha.rwu.edu.

Application contact Julie Cairns, Office of Admissions, Roger Williams University, 1 Old Ferry Road, Bristol, RI 02809. *Phone:* 401-254-3500. *E-mail:* admit@alpha.rwu.edu. *Web address:* http://www.rwu.edu/.

SACRED HEART UNIVERSITY
Fairfield, Connecticut

Students with LD Served by Program	47	ADD/ADHD Services	✓
Staff	1 full-time, 8 part-time	Summer Preparation Program	n/a
LD Program or Service Fee	varies	Alternative Test Arrangements	✓
LD Program Began	1996	LD Student Organization	n/a

Additional Jandrisevits Services (AJS) began offering services in 1996. The program serves approximately 47 undergraduate students. Faculty consists of 1 full-time and 8 part-time staff members. Services are provided by LD specialists, professional tutors, and adaptive technology.

Policies The college has written policies regarding course substitutions and grade forgiveness. Students with LD may take up to 17 credits per semester; 12 credits per semester are required to maintain full-time status and to be eligible for financial aid. LD services are also available to graduate students.

Fees *LD Program or Service Fee:* ranges from $800 to $1200 per year. *Diagnostic Testing Fee:* ranges from $400 to $900.

Special preparation or orientation Optional orientation held during registration and individually by special arrangement.

Diagnostic testing Available for auditory processing, spoken language, intelligence, reading, written language, visual processing, and math.

Basic skills remediation Available in study skills, reading, time management, learning strategies, and written language. Offered one-on-one by LD specialists.

Subject-area tutoring Available in some subjects. Offered one-on-one by professional tutors, graduate assistants/students, and LD specialists.

Counseling and advisement Career counseling, individual counseling, small-group counseling, and support groups are available.

Auxiliary aids and services *Aids:* scan and read programs (e.g., Kurzweil), screen-enlarging programs, speech recognition programs (e.g., Dragon), tape recorders, taped textbooks, recorders for books on tape. *Services and accommodations:* priority registration, alternative test arrangements, readers, note-takers, and scribes.

ADD/ADHD Students with ADD/ADHD are eligible for the same services available to students with LD, as well as distraction-free study areas, distraction-free testing environments and personal coach or mentors.

Application *Required:* high school transcript, ACT or SAT I (extended-time or untimed test accepted), interview, and personal statement. *Recommended:* psychoeducational report (3 years old or less), documentation of high school services (e.g., Individualized Education Program [IEP] or 504 plan), and transition plan. Upon application, documentation of need for special services should be sent only to your LD program or unit. Upon acceptance, documentation of need for special services should be sent only to your LD program or unit. *Application deadline (institutional):* rolling/continuous for fall and rolling/continuous for spring. *Application deadline (LD program):* rolling/continuous for fall and rolling/continuous for spring.

LD program contact Jill E. Angotta, Director of Special Services, 5151 Park Avenue, Fairfield, CT 06432-1000. *Phone:* 203-365-4730. *Fax:* 203-396-8049. *E-mail:* angottaj@sacredheart.edu.

Application contact Karen N. Guastelle, Dean of Undergraduate Admissions, Sacred Heart University, 5151 Park Avenue, Fairfield, CT 06432-1000. *Phone:* 203-371-7880. *E-mail:* enroll@sacredheart.edu. *Web address:* http://www.sacredheart.edu/.

THE SAGE COLLEGES
Troy, New York

Students with LD Served by Program	15	ADD/ADHD Services	✓
Staff	1 full-time, 2 part-time	Summer Preparation Program	✓
LD Program or Service Fee	varies	Alternative Test Arrangements	✓
LD Program Began	1998	LD Student Organization	n/a

Learning Success Program (LSP) began offering services in 1998. The program serves approximately 15 undergraduate students. Faculty consists of 1 full-time and 2 part-time staff members. Services are provided by counselors, remediation/learning specialists, graduate assistants/students, LD specialists, professional tutors, and Director.

Policies The college has written policies regarding course substitutions.

Fees *LD Program or Service Fee:* ranges from $1300 to $1700 per year.

Special preparation or orientation Optional summer program offered prior to entering college.

Basic skills remediation Available in auditory processing, study skills, computer skills, reading, time management, handwriting, social skills, visual processing, learning strategies, spelling, and written language. Offered one-on-one by computer-based instruction, LD specialists, and professional tutors.

Special courses Available in study skills, college survival skills, practical computer skills, test taking, reading, time management, learning strategies, self-advocacy, stress management, and written composition skills. Most courses are offered for credit; most enter into overall grade point average.

Counseling and advisement Career counseling and individual counseling are available.

Auxiliary aids and services *Aids:* personal computers, personal spelling/word-use assistants (e.g., Franklin Speller), scan and read programs (e.g., Kurzweil), screen-enlarging programs, screen readers, speech recognition programs (e.g., Dragon), tape recorders, taped textbooks. *Services and accommodations:* advocates, alternative test arrangements, readers, note-takers, and scribes.

ADD/ADHD Students with ADD/ADHD are eligible for the same services available to students with LD, as well as distraction-free study areas and distraction-free testing environments.

Application *Required:* high school transcript, interview, letter(s) of recommendation, separate application to your LD program or unit, psychoeducational report (3 years old or less), documentation of high school services (e.g., Individualized Education Program [IEP] or 504 plan), and signed release. *Recommended:* participation in extracurricular activities and ACT or SAT I (extended-time or untimed test accepted). Upon application, documentation of need for special services should be sent only to your LD program or unit. Upon acceptance, documentation of need for special services should be sent to both admissions and your LD program or unit. *Application deadline (institutional):* rolling/continuous for fall and rolling/continuous for spring. *Application deadline (LD program):* 8/15 for fall and 12/15 for spring.

LD program contact David Chowenhill, Director, 140 New Scotland Avenue, Albany, NY 12214. *Phone:* 518-292-8624. *Fax:* 578-292-1910. *E-mail:* chowed@sage.edu.

The Sage Colleges (continued)

Application contact The Sage Colleges, 45 Ferry Street, Troy, NY 12180-4115.

SAGINAW VALLEY STATE UNIVERSITY

University Center, Michigan

Students with LD Served by Program	n/a	ADD/ADHD Services	✓
Staff	2 part-time	Summer Preparation Program	n/a
LD Program or Service Fee	n/a	Alternative Test Arrangements	✓
LD Program Began	n/a	LD Student Organization	✓

Disability Services faculty consists of 2 part-time staff members. Services are provided by staff workers.

Policies Students with LD may take up to 18 credit hours per semester; 12 credit hours per semester are required to maintain full-time status. LD services are also available to graduate students.

Auxiliary aids and services *Aids:* scan and read programs (e.g., Kurzweil), screen-enlarging programs, screen readers. *Services and accommodations:* advocates, alternative test arrangements, and note-takers.

Student organization There is a student organization for students with LD.

ADD/ADHD Students with ADD/ADHD are eligible for the same services available to students with LD, as well as distraction-free testing environments.

Application *Required:* high school transcript and ACT (extended-time test accepted). Upon application, documentation of need for special services should be sent only to admissions. Upon acceptance, documentation of need for special services should be sent only to your LD program or unit. *Application deadline (institutional):* rolling/continuous for fall and rolling/continuous for spring. *Application deadline (LD program):* rolling/continuous for fall and rolling/continuous for spring.

LD program contact Cynthia L.B. Woiderski, Coordinator of Disability Services, 174 Wickes Hall, 7400 Bay Road, University Center, MI 48710. *Phone:* 517-790-4168.

Application contact Saginaw Valley State University, 7400 Bay Road, University Center, MI 48710. *E-mail:* admissions@tardis.svsu.edu. *Web address:* http://www.svsu.edu/.

ST. AMBROSE UNIVERSITY

Davenport, Iowa

Students with LD Served by Program	75	ADD/ADHD Services	✓
Staff	1 full-time, 2 part-time	Summer Preparation Program	✓
LD Program or Service Fee	n/a	Alternative Test Arrangements	✓
LD Program Began	1990	LD Student Organization	n/a

Services for Students with Disabilities began offering services in 1990. The program serves approximately 75 undergraduate students. Faculty consists of 1 full-time and 2 part-time staff members. Services are provided by academic advisers, graduate assistants/students, and LD specialists.

Policies 12 credit hours per semester are required to maintain full-time status and to be eligible for financial aid. LD services are also available to graduate students.

Special preparation or orientation Optional summer program offered prior to entering college.

Subject-area tutoring Available in all subjects. Offered one-on-one by graduate assistants/students and LD specialists.

Counseling and advisement Individual counseling is available. Academic advisement by a staff member affiliated with the program is available.

Auxiliary aids and services *Aids:* calculators, personal computers, personal spelling/word-use assistants (e.g., Franklin Speller), scan and read programs (e.g., Kurzweil), screen-enlarging programs, screen readers, speech recognition programs (e.g., Dragon), tape recorders, taped textbooks. *Services and accommodations:* advocates, alternative test arrangements, readers, note-takers, and scribes.

ADD/ADHD Students with ADD/ADHD are eligible for the same services available to students with LD, as well as distraction-free testing environments and medication management.

Application *Required:* high school transcript, ACT (extended-time or untimed test accepted), and psychoeducational report (3 years old or less). *Recommended:* participation in extracurricular activities, interview, personal statement, and letter(s) of recommendation. Upon application, documentation of need for special services should be sent only to your LD program or unit. Upon acceptance, documentation of need for special services should be sent only to your LD program or unit. *Application deadline (institutional):* rolling/continuous for fall and rolling/continuous for spring. *Application deadline (LD program):* rolling/continuous for fall and rolling/continuous for spring.

LD program contact Ann Austin, LD Specialist, 518 West Locust, Davenport, IA 52803. *Phone:* 319-333-6161. *Fax:* 319-333-6243.

Application contact St. Ambrose University, 518 West Locust Street, Davenport, IA 52803-2898. *Web address:* http://www.sau.edu/.

ST. ANDREWS PRESBYTERIAN COLLEGE

Laurinburg, North Carolina

Students with LD Served by Program	15	ADD/ADHD Services	✓
Staff	2 full-time, 15 part-time	Summer Preparation Program	n/a
LD Program or Service Fee	n/a	Alternative Test Arrangements	✓
LD Program Began	1994	LD Student Organization	n/a

Disability and Academic Support Services began offering services in 1994. The program serves approximately 15 undergraduate students. Faculty consists of 2 full-time and 15 part-time staff members. Services are provided by proctors, director, academic aide coordinator.

Policies The college has written policies regarding course substitutions. Students with LD may take up to 18 credit hours per semester; 9 credit hours per semester are required to maintain full-time status and to be eligible for financial aid.

Auxiliary aids and services *Aids:* calculators, personal computers, personal spelling/word-use assistants (e.g., Franklin Speller), scan and read programs (e.g., Kurzweil), screen-enlarging programs, screen readers, speech recognition programs (e.g., Dragon), tape recorders, taped textbooks, Alpha-Smart. *Services and accommodations:* alternative test arrangements, readers, note-takers, and scribes.

ADD/ADHD Students with ADD/ADHD are eligible for the same services available to students with LD, as well as distraction-free testing environments.

Application *Required:* high school transcript and ACT or SAT I (extended-time or untimed test accepted). *Recommended:* participation in extracurricular activities, interview, personal statement, and letter(s) of recommendation. Upon acceptance, documentation of need for special services should be sent only to your LD program or unit. *Application deadline (institutional):* rolling/continuous for fall and rolling/continuous for spring.

LD program contact Disability and Academic Support Services, 1700 Dogwood Mile, Laurinburg, NC 28387. *Phone:* 910-277-5331. *Fax:* 910-277-5020. *E-mail:* info@sapc.edu.
Application contact St. Andrews Presbyterian College, 1700 Dogwood Mile, Laurinburg, NC 28352-5598. *E-mail:* admission@sapc.edu. *Web address:* http://www.sapc.edu/.

ST. BONAVENTURE UNIVERSITY
St. Bonaventure, New York

Students with LD Served by Program	64	ADD/ADHD Services	✓
Staff	1 full-time, 2 part-time	Summer Preparation Program	n/a
LD Program or Service Fee	n/a	Alternative Test Arrangements	✓
LD Program Began	1985	LD Student Organization	n/a

The Teaching and Learning Center began offering services in 1985. The program serves approximately 64 undergraduate students. Faculty consists of 1 full-time and 2 part-time staff members. Services are provided by academic advisers, graduate assistants/students, and LD specialists.
Policies The college has written policies regarding course substitutions. Students with LD may take up to 18 credit hours per semester; 12 credit hours per semester are required to maintain full-time status and to be eligible for financial aid. LD services are also available to graduate students.
Special preparation or orientation Optional orientation held before registration, during registration, before classes begin, during summer prior to enrollment, and individually by special arrangement.
Counseling and advisement Individual counseling is available. Academic advisement by a staff member affiliated with the program is available.
Auxiliary aids and services *Services and accommodations:* advocates, alternative test arrangements, readers, note-takers, and scribes.
ADD/ADHD Students with ADD/ADHD are eligible for the same services available to students with LD, as well as distraction-free study areas, distraction-free testing environments and personal coach or mentors.
Application *Required:* high school transcript, ACT (extended-time test accepted), personal statement, letter(s) of recommendation, psychoeducational report (3 years old or less), documentation of high school services (e.g., Individualized Education Program [IEP] or 504 plan), and medical form. *Recommended:* participation in extracurricular activities, SAT I (extended-time test accepted), interview, and separate application to your LD program or unit. Upon application, documentation of need for special services should be sent only to your LD program or unit. Upon acceptance, documentation of need for special services should be sent only to your LD program or unit. *Application deadline (institutional):* rolling/continuous for fall and rolling/continuous for spring. *Application deadline (LD program):* rolling/continuous for fall and rolling/continuous for spring.
LD program contact Nancy A. Matthews, Coordinator of Services for Students with Disabilities, Teaching and Learning Center, St. Bonaventure, NY 14778. *Phone:* 716-375-2066. *Fax:* 716-375-2072. *E-mail:* nmatthew@sbu.edu.
Application contact St. Bonaventure University, Route 417, St. Bonaventure, NY 14778-2284. *E-mail:* admissions@sbu.edu. *Web address:* http://www.sbu.edu/.

ST. LAWRENCE UNIVERSITY
Canton, New York

Students with LD Served by Program	106	ADD/ADHD Services	✓
Staff	1 full-time	Summer Preparation Program	n/a
LD Program or Service Fee	n/a	Alternative Test Arrangements	✓
LD Program Began	1987	LD Student Organization	n/a

Office of Services for Students with Special Needs began offering services in 1987. The program serves approximately 106 undergraduate students. Faculty consists of 1 full-time staff member. Services are provided by academic advisers, regular education teachers, counselors, graduate assistants/students, and trained peer tutors.
Policies LD services are also available to graduate students.
Subject-area tutoring Available in all subjects. Offered one-on-one by graduate assistants/students and trained peer tutors.
Counseling and advisement Career counseling, individual counseling, and small-group counseling are available. Academic advisement by a staff member affiliated with the program is available.
Auxiliary aids and services *Aids:* scan and read programs (e.g., Kurzweil), screen-enlarging programs, screen readers, speech recognition programs (e.g., Dragon), tape recorders. *Services and accommodations:* advocates, priority registration, alternative test arrangements, readers, note-takers, and scribes.
ADD/ADHD Students with ADD/ADHD are eligible for the same services available to students with LD, as well as distraction-free study areas, distraction-free testing environments and medication management.
Application *Required:* high school transcript, ACT or SAT I (extended-time or untimed test accepted), personal statement, and letter(s) of recommendation. *Recommended:* participation in extracurricular activities and interview. Upon acceptance, documentation of need for special services should be sent only to your LD program or unit. *Application deadline (institutional):* 2/15 for fall and 12/1 for spring.
LD program contact John Meagher, Director, Canton, NY 13617. *Phone:* 315-229-5104. *Fax:* 315-229-5104. *E-mail:* jmeagher@stlawu.edu.
Application contact St. Lawrence University, Canton, NY 13617-1455. *E-mail:* admiss@music.stlawu.edu. *Web address:* http://www.stlawu.edu/.

SAINT LEO UNIVERSITY
Saint Leo, Florida

Students with LD Served by Program	30	ADD/ADHD Services	✓
Staff	1 full-time	Summer Preparation Program	n/a
LD Program or Service Fee	n/a	Alternative Test Arrangements	✓
LD Program Began	1998	LD Student Organization	n/a

ADA Student Support Services began offering services in 1998. The program serves approximately 30 undergraduate students. Faculty consists of 1 full-time staff member. Services are provided by academic advisers, LD specialists, and trained peer tutors.
Policies The college has written policies regarding course substitutions. Students with LD may take up to 18 credit hours per semester; 12 credit hours per semester are required to maintain full-time status and to be eligible for financial aid.
Counseling and advisement Academic advisement by a staff member affiliated with the program is available.

Saint Leo University (continued)

Auxiliary aids and services *Aids:* calculators, personal computers, scan and read programs (e.g., Kurzweil), speech recognition programs (e.g., Dragon), tape recorders, taped textbooks. *Services and accommodations:* alternative test arrangements, readers, note-takers, and scribes.

ADD/ADHD Students with ADD/ADHD are eligible for the same services available to students with LD, as well as distraction-free study areas and distraction-free testing environments.

Application *Required:* high school transcript, ACT or SAT I (extended-time or untimed test accepted), personal statement, letter(s) of recommendation, and psychoeducational report (3 years old or less). Upon acceptance, documentation of need for special services should be sent to both admissions and your LD program or unit. *Application deadline (institutional):* rolling/continuous for fall and rolling/continuous for spring.

LD program contact Karen A. Hahn, Director of ADA Student Support Services, PO Box 6665, MC 2010, Saint Leo, FL 33574. *Phone:* 352-588-8464. *Fax:* 352-588-8605. *E-mail:* karen.hahn@saintleo.edu.

Application contact Dr. Susan Hallenbeck, Director of Undergraduate Admission, Saint Leo University, PO Box 6665 MC 2008, Saint Leo, FL 33574-2008. *Phone:* 352-588-8283. *E-mail:* admissns@saintleo.edu. *Web address:* http://www.saintleo.edu/.

SAINT MARY'S COLLEGE OF CALIFORNIA
Moraga, California

Students with LD Served by Program	110	ADD/ADHD Services	✓
Staff	1 full-time, 1 part-time	Summer Preparation Program	n/a
LD Program or Service Fee	n/a	Alternative Test Arrangements	✓
LD Program Began	1990	LD Student Organization	n/a

Academic Support and Achievement Programs (ASAP) began offering services in 1990. The program serves approximately 110 undergraduate students. Faculty consists of 1 full-time and 1 part-time staff member. Services are provided by academic advisers, regular education teachers, and Director.

Policies Students with LD may take up to 14 hours per semester. LD services are also available to graduate students.

Special preparation or orientation Optional orientation held individually by special arrangement.

Special courses Available in self-advocacy. No courses are offered for credit; none enter into overall grade point average.

Counseling and advisement Support groups is available. Academic advisement by a staff member affiliated with the program is available.

Auxiliary aids and services *Aids:* calculators, personal computers, personal spelling/word-use assistants (e.g., Franklin Speller), screen-enlarging programs, speech recognition programs (e.g., Dragon), tape recorders. *Services and accommodations:* advocates, priority registration, alternative test arrangements, readers, note-takers, and scribes.

ADD/ADHD Students with ADD/ADHD are eligible for the same services available to students with LD, as well as distraction-free testing environments.

Application *Required:* high school transcript, ACT or SAT I (extended-time or untimed test accepted), personal statement, and letter(s) of recommendation. *Recommended:* participation in extracurricular activities. Upon application, documentation of need for special services should be sent only to your LD program or unit. Upon acceptance, documentation of need for

special services should be sent only to your LD program or unit. *Application deadline (institutional):* 2/1 for fall and 1/1 for spring.

LD program contact Jeannine Chavez-Parfitt, Director, Academic Support and Achievement Programs, 1928 Saint Mary's Road, Moraga, CA 94575. *Phone:* 925-631-4358. *Fax:* 925-631-4835. *E-mail:* jparfitt@stmarys-ca.edu.

Application contact Saint Mary's College of California, PO Box 4800, Moraga, CA 94575. *E-mail:* smcadmit@stmarys-ca.edu. *Web address:* http://www.stmarys-ca.edu/.

SAINT MARY'S UNIVERSITY
Halifax, Nova Scotia

Students with LD Served by Program	60	ADD/ADHD Services	✓
Staff	9 full-time	Summer Preparation Program	n/a
LD Program or Service Fee	n/a	Alternative Test Arrangements	✓
LD Program Began	1990	LD Student Organization	n/a

Atlantic Centre of Support for Students with Disabilities began offering services in 1990. The program serves approximately 60 undergraduate students. Faculty consists of 9 full-time staff members. Services are provided by counselors, LD specialists, and Examination coordinator .

Policies LD services are also available to graduate students.

Special preparation or orientation Required orientation held before registration.

Basic skills remediation Available in study skills, computer skills, reading, time management, social skills, learning strategies, written language, and use of adaptive technologies. Offered one-on-one and in small groups by computer-based instruction and LD specialists.

Counseling and advisement Career counseling and individual counseling are available.

Auxiliary aids and services *Aids:* calculators, personal computers, personal spelling/word-use assistants (e.g., Franklin Speller), scan and read programs (e.g., Kurzweil), screen-enlarging programs, screen readers, speech recognition programs (e.g., Dragon), tape recorders, taped textbooks. *Services and accommodations:* advocates, alternative test arrangements, readers, note-takers, and scribes.

ADD/ADHD Students with ADD/ADHD are eligible for the same services available to students with LD, as well as distraction-free study areas, distraction-free testing environments and personal coach or mentors.

Application *Required:* separate application to your LD program or unit and psychoeducational report (5 years old or less). *Recommended:* interview, personal statement, letter(s) of recommendation, and documentation of high school services (e.g., Individualized Education Program [IEP] or 504 plan). Upon application, documentation of need for special services should be sent only to your LD program or unit. Upon acceptance, documentation of need for special services should be sent only to your LD program or unit. *Application deadline (LD program):* rolling/continuous for fall and rolling/continuous for spring.

LD program contact Madeleine Lelievre, Counselor, Atlantic Centre of Support for Students with Disabilities, Halifax, NS B3H 3C3. *Phone:* 902-420-5452. *Fax:* 902-496-8122. *E-mail:* mlelievr@stmarys.ca.

Application contact Saint Mary's University, Halifax, NS B3H 3C3. *E-mail:* jimdunn@stmarys.ca. *Web address:* http://www.stmarys.ca/.

SAINT MARY'S UNIVERSITY OF MINNESOTA

Winona, Minnesota

Students with LD Served by Program	40	ADD/ADHD Services	✓
Staff	3 full-time, 1 part-time	Summer Preparation Program	n/a
LD Program or Service Fee	n/a	Alternative Test Arrangements	✓
LD Program Began	1980	LD Student Organization	n/a

Academic Skills Center began offering services in 1980. The program serves approximately 40 undergraduate students. Faculty consists of 3 full-time staff members and 1 part-time staff member. Services are provided by academic advisers, regular education teachers, and LD specialists.

Policies Students with LD may take up to 17 credit hours per semester; 12 credit hours per semester are required to maintain full-time status and to be eligible for financial aid. LD services are also available to graduate students.

Diagnostic testing Available for intelligence, personality, reading, written language, learning styles, and math.

Subject-area tutoring Available in most subjects. Offered in small groups by trained peer tutors.

Counseling and advisement Academic advisement by a staff member affiliated with the program is available.

Auxiliary aids and services *Aids:* calculators, personal spelling/word-use assistants (e.g., Franklin Speller), scan and read programs (e.g., Kurzweil), screen-enlarging programs, screen readers, speech recognition programs (e.g., Dragon), tape recorders, taped textbooks. *Services and accommodations:* advocates, priority registration, alternative test arrangements, readers, note-takers, and scribes.

ADD/ADHD Students with ADD/ADHD are eligible for the same services available to students with LD, as well as distraction-free study areas, distraction-free testing environments and personal coach or mentors.

Application *Required:* high school transcript and ACT or SAT I (extended-time or untimed test accepted). *Recommended:* psychoeducational report (4 years old or less) and documentation of high school services (e.g., Individualized Education Program [IEP] or 504 plan). Upon application, documentation of need for special services should be sent only to your LD program or unit. Upon acceptance, documentation of need for special services should be sent only to your LD program or unit. *Application deadline (institutional):* rolling/continuous for fall and rolling/continuous for spring. *Application deadline (LD program):* rolling/continuous for fall and rolling/continuous for spring.

LD program contact Bonnie M. Smith, Disability Services Coordinator, 700 Terrace Heights #1513, Winona, MN 55987. *Phone:* 507-457-1465. *Fax:* 507-457-1633. *E-mail:* bsmith@smumn.edu.

Application contact Saint Mary's University of Minnesota, 700 Terrace Heights, Winona, MN 55987-1399. *E-mail:* admissions@smumn.edu. *Web address:* http://www.smumn.edu/.

ST. NORBERT COLLEGE

De Pere, Wisconsin

Students with LD Served by Program	70	ADD/ADHD Services	✓
Staff	2 full-time	Summer Preparation Program	n/a
LD Program or Service Fee	n/a	Alternative Test Arrangements	✓
LD Program Began	1995	LD Student Organization	n/a

Academic Support Services began offering services in 1995. The program serves approximately 70 undergraduate students. Faculty consists of 2 full-time staff members. Services are provided by remediation/learning specialists and trained peer tutors.

Policies The college has written policies regarding course substitutions. Students with LD may take up to 16 semester hours per semester; 12 semester hours per semester are required to maintain full-time status; 8 semester hours per semester are required to be eligible for financial aid.

Subject-area tutoring Available in most subjects. Offered one-on-one and in small groups by trained peer tutors.

Special courses Available in college survival skills. All courses are offered for credit; all enter into overall grade point average.

Counseling and advisement Career counseling, individual counseling, and small-group counseling are available.

Auxiliary aids and services *Aids:* calculators, personal computers, personal spelling/word-use assistants (e.g., Franklin Speller), scan and read programs (e.g., Kurzweil), screen-enlarging programs, tape recorders, taped textbooks. *Services and accommodations:* advocates, priority registration, alternative test arrangements, readers, note-takers, and scribes.

ADD/ADHD Students with ADD/ADHD are eligible for the same services available to students with LD, as well as distraction-free study areas, distraction-free testing environments and personal coach or mentors.

Application *Required:* high school transcript, ACT (extended-time or untimed test accepted), personal statement, letter(s) of recommendation, and psychoeducational report (3 years old or less). Upon application, documentation of need for special services should be sent only to your LD program or unit. *Application deadline (institutional):* rolling/continuous for fall and rolling/continuous for spring.

LD program contact Karen Goode-Bartholomew, Director, Academic Support Services, 100 Grant Street, DePere, WI 54115. *Phone:* 920-403-1321. *Fax:* 920-403-4021. *E-mail:* bartkg@mail.snc.edu.

Application contact St. Norbert College, 100 Grant Street, Office of Admission, De Pere, WI 54115-2099. *E-mail:* admit@sncac.snc.edu. *Web address:* http://www.snc.edu/.

SANTA CLARA UNIVERSITY

Santa Clara, California

Students with LD Served by Program	50	ADD/ADHD Services	✓
Staff	1 full-time, 2 part-time	Summer Preparation Program	n/a
LD Program or Service Fee	n/a	Alternative Test Arrangements	✓
LD Program Began	1990	LD Student Organization	n/a

Disabilities Resources began offering services in 1990. The program serves approximately 50 undergraduate students. Faculty consists of 1 full-time and 2 part-time staff members. Services are provided by academic advisers, regular education teachers, counselors, graduate assistants/students, LD specialists, and trained peer tutors.

Policies The college has written policies regarding course substitutions and substitution and waivers of requirements for admission and graduation. Students with LD may take up to 19 credits per quarter. LD services are also available to graduate students.

Special preparation or orientation Optional orientation held before registration, during registration, before classes begin, and during summer prior to enrollment.

Basic skills remediation Available in study skills, time management, and learning strategies. Offered in small groups by LD specialists.

Santa Clara University (continued)

Subject-area tutoring Available in most subjects. Offered one-on-one by trained peer tutors.

Counseling and advisement Career counseling, individual counseling, and support groups are available. Academic advisement by a staff member affiliated with the program is available.

Auxiliary aids and services *Aids:* calculators, scan and read programs (e.g., Kurzweil), screen-enlarging programs, tape recorders, taped textbooks. *Services and accommodations:* priority registration, alternative test arrangements, readers, note-takers, and scribes.

ADD/ADHD Students with ADD/ADHD are eligible for the same services available to students with LD, as well as distraction-free study areas and distraction-free testing environments.

Application *Required:* high school transcript, ACT or SAT I (untimed tests accepted), personal statement, and letter(s) of recommendation. *Recommended:* participation in extracurricular activities, interview, psychoeducational report (3 years old or less), and documentation of high school services (e.g., Individualized Education Program [IEP] or 504 plan). Upon application, documentation of need for special services should be sent only to your LD program or unit. Upon acceptance, documentation of need for special services should be sent only to your LD program or unit. *Application deadline (institutional):* 1/15 for fall.

LD program contact Ann Ravenscroft, Coordinator, Disability Resources, 500 El Camino Real, Santa Clara, CA 95053. *Phone:* 408-554-4111. *E-mail:* eravenscroft@scu.edu.

Application contact Santa Clara University, 500 El Camino Real, Santa Clara, CA 95053-0001. *E-mail:* ugadmissions@scu.edu. *Web address:* http://www.scu.edu/.

SCHOOL OF THE ART INSTITUTE OF CHICAGO
Chicago, Illinois

Students with LD Served by Program	55	ADD/ADHD Services	✓
Staff	2 part-time	Summer Preparation Program	n/a
LD Program or Service Fee	n/a	Alternative Test Arrangements	✓
LD Program Began	1986	LD Student Organization	n/a

Learning Center Support Services began offering services in 1986. The program serves approximately 55 undergraduate students. Faculty consists of 2 part-time staff members. Services are provided by diagnostic specialists and LD specialists.

Policies Students with LD may take up to 18 credit hours per term; 9 credit hours per term are required to maintain full-time status and to be eligible for financial aid. LD services are also available to graduate students.

Fees *Diagnostic Testing Fee:* ranges from $150 to $200.

Diagnostic testing Available for auditory processing, motor skills, spelling, spoken language, intelligence, reading, written language, visual processing, and math.

Basic skills remediation Available in auditory processing, study skills, computer skills, reading, time management, visual processing, learning strategies, spelling, written language, math, and spoken language. Offered one-on-one, in small groups, and class-size groups by regular education teachers and LD specialists.

Subject-area tutoring Available in most subjects. Offered one-on-one and in small groups by LD specialists.

Special courses Available in reading and written composition skills. All courses are offered for credit; all enter into overall grade point average.

Auxiliary aids and services *Aids:* scan and read programs (e.g., Kurzweil), screen-enlarging programs, screen readers, speech recognition programs (e.g., Dragon), tape recorders. *Services and accommodations:* advocates, priority registration, alternative test arrangements, readers, note-takers, and scribes.

ADD/ADHD Students with ADD/ADHD are eligible for the same services available to students with LD, as well as distraction-free testing environments, personal coach or mentors, and support groups for ADD/ADHD.

Application *Required:* high school transcript, ACT or SAT I (extended-time tests accepted), interview, personal statement, and letter(s) of recommendation. *Recommended:* psychoeducational report (3 years old or less). Upon application, documentation of need for special services should be sent only to your LD program or unit. Upon acceptance, documentation of need for special services should be sent only to your LD program or unit. *Application deadline (institutional):* rolling/continuous for fall and rolling/continuous for spring. *Application deadline (LD program):* rolling/continuous for fall and rolling/continuous for spring.

LD program contact Judith S. Watson, Director, Learning Center Support Services, 112 South Michgian Avenue, Chicago, IL 60603. *Phone:* 312-345-3507. *Fax:* 312-541-8063. *E-mail:* jwatson@artic.edu.

Application contact School of the Art Institute of Chicago, 37 South Wabash, Chicago, IL 60603-3103. *E-mail:* admiss@artic.edu. *Web address:* http://www.artic.edu/saic/.

SEATTLE PACIFIC UNIVERSITY
Seattle, Washington

Students with LD Served by Program	90	ADD/ADHD Services	✓
Staff	1 full-time, 1 part-time	Summer Preparation Program	n/a
LD Program or Service Fee	n/a	Alternative Test Arrangements	✓
LD Program Began	1977	LD Student Organization	n/a

Disabled Student Services began offering services in 1977. The program serves approximately 90 undergraduate students. Faculty consists of 1 full-time and 1 part-time staff member. Services are provided by counselors, graduate assistants/students, LD specialists, and trained peer tutors.

Policies The college has written policies regarding course substitutions. Students with LD may take up to 20 credit hours per quarter; 12 credit hours per quarter are required to maintain full-time status. LD services are also available to graduate students.

Special courses Available in study skills, college survival skills, test taking, time management, learning strategies, math, and written composition skills. All courses are offered for credit; most enter into overall grade point average.

Counseling and advisement Individual counseling is available.

Auxiliary aids and services *Aids:* personal computers, screen-enlarging programs, speech recognition programs (e.g., Dragon), taped textbooks. *Services and accommodations:* priority registration, alternative test arrangements, readers, note-takers, and scribes.

ADD/ADHD Students with ADD/ADHD are eligible for the same services available to students with LD, as well as distraction-free study areas, distraction-free testing environments and personal coach or mentors.

Application *Required:* high school transcript, ACT or SAT I (extended-time or untimed test accepted), personal statement, and letter(s) of recommendation. *Recommended:* participation in extracurricular activities. Upon acceptance, documentation of need for special services should be sent only to your LD program or unit. *Application deadline (institutional):* 6/1 for fall and 2/15 for spring. *Application deadline (LD program):* rolling/continuous for fall and rolling/continuous for spring.

LD program contact Richard Okamoto, Assistant Director, Educational Services, 3307 Third Avenue West, Seattle, WA 98119. *Phone:* 206-281-2475. *Fax:* 206-286-7348. *E-mail:* rokamoto@spu.edu.

Application contact Seattle Pacific University, 3307 Third Avenue West, Seattle, WA 98119-1997. *E-mail:* admissions@spu.edu. *Web address:* http://www.spu.edu/.

SHAWNEE STATE UNIVERSITY
Portsmouth, Ohio

Students with LD Served by Program	70	ADD/ADHD Services	✓
Staff	1 full-time	Summer Preparation Program	n/a
LD Program or Service Fee	n/a	Alternative Test Arrangements	✓
LD Program Began	1986	LD Student Organization	n/a

Office of Special Needs Services began offering services in 1986. The program serves approximately 70 undergraduate students. Faculty consists of 1 full-time staff member. Services are provided by academic advisers, counselors, trained peer tutors, and professional tutors.

Policies Students with LD may take up to 18 credit hours per quarter; 12 credit hours per quarter are required to maintain full-time status; 6 credit hours per quarter are required to be eligible for financial aid.

Special preparation or orientation Optional orientation held before classes begin.

Basic skills remediation Available in reading. Offered one-on-one by trained peer tutors.

Subject-area tutoring Available in most subjects. Offered one-on-one by trained peer tutors.

Special courses Available in study skills. All courses are offered for credit; all enter into overall grade point average.

Counseling and advisement Career counseling and individual counseling are available. Academic advisement by a staff member affiliated with the program is available.

Auxiliary aids and services *Aids:* calculators, personal computers, personal spelling/word-use assistants (e.g., Franklin Speller), scan and read programs (e.g., Kurzweil), speech recognition programs (e.g., Dragon), tape recorders, taped textbooks. *Services and accommodations:* alternative test arrangements, readers, note-takers, and scribes.

ADD/ADHD Students with ADD/ADHD are eligible for the same services available to students with LD, as well as distraction-free study areas and distraction-free testing environments.

Application *Required:* high school transcript and psychoeducational report (7 years old or less). *Recommended:* documentation of high school services (e.g., Individualized Education Program [IEP] or 504 plan). Upon application, documentation of need for special services should be sent only to your LD program or unit. Upon acceptance, documentation of need for special services should be sent only to your LD program or unit. *Application deadline (institutional):* rolling/continuous for fall and rolling/continuous for spring. *Application deadline (LD program):* rolling/continuous for fall and rolling/continuous for spring.

LD program contact Royna Lattimore, Coordinator, Disability Services, 940 2nd Street, Portsmouth, OH 45662. *Phone:* 740-355-2276. *Fax:* 740-355-2107. *E-mail:* rlattimore@shawnee.edu.

Application contact Shawnee State University, 940 Second Street, Portsmouth, OH 45662-4344. *E-mail:* admsn@shawnee.edu. *Web address:* http://www.shawnee.edu/.

SHELDON JACKSON COLLEGE
Sitka, Alaska

Students with LD Served by Program	6	ADD/ADHD Services	✓
Staff	1 full-time, 5 part-time	Summer Preparation Program	n/a
LD Program or Service Fee	n/a	Alternative Test Arrangements	✓
LD Program Began	n/a	LD Student Organization	n/a

Learning Assistant Program serves approximately 6 undergraduate students. Faculty consists of 1 full-time and 5 part-time staff members. Services are provided by remediation/learning specialists, trained peer tutors, and Alaska Vocational Rehabilitation Counselor.

Policies Students with LD may take up to 15 credit hours per semester; 12 credit hours per semester are required to maintain full-time status and to be eligible for financial aid.

Diagnostic testing Available for intelligence, reading, and math.

Basic skills remediation Available in study skills, reading, time management, learning strategies, spelling, written language, and math. Offered one-on-one, in small groups, and class-size groups by LD specialists and trained peer tutors.

Subject-area tutoring Available in most subjects. Offered one-on-one and in small groups by trained peer tutors and LD specialists.

Special courses Available in oral communication skills, study skills, college survival skills, practical computer skills, test taking, health and nutrition, reading, time management, learning strategies, vocabulary development, math, and written composition skills. Some courses are offered for credit; some enter into overall grade point average.

Counseling and advisement Individual counseling is available.

Auxiliary aids and services *Aids:* personal spelling/word-use assistants (e.g., Franklin Speller), scan and read programs (e.g., Kurzweil), tape recorders, taped textbooks. *Services and accommodations:* alternative test arrangements, readers, and note-takers.

ADD/ADHD Students with ADD/ADHD are eligible for the same services available to students with LD

Application *Required:* personal statement, psychoeducational report (3 years old or less), and documentation of high school services (e.g., Individualized Education Program [IEP] or 504 plan). Upon application, documentation of need for special services should be sent only to your LD program or unit. Upon acceptance, documentation of need for special services should be sent only to your LD program or unit. *Application deadline (institutional):* rolling/continuous for fall and rolling/continuous for spring. *Application deadline (LD program):* rolling/continuous for fall and rolling/continuous for spring.

LD program contact Alice J. Smith, Learning Center Director, 801 Lincoln Street, Sitka, AK 99835. *Phone:* 907-747-5235. *Fax:* 907-747-5237. *E-mail:* chardsmith@hotmail.com.

Application contact Sheldon Jackson College, 801 Lincoln Street, Sitka, AK 99835-7699. *E-mail:* sombrozak@juno.com. *Web address:* http://www.sj-alaska.edu/.

SHIPPENSBURG UNIVERSITY OF PENNSYLVANIA

Shippensburg, Pennsylvania

Students with LD Served by Program	210	ADD/ADHD Services	n/a
Staff	1 full-time, 1 part-time	Summer Preparation Program	n/a
LD Program or Service Fee	n/a	Alternative Test Arrangements	n/a
LD Program Began	n/a	LD Student Organization	n/a

Office of Social Equity serves approximately 210 undergraduate students. Faculty consists of 1 full-time and 1 part-time staff member. Services are provided by remediation/learning specialists, graduate assistants/students, and professional tutors.
Policies 12 credit hours per semester are required to maintain full-time status and to be eligible for financial aid. LD services are also available to graduate students.
Special preparation or orientation Held before classes begin.
Auxiliary aids and services *Aids:* scan and read programs (e.g., Kurzweil), taped textbooks.
Application *Required:* high school transcript and ACT or SAT I (extended-time or untimed test accepted). *Recommended:* participation in extracurricular activities, interview, personal statement, letter(s) of recommendation, psychoeducational report (4 years old or less), and documentation of high school services (e.g., Individualized Education Program [IEP] or 504 plan). Upon application, documentation of need for special services should be sent only to your LD program or unit. Upon acceptance, documentation of need for special services should be sent only to your LD program or unit. *Application deadline (institutional):* rolling/continuous for fall and rolling/continuous for spring. *Application deadline (LD program):* rolling/continuous for fall and rolling/continuous for spring.
LD program contact Dr. Lois Waters, Director, Social Equity, 1871 Old Main Drive, Box 2, Shippensburg, PA 17257. *Phone:* 717-477-1161. *Fax:* 717-477-4001. *E-mail:* lawate@wharf.ship.edu.
Application contact Shippensburg University of Pennsylvania, 1871 Old Main Drive, Shippensburg, PA 17257-2299. *E-mail:* admiss@ark.ship.edu. *Web address:* http://www.ship.edu/.

SIENA COLLEGE

Loudonville, New York

Students with LD Served by Program	55	ADD/ADHD Services	✓
Staff	1 full-time	Summer Preparation Program	n/a
LD Program or Service Fee	n/a	Alternative Test Arrangements	✓
LD Program Began	n/a	LD Student Organization	n/a

Office of Tutoring and Services for Students with Disabilities serves approximately 55 undergraduate students. Faculty consists of 1 full-time staff member. Services are provided by counselors, trained peer tutors, and professional tutors.
Policies The college has written policies regarding substitution and waivers of requirements for admission. 12 credit hours per semester are required to maintain full-time status; 6 credit hours per semester are required to be eligible for financial aid.
Basic skills remediation Available in study skills, time management, and learning strategies. Offered in small group workshops.
Subject-area tutoring Available in all subjects. Offered one-on-one and in small groups by professional tutors and trained peer tutors.
Counseling and advisement Individual counseling is available.

Auxiliary aids and services *Aids:* calculators, personal spelling/word-use assistants (e.g., Franklin Speller), screen-enlarging programs, speech recognition programs (e.g., Dragon), tape recorders, taped textbooks. *Services and accommodations:* advocates, priority registration, alternative test arrangements, readers, note-takers, and scribes.
ADD/ADHD Students with ADD/ADHD are eligible for the same services available to students with LD, as well as distraction-free testing environments.
Application *Required:* high school transcript, ACT or SAT I (extended-time or untimed test accepted), personal statement, and letter(s) of recommendation. *Recommended:* participation in extracurricular activities, ACT (extended-time or untimed test accepted), SAT I (extended-time or untimed test accepted), and interview. Upon application, documentation of need for special services should be sent to both admissions and your LD program or unit. Upon acceptance, documentation of need for special services should be sent only to your LD program or unit. *Application deadline (institutional):* rolling/continuous for spring and 3/1 for fall. *Application deadline (LD program):* rolling/continuous for spring and 3/1 for fall.
LD program contact Renee D. Zullo, Director, 515 Loudon Road, Loudonville, NY 12211. *Phone:* 518-783-4239. *Fax:* 518-786-5013. *E-mail:* zullo@siena.edu.
Application contact Siena College, 515 Loudon Road, Loudonville, NY 12211-1462. *E-mail:* admit@siena.edu. *Web address:* http://www.siena.edu/.

SIERRA NEVADA COLLEGE

Incline Village, Nevada

Students with LD Served by Program	20	ADD/ADHD Services	✓
Staff	1 full-time	Summer Preparation Program	n/a
LD Program or Service Fee	n/a	Alternative Test Arrangements	✓
LD Program Began	1995	LD Student Organization	n/a

Disabled Student Services began offering services in 1995. The program serves approximately 20 undergraduate students. Faculty consists of 1 full-time staff member. Services are provided by academic advisers, regular education teachers, counselors, remediation/learning specialists, and professional tutors.
Policies Students with LD may take up to 15 credit hours per semester; 12 credit hours per semester are required to maintain full-time status and to be eligible for financial aid. LD services are also available to graduate students.
Special preparation or orientation Optional orientation held individually by special arrangement.
Subject-area tutoring Available in all subjects. Offered one-on-one and in small groups by professional tutors.
Counseling and advisement Career counseling and individual counseling are available. Academic advisement by a staff member affiliated with the program is available.
Auxiliary aids and services *Aids:* calculators, personal computers, tape recorders, taped textbooks. *Services and accommodations:* advocates, priority registration, alternative test arrangements, and note-takers.
ADD/ADHD Students with ADD/ADHD are eligible for the same services available to students with LD, as well as distraction-free study areas, distraction-free testing environments and personal counseling.
Application *Required:* high school transcript, ACT or SAT I (extended-time tests accepted), personal statement, psychoeducational report (3 years old or less), and documentation of high school services (e.g., Individualized Education Program [IEP] or 504 plan). *Recommended:* participation in extracurricular activi-

ties and interview. Upon application, documentation of need for special services should be sent only to admissions. Upon acceptance, documentation of need for special services should be sent only to your LD program or unit. *Application deadline (institutional):* 3/15 for fall and 11/15 for spring. *Application deadline (LD program):* 3/15 for fall and 11/15 for spring.
LD program contact Janey Muccio, Student Assistance Services Coordinator, PO Box 4269, Incline Village, NV 89450. *Phone:* 775-831-1314 Ext. 1637. *Fax:* 775-831-1347. *E-mail:* jmuccio@sierranevada.edu.
Application contact Sierra Nevada College, 800 College Drive, PO Box 4269, Incline Village, NV 89450-4269. *Web address:* http://www.sierranevada.edu/.

SONOMA STATE UNIVERSITY
Rohnert Park, California

Students with LD Served by Program	200	ADD/ADHD Services	✓
Staff	1 full-time	Summer Preparation Program	n/a
LD Program or Service Fee	n/a	Alternative Test Arrangements	✓
LD Program Began	1985	LD Student Organization	✓

Disability Resource Center began offering services in 1985. The program serves approximately 200 undergraduate students. Faculty consists of 1 full-time staff member. Services are provided by counselors, remediation/learning specialists, trained peer tutors, and professional tutors.
Policies The college has written policies regarding course substitutions, grade forgiveness, and substitution and waivers of requirements for admission and graduation. Students with LD may take up to 19 credit hours per semester; 12 credit hours per semester are required to maintain full-time status and to be eligible for financial aid. LD services are also available to graduate students.
Special preparation or orientation Optional orientation held individually by special arrangement.
Basic skills remediation Available in reading, learning strategies, written language, and math. Offered one-on-one and in small groups by professional tutors and trained peer tutors.
Subject-area tutoring Available in some subjects. Offered one-on-one and in small groups by computer-based instruction, professional tutors, and trained peer tutors.
Auxiliary aids and services *Aids:* calculators, personal computers, personal spelling/word-use assistants (e.g., Franklin Speller), scan and read programs (e.g., Kurzweil), screen-enlarging programs, screen readers, speech recognition programs (e.g., Dragon), tape recorders, taped textbooks. *Services and accommodations:* advocates, priority registration, alternative test arrangements, readers, note-takers, and scribes.
Student organization There is a student organization for students with LD.
ADD/ADHD Students with ADD/ADHD are eligible for the same services available to students with LD, as well as distraction-free study areas and distraction-free testing environments.
Application *Required:* high school transcript, SAT I (extended-time or untimed test accepted), and psychoeducational report (3 years old or less). Upon application, documentation of need for special services should be sent only to your LD program or unit. Upon acceptance, documentation of need for special services should be sent only to your LD program or unit. *Application deadline (institutional):* 11/30 for fall and 8/30 for spring. *Application deadline (LD program):* rolling/continuous for fall and rolling/continuous for spring.

LD program contact Bill Clopton, Disability Management Advisor, 1801 East Cotati Avenue, Rohnert Park, CA 94928. *Phone:* 707-664-2677. *Fax:* 707-664-2505. *E-mail:* bill.clopton@sonoma.edu.
Application contact Margo Axsom, Registrar, Sonoma State University, 1801 East Cotati Avenue, Rohnert Park, CA 94928-3609. *Phone:* 707-664-3129. *E-mail:* admitme@sonoma.edu. *Web address:* http://www.sonoma.edu/.

SOUTH CAROLINA STATE UNIVERSITY
Orangeburg, South Carolina

Students with LD Served by Program	10	ADD/ADHD Services	✓
Staff	1 full-time, 3 part-time	Summer Preparation Program	n/a
LD Program or Service Fee	n/a	Alternative Test Arrangements	✓
LD Program Began	n/a	LD Student Organization	n/a

Disabled Student Services serves approximately 10 undergraduate students. Faculty consists of 1 full-time and 3 part-time staff members. Services are provided by academic advisers, counselors, graduate assistants/students, LD specialists, and professional tutors.
Policies The college has written policies regarding substitution and waivers of requirements for admission. LD services are also available to graduate students.
Diagnostic testing Available for intelligence, learning strategies, reading, learning styles, and social skills.
Basic skills remediation Available in study skills, computer skills, reading, time management, social skills, learning strategies, and math. Offered one-on-one.
Subject-area tutoring Available in most subjects. Offered one-on-one by graduate assistants/students, trained peer tutors, and LD specialists.
Counseling and advisement Career counseling, individual counseling, and small-group counseling are available. Academic advisement by a staff member affiliated with the program is available.
Auxiliary aids and services *Aids:* tape recorders. *Services and accommodations:* advocates, priority registration, alternative test arrangements, readers, and note-takers.
ADD/ADHD Students with ADD/ADHD are eligible for the same services available to students with LD, as well as personal coach or mentors.
Application *Required:* high school transcript, ACT or SAT I (extended-time tests accepted), letter(s) of recommendation, and documentation of high school services (e.g., Individualized Education Program [IEP] or 504 plan). *Recommended:* interview. Upon application, documentation of need for special services should be sent to both admissions and your LD program or unit. Upon acceptance, documentation of need for special services should be sent to both admissions and your LD program or unit.
LD program contact Dr. Imogene L. Gouveia, Chief Psychologist, Counsel and Self Development Center, Campus PO Box 7508, Orangeburg, SC 29115. *Phone:* 803-536-8670. *Fax:* 803-536-8702. *E-mail:* gouveia@scsu.edu.
Application contact South Carolina State University, 300 College Street Northeast, Orangeburg, SC 29117-0001. *E-mail:* carolyn-free@scsu.scsu.edu. *Web address:* http://www.scsu.edu/.

SOUTH DAKOTA SCHOOL OF MINES AND TECHNOLOGY
Rapid City, South Dakota

Students with LD Served by Program	10	ADD/ADHD Services	✓
Staff	2 full-time, 4 part-time	Summer Preparation Program	n/a
LD Program or Service Fee	n/a	Alternative Test Arrangements	✓
LD Program Began	1992	LD Student Organization	n/a

ADA Support Services began offering services in 1992. The program serves approximately 10 undergraduate students. Faculty consists of 2 full-time and 4 part-time staff members. Services are provided by academic advisers, counselors, diagnostic specialists, and trained peer tutors.

Policies Students with LD may take up to 18 credit hours per semester; 12 credit hours per semester are required to maintain full-time status; 6 credit hours per semester are required to be eligible for financial aid. LD services are also available to graduate students.

Fees *Diagnostic Testing Fee:* $150.

Special preparation or orientation Optional orientation held individually by special arrangement.

Diagnostic testing Available for auditory processing, intelligence, reading, written language, and visual processing.

Subject-area tutoring Available in all subjects. Offered one-on-one by trained peer tutors.

Counseling and advisement Career counseling, individual counseling, small-group counseling, and support groups are available. Academic advisement by a staff member affiliated with the program is available.

Auxiliary aids and services *Aids:* screen-enlarging programs, tape recorders, taped textbooks. *Services and accommodations:* alternative test arrangements and note-takers.

ADD/ADHD Students with ADD/ADHD are eligible for the same services available to students with LD, as well as distraction-free testing environments.

Application *Required:* high school transcript and ACT (extended-time or untimed test accepted). Upon application, documentation of need for special services should be sent only to your LD program or unit. Upon acceptance, documentation of need for special services should be sent only to your LD program or unit. *Application deadline (institutional):* rolling/continuous for fall and rolling/continuous for spring.

LD program contact Dr. Francine Campone, Associate Dean of Students, 501 East Saint Joseph Street, OH 201, Rapid City, SD 57701. *Phone:* 605-394-2416. *Fax:* 605-394-2914. *E-mail:* fcampone@silver.sdsmt.edu.

Application contact South Dakota School of Mines and Technology, 501 East Saint Joseph, Rapid City, SD 57701-3995. *E-mail:* undergraduate_admissions@silver.sdsmt.ed. *Web address:* http://www.sdsmt.edu/.

SOUTHEASTERN COLLEGE OF THE ASSEMBLIES OF GOD
Lakeland, Florida

Students with LD Served by Program	26	ADD/ADHD Services	✓
Staff	1 full-time	Summer Preparation Program	n/a
LD Program or Service Fee	n/a	Alternative Test Arrangements	✓
LD Program Began	1990	LD Student Organization	n/a

Disabled Student Services began offering services in 1990. The program serves approximately 26 undergraduate students. Faculty consists of 1 full-time staff member. Services are provided by counselors, teacher trainees, and trained peer tutors.

Policies The college has written policies regarding course substitutions and substitution and waivers of requirements for admission and graduation. Students with LD may take up to 18 credit hours per semester; 12 credit hours per semester are required to maintain full-time status and to be eligible for financial aid.

Basic skills remediation Available in reading, written language, and math. Offered one-on-one and in class-size groups by computer-based instruction, regular education teachers, teacher trainees, and trained peer tutors.

Subject-area tutoring Available in all subjects. Offered one-on-one by trained peer tutors and teacher trainees.

Counseling and advisement Career counseling and individual counseling are available.

Auxiliary aids and services *Aids:* calculators, personal computers, personal spelling/word-use assistants (e.g., Franklin Speller), scan and read programs (e.g., Kurzweil). *Services and accommodations:* priority registration, alternative test arrangements, readers, note-takers, and scribes.

ADD/ADHD Students with ADD/ADHD are eligible for the same services available to students with LD, as well as distraction-free study areas and distraction-free testing environments.

Application *Required:* high school transcript, ACT or SAT I (extended-time or untimed test accepted), letter(s) of recommendation, psychoeducational report (3 years old or less), and documentation of high school services (e.g., Individualized Education Program [IEP] or 504 plan). Upon acceptance, documentation of need for special services should be sent only to your LD program or unit. *Application deadline (institutional):* rolling/continuous for fall and rolling/continuous for spring. *Application deadline (LD program):* rolling/continuous for fall and rolling/continuous for spring.

LD program contact Gary Yost, Career Development Director, 1000 Longfellow Boulevard, Lakeland, FL 33801. *Phone:* 863-667-5064. *Fax:* 863-667-5200. *E-mail:* gyost@secollege.edu.

Application contact Sandy Markharn, Admission Secretary, Southeastern College of the Assemblies of God, 1000 Longfellow Boulevard, Lakeland, FL 33801-6099. *Phone:* 863-667-5018. *E-mail:* rmshelto@secollege.edu. *Web address:* http://www.secollege.edu/.

SOUTHEASTERN LOUISIANA UNIVERSITY
Hammond, Louisiana

Students with LD Served by Program	100	ADD/ADHD Services	✓
Staff	2 full-time, 3 part-time	Summer Preparation Program	n/a
LD Program or Service Fee	n/a	Alternative Test Arrangements	✓
LD Program Began	n/a	LD Student Organization	n/a

Office of Student Life serves approximately 100 undergraduate students. Faculty consists of 2 full-time and 3 part-time staff members. Services are provided by graduate assistants/students and administrator.

Policies The college has written policies regarding course substitutions. Students with LD may take up to 18 credit hours per semester; 12 credit hours per semester are required to maintain full-time status and to be eligible for financial aid. LD services are also available to graduate students.

Subject-area tutoring Available in most subjects. Offered one-on-one and in small groups by trained peer tutors.

Counseling and advisement Career counseling and individual counseling are available.

Auxiliary aids and services *Aids:* screen-enlarging programs, screen readers, speech recognition programs (e.g., Dragon). *Services and accommodations:* priority registration, alternative test arrangements, readers, note-takers, and scribes.

ADD/ADHD Students with ADD/ADHD are eligible for the same services available to students with LD, as well as distraction-free testing environments.

Application *Required:* high school transcript and ACT or SAT I (extended-time or untimed ACT test accepted). Upon acceptance, documentation of need for special services should be sent only to your LD program or unit. *Application deadline (institutional):* 7/15 for fall and 12/5 for spring. *Application deadline (LD program):* rolling/continuous for fall and rolling/continuous for spring.

LD program contact Dr. Michelle Hall, Interim Director, Office of Institutional Research and Assessment, SLU 11851, Hammond, LA 70402. *Phone:* 504-549-2077. *Fax:* 504-549-3640. *E-mail:* mhall@selu.edu.

Application contact Pat Duplessis, University Admissions Analyst, Southeastern Louisiana University, SLU 752, Hammond, LA 70402. *Phone:* 504-549-2066. *E-mail:* ssoutullo@selu.edu. *Web address:* http://www.selu.edu/.

SOUTHEASTERN OKLAHOMA STATE UNIVERSITY
Durant, Oklahoma

Students with LD Served by Program	30	ADD/ADHD Services	✓
Staff	2 part-time	Summer Preparation Program	n/a
LD Program or Service Fee	n/a	Alternative Test Arrangements	✓
LD Program Began	n/a	LD Student Organization	n/a

Office for Student Disability Services serves approximately 30 undergraduate students. Faculty consists of 2 part-time staff members. Services are provided by academic advisers, counselors, and LD specialists.

Policies The college has written policies regarding course substitutions. 12 credit hours per semester are required to maintain full-time status; 6 credit hours per semester are required to be eligible for financial aid. LD services are also available to graduate students.

Subject-area tutoring Available in most subjects. Offered by trained peer tutors.

Counseling and advisement Career counseling and individual counseling are available. Academic advisement by a staff member affiliated with the program is available.

Auxiliary aids and services *Aids:* tape recorders, taped textbooks. *Services and accommodations:* advocates, alternative test arrangements, readers, note-takers, and scribes.

ADD/ADHD Students with ADD/ADHD are eligible for the same services available to students with LD, as well as distraction-free testing environments.

Application *Required:* high school transcript and ACT or SAT I (extended-time or untimed test accepted). Upon acceptance, documentation of need for special services should be sent only to your LD program or unit. *Application deadline (institutional):* rolling/continuous for fall and rolling/continuous for spring. *Application deadline (LD program):* rolling/continuous for fall and rolling/continuous for spring.

LD program contact Jan Anderson, Director, Student Support Services, Box 4112, Durant, OK 74701. *Phone:* 580-745-2394. *Fax:* 580-745-7470.

Application contact Southeastern Oklahoma State University, Fifth and University, Durant, OK 74701-0609. *Web address:* http://www.sosu.edu/.

SOUTHERN METHODIST UNIVERSITY
Dallas, Texas

Students with LD Served by Program	300	ADD/ADHD Services	✓
Staff	2 full-time, 1 part-time	Summer Preparation Program	n/a
LD Program or Service Fee	n/a	Alternative Test Arrangements	✓
LD Program Began	n/a	LD Student Organization	n/a

Services for Students with Disabilities serves approximately 300 undergraduate students. Faculty consists of 2 full-time staff members and 1 part-time staff member. Services are provided by counselors, diagnostic specialists, and LD specialists.

Policies Students with LD may take up to 18 credit hours per semester; 12 credit hours per semester are required to maintain full-time status and to be eligible for financial aid. LD services are also available to graduate students.

Fees *Diagnostic Testing Fee:* $200.

Diagnostic testing Available for auditory processing, motor skills, spelling, handwriting, neuropsychological, spoken language, intelligence, personality, study skills, learning strategies, reading, written language, learning styles, social skills, visual processing, math, and foreign language aptitude, Connors CPT.

Basic skills remediation Available in auditory processing, study skills, time management, and learning strategies. Offered one-on-one and in small groups by LD specialists.

Subject-area tutoring Available in some subjects. Offered one-on-one and in small groups by graduate assistants/students, trained peer tutors, and LD specialists.

Special courses Available in study skills, college survival skills, test taking, time management, learning strategies, and self-advocacy. No courses are offered for credit; none enter into overall grade point average.

Auxiliary aids and services *Aids:* personal spelling/word-use assistants (e.g., Franklin Speller), scan and read programs (e.g., Kurzweil), screen-enlarging programs, screen readers, speech recognition programs (e.g., Dragon), taped textbooks. *Services and accommodations:* priority registration, alternative test arrangements, readers, note-takers, and scribes.

ADD/ADHD Students with ADD/ADHD are eligible for the same services available to students with LD, as well as distraction-free testing environments and personal coach or mentors.

Application *Required:* high school transcript, ACT or SAT I (extended-time or untimed test accepted), personal statement, and letter(s) of recommendation. *Recommended:* participation in extracurricular activities and interview. Upon acceptance, documentation of need for special services should be sent only to your LD program or unit. *Application deadline (institutional):* 11/1 for spring.

LD program contact Rebecca Marin, Coordinator, Services for Students with Disabilities, Box 355, Dallas, TX 75275-0355. *Phone:* 214-768-4563. *Fax:* 214-768-4572. *E-mail:* rmarin@mail.smu.edu.

Application contact Southern Methodist University, 6425 Boaz, Dallas, TX 75275. *E-mail:* ugadmission@smu.edu. *Web address:* http://www.smu.edu/.

SOUTHERN POLYTECHNIC STATE UNIVERSITY
Marietta, Georgia

Students with LD Served by Program	45	ADD/ADHD Services	✓
Staff	1 part-time	Summer Preparation Program	n/a
LD Program or Service Fee	n/a	Alternative Test Arrangements	✓
LD Program Began	n/a	LD Student Organization	n/a

Counseling Services/Disability Services serves approximately 45 undergraduate students. Faculty consists of 1 part-time staff member. Services are provided by counselors and Regents Center for Learning Disorders.

Policies The college has written policies regarding course substitutions and substitution and waivers of requirements for admission and graduation. LD services are also available to graduate students.

Fees *Diagnostic Testing Fee: $300.*

Diagnostic testing Available for auditory processing, motor skills, spelling, neuropsychological, spoken language, intelligence, reading, written language, visual processing, math, and attention, memory, executive functions, fine motor skills, social-emotional.

Auxiliary aids and services *Aids:* personal spelling/word-use assistants (e.g., Franklin Speller), screen-enlarging programs, tape recorders, taped textbooks. *Services and accommodations:* advocates, priority registration, alternative test arrangements, readers, note-takers, scribes, and extended testing time.

ADD/ADHD Students with ADD/ADHD are eligible for the same services available to students with LD, as well as distraction-free testing environments.

Application *Required:* high school transcript, ACT or SAT I (extended-time or untimed test accepted), and Certificate of Immunization. *Recommended:* interview and personal statement. Upon application, documentation of need for special services should be sent only to your LD program or unit. Upon acceptance, documentation of need for special services should be sent only to your LD program or unit. *Application deadline (institutional):* 8/1 for fall and 12/1 for spring.

LD program contact Terri Cordle, Counselor/Disability Services Coordinator, 1100 South Marietta Parkway, Marietta, GA 30060-2896. *Phone:* 770-528-7226. *Fax:* 770-528-6855. *E-mail:* tcordle@spsu.edu.

Application contact Southern Polytechnic State University, 1100 South Marietta Parkway, Marietta, GA 30060-2896. *E-mail:* vhead@sct.edu. *Web address:* http://www.spsu.edu/.

SOUTHERN UTAH UNIVERSITY
Cedar City, Utah

Students with LD Served by Program	40	ADD/ADHD Services	✓
Staff	3 part-time	Summer Preparation Program	n/a
LD Program or Service Fee	n/a	Alternative Test Arrangements	✓
LD Program Began	1990	LD Student Organization	n/a

Student Support Services began offering services in 1990. The program serves approximately 40 undergraduate students. Faculty consists of 3 part-time staff members. Services are provided by academic advisers, remediation/learning specialists, and professional staff.

Policies Students with LD may take up to 19 credit hours per semester; 12 credit hours per semester are required to maintain full-time status and to be eligible for financial aid. LD services are also available to graduate students.

Basic skills remediation Available in study skills, reading, written language, and math. Offered in class-size groups by computer-based instruction and professional staff.

Counseling and advisement Academic advisement by a staff member affiliated with the program is available.

Auxiliary aids and services *Aids:* calculators, personal computers, personal spelling/word-use assistants (e.g., Franklin Speller), screen-enlarging programs, screen readers, speech recognition programs (e.g., Dragon), tape recorders, taped textbooks. *Services and accommodations:* advocates, priority registration, alternative test arrangements, readers, note-takers, and scribes.

ADD/ADHD Students with ADD/ADHD are eligible for the same services available to students with LD, as well as distraction-free study areas and distraction-free testing environments.

Application *Required:* high school transcript and ACT (extended-time or untimed test accepted). *Recommended:* participation in extracurricular activities and SAT I (extended-time or untimed test accepted). Upon acceptance, documentation of need for special services should be sent only to your LD program or unit. *Application deadline (institutional):* rolling/continuous for fall and rolling/continuous for spring. *Application deadline (LD program):* rolling/continuous for fall and rolling/continuous for spring.

LD program contact Georgia Thompson, ADA Coordinator, 351 West Center Street, Cedar City, UT 84720. *Phone:* 435-586-7710. *Fax:* 435-865-8393. *E-mail:* thompson@suu.edu.

Application contact Southern Utah University, 351 West Center Street, Cedar City, UT 84720-2498. *E-mail:* adminfo@suu.edu. *Web address:* http://www.suu.edu/.

SOUTHERN VERMONT COLLEGE
Bennington, Vermont

Students with LD Served by Program	65	ADD/ADHD Services	✓
Staff	2 full-time	Summer Preparation Program	n/a
LD Program or Service Fee	n/a	Alternative Test Arrangements	✓
LD Program Began	1984	LD Student Organization	n/a

Disabilities Support Program began offering services in 1984. The program serves approximately 65 undergraduate students. Faculty consists of 2 full-time staff members. Services are provided by diagnostic specialists, LD specialists, and professional tutors.

Policies The college has written policies regarding course substitutions. Students with LD may take up to 18 credit hours per semester; 12 credit hours per semester are required to maintain full-time status; 6 credit hours per semester are required to be eligible for financial aid.

Special preparation or orientation Optional orientation held after classes begin.

Diagnostic testing Available for auditory processing, spelling, reading, written language, learning styles, visual processing, and math.

Subject-area tutoring Available in some subjects. Offered one-on-one by professional tutors and LD specialists.

Counseling and advisement Career counseling and individual counseling are available.

Auxiliary aids and services *Aids:* calculators, personal computers, personal spelling/word-use assistants (e.g., Franklin Speller), scan and read programs (e.g., Kurzweil), screen-enlarging programs, speech recognition programs (e.g., Dragon), tape recorders, taped textbooks. *Services and accommodations:* alternative test arrangements and note-takers.

ADD/ADHD Students with ADD/ADHD are eligible for the same services available to students with LD, as well as distraction-free study areas, distraction-free testing environments and personal coach or mentors.

Application *Required:* high school transcript, ACT or SAT I (extended-time or untimed test accepted), personal statement, letter(s) of recommendation, psychoeducational report (2 years old or less), documentation of high school services (e.g., Individualized Education Program [IEP] or 504 plan), and achievement tests in reading, math, writing. *Recommended:* interview. Upon application, documentation of need for special services should be sent only to your LD program or unit. Upon acceptance, documentation of need for special services should be sent only to your LD program or unit. *Application deadline (institutional):* rolling/continuous for fall and rolling/continuous for spring. *Application deadline (LD program):* rolling/continuous for fall and rolling/continuous for spring.

LD program contact Linda Crowe, Coordinator, Disability Services Program, 978 Mansion Drive, Bennington, VT 05201. *Phone:* 802-447-6360. *Fax:* 802-447-4695. *E-mail:* lcrowe@svc.edu.

Application contact Southern Vermont College, 982 Foothills Road, Bennington, VT 05201-2128. *E-mail:* admis@svc.edu. *Web address:* http://www.svc.edu/.

SPRINGFIELD COLLEGE
Springfield, Massachusetts

Students with LD Served by Program	90	ADD/ADHD Services	✓
Staff	1 full-time	Summer Preparation Program	n/a
LD Program or Service Fee	n/a	Alternative Test Arrangements	✓
LD Program Began	1993	LD Student Organization	n/a

Student Support Services began offering services in 1993. The program serves approximately 90 undergraduate students. Faculty consists of 1 full-time staff member. Services are provided by LD specialists.

Policies Students with LD may take up to 18 semester hours per semester ; 12 semester hours per semester are required to maintain full-time status and to be eligible for financial aid. LD services are also available to graduate students.

Basic skills remediation Available in study skills, time management, and learning strategies. Offered one-on-one by LD specialists.

Auxiliary aids and services *Aids:* personal spelling/word-use assistants (e.g., Franklin Speller), scan and read programs (e.g., Kurzweil), screen-enlarging programs, screen readers, speech recognition programs (e.g., Dragon), tape recorders. *Services and accommodations:* advocates, alternative test arrangements, readers, note-takers, and scribes.

ADD/ADHD Students with ADD/ADHD are eligible for the same services available to students with LD, as well as distraction-free testing environments.

Application *Required:* high school transcript, ACT or SAT I (extended-time or untimed test accepted), interview, personal statement, and letter(s) of recommendation. *Recommended:* participation in extracurricular activities. Upon acceptance, documentation of need for special services should be sent only to your LD program or unit. *Application deadline (institutional):* 4/1 for fall and 12/1 for spring.

LD program contact Deb Dickens, Director, Student Support Services, 263 Alden Street, Springfield, MA 01109. *Phone:* 413-748-3768. *Fax:* 413-748-3937. *E-mail:* ddickens@spfldcol.edu.

Application contact Springfield College, 263 Alden Street, Springfield, MA 01109-3797. *E-mail:* admissions@spfldcol.edu. *Web address:* http://www.spfldcol.edu/.

STATE UNIVERSITY OF NEW YORK AT ALBANY
Albany, New York

Students with LD Served by Program	120	ADD/ADHD Services	✓
Staff	2 full-time, 1 part-time	Summer Preparation Program	✓
LD Program or Service Fee	n/a	Alternative Test Arrangements	✓
LD Program Began	1980	LD Student Organization	n/a

Disabled Student Services began offering services in 1980. The program serves approximately 120 undergraduate students. Faculty consists of 2 full-time staff members and 1 part-time staff member. Services are provided by academic advisers, counselors, diagnostic specialists, graduate assistants/students, and trained peer tutors.

Policies Students with LD may take up to 18 credits per semester; 12 credits per semester are required to maintain full-time status. LD services are also available to graduate students.

Special preparation or orientation Optional summer program offered prior to entering college.

Diagnostic testing Available for auditory processing, neuropsychological, spoken language, intelligence, personality, study skills, learning strategies, reading, written language, and math.

Subject-area tutoring Available in most subjects. Offered one-on-one and in small groups by graduate assistants/students and trained peer tutors.

Counseling and advisement Career counseling, individual counseling, and support groups are available. Academic advisement by a staff member affiliated with the program is available.

Auxiliary aids and services *Aids:* calculators, personal computers, personal spelling/word-use assistants (e.g., Franklin Speller), scan and read programs (e.g., Kurzweil), screen-enlarging programs, screen readers, tape recorders, taped textbooks. *Services and accommodations:* advocates, priority registration, alternative test arrangements, readers, note-takers, and scribes.

ADD/ADHD Students with ADD/ADHD are eligible for the same services available to students with LD, as well as distraction-free study areas, distraction-free testing environments and medication management.

Application *Required:* high school transcript, SAT I (extended-time or untimed test accepted), personal statement, letter(s) of recommendation, psychoeducational report (2 years old or less), and documentation of high school services (e.g., Individualized Education Program [IEP] or 504 plan). *Recommended:* participation in extracurricular activities. Upon application, documentation of need for special services should be sent only to your LD program or unit. Upon acceptance, documentation of need for special services should be sent only to your LD program or unit. *Application deadline (institutional):* 3/1 for fall and 1/1 for spring. *Application deadline (LD program):* 3/1 for fall and 1/1 for spring.

LD program contact Nancy Belowich-Negron, Director, 1400 Washington Avenue, CC137, Albany, NY 12222. *Phone:* 518-442-5490. *Fax:* 518-442-3908.

Application contact State University of New York at Albany, 1400 Washington Avenue, Albany, NY 12222-0001. *E-mail:* ugadmit@safnet.albany.edu. *Web address:* http://www.albany.edu/.

STATE UNIVERSITY OF NEW YORK AT BINGHAMTON
Binghamton, New York

Students with LD Served by Program	95	ADD/ADHD Services	✓
Staff	3 full-time	Summer Preparation Program	n/a
LD Program or Service Fee	n/a	Alternative Test Arrangements	✓
LD Program Began	1988	LD Student Organization	n/a

Services for Students with Disabilities began offering services in 1988. The program serves approximately 95 undergraduate students. Faculty consists of 3 full-time staff members. Services are provided by LD specialists and director.

Policies 12 credit hours per semester are required to maintain full-time status. LD services are also available to graduate students.

Special preparation or orientation Optional orientation held before classes begin and individually by special arrangement.

Basic skills remediation Available in study skills, computer skills, time management, and learning strategies. Offered one-on-one, in small groups, and class-size groups by graduate assistants/students and LD specialists.

Subject-area tutoring Available in most subjects. Offered one-on-one by graduate assistants/students and trained peer tutors.

Special courses Available in career planning, study skills, college survival skills, test taking, reading, time management, learning strategies, self-advocacy, and stress management. All courses are offered for credit; all enter into overall grade point average.

Counseling and advisement Individual counseling and support groups are available.

Auxiliary aids and services *Aids:* calculators, personal spelling/word-use assistants (e.g., Franklin Speller), scan and read programs (e.g., Kurzweil), screen-enlarging programs, screen readers, speech recognition programs (e.g., Dragon), tape recorders, taped textbooks. *Services and accommodations:* advocates, priority registration, alternative test arrangements, readers, note-takers, and scribes.

ADD/ADHD Students with ADD/ADHD are eligible for the same services available to students with LD, as well as distraction-free testing environments and support groups for ADD/ADHD.

Application *Required:* high school transcript, ACT or SAT I (extended-time or untimed test accepted), and personal statement. *Recommended:* participation in extracurricular activities and letter(s) of recommendation. Upon application, documentation of need for special services should be sent only to your LD program or unit. Upon acceptance, documentation of need for special services should be sent only to your LD program or unit. *Application deadline (institutional):* rolling/continuous for fall and rolling/continuous for spring. *Application deadline (LD program):* rolling/continuous for fall and rolling/continuous for spring.

LD program contact Barbara Jean Fairbairn, Director, Services for Students with Disabilities, Box 6000, Binghamton, NY 13902-6000. *Phone:* 607-777-2686. *Fax:* 607-777-6893. *E-mail:* bjfairba@binghamton.edu.

Application contact State University of New York at Binghamton, PO Box 6001, Binghamton, NY 13902-6001. *E-mail:* admit@binghamton.edu. *Web address:* http://www.binghamton.edu/.

STATE UNIVERSITY OF NEW YORK AT OSWEGO
Oswego, New York

Students with LD Served by Program	250	ADD/ADHD Services	✓
Staff	1 full-time, 10 part-time	Summer Preparation Program	n/a
LD Program or Service Fee	n/a	Alternative Test Arrangements	✓
LD Program Began	1994	LD Student Organization	n/a

Office of Disabled Student Services began offering services in 1994. The program serves approximately 250 undergraduate students. Faculty consists of 1 full-time and 10 part-time staff members. Services are provided by counselors, graduate assistants/students, and trained peer tutors.

Policies Students with LD may take up to 17 credit hours per semester; 12 credit hours per semester are required to maintain full-time status and to be eligible for financial aid. LD services are also available to graduate students.

Special preparation or orientation Optional orientation held individually by special arrangement.

Counseling and advisement Career counseling and individual counseling are available.

Auxiliary aids and services *Aids:* calculators, personal computers, scan and read programs (e.g., Kurzweil), screen readers, speech recognition programs (e.g., Dragon), tape recorders. *Services and accommodations:* priority registration, alternative test arrangements, readers, note-takers, and scribes.

ADD/ADHD Students with ADD/ADHD are eligible for the same services available to students with LD, as well as distraction-free study areas, distraction-free testing environments and medication management.

Application *Required:* high school transcript, ACT or SAT I (extended-time tests accepted), personal statement, letter(s) of recommendation, and Documentation of Disability. *Recommended:* interview, separate application to your LD program or unit, psychoeducational report (5 years old or less), and documentation of high school services (e.g., Individualized Education Program [IEP] or 504 plan). Upon application, documentation of need for special services should be sent only to your LD program or unit. Upon acceptance, documentation of need for special services should be sent only to your LD program or unit. *Application deadline (institutional):* rolling/continuous for fall and rolling/continuous for spring. *Application deadline (LD program):* rolling/continuous for fall and rolling/continuous for spring.

LD program contact Bernardo F. DelSavio, DSS Coordinator, Office of Disabled Student Services, 210 Swetman Hall, Oswego, NY 13126. *Phone:* 315-341-3358. *Fax:* 315-341-2854. *E-mail:* delsavio@oswego.edu.

Application contact Robert Stewart, Senior Associate Director, State University of New York at Oswego, Oswego, NY 13126. *Phone:* 315-341-2250. *E-mail:* admiss@oswego.edu. *Web address:* http://www.oswego.edu/.

STATE UNIVERSITY OF NEW YORK AT STONY BROOK

Stony Brook, New York

Students with LD Served by Program	300	ADD/ADHD Services	✓
Staff	1 full-time, 1 part-time	Summer Preparation Program	n/a
LD Program or Service Fee	n/a	Alternative Test Arrangements	✓
LD Program Began	1980	LD Student Organization	✓

Disabled Student Services began offering services in 1980. The program serves approximately 300 undergraduate students. Faculty consists of 1 full-time and 1 part-time staff member. Services are provided by graduate assistants/students, LD specialists, and trained peer tutors.

Policies Students with LD may take up to 19 credit hours per semester; 12 credit hours per semester are required to maintain full-time status. LD services are also available to graduate students.

Special preparation or orientation Optional orientation held before classes begin.

Subject-area tutoring Available in some subjects. Offered one-on-one by trained peer tutors.

Special courses Available in study skills, test taking, time management, and learning strategies. No courses are offered for credit; none enter into overall grade point average.

Counseling and advisement Individual counseling is available.

Auxiliary aids and services *Aids:* scan and read programs (e.g., Kurzweil), screen-enlarging programs, taped textbooks. *Services and accommodations:* priority registration, alternative test arrangements, readers, note-takers, and scribes.

Student organization There is a student organization for students with LD.

ADD/ADHD Students with ADD/ADHD are eligible for the same services available to students with LD

Application *Required:* high school transcript. *Recommended:* SAT I (extended-time test accepted), interview, personal statement, and letter(s) of recommendation. Upon application, documentation of need for special services should be sent only to admissions. Upon acceptance, documentation of need for special services should be sent only to your LD program or unit. *Application deadline (institutional):* 7/10 for fall and 12/20 for spring. *Application deadline (LD program):* 7/10 for fall and 12/20 for spring.

LD program contact Disabled Student Services, Stony Brook, NY 11794-5328. *Phone:* 631-632-6748. *Fax:* 631-632-6749.

Application contact Gigi Lamens, Director of Admissions, State University of New York at Stony Brook, Nicolls Road, Stony Brook, NY 11794. *Phone:* 631-632-6868. *E-mail:* admiss@mail.upsa.sunysb.edu. *Web address:* http://www.sunysb.edu/.

STATE UNIVERSITY OF NEW YORK COLLEGE AT BROCKPORT

Brockport, New York

Students with LD Served by Program	162	ADD/ADHD Services	✓
Staff	1 full-time, 1 part-time	Summer Preparation Program	n/a
LD Program or Service Fee	n/a	Alternative Test Arrangements	✓
LD Program Began	1973	LD Student Organization	n/a

Office for Students with Disabilities began offering services in 1973. The program serves approximately 162 undergraduate students. Faculty consists of 1 full-time and 1 part-time staff member. Services are provided by Coordinator.

Policies Students with LD may take up to 18 credit hours per semester; 12 credit hours per semester are required to maintain full-time status; 6 credit hours per semester are required to be eligible for financial aid.

Special preparation or orientation Held before classes begin, after classes begin, and individually by special arrangement.

Auxiliary aids and services *Aids:* personal computers, tape recorders, taped textbooks. *Services and accommodations:* advocates, priority registration, alternative test arrangements, readers, note-takers, and scribes.

ADD/ADHD Students with ADD/ADHD are eligible for the same services available to students with LD, as well as distraction-free testing environments.

Application *Required:* high school transcript, ACT or SAT I (extended-time or untimed test accepted), and psychoeducational report (3 years old or less). *Recommended:* participation in extracurricular activities, personal statement, letter(s) of recommendation, and documentation of high school services (e.g., Individualized Education Program [IEP] or 504 plan). Upon application, documentation of need for special services should be sent only to your LD program or unit. Upon acceptance, documentation of need for special services should be sent only to your LD program or unit. *Application deadline (institutional):* rolling/continuous for fall and rolling/continuous for spring. *Application deadline (LD program):* rolling/continuous for fall and rolling/continuous for spring.

LD program contact Vivian L. Vanderzell, Coordinator, Office for Students with Disabilities, 350 New Campus Drive, Brockport, NY 14420-2914. *Phone:* 716-395-5409. *Fax:* 716-395-5291. *E-mail:* vvanderz@brockport.edu.

Application contact Bernie Valento, Assistant Director of Admission, State University of New York College at Brockport, 350 New Campus Drive, Brockport, NY 14420-2997. *Phone:* 716-395-5059 Ext. 5059. *Fax:* 716-395-5452. *E-mail:* ccasalin@brockuma.cc.brockport.edu. *Web address:* http://www.brockport.edu/.

STATE UNIVERSITY OF NEW YORK COLLEGE AT BUFFALO

Buffalo, New York

Students with LD Served by Program	300	ADD/ADHD Services	✓
Staff	2 full-time, 1 part-time	Summer Preparation Program	n/a
LD Program or Service Fee	n/a	Alternative Test Arrangements	✓
LD Program Began	n/a	LD Student Organization	n/a

Special Services for Students with Disabilities serves approximately 300 undergraduate students. Faculty consists of 2 full-time staff members and 1 part-time staff member. Services are provided by regular education teachers and coordinators.

Policies Students with LD may take up to 18 credit hours per semester; 12 credit hours per semester are required to maintain full-time status; 3 credit hours per semester are required to be eligible for financial aid. LD services are also available to graduate students.

Counseling and advisement Career counseling, individual counseling, small-group counseling, and support groups are available.

Auxiliary aids and services *Aids:* personal spelling/word-use assistants (e.g., Franklin Speller), scan and read programs (e.g., Kurzweil), screen-enlarging programs, screen readers, speech recognition programs (e.g., Dragon), taped textbooks. *Services and accommodations:* advocates, priority registration, alternative test arrangements, readers, note-takers, and scribes.

State University of New York College at Buffalo (continued)

ADD/ADHD Students with ADD/ADHD are eligible for the same services available to students with LD, as well as distraction-free study areas and distraction-free testing environments.

Application *Required:* high school transcript. *Recommended:* SAT I. Upon acceptance, documentation of need for special services should be sent only to your LD program or unit. *Application deadline (institutional):* rolling/continuous for fall and rolling/continuous for spring. *Application deadline (LD program):* rolling/continuous for fall and rolling/continuous for spring.

LD program contact Marianne Savino, Coordinator, 1300 Elmwood Avenue, Buffalo, NY 14222. *Phone:* 716-878-4500. *Fax:* 716-878-3473. *E-mail:* savinomr@buffalostate.edu.

Application contact State University of New York College at Buffalo, 1300 Elmwood Avenue, Buffalo, NY 14222-1095. *E-mail:* admissio@snybufaa.cs.snybuf.edu. *Web address:* http://www.buffalostate.edu/.

STATE UNIVERSITY OF NEW YORK COLLEGE AT FREDONIA

Fredonia, New York

Students with LD Served by Program	45	ADD/ADHD Services	✓
Staff	1 full-time	Summer Preparation Program	n/a
LD Program or Service Fee	n/a	Alternative Test Arrangements	✓
LD Program Began	1993	LD Student Organization	n/a

Disabled Student Support Services began offering services in 1993. The program serves approximately 45 undergraduate students. Faculty consists of 1 full-time staff member. Services are provided by trained peer tutors and DSS Coordinator.

Policies Students with LD may take up to 19 credit hours per semester; 12 credit hours per semester are required to maintain full-time status; 6 credit hours per semester are required to be eligible for financial aid. LD services are also available to graduate students.

Special preparation or orientation Optional orientation held individually by special arrangement.

Subject-area tutoring Available in most subjects. Offered one-on-one by trained peer tutors.

Auxiliary aids and services *Aids:* personal spelling/word-use assistants (e.g., Franklin Speller), scan and read programs (e.g., Kurzweil), screen-enlarging programs, screen readers, speech recognition programs (e.g., Dragon), tape recorders, taped textbooks. *Services and accommodations:* advocates, alternative test arrangements, readers, note-takers, and scribes.

ADD/ADHD Students with ADD/ADHD are eligible for the same services available to students with LD, as well as distraction-free study areas and distraction-free testing environments.

Application *Required:* high school transcript and ACT or SAT I (extended-time or untimed test accepted). *Recommended:* participation in extracurricular activities, personal statement, and letter(s) of recommendation. Upon application, documentation of need for special services should be sent only to your LD program or unit. Upon acceptance, documentation of need for special services should be sent only to your LD program or unit. *Application deadline (institutional):* rolling/continuous for fall and rolling/continuous for spring.

LD program contact Carolyn L. Boone, Coordinator, Disabled Student Support Services, 102A Hendrix Hall, Fredonia, NY 14063. *Phone:* 716-673-3270. *Fax:* 716-673-3801. *E-mail:* boone@fredonia.edu.

Application contact State University of New York College at Fredonia, Fredonia, NY 14063. *E-mail:* admissionsinq@fredonia.edu. *Web address:* http://www.fredonia.edu/.

STATE UNIVERSITY OF NEW YORK COLLEGE AT GENESEO

Geneseo, New York

Students with LD Served by Program	64	ADD/ADHD Services	✓
Staff	2 part-time	Summer Preparation Program	n/a
LD Program or Service Fee	n/a	Alternative Test Arrangements	✓
LD Program Began	1992	LD Student Organization	n/a

Office of Disability Services (ODS) began offering services in 1992. The program serves approximately 64 undergraduate students. Faculty consists of 2 part-time staff members. Services are provided by Staff Members of Office.

Policies Students with LD may take up to 18 credit hours per semester; 12 credit hours per semester are required to maintain full-time status and to be eligible for financial aid. LD services are also available to graduate students.

Counseling and advisement Career counseling, individual counseling, and support groups are available.

Auxiliary aids and services *Aids:* tape recorders, taped textbooks. *Services and accommodations:* alternative test arrangements, readers, note-takers, and scribes.

ADD/ADHD Students with ADD/ADHD are eligible for the same services available to students with LD, as well as distraction-free testing environments and support groups for ADD/ADHD.

Application *Required:* high school transcript and SAT I (extended-time or untimed test accepted). *Recommended:* interview, personal statement, and letter(s) of recommendation. Upon application, documentation of need for special services should be sent only to your LD program or unit. Upon acceptance, documentation of need for special services should be sent only to your LD program or unit. *Application deadline (institutional):* 1/15 for fall and 11/1 for spring. *Application deadline (LD program):* 1/15 for fall and 11/1 for spring.

LD program contact Charles K. Hartness, Coordinator of Disability Services, 105-D Erwin Hall, 1 College Circle, Geneseo, NY 14454. *Phone:* 716-245-5112. *Fax:* 716-245-5032. *E-mail:* hartness@geneseo.edu.

Application contact State University of New York College at Geneseo, 1 College Circle, Geneseo, NY 14454-1401. *E-mail:* admissions@sgenva.cc.geneseo.edu. *Web address:* http://www.geneseo.edu/.

STATE UNIVERSITY OF NEW YORK COLLEGE AT ONEONTA

Oneonta, New York

Students with LD Served by Program	150	ADD/ADHD Services	✓
Staff	1 full-time, 2 part-time	Summer Preparation Program	n/a
LD Program or Service Fee	n/a	Alternative Test Arrangements	✓
LD Program Began	1986	LD Student Organization	n/a

Student Disability Services(SDS) began offering services in 1986. The program serves approximately 150 undergraduate students. Faculty consists of 1 full-time and 2 part-time staff members. Services are provided by graduate assistants/students and LD specialists.

Policies Students with LD may take up to 17 credit hours per semester; 12 credit hours per semester are required to maintain full-time status and to be eligible for financial aid.

Subject-area tutoring Available in most subjects. Offered one-on-one by graduate assistants/students.

Auxiliary aids and services *Aids:* calculators, personal computers, personal spelling/word-use assistants (e.g., Franklin Speller), screen-enlarging programs, screen readers, speech recognition programs (e.g., Dragon), tape recorders, taped textbooks. *Services and accommodations:* advocates, priority registration, alternative test arrangements, readers, note-takers, and scribes.
ADD/ADHD Students with ADD/ADHD are eligible for the same services available to students with LD
Application *Required:* high school transcript, ACT or SAT I (extended-time or untimed test accepted), and personal statement. *Recommended:* participation in extracurricular activities, interview, and letter(s) of recommendation. Upon application, documentation of need for special services should be sent only to your LD program or unit. Upon acceptance, documentation of need for special services should be sent only to your LD program or unit. *Application deadline (institutional):* rolling/continuous for fall and rolling/continuous for spring. *Application deadline (LD program):* rolling/continuous for fall and rolling/continuous for spring.
LD program contact Craig Levins, Coordinator, Alumni Hall, Oneonta, NY 13820. *Phone:* 607-436-2137. *Fax:* 607-436-3167. *E-mail:* sds@oneonta.edu.
Application contact State University of New York College at Oneonta, Alumni Hall 116, Oneonta, NY 13820-4016. *E-mail:* admissions@oneontxa.edu. *Web address:* http://www.oneonta.edu/.

STATE UNIVERSITY OF NEW YORK COLLEGE AT POTSDAM
Potsdam, New York

Students with LD Served by Program	65	ADD/ADHD Services	✓
Staff	1 full-time	Summer Preparation Program	n/a
LD Program or Service Fee	n/a	Alternative Test Arrangements	✓
LD Program Began	1984	LD Student Organization	n/a

Office of Accommodative Services began offering services in 1984. The program serves approximately 65 undergraduate students. Faculty consists of 1 full-time staff member. Services are provided by academic advisers and trained peer tutors.
Policies Students with LD may take up to 19 credit hours per semester; 12 credit hours per semester are required to maintain full-time status. LD services are also available to graduate students.
Basic skills remediation Available in study skills, time management, and learning strategies. Offered one-on-one by tutor, coordinator, and student support services program counselor.
Subject-area tutoring Available in most subjects. Offered one-on-one and in small groups by trained peer tutors.
Special courses Available in learning strategies. All courses are offered for credit; all enter into overall grade point average.
Counseling and advisement Career counseling and individual counseling are available. Academic advisement by a staff member affiliated with the program is available.
Auxiliary aids and services *Aids:* calculators, personal computers, personal spelling/word-use assistants (e.g., Franklin Speller), scan and read programs (e.g., Kurzweil), screen-enlarging programs, screen readers, tape recorders, taped textbooks. *Services and accommodations:* alternative test arrangements, readers, note-takers, and scribes.
ADD/ADHD Students with ADD/ADHD are eligible for the same services available to students with LD, as well as distraction-free testing environments.
Application *Required:* high school transcript and ACT or SAT I (extended-time or untimed test accepted). *Recommended:* participation in extracurricular activities, interview, personal state-

ment, letter(s) of recommendation, psychoeducational report (3 years old or less), and documentation of high school services (e.g., Individualized Education Program [IEP] or 504 plan). Upon application, documentation of need for special services should be sent only to your LD program or unit. Upon acceptance, documentation of need for special services should be sent only to your LD program or unit. *Application deadline (institutional):* rolling/continuous for fall and rolling/continuous for spring. *Application deadline (LD program):* rolling/continuous for fall and rolling/continuous for spring.
LD program contact Sharon House, Academic Coordinator, 110/112 Sisson Hall, Potsdam, NY 13676. *Phone:* 315-267-3267. *Fax:* 315-267-3268. *E-mail:* housese@potsdam.edu.
Application contact State University of New York College at Potsdam, 44 Pierrepont Avenue, Potsdam, NY 13676. *E-mail:* admissions@potsdam.edu. *Web address:* http://www.potsdam.edu/.

STATE UNIVERSITY OF NEW YORK COLLEGE OF ENVIRONMENTAL SCIENCE AND FORESTRY
Syracuse, New York

Students with LD Served by Program	20	ADD/ADHD Services	✓
Staff	3 full-time, 3 part-time	Summer Preparation Program	n/a
LD Program or Service Fee	n/a	Alternative Test Arrangements	✓
LD Program Began	1980	LD Student Organization	✓

Office of Student Life began offering services in 1980. The program serves approximately 20 undergraduate students. Faculty consists of 3 full-time and 3 part-time staff members. Services are provided by counselors, diagnostic specialists, graduate assistants/students, LD specialists, and trained peer tutors.
Policies Students with LD may take up to 18 credit hours per semester; 12 credit hours per semester are required to maintain full-time status and to be eligible for financial aid. LD services are also available to graduate students.
Basic skills remediation Available in study skills, reading, time management, learning strategies, math, and spoken language. Offered one-on-one and in small groups by graduate assistants/students and LD specialists.
Subject-area tutoring Available in most subjects. Offered one-on-one and in small groups by graduate assistants/students, trained peer tutors, and LD specialists.
Counseling and advisement Individual counseling and support groups are available.
Auxiliary aids and services *Aids:* scan and read programs (e.g., Kurzweil), screen-enlarging programs, screen readers, tape recorders, taped textbooks. *Services and accommodations:* advocates, alternative test arrangements, readers, note-takers, and scribes.
Student organization There is a student organization for students with LD.
ADD/ADHD Students with ADD/ADHD are eligible for the same services available to students with LD, as well as distraction-free testing environments.
Application *Required:* high school transcript, ACT or SAT I (extended-time or untimed test accepted), personal statement, letter(s) of recommendation, and psychoeducational report (3 years old or less). *Recommended:* participation in extracurricular activities and interview. Upon acceptance, documentation of need for special services should be sent only to your LD program or unit. *Application deadline (institutional):* rolling/

State University of New York College of Environmental Science and Forestry (continued)

continuous for fall and rolling/continuous for spring. *Application deadline (LD program):* rolling/continuous for fall and rolling/continuous for spring.

LD program contact Thomas Slocum, Director of Career and Counseling Services, 110 Bray Hall, 1 Forestry Drive, Syracuse, NY 13210. *Phone:* 315-470-6660. *Fax:* 315-470-4728. *E-mail:* toslocum@esf.edu.

Application contact Susan Sanford, Director of Admissions, State University of New York College of Environmental Science and Forestry, 1 Forestry Drive, Syracuse, NY 13210-2779. *Phone:* 315-470-6600. *E-mail:* esfinfo@lmailbox.syr.edu. *Web address:* http://www.esf.edu/.

STATE UNIVERSITY OF NEW YORK COLLEGE OF TECHNOLOGY AT CANTON

Canton, New York

Students with LD Served by Program	108	ADD/ADHD Services	✓
Staff	3 part-time	Summer Preparation Program	n/a
LD Program or Service Fee	n/a	Alternative Test Arrangements	✓
LD Program Began	n/a	LD Student Organization	n/a

Accommodative Services serves approximately 108 undergraduate students. Faculty consists of 3 part-time staff members. Services are provided by counselors, trained peer tutors, and professional tutors.

Policies 12 credit hours per semester are required to maintain full-time status and to be eligible for financial aid.

Auxiliary aids and services *Aids:* calculators, personal spelling/word-use assistants (e.g., Franklin Speller), scan and read programs (e.g., Kurzweil), screen-enlarging programs, tape recorders. *Services and accommodations:* priority registration, alternative test arrangements, readers, note-takers, and scribes.

ADD/ADHD Students with ADD/ADHD are eligible for the same services available to students with LD, as well as distraction-free testing environments.

Application *Required:* high school transcript, psychoeducational report (3 years old or less), and documentation of high school services (e.g., Individualized Education Program [IEP] or 504 plan). Upon acceptance, documentation of need for special services should be sent only to your LD program or unit. *Application deadline (institutional):* rolling/continuous for fall and rolling/continuous for spring. *Application deadline (LD program):* rolling/continuous for fall and rolling/continuous for spring.

LD program contact Veigh Lee, Coordinator of Accommodative Services, FOB 232, 34 Cornell Drive, Canton, NY 13617. *Phone:* 315-386-7392. *E-mail:* leev@canton.edu.

Application contact David M. Gerlach, Interim Dean of Enrollment Management, State University of New York College of Technology at Canton, Cornell Drive, Canton, NY 13617. *Phone:* 315-386-7123. *Web address:* http://www.canton.edu/.

STATE UNIVERSITY OF NEW YORK INSTITUTE OF TECHNOLOGY AT UTICA/ROME

Utica, New York

Students with LD Served by Program	40	ADD/ADHD Services	✓
Staff	1 part-time	Summer Preparation Program	n/a
LD Program or Service Fee	n/a	Alternative Test Arrangements	✓
LD Program Began	1990	LD Student Organization	n/a

Disabled Student Services began offering services in 1990. The program serves approximately 40 undergraduate students. Faculty consists of 1 part-time staff member. Services are provided by counselors.

Policies LD services are also available to graduate students.

Special preparation or orientation Optional orientation held before registration, before classes begin, after classes begin, and individually by special arrangement.

Subject-area tutoring Available in most subjects. Offered one-on-one and in small groups by computer-based instruction, professional tutors, graduate assistants/students, trained peer tutors, and LD specialists.

Counseling and advisement Career counseling, individual counseling, and small-group counseling are available.

Auxiliary aids and services *Aids:* calculators, personal spelling/word-use assistants (e.g., Franklin Speller), scan and read programs (e.g., Kurzweil), screen-enlarging programs, tape recorders, taped textbooks. *Services and accommodations:* advocates, priority registration, alternative test arrangements, readers, and note-takers.

ADD/ADHD Students with ADD/ADHD are eligible for the same services available to students with LD, as well as distraction-free study areas, distraction-free testing environments and personal coach or mentors.

Application *Required:* Completion of 56 credit hours. Upon application, documentation of need for special services should be sent only to admissions. Upon acceptance, documentation of need for special services should be sent only to your LD program or unit. *Application deadline (institutional):* rolling/continuous for fall and rolling/continuous for spring. *Application deadline (LD program):* rolling/continuous for fall and rolling/continuous for spring.

LD program contact Mary Brown-DePass, Director of Counseling, PO Box 3050, Utica, NY 13504-3050. *Phone:* 315-792-7160. *Fax:* 315-792-7112. *E-mail:* smb2@sunyit.edu.

Application contact State University of New York Institute of Technology at Utica/Rome, PO Box 3050, Utica, NY 13504-3050. *E-mail:* admissions@sunyit.edu. *Web address:* http://www.sunyit.edu/.

STATE UNIVERSITY OF WEST GEORGIA

Carrollton, Georgia

Students with LD Served by Program	200	ADD/ADHD Services	✓
Staff	2 full-time, 4 part-time	Summer Preparation Program	✓
LD Program or Service Fee	n/a	Alternative Test Arrangements	✓
LD Program Began	n/a	LD Student Organization	n/a

Disabled Student Services serves approximately 200 undergraduate students. Faculty consists of 2 full-time and 4 part-time staff members. Services are provided by counselors, remediation/learning specialists, trained peer tutors, and professional tutors.

Policies The college has written policies regarding course substitutions, grade forgiveness, and substitution and waivers of requirements for admission and graduation. Students with LD may take up to 18 credit hours per semester; 12 credit hours per semester are required to maintain full-time status; 3 credit hours per semester are required to be eligible for financial aid. LD services are also available to graduate students.

Special preparation or orientation Optional summer program offered prior to entering college. Required orientation held after classes begin and individually by special arrangement.

Subject-area tutoring Available in all subjects. Offered one-on-one by professional tutors and trained peer tutors.

Counseling and advisement Career counseling, individual counseling, small-group counseling, support groups, and academic counseling are available.

Auxiliary aids and services *Aids:* personal computers, scan and read programs (e.g., Kurzweil), screen-enlarging programs, screen readers, speech recognition programs (e.g., Dragon), tape recorders, taped textbooks, hearing helper. *Services and accommodations:* advocates, priority registration, alternative test arrangements, readers, note-takers, and scribes.

ADD/ADHD Students with ADD/ADHD are eligible for the same services available to students with LD, as well as distraction-free study areas, distraction-free testing environments, personal coach or mentors, and support groups for ADD/ADHD.

Application *Required:* psychoeducational report (3 years old or less). *Recommended:* interview and documentation of high school services (e.g., Individualized Education Program [IEP] or 504 plan). Upon application, documentation of need for special services should be sent only to your LD program or unit. Upon acceptance, documentation of need for special services should be sent only to your LD program or unit. *Application deadline (institutional):* rolling/continuous for fall and rolling/continuous for spring. *Application deadline (LD program):* rolling/continuous for fall and rolling/continuous for spring.

LD program contact Shannon Peacock, Disability Coordinator, Student Development Center, 137 Parker Hall, Carrollton, GA 30118. *Phone:* 770-836-6428. *Fax:* 770-838-2562. *E-mail:* speacock@ westga.edu.

Application contact Dr. Robert Johnson, Director of Admissions, State University of West Georgia, 1600 Maple Street, Carrollton, GA 30118. *Phone:* 770-836-6416. *E-mail:* rjohnson@ westga.edu. *Web address:* http://www.westga.edu/.

SUFFOLK UNIVERSITY
Boston, Massachusetts

Students with LD Served by Program	100	ADD/ADHD Services	✓
Staff	1 full-time, 2 part-time	Summer Preparation Program	n/a
LD Program or Service Fee	n/a	Alternative Test Arrangements	✓
LD Program Began	1992	LD Student Organization	✓

Special Services for Students with Learning Disabilities began offering services in 1992. The program serves approximately 100 undergraduate students. Faculty consists of 1 full-time and 2 part-time staff members. Services are provided by counselors, LD specialists, and trained peer tutors.

Policies The college has written policies regarding course substitutions. Students with LD may take up to 16 credit hours per semester; 12 credit hours per semester are required to maintain full-time status and to be eligible for financial aid. LD services are also available to graduate students.

Special preparation or orientation Optional orientation held individually by special arrangement.

Basic skills remediation Available in study skills, reading, time management, learning strategies, written language, math, and spoken language. Offered one-on-one and in small groups by regular education teachers, graduate assistants/students, LD specialists, and ESL specialists.

Subject-area tutoring Available in most subjects. Offered one-on-one and in small groups by graduate assistants/students, trained peer tutors, and LD specialists.

Counseling and advisement Individual counseling and support groups are available.

Auxiliary aids and services *Aids:* scan and read programs (e.g., Kurzweil), screen readers, speech recognition programs (e.g., Dragon), taped textbooks. *Services and accommodations:* advocates, priority registration, alternative test arrangements, readers, and note-takers.

Student organization There is a student organization for students with LD.

ADD/ADHD Students with ADD/ADHD are eligible for the same services available to students with LD, as well as distraction-free testing environments, personal coach or mentors, and support groups for ADD/ADHD.

Application *Required:* high school transcript, ACT, SAT I, personal statement, and letter(s) of recommendation. *Recommended:* interview. Upon acceptance, documentation of need for special services should be sent only to your LD program or unit. *Application deadline (institutional):* rolling/continuous for fall and rolling/continuous for spring. *Application deadline (LD program):* rolling/continuous for fall and rolling/continuous for spring.

LD program contact Joyce Atkinson, Learning Disabilities Specialist, Ballotti Learning Center, 148 Cambridge Street, Boston, MA 02114. *Phone:* 617-573-8235. *Fax:* 617-742-6761. *E-mail:* jatkinso@admin.suffolk.edu.

Application contact Suffolk University, 8 Ashburton Place, Boston, MA 02108-2770. *Web address:* http://www.suffolk.edu/.

TARLETON STATE UNIVERSITY
Stephenville, Texas

Students with LD Served by Program	90	ADD/ADHD Services	✓
Staff	1 full-time, 6 part-time	Summer Preparation Program	n/a
LD Program or Service Fee	n/a	Alternative Test Arrangements	✓
LD Program Began	1991	LD Student Organization	n/a

Disability Services began offering services in 1991. The program serves approximately 90 undergraduate students. Faculty consists of 1 full-time and 6 part-time staff members. Services are provided by regular education teachers, special education teachers, and graduate assistants/students.

Policies Students with LD may take up to 18 credit hours per semester; 12 credit hours per semester are required to maintain full-time status. LD services are also available to graduate students.

Auxiliary aids and services *Aids:* scan and read programs (e.g., Kurzweil), screen-enlarging programs, screen readers, speech recognition programs (e.g., Dragon), tape recorders, taped textbooks. *Services and accommodations:* priority registration, alternative test arrangements, readers, note-takers, and scribes.

Tarleton State University (continued)

ADD/ADHD Students with ADD/ADHD are eligible for the same services available to students with LD, as well as distraction-free testing environments.

Application *Required:* high school transcript and ACT or SAT I (extended-time or untimed test accepted). Upon application, documentation of need for special services should be sent only to your LD program or unit. Upon acceptance, documentation of need for special services should be sent only to your LD program or unit. *Application deadline (institutional):* 8/10 for fall and 1/5 for spring. *Application deadline (LD program):* rolling/continuous for fall and rolling/continuous for spring.

LD program contact Dr. L. Dwayne Snider, Director of Disability Services, Academic Affairs, Box T-0010, Stephenville, TX 76402. *Phone:* 254-968-9103. *Fax:* 254-968-9703.

Application contact Tarleton State University, Stephenville, TX 76402. *Web address:* http://www.tarleton.edu/.

TAYLOR UNIVERSITY
Upland, Indiana

Students with LD Served by Program	20	ADD/ADHD Services	✓
Staff	1 full-time	Summer Preparation Program	n/a
LD Program or Service Fee	n/a	Alternative Test Arrangements	✓
LD Program Began	1993	LD Student Organization	n/a

Academic Support Services began offering services in 1993. The program serves approximately 20 undergraduate students. Faculty consists of 1 full-time staff member. Services are provided by trained peer tutors.

Policies The college has written policies regarding course substitutions. Students with LD may take up to 17 credit hours per semester; 12 credit hours per semester are required to maintain full-time status and to be eligible for financial aid.

Subject-area tutoring Available in most subjects. Offered one-on-one and in small groups by trained peer tutors.

Auxiliary aids and services *Aids:* screen-enlarging programs, screen readers, speech recognition programs (e.g., Dragon), tape recorders, taped textbooks. *Services and accommodations:* advocates, priority registration, alternative test arrangements, readers, note-takers, and scribes.

ADD/ADHD Students with ADD/ADHD are eligible for the same services available to students with LD, as well as distraction-free testing environments.

Application *Required:* high school transcript, ACT or SAT I (extended-time or untimed test accepted), interview, personal statement, and letter(s) of recommendation. *Recommended:* participation in extracurricular activities, separate application to your LD program or unit, psychoeducational report, and documentation of high school services (e.g., Individualized Education Program [IEP] or 504 plan). Upon application, documentation of need for special services should be sent only to your LD program or unit. Upon acceptance, documentation of need for special services should be sent only to your LD program or unit. *Application deadline (institutional):* 1/15 for fall and 1/15 for spring. *Application deadline (LD program):* rolling/continuous for fall and rolling/continuous for spring.

LD program contact Dr. R. Edwin Welch, Coordinator of Academic Support, 236 West Reade Avenue, Upland, IN 46989-1001. *Phone:* 765-998-5523. *Fax:* 765-998-5569. *E-mail:* edwelch@tayloru.edu.

Application contact Taylor University, 500 West Reade Avenue, Upland, IN 46989-1001. *E-mail:* admissions_u@tayloru.edu. *Web address:* http://www.tayloru.edu/.

TEMPLE UNIVERSITY
Philadelphia, Pennsylvania

Students with LD Served by Program	400	ADD/ADHD Services	✓
Staff	5 full-time, 1 part-time	Summer Preparation Program	n/a
LD Program or Service Fee	n/a	Alternative Test Arrangements	✓
LD Program Began	1977	LD Student Organization	n/a

Disability Resources Services (DRS) began offering services in 1977. The program serves approximately 400 undergraduate students. Faculty consists of 5 full-time staff members and 1 part-time staff member. Services are provided by graduate assistants/students, LD specialists, and trained peer tutors.

Policies Students with LD may take up to 16 credit hours per semester; 12 credit hours per semester are required to maintain full-time status; 6 credit hours per semester are required to be eligible for financial aid. LD services are also available to graduate students.

Special preparation or orientation Optional orientation held before classes begin, during summer prior to enrollment, and individually by special arrangement.

Counseling and advisement Career counseling, individual counseling, and peer coaching are available.

Auxiliary aids and services *Aids:* calculators, personal computers, personal spelling/word-use assistants (e.g., Franklin Speller), scan and read programs (e.g., Kurzweil), screen-enlarging programs, screen readers, speech recognition programs (e.g., Dragon), tape recorders, taped textbooks. *Services and accommodations:* alternative test arrangements, readers, note-takers, and scribes.

ADD/ADHD Students with ADD/ADHD are eligible for the same services available to students with LD, as well as distraction-free testing environments, personal coach or mentors, and support groups for ADD/ADHD.

Application *Required:* high school transcript, ACT or SAT I (extended-time or untimed test accepted), personal statement, and letter(s) of recommendation. *Recommended:* participation in extracurricular activities, interview, separate application to your LD program or unit, psychoeducational report, and documentation of high school services (e.g., Individualized Education Program [IEP] or 504 plan). Upon application, documentation of need for special services should be sent only to your LD program or unit. Upon acceptance, documentation of need for special services should be sent only to your LD program or unit. *Application deadline (institutional):* 4/1 for fall and 11/1 for spring. *Application deadline (LD program):* rolling/continuous for fall and rolling/continuous for spring.

LD program contact Megan M. Cunnane, Learning Disabilities Advisor, 100 Ritter Annex, 1301 C.B. Moore Avenue, Philadelphia, PA 19122. *Phone:* 215-204-1280. *Fax:* 215-204-6794. *E-mail:* mcunnane@unix.temple.edu.

Application contact Temple University, 1801 N. Broad St, Philadelphia, PA 19122-6096. *E-mail:* tuadm@vm.temple.edu. *Web address:* http://www.temple.edu/.

TEXAS A&M UNIVERSITY
College Station, Texas

Students with LD Served by Program	400	ADD/ADHD Services	✓
Staff	6 full-time, 1 part-time	Summer Preparation Program	n/a
LD Program or Service Fee	n/a	Alternative Test Arrangements	✓
LD Program Began	1981	LD Student Organization	✓

Services for Students with Disabilities (SSD) began offering services in 1981. The program serves approximately 400 undergraduate students. Faculty consists of 6 full-time staff members and 1 part-time staff member. Services are provided by counselors, special education teachers, and LD specialists.

Policies The college has written policies regarding course substitutions and grade forgiveness. Students with LD may take up to 19 credit hours per semester; 12 credit hours per semester are required to maintain full-time status and to be eligible for financial aid. LD services are also available to graduate students.

Auxiliary aids and services *Aids:* calculators, screen-enlarging programs, screen readers, speech recognition programs (e.g., Dragon), tape recorders, taped textbooks. *Services and accommodations:* advocates, priority registration, alternative test arrangements, readers, note-takers, and scribes.

Student organization There is a student organization for students with LD.

ADD/ADHD Students with ADD/ADHD are eligible for the same services available to students with LD, as well as distraction-free testing environments.

Application *Required:* high school transcript and personal statement. *Recommended:* participation in extracurricular activities, ACT or SAT I (extended-time tests accepted), letter(s) of recommendation, and community service, talents/awards, employment. Upon application, documentation of need for special services should be sent only to your LD program or unit. Upon acceptance, documentation of need for special services should be sent only to your LD program or unit. *Application deadline (institutional):* 2/15 for fall and 10/15 for spring. *Application deadline (LD program):* rolling/continuous for fall and rolling/continuous for spring.

LD program contact Dr. Anne Reber, Coordinator, 126 Koldus Building, College Station, TX 77843-1257. *Phone:* 409-845-1637. *Fax:* 409-458-1214. *E-mail:* anne@stulife2.tamu.edu.

Application contact Stephanie D. Hays, Associate Director of Admissions, Texas A&M University, 217 John J. Koldus Building, College Station, TX 77843-1265. *Phone:* 409-845-3741. *E-mail:* adminfo@tamu.edu. *Web address:* http://www.tamu.edu/.

TEXAS A&M UNIVERSITY-COMMERCE
Commerce, Texas

Students with LD Served by Program	69	ADD/ADHD Services	✓
Staff	1 full-time	Summer Preparation Program	n/a
LD Program or Service Fee	n/a	Alternative Test Arrangements	✓
LD Program Began	1980	LD Student Organization	n/a

Student Support Services—Mach III TRIO Programs began offering services in 1980. The program serves approximately 69 undergraduate students. Faculty consists of 1 full-time staff member. Services are provided by academic advisers, counselors, graduate assistants/students, and trained peer tutors.

Policies The college has written policies regarding course substitutions. Students with LD may take up to 21 hours per term; 3 hours per term are required to maintain full-time status; 6 hours per term are required to be eligible for financial aid. LD services are also available to graduate students.

Special preparation or orientation Optional orientation held individually by special arrangement.

Diagnostic testing Available for reading, written language, and math.

Basic skills remediation Available in study skills, computer skills, reading, time management, handwriting, learning strategies, spelling, written language, and math. Offered one-on-one and in small groups by computer-based instruction, graduate assistants/students, and trained peer tutors.

Subject-area tutoring Available in most subjects. Offered one-on-one and in small groups by computer-based instruction, graduate assistants/students, and trained peer tutors.

Counseling and advisement Academic advisement by a staff member affiliated with the program is available.

Auxiliary aids and services *Aids:* calculators, personal computers, personal spelling/word-use assistants (e.g., Franklin Speller), scan and read programs (e.g., Kurzweil), screen-enlarging programs, tape recorders, taped textbooks. *Services and accommodations:* priority registration, alternative test arrangements, readers, note-takers, and scribes.

ADD/ADHD Students with ADD/ADHD are eligible for the same services available to students with LD, as well as distraction-free testing environments and personal coach or mentors.

Application *Required:* high school transcript, ACT or SAT I (extended-time tests accepted), separate application to your LD program or unit, psychoeducational report (2 years old or less), and documentation of high school services (e.g., Individualized Education Program [IEP] or 504 plan). Upon application, documentation of need for special services should be sent only to your LD program or unit. Upon acceptance, documentation of need for special services should be sent only to your LD program or unit. *Application deadline (institutional):* 8/12 for fall and 1/10 for spring. *Application deadline (LD program):* 8/12 for fall and 1/10 for spring.

LD program contact Frank Perez, Assistant Director, TRIO Programs, Commerce, TX 75429. *Phone:* 903-886-5835. *Fax:* 903-468-3220. *E-mail:* frank_perez@tamu-commerce.edu.

Application contact Randy McDonald, Director of School Relations, Texas A&M University-Commerce, PO Box 3011, Commerce, TX 75429-3011. *Phone:* 903-886-5072. *E-mail:* cathy_griffin@tamu-commerce.edu. *Web address:* http://www.tamu-commerce.edu/.

TEXAS A&M UNIVERSITY-KINGSVILLE
Kingsville, Texas

Students with LD Served by Program	60	ADD/ADHD Services	✓
Staff	1 full-time, 11 part-time	Summer Preparation Program	n/a
LD Program or Service Fee	n/a	Alternative Test Arrangements	✓
LD Program Began	1990	LD Student Organization	n/a

Services for Students with Disabilities (SSD) began offering services in 1990. The program serves approximately 60 undergraduate students. Faculty consists of 1 full-time and 11 part-time staff members. Services are provided by counselors, graduate assistants/students, and SSD assistant coordinator.

Policies Students with LD may take up to 18 credit hours per semester; 12 credit hours per semester are required to maintain full-time status and to be eligible for financial aid. LD services are also available to graduate students.

Special preparation or orientation Optional orientation held after classes begin.

Basic skills remediation Available in study skills, computer skills, time management, and learning strategies. Offered one-on-one and in small groups by graduate assistants/students and SSD assistant coordinator.

Counseling and advisement Career counseling and individual counseling are available.

Texas A&M University-Kingsville (continued)

Auxiliary aids and services *Aids:* scan and read programs (e.g., Kurzweil), tape recorders. *Services and accommodations:* advocates, priority registration, alternative test arrangements, readers, note-takers, and scribes.

ADD/ADHD Students with ADD/ADHD are eligible for the same services available to students with LD, as well as distraction-free testing environments and personal coach or mentors.

Application *Required:* high school transcript, ACT or SAT I (extended-time or untimed test accepted), separate application to your LD program or unit, and Texas Academic Skills Program (TASP). *Recommended:* documentation of high school services (e.g., Individualized Education Program [IEP] or 504 plan). Upon application, documentation of need for special services should be sent only to your LD program or unit. Upon acceptance, documentation of need for special services should be sent only to your LD program or unit.

LD program contact Rachel A. Cox, Assistant Coordinator for Services for Students with Disabilities, 1210 Retama Drive, Kingsville, TX 78363. *Phone:* 361-593-3024. *Fax:* 361-593-2006. *E-mail:* karab02@tamuk.edu.

Application contact Ray Broglie, Director, School Relations, Texas A&M University-Kingsville, West Santa Gertrudis, Kingsville, TX 78363. *Phone:* 512-593-2315. *Web address:* http://www.tamuk.edu/.

THIEL COLLEGE
Greenville, Pennsylvania

Students with LD Served by Program	40	ADD/ADHD Services	✓
Staff	1 part-time	Summer Preparation Program	n/a
LD Program or Service Fee	n/a	Alternative Test Arrangements	✓
LD Program Began	1991	LD Student Organization	n/a

Academic Resource Center began offering services in 1991. The program serves approximately 40 undergraduate students. Faculty consists of 1 part-time staff member. Services are provided by academic advisers, remediation/learning specialists, and trained peer tutors.

Policies Students with LD may take up to 18 credit hours per semester; 12 credit hours per semester are required to maintain full-time status and to be eligible for financial aid.

Special preparation or orientation Required orientation held before registration, during registration, and individually by special arrangement.

Basic skills remediation Available in study skills, reading, time management, and learning strategies. Offered one-on-one and in small groups by professional tutors.

Subject-area tutoring Available in most subjects. Offered one-on-one and in small groups by professional tutors and trained peer tutors.

Counseling and advisement Academic advisement by a staff member affiliated with the program is available.

Auxiliary aids and services *Aids:* tape recorders, taped textbooks. *Services and accommodations:* alternative test arrangements, readers, and scribes.

ADD/ADHD Students with ADD/ADHD are eligible for the same services available to students with LD, as well as distraction-free testing environments.

Application *Required:* high school transcript, ACT or SAT I (extended-time or untimed test accepted), and psychoeducational report (5 years old or less). *Recommended:* participation in extracurricular activities, interview, letter(s) of recommendation, and documentation of high school services (e.g., Individualized Education Program [IEP] or 504 plan). Upon application, docu-

mentation of need for special services should be sent to both admissions and your LD program or unit. Upon acceptance, documentation of need for special services should be sent only to your LD program or unit. *Application deadline (institutional):* rolling/continuous for fall and rolling/continuous for spring. *Application deadline (LD program):* rolling/continuous for fall and rolling/continuous for spring.

LD program contact Linda B. Kahler, Director of academic Resource Center, 75 College Avenue, Greenville, PA 16125-2181. *Phone:* 724-589-2215. *Fax:* 724-589-2021. *E-mail:* arc@thiel.edu.

Application contact Thiel College, 75 College Avenue, Greenville, PA 16125-2181. *E-mail:* thieladmis@shrsys.hslc.org. *Web address:* http://www.thiel.edu/.

THOMAS MORE COLLEGE
Crestview Hills, Kentucky

Students with LD Served by Program	50	ADD/ADHD Services	✓
Staff	2 full-time, 1 part-time	Summer Preparation Program	n/a
LD Program or Service Fee	n/a	Alternative Test Arrangements	✓
LD Program Began	1980	LD Student Organization	n/a

Student Support Services began offering services in 1980. The program serves approximately 50 undergraduate students. Faculty consists of 2 full-time staff members and 1 part-time staff member. Services are provided by academic advisers, counselors, remediation/learning specialists, and trained peer tutors.

Policies The college has written policies regarding substitution and waivers of requirements for admission and graduation. Students with LD may take up to 18 credit hours per semester; 12 credit hours per semester are required to maintain full-time status; 3 credit hours per semester are required to be eligible for financial aid.

Special preparation or orientation Optional orientation held individually by special arrangement.

Basic skills remediation Available in study skills, computer skills, reading, time management, handwriting, social skills, learning strategies, spelling, written language, math, and spoken language. Offered one-on-one and in small groups by computer-based instruction, LD specialists, and professional tutors.

Subject-area tutoring Available in all subjects. Offered one-on-one and in small groups by computer-based instruction and trained peer tutors.

Special courses Available in career planning, study skills, college survival skills, test taking, reading, time management, vocabulary development, stress management, and written composition skills. All courses are offered for credit; all enter into overall grade point average.

Counseling and advisement Career counseling, individual counseling, and support groups are available. Academic advisement by a staff member affiliated with the program is available.

Auxiliary aids and services *Aids:* calculators, tape recorders, taped textbooks. *Services and accommodations:* alternative test arrangements, note-takers, and scribes.

ADD/ADHD Students with ADD/ADHD are eligible for the same services available to students with LD, as well as distraction-free testing environments.

Application *Required:* high school transcript, ACT or SAT I (extended-time or untimed test accepted), and psychoeducational report (3 years old or less). *Recommended:* participation in extracurricular activities, personal statement, letter(s) of recommendation, and documentation of high school services (e.g., Individualized Education Program [IEP] or 504 plan). Upon application, documentation of need for special services should be sent only to admissions. Upon acceptance, documentation of need for special services should be sent only to your LD program or unit. *Application deadline (institutional):* rolling/continuous for fall and rolling/continuous for spring. *Application deadline (LD program):* rolling/continuous for fall and rolling/continuous for spring.

LD program contact Barbara S. Davis, Director, 333 Thomas More Parkway, Crestview Hills, KY 41017. *Phone:* 606-344-3521. *Fax:* 606-344-3607. *E-mail:* barb.davis@thomasmore.edu.

Application contact Thomas More College, 333 Thomas More Parkway, Crestview Hills, KY 41017-3495. *E-mail:* cantralk@thomasmore.edu. *Web address:* http://www.thomasmore.edu/.

TOCCOA FALLS COLLEGE
Toccoa Falls, Georgia

Students with LD Served by Program	20	ADD/ADHD Services	✓
Staff	1 full-time, 1 part-time	Summer Preparation Program	n/a
LD Program or Service Fee	n/a	Alternative Test Arrangements	✓
LD Program Began	1999	LD Student Organization	n/a

Learning Support Services (LSS) began offering services in 1999. The program serves approximately 20 undergraduate students. Faculty consists of 1 full-time and 1 part-time staff member. Services are provided by academic advisers, regular education teachers, counselors, and trained peer tutors.
Policies Students with LD may take up to 18 credit hours per semester; 12 credit hours per semester are required to maintain full-time status and to be eligible for financial aid.
Subject-area tutoring Available in most subjects. Offered one-on-one by trained peer tutors.
Counseling and advisement Individual counseling is available. Academic advisement by a staff member affiliated with the program is available.
Auxiliary aids and services *Aids:* tape recorders, taped textbooks. *Services and accommodations:* advocates, priority registration, alternative test arrangements, readers, note-takers, and scribes.
ADD/ADHD Students with ADD/ADHD are eligible for the same services available to students with LD, as well as distraction-free study areas, distraction-free testing environments and personal coach or mentors.
Application *Required:* high school transcript, ACT or SAT I, personal statement, and letter(s) of recommendation. Upon application, documentation of need for special services should be sent only to admissions. Upon acceptance, documentation of need for special services should be sent to both admissions and your LD program or unit. *Application deadline (institutional):* rolling/continuous for fall and rolling/continuous for spring. *Application deadline (LD program):* rolling/continuous for fall and rolling/continuous for spring.
LD program contact Maily L. Heu, Director, PO Box 801060, Toccoa Falls, GA 30598. *Phone:* 706-886-6831 Ext. 5462. *Fax:* 706-886-6412. *E-mail:* mheu@toccoafalls.edu.
Application contact Paul G. Worley, Director of Admissions, Toccoa Falls College, PO Box 777, Toccoa Falls, GA 30598-1000. *Phone:* 706-886-6831 Ext. 5380. *E-mail:* admissio@toccoafalls.edu. *Web address:* http://www.toccoafalls.edu/.

TOWSON UNIVERSITY
Towson, Maryland

Students with LD Served by Program	435	ADD/ADHD Services	✓
Staff	2 full-time	Summer Preparation Program	n/a
LD Program or Service Fee	n/a	Alternative Test Arrangements	✓
LD Program Began	1979	LD Student Organization	n/a

Disability Support Services began offering services in 1979. The program serves approximately 435 undergraduate students. Faculty consists of 2 full-time staff members. Services are provided by graduate assistants/students and LD specialists.
Policies Students with LD may take up to 18 credit hours per semester; 12 credit hours per semester are required to maintain full-time status and to be eligible for financial aid. LD services are also available to graduate students.
Special preparation or orientation Required orientation held individually by special arrangement.
Diagnostic testing Available for spelling, reading, and math.
Basic skills remediation Available in study skills, reading, time management, learning strategies, and written language. Offered one-on-one by LD specialists.
Auxiliary aids and services *Aids:* scan and read programs (e.g., Kurzweil), screen-enlarging programs, speech recognition programs (e.g., Dragon), taped textbooks, phonic ear. *Services and accommodations:* priority registration, alternative test arrangements, readers, note-takers, and scribes.
ADD/ADHD Students with ADD/ADHD are eligible for the same services available to students with LD, as well as distraction-free testing environments.
Application *Required:* high school transcript, ACT or SAT I (extended-time or untimed test accepted), and psychoeducational report (3 years old or less). *Recommended:* interview, personal statement, letter(s) of recommendation, and documentation of high school services (e.g., Individualized Education Program [IEP] or 504 plan). Upon application, documentation of need for special services should be sent only to admissions. Upon acceptance, documentation of need for special services should be sent to both admissions and your LD program or unit. *Application deadline (institutional):* 5/1 for fall and 12/10 for spring.
LD program contact Ronni Uhland, Director, Disability Support Services, 8000 York Road, Towson, MD 21252-0001. *Phone:* 410-830-2638. *Fax:* 410-830-4247. *E-mail:* ruhland@towson.edu.
Application contact Towson University, 8000 York Road, Towson, MD 21252-0001. *E-mail:* jackson-a@towson.edu. *Web address:* http://www.towson.edu.

TRENT UNIVERSITY
Peterborough, Ontario

Students with LD Served by Program	150	ADD/ADHD Services	✓
Staff	3 full-time, 1 part-time	Summer Preparation Program	n/a
LD Program or Service Fee	n/a	Alternative Test Arrangements	✓
LD Program Began	1989	LD Student Organization	n/a

Special Needs Office began offering services in 1989. The program serves approximately 150 undergraduate students. Faculty consists of 3 full-time staff members and 1 part-time staff member. Services are provided by academic advisers, counselors, graduate assistants/students, teacher trainees, and LD specialists.
Policies LD services are also available to graduate students.

Trent University (continued)

Special preparation or orientation Optional orientation held during summer prior to enrollment.

Diagnostic testing Available for LD screen.

Basic skills remediation Available in study skills, time management, learning strategies, written language, and math. Offered one-on-one and in small groups by graduate assistants/students and LD specialists.

Special courses Available in study skills, test taking, reading, and written composition skills. No courses are offered for credit; none enter into overall grade point average.

Counseling and advisement Career counseling and individual counseling are available. Academic advisement by a staff member affiliated with the program is available.

Auxiliary aids and services *Aids:* calculators, personal computers, personal spelling/word-use assistants (e.g., Franklin Speller), scan and read programs (e.g., Kurzweil), screen-enlarging programs, screen readers, speech recognition programs (e.g., Dragon), tape recorders, taped textbooks. *Services and accommodations:* advocates, alternative test arrangements, readers, note-takers, and scribes.

ADD/ADHD Students with ADD/ADHD are eligible for the same services available to students with LD, as well as distraction-free testing environments.

Application *Required:* high school transcript and documentation of high school services (e.g., Individualized Education Program [IEP] or 504 plan). *Recommended:* psychoeducational report (3 years old or less). Upon application, documentation of need for special services should be sent to both admissions and your LD program or unit. *Application deadline (institutional):* rolling/continuous for fall and rolling/continuous for spring. *Application deadline (LD program):* rolling/continuous for fall and rolling/continuous for spring.

LD program contact Eunice Lund-Lucas, Coordinator, Special Needs, 1600 West Bank Drive, Peterborough, ON K9J 7B8. *Phone:* 705-748-1281. *Fax:* 705-748-1509. *E-mail:* specialneeds@trentu. ca.

Application contact Carol Murray, Admissions Officer, Trent University, Office of the Registrar, Peterborough, ON K9J 7B8. *Phone:* 705-748-1215. *E-mail:* liaison@trentu.ca. *Web address:* http://www.trentu.ca/.

TRINITY COLLEGE
Washington, District of Columbia

Students with LD Served by Program	25	ADD/ADHD Services	✓
Staff	1 full-time	Summer Preparation Program	n/a
LD Program or Service Fee	n/a	Alternative Test Arrangements	✓
LD Program Began	1985	LD Student Organization	n/a

Academic Support Services began offering services in 1985. The program serves approximately 25 undergraduate students. Faculty consists of 1 full-time staff member. Services are provided by academic advisers, regular education teachers, counselors, remediation/learning specialists, special education teachers, and trained peer tutors.

Policies Students with LD may take up to 18 credit hours per semester; 12 credit hours per semester are required to maintain full-time status and to be eligible for financial aid. LD services are also available to graduate students.

Diagnostic testing Available for study skills, learning strategies, reading, written language, learning styles, and math.

Basic skills remediation Available in study skills, computer skills, reading, time management, social skills, learning strategies, written language, and math. Offered one-on-one and in small groups by computer-based instruction, regular education teachers, special education teachers, trained peer tutors, and director.

Subject-area tutoring Available in most subjects. Offered one-on-one and in small groups by trained peer tutors and director.

Counseling and advisement Career counseling and individual counseling are available. Academic advisement by a staff member affiliated with the program is available.

Auxiliary aids and services *Aids:* calculators, personal computers. *Services and accommodations:* advocates, priority registration, alternative test arrangements, readers, note-takers, and scribes.

ADD/ADHD Students with ADD/ADHD are eligible for the same services available to students with LD, as well as distraction-free study areas and distraction-free testing environments.

Application *Required:* high school transcript, interview, personal statement, letter(s) of recommendation, and psychoeducational report (3 years old or less). *Recommended:* participation in extracurricular activities, ACT or SAT I (extended-time or untimed test accepted), and documentation of high school services (e.g., Individualized Education Program [IEP] or 504 plan). Upon application, documentation of need for special services should be sent only to admissions. Upon acceptance, documentation of need for special services should be sent only to your LD program or unit. *Application deadline (institutional):* rolling/continuous for fall and rolling/continuous for spring.

LD program contact Kimberly Harris, Director of Academic Support Services, 125 Michigan Avenue, NE, Washington, DC 20017. *Phone:* 202-884-9647. *Fax:* 202-884-9229. *E-mail:* harrisk@trinitydc.edu.

Application contact Trinity College, 125 Michigan Avenue, NE, Washington, DC 20017-1094. *Web address:* http://www.trinitydc.edu/.

TROY STATE UNIVERSITY MONTGOMERY
Montgomery, Alabama

Students with LD Served by Program	75	ADD/ADHD Services	✓
Staff	3 full-time, 2 part-time	Summer Preparation Program	n/a
LD Program or Service Fee	n/a	Alternative Test Arrangements	✓
LD Program Began	1988	LD Student Organization	n/a

Disability Services began offering services in 1988. The program serves approximately 75 undergraduate students. Faculty consists of 3 full-time and 2 part-time staff members. Services are provided by regular education teachers, counselors, remediation/learning specialists, and graduate assistants/students.

Policies Students with LD may take up to 23 credit hours per quarter; 12 credit hours per quarter are required to maintain full-time status; 6 credit hours per quarter are required to be eligible for financial aid. LD services are also available to graduate students.

Subject-area tutoring Available in some subjects. Offered one-on-one by computer-based instruction, professional tutors, and graduate assistants/students.

Counseling and advisement Individual counseling is available.

Auxiliary aids and services *Aids:* calculators, personal computers, personal spelling/word-use assistants (e.g., Franklin Speller), scan and read programs (e.g., Kurzweil), screen-enlarging programs, screen readers, speech recognition programs (e.g., Dragon), tape recorders, taped textbooks, videos. *Services and accommodations:* advocates, priority registration, alternative test arrangements, readers, note-takers, and scribes.

ADD/ADHD Students with ADD/ADHD are eligible for the same services available to students with LD, as well as distraction-free testing environments, extended time to test and on assignments and counseling.

Application *Required:* high school diploma or GED. *Application deadline (institutional):* rolling/continuous for fall and rolling/continuous for spring. *Application deadline (LD program):* rolling/continuous for fall and rolling/continuous for spring.

LD program contact Jane Rudick, Disability Services Coordinator, 231 Montgomery Street, Whitley Hall, Room 432, Montgomery, AL 36104. *Phone:* 334-241-9587. *Fax:* 334-241-5455. *E-mail:* jrudick@tsum.edu.

Application contact Troy State University Montgomery, PO Drawer 4419, Montgomery, AL 36103-4419. *Web address:* http://www.tsum.edu/.

TUFTS UNIVERSITY
Medford, Massachusetts

Students with LD Served by Program	75	ADD/ADHD Services	✓
Staff	1 part-time	Summer Preparation Program	n/a
LD Program or Service Fee	n/a	Alternative Test Arrangements	✓
LD Program Began	n/a	LD Student Organization	n/a

Academic Resource Center serves approximately 75 undergraduate students. Faculty consists of 1 part-time staff member. Services are provided by LD specialists.

Policies Students with LD may take up to 19 credit hours per semester; 9 credit hours per semester are required to maintain full-time status and to be eligible for financial aid. LD services are also available to graduate students.

Basic skills remediation Available in study skills, time management, and learning strategies. Offered one-on-one by LD specialists.

Subject-area tutoring Available in most subjects. Offered one-on-one by trained peer tutors.

Auxiliary aids and services *Aids:* scan and read programs (e.g., Kurzweil), tape recorders, taped textbooks. *Services and accommodations:* alternative test arrangements, readers, note-takers, and scribes.

ADD/ADHD Students with ADD/ADHD are eligible for the same services available to students with LD, as well as distraction-free study areas, distraction-free testing environments and medication management.

Application *Required:* high school transcript, ACT or SAT I (extended-time or untimed test accepted), personal statement, letter(s) of recommendation, and documentation of high school services (e.g., Individualized Education Program [IEP] or 504 plan). *Recommended:* participation in extracurricular activities and psychoeducational report (5 years old or less). Upon application, documentation of need for special services should be sent only to your LD program or unit. Upon acceptance, documentation of need for special services should be sent only to your LD program or unit. *Application deadline (institutional):* 1/1 for fall.

LD program contact Sandra Baer, Coordinator of Academic Services for Students with Disabilities, Dowling Center, Medford, MA 02155. *Phone:* 617-627-5571. *Fax:* 617-627-2367. *E-mail:* sbaer01@emerald.tufts.edu.

Application contact Tufts University, Medford, MA 02155. *E-mail:* uadmiss_inquiry@infonet.tufts.edu. *Web address:* http://www.tufts.edu/.

TULANE UNIVERSITY
New Orleans, Louisiana

Students with LD Served by Program	145	ADD/ADHD Services	✓
Staff	1 full-time, 1 part-time	Summer Preparation Program	n/a
LD Program or Service Fee	n/a	Alternative Test Arrangements	✓
LD Program Began	n/a	LD Student Organization	n/a

Office of Disability Services serves approximately 145 undergraduate students. Faculty consists of 1 full-time and 1 part-time staff member. Services are provided by academic advisers, regular education teachers, counselors, and graduate assistants/students.

Policies 12 credit hours per semester are required to maintain full-time status and to be eligible for financial aid. LD services are also available to graduate students.

Special preparation or orientation Optional orientation held before registration and before classes begin.

Counseling and advisement Career counseling, individual counseling, and small-group counseling are available. Academic advisement by a staff member affiliated with the program is available.

Auxiliary aids and services *Aids:* screen-enlarging programs, screen readers, speech recognition programs (e.g., Dragon), tape recorders, taped textbooks. *Services and accommodations:* alternative test arrangements, readers, note-takers, and scribes.

ADD/ADHD Students with ADD/ADHD are eligible for the same services available to students with LD, as well as distraction-free study areas and distraction-free testing environments.

Application *Required:* high school transcript, ACT or SAT I (extended-time or untimed test accepted), personal statement, and letter(s) of recommendation. *Recommended:* participation in extracurricular activities, interview, and separate application to your LD program or unit. Upon application, documentation of need for special services should be sent only to your LD program or unit. Upon acceptance, documentation of need for special services should be sent only to your LD program or unit. *Application deadline (institutional):* 1/15 for fall.

LD program contact Kelley Hunter Ellis, Coordinator of Disability Services, ERC, Mechanical Engineering Building, New Orleans, LA 70118. *Phone:* 504-865-5113. *Fax:* 504-862-8148. *E-mail:* khunter@mailhost.tcs.tulane.edu.

Application contact Tulane University, 6823 St Charles Avenue, New Orleans, LA 70118-5669. *E-mail:* undergrad.admission@tulane.edu. *Web address:* http://www.tulane.edu/.

UNITED STATES INTERNATIONAL UNIVERSITY
San Diego, California

Students with LD Served by Program	50	ADD/ADHD Services	✓
Staff	1 full-time	Summer Preparation Program	n/a
LD Program or Service Fee	n/a	Alternative Test Arrangements	✓
LD Program Began	1996	LD Student Organization	n/a

Disabled Student Services began offering services in 1996. The program serves approximately 50 undergraduate students. Faculty consists of 1 full-time staff member. Services are provided by academic advisers, regular education teachers, counselors, graduate assistants/students, and trained peer tutors.

United States International University (continued)

Policies Students with LD may take up to 20 credit hours per quarter; 12 credit hours per quarter are required to maintain full-time status and to be eligible for financial aid. LD services are also available to graduate students.

Special preparation or orientation Optional orientation held individually by special arrangement.

Basic skills remediation Available in computer skills, written language, and math. Offered in class-size groups by regular education teachers.

Subject-area tutoring Available in most subjects. Offered one-on-one and in small groups by graduate assistants/students and trained peer tutors.

Special courses Available in career planning, study skills, college survival skills, test taking, time management, learning strategies, and stress management. No courses are offered for credit; none enter into overall grade point average.

Counseling and advisement Career counseling, individual counseling, small-group counseling, and support groups are available. Academic advisement by a staff member affiliated with the program is available.

Auxiliary aids and services *Aids:* calculators, personal computers, tape recorders, taped textbooks. *Services and accommodations:* priority registration, alternative test arrangements, readers, note-takers, and scribes.

ADD/ADHD Students with ADD/ADHD are eligible for the same services available to students with LD, as well as distraction-free study areas, distraction-free testing environments and support groups for ADD/ADHD.

Application *Required:* high school transcript, ACT or SAT I (extended-time or untimed test accepted), psychoeducational report, and documentation of high school services (e.g., Individualized Education Program [IEP] or 504 plan). *Recommended:* participation in extracurricular activities. Upon application, documentation of need for special services should be sent only to your LD program or unit. Upon acceptance, documentation of need for special services should be sent only to your LD program or unit. *Application deadline (institutional):* rolling/continuous for fall and rolling/continuous for spring. *Application deadline (LD program):* rolling/continuous for fall and rolling/continuous for spring.

LD program contact Lorna Reese, Assistant Dean for Student Affairs, 10455 Pomerado Road, San Diego, CA 92131. *Phone:* 858-635-4598.

Application contact United States International University, 10455 Pomerado Road, San Diego, CA 92131-1799. *E-mail:* usiu_adm@sanac.usiu.edu. *Web address:* http://www.usiu.edu/.

UNIVERSITY COLLEGE OF THE CARIBOO
Kamloops, British Columbia

Students with LD Served by Program	60	ADD/ADHD Services	✓
Staff	3 full-time, 6 part-time	Summer Preparation Program	n/a
LD Program or Service Fee	n/a	Alternative Test Arrangements	✓
LD Program Began	n/a	LD Student Organization	n/a

Offices of Services for Students with Disabilities (OSSD) serves approximately 60 undergraduate students. Faculty consists of 3 full-time and 6 part-time staff members. Services are provided by academic advisers, counselors, remediation/learning specialists, diagnostic specialists, special education teachers, trained peer tutors, and professional tutors.

Policies Students with LD may take up to 18 credit hours per semester; 9 credit hours per semester are required to maintain full-time status; 6 credit hours per semester are required to be eligible for financial aid.

Special preparation or orientation Optional orientation held individually by special arrangement.

Diagnostic testing Available for auditory processing, spelling, intelligence, personality, learning strategies, reading, written language, learning styles, visual processing, and math.

Basic skills remediation Available in study skills, computer skills, reading, time management, social skills, visual processing, learning strategies, written language, and math. Offered one-on-one by LD specialists, professional tutors, and counselors.

Subject-area tutoring Available in most subjects. Offered one-on-one by professional tutors.

Counseling and advisement Career counseling and individual counseling are available. Academic advisement by a staff member affiliated with the program is available.

Auxiliary aids and services *Aids:* personal computers, screen-enlarging programs, screen readers, speech recognition programs (e.g., Dragon), tape recorders, taped textbooks. advocates, priority registration, alternative test arrangements, readers, and scribes.

ADD/ADHD Students with ADD/ADHD are eligible for the same services available to students with LD, as well as distraction-free testing environments and personal coach or mentors.

Application *Required:* interview and psychoeducational report (5 years old or less). *Recommended:* high school transcript and documentation of high school services (e.g., Individualized Education Program [IEP] or 504 plan). Upon application, documentation of need for special services should be sent only to your LD program or unit. Upon acceptance, documentation of need for special services should be sent only to your LD program or unit. *Application deadline (institutional):* 4/15 for fall.

LD program contact Joyce Henry, Coordinator of Services for Students with Disabilities, 850 McGill Road, Box 3010, Kamloops, BC V2C 5N3. *Phone:* 250-828-5085. *Fax:* 250-371-5772. *E-mail:* jhendry@cariboo.bc.ca.

Application contact University College of the Cariboo, PO Box 3010, Station Terminal, Kamloops, BC V2C 5N3. *Web address:* http://www.cariboo.bc.ca/.

UNIVERSITY COLLEGE OF THE FRASER VALLEY
Abbotsford, British Columbia

Students with LD Served by Program	55	ADD/ADHD Services	✓
Staff	2 full-time, 1 part-time	Summer Preparation Program	n/a
LD Program or Service Fee	n/a	Alternative Test Arrangements	✓
LD Program Began	1984	LD Student Organization	✓

Disability Resource Centre began offering services in 1984. The program serves approximately 55 undergraduate students. Faculty consists of 2 full-time staff members and 1 part-time staff member. Services are provided by LD specialists and ACCESS advisors.

Policies Students with LD may take up to 15 hours per semester; 9 hours per semester are required to maintain full-time status and to be eligible for financial aid.

Special preparation or orientation Optional orientation held before classes begin and individually by special arrangement.

Basic skills remediation Available in study skills, computer skills, reading, time management, learning strategies, spelling, and written language. Offered one-on-one by LD specialists.

Subject-area tutoring Available in some subjects. Offered one-on-one by trained peer tutors and LD specialists.

Counseling and advisement Career counseling and individual counseling are available.

Auxiliary aids and services *Aids:* calculators, personal computers, scan and read programs (e.g., Kurzweil), screen-enlarging programs, screen readers, speech recognition programs (e.g., Dragon), tape recorders, taped textbooks. *Services and accommodations:* advocates, priority registration, alternative test arrangements, readers, note-takers, and scribes.

Student organization There is a student organization for students with LD.

ADD/ADHD Students with ADD/ADHD are eligible for the same services available to students with LD, as well as distraction-free study areas, distraction-free testing environments and personal coach or mentors.

Application *Required:* high school transcript. *Recommended:* separate application to your LD program or unit, psychoeducational report (3 years old or less), and documentation of high school services (e.g., Individualized Education Program [IEP] or 504 plan). Upon application, documentation of need for special services should be sent only to your LD program or unit. Upon acceptance, documentation of need for special services should be sent only to your LD program or unit. *Application deadline (LD program):* rolling/continuous for fall and rolling/continuous for spring.

LD program contact Ellen Dixon, Access Advisor/Learning Assistant, Disability Resource Centre, 33844 King Road, Abbotsford, BC V2S 7M8. *Phone:* 604-864-4609. *Fax:* 604-855-7614. *E-mail:* dixone@ucfv.bc.ca.

Application contact Elaine Harris, Associate Registrar, University College of the Fraser Valley, 33844 King Road, Abbotsford, BC V2S 7M9. *Phone:* 604-864-4645. *Web address:* http://www.ucfv.bc.ca/.

THE UNIVERSITY OF ALABAMA
Tuscaloosa, Alabama

Students with LD Served by Program	450	ADD/ADHD Services	✓
Staff	2 full-time	Summer Preparation Program	n/a
LD Program or Service Fee	n/a	Alternative Test Arrangements	✓
LD Program Began	1985	LD Student Organization	n/a

Office of Disability Services began offering services in 1985. The program serves approximately 450 undergraduate students. Faculty consists of 2 full-time staff members. Services are provided by LD specialists.

Policies The college has written policies regarding substitution and waivers of requirements for admission and graduation. 12 semester hours per semester are required to maintain full-time status; 6 semester hours per semester are required to be eligible for financial aid. LD services are also available to graduate students.

Auxiliary aids and services *Aids:* calculators, scan and read programs (e.g., Kurzweil), screen-enlarging programs, screen readers, speech recognition programs (e.g., Dragon), tape recorders, taped textbooks. *Services and accommodations:* advocates, priority registration, alternative test arrangements, readers, note-takers, and scribes.

ADD/ADHD Students with ADD/ADHD are eligible for the same services available to students with LD

Application *Required:* high school transcript, ACT or SAT I (extended-time or untimed test accepted), personal statement, separate application to your LD program or unit, and psychoeducational report (3 years old or less). *Recommended:* partici-pation in extracurricular activities and documentation of high school services (e.g., Individualized Education Program [IEP] or 504 plan). Upon application, documentation of need for special services should be sent only to your LD program or unit. Upon acceptance, documentation of need for special services should be sent only to your LD program or unit. *Application deadline (institutional):* rolling/continuous for fall and rolling/continuous for spring. *Application deadline (LD program):* rolling/continuous for fall and rolling/continuous for spring.

LD program contact Dr. Jim Saski, Manager, LD and ADHD Services, Box 870304, Tuscaloosa, AL 35487-0304. *Phone:* 205-348-7966. *Fax:* 205-348-5291. *E-mail:* jsaski2@sa.ua.edu.

Application contact The University of Alabama, Tuscaloosa, AL 35487. *E-mail:* uaadmit@ua1vm.ua.edu. *Web address:* http://www.ua.edu/.

THE UNIVERSITY OF ALABAMA IN HUNTSVILLE
Huntsville, Alabama

Students with LD Served by Program	38	ADD/ADHD Services	✓
Staff	5 part-time	Summer Preparation Program	n/a
LD Program or Service Fee	n/a	Alternative Test Arrangements	✓
LD Program Began	1987	LD Student Organization	n/a

Student Development Services began offering services in 1987. The program serves approximately 38 undergraduate students. Faculty consists of 5 part-time staff members. Services are provided by regular education teachers, counselors, graduate assistants/students, trained peer tutors, and professional tutors.

Policies Students with LD may take up to 20 credit hours per semester; 12 credit hours per semester are required to maintain full-time status; 6 credit hours per semester are required to be eligible for financial aid. LD services are also available to graduate students.

Counseling and advisement Career counseling and individual counseling are available.

Auxiliary aids and services *Aids:* personal spelling/word-use assistants (e.g., Franklin Speller), scan and read programs (e.g., Kurzweil), screen-enlarging programs, screen readers, tape recorders, taped textbooks, video recording for classes. *Services and accommodations:* advocates, priority registration, alternative test arrangements, readers, note-takers, scribes, and special furniture.

ADD/ADHD Students with ADD/ADHD are eligible for the same services available to students with LD, as well as distraction-free testing environments.

Application *Required:* high school transcript and ACT (extended-time test accepted). *Recommended:* psychoeducational report (1 year old or less) and documentation of high school services (e.g., Individualized Education Program [IEP] or 504 plan). Upon application, documentation of need for special services should be sent only to your LD program or unit. Upon acceptance, documentation of need for special services should be sent only to your LD program or unit. *Application deadline (institutional):* rolling/continuous for fall and rolling/continuous for spring. *Application deadline (LD program):* rolling/continuous for fall and rolling/continuous for spring.

LD program contact Rosemary Robinson, Assistant Director, Student Development Services, Student Development, University Center, Room 113, Huntsville, AL 35899. *Phone:* 256-890-6203. *Fax:* 256-890-6672. *E-mail:* robinsr@email.uah.edu.

The University of Alabama in Huntsville (continued)

Application contact Sabrina Williams, Associate Director of Admissions, The University of Alabama in Huntsville, Enrollment Services, Huntsville, AL 35899. *Phone:* 256-890-6070. *E-mail:* admitme@email.uah.edu. *Web address:* http://www.uah.edu/.

UNIVERSITY OF ALASKA FAIRBANKS
Fairbanks, Alaska

Students with LD Served by Program	100	ADD/ADHD Services	✓
Staff	1 full-time	Summer Preparation Program	n/a
LD Program or Service Fee	n/a	Alternative Test Arrangements	✓
LD Program Began	1989	LD Student Organization	n/a

Disability Services began offering services in 1989. The program serves approximately 100 undergraduate students. Faculty consists of 1 full-time staff member. Services are provided by academic advisers and graduate assistants/students.

Policies The college has written policies regarding course substitutions. Students with LD may take up to 18 credit hours per semester; 12 credit hours per semester are required to maintain full-time status and to be eligible for financial aid. LD services are also available to graduate students.

Counseling and advisement Academic advisement by a staff member affiliated with the program is available.

Auxiliary aids and services *Aids:* scan and read programs (e.g., Kurzweil), screen-enlarging programs, screen readers, speech recognition programs (e.g., Dragon), tape recorders, taped textbooks. *Services and accommodations:* advocates, priority registration, alternative test arrangements, readers, note-takers, and scribes.

ADD/ADHD Students with ADD/ADHD are eligible for the same services available to students with LD, as well as distraction-free testing environments.

Application *Required:* high school transcript, ACT or SAT I (extended-time tests accepted), psychoeducational report (3 years old or less), and intake appointment with Coordinator of Disability Services. *Recommended:* documentation of high school services (e.g., Individualized Education Program [IEP] or 504 plan). Upon application, documentation of need for special services should be sent only to your LD program or unit. Upon acceptance, documentation of need for special services should be sent only to your LD program or unit. *Application deadline (institutional):* 8/2 for fall and 12/1 for spring. *Application deadline (LD program):* rolling/continuous for fall and rolling/continuous for spring.

LD program contact Jan Ohmstede, Coordinator, PO Box 755580, Fairbanks, AK 99775-5580. *Phone:* 907-474-7043. *Fax:* 907-474-5777. *E-mail:* fnjlo1@uaf.edu.

Application contact Nancy Dix, Admissions Counselor, University of Alaska Fairbanks, PO Box 757480, Fairbanks, AK 99775-7480. *Phone:* 907-474-7500. *E-mail:* fyapply@aurora.alaska.edu. *Web address:* http://www.uaf.edu/.

UNIVERSITY OF ARKANSAS AT LITTLE ROCK
Little Rock, Arkansas

Students with LD Served by Program	220	ADD/ADHD Services	✓
Staff	5 full-time	Summer Preparation Program	n/a
LD Program or Service Fee	n/a	Alternative Test Arrangements	✓
LD Program Began	1985	LD Student Organization	n/a

Disability Support Services began offering services in 1985. The program serves approximately 220 undergraduate students. Faculty consists of 5 full-time staff members. Services are provided by counselors, graduate assistants/students, and tutors.

Policies The college has written policies regarding course substitutions. Students with LD may take up to 18 credit hours per semester; 12 credit hours per semester are required to maintain full-time status; 6 credit hours per semester are required to be eligible for financial aid. LD services are also available to graduate students.

Special preparation or orientation Optional orientation held before classes begin.

Subject-area tutoring Available in most subjects. Offered one-on-one by undergrad students with training.

Counseling and advisement Career counseling and individual counseling are available.

Auxiliary aids and services *Aids:* personal spelling/word-use assistants (e.g., Franklin Speller), scan and read programs (e.g., Kurzweil), screen-enlarging programs, screen readers, speech recognition programs (e.g., Dragon), taped textbooks. *Services and accommodations:* advocates, priority registration, alternative test arrangements, readers, note-takers, and scribes.

ADD/ADHD Students with ADD/ADHD are eligible for the same services available to students with LD, as well as distraction-free testing environments.

Application *Required:* high school transcript, ACT or SAT I (extended-time or untimed ACT test accepted), separate application to your LD program or unit, and psychoeducational report (5 years old or less). Upon application, documentation of need for special services should be sent only to your LD program or unit. Upon acceptance, documentation of need for special services should be sent only to your LD program or unit. *Application deadline (institutional):* rolling/continuous for fall and rolling/continuous for spring. *Application deadline (LD program):* rolling/continuous for fall and rolling/continuous for spring.

LD program contact Susan Quelles, Director, Disability Support Services, 2801 South University Avenue, Little Rock, AR 72204. *Phone:* 501-569-3143. *Fax:* 501-569-8068. *E-mail:* slquelles@ualr.edu.

Application contact University of Arkansas at Little Rock, 2801 South University Avenue, Little Rock, AR 72204-1099. *E-mail:* dspine@ualr.edu. *Web address:* http://www.ualr.edu/.

UNIVERSITY OF CALGARY
Calgary, Alberta

Students with LD Served by Program	239	ADD/ADHD Services	✓
Staff	2 part-time	Summer Preparation Program	n/a
LD Program or Service Fee	n/a	Alternative Test Arrangements	✓
LD Program Began	1985	LD Student Organization	n/a

Disability Resource Centre (DRC) began offering services in 1985. The program serves approximately 239 undergraduate students. Faculty consists of 2 part-time staff members. Services are provided by counselors, remediation/learning specialists, LD specialists, professional tutors, and adaptive technology specialist.

Policies LD services are also available to graduate students.

Fees *Diagnostic Testing Fee:* ranges from $900 to $1200.

Special preparation or orientation Required orientation held after classes begin.

Diagnostic testing Available for spelling, intelligence, study skills, learning strategies, reading, written language, learning styles, and attention issues.

Subject-area tutoring Available in most subjects. Offered one-on-one by professional tutors and trained peer tutors.

Counseling and advisement Career counseling is available.

Auxiliary aids and services *Aids:* calculators, personal computers, personal spelling/word-use assistants (e.g., Franklin Speller), scan and read programs (e.g., Kurzweil), screen-enlarging programs, screen readers, speech recognition programs (e.g., Dragon), tape recorders, taped textbooks, software programs. *Services and accommodations:* advocates, alternative test arrangements, readers, note-takers, and scribes.

ADD/ADHD Students with ADD/ADHD are eligible for the same services available to students with LD, as well as distraction-free study areas, distraction-free testing environments, medication management and support groups for ADD/ADHD.

Application *Required:* high school transcript. Upon application, documentation of need for special services should be sent only to your LD program or unit. Upon acceptance, documentation of need for special services should be sent only to your LD program or unit. *Application deadline (LD program):* rolling/continuous for fall and rolling/continuous for spring.

LD program contact Marilyn Samuels, Learning Disability Specialist, Disability Resource Center, MSC 274, 2500 University Drive NW, Calgary, AB T2N 1N4. *Phone:* 403-220-8237. *Fax:* 403-210-1063. *E-mail:* msamuels@ucalgary.ca.

Application contact University of Calgary, Office of Admissions, Calgary, AB T2N 1N4. *Web address:* http://www.ucalgary.ca/.

UNIVERSITY OF CALIFORNIA, BERKELEY

Berkeley, California

Students with LD Served by Program	300	ADD/ADHD Services	✓
Staff	2 full-time, 2 part-time	Summer Preparation Program	n/a
LD Program or Service Fee	n/a	Alternative Test Arrangements	✓
LD Program Began	1980	LD Student Organization	n/a

Disabled Students Program began offering services in 1980. The program serves approximately 300 undergraduate students. Faculty consists of 2 full-time and 2 part-time staff members. Services are provided by diagnostic specialists and LD specialists.

Policies The college has written policies regarding course substitutions. LD services are also available to graduate students.

Special preparation or orientation Held after classes begin.

Special courses Available in study skills and learning strategies.

Counseling and advisement Career counseling and support groups are available.

Auxiliary aids and services *Aids:* personal spelling/word-use assistants (e.g., Franklin Speller), scan and read programs (e.g., Kurzweil), screen-enlarging programs, screen readers, speech recognition programs (e.g., Dragon), taped textbooks. *Services and accommodations:* priority registration, alternative test arrangements, readers, and note-takers.

ADD/ADHD Students with ADD/ADHD are eligible for the same services available to students with LD, as well as distraction-free testing environments and support groups for ADD/ADHD.

Application *Required:* high school transcript and ACT or SAT I (extended-time SAT I test accepted). Upon acceptance, documentation of need for special services should be sent only to your LD program or unit.

LD program contact Dr. Constance Chiba, Disability Services Coordinator, Disabled Students Program, 230 Cesar Chavez, Berkeley, CA 94720-4250. *Phone:* 510-642-0518. *Fax:* 510-643-9686. *E-mail:* cchiba@uclink4.berkeley.edu.

Application contact Pre-Admission Advising, Office of Undergraduate Admission and Relations With Schools, University of California, Berkeley, Berkeley, CA 94720-5800. *Phone:* 510-642-3175. *E-mail:* ouars@uclink.berkeley.edu. *Web address:* http://www.berkeley.edu/.

UNIVERSITY OF CALIFORNIA, LOS ANGELES

Los Angeles, California

Students with LD Served by Program	164	ADD/ADHD Services	✓
Staff	2 full-time, 2 part-time	Summer Preparation Program	n/a
LD Program or Service Fee	n/a	Alternative Test Arrangements	✓
LD Program Began	1992	LD Student Organization	✓

Office for Students with Disabilities (OSD) began offering services in 1992. The program serves approximately 164 undergraduate students. Faculty consists of 2 full-time and 2 part-time staff members. Services are provided by LD specialists.

Policies LD services are also available to graduate students.

Special preparation or orientation Optional orientation held before classes begin, during summer prior to enrollment, and individually by special arrangement.

Subject-area tutoring Available in most subjects. Offered one-on-one and in small groups by trained peer tutors.

Counseling and advisement Career counseling, individual counseling, small-group counseling, and support groups are available.

Auxiliary aids and services *Aids:* calculators, personal computers, personal spelling/word-use assistants (e.g., Franklin Speller), scan and read programs (e.g., Kurzweil), screen-enlarging programs, screen readers, speech recognition programs (e.g., Dragon), tape recorders, taped textbooks. *Services and accommodations:* priority registration, alternative test arrangements, readers, note-takers, and scribes.

Student organization There is a student organization for students with LD.

ADD/ADHD Students with ADD/ADHD are eligible for the same services available to students with LD, as well as distraction-free study areas, distraction-free testing environments and support groups for ADD/ADHD.

Application *Required:* high school transcript, ACT or SAT I (extended-time or untimed test accepted), and personal statement. Upon application, documentation of need for special services should be sent only to your LD program or unit. Upon acceptance, documentation of need for special services should be sent only to your LD program or unit. *Application deadline (institutional):* 11/30 for fall and 10/31 for spring.

LD program contact Dr. Arline Halper, Learning Disabilities Program Coordinator, PO Box 951426, Los Angeles, CA 90095-1426. *Phone:* 310-825-1501. *Fax:* 310-825-9656. *E-mail:* ahalper@saonet.ucla.edu.

University of California, Los Angeles (continued)

Application contact University of California, Los Angeles, 405 Hilgard Avenue, Los Angeles, CA 90095. *E-mail:* ugadm@saonet. ucla.edu. *Web address:* http://www.ucla.edu/.

UNIVERSITY OF COLORADO AT COLORADO SPRINGS

Colorado Springs, Colorado

Students with LD Served by Program	50	ADD/ADHD Services	✓
Staff	1 full-time	Summer Preparation Program	n/a
LD Program or Service Fee	n/a	Alternative Test Arrangements	✓
LD Program Began	1990	LD Student Organization	n/a

Disability Services began offering services in 1990. The program serves approximately 50 undergraduate students. Faculty consists of 1 full-time staff member. Services are provided by coordinator.

Policies The college has written policies regarding course substitutions. LD services are also available to graduate students.

Basic skills remediation Available in study skills, reading, time management, social skills, learning strategies, and written language. Offered one-on-one by LD specialists.

Auxiliary aids and services *Aids:* scan and read programs (e.g., Kurzweil), screen-enlarging programs, tape recorders, taped textbooks. *Services and accommodations:* advocates, alternative test arrangements, readers, note-takers, and scribes.

ADD/ADHD Students with ADD/ADHD are eligible for the same services available to students with LD

Application *Required:* high school transcript and ACT or SAT I (extended-time or untimed test accepted). Upon acceptance, documentation of need for special services should be sent only to admissions. *Application deadline (institutional):* rolling/continuous for fall and rolling/continuous for spring.

LD program contact JoAnne Hill, Coordinator, 1420 Austin Bluffs Parkway, PO Box 7150, Colorado Springs, CO 80933-7150. *Phone:* 800-990-UCCS. *Fax:* 719-262-3354. *E-mail:* jhill@mail.uccs.edu.

Application contact James Tidwell, Assistant Admissions Director, University of Colorado at Colorado Springs, PO Box 7150, Colorado Springs, CO 80933-7150. *Phone:* 719-262-3383. *E-mail:* admrec@mail.uccs.edu. *Web address:* http://www.uccs.edu/.

UNIVERSITY OF COLORADO AT DENVER

Denver, Colorado

Students with LD Served by Program	56	ADD/ADHD Services	✓
Staff	2 full-time, 1 part-time	Summer Preparation Program	n/a
LD Program or Service Fee	n/a	Alternative Test Arrangements	✓
LD Program Began	n/a	LD Student Organization	✓

Disability Services Office serves approximately 56 undergraduate students. Faculty consists of 2 full-time staff members and 1 part-time staff member. Services are provided by counselors and LD specialists.

Policies The college has written policies regarding course substitutions. LD services are also available to graduate students.

Auxiliary aids and services *Aids:* calculators, personal computers, personal spelling/word-use assistants (e.g., Franklin Speller), scan and read programs (e.g., Kurzweil), screen-enlarging programs, screen readers, speech recognition programs (e.g., Dragon), tape recorders, taped textbooks. *Services and accommodations:* advocates, priority registration, alternative test arrangements, readers, note-takers, scribes, and course substitution for foreign language for "qualified students with disabilities".

Student organization There is a student organization for students with LD.

ADD/ADHD Students with ADD/ADHD are eligible for the same services available to students with LD, as well as distraction-free study areas and distraction-free testing environments.

Application *Required:* high school transcript and ACT or SAT I. Upon acceptance, documentation of need for special services should be sent only to your LD program or unit. *Application deadline (institutional):* rolling/continuous for fall and rolling/continuous for spring.

LD program contact Lisa E. McGill, Director of Disability Services, Auraria Higher Education Center, PO Box 173361, Campus Box P, Denver, CO 80217-3361. *Phone:* 303-556-8387. *Fax:* 303-556-2074.

Application contact Alice Holman, Associate Director of Admissions, University of Colorado at Denver, PO Box 173364, Denver, CO 80217-3364. *Phone:* 303-556-2275. *E-mail:* admissions@castle.cudenver.edu. *Web address:* http://www.cudenver.edu/.

UNIVERSITY OF DAYTON

Dayton, Ohio

Students with LD Served by Program	150	ADD/ADHD Services	✓
Staff	3 full-time, 10 part-time	Summer Preparation Program	n/a
LD Program or Service Fee	n/a	Alternative Test Arrangements	✓
LD Program Began	1982	LD Student Organization	n/a

Office for Students with Disabilities (OSD) began offering services in 1982. The program serves approximately 150 undergraduate students. Faculty consists of 3 full-time and 10 part-time staff members. Services are provided by academic advisers, regular education teachers, counselors, diagnostic specialists, graduate assistants/students, teacher trainees, LD specialists, trained peer tutors, and professional tutors.

Policies The college has written policies regarding course substitutions. LD services are also available to graduate students.

Special preparation or orientation Held individually by special arrangement.

Subject-area tutoring Available in all subjects. Offered one-on-one and in small groups by computer-based instruction, professional tutors, graduate assistants/students, trained peer tutors, and LD specialists.

Special courses Available in study skills, college survival skills, practical computer skills, test taking, time management, learning strategies, vocabulary development, math, and written composition skills. Some courses are offered for credit; none enter into overall grade point average.

Counseling and advisement Career counseling and individual counseling are available. Academic advisement by a staff member affiliated with the program is available.

Auxiliary aids and services *Aids:* scan and read programs (e.g., Kurzweil), screen-enlarging programs, screen readers, speech recognition programs (e.g., Dragon), taped textbooks, adaptive computer lab for training/testing. *Services and accommodations:* advocates, priority registration, alternative test arrangements, readers, note-takers, and scribes.

ADD/ADHD Students with ADD/ADHD are eligible for the same services available to students with LD, as well as distraction-free study areas, distraction-free testing environments and personal coach or mentors.

Application *Required:* high school transcript, ACT or SAT I (extended-time or untimed test accepted), interview, personal statement, letter(s) of recommendation, separate application to your LD program or unit, psychoeducational report (3 years old or less), and documentation of high school services (e.g., Individualized Education Program [IEP] or 504 plan). Upon application, documentation of need for special services should be sent to both admissions and your LD program or unit. Upon acceptance, documentation of need for special services should be sent to both admissions and your LD program or unit.

LD program contact Bea Bedard, Coordinator, 300 College Park Avenue, Dayton, OH 45469-1352. *Phone:* 937-229-3684. *Fax:* 937-229-3270. *E-mail:* bea.bedard@notes.udayton.edu.

Application contact University of Dayton, 300 College Park, Dayton, OH 45469-1300. *E-mail:* admission@udayton.edu. *Web address:* http://www.udayton.edu/.

UNIVERSITY OF GUELPH

Guelph, Ontario

Students with LD Served by Program	160	ADD/ADHD Services	✓
Staff	3 full-time, 1 part-time	Summer Preparation Program	n/a
LD Program or Service Fee	n/a	Alternative Test Arrangements	✓
LD Program Began	1990	LD Student Organization	n/a

Centre for Students with Disabilities began offering services in 1990. The program serves approximately 160 undergraduate students. Faculty consists of 3 full-time staff members and 1 part-time staff member. Services are provided by counselors, graduate assistants/students, LD specialists, and trained peer tutors.

Policies LD services are also available to graduate students.

Special preparation or orientation Optional orientation held before registration, during registration, and before classes begin.

Diagnostic testing Available for auditory processing, motor skills, spelling, spoken language, intelligence, study skills, learning strategies, reading, written language, social skills, visual processing, and math.

Subject-area tutoring Available in most subjects. Offered one-on-one and in small groups by professional tutors and graduate assistants/students.

Special courses Available in study skills, practical computer skills, test taking, reading, time management, learning strategies, self-advocacy, and stress management. All courses are offered for credit; all enter into overall grade point average.

Counseling and advisement Career counseling, individual counseling, and support groups are available.

Auxiliary aids and services *Aids:* calculators, personal computers, scan and read programs (e.g., Kurzweil), screen-enlarging programs, speech recognition programs (e.g., Dragon), tape recorders, taped textbooks. *Services and accommodations:* advocates, priority registration, alternative test arrangements, readers, note-takers, and scribes.

ADD/ADHD Students with ADD/ADHD are eligible for the same services available to students with LD, as well as distraction-free study areas, distraction-free testing environments and support groups for ADD/ADHD.

Application *Required:* high school transcript. Upon application, documentation of need for special services should be sent only to your LD program or unit. Upon acceptance, documentation of need for special services should be sent only to your LD program or unit. *Application deadline (LD program):* rolling/continuous for fall.

LD program contact Bruno Mancini, Director, Centre for Students with Disabilities, University Centre, Guelph, ON N1H 4S6. *Phone:* 519-824-4120 Ext. 2386. *Fax:* 519-824-3432. *E-mail:* bmancini@uoguelph.ca.

Application contact Jock Phippen, Admissions Coordinator, University of Guelph, Guelph, ON N1G 2W1. *Phone:* 519-824-4120 Ext. 6066. *E-mail:* info@registrar.uoguelph.ca. *Web address:* http://www.uoguelph.ca/.

UNIVERSITY OF HARTFORD

West Hartford, Connecticut

Students with LD Served by Program	200	ADD/ADHD Services	✓
Staff	1 full-time, 6 part-time	Summer Preparation Program	n/a
LD Program or Service Fee	n/a	Alternative Test Arrangements	✓
LD Program Began	1986	LD Student Organization	n/a

Learning Plus began offering services in 1986. The program serves approximately 200 undergraduate students. Faculty consists of 1 full-time and 6 part-time staff members. Services are provided by professional tutors.

Policies Students with LD may take up to 18 credit hours per semester; 12 credit hours per semester are required to maintain full-time status and to be eligible for financial aid. LD services are also available to graduate students.

Auxiliary aids and services *Aids:* taped textbooks. *Services and accommodations:* alternative test arrangements.

ADD/ADHD Students with ADD/ADHD are eligible for the same services available to students with LD, as well as distraction-free testing environments.

Application *Required:* high school transcript and ACT or SAT I (extended-time tests accepted). *Recommended:* participation in extracurricular activities, interview, personal statement, letter(s) of recommendation, psychoeducational report (3 years old or less), and documentation of high school services (e.g., Individualized Education Program [IEP] or 504 plan). Upon application, documentation of need for special services should be sent only to your LD program or unit. Upon acceptance, documentation of need for special services should be sent only to your LD program or unit. *Application deadline (institutional):* rolling/continuous for fall. *Application deadline (LD program):* rolling/continuous for fall.

LD program contact Marcia Gilder Orcutt, Director, Learning Plus, A.209, 200 Bloomfield Avenue, West Hartford, CT 06117. *Phone:* 860-768-4312. *Fax:* 860-768-4183. *E-mail:* orcutt@mail.hartford.edu.

Application contact University of Hartford, 200 Bloomfield Avenue, West Hartford, CT 06117-1599. *E-mail:* admission@uhavax.hartford.edu. *Web address:* http://www.hartford.edu/.

UNIVERSITY OF HAWAII AT HILO

Hilo, Hawaii

Students with LD Served by Program	10	ADD/ADHD Services	✓
Staff	1 part-time	Summer Preparation Program	n/a
LD Program or Service Fee	n/a	Alternative Test Arrangements	✓
LD Program Began	1987	LD Student Organization	n/a

Student Support Services Program began offering services in 1987. The program serves approximately 10 undergraduate students. Faculty consists of 1 part-time staff member. Services are provided by counselors.

University of Hawaii at Hilo (continued)

Policies The college has written policies regarding course substitutions. Students with LD may take up to 18 credit hours per semester; 12 credit hours per semester are required to maintain full-time status; 6 credit hours per semester are required to be eligible for financial aid.

Basic skills remediation Available in study skills, computer skills, time management, written language, and math. Offered one-on-one by trained peer tutors.

Subject-area tutoring Available in some subjects. Offered one-on-one and in small groups by trained peer tutors.

Counseling and advisement Individual counseling is available.

Auxiliary aids and services *Aids:* calculators, personal spelling/word-use assistants (e.g., Franklin Speller), scan and read programs (e.g., Kurzweil), screen-enlarging programs, tape recorders, taped textbooks. *Services and accommodations:* advocates, priority registration, alternative test arrangements, readers, note-takers, and scribes.

ADD/ADHD Students with ADD/ADHD are eligible for the same services available to students with LD

Application *Required:* high school transcript and ACT or SAT I (extended-time tests accepted). Upon application, documentation of need for special services should be sent only to your LD program or unit. Upon acceptance, documentation of need for special services should be sent only to your LD program or unit. *Application deadline (institutional):* 7/1 for fall and 12/15 for spring. *Application deadline (LD program):* rolling/continuous for fall and rolling/continuous for spring.

LD program contact Barbara Lee, Disability Services Coordinator, 200 West Kawili Street, Hilo, HI 96720-4091. *Phone:* 808-974-7619. *Fax:* 808-974-7691.

Application contact University of Hawaii at Hilo, 200 West Kawili Street, Hilo, HI 96720-4091. *E-mail:* uhhao@uhhadc.uhh.hawaii.edu. *Web address:* http://www.uhh.hawaii.edu/.

UNIVERSITY OF HOUSTON-CLEAR LAKE
Houston, Texas

Students with LD Served by Program	100	ADD/ADHD Services	✓
Staff	1 full-time, 3 part-time	Summer Preparation Program	n/a
LD Program or Service Fee	n/a	Alternative Test Arrangements	✓
LD Program Began	n/a	LD Student Organization	✓

Disability Services serves approximately 100 undergraduate students. Faculty consists of 1 full-time and 3 part-time staff members. Services are provided by LD specialists.

Policies Students with LD may take up to 18 credit hours per semester; 12 credit hours per semester are required to maintain full-time status; 3 credit hours per semester are required to be eligible for financial aid. LD services are also available to graduate students.

Special preparation or orientation Optional orientation held individually by special arrangement.

Counseling and advisement Career counseling, individual counseling, small-group counseling, and support groups are available.

Auxiliary aids and services *Aids:* calculators, personal computers, personal spelling/word-use assistants (e.g., Franklin Speller), scan and read programs (e.g., Kurzweil), screen-enlarging programs, screen readers, speech recognition programs (e.g., Dragon), tape recorders, taped textbooks. *Services and accommodations:* advocates, alternative test arrangements, readers, note-takers, and scribes.

Student organization There is a student organization for students with LD.

ADD/ADHD Students with ADD/ADHD are eligible for the same services available to students with LD, as well as distraction-free testing environments, personal coach or mentors, and support groups for ADD/ADHD.

Application *Required:* Texas Academic Skills Program (TASP). Upon acceptance, documentation of need for special services should be sent only to your LD program or unit. *Application deadline (institutional):* rolling/continuous for fall and rolling/continuous for spring. *Application deadline (LD program):* rolling/continuous for fall and rolling/continuous for spring.

LD program contact Sean L. Murphy, Coordinator of Disability Services, 2700 Bay Area Boulevard, Houston, TX 77058. *Phone:* 281-283-2627. *Fax:* 281-283-2624.

Application contact University of Houston-Clear Lake, 2700 Bay Area Boulevard, Box 13, Houston, TX 77058-1098. *E-mail:* admissions@cl.uh.edu. *Web address:* http://www.cl.uh.edu/.

UNIVERSITY OF IDAHO
Moscow, Idaho

Students with LD Served by Program	100	ADD/ADHD Services	✓
Staff	2 full-time, 3 part-time	Summer Preparation Program	n/a
LD Program or Service Fee	n/a	Alternative Test Arrangements	✓
LD Program Began	1980	LD Student Organization	n/a

Student Support Services began offering services in 1980. The program serves approximately 100 undergraduate students. Faculty consists of 2 full-time and 3 part-time staff members. Services are provided by counselors, graduate assistants/students, trained peer tutors, professional tutors, and AmeriCorps member.

Policies 12 credits per semester are required to maintain full-time status; 6 credits per semester are required to be eligible for financial aid. LD services are also available to graduate students.

Fees *Diagnostic Testing Fee:* ranges from $10 to $50.

Special preparation or orientation Optional orientation held individually by special arrangement.

Diagnostic testing Available for auditory processing, spelling, neuropsychological, intelligence, reading, written language, visual processing, math, and ADD/ADHD.

Subject-area tutoring Available in all subjects. Offered one-on-one and in small groups by computer-based instruction, professional tutors, graduate assistants/students, trained peer tutors, and AmeriCorps member.

Special courses Available in math and Pre-internship class. All courses are offered for credit; some enter into overall grade point average.

Counseling and advisement Career counseling, individual counseling, and support groups are available.

Auxiliary aids and services *Aids:* personal computers, taped textbooks. *Services and accommodations:* advocates, priority registration, alternative test arrangements, readers, note-takers, and scribes.

ADD/ADHD Students with ADD/ADHD are eligible for the same services available to students with LD

Application *Required:* high school transcript and ACT or SAT I (extended-time or untimed test accepted). *Recommended:* personal statement, letter(s) of recommendation, psychoeducational report (3 years old or less), and documentation of high school services (e.g., Individualized Education Program [IEP] or 504 plan). Upon application, documentation of need for special services should be sent only to admissions. Upon acceptance, documentation of need for special services should be sent only to your LD program or unit. *Application deadline (institutional):*

rolling/continuous for fall and rolling/continuous for spring. *Application deadline (LD program):* rolling/continuous for fall and rolling/continuous for spring.

LD program contact Meredyth L. Goodwin, Director, Student Support Services, PO Box 443230, Idaho Commons 338, Moscow, ID 83844-3230. *Phone:* 208-895-6746. *Fax:* 208-895-9404. *E-mail:* sss@uidaho.edu.

Application contact University of Idaho, Moscow, ID 83844-4140. *E-mail:* admappl@uidaho.edu. *Web address:* http://www.uidaho.edu/.

UNIVERSITY OF ILLINOIS AT URBANA-CHAMPAIGN
Urbana, Illinois

Students with LD Served by Program	116	ADD/ADHD Services	✓
Staff	5 full-time, 1 part-time	Summer Preparation Program	n/a
LD Program or Service Fee	n/a	Alternative Test Arrangements	✓
LD Program Began	1988	LD Student Organization	✓

Division of Rehabilitation-Education Services (DRES) began offering services in 1988. The program serves approximately 116 undergraduate students. Faculty consists of 5 full-time staff members and 1 part-time staff member. Services are provided by remediation/learning specialists, diagnostic specialists, graduate assistants/students, LD specialists, and licensed clinical psychologist.

Policies Students with LD may take up to 18 credit hours per semester; 12 credit hours per semester are required to maintain full-time status; 6 credit hours per semester are required to be eligible for financial aid. LD services are also available to graduate students.

Special preparation or orientation Optional orientation held individually by special arrangement.

Diagnostic testing Available for auditory processing, motor skills, spelling, neuropsychological, spoken language, intelligence, personality, learning strategies, reading, written language, visual processing, and math.

Basic skills remediation Available in auditory processing, study skills, reading, time management, social skills, visual processing, learning strategies, spelling, written language, math, and spoken language. Offered one-on-one by graduate assistants/students and LD specialists.

Counseling and advisement Career counseling, individual counseling, small-group counseling, and support groups are available.

Auxiliary aids and services *Aids:* personal computers, personal spelling/word-use assistants (e.g., Franklin Speller), scan and read programs (e.g., Kurzweil), screen-enlarging programs, screen readers, speech recognition programs (e.g., Dragon). *Services and accommodations:* advocates, priority registration, alternative test arrangements, readers, note-takers, and scribes.

Student organization There is a student organization for students with LD.

ADD/ADHD Students with ADD/ADHD are eligible for the same services available to students with LD, as well as distraction-free testing environments, personal coach or mentors, and support groups for ADD/ADHD.

Application *Required:* high school transcript, participation in extracurricular activities, ACT or SAT I (extended-time or untimed test accepted), personal statement, letter(s) of recommendation, and separate application to your LD program or unit. Upon application, documentation of need for special services should be sent only to your LD program or unit. Upon acceptance, documentation of need for special services should be sent only to your LD program or unit. *Application deadline (institutional):* 1/2 for fall and 11/1 for spring. *Application deadline (LD program):* rolling/continuous for fall and rolling/continuous for spring.

LD program contact Dr. Kimberly Collins, Clinical Psychologist, Division of Rehabilitation-Education Services, 1207 South Oak Street, Champaign, IL 61820. *Phone:* 217-265-0775. *Fax:* 217-333-0248. *E-mail:* kdcollins@uiuc.edu.

Application contact Tammy Bouseman, Assistant Director of Admissions, University of Illinois at Urbana-Champaign, 10 Henry Administration Building, Urbana, IL 61820-5711. *Phone:* 217-333-0302. *E-mail:* admssion@uiuc.edu. *Web address:* http://www.uiuc.edu/.

UNIVERSITY OF LOUISIANA AT LAFAYETTE
Lafayette, Louisiana

Students with LD Served by Program	200	ADD/ADHD Services	✓
Staff	1 full-time, 9 part-time	Summer Preparation Program	n/a
LD Program or Service Fee	n/a	Alternative Test Arrangements	✓
LD Program Began	1972	LD Student Organization	✓

Services for Students with Disabilities began offering services in 1972. The program serves approximately 200 undergraduate students. Faculty consists of 1 full-time and 9 part-time staff members. Services are provided by academic advisers, counselors, graduate assistants/students, and trained peer tutors.

Policies 12 credit hours per semester are required to maintain full-time status. LD services are also available to graduate students.

Diagnostic testing Available for spelling, intelligence, reading, written language, and math.

Basic skills remediation Available in study skills, time management, and learning strategies. Offered one-on-one by coordinator.

Subject-area tutoring Available in some subjects. Offered one-on-one and in small groups by computer-based instruction and trained peer tutors.

Special courses Available in college survival skills. All courses are offered for credit; all enter into overall grade point average.

Counseling and advisement Career counseling and individual counseling are available. Academic advisement by a staff member affiliated with the program is available.

Auxiliary aids and services *Aids:* calculators, personal spelling/word-use assistants (e.g., Franklin Speller), scan and read programs (e.g., Kurzweil), screen-enlarging programs, screen readers, speech recognition programs (e.g., Dragon), tape recorders, taped textbooks. *Services and accommodations:* advocates, priority registration, alternative test arrangements, readers, note-takers, and scribes.

Student organization There is a student organization for students with LD.

ADD/ADHD Students with ADD/ADHD are eligible for the same services available to students with LD, as well as distraction-free testing environments and personal coach or mentors.

Application *Required:* high school transcript, ACT or SAT I (extended-time tests accepted), and separate application to your LD program or unit. Upon application, documentation of need for special services should be sent only to your LD program or unit. Upon acceptance, documentation of need for special services should be sent only to your LD program or unit. *Application deadline (institutional):* rolling/continuous for fall. *Application deadline (LD program):* rolling/continuous for fall.

University of Louisiana at Lafayette (continued)

LD program contact Page Salley, Coordinator of Services for Students with Disabilities, Junior Division, PO Drawer 41650, Lafayette, LA 70504-1650. *Phone:* 337-482-5252. *Fax:* 337-482-6195. *E-mail:* pts3792@louisiana.edu.

Application contact University of Louisiana at Lafayette, 104 University Circle, Lafayette, LA 70504. *Web address:* http://www. louisiana.edu/.

UNIVERSITY OF LOUISIANA AT MONROE
Monroe, Louisiana

Students with LD Served by Program	220	ADD/ADHD Services	✓
Staff	2 full-time	Summer Preparation Program	n/a
LD Program or Service Fee	n/a	Alternative Test Arrangements	n/a
LD Program Began	1982	LD Student Organization	n/a

The University of Louisiana at Monroe Counseling Center began offering services in 1982. The program serves approximately 220 undergraduate students. Faculty consists of 2 full-time staff members. Services are provided by academic advisers, counselors, diagnostic specialists, special education teachers, and LD specialists.

Policies LD services are also available to graduate students.

Counseling and advisement Career counseling, individual counseling, small-group counseling, and support groups are available. Academic advisement by a staff member affiliated with the program is available.

Auxiliary aids and services *Aids:* screen-enlarging programs, screen readers, taped textbooks.

ADD/ADHD Students with ADD/ADHD are eligible for the same services available to students with LD, as well as distraction-free study areas and distraction-free testing environments.

Application *Required:* high school transcript and ACT or SAT I (untimed tests accepted). Upon acceptance, documentation of need for special services should be sent only to your LD program or unit. *Application deadline (institutional):* 7/23 for fall and 12/11 for spring.

LD program contact Karen Foster, Director, 700 University Avenue, ULM Counseling Center, Monroe, LA 71209. *Phone:* 318-342-5220. *Fax:* 318-342-5228. *E-mail:* ccfoster@alpha.ulm.edu.

Application contact University of Louisiana at Monroe, Monroe, LA 71209-0001. *E-mail:* reweems@alpha.nlu.edu. *Web address:* http://www.nlu.edu/.

UNIVERSITY OF LOUISVILLE
Louisville, Kentucky

Students with LD Served by Program	300	ADD/ADHD Services	✓
Staff	1 full-time, 1 part-time	Summer Preparation Program	n/a
LD Program or Service Fee	n/a	Alternative Test Arrangements	✓
LD Program Began	1982	LD Student Organization	n/a

Disability Resource Center began offering services in 1982. The program serves approximately 300 undergraduate students. Faculty consists of 1 full-time and 1 part-time staff member. Services are provided by counselors.

Policies Students with LD may take up to 17 credit hours per semester; 12 credit hours per semester are required to maintain full-time status; 6 credit hours per semester are required to be eligible for financial aid. LD services are also available to graduate students.

Auxiliary aids and services *Aids:* scan and read programs (e.g., Kurzweil), screen-enlarging programs, screen readers, speech recognition programs (e.g., Dragon), tape recorders, taped textbooks. *Services and accommodations:* advocates, priority registration, alternative test arrangements, readers, note-takers, and scribes.

ADD/ADHD Students with ADD/ADHD are eligible for the same services available to students with LD, as well as distraction-free study areas and distraction-free testing environments.

Application *Required:* high school transcript, ACT (extended-time test accepted), and psychoeducational report. *Recommended:* documentation of high school services (e.g., Individualized Education Program [IEP] or 504 plan). Upon application, documentation of need for special services should be sent only to your LD program or unit. Upon acceptance, documentation of need for special services should be sent only to your LD program or unit. *Application deadline (institutional):* 8/1 for fall and 12/1 for spring. *Application deadline (LD program):* 8/1 for fall and 12/1 for spring.

LD program contact Kathy Pendleton, Coordinator, Services for Students with Learning Disabilities, Disability Resource Center, Robbins Hall, Louisville, KY 40292. *Phone:* 502-852-6938. *Fax:* 502-852-0924. *E-mail:* kjpend01@gwise.louisville.edu.

Application contact University of Louisville, 2301 South Third Street, Louisville, KY 40292-0001. *E-mail:* admitme@ulkyvm.louisville.edu. *Web address:* http://www.louisville.edu/.

UNIVERSITY OF MAINE AT MACHIAS
Machias, Maine

Students with LD Served by Program	60	ADD/ADHD Services	✓
Staff	1 full-time	Summer Preparation Program	n/a
LD Program or Service Fee	n/a	Alternative Test Arrangements	✓
LD Program Began	1994	LD Student Organization	n/a

Student Resources Coordinator began offering services in 1994. The program serves approximately 60 undergraduate students. Faculty consists of 1 full-time staff member. Services are provided by remediation/learning specialists, trained peer tutors, and student resources coordinator.

Policies The college has written policies regarding course substitutions.

Diagnostic testing Available for personality, study skills, learning strategies, and learning styles.

Basic skills remediation Available in reading, written language, and math. Offered in class-size groups by regular education teachers.

Subject-area tutoring Available in some subjects. Offered one-on-one by trained peer tutors.

Counseling and advisement Career counseling and individual counseling are available.

Auxiliary aids and services *Aids:* personal computers, scan and read programs (e.g., Kurzweil), speech recognition programs (e.g., Dragon), tape recorders, taped textbooks. *Services and accommodations:* advocates, alternative test arrangements, readers, note-takers, and scribes.

ADD/ADHD Students with ADD/ADHD are eligible for the same services available to students with LD, as well as distraction-free testing environments and personal coach or mentors.

Application *Required:* high school transcript, SAT I (extended-time or untimed test accepted), and personal statement. *Recommended:* participation in extracurricular activities, interview, letter(s) of recommendation, and psychoeducational report (2 years old or less). Upon application, documentation of need for special services should be sent only to admissions. Upon acceptance, documentation of need for special services should be sent only to your LD program or unit. *Application deadline (institutional):* rolling/continuous for fall and rolling/continuous for spring. *Application deadline (LD program):* rolling/continuous for fall and rolling/continuous for spring.

LD program contact Jean Schild, Student Resources Coordinator, Torrey Hall, 9 O'Brien Avenue, Machias, ME 04654. *Phone:* 207-255-1228. *Fax:* 207-255-4864.

Application contact University of Maine at Machias, 9 O'Brien Avenue, Machias, ME 04654-1321. *E-mail:* admissions@acad.umm.maine.edu. *Web address:* http://www.umm.maine.edu/.

UNIVERSITY OF MARY
Bismarck, North Dakota

Students with LD Served by Program	25	ADD/ADHD Services	✓
Staff	1 part-time	Summer Preparation Program	n/a
LD Program or Service Fee	n/a	Alternative Test Arrangements	✓
LD Program Began	1980	LD Student Organization	n/a

Learning Skills Center began offering services in 1980. The program serves approximately 25 undergraduate students. Faculty consists of 1 part-time staff member. Services are provided by LD specialists.

Policies 12 credits per semester are required to maintain full-time status and to be eligible for financial aid.

Diagnostic testing Available for study skills and learning styles.

Basic skills remediation Available in study skills, computer skills, time management, learning strategies, written language, and math. Offered one-on-one by computer-based instruction and LD specialists.

Subject-area tutoring Available in most subjects. Offered one-on-one by computer-based instruction, professional tutors, graduate assistants/students, trained peer tutors, and LD specialists.

Auxiliary aids and services *Aids:* calculators, personal spelling/word-use assistants (e.g., Franklin Speller), speech recognition programs (e.g., Dragon), tape recorders, taped textbooks. *Services and accommodations:* alternative test arrangements, readers, note-takers, and scribes.

ADD/ADHD Students with ADD/ADHD are eligible for the same services available to students with LD, as well as distraction-free testing environments.

Application *Required:* high school transcript, ACT (extended-time test accepted), personal statement, and letter(s) of recommendation. Upon application, documentation of need for special services should be sent only to your LD program or unit. Upon acceptance, documentation of need for special services should be sent only to your LD program or unit. *Application deadline (institutional):* rolling/continuous for fall and rolling/continuous for spring. *Application deadline (LD program):* rolling/continuous for fall and rolling/continuous for spring.

LD program contact Susan Miller, Director, Learning Skills Center, 7500 University Drive, Bismarck, ND 58504. *Phone:* 701-255-7500 Ext. 510. *Fax:* 701-255-7687. *E-mail:* smiller@umary.edu.

Application contact University of Mary, 7500 University Drive, Bismarck, ND 58504-9652. *Web address:* http://www.umary.edu/.

UNIVERSITY OF MARYLAND, BALTIMORE COUNTY
Baltimore, Maryland

Students with LD Served by Program	89	ADD/ADHD Services	✓
Staff	5 full-time, 2 part-time	Summer Preparation Program	n/a
LD Program or Service Fee	n/a	Alternative Test Arrangements	✓
LD Program Began	1984	LD Student Organization	n/a

Student Support Services Department began offering services in 1984. The program serves approximately 89 undergraduate students. Faculty consists of 5 full-time and 2 part-time staff members. Services are provided by counselors, remediation/learning specialists, graduate assistants/students, and trained peer tutors.

Policies The college has written policies regarding course substitutions. Students with LD may take up to 18 credit hours per semester; 12 credit hours per semester are required to maintain full-time status and to be eligible for financial aid. LD services are also available to graduate students.

Basic skills remediation Available in study skills, reading, time management, learning strategies, written language, math, and spoken language. Offered one-on-one and in small groups by academic skills specialists.

Subject-area tutoring Available in most subjects. Offered one-on-one and in small groups by trained peer tutors and academic skills specialist.

Counseling and advisement Career counseling and individual counseling are available.

Auxiliary aids and services *Aids:* calculators, personal computers, screen-enlarging programs, speech recognition programs (e.g., Dragon), tape recorders. *Services and accommodations:* advocates, alternative test arrangements, readers, note-takers, and scribes.

ADD/ADHD Students with ADD/ADHD are eligible for the same services available to students with LD, as well as distraction-free testing environments.

Application *Required:* high school transcript, ACT or SAT I (extended-time or untimed test accepted), interview, and separate application to your LD program or unit. Upon acceptance, documentation of need for special services should be sent only to your LD program or unit. *Application deadline (institutional):* 3/15 for fall and 12/1 for spring. *Application deadline (LD program):* rolling/continuous for fall and rolling/continuous for spring.

LD program contact Cynthia M. Hill, Director, Student Support Services, 211 Mathematics/Psychology Building, 1000 Hilltop Circle, Baltimore, MD 21250. *Phone:* 410-455-2459. *Fax:* 410-455-1028. *E-mail:* chill@umbc.edu.

Application contact University of Maryland, Baltimore County, 1000 Hilltop Circle, Baltimore, MD 21250-5398. *E-mail:* admissions@umbc.edu. *Web address:* http://www.umbc.edu/.

UNIVERSITY OF MARYLAND, COLLEGE PARK
College Park, Maryland

Students with LD Served by Program	550	ADD/ADHD Services	✓
Staff	2 full-time, 2 part-time	Summer Preparation Program	n/a
LD Program or Service Fee	n/a	Alternative Test Arrangements	✓
LD Program Began	1981	LD Student Organization	n/a

University of Maryland, College Park (continued)

Disability Support Services/Learning Assistance Service began offering services in 1981. The program serves approximately 550 undergraduate students. Faculty consists of 2 full-time and 2 part-time staff members. Services are provided by graduate assistants/students and LD specialists.

Policies The college has written policies regarding course substitutions. Students with LD may take up to 18 credit hours per semester. LD services are also available to graduate students.

Special preparation or orientation Optional orientation held before classes begin and individually by special arrangement.

Diagnostic testing Available for spelling, handwriting, spoken language, study skills, learning strategies, reading, written language, learning styles, and math.

Basic skills remediation Available in study skills, reading, time management, learning strategies, spelling, written language, math, and organization. Offered one-on-one by computer-based instruction, graduate assistants/students, and professional tutors.

Special courses Available in study skills, test taking, time management, and learning strategies. Most courses are offered for credit; all enter into overall grade point average.

Counseling and advisement Career counseling, individual counseling, small-group counseling, and support groups are available.

Auxiliary aids and services *Aids:* scan and read programs (e.g., Kurzweil), screen-enlarging programs, screen readers, speech recognition programs (e.g., Dragon), tape recorders, taped textbooks. *Services and accommodations:* advocates, priority registration, alternative test arrangements, readers, note-takers, and scribes.

ADD/ADHD Students with ADD/ADHD are eligible for the same services available to students with LD, as well as distraction-free testing environments, medication management, personal coach or mentors, and support groups for ADD/ADHD.

Application *Required:* high school transcript, participation in extracurricular activities, and SAT I (extended-time or untimed test accepted). *Recommended:* ACT (extended-time or untimed test accepted), personal statement, letter(s) of recommendation, psychoeducational report (5 years old or less), and documentation of high school services (e.g., Individualized Education Program [IEP] or 504 plan). Upon application, documentation of need for special services should be sent to both admissions and your LD program or unit. Upon acceptance, documentation of need for special services should be sent only to your LD program or unit.

LD program contact Peggy Hayeslip, Learning Disabilities Coordinator, 2111 Shoemaker, College Park, MD 20742. *Phone:* 301-314-9969. *Fax:* 301-314-9206. *E-mail:* mh185@umail.umd.edu.

Application contact University of Maryland, College Park, College Park, MD 20742. *Web address:* http://www.maryland.edu/.

UNIVERSITY OF MARYLAND EASTERN SHORE
Princess Anne, Maryland

Students with LD Served by Program	85	ADD/ADHD Services	✓
Staff	1 full-time, 2 part-time	Summer Preparation Program	n/a
LD Program or Service Fee	n/a	Alternative Test Arrangements	✓
LD Program Began	1980	LD Student Organization	✓

Office of Disabled Student Services began offering services in 1980. The program serves approximately 85 undergraduate students. Faculty consists of 1 full-time and 2 part-time staff members. Services are provided by academic advisers, remediation/learning specialists, and trained peer tutors.

Policies Students with LD may take up to 12 credit hours per semester; 9 credit hours per semester are required to maintain full-time status and to be eligible for financial aid.

Diagnostic testing Available for study skills, reading, written language, and math.

Basic skills remediation Available in study skills, reading, time management, written language, and math. Offered one-on-one by trained professional staff.

Subject-area tutoring Available in all subjects. Offered one-on-one by trained peer tutors.

Counseling and advisement Career counseling, individual counseling, and support groups are available. Academic advisement by a staff member affiliated with the program is available.

Auxiliary aids and services *Aids:* calculators, tape recorders, taped textbooks. *Services and accommodations:* alternative test arrangements and note-takers.

Student organization There is a student organization for students with LD.

ADD/ADHD Students with ADD/ADHD are eligible for the same services available to students with LD, as well as distraction-free testing environments.

Application *Required:* high school transcript, ACT or SAT I (untimed tests accepted), personal statement, and letter(s) of recommendation. *Recommended:* psychoeducational report (2 years old or less) and documentation of high school services (e.g., Individualized Education Program [IEP] or 504 plan). Upon application, documentation of need for special services should be sent to both admissions and your LD program or unit. Upon acceptance, documentation of need for special services should be sent to both admissions and your LD program or unit. *Application deadline (institutional):* 7/15 for fall and 12/1 for spring. *Application deadline (LD program):* 7/15 for fall and 12/1 for spring.

LD program contact Dr. Diann R. Showell, Director, Backbone Road, Princess Anne, MD 21853. *Phone:* 410-651-6456. *Fax:* 410-651-6322. *E-mail:* drshowell@mail.umes.edu.

Application contact University of Maryland Eastern Shore, Princess Anne, MD 21853-1299. *Web address:* http://www.umes.umd.edu/.

UNIVERSITY OF MASSACHUSETTS DARTMOUTH
North Dartmouth, Massachusetts

Students with LD Served by Program	200	ADD/ADHD Services	✓
Staff	1 full-time, 2 part-time	Summer Preparation Program	n/a
LD Program or Service Fee	n/a	Alternative Test Arrangements	✓
LD Program Began	1979	LD Student Organization	✓

Disabled Student Services began offering services in 1979. The program serves approximately 200 undergraduate students. Faculty consists of 1 full-time and 2 part-time staff members. Services are provided by academic advisers, counselors, graduate assistants/students, and trained peer tutors.

Policies The college has written policies regarding course substitutions and substitution and waivers of requirements for admission and graduation. Students with LD may take up to 12 credit hours per semester; 12 credit hours per semester are required to maintain full-time status and to be eligible for financial aid. LD services are also available to graduate students.

Subject-area tutoring Available in some subjects. Offered one-on-one and in small groups by graduate assistants/students and trained peer tutors.

Counseling and advisement Individual counseling and support groups are available. Academic advisement by a staff member affiliated with the program is available.

Auxiliary aids and services *Aids:* taped textbooks. *Services and accommodations:* advocates, priority registration, alternative test arrangements, readers, note-takers, and scribes.

Student organization There is a student organization for students with LD.

ADD/ADHD Students with ADD/ADHD are eligible for the same services available to students with LD, as well as distraction-free testing environments, personal coach or mentors, and support groups for ADD/ADHD.

Application *Required:* high school transcript, ACT or SAT I (extended-time tests accepted), and personal statement. *Recommended:* participation in extracurricular activities, interview, letter(s) of recommendation, psychoeducational report (3 years old or less), and documentation of high school services (e.g., Individualized Education Program [IEP] or 504 plan). Upon application, documentation of need for special services should be sent only to your LD program or unit. Upon acceptance, documentation of need for special services should be sent only to your LD program or unit.

LD program contact Carole J. Johnson, Director, 285 Old Westport Road, North Dartmouth, MA 02747-2300. *Phone:* 508-997-8711. *Fax:* 508-999-9257. *E-mail:* cjohnson@umassd.edu.

Application contact University of Massachusetts Dartmouth, 285 Old Westport Road, North Dartmouth, MA 02747-2300. *E-mail:* athompson@umassd.edu. *Web address:* http://www.umassd.edu/.

UNIVERSITY OF MIAMI
Coral Gables, Florida

Students with LD Served by Program	230	ADD/ADHD Services	✓
Staff	2 full-time	Summer Preparation Program	n/a
LD Program or Service Fee	n/a	Alternative Test Arrangements	✓
LD Program Began	1992	LD Student Organization	n/a

Office of Disability Services began offering services in 1992. The program serves approximately 230 undergraduate students. Faculty consists of 2 full-time staff members. Services are provided by graduate assistants/students and trained peer tutors.

Policies LD services are also available to graduate students.

Subject-area tutoring Available in some subjects. Offered one-on-one and in small groups by graduate assistants/students and trained peer tutors.

Counseling and advisement Career counseling and individual counseling are available.

Auxiliary aids and services *Services and accommodations:* alternative test arrangements, readers, and note-takers.

ADD/ADHD Students with ADD/ADHD are eligible for the same services available to students with LD, as well as distraction-free testing environments and support groups for ADD/ADHD.

Application *Required:* high school transcript, ACT or SAT I, personal statement, and letter(s) of recommendation. Upon application, documentation of need for special services should be sent only to your LD program or unit. Upon acceptance, documentation of need for special services should be sent only to your LD program or unit. *Application deadline (institutional):* 3/1 for fall and 11/15 for spring. *Application deadline (LD program):* rolling/continuous for fall and rolling/continuous for spring.

LD program contact Judith Antinarella, Director, Office of Disability Services, PO Box 248106, Coral Gables, FL 33124-6990. *Phone:* 305-284-2374. *Fax:* 305-284-1999.

Application contact Edward M. Gillis, Associate Dean of Enrollments, University of Miami, PO Box 248025, Coral Gables, FL 33124. *Phone:* 305-284-4323. *E-mail:* admission@admiss.msmail.miami.edu. *Web address:* http://www.miami.edu/.

UNIVERSITY OF MICHIGAN-DEARBORN
Dearborn, Michigan

Students with LD Served by Program	30	ADD/ADHD Services	✓
Staff	3 part-time	Summer Preparation Program	n/a
LD Program or Service Fee	n/a	Alternative Test Arrangements	✓
LD Program Began	1992	LD Student Organization	n/a

Disability Resource Services began offering services in 1992. The program serves approximately 30 undergraduate students. Faculty consists of 3 part-time staff members. Services are provided by counselors and assistant to coordinator, proctor.

Policies The college has written policies regarding course substitutions. Students with LD may take up to 18 credit hours per semester; 12 credit hours per semester are required to maintain full-time status; 6 credit hours per semester are required to be eligible for financial aid. LD services are also available to graduate students.

Special preparation or orientation Required orientation held after classes begin.

Subject-area tutoring Available in some subjects. Offered one-on-one, in small groups, and class-size groups by students.

Special courses Available in time management and stress management. No courses are offered for credit; none enter into overall grade point average.

Counseling and advisement Career counseling, individual counseling, and small-group counseling are available.

Auxiliary aids and services *Aids:* scan and read programs (e.g., Kurzweil), screen-enlarging programs, screen readers, taped textbooks. *Services and accommodations:* advocates, priority registration, alternative test arrangements, readers, note-takers, and scribes.

ADD/ADHD Students with ADD/ADHD are eligible for the same services available to students with LD, as well as distraction-free testing environments.

Application *Required:* high school transcript and ACT or SAT I (extended-time or untimed test accepted). *Recommended:* participation in extracurricular activities, personal statement, and letter(s) of recommendation. Upon acceptance, documentation of need for special services should be sent only to your LD program or unit. *Application deadline (institutional):* rolling/continuous for fall and rolling/continuous for spring. *Application deadline (LD program):* rolling/continuous for fall and rolling/continuous for spring.

LD program contact Dennis Underwood, Coordinator, 4901 Evergreen, Dearborn, MI 48128-1491. *Phone:* 313-593-5430. *Fax:* 313-593-3263. *E-mail:* dennisu@umd.umich.edu.

Application contact University of Michigan-Dearborn, 4901 Evergreen Road, Dearborn, MI 48128-1491. *E-mail:* umdgoblu@umd.umich.edu. *Web address:* http://www.umd.umich.edu/.

UNIVERSITY OF MICHIGAN-FLINT

Flint, Michigan

Students with LD Served by Program	100	ADD/ADHD Services	✓
Staff	1 full-time	Summer Preparation Program	n/a
LD Program or Service Fee	n/a	Alternative Test Arrangements	✓
LD Program Began	1990	LD Student Organization	n/a

Accessibility Services began offering services in 1990. The program serves approximately 100 undergraduate students. Faculty consists of 1 full-time staff member. Services are provided by academic advisers, counselors, and trained peer tutors.

Policies Students with LD may take up to 18 credit hours per semester; 12 credit hours per semester are required to maintain full-time status; 6 credit hours per semester are required to be eligible for financial aid. LD services are also available to graduate students.

Counseling and advisement Academic advisement by a staff member affiliated with the program is available.

Auxiliary aids and services *Aids:* scan and read programs (e.g., Kurzweil), screen-enlarging programs, screen readers, speech recognition programs (e.g., Dragon), taped textbooks, e-text materials and textbooks. *Services and accommodations:* advocates, priority registration, alternative test arrangements, readers, note-takers, and scribes.

ADD/ADHD Students with ADD/ADHD are eligible for the same services available to students with LD, as well as distraction-free testing environments.

Application *Required:* high school transcript and ACT or SAT I (extended-time or untimed test accepted). *Recommended:* participation in extracurricular activities and personal statement. Upon application, documentation of need for special services should be sent only to your LD program or unit. Upon acceptance, documentation of need for special services should be sent only to your LD program or unit. *Application deadline (institutional):* rolling/continuous for fall and rolling/continuous for spring. *Application deadline (LD program):* rolling/continuous for fall and rolling/continuous for spring.

LD program contact Trudie N. Hines, Accessibility Services Coordinator, 264 University Center, Flint, MI 48502-1950. *Phone:* 810-762-3456. *Fax:* 810-762-3498. *E-mail:* tnhines@umich.edu.

Application contact University of Michigan-Flint, 303 Kearsley Street, Flint, MI 48502-1950. *E-mail:* davis_m@pavilion.flint.umich.edu. *Web address:* http://www.flint.umich.edu/.

UNIVERSITY OF MINNESOTA, CROOKSTON

Crookston, Minnesota

Students with LD Served by Program	30	ADD/ADHD Services	✓
Staff	n/a	Summer Preparation Program	n/a
LD Program or Service Fee	n/a	Alternative Test Arrangements	✓
LD Program Began	1975	LD Student Organization	n/a

Office for Students with Disabilities began offering services in 1975. The program serves approximately 30 undergraduate students. Services are provided by regular education teachers, counselors, remediation/learning specialists, trained peer tutors, and professional tutors.

Policies The college has written policies regarding course substitutions.

Basic skills remediation Available in study skills, reading, and math. Offered in small groups by computer-based instruction and regular education teachers.

Subject-area tutoring Available in most subjects. Offered one-on-one and in small groups by computer-based instruction, professional tutors, and trained peer tutors.

Counseling and advisement Career counseling, individual counseling, and personal counseling are available.

Auxiliary aids and services *Aids:* calculators, personal computers, screen-enlarging programs, speech recognition programs (e.g., Dragon), tape recorders, taped textbooks. *Services and accommodations:* advocates, alternative test arrangements, readers, note-takers, and scribes.

ADD/ADHD Students with ADD/ADHD are eligible for the same services available to students with LD, as well as distraction-free study areas, distraction-free testing environments, extended time for exams, tutoring and scheduling assistance.

Application *Required:* high school transcript and ACT (extended-time or untimed test accepted). Upon acceptance, documentation of need for special services should be sent to both admissions and your LD program or unit. *Application deadline (institutional):* rolling/continuous for fall and rolling/continuous for spring.

LD program contact Laurie Wilson, Coordinator, 270 Owen Hall, 2900 University Avenue, Crookston, MN 56716. *Phone:* 218-281-8587. *Fax:* 218-281-8584. *E-mail:* lwilson@mail.crk.umn.edu.

Application contact University of Minnesota, Crookston, 2900 University Avenue, Crookston, MN 56716-5001. *E-mail:* info@crk.umn.edu. *Web address:* http://www.crk.umn.edu/.

UNIVERSITY OF MINNESOTA, MORRIS

Morris, Minnesota

Students with LD Served by Program	18	ADD/ADHD Services	✓
Staff	3 part-time	Summer Preparation Program	n/a
LD Program or Service Fee	n/a	Alternative Test Arrangements	✓
LD Program Began	1990	LD Student Organization	n/a

Disability Services began offering services in 1990. The program serves approximately 18 undergraduate students. Faculty consists of 3 part-time staff members. Services are provided by regular education teachers, remediation/learning specialists, and trained peer tutors.

Basic skills remediation Available in study skills, reading, time management, learning strategies, written language, and math. Offered one-on-one by computer-based instruction and regular education teachers.

Subject-area tutoring Available in most subjects. Offered one-on-one and in small groups by computer-based instruction and trained peer tutors.

Auxiliary aids and services *Aids:* calculators, personal computers, personal spelling/word-use assistants (e.g., Franklin Speller), scan and read programs (e.g., Kurzweil), screen-enlarging programs, screen readers, speech recognition programs (e.g., Dragon), tape recorders, taped textbooks. *Services and accommodations:* advocates, priority registration, alternative test arrangements, note-takers, and scribes.

ADD/ADHD Students with ADD/ADHD are eligible for the same services available to students with LD, as well as distraction-free testing environments and personal coach or mentors.

Application *Required:* high school transcript, ACT or SAT I (extended-time or untimed test accepted), and personal statement. *Recommended:* participation in extracurricular activities, ACT (extended-time or untimed test accepted), letter(s) of recommendation, and documentation of high school services (e.g., Individualized Education Program [IEP] or 504 plan). Upon application, documentation of need for special services should be sent only to your LD program or unit. Upon acceptance, documentation of need for special services should be sent only to your LD program or unit. *Application deadline (institutional):* rolling/continuous for fall and rolling/continuous for spring. *Application deadline (LD program):* rolling/continuous for fall and rolling/continuous for spring.

LD program contact Ferolyn Angell, Director, Academic Assistance/Disability Services, 600 East 4th, Morris, MN 56267. *Phone:* 320-589-6163. *Fax:* 320-589-6168. *E-mail:* angfa@mrs. umn.edu.

Application contact University of Minnesota, Morris, 600 East 4th Street, Morris, MN 56267-2134. *E-mail:* admissions@caa.mrs. umn.edu. *Web address:* http://www.mrs.umn.edu/.

UNIVERSITY OF MISSOURI-KANSAS CITY

Kansas City, Missouri

Students with LD Served by Program	40	ADD/ADHD Services	✓
Staff	1 full-time, 6 part-time	Summer Preparation Program	n/a
LD Program or Service Fee	n/a	Alternative Test Arrangements	✓
LD Program Began	1973	LD Student Organization	n/a

Office of Services for Students with Disabilities began offering services in 1973. The program serves approximately 40 undergraduate students. Faculty consists of 1 full-time and 6 part-time staff members. Services are provided by coordinator.

Policies Students with LD may take up to 17 credit hours per semester; 12 credit hours per semester are required to maintain full-time status; 6 credit hours per semester are required to be eligible for financial aid. LD services are also available to graduate students.

Subject-area tutoring Available in some subjects. Offered one-on-one and in small groups by trained peer tutors.

Counseling and advisement Career counseling and individual counseling are available.

Auxiliary aids and services *Aids:* screen-enlarging programs, screen readers, speech recognition programs (e.g., Dragon), tape recorders, taped textbooks. *Services and accommodations:* advocates, priority registration, alternative test arrangements, readers, and note-takers.

ADD/ADHD Students with ADD/ADHD are eligible for the same services available to students with LD, as well as reduced distraction testing area.

Application *Required:* high school transcript and ACT or SAT I (extended-time or untimed test accepted). Upon acceptance, documentation of need for special services should be sent only to your LD program or unit. *Application deadline (institutional):* rolling/continuous for fall and rolling/continuous for spring. *Application deadline (LD program):* rolling/continuous for fall and rolling/continuous for spring.

LD program contact Scott Laurent, Coordinator, 350 AC, 5100 Rockhill Road, Kansas City, MO 64110. *Phone:* 816-235-5696. *Fax:* 816-235-6537. *E-mail:* disability@umkc.edu.

Application contact University of Missouri-Kansas City, 5100 Rockhill Road, Kansas City, MO 64110-2499. *E-mail:* admit@ umkc.edu. *Web address:* http://www.umkc.edu/.

THE UNIVERSITY OF MONTANA-MISSOULA

Missoula, Montana

Students with LD Served by Program	300	ADD/ADHD Services	✓
Staff	8 full-time, 3 part-time	Summer Preparation Program	✓
LD Program or Service Fee	n/a	Alternative Test Arrangements	✓
LD Program Began	1978	LD Student Organization	✓

Disability Student Services (DSS) began offering services in 1978. The program serves approximately 300 undergraduate students. Faculty consists of 8 full-time and 3 part-time staff members. Services are provided by DSS coordinators.

Policies The college has written policies regarding course substitutions and substitution and waivers of requirements for admission and graduation. 12 credit hours per semester are required to maintain full-time status and to be eligible for financial aid. LD services are also available to graduate students.

Special preparation or orientation Optional summer program offered prior to entering college. Optional orientation held before registration, during registration, before classes begin, after classes begin, during summer prior to enrollment, and individually by special arrangement.

Counseling and advisement Career counseling, individual counseling, and counseling on first-class citizenship, personal responsibility, and individual rights are available.

Auxiliary aids and services *Aids:* calculators, personal computers, personal spelling/word-use assistants (e.g., Franklin Speller), scan and read programs (e.g., Kurzweil), screen-enlarging programs, screen readers, speech recognition programs (e.g., Dragon), tape recorders, taped textbooks. *Services and accommodations:* advocates, priority registration, alternative test arrangements, readers, note-takers, and scribes.

Student organization There is a student organization for students with LD.

ADD/ADHD Students with ADD/ADHD are eligible for the same services available to students with LD, as well as distraction-free study areas and distraction-free testing environments.

Application *Required:* high school transcript, ACT or SAT I (extended-time tests accepted), separate application to your LD program or unit, and psychoeducational report (5 years old or less). Upon application, documentation of need for special services should be sent to both admissions and your LD program or unit. Upon acceptance, documentation of need for special services should be sent only to your LD program or unit. *Application deadline (institutional):* rolling/continuous for fall and rolling/continuous for spring. *Application deadline (LD program):* rolling/continuous for fall and rolling/continuous for spring.

LD program contact Jim Marks, Director, 032 Corbin Hall, Missoula, MT 59812. *Phone:* 406-243-2243. *Fax:* 406-243-5330. *E-mail:* marks@selway.umt.edu.

Application contact Office of New Student Services, The University of Montana-Missoula, Missoula, MT 59812-0002. *Phone:* 406-243-6266. *E-mail:* admiss@selway.umt.edu. *Web address:* http://www.umt.edu/.

UNIVERSITY OF NEBRASKA-LINCOLN
Lincoln, Nebraska

Students with LD Served by Program	200	ADD/ADHD Services	✓
Staff	2 full-time, 4 part-time	Summer Preparation Program	n/a
LD Program or Service Fee	n/a	Alternative Test Arrangements	✓
LD Program Began	1985	LD Student Organization	n/a

Services for Students with Disabilities began offering services in 1985. The program serves approximately 200 undergraduate students. Faculty consists of 2 full-time and 4 part-time staff members. Services are provided by graduate assistants/students.

Policies The college has written policies regarding course substitutions and substitution and waivers of requirements for admission and graduation. Students with LD may take up to 18 credit hours per semester; 12 credit hours per semester are required to maintain full-time status; 6 credit hours per semester are required to be eligible for financial aid. LD services are also available to graduate students.

Counseling and advisement Support groups is available.

Auxiliary aids and services *Aids:* scan and read programs (e.g., Kurzweil), screen-enlarging programs, screen readers, tape recorders, taped textbooks. *Services and accommodations:* advocates, priority registration, alternative test arrangements, readers, note-takers, and scribes.

ADD/ADHD Students with ADD/ADHD are eligible for the same services available to students with LD, as well as distraction-free testing environments and support groups for ADD/ADHD.

Application *Required:* high school transcript, ACT (extended-time or untimed test accepted), separate application to your LD program or unit, psychoeducational report (3 years old or less), and documentation of high school services (e.g., Individualized Education Program [IEP] or 504 plan). Upon application, documentation of need for special services should be sent only to your LD program or unit. Upon acceptance, documentation of need for special services should be sent only to your LD program or unit. *Application deadline (LD program):* rolling/continuous for fall and rolling/continuous for spring.

LD program contact Director, Services for Students with Disabilities, 132 Administration, Lincoln, NE 68588-0401. *Phone:* 402-472-3787. *Fax:* 402-472-0080.

Application contact University of Nebraska-Lincoln, 14th and R Streets, Lincoln, NE 68588-0417. *E-mail:* lschmidt@unl.edu. *Web address:* http://www.unl.edu/.

UNIVERSITY OF NEW HAMPSHIRE
Durham, New Hampshire

Students with LD Served by Program	200	ADD/ADHD Services	✓
Staff	2 full-time	Summer Preparation Program	n/a
LD Program or Service Fee	n/a	Alternative Test Arrangements	✓
LD Program Began	n/a	LD Student Organization	✓

ACCESS serves approximately 200 undergraduate students. Faculty consists of 2 full-time staff members. Services are provided by counselors and diagnostic specialists.

Policies The college has written policies regarding course substitutions. Students with LD may take up to 20 credit hours per semester; 12 credit hours per semester are required to main-tain full-time status; 8 credit hours per semester are required to be eligible for financial aid. LD services are also available to graduate students.

Subject-area tutoring Available in some subjects. Offered one-on-one and in small groups by trained peer tutors.

Counseling and advisement Career counseling, individual counseling, small-group counseling, and support groups are available.

Auxiliary aids and services *Aids:* scan and read programs (e.g., Kurzweil), screen-enlarging programs, screen readers, speech recognition programs (e.g., Dragon), tape recorders, taped textbooks, texts on computer disk. *Services and accommodations:* advocates, priority registration, alternative test arrangements, readers, note-takers, and scribes.

Student organization There is a student organization for students with LD.

ADD/ADHD Students with ADD/ADHD are eligible for the same services available to students with LD, as well as distraction-free testing environments.

Application *Required:* high school transcript, SAT I (extended-time or untimed test accepted), documentation of high school services (e.g., Individualized Education Program [IEP] or 504 plan), and diagnostic tests. *Recommended:* participation in extracurricular activities, interview, and personal statement. Upon application, documentation of need for special services should be sent only to admissions. Upon acceptance, documentation of need for special services should be sent only to your LD program or unit. *Application deadline (institutional):* 2/1 for fall and 11/1 for spring.

LD program contact Margo W. Druschel, Director, ACCESS, Memorial Union Building, Room 118, Durham, NH 03824. *Phone:* 603-862-2648. *Fax:* 603-862-4043. *E-mail:* mwd@cisunix.unh.edu.

Application contact University of New Hampshire, Grant House, 4 Garrison Avenue, Durham, NH 03824. *E-mail:* admissions@unh.edu. *Web address:* http://www.unh.edu/.

UNIVERSITY OF NEW HAMPSHIRE AT MANCHESTER
Manchester, New Hampshire

Students with LD Served by Program	25	ADD/ADHD Services	✓
Staff	2 part-time	Summer Preparation Program	n/a
LD Program or Service Fee	n/a	Alternative Test Arrangements	✓
LD Program Began	1988	LD Student Organization	n/a

Academic Counseling Office and Learning Center began offering services in 1988. The program serves approximately 25 undergraduate students. Faculty consists of 2 part-time staff members. Services are provided by academic advisers, trained peer tutors, and professional tutors.

Policies The college has written policies regarding course substitutions. Students with LD may take up to 20 semester hours per semester; 12 semester hours per semester are required to maintain full-time status; 8 semester hours per semester are required to be eligible for financial aid. LD services are also available to graduate students.

Counseling and advisement Academic advisement by a staff member affiliated with the program is available.

Auxiliary aids and services *Aids:* calculators, scan and read programs (e.g., Kurzweil), screen-enlarging programs, screen readers, speech recognition programs (e.g., Dragon), tape recorders, taped textbooks. *Services and accommodations:* priority registration, alternative test arrangements, readers, note-takers, and scribes.

ADD/ADHD Students with ADD/ADHD are eligible for the same services available to students with LD, as well as distraction-free testing environments.

Application *Required:* high school transcript, ACT or SAT I (untimed tests accepted), personal statement, and letter(s) of recommendation. *Recommended:* participation in extracurricular activities and interview. Upon application, documentation of need for special services should be sent only to admissions. Upon acceptance, documentation of need for special services should be sent only to your LD program or unit. *Application deadline (institutional):* 11/1 for fall and 6/1 for spring.

LD program contact Carol A. Swiech, Academic Counselor, 220 Hackett Hill Road, Manchester, NH 03102. *Phone:* 603-629-4170. *Fax:* 603-629-4170. *E-mail:* c_swiech@cisvms.unh.edu.

Application contact Susan Miller, Admissions Secretary, University of New Hampshire at Manchester, 220 Hackett Hill Road, Manchester, NH 03102-8597. *Phone:* 603-629-4150. *E-mail:* unhm@unh.edu. *Web address:* http://www.unh.edu/unhm/.

UNIVERSITY OF NEW HAVEN
West Haven, Connecticut

Students with LD Served by Program	118	ADD/ADHD Services	✓
Staff	1 full-time	Summer Preparation Program	n/a
LD Program or Service Fee	n/a	Alternative Test Arrangements	✓
LD Program Began	1994	LD Student Organization	n/a

Disability Services and Resources began offering services in 1994. The program serves approximately 118 undergraduate students. Faculty consists of 1 full-time staff member. Services are provided by regular education teachers, counselors, diagnostic specialists, and graduate assistants/students.

Policies 12 credit hours per semester are required to maintain full-time status; 9 credit hours per semester are required to be eligible for financial aid. LD services are also available to graduate students.

Special preparation or orientation Required orientation held individually by special arrangement.

Basic skills remediation Available in study skills, computer skills, time management, social skills, learning strategies, written language, and math. Offered one-on-one by graduate assistants/students.

Subject-area tutoring Available in some subjects. Offered one-on-one by graduate assistants/students.

Counseling and advisement Career counseling and individual counseling are available.

Auxiliary aids and services *Aids:* calculators, personal computers, scan and read programs (e.g., Kurzweil), screen-enlarging programs, screen readers, speech recognition programs (e.g., Dragon), tape recorders, taped textbooks. *Services and accommodations:* advocates, alternative test arrangements, readers, note-takers, scribes, and proofreaders, transcriptionists.

ADD/ADHD Students with ADD/ADHD are eligible for the same services available to students with LD, as well as distraction-free study areas, distraction-free testing environments and personal coach or mentors.

Application *Required:* high school transcript and ACT or SAT I (extended-time or untimed test accepted). *Recommended:* interview, personal statement, and letter(s) of recommendation. Upon application, documentation of need for special services should be sent only to your LD program or unit. Upon acceptance, documentation of need for special services should be sent only to your LD program or unit. *Application deadline (institutional):*

rolling/continuous for fall and rolling/continuous for spring. *Application deadline (LD program):* rolling/continuous for fall and rolling/continuous for spring.

LD program contact Linda Copney-Okeke, Director, Disability Services and Resources, 300 Orange Avenue, New Haven, CT 06516. *Phone:* 203-932-7331. *Fax:* 203-931-6082. *E-mail:* lcokeke@newhaven.edu.

Application contact University of New Haven, 300 Orange Avenue, West Haven, CT 06516-1916. *Web address:* http://www.newhaven.edu/.

UNIVERSITY OF NEW MEXICO
Albuquerque, New Mexico

Students with LD Served by Program	260	ADD/ADHD Services	✓
Staff	3 full-time	Summer Preparation Program	n/a
LD Program or Service Fee	n/a	Alternative Test Arrangements	✓
LD Program Began	1990	LD Student Organization	n/a

Learning Support Services (LSS) began offering services in 1990. The program serves approximately 260 undergraduate students. Faculty consists of 3 full-time staff members. Services are provided by diagnostic specialists, LD specialists, and trained peer tutors.

Policies The college has written policies regarding substitution and waivers of requirements for admission. Students with LD may take up to 18 credit hours per semester; 9 credit hours per semester are required to maintain full-time status and to be eligible for financial aid. LD services are also available to graduate students.

Special preparation or orientation Optional orientation held individually by special arrangement.

Diagnostic testing Available for auditory processing, spelling, spoken language, intelligence, study skills, learning strategies, reading, written language, learning styles, visual processing, and math.

Basic skills remediation Available in study skills, reading, time management, learning strategies, spelling, and written language. Offered one-on-one by LD specialists.

Subject-area tutoring Available in most subjects. Offered one-on-one, in small groups, and class-size groups by trained peer tutors and LD specialists.

Special courses Available in introduction to learning strategies. All courses are offered for credit; all enter into overall grade point average.

Auxiliary aids and services *Aids:* scan and read programs (e.g., Kurzweil), screen-enlarging programs, speech recognition programs (e.g., Dragon), tape recorders, taped textbooks. *Services and accommodations:* advocates, alternative test arrangements, note-takers, and scribes.

ADD/ADHD Students with ADD/ADHD are eligible for the same services available to students with LD

Application *Required:* high school transcript, ACT or SAT I (extended-time or untimed test accepted), personal statement, letter(s) of recommendation, psychoeducational report (5 years old or less), and letter of approval. Upon application, documentation of need for special services should be sent only to admissions. Upon acceptance, documentation of need for special services should be sent only to your LD program or unit. *Application deadline (institutional):* 6/15 for fall and 11/15 for spring. *Application deadline (LD program):* rolling/continuous for fall and rolling/continuous for spring.

LD program contact Patricia Useem, Manager, Zimmerman Library Room 220, Albuquerque, NM 87131-1466. *Phone:* 505-277-8291. *Fax:* 505-277-7224. *E-mail:* lssunm@unm.edu.

University of New Mexico (continued)

Application contact Robin Ryan, Associate Director of Admissions, University of New Mexico, Albuquerque, NM 87131-2039. *Phone:* 505-277-2446. *E-mail:* apply@unm.edu. *Web address:* http://www.unm.edu/.

UNIVERSITY OF NEW ORLEANS
New Orleans, Louisiana

Students with LD Served by Program	55	ADD/ADHD Services	✓
Staff	2 full-time	Summer Preparation Program	n/a
LD Program or Service Fee	n/a	Alternative Test Arrangements	✓
LD Program Began	n/a	LD Student Organization	n/a

The Office of Disability Services (ODS) serves approximately 55 undergraduate students. Faculty consists of 2 full-time staff members. Services are provided by regular education teachers, graduate assistants/students, and professional office staff.

Policies The college has written policies regarding course substitutions. Students with LD may take up to 18 credit hours per semester; 12 credit hours per semester are required to maintain full-time status; 6 credit hours per semester are required to be eligible for financial aid. LD services are also available to graduate students.

Auxiliary aids and services *Aids:* calculators, personal computers, personal spelling/word-use assistants (e.g., Franklin Speller), scan and read programs (e.g., Kurzweil), screen-enlarging programs, screen readers, speech recognition programs (e.g., Dragon), tape recorders, taped textbooks. *Services and accommodations:* alternative test arrangements, readers, note-takers, and scribes.

ADD/ADHD Students with ADD/ADHD are eligible for the same services available to students with LD, as well as distraction-free testing environments.

Application *Required:* high school transcript and ACT or SAT I (extended-time or untimed test accepted). Upon acceptance, documentation of need for special services should be sent only to your LD program or unit. *Application deadline (institutional):* 7/1 for fall and 12/15 for spring. *Application deadline (LD program):* rolling/continuous for fall and rolling/continuous for spring.

LD program contact Amy A. King, Coordinator, Office of Disability Services, UC Room 260, New Orleans, LA 70148. *Phone:* 504-280-7284. *Fax:* 504-280-3975.

Application contact University of New Orleans, Lake Front, New Orleans, LA 70148. *E-mail:* ehs@uno.edu. *Web address:* http://www.uno.edu/.

UNIVERSITY OF NORTH ALABAMA
Florence, Alabama

Students with LD Served by Program	150	ADD/ADHD Services	✓
Staff	3 full-time, 2 part-time	Summer Preparation Program	n/a
LD Program or Service Fee	n/a	Alternative Test Arrangements	✓
LD Program Began	1990	LD Student Organization	n/a

Developmental Services began offering services in 1990. The program serves approximately 150 undergraduate students. Faculty consists of 3 full-time and 2 part-time staff members. Services are provided by academic advisers, counselors, remediation/learning specialists, graduate assistants/students, and trained peer tutors.

Policies The college has written policies regarding course substitutions. Students with LD may take up to 18 credit hours per semester; 12 credit hours per semester are required to maintain full-time status and to be eligible for financial aid. LD services are also available to graduate students.

Basic skills remediation Available in study skills, computer skills, reading, time management, handwriting, social skills, spelling, math, and memory/concentration, test preparation. Offered one-on-one, in small groups, and class-size groups by computer-based instruction, graduate assistants/students, trained peer tutors, and Developmental Services staff.

Subject-area tutoring Available in most subjects. Offered one-on-one, in small groups, and class-size groups by computer-based instruction, professional tutors, graduate assistants/students, and trained peer tutors.

Special courses Available in career planning, study skills, college survival skills, practical computer skills, test taking, reading, time management, learning strategies, math, stress management, and written composition skills. No courses are offered for credit.

Counseling and advisement Career counseling, individual counseling, and support groups are available. Academic advisement by a staff member affiliated with the program is available.

Auxiliary aids and services *Aids:* calculators, personal computers, personal spelling/word-use assistants (e.g., Franklin Speller), scan and read programs (e.g., Kurzweil), screen-enlarging programs, screen readers, speech recognition programs (e.g., Dragon), tape recorders, taped textbooks. *Services and accommodations:* advocates, priority registration, alternative test arrangements, readers, note-takers, and scribes.

ADD/ADHD Students with ADD/ADHD are eligible for the same services available to students with LD, as well as distraction-free testing environments.

Application *Required:* high school transcript, ACT or SAT I (extended-time tests accepted), separate application to your LD program or unit, and documentation of high school services (e.g., Individualized Education Program [IEP] or 504 plan). Upon application, documentation of need for special services should be sent only to your LD program or unit. Upon acceptance, documentation of need for special services should be sent only to your LD program or unit.

LD program contact Jennifer Adams, Associate Director of Student Life, Box 5008, Florence, AL 35630. *Phone:* 256-765-4248. *Fax:* 256-765-4904. *E-mail:* jadams@unanov.una.edu.

Application contact Kim O. Mauldin, Director of Admissions, University of North Alabama, University Station, Florence, AL 35632-0001. *Phone:* 256-765-4680. *E-mail:* admis1@unanov.una.edu. *Web address:* http://www.una.edu/.

THE UNIVERSITY OF NORTH CAROLINA AT GREENSBORO
Greensboro, North Carolina

Students with LD Served by Program	200	ADD/ADHD Services	✓
Staff	5 full-time, 2 part-time	Summer Preparation Program	n/a
LD Program or Service Fee	n/a	Alternative Test Arrangements	✓
LD Program Began	1985	LD Student Organization	✓

Disability Services began offering services in 1985. The program serves approximately 200 undergraduate students. Faculty consists of 5 full-time and 2 part-time staff members. Services are provided by counselors, graduate assistants/students, LD specialists, and trained peer tutors.

Policies The college has written policies regarding course substitutions. Students with LD may take up to 18 credit hours per semester; 12 credit hours per semester are required to maintain full-time status; 6 credit hours per semester are required to be eligible for financial aid. LD services are also available to graduate students.

Subject-area tutoring Available in some subjects. Offered one-on-one and in small groups by trained peer tutors and LD specialists.

Counseling and advisement Career counseling and individual counseling are available.

Auxiliary aids and services *Aids:* personal spelling/word-use assistants (e.g., Franklin Speller), scan and read programs (e.g., Kurzweil), screen-enlarging programs, screen readers, speech recognition programs (e.g., Dragon), tape recorders, taped textbooks. *Services and accommodations:* advocates, priority registration, alternative test arrangements, readers, note-takers, and scribes.

Student organization There is a student organization for students with LD.

ADD/ADHD Students with ADD/ADHD are eligible for the same services available to students with LD, as well as distraction-free testing environments and support groups for ADD/ADHD.

Application *Required:* high school transcript and ACT or SAT I (extended-time or untimed test accepted). *Recommended:* participation in extracurricular activities and interview. Upon acceptance, documentation of need for special services should be sent only to your LD program or unit. *Application deadline (institutional):* rolling/continuous for fall and rolling/continuous for spring.

LD program contact Dr. Patricia Bailey, Director, 157 EUC, Greensboro, NC 27402-6170. *Phone:* 336-334-5440. *Fax:* 336-334-4412. *E-mail:* plbailey@uncg.edu.

Application contact The University of North Carolina at Greensboro, 1000 Spring Garden Street, Greensboro, NC 27412-5001. *E-mail:* undergrad_admissions@uncg.edu. *Web address:* http://www.uncg.edu/.

UNIVERSITY OF NORTHERN IOWA
Cedar Falls, Iowa

Students with LD Served by Program	75	ADD/ADHD Services	✓
Staff	1 full-time, 7 part-time	Summer Preparation Program	n/a
LD Program or Service Fee	n/a	Alternative Test Arrangements	✓
LD Program Began	1986	LD Student Organization	n/a

Office of Disability Services began offering services in 1986. The program serves approximately 75 undergraduate students. Faculty consists of 1 full-time and 7 part-time staff members. Services are provided by academic advisers, regular education teachers, counselors, remediation/learning specialists, graduate assistants/students, and trained peer tutors.

Policies The college has written policies regarding course substitutions. Students with LD may take up to 18 credit hours per semester; 12 credit hours per semester are required to maintain full-time status; 6 credit hours per semester are required to be eligible for financial aid. LD services are also available to graduate students.

Basic skills remediation Available in study skills, reading, time management, learning strategies, written language, and math. Offered one-on-one by graduate assistants/students, teacher trainees, professional tutors, trained peer tutors, and reading/learning strategies coordinator.

Subject-area tutoring Available in some subjects. Offered one-on-one by graduate assistants/students and trained peer tutors.

Counseling and advisement Career counseling, individual counseling, small-group counseling, and support groups are available. Academic advisement by a staff member affiliated with the program is available.

Auxiliary aids and services *Aids:* tape recorders, taped textbooks. *Services and accommodations:* priority registration, alternative test arrangements, readers, note-takers, and scribes.

ADD/ADHD Students with ADD/ADHD are eligible for the same services available to students with LD, as well as distraction-free study areas and distraction-free testing environments.

Application *Required:* high school transcript, ACT (extended-time or untimed test accepted), separate application to your LD program or unit, and psychoeducational report (3 years old or less). *Recommended:* documentation of high school services (e.g., Individualized Education Program [IEP] or 504 plan). Upon acceptance, documentation of need for special services should be sent only to your LD program or unit. *Application deadline (LD program):* rolling/continuous for fall and rolling/continuous for spring.

LD program contact Jane Slykhuis, Coordinator, Office of Disability Services, 213 Student Services Center, Cedar Falls, IA 50614-0385. *Phone:* 319-273-2676. *Fax:* 319-273-6884. *E-mail:* jane.slykhuis@uni.edu.

Application contact University of Northern Iowa, 1222 West 27th Street, Cedar Falls, IA 50614. *E-mail:* admissions@uni.edu. *Web address:* http://www.uni.edu/.

UNIVERSITY OF NOTRE DAME
Notre Dame, Indiana

Students with LD Served by Program	80	ADD/ADHD Services	✓
Staff	1 full-time	Summer Preparation Program	n/a
LD Program or Service Fee	n/a	Alternative Test Arrangements	✓
LD Program Began	1995	LD Student Organization	n/a

Office for Students with Disabilities began offering services in 1995. The program serves approximately 80 undergraduate students. Faculty consists of 1 full-time staff member. Services are provided by Program Coordinator.

Policies The college has written policies regarding course substitutions. Students with LD may take up to 21 credit hours per semester; 12 credit hours per semester are required to maintain full-time status and to be eligible for financial aid. LD services are also available to graduate students.

Auxiliary aids and services *Aids:* scan and read programs (e.g., Kurzweil), screen-enlarging programs, screen readers, tape recorders, taped textbooks. *Services and accommodations:* advocates, priority registration, alternative test arrangements, readers, note-takers, and scribes.

ADD/ADHD Students with ADD/ADHD are eligible for the same services available to students with LD, as well as distraction-free testing environments.

Application *Required:* high school transcript, ACT or SAT I (extended-time tests accepted), personal statement, and letter(s) of recommendation. *Recommended:* participation in extracurricular activities. Upon application, documentation of need for special services should be sent only to your LD program or unit. Upon acceptance, documentation of need for special services should be sent only to your LD program or unit. *Application deadline (institutional):* 1/1 for fall.

LD program contact Scott Howland, Program Coordinator, Office for Students with Disabilities, Notre Dame, IN 46556. *Phone:* 219-631-7141. *Fax:* 219-631-7939. *E-mail:* showland@nd.edu.

University of Notre Dame (continued)

Application contact University of Notre Dame, Notre Dame, IN 46556. *E-mail:* admissions.admissio.1@nd.edu. *Web address:* http://www.nd.edu/.

UNIVERSITY OF OREGON
Eugene, Oregon

Students with LD Served by Program	200	ADD/ADHD Services	✓
Staff	3 full-time, 2 part-time	Summer Preparation Program	n/a
LD Program or Service Fee	n/a	Alternative Test Arrangements	✓
LD Program Began	1985	LD Student Organization	n/a

Disability Services began offering services in 1985. The program serves approximately 200 undergraduate students. Faculty consists of 3 full-time and 2 part-time staff members. Services are provided by academic advisers and counselors.

Policies The college has written policies regarding course substitutions. Students with LD may take up to 21 credits per quarter; 12 credits per quarter are required to maintain full-time status and to be eligible for financial aid. LD services are also available to graduate students.

Special preparation or orientation Optional orientation held during summer prior to enrollment and individually by special arrangement.

Counseling and advisement Individual counseling is available. Academic advisement by a staff member affiliated with the program is available.

Auxiliary aids and services *Aids:* scan and read programs (e.g., Kurzweil), screen-enlarging programs, screen readers, speech recognition programs (e.g., Dragon), taped textbooks. *Services and accommodations:* priority registration, alternative test arrangements, readers, note-takers, and scribes.

ADD/ADHD Students with ADD/ADHD are eligible for the same services available to students with LD, as well as distraction-free testing environments.

Application *Required:* high school transcript, ACT or SAT I (extended-time or untimed test accepted), separate application to your LD program or unit, and psychoeducational report (3 years old or less). *Recommended:* participation in extracurricular activities, interview, personal statement, letter(s) of recommendation, and documentation of high school services (e.g., Individualized Education Program [IEP] or 504 plan). Upon application, documentation of need for special services should be sent only to your LD program or unit. Upon acceptance, documentation of need for special services should be sent only to your LD program or unit. *Application deadline (institutional):* 2/1 for fall and 1/18 for spring. *Application deadline (LD program):* rolling/continuous for fall and rolling/continuous for spring.

LD program contact Molly Sirois, Assistant Counselor for Students with Disabilities, Eugene, OR 97405. *Phone:* 541-346-3211. *Fax:* 541-346-6048. *E-mail:* disabsrv@darkwing.uoregon.edu.

Application contact University of Oregon, Eugene, OR 97403. *E-mail:* uoadmit@oregon.uoregon.edu. *Web address:* http://www.uoregon.edu/.

UNIVERSITY OF PITTSBURGH
Pittsburgh, Pennsylvania

Students with LD Served by Program	425	ADD/ADHD Services	✓
Staff	3 full-time, 2 part-time	Summer Preparation Program	n/a
LD Program or Service Fee	n/a	Alternative Test Arrangements	✓
LD Program Began	1995	LD Student Organization	n/a

Disability Resources and Services began offering services in 1995. The program serves approximately 425 undergraduate students. Faculty consists of 3 full-time and 2 part-time staff members. Services are provided by graduate assistants/students and LD specialists.

Policies 12 credit hours per term are required to maintain full-time status and to be eligible for financial aid. LD services are also available to graduate students.

Counseling and advisement Career counseling and individual counseling are available.

Auxiliary aids and services *Aids:* calculators, personal computers, scan and read programs (e.g., Kurzweil), screen-enlarging programs, screen readers, speech recognition programs (e.g., Dragon), tape recorders, taped textbooks. *Services and accommodations:* alternative test arrangements, readers, and scribes.

ADD/ADHD Students with ADD/ADHD are eligible for the same services available to students with LD, as well as distraction-free testing environments and personal coach or mentors.

Application *Required:* high school transcript, ACT or SAT I (extended-time or untimed test accepted), and application fee. *Recommended:* participation in extracurricular activities and personal statement. Upon application, documentation of need for special services should be sent only to your LD program or unit. Upon acceptance, documentation of need for special services should be sent only to your LD program or unit. *Application deadline (institutional):* rolling/continuous for fall and rolling/continuous for spring.

LD program contact Lynnett Van Slyke, Director, 216 William Pitt Union, Pittsburgh, PA 15260. *Phone:* 412-648-7890. *Fax:* 412-624-3346. *E-mail:* vanslyke+@pitt.edu.

Application contact University of Pittsburgh, Bruce Hall, Second Floor, Pittsburgh, PA 15260. *E-mail:* oafa@pitt.edu. *Web address:* http://www.pitt.edu/.

UNIVERSITY OF PITTSBURGH AT BRADFORD
Bradford, Pennsylvania

Students with LD Served by Program	15	ADD/ADHD Services	✓
Staff	2 full-time, 8 part-time	Summer Preparation Program	n/a
LD Program or Service Fee	n/a	Alternative Test Arrangements	✓
LD Program Began	1989	LD Student Organization	n/a

Academic Development Center began offering services in 1989. The program serves approximately 15 undergraduate students. Faculty consists of 2 full-time and 8 part-time staff members. Services are provided by remediation/learning specialists and trained peer tutors.

Policies Students with LD may take up to 18 credit hours per semester; 12 credit hours per semester are required to maintain full-time status and to be eligible for financial aid.

Subject-area tutoring Available in some subjects. Offered one-on-one and in small groups by trained peer tutors and Director, Academic Development Center.

Auxiliary aids and services *Services and accommodations:* priority registration and alternative test arrangements.

ADD/ADHD Students with ADD/ADHD are eligible for the same services available to students with LD, as well as distraction-free study areas and distraction-free testing environments.

Application *Required:* high school transcript and ACT or SAT I (extended-time or untimed test accepted). *Recommended:* psychoeducational report and documentation of high school services (e.g., Individualized Education Program [IEP] or 504 plan). Upon acceptance, documentation of need for special services should be sent only to your LD program or unit. *Application deadline (institutional):* rolling/continuous for fall and rolling/continuous for spring. *Application deadline (LD program):* rolling/continuous for fall and rolling/continuous for spring.

LD program contact Director, Academic Development Center, 300 Campus Drive, Bradford, PA 16701. *Phone:* 814-362-7533. *Fax:* 814-362-7684.

Application contact Janet Shade, Administrative Secretary, University of Pittsburgh at Bradford, 300 Campus Drive, Bradford, PA 16701-2812. *Phone:* 814-362-7555. *Web address:* http://www.pitt.edu/~bradford/.

UNIVERSITY OF REDLANDS
Redlands, California

Students with LD Served by Program	100	ADD/ADHD Services	✓
Staff	1 full-time	Summer Preparation Program	n/a
LD Program or Service Fee	n/a	Alternative Test Arrangements	✓
LD Program Began	1990	LD Student Organization	n/a

Academic Support Services began offering services in 1990. The program serves approximately 100 undergraduate students. Faculty consists of 1 full-time staff member. Services are provided by Director of Academic Support Services.

Policies Students with LD may take up to 19 credit hours per semester; 12 credit hours per semester are required to maintain full-time status and to be eligible for financial aid. LD services are also available to graduate students.

Fees *Diagnostic Testing Fee:* ranges from $500 to $800.

Special preparation or orientation Optional orientation held during registration and individually by special arrangement.

Diagnostic testing Available for auditory processing, neuropsychological, intelligence, written language, visual processing, and math.

Subject-area tutoring Available in all subjects. Offered one-on-one and in small groups by trained peer tutors.

Counseling and advisement Career counseling, individual counseling, and academic counseling are available.

Auxiliary aids and services *Services and accommodations:* advocates, alternative test arrangements, readers, and note-takers.

ADD/ADHD Students with ADD/ADHD are eligible for the same services available to students with LD, as well as distraction-free study areas, distraction-free testing environments and personal coach or mentors.

Application *Required:* high school transcript, ACT or SAT I (extended-time or untimed test accepted), personal statement, and letter(s) of recommendation. *Recommended:* participation in extracurricular activities and interview. Upon application, documentation of need for special services should be sent only to admissions. Upon acceptance, documentation of need for special services should be sent only to your LD program or unit. *Application deadline (institutional):* rolling/continuous for fall and rolling/continuous for spring. *Application deadline (LD program):* rolling/continuous for fall and rolling/continuous for spring.

LD program contact Judy Bowman, Director, Academic Support Services, PO Box 3080, Redlands, CA 92373-0999. *Phone:* 909-335-4079. *Fax:* 909-335-5297. *E-mail:* jbowman@uor.edu.

Application contact University of Redlands, PO Box 3080, Redlands, CA 92373-0999. *E-mail:* adkwolf@ultrix.uor.edu. *Web address:* http://www.redlands.edu/.

UNIVERSITY OF REGINA
Regina, Saskatchewan

Students with LD Served by Program	55	ADD/ADHD Services	✓
Staff	1 full-time	Summer Preparation Program	n/a
LD Program or Service Fee	n/a	Alternative Test Arrangements	✓
LD Program Began	n/a	LD Student Organization	n/a

Special Needs Services serves approximately 55 undergraduate students. Faculty consists of 1 full-time staff member. Services are provided by Coordinator, Special Needs Services.

Policies Students with LD may take up to 15 credit hours per semester; 12 credit hours per semester are required to maintain full-time status; 9 credit hours per semester are required to be eligible for financial aid. LD services are also available to graduate students.

Special preparation or orientation Optional orientation held individually by special arrangement.

Counseling and advisement Career counseling, individual counseling, small-group counseling, and support groups are available.

Auxiliary aids and services *Aids:* calculators, personal computers, personal spelling/word-use assistants (e.g., Franklin Speller), scan and read programs (e.g., Kurzweil), screen-enlarging programs, screen readers, speech recognition programs (e.g., Dragon), tape recorders. *Services and accommodations:* priority registration, alternative test arrangements, and note-takers.

ADD/ADHD Students with ADD/ADHD are eligible for the same services available to students with LD, as well as distraction-free study areas and distraction-free testing environments.

Application *Required:* high school transcript. *Recommended:* psychoeducational report (5 years old or less) and documentation of high school services (e.g., Individualized Education Program [IEP] or 504 plan). Upon application, documentation of need for special services should be sent only to your LD program or unit. Upon acceptance, documentation of need for special services should be sent only to your LD program or unit. *Application deadline (institutional):* 8/13 for fall and 3/31 for spring.

LD program contact Dianne Mader, Coordinator, Special Needs Services, Room 251.15, Dr. William Riddell Centre, Regina, SK S4S 0A2. *Phone:* 306-585-4631. *Fax:* 306-585-5172. *E-mail:* dianne.mader@uregina.ca.

Application contact Clarence Gray, Assistant Registrar/Admissions and Awards, University of Regina, Regina, SK S4S 0A2. *Phone:* 306-585-4591. *E-mail:* admissions.office@uregina.ca. *Web address:* http://www.uregina.ca/.

UNIVERSITY OF RHODE ISLAND
Kingston, Rhode Island

Students with LD Served by Program	320	ADD/ADHD Services	✓
Staff	2 full-time, 4 part-time	Summer Preparation Program	n/a
LD Program or Service Fee	n/a	Alternative Test Arrangements	✓
LD Program Began	1986	LD Student Organization	✓

Disability Services for Students began offering services in 1986. The program serves approximately 320 undergraduate students. Faculty consists of 2 full-time and 4 part-time staff members. Services are provided by academic advisers, counselors, diagnostic specialists, and graduate assistants/students.

Policies The college has written policies regarding course substitutions and substitution and waivers of requirements for admission and graduation. Students with LD may take up to 18 credit hours per semester; 12 credit hours per semester are required to maintain full-time status and to be eligible for financial aid. LD services are also available to graduate students.

Special preparation or orientation Optional orientation held before registration and during summer prior to enrollment.

Counseling and advisement Career counseling, individual counseling, small-group counseling, and support groups are available. Academic advisement by a staff member affiliated with the program is available.

Auxiliary aids and services *Aids:* calculators, personal computers, personal spelling/word-use assistants (e.g., Franklin Speller), scan and read programs (e.g., Kurzweil), screen-enlarging programs, screen readers, speech recognition programs (e.g., Dragon), tape recorders, taped textbooks. *Services and accommodations:* advocates, priority registration, alternative test arrangements, readers, note-takers, and scribes.

Student organization There is a student organization for students with LD.

ADD/ADHD Students with ADD/ADHD are eligible for the same services available to students with LD, as well as distraction-free study areas, distraction-free testing environments and support groups for ADD/ADHD.

Application *Required:* high school transcript, participation in extracurricular activities, ACT or SAT I (extended-time or untimed test accepted), personal statement, and letter(s) of recommendation. *Recommended:* interview and psychoeducational report (3 years old or less). Upon application, documentation of need for special services should be sent only to admissions. Upon acceptance, documentation of need for special services should be sent only to your LD program or unit.

LD program contact Pamela Rohland, Director, Disability Services for Students, Office of Student Life, 330 Memorial Union, Kingston, RI 02881. *Phone:* 401-874-2098. *Fax:* 401-874-5574.

Application contact Catherine Zeiser, Assistant Dean of Admissions, University of Rhode Island, Kingston, RI 02881. *Phone:* 401-874-7100. *E-mail:* uriadmit@riacc.uri.edu. *Web address:* http://www.uri.edu/.

UNIVERSITY OF ROCHESTER
Rochester, New York

Students with LD Served by Program	120	ADD/ADHD Services	✓
Staff	3 full-time, 1 part-time	Summer Preparation Program	n/a
LD Program or Service Fee	n/a	Alternative Test Arrangements	✓
LD Program Began	1990	LD Student Organization	✓

Learning Assistance Services began offering services in 1990. The program serves approximately 120 undergraduate students. Faculty consists of 3 full-time staff members and 1 part-time staff member. Services are provided by Disability Support Coordinator, Assistant Dean, Academic Support Coordinator, Writing Center Manager.

Policies LD services are also available to graduate students.

Special preparation or orientation Optional orientation held before registration, before classes begin, and during summer prior to enrollment.

Subject-area tutoring Available in most subjects. Offered one-on-one and in small groups by graduate assistants/students and trained peer tutors.

Special courses Available in study skills, test taking, time management, and learning strategies. All courses are offered for credit; all enter into overall grade point average.

Counseling and advisement Individual counseling and support groups are available.

Auxiliary aids and services *Aids:* personal computers, scan and read programs (e.g., Kurzweil), screen-enlarging programs, speech recognition programs (e.g., Dragon), tape recorders, taped textbooks. *Services and accommodations:* advocates, alternative test arrangements, readers, note-takers, and scribes.

Student organization There is a student organization for students with LD.

ADD/ADHD Students with ADD/ADHD are eligible for the same services available to students with LD, as well as distraction-free study areas, distraction-free testing environments, medication management, personal coach or mentors, and support groups for ADD/ADHD.

Application *Required:* high school transcript, ACT or SAT I (extended-time or untimed test accepted), personal statement, and letter(s) of recommendation. *Recommended:* participation in extracurricular activities, interview, and documentation of high school services (e.g., Individualized Education Program [IEP] or 504 plan). Upon application, documentation of need for special services should be sent to both admissions and your LD program or unit. Upon acceptance, documentation of need for special services should be sent to both admissions and your LD program or unit. *Application deadline (institutional):* 1/31 for fall and 12/1 for spring.

LD program contact Linda Jennings, Disability Support Coordinator, Learning Assistance Services, 107 Lattimore Hall, Rochester, NY 14627. *Phone:* 716-275-9049. *Fax:* 716-273-1116. *E-mail:* linj@mail.rochester.edu.

Application contact University of Rochester, Meliora Hall, Intercampus Drive, Rochester, NY 14627-0001. *E-mail:* admit@macmail.cc.rochester.edu. *Web address:* http://www.rochester.edu/.

THE UNIVERSITY OF SCRANTON
Scranton, Pennsylvania

Students with LD Served by Program	50	ADD/ADHD Services	✓
Staff	2 full-time	Summer Preparation Program	n/a
LD Program or Service Fee	n/a	Alternative Test Arrangements	n/a
LD Program Began	1990	LD Student Organization	✓

Learning Resources Center began offering services in 1990. The program serves approximately 50 undergraduate students. Faculty consists of 2 full-time staff members. Services are provided by staff at Learning Resources Center.

Policies LD services are also available to graduate students.

Special preparation or orientation Optional orientation held after classes begin.

Auxiliary aids and services *Aids:* scan and read programs (e.g., Kurzweil), screen-enlarging programs, speech recognition programs (e.g., Dragon), tape recorders, taped textbooks.
Student organization There is a student organization for students with LD.
ADD/ADHD Students with ADD/ADHD are eligible for the same services available to students with LD, as well as distraction-free testing environments.
Application *Required:* high school transcript, participation in extracurricular activities, ACT or SAT I (extended-time or untimed test accepted), interview, personal statement, letter(s) of recommendation, psychoeducational report (3 years old or less), and documentation of high school services (e.g., Individualized Education Program [IEP] or 504 plan). Upon application, documentation of need for special services should be sent to both admissions and your LD program or unit. Upon acceptance, documentation of need for special services should be sent to both admissions and your LD program or unit. *Application deadline (institutional):* rolling/continuous for fall and rolling/continuous for spring.
LD program contact Mary Ann McAndrew, Assistant Director, Learning Resources Center, Alumni Memorial Hall, Scranton, PA 18510. *Phone:* 510-941-4038. *Fax:* 510-941-7899. *E-mail:* mcandrewmi@uofs.edu.
Application contact The University of Scranton, Scranton, PA 18510. *E-mail:* admissions@uofs.edu. *Web address:* http://www.uofs.edu/.

UNIVERSITY OF SOUTH CAROLINA
Columbia, South Carolina

Students with LD Served by Program	300	ADD/ADHD Services	✓
Staff	2 full-time, 5 part-time	Summer Preparation Program	n/a
LD Program or Service Fee	n/a	Alternative Test Arrangements	✓
LD Program Began	1990	LD Student Organization	n/a

Office of Disability Services began offering services in 1990. The program serves approximately 300 undergraduate students. Faculty consists of 2 full-time and 5 part-time staff members. Services are provided by counselors and graduate assistants/students.
Policies The college has written policies regarding course substitutions. Students with LD may take up to 17 credit hours per semester; 9 credit hours per semester are required to maintain full-time status and to be eligible for financial aid. LD services are also available to graduate students.
Auxiliary aids and services *Aids:* scan and read programs (e.g., Kurzweil), screen-enlarging programs, screen readers, taped textbooks. *Services and accommodations:* priority registration, alternative test arrangements, readers, and note-takers.
ADD/ADHD Students with ADD/ADHD are eligible for the same services available to students with LD, as well as distraction-free study areas and distraction-free testing environments.
Application *Required:* high school transcript and ACT or SAT I (extended-time or untimed test accepted). Upon acceptance, documentation of need for special services should be sent only to your LD program or unit. *Application deadline (institutional):* rolling/continuous for fall and rolling/continuous for spring. *Application deadline (LD program):* rolling/continuous for fall and rolling/continuous for spring.
LD program contact Karen Pettus, Director, Disability Services, Room 106 LeConte, Columbia, SC 29208. *Phone:* 803-777-6742. *Fax:* 803-777-6741. *E-mail:* kpettus@gwm.sc.edu.

Application contact University of South Carolina, Columbia, SC 29208. *E-mail:* admissions-ugrad@scarolina.edu. *Web address:* http://www.sc.edu/.

UNIVERSITY OF SOUTH CAROLINA SPARTANBURG
Spartanburg, South Carolina

Students with LD Served by Program	150	ADD/ADHD Services	✓
Staff	1 full-time, 1 part-time	Summer Preparation Program	n/a
LD Program or Service Fee	n/a	Alternative Test Arrangements	✓
LD Program Began	1992	LD Student Organization	n/a

Office of Disability Services began offering services in 1992. The program serves approximately 150 undergraduate students. Faculty consists of 1 full-time and 1 part-time staff member. Services are provided by regular education teachers, counselors, remediation/learning specialists, LD specialists, and trained peer tutors.
Policies The college has written policies regarding course substitutions and grade forgiveness. Students with LD may take up to 18 credit hours per semester; 12 credit hours per semester are required to maintain full-time status; 6 credit hours per semester are required to be eligible for financial aid.
Subject-area tutoring Available in all subjects. Offered one-on-one by trained peer tutors.
Counseling and advisement Career counseling and individual counseling are available.
Auxiliary aids and services *Aids:* taped textbooks. *Services and accommodations:* advocates, priority registration, alternative test arrangements, readers, note-takers, and scribes.
ADD/ADHD Students with ADD/ADHD are eligible for the same services available to students with LD, as well as distraction-free study areas and distraction-free testing environments.
Application *Required:* high school transcript, ACT or SAT I (extended-time or untimed test accepted), separate application to your LD program or unit, psychoeducational report (3 years old or less), and documentation of high school services (e.g., Individualized Education Program [IEP] or 504 plan). *Recommended:* participation in extracurricular activities, interview, personal statement, and letter(s) of recommendation. Upon acceptance, documentation of need for special services should be sent only to your LD program or unit. *Application deadline (institutional):* 8/23 for fall and 1/10 for spring. *Application deadline (LD program):* 8/23 for fall and 1/10 for spring.
LD program contact Stephanie G. Boyd, Assistant Director of Student Development, 800 University Way, Campus Life Center, Room 230, Spartanburg, SC 29303. *Phone:* 864-503-5123. *Fax:* 864-503-5100. *E-mail:* sboyd@gw.uscs.edu.
Application contact University of South Carolina Spartanburg, 800 University Way, Spartanburg, SC 29303-4999. *Web address:* http://www.uscs.edu/.

UNIVERSITY OF SOUTHERN CALIFORNIA
Los Angeles, California

Students with LD Served by Program	300	ADD/ADHD Services	✓
Staff	3 full-time, 25 part-time	Summer Preparation Program	n/a
LD Program or Service Fee	n/a	Alternative Test Arrangements	✓
LD Program Began	1984	LD Student Organization	n/a

University of Southern California (continued)

Disability Services and Programs (DSP) began offering services in 1984. The program serves approximately 300 undergraduate students. Faculty consists of 3 full-time and 25 part-time staff members. Services are provided by academic advisers, counselors, graduate assistants/students, LD specialists, and faculty.

Policies The college has written policies regarding course substitutions, grade forgiveness, and substitution and waivers of requirements for admission. 12 semester units per semester are required to maintain full-time status and to be eligible for financial aid. LD services are also available to graduate students.

Subject-area tutoring Available in some subjects. Offered one-on-one and in small groups by computer-based instruction, graduate assistants/students, and trained peer tutors.

Counseling and advisement Academic advisement by a staff member affiliated with the program is available.

Auxiliary aids and services *Aids:* scan and read programs (e.g., Kurzweil), screen-enlarging programs, screen readers, speech recognition programs (e.g., Dragon), tape recorders, taped textbooks. *Services and accommodations:* advocates, alternative test arrangements, readers, note-takers, and scribes.

ADD/ADHD Students with ADD/ADHD are eligible for the same services available to students with LD, as well as distraction-free testing environments, personal coach or mentors, and support groups for ADD/ADHD.

Application *Required:* high school transcript, ACT or SAT I (extended-time or untimed test accepted), and personal statement. *Recommended:* participation in extracurricular activities, letter(s) of recommendation, psychoeducational report, and documentation of high school services (e.g., Individualized Education Program [IEP] or 504 plan). Upon application, documentation of need for special services should be sent only to admissions. *Application deadline (institutional):* 1/10 for fall and 9/15 for spring. *Application deadline (LD program):* 1/10 for fall and 9/15 for spring.

LD program contact Dr. Janet Eddy, Director, Disability Services and Programs, STU 301, Los Angeles, CA 90089-0896. *Phone:* 213-740-0776. *Fax:* 213-740-8216. *E-mail:* jeddy@usc.edu.

Application contact University of Southern California, University Park Campus, Los Angeles, CA 90089-0911. *Web address:* http://www.usc.edu/.

UNIVERSITY OF SOUTHERN INDIANA
Evansville, Indiana

Students with LD Served by Program	73	ADD/ADHD Services	✓
Staff	3 part-time	Summer Preparation Program	n/a
LD Program or Service Fee	n/a	Alternative Test Arrangements	✓
LD Program Began	1987	LD Student Organization	✓

University of Southern Indiana Counseling Center began offering services in 1987. The program serves approximately 73 undergraduate students. Faculty consists of 3 part-time staff members. Services are provided by counselors and undergraduate student workers.

Policies The college has written policies regarding grade forgiveness. Students with LD may take up to 18 credit hours per semester; 12 credit hours per semester are required to maintain full-time status; 6 credit hours per semester are required to be eligible for financial aid. LD services are also available to graduate students.

Special preparation or orientation Required orientation held before registration, before classes begin, during summer prior to enrollment, and individually by special arrangement.

Diagnostic testing Available for study skills, reading, written language, and math.

Basic skills remediation Available in study skills, reading, written language, and math. Offered one-on-one and in class-size groups by computer-based instruction and regular education teachers.

Subject-area tutoring Available in some subjects. Offered one-on-one and in small groups by computer-based instruction and trained peer tutors.

Special courses Available in career planning, study skills, college survival skills, reading, math, and written composition skills. No courses are offered for credit; none enter into overall grade point average.

Counseling and advisement Career counseling, individual counseling, small-group counseling, support groups, and community referral are available.

Auxiliary aids and services *Aids:* scan and read programs (e.g., Kurzweil), screen-enlarging programs, screen readers, speech recognition programs (e.g., Dragon), taped textbooks, note taker supplies. *Services and accommodations:* advocates, priority registration, alternative test arrangements, readers, note-takers, scribes, and tutor referral.

Student organization There is a student organization for students with LD.

ADD/ADHD Students with ADD/ADHD are eligible for the same services available to students with LD, as well as distraction-free testing environments and medication management.

Application *Required:* high school transcript, ACT or SAT I (extended-time or untimed test accepted), separate application to your LD program or unit, and psychoeducational report (5 years old or less). *Recommended:* participation in extracurricular activities, interview, and documentation of high school services (e.g., Individualized Education Program [IEP] or 504 plan). Upon application, documentation of need for special services should be sent only to your LD program or unit. Upon acceptance, documentation of need for special services should be sent only to your LD program or unit. *Application deadline (institutional):* rolling/continuous for fall and rolling/continuous for spring. *Application deadline (LD program):* rolling/continuous for fall and rolling/continuous for spring.

LD program contact Leslie M. Swanson, Assistant Director of Counseling, USI Counseling Center OC 1022, 8600 University Boulevard, Evansville, IN 47712. *Phone:* 812-464-1867. *Fax:* 812-464-1960. *E-mail:* lswanson@usi.edu.

Application contact University of Southern Indiana, 8600 University Boulevard, Evansville, IN 47712-3590. *Web address:* http://www.usi.edu/.

UNIVERSITY OF SOUTHERN MISSISSIPPI
Hattiesburg, Mississippi

Students with LD Served by Program	40	ADD/ADHD Services	✓
Staff	4 full-time, 4 part-time	Summer Preparation Program	n/a
LD Program or Service Fee	n/a	Alternative Test Arrangements	✓
LD Program Began	n/a	LD Student Organization	n/a

Office for Disability Accommodations (ODA) serves approximately 40 undergraduate students. Faculty consists of 4 full-time and 4 part-time staff members. Services are provided by academic advisers, counselors, graduate assistants/students, and LD specialists.

Policies Students with LD may take up to 19 credit hours per semester; 12 credit hours per semester are required to maintain full-time status and to be eligible for financial aid. LD services are also available to graduate students.

Special courses Available in career planning, study skills, and stress management. No courses are offered for credit; none enter into overall grade point average.

Counseling and advisement Academic advisement by a staff member affiliated with the program is available.

Auxiliary aids and services *Aids:* screen-enlarging programs, screen readers, speech recognition programs (e.g., Dragon), tape recorders, taped textbooks. *Services and accommodations:* alternative test arrangements and note-takers.

ADD/ADHD Students with ADD/ADHD are eligible for the same services available to students with LD, as well as distraction-free study areas and distraction-free testing environments.

Application *Required:* high school transcript, ACT or SAT I (extended-time or untimed test accepted), and completion of college prep courses. Upon application, documentation of need for special services should be sent only to your LD program or unit. Upon acceptance, documentation of need for special services should be sent only to your LD program or unit. *Application deadline (LD program):* rolling/continuous for fall and rolling/continuous for spring.

LD program contact Dr. Valerie DeCoux, Coordinator, Office for Disability Accommodations, Box 8586, Hattiesburg, MS 39406. *Phone:* 601-266-5024. *Fax:* 601-266-6035.

Application contact University of Southern Mississippi, 2701 Hardy Street, Hattiesburg, MS 39406. *Web address:* http://www.usm.edu/.

THE UNIVERSITY OF TENNESSEE KNOXVILLE
Knoxville, Tennessee

Students with LD Served by Program	360	ADD/ADHD Services	✓
Staff	8 full-time, 1 part-time	Summer Preparation Program	n/a
LD Program or Service Fee	n/a	Alternative Test Arrangements	✓
LD Program Began	1978	LD Student Organization	n/a

Disability Services began offering services in 1978. The program serves approximately 360 undergraduate students. Faculty consists of 8 full-time staff members and 1 part-time staff member. Services are provided by LD specialists and career services specialist, staff interpreters.

Policies Students with LD may take up to 15 credit hours per semester; 12 credit hours per semester are required to maintain full-time status and to be eligible for financial aid. LD services are also available to graduate students.

Special preparation or orientation Optional orientation held before classes begin.

Subject-area tutoring Available in most subjects. Offered in small groups by trained peer tutors.

Special courses Available in various courses. All courses are offered for credit; all enter into overall grade point average.

Auxiliary aids and services *Aids:* calculators, personal spelling/word-use assistants (e.g., Franklin Speller), scan and read programs (e.g., Kurzweil), screen readers, speech recognition programs (e.g., Dragon), tape recorders, taped textbooks. *Services and accommodations:* alternative test arrangements, readers, note-takers, and scribes.

ADD/ADHD Students with ADD/ADHD are eligible for the same services available to students with LD, as well as distraction-free testing environments and medication management.

Application *Required:* high school transcript, ACT or SAT I (extended-time or untimed test accepted), and psychoeducational report. Upon application, documentation of need for special services should be sent only to your LD program or unit. Upon acceptance, documentation of need for special services should be sent only to your LD program or unit. *Application deadline (institutional):* 1/15 for fall and 11/1 for spring.

LD program contact Jan Howard, Director of Disability Services, 191 Hoskins Library, Knoxville, TN 37996-4007. *Phone:* 865-974-6087. *Fax:* 865-974-9552. *E-mail:* jhoward5@utk.edu.

Application contact The University of Tennessee Knoxville, Knoxville, TN 37996. *Web address:* http://www.utk.edu/.

THE UNIVERSITY OF TEXAS AT AUSTIN
Austin, Texas

Students with LD Served by Program	275	ADD/ADHD Services	✓
Staff	2 full-time, 1 part-time	Summer Preparation Program	n/a
LD Program or Service Fee	n/a	Alternative Test Arrangements	✓
LD Program Began	1988	LD Student Organization	n/a

Services for Students with Disabilities (SSD) began offering services in 1988. The program serves approximately 275 undergraduate students. Faculty consists of 2 full-time staff members and 1 part-time staff member. Services are provided by graduate assistants/students and LD specialists.

Policies The college has written policies regarding course substitutions. Students with LD may take up to 17 credit hours per semester; 12 credit hours per semester are required to maintain full-time status and to be eligible for financial aid. LD services are also available to graduate students.

Counseling and advisement Support groups is available.

Auxiliary aids and services *Aids:* taped textbooks. *Services and accommodations:* priority registration, alternative test arrangements, readers, and scribes.

ADD/ADHD Students with ADD/ADHD are eligible for the same services available to students with LD, as well as distraction-free testing environments and support groups for ADD/ADHD.

Application *Required:* high school transcript, personal statement, letter(s) of recommendation, separate application to your LD program or unit, and psychoeducational report (3 years old or less). *Recommended:* participation in extracurricular activities and ACT or SAT I (extended-time or untimed test accepted). Upon application, documentation of need for special services should be sent to both admissions and your LD program or unit. Upon acceptance, documentation of need for special services should be sent only to your LD program or unit. *Application deadline (institutional):* 2/1 for fall and 10/1 for spring.

LD program contact Dr. Sherri Sanders, Associate Dean of Students, 100-B West Dean Keeton, Suite 4.400, Austin, TX 78712. *Phone:* 512-471-6259. *Fax:* 512-232-3963. *E-mail:* sl.sanders@mail.utexas.edu.

Application contact Freshman Admissions Center, The University of Texas at Austin, Austin, TX 78712-1111. *Phone:* 512-475-7440. *E-mail:* adfre@utxdp.dp.utexas.edu. *Web address:* http://www.utexas.edu/.

THE UNIVERSITY OF TEXAS AT EL PASO

El Paso, Texas

Students with LD Served by Program	63	ADD/ADHD Services	✓
Staff	4 full-time, 14 part-time	Summer Preparation Program	n/a
LD Program or Service Fee	n/a	Alternative Test Arrangements	✓
LD Program Began	1995	LD Student Organization	n/a

Disabled Student Services Office began offering services in 1995. The program serves approximately 63 undergraduate students. Faculty consists of 4 full-time and 14 part-time staff members. Services are provided by director, assistant to director.

Policies Students with LD may take up to 21 credit hours per semester; 9 credit hours per semester are required to maintain full-time status; 12 credit hours per semester are required to be eligible for financial aid. LD services are also available to graduate students.

Diagnostic testing Available for auditory processing, spelling, spoken language, intelligence, reading, written language, visual processing, and math.

Subject-area tutoring Available in most subjects. Offered one-on-one by trained peer tutors.

Auxiliary aids and services *Aids:* calculators, personal computers, scan and read programs (e.g., Kurzweil), screen-enlarging programs, screen readers, speech recognition programs (e.g., Dragon), tape recorders, taped textbooks, closed circuit TV. *Services and accommodations:* advocates, priority registration, alternative test arrangements, readers, note-takers, and scribes.

ADD/ADHD Students with ADD/ADHD are eligible for the same services available to students with LD, as well as distraction-free testing environments.

Application *Required:* high school transcript and ACT or SAT I. Upon application, documentation of need for special services should be sent only to your LD program or unit. Upon acceptance, documentation of need for special services should be sent only to your LD program or unit. *Application deadline (institutional):* 7/1 for fall and 11/30 for spring.

LD program contact Susan J. Lopez, Director, 500 West University Avenue, Room 106E Union Building, El Paso, TX 79968-0609. *Phone:* 915-747-5145. *Fax:* 915-747-8712. *E-mail:* dss@utep.edu.

Application contact The University of Texas at El Paso, 500 West University Avenue, El Paso, TX 79968-0001. *Web address:* http://www.utep.edu/.

THE UNIVERSITY OF TEXAS AT SAN ANTONIO

San Antonio, Texas

Students with LD Served by Program	75	ADD/ADHD Services	✓
Staff	1 full-time	Summer Preparation Program	n/a
LD Program or Service Fee	n/a	Alternative Test Arrangements	✓
LD Program Began	n/a	LD Student Organization	n/a

Disability Services serves approximately 75 undergraduate students. Faculty consists of 1 full-time staff member. Services are provided by Director of Disability Services.

Policies 12 credit hours per semester are required to maintain full-time status; 6 credit hours per semester are required to be eligible for financial aid. LD services are also available to graduate students.

Counseling and advisement Individual counseling and small-group counseling are available.

Auxiliary aids and services *Aids:* personal spelling/word-use assistants (e.g., Franklin Speller), scan and read programs (e.g., Kurzweil), screen-enlarging programs, screen readers, speech recognition programs (e.g., Dragon), tape recorders, taped textbooks. *Services and accommodations:* advocates, alternative test arrangements, readers, note-takers, and scribes.

ADD/ADHD Students with ADD/ADHD are eligible for the same services available to students with LD, as well as distraction-free testing environments.

Application *Required:* high school transcript, ACT or SAT I (extended-time tests accepted), and psychoeducational report (3 years old or less). Upon application, documentation of need for special services should be sent only to your LD program or unit. Upon acceptance, documentation of need for special services should be sent only to admissions. *Application deadline (institutional):* 7/1 for fall and 12/1 for spring. *Application deadline (LD program):* rolling/continuous for fall and rolling/continuous for spring.

LD program contact Lorraine Harrison, Director, 6900 North Loop 1604 West, San Antonio, TX 78249. *Phone:* 210-458-4157. *Fax:* 210-458-4980. *E-mail:* lharrison@utsa.edu.

Application contact Sandy Speed, Interim Director, The University of Texas at San Antonio, 6900 North Loop 1604 West, San Antonio, TX 78249-0617. *Phone:* 210-458-4530. *Web address:* http://www.utsa.edu/.

UNIVERSITY OF THE DISTRICT OF COLUMBIA

Washington, District of Columbia

Students with LD Served by Program	19	ADD/ADHD Services	✓
Staff	3 part-time	Summer Preparation Program	n/a
LD Program or Service Fee	n/a	Alternative Test Arrangements	✓
LD Program Began	1974	LD Student Organization	n/a

Student Support Services began offering services in 1974. The program serves approximately 19 undergraduate students. Faculty consists of 3 part-time staff members. Services are provided by regular education teachers, counselors, diagnostic specialists, and professional tutors.

Policies Students with LD may take up to 18 semester hours per semester; 12 semester hours per semester are required to maintain full-time status; 6 semester hours per semester are required to be eligible for financial aid. LD services are also available to graduate students.

Special preparation or orientation Optional orientation held before registration.

Diagnostic testing Available for spelling, intelligence, personality, study skills, learning strategies, reading, learning styles, social skills, and math.

Basic skills remediation Available in study skills, reading, time management, social skills, learning strategies, spelling, and math. Offered one-on-one by computer-based instruction and professional tutors.

Subject-area tutoring Available in some subjects. Offered one-on-one and in small groups by computer-based instruction and professional tutors.

Counseling and advisement Career counseling, individual counseling, and small-group counseling are available.

Auxiliary aids and services *Aids:* scan and read programs (e.g., Kurzweil), tape recorders, taped textbooks. *Services and accommodations:* alternative test arrangements, readers, note-takers, and scribes.

ADD/ADHD Students with ADD/ADHD are eligible for the same services available to students with LD, as well as distraction-free testing environments.

Application *Required:* high school transcript and documentation of high school services (e.g., Individualized Education Program [IEP] or 504 plan). Upon acceptance, documentation of need for special services should be sent only to your LD program or unit.

LD program contact Dr. Madhuker Ohal, Senior Director for Student Life and Services, 4200 Connecticut Avenue, NW, Building 38, Room A-10, Washington, DC 20008. *Phone:* 202-274-5336.

Application contact LaHugh Bankston, Registrar and Enrollment Management, University of the District of Columbia, 4200 Connecticut Avenue, NW, Washington, DC 20008-1175. *Phone:* 202-274-6200. *Web address:* http://www.udc.edu/.

UNIVERSITY OF THE INCARNATE WORD
San Antonio, Texas

Students with LD Served by Program	30	ADD/ADHD Services	✓
Staff	n/a	Summer Preparation Program	n/a
LD Program or Service Fee	n/a	Alternative Test Arrangements	✓
LD Program Began	1998	LD Student Organization	✓

Student Disability Support Services (SDSS) began offering services in 1998. The program serves approximately 30 undergraduate students. Services are provided by graduate assistants/students.

Policies The college has written policies regarding course substitutions. Students with LD may take up to 18 credit hours per semester; 12 credit hours per semester are required to maintain full-time status; 6 credit hours per semester are required to be eligible for financial aid. LD services are also available to graduate students.

Basic skills remediation Available in auditory processing, study skills, reading, time management, social skills, visual processing, learning strategies, and written language. Offered one-on-one and in small groups by graduate assistants/students, trained peer tutors, and trained staff in SDSS office.

Subject-area tutoring Available in all subjects. Offered one-on-one and in small groups by graduate assistants/students and trained peer tutors.

Counseling and advisement Support groups is available.

Auxiliary aids and services *Aids:* screen readers, tape recorders, taped textbooks. *Services and accommodations:* advocates, alternative test arrangements, readers, and scribes.

Student organization There is a student organization for students with LD.

ADD/ADHD Students with ADD/ADHD are eligible for the same services available to students with LD, as well as distraction-free study areas and distraction-free testing environments.

Application *Required:* high school transcript, ACT or SAT I (extended-time or untimed test accepted), and letter(s) of recommendation. *Recommended:* participation in extracurricular activities and interview. Upon application, documentation of need for special services should be sent only to your LD program or unit. Upon acceptance, documentation of need for special services should be sent only to your LD program or unit. *Application deadline (institutional):* rolling/continuous for fall and rolling/continuous for spring. *Application deadline (LD program):* rolling/continuous for fall and rolling/continuous for spring.

LD program contact Lorena Fritz Novak, Coordinator, Student Disability Support Services, 4301 Broadway, UPO 22, San Antonio, TX 78209. *Phone:* 210-283-5056. *Fax:* 210-283-5021. *E-mail:* novak@universe.uiwtx.edu.

Application contact University of the Incarnate Word, 4301 Broadway, San Antonio, TX 78209-6397. *E-mail:* admis@universe.viwtx.edu. *Web address:* http://www.uiw.edu/.

UNIVERSITY OF TULSA
Tulsa, Oklahoma

Students with LD Served by Program	60	ADD/ADHD Services	✓
Staff	3 full-time, 7 part-time	Summer Preparation Program	n/a
LD Program or Service Fee	n/a	Alternative Test Arrangements	✓
LD Program Began	n/a	LD Student Organization	✓

Center for Student Academic Support (CSAS) serves approximately 60 undergraduate students. Faculty consists of 3 full-time and 7 part-time staff members. Services are provided by academic advisers, graduate assistants/students, and LD specialists.

Policies The college has written policies regarding course substitutions. Students with LD may take up to 18 credit hours per semester; 12 credit hours per semester are required to maintain full-time status and to be eligible for financial aid. LD services are also available to graduate students.

Special preparation or orientation Held during summer prior to enrollment and individually by special arrangement.

Basic skills remediation Available in study skills, time management, social skills, learning strategies, and written language. Offered one-on-one by graduate assistants/students and professional tutors.

Subject-area tutoring Available in all subjects. Offered one-on-one and in small groups by professional tutors, graduate assistants/students, and trained peer tutors.

Special courses Available in career planning, study skills, college survival skills, test taking, time management, learning strategies, stress management, and written composition skills. No courses are offered for credit; none enter into overall grade point average.

Counseling and advisement Career counseling and individual counseling are available. Academic advisement by a staff member affiliated with the program is available.

Auxiliary aids and services *Aids:* personal spelling/word-use assistants (e.g., Franklin Speller), scan and read programs (e.g., Kurzweil), screen-enlarging programs, speech recognition programs (e.g., Dragon), tape recorders, taped textbooks. *Services and accommodations:* priority registration, alternative test arrangements, readers, note-takers, and scribes.

Student organization There is a student organization for students with LD.

ADD/ADHD Students with ADD/ADHD are eligible for the same services available to students with LD, as well as distraction-free testing environments.

Application *Required:* high school transcript and personal statement. Upon application, documentation of need for special services should be sent only to your LD program or unit. Upon acceptance, documentation of need for special services should be sent only to your LD program or unit. *Application deadline (institutional):* rolling/continuous for fall and rolling/continuous for spring. *Application deadline (LD program):* rolling/continuous for fall and rolling/continuous for spring.

LD program contact Jane Corso, Director, Center for Student Academic Support, 600 South College, Holmes Student Center #59, Tulsa, OK 74104. *Phone:* 918-631-2334. *Fax:* 918-631-3459. *E-mail:* jane-corso@utulsa.edu.

University of Tulsa (continued)

Application contact University of Tulsa, 600 South College Avenue, Tulsa, OK 74104-3189. *E-mail:* admission@utulsa.edu. *Web address:* http://www.utulsa.edu/.

UNIVERSITY OF UTAH
Salt Lake City, Utah

Students with LD Served by Program	325	ADD/ADHD Services	✓
Staff	5 full-time, 2 part-time	Summer Preparation Program	n/a
LD Program or Service Fee	n/a	Alternative Test Arrangements	✓
LD Program Began	1985	LD Student Organization	n/a

Center for Disability Services began offering services in 1985. The program serves approximately 325 undergraduate students. Faculty consists of 5 full-time and 2 part-time staff members. Services are provided by academic advisers, counselors, diagnostic specialists, and LD specialists.

Policies The college has written policies regarding substitution and waivers of requirements for admission and graduation. 12 credit hours per semester are required to maintain full-time status and to be eligible for financial aid. LD services are also available to graduate students.

Fees *Diagnostic Testing Fee:* $115.

Special preparation or orientation Optional orientation held individually by special arrangement.

Diagnostic testing Available for spelling, neuropsychological, intelligence, study skills, learning strategies, reading, written language, visual processing, and math.

Subject-area tutoring Available in most subjects. Offered one-on-one and in small groups by trained peer tutors.

Counseling and advisement Career counseling and individual counseling are available. Academic advisement by a staff member affiliated with the program is available.

Auxiliary aids and services *Aids:* scan and read programs (e.g., Kurzweil), screen-enlarging programs, screen readers, speech recognition programs (e.g., Dragon), tape recorders, taped textbooks. *Services and accommodations:* advocates, priority registration, alternative test arrangements, readers, note-takers, and scribes.

ADD/ADHD Students with ADD/ADHD are eligible for the same services available to students with LD, as well as distraction-free study areas, distraction-free testing environments, one-on-one support, guidance and skills training by disability advisors.

Application *Required:* high school transcript, ACT or SAT I (extended-time tests accepted), separate application to your LD program or unit, and psychoeducational report (3 years old or less). *Recommended:* interview, personal statement, and documentation of high school services (e.g., Individualized Education Program [IEP] or 504 plan). Upon application, documentation of need for special services should be sent only to your LD program or unit. Upon acceptance, documentation of need for special services should be sent only to your LD program or unit. *Application deadline (institutional):* 6/1 for fall and 11/15 for spring. *Application deadline (LD program):* rolling/continuous for fall and rolling/continuous for spring.

LD program contact Olga Nadeau, Director, Center for Disability Services, 200 South Central Campus Drive, Room 162, Salt Lake City, UT 84112-9107. *Phone:* 801-581-5020. *Fax:* 801-581-5487. *E-mail:* onadeau@saff.utah.edu.

Application contact Suzanne Espinoza, Director of High School Services, University of Utah, 250 South Student Services Building, Salt Lake City, UT 84112. *Phone:* 801-581-8761. *Web address:* http://www.utah.edu/.

UNIVERSITY OF WATERLOO
Waterloo, Ontario

Students with LD Served by Program	290	ADD/ADHD Services	✓
Staff	1 full-time, 3 part-time	Summer Preparation Program	n/a
LD Program or Service Fee	n/a	Alternative Test Arrangements	✓
LD Program Began	1989	LD Student Organization	n/a

Office for Persons with Disabilities began offering services in 1989. The program serves approximately 290 undergraduate students. Faculty consists of 1 full-time and 3 part-time staff members. Services are provided by counselors, diagnostic specialists, graduate assistants/students, LD specialists, and trained peer tutors.

Policies LD services are also available to graduate students.

Fees *Diagnostic Testing Fee:* ranges from $0 to $1800.

Special preparation or orientation Held after classes begin, individually by special arrangement, and Student Life 101 Day.

Diagnostic testing Available for auditory processing, motor skills, spelling, handwriting, neuropsychological, spoken language, intelligence, personality, study skills, learning strategies, reading, written language, learning styles, social skills, visual processing, and math.

Subject-area tutoring Available in most subjects. Offered one-on-one and in small groups by professional tutors, graduate assistants/students, trained peer tutors, and LD specialists.

Special courses Available in learning strategies and employment strategies. No courses are offered for credit; none enter into overall grade point average.

Counseling and advisement Career counseling, individual counseling, and support groups are available.

Auxiliary aids and services *Aids:* calculators, personal computers, personal spelling/word-use assistants (e.g., Franklin Speller), scan and read programs (e.g., Kurzweil), screen-enlarging programs, screen readers, speech recognition programs (e.g., Dragon), tape recorders, taped textbooks. *Services and accommodations:* alternative test arrangements, readers, note-takers, and scribes.

ADD/ADHD Students with ADD/ADHD are eligible for the same services available to students with LD, as well as distraction-free study areas, distraction-free testing environments, personal coach or mentors, and support groups for ADD/ADHD.

Application *Required:* high school transcript and documentation of high school services (e.g., Individualized Education Program [IEP] or 504 plan). *Recommended:* participation in extracurricular activities, personal statement, letter(s) of recommendation, and psychoeducational report (5 years old or less). Upon application, documentation of need for special services should be sent only to your LD program or unit. Upon acceptance, documentation of need for special services should be sent only to your LD program or unit. *Application deadline (institutional):* rolling/continuous for fall and rolling/continuous for spring. *Application deadline (LD program):* rolling/continuous for fall and rolling/continuous for spring.

LD program contact Dr. Virginia Nusca, Learning Specialist, Office for Persons with Disabilities, Needles Hall #2051, 200 University Avenue W, Waterloo, ON N2L 3G1. *Phone:* 519-888-4567 Ext. 5231. *Fax:* 519-746-2401. *E-mail:* vnusca@uwaterloo.ca.

Application contact University of Waterloo, 200 University Avenue West, Waterloo, ON N2L 3G1. *E-mail:* registrar@nhladm.uwaterloo.ca. *Web address:* http://www.findoutmore.uwaterloo.ca.

THE UNIVERSITY OF WESTERN ONTARIO
London, Ontario

Students with LD Served by Program	280	ADD/ADHD Services	✓
Staff	5 full-time, 18 part-time	Summer Preparation Program	n/a
LD Program or Service Fee	n/a	Alternative Test Arrangements	✓
LD Program Began	1980	LD Student Organization	n/a

Services for Students with Disabilities (SSD) began offering services in 1980. The program serves approximately 280 undergraduate students. Faculty consists of 5 full-time and 18 part-time staff members. Services are provided by counselors, remediation/learning specialists, diagnostic specialists, and graduate assistants/students.
Policies LD services are also available to graduate students.
Special preparation or orientation Optional orientation held before classes begin and individually by special arrangement.
Diagnostic testing Available for spelling, intelligence, personality, study skills, learning strategies, reading, written language, math, and memory.
Basic skills remediation Available in study skills, reading, time management, learning strategies, written language, math, and note taking, exam preparation and writing. Offered one-on-one and in small groups by learning skills counselors and western effective writing instructors.
Counseling and advisement Individual counseling is available.
Auxiliary aids and services *Aids:* personal spelling/word-use assistants (e.g., Franklin Speller), scan and read programs (e.g., Kurzweil), screen-enlarging programs, screen readers, tape recorders, taped textbooks. *Services and accommodations:* advocates, alternative test arrangements, and note-takers.
ADD/ADHD Students with ADD/ADHD are eligible for the same services available to students with LD, as well as distraction-free testing environments and support groups for ADD/ADHD.
Application *Required:* high school transcript, SAT I, personal statement, and documentation of high school services (e.g., Individualized Education Program [IEP] or 504 plan). *Recommended:* letter(s) of recommendation, psychoeducational report (3 years old or less), and letter from student. Upon application, documentation of need for special services should be sent only to admissions. Upon acceptance, documentation of need for special services should be sent only to your LD program or unit. *Application deadline (institutional):* rolling/continuous for fall.
LD program contact Dr. Wendy Dickinson, Office Manager, Services for Students with Disabilities, Student Development Centre, University Community Centre, Room 210, London, ON N6A 3K7. *Phone:* 519-661-2147. *Fax:* 519-661-3949. *E-mail:* wendyd@sdc.uwo.ca.
Application contact The University of Western Ontario, London, ON N6A 5B8. *E-mail:* reguwo@uwoadmin.uwo.ca. *Web address:* http://www.uwo.ca/.

UNIVERSITY OF WEST FLORIDA
Pensacola, Florida

Students with LD Served by Program	95	ADD/ADHD Services	✓
Staff	2 full-time, 2 part-time	Summer Preparation Program	n/a
LD Program or Service Fee	n/a	Alternative Test Arrangements	✓
LD Program Began	1978	LD Student Organization	✓

Disabled Student Services began offering services in 1978. The program serves approximately 95 undergraduate students. Faculty consists of 2 full-time and 2 part-time staff members. Services are provided by academic advisers, counselors, and trained peer tutors.
Policies The college has written policies regarding course substitutions, grade forgiveness, and substitution and waivers of requirements for admission and graduation. Students with LD may take up to 18 credit hours per semester; 12 credit hours per semester are required to maintain full-time status and to be eligible for financial aid. LD services are also available to graduate students.
Special preparation or orientation Optional orientation held before registration, during registration, before classes begin, during summer prior to enrollment, and individually by special arrangement.
Subject-area tutoring Available in all subjects. Offered one-on-one and in small groups by graduate assistants/students and trained peer tutors.
Counseling and advisement Career counseling and individual counseling are available. Academic advisement by a staff member affiliated with the program is available.
Auxiliary aids and services *Aids:* scan and read programs (e.g., Kurzweil), screen-enlarging programs, screen readers, speech recognition programs (e.g., Dragon), tape recorders. *Services and accommodations:* alternative test arrangements, readers, and note-takers.
Student organization There is a student organization for students with LD.
ADD/ADHD Students with ADD/ADHD are eligible for the same services available to students with LD, as well as distraction-free testing environments, tutors and extra time on tests.
Application *Required:* high school transcript, ACT or SAT I (extended-time or untimed test accepted), personal statement, letter(s) of recommendation, separate application to your LD program or unit, psychoeducational report (5 years old or less), and documentation of high school services (e.g., Individualized Education Program [IEP] or 504 plan). *Recommended:* participation in extracurricular activities and interview. Upon application, documentation of need for special services should be sent to both admissions and your LD program or unit. Upon acceptance, documentation of need for special services should be sent only to your LD program or unit. *Application deadline (institutional):* 6/30 for fall and 11/1 for spring. *Application deadline (LD program):* rolling/continuous for fall and rolling/continuous for spring.
LD program contact Barbara Fitzpatrick, Assistant Director, Student Affairs, 11000 University Parkway, Pensacola, FL 32514-5750. *Phone:* 850-474-2387. *Fax:* 850-857-6188. *E-mail:* bfitzpat@uwf.edu.
Application contact University of West Florida, 11000 University Parkway, Pensacola, FL 32514-5750. *E-mail:* sneeley@uwf.edu. *Web address:* http://www.uwf.edu/.

UNIVERSITY OF WISCONSIN-EAU CLAIRE
Eau Claire, Wisconsin

Students with LD Served by Program	60	ADD/ADHD Services	✓
Staff	3 part-time	Summer Preparation Program	n/a
LD Program or Service Fee	n/a	Alternative Test Arrangements	✓
LD Program Began	1987	LD Student Organization	n/a

University of Wisconsin-Eau Claire (continued)

Services for Students with Disabilities began offering services in 1987. The program serves approximately 60 undergraduate students. Faculty consists of 3 part-time staff members. Services are provided by remediation/learning specialists and trained peer tutors.

Policies The college has written policies regarding course substitutions and substitution and waivers of requirements for admission and graduation. Students with LD may take up to 18 credits per semester; 12 credits per semester are required to maintain full-time status. LD services are also available to graduate students.

Special preparation or orientation Held during registration.

Basic skills remediation Available in study skills, computer skills, reading, time management, learning strategies, written language, and math. Offered one-on-one by trained peer tutors.

Subject-area tutoring Available in most subjects. Offered one-on-one by trained peer tutors.

Counseling and advisement Career counseling and individual counseling are available.

Auxiliary aids and services *Aids:* screen-enlarging programs, screen readers, speech recognition programs (e.g., Dragon), taped textbooks. *Services and accommodations:* priority registration, alternative test arrangements, readers, note-takers, and scribes.

ADD/ADHD Students with ADD/ADHD are eligible for the same services available to students with LD, as well as distraction-free study areas and distraction-free testing environments.

Application *Required:* high school transcript, ACT or SAT I (extended-time or untimed test accepted), and personal statement. *Recommended:* participation in extracurricular activities. Upon acceptance, documentation of need for special services should be sent only to your LD program or unit.

LD program contact Joseph C. Hisrich, Coordinator of services for Students with Disabilities, 105 Garfield Avenue, PO Box 4004, Eau Claire, WI 54702-4004. *Phone:* 715-836-4542. *Fax:* 715-836-3712. *E-mail:* hisricjc@uwec.edu.

Application contact University of Wisconsin-Eau Claire, PO Box 4004, Eau Claire, WI 54702-4004. *E-mail:* ask-uwec@uwec.edu. *Web address:* http://www.uwec.edu/.

UNIVERSITY OF WISCONSIN-LA CROSSE

La Crosse, Wisconsin

Students with LD Served by Program	150	ADD/ADHD Services	✓
Staff	6 full-time	Summer Preparation Program	n/a
LD Program or Service Fee	n/a	Alternative Test Arrangements	✓
LD Program Began	1981	LD Student Organization	✓

Disability Resource Services began offering services in 1981. The program serves approximately 150 undergraduate students. Faculty consists of 6 full-time staff members. Services are provided by counselors and LD specialists.

Policies 12 credit hours per semester are required to maintain full-time status. LD services are also available to graduate students.

Special preparation or orientation Required orientation held before classes begin.

Auxiliary aids and services *Aids:* calculators, scan and read programs (e.g., Kurzweil), screen-enlarging programs, screen readers, taped textbooks. *Services and accommodations:* priority registration, alternative test arrangements, readers, note-takers, and scribes.

Student organization There is a student organization for students with LD.

ADD/ADHD Students with ADD/ADHD are eligible for the same services available to students with LD, as well as distraction-free testing environments.

Application *Required:* high school transcript, ACT (untimed test accepted), psychoeducational report (3 years old or less), and documentation of high school services (e.g., Individualized Education Program [IEP] or 504 plan). *Recommended:* interview. Upon application, documentation of need for special services should be sent only to your LD program or unit. Upon acceptance, documentation of need for special services should be sent only to your LD program or unit. *Application deadline (institutional):* rolling/continuous for spring and 1/3 for fall. *Application deadline (LD program):* rolling/continuous for fall and rolling/continuous for spring.

LD program contact June Reinert, Coordinator, Disability Resource Services, 165 Murphy Library, 1725 State Street, LaCrosse, WI 54601. *Phone:* 608-785-6900. *Fax:* 608-785-6910. *E-mail:* reinert.june@uwlax.edu.

Application contact University of Wisconsin-La Crosse, 1725 State Street, La Crosse, WI 54601-3742. *E-mail:* admissions@post.uwlax.edu. *Web address:* http://www.uwlax.edu/.

UNIVERSITY OF WISCONSIN-MADISON

Madison, Wisconsin

Students with LD Served by Program	300	ADD/ADHD Services	✓
Staff	1 full-time	Summer Preparation Program	n/a
LD Program or Service Fee	n/a	Alternative Test Arrangements	✓
LD Program Began	1986	LD Student Organization	n/a

McBurney Disability Resource Center began offering services in 1986. The program serves approximately 300 undergraduate students. Faculty consists of 1 full-time staff member. Services are provided by LD specialists.

Policies The college has written policies regarding course substitutions. Students with LD may take up to 18 credits per semester; 12 credits per semester are required to maintain full-time status and to be eligible for financial aid. LD services are also available to graduate students.

Special preparation or orientation Required orientation held before classes begin and individually by special arrangement.

Basic skills remediation Available in study skills, time management, and learning strategies. Offered one-on-one and in small groups by LD specialists.

Counseling and advisement Individual counseling is available.

Auxiliary aids and services *Aids:* taped textbooks. *Services and accommodations:* advocates, alternative test arrangements, readers, note-takers, and scribes.

ADD/ADHD Students with ADD/ADHD are eligible for the same services available to students with LD, as well as distraction-free testing environments and support groups for ADD/ADHD.

Application *Required:* high school transcript and ACT or SAT I (extended-time tests accepted). *Recommended:* personal statement, letter(s) of recommendation, psychoeducational report, and documentation of high school services (e.g., Individualized Education Program [IEP] or 504 plan). Upon application, documentation of need for special services should be sent to both admissions and your LD program or unit. Upon acceptance, documentation of need for special services should be sent only to your LD program or unit. *Application deadline (institutional):* 1/2 for fall.

LD program contact McBurney Disability Resource Center, 905 University Avenue, Madison, WI 53715. *Phone:* 608-263-2741. *Fax:* 608-256-2998.

Application contact Thomas Reason, Office of Admissions, University of Wisconsin-Madison, 140 Peterson Office Building, 750 University Avenue, Madison, WI 53706-1490. *Phone:* 608-262-3961. *E-mail:* on.wisconsin@mail.admin.wisc.edu. *Web address:* http://www.wisc.edu/.

UNIVERSITY OF WISCONSIN-PARKSIDE
Kenosha, Wisconsin

Students with LD Served by Program	75	ADD/ADHD Services	✓
Staff	1 full-time	Summer Preparation Program	n/a
LD Program or Service Fee	n/a	Alternative Test Arrangements	✓
LD Program Began	1991	LD Student Organization	n/a

Disabled Student Services began offering services in 1991. The program serves approximately 75 undergraduate students. Faculty consists of 1 full-time staff member. Services are provided by coordinator.

Policies The college has written policies regarding course substitutions and grade forgiveness. Students with LD may take up to 21 credit hours per term; 12 credit hours per term are required to maintain full-time status; 6 credit hours per term are required to be eligible for financial aid. LD services are also available to graduate students.

Auxiliary aids and services *Aids:* scan and read programs (e.g., Kurzweil), taped textbooks, visual enlarger machine. *Services and accommodations:* priority registration, alternative test arrangements, readers, note-takers, and scribes.

ADD/ADHD Students with ADD/ADHD are eligible for the same services available to students with LD, as well as distraction-free study areas and distraction-free testing environments.

Application *Required:* high school transcript and ACT (extended-time or untimed test accepted). *Recommended:* psychoeducational report (5 years old or less) and documentation of high school services (e.g., Individualized Education Program [IEP] or 504 plan). Upon application, documentation of need for special services should be sent only to your LD program or unit. Upon acceptance, documentation of need for special services should be sent only to your LD program or unit.

LD program contact Renee Sartin Kirby, Coordinator, Disability Services, 900 Wood Road, Box 2000, Kenosha, WI 53141. *Phone:* 262-595-2610. *Fax:* 262-595-2716. *E-mail:* renee.kirby@uwp.edu.

Application contact University of Wisconsin-Parkside, 900 Wood Road, Box 2000, Kenosha, WI 53141-2000. *E-mail:* jucha@it.uwp.edu. *Web address:* http://www.uwp.edu/.

UNIVERSITY OF WISCONSIN-PLATTEVILLE
Platteville, Wisconsin

Students with LD Served by Program	50	ADD/ADHD Services	✓
Staff	1 full-time, 1 part-time	Summer Preparation Program	n/a
LD Program or Service Fee	n/a	Alternative Test Arrangements	✓
LD Program Began	1991	LD Student Organization	✓

Services for Students with Disabilities began offering services in 1991. The program serves approximately 50 undergraduate students. Faculty consists of 1 full-time and 1 part-time staff member. Services are provided by counselors, graduate assistants/students, LD specialists, and trained peer tutors.

Policies Students with LD may take up to 18 credit hours per semester; 12 credit hours per semester are required to maintain full-time status and to be eligible for financial aid. LD services are also available to graduate students.

Basic skills remediation Available in study skills, computer skills, time management, learning strategies, and math. Offered one-on-one and in small groups by regular education teachers and LD specialists.

Subject-area tutoring Available in most subjects. Offered one-on-one and in small groups by trained peer tutors.

Counseling and advisement Individual counseling is available.

Auxiliary aids and services *Aids:* calculators, tape recorders, taped textbooks. *Services and accommodations:* priority registration, alternative test arrangements, note-takers, and scribes.

Student organization There is a student organization for students with LD.

ADD/ADHD Students with ADD/ADHD are eligible for the same services available to students with LD, as well as distraction-free testing environments.

Application *Required:* high school transcript and ACT (extended-time or untimed test accepted). *Recommended:* participation in extracurricular activities. Upon application, documentation of need for special services should be sent to both admissions and your LD program or unit. Upon acceptance, documentation of need for special services should be sent to both admissions and your LD program or unit. *Application deadline (institutional):* rolling/continuous for fall and rolling/continuous for spring. *Application deadline (LD program):* rolling/continuous for fall and rolling/continuous for spring.

LD program contact Rebecca L. Peters, Coordinator, 116 Warner Hall, Platteville, WI 53818. *Phone:* 608-342-1818. *Fax:* 608-342-1232. *E-mail:* petersre@uwplatt.edu.

Application contact University of Wisconsin-Platteville, 1 University Plaza, Platteville, WI 53818-3099. *E-mail:* admit@uwplatt.edu. *Web address:* http://www.uwplatt.edu/.

UNIVERSITY OF WISCONSIN-RIVER FALLS
River Falls, Wisconsin

Students with LD Served by Program	50	ADD/ADHD Services	✓
Staff	2 part-time	Summer Preparation Program	n/a
LD Program or Service Fee	n/a	Alternative Test Arrangements	✓
LD Program Began	n/a	LD Student Organization	n/a

Disability Services serves approximately 50 undergraduate students. Faculty consists of 2 part-time staff members. Services are provided by academic advisers, counselors, and trained peer tutors.

Policies Students with LD may take up to 17 credit hours per semester; 12 credit hours per semester are required to maintain full-time status; 6 credit hours per semester are required to be eligible for financial aid. LD services are also available to graduate students.

Subject-area tutoring Available in most subjects. Offered one-on-one and in small groups by trained peer tutors.

Counseling and advisement Career counseling and individual counseling are available. Academic advisement by a staff member affiliated with the program is available.

Auxiliary aids and services *Aids:* calculators, personal computers, tape recorders, taped textbooks. *Services and accommodations:* alternative test arrangements, readers, note-takers, and scribes.

University of Wisconsin-River Falls (continued)

ADD/ADHD Students with ADD/ADHD are eligible for the same services available to students with LD, as well as distraction-free testing environments, medication management and personal coach or mentors.

Application *Required:* high school transcript and ACT (extended-time or untimed test accepted). Upon application, documentation of need for special services should be sent only to your LD program or unit. Upon acceptance, documentation of need for special services should be sent only to your LD program or unit. *Application deadline (institutional):* 1/1 for fall and 12/1 for spring.

LD program contact Wade Warner, Coordinator, 410 South Third Street, River Falls, WI 54022. *Phone:* 715-425-3531. *Fax:* 715-425-3277. *E-mail:* wade.w.warner@uwrf.edu.

Application contact University of Wisconsin-River Falls, 410 South Third Street, River Falls, WI 54022-5001. *E-mail:* admit@uwrf.edu. *Web address:* http://www.uwrf.edu/.

UNIVERSITY OF WISCONSIN-SUPERIOR
Superior, Wisconsin

Students with LD Served by Program	30	ADD/ADHD Services	✓
Staff	n/a	Summer Preparation Program	n/a
LD Program or Service Fee	n/a	Alternative Test Arrangements	✓
LD Program Began	1990	LD Student Organization	n/a

Academic Support Center began offering services in 1990. The program serves approximately 30 undergraduate students. Services are provided by academic advisers, regular education teachers, counselors, remediation/learning specialists, special education teachers, graduate assistants/students, LD specialists, and trained peer tutors.

Policies Students with LD may take up to 18 credit hours per semester; 12 credit hours per semester are required to maintain full-time status; 6 credit hours per semester are required to be eligible for financial aid. LD services are also available to graduate students.

Diagnostic testing Available for spelling, neuropsychological, spoken language, intelligence, personality, learning strategies, reading, written language, and learning styles.

Basic skills remediation Available in study skills, reading, time management, social skills, learning strategies, spelling, written language, and math. Offered one-on-one, in small groups, and class-size groups by computer-based instruction, regular education teachers, graduate assistants/students, LD specialists, and trained peer tutors.

Subject-area tutoring Available in most subjects. Offered one-on-one, in small groups, and class-size groups by computer-based instruction, professional tutors, graduate assistants/students, trained peer tutors, and LD specialists.

Special courses Available in career planning, oral communication skills, study skills, college survival skills, practical computer skills, test taking, reading, time management, learning strategies, self-advocacy, vocabulary development, math, stress management, and written composition skills. All courses are offered for credit; all enter into overall grade point average.

Counseling and advisement Career counseling and individual counseling are available. Academic advisement by a staff member affiliated with the program is available.

Auxiliary aids and services *Aids:* calculators, personal computers, personal spelling/word-use assistants (e.g., Franklin Speller), scan and read programs (e.g., Kurzweil), screen-enlarging programs, screen readers, tape recorders, taped textbooks. *Services and accommodations:* advocates, priority registration, alternative test arrangements, readers, note-takers, and scribes.

ADD/ADHD Students with ADD/ADHD are eligible for the same services available to students with LD, as well as distraction-free testing environments and personal coach or mentors.

Application *Required:* high school transcript and ACT or SAT I.

LD program contact Karen Strewler, Study Skills and Disabilities Specialist, Belknap and Catlin, Box 2000, Superior, WI 54880. *Phone:* 715-394-8288. *Fax:* 715-394-8107. *E-mail:* kstrewle@staff.uwsuper.edu.

Application contact Lorraine Washa, Student Application Contact, University of Wisconsin-Superior, Belknap and Catlin, PO Box 2000, Superior, WI 54880-4500. *Phone:* 715-394-8230. *E-mail:* admissions@uwsuper.edu. *Web address:* http://www.uwsuper.edu/.

UTAH STATE UNIVERSITY
Logan, Utah

Students with LD Served by Program	200	ADD/ADHD Services	✓
Staff	3 full-time	Summer Preparation Program	n/a
LD Program or Service Fee	n/a	Alternative Test Arrangements	✓
LD Program Began	n/a	LD Student Organization	n/a

Disability Resource Center serves approximately 200 undergraduate students. Faculty consists of 3 full-time staff members. Services are provided by academic advisers, diagnostic specialists, graduate assistants/students, and LD specialists.

Policies 12 credit hours per semester are required to maintain full-time status. LD services are also available to graduate students.

Counseling and advisement Career counseling, individual counseling, and support groups are available. Academic advisement by a staff member affiliated with the program is available.

Auxiliary aids and services *Aids:* scan and read programs (e.g., Kurzweil), screen-enlarging programs, screen readers, speech recognition programs (e.g., Dragon), taped textbooks. *Services and accommodations:* advocates, priority registration, alternative test arrangements, readers, note-takers, and scribes.

ADD/ADHD Students with ADD/ADHD are eligible for the same services available to students with LD, as well as distraction-free testing environments and support groups for ADD/ADHD.

Application *Required:* high school transcript, ACT (extended-time or untimed test accepted), and psychoeducational report (3 years old or less). Upon application, documentation of need for special services should be sent only to your LD program or unit. Upon acceptance, documentation of need for special services should be sent only to your LD program or unit. *Application deadline (institutional):* rolling/continuous for fall and rolling/continuous for spring. *Application deadline (LD program):* rolling/continuous for fall and rolling/continuous for spring.

LD program contact Diane Craig Hardman, Director, Disability Resource Center, 0101 Old Main Hill, Logan, UT 84322-0101. *Phone:* 435-797-2444. *Fax:* 435-797-0130. *E-mail:* dhardman@admissions.usu.edu.

Application contact Utah State University, Old Main Hill, Logan, UT 84322. *E-mail:* admit@admission.usu.edu. *Web address:* http://www.usu.edu/.

VALDOSTA STATE UNIVERSITY
Valdosta, Georgia

Students with LD Served by Program	150	ADD/ADHD Services	✓
Staff	3 full-time	Summer Preparation Program	n/a
LD Program or Service Fee	n/a	Alternative Test Arrangements	✓
LD Program Began	1991	LD Student Organization	✓

Special Services Program began offering services in 1991. The program serves approximately 150 undergraduate students. Faculty consists of 3 full-time staff members. Services are provided by counselors, special education teachers, and graduate assistants/students.

Policies The college has written policies regarding course substitutions and grade forgiveness. Students with LD may take up to 18 credit hours per semester; 12 credit hours per semester are required to maintain full-time status; 6 credit hours per semester are required to be eligible for financial aid. LD services are also available to graduate students.

Subject-area tutoring Available in some subjects. Offered one-on-one by graduate assistants/students.

Counseling and advisement Individual counseling and support groups are available.

Auxiliary aids and services *Aids:* scan and read programs (e.g., Kurzweil), screen-enlarging programs, screen readers, speech recognition programs (e.g., Dragon), tape recorders, taped textbooks. *Services and accommodations:* priority registration, alternative test arrangements, and note-takers.

Student organization There is a student organization for students with LD.

ADD/ADHD Students with ADD/ADHD are eligible for the same services available to students with LD, as well as distraction-free testing environments and support groups for ADD/ADHD.

Application *Required:* high school transcript, ACT or SAT I (extended-time or untimed ACT test accepted), separate application to your LD program or unit, and psychoeducational report (3 years old or less). Upon application, documentation of need for special services should be sent only to your LD program or unit. Upon acceptance, documentation of need for special services should be sent only to your LD program or unit. *Application deadline (institutional):* rolling/continuous for fall and rolling/continuous for spring. *Application deadline (LD program):* rolling/continuous for fall and rolling/continuous for spring.

LD program contact Maggie J. Viverette, Coordinator, 1500 North Patterson Street, Valdosta, GA 31698. *Phone:* 912-245-2498. *Fax:* 912-245-3788. *E-mail:* mviveret@valdosta.edu.

Application contact Valdosta State University, 1500 North Patterson Street, Valdosta, GA 31698. *E-mail:* btillman@grits.valdosta.peachnet.edu. *Web address:* http://www.valdosta.edu/.

VALPARAISO UNIVERSITY
Valparaiso, Indiana

Students with LD Served by Program	60	ADD/ADHD Services	✓
Staff	n/a	Summer Preparation Program	n/a
LD Program or Service Fee	n/a	Alternative Test Arrangements	✓
LD Program Began	1995	LD Student Organization	n/a

The Bridges Program began offering services in 1995. The program serves approximately 60 undergraduate students. Services are provided by academic advisers, counselors, and trained peer tutors.

Policies Students with LD may take up to 18 credit hours per semester; 12 credit hours per semester are required to maintain full-time status and to be eligible for financial aid. LD services are also available to graduate students.

Special preparation or orientation Held before registration and individually by special arrangement.

Subject-area tutoring Available in all subjects. Offered one-on-one and in small groups by a professor.

Special courses Available in study skills, college survival skills, test taking, time management, learning strategies, self-advocacy, stress management, and written composition skills. No courses are offered for credit.

Counseling and advisement Career counseling and individual counseling are available. Academic advisement by a staff member affiliated with the program is available.

Auxiliary aids and services *Aids:* personal computers, scan and read programs (e.g., Kurzweil), screen-enlarging programs. *Services and accommodations:* advocates, priority registration, alternative test arrangements, readers, note-takers, and scribes.

ADD/ADHD Students with ADD/ADHD are eligible for the same services available to students with LD, as well as distraction-free study areas, distraction-free testing environments and medication management.

Application *Recommended:* high school transcript, ACT or SAT I (extended-time or untimed test accepted), and separate application to your LD program or unit. Upon application, documentation of need for special services should be sent only to your LD program or unit. Upon acceptance, documentation of need for special services should be sent only to your LD program or unit. *Application deadline (institutional):* rolling/continuous for fall and rolling/continuous for spring.

LD program contact Barbara Gaebel-Morgan, Director, Bridges Program, Huegli Hall, Valparaiso, IN 46383. *Phone:* 219-464-6833. *Fax:* 219-464-5395.

Application contact Karen Foust, Director of Admissions, Valparaiso University, 651 South College Avenue, Valparaiso, IN 46383-6493. *Phone:* 219-464-5011. *E-mail:* undergrad_admissions@valpo.edu. *Web address:* http://www.valpo.edu/.

VANDERBILT UNIVERSITY
Nashville, Tennessee

Students with LD Served by Program	275	ADD/ADHD Services	✓
Staff	3 full-time, 16 part-time	Summer Preparation Program	n/a
LD Program or Service Fee	n/a	Alternative Test Arrangements	✓
LD Program Began	1977	LD Student Organization	n/a

Opportunity Development Center began offering services in 1977. The program serves approximately 275 undergraduate students. Faculty consists of 3 full-time and 16 part-time staff members. Services are provided by counselors, graduate assistants/students, LD specialists, and professional tutors.

Policies 15 hours per semester are required to maintain full-time status and to be eligible for financial aid. LD services are also available to graduate students.

Fees *Diagnostic Testing Fee:* $350.

Diagnostic testing Available for auditory processing, motor skills, spelling, handwriting, neuropsychological, spoken language, intelligence, personality, study skills, learning strategies, reading, written language, learning styles, social skills, visual processing, and math.

Subject-area tutoring Available in most subjects. Offered one-on-one and in small groups by professional tutors and graduate assistants/students.

Vanderbilt University (continued)

Counseling and advisement Career counseling, individual counseling, small-group counseling, and support groups are available.

Auxiliary aids and services *Aids:* scan and read programs (e.g., Kurzweil), tape recorders, taped textbooks. *Services and accommodations:* advocates, priority registration, alternative test arrangements, readers, note-takers, and interpreters, classroom re-assignment.

ADD/ADHD Students with ADD/ADHD are eligible for the same services available to students with LD, as well as distraction-free testing environments.

Application *Required:* high school transcript, participation in extracurricular activities, SAT I (extended-time test accepted), personal statement, and letter(s) of recommendation. Upon application, documentation of need for special services should be sent only to your LD program or unit. Upon acceptance, documentation of need for special services should be sent only to your LD program or unit.

LD program contact Sara Ezell, Assistant Director for Disability Services, 110 21st Avenue South, Box 1809, Station B, Nashville, TN 37235. *Phone:* 615-322-4705. *Fax:* 615-343-0671.

Application contact Vanderbilt University, 2305 West End Avenue, Nashville, TN 37203-1700. *E-mail:* admissions@vanderbilt.edu. *Web address:* http://www.vanderbilt.edu/.

VANGUARD UNIVERSITY OF SOUTHERN CALIFORNIA
Costa Mesa, California

Students with LD Served by Program	30	ADD/ADHD Services	✓
Staff	2 part-time	Summer Preparation Program	n/a
LD Program or Service Fee	n/a	Alternative Test Arrangements	✓
LD Program Began	1977	LD Student Organization	n/a

Learning Assistance began offering services in 1977. The program serves approximately 30 undergraduate students. Faculty consists of 2 part-time staff members. Services are provided by academic advisers, regular education teachers, counselors, graduate assistants/students, and director of learning skills.

Policies 12 units per semester are required to maintain full-time status and to be eligible for financial aid. LD services are also available to graduate students.

Special preparation or orientation Required orientation held before classes begin and during orientation, "Welcome Week".

Basic skills remediation Available in study skills, time management, learning strategies, and English grammar and composition. Offered one-on-one, in small groups, and class-size groups by regular education teachers and Director of Learning Skills, University Writing Center.

Subject-area tutoring Available in most subjects. Offered one-on-one, in small groups, and class-size groups by graduate assistants/students, trained peer tutors, and University Writing Center.

Counseling and advisement Individual counseling is available. Academic advisement by a staff member affiliated with the program is available.

Auxiliary aids and services *Aids:* personal computers, taped textbooks. *Services and accommodations:* alternative test arrangements, note-takers, scribes, and Director of Leanings Skills advocating.

ADD/ADHD Students with ADD/ADHD are eligible for the same services available to students with LD, as well as distraction-free study areas, distraction-free testing environments and personal coach or mentors.

Application *Required:* high school transcript, ACT or SAT I (extended-time or untimed test accepted), personal statement, letter(s) of recommendation, separate application to your LD program or unit, psychoeducational report (4 years old or less), and documentation of high school services (e.g., Individualized Education Program [IEP] or 504 plan). Upon application, documentation of need for special services should be sent only to your LD program or unit. Upon acceptance, documentation of need for special services should be sent only to your LD program or unit. *Application deadline (institutional):* rolling/continuous for fall and rolling/continuous for spring. *Application deadline (LD program):* rolling/continuous for fall and rolling/continuous for spring.

LD program contact Jessica Mireles, Director of Admissions, 55 Fair Drive, Costa Mesa, CA 92626. *Phone:* 714-556-3610. *Fax:* 714-966-5471. *E-mail:* jmireles@vanguard.edu.

Application contact Jessica Mireles, Associate Director of Admissions, Vanguard University of Southern California, 55 Fair Drive, Costa Mesa, CA 92626-6597. *Phone:* 714-556-3610 Ext. 327. *E-mail:* admissions@sccu.edu. *Web address:* http://www.vanguard.edu/.

VASSAR COLLEGE
Poughkeepsie, New York

Students with LD Served by Program	56	ADD/ADHD Services	✓
Staff	1 full-time	Summer Preparation Program	n/a
LD Program or Service Fee	n/a	Alternative Test Arrangements	✓
LD Program Began	1995	LD Student Organization	✓

Office of Disability and Support Services began offering services in 1995. The program serves approximately 56 undergraduate students. Faculty consists of 1 full-time staff member.

Policies The college has written policies regarding course substitutions.

Basic skills remediation Available in study skills, reading, time management, learning strategies, written language, math, and test taking skills. Offered one-on-one by writing, reading, math, time management, and organization specialists.

Counseling and advisement Individual counseling is available.

Auxiliary aids and services *Aids:* calculators, personal computers, personal spelling/word-use assistants (e.g., Franklin Speller), scan and read programs (e.g., Kurzweil), screen-enlarging programs, tape recorders, taped textbooks, enlarged print for texts, class hand-outs, journal articles. *Services and accommodations:* priority registration, alternative test arrangements, readers, note-takers, and scribes.

Student organization There is a student organization for students with LD.

ADD/ADHD Students with ADD/ADHD are eligible for the same services available to students with LD, as well as distraction-free testing environments.

Application *Required:* high school transcript, ACT or SAT I (extended-time tests accepted), personal statement, and letter(s) of recommendation. *Recommended:* participation in extracurricular activities. Upon acceptance, documentation of need for special services should be sent only to your LD program or unit. *Application deadline (institutional):* 1/1 for fall.

LD program contact Belinda M. Guthrie, Director of Disability and Support Services, 124 Raymond Avenue, Box 164, Poughkeepsie, NY 12604-0164. *Phone:* 914-437-7584. *Fax:* 914-437-5715. *E-mail:* guthrie@vassar.edu.

Application contact Vassar College, 124 Raymond Avenue, Poughkeepsie, NY 12604. *Web address:* http://www.vassar.edu/.

VILLANOVA UNIVERSITY

Villanova, Pennsylvania

Students with LD Served by Program	110	ADD/ADHD Services	✓
Staff	1 full-time	Summer Preparation Program	n/a
LD Program or Service Fee	n/a	Alternative Test Arrangements	✓
LD Program Began	1994	LD Student Organization	n/a

Office of Learning Support Services began offering services in 1994. The program serves approximately 110 undergraduate students. Faculty consists of 1 full-time staff member. Services are provided by LD specialists and trained peer tutors.

Policies Students with LD may take up to 18 credit hours per semester; 12 credit hours per semester are required to maintain full-time status and to be eligible for financial aid. LD services are also available to graduate students.

Special preparation or orientation Optional orientation held during general New Student Orientation.

Subject-area tutoring Available in most subjects. Offered one-on-one and in small groups by graduate assistants/students, trained peer tutors, and LD specialists.

Counseling and advisement Career counseling and individual counseling are available.

Auxiliary aids and services *Aids:* speech recognition programs (e.g., Dragon), tape recorders, taped textbooks. *Services and accommodations:* advocates, alternative test arrangements, readers, note-takers, and scribes.

ADD/ADHD Students with ADD/ADHD are eligible for the same services available to students with LD, as well as distraction-free study areas and distraction-free testing environments.

Application *Required:* high school transcript and ACT or SAT I (extended-time or untimed test accepted). *Recommended:* participation in extracurricular activities. Upon acceptance, documentation of need for special services should be sent only to your LD program or unit.

LD program contact Nancy Mott, Learning Disabilities Coordinator, Learning Support Services, 800 Lancaster Avenue, Villanova, PA 19085-1699. *Phone:* 610-519-5636. *Fax:* 610-519-7649. *E-mail:* nancy.mott@villanova.edu.

Application contact Villanova University, 800 Lancaster Avenue, Villanova, PA 19085-1699. *E-mail:* gotovu@ucis.vill.edu. *Web address:* http://www.villanova.edu/.

VIRGINIA COMMONWEALTH UNIVERSITY

Richmond, Virginia

Students with LD Served by Program	325	ADD/ADHD Services	✓
Staff	2 full-time, 17 part-time	Summer Preparation Program	n/a
LD Program or Service Fee	n/a	Alternative Test Arrangements	✓
LD Program Began	1989	LD Student Organization	n/a

Services for Students with Disabilities (SSD) began offering services in 1989. The program serves approximately 325 undergraduate students. Faculty consists of 2 full-time and 17 part-time staff members. Services are provided by academic advisers, counselors, and graduate assistants/students.

Policies Students with LD may take up to 19 credits per semester; 12 credits per semester are required to maintain full-time status; 6 credits per semester are required to be eligible for financial aid. LD services are also available to graduate students.

Subject-area tutoring Available in most subjects. Offered one-on-one by trained peer tutors.

Counseling and advisement Academic advisement by a staff member affiliated with the program is available.

Auxiliary aids and services *Aids:* screen-enlarging programs, screen readers, speech recognition programs (e.g., Dragon), taped textbooks. *Services and accommodations:* priority registration, alternative test arrangements, readers, note-takers, and scribes.

ADD/ADHD Students with ADD/ADHD are eligible for the same services available to students with LD, as well as distraction-free testing environments and medication management.

Application *Required:* high school transcript and ACT or SAT I (extended-time or untimed test accepted). *Recommended:* participation in extracurricular activities. Upon application, documentation of need for special services should be sent only to your LD program or unit. Upon acceptance, documentation of need for special services should be sent only to your LD program or unit. *Application deadline (institutional):* 2/1 for fall and 12/1 for spring. *Application deadline (LD program):* 2/1 for fall and 12/1 for spring.

LD program contact Dr. Shyla M. Ipsen, Coordinator, Services for Students with Disabilities, 109 North Harrison Street, Richmond, VA 23284-2500. *Phone:* 804-828-1139. *Fax:* 804-828-1944. *E-mail:* sipsen@saturn.vcu.edu.

Application contact Counseling Staff, Virginia Commonwealth University, 821 West Franklin Street, Box 842526, Richmond, VA 23284-9005. *Phone:* 804-828-1222. *E-mail:* vcuinfo@vcu.edu. *Web address:* http://www.vcu.edu/.

VIRGINIA INTERMONT COLLEGE

Bristol, Virginia

Students with LD Served by Program	23	ADD/ADHD Services	✓
Staff	3 full-time	Summer Preparation Program	n/a
LD Program or Service Fee	n/a	Alternative Test Arrangements	✓
LD Program Began	1987	LD Student Organization	n/a

Student Support Services began offering services in 1987. The program serves approximately 23 undergraduate students. Faculty consists of 3 full-time staff members. Services are provided by academic advisers, counselors, diagnostic specialists, LD specialists, and trained peer tutors.

Policies Students with LD may take up to 18 credit hours per semester; 12 credit hours per semester are required to maintain full-time status and to be eligible for financial aid.

Diagnostic testing Available for auditory processing, motor skills, spelling, handwriting, spoken language, intelligence, study skills, learning strategies, reading, written language, learning styles, visual processing, and math.

Basic skills remediation Available in study skills, time management, and learning strategies. Offered one-on-one.

Subject-area tutoring Available in most subjects. Offered one-on-one and in small groups by trained peer tutors.

Counseling and advisement Individual counseling and support groups are available. Academic advisement by a staff member affiliated with the program is available.

Auxiliary aids and services *Aids:* scan and read programs (e.g., Kurzweil), taped textbooks. *Services and accommodations:* advocates, alternative test arrangements, readers, note-takers, scribes, and secondary advisor.

ADD/ADHD Students with ADD/ADHD are eligible for the same services available to students with LD, as well as distraction-free testing environments and support groups for ADD/ADHD.

Virginia Intermont College (continued)

Application *Required:* high school transcript and ACT or SAT I (extended-time or untimed test accepted). Upon acceptance, documentation of need for special services should be sent only to your LD program or unit. *Application deadline (institutional):* rolling/continuous for fall and rolling/continuous for spring.
LD program contact Barbara Holbrook, School Psychologist, Student Support Services, Campus Box 380, Bristol, VA 24201. *Phone:* 540-466-7906. *Fax:* 540-669-5763. *E-mail:* bholbroo@vic,edu.
Application contact Robin B. Cozart, Director of Admissions, Virginia Intermont College, 1013 Moore Street, Bristol, VA 24201-4298. *Phone:* 540-466-7854. *E-mail:* viadmit@vic.edu. *Web address:* http://www.vic.edu/.

VOORHEES COLLEGE
Denmark, South Carolina

Students with LD Served by Program	10	ADD/ADHD Services	✓
Staff	1 full-time	Summer Preparation Program	n/a
LD Program or Service Fee	n/a	Alternative Test Arrangements	✓
LD Program Began	n/a	LD Student Organization	n/a

Student Testing and Retention (STAR) Center serves approximately 10 undergraduate students. Faculty consists of 1 full-time staff member. Services are provided by Director of STAR Center.
Special preparation or orientation Optional orientation held individually by special arrangement.
Diagnostic testing Available for neuropsychological, intelligence, personality, study skills, reading, and learning styles.
Subject-area tutoring Available in all subjects. Offered one-on-one and in small groups by computer-based instruction and professional tutors.
Counseling and advisement Career counseling and individual counseling are available.
Auxiliary aids and services *Services and accommodations:* alternative test arrangements.
ADD/ADHD Students with ADD/ADHD are eligible for the same services available to students with LD, as well as distraction-free study areas and distraction-free testing environments.
Application *Required:* high school transcript, ACT or SAT I (extended-time or untimed test accepted), and letter(s) of recommendation. Upon application, documentation of need for special services should be sent only to your LD program or unit. Upon acceptance, documentation of need for special services should be sent only to your LD program or unit. *Application deadline (institutional):* rolling/continuous for fall and rolling/continuous for spring.
LD program contact Dr. Adeleri Onisegun, Director of Assessment and Student Achievement, PO Box 678, Denmark, SC 29042. *Phone:* 803-703-7131. *E-mail:* onisegun@voorhees.edu.
Application contact Voorhees College, 1411 Voorhees Road, Denmark, SC 29042.

WASHINGTON STATE UNIVERSITY
Pullman, Washington

Students with LD Served by Program	300	ADD/ADHD Services	✓
Staff	6 full-time, 1 part-time	Summer Preparation Program	n/a
LD Program or Service Fee	n/a	Alternative Test Arrangements	✓
LD Program Began	1986	LD Student Organization	✓

Disability Resource Center (DRC) began offering services in 1986. The program serves approximately 300 undergraduate students. Faculty consists of 6 full-time staff members and 1 part-time staff member. Services are provided by LD specialists.
Policies The college has written policies regarding course substitutions. Students with LD may take up to 18 credit hours per semester; 12 credit hours per semester are required to maintain full-time status and to be eligible for financial aid. LD services are also available to graduate students.
Fees *Diagnostic Testing Fee:* $200.
Diagnostic testing Available for learning disability/ADD.
Counseling and advisement Career counseling, individual counseling, small-group counseling, and support groups are available.
Auxiliary aids and services *Aids:* scan and read programs (e.g., Kurzweil), screen readers, speech recognition programs (e.g., Dragon), taped textbooks. *Services and accommodations:* advocates, priority registration, alternative test arrangements, readers, note-takers, and scribes.
Student organization There is a student organization for students with LD.
ADD/ADHD Students with ADD/ADHD are eligible for the same services available to students with LD, as well as distraction-free testing environments.
Application *Required:* high school transcript and ACT or SAT I (extended-time or untimed test accepted). Upon acceptance, documentation of need for special services should be sent only to your LD program or unit. *Application deadline (institutional):* rolling/continuous for fall and rolling/continuous for spring. *Application deadline (LD program):* rolling/continuous for fall and rolling/continuous for spring.
LD program contact Susan Schaeffer, Assistant Director, AD Annex 206, Pullman, WA 99164-4122. *Phone:* 509-335-1566. *Fax:* 509-335-8511. *E-mail:* schaeff@wsu.edu.
Application contact Washington State University, Office of Admissions, PO Box 641067, Pullman, WA 99164-1067. *E-mail:* admiss@wsu.edu. *Web address:* http://www.wsu.edu/.

WASHINGTON UNIVERSITY IN ST. LOUIS
St. Louis, Missouri

Students with LD Served by Program	71	ADD/ADHD Services	✓
Staff	2 full-time	Summer Preparation Program	n/a
LD Program or Service Fee	n/a	Alternative Test Arrangements	✓
LD Program Began	1987	LD Student Organization	n/a

Disability Resource Center began offering services in 1987. The program serves approximately 71 undergraduate students. Faculty consists of 2 full-time staff members.
Policies Students with LD may take up to 21 credit hours per semester; 12 credit hours per semester are required to maintain full-time status and to be eligible for financial aid. LD services are also available to graduate students.
Special preparation or orientation Optional orientation held before classes begin.
Counseling and advisement Individual counseling is available.
Auxiliary aids and services *Aids:* scan and read programs (e.g., Kurzweil), screen-enlarging programs, screen readers, speech recognition programs (e.g., Dragon), tape recorders, taped textbooks. *Services and accommodations:* advocates, alternative test arrangements, readers, note-takers, and scribes.
ADD/ADHD Students with ADD/ADHD are eligible for the same services available to students with LD, as well as distraction-free testing environments.

Application *Required:* high school transcript, ACT or SAT I (extended-time or untimed test accepted), personal statement, and letter(s) of recommendation. *Recommended:* participation in extracurricular activities. Upon acceptance, documentation of need for special services should be sent only to your LD program or unit. *Application deadline (institutional):* 1/15 for fall. **LD program contact** Dr. Fran Lang, Director, Campus Box 1136, One Brookings Drive, St. Louis, MO 63130-4899. *Phone:* 314-935-4062. *Fax:* 314-935-8272. *E-mail:* drc@dosa.wustl.edu. **Application contact** Washington University in St. Louis, Campus Box 1089, 1 Brookings Drive, St. Louis, MO 63130-4899. *E-mail:* admission@wustl.edu. *Web address:* http://www.wustl.edu/.

WAYNE STATE UNIVERSITY
Detroit, Michigan

Students with LD Served by Program	45	ADD/ADHD Services	✓
Staff	3 full-time, 5 part-time	Summer Preparation Program	n/a
LD Program or Service Fee	n/a	Alternative Test Arrangements	✓
LD Program Began	1991	LD Student Organization	n/a

Educational Accessibility Services (EAS) began offering services in 1991. The program serves approximately 45 undergraduate students. Faculty consists of 3 full-time and 5 part-time staff members. Services are provided by academic advisers, counselors, graduate assistants/students, and LD specialists.
Policies The college has written policies regarding course substitutions. Students with LD may take up to 12 credits per semester; 12 credits per semester are required to be eligible for financial aid. LD services are also available to graduate students.
Basic skills remediation Available in study skills, reading, time management, visual processing, learning strategies, spelling, written language, and math. Offered one-on-one and in small groups by computer-based instruction, graduate assistants/students, LD specialists, and books, audio tapes.
Subject-area tutoring Available in most subjects. Offered one-on-one and in small groups by graduate assistants/students.
Special courses Available in career planning, oral communication skills, study skills, college survival skills, practical computer skills, test taking, reading, time management, learning strategies, self-advocacy, vocabulary development, math, stress management, and written composition skills. No courses are offered for credit; none enter into overall grade point average.
Counseling and advisement Career counseling, individual counseling, small-group counseling, and support groups are available. Academic advisement by a staff member affiliated with the program is available.
Auxiliary aids and services *Aids:* calculators, personal spelling/word-use assistants (e.g., Franklin Speller), scan and read programs (e.g., Kurzweil), screen-enlarging programs, screen readers, speech recognition programs (e.g., Dragon), tape recorders, taped textbooks. *Services and accommodations:* advocates, priority registration, alternative test arrangements, readers, note-takers, and scribes.
ADD/ADHD Students with ADD/ADHD are eligible for the same services available to students with LD, as well as distraction-free study areas and distraction-free testing environments.
Application *Required:* high school transcript and ACT (extended-time or untimed test accepted). *Recommended:* separate application to your LD program or unit. Upon application, documentation of need for special services should be sent only to your LD program or unit. Upon acceptance, documentation of need

for special services should be sent only to your LD program or unit. *Application deadline (institutional):* 8/1 for fall and 4/1 for spring.
LD program contact Donald Anderson, University Counselor II, 652 Student Center Building, Detroit, MI 48202. *Phone:* 313-577-1851. *Fax:* 313-577-0617. *E-mail:* ad3245@wayne.edu.
Application contact Wayne State University, 656 West Kirby Street, Detroit, MI 48202. *E-mail:* credwine@cms.cc.wayne.edu. *Web address:* http://www.wayne.edu/.

WESTERN BAPTIST COLLEGE
Salem, Oregon

Students with LD Served by Program	5	ADD/ADHD Services	✓
Staff	1 full-time	Summer Preparation Program	n/a
LD Program or Service Fee	n/a	Alternative Test Arrangements	✓
LD Program Began	1996	LD Student Organization	n/a

Academic Services began offering services in 1996. The program serves approximately 5 undergraduate students. Faculty consists of 1 full-time staff member. Services are provided by academic advisers, regular education teachers, and diagnostic specialists.
Policies The college has written policies regarding course substitutions. Students with LD may take up to 17 semester hours per semester; 12 semester hours per semester are required to maintain full-time status and to be eligible for financial aid.
Counseling and advisement Academic advisement by a staff member affiliated with the program is available.
Auxiliary aids and services *Aids:* tape recorders, taped textbooks. *Services and accommodations:* advocates, alternative test arrangements, readers, note-takers, and scribes.
ADD/ADHD Students with ADD/ADHD are eligible for the same services available to students with LD, as well as distraction-free testing environments and medication management.
Application *Required:* high school transcript, ACT or SAT I (extended-time or untimed test accepted), personal statement, letter(s) of recommendation, separate application to your LD program or unit, and psychoeducational report (3 years old or less). Upon application, documentation of need for special services should be sent only to your LD program or unit. Upon acceptance, documentation of need for special services should be sent only to your LD program or unit. *Application deadline (institutional):* rolling/continuous for fall and rolling/continuous for spring. *Application deadline (LD program):* rolling/continuous for fall and rolling/continuous for spring.
LD program contact Faythe Moore, Director of Academic and Career Services, 5000 Deer Park Drive SE, Salem, OR 97301. *Phone:* 503-375-7012. *Fax:* 503-585-4316. *E-mail:* fmoore@wbc.edu.
Application contact Daren Milionis, Dean of Admissions, Western Baptist College, 5000 Deer Park Drive, SE, Salem, OR 97301-9392. *Phone:* 503-375-7005. *E-mail:* dmilionis@wbc.edu. *Web address:* http://www.wbc.edu/.

WESTERN CAROLINA UNIVERSITY
Cullowhee, North Carolina

Students with LD Served by Program	100	ADD/ADHD Services	✓
Staff	4 full-time, 1 part-time	Summer Preparation Program	n/a
LD Program or Service Fee	n/a	Alternative Test Arrangements	✓
LD Program Began	1980	LD Student Organization	n/a

Western Carolina University (continued)

Student Support Services began offering services in 1980. The program serves approximately 100 undergraduate students. Faculty consists of 4 full-time staff members and 1 part-time staff member. Services are provided by academic advisers, regular education teachers, counselors, graduate assistants/students, trained peer tutors, and professional tutors.

Policies The college has written policies regarding course substitutions and grade forgiveness. Students with LD may take up to 19 credit hours per semester; 12 credit hours per semester are required to maintain full-time status and to be eligible for financial aid. LD services are also available to graduate students.

Subject-area tutoring Available in most subjects. Offered one-on-one and in small groups by professional tutors, graduate assistants/students, and trained peer tutors.

Counseling and advisement Career counseling, individual counseling, small-group counseling, and support groups are available. Academic advisement by a staff member affiliated with the program is available.

Auxiliary aids and services *Aids:* calculators, personal spelling/word-use assistants (e.g., Franklin Speller), scan and read programs (e.g., Kurzweil), screen-enlarging programs, screen readers, speech recognition programs (e.g., Dragon), tape recorders, taped textbooks. *Services and accommodations:* advocates, priority registration, alternative test arrangements, readers, notetakers, and scribes.

ADD/ADHD Students with ADD/ADHD are eligible for the same services available to students with LD, as well as distraction-free study areas and distraction-free testing environments.

Application *Required:* high school transcript, SAT I (extended-time test accepted), and letter(s) of recommendation. *Recommended:* separate application to your LD program or unit, psychoeducational report, and documentation of high school services (e.g., Individualized Education Program [IEP] or 504 plan). Upon acceptance, documentation of need for special services should be sent only to your LD program or unit.

LD program contact Carol Mellen, Director, Student Support Services, 20 McKee, Cullowhee, NC 28723. *Phone:* 828-227-7127. *Fax:* 828-227-7344. *E-mail:* mellen@wcu.edu.

Application contact Western Carolina University, Cullowhee, NC 28723. *E-mail:* cauley@wcu.edu. *Web address:* http://www.wcu.edu/.

WESTERN ILLINOIS UNIVERSITY
Macomb, Illinois

Students with LD Served by Program	101	ADD/ADHD Services	✓
Staff	3 full-time, 4 part-time	Summer Preparation Program	n/a
LD Program or Service Fee	n/a	Alternative Test Arrangements	✓
LD Program Began	1982	LD Student Organization	✓

Disability Support Services (DSS) began offering services in 1982. The program serves approximately 101 undergraduate students. Faculty consists of 3 full-time and 4 part-time staff members. Services are provided by LD specialists.

Policies The college has written policies regarding course substitutions. Students with LD may take up to 18 credit hours per semester; 12 credit hours per semester are required to maintain full-time status; 6 credit hours per semester are required to be eligible for financial aid. LD services are also available to graduate students.

Special preparation or orientation Optional orientation held before classes begin and individually by special arrangement.

Auxiliary aids and services *Aids:* scan and read programs (e.g., Kurzweil), screen-enlarging programs, screen readers, speech recognition programs (e.g., Dragon), tape recorders, taped textbooks. *Services and accommodations:* advocates, priority registration, alternative test arrangements, readers, notetakers, and scribes.

Student organization There is a student organization for students with LD.

ADD/ADHD Students with ADD/ADHD are eligible for the same services available to students with LD, as well as distraction-free testing environments.

Application *Required:* high school transcript and ACT or SAT I (extended-time or untimed test accepted). Upon acceptance, documentation of need for special services should be sent only to your LD program or unit. *Application deadline (institutional):* rolling/continuous for fall and rolling/continuous for spring. *Application deadline (LD program):* rolling/continuous for fall and rolling/continuous for spring.

LD program contact Joan Green, Director, Disability Support Services, 1 University Circle, Macomb, IL 61455-1390. *Phone:* 309-298-2512. *Fax:* 309-298-2361. *E-mail:* joan_green@ccmail.wiu.edu.

Application contact Western Illinois University, 1 University Circle, Macomb, IL 61455-1390. *E-mail:* karen_helmers@uniu.edu. *Web address:* http://www.wiu.edu/.

WESTERN NEW ENGLAND COLLEGE
Springfield, Massachusetts

Students with LD Served by Program	50	ADD/ADHD Services	✓
Staff	2 full-time, 5 part-time	Summer Preparation Program	n/a
LD Program or Service Fee	varies	Alternative Test Arrangements	✓
LD Program Began	1998	LD Student Organization	n/a

Student Disability Services began offering services in 1998. The program serves approximately 50 undergraduate students. Faculty consists of 2 full-time and 5 part-time staff members. Services are provided by remediation/learning specialists, LD specialists, trained peer tutors, and professional tutors.

Policies Students with LD may take up to 18 credit hours per semester; 9 credit hours per semester are required to maintain full-time status; 12 credit hours per semester are required to be eligible for financial aid.

Fees *LD Program or Service Fee:* ranges from $1400 to $2500 per year.

Special preparation or orientation Optional orientation held during registration, during summer prior to enrollment, and individually by special arrangement.

Diagnostic testing Available for study skills, learning strategies, and learning styles.

Basic skills remediation Available in auditory processing, study skills, computer skills, reading, time management, visual processing, learning strategies, written language, and math. Offered one-on-one by LD specialists, professional tutors, and trained peer tutors.

Subject-area tutoring Available in all subjects. Offered one-on-one by professional tutors, trained peer tutors, and LD specialists.

Counseling and advisement Individual counseling and support groups are available.

Auxiliary aids and services *Aids:* calculators, scan and read programs (e.g., Kurzweil), screen-enlarging programs, screen readers, speech recognition programs (e.g., Dragon), tape recorders, taped textbooks. *Services and accommodations:* advocates, priority registration, alternative test arrangements, readers, note-takers, and scribes.

ADD/ADHD Students with ADD/ADHD are eligible for the same services available to students with LD, as well as distraction-free study areas, distraction-free testing environments and personal coach or mentors.

Application *Required:* high school transcript, ACT or SAT I (extended-time or untimed SAT I test accepted), and letter(s) of recommendation. *Recommended:* participation in extracurricular activities, interview, personal statement, and separate application to your LD program or unit. Upon application, documentation of need for special services should be sent only to your LD program or unit. Upon acceptance, documentation of need for special services should be sent only to your LD program or unit. *Application deadline (institutional):* rolling/continuous for fall and rolling/continuous for spring. *Application deadline (LD program):* rolling/continuous for fall and rolling/continuous for spring.

LD program contact Dr. Bonni Alpert, Director, Student Disability Services, 1215 Wilbraham Road, Springfield, MA 01119. *Phone:* 413-782-1257. *Fax:* 413-782-1746. *E-mail:* balpert@wnec. edu.

Application contact Western New England College, 1215 Wilbraham Road, Springfield, MA 01119-2654. *E-mail:* ugradmis@wnec.edu. *Web address:* http://www.wnec.edu/.

WESTERN WASHINGTON UNIVERSITY
Bellingham, Washington

Students with LD Served by Program	175	ADD/ADHD Services	✓
Staff	1 full-time, 1 part-time	Summer Preparation Program	n/a
LD Program or Service Fee	n/a	Alternative Test Arrangements	✓
LD Program Began	1985	LD Student Organization	n/a

Student Life/Disability Resources for Students began offering services in 1985. The program serves approximately 175 undergraduate students. Faculty consists of 1 full-time and 1 part-time staff member.

Policies The college has written policies regarding course substitutions, grade forgiveness, and substitution and waivers of requirements for admission and graduation. LD services are also available to graduate students.

Counseling and advisement Career counseling, individual counseling, small-group counseling, and support groups are available.

Auxiliary aids and services *Aids:* calculators, personal computers, personal spelling/word-use assistants (e.g., Franklin Speller), scan and read programs (e.g., Kurzweil), screen-enlarging programs, screen readers, speech recognition programs (e.g., Dragon), tape recorders, taped textbooks. *Services and accommodations:* advocates, priority registration, alternative test arrangements, readers, note-takers, and scribes.

ADD/ADHD Students with ADD/ADHD are eligible for the same services available to students with LD, as well as distraction-free testing environments and support groups for ADD/ADHD.

Application *Required:* high school transcript, participation in extracurricular activities, ACT or SAT I (extended-time or untimed test accepted), personal statement, and letter(s) of recommendation. Upon application, documentation of need for special services should be sent only to your LD program or unit. Upon acceptance, documentation of need for special services should be sent only to your LD program or unit.

LD program contact David Brunnemer, Associate Director/Disability Specialist, Student Life/Disability Resources for Students, Old Main 110, Bellingham, WA 98225-9019. *Phone:* 360-650-3844. *Fax:* 360-650-3715. *E-mail:* david.brunnemer@wwu. edu.

Application contact Western Washington University, 516 High Street, Bellingham, WA 98225-9009. *E-mail:* admit@cc.wwu.edu. *Web address:* http://www.wwu.edu/.

WEST VIRGINIA STATE COLLEGE
Institute, West Virginia

Students with LD Served by Program	75	ADD/ADHD Services	✓
Staff	1 full-time, 6 part-time	Summer Preparation Program	n/a
LD Program or Service Fee	n/a	Alternative Test Arrangements	✓
LD Program Began	n/a	LD Student Organization	n/a

Disability Services Office serves approximately 75 undergraduate students. Faculty consists of 1 full-time and 6 part-time staff members. Services are provided by counselors and trained peer tutors.

Policies Students with LD may take up to 18 credit hours per semester; 12 credit hours per semester are required to maintain full-time status; 6 credit hours per semester are required to be eligible for financial aid.

Basic skills remediation Available in study skills, reading, time management, learning strategies, spelling, and math. Offered one-on-one and in small groups by trained peer tutors.

Subject-area tutoring Available in most subjects. Offered one-on-one and in small groups by trained peer tutors.

Special courses Available in college survival skills and time management. All courses are offered for credit; all enter into overall grade point average.

Counseling and advisement Career counseling and individual counseling are available.

Auxiliary aids and services *Aids:* calculators, personal computers, scan and read programs (e.g., Kurzweil), screen-enlarging programs, screen readers, speech recognition programs (e.g., Dragon), tape recorders, taped textbooks. *Services and accommodations:* advocates, alternative test arrangements, readers, note-takers, and scribes.

ADD/ADHD Students with ADD/ADHD are eligible for the same services available to students with LD, as well as distraction-free testing environments.

Application *Required:* high school transcript and ACT or SAT I (extended-time or untimed test accepted). Upon application, documentation of need for special services should be sent only to your LD program or unit. Upon acceptance, documentation of need for special services should be sent only to your LD program or unit. *Application deadline (institutional):* 8/20 for fall and 1/5 for spring. *Application deadline (LD program):* rolling/continuous for fall and rolling/continuous for spring.

LD program contact Kellie Dunlap, Disability Services Counselor, PO Box 1000, Campus Box 178, Institute, WV 25112. *Phone:* 304-766-3083. *Fax:* 304-766-4158. *E-mail:* dunlopke@mail.wvsc.edu.

Application contact Alice Ruhnke, Interim Director of Admissions, West Virginia State College, WVSC, Campus Box 188, PO Box 1000, Institute, WV 25112-1000. *Phone:* 304-766-3221. *E-mail:* greenrl@ernie.wvsc.wvnet.edu. *Web address:* http://www.wvsc. edu/.

WEST VIRGINIA WESLEYAN COLLEGE

Buckhannon, West Virginia

Students with LD Served by Program	115	ADD/ADHD Services	✓
Staff	8 full-time, 5 part-time	Summer Preparation Program	n/a
LD Program or Service Fee	n/a	Alternative Test Arrangements	✓
LD Program Began	n/a	LD Student Organization	n/a

Student Academic Support Services serves approximately 115 undergraduate students. Faculty consists of 8 full-time and 5 part-time staff members. Services are provided by regular education teachers, counselors, remediation/learning specialists, LD specialists, trained peer tutors, and reading specialists.

Policies 12 credit hours per semester are required to maintain full-time status and to be eligible for financial aid.

Special preparation or orientation Required orientation held first day of freshmen orientation.

Auxiliary aids and services *Aids:* calculators, personal computers, personal spelling/word-use assistants (e.g., Franklin Speller), scan and read programs (e.g., Kurzweil), screen-enlarging programs, speech recognition programs (e.g., Dragon), tape recorders, taped textbooks, assistive technology lab, testing lab. *Services and accommodations:* advocates, priority registration, alternative test arrangements, readers, note-takers, and scribes.

ADD/ADHD Students with ADD/ADHD are eligible for the same services available to students with LD, as well as distraction-free study areas, distraction-free testing environments, medication management and personal coach or mentors.

Application *Required:* high school transcript and ACT or SAT I (extended-time or untimed test accepted). *Recommended:* participation in extracurricular activities, interview, personal statement, letter(s) of recommendation, psychoeducational report (3 years old or less), and documentation of high school services (e.g., Individualized Education Program [IEP] or 504 plan). Upon application, documentation of need for special services should be sent only to your LD program or unit. Upon acceptance, documentation of need for special services should be sent only to your LD program or unit. *Application deadline (institutional):* 3/1 for fall and 12/1 for spring. *Application deadline (LD program):* 3/1 for fall and 12/1 for spring.

LD program contact Carolyn Baisden, Administrative Assistant, 59 College Avenue, Buckhannon, WV 26201. *Phone:* 304-473-8563. *Fax:* 304-473-8497. *E-mail:* baisden_c@wvwc.edu.

Application contact West Virginia Wesleyan College, 59 College Avenue, Buckhannon, WV 26201. *E-mail:* admissions@academ.wvwc.edu. *Web address:* http://www.wvwc.edu/.

WHEELOCK COLLEGE

Boston, Massachusetts

Students with LD Served by Program	45	ADD/ADHD Services	✓
Staff	3 full-time, 1 part-time	Summer Preparation Program	n/a
LD Program or Service Fee	n/a	Alternative Test Arrangements	✓
LD Program Began	1991	LD Student Organization	n/a

Office of Academic Advising and Assistance (OAAA) began offering services in 1991. The program serves approximately 45 undergraduate students. Faculty consists of 3 full-time staff members and 1 part-time staff member. Services are provided by academic advisers, remediation/learning specialists, LD specialists, and trained peer tutors.

Policies Students with LD may take up to 20 credit hours per semester; 12 credit hours per semester are required to maintain full-time status; 6 credit hours per semester are required to be eligible for financial aid. LD services are also available to graduate students.

Special preparation or orientation Required orientation held during registration, after classes begin, and individually by special arrangement.

Basic skills remediation Available in study skills, reading, time management, learning strategies, spelling, written language, and math. Offered one-on-one and in small groups by regular education teachers, LD specialists, and trained peer tutors.

Subject-area tutoring Available in all subjects. Offered one-on-one and in small groups by trained peer tutors and LD specialists.

Counseling and advisement Career counseling, individual counseling, and small-group counseling are available. Academic advisement by a staff member affiliated with the program is available.

Auxiliary aids and services *Aids:* calculators, personal computers, tape recorders, taped textbooks. *Services and accommodations:* advocates, priority registration, alternative test arrangements, readers, note-takers, and scribes.

ADD/ADHD Students with ADD/ADHD are eligible for the same services available to students with LD, as well as distraction-free study areas, distraction-free testing environments and medication management.

Application *Required:* high school transcript, ACT or SAT I (extended-time or untimed test accepted), personal statement, and letter(s) of recommendation. *Recommended:* participation in extracurricular activities, interview, psychoeducational report, and documentation of high school services (e.g., Individualized Education Program [IEP] or 504 plan). Upon application, documentation of need for special services should be sent only to your LD program or unit. Upon acceptance, documentation of need for special services should be sent only to your LD program or unit. *Application deadline (institutional):* 4/1 for fall and 12/1 for spring.

LD program contact Coordinator of Disability Services, 200 The Riverway, Boston, MA 02215. *Phone:* 617-879-2305.

Application contact Wheelock College, 200 The Riverway, Boston, MA 02215. *E-mail:* undergrad@wheelock.edu. *Web address:* http://www.wheelock.edu/.

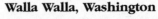

WHITMAN COLLEGE

Walla Walla, Washington

Students with LD Served by Program	25	ADD/ADHD Services	✓
Staff	1 full-time, 1 part-time	Summer Preparation Program	n/a
LD Program or Service Fee	n/a	Alternative Test Arrangements	✓
LD Program Began	1985	LD Student Organization	n/a

Academic Resource Center began offering services in 1985. The program serves approximately 25 undergraduate students. Faculty consists of 1 full-time and 1 part-time staff member. Services are provided by Director.

Diagnostic testing Available for auditory processing, visual processing, and learning disabilities screening.

Counseling and advisement Individual counseling is available.

Auxiliary aids and services *Aids:* personal computers, scan and read programs (e.g., Kurzweil), screen-enlarging programs, speech recognition programs (e.g., Dragon), tape recorders, taped textbooks. *Services and accommodations:* advocates, priority registration, alternative test arrangements, readers, note-takers, and scribes.

ADD/ADHD Students with ADD/ADHD are eligible for the same services available to students with LD, as well as distraction-free study areas, distraction-free testing environments and medication management.

Application *Required:* high school transcript, personal statement, and letter(s) of recommendation. *Recommended:* participation in extracurricular activities, ACT (extended-time or untimed test accepted), and interview. Upon acceptance, documentation of need for special services should be sent only to your LD program or unit. *Application deadline (institutional):* 2/1 for fall and 12/1 for spring.

LD program contact Clare Carson, Director of Academic Resources, 345 Boyer Avenue, Walla Walla, WA 99362. *Phone:* 509-527-5213. *Fax:* 509-526-4770. *E-mail:* carsonc@whitman. edu.

Application contact Whitman College, 345 Boyer Avenue, Walla Walla, WA 99362-2083. *E-mail:* admission@whitman.edu. *Web address:* http://www.whitman.edu/.

WHITTIER COLLEGE
Whittier, California

Students with LD Served by Program	61	ADD/ADHD Services	✓
Staff	1 full-time, 1 part-time	Summer Preparation Program	n/a
LD Program or Service Fee	n/a	Alternative Test Arrangements	✓
LD Program Began	1994	LD Student Organization	n/a

Learning Support Services began offering services in 1994. The program serves approximately 61 undergraduate students. Faculty consists of 1 full-time and 1 part-time staff member. Services are provided by counselors.

Policies Students with LD may take up to 15 units per semester; 12 units per semester are required to maintain full-time status and to be eligible for financial aid.

Special preparation or orientation Optional orientation held during registration and individually by special arrangement.

Counseling and advisement Individual counseling is available.

Auxiliary aids and services *Aids:* scan and read programs (e.g., Kurzweil), speech recognition programs (e.g., Dragon), taped textbooks. *Services and accommodations:* priority registration, alternative test arrangements, readers, and note-takers.

ADD/ADHD Students with ADD/ADHD are eligible for the same services available to students with LD, as well as distraction-free testing environments.

Application *Required:* high school transcript, ACT or SAT I (extended-time or untimed test accepted), and letter(s) of recommendation. *Recommended:* participation in extracurricular activities, interview, and personal statement. Upon acceptance, documentation of need for special services should be sent only to your LD program or unit. *Application deadline (institutional):* 2/1 for fall.

LD program contact Jamie Shepherd, Director of Learning Support Services, 13406 Philadelphia Street, PO Box 634, Whittier, CA 90608. *Phone:* 562-907-4233. *Fax:* 562-907-4980. *E-mail:* jshepherd@whittier.edu.

Application contact Whittier College, 13406 E Philadelphia Street, Whittier, CA 90608-0634. *Web address:* http://www.whittier.edu/.

WINGATE UNIVERSITY
Wingate, North Carolina

Students with LD Served by Program	80	ADD/ADHD Services	✓
Staff	1 full-time, 2 part-time	Summer Preparation Program	n/a
LD Program or Service Fee	n/a	Alternative Test Arrangements	✓
LD Program Began	1985	LD Student Organization	n/a

Support Services for Students with Disabilities began offering services in 1985. The program serves approximately 80 undergraduate students. Faculty consists of 1 full-time and 2 part-time staff members. Services are provided by academic advisers, regular education teachers, and counselors.

Policies The college has written policies regarding course substitutions and substitution and waivers of requirements for admission and graduation. Students with LD may take up to 18 credit hours per semester; 12 credit hours per semester are required to maintain full-time status and to be eligible for financial aid. LD services are also available to graduate students.

Special preparation or orientation Required orientation held before classes begin, after classes begin, and individually by special arrangement.

Subject-area tutoring Available in most subjects. Offered one-on-one, in small groups, and class-size groups by trained peer tutors.

Counseling and advisement Academic advisement by a staff member affiliated with the program is available.

Auxiliary aids and services *Aids:* tape recorders, taped textbooks. *Services and accommodations:* priority registration, alternative test arrangements, and note-takers.

ADD/ADHD Students with ADD/ADHD are eligible for the same services available to students with LD, as well as distraction-free study areas and distraction-free testing environments.

Application *Required:* high school transcript, ACT or SAT I (extended-time or untimed test accepted), personal statement, letter(s) of recommendation, and psychoeducational report (3 years old or less). Upon application, documentation of need for special services should be sent only to admissions. Upon acceptance, documentation of need for special services should be sent only to your LD program or unit. *Application deadline (institutional):* rolling/continuous for fall and rolling/continuous for spring.

LD program contact Linda Stedje-Larsen, Director of Support Services, CB 3068, Wingate, NC 28174. *Phone:* 704-233-8269. *Fax:* 704-233-8290. *E-mail:* stedje@wingate.edu.

Application contact Wingate University, Wingate, NC 28174-0159. *E-mail:* admit@wingate.edu. *Web address:* http://www.wingate.edu/.

XAVIER UNIVERSITY
Cincinnati, Ohio

Students with LD Served by Program	90	ADD/ADHD Services	✓
Staff	1 full-time, 15 part-time	Summer Preparation Program	n/a
LD Program or Service Fee	n/a	Alternative Test Arrangements	✓
LD Program Began	1989	LD Student Organization	n/a

Learning Assistance Center (LAC) began offering services in 1989. The program serves approximately 90 undergraduate students. Faculty consists of 1 full-time and 15 part-time staff members. Services are provided by academic advisers, counselors, diagnostic specialists, graduate assistants/students, and trained peer tutors.

Xavier University (continued)

Policies The college has written policies regarding course substitutions. Students with LD may take up to 18 credit hours per semester; 12 credit hours per semester are required to maintain full-time status; 6 credit hours per semester are required to be eligible for financial aid. LD services are also available to graduate students.

Diagnostic testing Available for neuropsychological, intelligence, study skills, and learning styles.

Basic skills remediation Available in auditory processing, study skills, time management, visual processing, learning strategies, written language, and math. Offered one-on-one and in small groups by graduate assistants/students and trained peer tutors.

Subject-area tutoring Available in most subjects. Offered one-on-one and in small groups by graduate assistants/students and trained peer tutors.

Counseling and advisement Support groups is available. Academic advisement by a staff member affiliated with the program is available.

Auxiliary aids and services *Aids:* speech recognition programs (e.g., Dragon), tape recorders, taped textbooks. *Services and accommodations:* priority registration, alternative test arrangements, readers, note-takers, scribes, and interpreters.

ADD/ADHD Students with ADD/ADHD are eligible for the same services available to students with LD, as well as distraction-free study areas, distraction-free testing environments, medication management, personal coach or mentors, and support groups for ADD/ADHD.

Application *Required:* high school transcript, ACT or SAT I (extended-time or untimed test accepted), letter(s) of recommendation, and psychoeducational report. *Recommended:* participation in extracurricular activities, interview, and personal statement. Upon acceptance, documentation of need for special services should be sent only to your LD program or unit. *Application deadline (institutional):* rolling/continuous for fall and rolling/continuous for spring. *Application deadline (LD program):* rolling/continuous for fall and rolling/continuous for spring.

LD program contact Sarah M. Kelly, Director, Learning Assistance Center, 3800 Victory Parkway, Cincinnati, OH 45207-2612. *Phone:* 513-745-3280. *Fax:* 513-745-3387. *E-mail:* kellys@admin. xu.edu.

Application contact Xavier University, 3800 Victory Parkway, Cincinnati, OH 45207-2111. *E-mail:* xuadmit@admin.xu.edu. *Web address:* http://www.xu.edu/.

► TWO-YEAR COLLEGES ◄

WITH COMPREHENSIVE PROGRAMS

ADIRONDACK COMMUNITY COLLEGE

Queensbury, New York

Students with LD Served by Program	98	ADD/ADHD Services	✓
Staff	1 full-time	Summer Preparation Program	n/a
LD Program or Service Fee	n/a	Alternative Test Arrangements	✓
LD Program Began	1984	LD Student Organization	n/a

Special Services Office began offering services in 1984. The program serves approximately 98 undergraduate students. Faculty consists of 1 full-time staff member. Services are provided by LD specialists.

Policies The college has written policies regarding substitution and waivers of requirements for admission. Students with LD may take up to 16 credit hours per semester; 12 credit hours per semester are required to maintain full-time status; 3 credit hours per semester are required to be eligible for financial aid.

Special preparation or orientation Optional orientation held before classes begin.

Basic skills remediation Available in study skills, computer skills, reading, time management, visual processing, learning strategies, spelling, written language, and math. Offered one-on-one and in class-size groups by computer-based instruction, regular education teachers, and LD specialists.

Subject-area tutoring Available in most subjects. Offered one-on-one by computer-based instruction, professional tutors, trained peer tutors, and LD specialists.

Special courses Available in career planning, oral communication skills, study skills, college survival skills, practical computer skills, test taking, reading, time management, learning strategies, self-advocacy, vocabulary development, math, stress management, and written composition skills. Some courses are offered for credit; some enter into overall grade point average.

Counseling and advisement Career counseling, individual counseling, and support groups are available.

Auxiliary aids and services *Aids:* calculators, personal computers, personal spelling/word-use assistants (e.g., Franklin Speller), scan and read programs (e.g., Kurzweil), screen-enlarging programs, screen readers, speech recognition programs (e.g., Dragon), tape recorders, taped textbooks. *Services and accommodations:* advocates, priority registration, alternative test arrangements, readers, note-takers, scribes, and tutors.

ADD/ADHD Students with ADD/ADHD are eligible for the same services available to students with LD, as well as distraction-free study areas and distraction-free testing environments.

Application *Required:* high school transcript, psychoeducational report (3 years old or less), and documentation of high school services (e.g., Individualized Education Program [IEP] or 504 plan). *Recommended:* participation in extracurricular activities, ACT or SAT I (extended-time tests accepted), interview, and letter(s) of recommendation. Upon application, documentation of need for special services should be sent to both admissions and your LD program or unit. Upon acceptance, documentation of need for special services should be sent only to your LD program or unit. *Application deadline (institutional):* rolling/continuous for fall and rolling/continuous for spring. *Application deadline (LD program):* rolling/continuous for fall and rolling/continuous for spring.

LD program contact Deborah Guy, Director of Special Services, 640 Bay Road, Queensbury, NY 12804. *Phone:* 518-743-2282. *Fax:* 518-745-1433. *E-mail:* guyd@acc.sunyacc.edu.

Application contact Sarah Jane Linehan, Director of Enrollment Management, Adirondack Community College, Bay Road, Queensbury, NY 12804. *Phone:* 518-743-2264. *Web address:* http://www.crisny.org/business/companies/acc/.

ANDREW COLLEGE

Cuthbert, Georgia

Students with LD Served by Program	20	ADD/ADHD Services	✓
Staff	1 full-time, 5 part-time	Summer Preparation Program	n/a
LD Program or Service Fee	✓	Alternative Test Arrangements	✓
LD Program Began	1994	LD Student Organization	n/a

Learning Disability Support Services began offering services in 1994. The program serves approximately 20 undergraduate students. Faculty consists of 1 full-time and 5 part-time staff members. Services are provided by regular education teachers and professional tutors.

Policies The college has written policies regarding course substitutions. Students with LD may take up to 18 credit hours per semester; 12 credit hours per semester are required to maintain full-time status and to be eligible for financial aid.

Fees *LD Program or Service Fee:* $5000 per year.

Special preparation or orientation Held before classes begin and individually by special arrangement.

Basic skills remediation Available in study skills, computer skills, reading, time management, social skills, visual processing, learning strategies, spelling, written language, and math. Offered one-on-one and in class-size groups by computer-based instruction, regular education teachers, professional tutors, and classes.

Subject-area tutoring Available in all subjects. Offered one-on-one and in small groups by professional tutors, trained peer tutors, and professors.

Auxiliary aids and services *Aids:* calculators, personal computers, personal spelling/word-use assistants (e.g., Franklin Speller), scan and read programs (e.g., Kurzweil), tape recorders, taped textbooks. *Services and accommodations:* advocates, priority registration, alternative test arrangements, readers, note-takers, scribes, and designated extended hours study lab.

ADD/ADHD Students with ADD/ADHD are eligible for the same services available to students with LD, as well as distraction-free study areas, distraction-free testing environments and personal coach or mentors.

Application *Required:* high school transcript, ACT or SAT I (extended-time or untimed test accepted), interview, separate application to your LD program or unit, psychoeducational report (3 years old or less), and documentation of high school services (e.g., Individualized Education Program [IEP] or 504 plan). *Recommended:* participation in extracurricular activities and letter(s) of recommendation. Upon application, documentation of need for special services should be sent to both admissions and your LD program or unit. Upon acceptance, documentation of need for special services should be sent only to your LD program or unit. *Application deadline (institutional):* rolling/continuous for fall and rolling/continuous for spring. *Application deadline (LD program):* 7/30 for fall and 12/1 for spring.

LD program contact Claudia Seyle, Director, Learning Disability Support Services, 413 College Street, Cuthbert, GA 31740. *Phone:* 912-732-5908. *Fax:* 912-732-5969. *E-mail:* claudiaseyle@andrewcollege.edu.

Application contact Andrew College, 413 College Street, Cuthbert, GA 31740-1395. *E-mail:* andrewco@sowega.net.

ANTELOPE VALLEY COLLEGE
Lancaster, California

Students with LD Served by Program	225	ADD/ADHD Services	✓
Staff	1 full-time, 2 part-time	Summer Preparation Program	n/a
LD Program or Service Fee	n/a	Alternative Test Arrangements	✓
LD Program Began	1980	LD Student Organization	n/a

Disabled Student Services-Learning Disabilities began offering services in 1980. The program serves approximately 225 undergraduate students. Faculty consists of 1 full-time and 2 part-time staff members. Services are provided by remediation/learning specialists, LD specialists, and trained peer tutors.

Policies The college has written policies regarding course substitutions. Students with LD may take up to 18 units per semester; 12 units per semester are required to maintain full-time status; 6 units per semester are required to be eligible for financial aid.

Special preparation or orientation Optional orientation held before registration.

Diagnostic testing Available for auditory processing, spelling, spoken language, intelligence, study skills, learning strategies, reading, written language, learning styles, visual processing, and math.

Basic skills remediation Available in computer skills, reading, visual processing, learning strategies, spelling, written language, and math. Offered one-on-one, in small groups, and class-size groups by computer-based instruction and regular education teachers.

Subject-area tutoring Available in most subjects. Offered one-on-one, in small groups, and class-size groups by computer-based instruction and trained peer tutors.

Special courses Available in career planning, college survival skills, math, and stress management.

Auxiliary aids and services *Aids:* personal spelling/word-use assistants (e.g., Franklin Speller), scan and read programs (e.g., Kurzweil), screen-enlarging programs, screen readers, speech recognition programs (e.g., Dragon), tape recorders, taped textbooks. *Services and accommodations:* priority registration, alternative test arrangements, and note-takers.

ADD/ADHD Students with ADD/ADHD are eligible for the same services available to students with LD, as well as distraction-free study areas and distraction-free testing environments.

Application *Required:* documentation of high school services (e.g., Individualized Education Program [IEP] or 504 plan). *Recommended:* high school transcript and psychoeducational report. Upon application, documentation of need for special services should be sent only to your LD program or unit. *Application deadline (institutional):* 9/8 for fall and 2/4 for spring. *Application deadline (LD program):* 9/8 for fall and 2/4 for spring.

LD program contact David W. Greenleaf, Learning Disability Specialist, 3041 West Avenue K, Lancaster, CA 93536. *Phone:* 661-722-6300 Ext. 6162. *Fax:* 661-722-6361. *E-mail:* dgreenleaf@avc.edu.

Application contact Antelope Valley College, 3041 West Avenue K, Lancaster, CA 93536-5426.

CABRILLO COLLEGE
Aptos, California

Students with LD Served by Program	450	ADD/ADHD Services	✓
Staff	4 full-time, 5 part-time	Summer Preparation Program	n/a
LD Program or Service Fee	n/a	Alternative Test Arrangements	✓
LD Program Began	1974	LD Student Organization	n/a

Disabled Student Services, Learning Skills Program began offering services in 1974. The program serves approximately 450 undergraduate students. Faculty consists of 4 full-time and 5 part-time staff members. Services are provided by counselors, diagnostic specialists, LD specialists, trained peer tutors, and professional tutors.

Policies The college has written policies regarding course substitutions, grade forgiveness, and substitution and waivers of requirements for admission and graduation. 12 credit per semester are required to maintain full-time status; 6 credit per semester are required to be eligible for financial aid.

Special preparation or orientation Required orientation held individually by special arrangement and prior to receiving any services.

Diagnostic testing Available for auditory processing, spelling, handwriting, intelligence, study skills, learning strategies, reading, learning styles, visual processing, and math.

Basic skills remediation Available in motor skills, study skills, computer skills, reading, time management, visual processing, learning strategies, spelling, written language, and math. Offered in class-size groups by regular education teachers and LD specialists.

Subject-area tutoring Available in most subjects. Offered in small groups by professional tutors and LD specialists.

Special courses Available in career planning, study skills, college survival skills, test taking, time management, learning strategies, self-advocacy, math, stress management, and written composition skills. All courses are offered for credit; all enter into overall grade point average.

Counseling and advisement Career counseling, individual counseling, small-group counseling, and support groups are available.

Auxiliary aids and services *Aids:* personal computers, personal spelling/word-use assistants (e.g., Franklin Speller), scan and read programs (e.g., Kurzweil), screen-enlarging programs, screen readers, speech recognition programs (e.g., Dragon), tape recorders, taped textbooks. *Services and accommodations:* priority registration, alternative test arrangements, readers, note-takers, and counseling.

ADD/ADHD Students with ADD/ADHD are eligible for the same services available to students with LD, as well as distraction-free testing environments.

Application *Required:* personal statement and separate application to your LD program or unit. *Recommended:* high school transcript, psychoeducational report (3 years old or less), and documentation of high school services (e.g., Individualized Education Program [IEP] or 504 plan). Upon application, documentation of need for special services should be sent only to your LD program or unit.

LD program contact Frank Lynch, Director, 6500 Soquel Drive, Aptos, CA 95003. *Phone:* 831-479-6390. *Fax:* 831-479-6393. *E-mail:* frlynch@cabrillo.cc.ca.us.

Application contact Gloria Garing, Director of Admissions and Records, Cabrillo College, 6500 Soquel Drive, Aptos, CA 95003-3194. *Phone:* 408-479-6201. *Web address:* http://www.cabrillo.cc.ca.us/.

CAMDEN COUNTY COLLEGE

Blackwood, New Jersey

Students with LD Served by Program	350	ADD/ADHD Services	✓
Staff	3 full-time	Summer Preparation Program	✓
LD Program or Service Fee	n/a	Alternative Test Arrangements	✓
LD Program Began	1988	LD Student Organization	✓

Program for the Academically Challenged Student (PACS) began offering services in 1988. The program serves approximately 350 undergraduate students. Faculty consists of 3 full-time staff members.

Policies The college has written policies regarding course substitutions.

Special preparation or orientation Required summer program offered prior to entering college. Required orientation held before registration, before classes begin, and during summer prior to enrollment.

Basic skills remediation Available in study skills, computer skills, reading, time management, learning strategies, written language, and math. Offered in small groups by regular education teachers.

Subject-area tutoring Available in some subjects. Offered in small groups by professional tutors and trained peer tutors.

Special courses Available in career planning, study skills, college survival skills, practical computer skills, test taking, reading, time management, math, and written composition skills. Some courses are offered for credit; some enter into overall grade point average.

Counseling and advisement Career counseling is available.

Auxiliary aids and services *Aids:* calculators, screen-enlarging programs, screen readers, speech recognition programs (e.g., Dragon), tape recorders. *Services and accommodations:* priority registration, alternative test arrangements, readers, note-takers, and scribes.

Student organization There is a student organization for students with LD.

ADD/ADHD Students with ADD/ADHD are eligible for the same services available to students with LD, as well as distraction-free testing environments.

Application *Required:* high school transcript, interview, psychoeducational report (5 years old or less), and documentation of high school services (e.g., Individualized Education Program [IEP] or 504 plan). Upon application, documentation of need for special services should be sent only to your LD program or unit. Upon acceptance, documentation of need for special services should be sent only to your LD program or unit. *Application deadline (institutional):* rolling/continuous for fall and rolling/continuous for spring. *Application deadline (LD program):* rolling/continuous for fall and rolling/continuous for spring.

LD program contact Joanne Kinzy, Coordinator, PO Box 200, College Drive, Blackwood, NJ 08012. *Phone:* 856-227-7200 Ext. 4430. *Fax:* 856-374-4975. *E-mail:* jkinzy@camdencc.edu.

Application contact Sharon Kohl, Director of Student Records and Registration, Camden County College, PO Box 200, Blackwood, NJ 08012-0200. *Phone:* 609-227-7200 Ext. 4528. *Web address:* http://www.camdencc.edu/.

CAPE COD COMMUNITY COLLEGE

West Barnstable, Massachusetts

Students with LD Served by Program	185	ADD/ADHD Services	✓
Staff	n/a	Summer Preparation Program	n/a
LD Program or Service Fee	n/a	Alternative Test Arrangements	✓
LD Program Began	1987	LD Student Organization	✓

Learning Disabilities Support Services Program began offering services in 1987. The program serves approximately 185 undergraduate students. Services are provided by LD specialists.

Policies Students with LD may take up to 16 credit hours per semester; 12 credit hours per semester are required to maintain full-time status; 6 credit hours per semester are required to be eligible for financial aid.

Special preparation or orientation Required orientation held before classes begin and individually by special arrangement.

Basic skills remediation Available in study skills, computer skills, reading, learning strategies, spelling, written language, and math. Offered one-on-one and in class-size groups by computer-based instruction, regular education teachers, LD specialists, and professional tutors.

Subject-area tutoring Available in most subjects. Offered one-on-one and in small groups by computer-based instruction, professional tutors, trained peer tutors, and LD specialists.

Counseling and advisement Career counseling, individual counseling, and support groups are available.

Auxiliary aids and services *Aids:* calculators, personal spelling/word-use assistants (e.g., Franklin Speller), scan and read programs (e.g., Kurzweil), screen-enlarging programs, screen readers, speech recognition programs (e.g., Dragon), tape recorders, taped textbooks. *Services and accommodations:* advocates, priority registration, alternative test arrangements, and note-takers.

Student organization There is a student organization for students with LD.

ADD/ADHD Students with ADD/ADHD are eligible for the same services available to students with LD, as well as distraction-free testing environments and support groups for ADD/ADHD.

Application *Required:* high school transcript. Upon application, documentation of need for special services should be sent only to your LD program or unit. Upon acceptance, documentation of need for special services should be sent only to your LD program or unit. *Application deadline (institutional):* rolling/continuous for fall and rolling/continuous for spring. *Application deadline (LD program):* rolling/continuous for fall and rolling/continuous for spring.

LD program contact Dr. Richard H. Sommers, Learning Disabilities Specialist, 2240 Iyanough Road, West Barnstable, MA 02668-1599. *Phone:* 508-362-2131 Ext. 4317. *Fax:* 508-375-4020. *E-mail:* rsommers@capecod.mass.edu.

Application contact Susan Kline-Symington, Director of Admissions, Cape Cod Community College, 2240 Iyanough Road, West Barnstable, MA 02668-1599. *Phone:* 508-362-2131 Ext. 4311. *Web address:* http://www.capecod.mass.edu/.

CEDAR VALLEY COLLEGE

Lancaster, Texas

Students with LD Served by Program	60	ADD/ADHD Services	✓
Staff	1 full-time, 1 part-time	Summer Preparation Program	n/a
LD Program or Service Fee	n/a	Alternative Test Arrangements	✓
LD Program Began	1977	LD Student Organization	✓

Cedar Valley College (continued)

Special Services Office began offering services in 1977. The program serves approximately 60 undergraduate students. Faculty consists of 1 full-time and 1 part-time staff member. Services are provided by academic advisers and disabled student specialist.

Special preparation or orientation Optional orientation held before registration.

Subject-area tutoring Available in most subjects. Offered one-on-one, in small groups, and class-size groups by computer-based instruction and professional tutors.

Special courses Available in human development.

Counseling and advisement Career counseling and individual counseling are available. Academic advisement by a staff member affiliated with the program is available.

Auxiliary aids and services *Aids:* calculators, personal computers, personal spelling/word-use assistants (e.g., Franklin Speller), scan and read programs (e.g., Kurzweil), screen-enlarging programs, tape recorders, taped textbooks. *Services and accommodations:* priority registration, alternative test arrangements, note-takers, and scribes.

Student organization There is a student organization for students with LD.

ADD/ADHD Students with ADD/ADHD are eligible for the same services available to students with LD

Application *Required:* high school transcript, interview, separate application to your LD program or unit, psychoeducational report (5 years old or less), documentation of high school services (e.g., Individualized Education Program [IEP] or 504 plan), and Texas Academic Skills Program (TASP). *Recommended:* ACT or SAT I (extended-time or untimed test accepted). Upon application, documentation of need for special services should be sent only to your LD program or unit. Upon acceptance, documentation of need for special services should be sent only to your LD program or unit.

LD program contact Grenna Fynn, Director, 3030 North Dallas Avenue, Lancaster, TX 75134-3799. *Phone:* 972-860-8119. *Fax:* 972-860-8014. *E-mail:* gcf3787@dcccd.edu.

Application contact John W. Williamson, Director of Admissions/ Registrar, Cedar Valley College, 3030 North Dallas Avenue, Lancaster, TX 75134-3799. *Phone:* 972-860-8201. *Web address:* http://www.dcccd.edu/cvc.

CENTRAL PIEDMONT COMMUNITY COLLEGE
Charlotte, North Carolina

Students with LD Served by Program	150	ADD/ADHD Services	✓
Staff	2 full-time	Summer Preparation Program	n/a
LD Program or Service Fee	n/a	Alternative Test Arrangements	✓
LD Program Began	1981	LD Student Organization	✓

Services for Students with Disabilities began offering services in 1981. The program serves approximately 150 undergraduate students. Faculty consists of 2 full-time staff members. Services are provided by academic advisers, remediation/learning specialists, counselors, regular education teachers, LD specialists, and trained peer tutors.

Special preparation or orientation Held interview with learning disability counselor prior to enroll.

Basic skills remediation Available in study skills, reading, time management, written language, and math. Offered by computer-based instruction, regular education teachers, and trained peer tutors.

Subject-area tutoring Available in most subjects. Offered one-on-one and in small groups by trained peer tutors.

Counseling and advisement Career counseling, individual counseling, and support groups are available. Academic advisement by a staff member affiliated with the program is available.

Auxiliary aids and services *Aids:* scan and read programs (e.g., Kurzweil). advocates, priority registration, alternative test arrangements, readers, note-takers, and scribes.

Student organization There is a student organization for students with LD.

ADD/ADHD Students with ADD/ADHD are eligible for the same services available to students with LD, as well as distraction-free study areas, distraction-free testing environments and support groups for ADD/ADHD.

Application *Recommended:* high school transcript, psychoeducational report (3 years old or less), and documentation of high school services (e.g., Individualized Education Program [IEP] or 504 plan). Upon application, documentation of need for special services should be sent only to your LD program or unit. Upon acceptance, documentation of need for special services should be sent only to your LD program or unit.

LD program contact Pat Adams, Counselor/Acting Director, PO Box 10136, Charlotte, NC 28235. *Phone:* 704-330-6556. *Fax:* 704-330-4020. *E-mail:* patricia_adams@cpcc.cc.nc.us.

Application contact Central Piedmont Community College, PO Box 35009, Charlotte, NC 28235-5009. *Web address:* http:// www.cpcc.cc.nc.us/.

CERRO COSO COMMUNITY COLLEGE
Ridgecrest, California

Students with LD Served by Program	240	ADD/ADHD Services	✓
Staff	3 full-time, 8 part-time	Summer Preparation Program	n/a
LD Program or Service Fee	n/a	Alternative Test Arrangements	✓
LD Program Began	n/a	LD Student Organization	✓

Special Services-Disabled Student Services Learning Skills Program serves approximately 240 undergraduate students. Faculty consists of 3 full-time and 8 part-time staff members. Services are provided by counselors, remediation/learning specialists, diagnostic specialists, LD specialists, and learning assistants.

Policies The college has written policies regarding course substitutions. 12 credit hours per semester are required to maintain full-time status and to be eligible for financial aid.

Fees *Diagnostic Testing Fee:* $5.50.

Special preparation or orientation Required orientation held before registration, before classes begin, and individually by special arrangement.

Diagnostic testing Available for auditory processing, spelling, intelligence, reading, written language, visual processing, and math.

Basic skills remediation Available in auditory processing, study skills, computer skills, reading, time management, visual processing, learning strategies, spelling, written language, and math. Offered one-on-one by computer-based instruction and learning assistants.

Subject-area tutoring Available in most subjects. Offered one-on-one and in small groups by computer-based instruction, professional tutors, trained peer tutors, and LD specialists.

Special courses Available in study skills, learning strategies, written composition skills, and word processing, basic thinking skills. All courses are offered for credit; all enter into overall grade point average.

Counseling and advisement Career counseling, individual counseling, and partners are available.

Auxiliary aids and services *Aids:* calculators, personal computers, personal spelling/word-use assistants (e.g., Franklin Speller), scan and read programs (e.g., Kurzweil), screen-enlarging programs, screen readers, speech recognition programs (e.g., Dragon), tape recorders, taped textbooks, remote microphone, computer software. *Services and accommodations:* advocates, priority registration, alternative test arrangements, readers, note-takers, scribes, and letters to instructors that indicate needed accommodations.

Student organization There is a student organization for students with LD.

ADD/ADHD Students with ADD/ADHD are eligible for the same services available to students with LD, as well as distraction-free testing environments, personal coach or mentors, and support groups for ADD/ADHD.

Application *Required:* separate application to your LD program or unit and psychoeducational report (3 years old or less). Upon application, documentation of need for special services should be sent only to your LD program or unit. Upon acceptance, documentation of need for special services should be sent only to your LD program or unit.

LD program contact Bonita Robison, Learning Disabilities/Remediation Specialist, 3000 College Heights Boulevard, Ridgecrest, CA 93555. *Phone:* 760-384-6302. *Fax:* 760-375-4776. *E-mail:* brobison@cc.cc.ca.us.

Application contact Cerro Coso Community College, 3000 College Heights Boulevard, Ridgecrest, CA 93555-9571. *Web address:* http://www.cc.cc.ca.us/.

COLLEGE OF SAN MATEO
San Mateo, California

Students with LD Served by Program	120	ADD/ADHD Services	✓
Staff	1 full-time, 1 part-time	Summer Preparation Program	n/a
LD Program or Service Fee	n/a	Alternative Test Arrangements	✓
LD Program Began	1980	LD Student Organization	n/a

Learning Disabilities Assessment Center began offering services in 1980. The program serves approximately 120 undergraduate students. Faculty consists of 1 full-time and 1 part-time staff member. Services are provided by LD specialists and paraprofessional staff.

Policies Students with LD may take up to 18 credit hours per semester; 12 credit hours per semester are required to maintain full-time status and to be eligible for financial aid.

Special preparation or orientation Optional orientation held before registration and during summer prior to enrollment.

Diagnostic testing Available for spelling, intelligence, reading, written language, and math.

Subject-area tutoring Available in some subjects. Offered one-on-one and in small groups by trained peer tutors.

Special courses Available in study skills, college survival skills, practical computer skills, and learning strategies. All courses are offered for credit; all enter into overall grade point average.

Auxiliary aids and services *Aids:* calculators, personal computers, personal spelling/word-use assistants (e.g., Franklin Speller), scan and read programs (e.g., Kurzweil), screen-enlarging programs, screen readers, speech recognition programs (e.g., Dragon), tape recorders, taped textbooks. *Services and accommodations:* priority registration, alternative test arrangements, note-takers, and readers/scribes for exams/tests.

ADD/ADHD Students with ADD/ADHD are eligible for the same services available to students with LD, as well as distraction-free study areas, distraction-free testing environments and personal coach or mentors.

Application *Required:* high school transcript. Upon application, documentation of need for special services should be sent only to your LD program or unit. Upon acceptance, documentation of need for special services should be sent only to your LD program or unit. *Application deadline (institutional):* rolling/continuous for fall and rolling/continuous for spring. *Application deadline (LD program):* rolling/continuous for fall and rolling/continuous for spring.

LD program contact Marie Paparelli, Learning Disabilities Specialist, 1700 West Hillsdale Boulevard, San Mateo, CA 94402. *Phone:* 650-574-6433. *Fax:* 650-358-6806. *E-mail:* paparelli@smcccd.cc.ca.us.

Application contact College of San Mateo, 1700 West Hillsdale Boulevard, San Mateo, CA 94402-3784. *E-mail:* csmadmission@smcccd.cc.ca.us. *Web address:* http://www.smcccd.cc.ca.us/smcccd/csm/csm.html.

COLLEGE OF THE CANYONS
Santa Clarita, California

Students with LD Served by Program	96	ADD/ADHD Services	✓
Staff	3 full-time, 4 part-time	Summer Preparation Program	✓
LD Program or Service Fee	n/a	Alternative Test Arrangements	✓
LD Program Began	1980	LD Student Organization	n/a

Disabled Students Programs and Services (DSPS) began offering services in 1980. The program serves approximately 96 undergraduate students. Faculty consists of 3 full-time and 4 part-time staff members. Services are provided by counselors, diagnostic specialists, LD specialists, and professional tutors.

Policies 6 units per semester are required to be eligible for financial aid.

Fees *Diagnostic Testing Fee:* $6.

Special preparation or orientation Optional summer program offered prior to entering college. Held after classes begin and individually by special arrangement.

Diagnostic testing Available for spelling, written language, math, and cognitive and achievement.

Basic skills remediation Available in computer skills, reading, time management, learning strategies, spelling, and math. Offered in small groups by computer-based instruction and professional tutors.

Subject-area tutoring Available in some subjects. Offered in small groups by computer-based instruction and professional tutors.

Special courses Available in career planning, practical computer skills, test taking, time management, and stress management. All courses are offered for credit; all enter into overall grade point average.

Counseling and advisement Career counseling, individual counseling, and small-group counseling are available.

Auxiliary aids and services *Aids:* scan and read programs (e.g., Kurzweil), screen-enlarging programs, screen readers, speech recognition programs (e.g., Dragon), tape recorders, taped textbooks, computer lab. *Services and accommodations:* priority registration, alternative test arrangements, and note-takers.

ADD/ADHD Students with ADD/ADHD are eligible for the same services available to students with LD, as well as distraction-free study areas and distraction-free testing environments.

Application *Required:* separate application to your LD program or unit. *Recommended:* psychoeducational report (3 years old or less), documentation of high school services (e.g., Individualized Education Program [IEP] or 504 plan), and LD testing at this institution. Upon application, documentation of need for

College of the Canyons (continued)

special services should be sent only to your LD program or unit. Upon acceptance, documentation of need for special services should be sent only to your LD program or unit. *Application deadline (institutional):* rolling/continuous for fall and rolling/continuous for spring. *Application deadline (LD program):* rolling/continuous for fall and rolling/continuous for spring.

LD program contact Dr. Jane A. Feuerhelm, Director, Disabled Students Programs and Services, 26455 North Rockwell Canyon Road, Santa Clarita, CA 91355. *Phone:* 661-257-7800 Ext. 3341. *Fax:* 661-254-5716.

Application contact Deborah Rio, Director, Admissions and Records, College of the Canyons, 26455 Rockwell Canyon Road, Santa Clarita, CA 91355-1899. *Phone:* 661-259-7800 Ext. 3280. *Web address:* http://www.coc.cc.ca.us/.

COLLEGE OF THE DESERT
Palm Desert, California

Students with LD Served by Program	100	ADD/ADHD Services	✓
Staff	1 full-time, 3 part-time	Summer Preparation Program	n/a
LD Program or Service Fee	n/a	Alternative Test Arrangements	✓
LD Program Began	1985	LD Student Organization	n/a

Disabled Students Programs and Services (DSPS) began offering services in 1985. The program serves approximately 100 undergraduate students. Faculty consists of 1 full-time and 3 part-time staff members. Services are provided by special education teachers, LD specialists, and trained peer tutors.

Policies The college has written policies regarding grade forgiveness. Students with LD may take up to 18 credit hours per semester; 3 credit hours per semester are required to be eligible for financial aid.

Special preparation or orientation Required orientation held before classes begin.

Diagnostic testing Available for auditory processing, spelling, spoken language, intelligence, learning strategies, reading, written language, learning styles, visual processing, and math.

Basic skills remediation Available in motor skills, study skills, computer skills, reading, time management, visual processing, learning strategies, spelling, written language, and math. Offered in small groups by computer-based instruction, special education teachers, LD specialists, and instructional support assistant.

Subject-area tutoring Available in most subjects. Offered one-on-one and in small groups by professional tutors and trained peer tutors.

Counseling and advisement Individual counseling is available.

Auxiliary aids and services *Aids:* calculators, personal spelling/word-use assistants (e.g., Franklin Speller), scan and read programs (e.g., Kurzweil), screen-enlarging programs, screen readers, speech recognition programs (e.g., Dragon), tape recorders, taped textbooks. *Services and accommodations:* priority registration, alternative test arrangements, readers, note-takers, and scribes.

ADD/ADHD Students with ADD/ADHD are eligible for the same services available to students with LD, as well as distraction-free testing environments.

Application *Required:* separate application to your LD program or unit. *Recommended:* psychoeducational report (3 years old or less) and documentation of high school services (e.g., Individualized Education Program [IEP] or 504 plan). Upon application, documentation of need for special services should be sent only to your LD program or unit. Upon acceptance, docu-

mentation of need for special services should be sent only to your LD program or unit. *Application deadline (LD program):* rolling/continuous for fall and rolling/continuous for spring.

LD program contact Michael O'Neill, Coordinator/Learning Specialist, 43-500 Monterey Avenue, Palm Desert, CA 92260. *Phone:* 760-773-2534. *Fax:* 760-776-0198.

Application contact Kathi Westerfield, Registrar, College of the Desert, 43-500 Monterey Avenue, Palm Desert, CA 92260-9305. *Phone:* 760-773-2519. *Web address:* http://desert.cc.ca.us/.

COLLEGE OF THE SISKIYOUS
Weed, California

Students with LD Served by Program	95	ADD/ADHD Services	✓
Staff	2 part-time	Summer Preparation Program	n/a
LD Program or Service Fee	n/a	Alternative Test Arrangements	✓
LD Program Began	1985	LD Student Organization	✓

Disabled Student Programs and Services began offering services in 1985. The program serves approximately 95 undergraduate students. Faculty consists of 2 part-time staff members. Services are provided by academic advisers, regular education teachers, diagnostic specialists, LD specialists, and trained peer tutors.

Policies 12 units per semester are required to maintain full-time status; 3 units per semester are required to be eligible for financial aid.

Diagnostic testing Available for auditory processing, spelling, intelligence, learning strategies, reading, written language, learning styles, visual processing, and math.

Basic skills remediation Available in study skills, computer skills, reading, time management, spelling, written language, and math. Offered one-on-one, in small groups, and class-size groups by computer-based instruction, regular education teachers, special education teachers, LD specialists, professional tutors, and trained peer tutors.

Subject-area tutoring Available in all subjects. Offered one-on-one and in small groups by computer-based instruction, professional tutors, trained peer tutors, and in-class tutors.

Counseling and advisement Career counseling and individual counseling are available. Academic advisement by a staff member affiliated with the program is available.

Auxiliary aids and services *Aids:* calculators, personal computers, personal spelling/word-use assistants (e.g., Franklin Speller), scan and read programs (e.g., Kurzweil), screen-enlarging programs, screen readers, speech recognition programs (e.g., Dragon), tape recorders. *Services and accommodations:* advocates, alternative test arrangements, readers, note-takers, scribes, and registration assistants.

Student organization There is a student organization for students with LD.

ADD/ADHD Students with ADD/ADHD are eligible for the same services available to students with LD, as well as distraction-free study areas, distraction-free testing environments and personal coach or mentors.

Application *Recommended:* psychoeducational report (3 years old or less). Upon application, documentation of need for special services should be sent only to your LD program or unit. Upon acceptance, documentation of need for special services should be sent only to your LD program or unit. *Application deadline (institutional):* rolling/continuous for fall and rolling/continuous for spring. *Application deadline (LD program):* rolling/continuous for fall and rolling/continuous for spring.

LD program contact Marly Cordoba, Learning Disabilities Specialist, 800 College Avenue, Weed, CA 96094. *Phone:* 530-938-5300. *E-mail:* cordoba@siskiyous.edu.

Application contact College of the Siskiyous, 800 College Avenue, Weed, CA 96094-2899. *E-mail:* a-r@siskiyous.edu. *Web address:* http://www.siskiyous.edu/.

COMMUNITY COLLEGE OF ALLEGHENY COUNTY
Pittsburgh, Pennsylvania

Students with LD Served by Program	400	ADD/ADHD Services	✓
Staff	9 full-time, 10 part-time	Summer Preparation Program	✓
LD Program or Service Fee	n/a	Alternative Test Arrangements	✓
LD Program Began	1978	LD Student Organization	✓

Supportive Services for Students with Disabilities began offering services in 1978. The program serves approximately 400 undergraduate students. Faculty consists of 9 full-time and 10 part-time staff members. Services are provided by academic advisers and LD specialists.

Policies The college has written policies regarding course substitutions, grade forgiveness, and substitution and waivers of requirements for admission. Students with LD may take up to 18 credit hours per semester; 12 credit hours per semester are required to maintain full-time status; 1 credit hour per semester is required to be eligible for financial aid.

Special preparation or orientation Optional summer program offered prior to entering college. Optional orientation held individually by special arrangement.

Basic skills remediation Available in study skills, reading, learning strategies, written language, and math. Offered in class-size groups by regular education teachers.

Subject-area tutoring Available in some subjects. Offered one-on-one and in small groups by professional tutors and trained peer tutors.

Special courses Available in job seeking. All courses are offered for credit; all enter into overall grade point average.

Counseling and advisement Academic advisement by a staff member affiliated with the program is available.

Auxiliary aids and services *Aids:* scan and read programs (e.g., Kurzweil), screen-enlarging programs, screen readers, speech recognition programs (e.g., Dragon), tape recorders, taped textbooks. *Services and accommodations:* advocates, priority registration, alternative test arrangements, readers, note-takers, and scribes.

Student organization There is a student organization for students with LD.

ADD/ADHD Students with ADD/ADHD are eligible for the same services available to students with LD, as well as distraction-free study areas, distraction-free testing environments and personal coach or mentors.

Application *Required:* high school transcript, separate application to your LD program or unit, and psychoeducational report (3 years old or less). *Recommended:* ACT or SAT I (extended-time tests accepted) and documentation of high school services (e.g., Individualized Education Program [IEP] or 504 plan). Upon application, documentation of need for special services should be sent only to your LD program or unit. Upon acceptance, documentation of need for special services should be sent only to your LD program or unit. *Application deadline (institutional):* 9/20 for fall and 1/10 for spring. *Application deadline (LD program):* rolling/continuous for fall and rolling/continuous for spring.

LD program contact Mary Beth Doyle, Director, 808 Ridge Avenue, Room L114, Pittsburgh, PA 15212. *Phone:* 412-237-4612. *Fax:* 412-237-2721.

Application contact Community College of Allegheny County, 808 Ridge Avenue, Pittsburgh, PA 15233. *E-mail:* mgra7@ccac.edu. *Web address:* http://www.ccac.edu/.

COPIAH-LINCOLN COMMUNITY COLLEGE
Wesson, Mississippi

Students with LD Served by Program	225	ADD/ADHD Services	✓
Staff	3 full-time, 3 part-time	Summer Preparation Program	n/a
LD Program or Service Fee	n/a	Alternative Test Arrangements	✓
LD Program Began	1949	LD Student Organization	n/a

Disability Support Services began offering services in 1949. The program serves approximately 225 undergraduate students. Faculty consists of 3 full-time and 3 part-time staff members. Services are provided by academic advisers, regular education teachers, counselors, remediation/learning specialists, and professional tutors.

Policies Students with LD may take up to 18 credit hours per semester; 12 credit hours per semester are required to maintain full-time status and to be eligible for financial aid.

Diagnostic testing Available for reading, written language, and math.

Basic skills remediation Available in reading, written language, and math. Offered in class-size groups by computer-based instruction, LD specialists, and professional tutors.

Subject-area tutoring Available in some subjects. Offered one-on-one and in small groups by computer-based instruction, professional tutors, and trained peer tutors.

Special courses Available in study skills. All courses are offered for credit; all enter into overall grade point average.

Counseling and advisement Career counseling and individual counseling are available. Academic advisement by a staff member affiliated with the program is available.

Auxiliary aids and services *Aids:* personal computers, screen-enlarging programs, tape recorders. *Services and accommodations:* alternative test arrangements and note-takers.

ADD/ADHD Students with ADD/ADHD are eligible for the same services available to students with LD, as well as counseling.

Application *Required:* high school transcript, ACT (extended-time test accepted), and immunization form and college application for admission. Upon acceptance, documentation of need for special services should be sent only to your LD program or unit. *Application deadline (LD program):* rolling/continuous for fall and rolling/continuous for spring.

LD program contact Jane Hulon, Director, Planning and Research, PO Box 649, Wesson, MS 39191-0649. *Phone:* 601-643-8411. *Fax:* 601-643-8212. *E-mail:* jane.hulon@colin.cc.ms.us.

Application contact Copiah-Lincoln Community College, PO Box 371, Wesson, MS 39191-0457. *Web address:* http://www.colin.cc.ms.us/.

COUNTY COLLEGE OF MORRIS
Randolph, New Jersey

Students with LD Served by Program	500	ADD/ADHD Services	✓
Staff	5 full-time, 1 part-time	Summer Preparation Program	✓
LD Program or Service Fee	n/a	Alternative Test Arrangements	✓
LD Program Began	1989	LD Student Organization	✓

County College of Morris (continued)

Center for Academic Support and Enrichment (CASE), Horizons Program began offering services in 1989. The program serves approximately 500 undergraduate students. Faculty consists of 5 full-time staff members and 1 part-time staff member. Services are provided by diagnostic specialists, LD specialists, and professional tutors.

Policies The college has written policies regarding course substitutions and substitution and waivers of requirements for admission and graduation. Students with LD may take up to 18 credit hours per semester; 12 credit hours per semester are required to maintain full-time status and to be eligible for financial aid.

Special preparation or orientation Optional summer program offered prior to entering college. Required orientation held before classes begin, during summer prior to enrollment, and individually by special arrangement.

Basic skills remediation Available in study skills, computer skills, reading, learning strategies, written language, and math. Offered in small groups and class-size groups by computer-based instruction, regular education teachers, and professional tutors.

Subject-area tutoring Available in most subjects. Offered one-on-one and in small groups by computer-based instruction, professional tutors, and LD specialists.

Special courses Available in career planning, oral communication skills, study skills, college survival skills, practical computer skills, test taking, health and nutrition, reading, time management, learning strategies, self-advocacy, vocabulary development, math, stress management, and written composition skills. Some courses are offered for credit; some enter into overall grade point average.

Auxiliary aids and services *Aids:* calculators, personal computers, personal spelling/word-use assistants (e.g., Franklin Speller), scan and read programs (e.g., Kurzweil), screen-enlarging programs, screen readers, speech recognition programs (e.g., Dragon), tape recorders, taped textbooks. *Services and accommodations:* advocates, priority registration, and alternative test arrangements.

Student organization There is a student organization for students with LD.

ADD/ADHD Students with ADD/ADHD are eligible for the same services available to students with LD, as well as as determined by Counseling Office.

Application *Required:* high school transcript, personal statement, letter(s) of recommendation, separate application to your LD program or unit, psychoeducational report (3 years old or less), and self-assessment, basic skills placement tests. *Recommended:* interview. Upon application, documentation of need for special services should be sent only to your LD program or unit. *Application deadline (LD program):* 4/15 for fall and 10/15 for spring.

LD program contact Dr. Judith S. Kuperstein, Coordinator, 214 Center Grove Road, Sheffield Hall-A105, Randolph, NJ 07869-2086. *Phone:* 973-328-5284. *Fax:* 973-328-5286. *E-mail:* jkuperstein@ccm.edu.

Application contact County College of Morris, 214 Center Grove Road, Randolph, NJ 07869-2086. *E-mail:* admiss@ccm.edu. *Web address:* http://www.ccm.edu/.

CRAFTON HILLS COLLEGE
Yucaipa, California

Students with LD Served by Program	120	ADD/ADHD Services	✓
Staff	2 full-time, 4 part-time	Summer Preparation Program	n/a
LD Program or Service Fee	n/a	Alternative Test Arrangements	✓
LD Program Began	1981	LD Student Organization	n/a

Disabled Student Services began offering services in 1981. The program serves approximately 120 undergraduate students. Faculty consists of 2 full-time and 4 part-time staff members. Services are provided by counselors, LD specialists, and trained peer tutors.

Policies 12 units per semester are required to maintain full-time status; 1 unit per semester is required to be eligible for financial aid.

Fees *Diagnostic Testing Fee:* ranges from $3 to $15.

Special preparation or orientation Required orientation held individually by special arrangement.

Diagnostic testing Available for auditory processing, spelling, intelligence, reading, written language, visual processing, and math.

Basic skills remediation Available in study skills, computer skills, reading, learning strategies, spelling, written language, and math. Offered one-on-one and in small groups by LD specialists, professional tutors, and trained peer tutors.

Subject-area tutoring Available in some subjects. Offered one-on-one and in small groups by professional tutors, trained peer tutors, and LD specialists.

Counseling and advisement Individual counseling is available.

Auxiliary aids and services *Aids:* calculators, personal computers, personal spelling/word-use assistants (e.g., Franklin Speller), scan and read programs (e.g., Kurzweil), screen-enlarging programs, screen readers, speech recognition programs (e.g., Dragon), tape recorders, taped textbooks. *Services and accommodations:* advocates, priority registration, alternative test arrangements, readers, note-takers, scribes, and distraction-free environment.

ADD/ADHD Students with ADD/ADHD are eligible for the same services available to students with LD, as well as distraction-free testing environments.

Application *Recommended:* high school transcript and psycho-educational report (3 years old or less). Upon application, documentation of need for special services should be sent only to your LD program or unit. Upon acceptance, documentation of need for special services should be sent only to your LD program or unit. *Application deadline (institutional):* rolling/continuous for fall and rolling/continuous for spring. *Application deadline (LD program):* rolling/continuous for fall and rolling/continuous for spring.

LD program contact Kirsten Colvey, Learning Disabilities Specialist, 11711 Sand Canyon Road, Yucaipa, CA 92399. *Phone:* 909-389-3325. *Fax:* 909-794-3684. *E-mail:* kcolvey@crafton.sbccd.cc.ca.us.

Application contact Ellen Edgar, Registrar, Crafton Hills College, 11711 Sand Canyon Road, Yucaipa, CA 92399-1799. *Phone:* 909-389-3372.

CUESTA COLLEGE
San Luis Obispo, California

Students with LD Served by Program	600	ADD/ADHD Services	✓
Staff	14 full-time, 7 part-time	Summer Preparation Program	n/a
LD Program or Service Fee	n/a	Alternative Test Arrangements	✓
LD Program Began	1973	LD Student Organization	n/a

Disabled Student Programs and Services began offering services in 1973. The program serves approximately 600 undergraduate students. Faculty consists of 14 full-time and 7 part-time staff members. Services are provided by remediation/learning specialists, counselors, diagnostic specialists, graduate assistants/students, LD specialists, trained peer tutors, and professional tutors.

Policies The college has written policies regarding course substitutions. 12 credit per semester are required to maintain full-time status.

Special preparation or orientation Optional orientation held individually by special arrangement and in the spring, prior to fall enrollment.

Diagnostic testing Available for auditory processing, spelling, reading, written language, visual processing, and math.

Basic skills remediation Available in auditory processing, study skills, computer skills, reading, spelling, written language, and math. Offered in class-size groups by LD specialists.

Subject-area tutoring Available in some subjects. Offered one-on-one and in small groups by professional tutors.

Special courses Available in practical computer skills, reading, math, and written composition skills. All courses are offered for credit; all enter into overall grade point average.

Counseling and advisement Individual counseling is available.

Auxiliary aids and services *Aids:* calculators, personal computers, personal spelling/word-use assistants (e.g., Franklin Speller), scan and read programs (e.g., Kurzweil), screen-enlarging programs, screen readers, speech recognition programs (e.g., Dragon), tape recorders, taped textbooks. *Services and accommodations:* priority registration, alternative test arrangements, readers, note-takers, scribes, and tutoring.

ADD/ADHD Students with ADD/ADHD are eligible for the same services available to students with LD, as well as distraction-free study areas and distraction-free testing environments.

Application *Required:* high school transcript and separate application to your LD program or unit. *Recommended:* documentation of high school services (e.g., Individualized Education Program [IEP] or 504 plan) and secial 1.5 day admission/orientation/registration (A/0/2) available in spring. Upon application, documentation of need for special services should be sent only to your LD program or unit. Upon acceptance, documentation of need for special services should be sent only to your LD program or unit. *Application deadline (LD program):* rolling/continuous for fall and rolling/continuous for spring.

LD program contact Dr. Lynn Frady, Director, PO Box 8106, San Luis Obispo, CA 93403-8106. *Phone:* 805-546-3148. *Fax:* 805-546-3930. *E-mail:* lfrady@bass.cuesta.cc.ca.us.

Application contact Juileta Siu, Admissions Clerk, Cuesta College, PO Box 8106, San Luis Obispo, CA 93403-8106. *Phone:* 805-546-3140. *Web address:* http://www.cuesta.cc.ca.us/.

CUMBERLAND COUNTY COLLEGE
Vineland, New Jersey

Students with LD Served by Program	90	ADD/ADHD Services	✓
Staff	2 full-time	Summer Preparation Program	✓
LD Program or Service Fee	n/a	Alternative Test Arrangements	✓
LD Program Began	1987	LD Student Organization	✓

Student Support Services Project Assistant began offering services in 1987. The program serves approximately 90 undergraduate students. Faculty consists of 2 full-time staff members. Services are provided by academic advisers, counselors, regular education teachers, diagnostic specialists, LD specialists, trained peer tutors, and professional tutors.

Special preparation or orientation Optional summer program offered prior to entering college. Optional orientation held during summer prior to enrollment.

Basic skills remediation Available in reading, written language, and math. Offered in class-size groups by computer-based instruction, regular education teachers, and teacher trainees.

Subject-area tutoring Available in most subjects. Offered one-on-one, in small groups, and class-size groups by computer-based instruction, professional tutors, and trained peer tutors.

Special courses Available in learning strategies. All courses are offered for credit; all enter into overall grade point average.

Counseling and advisement Career counseling, individual counseling, small-group counseling, and support groups are available. Academic advisement by a staff member affiliated with the program is available.

Auxiliary aids and services *Aids:* calculators, personal computers, personal spelling/word-use assistants (e.g., Franklin Speller), scan and read programs (e.g., Kurzweil), screen-enlarging programs, screen readers, tape recorders, taped textbooks. *Services and accommodations:* advocates, alternative test arrangements, readers, note-takers, and scribes.

Student organization There is a student organization for students with LD.

ADD/ADHD Students with ADD/ADHD are eligible for the same services available to students with LD, as well as distraction-free study areas and distraction-free testing environments.

Application *Required:* high school transcript, interview, separate application to your LD program or unit, psychoeducational report (3 years old or less), documentation of high school services (e.g., Individualized Education Program [IEP] or 504 plan), and learning disability evaluation. *Recommended:* participation in extracurricular activities, personal statement, and letter(s) of recommendation. Upon application, documentation of need for special services should be sent only to your LD program or unit. Upon acceptance, documentation of need for special services should be sent only to your LD program or unit.

LD program contact Patricia Martinez-Maseri, Assistant Director, PO Box 517, 3322 College Drive, Vineland, NJ 08362-0517. *Phone:* 856-691-8600. *Fax:* 856-690-0059. *E-mail:* pmmaseri@cccnj.net.

Application contact Maud Fried-Goodnight, Director of Enrollment Services, Cumberland County College, PO Box 517, College Drive, Vineland, NJ 08362-0517. *Phone:* 609-691-8600 Ext. 220. *Web address:* http://www.cccnj.net/.

CUYAHOGA COMMUNITY COLLEGE, EASTERN CAMPUS
Highland Hills, Ohio

Students with LD Served by Program	210	ADD/ADHD Services	✓
Staff	2 full-time, 7 part-time	Summer Preparation Program	✓
LD Program or Service Fee	n/a	Alternative Test Arrangements	✓
LD Program Began	1991	LD Student Organization	✓

ACCESS/Vocational Education began offering services in 1991. The program serves approximately 210 undergraduate students. Faculty consists of 2 full-time and 7 part-time staff members. Services are provided by remediation/learning specialists, teacher trainees, LD specialists, trained peer tutors, and professional tutors.

Policies The college has written policies regarding course substitutions and substitution and waivers of requirements for admission. 12 credit hours per semester are required to maintain full-time status; 6 credit hours per semester are required to be eligible for financial aid.

Special preparation or orientation Optional summer program offered prior to entering college. Optional orientation held before registration, before classes begin, during summer prior to enrollment, and individually by special arrangement.

Diagnostic testing Available for spelling, intelligence, study skills, learning strategies, reading, written language, learning styles, and math.

Basic skills remediation Available in study skills, reading, time management, handwriting, social skills, learning strategies, spelling, written language, math, and spoken language. Offered one-on-one by LD specialists and professional tutors.

Subject-area tutoring Available in most subjects. Offered one-on-one and in small groups by computer-based instruction, professional tutors, trained peer tutors, and LD specialists.

Special courses Available in career planning, study skills, college survival skills, test taking, time management, learning strategies, self-advocacy, and stress management. No courses are offered for credit; none enter into overall grade point average.

Counseling and advisement Career counseling, individual counseling, small-group counseling, and support groups are available.

Auxiliary aids and services *Aids:* calculators, personal computers, personal spelling/word-use assistants (e.g., Franklin Speller), scan and read programs (e.g., Kurzweil), screen-enlarging programs, screen readers, speech recognition programs (e.g., Dragon), tape recorders, taped textbooks. *Services and accommodations:* advocates, priority registration, alternative test arrangements, readers, note-takers, and scribes.

Student organization There is a student organization for students with LD.

ADD/ADHD Students with ADD/ADHD are eligible for the same services available to students with LD, as well as distraction-free study areas, distraction-free testing environments, medication management, personal coach or mentors, and support groups for ADD/ADHD.

Application *Required:* high school transcript, psychoeducational report (3 years old or less), and documentation of high school services (e.g., Individualized Education Program [IEP] or 504 plan). Upon application, documentation of need for special services should be sent only to your LD program or unit. Upon acceptance, documentation of need for special services should be sent only to your LD program or unit. *Application deadline (institutional):* rolling/continuous for fall and rolling/continuous for spring. *Application deadline (LD program):* rolling/continuous for fall and rolling/continuous for spring.

LD program contact Mary Syarto, Program Manager, 4250 Richmond Road, Room E3 2405, Highland Hills, OH 44122. *Phone:* 216-987-2034. *Fax:* 216-987-2423. *E-mail:* maryann. syarto@tri-c.cc.oh.us.

Application contact Cuyahoga Community College, Eastern Campus, 4250 Richmond Road, Highland Hills, OH 44122-6104. *Web address:* http://www.tri-c.cc.oh.us/east/.

DE ANZA COLLEGE
Cupertino, California

Students with LD Served by Program	400	ADD/ADHD Services	✓
Staff	6 full-time, 13 part-time	Summer Preparation Program	✓
LD Program or Service Fee	n/a	Alternative Test Arrangements	✓
LD Program Began	1973	LD Student Organization	✓

Educational Diagnostic Center (EDC) began offering services in 1973. The program serves approximately 400 undergraduate students. Faculty consists of 6 full-time and 13 part-time staff members. Services are provided by LD specialists, trained peer tutors, and professional tutors.

Policies The college has written policies regarding course substitutions and substitution and waivers of requirements for admission and graduation.

Fees *Diagnostic Testing Fee:* $4.50.

Special preparation or orientation Optional summer program offered prior to entering college. Optional orientation held spring prior to summer program.

Diagnostic testing Available for auditory processing, spelling, reading, written language, visual processing, and math.

Basic skills remediation Available in study skills, computer skills, reading, time management, visual processing, learning strategies, spelling, written language, and math. Offered in class-size groups by computer-based instruction, LD specialists, and professional tutors.

Subject-area tutoring Offered one-on-one and in small groups by professional tutors, trained peer tutors, and LD specialists.

Special courses Available in career planning, study skills, college survival skills, practical computer skills, time management, self-advocacy, math, written composition skills, and spelling/decoding/word attack. All courses are offered for credit; some enter into overall grade point average.

Counseling and advisement Career counseling is available.

Auxiliary aids and services *Aids:* scan and read programs (e.g., Kurzweil), screen-enlarging programs, screen readers, speech recognition programs (e.g., Dragon), tape recorders, assistance in obtaining taped textbooks. *Services and accommodations:* advocates, priority registration, alternative test arrangements, readers, note-takers, and scribes.

Student organization There is a student organization for students with LD.

ADD/ADHD Students with ADD/ADHD are eligible for the same services available to students with LD, as well as distraction-free study areas and distraction-free testing environments.

Application *Recommended:* high school transcript, interview, and documentation of high school services (e.g., Individualized Education Program [IEP] or 504 plan). Upon application, documentation of need for special services should be sent only to your LD program or unit. *Application deadline (institutional):* rolling/continuous for fall and rolling/continuous for spring. *Application deadline (LD program):* rolling/continuous for fall and rolling/continuous for spring.

LD program contact Pauline Waathiq, Director, 21250 Stevens Creek Boulevard, Cupertino, CA 95014. *Phone:* 408-864-8839. *Fax:* 408-864-5492. *E-mail:* waathiq@mercury.fhda.edu.

Application contact De Anza College, 21250 Stevens Creek Boulevard, Cupertino, CA 95014-5793. *E-mail:* webregda@mercury.fhda.edu. *Web address:* http://www.deanza.fhda.edu/.

DELAWARE COUNTY COMMUNITY COLLEGE
Media, Pennsylvania

Students with LD Served by Program	285	ADD/ADHD Services	✓
Staff	1 full-time, 1 part-time	Summer Preparation Program	n/a
LD Program or Service Fee	n/a	Alternative Test Arrangements	✓
LD Program Began	n/a	LD Student Organization	n/a

Special Needs Services serves approximately 285 undergraduate students. Faculty consists of 1 full-time and 1 part-time staff member. Services are provided by academic advisers, regular education teachers, counselors, LD specialists, trained peer tutors, and professional tutors.

Policies Students with LD may take up to 18 credits per semester; 12 credits per semester are required to maintain full-time status; 6 credits per semester are required to be eligible for financial aid.

Special preparation or orientation Optional orientation held individually by special arrangement.

Basic skills remediation Available in auditory processing, study skills, computer skills, reading, time management, visual processing, learning strategies, spelling, written language, and math. Offered one-on-one, in small groups, and class-size groups by computer-based instruction, regular education teachers, professional tutors, and trained peer tutors.

Subject-area tutoring Available in most subjects. Offered one-on-one and in small groups by computer-based instruction, professional tutors, and trained peer tutors.

Special courses Available in career planning, oral communication skills, study skills, college survival skills, practical computer skills, test taking, reading, time management, learning strategies, self-advocacy, vocabulary development, math, stress management, and written composition skills. Some courses are offered for credit; some enter into overall grade point average.

Counseling and advisement Career counseling, individual counseling, and small-group counseling are available. Academic advisement by a staff member affiliated with the program is available.

Auxiliary aids and services *Aids:* calculators, personal computers, scan and read programs (e.g., Kurzweil), screen-enlarging programs, screen readers, speech recognition programs (e.g., Dragon), tape recorders, taped textbooks. *Services and accommodations:* advocates, priority registration, alternative test arrangements, readers, and note-takers.

ADD/ADHD Students with ADD/ADHD are eligible for the same services available to students with LD, as well as distraction-free testing environments.

Application *Required:* high school transcript, psychoeducational report (3 years old or less), and documentation of high school services (e.g., Individualized Education Program [IEP] or 504 plan). Upon acceptance, documentation of need for special services should be sent only to your LD program or unit. *Application deadline (institutional):* rolling/continuous for fall and rolling/continuous for spring. *Application deadline (LD program):* rolling/continuous for fall and rolling/continuous for spring.

LD program contact Ann S. Binder, Director of Special Needs Services, 901 South Media Line Road, Media, PA 19063-1094. *Phone:* 610-325-2748. *Fax:* 610-359-5351. *E-mail:* abinder@dcccnet.dccc.edu.

Application contact Delaware County Community College, 901 South Media Line Road, Media, PA 19063-1094. *E-mail:* admiss@dcccnet.dccc.edu. *Web address:* http://www.dccc.edu/.

DIABLO VALLEY COLLEGE
Pleasant Hill, California

Students with LD Served by Program	600	ADD/ADHD Services	✓
Staff	8 full-time, 25 part-time	Summer Preparation Program	n/a
LD Program or Service Fee	n/a	Alternative Test Arrangements	✓
LD Program Began	1986	LD Student Organization	n/a

Disabled Student Programs and Services began offering services in 1986. The program serves approximately 600 undergraduate students. Faculty consists of 8 full-time and 25 part-time staff members. Services are provided by academic advisers, regular education teachers, counselors, remediation/learning specialists, diagnostic specialists, LD specialists, and professional tutors.

Policies The college has written policies regarding course substitutions. Students with LD may take up to 18 units per semester; 12 units per semester are required to maintain full-time status; 6 units per semester are required to be eligible for financial aid.

Fees *Diagnostic Testing Fee:* $15.

Special preparation or orientation Optional orientation held before registration, before classes begin, and during summer prior to enrollment.

Diagnostic testing Available for auditory processing, spelling, intelligence, reading, learning styles, visual processing, and math.

Basic skills remediation Available in auditory processing, study skills, computer skills, reading, time management, visual processing, learning strategies, written language, and math. Offered in class-size groups by computer-based instruction and LD specialists.

Subject-area tutoring Available in some subjects. Offered one-on-one and in small groups by professional tutors and trained peer tutors.

Special courses Available in study skills, time management, learning strategies, math, and written composition skills. Some courses are offered for credit; most enter into overall grade point average.

Counseling and advisement Career counseling, individual counseling, and mentorship program are available. Academic advisement by a staff member affiliated with the program is available.

Auxiliary aids and services *Aids:* calculators, personal computers, personal spelling/word-use assistants (e.g., Franklin Speller), scan and read programs (e.g., Kurzweil), screen-enlarging programs, screen readers, speech recognition programs (e.g., Dragon), tape recorders, taped textbooks, Alpha Smart Pro notetakers. *Services and accommodations:* advocates, priority registration, alternative test arrangements, readers, note-takers, and scribes.

ADD/ADHD Students with ADD/ADHD are eligible for the same services available to students with LD, as well as distraction-free study areas and distraction-free testing environments.

Application *Recommended:* psychoeducational report and documentation of high school services (e.g., Individualized Education Program [IEP] or 504 plan). Upon application, documentation of need for special services should be sent only to your LD program or unit. *Application deadline (institutional):* 8/1 for fall and 1/8 for spring.

Diablo Valley College (continued)

LD program contact Terry Armstrong, Academic/Student Services Manager, 321 Golf Club Road, Pleasant Hill, CA 94523. *Phone:* 925-685-1230 Ext. 607. *Fax:* 925-687-1829. *E-mail:* tarmstro@dvc.edu.

Application contact John Dravland, Director of Admissions and Records, Diablo Valley College, 321 Golf Club Road, Pleasant Hill, CA 94523-1544. *Phone:* 925-685-1230 Ext. 330.

DONA ANA BRANCH COMMUNITY COLLEGE

Las Cruces, New Mexico

Students with LD Served by Program	150	ADD/ADHD Services	✓
Staff	3 full-time, 10 part-time	Summer Preparation Program	n/a
LD Program or Service Fee	n/a	Alternative Test Arrangements	✓
LD Program Began	1981	LD Student Organization	n/a

Services for Students with Disabilities began offering services in 1981. The program serves approximately 150 undergraduate students. Faculty consists of 3 full-time and 10 part-time staff members. Services are provided by academic advisers, counselors, LD specialists, and student employees and service providers.

Policies The college has written policies regarding course substitutions and substitution and waivers of requirements for admission and graduation. Students with LD may take up to 18 credit hours per semester; 12 credit hours per semester are required to maintain full-time status; 6 credit hours per semester are required to be eligible for financial aid.

Counseling and advisement Career counseling and individual counseling are available. Academic advisement by a staff member affiliated with the program is available.

Auxiliary aids and services *Aids:* personal spelling/word-use assistants (e.g., Franklin Speller), scan and read programs (e.g., Kurzweil), screen-enlarging programs, screen readers, speech recognition programs (e.g., Dragon), tape recorders, taped textbooks, FM transmitter. *Services and accommodations:* advocates, priority registration, alternative test arrangements, readers, note-takers, scribes, and interpreter services for the deaf.

ADD/ADHD Students with ADD/ADHD are eligible for the same services available to students with LD, as well as distraction-free study areas, distraction-free testing environments and personal coach or mentors.

Application *Required:* high school transcript and COMPASS testing. *Recommended:* separate application to your LD program or unit, psychoeducational report, and documentation of high school services (e.g., Individualized Education Program [IEP] or 504 plan). Upon application, documentation of need for special services should be sent only to your LD program or unit. Upon acceptance, documentation of need for special services should be sent only to your LD program or unit. *Application deadline (LD program):* rolling/continuous for fall and rolling/continuous for spring.

LD program contact Dr. G. Lawrence Sharp, Coordinator, MSC 3DA PO Box 30001, 3400 South Espina Street, Las Cruces, NM 88003-8001. *Phone:* 505-527-7548. *Fax:* 505-527-7515. *E-mail:* lsharp@nmsu.edu.

Application contact Rosemary Gonzalez, Admissions Counselor, Dona Ana Branch Community College, MSC-3DA, Box 30001, 3400 South Espina Street, Las Cruces, NM 88003-8001. *Phone:* 505-527-7532. *Web address:* http://dabcc-www.nmsu.edu/.

EASTERN NEW MEXICO UNIVERSITY-ROSWELL

Roswell, New Mexico

Students with LD Served by Program	100	ADD/ADHD Services	✓
Staff	7 full-time, 15 part-time	Summer Preparation Program	n/a
LD Program or Service Fee	n/a	Alternative Test Arrangements	✓
LD Program Began	1985	LD Student Organization	n/a

Special Services began offering services in 1985. The program serves approximately 100 undergraduate students. Faculty consists of 7 full-time and 15 part-time staff members. Services are provided by academic advisers, remediation/learning specialists, counselors, diagnostic specialists, and LD specialists.

Policies The college has written policies regarding course substitutions. Students with LD may take up to 18 credit hours per semester; 12 credit hours per semester are required to maintain full-time status; 6 credit hours per semester are required to be eligible for financial aid.

Special preparation or orientation Optional orientation held individually by special arrangement.

Diagnostic testing Available for motor skills, spelling, spoken language, learning strategies, reading, written language, learning styles, visual processing, and math.

Basic skills remediation Available in reading, time management, spelling, written language, and math. Offered one-on-one, in small groups, and class-size groups by regular education teachers and LD specialists.

Subject-area tutoring Available in most subjects. Offered one-on-one and in small groups by trained peer tutors and LD specialists.

Special courses Available in vocational certificate courses. All courses are offered for credit; all enter into overall grade point average.

Counseling and advisement Career counseling and individual counseling are available. Academic advisement by a staff member affiliated with the program is available.

Auxiliary aids and services *Aids:* calculators, personal computers, personal spelling/word-use assistants (e.g., Franklin Speller), scan and read programs (e.g., Kurzweil), speech recognition programs (e.g., Dragon), tape recorders, taped textbooks. *Services and accommodations:* alternative test arrangements, readers, note-takers, and scribes.

ADD/ADHD Students with ADD/ADHD are eligible for the same services available to students with LD, as well as distraction-free study areas and distraction-free testing environments.

Application *Required:* high school transcript, separate application to your LD program or unit, and psychoeducational report (5 years old or less). *Recommended:* participation in extracurricular activities and documentation of high school services (e.g., Individualized Education Program [IEP] or 504 plan). Upon acceptance, documentation of need for special services should be sent only to your LD program or unit. *Application deadline (institutional):* rolling/continuous for fall and rolling/continuous for spring. *Application deadline (LD program):* rolling/continuous for fall and rolling/continuous for spring.

LD program contact Linda Green, Director, Special Services, PO Box 6000, Roswell, NM 88202-6000. *Phone:* 505-624-7289. *Fax:* 505-624-7100. *E-mail:* greenl@lib.enmuros.cc.nm.us.

Application contact James Mares, Assistant Director, Eastern New Mexico University-Roswell, PO Box 6000, Roswell, NM 88202-6000. *Phone:* 505-624-7149. *Web address:* http://www.enmu.edu/roswell/buchanaj/ENMU-R/.

ELLSWORTH COMMUNITY COLLEGE
Iowa Falls, Iowa

Students with LD Served by Program	20	ADD/ADHD Services	✓
Staff	2 full-time	Summer Preparation Program	✓
LD Program or Service Fee	✓	Alternative Test Arrangements	✓
LD Program Began	1986	LD Student Organization	n/a

Community Based Vocational Training Program (CBVT) began offering services in 1986. The program serves approximately 20 undergraduate students. Faculty consists of 2 full-time staff members. Services are provided by coordinator, Assistant Director.

Policies Students with LD may take up to 12 credit hours per semester; 12 credit hours per semester are required to maintain full-time status; 6 credit hours per semester are required to be eligible for financial aid.

Fees *LD Program or Service Fee:* $4000 per year.

Special preparation or orientation Required summer program offered prior to entering college. Held during summer prior to enrollment.

Diagnostic testing Available for spelling, reading, written language, and math.

Basic skills remediation Available in study skills, reading, written language, and math. Offered in class-size groups by regular education teachers.

Subject-area tutoring Available in most subjects. Offered in small groups by staff/professional teachers.

Counseling and advisement Career counseling and individual counseling are available.

Auxiliary aids and services *Aids:* calculators, personal spelling/word-use assistants (e.g., Franklin Speller), tape recorders, taped textbooks. *Services and accommodations:* alternative test arrangements and note-takers.

ADD/ADHD Students with ADD/ADHD are eligible for the same services available to students with LD, as well as distraction-free study areas.

Application *Required:* high school transcript, interview, and documentation of high school services (e.g., Individualized Education Program [IEP] or 504 plan). Upon application, documentation of need for special services should be sent only to your LD program or unit. *Application deadline (institutional):* rolling/continuous for fall and rolling/continuous for spring. *Application deadline (LD program):* 7/1 for fall.

LD program contact Lori Mulford, Coordinator, 1100 College Avenue, Iowa Falls, IA 50126-1199. *Phone:* 515-648-3128. *E-mail:* lmulford@iavalley.cc.ia.us.

Application contact Philip Rusley, Director of Admissions/Registrar, Ellsworth Community College, 1100 College Avenue, Iowa Falls, IA 50126-1199. *Phone:* 515-648-4611. *Web address:* http://www.iavalley.cc.ia.us/ecc/index.html.

FIORELLO H. LAGUARDIA COMMUNITY COLLEGE OF THE CITY UNIVERSITY OF NEW YORK
Long Island City, New York

Students with LD Served by Program	225	ADD/ADHD Services	✓
Staff	4 full-time, 15 part-time	Summer Preparation Program	n/a
LD Program or Service Fee	n/a	Alternative Test Arrangements	✓
LD Program Began	1979	LD Student Organization	n/a

The Learning Project began offering services in 1979. The program serves approximately 225 undergraduate students. Faculty consists of 4 full-time and 15 part-time staff members. Services are provided by counselors, remediation/learning specialists, diagnostic specialists, LD specialists, and trained peer tutors.

Policies Students with LD may take up to 18 tuition units per semester; 12 tuition units per semester are required to maintain full-time status.

Special preparation or orientation Optional orientation held before registration, during summer prior to enrollment, and individually by special arrangement.

Diagnostic testing Available for auditory processing, motor skills, spelling, spoken language, intelligence, learning strategies, reading, written language, learning styles, visual processing, and math.

Basic skills remediation Available in study skills, reading, time management, learning strategies, written language, and math. Offered one-on-one, in small groups, and class-size groups by LD specialists, professional tutors, and trained peer tutors.

Subject-area tutoring Available in most subjects. Offered one-on-one, in small groups, and class-size groups by professional tutors, trained peer tutors, and LD specialists.

Counseling and advisement Career counseling and individual counseling are available.

Auxiliary aids and services *Aids:* calculators, personal computers, scan and read programs (e.g., Kurzweil), screen-enlarging programs, screen readers, speech recognition programs (e.g., Dragon), tape recorders, taped textbooks. *Services and accommodations:* advocates, priority registration, alternative test arrangements, readers, note-takers, and scribes.

ADD/ADHD Students with ADD/ADHD are eligible for the same services available to students with LD, as well as distraction-free study areas and distraction-free testing environments.

Application *Required:* high school transcript. *Recommended:* interview, separate application to your LD program or unit, psychoeducational report (5 years old or less), and documentation of high school services (e.g., Individualized Education Program [IEP] or 504 plan). Upon application, documentation of need for special services should be sent only to your LD program or unit. Upon acceptance, documentation of need for special services should be sent only to your LD program or unit.

LD program contact Matthew S. Joffe, Director, Office for Students with Disabilities, 31-10 Thomson Avenue, Room M120B, Long Island City, NY 11101-3071. *Phone:* 718-482-5278. *Fax:* 718-482-6055. *E-mail:* matthewj@lagcc.cuny.edu.

Application contact LaVora Desvigne, Director of Admissions, Fiorello H. LaGuardia Community College of the City University of New York, 31-10 Thomson Avenue, Long Island City, NY 11101-3071. *Phone:* 718-482-7206. *Web address:* http://www.lagcc.cuny.edu/.

FLATHEAD VALLEY COMMUNITY COLLEGE
Kalispell, Montana

Students with LD Served by Program	43	ADD/ADHD Services	✓
Staff	1 full-time, 4 part-time	Summer Preparation Program	n/a
LD Program or Service Fee	n/a	Alternative Test Arrangements	✓
LD Program Began	1989	LD Student Organization	✓

Educational Disability Services began offering services in 1989. The program serves approximately 43 undergraduate students. Faculty consists of 1 full-time and 4 part-time staff members. Services are provided by academic advisers, remediation/learning specialists, counselors, regular education teachers, diagnostic specialists, LD specialists, and trained peer tutors.

Policies The college has written policies regarding course substitutions. 12 credit hours per semester are required to maintain full-time status; 6 credit hours per semester are required to be eligible for financial aid.

Special preparation or orientation Optional orientation held individually by special arrangement.

Diagnostic testing Available for auditory processing, spelling, intelligence, learning strategies, reading, written language, learning styles, visual processing, and math.

Basic skills remediation Available in study skills, reading, learning strategies, spelling, written language, and math. Offered in small groups and class-size groups by regular education teachers and LD specialists.

Subject-area tutoring Available in all subjects. Offered one-on-one by trained peer tutors.

Special courses Available in career planning, study skills, college survival skills, reading, vocabulary development, math, and written composition skills. All courses are offered for credit; all enter into overall grade point average.

Counseling and advisement Career counseling, individual counseling, and support groups are available. Academic advisement by a staff member affiliated with the program is available.

Auxiliary aids and services *Aids:* calculators, personal computers, personal spelling/word-use assistants (e.g., Franklin Speller), scan and read programs (e.g., Kurzweil), screen-enlarging programs, speech recognition programs (e.g., Dragon), tape recorders, taped textbooks. *Services and accommodations:* advocates, priority registration, alternative test arrangements, readers, note-takers, and scribes.

Student organization There is a student organization for students with LD.

ADD/ADHD Students with ADD/ADHD are eligible for the same services available to students with LD, as well as distraction-free study areas, distraction-free testing environments and personal coach or mentors.

Application *Required:* ASSET test (changing soon to COMPASS) for degree-seeking students. *Recommended:* interview, psychoeducational report (3 years old or less), and documentation of high school services (e.g., Individualized Education Program [IEP] or 504 plan). Upon application, documentation of need for special services should be sent only to your LD program or unit. Upon acceptance, documentation of need for special services should be sent only to your LD program or unit. *Application deadline (LD program):* rolling/continuous for fall and rolling/continuous for spring.

LD program contact Lynn Farris, TRIO Director, 777 Grandview Drive, Kalispell, MT 59901. *Phone:* 406-756-3849. *Fax:* 406-756-3911. *E-mail:* lfarris@fvcc.cc.mt.us.

Application contact Marlene C. Stoltz, Admissions/Graduation Coordinator, Flathead Valley Community College, 777 Grandview Drive, Kalispell, MT 59901-2622. *Phone:* 406-756-3846. *E-mail:* mstoltz@fvcc.cc.mt.us. *Web address:* http://www.fvcc.cc.mt.us/.

FOND DU LAC TRIBAL AND COMMUNITY COLLEGE
Cloquet, Minnesota

Students with LD Served by Program	10	ADD/ADHD Services	✓
Staff	1 part-time	Summer Preparation Program	n/a
LD Program or Service Fee	n/a	Alternative Test Arrangements	✓
LD Program Began	n/a	LD Student Organization	n/a

Office for Students with Disabilities (OSD) serves approximately 10 undergraduate students. Faculty consists of 1 part-time staff member. Services are provided by academic advisers, remediation/learning specialists, counselors, trained peer tutors, and professional tutors.

Policies The college has written policies regarding substitution and waivers of requirements for admission. Students with LD may take up to 18 credits per semester; 12 credits per semester are required to maintain full-time status.

Basic skills remediation Available in auditory processing, study skills, reading, time management, social skills, learning strategies, and math. Offered one-on-one, in small groups, and class-size groups by classes.

Subject-area tutoring Available in all subjects. Offered one-on-one and in small groups by professional tutors and trained peer tutors.

Counseling and advisement Career counseling and individual counseling are available. Academic advisement by a staff member affiliated with the program is available.

Auxiliary aids and services *Aids:* calculators, personal spelling/word-use assistants (e.g., Franklin Speller), scan and read programs (e.g., Kurzweil), screen-enlarging programs, screen readers, speech recognition programs (e.g., Dragon), tape recorders, taped textbooks. *Services and accommodations:* priority registration, alternative test arrangements, readers, note-takers, and scribes.

ADD/ADHD Students with ADD/ADHD are eligible for the same services available to students with LD, as well as distraction-free testing environments.

Application *Required:* high school transcript, psychoeducational report (3 years old or less), and documentation of disability, interview with OSD counselor. *Recommended:* documentation of high school services (e.g., Individualized Education Program [IEP] or 504 plan). Upon application, documentation of need for special services should be sent only to your LD program or unit. Upon acceptance, documentation of need for special services should be sent only to your LD program or unit. *Application deadline (institutional):* rolling/continuous for fall and rolling/continuous for spring. *Application deadline (LD program):* rolling/continuous for fall and rolling/continuous for spring.

LD program contact Patricia Grace, OSD Counselor, 2101 14th Street, Cloquet, MN 55720. *Phone:* 218-879-0805. *Fax:* 218-879-0814. *E-mail:* pgrace@ezigaa.fdl.cc.mn.us.

Application contact Fond du Lac Tribal and Community College, 2101 14th Street, Cloquet, MN 55720. *E-mail:* darla@asab.fdl.cc.mn.us. *Web address:* http://www.fdl.cc.mn.us/.

FOOTHILL COLLEGE
Los Altos Hills, California

Students with LD Served by Program	150	ADD/ADHD Services	✓
Staff	1 full-time, 2 part-time	Summer Preparation Program	✓
LD Program or Service Fee	n/a	Alternative Test Arrangements	✓
LD Program Began	1986	LD Student Organization	n/a

Student Tutorial Educational Program (Step) began offering services in 1986. The program serves approximately 150 undergraduate students. Faculty consists of 1 full-time and 2 part-time staff members. Services are provided by academic advisers, counselors, LD specialists, and professional tutors.

Policies The college has written policies regarding course substitutions and substitution and waivers of requirements for admission and graduation. Students with LD may take up to 18 units per quarter; 9 units per quarter are required to maintain full-time status; 12 units per quarter are required to be eligible for financial aid.

Special preparation or orientation Optional summer program offered prior to entering college. Held before classes begin.

Subject-area tutoring Available in some subjects. Offered in small groups by professional tutors.

Special courses Available in reading and comprehension. No courses are offered for credit; none enter into overall grade point average.

Counseling and advisement Individual counseling and small-group counseling are available. Academic advisement by a staff member affiliated with the program is available.

Auxiliary aids and services *Aids:* calculators, personal computers, scan and read programs (e.g., Kurzweil), screen readers, tape recorders, taped textbooks. *Services and accommodations:* priority registration, alternative test arrangements, and note-takers.

ADD/ADHD Students with ADD/ADHD are eligible for the same services available to students with LD, as well as distraction-free study areas and distraction-free testing environments.

Application *Required:* high school transcript and documentation of high school services (e.g., Individualized Education Program [IEP] or 504 plan). *Recommended:* separate application to your LD program or unit. Upon application, documentation of need for special services should be sent only to your LD program or unit. Upon acceptance, documentation of need for special services should be sent only to your LD program or unit. *Application deadline (institutional):* rolling/continuous for fall and rolling/continuous for spring.

LD program contact Diana Lydgate, Director, Student Tutorial Education Program, 12345 El Monte Road, Los Altos, CA 94022. *Phone:* 650-949-7377. *Fax:* 650-941-3767.

Application contact Foothill College, 12345 El Monte Road, Los Altos Hills, CA 94022-4599. *Web address:* http://www.foothill.fhda.edu/.

FULTON-MONTGOMERY COMMUNITY COLLEGE
Johnstown, New York

Students with LD Served by Program	75	ADD/ADHD Services	✓
Staff	3 full-time, 2 part-time	Summer Preparation Program	n/a
LD Program or Service Fee	n/a	Alternative Test Arrangements	✓
LD Program Began	1988	LD Student Organization	n/a

The Learning Center began offering services in 1988. The program serves approximately 75 undergraduate students. Faculty consists of 3 full-time and 2 part-time staff members. Services are provided by academic advisers, counselors, graduate assistants/students, trained peer tutors, professional tutors, and volunteer tutors.

Diagnostic testing Available for reading, written language, and math.

Subject-area tutoring Available in most subjects. Offered one-on-one and in small groups by professional tutors, graduate assistants/students, and trained peer tutors.

Special courses Available in career planning, college survival skills, test taking, reading, time management, learning strategies, math, and written composition skills. Most courses are offered for credit; some enter into overall grade point average.

Counseling and advisement Individual counseling is available. Academic advisement by a staff member affiliated with the program is available.

Auxiliary aids and services *Aids:* personal computers, screen-enlarging programs, speech recognition programs (e.g., Dragon), tape recorders. *Services and accommodations:* alternative test arrangements, readers, note-takers, and scribes.

ADD/ADHD Students with ADD/ADHD are eligible for the same services available to students with LD, as well as distraction-free study areas and distraction-free testing environments.

Application *Required:* high school transcript, psychoeducational report (3 years old or less), and documentation of high school services (e.g., Individualized Education Program [IEP] or 504 plan). Upon application, documentation of need for special services should be sent to both admissions and your LD program or unit. Upon acceptance, documentation of need for special services should be sent to both admissions and your LD program or unit.

LD program contact Ellie Fosmire, Learning Center Coordinator, Learning Center, 2805 State Highway 67, Johnstown, NY 12095. *Phone:* 518-762-4651 Ext. 5502. *Fax:* 518-762-4334. *E-mail:* efosmire@fmcc.suny.edu.

Application contact Fulton-Montgomery Community College, 2805 State Highway 67, Johnstown, NY 12095-3790. *E-mail:* dczechow@fmcc.suny.edu. *Web address:* http://fmcc.suny.edu/.

GAVILAN COLLEGE
Gilroy, California

Students with LD Served by Program	150	ADD/ADHD Services	✓
Staff	4 full-time, 1 part-time	Summer Preparation Program	n/a
LD Program or Service Fee	n/a	Alternative Test Arrangements	✓
LD Program Began	1980	LD Student Organization	n/a

Disabled Students Programs and Services began offering services in 1980. The program serves approximately 150 undergraduate students. Faculty consists of 4 full-time staff members and 1 part-time staff member. Services are provided by remediation/learning specialists, counselors, diagnostic specialists, LD specialists, and professional tutors.

Policies The college has written policies regarding course substitutions and substitution and waivers of requirements for admission and graduation.

Diagnostic testing Available for auditory processing, spelling, intelligence, reading, written language, visual processing, and math.

Basic skills remediation Available in reading, spelling, written language, and math. Offered one-on-one, in small groups, and class-size groups by LD specialists, professional tutors, and trained peer tutors.

Gavilan College (continued)

Subject-area tutoring Available in most subjects. Offered one-on-one, in small groups, and class-size groups by professional tutors, trained peer tutors, and LD specialists.

Special courses Available in practical computer skills, vocabulary development, math, and written composition skills. All courses are offered for credit; all enter into overall grade point average.

Counseling and advisement Individual counseling is available.

Auxiliary aids and services *Aids:* calculators, personal computers, personal spelling/word-use assistants (e.g., Franklin Speller), scan and read programs (e.g., Kurzweil), screen-enlarging programs, speech recognition programs (e.g., Dragon), tape recorders. priority registration, alternative test arrangements, readers, note-takers, and scribes.

ADD/ADHD Students with ADD/ADHD are eligible for the same services available to students with LD

Application *Required:* separate application to your LD program or unit and psychoeducational report (3 years old or less). Upon acceptance, documentation of need for special services should be sent only to your LD program or unit. *Application deadline (LD program):* rolling/continuous for fall and rolling/continuous for spring.

LD program contact Fran Lopez, Disabled Students Programs and Services Director, 5055 Santa Terese Boulevard, Gilroy, CA 95020. *Phone:* 408-848-4871. *Fax:* 408-846-9814. *E-mail:* flopez@gavilan.cc.ca.us.

Application contact Joy Parker, Director of Admissions, Gavilan College, 5055 Santa Teresa Boulevard, Gilroy, CA 95020-9599. *Phone:* 408-848-4735. *Web address:* http://www.gavilan.cc.ca.us/.

GLENDALE COMMUNITY COLLEGE
Glendale, California

Students with LD Served by Program	350	ADD/ADHD Services	✓
Staff	4 full-time, 3 part-time	Summer Preparation Program	n/a
LD Program or Service Fee	n/a	Alternative Test Arrangements	✓
LD Program Began	1973	LD Student Organization	n/a

Disabled Student Services began offering services in 1973. The program serves approximately 350 undergraduate students. Faculty consists of 4 full-time and 3 part-time staff members. Services are provided by counselors, diagnostic specialists, teacher trainees, LD specialists, and professional tutors.

Policies The college has written policies regarding course substitutions. Students with LD may take up to 18 credit hours per term; 12 credit hours per term are required to maintain full-time status; 3 credit hours per term are required to be eligible for financial aid.

Special preparation or orientation Optional orientation held before classes begin.

Diagnostic testing Available for auditory processing, spelling, learning strategies, reading, written language, learning styles, visual processing, and math.

Subject-area tutoring Available in most subjects. Offered one-on-one and in small groups by computer-based instruction, professional tutors, graduate assistants/students, and LD specialists.

Special courses Available in career planning, study skills, college survival skills, practical computer skills, health and nutrition, reading, and learning strategies. All courses are offered for credit; all enter into overall grade point average.

Counseling and advisement Career counseling, individual counseling, support groups, and personal counseling are available.

Auxiliary aids and services *Aids:* calculators, personal computers, scan and read programs (e.g., Kurzweil), screen-enlarging programs, screen readers, speech recognition programs (e.g., Dragon), tape recorders, taped textbooks. *Services and accommodations:* priority registration, alternative test arrangements, readers, note-takers, and scribes.

ADD/ADHD Students with ADD/ADHD are eligible for the same services available to students with LD, as well as distraction-free study areas, distraction-free testing environments and support groups for ADD/ADHD.

Application *Required:* interview, separate application to your LD program or unit, psychoeducational report (3 years old or less), and verification of LD. *Recommended:* high school transcript and documentation of high school services (e.g., Individualized Education Program [IEP] or 504 plan). Upon application, documentation of need for special services should be sent only to your LD program or unit. Upon acceptance, documentation of need for special services should be sent only to your LD program or unit. *Application deadline (institutional):* rolling/continuous for fall and rolling/continuous for spring. *Application deadline (LD program):* rolling/continuous for fall and rolling/continuous for spring.

LD program contact Ellen Oppenberg, LD Specialist, 1500 North Verdugo Road, Glendale, CA 91208. *Phone:* 818-240-1000 Ext. 5530. *Fax:* 818-551-5283. *E-mail:* elleno@glendale.cc.ca.us.

Application contact Sharon Combs, Acting Dean, Admissions and Records, Glendale Community College, 1500 North Verdugo Road, Glendale, CA 91208-2894. *Phone:* 818-551-5115. *Web address:* http://glendale.cc.ca.us.

HARCUM COLLEGE
Bryn Mawr, Pennsylvania

Students with LD Served by Program	20	ADD/ADHD Services	✓
Staff	1 full-time	Summer Preparation Program	✓
LD Program or Service Fee	varies	Alternative Test Arrangements	✓
LD Program Began	1990	LD Student Organization	✓

The PLUS Program (Personalized Learning Strategies) began offering services in 1990. The program serves approximately 20 undergraduate students. Faculty consists of 1 full-time staff member. Services are provided by academic advisers, remediation/learning specialists, counselors, regular education teachers, diagnostic specialists, special education teachers, LD specialists, trained peer tutors, and professional tutors.

Policies 12 hours per semester are required to maintain full-time status.

Fees *LD Program or Service Fee:* ranges from $1762 to $3522 per year.

Special preparation or orientation Optional summer program offered prior to entering college. Optional orientation held individually by special arrangement.

Basic skills remediation Offered one-on-one and in small groups by special education teachers, LD specialists, and professional tutors.

Subject-area tutoring Available in most subjects. Offered one-on-one and in small groups by computer-based instruction, professional tutors, trained peer tutors, and LD specialists.

Counseling and advisement Career counseling, individual counseling, and support groups are available. Academic advisement by a staff member affiliated with the program is available.

Auxiliary aids and services *Aids:* calculators, personal spelling/word-use assistants (e.g., Franklin Speller), scan and read programs (e.g., Kurzweil), speech recognition programs (e.g.,

Dragon), tape recorders, taped textbooks. *Services and accommodations:* advocates, alternative test arrangements, readers, note-takers, and scribes.

Student organization There is a student organization for students with LD.

ADD/ADHD Students with ADD/ADHD are eligible for the same services available to students with LD, as well as distraction-free study areas, distraction-free testing environments and personal coach or mentors.

Application *Required:* high school transcript, interview, personal statement, letter(s) of recommendation, separate application to your LD program or unit, psychoeducational report (3 years old or less), and documentation of high school services (e.g., Individualized Education Program [IEP] or 504 plan). *Recommended:* participation in extracurricular activities and ACT or SAT I (extended-time or untimed test accepted). Upon application, documentation of need for special services should be sent only to admissions. Upon acceptance, documentation of need for special services should be sent only to admissions. *Application deadline (institutional):* rolling/continuous for fall and rolling/continuous for spring. *Application deadline (LD program):* rolling/continuous for fall and rolling/continuous for spring.

LD program contact Nancy S. O'Connor, Director, PLUS Program, 750 Montgomery Avenue, Bryn Mawr, PA 19010. *Phone:* 610-526-6027. *Fax:* 610-526-6147. *E-mail:* enroll@harcum.edu.

Application contact Harcum College, 750 Montgomery Avenue, Bryn Mawr, PA 19010-3476. *Web address:* http://www.harcum.edu/.

HILLSBOROUGH COMMUNITY COLLEGE
Tampa, Florida

Students with LD Served by Program	400	ADD/ADHD Services	✓
Staff	53 part-time	Summer Preparation Program	n/a
LD Program or Service Fee	n/a	Alternative Test Arrangements	✓
LD Program Began	1981	LD Student Organization	n/a

Office of Services for Students with Disabilities began offering services in 1981. The program serves approximately 400 undergraduate students. Faculty consists of 53 part-time staff members. Services are provided by regular education teachers, special education teachers, LD specialists, and tutors.

Policies The college has written policies regarding course substitutions, grade forgiveness, and substitution and waivers of requirements for admission and graduation. Students with LD may take up to 18 credit hours per semester; 12 credit hours per semester are required to maintain full-time status; 6 credit hours per semester are required to be eligible for financial aid.

Diagnostic testing Available for learning strategies and learning styles.

Basic skills remediation Available in reading, written language, and math. Offered in class-size groups by computer-based instruction and regular education teachers.

Subject-area tutoring Available in most subjects. Offered one-on-one and in small groups by professional tutors and LD specialists.

Counseling and advisement Individual counseling is available.

Auxiliary aids and services *Aids:* calculators, personal spelling/word-use assistants (e.g., Franklin Speller), scan and read programs (e.g., Kurzweil), screen-enlarging programs, screen readers, speech recognition programs (e.g., Dragon), tape recorders, taped textbooks. *Services and accommodations:* priority registration, alternative test arrangements, readers, note-takers, and scribes.

ADD/ADHD Students with ADD/ADHD are eligible for the same services available to students with LD, as well as distraction-free study areas and distraction-free testing environments.

Application *Required:* high school transcript, separate application to your LD program or unit, psychoeducational report, and documentation of high school services (e.g., Individualized Education Program [IEP] or 504 plan). Upon application, documentation of need for special services should be sent only to your LD program or unit. Upon acceptance, documentation of need for special services should be sent only to your LD program or unit. *Application deadline (institutional):* rolling/continuous for fall and rolling/continuous for spring. *Application deadline (LD program):* rolling/continuous for fall and rolling/continuous for spring.

LD program contact Joseph A. Bentrovato, Coordinator of Services for Students with Disabilities, 10414 East Columbus Drive, Tampa, FL 33567-9640. *Phone:* 813-253-7914. *Fax:* 813-253-7910. *E-mail:* jbentrovato@hcc.cc.fl.us.

Application contact Hillsborough Community College, PO Box 31127, Tampa, FL 33606. *Web address:* http://www.hcc.fl.us/.

HIRAM G. ANDREWS CENTER
Johnstown, Pennsylvania

Students with LD Served by Program	125	ADD/ADHD Services	✓
Staff	40 full-time	Summer Preparation Program	n/a
LD Program or Service Fee	n/a	Alternative Test Arrangements	✓
LD Program Began	1959	LD Student Organization	n/a

Commonwealth Technical Institute began offering services in 1959. The program serves approximately 125 undergraduate students. Faculty consists of 40 full-time staff members. Services are provided by academic advisers, remediation/learning specialists, counselors, regular education teachers, diagnostic specialists, special education teachers, graduate assistants/students, LD specialists, trained peer tutors, and professional tutors.

Policies Students with LD may take up to 18 credits per term; 12 credits per term are required to maintain full-time status and to be eligible for financial aid.

Fees *Diagnostic Testing Fee:* $130.

Diagnostic testing Available for auditory processing, motor skills, spelling, handwriting, neuropsychological, spoken language, intelligence, personality, study skills, learning strategies, reading, written language, learning styles, social skills, visual processing, and math.

Basic skills remediation Available in auditory processing, motor skills, study skills, computer skills, reading, time management, handwriting, social skills, visual processing, learning strategies, spelling, written language, math, and spoken language. Offered one-on-one and in small groups by computer-based instruction, regular education teachers, special education teachers, LD specialists, professional tutors, and trained peer tutors.

Subject-area tutoring Available in all subjects. Offered one-on-one and in small groups by computer-based instruction, professional tutors, trained peer tutors, and LD specialists.

Special courses Available in career planning, oral communication skills, study skills, college survival skills, practical computer skills, test taking, health and nutrition, reading, time management, learning strategies, self-advocacy, vocabulary development, math, stress management, and written composition skills. Some courses are offered for credit; some enter into overall grade point average.

Hiram G. Andrews Center (continued)

Counseling and advisement Career counseling, individual counseling, and small-group counseling are available. Academic advisement by a staff member affiliated with the program is available.

Auxiliary aids and services *Aids:* calculators, personal computers, personal spelling/word-use assistants (e.g., Franklin Speller), scan and read programs (e.g., Kurzweil), screen-enlarging programs, screen readers, speech recognition programs (e.g., Dragon), tape recorders, taped textbooks. *Services and accommodations:* advocates, alternative test arrangements, and note-takers.

ADD/ADHD Students with ADD/ADHD are eligible for the same services available to students with LD, as well as distraction-free testing environments, medication management and personal coach or mentors.

Application *Required:* interview. *Recommended:* high school transcript, psychoeducational report, and documentation of high school services (e.g., Individualized Education Program [IEP] or 504 plan). Upon application, documentation of need for special services should be sent only to admissions. Upon acceptance, documentation of need for special services should be sent only to admissions. *Application deadline (institutional):* rolling/continuous for fall and rolling/continuous for spring. *Application deadline (LD program):* rolling/continuous for fall and rolling/continuous for spring.

LD program contact Carol Cooney, Administrative Assistant, 727 Goucher Street, Johnstown, PA 15905. *Phone:* 814-255-8232. *Fax:* 814-255-1992. *E-mail:* ccooney@dli.state.pa.us.

Application contact Albert Hromulak, Director of Admissions, Hiram G. Andrews Center, 727 Goucher Street, Johnstown, PA 15905-3092. *Phone:* 814-255-8200 Ext. 8237. *Web address:* http://www.hgac.org.

HOLY CROSS COLLEGE
Notre Dame, Indiana

Students with LD Served by Program	40	ADD/ADHD Services	✓
Staff	2 full-time, 2 part-time	Summer Preparation Program	✓
LD Program or Service Fee	✓	Alternative Test Arrangements	n/a
LD Program Began	1991	LD Student Organization	n/a

Conditional Acceptance Program (CAP) began offering services in 1991. The program serves approximately 40 undergraduate students. Faculty consists of 2 full-time and 2 part-time staff members. Services are provided by academic advisers, counselors, regular education teachers, diagnostic specialists, and trained peer tutors.

Policies The college has written policies regarding course substitutions. Students with LD may take up to 15 semester hours per semester; 12 semester hours per semester are required to maintain full-time status and to be eligible for financial aid. LD services are also available to graduate students.

Fees *LD Program or Service Fee:* $600 per year. *Diagnostic Testing Fee:* $600.

Special preparation or orientation Required summer program offered prior to entering college.

Diagnostic testing Available for auditory processing, motor skills, handwriting, neuropsychological, intelligence, personality, learning strategies, reading, written language, learning styles, social skills, visual processing, and math.

Basic skills remediation Available in study skills, computer skills, reading, time management, learning strategies, written language, and math. Offered in class-size groups by regular education teachers.

Subject-area tutoring Available in most subjects. Offered one-on-one and in small groups by professional tutors and trained peer tutors.

Special courses Available in study skills, college survival skills, practical computer skills, reading, time management, learning strategies, math, and written composition skills. Most courses are offered for credit; all enter into overall grade point average.

Counseling and advisement Career counseling, individual counseling, small-group counseling, and support groups are available. Academic advisement by a staff member affiliated with the program is available.

Auxiliary aids and services *Aids:* calculators, personal computers, tape recorders, taped textbooks.

ADD/ADHD Students with ADD/ADHD are eligible for the same services available to students with LD, as well as support groups for ADD/ADHD.

Application *Required:* high school transcript, ACT or SAT I (extended-time tests accepted), interview, and personal statement. *Recommended:* participation in extracurricular activities, letter(s) of recommendation, psychoeducational report (2 years old or less), documentation of high school services (e.g., Individualized Education Program [IEP] or 504 plan), and placement testing. Upon application, documentation of need for special services should be sent to both admissions and your LD program or unit. Upon acceptance, documentation of need for special services should be sent only to your LD program or unit. *Application deadline (institutional):* rolling/continuous for fall and rolling/continuous for spring. *Application deadline (LD program):* rolling/continuous for fall and rolling/continuous for spring.

LD program contact Director of Academic Advising, PO Box 308, Notre Dame, IN 46556. *Phone:* 219-239-8383. *Fax:* 219-233-7427. *E-mail:* uduke@hcc-nd.edu.

Application contact Holy Cross College, PO Box 308, Notre Dame, IN 46556-0308. *E-mail:* hccadmis@gnn.com. *Web address:* http://www.hcc-nd.edu/.

HOWARD COMMUNITY COLLEGE
Columbia, Maryland

Students with LD Served by Program	150	ADD/ADHD Services	✓
Staff	5 full-time, 3 part-time	Summer Preparation Program	✓
LD Program or Service Fee	n/a	Alternative Test Arrangements	✓
LD Program Began	1979	LD Student Organization	✓

Student Support Services Program/Disability Services began offering services in 1979. The program serves approximately 150 undergraduate students. Faculty consists of 5 full-time and 3 part-time staff members. Services are provided by remediation/learning specialists, counselors, diagnostic specialists, LD specialists, trained peer tutors, and professional tutors.

Policies The college has written policies regarding course substitutions. 6 credit hours per semester are required to be eligible for financial aid.

Special preparation or orientation Optional summer program offered prior to entering college. Optional orientation held before classes begin, during summer prior to enrollment, and individually by special arrangement.

Basic skills remediation Available in study skills, computer skills, reading, time management, learning strategies, and math. Offered one-on-one and in small groups by computer-based instruction, LD specialists, professional tutors, and trained peer tutors.

Subject-area tutoring Available in most subjects. Offered one-on-one and in small groups by professional tutors, trained peer tutors, LD specialists, and specialist in reading and math.

Counseling and advisement Career counseling and individual counseling are available.

Auxiliary aids and services *Aids:* calculators, personal spelling/word-use assistants (e.g., Franklin Speller), scan and read programs (e.g., Kurzweil), screen-enlarging programs, speech recognition programs (e.g., Dragon), tape recorders. *Services and accommodations:* advocates, priority registration, alternative test arrangements, readers, note-takers, and scribes.

Student organization There is a student organization for students with LD.

ADD/ADHD Students with ADD/ADHD are eligible for the same services available to students with LD, as well as distraction-free testing environments.

Application *Required:* high school transcript, separate application to your LD program or unit, psychoeducational report, and documentation of high school services (e.g., Individualized Education Program [IEP] or 504 plan). *Recommended:* participation in extracurricular activities, ACT or SAT I (extended-time or untimed test accepted), and interview. Upon application, documentation of need for special services should be sent only to your LD program or unit. Upon acceptance, documentation of need for special services should be sent only to your LD program or unit. *Application deadline (institutional):* 8/31 for fall and 2/1 for spring. *Application deadline (LD program):* rolling/continuous for fall and rolling/continuous for spring.

LD program contact Janice Marks, Director, Academic Support and Career Services, 10901 Little Patuxent Parkway, Columbia, MD 21044. *Phone:* 410-772-4822. *Fax:* 410-772-4276. *E-mail:* jmarks@howardcc.edu.

Application contact Howard Community College, 10901 Little Patuxent Parkway, Columbia, MD 21044-3197. *E-mail:* mamiller@ccm.howardcc.edu. *Web address:* http://www.howardcc.edu/.

IMPERIAL VALLEY COLLEGE
Imperial, California

Students with LD Served by Program	100	ADD/ADHD Services	✓
Staff	4 full-time, 8 part-time	Summer Preparation Program	n/a
LD Program or Service Fee	n/a	Alternative Test Arrangements	✓
LD Program Began	n/a	LD Student Organization	n/a

Disabled Student Programs and Services serves approximately 100 undergraduate students. Faculty consists of 4 full-time and 8 part-time staff members. Services are provided by regular education teachers, counselors, and LD specialists.

Policies The college has written policies regarding course substitutions and grade forgiveness.

Special preparation or orientation Optional orientation held before registration.

Diagnostic testing Available for spelling, reading, and written language.

Basic skills remediation Available in computer skills, reading, time management, spelling, written language, and math. Offered one-on-one by computer-based instruction and trained peer tutors.

Subject-area tutoring Available in some subjects. Offered one-on-one by trained peer tutors.

Special courses Available in study skills, college survival skills, practical computer skills, test taking, health and nutrition, reading, and math. Some courses are offered for credit; none enter into overall grade point average.

Counseling and advisement Career counseling and individual counseling are available.

Auxiliary aids and services *Aids:* calculators, personal computers, personal spelling/word-use assistants (e.g., Franklin Speller), scan and read programs (e.g., Kurzweil), screen-enlarging programs, screen readers, speech recognition programs (e.g., Dragon), tape recorders. *Services and accommodations:* priority registration, alternative test arrangements, readers, note-takers, and scribes.

ADD/ADHD Students with ADD/ADHD are eligible for the same services available to students with LD, as well as distraction-free study areas and distraction-free testing environments.

Application *Required:* high school transcript. *Recommended:* separate application to your LD program or unit, psychoeducational report (3 years old or less), and documentation of high school services (e.g., Individualized Education Program [IEP] or 504 plan). Upon application, documentation of need for special services should be sent only to your LD program or unit. Upon acceptance, documentation of need for special services should be sent only to your LD program or unit. *Application deadline (LD program):* rolling/continuous for fall and rolling/continuous for spring.

LD program contact Raquel Garcia, Instructional Specialist/Counselor, PO Box 158, Imperial, CA 92251. *Phone:* 760-355-6316. *Fax:* 760-355-6132. *E-mail:* raquel@imperial.cc.ca.us.

Application contact Imperial Valley College, PO Box 158, 380 East Aten Road, Imperial, CA 92251-0158. *Web address:* http://www.imperial.cc.ca.us/.

IOWA WESTERN COMMUNITY COLLEGE
Council Bluffs, Iowa

Students with LD Served by Program	46	ADD/ADHD Services	✓
Staff	1 full-time, 1 part-time	Summer Preparation Program	n/a
LD Program or Service Fee	n/a	Alternative Test Arrangements	✓
LD Program Began	n/a	LD Student Organization	n/a

Office of Disability Services serves approximately 46 undergraduate students. Faculty consists of 1 full-time and 1 part-time staff member. Services are provided by academic advisers, remediation/learning specialists, counselors, regular education teachers, trained peer tutors, and professional tutors.

Policies The college has written policies regarding course substitutions, grade forgiveness, and substitution and waivers of requirements for admission and graduation. 12 credit per semester are required to maintain full-time status; 6 credit per semester are required to be eligible for financial aid.

Special preparation or orientation Required orientation held before registration, during registration, before classes begin, after classes begin, during summer prior to enrollment, and individually by special arrangement.

Basic skills remediation Available in study skills, reading, time management, social skills, learning strategies, spelling, written language, and math. Offered one-on-one and in class-size groups by computer-based instruction, regular education teachers, graduate assistants/students, professional tutors, and trained peer tutors.

Subject-area tutoring Available in most subjects. Offered one-on-one by computer-based instruction, professional tutors, graduate assistants/students, and trained peer tutors.

Special courses Available in career planning, study skills, practical computer skills, test taking, reading, time management, learning strategies, self-advocacy, vocabulary development, math, stress management, and written composition skills. Some courses are offered for credit; most enter into overall grade point average.

Iowa Western Community College (continued)

Counseling and advisement Career counseling, individual counseling, small-group counseling, and support groups are available. Academic advisement by a staff member affiliated with the program is available.

Auxiliary aids and services *Aids:* personal computers, screen-enlarging programs, speech recognition programs (e.g., Dragon), tape recorders, taped textbooks. *Services and accommodations:* alternative test arrangements, readers, note-takers, and scribes.

ADD/ADHD Students with ADD/ADHD are eligible for the same services available to students with LD, as well as distraction-free study areas and distraction-free testing environments.

Application *Required:* high school transcript, interview, separate application to your LD program or unit, psychoeducational report (3 years old or less), and documentation of high school services (e.g., Individualized Education Program [IEP] or 504 plan). Upon application, documentation of need for special services should be sent only to your LD program or unit. Upon acceptance, documentation of need for special services should be sent only to your LD program or unit. *Application deadline (institutional):* rolling/continuous for fall and rolling/continuous for spring. *Application deadline (LD program):* rolling/continuous for fall and rolling/continuous for spring.

LD program contact Chris Holst, Coordinator of Disability Services, 2700 College Road, Box 4-C, Council Bluffs, IA 51502. *Phone:* 712-325-3390. *Fax:* 712-388-0123. *E-mail:* cholst@iwcc.cc.ia.us.

Application contact Todd Douglas Jones, Director of Admissions, Iowa Western Community College, 2700 College Road, Box 4-C, Council Bluffs, IA 51502. *Phone:* 712-325-3288. *Web address:* http://iwcc.cc.ia.us.

LAKE CITY COMMUNITY COLLEGE
Lake City, Florida

Students with LD Served by Program	120	ADD/ADHD Services	✓
Staff	1 full-time, 6 part-time	Summer Preparation Program	n/a
LD Program or Service Fee	n/a	Alternative Test Arrangements	✓
LD Program Began	1981	LD Student Organization	n/a

Disabled Student Services began offering services in 1981. The program serves approximately 120 undergraduate students. Faculty consists of 1 full-time and 6 part-time staff members. Services are provided by academic advisers, regular education teachers, counselors, remediation/learning specialists, and trained peer tutors.

Policies The college has written policies regarding course substitutions, grade forgiveness, and substitution and waivers of requirements for admission and graduation. Students with LD may take up to 12 credit hours per semester; 12 credit hours per semester are required to maintain full-time status; 6 credit hours per semester are required to be eligible for financial aid.

Basic skills remediation Available in study skills, time management, and math. Offered one-on-one by computer-based instruction, regular education teachers, and trained peer tutors.

Subject-area tutoring Available in all subjects. Offered one-on-one by trained peer tutors.

Counseling and advisement Career counseling, individual counseling, support groups, and academic counseling are available. Academic advisement by a staff member affiliated with the program is available.

Auxiliary aids and services *Aids:* calculators, personal computers, personal spelling/word-use assistants (e.g., Franklin Speller), screen readers, speech recognition programs (e.g.,

Dragon), tape recorders, taped textbooks. *Services and accommodations:* advocates, priority registration, alternative test arrangements, readers, note-takers, and scribes.

ADD/ADHD Students with ADD/ADHD are eligible for the same services available to students with LD, as well as distraction-free study areas, distraction-free testing environments and extended time on tests.

Application *Required:* high school transcript, interview, letter(s) of recommendation, separate application to your LD program or unit, and GED. *Recommended:* ACT or SAT I (extended-time or untimed test accepted) and documentation of high school services (e.g., Individualized Education Program [IEP] or 504 plan). Upon application, documentation of need for special services should be sent only to your LD program or unit. Upon acceptance, documentation of need for special services should be sent only to your LD program or unit. *Application deadline (institutional):* rolling/continuous for fall and rolling/continuous for spring. *Application deadline (LD program):* rolling/continuous for fall and rolling/continuous for spring.

LD program contact Natasha R. Mitchell, Coordinator of Disabled Student Services, Route 19, Box 1030, Lake City, FL 32025. *Phone:* 904-752-1822 Ext. 1393. *Fax:* 904-755-3144. *E-mail:* mitchelln@mail.lakecity.cc.fl.us.

Application contact Lake City Community College, Route 19, Box 1030, Lake City, FL 32025-8703. *E-mail:* admissions@mail.lakecity.cc.fl.us. *Web address:* http://www.lakecity.cc.fl.us/.

LAKESHORE TECHNICAL COLLEGE
Cleveland, Wisconsin

Students with LD Served by Program	50	ADD/ADHD Services	✓
Staff	1 full-time, 2 part-time	Summer Preparation Program	n/a
LD Program or Service Fee	n/a	Alternative Test Arrangements	✓
LD Program Began	1987	LD Student Organization	n/a

Special Needs/Instructional Support began offering services in 1987. The program serves approximately 50 undergraduate students. Faculty consists of 1 full-time and 2 part-time staff members. Services are provided by remediation/learning specialists, counselors, regular education teachers, special education teachers, LD specialists, and trained peer tutors.

Policies The college has written policies regarding substitution and waivers of requirements for admission. 6 credits per semester are required to maintain full-time status and to be eligible for financial aid.

Diagnostic testing Available for study skills and learning styles.

Basic skills remediation Available in study skills, computer skills, reading, time management, learning strategies, spelling, and written language. Offered by computer-based instruction and regular education teachers.

Subject-area tutoring Available in some subjects. Offered one-on-one and in small groups by trained peer tutors and LD specialists.

Special courses Available in career planning, study skills, college survival skills, practical computer skills, test taking, reading, time management, learning strategies, self-advocacy, vocabulary development, math, stress management, and written composition skills. Some courses are offered for credit.

Counseling and advisement Career counseling and individual counseling are available.

Auxiliary aids and services *Aids:* calculators, personal computers, personal spelling/word-use assistants (e.g., Franklin Speller), scan and read programs (e.g., Kurzweil), screen-enlarging programs, screen readers, speech recognition pro-

grams (e.g., Dragon), tape recorders, taped textbooks. *Services and accommodations:* advocates, alternative test arrangements, readers, note-takers, scribes, and peer tutors.

ADD/ADHD Students with ADD/ADHD are eligible for the same services available to students with LD, as well as distraction-free study areas, distraction-free testing environments and personal coach or mentors.

Application *Required:* high school transcript and ASSET or COMPASS test. *Recommended:* interview, separate application to your LD program or unit, psychoeducational report (3 years old or less), and documentation of high school services (e.g., Individualized Education Program [IEP] or 504 plan). Upon application, documentation of need for special services should be sent only to your LD program or unit. Upon acceptance, documentation of need for special services should be sent only to your LD program or unit. *Application deadline (institutional):* rolling/continuous for fall and rolling/continuous for spring. *Application deadline (LD program):* rolling/continuous for fall and rolling/continuous for spring.

LD program contact Vicki Wiese, Special Needs Instructor, 1290 North Avenue, Cleveland, WI 53015. *Phone:* 920-458-4183 Ext. 160. *Fax:* 920-457-6211. *E-mail:* viwi@ltc.tec.wi.us.

Application contact Corinne Demler, Enrollment Specialist, Lakeshore Technical College, 1290 North Avenue, Cleveland, WI 53015-1414. *Phone:* 920-458-4183 Ext. 112. *Web address:* http://www.ltc.tec.wi.us/.

LAKE SUPERIOR COLLEGE
Duluth, Minnesota

Students with LD Served by Program	100	ADD/ADHD Services	✓
Staff	3 full-time	Summer Preparation Program	n/a
LD Program or Service Fee	n/a	Alternative Test Arrangements	✓
LD Program Began	n/a	LD Student Organization	✓

The Office for Students with Disabilities serves approximately 100 undergraduate students. Faculty consists of 3 full-time staff members. Services are provided by academic advisers, counselors, LD specialists, and student advocates.

Special preparation or orientation Optional orientation held individually by special arrangement.

Counseling and advisement Academic advisement by a staff member affiliated with the program is available.

Auxiliary aids and services *Aids:* calculators, personal spelling/word-use assistants (e.g., Franklin Speller), scan and read programs (e.g., Kurzweil), screen-enlarging programs, screen readers, speech recognition programs (e.g., Dragon), tape recorders, taped textbooks. *Services and accommodations:* advocates, priority registration, alternative test arrangements, readers, note-takers, and scribes.

Student organization There is a student organization for students with LD.

ADD/ADHD Students with ADD/ADHD are eligible for the same services available to students with LD, as well as distraction-free study areas, distraction-free testing environments and support groups for ADD/ADHD.

Application *Required:* high school transcript, psychoeducational report (3 years old or less), and documentation of high school services (e.g., Individualized Education Program [IEP] or 504 plan). Upon application, documentation of need for special services should be sent only to your LD program or unit. Upon acceptance, documentation of need for special services should be sent only to your LD program or unit.

LD program contact Amada Delich, Disabilities Coordinator, 2101 Trinity Road, Duluth, MN 55811. *Phone:* 218-733-7650. *Fax:* 218-733-5945. *E-mail:* a.delich@lsc.mnscu.edu.

Application contact Kathy TanskiLake Superior College, 2101 Trinity Road, Duluth, MN 55811. *Phone:* 218-733-7617. *Web address:* http://lsc.cc.mn-us/.

LEEWARD COMMUNITY COLLEGE
Pearl City, Hawaii

Students with LD Served by Program	75	ADD/ADHD Services	✓
Staff	1 full-time, 2 part-time	Summer Preparation Program	n/a
LD Program or Service Fee	n/a	Alternative Test Arrangements	✓
LD Program Began	1988	LD Student Organization	✓

Program for Adult Achievement began offering services in 1988. The program serves approximately 75 undergraduate students. Faculty consists of 1 full-time and 2 part-time staff members. Services are provided by counselors, diagnostic specialists, LD specialists, and trained peer tutors.

Policies The college has written policies regarding course substitutions.

Diagnostic testing Available for auditory processing, motor skills, spelling, handwriting, spoken language, intelligence, personality, learning strategies, reading, written language, learning styles, visual processing, and math.

Basic skills remediation Available in study skills, reading, spelling, written language, and math. Offered one-on-one by trained peer tutors.

Subject-area tutoring Available in most subjects. Offered one-on-one by trained peer tutors.

Counseling and advisement Career counseling, individual counseling, and support groups are available.

Auxiliary aids and services *Aids:* calculators, personal computers, personal spelling/word-use assistants (e.g., Franklin Speller), tape recorders, taped textbooks. *Services and accommodations:* advocates, priority registration, alternative test arrangements, readers, note-takers, and scribes.

Student organization There is a student organization for students with LD.

ADD/ADHD Students with ADD/ADHD are eligible for the same services available to students with LD, as well as distraction-free study areas, distraction-free testing environments and support groups for ADD/ADHD.

Application *Required:* separate application to your LD program or unit and psychoeducational report (5 years old or less). *Recommended:* documentation of high school services (e.g., Individualized Education Program [IEP] or 504 plan). Upon application, documentation of need for special services should be sent only to your LD program or unit. Upon acceptance, documentation of need for special services should be sent only to your LD program or unit. *Application deadline (institutional):* rolling/continuous for fall and rolling/continuous for spring. *Application deadline (LD program):* rolling/continuous for fall and rolling/continuous for spring.

LD program contact Patricia Ewins, Coordinator, 96-045 Ala Ike, Pearl City, HI 96821. *Phone:* 808-455-0421. *Fax:* 808-455-0471. *E-mail:* ewins@hawaii.edu.

Application contact Veda Tokashiki, Clerk, Leeward Community College, 96-045 Ala Ike, Pearl City, HI 96782-3393. *Phone:* 808-455-0217. *Web address:* http://www.lcc.hawaii.edu.

LON MORRIS COLLEGE

Jacksonville, Texas

Students with LD Served by Program	38	ADD/ADHD Services	✓
Staff	1 full-time, 2 part-time	Summer Preparation Program	✓
LD Program or Service Fee	n/a	Alternative Test Arrangements	✓
LD Program Began	1999	LD Student Organization	✓

Learning Enrichment Program began offering services in 1999. The program serves approximately 38 undergraduate students. Faculty consists of 1 full-time and 2 part-time staff members. Services are provided by counselors, regular education teachers, and trained peer tutors.
Policies The college has written policies regarding substitution and waivers of requirements for admission. Students with LD may take up to 17 semester hours per semester; 12 semester hours per semester are required to maintain full-time status; 6 semester hours per semester are required to be eligible for financial aid.
Special preparation or orientation Optional summer program offered prior to entering college. Optional orientation held individually by special arrangement.
Diagnostic testing Available for spelling, spoken language, intelligence, reading, written language, math, and career assessments.
Basic skills remediation Available in reading, written language, and math. Offered one-on-one and in class-size groups by computer-based instruction and regular education teachers.
Subject-area tutoring Available in most subjects. Offered one-on-one and in small groups by computer-based instruction and trained peer tutors.
Special courses Available in study skills and college survival skills. All courses are offered for credit; all enter into overall grade point average.
Counseling and advisement Career counseling, individual counseling, and support groups are available.
Auxiliary aids and services *Aids:* calculators, personal spelling/word-use assistants (e.g., Franklin Speller), scan and read programs (e.g., Kurzweil), speech recognition programs (e.g., Dragon), tape recorders, taped textbooks. *Services and accommodations:* alternative test arrangements, readers, and note-takers.
Student organization There is a student organization for students with LD.
ADD/ADHD Students with ADD/ADHD are eligible for the same services available to students with LD, as well as distraction-free study areas and distraction-free testing environments.
Application *Required:* high school transcript. *Recommended:* ACT or SAT I (extended-time or untimed test accepted), psycho-educational report, and documentation of high school services (e.g., Individualized Education Program [IEP] or 504 plan). Upon application, documentation of need for special services should be sent only to your LD program or unit. Upon acceptance, documentation of need for special services should be sent only to your LD program or unit. *Application deadline (institutional):* rolling/continuous for fall and rolling/continuous for spring.
LD program contact Dr. Deborah P. Kelley, Director, 800 College Avenue, Jacksonville, TX 75766. *Phone:* 903-589-4000. *Fax:* 903-589-4065. *E-mail:* dkelley@lonmorris.edu.
Application contact Shelly Gibson, Director of Admissions, Lon Morris College, 800 College Avenue, Jacksonville, TX 75766-2900. *Phone:* 903-589-4000 Ext. 4062. *Web address:* http://www.lonmorris.edu/.

LOUISBURG COLLEGE

Louisburg, North Carolina

Students with LD Served by Program	12	ADD/ADHD Services	✓
Staff	2 full-time, 1 part-time	Summer Preparation Program	✓
LD Program or Service Fee	✓	Alternative Test Arrangements	n/a
LD Program Began	1999	LD Student Organization	n/a

Louisburg Learning Partners (LLP) began offering services in 1999. The program serves approximately 12 undergraduate students. Faculty consists of 2 full-time staff members and 1 part-time staff member. Services are provided by LD specialists.
Policies The college has written policies regarding course substitutions. Students with LD may take up to 18 credit hours per semester; 12 credit hours per semester are required to maintain full-time status and to be eligible for financial aid.
Fees *LD Program or Service Fee:* $3500 per year.
Special preparation or orientation Optional summer program offered prior to entering college.
Subject-area tutoring Available in most subjects. Offered one-on-one, in small groups, and class-size groups by LD specialists.
Special courses Available in study skills and educational psychology. All courses are offered for credit; all enter into overall grade point average.
ADD/ADHD Students with ADD/ADHD are eligible for the same services available to students with LD
Application *Required:* high school transcript, ACT or SAT I (extended-time tests accepted), and separate application to your LD program or unit. Upon application, documentation of need for special services should be sent only to your LD program or unit. Upon acceptance, documentation of need for special services should be sent only to your LD program or unit. *Application deadline (institutional):* rolling/continuous for fall and rolling/continuous for spring. *Application deadline (LD program):* 4/1 for fall and 11/15 for spring.
LD program contact Jayne Davis, Director, 501 North Main Street, Louisburg, NC 27587. *Phone:* 919-497-3216. *Fax:* 919-496-1788.
Application contact Louisburg College, 501 North Main Street, Louisburg, NC 27549-2399. *Web address:* http://www.louisburg.edu/.

LOUISIANA STATE UNIVERSITY AT EUNICE

Eunice, Louisiana

Students with LD Served by Program	400	ADD/ADHD Services	✓
Staff	6 full-time	Summer Preparation Program	✓
LD Program or Service Fee	n/a	Alternative Test Arrangements	✓
LD Program Began	1973	LD Student Organization	n/a

Student Support Services began offering services in 1973. The program serves approximately 400 undergraduate students. Faculty consists of 6 full-time staff members. Services are provided by counselors.
Policies The college has written policies regarding grade forgiveness. Students with LD may take up to 12 credits per semester; 3 credits per semester are required to maintain full-time status; 12 credits per semester are required to be eligible for financial aid.
Special preparation or orientation Optional summer program offered prior to entering college. Optional orientation held individually by special arrangement.

Basic skills remediation Available in study skills and math. Offered in small groups by LD specialists and trained peer tutors.

Subject-area tutoring Available in most subjects. Offered one-on-one by trained peer tutors.

Special courses Available in career planning, oral communication skills, study skills, college survival skills, learning strategies, and stress management. No courses are offered for credit; all enter into overall grade point average.

Counseling and advisement Individual counseling and support groups are available.

Auxiliary aids and services *Aids:* screen-enlarging programs, tape recorders, taped textbooks. *Services and accommodations:* alternative test arrangements, readers, and note-takers.

ADD/ADHD Students with ADD/ADHD are eligible for the same services available to students with LD, as well as distraction-free study areas and distraction-free testing environments.

Application *Required:* ACT (extended-time test accepted), interview, and documentation of high school services (e.g., Individualized Education Program [IEP] or 504 plan). Upon application, documentation of need for special services should be sent only to your LD program or unit. Upon acceptance, documentation of need for special services should be sent to both admissions and your LD program or unit. *Application deadline (LD program):* rolling/continuous for fall and rolling/continuous for spring.

LD program contact Timika W. Tilford, Student Support Counselor, PO Box 1129, Eunice, LA 70535. *Phone:* 337-550-1254. *Fax:* 337-546-6620. *E-mail:* ttilford@lsue.edu.

Application contact Gracie Guillory, Director of Financial Aid, Louisiana State University at Eunice, PO Box 1129, Eunice, LA 70535-1129. *Phone:* 318-550-1282. *Web address:* http://www.lsue.edu/.

LUNA VOCATIONAL TECHNICAL INSTITUTE
Las Vegas, New Mexico

Students with LD Served by Program	25	ADD/ADHD Services	✓
Staff	1 full-time	Summer Preparation Program	✓
LD Program or Service Fee	n/a	Alternative Test Arrangements	✓
LD Program Began	1971	LD Student Organization	n/a

Special Needs Office began offering services in 1971. The program serves approximately 25 undergraduate students. Faculty consists of 1 full-time staff member. Services are provided by academic advisers, counselors, and regular education teachers.

Policies Students with LD may take up to 16 credit hours per semester; 12 credit hours per semester are required to maintain full-time status; 6 credit hours per semester are required to be eligible for financial aid. LD services are also available to graduate students.

Special preparation or orientation Optional summer program offered prior to entering college. Optional orientation held before registration, during registration, before classes begin, after classes begin, during summer prior to enrollment, and individually by special arrangement.

Basic skills remediation Available in study skills, reading, handwriting, learning strategies, spelling, written language, and math. Offered one-on-one by regular education teachers and trained peer tutors.

Subject-area tutoring Available in all subjects. Offered one-on-one by trained peer tutors and special needs counselor.

Special courses Available in college survival skills. All courses are offered for credit; all enter into overall grade point average.

Counseling and advisement Career counseling and individual counseling are available. Academic advisement by a staff member affiliated with the program is available.

Auxiliary aids and services *Aids:* calculators, personal spelling/word-use assistants (e.g., Franklin Speller), tape recorders. *Services and accommodations:* advocates, priority registration, alternative test arrangements, and note-takers.

ADD/ADHD Students with ADD/ADHD are eligible for the same services available to students with LD, as well as distraction-free testing environments and tutoral assistance.

Application *Required:* high school transcript, documentation of high school services (e.g., Individualized Education Program [IEP] or 504 plan), and COMPASS exam. *Recommended:* ACT (extended-time or untimed test accepted). Upon application, documentation of need for special services should be sent only to your LD program or unit. Upon acceptance, documentation of need for special services should be sent only to your LD program or unit.

LD program contact Emilio Roybal, Counselor, PO Box 1510, Las Veyas, NM 87702. *Phone:* 505-454-2533. *Fax:* 505-454-2588. *E-mail:* eroybal@lvti.cc.nm.us.

Application contact Luna Vocational Technical Institute, PO Box 1510, Las Vegas, NM 87701.

MARSHALLTOWN COMMUNITY COLLEGE
Marshalltown, Iowa

Students with LD Served by Program	22	ADD/ADHD Services	✓
Staff	4 full-time	Summer Preparation Program	✓
LD Program or Service Fee	✓	Alternative Test Arrangements	✓
LD Program Began	1982	LD Student Organization	n/a

Individualized Resource Program (IRP) began offering services in 1982. The program serves approximately 22 undergraduate students. Faculty consists of 4 full-time staff members. Services are provided by remediation/learning specialists, counselors, diagnostic specialists, and Coordinator and Assistant Director.

Policies The college has written policies regarding substitution and waivers of requirements for admission. Students with LD may take up to 14 credit hours per semester; 12 credit hours per semester are required to maintain full-time status; 6 credit hours per semester are required to be eligible for financial aid.

Fees *LD Program or Service Fee:* $4000 per year.

Special preparation or orientation Required summer program offered prior to entering college. Required orientation held before classes begin.

Diagnostic testing Available for motor skills, spelling, spoken language, personality, study skills, learning strategies, reading, written language, math, and perceptual skills; social skills.

Basic skills remediation Available in motor skills, study skills, computer skills, reading, time management, social skills, learning strategies, spelling, math, and perceptual skills. Offered one-on-one and in small groups by regular education teachers.

Subject-area tutoring Available in most subjects. Offered one-on-one and in small groups by trained peer tutors and professional teachers.

Special courses Available in career planning, oral communication skills, study skills, college survival skills, reading, time management, learning strategies, vocabulary development, math, and word processing. Some courses are offered for credit; some enter into overall grade point average.

Counseling and advisement Career counseling, individual counseling, small-group counseling, and self-advocacy are available.

Marshalltown Community College (continued)

Auxiliary aids and services *Aids:* calculators, personal computers, speech recognition programs (e.g., Dragon), tape recorders, taped textbooks, typewriters. *Services and accommodations:* advocates, priority registration, alternative test arrangements, and note-takers.

ADD/ADHD Students with ADD/ADHD are eligible for the same services available to students with LD, as well as distraction-free study areas and distraction-free testing environments.

Application *Required:* high school transcript, letter(s) of recommendation, psychoeducational report (1 year old or less), documentation of high school services (e.g., Individualized Education Program [IEP] or 504 plan), and psychological evaluation. *Recommended:* ACT (untimed test accepted) and interview. Upon application, documentation of need for special services should be sent only to your LD program or unit. Upon acceptance, documentation of need for special services should be sent only to your LD program or unit. *Application deadline (LD program):* rolling/continuous for fall and rolling/continuous for spring.

LD program contact Regina West, Coordinator/Instructor, Individualized Resource Program, Iowa Valley Community College District, 3702 South Center Street, Marshalltown, IA 50158. *Phone:* 515-752-7106 Ext. 420. *Fax:* 515-752-8149. *E-mail:* rwest@iavalley.cc.ia.us.

Application contact Sylvia Grandgeorge, Dean of Student Services, Marshalltown Community College, 3700 South Center Street, Marshalltown, IA 50158-4760. *Phone:* 515-752-7106 Ext. 232. *Web address:* http://voyager.iavalley.cc.ia.us/mcc/.

MCDOWELL TECHNICAL COMMUNITY COLLEGE
Marion, North Carolina

Students with LD Served by Program	25	ADD/ADHD Services	✓
Staff	3 full-time, 10 part-time	Summer Preparation Program	✓
LD Program or Service Fee	n/a	Alternative Test Arrangements	✓
LD Program Began	1988	LD Student Organization	n/a

Student Services began offering services in 1988. The program serves approximately 25 undergraduate students. Faculty consists of 3 full-time and 10 part-time staff members. Services are provided by academic advisers, remediation/learning specialists, counselors, regular education teachers, diagnostic specialists, LD specialists, and trained peer tutors.

Policies Students with LD may take up to 18 semester hours per semester; 6 semester hours per semester are required to be eligible for financial aid.

Special preparation or orientation Optional summer program offered prior to entering college.

Diagnostic testing Available for auditory processing, motor skills, spelling, handwriting, spoken language, study skills, learning strategies, reading, written language, learning styles, visual processing, and math.

Basic skills remediation Available in reading, written language, and math. Offered in class-size groups by regular education teachers.

Subject-area tutoring Available in all subjects. Offered one-on-one and in small groups by trained peer tutors.

Special courses Available in career planning, oral communication skills, study skills, college survival skills, practical computer skills, test taking, reading, time management, learning strategies, self-advocacy, vocabulary development, math, stress management, written composition skills, and Self esteem. Some courses are offered for credit; some enter into overall grade point average.

Counseling and advisement Career counseling and individual counseling are available. Academic advisement by a staff member affiliated with the program is available.

Auxiliary aids and services *Aids:* calculators, scan and read programs (e.g., Kurzweil), screen-enlarging programs, tape recorders, taped textbooks. *Services and accommodations:* advocates, alternative test arrangements, readers, note-takers, and scribes.

ADD/ADHD Students with ADD/ADHD are eligible for the same services available to students with LD, as well as distraction-free study areas and distraction-free testing environments.

Application *Required:* high school transcript and Placement Test (CPT-Computerized Placement Test). *Recommended:* psychoeducational report (3 years old or less) and documentation of high school services (e.g., Individualized Education Program [IEP] or 504 plan). Upon application, documentation of need for special services should be sent only to admissions. Upon acceptance, documentation of need for special services should be sent only to admissions. *Application deadline (institutional):* rolling/continuous for fall and rolling/continuous for spring. *Application deadline (LD program):* rolling/continuous for fall and rolling/continuous for spring.

LD program contact Jim Biddix, Dean of Students, Route 1, Box 170, Marion, NC 28752. *Phone:* 828-652-6021 Ext. 400.

Application contact McDowell Technical Community College, Route 1, Box 170, Marion, NC 28752-9724. *Web address:* http://www.mcdowelltech.cc.nc.us/.

MENDOCINO COLLEGE
Ukiah, California

Students with LD Served by Program	100	ADD/ADHD Services	✓
Staff	2 full-time	Summer Preparation Program	n/a
LD Program or Service Fee	n/a	Alternative Test Arrangements	✓
LD Program Began	1986	LD Student Organization	n/a

Learning Disabilities Program began offering services in 1986. The program serves approximately 100 undergraduate students. Faculty consists of 2 full-time staff members. Services are provided by LD specialists and LD Instructional assistant.

Policies The college has written policies regarding course substitutions and grade forgiveness. 12 units per semester are required to maintain full-time status and to be eligible for financial aid.

Special preparation or orientation Optional orientation held after classes begin.

Diagnostic testing Available for auditory processing, neuropsychological, reading, written language, visual processing, and math.

Basic skills remediation Available in study skills, computer skills, reading, time management, learning strategies, spelling, written language, and math. Offered one-on-one and in small groups by LD specialists and trained peer tutors.

Subject-area tutoring Available in all subjects. Offered in small groups by trained peer tutors and LD specialists.

Special courses Available in career planning, study skills, college survival skills, practical computer skills, test taking, reading, time management, learning strategies, self-advocacy, vocabulary development, math, stress management, and written composition skills. All courses are offered for credit; none enter into overall grade point average.

Counseling and advisement Career counseling and support groups are available.

Auxiliary aids and services *Aids:* calculators, personal spelling/word-use assistants (e.g., Franklin Speller), scan and read programs (e.g., Kurzweil), screen-enlarging programs, screen readers, speech recognition programs (e.g., Dragon), tape recorders, taped textbooks. *Services and accommodations:* advocates, priority registration, alternative test arrangements, and note-takers.
ADD/ADHD Students with ADD/ADHD are eligible for the same services available to students with LD, as well as distraction-free study areas and distraction-free testing environments.
Application *Recommended:* high school transcript, psychoeducational report (5 years old or less), and documentation of high school services (e.g., Individualized Education Program [IEP] or 504 plan). Upon application, documentation of need for special services should be sent only to your LD program or unit. Upon acceptance, documentation of need for special services should be sent only to your LD program or unit. *Application deadline (institutional):* rolling/continuous for fall and rolling/continuous for spring. *Application deadline (LD program):* rolling/continuous for fall and rolling/continuous for spring.
LD program contact Kathleen A. Daigle, Learning Disabilities Specialist, PO Box 3000, Ukiah, CA 95482. *Phone:* 707-468-3151. *Fax:* 707-468-3120. *E-mail:* kdaigle@mendocino.cc.ca.us.
Application contact Mendocino College, PO Box 3000, Ukiah, CA 95482-0300. *E-mail:* ktaylor@mendocino.cc.ca.us. *Web address:* http://www.mendocino.cc.ca.us/.

MERRITT COLLEGE
Oakland, California

Students with LD Served by Program	150	ADD/ADHD Services	✓
Staff	1 full-time, 1 part-time	Summer Preparation Program	n/a
LD Program or Service Fee	n/a	Alternative Test Arrangements	✓
LD Program Began	n/a	LD Student Organization	✓

Learning Opportunity Program for Students with Learning Differences serves approximately 150 undergraduate students. Faculty consists of 1 full-time and 1 part-time staff member. Services are provided by academic advisers, counselors, diagnostic specialists, LD specialists, and trained paraprofessionals.
Policies The college has written policies regarding course substitutions.
Diagnostic testing Available for auditory processing, motor skills, spelling, spoken language, study skills, learning strategies, reading, written language, learning styles, visual processing, math, and cognitive processing.
Special courses Available in career planning, study skills, college survival skills, practical computer skills, test taking, health and nutrition, reading, time management, learning strategies, self-advocacy, vocabulary development, math, and written composition skills. Most courses are offered for credit.
Counseling and advisement Career counseling, individual counseling, small-group counseling, and support groups are available. Academic advisement by a staff member affiliated with the program is available.
Auxiliary aids and services *Aids:* calculators, personal spelling/word-use assistants (e.g., Franklin Speller), scan and read programs (e.g., Kurzweil), screen-enlarging programs, screen readers, speech recognition programs (e.g., Dragon), tape recorders, taped textbooks. *Services and accommodations:* advocates, priority registration, alternative test arrangements, readers, note-takers, and scribes.
Student organization There is a student organization for students with LD.

ADD/ADHD Students with ADD/ADHD are eligible for the same services available to students with LD, as well as distraction-free testing environments.
Application *Required:* psychoeducational report (3 years old or less) and documentation of high school services (e.g., Individualized Education Program [IEP] or 504 plan). Upon application, documentation of need for special services should be sent only to your LD program or unit. Upon acceptance, documentation of need for special services should be sent only to your LD program or unit.
LD program contact Barbara A. Dimopoulos, Learning Disabilities Specialist, 12500 Campus Drive, Oakland, CA 94619. *Phone:* 510-436-2579. *Fax:* 510-436-2405. *E-mail:* bdimopoulos@peralta.cc.ca.us.
Application contact Barbara Simmons, District Admissions Officer, Merritt College, 12500 Campus Drive, Oakland, CA 94619-3196. *Phone:* 510-466-7369. *E-mail:* hperdue@peralta.cc.ca.us.

MIDDLESEX COUNTY COLLEGE
Edison, New Jersey

Students with LD Served by Program	160	ADD/ADHD Services	n/a
Staff	4 full-time, 2 part-time	Summer Preparation Program	n/a
LD Program or Service Fee	n/a	Alternative Test Arrangements	✓
LD Program Began	1984	LD Student Organization	✓

Project Connections began offering services in 1984. The program serves approximately 160 undergraduate students. Faculty consists of 4 full-time and 2 part-time staff members. Services are provided by counselors, diagnostic specialists, LD specialists, and professional tutors.
Policies 6 credit hours per semester are required to be eligible for financial aid.
Special preparation or orientation Required orientation held before classes begin and during summer prior to enrollment.
Diagnostic testing Available for spelling, intelligence, study skills, learning strategies, reading, written language, learning styles, visual processing, and math.
Basic skills remediation Available in computer skills, reading, learning strategies, written language, and math. Offered one-on-one, in small groups, and class-size groups by regular education teachers, LD specialists, and professional tutors.
Subject-area tutoring Available in most subjects. Offered one-on-one and in small groups by professional tutors and LD specialists.
Special courses Available in career planning, study skills, college survival skills, practical computer skills, test taking, time management, learning strategies, and stress management. No courses are offered for credit; some enter into overall grade point average.
Counseling and advisement Career counseling, individual counseling, small-group counseling, and support groups are available.
Auxiliary aids and services *Aids:* calculators, personal computers, personal spelling/word-use assistants (e.g., Franklin Speller), scan and read programs (e.g., Kurzweil), screen-enlarging programs, screen readers, speech recognition programs (e.g., Dragon), tape recorders, taped textbooks. *Services and accommodations:* priority registration, alternative test arrangements, readers, note-takers, and scribes.
Student organization There is a student organization for students with LD.
Application *Required:* high school transcript. *Recommended:* separate application to your LD program or unit, psychoeducational report (3 years old or less), and documentation of high

Middlesex County College (continued)

school services (e.g., Individualized Education Program [IEP] or 504 plan). Upon application, documentation of need for special services should be sent only to your LD program or unit. Upon acceptance, documentation of need for special services should be sent only to your LD program or unit. *Application deadline (institutional):* rolling/continuous for fall and rolling/continuous for spring. *Application deadline (LD program):* rolling/continuous for spring and 2/15 for fall.

LD program contact Elaine Weir-Daidone, Counselor for Students with Disabilities, 2600 Woodbridge Avenue, PO Box 3050, Edison, NJ 08818. *Phone:* 732-906-2546. *Fax:* 732-906-2506. *E-mail:* elaine_weir_daidone@middlesex.cc.nj.us.

Application contact Diane E. Lemcoe, Director of Admissions and Recruitment, Middlesex County College, 2600 Woodbridge Avenue, PO Box 3050, Edison, NJ 08818-3050. *Phone:* 732-906-2510. *Web address:* http://www.middlesex.cc.nj.us/.

MILWAUKEE AREA TECHNICAL COLLEGE
Milwaukee, Wisconsin

Students with LD Served by Program	275	ADD/ADHD Services	✓
Staff	12 full-time	Summer Preparation Program	n/a
LD Program or Service Fee	n/a	Alternative Test Arrangements	✓
LD Program Began	1984	LD Student Organization	n/a

Center for Special Needs began offering services in 1984. The program serves approximately 275 undergraduate students. Faculty consists of 12 full-time staff members. Services are provided by remediation/learning specialists, LD specialists, and professional tutors.

Policies 12 credit hours per semester are required to maintain full-time status; 6 credit hours per semester are required to be eligible for financial aid.

Special preparation or orientation Optional orientation held before registration, during registration, after classes begin, and individually by special arrangement.

Basic skills remediation Available in computer skills, reading, written language, and math. Offered in small groups and class-size groups by computer-based instruction, special education teachers, and LD specialists.

Subject-area tutoring Available in most subjects. Offered one-on-one and in small groups by professional tutors and trained peer tutors.

Special courses Available in career planning, study skills, college survival skills, test taking, time management, learning strategies, and stress management. Some courses are offered for credit; some enter into overall grade point average.

Auxiliary aids and services *Aids:* calculators, personal computers, personal spelling/word-use assistants (e.g., Franklin Speller), scan and read programs (e.g., Kurzweil), screen-enlarging programs, screen readers, speech recognition programs (e.g., Dragon), tape recorders, taped textbooks. *Services and accommodations:* priority registration, alternative test arrangements, readers, note-takers, and scribes.

ADD/ADHD Students with ADD/ADHD are eligible for the same services available to students with LD, as well as distraction-free study areas and distraction-free testing environments.

Application *Required:* high school transcript, psychoeducational report (3 years old or less), and documentation of high school services (e.g., Individualized Education Program [IEP] or 504 plan). Upon application, documentation of need for special services should be sent only to your LD program or unit. *Appli-*

cation deadline (institutional): rolling/continuous for fall and rolling/continuous for spring. *Application deadline (LD program):* rolling/continuous for fall and rolling/continuous for spring.

LD program contact Kathy Bohte, Instructor/Coordinator, Learning Center, 700 West State Street, Milwaukee, WI 53233. *Phone:* 414-297-6245. *Fax:* 414-297-7705. *E-mail:* bohtek@matc.edu.

Application contact Richard Crombie, Director of Enrollment Management, Milwaukee Area Technical College, 700 West State Street, Milwaukee, WI 53233-1443. *Phone:* 414-297-6301.

MIRACOSTA COLLEGE
Oceanside, California

Students with LD Served by Program	150	ADD/ADHD Services	✓
Staff	1 full-time	Summer Preparation Program	n/a
LD Program or Service Fee	n/a	Alternative Test Arrangements	✓
LD Program Began	1983	LD Student Organization	n/a

Disabled Student Programs and Services-Learning Disabilities Program began offering services in 1983. The program serves approximately 150 undergraduate students. Faculty consists of 1 full-time staff member. Services are provided by counselors, diagnostic specialists, special education teachers, and LD specialists.

Policies 12 units per semester are required to maintain full-time status.

Diagnostic testing Available for auditory processing, spelling, intelligence, reading, written language, learning styles, visual processing, and math.

Basic skills remediation Available in learning strategies, written language, and math. Offered one-on-one, in small groups, and class-size groups by computer-based instruction, LD specialists, and professional tutors.

Subject-area tutoring Available in most subjects. Offered one-on-one and in small groups by trained peer tutors.

Special courses Available in math and written composition skills. All courses are offered for credit; all enter into overall grade point average.

Counseling and advisement Individual counseling and academic counseling are available.

Auxiliary aids and services *Aids:* calculators, personal computers, personal spelling/word-use assistants (e.g., Franklin Speller), scan and read programs (e.g., Kurzweil), screen-enlarging programs, screen readers, speech recognition programs (e.g., Dragon), tape recorders, taped textbooks. *Services and accommodations:* advocates, priority registration, alternative test arrangements, readers, note-takers, scribes, and tape recording of lectures.

ADD/ADHD Students with ADD/ADHD are eligible for the same services available to students with LD, as well as distraction-free testing environments.

Application *Required:* separate application to your LD program or unit, psychoeducational report (3 years old or less), and documentation of high school services (e.g., Individualized Education Program [IEP] or 504 plan). *Recommended:* high school transcript and interview. Upon application, documentation of need for special services should be sent only to your LD program or unit. Upon acceptance, documentation of need for special services should be sent only to your LD program or unit.

LD program contact Nancy Schaefer, Learning Disabilities Specialist, One Barnard Drive, Oceanside, CA 92056-3899. *Phone:* 760-757-2121 Ext. 6658. *Fax:* 760-967-6420. *E-mail:* nschaefer@yar.miracosta.cc.ca.us.

Application contact Admissions and Records Assistant, Mira-Costa College, One Barnard Drive, Oceanside, CA 92056-3899. *Phone:* 760-795-6620. *Web address:* http://www.miracosta.cc.ca.us/.

MITCHELL COLLEGE
New London, Connecticut

Students with LD Served by Program	150	ADD/ADHD Services	✓
Staff 12 full-time, 3 part-time		Summer Preparation Program	✓
LD Program or Service Fee	✓	Alternative Test Arrangements	✓
LD Program Began	1981	LD Student Organization	n/a

Learning Resource Center (LRC) began offering services in 1981. The program serves approximately 150 undergraduate students. Faculty consists of 12 full-time and 3 part-time staff members. Services are provided by LD specialists.

Policies The college has written policies regarding course substitutions and substitution and waivers of requirements for admission and graduation. Students with LD may take up to 18 credit hours per semester.

Fees *LD Program or Service Fee:* $4900 per year.

Special preparation or orientation Optional summer program offered prior to entering college. Required orientation held before classes begin.

Subject-area tutoring Available in most subjects. Offered one-on-one and in small groups by professional tutors.

Special courses Available in study skills, college survival skills, test taking, reading, time management, learning strategies, self-advocacy, vocabulary development, stress management, and written composition skills. No courses are offered for credit; none enter into overall grade point average.

Auxiliary aids and services *Aids:* speech recognition programs (e.g., Dragon), tape recorders, taped textbooks. *Services and accommodations:* priority registration, alternative test arrangements, readers, note-takers, and scribes.

ADD/ADHD Students with ADD/ADHD are eligible for the same services available to students with LD, as well as distraction-free study areas, distraction-free testing environments and personal coach or mentors.

Application *Required:* high school transcript, ACT or SAT I (extended-time or untimed test accepted), interview, personal statement, letter(s) of recommendation, psychoeducational report (3 years old or less), documentation of high school services (e.g., Individualized Education Program [IEP] or 504 plan), and academic achievement test in reading, writing, math. *Recommended:* participation in extracurricular activities. Upon application, documentation of need for special services should be sent only to admissions. Upon acceptance, documentation of need for special services should be sent only to your LD program or unit.

LD program contact Dr. Patricia A. Pezzullo, Learning Resource Center Director, 437 Pequot Avenue, New London, CT 06320-4498. *Phone:* 860-701-5144. *Fax:* 860-701-5090. *E-mail:* pezzullo_p@mitchell.edu.

Application contact Mitchell College, 437 Pequot Avenue, New London, CT 06320-4498. *Web address:* http://www.mitchell.edu/.

MODESTO JUNIOR COLLEGE
Modesto, California

Students with LD Served by Program	250	ADD/ADHD Services	✓
Staff 9 full-time, 8 part-time		Summer Preparation Program	n/a
LD Program or Service Fee	n/a	Alternative Test Arrangements	✓
LD Program Began	1974	LD Student Organization	n/a

Disability Services Center began offering services in 1974. The program serves approximately 250 undergraduate students. Faculty consists of 9 full-time and 8 part-time staff members. Services are provided by regular education teachers, counselors, special education teachers, and LD specialists.

Policies The college has written policies regarding course substitutions. Students with LD may take up to 18 semester hours per semester; 12 semester hours per semester are required to maintain full-time status and to be eligible for financial aid.

Diagnostic testing Available for auditory processing, spelling, intelligence, learning strategies, reading, learning styles, visual processing, and math.

Basic skills remediation Available in auditory processing, study skills, computer skills, reading, time management, visual processing, learning strategies, spelling, written language, and math. Offered one-on-one, in small groups, and class-size groups by computer-based instruction, regular education teachers, and learning labs, individual instruction classes.

Subject-area tutoring Available in most subjects. Offered one-on-one and in small groups by trained peer tutors.

Special courses Available in career planning, college survival skills, practical computer skills, test taking, reading, time management, learning strategies, self-advocacy, vocabulary development, and math. All courses are offered for credit; some enter into overall grade point average.

Counseling and advisement Career counseling, individual counseling, and personal counseling are available.

Auxiliary aids and services *Aids:* calculators, personal spelling/word-use assistants (e.g., Franklin Speller), scan and read programs (e.g., Kurzweil), screen-enlarging programs, screen readers, speech recognition programs (e.g., Dragon), tape recorders, taped textbooks. *Services and accommodations:* advocates, priority registration, alternative test arrangements, readers, note-takers, and scribes.

ADD/ADHD Students with ADD/ADHD are eligible for the same services available to students with LD, as well as distraction-free study areas, distraction-free testing environments and note takers.

Application *Required:* separate application to your LD program or unit. Upon application, documentation of need for special services should be sent only to your LD program or unit. Upon acceptance, documentation of need for special services should be sent only to your LD program or unit. *Application deadline (institutional):* rolling/continuous for fall and rolling/continuous for spring. *Application deadline (LD program):* rolling/continuous for fall and rolling/continuous for spring.

LD program contact Derek Waring, Dean, Special Programs, 435 College Avenue, Modesto, CA 95350. *Phone:* 209-575-6861. *E-mail:* waringd@yosemite.cc.ca.us.

Application contact Susie Agostini, Director of Matriculation, Admissions, and Records, Modesto Junior College, 435 College Avenue, Modesto, CA 95350-5800. *Phone:* 209-575-6470. *Web address:* http://mjc.yosemite.cc.ca.us/.

MONTGOMERY COLLEGE-ROCKVILLE CAMPUS
Rockville, Maryland

Students with LD Served by Program	650	ADD/ADHD Services	✓
Staff	6 full-time, 12 part-time	Summer Preparation Program	n/a
LD Program or Service Fee	n/a	Alternative Test Arrangements	✓
LD Program Began	1978	LD Student Organization	n/a

Learning Center Program began offering services in 1978. The program serves approximately 650 undergraduate students. Faculty consists of 6 full-time and 12 part-time staff members. Services are provided by academic advisers, counselors, remediation/learning specialists, diagnostic specialists, LD specialists, and trained peer tutors.

Policies The college has written policies regarding course substitutions. Students with LD may take up to 15 credit hours per semester; 12 credit hours per semester are required to maintain full-time status; 6 credit hours per semester are required to be eligible for financial aid.

Special preparation or orientation Optional orientation held before classes begin.

Diagnostic testing Available for reading, written language, and learning styles.

Basic skills remediation Available in study skills, computer skills, reading, time management, learning strategies, spelling, and written language. Offered one-on-one, in small groups, and class-size groups by computer-based instruction, LD specialists, and trained peer tutors.

Special courses Available in study skills, college survival skills, practical computer skills, test taking, reading, time management, learning strategies, self-advocacy, vocabulary development, stress management, and written composition skills. Some courses are offered for credit; some enter into overall grade point average.

Counseling and advisement Career counseling and individual counseling are available. Academic advisement by a staff member affiliated with the program is available.

Auxiliary aids and services *Aids:* calculators, personal spelling/word-use assistants (e.g., Franklin Speller), scan and read programs (e.g., Kurzweil), screen-enlarging programs, screen readers, speech recognition programs (e.g., Dragon), tape recorders, taped textbooks. *Services and accommodations:* alternative test arrangements, readers, note-takers, and scribes.

ADD/ADHD Students with ADD/ADHD are eligible for the same services available to students with LD, as well as distraction-free testing environments.

Application *Required:* high school transcript, interview, separate application to your LD program or unit, psychoeducational report (4 years old or less), and documentation of high school services (e.g., Individualized Education Program [IEP] or 504 plan). Upon application, documentation of need for special services should be sent only to your LD program or unit. Upon acceptance, documentation of need for special services should be sent only to your LD program or unit. *Application deadline (institutional):* rolling/continuous for fall and rolling/continuous for spring. *Application deadline (LD program):* rolling/continuous for fall and rolling/continuous for spring.

LD program contact Rose Sachs, Chair/Counselor, 51 Mannakee Street, CAB Building, Room 122, Rockville, MD 20850. *Phone:* 301-279-5077.

Application contact Montgomery College-Rockville Campus, 51 Mannakee Street, Rockville, MD 20850-1196. *Web address:* http://www.mc.cc.md.us/.

MOORPARK COLLEGE
Moorpark, California

Students with LD Served by Program	1000	ADD/ADHD Services	✓
Staff	12 full-time, 10 part-time	Summer Preparation Program	✓
LD Program or Service Fee	n/a	Alternative Test Arrangements	✓
LD Program Began	1974	LD Student Organization	✓

Disabled Students Program and Services (DSPS) began offering services in 1974. The program serves approximately 1000 undergraduate students. Faculty consists of 12 full-time and 10 part-time staff members. Services are provided by academic advisers, counselors, remediation/learning specialists, diagnostic specialists, special education teachers, LD specialists, trained peer tutors, professional tutors, and job developer, psychologist, high tech computer center specialist.

Policies The college has written policies regarding course substitutions. Students with LD may take up to 18 units per semester; 12 units per semester are required to be eligible for financial aid.

Special preparation or orientation Optional summer program offered prior to entering college. Optional orientation held before registration, before classes begin, during summer prior to enrollment, and individually by special arrangement.

Diagnostic testing Available for auditory processing, motor skills, spelling, handwriting, intelligence, reading, written language, learning styles, visual processing, math, and attention deficit/hyperactive disorder.

Basic skills remediation Available in study skills, computer skills, reading, time management, learning strategies, spelling, written language, and math. Offered in class-size groups by computer-based instruction, regular education teachers, special education teachers, and LD specialists.

Subject-area tutoring Available in most subjects. Offered one-on-one and in small groups by computer-based instruction, professional tutors, and trained peer tutors.

Special courses Available in career planning, study skills, college survival skills, practical computer skills, test taking, reading, time management, learning strategies, self-advocacy, vocabulary development, math, stress management, written composition skills, and self-esteem. No courses are offered for credit; none enter into overall grade point average.

Counseling and advisement Career counseling, individual counseling, small-group counseling, and support groups are available. Academic advisement by a staff member affiliated with the program is available.

Auxiliary aids and services *Aids:* calculators, personal computers, personal spelling/word-use assistants (e.g., Franklin Speller), scan and read programs (e.g., Kurzweil), screen-enlarging programs, screen readers, speech recognition programs (e.g., Dragon), tape recorders, taped textbooks. *Services and accommodations:* priority registration, alternative test arrangements, readers, note-takers, and scribes.

Student organization There is a student organization for students with LD.

ADD/ADHD Students with ADD/ADHD are eligible for the same services available to students with LD, as well as distraction-free testing environments and medication management.

Application *Required:* separate application to your LD program or unit, psychoeducational report (3 years old or less), and documentation of high school services (e.g., Individualized Education Program [IEP] or 504 plan). *Recommended:* high school transcript and interview. Upon application, documentation of need for special services should be sent only to your LD program or unit. Upon acceptance, documentation of need for special services should be sent only to your LD program or unit.

LD program contact Sherry D'Attile, Learning Disabilities Specialist, 7075 Campus Road, Moorpark, CA 93021. *Phone:* 805-378-1461. *Fax:* 805-378-1594. *E-mail:* sdattile@vcccd.cc.ca.us.

Application contact Kathy C. Colborn, Registrar, Moorpark College, 7075 Campus Road, Moorpark, CA 93021-2899. *Phone:* 805-378-1415. *Web address:* http://www.moorpark.cc.ca.us/.

NAPA VALLEY COLLEGE
Napa, California

Students with LD Served by Program	730	ADD/ADHD Services	✓
Staff	3 full-time, 10 part-time	Summer Preparation Program	n/a
LD Program or Service Fee	n/a	Alternative Test Arrangements	✓
LD Program Began	1977	LD Student Organization	n/a

Office of Special Services began offering services in 1977. The program serves approximately 730 undergraduate students. Faculty consists of 3 full-time and 10 part-time staff members. Services are provided by counselors, diagnostic specialists, LD specialists, and professional tutors.

Policies 12 units per semester are required to maintain full-time status; 6 units per semester are required to be eligible for financial aid. LD services are also available to graduate students.

Diagnostic testing Available for auditory processing, spelling, handwriting, spoken language, reading, written language, visual processing, and math.

Basic skills remediation Available in study skills, reading, time management, spelling, and math. Offered in class-size groups by computer-based instruction, LD specialists, professional tutors, and trained peer tutors.

Subject-area tutoring Available in some subjects. Offered one-on-one and in small groups by computer-based instruction, professional tutors, and trained peer tutors.

Special courses Available in reading, math, and written composition skills. All courses are offered for credit; all enter into overall grade point average.

Counseling and advisement Career counseling, individual counseling, and support groups are available.

Auxiliary aids and services *Aids:* calculators, scan and read programs (e.g., Kurzweil), screen-enlarging programs, screen readers, speech recognition programs (e.g., Dragon), tape recorders, taped textbooks. *Services and accommodations:* advocates, priority registration, alternative test arrangements, readers, note-takers, and scribes.

ADD/ADHD Students with ADD/ADHD are eligible for the same services available to students with LD, as well as distraction-free study areas and distraction-free testing environments.

Application *Required:* high school transcript, interview, and documentation of high school services (e.g., Individualized Education Program [IEP] or 504 plan). Upon application, documentation of need for special services should be sent to both admissions and your LD program or unit. Upon acceptance, documentation of need for special services should be sent to both admissions and your LD program or unit.

LD program contact JoAnn Busenbark, Associate Dean, Napa Valley College, 2277 Napa-Vallejo Highway, Napa, CA 94558. *Phone:* 707-253-3080. *Fax:* 707-253-3083. *E-mail:* jbusenbark@campus.nvc.cc.ca.us.

Application contact Napa Valley College, 2277 Napa-Vallejo Highway, Napa, CA 94558-6236. *E-mail:* yvongrab@admin.nvc.cc.ca.us. *Web address:* http://www.nvc.cc.ca.us/.

NASHVILLE STATE TECHNICAL INSTITUTE
Nashville, Tennessee

Students with LD Served by Program	130	ADD/ADHD Services	✓
Staff	n/a	Summer Preparation Program	✓
LD Program or Service Fee	n/a	Alternative Test Arrangements	✓
LD Program Began	1996	LD Student Organization	n/a

Student Disability Services (SDS) began offering services in 1996. The program serves approximately 130 undergraduate students. Services are provided by academic advisers, counselors, remediation/learning specialists, special education teachers, trained peer tutors, and professional tutors.

Policies The college has written policies regarding course substitutions and grade forgiveness.

Special preparation or orientation Optional summer program offered prior to entering college. Optional orientation Yes.

Basic skills remediation Available in reading and math. Offered in class-size groups by computer-based instruction, regular education teachers, and special education teachers.

Subject-area tutoring Available in most subjects. Offered one-on-one by professional tutors and trained peer tutors.

Special courses Available in study skills, reading, self-advocacy, math, and written composition skills. All courses are offered for credit; some enter into overall grade point average.

Counseling and advisement Individual counseling is available. Academic advisement by a staff member affiliated with the program is available.

Auxiliary aids and services *Aids:* calculators, scan and read programs (e.g., Kurzweil), screen-enlarging programs, speech recognition programs (e.g., Dragon), tape recorders. *Services and accommodations:* priority registration, alternative test arrangements, readers, note-takers, and scribes.

ADD/ADHD Students with ADD/ADHD are eligible for the same services available to students with LD, as well as distraction-free testing environments.

Application *Required:* high school transcript, ACT (extended-time or untimed test accepted), separate application to your LD program or unit, psychoeducational report (3 years old or less), and documentation of high school services (e.g., Individualized Education Program [IEP] or 504 plan). Upon application, documentation of need for special services should be sent only to your LD program or unit. Upon acceptance, documentation of need for special services should be sent only to your LD program or unit. *Application deadline (institutional):* rolling/continuous for fall and rolling/continuous for spring. *Application deadline (LD program):* rolling/continuous for fall and rolling/continuous for spring.

LD program contact Diane Wood, Director, 120 White Bridge Road, Nashville, TN 37209. *Phone:* 615-353-3720. *Fax:* 615-353-3376. *E-mail:* wood_d@nsti.tec.tn.us.

Application contact Nancy Jewell, Assistant Director of Admissions, Nashville State Technical Institute, 120 White Bridge Road, Nashville, TN 37209-4515. *Phone:* 615-353-3214. *Web address:* http://www.nsti.tec.tn.us/.

NEW RIVER COMMUNITY COLLEGE
Dublin, Virginia

Students with LD Served by Program	150	ADD/ADHD Services	✓
Staff	1 full-time, 1 part-time	Summer Preparation Program	✓
LD Program or Service Fee	n/a	Alternative Test Arrangements	✓
LD Program Began	1985	LD Student Organization	✓

Learning Enrichment Achievement Program (Leap) Center to Serve Students with Learning Disabilities and ADHD began offering services in 1985. The program serves approximately 150 undergraduate students. Faculty consists of 1 full-time and 1 part-time staff member. Services are provided by academic advisers, counselors, remediation/learning specialists, LD specialists, trained peer tutors, and professional tutors.

Policies The college has written policies regarding course substitutions.

Special preparation or orientation Optional summer program offered prior to entering college. Optional orientation held during summer prior to enrollment.

Basic skills remediation Available in study skills, computer skills, time management, learning strategies, written language, and math. Offered one-on-one and in class-size groups by computer-based instruction, LD specialists, professional tutors, and trained peer tutors.

Subject-area tutoring Available in most subjects. Offered one-on-one by computer-based instruction, professional tutors, and trained peer tutors.

Special courses Available in career planning and study skills. Most courses are offered for credit; most enter into overall grade point average.

Counseling and advisement Career counseling, individual counseling, and support groups are available. Academic advisement by a staff member affiliated with the program is available.

Auxiliary aids and services *Aids:* calculators, personal computers, personal spelling/word-use assistants (e.g., Franklin Speller), scan and read programs (e.g., Kurzweil), screen-enlarging programs, screen readers, speech recognition programs (e.g., Dragon), tape recorders, taped textbooks. *Services and accommodations:* priority registration, alternative test arrangements, readers, note-takers, and scribes.

Student organization There is a student organization for students with LD.

ADD/ADHD Students with ADD/ADHD are eligible for the same services available to students with LD, as well as distraction-free study areas, distraction-free testing environments and support groups for ADD/ADHD.

Application *Required:* high school transcript, interview, separate application to your LD program or unit, psychoeducational report, and documentation of high school services (e.g., Individualized Education Program [IEP] or 504 plan). Upon application, documentation of need for special services should be sent only to your LD program or unit. *Application deadline (institutional):* rolling/continuous for fall and rolling/continuous for spring. *Application deadline (LD program):* rolling/continuous for fall and rolling/continuous for spring.

LD program contact Jeananne Dixon, Coordinator, Box 1127, Dublin, VA 24084. *Phone:* 540-674-3600 Ext. 4358. *Fax:* 540-674-3644. *E-mail:* nrdixoj@nr.cc.va.us.

Application contact New River Community College, PO Box 1127, Dublin, VA 24084-1127. *E-mail:* nrchrim@vccscent.bitnet. *Web address:* http://www.nr.cc.va.us/.

NORMANDALE COMMUNITY COLLEGE
Bloomington, Minnesota

Students with LD Served by Program	100	ADD/ADHD Services	✓
Staff	1 full-time, 3 part-time	Summer Preparation Program	n/a
LD Program or Service Fee	n/a	Alternative Test Arrangements	✓
LD Program Began	1975	LD Student Organization	n/a

Office for Students with Disabilities (OSD) began offering services in 1975. The program serves approximately 100 undergraduate students. Faculty consists of 1 full-time and 3 part-time staff members. Services are provided by regular education teachers, special education teachers, and LD specialists.

Policies Students with LD may take up to 18 credit hours per semester; 12 credit hours per semester are required to maintain full-time status and to be eligible for financial aid.

Auxiliary aids and services *Aids:* calculators, personal computers, personal spelling/word-use assistants (e.g., Franklin Speller), scan and read programs (e.g., Kurzweil), screen-enlarging programs, screen readers, speech recognition programs (e.g., Dragon), tape recorders, taped textbooks. *Services and accommodations:* advocates, priority registration, alternative test arrangements, readers, note-takers, and scribes.

ADD/ADHD Students with ADD/ADHD are eligible for the same services available to students with LD, as well as distraction-free study areas, distraction-free testing environments and personal coach or mentors.

Application *Required:* high school transcript and psychoeducational report (3 years old or less). *Recommended:* documentation of high school services (e.g., Individualized Education Program [IEP] or 504 plan). Upon application, documentation of need for special services should be sent only to your LD program or unit. Upon acceptance, documentation of need for special services should be sent only to your LD program or unit. *Application deadline (institutional):* rolling/continuous for fall and rolling/continuous for spring. *Application deadline (LD program):* rolling/continuous for fall and rolling/continuous for spring.

LD program contact Mary Jibben, Coordinator, Office for Students with Disabilities, 9700 France Avenue S, Bloomington, MN 55431. *Phone:* 952-832-6422. *Fax:* 952-832-6391.

Application contact Information Center, Normandale Community College, 9700 France Avenue South, Bloomington, MN 55431-4399. *Phone:* 612-832-6320. *Web address:* http://www.nr.cc.mn.us/.

NORTHAMPTON COUNTY AREA COMMUNITY COLLEGE
Bethlehem, Pennsylvania

Students with LD Served by Program	250	ADD/ADHD Services	✓
Staff	1 full-time, 3 part-time	Summer Preparation Program	n/a
LD Program or Service Fee	n/a	Alternative Test Arrangements	✓
LD Program Began	1982	LD Student Organization	n/a

Disability Services began offering services in 1982. The program serves approximately 250 undergraduate students. Faculty consists of 1 full-time and 3 part-time staff members. Services are provided by academic advisers, counselors, remediation/learning specialists, LD specialists, trained peer tutors, and professional tutors.

Policies Students with LD may take up to 18 credit hours per semester; 12 credit hours per semester are required to maintain full-time status; 6 credit hours per semester are required to be eligible for financial aid.

Special preparation or orientation Optional orientation held during registration, before classes begin, and during summer prior to enrollment.

Basic skills remediation Available in study skills, time management, social skills, learning strategies, and written language. Offered one-on-one by LD specialists.

Subject-area tutoring Available in most subjects. Offered one-on-one by professional tutors and trained peer tutors.

Special courses Available in career planning, college survival skills, practical computer skills, test taking, reading, time management, learning strategies, self-advocacy, and stress management. Some courses are offered for credit; some enter into overall grade point average.

Counseling and advisement Career counseling, individual counseling, and small-group counseling are available. Academic advisement by a staff member affiliated with the program is available.

Auxiliary aids and services *Aids:* calculators, personal spelling/word-use assistants (e.g., Franklin Speller), scan and read programs (e.g., Kurzweil), screen-enlarging programs, screen readers, speech recognition programs (e.g., Dragon), tape recorders, taped textbooks. *Services and accommodations:* advocates, priority registration, alternative test arrangements, readers, note-takers, and scribes.

ADD/ADHD Students with ADD/ADHD are eligible for the same services available to students with LD, as well as distraction-free testing environments and personal coach or mentors.

Application *Required:* high school transcript, interview, and psychoeducational report (3 years old or less). Upon application, documentation of need for special services should be sent only to your LD program or unit. Upon acceptance, documentation of need for special services should be sent only to your LD program or unit. *Application deadline (institutional):* rolling/continuous for fall and rolling/continuous for spring. *Application deadline (LD program):* rolling/continuous for fall and rolling/continuous for spring.

LD program contact Laraine A. Demshock, Coordinator of Disability Services, 3825 Green Pond Road, Bethlehem, PA 18020. *Phone:* 610-861-5318. *E-mail:* ldemshock@northhampton.edu.

Application contact Northampton County Area Community College, 3835 Green Pond Road, Bethlehem, PA 18020-7599. *E-mail:* adminfo@pmail.nhrm.cc.pa.us. *Web address:* http://www.northampton.edu/.

NORTH IDAHO COLLEGE
Coeur d'Alene, Idaho

Students with LD Served by Program	60	ADD/ADHD Services	✓
Staff	1 full-time, 4 part-time	Summer Preparation Program	n/a
LD Program or Service Fee	n/a	Alternative Test Arrangements	✓
LD Program Began	1998	LD Student Organization	✓

Disability Support Services began offering services in 1998. The program serves approximately 60 undergraduate students. Faculty consists of 1 full-time and 4 part-time staff members. Services are provided by academic advisers, counselors, special education teachers, trained peer tutors, and professional tutors.

Policies Students with LD may take up to 18 credit hours per semester; 12 credit hours per semester are required to maintain full-time status; 6 credit hours per semester are required to be eligible for financial aid.

Special preparation or orientation Optional orientation held before classes begin.

Basic skills remediation Available in study skills, reading, time management, learning strategies, spelling, written language, and math. Offered in small groups by regular education teachers and special education teachers.

Subject-area tutoring Available in most subjects. Offered one-on-one.

Counseling and advisement Career counseling, individual counseling, and support groups are available. Academic advisement by a staff member affiliated with the program is available.

Auxiliary aids and services *Aids:* calculators, scan and read programs (e.g., Kurzweil), screen-enlarging programs, screen readers, tape recorders, taped textbooks. *Services and accommodations:* advocates, priority registration, alternative test arrangements, readers, note-takers, and scribes.

Student organization There is a student organization for students with LD.

ADD/ADHD Students with ADD/ADHD are eligible for the same services available to students with LD, as well as distraction-free study areas, distraction-free testing environments, personal coach or mentors, and support groups for ADD/ADHD.

Application *Required:* high school transcript, separate application to your LD program or unit, and psychoeducational report. *Recommended:* documentation of high school services (e.g., Individualized Education Program [IEP] or 504 plan). Upon acceptance, documentation of need for special services should be sent only to your LD program or unit. *Application deadline (institutional):* 8/5 for fall and 1/4 for spring. *Application deadline (LD program):* rolling/continuous for fall and rolling/continuous for spring.

LD program contact Sharon Daniels-Bullock, Disability Support Services Coordinator, 1000 West Garden Avenue, Coeur d'Alene, ID 83814. *Phone:* 208-769-7794. *E-mail:* sharon_daniels@nic.edu.

Application contact North Idaho College, 1000 West Garden Avenue, Coeur d'Alene, ID 83814-2199. *E-mail:* admit@nidc.edu. *Web address:* http://www.nic.edu/.

NORTH LAKE COLLEGE
Irving, Texas

Students with LD Served by Program	300	ADD/ADHD Services	✓
Staff	3 full-time, 1 part-time	Summer Preparation Program	n/a
LD Program or Service Fee	n/a	Alternative Test Arrangements	✓
LD Program Began	1977	LD Student Organization	n/a

Disability and Supplemental Services began offering services in 1977. The program serves approximately 300 undergraduate students. Faculty consists of 3 full-time staff members and 1 part-time staff member. Services are provided by academic advisers, regular education teachers, counselors, and graduate assistants/students.

Basic skills remediation Available in reading, written language, and math. Offered one-on-one and in class-size groups by computer-based instruction and regular education teachers.

Special courses Available in reading. No courses are offered for credit; some enter into overall grade point average.

Counseling and advisement Career counseling and individual counseling are available. Academic advisement by a staff member affiliated with the program is available.

Auxiliary aids and services *Aids:* calculators, personal computers, personal spelling/word-use assistants (e.g., Franklin Speller), scan and read programs (e.g., Kurzweil), screen-enlarging programs, screen readers, speech recognition pro-

North Lake College (continued)

grams (e.g., Dragon), tape recorders, taped textbooks. *Services and accommodations:* advocates, alternative test arrangements, readers, note-takers, and scribes.

ADD/ADHD Students with ADD/ADHD are eligible for the same services available to students with LD, as well as distraction-free study areas and distraction-free testing environments.

Application *Required:* high school transcript, interview, separate application to your LD program or unit, psychoeducational report (2 years old or less), and documentation of high school services (e.g., Individualized Education Program [IEP] or 504 plan). Upon application, documentation of need for special services should be sent only to your LD program or unit. Upon acceptance, documentation of need for special services should be sent only to your LD program or unit. *Application deadline (institutional):* rolling/continuous for fall and rolling/continuous for spring. *Application deadline (LD program):* rolling/continuous for fall and rolling/continuous for spring.

LD program contact Carole Gray, Coordinator, Special Populations, 5001 North MacArthur Boulevard, Irving, TX 75038-3899. *Phone:* 972-273-3165. *Fax:* 972-273-3164. *E-mail:* cag7341@dcccd.edu.

Application contact North Lake College, 5001 North MacArthur Boulevard, Irving, TX 75038-3899.

NORTHWEST COLLEGE
Powell, Wyoming

Students with LD Served by Program	50	ADD/ADHD Services	✓
Staff	3 full-time, 1 part-time	Summer Preparation Program	n/a
LD Program or Service Fee	n/a	Alternative Test Arrangements	✓
LD Program Began	1990	LD Student Organization	n/a

Success Center began offering services in 1990. The program serves approximately 50 undergraduate students. Faculty consists of 3 full-time staff members and 1 part-time staff member. Services are provided by remediation/learning specialists, LD specialists, and trained peer tutors.

Policies Students with LD may take up to 15 credit hours per term; 12 credit hours per term are required to maintain full-time status and to be eligible for financial aid.

Special preparation or orientation Optional orientation held During orientation.

Basic skills remediation Available in study skills, reading, time management, written language, and math. Offered in class-size groups by computer-based instruction and LD specialists.

Subject-area tutoring Available in all subjects. Offered one-on-one and in small groups by computer-based instruction, trained peer tutors, and LD specialists.

Counseling and advisement Career counseling, individual counseling, and support groups are available.

Auxiliary aids and services *Aids:* calculators, personal computers, personal spelling/word-use assistants (e.g., Franklin Speller), scan and read programs (e.g., Kurzweil), screen-enlarging programs, screen readers, speech recognition programs (e.g., Dragon), tape recorders, taped textbooks. *Services and accommodations:* priority registration, alternative test arrangements, readers, note-takers, and scribes.

ADD/ADHD Students with ADD/ADHD are eligible for the same services available to students with LD, as well as distraction-free study areas and distraction-free testing environments.

Application *Required:* high school transcript and psychoeducational report (5 years old or less). *Recommended:* ACT (extended-time test accepted), interview, personal statement, and documentation of high school services (e.g., Individualized

Education Program [IEP] or 504 plan). Upon application, documentation of need for special services should be sent only to your LD program or unit. Upon acceptance, documentation of need for special services should be sent only to your LD program or unit. *Application deadline (institutional):* rolling/continuous for fall and rolling/continuous for spring. *Application deadline (LD program):* rolling/continuous for fall and rolling/continuous for spring.

LD program contact Lyn Pizor, Director, 231 West Sixth Street, Powell, WY 82435. *Phone:* 307-754-6695. *Fax:* 307-754-6700. *E-mail:* pizorl@nwc.cc.wy.us.

Application contact Northwest College, 231 West 6th Street, Powell, WY 82435-1898. *E-mail:* beark@adm.nwc.whecn.edu. *Web address:* http://www.nwc.cc.wy.us.

OCEAN COUNTY COLLEGE
Toms River, New Jersey

Students with LD Served by Program	280	ADD/ADHD Services	✓
Staff	7 full-time, 10 part-time	Summer Preparation Program	✓
LD Program or Service Fee	n/a	Alternative Test Arrangements	✓
LD Program Began	1987	LD Student Organization	✓

Disability Resource Center, Project Academic Skill Support (PASS) began offering services in 1987. The program serves approximately 280 undergraduate students. Faculty consists of 7 full-time and 10 part-time staff members. Services are provided by academic advisers, counselors, diagnostic specialists, LD specialists, trained peer tutors, and professional tutors.

Policies Students with LD may take up to 18 credit hours per semester; 12 credit hours per semester are required to maintain full-time status; 6 credit hours per semester are required to be eligible for financial aid.

Special preparation or orientation Optional summer program offered prior to entering college. Optional orientation held before classes begin.

Diagnostic testing Available for auditory processing, spelling, spoken language, intelligence, learning strategies, reading, written language, learning styles, visual processing, and math.

Basic skills remediation Available in reading, learning strategies, written language, and math. Offered in class-size groups by regular education teachers.

Subject-area tutoring Available in most subjects. Offered one-on-one and in small groups by professional tutors and trained peer tutors.

Special courses Available in career planning, study skills, college survival skills, time management, learning strategies, self-advocacy, stress management, and written composition skills. No courses are offered for credit; all enter into overall grade point average.

Counseling and advisement Career counseling, individual counseling, small-group counseling, and support groups are available. Academic advisement by a staff member affiliated with the program is available.

Auxiliary aids and services *Aids:* calculators, personal spelling/word-use assistants (e.g., Franklin Speller), scan and read programs (e.g., Kurzweil), screen-enlarging programs, screen readers, tape recorders, taped textbooks. *Services and accommodations:* priority registration, alternative test arrangements, readers, note-takers, and scribes.

Student organization There is a student organization for students with LD.

ADD/ADHD Students with ADD/ADHD are eligible for the same services available to students with LD, as well as distraction-free testing environments and support groups for ADD/ADHD.

Application *Required:* separate application to your LD program or unit, psychoeducational report (3 years old or less), and documentation of high school services (e.g., Individualized Education Program [IEP] or 504 plan). *Recommended:* high school transcript. Upon application, documentation of need for special services should be sent only to your LD program or unit. Upon acceptance, documentation of need for special services should be sent only to your LD program or unit. *Application deadline (institutional):* rolling/continuous for fall and rolling/continuous for spring. *Application deadline (LD program):* rolling/continuous for fall and rolling/continuous for spring.

LD program contact Maureen Reustle, Director, College Drive, Toms River, NJ 08753. *Phone:* 732-255-0456. *Fax:* 732-255-0458. *E-mail:* mreustle@ocean.cc.nj.us.

Application contact Ocean County College, College Drive, PO Box 2001, Toms River, NJ 08754-2001. *Web address:* http://www.ocean.cc.nj.us/.

PENNSYLVANIA STATE UNIVERSITY DELAWARE COUNTY CAMPUS OF THE COMMONWEALTH COLLEGE

Media, Pennsylvania

Students with LD Served by Program	40	ADD/ADHD Services	✓
Staff	1 full-time, 10 part-time	Summer Preparation Program	✓
LD Program or Service Fee	n/a	Alternative Test Arrangements	✓
LD Program Began	1994	LD Student Organization	n/a

Success from the Start began offering services in 1994. The program serves approximately 40 undergraduate students. Faculty consists of 1 full-time and 10 part-time staff members. Services are provided by remediation/learning specialists, LD specialists, trained peer tutors, and professional tutors.

Policies The college has written policies regarding course substitutions and substitution and waivers of requirements for admission and graduation. Students with LD may take up to 18 credit hours per semester; 12 credit hours per semester are required to maintain full-time status and to be eligible for financial aid.

Special preparation or orientation Optional summer program offered prior to entering college. Optional orientation held individually by special arrangement.

Diagnostic testing Available for reading and learning styles.

Basic skills remediation Available in study skills, reading, time management, written language, and math. Offered one-on-one, in small groups, and class-size groups by LD specialists, professional tutors, and trained peer tutors.

Subject-area tutoring Available in all subjects. Offered one-on-one and in small groups by professional tutors, trained peer tutors, and LD specialists.

Special courses Available in career planning, oral communication skills, study skills, college survival skills, practical computer skills, test taking, reading, time management, learning strategies, vocabulary development, math, stress management, and written composition skills. Some courses are offered for credit; some enter into overall grade point average.

Counseling and advisement Career counseling and individual counseling are available.

Auxiliary aids and services *Aids:* calculators, personal computers, scan and read programs (e.g., Kurzweil), tape recorders, taped textbooks. *Services and accommodations:* alternative test arrangements, readers, note-takers, and scribes.

ADD/ADHD Students with ADD/ADHD are eligible for the same services available to students with LD, as well as distraction-free testing environments and personal coach or mentors.

Application *Required:* high school transcript and ACT or SAT I (extended-time or untimed test accepted). *Recommended:* participation in extracurricular activities, personal statement, and letter(s) of recommendation. Upon application, documentation of need for special services should be sent only to your LD program or unit. Upon acceptance, documentation of need for special services should be sent only to your LD program or unit. *Application deadline (institutional):* rolling/continuous for fall and rolling/continuous for spring. *Application deadline (LD program):* rolling/continuous for fall and rolling/continuous for spring.

LD program contact Sharon Manco, Disability Contact Liaison, 25 Yearsley Mill Road, Media, PA 19063. *Phone:* 610-892-1461. *Fax:* 610-892-1357. *E-mail:* sam26@psu.edu.

Application contact Pennsylvania State University Delaware County Campus of the Commonwealth College, 25 Yearsley Mill Road, Media, PA 19063-5596. *E-mail:* admissions@psu.edu. *Web address:* http://www.psu.edu/.

PHOENIX COLLEGE

Phoenix, Arizona

Students with LD Served by Program	85	ADD/ADHD Services	✓
Staff	1 full-time, 3 part-time	Summer Preparation Program	n/a
LD Program or Service Fee	n/a	Alternative Test Arrangements	✓
LD Program Began	n/a	LD Student Organization	n/a

Disability Support Services serves approximately 85 undergraduate students. Faculty consists of 1 full-time and 3 part-time staff members. Services are provided by academic advisers, remediation/learning specialists, counselors, trained peer tutors, and professional tutors.

Policies The college has written policies regarding course substitutions. Students with LD may take up to 18 credit hours per semester; 12 credit hours per semester are required to maintain full-time status; 3 credit hours per semester are required to be eligible for financial aid.

Special preparation or orientation Optional orientation held before registration, during registration, before classes begin, and individually by special arrangement.

Basic skills remediation Available in auditory processing, study skills, computer skills, reading, time management, learning strategies, and written language. Offered one-on-one, in small groups, and class-size groups by graduate assistants/students, LD specialists, and professional tutors.

Subject-area tutoring Available in some subjects. Offered one-on-one by professional tutors and LD specialists.

Counseling and advisement Career counseling, individual counseling, small-group counseling, and support groups are available. Academic advisement by a staff member affiliated with the program is available.

Auxiliary aids and services *Aids:* personal computers, personal spelling/word-use assistants (e.g., Franklin Speller), scan and read programs (e.g., Kurzweil), screen-enlarging programs, screen readers, speech recognition programs (e.g., Dragon), tape recorders, taped textbooks. *Services and accommodations:* advocates, priority registration, alternative test arrangements, readers, note-takers, and scribes.

ADD/ADHD Students with ADD/ADHD are eligible for the same services available to students with LD, as well as distraction-free study areas and distraction-free testing environments.

Application *Required:* separate application to your LD program or unit and psychoeducational report (3 years old or less). *Recommended:* high school transcript and interview. Upon application, documentation of need for special services should be

Phoenix College (continued)

sent only to your LD program or unit. Upon acceptance, documentation of need for special services should be sent only to your LD program or unit. *Application deadline (institutional):* 8/23 for fall and 1/18 for spring. *Application deadline (LD program):* 8/7 for fall and 1/10 for spring.

LD program contact Ramona Shingler, Coordinator, Disability Support Services, 1202 West Thomas Road, Phoenix, AZ 85013. *Phone:* 602-285-7477. *Fax:* 602-285-7663. *E-mail:* r.shingler@pc. mail.maricopa.edu.

Application contact Donna Fischer, Supervisor of Admissions and Records, Phoenix College, 1202 West Thomas Road, Phoenix, AZ 85013-4234. *Phone:* 602-285-7500. *Web address:* http://www.pc.maricopa.edu/.

PIMA COMMUNITY COLLEGE
Tucson, Arizona

Students with LD Served by Program	225	ADD/ADHD Services	✓
Staff	8 full-time	Summer Preparation Program	n/a
LD Program or Service Fee	n/a	Alternative Test Arrangements	✓
LD Program Began	1979	LD Student Organization	n/a

Disabled Student Resources (DSR) began offering services in 1979. The program serves approximately 225 undergraduate students. Faculty consists of 8 full-time staff members. Services are provided by counselors, remediation/learning specialists, diagnostic specialists, LD specialists, and disabilities specialist.

Policies Students with LD may take up to 18 credit hours per semester; 12 credit hours per semester are required to maintain full-time status; 6 credit hours per semester are required to be eligible for financial aid.

Basic skills remediation Available in study skills, time management, learning strategies, and spelling. Offered one-on-one by LD specialists and disabilities specialist.

Subject-area tutoring Available in some subjects. Offered one-on-one by student tutors.

Counseling and advisement Individual counseling is available.

Auxiliary aids and services *Aids:* calculators, personal computers, personal spelling/word-use assistants (e.g., Franklin Speller), scan and read programs (e.g., Kurzweil), screen-enlarging programs, screen readers, speech recognition programs (e.g., Dragon), tape recorders, taped textbooks. *Services and accommodations:* advocates, priority registration, alternative test arrangements, readers, note-takers, and scribes.

ADD/ADHD Students with ADD/ADHD are eligible for the same services available to students with LD, as well as distraction-free testing environments.

Application *Required:* interview, psychoeducational report, documentation of high school services (e.g., Individualized Education Program [IEP] or 504 plan), and medical doctor's report. Upon application, documentation of need for special services should be sent only to your LD program or unit. Upon acceptance, documentation of need for special services should be sent only to your LD program or unit. *Application deadline (institutional):* rolling/continuous for fall and rolling/continuous for spring. *Application deadline (LD program):* rolling/continuous for fall and rolling/continuous for spring.

LD program contact Eric Morrison, Faculty Lead, 2202 West Anklam Road, Tucson, AZ 85709-0095. *Phone:* 520-206-6688. *Fax:* 520-206-6071. *E-mail:* emorrison@pimaacc.pima.edu.

Application contact Pima Community College, 4905 East Broadway, Tucson, AZ 85709-1010. *Web address:* http://www.pima.edu/.

QUEENSBOROUGH COMMUNITY COLLEGE OF THE CITY UNIVERSITY OF NEW YORK
Bayside, New York

Students with LD Served by Program	500	ADD/ADHD Services	✓
Staff	4 full-time, 5 part-time	Summer Preparation Program	n/a
LD Program or Service Fee	n/a	Alternative Test Arrangements	✓
LD Program Began	1989	LD Student Organization	✓

Services for Students with Disabilities began offering services in 1989. The program serves approximately 500 undergraduate students. Faculty consists of 4 full-time and 5 part-time staff members. Services are provided by academic advisers, remediation/learning specialists, counselors, regular education teachers, LD specialists, and trained peer tutors.

Policies Students with LD may take up to 18 credit hours per semester; 12 credit hours per semester are required to maintain full-time status and to be eligible for financial aid.

Special preparation or orientation Required orientation held before registration, after classes begin, and individually by special arrangement.

Basic skills remediation Available in study skills, computer skills, reading, time management, social skills, learning strategies, math, and writing comprehension. Offered in small groups and class-size groups by computer-based instruction, regular education teachers, LD specialists, and professional tutors.

Subject-area tutoring Available in some subjects. Offered one-on-one, in small groups, and class-size groups by computer-based instruction, professional tutors, graduate assistants/students, trained peer tutors, and LD specialists.

Special courses Available in career planning, study skills, college survival skills, test taking, reading, time management, learning strategies, vocabulary development, math, and written composition skills. Some courses are offered for credit; some enter into overall grade point average.

Counseling and advisement Career counseling, individual counseling, and small-group counseling are available. Academic advisement by a staff member affiliated with the program is available.

Auxiliary aids and services *Aids:* calculators, scan and read programs (e.g., Kurzweil), screen-enlarging programs, tape recorders, taped textbooks. *Services and accommodations:* priority registration, alternative test arrangements, readers, note-takers, and scribes.

Student organization There is a student organization for students with LD.

ADD/ADHD Students with ADD/ADHD are eligible for the same services available to students with LD, as well as distraction-free study areas and distraction-free testing environments.

Application *Required:* high school transcript. *Recommended:* psychoeducational report (3 years old or less), documentation of high school services (e.g., Individualized Education Program [IEP] or 504 plan), and medical letter from physician. Upon acceptance, documentation of need for special services should be sent only to your LD program or unit. *Application deadline (LD program):* rolling/continuous for fall and rolling/continuous for spring.

LD program contact Elliot L. Rosman, Director, 222-05 56th Avenue, Room S 132, Bayside, NY 11364. *Phone:* 718-631-6257. *Fax:* 718-229-1733. *E-mail:* erosman@qcc.cuny.edu.

Application contact Guy Hildebrandt, Director of Registration, Queensborough Community College of the City University of New York, 222-05 56th Avenue, Bayside, NY 11364. *Phone:* 718-631-6307.

RANDOLPH COMMUNITY COLLEGE
Asheboro, North Carolina

Students with LD Served by Program	90	ADD/ADHD Services	✓
Staff	5 full-time	Summer Preparation Program	✓
LD Program or Service Fee	n/a	Alternative Test Arrangements	✓
LD Program Began	1981	LD Student Organization	n/a

Special Services Project began offering services in 1981. The program serves approximately 90 undergraduate students. Faculty consists of 5 full-time staff members. Services are provided by academic advisers, remediation/learning specialists, counselors, and trained peer tutors.

Policies The college has written policies regarding course substitutions and grade forgiveness. 12 credit hours per semester are required to maintain full-time status; 3 credit hours per semester are required to be eligible for financial aid.

Special preparation or orientation Optional summer program offered prior to entering college.

Basic skills remediation Available in study skills, computer skills, reading, spelling, written language, and math. Offered one-on-one and in small groups by professional tutors and trained peer tutors.

Subject-area tutoring Available in all subjects. Offered one-on-one and in small groups by professional tutors and trained peer tutors.

Counseling and advisement Career counseling, individual counseling, small-group counseling, and coaching are available. Academic advisement by a staff member affiliated with the program is available.

Auxiliary aids and services *Aids:* calculators, personal computers, screen-enlarging programs, speech recognition programs (e.g., Dragon), tape recorders, taped textbooks. *Services and accommodations:* advocates, priority registration, alternative test arrangements, readers, note-takers, and scribes.

ADD/ADHD Students with ADD/ADHD are eligible for the same services available to students with LD, as well as distraction-free study areas, distraction-free testing environments and personal coach or mentors.

Application *Required:* high school transcript and separate application to your LD program or unit. *Recommended:* psychoeducational report and letter from qualified professional. Upon acceptance, documentation of need for special services should be sent only to your LD program or unit.

LD program contact Dr. Rebekah Megerian, Dean, Developmental and Basic Skills Program, Box 1009, Asheboro, NC 27204. *Phone:* 336-633-0227. *Fax:* 336-629-4695. *E-mail:* rhmegerian@randolph.cc.nc.us.

Application contact Carol M. Elmore, Registrar, Randolph Community College, PO Box 1009, Asheboro, NC 27204-1009. *Phone:* 336-633-0213.

REEDLEY COLLEGE
Reedley, California

Students with LD Served by Program	150	ADD/ADHD Services	✓
Staff	1 full-time, 2 part-time	Summer Preparation Program	n/a
LD Program or Service Fee	n/a	Alternative Test Arrangements	✓
LD Program Began	1993	LD Student Organization	n/a

Disabled Student Services began offering services in 1993. The program serves approximately 150 undergraduate students. Faculty consists of 1 full-time and 2 part-time staff members. Services are provided by academic advisers, counselors, diagnostic specialists, and LD specialists.

Special preparation or orientation Optional orientation held before classes begin.

Diagnostic testing Available for auditory processing, spelling, spoken language, intelligence, learning strategies, reading, written language, learning styles, social skills, visual processing, and math.

Counseling and advisement Career counseling, individual counseling, small-group counseling, and support groups are available. Academic advisement by a staff member affiliated with the program is available.

Auxiliary aids and services *Aids:* calculators, personal computers, personal spelling/word-use assistants (e.g., Franklin Speller), scan and read programs (e.g., Kurzweil), screen-enlarging programs, screen readers, tape recorders, taped textbooks. *Services and accommodations:* advocates, priority registration, alternative test arrangements, readers, note-takers, and scribes.

ADD/ADHD Students with ADD/ADHD are eligible for the same services available to students with LD, as well as distraction-free testing environments and personal coach or mentors.

Application *Recommended:* high school transcript. Upon acceptance, documentation of need for special services should be sent only to your LD program or unit. *Application deadline (institutional):* rolling/continuous for fall and rolling/continuous for spring. *Application deadline (LD program):* rolling/continuous for fall and rolling/continuous for spring.

LD program contact Lynn Mancini, Director, Disabled Student Services, 995 North Reed Avenue, Reedley, CA 93654. *Phone:* 559-638-0332. *Fax:* 559-638-0382. *E-mail:* lynn.mancini@dol.scccd.cc.ca.us.

Application contact Leticia Alvarez, Admissions and Records Manager, Reedley College, 995 North Reed Avenue, Reedley, CA 93654-2099. *Phone:* 559-638-3641 Ext. 3624.

RIVERSIDE COMMUNITY COLLEGE
Riverside, California

Students with LD Served by Program	300	ADD/ADHD Services	✓
Staff	3 full-time, 3 part-time	Summer Preparation Program	n/a
LD Program or Service Fee	n/a	Alternative Test Arrangements	✓
LD Program Began	1980	LD Student Organization	n/a

Disabled Students Programs and Services/Learning Disabilities Program began offering services in 1980. The program serves approximately 300 undergraduate students. Faculty consists of 3 full-time and 3 part-time staff members. Services are provided by academic advisers and LD specialists.

Policies Students with LD may take up to 18 credit hours per semester; 12 credits per semester are required to maintain full-time status; 1 credit per semester is required to be eligible for financial aid.

Special preparation or orientation Optional orientation held individually by special arrangement.

Diagnostic testing Available for spelling, intelligence, study skills, reading, learning styles, and math.

Basic skills remediation Available in reading, learning strategies, spelling, written language, and math. Offered in class-size groups by computer-based instruction, regular education teachers, and LD specialists.

Riverside Community College (continued)

Subject-area tutoring Available in some subjects. Offered one-on-one and in small groups by trained peer tutors.

Special courses Available in reading and learning strategies. All courses are offered for credit; none enter into overall grade point average.

Counseling and advisement Individual counseling is available. Academic advisement by a staff member affiliated with the program is available.

Auxiliary aids and services *Aids:* calculators, personal computers, personal spelling/word-use assistants (e.g., Franklin Speller), scan and read programs (e.g., Kurzweil), screen-enlarging programs, screen readers, speech recognition programs (e.g., Dragon), tape recorders, taped textbooks. *Services and accommodations:* priority registration, alternative test arrangements, readers, note-takers, and scribes.

ADD/ADHD Students with ADD/ADHD are eligible for the same services available to students with LD, as well as distraction-free testing environments.

Application *Recommended:* psychoeducational report (3 years old or less) and documentation of high school services (e.g., Individualized Education Program [IEP] or 504 plan). Upon application, documentation of need for special services should be sent only to your LD program or unit. Upon acceptance, documentation of need for special services should be sent only to your LD program or unit. *Application deadline (institutional):* rolling/continuous for fall and rolling/continuous for spring. *Application deadline (LD program):* rolling/continuous for fall and rolling/continuous for spring.

LD program contact Maureen Fry, Learning Disabilities Specialist, 4800 Magnolia Avenue, Riverside, CA 92506-1299. *Phone:* 909-222-8641. *Fax:* 909-222-8790. *E-mail:* mfry@rccd.cc.ca.us.

Application contact Riverside Community College, 4800 Magnolia Avenue, Riverside, CA 92506-1293. *Web address:* http://www.rccd.cc.ca.us/.

ROCKLAND COMMUNITY COLLEGE
Suffern, New York

Students with LD Served by Program			
Students with LD Served by Program	300	ADD/ADHD Services	✓
Staff	3 full-time, 1 part-time	Summer Preparation Program	✓
LD Program or Service Fee	n/a	Alternative Test Arrangements	✓
LD Program Began	1987	LD Student Organization	n/a

Office of Disability Services began offering services in 1987. The program serves approximately 300 undergraduate students. Faculty consists of 3 full-time staff members and 1 part-time staff member. Services are provided by academic advisers, counselors, regular education teachers, and LD specialists.

Policies Students with LD may take up to 18 credit hours per semester; 12 credit hours per semester are required to maintain full-time status; 6 credit hours per semester are required to be eligible for financial aid.

Special preparation or orientation Optional summer program offered prior to entering college. Optional orientation held individually by special arrangement.

Counseling and advisement Career counseling and individual counseling are available. Academic advisement by a staff member affiliated with the program is available.

Auxiliary aids and services *Aids:* calculators, personal computers, personal spelling/word-use assistants (e.g., Franklin Speller), scan and read programs (e.g., Kurzweil), screen-enlarging programs, screen readers, speech recognition pro-

grams (e.g., Dragon), tape recorders, taped textbooks. *Services and accommodations:* advocates, priority registration, alternative test arrangements, readers, note-takers, and scribes.

ADD/ADHD Students with ADD/ADHD are eligible for the same services available to students with LD, as well as distraction-free study areas and distraction-free testing environments.

Application *Required:* high school transcript. Upon application, documentation of need for special services should be sent only to your LD program or unit. Upon acceptance, documentation of need for special services should be sent only to your LD program or unit. *Application deadline (institutional):* 9/1 for fall and 1/24 for spring. *Application deadline (LD program):* 9/1 for fall and 1/24 for spring.

LD program contact Marge Zemek, Learning Disabilities Specialist, 145 College Road, Suffern, NY 10901. *Phone:* 914-574-4316. *Fax:* 914-574-4462. *E-mail:* mzemek@sunyrockland.edu.

Application contact Rockland Community College, 145 College Road, Suffern, NY 10901-3699. *E-mail:* info@sunyrockland.edu. *Web address:* http://www.sunyrockland.edu/.

SAN BERNARDINO VALLEY COLLEGE
San Bernardino, California

Students with LD Served by Program			
Students with LD Served by Program	80	ADD/ADHD Services	✓
Staff	2 full-time, 3 part-time	Summer Preparation Program	n/a
LD Program or Service Fee	n/a	Alternative Test Arrangements	✓
LD Program Began	n/a	LD Student Organization	n/a

Disabled Student Programs and Services serves approximately 80 undergraduate students. Faculty consists of 2 full-time and 3 part-time staff members. Services are provided by counselors, LD specialists, and trained peer tutors.

Policies Students with LD may take up to 18 credits per semester; 6 credits per semester are required to be eligible for financial aid.

Special preparation or orientation Optional orientation held after classes begin.

Diagnostic testing Available for spelling, intelligence, reading, written language, and math.

Basic skills remediation Available in computer skills, reading, spelling, and math. Offered in small groups by teaching paraprofessional.

Subject-area tutoring Available in some subjects. Offered one-on-one, in small groups, and class-size groups by computer-based instruction and trained peer tutors.

Special courses Available in reading and math. All courses are offered for credit; none enter into overall grade point average.

Counseling and advisement Individual counseling is available.

Auxiliary aids and services *Aids:* personal computers, personal spelling/word-use assistants (e.g., Franklin Speller), scan and read programs (e.g., Kurzweil), screen-enlarging programs, speech recognition programs (e.g., Dragon), tape recorders, taped textbooks. *Services and accommodations:* priority registration, alternative test arrangements, readers, note-takers, scribes, and academic counseling.

ADD/ADHD Students with ADD/ADHD are eligible for the same services available to students with LD

Application *Recommended:* high school transcript. Upon application, documentation of need for special services should be sent only to your LD program or unit. Upon acceptance, documentation of need for special services should be sent only to your LD program or unit. *Application deadline (institutional):*

rolling/continuous for fall and rolling/continuous for spring. *Application deadline (LD program):* rolling/continuous for fall and rolling/continuous for spring.

LD program contact Marty Milligan, Learning Disabilities Specialist, 701 South Mount Vernon Avenue, San Bernardino, CA 92410. *Phone:* 909-888-6511 Ext. 1181. *Fax:* 909-884-9072. *E-mail:* marty_milligan@sbccd.cc.ca.us.

Application contact Daniel T. Angelo, Director of Admissions and Records, San Bernardino Valley College, 701 South Mt Vernon Avenue, San Bernardino, CA 92410-2748. *Phone:* 909-888-6511 Ext. 1656.

SAN DIEGO CITY COLLEGE
San Diego, California

Students with LD Served by Program	230	ADD/ADHD Services	✓
Staff	6 full-time, 3 part-time	Summer Preparation Program	n/a
LD Program or Service Fee	n/a	Alternative Test Arrangements	✓
LD Program Began	1973	LD Student Organization	n/a

Disabled Student Programs and Services (DSPS) began offering services in 1973. The program serves approximately 230 undergraduate students. Faculty consists of 6 full-time and 3 part-time staff members. Services are provided by remediation/learning specialists, counselors, LD specialists, and trained peer tutors.

Policies Students with LD may take up to 20 credit units per semester; 12 credit units per semester are required to maintain full-time status and to be eligible for financial aid.

Special preparation or orientation Required orientation held before registration, during registration, before classes begin, after classes begin, during summer prior to enrollment, and individually by special arrangement.

Diagnostic testing Available for auditory processing, spelling, intelligence, reading, written language, visual processing, and math.

Subject-area tutoring Available in most subjects. Offered one-on-one and in small groups by computer-based instruction and trained peer tutors.

Special courses Available in career planning, college survival skills, practical computer skills, learning strategies, math, and written composition skills. All courses are offered for credit; most enter into overall grade point average.

Counseling and advisement Career counseling and individual counseling are available.

Auxiliary aids and services *Aids:* calculators, personal spelling/word-use assistants (e.g., Franklin Speller), scan and read programs (e.g., Kurzweil), screen-enlarging programs, screen readers, speech recognition programs (e.g., Dragon), tape recorders, taped textbooks. *Services and accommodations:* priority registration, alternative test arrangements, readers, note-takers, and scribes.

ADD/ADHD Students with ADD/ADHD are eligible for the same services available to students with LD, as well as distraction-free testing environments.

Application Upon acceptance, documentation of need for special services should be sent only to your LD program or unit. *Application deadline (institutional):* 9/13 for fall and 2/17 for spring. *Application deadline (LD program):* rolling/continuous for fall and rolling/continuous for spring.

LD program contact Barbara J. Mason, Learning Disabilities Specialist, 1313 Twelfth Street, San Diego, CA 92101. *Phone:* 619-230-2195. *Fax:* 619-230-2801. *E-mail:* bmason@sdccd.net.

Application contact San Diego City College, 1313 Twelfth Avenue, San Diego, CA 92101-4787.

SAN DIEGO MIRAMAR COLLEGE
San Diego, California

Students with LD Served by Program	140	ADD/ADHD Services	✓
Staff	2 full-time, 1 part-time	Summer Preparation Program	n/a
LD Program or Service Fee	n/a	Alternative Test Arrangements	✓
LD Program Began	1993	LD Student Organization	n/a

Disabled Students Programs and Services (DSPS) began offering services in 1993. The program serves approximately 140 undergraduate students. Faculty consists of 2 full-time staff members and 1 part-time staff member. Services are provided by academic advisers, counselors, diagnostic specialists, special education teachers, LD specialists, trained peer tutors, and assistive technology instructor.

Policies Students with LD may take up to 20 units per semester; 12 units per semester are required to maintain full-time status and to be eligible for financial aid.

Special preparation or orientation Optional orientation held individually by special arrangement.

Diagnostic testing Available for auditory processing, spelling, intelligence, reading, written language, learning styles, visual processing, and math.

Subject-area tutoring Available in most subjects. Offered one-on-one by computer-based instruction and trained peer tutors.

Special courses Available in practical computer skills and learning strategies. All courses are offered for credit; none enter into overall grade point average.

Counseling and advisement Career counseling, individual counseling, and academic advising are available. Academic advisement by a staff member affiliated with the program is available.

Auxiliary aids and services *Aids:* calculators, personal computers, personal spelling/word-use assistants (e.g., Franklin Speller), scan and read programs (e.g., Kurzweil), screen-enlarging programs, screen readers, speech recognition programs (e.g., Dragon), tape recorders, taped textbooks, computerized whiteboards. *Services and accommodations:* advocates, priority registration, alternative test arrangements, readers, note-takers, and scribes.

ADD/ADHD Students with ADD/ADHD are eligible for the same services available to students with LD, as well as distraction-free testing environments.

Application *Recommended:* high school transcript. Upon application, documentation of need for special services should be sent only to your LD program or unit. Upon acceptance, documentation of need for special services should be sent only to your LD program or unit. *Application deadline (institutional):* rolling/continuous for fall and rolling/continuous for spring. *Application deadline (LD program):* rolling/continuous for fall and rolling/continuous for spring.

LD program contact Sandra J. Smith, Educational Psychologist, 10440 Black Mountain Road, San Diego, CA 92126. *Phone:* 858-536-7212. *Fax:* 858-536-4302. *E-mail:* ssmith@sdccd.net.

Application contact Dana Andras, Admissions Supervisor, San Diego Miramar College, 10440 Black Mountain Road, San Diego, CA 92126-2999. *Phone:* 619-536-7854. *E-mail:* dmaxwell@sdccd.cc.ca.us. *Web address:* http://www.miramar.sdccd.cc.ca.us/.

SANTA ANA COLLEGE
Santa Ana, California

Students with LD Served by Program	290	ADD/ADHD Services	✓
Staff	5 full-time, 20 part-time	Summer Preparation Program	n/a
LD Program or Service Fee	n/a	Alternative Test Arrangements	✓
LD Program Began	1976	LD Student Organization	n/a

Learning Disabilities Program began offering services in 1976. The program serves approximately 290 undergraduate students. Faculty consists of 5 full-time and 20 part-time staff members. Services are provided by graduate assistants/students, LD specialists, and professional tutors.

Policies The college has written policies regarding course substitutions and substitution and waivers of requirements for admission. Students with LD may take up to 18 credit hours per semester; 12 credit hours per semester are required to be eligible for financial aid.

Special preparation or orientation Optional orientation held during registration and individually by special arrangement.

Diagnostic testing Available for auditory processing, spelling, handwriting, neuropsychological, spoken language, intelligence, learning strategies, reading, written language, learning styles, social skills, visual processing, and math.

Basic skills remediation Available in auditory processing, study skills, computer skills, reading, time management, handwriting, visual processing, learning strategies, spelling, written language, and math. Offered one-on-one and in small groups by computer-based instruction, LD specialists, and professional tutors.

Subject-area tutoring Available in some subjects. Offered one-on-one and in small groups by computer-based instruction, professional tutors, and LD specialists.

Counseling and advisement Career counseling, individual counseling, small-group counseling, and support groups are available.

Auxiliary aids and services *Aids:* calculators, personal spelling/word-use assistants (e.g., Franklin Speller), scan and read programs (e.g., Kurzweil), screen-enlarging programs, screen readers, speech recognition programs (e.g., Dragon), tape recorders, taped textbooks. *Services and accommodations:* priority registration, alternative test arrangements, readers, note-takers, and scribes.

ADD/ADHD Students with ADD/ADHD are eligible for the same services available to students with LD, as well as distraction-free study areas and distraction-free testing environments.

Application *Required:* interview, separate application to your LD program or unit, and psychoeducational report (3 years old or less). *Recommended:* high school transcript, participation in extracurricular activities, ACT or SAT I, and documentation of high school services (e.g., Individualized Education Program [IEP] or 504 plan). Upon application, documentation of need for special services should be sent only to your LD program or unit. Upon acceptance, documentation of need for special services should be sent only to your LD program or unit.

LD program contact Dr. Cheryl Dunn, Coordinator of Special Services, 1530 West 17th Street, Santa Ana, CA 92706. *Phone:* 714-564-6277. *Fax:* 714-285-9619. *E-mail:* dunn_cheryl@rsccd.org.

Application contact Chris Steward, Admissions Clerk, Santa Ana College, 1530 West 17th Street, Santa Ana, CA 92706-3398. *Phone:* 714-564-6053. *Web address:* http://www.rsccd.org/.

SANTA BARBARA CITY COLLEGE
Santa Barbara, California

Students with LD Served by Program	600	ADD/ADHD Services	✓
Staff	6 full-time, 8 part-time	Summer Preparation Program	n/a
LD Program or Service Fee	n/a	Alternative Test Arrangements	✓
LD Program Began	1977	LD Student Organization	n/a

Programs and Services for Students with Disabilities (DSPS) began offering services in 1977. The program serves approximately 600 undergraduate students. Faculty consists of 6 full-time and 8 part-time staff members. Services are provided by counselors, diagnostic specialists, LD specialists, and professional tutors.

Policies The college has written policies regarding course substitutions. Students with LD may take up to 18 credits per semester; 12 credits per semester are required to maintain full-time status and to be eligible for financial aid.

Special preparation or orientation Optional orientation held before registration and individually by special arrangement.

Diagnostic testing Available for auditory processing, spelling, reading, visual processing, math, and academic aptitude (Woodcock-Johnson PEBI).

Special courses Available in practical computer skills, reading, learning strategies, and self-advocacy. All courses are offered for credit; none enter into overall grade point average.

Counseling and advisement Career counseling, individual counseling, small-group counseling, and support groups are available.

Auxiliary aids and services *Aids:* scan and read programs (e.g., Kurzweil), screen-enlarging programs, screen readers, speech recognition programs (e.g., Dragon), taped textbooks. *Services and accommodations:* priority registration, alternative test arrangements, and shared notes, strategies tutoring, drop-in lab.

ADD/ADHD Students with ADD/ADHD are eligible for the same services available to students with LD

Application *Required:* separate application to your LD program or unit, psychoeducational report (3 years old or less), and proof of California residency if claiming such. *Recommended:* high school transcript and documentation of high school services (e.g., Individualized Education Program [IEP] or 504 plan). Upon application, documentation of need for special services should be sent only to your LD program or unit. *Application deadline (institutional):* 8/14 for fall and 1/14 for spring. *Application deadline (LD program):* rolling/continuous for fall and rolling/continuous for spring.

LD program contact Mary Lawson, Learning Disabilities Specialist, 721 Cliff Drive, Santa Barbara, CA 93109. *Phone:* 805-965-0581 Ext. 2374. *Fax:* 805-884-4966. *E-mail:* lawson@sbcc.net.

Application contact Santa Barbara City College, 721 Cliff Drive, Santa Barbara, CA 93109-2394. *E-mail:* info@gate1.sbcc.cc.ca.us. *Web address:* http://www.sbcc.net/.

SCHOOLCRAFT COLLEGE
Livonia, Michigan

Students with LD Served by Program	325	ADD/ADHD Services	✓
Staff	3 full-time, 6 part-time	Summer Preparation Program	n/a
LD Program or Service Fee	n/a	Alternative Test Arrangements	✓
LD Program Began	1985	LD Student Organization	n/a

Peterson's Colleges for Students with Learning Disabilities or Attention Deficit Disorders

Learning Assistance Center began offering services in 1985. The program serves approximately 325 undergraduate students. Faculty consists of 3 full-time and 6 part-time staff members. Services are provided by counselors, remediation/learning specialists, LD specialists, trained peer tutors, professional tutors, and faculty facilitators.

Special preparation or orientation Optional orientation held before classes begin.

Basic skills remediation Available in study skills, reading, time management, learning strategies, written language, and math. Offered one-on-one by computer-based instruction, LD specialists, professional tutors, and trained peer tutors.

Subject-area tutoring Available in most subjects. Offered one-on-one by computer-based instruction, professional tutors, trained peer tutors, and LD specialists.

Special courses Available in study skills, college survival skills, test taking, reading, time management, learning strategies, vocabulary development, and stress management. All courses are offered for credit; all enter into overall grade point average.

Counseling and advisement Career counseling and individual counseling are available.

Auxiliary aids and services *Aids:* personal spelling/word-use assistants (e.g., Franklin Speller), scan and read programs (e.g., Kurzweil), screen-enlarging programs, screen readers, speech recognition programs (e.g., Dragon), tape recorders, taped textbooks. *Services and accommodations:* advocates, alternative test arrangements, readers, note-takers, and scribes.

ADD/ADHD Students with ADD/ADHD are eligible for the same services available to students with LD, as well as distraction-free study areas, distraction-free testing environments and personal coach or mentors.

Application *Required:* interview and psychoeducational report (3 years old or less). *Recommended:* high school transcript and placement test. Upon application, documentation of need for special services should be sent only to your LD program or unit. Upon acceptance, documentation of need for special services should be sent only to your LD program or unit. *Application deadline (institutional):* rolling/continuous for fall and rolling/continuous for spring. *Application deadline (LD program):* rolling/continuous for fall and rolling/continuous for spring.

LD program contact Patricia Hurick, Learning Disabilities Counselor, 18600 Haggerty Road, Livonia, MI 48152. *Phone:* 734-462-4436. *Fax:* 734-462-4542. *E-mail:* phurick@schoolcraft.cc.mi.us.

Application contact Schoolcraft College, 18600 Haggerty Road, Livonia, MI 48152-2696. *Web address:* http://www.schoolcraft.cc.mi.us/.

SHELBY STATE COMMUNITY COLLEGE

Memphis, Tennessee

Students with LD Served by Program	50	ADD/ADHD Services	n/a
Staff	2 full-time, 1 part-time	Summer Preparation Program	n/a
LD Program or Service Fee	n/a	Alternative Test Arrangements	✓
LD Program Began	1991	LD Student Organization	n/a

Office of Disabled Student Services (ODSS) began offering services in 1991. The program serves approximately 50 undergraduate students. Faculty consists of 2 full-time staff members and 1 part-time staff member. Services are provided by academic advisers, regular education teachers, counselors, remediation/learning specialists, special education teachers, LD specialists, and professional tutors.

Policies Students with LD may take up to 15 credits per semester; 12 credits per semester are required to maintain full-time status and to be eligible for financial aid.

Special preparation or orientation Required orientation held before registration.

Basic skills remediation Available in study skills, reading, time management, written language, and math. Offered in class-size groups by regular education teachers.

Subject-area tutoring Available in most subjects. Offered one-on-one by trained peer tutors and LD specialists.

Counseling and advisement Career counseling and individual counseling are available. Academic advisement by a staff member affiliated with the program is available.

Auxiliary aids and services *Aids:* personal spelling/word-use assistants (e.g., Franklin Speller), scan and read programs (e.g., Kurzweil), screen-enlarging programs, screen readers. *Services and accommodations:* advocates, alternative test arrangements, note-takers, and scribes.

Application *Required:* high school transcript, interview, separate application to your LD program or unit, and psychoeducational report. *Recommended:* participation in extracurricular activities, ACT or SAT I, and documentation of high school services (e.g., Individualized Education Program [IEP] or 504 plan).

LD program contact Jimmy Wiley, Director of Counseling and Advising, 737 Union Avenue, Memphis, TN 38174-5087. *Phone:* 901-333-5087. *Fax:* 901-333-5711. *E-mail:* jwiley@sscc.cc.tn.us.

Application contact Shelby State Community College, PO Box 40568, Memphis, TN 38174-0568. *E-mail:* chinn-jones@sscc.cc.tn.us. *Web address:* http://www.sscc.cc.tn.us/.

SULLIVAN COUNTY COMMUNITY COLLEGE

Loch Sheldrake, New York

LD& ADD

Students with LD Served by Program	100	ADD/ADHD Services	✓
Staff	3 full-time, 10 part-time	Summer Preparation Program	n/a
LD Program or Service Fee	n/a	Alternative Test Arrangements	✓
LD Program Began	n/a	LD Student Organization	n/a

Center for Learning Assistance serves approximately 100 undergraduate students. Faculty consists of 3 full-time and 10 part-time staff members. Services are provided by academic advisers, counselors, LD specialists, trained peer tutors, and professional tutors.

Policies Students with LD may take up to 18 credit hours per semester; 12 credit hours per semester are required to maintain full-time status and to be eligible for financial aid.

Special preparation or orientation Optional orientation held individually by special arrangement.

Basic skills remediation Available in study skills, computer skills, reading, time management, learning strategies, spelling, written language, math, and spoken language. Offered one-on-one, in small groups, and class-size groups by computer-based instruction, regular education teachers, LD specialists, professional tutors, and trained peer tutors.

Subject-area tutoring Available in most subjects. Offered one-on-one and in small groups by computer-based instruction, professional tutors, trained peer tutors, and LD specialists.

Counseling and advisement Career counseling and individual counseling are available. Academic advisement by a staff member affiliated with the program is available.

Auxiliary aids and services *Aids:* calculators, personal computers, personal spelling/word-use assistants (e.g., Franklin Speller), scan and read programs (e.g., Kurzweil), screen-

Sullivan County Community College (continued)

enlarging programs, speech recognition programs (e.g., Dragon), tape recorders, taped textbooks. *Services and accommodations:* advocates, alternative test arrangements, readers, note-takers, and scribes.

ADD/ADHD Students with ADD/ADHD are eligible for the same services available to students with LD, as well as distraction-free study areas and distraction-free testing environments.

Application *Recommended:* psychoeducational report (3 years old or less) and documentation of high school services (e.g., Individualized Education Program [IEP] or 504 plan). Upon acceptance, documentation of need for special services should be sent only to your LD program or unit. *Application deadline (institutional):* rolling/continuous for fall and rolling/continuous for spring. *Application deadline (LD program):* rolling/continuous for fall and rolling/continuous for spring.

LD program contact Margaret DiCarlo, Coordinator, 112 College Road, Loch Sheldrake, NY 12759. *Phone:* 914-434-5750 Ext. 4229. *Fax:* 914-434-4806. *E-mail:* mdicarlo@sullivan.suny.edu.

Application contact Sullivan County Community College, 1000 Leroy Road, Loch Sheldrake, NY 12759. *E-mail:* lbarrett@sullivan.suny.edu. *Web address:* http://www.sullivan.suny.edu/.

TAFT COLLEGE
Taft, California

Students with LD Served by Program	80	ADD/ADHD Services	✓
Staff	3 full-time, 2 part-time	Summer Preparation Program	n/a
LD Program or Service Fee	n/a	Alternative Test Arrangements	✓
LD Program Began	1980	LD Student Organization	n/a

Student Support Services began offering services in 1980. The program serves approximately 80 undergraduate students. Faculty consists of 3 full-time and 2 part-time staff members. Services are provided by academic advisers and LD specialists.

Policies 12 units per semester are required to maintain full-time status; 6 units per semester are required to be eligible for financial aid.

Diagnostic testing Available for auditory processing, neuropsychological, spoken language, intelligence, reading, written language, learning styles, visual processing, and math.

Basic skills remediation Available in study skills, computer skills, reading, time management, and math. Offered one-on-one and in small groups by LD specialists and teacher trainees.

Subject-area tutoring Available in most subjects. Offered one-on-one by computer-based instruction and trained peer tutors.

Special courses Available in reading, learning strategies, and math. Most courses are offered for credit; most enter into overall grade point average.

Counseling and advisement Academic advisement by a staff member affiliated with the program is available.

Auxiliary aids and services *Aids:* calculators, personal computers, personal spelling/word-use assistants (e.g., Franklin Speller), scan and read programs (e.g., Kurzweil), screen-enlarging programs, speech recognition programs (e.g., Dragon), taped textbooks. *Services and accommodations:* priority registration, alternative test arrangements, and note-takers.

ADD/ADHD Students with ADD/ADHD are eligible for the same services available to students with LD

Application *Required:* high school transcript, psychoeducational report (3 years old or less), and documentation of high school services (e.g., Individualized Education Program [IEP] or 504 plan). Upon application, documentation of need for special services should be sent to both admissions and your LD program or unit. Upon acceptance, documentation of need for

special services should be sent to both admissions and your LD program or unit. *Application deadline (institutional):* rolling/continuous for fall and rolling/continuous for spring. *Application deadline (LD program):* rolling/continuous for fall and rolling/continuous for spring.

LD program contact Jeff Ross, Coordinator, Student Support Services, 29 Emmons Park Drive, Taft, CA 93268. *Phone:* 661-763-7776. *Fax:* 661-763-7705. *E-mail:* jross@taft.org.

Application contact Gayle Roberts, Director of Financial Aid and Admissions, Taft College, 29 Emmons Park Drive, Taft, CA 93268-2317. *Phone:* 661-763-7763. *Web address:* http://www.taft.cc.ca.us/.

TIDEWATER COMMUNITY COLLEGE
Norfolk, Virginia

Students with LD Served by Program	280	ADD/ADHD Services	✓
Staff	1 full-time, 4 part-time	Summer Preparation Program	n/a
LD Program or Service Fee	n/a	Alternative Test Arrangements	✓
LD Program Began	1993	LD Student Organization	n/a

Learning Disabilities Services began offering services in 1993. The program serves approximately 280 undergraduate students. Faculty consists of 1 full-time and 4 part-time staff members. Services are provided by academic advisers, counselors, remediation/learning specialists, diagnostic specialists, LD specialists, trained peer tutors, and professional tutors.

Policies The college has written policies regarding grade forgiveness.

Diagnostic testing Available for auditory processing, motor skills, spelling, handwriting, neuropsychological, spoken language, intelligence, study skills, learning strategies, reading, written language, learning styles, visual processing, and math.

Basic skills remediation Available in study skills, reading, time management, learning strategies, written language, and math. Offered in class-size groups by regular education teachers and LD specialists.

Subject-area tutoring Available in most subjects. Offered one-on-one and in small groups by trained peer tutors, LD specialists, and Instructors.

Special courses Available in career planning, oral communication skills, study skills, college survival skills, practical computer skills, test taking, health and nutrition, reading, time management, learning strategies, self-advocacy, vocabulary development, math, stress management, and written composition skills. Most courses are offered for credit; all enter into overall grade point average.

Counseling and advisement Career counseling, individual counseling, and small-group counseling are available. Academic advisement by a staff member affiliated with the program is available.

Auxiliary aids and services *Aids:* personal spelling/word-use assistants (e.g., Franklin Speller), scan and read programs (e.g., Kurzweil), screen-enlarging programs, screen readers, speech recognition programs (e.g., Dragon), tape recorders, taped textbooks. *Services and accommodations:* advocates, priority registration, alternative test arrangements, readers, note-takers, and scribes.

ADD/ADHD Students with ADD/ADHD are eligible for the same services available to students with LD, as well as distraction-free testing environments, medication management and personal coach or mentors.

Application *Required:* psychoeducational report (3 years old or less). Upon application, documentation of need for special services should be sent only to your LD program or unit. Upon acceptance, documentation of need for special services should be sent only to your LD program or unit.

LD program contact Sue R. Rice, Coordinator, Learning Disabilities Services, 300 Granby Street, Norfolk, VA 23510. *Phone:* 757-822-1213. *Fax:* 767-822-1214. *E-mail:* tcrices@tc.cc.va.us.

Application contact Tidewater Community College, 7000 College Drive, Portsmouth, VA 23703. *Web address:* http://www.tc.cc.va.us/.

TRUCKEE MEADOWS COMMUNITY COLLEGE
Reno, Nevada

Students with LD Served by Program	130	ADD/ADHD Services	✓
Staff	3 full-time, 2 part-time	Summer Preparation Program	n/a
LD Program or Service Fee	n/a	Alternative Test Arrangements	✓
LD Program Began	1986	LD Student Organization	n/a

Disabled Student Services began offering services in 1986. The program serves approximately 130 undergraduate students. Faculty consists of 3 full-time and 2 part-time staff members. Services are provided by LD specialists and professional tutors.
Policies Students with LD may take up to 18 credit hour per semester; 12 credit hour per semester are required to maintain full-time status and to be eligible for financial aid.
Basic skills remediation Available in reading, spelling, and math. Offered in class-size groups by regular education teachers.
Subject-area tutoring Available in most subjects. Offered one-on-one by professional tutors.
Special courses Available in college survival skills. All courses are offered for credit; all enter into overall grade point average.
Counseling and advisement Individual counseling is available.
Auxiliary aids and services *Aids:* scan and read programs (e.g., Kurzweil), screen-enlarging programs, taped textbooks. *Services and accommodations:* priority registration, alternative test arrangements, readers, note-takers, and scribes.
ADD/ADHD Students with ADD/ADHD are eligible for the same services available to students with LD, as well as distraction-free testing environments.
Application *Required:* high school transcript and psychoeducational report (3 years old or less). *Recommended:* ACT or SAT I (extended-time tests accepted), interview, and documentation of high school services (e.g., Individualized Education Program [IEP] or 504 plan). Upon application, documentation of need for special services should be sent only to your LD program or unit. Upon acceptance, documentation of need for special services should be sent only to your LD program or unit. *Application deadline (institutional):* rolling/continuous for fall and rolling/continuous for spring. *Application deadline (LD program):* rolling/continuous for fall and rolling/continuous for spring.
LD program contact Harry Heiser, Learning Disabilities Specialist, 7000 Dandini Boulevard, Reno, NV 89512. *Phone:* 775-673-7286.
Application contact Truckee Meadows Community College, Mail Station #15, Reno, NV 89512-3901. *Web address:* http://www.tmcc.edu/.

VENTURA COLLEGE
Ventura, California

Students with LD Served by Program	600	ADD/ADHD Services	✓
Staff	2 full-time, 6 part-time	Summer Preparation Program	n/a
LD Program or Service Fee	n/a	Alternative Test Arrangements	✓
LD Program Began	n/a	LD Student Organization	✓

Educational Assistance Center, Learning Skills Program serves approximately 600 undergraduate students. Faculty consists of 2 full-time and 6 part-time staff members. Services are provided by academic advisers, regular education teachers, counselors, remediation/learning specialists, diagnostic specialists, special education teachers, LD specialists, and trained peer tutors.
Policies The college has written policies regarding course substitutions. 12 units per semester are required to maintain full-time status and to be eligible for financial aid.
Diagnostic testing Available for auditory processing, spelling, intelligence, reading, written language, learning styles, visual processing, and math.
Basic skills remediation Available in auditory processing, study skills, computer skills, reading, time management, social skills, visual processing, learning strategies, spelling, written language, and math. Offered in class-size groups by LD specialists.
Subject-area tutoring Available in all subjects. Offered one-on-one, in small groups, and class-size groups by trained peer tutors and LD specialists.
Special courses Available in career planning, study skills, practical computer skills, test taking, reading, time management, learning strategies, vocabulary development, math, stress management, and written composition skills. All courses are offered for credit; all enter into overall grade point average.
Counseling and advisement Career counseling, individual counseling, and support groups are available. Academic advisement by a staff member affiliated with the program is available.
Auxiliary aids and services *Aids:* calculators, personal computers, personal spelling/word-use assistants (e.g., Franklin Speller), scan and read programs (e.g., Kurzweil), screen-enlarging programs, screen readers, speech recognition programs (e.g., Dragon), tape recorders, taped textbooks. *Services and accommodations:* priority registration, alternative test arrangements, readers, note-takers, and scribes.
Student organization There is a student organization for students with LD.
ADD/ADHD Students with ADD/ADHD are eligible for the same services available to students with LD, as well as distraction-free testing environments.
Application *Required:* separate application to your LD program or unit, psychoeducational report, and documentation of high school services (e.g., Individualized Education Program [IEP] or 504 plan). *Recommended:* high school transcript. Upon application, documentation of need for special services should be sent only to your LD program or unit. Upon acceptance, documentation of need for special services should be sent only to your LD program or unit. *Application deadline (institutional):* 8/15 for fall and 1/11 for spring. *Application deadline (LD program):* rolling/continuous for fall and rolling/continuous for spring.
LD program contact Nancy Latham, Coordinator, 4667 Telegraph Road, Ventura, CA 93003. *Phone:* 805-654-6300. *Fax:* 805-648-8915. *E-mail:* nlatham@vcccd.net.
Application contact Ventura College, 4667 Telegraph Road, Ventura, CA 93003-3899. *E-mail:* jhalk@server.vcccd.cc.ca.us. *Web address:* http://www.ventura.cc.ca.us/.

VINCENNES UNIVERSITY
Vincennes, Indiana

Students with LD Served by Program	80	ADD/ADHD Services	✓
Staff	4 full-time	Summer Preparation Program	n/a
LD Program or Service Fee	✓	Alternative Test Arrangements	✓
LD Program Began	1994	LD Student Organization	✓

Student Transition into Educational Programs (STEP) began offering services in 1994. The program serves approximately 80 undergraduate students. Faculty consists of 4 full-time staff members. Services are provided by academic advisers, regular education teachers, LD specialists, and professional tutors.

Policies The college has written policies regarding course substitutions and grade forgiveness. 12 credit hours per term are required to maintain full-time status and to be eligible for financial aid.

Fees *LD Program or Service Fee:* $700 per year.

Basic skills remediation Available in study skills, reading, social skills, learning strategies, spelling, written language, and math. Offered one-on-one and in class-size groups by computer-based instruction, regular education teachers, special education teachers, LD specialists, and professional tutors.

Subject-area tutoring Available in all subjects. Offered one-on-one and in class-size groups by computer-based instruction, professional tutors, and LD specialists.

Special courses Available in study skills, reading, math, and written composition skills. All courses are offered for credit; all enter into overall grade point average.

Counseling and advisement Individual counseling and support groups are available. Academic advisement by a staff member affiliated with the program is available.

Auxiliary aids and services *Aids:* scan and read programs (e.g., Kurzweil), screen-enlarging programs, screen readers. *Services and accommodations:* advocates, alternative test arrangements, and readers.

Student organization There is a student organization for students with LD.

ADD/ADHD Students with ADD/ADHD are eligible for the same services available to students with LD, as well as distraction-free testing environments and personal coach or mentors.

Application *Required:* high school transcript, interview, separate application to your LD program or unit, and psychoeducational report (3 years old or less). Upon application, documentation of need for special services should be sent to both admissions and your LD program or unit. Upon acceptance, documentation of need for special services should be sent only to your LD program or unit. *Application deadline (institutional):* rolling/continuous for fall and rolling/continuous for spring. *Application deadline (LD program):* 3/1 for fall and 12/1 for spring.

LD program contact Susan Laue, Director, 1002 North First Street, Vincennes, IN 47591. *Phone:* 800-742-9198. *Fax:* 812-888-5531. *E-mail:* slaue@indian.vinu.edu.

Application contact Vincennes University, 1002 North First Street, Vincennes, IN 47591-5202. *E-mail:* simonds@vunet.vinu.edu. *Web address:* http://www.vinu.edu/.

WALDORF COLLEGE
Forest City, Iowa

Students with LD Served by Program	20	ADD/ADHD Services	✓
Staff	1 full-time, 25 part-time	Summer Preparation Program	n/a
LD Program or Service Fee	✓	Alternative Test Arrangements	✓
LD Program Began	1986	LD Student Organization	n/a

Academic Achievement Center, Learning Disabilities Program began offering services in 1986. The program serves approximately 20 undergraduate students. Faculty consists of 1 full-time and 25 part-time staff members. Services are provided by academic advisers, regular education teachers, special education teachers, LD specialists, and trained peer tutors.

Policies Students with LD may take up to 18 credit hours per semester; 12 credits per semester are required to maintain full-time status and to be eligible for financial aid.

Fees *LD Program or Service Fee:* $800 per year.

Special preparation or orientation Optional orientation held before classes begin.

Diagnostic testing Available for personality, study skills, learning strategies, reading, written language, learning styles, and math.

Basic skills remediation Available in study skills, computer skills, reading, time management, learning strategies, written language, and math. Offered one-on-one, in small groups, and class-size groups by computer-based instruction, regular education teachers, special education teachers, LD specialists, professional tutors, and trained peer tutors.

Subject-area tutoring Available in most subjects. Offered one-on-one and in small groups by computer-based instruction, professional tutors, trained peer tutors, and LD specialists.

Special courses Available in college survival skills, learning strategies, math, and written composition skills. Some courses are offered for credit; some enter into overall grade point average.

Counseling and advisement Career counseling and individual counseling are available. Academic advisement by a staff member affiliated with the program is available.

Auxiliary aids and services *Aids:* calculators, personal computers, speech recognition programs (e.g., Dragon), tape recorders, taped textbooks. *Services and accommodations:* advocates, alternative test arrangements, and note-takers.

ADD/ADHD Students with ADD/ADHD are eligible for the same services available to students with LD, as well as distraction-free testing environments.

Application *Required:* high school transcript, ACT (extended-time or untimed test accepted), letter(s) of recommendation, and documentation of high school services (e.g., Individualized Education Program [IEP] or 504 plan). *Recommended:* participation in extracurricular activities, ACT or SAT I (extended-time or untimed test accepted), interview, personal statement, separate application to your LD program or unit, and psychoeducational report (3 years old or less). Upon acceptance, documentation of need for special services should be sent to both admissions and your LD program or unit. *Application deadline (institutional):* rolling/continuous for fall and rolling/continuous for spring. *Application deadline (LD program):* rolling/continuous for fall and rolling/continuous for spring.

LD program contact Rebecca S. Hill, Learning Disabilities Program Director, 106 South 6th Street, Forest City, IA 50436. *Phone:* 515-582-8207. *Fax:* 515-582-8194. *E-mail:* hillb@waldorf.edu.

Application contact Steve Hall, Assistant Dean of Admission, Waldorf College, 106 South 6th Street, Forest City, IA 50436-1713. *Phone:* 515-582-8119. *E-mail:* admissions@waldorf.edu. *Web address:* http://www.waldorf.edu/.

WASHTENAW COMMUNITY COLLEGE
Ann Arbor, Michigan

Students with LD Served by Program	47	ADD/ADHD Services	✓
Staff	3 full-time, 3 part-time	Summer Preparation Program	n/a
LD Program or Service Fee	n/a	Alternative Test Arrangements	✓
LD Program Began	1987	LD Student Organization	n/a

Learning Support Services began offering services in 1987. The program serves approximately 47 undergraduate students. Faculty consists of 3 full-time and 3 part-time staff members. Services are provided by academic advisers, counselors, diagnostic specialists, special education teachers, LD specialists, trained peer tutors, professional tutors, and ESL Specialists.

Policies Students with LD may take up to 14 credit hours per semester; 9 credit hours per semester are required to maintain full-time status; 6 credit hours per semester are required to be eligible for financial aid.

Diagnostic testing Available for spelling, intelligence, reading, written language, and math.

Basic skills remediation Available in study skills, reading, time management, learning strategies, spelling, written language, and math. Offered one-on-one by LD specialists.

Subject-area tutoring Available in most subjects. Offered one-on-one by professional tutors, trained peer tutors, and LD specialists.

Counseling and advisement Career counseling, individual counseling, and small-group counseling are available. Academic advisement by a staff member affiliated with the program is available.

Auxiliary aids and services *Aids:* calculators, personal computers, scan and read programs (e.g., Kurzweil), screen-enlarging programs, screen readers, speech recognition programs (e.g., Dragon), tape recorders. *Services and accommodations:* advocates, priority registration, alternative test arrangements, readers, note-takers, and scribes.

ADD/ADHD Students with ADD/ADHD are eligible for the same services available to students with LD, as well as distraction-free study areas, distraction-free testing environments and personal coach or mentors.

Application *Required:* separate application to your LD program or unit, psychoeducational report, and documentation of high school services (e.g., Individualized Education Program [IEP] or 504 plan). *Recommended:* interview. Upon application, documentation of need for special services should be sent only to your LD program or unit. Upon acceptance, documentation of need for special services should be sent only to your LD program or unit. *Application deadline (institutional):* rolling/continuous for fall and rolling/continuous for spring. *Application deadline (LD program):* rolling/continuous for fall and rolling/continuous for spring.

LD program contact Cheryl L. Chesney, Coordinator, Learning Support Services, 4800 East Huron River, PO Box D-1 LA Room 104, Ann Arbor, MI 48106-1610. *Phone:* 734-973-3342. *Fax:* 734-677-5414. *E-mail:* cchesney@wccnet.org.

Application contact Admissions Call Center, Admissions Representative, Washtenaw Community College, 4800 E Huron River Dr, PO Box D-1, Ann Arbor, MI 48106. *Phone:* 734-973-3543. *E-mail:* wccinfo@orchard.washtenaw.cc.mi.us. *Web address:* http://www.wccnet.org/.

WAUKESHA COUNTY TECHNICAL COLLEGE
Pewaukee, Wisconsin

Students with LD Served by Program	15	ADD/ADHD Services	n/a
Staff	3 full-time, 1 part-time	Summer Preparation Program	✓
LD Program or Service Fee	n/a	Alternative Test Arrangements	✓
LD Program Began	n/a	LD Student Organization	n/a

Special Services Department serves approximately 15 undergraduate students. Faculty consists of 3 full-time staff members and 1 part-time staff member. Services are provided by academic advisers, counselors, and LD specialists.

Policies Students with LD may take up to 12 credit hours per semester; 9 credit hours per semester are required to maintain full-time status; 6 credit hours per semester are required to be eligible for financial aid.

Special preparation or orientation Optional summer program offered prior to entering college. Optional orientation held during summer prior to enrollment.

Diagnostic testing Available for learning styles and math.

Basic skills remediation Available in reading, spelling, and math. Offered one-on-one by computer-based instruction and regular education teachers.

Subject-area tutoring Available in most subjects. Offered one-on-one and in small groups by LD specialists.

Special courses Available in self-advocacy and workplace success. No courses are offered for credit; none enter into overall grade point average.

Counseling and advisement Career counseling is available. Academic advisement by a staff member affiliated with the program is available.

Auxiliary aids and services *Aids:* screen-enlarging programs, speech recognition programs (e.g., Dragon). *Services and accommodations:* alternative test arrangements, note-takers, and scribes.

Application *Required:* high school transcript, interview, personal statement, letter(s) of recommendation, psychoeducational report, and documentation of high school services (e.g., Individualized Education Program [IEP] or 504 plan). *Recommended:* participation in extracurricular activities. Upon application, documentation of need for special services should be sent only to your LD program or unit. Upon acceptance, documentation of need for special services should be sent only to your LD program or unit.

LD program contact Deb Jilbert, Coordinator of Special Services, 800 Main Street, Pewaukee, WI 53072. *Phone:* 262-691-5210. *Fax:* 262-691-5089. *E-mail:* djilbert@waukesha.tec.wi.us.

Application contact Dr. Stanley P. Goran, Director of Admissions, Waukesha County Technical College, 800 Main Street, Pewaukee, WI 53072-4601. *Phone:* 414-691-5271.

WESTERN DAKOTA TECHNICAL INSTITUTE
Rapid City, South Dakota

Students with LD Served by Program	50	ADD/ADHD Services	✓
Staff	1 full-time, 5 part-time	Summer Preparation Program	✓
LD Program or Service Fee	n/a	Alternative Test Arrangements	✓
LD Program Began	1988	LD Student Organization	n/a

Western Dakota Technical Institute (continued)

Student Assistance Center began offering services in 1988. The program serves approximately 50 undergraduate students. Faculty consists of 1 full-time and 5 part-time staff members. Services are provided by remediation/learning specialists and trained peer tutors.

Policies 12 credits per semester are required to maintain full-time status; 12 credits per semester are required to be eligible for financial aid.

Special preparation or orientation Optional summer program offered prior to entering college. Held before classes begin.

Basic skills remediation Available in reading, time management, learning strategies, written language, and math. Offered one-on-one, in small groups, and class-size groups by LD specialists.

Subject-area tutoring Available in all subjects. Offered one-on-one, in small groups, and class-size groups by computer-based instruction, trained peer tutors, and LD specialists.

Special courses Available in career planning, study skills, college survival skills, practical computer skills, test taking, reading, time management, learning strategies, vocabulary development, math, stress management, and written composition skills. No courses are offered for credit; none enter into overall grade point average.

Counseling and advisement Career counseling, individual counseling, small-group counseling, and support groups are available.

Auxiliary aids and services *Aids:* calculators, scan and read programs (e.g., Kurzweil), tape recorders, taped textbooks. *Services and accommodations:* alternative test arrangements, readers, and note-takers.

ADD/ADHD Students with ADD/ADHD are eligible for the same services available to students with LD, as well as distraction-free study areas and distraction-free testing environments.

Application *Required:* high school transcript, letter(s) of recommendation, psychoeducational report, and documentation of high school services (e.g., Individualized Education Program [IEP] or 504 plan). Upon application, documentation of need for special services should be sent only to your LD program or unit. Upon acceptance, documentation of need for special services should be sent only to your LD program or unit. *Application deadline (institutional):* rolling/continuous for fall and rolling/continuous for spring.

LD program contact Mary Ann Slanina, Special Needs Coordinator, 800 Mickelson Drive, Rapid City, SD 57702. *Phone:* 605-394-4034. *Fax:* 605-394-1789. *E-mail:* mslanina@wdti.tec.sd.us.

Application contact Tom Allen, Admissions Coordinator, Western Dakota Technical Institute, 800 Mickelson Drive, Rapid City, SD 57701. *Phone:* 605-394-4034 Ext. 113. *Web address:* http://www.westerndakotatech.org.

WEST HILLS COMMUNITY COLLEGE
Coalinga, California

Students with LD Served by Program	100	ADD/ADHD Services	✓
Staff	3 full-time, 2 part-time	Summer Preparation Program	n/a
LD Program or Service Fee	n/a	Alternative Test Arrangements	✓
LD Program Began	n/a	LD Student Organization	n/a

Disabled Students' Program and Services (DSPS) serves approximately 100 undergraduate students. Faculty consists of 3 full-time and 2 part-time staff members. Services are provided by counselors, diagnostic specialists, special education teachers, LD specialists, and trained peer tutors.

Policies 12 units per semester are required to maintain full-time status.

Diagnostic testing Available for auditory processing, spelling, intelligence, reading, written language, visual processing, and math.

Basic skills remediation Available in study skills, reading, spelling, and written language. Offered in small groups and class-size groups by special education teachers and trained peer tutors.

Subject-area tutoring Available in most subjects. Offered one-on-one by trained peer tutors.

Special courses Available in practical computer skills, test taking, and learning strategies. All courses are offered for credit; all enter into overall grade point average.

Counseling and advisement Career counseling and individual counseling are available.

Auxiliary aids and services *Aids:* personal computers, scan and read programs (e.g., Kurzweil), screen-enlarging programs, screen readers, speech recognition programs (e.g., Dragon), tape recorders, taped textbooks. *Services and accommodations:* advocates, priority registration, alternative test arrangements, and note-takers.

ADD/ADHD Students with ADD/ADHD are eligible for the same services available to students with LD, as well as distraction-free study areas and distraction-free testing environments.

Application *Required:* interview and separate application to your LD program or unit. *Recommended:* high school transcript and documentation of high school services (e.g., Individualized Education Program [IEP] or 504 plan). Upon application, documentation of need for special services should be sent only to your LD program or unit. Upon acceptance, documentation of need for special services should be sent only to your LD program or unit. *Application deadline (institutional):* rolling/continuous for fall and rolling/continuous for spring. *Application deadline (LD program):* rolling/continuous for fall and rolling/continuous for spring.

LD program contact Joyce Smyers, Director, 300 Cherry Lane, Coalinga, CA 93230. *Phone:* 800-266-1114 Ext. 3225. *Fax:* 559-935-3788. *E-mail:* smyersjk@whccd.cc.ca.us.

Application contact Darlene Georgatos, Registrar, West Hills Community College, 300 Cherry Lane, Coalinga, CA 93210-1399. *Phone:* 559-935-0801 Ext. 3217. *E-mail:* georgada@whccd.cc.ca.us. *Web address:* http://www.westhills.cc.ca.us/.

WEST VALLEY COLLEGE
Saratoga, California

Students with LD Served by Program	500	ADD/ADHD Services	✓
Staff	4 full-time, 4 part-time	Summer Preparation Program	✓
LD Program or Service Fee	n/a	Alternative Test Arrangements	✓
LD Program Began	1975	LD Student Organization	n/a

Supported Education Services (SEP) began offering services in 1975. The program serves approximately 500 undergraduate students. Faculty consists of 4 full-time and 4 part-time staff members. Services are provided by counselors, remediation/learning specialists, LD specialists, and professional tutors.

Policies Students with LD may take up to 18 credit hours per semester; 8 credit hours per semester are required to maintain full-time status and to be eligible for financial aid.

Special preparation or orientation Optional summer program offered prior to entering college. Optional orientation held before registration, before classes begin, and during summer prior to enrollment.

Diagnostic testing Available for auditory processing, spelling, spoken language, intelligence, study skills, learning strategies, reading, written language, learning styles, visual processing, math, and speech and language.

Basic skills remediation Available in auditory processing, study skills, computer skills, reading, time management, visual processing, learning strategies, spelling, written language, math, and spoken language. Offered one-on-one, in small groups, and class-size groups by computer-based instruction, regular education teachers, special education teachers, LD specialists, and professional tutors.

some subjects. Offered one-on-one and in small groups by computer-based instruction, professional tutors, and LD specialists.

Special courses Available in oral communication skills, study skills, college survival skills, practical computer skills, test taking, reading, time management, learning strategies, vocabulary development, math, and written composition skills. Some courses are offered for credit; some enter into overall grade point average.

Counseling and advisement Career counseling, individual counseling, small-group counseling, and academic counseling, personal counseling are available.

Auxiliary aids and services *Aids:* personal spelling/word-use assistants (e.g., Franklin Speller), scan and read programs (e.g., Kurzweil), screen-enlarging programs, speech recognition programs (e.g., Dragon), tape recorders, taped textbooks. *Services and accommodations:* advocates, priority registration, alternative test arrangements, readers, note-takers, and scribes.

ADD/ADHD Students with ADD/ADHD are eligible for the same services available to students with LD, as well as distraction-free testing environments.

Application *Required:* interview. *Recommended:* psychoeducational report (2 years old or less) and documentation of high school services (e.g., Individualized Education Program [IEP] or 504 plan). Upon application, documentation of need for special services should be sent only to your LD program or unit. Upon acceptance, documentation of need for special services should be sent only to your LD program or unit. *Application deadline (institutional):* 8/21 for fall and 1/15 for spring. *Application deadline (LD program):* rolling/continuous for fall and rolling/continuous for spring.

LD program contact Colleen Butterfield 14000 Fruitvale Avenue, Saratoga, CA 95070. *Phone:* 408-971-2010. *E-mail:* colleen_butterfield@wvmccd.cc.ca.us.

Application contact Albert Moore, Admissions and Records Supervisor, West Valley College, 14000 Fruitvale Avenue, Saratoga, CA 95070-5698. *Phone:* 408-741-2533. *Web address:* http://www.westvalley.edu/.

WEST VIRGINIA UNIVERSITY AT PARKERSBURG

Parkersburg, West Virginia

Students with LD Served by Program	40	ADD/ADHD Services	✓
Staff	1 full-time, 5 part-time	Summer Preparation Program	n/a
LD Program or Service Fee	n/a	Alternative Test Arrangements	✓
LD Program Began	1995	LD Student Organization	n/a

ADA Educational Services began offering services in 1995. The program serves approximately 40 undergraduate students. Faculty consists of 1 full-time and 5 part-time staff members. Services are provided by counselors and Supervised psychologist.

Policies Students with LD may take up to 18 credit hours per semester; 12 credit hours per semester are required to maintain full-time status.

Special preparation or orientation Optional orientation held individually by special arrangement.

Counseling and advisement Individual counseling is available.

Auxiliary aids and services *Aids:* scan and read programs (e.g., Kurzweil), screen-enlarging programs, tape recorders, taped textbooks. *Services and accommodations:* priority registration, alternative test arrangements, readers, note-takers, and scribes.

ADD/ADHD Students with ADD/ADHD are eligible for the same services available to students with LD, as well as distraction-free testing environments.

Application *Required:* high school transcript and ACT or SAT I (extended-time or untimed test accepted). Upon acceptance, documentation of need for special services should be sent only to your LD program or unit. *Application deadline (institutional):* rolling/continuous for fall and rolling/continuous for spring. *Application deadline (LD program):* rolling/continuous for fall and rolling/continuous for spring.

LD program contact Catherine A. Mutz, Coordinator, 300 Campus Drive, Parkersburg, WV 26101-9577. *Phone:* 304-424-8320. *Fax:* 304-424-8350. *E-mail:* cmutz@wvu.edu.

Application contact Director of Enrollment Retention Management, West Virginia University at Parkersburg, 300 Campus Drive, Parkersburg, WV 26101-9577. *Phone:* 304-424-8220. *Web address:* http://www.wvup.wvunet.edu/.

WILKES COMMUNITY COLLEGE

Wilkesboro, North Carolina

Students with LD Served by Program	20	ADD/ADHD Services	✓
Staff	1 part-time	Summer Preparation Program	n/a
LD Program or Service Fee	n/a	Alternative Test Arrangements	✓
LD Program Began	n/a	LD Student Organization	n/a

Student Support Services serves approximately 20 undergraduate students. Faculty consists of 1 part-time staff member. Services are provided by counselors and trained peer tutors.

Policies Students with LD may take up to 14 credit hours per semester; 6 credit hours per semester are required to be eligible for financial aid.

Special preparation or orientation Held before classes begin.

Diagnostic testing Available for neuropsychological, intelligence, learning strategies, and learning styles.

Basic skills remediation Available in reading, written language, and math. Offered in class-size groups by regular education teachers.

Subject-area tutoring Available in most subjects. Offered one-on-one by trained peer tutors.

Special courses Available in career planning, study skills, college survival skills, test taking, health and nutrition, reading, time management, learning strategies, self-advocacy, math, stress management, and written composition skills. Most courses are offered for credit; some enter into overall grade point average.

Counseling and advisement Career counseling, individual counseling, and support groups are available.

Auxiliary aids and services *Aids:* calculators, personal computers, screen-enlarging programs, tape recorders, taped textbooks. *Services and accommodations:* advocates, alternative test arrangements, readers, note-takers, and scribes.

ADD/ADHD Students with ADD/ADHD are eligible for the same services available to students with LD, as well as distraction-free study areas, distraction-free testing environments and personal coach or mentors.

Application *Required:* high school transcript, psychoeducational report (3 years old or less), and documentation of high school services (e.g., Individualized Education Program [IEP] or 504

Wilkes Community College (continued)

plan). Upon application, documentation of need for special services should be sent only to your LD program or unit. Upon acceptance, documentation of need for special services should be sent only to your LD program or unit. *Application deadline (LD program):* rolling/continuous for fall.

LD program contact Nancy Sizemore, Counselor, Student Support Services, PO Box 120, Collegiate Drive, Wilkesboro, NC 28697. *Phone:* 336-838-6560. *E-mail:* sizemore@wilkes.cc.nc.us.

Application contact Wilkes Community College, PO Box 120, Wilkesboro, NC 28697. *Web address:* http://www.wilkes.cc.nc. us/.

WILLIAM RAINEY HARPER COLLEGE
Palatine, Illinois

Students with LD Served by Program	150	ADD/ADHD Services	✓
Staff	1 full-time, 6 part-time	Summer Preparation Program	✓
LD Program or Service Fee	✓	Alternative Test Arrangements	✓
LD Program Began	1981	LD Student Organization	✓

Program to Achieve Student Success (PASS) began offering services in 1981. The program serves approximately 150 undergraduate students. Faculty consists of 1 full-time and 6 part-time staff members. Services are provided by diagnostic specialists, LD specialists, trained peer tutors, and professional tutors.

Policies The college has written policies regarding course substitutions. Students with LD may take up to 18 credit hours per semester; 9 credit hours per semester are required to maintain full-time status; 6 credit hours per semester are required to be eligible for financial aid.

Fees *LD Program or Service Fee:* $1000 per year. *Diagnostic Testing Fee:* ranges from $300 to $450.

Special preparation or orientation Optional summer program offered prior to entering college. Required orientation held before registration.

Diagnostic testing Available for auditory processing, intelligence, reading, visual processing, and Woodcock Johnson battery.

Subject-area tutoring Available in most subjects. Offered one-on-one and in small groups by professional tutors, trained peer tutors, and LD specialists.

Special courses Available in career planning, study skills, reading, and written composition skills. All courses are offered for credit; some enter into overall grade point average.

Counseling and advisement Career counseling and individual counseling are available.

Auxiliary aids and services *Aids:* calculators, personal computers, personal spelling/word-use assistants (e.g., Franklin Speller), scan and read programs (e.g., Kurzweil), screen-enlarging programs, screen readers, speech recognition programs (e.g., Dragon), tape recorders, taped textbooks. *Services and accommodations:* priority registration, alternative test arrangements, readers, note-takers, and scribes.

Student organization There is a student organization for students with LD.

ADD/ADHD Students with ADD/ADHD are eligible for the same services available to students with LD, as well as distraction-free testing environments.

Application *Required:* high school transcript, ACT (extended-time test accepted), interview, separate application to your LD program or unit, psychoeducational report (5 years old or less), and documentation of high school services (e.g., Individualized Education Program [IEP] or 504 plan). Upon application, documentation of need for special services should be sent only to your LD program or unit. Upon acceptance, documentation of need for special services should be sent only to your LD program or unit. *Application deadline (institutional):* rolling/continuous for fall and rolling/continuous for spring. *Application deadline (LD program):* 8/15 for fall and 12/15 for spring.

LD program contact Pascuala Herrera, LD Specialist/Team Leader, 1200 West Algonquin Road, Palatine, IL 60067-7398. *Phone:* 847-925-6266. *Fax:* 847-925-6036. *E-mail:* pherrera@harper.cc.il.us.

Application contact Debbie Michelini, Student Recruitment Coordinator, William Rainey Harper College, 1200 West Algonquin Road, Palatine, IL 60067-7398. *Phone:* 847-925-6247. *E-mail:* info@harper.cc.il.us. *Web address:* http://www.harper.cc.il.us/.

► TWO-YEAR COLLEGES ◄

WITH SPECIAL SERVICES

ABRAHAM BALDWIN AGRICULTURAL COLLEGE
Tifton, Georgia

Students with LD Served by Program	50	ADD/ADHD Services	✓
Staff	2 full-time	Summer Preparation Program	n/a
LD Program or Service Fee	n/a	Alternative Test Arrangements	✓
LD Program Began	1993	LD Student Organization	n/a

Learning Disability Services began offering services in 1993. The program serves approximately 50 undergraduate students. Faculty consists of 2 full-time staff members. Services are provided by academic advisers, counselors, diagnostic specialists, LD specialists, and professional tutors.

Policies The college has written policies regarding course substitutions and substitution and waivers of requirements for admission. Students with LD may take up to 18 hours per semester; 12 hours per semester are required to maintain full-time status; 6 hours per semester are required to be eligible for financial aid.

Fees *Diagnostic Testing Fee:* ranges from $250 to $300.

Special preparation or orientation Held during registration, before classes begin, and individually by special arrangement.

Diagnostic testing Available for auditory processing, motor skills, spelling, handwriting, neuropsychological, spoken language, intelligence, personality, study skills, learning strategies, reading, written language, learning styles, social skills, visual processing, and math.

Subject-area tutoring Available in some subjects. Offered one-on-one by LD specialists.

Counseling and advisement Career counseling and individual counseling are available. Academic advisement by a staff member affiliated with the program is available.

Auxiliary aids and services *Aids:* calculators, personal computers, scan and read programs (e.g., Kurzweil), screen-enlarging programs, tape recorders, taped textbooks. *Services and accommodations:* priority registration, alternative test arrangements, readers, and scribes.

ADD/ADHD Students with ADD/ADHD are eligible for the same services available to students with LD, as well as distraction-free testing environments.

Application *Required:* high school transcript, ACT or SAT I (extended-time or untimed test accepted), and psychoeducational report (3 years old or less). *Recommended:* documentation of high school services (e.g., Individualized Education Program [IEP] or 504 plan). Upon application, documentation of need for special services should be sent only to your LD program or unit. Upon acceptance, documentation of need for special services should be sent only to your LD program or unit. *Application deadline (institutional):* rolling/continuous for fall and rolling/continuous for spring. *Application deadline (LD program):* rolling/continuous for fall and rolling/continuous for spring.

LD program contact Rita Wade, Learning Disability Service Provider, 2802 Moore Highway, ABAC Box #21, Tifton, GA 31794. *Phone:* 912-386-3489. *Fax:* 912-386-3579. *E-mail:* rwade@ abac.peachnet.edu.

Application contact Abraham Baldwin Agricultural College, ABAC 4 2802 Moore Highway, Tifton, GA 31794-2601. *Web address:* http://stallion.aback.peachnet.edu/.

ACADEMY OF MEDICAL ARTS AND BUSINESS
Harrisburg, Pennsylvania

Students with LD Served by Program	4	ADD/ADHD Services	✓
Staff	3 full-time	Summer Preparation Program	n/a
LD Program or Service Fee	n/a	Alternative Test Arrangements	✓
LD Program Began	1989	LD Student Organization	✓

The college began offering services in 1989. The program serves approximately 4 undergraduate students. Faculty consists of 3 full-time staff members. Services are provided by academic advisers, regular education teachers, and teacher trainees.

Policies Students with LD may take up to 12 credit hours per semester; 12 credit hours per semester are required to maintain full-time status; 6 credit hours per semester are required to be eligible for financial aid.

Basic skills remediation Available in study skills, computer skills, reading, time management, social skills, learning strategies, spelling, written language, math, and spoken language. Offered one-on-one and in small groups by computer-based instruction.

Subject-area tutoring Available in all subjects. Offered one-on-one and in small groups by computer-based instruction and regular education teachers.

Counseling and advisement Academic advisement by a staff member affiliated with the program is available.

Auxiliary aids and services *Aids:* calculators, personal computers, tape recorders. *Services and accommodations:* advocates, priority registration, alternative test arrangements, readers, note-takers, and scribes.

Student organization There is a student organization for students with LD.

ADD/ADHD Students with ADD/ADHD are eligible for the same services available to students with LD, as well as distraction-free study areas, distraction-free testing environments and personal coach or mentors.

Application *Required:* high school transcript, interview, and Wonderlic Examination. *Recommended:* documentation of high school services (e.g., Individualized Education Program [IEP] or 504 plan). Upon application, documentation of need for special services should be sent only to admissions. Upon acceptance, documentation of need for special services should be sent only to admissions. *Application deadline (institutional):* rolling/continuous for fall and rolling/continuous for spring. *Application deadline (LD program):* rolling/continuous for fall and rolling/continuous for spring.

LD program contact Gary Kay, President, 2301 Academy Drive, Harrisburg, PA 17112. *Phone:* 717-545-4747. *Fax:* 717-901-9090. *E-mail:* info@acadcampus.com.

Application contact Gary Kay, Director of Admissions, Academy of Medical Arts and Business, 2301 Academy Drive, Harrisburg, PA 17112-1012. *Phone:* 717-545-4747. *Web address:* http://www.acadcampus.com/.

ALBUQUERQUE TECHNICAL VOCATIONAL INSTITUTE
Albuquerque, New Mexico

Students with LD Served by Program	125	ADD/ADHD Services	✓
Staff	6 full-time	Summer Preparation Program	n/a
LD Program or Service Fee	n/a	Alternative Test Arrangements	✓
LD Program Began	1979	LD Student Organization	n/a

Special Services began offering services in 1979. The program serves approximately 125 undergraduate students. Faculty consists of 6 full-time staff members. Services are provided by counselors and diagnostic specialists.

Policies 12 credit hours per term are required to maintain full-time status.

Diagnostic testing Available for auditory processing, spelling, handwriting, spoken language, intelligence, reading, written language, learning styles, and math.

Counseling and advisement Career counseling and individual counseling are available.

Auxiliary aids and services *Aids:* calculators, personal spelling/word-use assistants (e.g., Franklin Speller), scan and read programs (e.g., Kurzweil), screen-enlarging programs, screen readers, speech recognition programs (e.g., Dragon), tape recorders, taped textbooks. *Services and accommodations:* alternative test arrangements, readers, note-takers, and scribes.

ADD/ADHD Students with ADD/ADHD are eligible for the same services available to students with LD, as well as distraction-free testing environments.

Application *Required:* interview and psychoeducational report. *Recommended:* documentation of high school services (e.g., Individualized Education Program [IEP] or 504 plan). Upon application, documentation of need for special services should be sent only to your LD program or unit. *Application deadline (institutional):* rolling/continuous for fall and rolling/continuous for spring. *Application deadline (LD program):* rolling/continuous for fall and rolling/continuous for spring.

LD program contact A. Paul Smarrella, Director, Special Services, 525 Buena Vista SE, Albuquerque, NM 87059. *Phone:* 505-224-3259. *Fax:* 505-224-3261. *E-mail:* pauls@tvi.cc.nm.us.

Application contact Jane Campbell, Director of Admissions and Records, Albuquerque Technical Vocational Institute, 525 Buena Vista, SE, Albuquerque, NM 87106-4096. *Phone:* 505-224-3210. *Web address:* http://www.tvi.cc.nm.us/.

ALEXANDRIA TECHNICAL COLLEGE
Alexandria, Minnesota

Students with LD Served by Program	30	ADD/ADHD Services	n/a
Staff	4 part-time	Summer Preparation Program	n/a
LD Program or Service Fee	n/a	Alternative Test Arrangements	✓
LD Program Began	1990	LD Student Organization	n/a

Support Services began offering services in 1990. The program serves approximately 30 undergraduate students. Faculty consists of 4 part-time staff members. Services are provided by trained peer tutors and professional tutors.

Policies 12 credit hours per semester are required to maintain full-time status; 1 credit hour per semester is required to be eligible for financial aid.

Auxiliary aids and services *Aids:* scan and read programs (e.g., Kurzweil), screen-enlarging programs, screen readers, speech recognition programs (e.g., Dragon), tape recorders,

taped textbooks. *Services and accommodations:* priority registration, alternative test arrangements, readers, note-takers, and scribes.

Application *Required:* high school transcript and interview. *Recommended:* psychoeducational report and documentation of high school services (e.g., Individualized Education Program [IEP] or 504 plan). Upon acceptance, documentation of need for special services should be sent only to your LD program or unit. *Application deadline (institutional):* rolling/continuous for fall and rolling/continuous for spring.

LD program contact Mary Ackerman, Support Services Coordinator, 1601 Jefferson Street, Alexandria, MN 56308. *Phone:* 320-762-0221. *Fax:* 320-762-4501. *E-mail:* marya@alx.tec.mn.us.

Application contact Alexandria Technical College, 1601 Jefferson Street, Alexandria, MN 56308-3707. *E-mail:* actinfo@alx.tec.mn.us. *Web address:* http://www.atc.tec.mn.us/.

AMARILLO COLLEGE
Amarillo, Texas

Students with LD Served by Program	150	ADD/ADHD Services	✓
Staff	2 full-time, 1 part-time	Summer Preparation Program	n/a
LD Program or Service Fee	n/a	Alternative Test Arrangements	✓
LD Program Began	1984	LD Student Organization	✓

Accessibility Department of the Access Services Division began offering services in 1984. The program serves approximately 150 undergraduate students. Faculty consists of 2 full-time staff members and 1 part-time staff member. Services are provided by academic advisers, remediation/learning specialists, counselors, regular education teachers, trained peer tutors, and professional tutors.

Policies Students with LD may take up to 18 credit hours per semester; 12 credit hours per semester are required to maintain full-time status; 6 credit hours per semester are required to be eligible for financial aid.

Basic skills remediation Available in auditory processing, study skills, computer skills, reading, time management, handwriting, visual processing, learning strategies, written language, math, and spoken language. Offered one-on-one, in small groups, and class-size groups by computer-based instruction, regular education teachers, LD specialists, professional tutors, and trained peer tutors.

Subject-area tutoring Available in most subjects. Offered one-on-one, in small groups, and class-size groups by computer-based instruction, professional tutors, trained peer tutors, and LD specialists.

Special courses Available in career planning, study skills, test taking, reading, time management, learning strategies, math, stress management, and written composition skills. Most courses are offered for credit; most enter into overall grade point average.

Counseling and advisement Career counseling, individual counseling, small-group counseling, and support groups are available. Academic advisement by a staff member affiliated with the program is available.

Auxiliary aids and services *Aids:* calculators, personal spelling/word-use assistants (e.g., Franklin Speller), screen-enlarging programs, tape recorders, taped textbooks. *Services and accommodations:* alternative test arrangements and scribes.

Student organization There is a student organization for students with LD.

ADD/ADHD Students with ADD/ADHD are eligible for the same services available to students with LD, as well as distraction-free study areas and distraction-free testing environments.

Application *Required:* interview, psychoeducational report (5 years old or less), and documentation of high school services (e.g., Individualized Education Program [IEP] or 504 plan). *Recommended:* high school transcript. Upon application, documentation of need for special services should be sent only to your LD program or unit. Upon acceptance, documentation of need for special services should be sent only to your LD program or unit. *Application deadline (institutional):* rolling/continuous for fall and rolling/continuous for spring. *Application deadline (LD program):* rolling/continuous for fall and rolling/continuous for spring.
LD program contact Brenda Wilkes, Accessibility Coordinator, PO Box 447, Amarillo, TX 79178. *Phone:* 806-371-5436. *Fax:* 806-345-5570. *E-mail:* bjwilkes@actx.edu.
Application contact Amarillo College, PO Box 447, Amarillo, TX 79178-0001. *Web address:* http://www.actx.edu/.

ANNE ARUNDEL COMMUNITY COLLEGE
Arnold, Maryland

Students with LD Served by Program	143	ADD/ADHD Services	✓
Staff	2 full-time	Summer Preparation Program	n/a
LD Program or Service Fee	n/a	Alternative Test Arrangements	✓
LD Program Began	1983	LD Student Organization	✓

Disabled Student Services Office began offering services in 1983. The program serves approximately 143 undergraduate students. Faculty consists of 2 full-time staff members. Services are provided by academic advisers, remediation/learning specialists, counselors, and regular education teachers.
Policies The college has written policies regarding course substitutions. Students with LD may take up to 18 credit hours per semester; 12 credit hours per semester are required to maintain full-time status; 3 credit hours per semester are required to be eligible for financial aid.
Counseling and advisement Career counseling and individual counseling are available. Academic advisement by a staff member affiliated with the program is available.
Auxiliary aids and services *Aids:* screen-enlarging programs, screen readers, speech recognition programs (e.g., Dragon), taped textbooks. *Services and accommodations:* alternative test arrangements, readers, note-takers, and scribes.
Student organization There is a student organization for students with LD.
ADD/ADHD Students with ADD/ADHD are eligible for the same services available to students with LD, as well as distraction-free testing environments.
Application *Required:* high school transcript, ACT or SAT I (extended-time tests accepted), psychoeducational report (4 years old or less), documentation of high school services (e.g., Individualized Education Program [IEP] or 504 plan), and College Placement Test in place of SAT or ACT. Upon application, documentation of need for special services should be sent only to your LD program or unit. Upon acceptance, documentation of need for special services should be sent only to your LD program or unit. *Application deadline (institutional):* rolling/continuous for fall and rolling/continuous for spring. *Application deadline (LD program):* rolling/continuous for fall and rolling/continuous for spring.
LD program contact Lyn Williams, Assistant Director, Special Populations, SSVC 134, Arnold, MD 21012. *Phone:* 410-541-2307. *Fax:* 410-541-2494. *E-mail:* ldwilliams@mail.aacc.cc.md.us.

Application contact Anne Arundel Community College, 101 College Parkway, Arnold, MD 21012-1895. *Web address:* http://www.aacc.md.us/.

ARAPAHOE COMMUNITY COLLEGE
Littleton, Colorado

Students with LD Served by Program	200	ADD/ADHD Services	✓
Staff	4 full-time	Summer Preparation Program	n/a
LD Program or Service Fee	n/a	Alternative Test Arrangements	✓
LD Program Began	1986	LD Student Organization	n/a

Disability Services began offering services in 1986. The program serves approximately 200 undergraduate students. Faculty consists of 4 full-time staff members. Services are provided by LD specialists.
Policies The college has written policies regarding course substitutions and grade forgiveness. Students with LD may take up to 12 credit hours per semester; 6 credit hours per semester are required to maintain full-time status and to be eligible for financial aid.
Special preparation or orientation Optional orientation held individually by special arrangement.
Basic skills remediation Available in computer skills, reading, spelling, written language, and math. Offered one-on-one and in class-size groups by computer-based instruction, regular education teachers, and LD specialists.
Auxiliary aids and services *Aids:* personal spelling/word-use assistants (e.g., Franklin Speller), scan and read programs (e.g., Kurzweil), screen-enlarging programs, screen readers, speech recognition programs (e.g., Dragon), taped textbooks, Alpha Smart. *Services and accommodations:* advocates, alternative test arrangements, readers, note-takers, and scribes.
ADD/ADHD Students with ADD/ADHD are eligible for the same services available to students with LD, as well as distraction-free testing environments.
Application Upon application, documentation of need for special services should be sent only to your LD program or unit. *Application deadline (institutional):* rolling/continuous for fall and rolling/continuous for spring. *Application deadline (LD program):* rolling/continuous for fall and rolling/continuous for spring.
LD program contact Linda Heesch, Director, Disability Services, 5900 South Santa Fe, PO Box 9002, Littleton, CO 80160-9002. *Phone:* 303-797-5806. *Fax:* 303-797-5810. *E-mail:* lheesch@arapahoe.edu.
Application contact Karen Funston, Admissions Specialist, Arapahoe Community College, 2500 West College Dr, PO Box 9002, Littleton, CO 80160-9002. *Phone:* 303-797-5622. *E-mail:* kfunston@arapahoe.edu.

THE ART INSTITUTE OF PITTSBURGH
Pittsburgh, Pennsylvania

Students with LD Served by Program	n/a	ADD/ADHD Services	✓
Staff	2 full-time, 5 part-time	Summer Preparation Program	n/a
LD Program or Service Fee	n/a	Alternative Test Arrangements	✓
LD Program Began	1996	LD Student Organization	n/a

The Art Institute of Pittsburgh (continued)

Special Needs and Remediation began offering services in 1996. Faculty consists of 2 full-time and 5 part-time staff members. Services are provided by academic advisers, counselors, regular education teachers, and trained peer tutors.

Policies Students with LD may take up to 18 credits per quarter; 12 credits per quarter are required to maintain full-time status; 6 credits per quarter are required to be eligible for financial aid.

Basic skills remediation Available in reading, spelling, written language, and math. Offered in class-size groups by regular education teachers.

Subject-area tutoring Available in all subjects. Offered one-on-one and in small groups by trained peer tutors and instructors.

Counseling and advisement Career counseling and individual counseling are available. Academic advisement by a staff member affiliated with the program is available.

Auxiliary aids and services *Aids:* calculators, personal computers, tape recorders, taped textbooks. *Services and accommodations:* priority registration, alternative test arrangements, and readers.

ADD/ADHD Students with ADD/ADHD are eligible for the same services available to students with LD, as well as distraction-free testing environments.

Application *Required:* high school transcript. *Recommended:* interview, psychoeducational report (5 years old or less), and documentation of high school services (e.g., Individualized Education Program [IEP] or 504 plan). Upon application, documentation of need for special services should be sent only to your LD program or unit. Upon acceptance, documentation of need for special services should be sent only to your LD program or unit.

LD program contact Jenna Templeton, Director of Student Life, 526 Penn Avenue, Pittsburgh, PA 15222. *Phone:* 412-263-6600. *Fax:* 412-263-3715.

Application contact The Art Institute of Pittsburgh, 526 Penn Avenue, Pittsburgh, PA 15222-3269. *E-mail:* colkerl@aii.edu. *Web address:* http://www.aip.aii.edu/.

ASHLAND COMMUNITY COLLEGE
Ashland, Kentucky

Students with LD Served by Program	100	ADD/ADHD Services	✓
Staff	1 full-time, 5 part-time	Summer Preparation Program	n/a
LD Program or Service Fee	n/a	Alternative Test Arrangements	✓
LD Program Began	1997	LD Student Organization	n/a

Disability Services began offering services in 1997. The program serves approximately 100 undergraduate students. Faculty consists of 1 full-time and 5 part-time staff members. Services are provided by academic advisers, counselors, and trained peer tutors.

Policies The college has written policies regarding course substitutions. Students with LD may take up to 18 credit hours per semester; 12 credit hours per semester are required to maintain full-time status; 6 credit hours per semester are required to be eligible for financial aid.

Special preparation or orientation Optional orientation held individually by special arrangement.

Basic skills remediation Available in study skills, computer skills, reading, time management, learning strategies, written language, and math. Offered in class-size groups by computer-based instruction, regular education teachers, and trained peer tutors.

Subject-area tutoring Available in all subjects. Offered one-on-one by computer-based instruction, professional tutors, and trained peer tutors.

Special courses Available in career planning, study skills, college survival skills, test taking, time management, learning strategies, and self-advocacy. No courses are offered for credit; none enter into overall grade point average.

Counseling and advisement Career counseling, individual counseling, and support groups are available. Academic advisement by a staff member affiliated with the program is available.

Auxiliary aids and services *Aids:* screen-enlarging programs, screen readers, tape recorders, taped textbooks. *Services and accommodations:* advocates, priority registration, alternative test arrangements, readers, note-takers, scribes, and special advising/supportive counseling/referral service.

ADD/ADHD Students with ADD/ADHD are eligible for the same services available to students with LD, as well as distraction-free study areas and distraction-free testing environments.

Application *Required:* high school transcript, ACT or SAT I (extended-time or untimed test accepted), psychoeducational report (3 years old or less), and documentation of high school services (e.g., Individualized Education Program [IEP] or 504 plan). Upon application, documentation of need for special services should be sent only to your LD program or unit. Upon acceptance, documentation of need for special services should be sent only to your LD program or unit. *Application deadline (institutional):* rolling/continuous for fall and rolling/continuous for spring. *Application deadline (LD program):* rolling/continuous for fall and rolling/continuous for spring.

LD program contact Nancy C. Preston, Disability Services Coordinator, 1400 College Drive, Ashland, KY 41101. *Phone:* 606-326-2051. *Fax:* 606-326-2192. *E-mail:* nancy.preston@kctcs.net.

Application contact Ashland Community College, 1400 College Drive, Ashland, KY 41101-3683. *E-mail:* ccsashsa@ukcc.uky.edu. *Web address:* http://www.ashlandcc.org/.

ATLANTIC CAPE COMMUNITY COLLEGE
Mays Landing, New Jersey

Students with LD Served by Program	48	ADD/ADHD Services	✓
Staff	1 full-time, 10 part-time	Summer Preparation Program	n/a
LD Program or Service Fee	n/a	Alternative Test Arrangements	✓
LD Program Began	1990	LD Student Organization	n/a

Disabled Student Services began offering services in 1990. The program serves approximately 48 undergraduate students. Faculty consists of 1 full-time and 10 part-time staff members. Services are provided by academic advisers, regular education teachers, counselors, diagnostic specialists, and professional tutors.

Policies The college has written policies regarding substitution and waivers of requirements for admission and graduation. LD services are also available to graduate students.

Fees *Diagnostic Testing Fee:* $150.

Diagnostic testing Available for spelling, intelligence, personality, reading, written language, and math.

Subject-area tutoring Available in most subjects. Offered one-on-one by professional tutors.

Counseling and advisement Career counseling, individual counseling, and support groups are available. Academic advisement by a staff member affiliated with the program is available.

Auxiliary aids and services *Aids:* screen-enlarging programs, Dragon Dictate. *Services and accommodations:* alternative test arrangements, readers, note-takers, and scribes.

ADD/ADHD Students with ADD/ADHD are eligible for the same services available to students with LD, as well as distraction-free study areas, distraction-free testing environments and support groups for ADD/ADHD.

Application *Required:* psychoeducational report (3 years old or less). *Recommended:* high school transcript and documentation of high school services (e.g., Individualized Education Program [IEP] or 504 plan). Upon application, documentation of need for special services should be sent only to your LD program or unit. Upon acceptance, documentation of need for special services should be sent only to your LD program or unit. *Application deadline (institutional):* rolling/continuous for fall and rolling/continuous for spring. *Application deadline (LD program):* rolling/continuous for fall and rolling/continuous for spring.

LD program contact Stanley Wiley, Coordinator, Disabled Student Services, 5100 Black Horse Pike, Mays Landing, NJ 08330. *Phone:* 609-343-5090. *Fax:* 609-343-4926. *E-mail:* swiley@atlantic.edu.

Application contact Linda McLeod, College Recruiter, Atlantic Cape Community College, 5100 Black Horse Pike, Mays Landing, NJ 08330-2699. *Phone:* 609-343-5000. *E-mail:* accadmit@nsvm.atlantic.edu. *Web address:* http://www.atlantic.edu/.

BAINBRIDGE COLLEGE
Bainbridge, Georgia

Students with LD Served by Program	20	ADD/ADHD Services	✓
Staff	1 full-time	Summer Preparation Program	n/a
LD Program or Service Fee	n/a	Alternative Test Arrangements	✓
LD Program Began	1973	LD Student Organization	n/a

Career Development and Counseling Center began offering services in 1973. The program serves approximately 20 undergraduate students. Faculty consists of 1 full-time staff member. Services are provided by academic advisers, regular education teachers, counselors, and diagnostic specialists.

Policies The college has written policies regarding course substitutions, grade forgiveness, and substitution and waivers of requirements for admission and graduation. Students with LD may take up to 18 credit hours per semester; 12 credit hours per semester are required to maintain full-time status; 6 credit hours per semester are required to be eligible for financial aid.

Fees *Diagnostic Testing Fee:* $300.

Diagnostic testing Available for auditory processing, spelling, intelligence, personality, learning strategies, reading, written language, learning styles, visual processing, and math.

Basic skills remediation Available in reading, spelling, and math. Offered in class-size groups by regular education teachers.

Subject-area tutoring Available in all subjects. Offered one-on-one by computer-based instruction and trained peer tutors.

Counseling and advisement Career counseling, individual counseling, small-group counseling, and support groups are available. Academic advisement by a staff member affiliated with the program is available.

Auxiliary aids and services *Aids:* calculators, personal computers, personal spelling/word-use assistants (e.g., Franklin Speller), screen-enlarging programs, tape recorders, taped textbooks. *Services and accommodations:* priority registration, alternative test arrangements, readers, note-takers, and scribes.

ADD/ADHD Students with ADD/ADHD are eligible for the same services available to students with LD, as well as distraction-free study areas and distraction-free testing environments.

Application *Required:* high school transcript, ACT or SAT I (extended-time tests accepted), psychoeducational report (3 years old or less), and COMPASS, entrance exam. *Recommended:* documentation of high school services (e.g., Individualized Education Program [IEP] or 504 plan). Upon application, documentation of need for special services should be sent to both admissions and your LD program or unit. Upon acceptance, documentation of need for special services should be sent to both admissions and your LD program or unit. *Application deadline (institutional):* rolling/continuous for fall and rolling/continuous for spring. *Application deadline (LD program):* rolling/continuous for fall and rolling/continuous for spring.

LD program contact Joan Fryer, Counselor, 2500 East Shotwell Street, Bainbridge, GA 31717. *Phone:* 912-248-2560. *Fax:* 912-248-2589. *E-mail:* jfryer@catfish.bbc.peachnet.edu.

Application contact Connie Snyder, Assistant Director of Admissions, Bainbridge College, 2500 East Shotwell Street, Bainbridge, GA 31717. *Phone:* 912-248-2500. *E-mail:* cboyd@catfish.bbc.peachnet.edu. *Web address:* http://www.bbc.peachnet.edu/.

BARTON COUNTY COMMUNITY COLLEGE
Great Bend, Kansas

Students with LD Served by Program	43	ADD/ADHD Services	✓
Staff	5 full-time, 10 part-time	Summer Preparation Program	✓
LD Program or Service Fee	n/a	Alternative Test Arrangements	✓
LD Program Began	1995	LD Student Organization	n/a

Special Support Services began offering services in 1995. The program serves approximately 43 undergraduate students. Faculty consists of 5 full-time and 10 part-time staff members. Services are provided by counselors, remediation/learning specialists, trained peer tutors, and professional tutors.

Fees *Diagnostic Testing Fee:* ranges from $40 to $150.

Special preparation or orientation Optional summer program offered prior to entering college. Required orientation held individually by special arrangement.

Diagnostic testing Available for auditory processing, motor skills, spelling, spoken language, intelligence, personality, study skills, learning strategies, reading, written language, learning styles, visual processing, and math.

Basic skills remediation Available in study skills, computer skills, reading, time management, learning strategies, spelling, written language, and math. Offered one-on-one and in small groups by computer-based instruction, LD specialists, professional tutors, and trained peer tutors.

Subject-area tutoring Available in most subjects. Offered one-on-one and in small groups by computer-based instruction, professional tutors, graduate assistants/students, trained peer tutors, and LD specialists.

Special courses Available in study skills, college survival skills, test taking, and vocabulary development. Some courses are offered for credit; most enter into overall grade point average.

Counseling and advisement Career counseling, individual counseling, and support groups are available.

Auxiliary aids and services *Aids:* calculators, personal computers, personal spelling/word-use assistants (e.g., Franklin Speller), scan and read programs (e.g., Kurzweil), screen-enlarging programs, screen readers, speech recognition pro-

Barton County Community College (continued)

grams (e.g., Dragon), tape recorders, taped textbooks. *Services and accommodations:* advocates, alternative test arrangements, readers, note-takers, and scribes.

ADD/ADHD Students with ADD/ADHD are eligible for the same services available to students with LD, as well as distraction-free study areas, distraction-free testing environments and personal coach or mentors.

Application *Required:* psychoeducational report (7 years old or less) and documentation of high school services (e.g., Individualized Education Program [IEP] or 504 plan). *Recommended:* separate application to your LD program or unit. Upon application, documentation of need for special services should be sent only to your LD program or unit. Upon acceptance, documentation of need for special services should be sent only to your LD program or unit. *Application deadline (institutional):* rolling/continuous for fall and rolling/continuous for spring. *Application deadline (LD program):* rolling/continuous for fall and rolling/continuous for spring.

LD program contact Jackie Elliott, Director of Student Support Services, 245 Northeast 30th Road, Great Bend, KS 67530. *Phone:* 316-792-9322. *Fax:* 316-792-3238. *E-mail:* elliottj@barton.cc.ks.us.

Application contact Lori Crowther, Director of Admissions, Barton County Community College, 245 Northeast 30th Road, Great Bend, KS 67530-9283. *Phone:* 316-792-9241. *E-mail:* crowtherl@cougar.barton.cc.ks.us. *Web address:* http://www.barton.cc.ks.us/.

BIG BEND COMMUNITY COLLEGE
Moses Lake, Washington

Students with LD Served by Program	60	ADD/ADHD Services	✓
Staff	1 part-time	Summer Preparation Program	n/a
LD Program or Service Fee	n/a	Alternative Test Arrangements	✓
LD Program Began	1974	LD Student Organization	n/a

Disabled Student Services began offering services in 1974. The program serves approximately 60 undergraduate students. Faculty consists of 1 part-time staff member. Services are provided by counselors, remediation/learning specialists, and trained peer tutors.

Policies Students with LD may take up to 18 credit hours per quarter; 12 credit hours per quarter are required to maintain full-time status; 6 credit hours per quarter are required to be eligible for financial aid.

Special preparation or orientation Optional orientation held individually by special arrangement.

Basic skills remediation Available in study skills, computer skills, reading, time management, learning strategies, spelling, written language, and math. Offered in small groups and class-size groups by regular education teachers.

Subject-area tutoring Available in most subjects. Offered one-on-one and in small groups by trained peer tutors.

Special courses Available in study skills, college survival skills, practical computer skills, test taking, reading, time management, learning strategies, vocabulary development, stress management, and written composition skills. All courses are offered for credit; all enter into overall grade point average.

Counseling and advisement Career counseling and individual counseling are available.

Auxiliary aids and services *Aids:* personal computers, screen-enlarging programs, screen readers, tape recorders, taped textbooks. *Services and accommodations:* priority registration, alternative test arrangements, readers, note-takers, and scribes.

ADD/ADHD Students with ADD/ADHD are eligible for the same services available to students with LD, as well as distraction-free testing environments.

Application *Required:* psychoeducational report (3 years old or less). *Recommended:* documentation of high school services (e.g., Individualized Education Program [IEP] or 504 plan). Upon application, documentation of need for special services should be sent only to your LD program or unit. Upon acceptance, documentation of need for special services should be sent only to your LD program or unit. *Application deadline (institutional):* rolling/continuous for fall and rolling/continuous for spring. *Application deadline (LD program):* rolling/continuous for fall and rolling/continuous for spring.

LD program contact Jean Fitzgerald, Disabled Student Liaison, 7662 Chanute, Moses Lake, WA 98837. *Phone:* 509-762-5351 Ext. 316. *E-mail:* jeanf@bbcc.ctc.edu.

Application contact Big Bend Community College, 7662 Chanute Street, Moses Lake, WA 98837-3299. *E-mail:* candyl@bbcc.ctc.edu. *Web address:* http://www.bbcc.ctc.edu/.

BLACKHAWK TECHNICAL COLLEGE
Janesville, Wisconsin

Students with LD Served by Program	50	ADD/ADHD Services	✓
Staff	3 full-time, 2 part-time	Summer Preparation Program	✓
LD Program or Service Fee	n/a	Alternative Test Arrangements	✓
LD Program Began	1984	LD Student Organization	n/a

Services for Students with Disabilities began offering services in 1984. The program serves approximately 50 undergraduate students. Faculty consists of 3 full-time and 2 part-time staff members. Services are provided by counselors, special education teachers, and trained peer tutors.

Policies 12 credits per semester are required to maintain full-time status; 6 credits per semester are required to be eligible for financial aid.

Special preparation or orientation Optional summer program offered prior to entering college.

Basic skills remediation Available in study skills, computer skills, reading, time management, learning strategies, spelling, written language, and math. Offered in class-size groups by computer-based instruction, regular education teachers, and special education teachers.

Subject-area tutoring Available in most subjects. Offered one-on-one by computer-based instruction, trained peer tutors, and special education teachers.

Special courses Available in study skills, college survival skills, test taking, time management, learning strategies, and self-advocacy. No courses are offered for credit; none enter into overall grade point average.

Counseling and advisement Individual counseling is available.

Auxiliary aids and services *Aids:* calculators, personal spelling/word-use assistants (e.g., Franklin Speller), scan and read programs (e.g., Kurzweil), screen-enlarging programs, screen readers, speech recognition programs (e.g., Dragon), tape recorders, taped textbooks. *Services and accommodations:* priority registration, alternative test arrangements, readers, note-takers, and scribes.

ADD/ADHD Students with ADD/ADHD are eligible for the same services available to students with LD, as well as distraction-free study areas and distraction-free testing environments.

Application *Required:* high school transcript, psychoeducational report, and documentation of high school services (e.g., Individualized Education Program [IEP] or 504 plan). Upon application, documentation of need for special services should be sent only to your LD program or unit. Upon acceptance, documentation of need for special services should be sent only to your LD program or unit. *Application deadline (institutional):* rolling/continuous for fall and rolling/continuous for spring. *Application deadline (LD program):* rolling/continuous for fall and rolling/continuous for spring.

LD program contact Christine Flottum, Special Populations Instructor/Project Manager, 6004 Prairie Avenue, PO Box 5009, Janesville, WI 53547. *Phone:* 608-757-7796. *Fax:* 608-743-4409.

Application contact Blackhawk Technical College, PO Box 5009, Janesville, WI 53547-5009. *Web address:* http://www.blackhawk.tec.wi.us/.

BLINN COLLEGE
Brenham, Texas

Students with LD Served by Program	600	ADD/ADHD Services	✓
Staff	3 full-time	Summer Preparation Program	n/a
LD Program or Service Fee	n/a	Alternative Test Arrangements	✓
LD Program Began	1995	LD Student Organization	n/a

Office of Disability Services began offering services in 1995. The program serves approximately 600 undergraduate students. Faculty consists of 3 full-time staff members. Services are provided by counselors.

Policies The college has written policies regarding course substitutions and substitution and waivers of requirements for admission and graduation. Students with LD may take up to 18 credit hours per semester; 12 credit hours per semester are required to maintain full-time status; 6 credit hours per semester are required to be eligible for financial aid.

Counseling and advisement Career counseling and individual counseling are available.

Auxiliary aids and services *Aids:* screen-enlarging programs, tape recorders, taped textbooks. *Services and accommodations:* advocates, alternative test arrangements, readers, note-takers, and scribes.

ADD/ADHD Students with ADD/ADHD are eligible for the same services available to students with LD, as well as distraction-free testing environments.

Application *Required:* high school transcript and Texas Academic Skills Program. Upon application, documentation of need for special services should be sent only to your LD program or unit. Upon acceptance, documentation of need for special services should be sent only to your LD program or unit. *Application deadline (institutional):* 9/21 for fall and 1/24 for spring. *Application deadline (LD program):* rolling/continuous for fall and rolling/continuous for spring.

LD program contact Patricia E. Moran, Director, 902 College Avenue, Brenham, TX 77833. *Phone:* 409-830-4157. *Fax:* 409-830-4110. *E-mail:* pmoran@mailroom.blinncol.edu.

Application contact Ashley Brinkoeter, Coordinator, Recruitment and Admissions, Blinn College, 902 College Avenue, Brenham, TX 77833-4049. *Phone:* 409-830-4152. *Web address:* http://www.blinncol.edu/.

BREVARD COMMUNITY COLLEGE
Cocoa, Florida

Students with LD Served by Program	300	ADD/ADHD Services	✓
Staff	3 full-time, 4 part-time	Summer Preparation Program	n/a
LD Program or Service Fee	n/a	Alternative Test Arrangements	✓
LD Program Began	1984	LD Student Organization	n/a

Office for Students with Disabilities began offering services in 1984. The program serves approximately 300 undergraduate students. Faculty consists of 3 full-time and 4 part-time staff members. Services are provided by academic advisers, LD specialists, and professional tutors.

Policies The college has written policies regarding course substitutions and substitution and waivers of requirements for admission and graduation. Students with LD may take up to 18 credit hours per semester; 12 credit hours per semester are required to maintain full-time status; 6 credit hours per semester are required to be eligible for financial aid.

Diagnostic testing Available for auditory processing, spelling, handwriting, spoken language, intelligence, learning strategies, reading, written language, learning styles, visual processing, math, and short and long term memory, processing speed, fluid reasoning.

Subject-area tutoring Available in some subjects. Offered one-on-one by professional tutors.

Counseling and advisement Academic advisement by a staff member affiliated with the program is available.

Auxiliary aids and services *Aids:* calculators, personal computers, personal spelling/word-use assistants (e.g., Franklin Speller), scan and read programs (e.g., Kurzweil), screen-enlarging programs, screen readers, speech recognition programs (e.g., Dragon), tape recorders. *Services and accommodations:* advocates, priority registration, and alternative test arrangements.

ADD/ADHD Students with ADD/ADHD are eligible for the same services available to students with LD, as well as distraction-free study areas and distraction-free testing environments.

Application *Required:* high school transcript and documentation of high school services (e.g., Individualized Education Program [IEP] or 504 plan). *Recommended:* ACT or SAT I (extended-time or untimed test accepted) and psychoeducational report. Upon application, documentation of need for special services should be sent only to your LD program or unit. Upon acceptance, documentation of need for special services should be sent only to your LD program or unit. *Application deadline (institutional):* rolling/continuous for fall and rolling/continuous for spring. *Application deadline (LD program):* rolling/continuous for fall and rolling/continuous for spring.

LD program contact Lyndi K. Fertel, Director, Office for Students with Disabilities, 1519 Clearlake Road, Cocoa, FL 32922. *Phone:* 321-632-1111 Ext. 63606. *Fax:* 321-633-4565. *E-mail:* fertell@brevard.cc.fl.us.

Application contact Margaret Thurman, Supervisor of Admissions, Brevard Community College, 1519 Clearlake Road, Cocoa, FL 32922-6597. *Phone:* 407-632-1111. *Web address:* http://www.brevard.cc.fl.us/.

BRIARWOOD COLLEGE

Southington, Connecticut

Students with LD Served by Program	50	ADD/ADHD Services	✓
Staff	2 part-time	Summer Preparation Program	n/a
LD Program or Service Fee	n/a	Alternative Test Arrangements	✓
LD Program Began	1991	LD Student Organization	n/a

Disability Services began offering services in 1991. The program serves approximately 50 undergraduate students. Faculty consists of 2 part-time staff members. Services are provided by academic advisers, regular education teachers, trained peer tutors, and professional tutors.

Policies Students with LD may take up to 18 credit hours per semester; 12 credit hours per semester are required to maintain full-time status and to be eligible for financial aid.

Basic skills remediation Available in study skills, reading, learning strategies, written language, and math. Offered one-on-one, in small groups, and class-size groups by computer-based instruction, regular education teachers, and trained peer tutors.

Subject-area tutoring Available in most subjects. Offered one-on-one, in small groups, and class-size groups by computer-based instruction, professional tutors, and trained peer tutors.

Counseling and advisement Career counseling and individual counseling are available. Academic advisement by a staff member affiliated with the program is available.

Auxiliary aids and services *Services and accommodations:* alternative test arrangements, readers, note-takers, and scribes.

ADD/ADHD Students with ADD/ADHD are eligible for the same services available to students with LD, as well as distraction-free testing environments.

Application *Required:* high school transcript and psychoeducational report. *Recommended:* participation in extracurricular activities, ACT or SAT I, interview, personal statement, letter(s) of recommendation, and documentation of high school services (e.g., Individualized Education Program [IEP] or 504 plan). Upon application, documentation of need for special services should be sent only to your LD program or unit. Upon acceptance, documentation of need for special services should be sent only to your LD program or unit. *Application deadline (institutional):* rolling/continuous for fall and rolling/continuous for spring. *Application deadline (LD program):* rolling/continuous for fall and rolling/continuous for spring.

LD program contact Cynthia Clark, Coordinator, Disability Services, 2279 Mount Vernon Road, Southington, CT 06489. *Phone:* 860-628-4751. *Fax:* 860-276-8838.

Application contact Briarwood College, 2279 Mount Vernon Road, Southington, CT 06489-1057. *Web address:* http://www.briarwood.edu/.

BRISTOL COMMUNITY COLLEGE

Fall River, Massachusetts

Students with LD Served by Program	160	ADD/ADHD Services	✓
Staff	2 full-time, 1 part-time	Summer Preparation Program	✓
LD Program or Service Fee	n/a	Alternative Test Arrangements	✓
LD Program Began	1975	LD Student Organization	✓

McNair Program for Academic Support and Success (PASS) began offering services in 1975. The program serves approximately 160 undergraduate students. Faculty consists of 2 full-

time staff members and 1 part-time staff member. Services are provided by academic advisers, LD specialists, and trained peer tutors.

Policies The college has written policies regarding course substitutions. Students with LD may take up to 18 credit hours per semester; 12 credit hours per semester are required to maintain full-time status; 6 credit hours per semester are required to be eligible for financial aid.

Special preparation or orientation Optional summer program offered prior to entering college. Optional orientation held during summer prior to enrollment.

Diagnostic testing Available for study skills, reading, written language, and learning styles.

Subject-area tutoring Available in most subjects. Offered one-on-one and in small groups by trained peer tutors.

Special courses Available in study skills, reading, math, and student development seminar. Most courses are offered for credit; most enter into overall grade point average.

Counseling and advisement Individual counseling, small-group counseling, and support groups are available. Academic advisement by a staff member affiliated with the program is available.

Auxiliary aids and services *Aids:* calculators, personal spelling/word-use assistants (e.g., Franklin Speller), scan and read programs (e.g., Kurzweil), screen-enlarging programs, screen readers, speech recognition programs (e.g., Dragon), tape recorders, taped textbooks. *Services and accommodations:* alternative test arrangements, readers, note-takers, and scribes.

Student organization There is a student organization for students with LD.

ADD/ADHD Students with ADD/ADHD are eligible for the same services available to students with LD, as well as distraction-free testing environments.

Application *Required:* high school transcript. *Recommended:* participation in extracurricular activities, ACT or SAT I (extended-time or untimed test accepted), interview, personal statement, letter(s) of recommendation, separate application to your LD program or unit, psychoeducational report (3 years old or less), and documentation of high school services (e.g., Individualized Education Program [IEP] or 504 plan). Upon application, documentation of need for special services should be sent only to your LD program or unit. Upon acceptance, documentation of need for special services should be sent only to your LD program or unit. *Application deadline (institutional):* 6/5 for fall and 12/15 for spring. *Application deadline (LD program):* rolling/continuous for fall and rolling/continuous for spring.

LD program contact Denyse Oliveira, Programs Specialist, 777 Elsbree Street, Fall River, MA 02720. *Phone:* 508-678-2811 Ext. 2589. *Fax:* 508-730-3297. *E-mail:* doliveir@bristol.mass.edu.

Application contact Bristol Community College, 777 Elsbree Street, Fall River, MA 02720-7395. *Web address:* http://www.bristol.mass.edu/.

BROOME COMMUNITY COLLEGE

Binghamton, New York

Students with LD Served by Program	150	ADD/ADHD Services	✓
Staff	8 full-time, 8 part-time	Summer Preparation Program	n/a
LD Program or Service Fee	n/a	Alternative Test Arrangements	✓
LD Program Began	1979	LD Student Organization	✓

Student Support Services began offering services in 1979. The program serves approximately 150 undergraduate students. Faculty consists of 8 full-time and 8 part-time staff members. Services are provided by academic advisers, remediation/learning specialists, counselors, diagnostic specialists, LD specialists, trained peer tutors, and professional tutors.

Policies The college has written policies regarding course substitutions and substitution and waivers of requirements for admission and graduation. Students with LD may take up to 21 credit hours per semester; 3 credit hours per semester are required to be eligible for financial aid.

Special preparation or orientation Optional orientation held before classes begin, after classes begin, during summer prior to enrollment, and individually by special arrangement.

Diagnostic testing Available for auditory processing, motor skills, spelling, spoken language, personality, study skills, learning strategies, reading, written language, learning styles, social skills, visual processing, and math.

Basic skills remediation Available in study skills, computer skills, reading, time management, visual processing, learning strategies, spelling, written language, math, and spoken language. Offered one-on-one, in small groups, and class-size groups by computer-based instruction, regular education teachers, professional tutors, and trained peer tutors.

Subject-area tutoring Available in all subjects. Offered one-on-one, in small groups, and class-size groups by computer-based instruction, professional tutors, and trained peer tutors.

Special courses Available in career planning, oral communication skills, study skills, college survival skills, practical computer skills, test taking, reading, time management, learning strategies, math, stress management, and written composition skills. Some courses are offered for credit; some enter into overall grade point average.

Counseling and advisement Career counseling, individual counseling, and support groups are available. Academic advisement by a staff member affiliated with the program is available.

Auxiliary aids and services *Aids:* calculators, personal spelling/word-use assistants (e.g., Franklin Speller), scan and read programs (e.g., Kurzweil), screen-enlarging programs, screen readers, speech recognition programs (e.g., Dragon), tape recorders, taped textbooks. *Services and accommodations:* priority registration, alternative test arrangements, readers, note-takers, and scribes.

Student organization There is a student organization for students with LD.

ADD/ADHD Students with ADD/ADHD are eligible for the same services available to students with LD, as well as distraction-free testing environments and support groups for ADD/ADHD.

Application *Required:* high school transcript. Upon application, documentation of need for special services should be sent only to your LD program or unit. *Application deadline (institutional):* rolling/continuous for fall and rolling/continuous for spring. *Application deadline (LD program):* rolling/continuous for fall and rolling/continuous for spring.

LD program contact Bruce E. Pomeroy, Director, Student Support Services, PO Box 1017, Binghamton, NY 13760. *Phone:* 607-778-5234. *Fax:* 607-778-5562. *E-mail:* pomeroy_b@sunybroome.edu.

Application contact Anthony Fiorelli, Director of Admissions, Broome Community College, PO Box 1017, Binghamton, NY 13902-1017. *Phone:* 607-778-5001. *Web address:* http://www.sunybroome.edu/.

BROWARD COMMUNITY COLLEGE
Fort Lauderdale, Florida

Students with LD Served by Program	300	ADD/ADHD Services	✓
Staff	6 full-time, 54 part-time	Summer Preparation Program	n/a
LD Program or Service Fee	n/a	Alternative Test Arrangements	✓
LD Program Began	1975	LD Student Organization	✓

Office of Disability Services began offering services in 1975. The program serves approximately 300 undergraduate students. Faculty consists of 6 full-time and 54 part-time staff members. Services are provided by graduate assistants/students, LD specialists, trained peer tutors, professional tutors, and Disability Services advisors and specialists.

Policies The college has written policies regarding course substitutions and substitution and waivers of requirements for admission and graduation. Students with LD may take up to 18 semester hours per semester; 12 semester hours per semester are required to maintain full-time status. LD services are also available to graduate students.

Subject-area tutoring Available in all subjects. Offered one-on-one by professional tutors, graduate assistants/students, trained peer tutors, and LD specialists.

Auxiliary aids and services *Aids:* calculators, personal spelling/word-use assistants (e.g., Franklin Speller), scan and read programs (e.g., Kurzweil), screen-enlarging programs, screen readers, speech recognition programs (e.g., Dragon), tape recorders, taped textbooks. *Services and accommodations:* advocates, alternative test arrangements, readers, note-takers, scribes, and extra time for completion of assignments.

Student organization There is a student organization for students with LD.

ADD/ADHD Students with ADD/ADHD are eligible for the same services available to students with LD, as well as distraction-free study areas and distraction-free testing environments.

Application *Required:* high school transcript and high school diploma or GED. *Recommended:* interview. Upon application, documentation of need for special services should be sent only to your LD program or unit. Upon acceptance, documentation of need for special services should be sent only to your LD program or unit. *Application deadline (institutional):* rolling/continuous for fall and rolling/continuous for spring. *Application deadline (LD program):* rolling/continuous for fall and rolling/continuous for spring.

LD program contact Jean L. McCormick, Director of Disability Services, 225 East Las Olas Boulevard, Fort Lauderdale, FL 33301. *Phone:* 954-761-7555. *Fax:* 954-761-7492. *E-mail:* jmccormi@broward.cc.fl.us.

Application contact Broward Community College, 225 East Las Olas Boulevard, Fort Lauderdale, FL 33301-2298. *Web address:* http://www.broward.cc.fl.us/.

BUNKER HILL COMMUNITY COLLEGE
Boston, Massachusetts

Students with LD Served by Program	80	ADD/ADHD Services	✓
Staff	1 full-time, 2 part-time	Summer Preparation Program	✓
LD Program or Service Fee	n/a	Alternative Test Arrangements	✓
LD Program Began	1995	LD Student Organization	✓

Bunker Hill Community College (continued)

Disability Support Services began offering services in 1995. The program serves approximately 80 undergraduate students. Faculty consists of 1 full-time and 2 part-time staff members. Services are provided by counselors, diagnostic specialists, and graduate assistants/students.

Policies Students with LD may take up to 12 credits per semester; 6 credits per semester are required to be eligible for financial aid.

Special preparation or orientation Optional summer program offered prior to entering college. Optional orientation held individually by special arrangement.

Basic skills remediation Available in reading, learning strategies, and written language. Offered in class-size groups by regular education teachers and trained peer tutors.

Subject-area tutoring Available in most subjects. Offered one-on-one by computer-based instruction and trained peer tutors.

Counseling and advisement Individual counseling is available.

Auxiliary aids and services *Aids:* scan and read programs (e.g., Kurzweil), screen-enlarging programs, tape recorders, taped textbooks. *Services and accommodations:* advocates, alternative test arrangements, readers, note-takers, and scribes.

Student organization There is a student organization for students with LD.

ADD/ADHD Students with ADD/ADHD are eligible for the same services available to students with LD

Application *Required:* high school transcript and documentation of high school services (e.g., Individualized Education Program [IEP] or 504 plan). Upon application, documentation of need for special services should be sent only to your LD program or unit. Upon acceptance, documentation of need for special services should be sent only to your LD program or unit. *Application deadline (institutional):* rolling/continuous for fall and rolling/continuous for spring. *Application deadline (LD program):* rolling/continuous for fall and rolling/continuous for spring.

LD program contact Dr. Albert B. Curtis, Coordinator of Disability Support Services, 250 New Rutherford Avenue, Boston, MA 02129-2956. *Phone:* 617-228-2234. *Fax:* 617-228-3407. *E-mail:* acurtis@bhcc.state.ma.us.

Application contact Chris Jones, Admissions Recruiter, Bunker Hill Community College, 250 New Rutherford Avenue, Boston, MA 02129. *Phone:* 617-228-2000. *Web address:* http://www.bhcc.state.ma.us/.

BUTLER COUNTY COMMUNITY COLLEGE

El Dorado, Kansas

Students with LD Served by Program	351	ADD/ADHD Services	n/a
Staff	1 full-time, 1 part-time	Summer Preparation Program	n/a
LD Program or Service Fee	n/a	Alternative Test Arrangements	✓
LD Program Began	1991	LD Student Organization	n/a

Special Needs Office began offering services in 1991. The program serves approximately 351 undergraduate students. Faculty consists of 1 full-time and 1 part-time staff member. Services are provided by LD specialists.

Policies Students with LD may take up to 18 credit hours per semester; 9 credit hours per semester are required to be eligible for financial aid.

Special preparation or orientation Required orientation held individually by special arrangement.

Basic skills remediation Available in reading, time management, visual processing, learning strategies, spelling, written language, and math. Offered one-on-one by regular education teachers and trained peer tutors.

Subject-area tutoring Available in most subjects. Offered one-on-one and in small groups by trained peer tutors.

Counseling and advisement Individual counseling is available.

Auxiliary aids and services *Aids:* scan and read programs (e.g., Kurzweil), tape recorders. *Services and accommodations:* alternative test arrangements, readers, and note-takers.

Application *Required:* high school transcript and psychoeducational report. Upon application, documentation of need for special services should be sent only to your LD program or unit. Upon acceptance, documentation of need for special services should be sent only to your LD program or unit. *Application deadline (institutional):* rolling/continuous for fall and rolling/continuous for spring. *Application deadline (LD program):* rolling/continuous for fall and rolling/continuous for spring.

LD program contact Liane Fowler, Director, Special Needs, 901 South Haverhill Road, El Dorado, KS 67042. *Fax:* 316-322-3109. *E-mail:* lfowler@butler.buccc.cc.ks.us.

Application contact Paul Kyle, Director of Enrollment Management, Butler County Community College, 901 South Haverhill Road, El Dorado, KS 67042-3280. *Phone:* 316-321-2222 Ext. 163. *Web address:* http://www.buccc.cc.ks.us/.

CALHOUN COMMUNITY COLLEGE

Decatur, Alabama

Students with LD Served by Program	100	ADD/ADHD Services	✓
Staff	1 full-time, 1 part-time	Summer Preparation Program	n/a
LD Program or Service Fee	n/a	Alternative Test Arrangements	✓
LD Program Began	1980	LD Student Organization	✓

Services for Students with Disabilities began offering services in 1980. The program serves approximately 100 undergraduate students. Faculty consists of 1 full-time and 1 part-time staff member. Services are provided by counselors and LD specialists.

Policies The college has written policies regarding course substitutions. 6 credit hours per semester are required to be eligible for financial aid.

Special preparation or orientation Optional orientation held individually by special arrangement.

Counseling and advisement Career counseling, individual counseling, and support groups are available.

Auxiliary aids and services *Aids:* calculators, personal spelling/word-use assistants (e.g., Franklin Speller), scan and read programs (e.g., Kurzweil), screen-enlarging programs, screen readers, speech recognition programs (e.g., Dragon), tape recorders, taped textbooks, lap-top word processors. *Services and accommodations:* priority registration, alternative test arrangements, readers, note-takers, and scribes.

Student organization There is a student organization for students with LD.

ADD/ADHD Students with ADD/ADHD are eligible for the same services available to students with LD, as well as distraction-free testing environments and support groups for ADD/ADHD.

Application *Required:* high school transcript, separate application to your LD program or unit, psychoeducational report, and documentation of high school services (e.g., Individualized Education Program [IEP] or 504 plan). Upon application, documentation of need for special services should be sent only to your LD program or unit. Upon acceptance, documentation of need for special services should be sent only to your LD program or unit. *Application deadline (institutional):* rolling/continuous for fall and rolling/continuous for spring. *Application deadline (LD program):* rolling/continuous for fall and rolling/continuous for spring.

LD program contact Virginia H. Smith, Counselor, PO Box 2216, Decatur, AL 35609-2216. *Phone:* 256-306-2633. *Fax:* 256-350-2656. *E-mail:* vhs@calhoun.cc.al.us.

Application contact Patricia Landers, Admissions Receptionist, Calhoun Community College, PO Box 2216, Decatur, AL 35609-2216. *Phone:* 256-306-2593.

CASPER COLLEGE
Casper, Wyoming

Students with LD Served by Program	50	ADD/ADHD Services	✓
Staff	1 full-time, 1 part-time	Summer Preparation Program	n/a
LD Program or Service Fee	n/a	Alternative Test Arrangements	✓
LD Program Began	1988	LD Student Organization	n/a

Student Services began offering services in 1988. The program serves approximately 50 undergraduate students. Faculty consists of 1 full-time and 1 part-time staff member. Services are provided by academic advisers, counselors, regular education teachers, diagnostic specialists, and trained peer tutors.

Policies 12 credit hours per semester are required to maintain full-time status; 6 credit hours per semester are required to be eligible for financial aid.

Basic skills remediation Available in study skills, computer skills, reading, time management, learning strategies, spelling, written language, and math. Offered one-on-one and in class-size groups by computer-based instruction, regular education teachers, and special education teachers.

Subject-area tutoring Available in most subjects. Offered one-on-one by trained peer tutors.

Counseling and advisement Career counseling and individual counseling are available. Academic advisement by a staff member affiliated with the program is available.

Auxiliary aids and services *Aids:* calculators, personal spelling/word-use assistants (e.g., Franklin Speller), scan and read programs (e.g., Kurzweil), screen-enlarging programs, screen readers, speech recognition programs (e.g., Dragon), tape recorders, taped textbooks. *Services and accommodations:* advocates, priority registration, alternative test arrangements, readers, note-takers, and scribes.

ADD/ADHD Students with ADD/ADHD are eligible for the same services available to students with LD, as well as distraction-free testing environments.

Application *Required:* high school transcript and GED. Upon acceptance, documentation of need for special services should be sent only to your LD program or unit. *Application deadline (institutional):* rolling/continuous for fall and rolling/continuous for spring. *Application deadline (LD program):* rolling/continuous for fall and rolling/continuous for spring.

LD program contact Ann Loader, Individual Learning Specialist, 125 College Drive, Casper, WY 82601. *Phone:* 307-268-2557. *Fax:* 307-268-2444. *E-mail:* aloader@admin.cc.whcn.edu.

Application contact Casper College, 125 College Drive, Casper, WY 82601-4699. *Web address:* http://www.cc.whecn.edu/.

CATAWBA VALLEY COMMUNITY COLLEGE
Hickory, North Carolina

Students with LD Served by Program	20	ADD/ADHD Services	✓
Staff	1 part-time	Summer Preparation Program	✓
LD Program or Service Fee	n/a	Alternative Test Arrangements	✓
LD Program Began	n/a	LD Student Organization	n/a

Program for Students with Disabilities serves approximately 20 undergraduate students. Faculty consists of 1 part-time staff member. Services are provided by academic advisers, counselors, and LD specialists.

Policies Students with LD may take up to 18 credit hours per semester; 12 credit hours per semester are required to maintain full-time status and to be eligible for financial aid.

Special preparation or orientation Optional summer program offered prior to entering college. Required orientation held individually by special arrangement.

Basic skills remediation Available in study skills, computer skills, reading, time management, learning strategies, spelling, written language, and math. Offered in class-size groups by regular education teachers.

Subject-area tutoring Available in most subjects. Offered one-on-one by computer-based instruction, professional tutors, and trained peer tutors.

Special courses Available in college survival skills, reading, math, and written composition skills. Some courses are offered for credit; some enter into overall grade point average.

Counseling and advisement Career counseling and individual counseling are available. Academic advisement by a staff member affiliated with the program is available.

Auxiliary aids and services *Aids:* personal computers, tape recorders, taped textbooks. *Services and accommodations:* alternative test arrangements, readers, and note-takers.

ADD/ADHD Students with ADD/ADHD are eligible for the same services available to students with LD, as well as distraction-free testing environments.

Application *Required:* high school transcript, interview, and psychoeducational report (3 years old or less). *Recommended:* documentation of high school services (e.g., Individualized Education Program [IEP] or 504 plan). Upon application, documentation of need for special services should be sent only to your LD program or unit. Upon acceptance, documentation of need for special services should be sent only to your LD program or unit. *Application deadline (institutional):* rolling/continuous for fall and rolling/continuous for spring. *Application deadline (LD program):* rolling/continuous for fall and rolling/continuous for spring.

LD program contact LaDonna T. Goodson, Director of Counseling Services, 2550 Highway 70 SE, Hickory, NC 28602. *Phone:* 828-327-7000 Ext. 4266. *Fax:* 828-327-7276. *E-mail:* lgoodson@cvcc.cc.nc.us.

Application contact Catawba Valley Community College, 2550 Highway 70 SE, Hickory, NC 28602-9699. *Web address:* http://www.cvcc.cc.nc.us/.

CENTRAL COMMUNITY COLLEGE-HASTINGS CAMPUS

Hastings, Nebraska

Students with LD Served by Program	115	ADD/ADHD Services	✓
Staff	1 full-time, 1 part-time	Summer Preparation Program	✓
LD Program or Service Fee	n/a	Alternative Test Arrangements	✓
LD Program Began	1994	LD Student Organization	n/a

Educational Support Services began offering services in 1994. The program serves approximately 115 undergraduate students. Faculty consists of 1 full-time and 1 part-time staff member. Services are provided by academic advisers, counselors, regular education teachers, graduate assistants/students, trained peer tutors, and professional tutors.

Policies 6 credit hours per semester are required to be eligible for financial aid.

Special preparation or orientation Optional summer program offered prior to entering college. Held before classes begin.

Diagnostic testing Available for personality, reading, written language, learning styles, and math.

Subject-area tutoring Available in all subjects. Offered one-on-one and in small groups by trained peer tutors.

Counseling and advisement Career counseling and individual counseling are available. Academic advisement by a staff member affiliated with the program is available.

Auxiliary aids and services *Aids:* calculators, personal computers, personal spelling/word-use assistants (e.g., Franklin Speller), scan and read programs (e.g., Kurzweil), screen-enlarging programs, screen readers, speech recognition programs (e.g., Dragon), tape recorders, taped textbooks. *Services and accommodations:* alternative test arrangements and note-takers.

ADD/ADHD Students with ADD/ADHD are eligible for the same services available to students with LD

Application *Required:* high school transcript, separate application to your LD program or unit, psychoeducational report, documentation of high school services (e.g., Individualized Education Program [IEP] or 504 plan), and medical documentation if appropriate. *Recommended:* interview and personal statement. Upon application, documentation of need for special services should be sent only to your LD program or unit. Upon acceptance, documentation of need for special services should be sent only to your LD program or unit. *Application deadline (institutional):* rolling/continuous for fall and rolling/continuous for spring. *Application deadline (LD program):* rolling/continuous for fall and rolling/continuous for spring.

LD program contact Robert Shields, Counselor, PO Box 1024, Hastings, NE 68902-1024. *Phone:* 402-461-2423. *Fax:* 402-460-2138. *E-mail:* rshields@cccneb.edu.

Application contact Central Community College-Hastings Campus, PO Box 1024, Hastings, NE 68902-1024. *E-mail:* myehsts@cccadm.cccneb.edu. *Web address:* http://www.cccneb.edu/.

CENTRAL COMMUNITY COLLEGE-PLATTE CAMPUS

Columbus, Nebraska

Students with LD Served by Program	80	ADD/ADHD Services	✓
Staff	1 full-time, 2 part-time	Summer Preparation Program	n/a
LD Program or Service Fee	n/a	Alternative Test Arrangements	✓
LD Program Began	1990	LD Student Organization	n/a

Special Populations Office began offering services in 1990. The program serves approximately 80 undergraduate students. Faculty consists of 1 full-time and 2 part-time staff members. Services are provided by academic advisers, regular education teachers, counselors, remediation/learning specialists, and trained peer tutors.

Special preparation or orientation Optional orientation held before registration, before classes begin, and during summer prior to enrollment.

Diagnostic testing Available for auditory processing, motor skills, spelling, handwriting, neuropsychological, spoken language, intelligence, personality, study skills, learning strategies, reading, written language, learning styles, social skills, visual processing, and math.

Basic skills remediation Available in study skills, computer skills, reading, time management, social skills, learning strategies, written language, math, and college survival. Offered in class-size groups by computer-based instruction and regular education teachers.

Subject-area tutoring Available in all subjects. Offered one-on-one and in small groups by computer-based instruction, trained peer tutors, and developmental education faculty.

Special courses Available in career planning, oral communication skills, study skills, college survival skills, practical computer skills, test taking, reading, time management, learning strategies, self-advocacy, and stress management. Some courses are offered for credit; some enter into overall grade point average.

Counseling and advisement Career counseling and small-group counseling are available. Academic advisement by a staff member affiliated with the program is available.

Auxiliary aids and services *Aids:* calculators, personal computers, personal spelling/word-use assistants (e.g., Franklin Speller), scan and read programs (e.g., Kurzweil), screen-enlarging programs, screen readers, speech recognition programs (e.g., Dragon), tape recorders, taped textbooks, large print dictionaries/thesaurus. *Services and accommodations:* advocates, alternative test arrangements, readers, note-takers, and scribes.

ADD/ADHD Students with ADD/ADHD are eligible for the same services available to students with LD, as well as distraction-free study areas and distraction-free testing environments.

Application *Required:* high school transcript, interview, separate application to your LD program or unit, psychoeducational report (3 years old or less), and documentation of high school services (e.g., Individualized Education Program [IEP] or 504 plan). Upon application, documentation of need for special services should be sent only to your LD program or unit. Upon acceptance, documentation of need for special services should be sent only to your LD program or unit. *Application deadline (institutional):* rolling/continuous for fall and rolling/continuous for spring. *Application deadline (LD program):* rolling/continuous for fall and rolling/continuous for spring.

LD program contact Michele Lutz, Assessment Coordinator, 4500 63rd Street, Columbus, NE 68602-1027. *Phone:* 402-562-1240. *Fax:* 402-562-1201. *E-mail:* mlutz@cccneb.edu.

Application contact Central Community College-Platte Campus, PO Box 1027, Columbus, NE 68602-1027. *E-mail:* augpsts@cccadm.gi.cccneb.edu. *Web address:* http://www.cccneb.edu/.

CENTRAL OHIO TECHNICAL COLLEGE
Newark, Ohio

Students with LD Served by Program	70	ADD/ADHD Services	✓
Staff	4 full-time	Summer Preparation Program	n/a
LD Program or Service Fee	n/a	Alternative Test Arrangements	✓
LD Program Began	1983	LD Student Organization	n/a

Office for Disability Services began offering services in 1983. The program serves approximately 70 undergraduate students. Faculty consists of 4 full-time staff members. Services are provided by LD specialists and trained peer tutors.

Policies The college has written policies regarding course substitutions. 12 quarter hours per quarter are required to maintain full-time status; 4 credit hours per quarter are required to be eligible for financial aid. LD services are also available to graduate students.

Diagnostic testing Available for auditory processing, spelling, neuropsychological, intelligence, study skills, learning strategies, reading, written language, learning styles, and visual processing.

Subject-area tutoring Available in most subjects. Offered one-on-one and in small groups by trained peer tutors and LD specialists.

Auxiliary aids and services *Aids:* calculators, scan and read programs (e.g., Kurzweil), screen-enlarging programs, screen readers, speech recognition programs (e.g., Dragon), tape recorders, taped textbooks. *Services and accommodations:* priority registration, alternative test arrangements, readers, note-takers, and scribes.

ADD/ADHD Students with ADD/ADHD are eligible for the same services available to students with LD, as well as distraction-free study areas and distraction-free testing environments.

Application *Recommended:* high school transcript, psychoeducational report, and documentation of high school services (e.g., Individualized Education Program [IEP] or 504 plan). Upon acceptance, documentation of need for special services should be sent only to your LD program or unit. *Application deadline (institutional):* rolling/continuous for fall and rolling/continuous for spring. *Application deadline (LD program):* rolling/continuous for fall and rolling/continuous for spring.

LD program contact Dr. Phyllis E. Thompson, Program Manager, 1179 University Drive, Newark, OH 43055. *Phone:* 740-366-9246. *Fax:* 740-364-9641. *E-mail:* thompson.33@osu.edu.

Application contact Admissions Representative, Central Ohio Technical College, 1179 University Drive, Newark, OH 43055-1767. *Phone:* 740-366-9222. *E-mail:* lnelson@bigvax.newark.ohio-state.edu. *Web address:* http://www.cotc.tec.oh.us/.

CHARLES STEWART MOTT COMMUNITY COLLEGE
Flint, Michigan

Students with LD Served by Program	90	ADD/ADHD Services	✓
Staff	n/a	Summer Preparation Program	n/a
LD Program or Service Fee	n/a	Alternative Test Arrangements	✓
LD Program Began	1977	LD Student Organization	n/a

Disability Services began offering services in 1977. The program serves approximately 90 undergraduate students. Services are provided by counselors, trained peer tutors, professional tutors, and Support Service Coordinator.

Policies Students with LD may take up to 18 credits per semester; 12 credits per semester are required to maintain full-time status.

Counseling and advisement Career counseling, individual counseling, and coping with disability are available.

Auxiliary aids and services *Aids:* calculators, personal computers, personal spelling/word-use assistants (e.g., Franklin Speller), scan and read programs (e.g., Kurzweil), screen-enlarging programs, screen readers, speech recognition programs (e.g., Dragon), tape recorders, taped textbooks. *Services and accommodations:* advocates, alternative test arrangements, readers, note-takers, scribes, and course modifications.

ADD/ADHD Students with ADD/ADHD are eligible for the same services available to students with LD, as well as distraction-free testing environments.

Application *Required:* separate application to your LD program or unit, psychoeducational report (3 years old or less), and documentation of high school services (e.g., Individualized Education Program [IEP] or 504 plan). Upon application, documentation of need for special services should be sent only to your LD program or unit. *Application deadline (institutional):* rolling/continuous for fall and rolling/continuous for spring. *Application deadline (LD program):* rolling/continuous for fall and rolling/continuous for spring.

LD program contact Julie Dudis, Support Services Coordinator, 1401 East Court Street, Flint, MI 48503. *Phone:* 810-762-0399. *Fax:* 810-232-9520.

Application contact Executive Director of Admissions, Recruitment, and Articulation, Charles Stewart Mott Community College, 1401 East Court Street, Flint, MI 48503-2089. *Phone:* 810-762-0316. *Web address:* http://www.mcc.edu/.

CHATTANOOGA STATE TECHNICAL COMMUNITY COLLEGE
Chattanooga, Tennessee

Students with LD Served by Program	250	ADD/ADHD Services	✓
Staff	5 full-time, 1 part-time	Summer Preparation Program	n/a
LD Program or Service Fee	n/a	Alternative Test Arrangements	✓
LD Program Began	1990	LD Student Organization	✓

Disabilities Support Services began offering services in 1990. The program serves approximately 250 undergraduate students. Faculty consists of 5 full-time staff members and 1 part-time staff member. Services are provided by academic advisers, remediation/learning specialists, counselors, special education teachers, LD specialists, and trained peer tutors.

Chattanooga State Technical Community College (continued)

Policies Students with LD may take up to 19 credit hours per semester; 12 credit hours per semester are required to maintain full-time status and to be eligible for financial aid.

Special preparation or orientation Optional orientation held before registration and individually by special arrangement.

Subject-area tutoring Available in most subjects. Offered one-on-one and in small groups by trained peer tutors and LD specialists.

Counseling and advisement Career counseling, individual counseling, small-group counseling, and support groups are available. Academic advisement by a staff member affiliated with the program is available.

Auxiliary aids and services *Aids:* calculators, personal computers, scan and read programs (e.g., Kurzweil), screen-enlarging programs, screen readers, speech recognition programs (e.g., Dragon), tape recorders, taped textbooks. *Services and accommodations:* alternative test arrangements, readers, note-takers, and scribes.

Student organization There is a student organization for students with LD.

ADD/ADHD Students with ADD/ADHD are eligible for the same services available to students with LD, as well as distraction-free study areas, distraction-free testing environments, personal coach or mentors, and support groups for ADD/ADHD.

Application *Required:* high school transcript, ACT or SAT I (extended-time or untimed test accepted), separate application to your LD program or unit, and psychoeducational report (5 years old or less). *Recommended:* documentation of high school services (e.g., Individualized Education Program [IEP] or 504 plan). Upon application, documentation of need for special services should be sent only to your LD program or unit. Upon acceptance, documentation of need for special services should be sent only to your LD program or unit. *Application deadline (institutional):* rolling/continuous for fall and rolling/continuous for spring. *Application deadline (LD program):* rolling/continuous for fall and rolling/continuous for spring.

LD program contact Kathy Lutes, Director, Disabilities Support Services, 4501 Amnicola Highway, Chattanooga, TN 37406. *Phone:* 423-697-4452. *Fax:* 423-697-3132. *E-mail:* lutes@cstcc.cc.tn.us.

Application contact Chattanooga State Technical Community College, 4501 Amnicola Highway, Chattanooga, TN 37406-1097. *E-mail:* admsis@cstcc.cc.tn.us. *Web address:* http://www.cstcc.cc.tn.us/.

CHEMEKETA COMMUNITY COLLEGE
Salem, Oregon

Students with LD Served by Program	150	ADD/ADHD Services	✓
Staff	2 full-time, 1 part-time	Summer Preparation Program	n/a
LD Program or Service Fee	n/a	Alternative Test Arrangements	✓
LD Program Began	1975	LD Student Organization	n/a

Services for Students with Disabilities began offering services in 1975. The program serves approximately 150 undergraduate students. Faculty consists of 2 full-time staff members and 1 part-time staff member. Services are provided by academic advisers, remediation/learning specialists, counselors, diagnostic specialists, and trained peer tutors.

Policies The college has written policies regarding course substitutions, grade forgiveness, and substitution and waivers of requirements for admission and graduation.

Subject-area tutoring Available in most subjects. Offered one-on-one, in small groups, and class-size groups by computer-based instruction, professional tutors, and trained peer tutors.

Counseling and advisement Career counseling and individual counseling are available. Academic advisement by a staff member affiliated with the program is available.

Auxiliary aids and services *Aids:* calculators, personal spelling/word-use assistants (e.g., Franklin Speller), scan and read programs (e.g., Kurzweil), screen-enlarging programs, screen readers, speech recognition programs (e.g., Dragon), tape recorders, taped textbooks. *Services and accommodations:* advocates, priority registration, alternative test arrangements, readers, note-takers, and scribes.

ADD/ADHD Students with ADD/ADHD are eligible for the same services available to students with LD, as well as distraction-free study areas, distraction-free testing environments and personal coach or mentors.

Application *Recommended:* high school transcript and participation in extracurricular activities. Upon application, documentation of need for special services should be sent only to your LD program or unit. Upon acceptance, documentation of need for special services should be sent only to your LD program or unit.

LD program contact Michael Duggan, Program Chair of Disability Services, 4000 Lancaster Drive NE, PO Box 14007, Salem, OR 97309. *Phone:* 503-399-5192. *Fax:* 503-399-2519. *E-mail:* dugm@chemeketa.edu.

Application contact Carolyn Brownell, Admissions Specialist, Chemeketa Community College, 4000 Lancaster Drive, NE, Salem, OR 97309-7070. *Phone:* 503-399-5006. *E-mail:* broc@chemek.cc.or.us. *Web address:* http://www.chemek.cc.or.us/.

CHESAPEAKE COLLEGE
Wye Mills, Maryland

Students with LD Served by Program	60	ADD/ADHD Services	✓
Staff	1 full-time	Summer Preparation Program	n/a
LD Program or Service Fee	n/a	Alternative Test Arrangements	✓
LD Program Began	1983	LD Student Organization	n/a

Services for Students with Disabilities began offering services in 1983. The program serves approximately 60 undergraduate students. Faculty consists of 1 full-time staff member. Services are provided by regular education teachers, counselors, and professional tutors.

Policies Students with LD may take up to 18 credit/load hours per semester; 12 credit/load hours per semester are required to maintain full-time status; 3 credit/load hours per semester are required to be eligible for financial aid.

Subject-area tutoring Available in all subjects. Offered one-on-one by professional tutors.

Counseling and advisement Career counseling, individual counseling, and transfer counseling are available.

Auxiliary aids and services *Aids:* scan and read programs (e.g., Kurzweil), screen-enlarging programs, speech recognition programs (e.g., Dragon), tape recorders. *Services and accommodations:* advocates, priority registration, alternative test arrangements, readers, note-takers, and scribes.

ADD/ADHD Students with ADD/ADHD are eligible for the same services available to students with LD, as well as distraction-free study areas and distraction-free testing environments.

Application *Required:* high school transcript. Upon application, documentation of need for special services should be sent only to your LD program or unit. Upon acceptance, documentation of need for special services should be sent only to your

LD program or unit. *Application deadline (institutional):* rolling/continuous for fall and rolling/continuous for spring. *Application deadline (LD program):* rolling/continuous for fall and rolling/continuous for spring.

LD program contact Joan M. Seitzer, Counselor/Director of Learning Assistance, PO Box 8, Wye Mills, MD 21679. *Phone:* 410-822-5400. *Fax:* 410-827-9466. *E-mail:* www.chesapeake.edu.

Application contact Chesapeake College, PO Box 8, Wye Mills, MD 21679-0008. *E-mail:* richard_midcap@crabpot.chesapeake.edu. *Web address:* http://www.chesapeake.edu/.

CITY COLLEGES OF CHICAGO, HAROLD WASHINGTON COLLEGE
Chicago, Illinois

Students with LD Served by Program	15	ADD/ADHD Services	✓
Staff	1 full-time, 5 part-time	Summer Preparation Program	n/a
LD Program or Service Fee	n/a	Alternative Test Arrangements	✓
LD Program Began	n/a	LD Student Organization	n/a

Special Needs Center serves approximately 15 undergraduate students. Faculty consists of 1 full-time and 5 part-time staff members. Services are provided by Director of Special Needs Center.

Special preparation or orientation Optional orientation held individually by special arrangement.

Auxiliary aids and services *Aids:* personal spelling/word-use assistants (e.g., Franklin Speller), scan and read programs (e.g., Kurzweil), screen-enlarging programs, screen readers, speech recognition programs (e.g., Dragon), tape recorders, taped textbooks. *Services and accommodations:* priority registration, alternative test arrangements, readers, note-takers, and scribes.

ADD/ADHD Students with ADD/ADHD are eligible for the same services available to students with LD, as well as distraction-free testing environments.

Application *Recommended:* high school transcript and ACT or SAT I (extended-time or untimed test accepted). Upon acceptance, documentation of need for special services should be sent only to your LD program or unit. *Application deadline (institutional):* rolling/continuous for fall and rolling/continuous for spring. *Application deadline (LD program):* rolling/continuous for fall and rolling/continuous for spring.

LD program contact Deborah Miles, Director of Special Needs Center, 30 East Lake Street, Chicago, IL 60601. *Phone:* 312-553-6096.

Application contact City Colleges of Chicago, Harold Washington College, 30 East Lake Street, Chicago, IL 60601-2449. *Web address:* http://www.ccc.edu/.

CITY COLLEGES OF CHICAGO, RICHARD J. DALEY COLLEGE
Chicago, Illinois

Students with LD Served by Program	10	ADD/ADHD Services	✓
Staff	1 full-time, 1 part-time	Summer Preparation Program	n/a
LD Program or Service Fee	n/a	Alternative Test Arrangements	✓
LD Program Began	1975	LD Student Organization	✓

Special Needs Program began offering services in 1975. The program serves approximately 10 undergraduate students. Faculty consists of 1 full-time and 1 part-time staff member. Services are provided by academic advisers, counselors, professional tutors, and Special Needs Advisor.

Policies Students with LD may take up to 18 credit hours per semester; 12 credit hours per semester are required to maintain full-time status; 3 credit hours per semester are required to be eligible for financial aid.

Special preparation or orientation Optional orientation held individually by special arrangement.

Basic skills remediation Available in study skills, time management, social skills, and learning strategies. Offered one-on-one by special needs advisor.

Subject-area tutoring Available in all subjects. Offered one-on-one by professional tutors and trained peer tutors.

Counseling and advisement Career counseling, individual counseling, small-group counseling, support groups, and peer counseling are available. Academic advisement by a staff member affiliated with the program is available.

Auxiliary aids and services *Aids:* calculators, scan and read programs (e.g., Kurzweil), screen-enlarging programs, tape recorders. *Services and accommodations:* advocates, priority registration, alternative test arrangements, readers, and note-takers.

Student organization There is a student organization for students with LD.

ADD/ADHD Students with ADD/ADHD are eligible for the same services available to students with LD, as well as distraction-free study areas, distraction-free testing environments and one-on-one tutoring.

Application *Recommended:* high school transcript and participation in extracurricular activities. Upon application, documentation of need for special services should be sent only to your LD program or unit. Upon acceptance, documentation of need for special services should be sent only to your LD program or unit. *Application deadline (institutional):* rolling/continuous for fall and rolling/continuous for spring. *Application deadline (LD program):* rolling/continuous for fall and rolling/continuous for spring.

LD program contact Karen L. Barnett, Special Needs Coordinator, 7500 South Pulaski Road, Room 1111-A1, Chicago, IL 60652. *Phone:* 773-838-7578. *Fax:* 773-838-7524. *E-mail:* kbarnett@cc.edu.

Application contact Karla Reynolds, Registrar, City Colleges of Chicago, Richard J. Daley College, 7500 South Pulaski Road, Chicago, IL 60652-1242. *Phone:* 773-838-7599. *E-mail:* kreynolds@ccc.edu. *Web address:* http://cccweb.cc.edu/daley/home.htm.

CLINTON COMMUNITY COLLEGE
Plattsburgh, New York

Students with LD Served by Program	36	ADD/ADHD Services	✓
Staff	1 full-time, 2 part-time	Summer Preparation Program	n/a
LD Program or Service Fee	n/a	Alternative Test Arrangements	✓
LD Program Began	n/a	LD Student Organization	n/a

Academic Advance Center serves approximately 36 undergraduate students. Faculty consists of 1 full-time and 2 part-time staff members. Services are provided by counselors, remediation/learning specialists, LD specialists, trained peer tutors, and professional tutors.

Clinton Community College (continued)

Auxiliary aids and services *Aids:* calculators, scan and read programs (e.g., Kurzweil), screen-enlarging programs, tape recorders, taped textbooks. *Services and accommodations:* advocates, priority registration, alternative test arrangements, readers, note-takers, and scribes.

ADD/ADHD Students with ADD/ADHD are eligible for the same services available to students with LD, as well as distraction-free testing environments.

Application *Required:* high school transcript. *Recommended:* ACT or SAT I (extended-time or untimed test accepted). Upon application, documentation of need for special services should be sent only to your LD program or unit. Upon acceptance, documentation of need for special services should be sent only to your LD program or unit. *Application deadline (institutional):* rolling/continuous for fall and rolling/continuous for spring. *Application deadline (LD program):* rolling/continuous for fall and rolling/continuous for spring.

LD program contact Laurie Bethka, Learning Resource Specialist, 136 Clinton Point Drive, Plattsburgh, NY 12901. *Phone:* 518-562-4252. *Fax:* 518-562-4178. *E-mail:* racila@clintoncc.suny.edu.

Application contact Robert C. Wood, Associate Dean for Enrollment Management, Clinton Community College, 136 Clinton Point Drive, Plattsburgh, NY 12901-9573. *Phone:* 518-562-4170. *Web address:* http://137.142.42.95/clintoncounty/CCC/ccc.html.

CLOUD COUNTY COMMUNITY COLLEGE
Concordia, Kansas

Students with LD Served by Program	15	ADD/ADHD Services	✓
Staff	2 full-time, 1 part-time	Summer Preparation Program	n/a
LD Program or Service Fee	n/a	Alternative Test Arrangements	✓
LD Program Began	1991	LD Student Organization	n/a

Learning Skills Center began offering services in 1991. The program serves approximately 15 undergraduate students. Faculty consists of 2 full-time staff members and 1 part-time staff member. Services are provided by academic advisers, counselors, regular education teachers, and developmental education specialist.

Policies Students with LD may take up to 18 credit hours per semester; 12 credit hours per semester are required to maintain full-time status; 3 credit hours per semester are required to be eligible for financial aid. LD services are also available to graduate students.

Diagnostic testing Available for study skills, reading, learning styles, and math.

Basic skills remediation Available in study skills, reading, spelling, written language, and math. Offered one-on-one and in small groups by regular education teachers.

Subject-area tutoring Available in most subjects. Offered one-on-one and in small groups by trained peer tutors.

Counseling and advisement Academic advisement by a staff member affiliated with the program is available.

Auxiliary aids and services *Aids:* calculators, personal computers, screen-enlarging programs, screen readers, tape recorders, taped textbooks. *Services and accommodations:* alternative test arrangements, readers, note-takers, and scribes.

ADD/ADHD Students with ADD/ADHD are eligible for the same services available to students with LD, as well as distraction-free study areas and distraction-free testing environments.

Application *Required:* high school transcript. *Recommended:* ACT (extended-time or untimed test accepted), interview, psychoeducational report (3 years old or less), documentation of high school services (e.g., Individualized Education Program [IEP] or 504 plan), and ASSET or ACT. Upon application, documentation of need for special services should be sent only to your LD program or unit. Upon acceptance, documentation of need for special services should be sent only to your LD program or unit. *Application deadline (institutional):* rolling/continuous for fall and rolling/continuous for spring. *Application deadline (LD program):* rolling/continuous for fall and rolling/continuous for spring.

LD program contact Les Hemphill, Director of Advisement and Counseling, 2221 Campus Drive, Concordia, KS 66901. *Phone:* 785-243-1435. *Fax:* 785-243-1043. *E-mail:* llmphill@cloudccc.cc.ks.us.

Application contact Cloud County Community College, 2221 Campus Drive, PO Box 1002, Concordia, KS 66901-1002. *E-mail:* thayer@mg.cloudccc.cc.ks.us. *Web address:* http://www.cloudccc.cc.ks.us/.

COCHISE COLLEGE
Douglas, Arizona

Students with LD Served by Program	60	ADD/ADHD Services	✓
Staff	1 full-time	Summer Preparation Program	n/a
LD Program or Service Fee	n/a	Alternative Test Arrangements	✓
LD Program Began	1990	LD Student Organization	n/a

Special Needs Office began offering services in 1990. The program serves approximately 60 undergraduate students. Faculty consists of 1 full-time staff member. Services are provided by trained peer tutors and ADA coordinator.

Policies The college has written policies regarding course substitutions. Students with LD may take up to 18 credit hours per semester; 12 credit hours per semester are required to maintain full-time status; 6 credit hours per semester are required to be eligible for financial aid.

Special preparation or orientation Optional orientation held individually by special arrangement.

Subject-area tutoring Available in most subjects. Offered one-on-one by trained peer tutors.

Auxiliary aids and services *Aids:* calculators, personal spelling/word-use assistants (e.g., Franklin Speller), screen-enlarging programs, screen readers, speech recognition programs (e.g., Dragon), tape recorders, taped textbooks. *Services and accommodations:* alternative test arrangements, readers, note-takers, and scribes.

ADD/ADHD Students with ADD/ADHD are eligible for the same services available to students with LD, as well as distraction-free testing environments.

Application *Recommended:* psychoeducational report (3 years old or less) and documentation of high school services (e.g., Individualized Education Program [IEP] or 504 plan). Upon application, documentation of need for special services should be sent only to your LD program or unit. Upon acceptance, documentation of need for special services should be sent only to your LD program or unit. *Application deadline (institutional):* rolling/continuous for fall and rolling/continuous for spring. *Application deadline (LD program):* rolling/continuous for fall and rolling/continuous for spring.

LD program contact Mary Kelly, ADA Coordinator, 901 North Colombo Avenue, Sierra Vista, AZ 85635. *Phone:* 520-515-5237. *Fax:* 520-515-5452. *E-mail:* kellym@cochise.cc.az.us.

Application contact Pati Mapp, Admissions Counselor, Cochise College, 4190 West Highway 80, Douglas, AZ 85607-9724. *Phone:* 520-364-0336. *E-mail:* info@tron.cochise.cc.az.us. *Web address:* http://www.cochise.cc.az.us/.

COLLEGE OF LAKE COUNTY
Grayslake, Illinois

Students with LD Served by Program	175	ADD/ADHD Services	✓
Staff	1 full-time, 4 part-time	Summer Preparation Program	n/a
LD Program or Service Fee	n/a	Alternative Test Arrangements	✓
LD Program Began	1985	LD Student Organization	n/a

Special Needs Office began offering services in 1985. The program serves approximately 175 undergraduate students. Faculty consists of 1 full-time and 4 part-time staff members. Services are provided by regular education teachers, LD specialists, and trained peer tutors.

Policies The college has written policies regarding course substitutions. Students with LD may take up to 18 credit hours per semester; 12 credit hours per semester are required to maintain full-time status; 6 credit hours per semester are required to be eligible for financial aid.

Subject-area tutoring Available in most subjects. Offered one-on-one and in small groups by professional tutors, trained peer tutors, and LD specialists.

Auxiliary aids and services *Aids:* calculators, personal computers, personal spelling/word-use assistants (e.g., Franklin Speller), scan and read programs (e.g., Kurzweil), screen-enlarging programs, screen readers, speech recognition programs (e.g., Dragon), tape recorders, taped textbooks. *Services and accommodations:* advocates, alternative test arrangements, readers, note-takers, and scribes.

ADD/ADHD Students with ADD/ADHD are eligible for the same services available to students with LD, as well as distraction-free testing environments.

Application *Required:* interview, separate application to your LD program or unit, psychoeducational report (3 years old or less), and documentation of high school services (e.g., Individualized Education Program [IEP] or 504 plan). *Recommended:* high school transcript. Upon application, documentation of need for special services should be sent only to your LD program or unit. Upon acceptance, documentation of need for special services should be sent only to your LD program or unit. *Application deadline (institutional):* rolling/continuous for fall and rolling/continuous for spring. *Application deadline (LD program):* rolling/continuous for fall and rolling/continuous for spring.

LD program contact Bill Freitag, Coordinator of Special Needs, 19351 West Washington Street, Grayslake, IL 60030. *Phone:* 847-543-2474. *Fax:* 847-223-7690. *E-mail:* lac271@clc.cc.il.us.

Application contact College of Lake County, 19351 West Washington Street, Grayslake, IL 60030-1198. *E-mail:* curtdenny@clc.cc.il.us. *Web address:* http://www.clc.cc.il.us/.

COLLIN COUNTY COMMUNITY COLLEGE DISTRICT
Plano, Texas

Students with LD Served by Program	265	ADD/ADHD Services	✓
Staff	5 full-time	Summer Preparation Program	n/a
LD Program or Service Fee	n/a	Alternative Test Arrangements	✓
LD Program Began	1991	LD Student Organization	n/a

Accommodations at Collin County for Equal Support Services (ACCESS) began offering services in 1991. The program serves approximately 265 undergraduate students. Faculty consists of 5 full-time staff members. Services are provided by academic advisers, remediation/learning specialists, diagnostic specialists, LD specialists, trained peer tutors, and professional tutors.

Policies Students with LD may take up to 18 credit hours per semester; 12 credit hours per semester are required to maintain full-time status; 6 credit hours per semester are required to be eligible for financial aid.

Special preparation or orientation Required orientation held individually by special arrangement.

Diagnostic testing Available for spelling, intelligence, reading, written language, and math.

Basic skills remediation Available in study skills, reading, written language, and math. Offered one-on-one and in class-size groups by computer-based instruction, regular education teachers, and professional tutors.

Subject-area tutoring Available in most subjects. Offered one-on-one by trained peer tutors.

Counseling and advisement Career counseling, individual counseling, small-group counseling, and support groups are available. Academic advisement by a staff member affiliated with the program is available.

Auxiliary aids and services *Aids:* calculators, personal computers, scan and read programs (e.g., Kurzweil), screen-enlarging programs, screen readers, speech recognition programs (e.g., Dragon), tape recorders, taped textbooks. *Services and accommodations:* advocates, priority registration, alternative test arrangements, readers, note-takers, and scribes.

ADD/ADHD Students with ADD/ADHD are eligible for the same services available to students with LD, as well as distraction-free testing environments.

Application *Required:* high school transcript, interview, separate application to your LD program or unit, and psychoeducational report (5 years old or less). *Recommended:* documentation of high school services (e.g., Individualized Education Program [IEP] or 504 plan). Upon application, documentation of need for special services should be sent only to your LD program or unit. Upon acceptance, documentation of need for special services should be sent only to your LD program or unit. *Application deadline (institutional):* rolling/continuous for fall and rolling/continuous for spring. *Application deadline (LD program):* rolling/continuous for fall and rolling/continuous for spring.

LD program contact Dawn Alexander, Learning Disabilities Specialist/Adviser, 2800 East Spring Creek Parkway, Plano, TX 75074. *Phone:* 972-881-5109. *Fax:* 972-881-5896. *E-mail:* dalexander@ccccd.edu.

Application contact Collin County Community College District, 2200 West University Drive, McKinney, TX 75070-2906. *E-mail:* zsbhill@express.ccccd.edu. *Web address:* http://www.ccccd.edu/ccccd.html.

COLORADO NORTHWESTERN COMMUNITY COLLEGE
Rangely, Colorado

Students with LD Served by Program	8	ADD/ADHD Services	✓
Staff	2 full-time	Summer Preparation Program	n/a
LD Program or Service Fee	n/a	Alternative Test Arrangements	✓
LD Program Began	1994	LD Student Organization	n/a

Colorado Northwestern Community College (continued)

Learning Assistance Center began offering services in 1994. The program serves approximately 8 undergraduate students. Faculty consists of 2 full-time staff members. Services are provided by academic advisers, counselors, regular education teachers, special education teachers, trained peer tutors, and professional tutors.

Policies Students with LD may take up to 18 credit hours per semester; 12 credit hours per semester are required to maintain full-time status and to be eligible for financial aid.

Special preparation or orientation Optional orientation held before registration, before classes begin, during summer prior to enrollment, and individually by special arrangement.

Diagnostic testing Available for personality, reading, and math.

Basic skills remediation Available in study skills, reading, time management, learning strategies, written language, and math. Offered one-on-one, in small groups, and class-size groups by regular education teachers, special education teachers, and trained peer tutors.

Subject-area tutoring Available in all subjects. Offered one-on-one and in small groups by computer-based instruction, professional tutors, and trained peer tutors.

Counseling and advisement Career counseling and individual counseling are available. Academic advisement by a staff member affiliated with the program is available.

Auxiliary aids and services *Aids:* calculators, personal computers, speech recognition programs (e.g., Dragon), tape recorders, taped textbooks. *Services and accommodations:* advocates, alternative test arrangements, readers, and note-takers.

ADD/ADHD Students with ADD/ADHD are eligible for the same services available to students with LD, as well as distraction-free study areas and distraction-free testing environments.

Application *Required:* high school transcript. *Recommended:* interview, psychoeducational report, and documentation of high school services (e.g., Individualized Education Program [IEP] or 504 plan). Upon application, documentation of need for special services should be sent only to your LD program or unit. Upon acceptance, documentation of need for special services should be sent only to your LD program or unit. *Application deadline (institutional):* rolling/continuous for fall and rolling/continuous for spring. *Application deadline (LD program):* rolling/continuous for fall and rolling/continuous for spring.

LD program contact Dana Gunderson, Director, 500 Kennedy Drive, Rangely, CO 81648. *Phone:* 970-675-3238. *Fax:* 970-675-3330. *E-mail:* dgunderson@cncc.cc.co.us.

Application contact Colorado Northwestern Community College, 500 Kennedy Drive, Rangely, CO 81648-3598. *E-mail:* thercug@cncc.cc.co.us. *Web address:* http://www.cncc.cc.co.us/.

COLUMBIA BASIN COLLEGE

Pasco, Washington

Students with LD Served by Program	189	ADD/ADHD Services	✓
Staff	2 full-time, 2 part-time	Summer Preparation Program	n/a
LD Program or Service Fee	n/a	Alternative Test Arrangements	✓
LD Program Began	1989	LD Student Organization	n/a

Education Access Disability Resource Center, LD Program began offering services in 1989. The program serves approximately 189 undergraduate students. Faculty consists of 2 full-time and 2 part-time staff members. Services are provided by counselors, regular education teachers, and trained peer tutors.

Policies The college has written policies regarding course substitutions and substitution and waivers of requirements for admission and graduation. Students with LD may take up to 20 credit hours per quarter; 12 credit hours per quarter are required to maintain full-time status; 6 credit hours per quarter are required to be eligible for financial aid.

Special preparation or orientation Optional orientation held before registration.

Basic skills remediation Available in study skills, reading, learning strategies, spelling, written language, math, and vocabulary improvement. Offered in class-size groups by computer-based instruction and regular education teachers.

Subject-area tutoring Available in most subjects. Offered one-on-one by trained peer tutors.

Counseling and advisement Career counseling, individual counseling, and support groups are available.

Auxiliary aids and services *Aids:* scan and read programs (e.g., Kurzweil), screen-enlarging programs, screen readers, speech recognition programs (e.g., Dragon), tape recorders, taped textbooks, specialized software. *Services and accommodations:* advocates, priority registration, alternative test arrangements, readers, note-takers, and scribes.

ADD/ADHD Students with ADD/ADHD are eligible for the same services available to students with LD, as well as distraction-free testing environments and support groups for ADD/ADHD.

Application *Required:* high school transcript, separate application to your LD program or unit, and psychoeducational report. *Recommended:* ASSET test of basic skills. Upon application, documentation of need for special services should be sent only to your LD program or unit. Upon acceptance, documentation of need for special services should be sent only to your LD program or unit. *Application deadline (institutional):* rolling/continuous for fall and rolling/continuous for spring. *Application deadline (LD program):* rolling/continuous for fall and rolling/continuous for spring.

LD program contact Peggy Buchmiller, Director, Diversity Services, 2600 North 20th Avenue, Pasco, WA 99301. *Phone:* 509-547-0511 Ext. 2252. *Fax:* 509-546-0401. *E-mail:* pbuchmiller@cbc2.org.

Application contact Columbia Basin College, 2600 North 20th Avenue, Pasco, WA 99301-3397. *Web address:* http://www.ctc.edu/~cbcwww/.

COLUMBUS STATE COMMUNITY COLLEGE

Columbus, Ohio

Students with LD Served by Program	545	ADD/ADHD Services	✓
Staff	11 full-time	Summer Preparation Program	n/a
LD Program or Service Fee	n/a	Alternative Test Arrangements	✓
LD Program Began	1973	LD Student Organization	n/a

Department of Disability Services began offering services in 1973. The program serves approximately 545 undergraduate students. Faculty consists of 11 full-time staff members. Services are provided by counselors and LD specialists.

Policies Students with LD may take up to 18 credit hours per quarter; 12 credit hours per quarter are required to maintain full-time status; 6 credit hours per quarter are required to be eligible for financial aid.

Special preparation or orientation Optional orientation held before classes begin.

Basic skills remediation Available in study skills, reading, spelling, and math. Offered in class-size groups by regular education teachers and trained peer tutors.

Counseling and advisement Career counseling and individual counseling are available.

Auxiliary aids and services *Aids:* personal computers, scan and read programs (e.g., Kurzweil), screen-enlarging programs, screen readers, tape recorders, taped textbooks. *Services and accommodations:* alternative test arrangements, readers, note-takers, and scribes.

ADD/ADHD Students with ADD/ADHD are eligible for the same services available to students with LD, as well as distraction-free testing environments.

Application *Required:* high school transcript and GED in place of high school transcript. Upon application, documentation of need for special services should be sent only to your LD program or unit. Upon acceptance, documentation of need for special services should be sent only to your LD program or unit. *Application deadline (institutional):* rolling/continuous for fall and rolling/continuous for spring. *Application deadline (LD program):* rolling/continuous for fall and rolling/continuous for spring.

LD program contact Wayne Cocchi, Director, Department of Disability Services, 550 East Spring Street, Columbus, OH 43215. *Phone:* 614-287-2629. *Fax:* 614-287-2558. *E-mail:* wcocchi@cscc.edu.

Application contact Columbus State Community College, Box 1609, Columbus, OH 43216-1609. *Web address:* http://www.cscc.edu/.

COMMUNITY COLLEGE OF AURORA
Aurora, Colorado

Students with LD Served by Program	50	ADD/ADHD Services	✓
Staff	1 full-time, 4 part-time	Summer Preparation Program	n/a
LD Program or Service Fee	n/a	Alternative Test Arrangements	✓
LD Program Began	1983	LD Student Organization	n/a

Disability Services began offering services in 1983. The program serves approximately 50 undergraduate students. Faculty consists of 1 full-time and 4 part-time staff members. Services are provided by academic advisers, remediation/learning specialists, graduate assistants/students, and professional tutors.

Special preparation or orientation Optional orientation held study skills class/Brain Gym.

Subject-area tutoring Available in most subjects. Offered one-on-one and in small groups by professional tutors.

Counseling and advisement Career counseling and individual counseling are available. Academic advisement by a staff member affiliated with the program is available.

Auxiliary aids and services *Aids:* calculators, personal computers, personal spelling/word-use assistants (e.g., Franklin Speller), screen-enlarging programs, screen readers, speech recognition programs (e.g., Dragon), tape recorders, taped textbooks. *Services and accommodations:* alternative test arrangements, readers, note-takers, and scribes.

ADD/ADHD Students with ADD/ADHD are eligible for the same services available to students with LD, as well as distraction-free study areas, distraction-free testing environments and personal coach or mentors.

Application *Required:* high school transcript, interview, and documentation of disability. *Recommended:* participation in extracurricular activities, ACT or SAT I (extended-time or untimed test accepted), psychoeducational report (5 years old or less), and documentation of high school services (e.g., Individualized Education Program [IEP] or 504 plan). Upon application, documentation of need for special services should be sent only to your LD program or unit. Upon acceptance, documentation of

need for special services should be sent only to your LD program or unit. *Application deadline (institutional):* rolling/continuous for fall and rolling/continuous for spring.

LD program contact Reniece Jones, Disability Services Coordinator, 16000 East Centretech Parkway, Suite S-202, Aurora, CO 80011-9036. *Phone:* 303-361-7395. *Fax:* 303-361-4791. *E-mail:* reniece.jones@cca.cccoes.edu.

Application contact Community College of Aurora, 16000 East Centre Tech Parkway, Aurora, CO 80011-9036. *Web address:* http://www.cca.cccoes.edu/.

THE COMMUNITY COLLEGE OF BALTIMORE COUNTY-CATONSVILLE CAMPUS
Catonsville, Maryland

Students with LD Served by Program	185	ADD/ADHD Services	✓
Staff	4 part-time	Summer Preparation Program	n/a
LD Program or Service Fee	n/a	Alternative Test Arrangements	✓
LD Program Began	n/a	LD Student Organization	n/a

Counseling Center, Support Services for Students with Disabilities serves approximately 185 undergraduate students. Faculty consists of 4 part-time staff members. Services are provided by counselors, LD specialists, trained peer tutors, and professional tutors.

Policies Students with LD may take up to 18 credit hours per semester; 12 credit hours per semester are required to maintain full-time status; 6 credit hours per semester are required to be eligible for financial aid.

Subject-area tutoring Available in most subjects. Offered one-on-one by professional tutors and trained peer tutors.

Counseling and advisement Career counseling and individual counseling are available.

Auxiliary aids and services *Aids:* calculators, personal computers, personal spelling/word-use assistants (e.g., Franklin Speller), scan and read programs (e.g., Kurzweil), screen-enlarging programs, screen readers, speech recognition programs (e.g., Dragon), tape recorders, taped textbooks. *Services and accommodations:* advocates, alternative test arrangements, readers, note-takers, and scribes.

ADD/ADHD Students with ADD/ADHD are eligible for the same services available to students with LD, as well as distraction-free testing environments and phonic ear.

Application *Required:* high school transcript and psychoeducational report (3 years old or less). *Recommended:* interview and documentation of high school services (e.g., Individualized Education Program [IEP] or 504 plan). Upon application, documentation of need for special services should be sent only to your LD program or unit. Upon acceptance, documentation of need for special services should be sent only to your LD program or unit. *Application deadline (institutional):* rolling/continuous for fall and rolling/continuous for spring. *Application deadline (LD program):* rolling/continuous for fall and rolling/continuous for spring.

LD program contact Jill B. Hodge, Coordinator of Student Support Services, K Building, Catonsville, MD 21228. *Phone:* 410-455-4718. *Fax:* 410-455-4185.

Application contact The Community College of Baltimore County-Catonsville Campus, 800 South Rolling Road, Catonsville, MD 21228-5381. *E-mail:* aamo@catcc.bitnet. *Web address:* http://www.catmus.cat.ccmd.us/.

THE COMMUNITY COLLEGE OF BALTIMORE COUNTY-ESSEX CAMPUS

Baltimore, Maryland

Students with LD Served by Program	125	ADD/ADHD Services	✓
Staff	2 full-time	Summer Preparation Program	n/a
LD Program or Service Fee	n/a	Alternative Test Arrangements	✓
LD Program Began	1983	LD Student Organization	n/a

Office of Special Services began offering services in 1983. The program serves approximately 125 undergraduate students. Faculty consists of 2 full-time staff members. Services are provided by LD specialists.

Policies The college has written policies regarding course substitutions.

Special preparation or orientation Optional orientation held before classes begin.

Counseling and advisement Individual counseling and support groups are available.

Auxiliary aids and services *Aids:* personal spelling/word-use assistants (e.g., Franklin Speller), scan and read programs (e.g., Kurzweil), screen-enlarging programs, screen readers, speech recognition programs (e.g., Dragon), tape recorders, taped textbooks. *Services and accommodations:* alternative test arrangements, readers, note-takers, and scribes.

ADD/ADHD Students with ADD/ADHD are eligible for the same services available to students with LD, as well as distraction-free testing environments.

Application *Required:* high school transcript and application to CCBC. Upon acceptance, documentation of need for special services should be sent only to your LD program or unit. *Application deadline (institutional):* rolling/continuous for fall and rolling/continuous for spring.

LD program contact Beth Hunsinger, Director, Office of Special Services, 7201 Rossville Boulevard, Baltimore, MD 21237. *Phone:* 410-780-6741. *Fax:* 410-780-6754. *E-mail:* bhunsinger@ccbc.cc.md.us.

Application contact The Community College of Baltimore County-Essex Campus, 7201 Rossville Boulevard, Baltimore, MD 21237-3899. *Web address:* http://www.essex.cc.md.us/.

COMMUNITY COLLEGE OF RHODE ISLAND

Warwick, Rhode Island

Students with LD Served by Program	250	ADD/ADHD Services	✓
Staff	2 full-time, 4 part-time	Summer Preparation Program	n/a
LD Program or Service Fee	n/a	Alternative Test Arrangements	✓
LD Program Began	1980	LD Student Organization	n/a

Office of Academic Accommodations, Access to Opportunity, Linkages and Transitions began offering services in 1980. The program serves approximately 250 undergraduate students. Faculty consists of 2 full-time and 4 part-time staff members. Services are provided by academic advisers and professional tutors.

Policies The college has written policies regarding course substitutions. Students with LD may take up to 18 credit hours per semester; 9 credit hours per semester are required to maintain full-time status; 3 credits per semester are required to be eligible for financial aid.

Subject-area tutoring Available in most subjects. Offered one-on-one by professional tutors.

Counseling and advisement Career counseling and individual counseling are available. Academic advisement by a staff member affiliated with the program is available.

Auxiliary aids and services *Aids:* calculators, personal spelling/word-use assistants (e.g., Franklin Speller), scan and read programs (e.g., Kurzweil), screen-enlarging programs, screen readers, speech recognition programs (e.g., Dragon), tape recorders, assistive listening equipment. *Services and accommodations:* alternative test arrangements, readers, and scribes.

ADD/ADHD Students with ADD/ADHD are eligible for the same services available to students with LD, as well as distraction-free study areas and distraction-free testing environments.

Application *Recommended:* high school transcript. Upon acceptance, documentation of need for special services should be sent only to your LD program or unit. *Application deadline (institutional):* rolling/continuous for fall and rolling/continuous for spring. *Application deadline (LD program):* rolling/continuous for fall and rolling/continuous for spring.

LD program contact Tracy Karasinski400 East Avenue, Warwick, RI 02886. *Phone:* 401-825-2305. *Fax:* 401-825-2282. *E-mail:* tkarasinski@ccri.cc.ri.us.

Application contact Donnamarie Allen, Senior Admissions Officer/Financial Aid Officer, Community College of Rhode Island, 400 East Avenue, Warwick, RI 02886-1807. *Phone:* 401-333-7080. *Web address:* http://www.ccri.cc.ri.us/.

CORNING COMMUNITY COLLEGE

Corning, New York

Students with LD Served by Program	100	ADD/ADHD Services	✓
Staff	1 full-time, 1 part-time	Summer Preparation Program	✓
LD Program or Service Fee	n/a	Alternative Test Arrangements	✓
LD Program Began	1988	LD Student Organization	n/a

Student Disability Services began offering services in 1988. The program serves approximately 100 undergraduate students. Faculty consists of 1 full-time and 1 part-time staff member. Services are provided by academic advisers, remediation/learning specialists, counselors, diagnostic specialists, LD specialists, and trained peer tutors.

Policies 12 credit hours per semester are required to maintain full-time status; 6 credit hours per semester are required to be eligible for financial aid.

Special preparation or orientation Optional summer program offered prior to entering college.

Diagnostic testing Available for auditory processing, spelling, spoken language, intelligence, learning strategies, reading, written language, learning styles, visual processing, and math.

Counseling and advisement Academic advisement by a staff member affiliated with the program is available.

Auxiliary aids and services *Aids:* calculators, personal computers, scan and read programs (e.g., Kurzweil), screen-enlarging programs, screen readers, speech recognition programs (e.g., Dragon), tape recorders, taped textbooks. *Services and accommodations:* advocates, priority registration, alternative test arrangements, readers, note-takers, and scribes.

ADD/ADHD Students with ADD/ADHD are eligible for the same services available to students with LD, as well as distraction-free study areas and distraction-free testing environments.

Application *Required:* high school transcript. Upon application, documentation of need for special services should be sent only to your LD program or unit. Upon acceptance, documentation of need for special services should be sent only to your

LD program or unit. *Application deadline (institutional):* rolling/continuous for fall and rolling/continuous for spring. *Application deadline (LD program):* rolling/continuous for fall and rolling/continuous for spring.

LD program contact Judy Northrop, Coordinator, Student Disability Services, 1 Academic Drive, Corning, NY 14830. *Phone:* 607-962-9262. *Fax:* 607-962-9006. *E-mail:* northrop@corning-cc.edu.

Application contact Corning Community College, One Academic Drive, Corning, NY 14830-3297. *E-mail:* admissions@corning-cc.edu. *Web address:* http://www.corning-cc.edu/.

CRAVEN COMMUNITY COLLEGE
New Bern, North Carolina

Students with LD Served by Program	25	ADD/ADHD Services	✓
Staff	1 full-time, 1 part-time	Summer Preparation Program	n/a
LD Program or Service Fee	n/a	Alternative Test Arrangements	✓
LD Program Began	1985	LD Student Organization	n/a

Academic Skills Center began offering services in 1985. The program serves approximately 25 undergraduate students. Faculty consists of 1 full-time and 1 part-time staff member. Services are provided by academic advisers, trained peer tutors, and professional tutors.

Policies Students with LD may take up to 21 credits per semester; 12 credit hours per semester are required to maintain full-time status and to be eligible for financial aid.

Subject-area tutoring Available in most subjects. Offered one-on-one and in small groups by computer-based instruction, graduate assistants/students, and trained peer tutors.

Counseling and advisement Academic advisement by a staff member affiliated with the program is available.

Auxiliary aids and services *Aids:* personal spelling/word-use assistants (e.g., Franklin Speller), screen-enlarging programs, speech recognition programs (e.g., Dragon), tape recorders. *Services and accommodations:* alternative test arrangements, readers, and note-takers.

ADD/ADHD Students with ADD/ADHD are eligible for the same services available to students with LD, as well as distraction-free testing environments.

Application *Required:* high school transcript and psychoeducational report. Upon application, documentation of need for special services should be sent only to your LD program or unit. Upon acceptance, documentation of need for special services should be sent only to your LD program or unit.

LD program contact Betty Soltow, Director of the Academic Skills Center, 800 College Court, New Bern, NC 28562. *Phone:* 252-638-7294. *Fax:* 252-638-4232. *E-mail:* soltowb@admin.craven.cc.nc.us.

Application contact Millicent Fulford, Recruiter, Craven Community College, 800 College Court, New Bern, NC 28562-4984. *Phone:* 252-638-7232. *Web address:* http://www.craven.cc.nc.us/.

DAWSON COMMUNITY COLLEGE
Glendive, Montana

Students with LD Served by Program	17	ADD/ADHD Services	✓
Staff	4 full-time, 4 part-time	Summer Preparation Program	n/a
LD Program or Service Fee	n/a	Alternative Test Arrangements	✓
LD Program Began	1974	LD Student Organization	n/a

Student Support Services began offering services in 1974. The program serves approximately 17 undergraduate students. Faculty consists of 4 full-time and 4 part-time staff members. Services are provided by academic advisers, remediation/learning specialists, counselors, regular education teachers, and professional tutors.

Policies The college has written policies regarding course substitutions, grade forgiveness, and substitution and waivers of requirements for admission and graduation. Students with LD may take up to 18 credit hours per semester; 12 credit hours per semester are required to maintain full-time status; 6 credit hours per semester are required to be eligible for financial aid.

Basic skills remediation Available in study skills, reading, time management, learning strategies, written language, and math. Offered one-on-one, in small groups, and class-size groups by computer-based instruction, regular education teachers, and professional tutors.

Subject-area tutoring Available in most subjects. Offered one-on-one, in small groups, and class-size groups by professional tutors.

Special courses Available in career planning, study skills, college survival skills, reading, learning strategies, math, stress management, and written composition skills. Most courses are offered for credit; some enter into overall grade point average.

Counseling and advisement Career counseling and individual counseling are available. Academic advisement by a staff member affiliated with the program is available.

Auxiliary aids and services *Aids:* calculators, personal computers, tape recorders, taped textbooks. *Services and accommodations:* advocates, alternative test arrangements, readers, note-takers, and scribes.

ADD/ADHD Students with ADD/ADHD are eligible for the same services available to students with LD, as well as distraction-free study areas and distraction-free testing environments.

Application *Required:* high school transcript and ACT (extended-time or untimed test accepted). *Recommended:* participation in extracurricular activities, interview, personal statement, psycho-educational report (3 years old or less), and documentation of high school services (e.g., Individualized Education Program [IEP] or 504 plan). Upon application, documentation of need for special services should be sent only to admissions. Upon acceptance, documentation of need for special services should be sent to both admissions and your LD program or unit. *Application deadline (institutional):* rolling/continuous for fall and rolling/continuous for spring. *Application deadline (LD program):* rolling/continuous for fall and rolling/continuous for spring.

LD program contact Kent Dion, Director, Student Support Services, 300 College Drive, Box 421, Glendive, MT 59330. *Phone:* 406-377-3396. *Fax:* 406-377-8132. *E-mail:* kent_d@dawson.cc.mt.us.

Application contact Dawson Community College, Box 421, Glendive, MT 59330-0421. *Web address:* http://www.dawson.cc.mt.us/.

DAYTONA BEACH COMMUNITY COLLEGE
Daytona Beach, Florida

Students with LD Served by Program	200	ADD/ADHD Services	✓
Staff	2 full-time, 2 part-time	Summer Preparation Program	n/a
LD Program or Service Fee	n/a	Alternative Test Arrangements	✓
LD Program Began	n/a	LD Student Organization	n/a

Daytona Beach Community College (continued)

Student Disability Services serves approximately 200 undergraduate students. Faculty consists of 2 full-time and 2 part-time staff members. Services are provided by diagnostic specialists, teacher trainees, and student disability specialists, director.

Policies The college has written policies regarding course substitutions and substitution and waivers of requirements for admission and graduation.

Special preparation or orientation Optional orientation held before registration and after classes begin.

Diagnostic testing Available for auditory processing, spelling, intelligence, reading, written language, visual processing, and math.

Subject-area tutoring Available in some subjects. Offered one-on-one and in small groups by trained peer tutors.

Auxiliary aids and services *Aids:* personal computers, personal spelling/word-use assistants (e.g., Franklin Speller), scan and read programs (e.g., Kurzweil), screen-enlarging programs, screen readers, speech recognition programs (e.g., Dragon), tape recorders, taped textbooks. *Services and accommodations:* advocates, priority registration, alternative test arrangements, readers, note-takers, and scribes.

ADD/ADHD Students with ADD/ADHD are eligible for the same services available to students with LD, as well as distraction-free study areas and distraction-free testing environments.

Application *Required:* high school transcript and psychoeducational report (3 years old or less). *Recommended:* documentation of high school services (e.g., Individualized Education Program [IEP] or 504 plan). Upon acceptance, documentation of need for special services should be sent only to your LD program or unit.

LD program contact Judy Mathis, Director, Student Disability Services, PO Box 2811, 1200 West International Speedway Boulevard, Daytona Beach, FL 32120-2811. *Phone:* 904-255-8131 Ext. 3807. *Fax:* 904-947-3152.

Application contact Daytona Beach Community College, PO Box 2811, Daytona Beach, FL 32120-2811. *Phone:* 904-255-8131 Ext. 3322. *Web address:* http://www.dbcc.cc.fl.us/.

DELTA COLLEGE
University Center, Michigan

Students with LD Served by Program	65	ADD/ADHD Services	✓
Staff	1 full-time, 2 part-time	Summer Preparation Program	n/a
LD Program or Service Fee	n/a	Alternative Test Arrangements	✓
LD Program Began	1984	LD Student Organization	n/a

Office of Disability Concerns began offering services in 1984. The program serves approximately 65 undergraduate students. Faculty consists of 1 full-time and 2 part-time staff members. Services are provided by academic advisers, counselors, special education teachers, LD specialists, and professional tutors.

Policies Students with LD may take up to 18 credit hours per semester; 6 credit hours per semester are required to maintain full-time status; 1 credit hour per semester is required to be eligible for financial aid.

Special preparation or orientation Optional orientation held before registration, before classes begin, after classes begin, and individually by special arrangement.

Basic skills remediation Available in study skills, computer skills, reading, time management, learning strategies, spelling, written language, math, and spoken language. Offered one-on-one, in small groups, and class-size groups by computer-based instruction, special education teachers, and LD specialists.

Subject-area tutoring Available in all subjects. Offered one-on-one, in small groups, and class-size groups by computer-based instruction, professional tutors, trained peer tutors, and LD specialists.

Counseling and advisement Career counseling and individual counseling are available. Academic advisement by a staff member affiliated with the program is available.

Auxiliary aids and services *Aids:* calculators, personal computers, personal spelling/word-use assistants (e.g., Franklin Speller), scan and read programs (e.g., Kurzweil), screen-enlarging programs, screen readers, speech recognition programs (e.g., Dragon), tape recorders, taped textbooks. *Services and accommodations:* alternative test arrangements, readers, note-takers, and scribes.

ADD/ADHD Students with ADD/ADHD are eligible for the same services available to students with LD, as well as distraction-free study areas and distraction-free testing environments.

Application *Required:* psychoeducational report (3 years old or less) and documentation of high school services (e.g., Individualized Education Program [IEP] or 504 plan). Upon application, documentation of need for special services should be sent only to your LD program or unit. Upon acceptance, documentation of need for special services should be sent only to your LD program or unit. *Application deadline (institutional):* rolling/continuous for fall and rolling/continuous for spring. *Application deadline (LD program):* rolling/continuous for fall and rolling/continuous for spring.

LD program contact David Murley, Director of Disability Concerns, 1961 Delta Road, University Center, MI 48710. *Phone:* 517-686-9322. *Fax:* 517-667-2202. *E-mail:* damurley@alpha.delta.edu.

Application contact Delta College, 1961 Delta Road, University Center, MI 48710. *Web address:* http://www.delta.edu/.

DYERSBURG STATE COMMUNITY COLLEGE
Dyersburg, Tennessee

Students with LD Served by Program	15	ADD/ADHD Services	✓
Staff	1 full-time	Summer Preparation Program	n/a
LD Program or Service Fee	n/a	Alternative Test Arrangements	✓
LD Program Began	1995	LD Student Organization	n/a

Office of Student Disability Services (OSDS) began offering services in 1995. The program serves approximately 15 undergraduate students. Faculty consists of 1 full-time staff member. Services are provided by remediation/learning specialists and ADA coordinator, student tutors, instructors.

Policies Students with LD may take up to 15 credits per semester; 12 credits per semester are required to maintain full-time status.

Special preparation or orientation Required orientation held individually by special arrangement.

Basic skills remediation Available in study skills, reading, time management, written language, and math. Offered one-on-one and in class-size groups by regular education teachers.

Subject-area tutoring Available in all subjects. Offered one-on-one and in small groups by trained peer tutors.

Special courses Available in study skills, reading, and math. All courses are offered for credit; all enter into overall grade point average.

Counseling and advisement Career counseling and individual counseling are available.

Auxiliary aids and services *Aids:* personal spelling/word-use assistants (e.g., Franklin Speller), screen-enlarging programs, speech recognition programs (e.g., Dragon), taped textbooks. *Services and accommodations:* advocates, priority registration, alternative test arrangements, readers, note-takers, and scribes.
ADD/ADHD Students with ADD/ADHD are eligible for the same services available to students with LD, as well as distraction-free study areas and distraction-free testing environments.
Application *Required:* high school transcript, ACT (extended-time or untimed test accepted), separate application to your LD program or unit, psychoeducational report (3 years old or less), and documentation of high school services (e.g., Individualized Education Program [IEP] or 504 plan). *Recommended:* participation in extracurricular activities. Upon application, documentation of need for special services should be sent only to your LD program or unit. Upon acceptance, documentation of need for special services should be sent only to your LD program or unit. *Application deadline (institutional):* 8/15 for fall and 1/24 for spring.
LD program contact Pam Dahl, Counselor/ADA Coordinator, 1510 Lake Road, Dyersburg, TN 38024. *Phone:* 901-286-3242. *Fax:* 901-286-3354. *E-mail:* dahl@dscclan.dscc.cc.tn.us.
Application contact Dyersburg State Community College, 1510 Lake Road, Dyersburg, TN 38024. *Web address:* http://www.dscc.cc.tn.us/.

EAST LOS ANGELES COLLEGE
Monterey Park, California

Students with LD Served by Program	135	ADD/ADHD Services	n/a
Staff	1 full-time, 2 part-time	Summer Preparation Program	n/a
LD Program or Service Fee	n/a	Alternative Test Arrangements	✓
LD Program Began	1989	LD Student Organization	n/a

Disabled Student Program and Services began offering services in 1989. The program serves approximately 135 undergraduate students. Faculty consists of 1 full-time and 2 part-time staff members. Services are provided by regular education teachers, counselors, graduate assistants/students, LD specialists, and trained peer tutors.
Policies 12 units per semester are required to maintain full-time status; 3 units per semester are required to be eligible for financial aid.
Special preparation or orientation Optional orientation held during registration, before classes begin, and individually by special arrangement.
Diagnostic testing Available for auditory processing, spelling, spoken language, intelligence, study skills, reading, written language, visual processing, and math.
Basic skills remediation Available in study skills, computer skills, reading, time management, learning strategies, spelling, and written language. Offered in class-size groups by LD specialists.
Subject-area tutoring Available in most subjects. Offered one-on-one by computer-based instruction and trained peer tutors.
Special courses Available in study skills, practical computer skills, test taking, reading, learning strategies, and vocabulary development. Some courses are offered for credit; some enter into overall grade point average.
Counseling and advisement Career counseling and individual counseling are available.
Auxiliary aids and services *Aids:* calculators, personal computers, personal spelling/word-use assistants (e.g., Franklin Speller), scan and read programs (e.g., Kurzweil), screen-enlarging programs, screen readers, speech recognition pro-

grams (e.g., Dragon), tape recorders. *Services and accommodations:* advocates, priority registration, alternative test arrangements, readers, and note-takers.
Application *Required:* interview and separate application to your LD program or unit. *Recommended:* psychoeducational report and documentation of high school services (e.g., Individualized Education Program [IEP] or 504 plan). Upon acceptance, documentation of need for special services should be sent only to your LD program or unit. *Application deadline (institutional):* 9/3 for fall and 1/5 for spring. *Application deadline (LD program):* rolling/continuous for fall and rolling/continuous for spring.
LD program contact Mary Seneker, Learning Disabilities Specialist, 1301 Avenida Cesar Chavez, Monterey Park, CA 91754-6099. *Phone:* 323-265-8785. *Fax:* 323-265-8174. *E-mail:* mseneker@juno.com.
Application contact East Los Angeles College, 1301 Cesar Chavez Avenue, Monterey Park, CA 91754-6001.

EDMONDS COMMUNITY COLLEGE
Lynnwood, Washington

Students with LD Served by Program	950	ADD/ADHD Services	✓
Staff	3 full-time, 2 part-time	Summer Preparation Program	n/a
LD Program or Service Fee	n/a	Alternative Test Arrangements	✓
LD Program Began	1971	LD Student Organization	n/a

Services for Students with Disabilities (SSD) began offering services in 1971. The program serves approximately 950 undergraduate students. Faculty consists of 3 full-time and 2 part-time staff members. Services are provided by academic advisers, remediation/learning specialists, counselors, regular education teachers, diagnostic specialists, graduate assistants/students, teacher trainees, trained peer tutors, and professional tutors.
Policies The college has written policies regarding course substitutions. 10 credit hours per quarter are required to maintain full-time status; 6 credit hours per quarter are required to be eligible for financial aid.
Special preparation or orientation Optional orientation held individually by special arrangement.
Diagnostic testing Available for learning styles.
Basic skills remediation Available in study skills, computer skills, reading, social skills, learning strategies, spelling, written language, and math. Offered one-on-one and in small groups by regular education teachers, teacher trainees, professional tutors, and trained peer tutors.
Subject-area tutoring Available in most subjects. Offered one-on-one by professional tutors and trained peer tutors.
Counseling and advisement Individual counseling is available. Academic advisement by a staff member affiliated with the program is available.
Auxiliary aids and services *Aids:* calculators, personal spelling/word-use assistants (e.g., Franklin Speller), scan and read programs (e.g., Kurzweil), screen-enlarging programs, screen readers, speech recognition programs (e.g., Dragon), tape recorders, taped textbooks. *Services and accommodations:* advocates, priority registration, alternative test arrangements, readers, note-takers, and scribes.
ADD/ADHD Students with ADD/ADHD are eligible for the same services available to students with LD, as well as distraction-free study areas and distraction-free testing environments.
Application *Recommended:* separate application to your LD program or unit and psychoeducational report. Upon application, documentation of need for special services should be sent only to your LD program or unit. Upon acceptance, documen-

Edmonds Community College (continued)

tation of need for special services should be sent only to your LD program or unit. *Application deadline (institutional):* rolling/continuous for fall and rolling/continuous for spring. *Application deadline (LD program):* rolling/continuous for fall and rolling/continuous for spring.

LD program contact Dee Olson, Director, 20000 68th Avenue W, Lynnewood, WA 98036. *Phone:* 425-640-1318. *Fax:* 425-640-1622. *E-mail:* dolson@edcc.edu.

Application contact Sharon Bench, Admissions Director, Edmonds Community College, 20000 68th Avenue West, Lynnwood, WA 98036-5999. *Phone:* 425-640-1416. *Web address:* http://www.edcc.edu/.

EL CENTRO COLLEGE
Dallas, Texas

Students with LD Served by Program	61	ADD/ADHD Services	✓
Staff	1 full-time, 17 part-time	Summer Preparation Program	n/a
LD Program or Service Fee	n/a	Alternative Test Arrangements	✓
LD Program Began	1978	LD Student Organization	n/a

Disability Services Office began offering services in 1978. The program serves approximately 61 undergraduate students. Faculty consists of 1 full-time and 17 part-time staff members. Services are provided by academic advisers, remediation/learning specialists, counselors, regular education teachers, diagnostic specialists, special education teachers, trained peer tutors, and professional tutors.

Policies Students with LD may take up to 18 credit hours per semester; 12 credit hours per semester are required to maintain full-time status; 6 credit hours per semester are required to be eligible for financial aid.

Special preparation or orientation Optional orientation held individually by special arrangement.

Diagnostic testing Available for spelling, intelligence, personality, study skills, learning strategies, reading, written language, learning styles, and math.

Basic skills remediation Available in reading, written language, and math. Offered in class-size groups by computer-based instruction and special education teachers.

Subject-area tutoring Available in most subjects. Offered one-on-one and in small groups by computer-based instruction, professional tutors, and trained peer tutors.

Counseling and advisement Career counseling, individual counseling, and support groups are available. Academic advisement by a staff member affiliated with the program is available.

Auxiliary aids and services *Aids:* calculators, personal computers, scan and read programs (e.g., Kurzweil), screen-enlarging programs, screen readers, speech recognition programs (e.g., Dragon), tape recorders, taped textbooks. *Services and accommodations:* advocates, priority registration, alternative test arrangements, readers, note-takers, and scribes.

ADD/ADHD Students with ADD/ADHD are eligible for the same services available to students with LD, as well as distraction-free study areas, distraction-free testing environments and personal coach or mentors.

Application *Required:* psychoeducational report (5 years old or less). *Recommended:* high school transcript and documentation of high school services (e.g., Individualized Education Program [IEP] or 504 plan). Upon application, documentation of need for special services should be sent only to your LD program or unit. Upon acceptance, documentation of need for special services should be sent only to your LD program or unit. *Application deadline (institutional):* rolling/continuous for fall

and rolling/continuous for spring. *Application deadline (LD program):* rolling/continuous for fall and rolling/continuous for spring.

LD program contact Sharon James, Taping Coordinator/DART Liaison, Main and Lamar, Dallas, TX 75202. *Phone:* 214-860-2411. *Fax:* 214-860-2233. *E-mail:* sdj5321@dcccd.edu.

Application contact El Centro College, Main and Lamar Streets, Dallas, TX 75202-3604. *E-mail:* rcb@dcccd.edu.

EUGENIO MARIA DE HOSTOS COMMUNITY COLLEGE OF THE CITY UNIVERSITY OF NEW YORK
Bronx, New York

Students with LD Served by Program	20	ADD/ADHD Services	✓
Staff	2 full-time, 8 part-time	Summer Preparation Program	n/a
LD Program or Service Fee	n/a	Alternative Test Arrangements	✓
LD Program Began	1991	LD Student Organization	n/a

Services for Students with Disabilities began offering services in 1991. The program serves approximately 20 undergraduate students. Faculty consists of 2 full-time and 8 part-time staff members. Services are provided by academic advisers, counselors, and assistive technology specialist.

Policies Students with LD may take up to 18 credit hours per semester; 12 credit hours per semester are required to maintain full-time status; 3 credit hours per semester are required to be eligible for financial aid.

Special preparation or orientation Optional orientation held individually by special arrangement.

Subject-area tutoring Available in some subjects. Offered one-on-one and in small groups by computer-based instruction and trained peer tutors.

Counseling and advisement Individual counseling and small-group counseling are available. Academic advisement by a staff member affiliated with the program is available.

Auxiliary aids and services *Aids:* calculators, scan and read programs (e.g., Kurzweil), screen-enlarging programs, screen readers, tape recorders, taped textbooks. *Services and accommodations:* priority registration, alternative test arrangements, readers, note-takers, scribes, and assistive technology.

ADD/ADHD Students with ADD/ADHD are eligible for the same services available to students with LD, as well as distraction-free testing environments.

Application *Required:* high school transcript and placement exams. *Recommended:* interview and psychoeducational report (5 years old or less). Upon application, documentation of need for special services should be sent only to your LD program or unit. Upon acceptance, documentation of need for special services should be sent only to your LD program or unit. *Application deadline (institutional):* rolling/continuous for fall and rolling/continuous for spring. *Application deadline (LD program):* rolling/continuous for fall and rolling/continuous for spring.

LD program contact Prof. Michael R. Stimola, Coordinator, Services for Students with Disabilities, 500 Grand Concourse Room, D101K, Bronx, NY 10451. *Phone:* 718-518-4454. *Fax:* 718-518-4252. *E-mail:* mrsho@mail.hostos.cuny.edu.

Application contact Eugenio Maria de Hostos Community College of the City University of New York, 500 Grand Concourse, Bronx, NY 10451. *E-mail:* nreho@cunyvm.cuny.edu. *Web address:* http://www.hostos.cuny.edu/.

EVERETT COMMUNITY COLLEGE

Everett, Washington

Students with LD Served by Program	85	ADD/ADHD Services	✓
Staff	2 full-time, 1 part-time	Summer Preparation Program	n/a
LD Program or Service Fee	n/a	Alternative Test Arrangements	✓
LD Program Began	1977	LD Student Organization	n/a

Center for Disability Services began offering services in 1977. The program serves approximately 85 undergraduate students. Faculty consists of 2 full-time staff members and 1 part-time staff member. Services are provided by counselors and diagnostic specialists.
Policies The college has written policies regarding course substitutions.
Fees *Diagnostic Testing Fee:* $95.
Special preparation or orientation Optional orientation held after classes begin.
Diagnostic testing Available for auditory processing, motor skills, intelligence, reading, written language, visual processing, and math.
Counseling and advisement Career counseling, individual counseling, and small-group counseling are available.
Auxiliary aids and services *Aids:* calculators, personal computers, scan and read programs (e.g., Kurzweil), screen-enlarging programs, screen readers, speech recognition programs (e.g., Dragon), tape recorders, taped textbooks. *Services and accommodations:* advocates, priority registration, alternative test arrangements, readers, note-takers, and scribes.
ADD/ADHD Students with ADD/ADHD are eligible for the same services available to students with LD, as well as distraction-free testing environments.
Application *Recommended:* interview, separate application to your LD program or unit, psychoeducational report (3 years old or less), and documentation of high school services (e.g., Individualized Education Program [IEP] or 504 plan). Upon application, documentation of need for special services should be sent only to your LD program or unit. Upon acceptance, documentation of need for special services should be sent only to your LD program or unit. *Application deadline (LD program):* rolling/continuous for fall and rolling/continuous for spring.
LD program contact Barbara Oswald, Coordinator, Center for Disability Services, 2000 Tower Street, Everett, WA 98201. *Phone:* 425-388-9272. *Fax:* 425-388-9109. *E-mail:* boswald@evcc.ctc.edu.
Application contact Linda Baca, Admissions Manager, Everett Community College, 801 Wetmore Avenue, Everett, WA 98201-1327. *Phone:* 425-388-9219. *Web address:* http://www.evcc.ctc.edu/.

FINGER LAKES COMMUNITY COLLEGE

Canandaigua, New York

Students with LD Served by Program	200	ADD/ADHD Services	✓
Staff	1 full-time	Summer Preparation Program	n/a
LD Program or Service Fee	n/a	Alternative Test Arrangements	✓
LD Program Began	n/a	LD Student Organization	n/a

Services to Students with a Learning Disability serves approximately 200 undergraduate students. Faculty consists of 1 full-time staff member. Services are provided by LD specialists, trained peer tutors, and professional tutors.

Policies The college has written policies regarding course substitutions and substitution and waivers of requirements for admission and graduation. Students with LD may take up to 18 credit hours per semester; 12 credit hours per semester are required to maintain full-time status and to be eligible for financial aid.
Special preparation or orientation Optional orientation held first year seminar.
Subject-area tutoring Available in all subjects. Offered one-on-one, in small groups, and class-size groups by computer-based instruction, professional tutors, trained peer tutors, and LD specialists.
Special courses Available in study skills and first year seminar. All courses are offered for credit; all enter into overall grade point average.
Counseling and advisement Career counseling, individual counseling, small-group counseling, and support groups are available.
Auxiliary aids and services *Aids:* calculators, personal computers, personal spelling/word-use assistants (e.g., Franklin Speller), scan and read programs (e.g., Kurzweil), screen-enlarging programs, screen readers, tape recorders, taped textbooks. *Services and accommodations:* alternative test arrangements, readers, note-takers, and scribes.
ADD/ADHD Students with ADD/ADHD are eligible for the same services available to students with LD, as well as distraction-free study areas and distraction-free testing environments.
Application *Required:* high school transcript and psychoeducational report (5 years old or less). *Recommended:* participation in extracurricular activities and interview. Upon application, documentation of need for special services should be sent only to your LD program or unit. Upon acceptance, documentation of need for special services should be sent only to your LD program or unit. *Application deadline (institutional):* rolling/continuous for fall and rolling/continuous for spring. *Application deadline (LD program):* rolling/continuous for fall and rolling/continuous for spring.
LD program contact Amy Nichols, Coordinator of Services to Students with a Learning Disability, 4355 Lakeshore Drive, Canandaigua, NY 14424-8395. *Phone:* 716-394-3500 Ext. 390. *Fax:* 716-394-5005. *E-mail:* nicholal@snyflcc.fingerlakes.edu.
Application contact Finger Lakes Community College, 4355 Lakeshore Drive, Canandaigua, NY 14424-8395. *E-mail:* admissions@snyflcc.fingerlakes.edu. *Web address:* http://www.fingerlakes.edu/.

FLORIDA COMMUNITY COLLEGE AT JACKSONVILLE

Jacksonville, Florida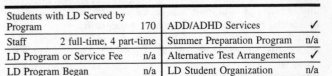

Students with LD Served by Program	170	ADD/ADHD Services	✓
Staff	2 full-time, 4 part-time	Summer Preparation Program	n/a
LD Program or Service Fee	n/a	Alternative Test Arrangements	✓
LD Program Began	n/a	LD Student Organization	n/a

Services for Students with Disabilities Program serves approximately 170 undergraduate students. Faculty consists of 2 full-time and 4 part-time staff members. Services are provided by LD specialists, trained peer tutors, and disabilities specialists.
Policies The college has written policies regarding course substitutions and grade forgiveness. Students with LD may take up to 18 credit hours per semester; 12 credit hours per semester are required to maintain full-time status; 6 credit hours per semester are required to be eligible for financial aid.
Special preparation or orientation Required orientation held during registration and before classes begin.

Florida Community College at Jacksonville (continued)

Basic skills remediation Available in auditory processing, study skills, reading, visual processing, learning strategies, spelling, written language, and math. Offered one-on-one by LD specialists and trained peer tutors.

Subject-area tutoring Available in all subjects. Offered one-on-one by trained peer tutors and LD specialists.

Counseling and advisement Career counseling and individual counseling are available.

Auxiliary aids and services *Aids:* calculators, personal spelling/word-use assistants (e.g., Franklin Speller), scan and read programs (e.g., Kurzweil), screen-enlarging programs, screen readers, speech recognition programs (e.g., Dragon), tape recorders, taped textbooks. *Services and accommodations:* priority registration, alternative test arrangements, readers, note-takers, and scribes.

ADD/ADHD Students with ADD/ADHD are eligible for the same services available to students with LD, as well as distraction-free testing environments.

Application *Required:* high school transcript, separate application to your LD program or unit, and documentation of disability. *Recommended:* interview, psychoeducational report (5 years old or less), and documentation of high school services (e.g., Individualized Education Program [IEP] or 504 plan). Upon application, documentation of need for special services should be sent only to your LD program or unit. Upon acceptance, documentation of need for special services should be sent only to your LD program or unit. *Application deadline (institutional):* 8/23 for fall and 1/10 for spring. *Application deadline (LD program):* rolling/continuous for fall and rolling/continuous for spring.

LD program contact Cecilia Sumner, Director, Services for Students with Disabilities, 4501 Capper Road, Jacksonville, FL 32218. *Phone:* 904-766-6607. *Fax:* 904-766-6654. *E-mail:* mcsumner@fccjmail.fccj.cc.fl.us.

Application contact Florida Community College at Jacksonville, 501 West State Street, Jacksonville, FL 32202-4030. *Web address:* http://www.fccj.cc.fl.us/.

FOX VALLEY TECHNICAL COLLEGE
Appleton, Wisconsin

Students with LD Served by Program	100	ADD/ADHD Services	✓
Staff	5 full-time	Summer Preparation Program	n/a
LD Program or Service Fee	n/a	Alternative Test Arrangements	✓
LD Program Began	1985	LD Student Organization	n/a

Special Needs Center began offering services in 1985. The program serves approximately 100 undergraduate students. Faculty consists of 5 full-time staff members. Services are provided by special education teachers and LD specialists.

Policies 12 credits per semester are required to maintain full-time status; 6 credits per semester are required to be eligible for financial aid.

Basic skills remediation Available in study skills, reading, written language, and math. Offered one-on-one by computer-based instruction and regular education teachers.

Auxiliary aids and services *Aids:* calculators, personal spelling/word-use assistants (e.g., Franklin Speller), scan and read programs (e.g., Kurzweil), screen-enlarging programs, screen readers, speech recognition programs (e.g., Dragon), tape recorders, taped textbooks. *Services and accommodations:* alternative test arrangements, readers, note-takers, and scribes.

ADD/ADHD Students with ADD/ADHD are eligible for the same services available to students with LD, as well as distraction-free testing environments.

Application *Required:* high school transcript. *Recommended:* ACT (extended-time or untimed test accepted). Upon application, documentation of need for special services should be sent only to your LD program or unit. Upon acceptance, documentation of need for special services should be sent only to your LD program or unit.

LD program contact Shary Schwabenlender, Special Needs Support Instructor-Coordinator, 1825 North Bluemound Drive, Appleton, WI 54912-2277. *Phone:* 920-735-5679. *Fax:* 920-831-4392. *E-mail:* schwoben@foxvalley.tec.wi.us.

Application contact Fox Valley Technical College, 1825 North Bluemound, PO Box 2277, Appleton, WI 54912-2277. *Web address:* http://www.foxvalley.tec.wi.us/.

FREDERICK COMMUNITY COLLEGE
Frederick, Maryland

Students with LD Served by Program	200	ADD/ADHD Services	✓
Staff	1 full-time	Summer Preparation Program	n/a
LD Program or Service Fee	n/a	Alternative Test Arrangements	✓
LD Program Began	1990	LD Student Organization	n/a

System for Student Success began offering services in 1990. The program serves approximately 200 undergraduate students. Faculty consists of 1 full-time staff member. Services are provided by academic advisers, regular education teachers, counselors, remediation/learning specialists, diagnostic specialists, LD specialists, trained peer tutors, professional tutors, and Testing Center director.

Policies 12 credits per semester are required to maintain full-time status; 6 credits per semester are required to be eligible for financial aid.

Special preparation or orientation Optional orientation held before registration.

Diagnostic testing Available for auditory processing, spelling, reading, written language, learning styles, visual processing, and math.

Subject-area tutoring Available in all subjects. Offered one-on-one by professional tutors, trained peer tutors, and LD specialists.

Counseling and advisement Individual counseling is available. Academic advisement by a staff member affiliated with the program is available.

Auxiliary aids and services *Aids:* calculators, personal computers, personal spelling/word-use assistants (e.g., Franklin Speller), scan and read programs (e.g., Kurzweil), screen-enlarging programs, screen readers, speech recognition programs (e.g., Dragon), tape recorders, taped textbooks. *Services and accommodations:* advocates, alternative test arrangements, readers, note-takers, and scribes.

ADD/ADHD Students with ADD/ADHD are eligible for the same services available to students with LD, as well as distraction-free testing environments.

Application *Required:* high school transcript, psychoeducational report, and documentation of high school services (e.g., Individualized Education Program [IEP] or 504 plan). Upon application, documentation of need for special services should be sent only to your LD program or unit. Upon acceptance, documentation of need for special services should be sent only to your LD program or unit. *Application deadline (institutional):* rolling/continuous for fall and rolling/continuous for spring. *Application deadline (LD program):* rolling/continuous for fall and rolling/continuous for spring.

LD program contact Dr. Rosemary Watkins, Learning Specialist, 7932 Opossumtown Pike, Frederick, MD 21702. *Phone:* 301-846-2409. *Fax:* 301-846-2498. *E-mail:* rwatson@fcc.cc.md.us.

Application contact Frederick Community College, 7932 Opossumtown Pike, Frederick, MD 21702-2097. *Web address:* http://www.fcc.cc.md.us/.

GALVESTON COLLEGE

Galveston, Texas

Students with LD Served by Program	50	ADD/ADHD Services	✓
Staff	1 full-time	Summer Preparation Program	n/a
LD Program or Service Fee	n/a	Alternative Test Arrangements	✓
LD Program Began	1990	LD Student Organization	✓

Office of Special Services began offering services in 1990. The program serves approximately 50 undergraduate students. Faculty consists of 1 full-time staff member. Services are provided by counselors.

Policies 12 credit hours per semester are required to maintain full-time status; 6 credits per semester are required to be eligible for financial aid.

Basic skills remediation Available in study skills, computer skills, reading, social skills, learning strategies, spelling, written language, and math. Offered in class-size groups by regular education teachers and special education teachers.

Subject-area tutoring Available in all subjects. Offered one-on-one by professional tutors, trained peer tutors, and LD specialists.

Counseling and advisement Career counseling, individual counseling, and support groups are available.

Auxiliary aids and services *Aids:* calculators, personal computers, tape recorders, taped textbooks. *Services and accommodations:* priority registration, alternative test arrangements, readers, note-takers, and scribes.

Student organization There is a student organization for students with LD.

ADD/ADHD Students with ADD/ADHD are eligible for the same services available to students with LD, as well as distraction-free testing environments, personal coach or mentors, and support groups for ADD/ADHD.

Application *Required:* high school transcript, interview, separate application to your LD program or unit, psychoeducational report (5 years old or less), and documentation of high school services (e.g., Individualized Education Program [IEP] or 504 plan). *Recommended:* participation in extracurricular activities. Upon application, documentation of need for special services should be sent only to your LD program or unit. Upon acceptance, documentation of need for special services should be sent only to your LD program or unit.

LD program contact Angela Foote, Counselor, Special Services, 4015 Avenue Q, Galveston, TX 77550. *Phone:* 409-763-6551 Ext. 225. *Fax:* 409-762-0667. *E-mail:* afoote@gc.edu.

Application contact Galveston College, 4015 Avenue Q, Galveston, TX 77550-7496. *Web address:* http://www.gc.edu/.

GEORGE C. WALLACE COMMUNITY COLLEGE

Dothan, Alabama

Students with LD Served by Program	30	ADD/ADHD Services	✓
Staff	1 full-time	Summer Preparation Program	n/a
LD Program or Service Fee	n/a	Alternative Test Arrangements	✓
LD Program Began	1980	LD Student Organization	n/a

Disabled Student Services began offering services in 1980. The program serves approximately 30 undergraduate students. Faculty consists of 1 full-time staff member. Services are provided by regular education teachers and ADA coordinator.

Policies Students with LD may take up to 19 credit hours per semester; 12 credit hours per semester are required to maintain full-time status and to be eligible for financial aid.

Basic skills remediation Available in reading, written language, and math. Offered in class-size groups by regular education teachers.

Subject-area tutoring Available in most subjects. Offered one-on-one by professional tutors and trained peer tutors.

Special courses Available in reading, math, and written composition skills. No courses are offered for credit; none enter into overall grade point average.

Counseling and advisement Career counseling and individual counseling are available.

Auxiliary aids and services *Aids:* tape recorders. *Services and accommodations:* priority registration, alternative test arrangements, and note-takers.

ADD/ADHD Students with ADD/ADHD are eligible for the same services available to students with LD, as well as distraction-free testing environments.

Application *Required:* high school transcript and psychoeducational report (3 years old or less). Upon application, documentation of need for special services should be sent only to your LD program or unit. Upon acceptance, documentation of need for special services should be sent only to your LD program or unit. *Application deadline (institutional):* rolling/continuous for fall and rolling/continuous for spring. *Application deadline (LD program):* rolling/continuous for fall and rolling/continuous for spring.

LD program contact Dr. Jane McMurtry, ADA Coordinator, Route 6, Box 62, Dothan, AL 36303. *Phone:* 334-983-3521 Ext. 287. *Fax:* 334-983-6066. *E-mail:* mcmurtry@wallace.edu.

Application contact Brenda Barnes, Assistant Dean of Student Affairs, George C. Wallace Community College, Route 6, Box 62, Dothan, AL 36303-9234. *Phone:* 334-983-3521 Ext. 283. *Web address:* http://dns1.wallace.edu/.

GLEN OAKS COMMUNITY COLLEGE

Centreville, Michigan

Students with LD Served by Program	25	ADD/ADHD Services	✓
Staff	1 full-time, 1 part-time	Summer Preparation Program	n/a
LD Program or Service Fee	n/a	Alternative Test Arrangements	✓
LD Program Began	1985	LD Student Organization	n/a

Occupational Student Support Program (OSSP) began offering services in 1985. The program serves approximately 25 undergraduate students. Faculty consists of 1 full-time and 1 part-time staff member. Services are provided by academic advisers, regular education teachers, counselors, remediation/learning specialists, diagnostic specialists, trained peer tutors, and professional tutors.

Policies Students with LD may take up to 18 credit hours per semester; 12 credit hours per semester are required to maintain full-time status; 12 credit hours per semester are required to be eligible for financial aid.

Diagnostic testing Available for spelling, reading, written language, visual processing, and math.

Subject-area tutoring Available in all subjects. Offered one-on-one by trained peer tutors.

Glen Oaks Community College (continued)

Counseling and advisement Career counseling and individual counseling are available. Academic advisement by a staff member affiliated with the program is available.

Auxiliary aids and services *Aids:* scan and read programs (e.g., Kurzweil), tape recorders. *Services and accommodations:* alternative test arrangements, readers, note-takers, and scribes.

ADD/ADHD Students with ADD/ADHD are eligible for the same services available to students with LD, as well as distraction-free study areas and distraction-free testing environments.

Application *Required:* high school transcript, interview, separate application to your LD program or unit, psychoeducational report (3 years old or less), and ASSET test. *Recommended:* documentation of high school services (e.g., Individualized Education Program [IEP] or 504 plan). Upon application, documentation of need for special services should be sent only to your LD program or unit. Upon acceptance, documentation of need for special services should be sent only to your LD program or unit. *Application deadline (institutional):* rolling/continuous for fall and rolling/continuous for spring. *Application deadline (LD program):* rolling/continuous for fall and rolling/continuous for spring.

LD program contact Donna Austin, Special Populations Counselor, 62249 Shimmel Road, Centreville, MI 49032. *Phone:* 616-467-9945. *Fax:* 616-467-9068. *E-mail:* daustin@glenoaks.cc.mi.us.

Application contact Beverly M. Andrews, Registrar and Coordinator of Institutional Research, Glen Oaks Community College, 62249 Shimmel Road, Centreville, MI 49032-9719. *Phone:* 616-467-9945 Ext. 243. *Web address:* http://www.glenoaks.cc.mi.us/.

GLOUCESTER COUNTY COLLEGE
Sewell, New Jersey

Students with LD Served by Program	265	ADD/ADHD Services	✓
Staff	2 full-time, 1 part-time	Summer Preparation Program	✓
LD Program or Service Fee	n/a	Alternative Test Arrangements	✓
LD Program Began	1979	LD Student Organization	n/a

Department of Special Needs Services began offering services in 1979. The program serves approximately 265 undergraduate students. Faculty consists of 2 full-time staff members and 1 part-time staff member. Services are provided by trained peer tutors and professional tutors.

Policies Students with LD may take up to 12 credit hours per semester; 12 credit hours per semester are required to maintain full-time status; 6 credit hours per semester are required to be eligible for financial aid.

Special preparation or orientation Optional summer program offered prior to entering college. Optional orientation held during summer prior to enrollment.

Basic skills remediation Available in reading, written language, and math. Offered one-on-one and in small groups by computer-based instruction and professional tutors.

Subject-area tutoring Available in most subjects. Offered one-on-one and in small groups by professional tutors and trained peer tutors.

Auxiliary aids and services *Aids:* calculators, personal spelling/word-use assistants (e.g., Franklin Speller), scan and read programs (e.g., Kurzweil), screen-enlarging programs, screen readers, speech recognition programs (e.g., Dragon), tape recorders, taped textbooks. *Services and accommodations:* alternative test arrangements, readers, note-takers, and scribes.

ADD/ADHD Students with ADD/ADHD are eligible for the same services available to students with LD, as well as distraction-free testing environments.

Application *Required:* high school transcript, separate application to your LD program or unit, and psychoeducational report (4 years old or less). *Recommended:* participation in extracurricular activities, interview, and personal statement. Upon acceptance, documentation of need for special services should be sent only to your LD program or unit. *Application deadline (institutional):* rolling/continuous for fall and rolling/continuous for spring. *Application deadline (LD program):* 8/1 for fall and 12/1 for spring.

LD program contact Dennis Cook, Director, 1400 Tanyard Road, Sewell, NJ 08080. *Phone:* 856-415-2281. *Fax:* 856-468-7381. *E-mail:* dcook@gccnj.edu.

Application contact Carol L. Lange, Admissions and Recruitment Coordinator, Gloucester County College, Deptford Township, Tanyard Road, RR 4, Box 203, Sewell, NJ 08080. *Phone:* 609-468-5000. *Web address:* http://www.gccnj.edu/.

GUILFORD TECHNICAL COMMUNITY COLLEGE
Jamestown, North Carolina

Students with LD Served by Program	90	ADD/ADHD Services	✓
Staff	3 full-time	Summer Preparation Program	n/a
LD Program or Service Fee	n/a	Alternative Test Arrangements	n/a
LD Program Began	1992	LD Student Organization	n/a

disAbility Access Services began offering services in 1992. The program serves approximately 90 undergraduate students. Faculty consists of 3 full-time staff members. Services are provided by regular education teachers and LD specialists.

Auxiliary aids and services *Aids:* personal spelling/word-use assistants (e.g., Franklin Speller).

ADD/ADHD Students with ADD/ADHD are eligible for the same services available to students with LD, as well as distraction-free testing environments.

Application *Required:* high school transcript and psychoeducational report (3 years old or less). *Recommended:* interview and documentation of high school services (e.g., Individualized Education Program [IEP] or 504 plan). Upon application, documentation of need for special services should be sent only to your LD program or unit. Upon acceptance, documentation of need for special services should be sent only to your LD program or unit. *Application deadline (institutional):* rolling/continuous for fall and rolling/continuous for spring. *Application deadline (LD program):* rolling/continuous for fall and rolling/continuous for spring.

LD program contact Angela Chasten Leak, Director of disAbility Access Services, 601 High Point Road, PO Box 309, Jamestown, NC 27282. *Phone:* 336-334-4822 Ext. 2325. *E-mail:* chastena@gtcc.cc.nc.us.

Application contact Herbert Curkin, Director of Admissions, Guilford Technical Community College, PO Box 309, Jamestown, NC 27282-0309. *Phone:* 336-334-4822 Ext. 2338. *Web address:* http://technet.gtcc.cc.nc.us/.

HARRISBURG AREA COMMUNITY COLLEGE
Harrisburg, Pennsylvania

Students with LD Served by Program	250	ADD/ADHD Services	✓
Staff	4 full-time, 20 part-time	Summer Preparation Program	n/a
LD Program or Service Fee	n/a	Alternative Test Arrangements	✓
LD Program Began	1990	LD Student Organization	n/a

Learning Support Services began offering services in 1990. The program serves approximately 250 undergraduate students. Faculty consists of 4 full-time and 20 part-time staff members. Services are provided by counselors and professional tutors.
Counseling and advisement Career counseling and individual counseling are available.
Auxiliary aids and services *Aids:* personal spelling/word-use assistants (e.g., Franklin Speller), scan and read programs (e.g., Kurzweil), screen-enlarging programs, screen readers, speech recognition programs (e.g., Dragon), tape recorders, taped textbooks. *Services and accommodations:* advocates, alternative test arrangements, readers, note-takers, scribes, and spell checkers.
ADD/ADHD Students with ADD/ADHD are eligible for the same services available to students with LD, as well as distraction-free testing environments.
Application *Required:* high school transcript, psychoeducational report (3 years old or less), and comprehensive evaluation report. *Recommended:* documentation of high school services (e.g., Individualized Education Program [IEP] or 504 plan). Upon application, documentation of need for special services should be sent only to your LD program or unit. Upon acceptance, documentation of need for special services should be sent only to your LD program or unit. *Application deadline (institutional):* rolling/continuous for fall and rolling/continuous for spring. *Application deadline (LD program):* rolling/continuous for fall and rolling/continuous for spring.
LD program contact Clare Koerner, Coordinator, Disability Services, One HACC Drive, Harrisburg, PA 17110. *Phone:* 717-780-2614. *Fax:* 717-236-0709. *E-mail:* cmkoerne@hacc.edu.
Application contact Vanita Cowan, Administrative Clerk, Admissions, Harrisburg Area Community College, 1 HACC Drive, Harrisburg, PA 17110-2999. *Phone:* 717-780-2406. *Web address:* http://www.hacc.edu/.

HAWAII COMMUNITY COLLEGE
Hilo, Hawaii

Students with LD Served by Program	40	ADD/ADHD Services	✓
Staff	1 full-time, 6 part-time	Summer Preparation Program	n/a
LD Program or Service Fee	n/a	Alternative Test Arrangements	✓
LD Program Began	1994	LD Student Organization	n/a

Ha'awi Kokua, Program for Students with Disabilities began offering services in 1994. The program serves approximately 40 undergraduate students. Faculty consists of 1 full-time and 6 part-time staff members. Services are provided by counselors and trained peer tutors.
Special courses Available in study skills. All courses are offered for credit; none enter into overall grade point average.
Counseling and advisement Career counseling and individual counseling are available.

Auxiliary aids and services *Aids:* calculators, personal spelling/word-use assistants (e.g., Franklin Speller), scan and read programs (e.g., Kurzweil), screen-enlarging programs, tape recorders. *Services and accommodations:* priority registration, alternative test arrangements, readers, note-takers, and scribes.
ADD/ADHD Students with ADD/ADHD are eligible for the same services available to students with LD, as well as distraction-free study areas and distraction-free testing environments.
Application *Required:* documentation of high school services (e.g., Individualized Education Program [IEP] or 504 plan). Upon application, documentation of need for special services should be sent only to your LD program or unit. Upon acceptance, documentation of need for special services should be sent only to your LD program or unit. *Application deadline (institutional):* 7/1 for fall and 12/1 for spring.
LD program contact Karen Kane, Coordinator/Counselor, 200 West Kawili Street, Manono Campus, Building 379, Hilo, HI 96720. *Phone:* 808-974-7741. *Fax:* 808-974-7692. *E-mail:* kkane@hawaii.edu.
Application contact Hawaii Community College, 200 West Kawili Street, Hilo, HI 96720-4091. *E-mail:* loeding@hawada.hawcc.hawaii.edu. *Web address:* http://www.hawcc.hawaii.edu/.

HAWKEYE COMMUNITY COLLEGE
Waterloo, Iowa

Students with LD Served by Program	105	ADD/ADHD Services	✓
Staff	2 full-time	Summer Preparation Program	n/a
LD Program or Service Fee	n/a	Alternative Test Arrangements	✓
LD Program Began	n/a	LD Student Organization	n/a

Student Development Department serves approximately 105 undergraduate students. Faculty consists of 2 full-time staff members. Services are provided by academic advisers, remediation/learning specialists, counselors, and trained peer tutors.
Policies The college has written policies regarding course substitutions and grade forgiveness. Students with LD may take up to 18 credit hours per semester; 12 credit hours per semester are required to maintain full-time status; 6 credit hours per semester are required to be eligible for financial aid.
Special preparation or orientation Optional orientation held before classes begin, during summer prior to enrollment, and individually by special arrangement.
Diagnostic testing Available for reading, written language, and math.
Basic skills remediation Available in study skills, reading, time management, written language, and math. Offered one-on-one, in small groups, and class-size groups by regular education teachers.
Subject-area tutoring Available in some subjects. Offered one-on-one and in small groups by computer-based instruction and trained peer tutors.
Counseling and advisement Career counseling and individual counseling are available. Academic advisement by a staff member affiliated with the program is available.
Auxiliary aids and services *Aids:* scan and read programs (e.g., Kurzweil), screen-enlarging programs, tape recorders, taped textbooks. *Services and accommodations:* advocates, priority registration, alternative test arrangements, readers, and note-takers.
ADD/ADHD Students with ADD/ADHD are eligible for the same services available to students with LD, as well as distraction-free testing environments.

Hawkeye Community College (continued)

Application *Required:* high school transcript and documentation of high school services (e.g., Individualized Education Program [IEP] or 504 plan). *Recommended:* ACT or SAT I (extended-time or untimed test accepted) and psychoeducational report (3 years old or less). Upon application, documentation of need for special services should be sent only to your LD program or unit. Upon acceptance, documentation of need for special services should be sent only to your LD program or unit. *Application deadline (institutional):* rolling/continuous for fall and rolling/continuous for spring. *Application deadline (LD program):* rolling/continuous for fall and rolling/continuous for spring.

LD program contact Dianne Shoultz, Director of Student Development, PO Box 8015, Waterloo, IA 50704-8015. *Phone:* 319-296-4014. *Fax:* 319-296-1028. *E-mail:* dshoultz@hawkeye.cc.ia.us.

Application contact Susan Mixdorf, Admissions Coordinator, Hawkeye Community College, PO Box 8015, Waterloo, IA 50704-8015. *Phone:* 319-296-4000. *Web address:* http://www.hawkeye.cc.ia.us/.

HENNEPIN TECHNICAL COLLEGE
Brooklyn Park, Minnesota

Students with LD Served by Program	250	ADD/ADHD Services	✓
Staff	6 full-time, 14 part-time	Summer Preparation Program	n/a
LD Program or Service Fee	n/a	Alternative Test Arrangements	✓
LD Program Began	1975	LD Student Organization	n/a

Learning Resource Center/Accommodating Disabilities began offering services in 1975. The program serves approximately 250 undergraduate students. Faculty consists of 6 full-time and 14 part-time staff members. Services are provided by regular education teachers, trained peer tutors, and professional tutors.

Policies The college has written policies regarding substitution and waivers of requirements for admission. Students with LD may take up to 16 credit hours per semester; 12 credit hours per semester are required to maintain full-time status; 6 credit hours per semester are required to be eligible for financial aid.

Basic skills remediation Available in study skills, computer skills, reading, time management, learning strategies, and math. Offered in small groups by professional tutors.

Subject-area tutoring Available in all subjects. Offered in small groups by computer-based instruction and professional tutors.

Special courses Available in oral communication skills, study skills, reading, time management, learning strategies, and math. Some courses are offered for credit; none enter into overall grade point average.

Counseling and advisement Career counseling, individual counseling, and support groups are available.

Auxiliary aids and services *Aids:* calculators, personal computers, personal spelling/word-use assistants (e.g., Franklin Speller), scan and read programs (e.g., Kurzweil), screen-enlarging programs, tape recorders, taped textbooks. *Services and accommodations:* advocates, alternative test arrangements, readers, note-takers, and scribes.

ADD/ADHD Students with ADD/ADHD are eligible for the same services available to students with LD, as well as distraction-free study areas and distraction-free testing environments.

Application *Required:* interview and documentation of high school services (e.g., Individualized Education Program [IEP] or 504 plan). Upon application, documentation of need for special services should be sent only to admissions. Upon acceptance, documentation of need for special services should be sent only to admissions. *Application deadline (institutional):* rolling/continuous for fall and rolling/continuous for spring. *Application deadline (LD program):* rolling/continuous for fall and rolling/continuous for spring.

LD program contact David Cook, Support Services Manager, 9200 Flying Cloud Drive, Eden Prairie, MN 55347. *Phone:* 612-550-3119. *Fax:* 612-550-3147. *E-mail:* dcook@htc.mnscu.edu.

Application contact Ron Kraft, Dean of Student Services, Hennepin Technical College, 9000 Brooklyn Boulevard, Brooklyn Park, MN 55445. *Phone:* 612-425-3800 Ext. 2110. *Web address:* http://www.htc.mnscu.edu/.

HERKIMER COUNTY COMMUNITY COLLEGE
Herkimer, New York

Students with LD Served by Program	150	ADD/ADHD Services	✓
Staff	1 full-time, 3 part-time	Summer Preparation Program	n/a
LD Program or Service Fee	n/a	Alternative Test Arrangements	✓
LD Program Began	1989	LD Student Organization	n/a

Office of Special Services (OSS) began offering services in 1989. The program serves approximately 150 undergraduate students. Faculty consists of 1 full-time and 3 part-time staff members. Services are provided by academic advisers, regular education teachers, counselors, remediation/learning specialists, special education teachers, LD specialists, trained peer tutors, and professional tutors.

Policies 12 credit hours per semester are required to maintain full-time status; 3 credits per semester are required to be eligible for financial aid.

Counseling and advisement Academic advisement by a staff member affiliated with the program is available.

Auxiliary aids and services *Aids:* calculators, personal computers, personal spelling/word-use assistants (e.g., Franklin Speller), scan and read programs (e.g., Kurzweil), screen-enlarging programs, speech recognition programs (e.g., Dragon), tape recorders. *Services and accommodations:* alternative test arrangements, readers, and scribes.

ADD/ADHD Students with ADD/ADHD are eligible for the same services available to students with LD, as well as distraction-free study areas and distraction-free testing environments.

Application *Required:* high school transcript, psychoeducational report, and documentation of high school services (e.g., Individualized Education Program [IEP] or 504 plan). *Recommended:* interview. Upon application, documentation of need for special services should be sent only to your LD program or unit. Upon acceptance, documentation of need for special services should be sent only to your LD program or unit. *Application deadline (institutional):* rolling/continuous for fall and rolling/continuous for spring.

LD program contact Leslie Cornish, Special Services Coordinator, 100 Reservoir Road, Herkimer, NY 13350. *Phone:* 315-866-0300 Ext. 331. *Fax:* 315-866-6957. *E-mail:* cornishld@hccc.suny.edu.

Application contact Herkimer County Community College, Reservoir Road, Herkimer, NY 13350. *E-mail:* admissionhccva@itec.suny.edu. *Web address:* http://www.hccc.ntcnet.com/.

HOCKING COLLEGE
Nelsonville, Ohio

Students with LD Served by Program	150	ADD/ADHD Services	✓
Staff	2 full-time, 1 part-time	Summer Preparation Program	✓
LD Program or Service Fee	n/a	Alternative Test Arrangements	✓
LD Program Began	1987	LD Student Organization	n/a

Access Center, Office of Disability Services began offering services in 1987. The program serves approximately 150 undergraduate students. Faculty consists of 2 full-time staff members and 1 part-time staff member. Services are provided by LD specialists and professional tutors.

Policies 12 credit hours per quarter are required to maintain full-time status; 1 credit hour per quarter is required to be eligible for financial aid.

Special preparation or orientation Optional summer program offered prior to entering college.

Subject-area tutoring Available in most subjects. Offered one-on-one and in small groups by computer-based instruction, professional tutors, and LD specialists.

Counseling and advisement Career counseling is available.

Auxiliary aids and services *Aids:* scan and read programs (e.g., Kurzweil), screen-enlarging programs, speech recognition programs (e.g., Dragon). *Services and accommodations:* advocates, priority registration, alternative test arrangements, readers, note-takers, and scribes.

ADD/ADHD Students with ADD/ADHD are eligible for the same services available to students with LD, as well as distraction-free study areas and distraction-free testing environments.

Application *Required:* documentation of high school services (e.g., Individualized Education Program [IEP] or 504 plan) and documentation from other sources if high school information not available. *Recommended:* psychoeducational report. Upon application, documentation of need for special services should be sent only to your LD program or unit. Upon acceptance, documentation of need for special services should be sent only to your LD program or unit. *Application deadline (institutional):* rolling/continuous for fall and rolling/continuous for spring. *Application deadline (LD program):* rolling/continuous for fall and rolling/continuous for spring.

LD program contact Kim Forbes Powell, Educational Coordinator for Students with Disabilities, 3301 Hocking Parkway, Nelsonville, OH 45764. *Phone:* 740-753-3591 Ext. 2230. *Fax:* 740-753-4097. *E-mail:* forbes_k@hocking.edu.

Application contact Hocking College, 3301 Hocking Parkway, Nelsonville, OH 45764-9588. *E-mail:* ralph_b@ccmgate.hocking.cc.oh.us/. *Web address:* http://www.hocking.edu/.

HOLYOKE COMMUNITY COLLEGE
Holyoke, Massachusetts

Students with LD Served by Program	200	ADD/ADHD Services	✓
Staff	2 full-time, 2 part-time	Summer Preparation Program	n/a
LD Program or Service Fee	n/a	Alternative Test Arrangements	✓
LD Program Began	1988	LD Student Organization	n/a

Office for Students with Disabilities and Deaf Services began offering services in 1988. The program serves approximately 200 undergraduate students. Faculty consists of 2 full-time and 2 part-time staff members. Services are provided by academic advisers, counselors, special education teachers, graduate assistants/students, trained peer tutors, and professional tutors.

Policies Students with LD may take up to 18 credit hours per semester; 3 credit hours per semester are required to maintain full-time status and to be eligible for financial aid.

Special preparation or orientation Required orientation held individually by special arrangement.

Subject-area tutoring Available in most subjects. Offered one-on-one, in small groups, and class-size groups by computer-based instruction, professional tutors, graduate assistants/students, and trained peer tutors.

Counseling and advisement Career counseling and individual counseling are available. Academic advisement by a staff member affiliated with the program is available.

Auxiliary aids and services *Aids:* scan and read programs (e.g., Kurzweil), screen-enlarging programs, speech recognition programs (e.g., Dragon), taped textbooks. *Services and accommodations:* advocates, priority registration, alternative test arrangements, readers, note-takers, and scribes.

ADD/ADHD Students with ADD/ADHD are eligible for the same services available to students with LD, as well as distraction-free testing environments.

Application *Required:* high school transcript and psychoeducational report (5 years old or less). Upon application, documentation of need for special services should be sent only to your LD program or unit. Upon acceptance, documentation of need for special services should be sent only to your LD program or unit. *Application deadline (institutional):* rolling/continuous for fall and rolling/continuous for spring. *Application deadline (LD program):* rolling/continuous for fall and rolling/continuous for spring.

LD program contact Maureen Conroy, Director, Office for Students with Disabilities and Deaf Services, 303 Homestead Avenue, Holyoke, MA 01040. *Phone:* 413-522-2417. *Fax:* 413-534-8975. *E-mail:* mconroy@hcc.mass.edu.

Application contact Holyoke Community College, 303 Homestead Avenue, Holyoke, MA 01040-1099. *Web address:* http://www.hcc.mass.edu/.

HOUSATONIC COMMUNITY COLLEGE
Bridgeport, Connecticut

Students with LD Served by Program	250	ADD/ADHD Services	✓
Staff	1 full-time, 1 part-time	Summer Preparation Program	n/a
LD Program or Service Fee	n/a	Alternative Test Arrangements	✓
LD Program Began	1990	LD Student Organization	n/a

Disability Support Services began offering services in 1990. The program serves approximately 250 undergraduate students. Faculty consists of 1 full-time and 1 part-time staff member. Services are provided by academic advisers, counselors, regular education teachers, graduate assistants/students, trained peer tutors, and professional tutors.

Policies Students with LD may take up to 18 credit hours per term; 6 credit hours per term are required to maintain full-time status and to be eligible for financial aid.

Special preparation or orientation Optional orientation held before registration, during registration, before classes begin, after classes begin, during summer prior to enrollment, and individually by special arrangement.

Basic skills remediation Available in study skills, reading, time management, learning strategies, spelling, written language, math, and spoken language. Offered one-on-one, in small groups, and class-size groups by regular education teachers, graduate assistants/students, professional tutors, and trained peer tutors.

Housatonic Community College (continued)

Subject-area tutoring Available in most subjects. Offered one-on-one, in small groups, and class-size groups by professional tutors, graduate assistants/students, trained peer tutors, and LD specialists.

Counseling and advisement Career counseling, individual counseling, small-group counseling, and support groups are available. Academic advisement by a staff member affiliated with the program is available.

Auxiliary aids and services *Aids:* calculators, screen-enlarging programs, screen readers, speech recognition programs (e.g., Dragon), tape recorders. *Services and accommodations:* advocates, alternative test arrangements, and readers.

ADD/ADHD Students with ADD/ADHD are eligible for the same services available to students with LD, as well as distraction-free study areas and distraction-free testing environments.

Application *Required:* high school transcript and accuplacer test. Upon application, documentation of need for special services should be sent only to your LD program or unit. Upon acceptance, documentation of need for special services should be sent only to your LD program or unit. *Application deadline (institutional):* rolling/continuous for fall and rolling/continuous for spring. *Application deadline (LD program):* rolling/continuous for fall and rolling/continuous for spring.

LD program contact Lynne Langella, Coordinator of Disability Support Services, 900 Lafayette Boulevard, Bridgeport, CT 06604-4704. *Phone:* 203-332-5018. *Fax:* 203-332-5250. *E-mail:* ho_llangella@commnet.edu.

Application contact Housatonic Community College, 900 Lafayette Boulevard, Bridgeport, CT 06604-4704. *Web address:* http://www.hctc.commnet.edu/.

ILLINOIS CENTRAL COLLEGE
East Peoria, Illinois

Students with LD Served by Program	75	ADD/ADHD Services	✓
Staff	1 full-time	Summer Preparation Program	n/a
LD Program or Service Fee	n/a	Alternative Test Arrangements	✓
LD Program Began	1980	LD Student Organization	n/a

Disability Services began offering services in 1980. The program serves approximately 75 undergraduate students. Faculty consists of 1 full-time staff member. Services are provided by academic advisers, counselors, regular education teachers, teacher trainees, trained peer tutors, and professional tutors.

Policies 12 credit hours per semester are required to maintain full-time status.

Special preparation or orientation Required orientation held before registration, during registration, before classes begin, after classes begin, and individually by special arrangement.

Diagnostic testing Available for reading, written language, and math.

Basic skills remediation Available in reading, spelling, written language, math, and spoken language. Offered one-on-one and in small groups by computer-based instruction, graduate assistants/students, professional tutors, and trained peer tutors.

Subject-area tutoring Available in most subjects. Offered one-on-one and in small groups by professional tutors, graduate assistants/students, and trained peer tutors.

Counseling and advisement Career counseling and individual counseling are available. Academic advisement by a staff member affiliated with the program is available.

Auxiliary aids and services *Aids:* calculators, personal computers, personal spelling/word-use assistants (e.g., Franklin Speller), scan and read programs (e.g., Kurzweil), screen-

enlarging programs, tape recorders, taped textbooks. *Services and accommodations:* priority registration, alternative test arrangements, readers, note-takers, and scribes.

ADD/ADHD Students with ADD/ADHD are eligible for the same services available to students with LD, as well as distraction-free testing environments.

Application *Required:* high school transcript, interview, separate application to your LD program or unit, psychoeducational report (3 years old or less), and documentation of high school services (e.g., Individualized Education Program [IEP] or 504 plan). Upon application, documentation of need for special services should be sent only to your LD program or unit. Upon acceptance, documentation of need for special services should be sent only to your LD program or unit. *Application deadline (institutional):* rolling/continuous for fall and rolling/continuous for spring. *Application deadline (LD program):* rolling/continuous for fall and rolling/continuous for spring.

LD program contact Pam Wilfinger, Coordinator, Disability Services, Room 238D, One College Drive, East Peoria, IL 61635. *Phone:* 309-694-5749. *Fax:* 309-694-5450. *E-mail:* pwilfinger@icc.cc.il.us.

Application contact Illinois Central College, Admissions Office, 1 College Drive, East Peoria, IL 61635-0001. *Web address:* http://www.icc.cc.il.us/.

IVY TECH STATE COLLEGE-CENTRAL INDIANA
Indianapolis, Indiana

Students with LD Served by Program	110	ADD/ADHD Services	✓
Staff	4 full-time, 3 part-time	Summer Preparation Program	n/a
LD Program or Service Fee	n/a	Alternative Test Arrangements	✓
LD Program Began	1985	LD Student Organization	n/a

Special Needs Services began offering services in 1985. The program serves approximately 110 undergraduate students. Faculty consists of 4 full-time and 3 part-time staff members. Services are provided by counselors, remediation/learning specialists, LD specialists, and professional tutors.

Policies Students with LD may take up to 15 credit hours per semester; 12 credit hours per semester are required to maintain full-time status; 6 credit hours per semester are required to be eligible for financial aid.

Special preparation or orientation Held before classes begin.

Subject-area tutoring Available in most subjects. Offered one-on-one and in small groups by professional tutors and LD specialists.

Counseling and advisement Career counseling and individual counseling are available.

Auxiliary aids and services *Aids:* calculators, scan and read programs (e.g., Kurzweil), screen-enlarging programs, screen readers, speech recognition programs (e.g., Dragon), tape recorders, taped textbooks. *Services and accommodations:* priority registration and alternative test arrangements.

ADD/ADHD Students with ADD/ADHD are eligible for the same services available to students with LD, as well as distraction-free study areas and distraction-free testing environments.

Application *Required:* high school transcript, psychoeducational report, documentation of high school services (e.g., Individualized Education Program [IEP] or 504 plan), and college placement exam. Upon application, documentation of need for special services should be sent only to your LD program or unit. Upon acceptance, documentation of need for special services should be sent only to your LD program or unit. *Application deadline* *(institutional)*: rolling/continuous for fall and rolling/continuous for spring. *Application deadline (LD program)*: rolling/continuous for fall and rolling/continuous for spring.

LD program contact Sharon Dunn, Manager of ACCESS Counseling and Support Services, 1 West 26th Street, PO Box 1763, Indianapolis, IN 46206. *Phone:* 317-921-4908. *Fax:* 317-921-4753. *E-mail:* sdunn@ivy.tec.in.us.

Application contact Ivy Tech State College-Central Indiana, 1 West 26th Street, PO Box 1763, Indianapolis, IN 46206-1763. *Web address:* http://www.ivy.tec.in.us/.

IVY TECH STATE COLLEGE-COLUMBUS
Columbus, Indiana

Students with LD Served by Program	30	ADD/ADHD Services	✓
Staff	1 full-time	Summer Preparation Program	n/a
LD Program or Service Fee	n/a	Alternative Test Arrangements	✓
LD Program Began	n/a	LD Student Organization	n/a

Office of Disability Services serves approximately 30 undergraduate students. Faculty consists of 1 full-time staff member. Services are provided by academic advisers, remediation/learning specialists, counselors, and regular education teachers.

Policies Students with LD may take up to 15 credit hours per semester; 12 credit hours per semester are required to maintain full-time status and to be eligible for financial aid.

Basic skills remediation Available in study skills, reading, time management, spelling, written language, and math. Offered in class-size groups by regular education teachers.

Subject-area tutoring Available in some subjects. Offered one-on-one and in small groups by any person with experience in the subject matter.

Counseling and advisement Career counseling and individual counseling are available. Academic advisement by a staff member affiliated with the program is available.

Auxiliary aids and services *Aids:* calculators, screen-enlarging programs, speech recognition programs (e.g., Dragon), tape recorders, taped textbooks. *Services and accommodations:* alternative test arrangements, readers, note-takers, and scribes.

ADD/ADHD Students with ADD/ADHD are eligible for the same services available to students with LD, as well as distraction-free study areas and distraction-free testing environments.

Application *Required:* high school transcript, interview, separate application to your LD program or unit, psychoeducational report (5 years old or less), and documentation of high school services (e.g., Individualized Education Program [IEP] or 504 plan). Upon application, documentation of need for special services should be sent only to your LD program or unit. Upon acceptance, documentation of need for special services should be sent only to your LD program or unit. *Application deadline (institutional):* rolling/continuous for fall and rolling/continuous for spring. *Application deadline (LD program):* rolling/continuous for fall and rolling/continuous for spring.

LD program contact Linn L. Jorgenson, Counselor, 4475 Central Avenue, Columbus, IN 47203. *Phone:* 812-372-9925 Ext. 132. *Fax:* 812-372-0311. *E-mail:* ljorgens@ivy.tec.in.us.

Application contact Ivy Tech State College-Columbus, 4475 Central Avenue, Columbus, IN 47203-1868. *Web address:* http://www.ivy.tec.in.us/.

IVY TECH STATE COLLEGE-NORTHEAST
Fort Wayne, Indiana

Students with LD Served by Program	100	ADD/ADHD Services	✓
Staff	9 part-time	Summer Preparation Program	n/a
LD Program or Service Fee	n/a	Alternative Test Arrangements	✓
LD Program Began	1994	LD Student Organization	n/a

Disability Services began offering services in 1994. The program serves approximately 100 undergraduate students. Faculty consists of 9 part-time staff members. Services are provided by academic advisers, counselors, and LD specialists.

Policies Students with LD may take up to 12 credit hours per semester; 12 credit hours per semester are required to maintain full-time status; 6 credit hours per semester are required to be eligible for financial aid.

Special preparation or orientation Optional orientation held individually by special arrangement.

Basic skills remediation Available in study skills, computer skills, reading, time management, learning strategies, spelling, written language, and math. Offered in class-size groups by regular education teachers.

Counseling and advisement Career counseling and individual counseling are available. Academic advisement by a staff member affiliated with the program is available.

Auxiliary aids and services *Aids:* calculators, personal computers, personal spelling/word-use assistants (e.g., Franklin Speller), scan and read programs (e.g., Kurzweil), screen-enlarging programs, screen readers, speech recognition programs (e.g., Dragon), tape recorders, taped textbooks. *Services and accommodations:* advocates, alternative test arrangements, readers, note-takers, and scribes.

ADD/ADHD Students with ADD/ADHD are eligible for the same services available to students with LD, as well as distraction-free study areas and distraction-free testing environments.

Application *Required:* high school transcript, psychoeducational report (3 years old or less), and documentation of high school services (e.g., Individualized Education Program [IEP] or 504 plan). *Recommended:* interview, personal statement, and separate application to your LD program or unit. Upon application, documentation of need for special services should be sent only to your LD program or unit. Upon acceptance, documentation of need for special services should be sent only to your LD program or unit. *Application deadline (institutional):* rolling/continuous for fall and rolling/continuous for spring. *Application deadline (LD program):* rolling/continuous for fall and rolling/continuous for spring.

LD program contact Rex A. Oechsle, Coordinator, 3800 North Anthony Boulevard, Fort Wayne, IN 46805. *Phone:* 219-482-9171. *Fax:* 219-480-4177. *E-mail:* roechsle@ivy.tec.in.us.

Application contact Neal Davis, Admissions Coordinator, Ivy Tech State College-Northeast, 3800 North Anthony Boulevard, Fort Wayne, IN 46805-1430. *Phone:* 219-480-4211. *Web address:* http://www.ivy.tec.in.us/.

IVY TECH STATE COLLEGE-SOUTHCENTRAL

Sellersburg, Indiana

Students with LD Served by Program	20	ADD/ADHD Services	✓
Staff	1 full-time	Summer Preparation Program	n/a
LD Program or Service Fee	n/a	Alternative Test Arrangements	✓
LD Program Began	n/a	LD Student Organization	✓

The college serves approximately 20 undergraduate students. Faculty consists of 1 full-time staff member. Services are provided by regular education teachers and counselors.

Policies 12 credit hours per semester are required to maintain full-time status; 3 credit hours per semester are required to be eligible for financial aid.

Special preparation or orientation Optional orientation held individually by special arrangement.

Subject-area tutoring Available in some subjects. Offered one-on-one by computer-based instruction and professional tutors.

Counseling and advisement Career counseling and individual counseling are available.

Auxiliary aids and services *Aids:* calculators, scan and read programs (e.g., Kurzweil), screen-enlarging programs. *Services and accommodations:* priority registration, alternative test arrangements, readers, note-takers, and scribes.

Student organization There is a student organization for students with LD.

ADD/ADHD Students with ADD/ADHD are eligible for the same services available to students with LD, as well as distraction-free study areas and distraction-free testing environments.

Application *Required:* high school transcript, psychoeducational report, and complete ASSET placement test. *Recommended:* participation in extracurricular activities, interview, and documentation of high school services (e.g., Individualized Education Program [IEP] or 504 plan). Upon application, documentation of need for special services should be sent only to your LD program or unit. Upon acceptance, documentation of need for special services should be sent only to your LD program or unit. *Application deadline (institutional):* 8/28 for fall and 1/10 for spring. *Application deadline (LD program):* 8/28 for fall and 1/10 for spring.

LD program contact Denise Shaw, Special Needs Counselor, 8204 Highway 311, Sellersburg, IN 47172. *Phone:* 812-246-3301. *Fax:* 812-246-9905. *E-mail:* dshaw@ivy.tec.in.us.

Application contact Ivy Tech State College-Southcentral, 8204 Highway 311, Sellersburg, IN 47172-1829. *Web address:* http://www.ivy.tec.in.us/.

IVY TECH STATE COLLEGE-SOUTHWEST

Evansville, Indiana

Students with LD Served by Program	35	ADD/ADHD Services	✓
Staff	1 part-time	Summer Preparation Program	n/a
LD Program or Service Fee	n/a	Alternative Test Arrangements	✓
LD Program Began	1991	LD Student Organization	n/a

Disability Services began offering services in 1991. The program serves approximately 35 undergraduate students. Faculty consists of 1 part-time staff member. Services are provided by academic advisers, regular education teachers, LD specialists, trained peer tutors, and professional tutors.

Basic skills remediation Available in study skills, reading, time management, learning strategies, spelling, written language, math, and spoken language. Offered one-on-one and in class-size groups by regular education teachers, LD specialists, and professional tutors.

Subject-area tutoring Available in some subjects. Offered one-on-one and in small groups by professional tutors, trained peer tutors, and LD specialists.

Special courses Available in math. All courses are offered for credit; none enter into overall grade point average.

Counseling and advisement Career counseling and academic counseling are available. Academic advisement by a staff member affiliated with the program is available.

Auxiliary aids and services *Aids:* calculators, personal computers, personal spelling/word-use assistants (e.g., Franklin Speller), scan and read programs (e.g., Kurzweil), screen-enlarging programs, screen readers, speech recognition programs (e.g., Dragon), tape recorders, taped textbooks. *Services and accommodations:* advocates, alternative test arrangements, readers, note-takers, and scribes.

ADD/ADHD Students with ADD/ADHD are eligible for the same services available to students with LD, as well as distraction-free testing environments.

Application *Required:* high school transcript and psychoeducational report (3 years old or less). *Recommended:* ACT (extended-time or untimed test accepted), SAT I (extended-time or untimed test accepted), interview, and documentation of high school services (e.g., Individualized Education Program [IEP] or 504 plan). Upon application, documentation of need for special services should be sent only to your LD program or unit. Upon acceptance, documentation of need for special services should be sent only to your LD program or unit. *Application deadline (institutional):* rolling/continuous for fall and rolling/continuous for spring. *Application deadline (LD program):* 6/15 for fall and 11/5 for spring.

LD program contact Peg Ehlen, Special Needs Coordinator/Associate Professor, 3501 First Avenue, Evansville, IN 47710. *Phone:* 812-429-1386. *Fax:* 812-429-1483. *E-mail:* pehlen@ivy.tec.in.us.

Application contact Ivy Tech State College-Southwest, 3501 First Avenue, Evansville, IN 47710-3398. *Web address:* http://www.ivy.tec.in.us/.

IVY TECH STATE COLLEGE-WABASH VALLEY

Terre Haute, Indiana

Students with LD Served by Program	48	ADD/ADHD Services	✓
Staff	1 full-time	Summer Preparation Program	n/a
LD Program or Service Fee	n/a	Alternative Test Arrangements	✓
LD Program Began	1994	LD Student Organization	n/a

Access Disability Services began offering services in 1994. The program serves approximately 48 undergraduate students. Faculty consists of 1 full-time staff member. Services are provided by academic advisers, counselors, regular education teachers, trained peer tutors, and professional tutors.

Policies Students with LD may take up to 18 credits per semester; 12 credits per semester are required to maintain full-time status; 3 credits per semester are required to be eligible for financial aid.

Special preparation or orientation Optional orientation held before classes begin, during summer prior to enrollment, and individually by special arrangement.

Diagnostic testing Available for reading, written language, and math.

Basic skills remediation Available in study skills, computer skills, reading, time management, spelling, written language, and math. Offered one-on-one, in small groups, and class-size groups by regular education teachers, professional tutors, and trained peer tutors.

Subject-area tutoring Available in most subjects. Offered one-on-one and in small groups by professional tutors, trained peer tutors, and instructors.

Special courses Available in career planning, study skills, college survival skills, practical computer skills, test taking, reading, time management, learning strategies, vocabulary development, math, stress management, and written composition skills. Some courses are offered for credit; none enter into overall grade point average.

Counseling and advisement Career counseling, individual counseling, and support groups are available. Academic advisement by a staff member affiliated with the program is available.

Auxiliary aids and services *Aids:* personal computers, personal spelling/word-use assistants (e.g., Franklin Speller), screen-enlarging programs, tape recorders, taped textbooks. *Services and accommodations:* advocates, priority registration, alternative test arrangements, readers, note-takers, and scribes.

ADD/ADHD Students with ADD/ADHD are eligible for the same services available to students with LD, as well as distraction-free study areas and distraction-free testing environments.

Application *Required:* high school transcript, separate application to your LD program or unit, psychoeducational report (3 years old or less), and medical experts' records. *Recommended:* ACT or SAT I (extended-time or untimed ACT test accepted) and documentation of high school services (e.g., Individualized Education Program [IEP] or 504 plan). Upon application, documentation of need for special services should be sent to both admissions and your LD program or unit. Upon acceptance, documentation of need for special services should be sent only to your LD program or unit. *Application deadline (institutional):* rolling/continuous for fall and rolling/continuous for spring.

LD program contact Lynn C. Foster, Outreach Counselor, 7999 US Highway 41 South, Terre Haute, IN 47802. *Phone:* 812-299-1121. *Fax:* 812-299-5723. *E-mail:* lfoster@ivy.tec.in.us.

Application contact Ron Maxwell, Director of Student Services, Ivy Tech State College-Wabash Valley, 7999 US Highway 41, South, Terre Haute, IN 47802. *Phone:* 812-299-1121. *Web address:* http://www.ivy.tec.in.us/.

JAMESTOWN COMMUNITY COLLEGE

Jamestown, New York

Students with LD Served by Program	60	ADD/ADHD Services	✓
Staff	1 part-time	Summer Preparation Program	n/a
LD Program or Service Fee	n/a	Alternative Test Arrangements	✓
LD Program Began	1985	LD Student Organization	n/a

Disability Support Services began offering services in 1985. The program serves approximately 60 undergraduate students. Faculty consists of 1 part-time staff member. Services are provided by remediation/learning specialists, trained peer tutors, and professional tutors.

Policies The college has written policies regarding course substitutions. Students with LD may take up to 19 credit hours per semester; 12 credit hours per semester are required to maintain full-time status; 6 credit hours per semester are required to be eligible for financial aid.

Auxiliary aids and services *Aids:* calculators, personal spelling/word-use assistants (e.g., Franklin Speller), scan and read programs (e.g., Kurzweil), screen-enlarging programs, screen readers, tape recorders, taped textbooks. *Services and accommodations:* advocates, alternative test arrangements, readers, note-takers, and scribes.

ADD/ADHD Students with ADD/ADHD are eligible for the same services available to students with LD, as well as distraction-free study areas and distraction-free testing environments.

Application *Required:* high school transcript. Upon application, documentation of need for special services should be sent only to your LD program or unit. *Application deadline (institutional):* rolling/continuous for fall and rolling/continuous for spring. *Application deadline (LD program):* rolling/continuous for fall and rolling/continuous for spring.

LD program contact Nancy Callahan, Coordinator, Disability Support Services, 525 Falconer Street, Jamestown, NY 14702-0020. *Phone:* 716-665-5220 Ext. 2459. *Fax:* 716-487-2626. *E-mail:* nancycallahan@mail.sunyjcc.edu.

Application contact Jamestown Community College, 525 Falconer Street, Jamestown, NY 14701-1999. *E-mail:* devneyjf@jccw22.cc.sunyjcc.edu. *Web address:* http://www.sunyjcc.edu/.

JOHNSON & WALES UNIVERSITY

Vail, Colorado

Students with LD Served by Program	550	ADD/ADHD Services	✓
Staff	3 full-time, 1 part-time	Summer Preparation Program	n/a
LD Program or Service Fee	n/a	Alternative Test Arrangements	✓
LD Program Began	1987	LD Student Organization	✓

Student Success began offering services in 1987. The program serves approximately 550 undergraduate students. Faculty consists of 3 full-time staff members and 1 part-time staff member. Services are provided by academic advisers, remediation/learning specialists, counselors, special education teachers, LD specialists, trained peer tutors, and professional tutors.

Policies The college has written policies regarding course substitutions. Students with LD may take up to 19 credit hours per quarter. LD services are also available to graduate students.

Special preparation or orientation Optional orientation held during registration.

Basic skills remediation Available in study skills, reading, time management, social skills, learning strategies, math, and spoken language. Offered one-on-one and in small groups by regular education teachers, LD specialists, and professional tutors.

Subject-area tutoring Available in most subjects. Offered one-on-one and in small groups by professional tutors, graduate assistants/students, trained peer tutors, and LD specialists.

Counseling and advisement Career counseling, individual counseling, small-group counseling, and support groups are available. Academic advisement by a staff member affiliated with the program is available.

Auxiliary aids and services *Aids:* taped textbooks. *Services and accommodations:* advocates, priority registration, alternative test arrangements, readers, note-takers, and scribes.

Student organization There is a student organization for students with LD.

ADD/ADHD Students with ADD/ADHD are eligible for the same services available to students with LD, as well as distraction-free testing environments and personal coach or mentors.

Application *Required:* high school transcript. *Recommended:* participation in extracurricular activities. Upon acceptance, documentation of need for special services should be sent only to your LD program or unit. *Application deadline (institutional):*

Johnson & Wales University (continued)

rolling/continuous for fall and rolling/continuous for spring. *Application deadline (LD program):* rolling/continuous for fall and rolling/continuous for spring.

LD program contact Meryl Berstein, Director of Student Success, 8 Abbott Park Place, Providence, RI 02903. *Phone:* 401-598-4689. *Fax:* 401-598-4657. *E-mail:* mberstein@jwu.edu.

Application contact Johnson & Wales University, 8 Abbot Park Place, Providence, RI 02903. *E-mail:* admissions@jwu.edu. *Web address:* http://www.jwu.edu/.

JOHNSON COUNTY COMMUNITY COLLEGE
Overland Park, Kansas

Students with LD Served by Program	300	ADD/ADHD Services	✓
Staff	3 full-time, 8 part-time	Summer Preparation Program	✓
LD Program or Service Fee	n/a	Alternative Test Arrangements	✓
LD Program Began	1972	LD Student Organization	n/a

Access Services began offering services in 1972. The program serves approximately 300 undergraduate students. Faculty consists of 3 full-time and 8 part-time staff members. Services are provided by academic advisers, counselors, and trained peer tutors.

Policies The college has written policies regarding grade forgiveness. 12 credit hours per semester are required to maintain full-time status; 6 credit hours per semester are required to be eligible for financial aid.

Special preparation or orientation Optional summer program offered prior to entering college. Optional orientation held during summer prior to enrollment.

Subject-area tutoring Available in most subjects. Offered one-on-one by professional tutors and trained peer tutors.

Counseling and advisement Career counseling and individual counseling are available. Academic advisement by a staff member affiliated with the program is available.

Auxiliary aids and services *Aids:* calculators, personal computers, scan and read programs (e.g., Kurzweil), screen-enlarging programs, screen readers, speech recognition programs (e.g., Dragon), tape recorders, taped textbooks. *Services and accommodations:* advocates, priority registration, alternative test arrangements, readers, note-takers, and scribes.

ADD/ADHD Students with ADD/ADHD are eligible for the same services available to students with LD, as well as distraction-free testing environments and process tutoring.

Application *Required:* high school transcript, separate application to your LD program or unit, and psychoeducational report (3 years old or less). *Recommended:* documentation of high school services (e.g., Individualized Education Program [IEP] or 504 plan). Upon application, documentation of need for special services should be sent only to your LD program or unit. *Application deadline (institutional):* 8/21 for fall and 1/21 for spring. *Application deadline (LD program):* rolling/continuous for fall and rolling/continuous for spring.

LD program contact Holly Kopplin Dressler, Access Advisor/Program Facilitator, 12345 College Boulevard, Overland Park, KS 66210-1299. *Phone:* 913-469-8500. *E-mail:* dressler@jccc.net.

Application contact Dr. Pat Long, Dean of Student Services, Johnson County Community College, 12345 College Boulevard, Overland Park, KS 66210-1299. *Phone:* 913-469-8500 Ext. 3806. *Web address:* http://www.johnco.cc.ks.us/.

JOHNSON TECHNICAL INSTITUTE
Scranton, Pennsylvania

Students with LD Served by Program	15	ADD/ADHD Services	✓
Staff	8 part-time	Summer Preparation Program	✓
LD Program or Service Fee	n/a	Alternative Test Arrangements	✓
LD Program Began	1991	LD Student Organization	n/a

Special Populations began offering services in 1991. The program serves approximately 15 undergraduate students. Faculty consists of 8 part-time staff members. Services are provided by counselors, regular education teachers, diagnostic specialists, and trained peer tutors.

Policies Students with LD may take up to 21 credit hours per semester; 12 credit hours per semester are required to maintain full-time status; 6 credit hours per semester are required to be eligible for financial aid.

Special preparation or orientation Optional summer program offered prior to entering college. Required orientation held before registration, during registration, before classes begin, after classes begin, during summer prior to enrollment, and individually by special arrangement.

Diagnostic testing Available for auditory processing, motor skills, spelling, handwriting, neuropsychological, spoken language, intelligence, personality, study skills, learning strategies, reading, written language, learning styles, social skills, visual processing, and math.

Basic skills remediation Available in auditory processing, motor skills, study skills, computer skills, reading, time management, handwriting, social skills, visual processing, learning strategies, spelling, written language, math, and spoken language. Offered one-on-one and in small groups by computer-based instruction, regular education teachers, trained peer tutors, and counselors.

Subject-area tutoring Available in all subjects. Offered one-on-one by computer-based instruction and trained peer tutors.

Special courses Available in study skills, practical computer skills, test taking, reading, time management, learning strategies, self-advocacy, vocabulary development, math, stress management, and written composition skills. Some courses are offered for credit; none enter into overall grade point average.

Counseling and advisement Career counseling, individual counseling, small-group counseling, and support groups are available.

Auxiliary aids and services *Aids:* calculators, personal spelling/word-use assistants (e.g., Franklin Speller), scan and read programs (e.g., Kurzweil), tape recorders, taped textbooks. *Services and accommodations:* advocates, priority registration, alternative test arrangements, readers, and note-takers.

ADD/ADHD Students with ADD/ADHD are eligible for the same services available to students with LD, as well as distraction-free study areas, distraction-free testing environments, medication management, personal coach or mentors, and support groups for ADD/ADHD.

Application *Required:* high school transcript, SAT I (extended-time test accepted), interview, personal statement, letter(s) of recommendation, psychoeducational report (4 years old or less), and documentation of high school services (e.g., Individualized Education Program [IEP] or 504 plan). *Recommended:* participation in extracurricular activities. Upon application, documentation of need for special services should be sent only to admissions. Upon acceptance, documentation of need for special services should be sent to both admissions and your LD program or unit. *Application deadline (institutional):* rolling/continuous for fall. *Application deadline (LD program):* rolling/continuous for fall.

LD program contact Susan L. Gardner, Assistant Director, Student Support Services, 3427 North Main Avenue, Scranton, PA 18508-1495. *Phone:* 570-342-6404 Ext. 134. *Fax:* 570-348-2181. **Application contact** Johnson Technical Institute, 3427 North Main Avenue, Scranton, PA 18508-1495. *Web address:* http://www.jti.org/.

JOHN TYLER COMMUNITY COLLEGE
Chester, Virginia

Students with LD Served by Program	350	ADD/ADHD Services	✓
Staff	2 full-time	Summer Preparation Program	n/a
LD Program or Service Fee	n/a	Alternative Test Arrangements	✓
LD Program Began	1998	LD Student Organization	n/a

Counseling, Disabilities Support began offering services in 1998. The program serves approximately 350 undergraduate students. Faculty consists of 2 full-time staff members. Services are provided by regular education teachers, counselors, remediation/learning specialists, trained peer tutors, and professional tutors.
Basic skills remediation Available in study skills, computer skills, reading, time management, learning strategies, and written language. Offered in small groups and class-size groups by regular education teachers.
Subject-area tutoring Available in most subjects. Offered one-on-one by professional tutors and trained peer tutors.
Counseling and advisement Career counseling and individual counseling are available.
Auxiliary aids and services *Aids:* calculators, scan and read programs (e.g., Kurzweil), screen-enlarging programs, screen readers, speech recognition programs (e.g., Dragon), tape recorders, taped textbooks. *Services and accommodations:* advocates, priority registration, alternative test arrangements, readers, note-takers, and scribes.
ADD/ADHD Students with ADD/ADHD are eligible for the same services available to students with LD, as well as distraction-free testing environments.
Application *Required:* psychoeducational report (3 years old or less). *Recommended:* high school transcript and interview. Upon application, documentation of need for special services should be sent only to your LD program or unit. Upon acceptance, documentation of need for special services should be sent only to your LD program or unit.
LD program contact Dr. Kerren McDougal, Counselor, 13801 Jefferson Davis Highway, Chester, VA 23831. *Phone:* 804-796-4202. *Fax:* 804-796-4362. *E-mail:* kmcdougal@jt.cc.va.us.
Application contact John Tyler Community College, 13101 Jefferson Davis Highway, Chester, VA 23831-5316. *Web address:* http://www.jt.cc.va.us/.

JOLIET JUNIOR COLLEGE
Joliet, Illinois

Students with LD Served by Program	250	ADD/ADHD Services	✓
Staff	7 part-time	Summer Preparation Program	n/a
LD Program or Service Fee	n/a	Alternative Test Arrangements	✓
LD Program Began	1975	LD Student Organization	n/a

Special Needs began offering services in 1975. The program serves approximately 250 undergraduate students. Faculty consists of 7 part-time staff members. Services are provided by LD specialists, professional tutors, and reading specialists.
Policies 12 credit hours per semester are required to maintain full-time status; 6 credit hours per semester are required to be eligible for financial aid.
Special preparation or orientation Required orientation held before classes begin.
Diagnostic testing Available for auditory processing and learning styles.
Subject-area tutoring Available in most subjects. Offered one-on-one and in small groups by computer-based instruction, professional tutors, and LD specialists.
Auxiliary aids and services *Aids:* personal spelling/word-use assistants (e.g., Franklin Speller), scan and read programs (e.g., Kurzweil), screen-enlarging programs, screen readers, speech recognition programs (e.g., Dragon), tape recorders, taped textbooks. *Services and accommodations:* alternative test arrangements, note-takers, and scribes.
ADD/ADHD Students with ADD/ADHD are eligible for the same services available to students with LD, as well as distraction-free testing environments.
Application Upon acceptance, documentation of need for special services should be sent only to your LD program or unit.
LD program contact Carol L. Smith, Special Needs Coordinator, 1215 Houbolt Road, Joliet, IL 60431-8938. *Phone:* 815-729-9020 Ext. 2230. *Fax:* 815-729-4256. *E-mail:* csmith@jjc.cc.il.us.
Application contact Joliet Junior College, 1215 Houbolt Road, Joliet, IL 60431-8938. *E-mail:* gmaniate@jjc.cc.il.us. *Web address:* http://www.jjc.cc.il.us/.

KALAMAZOO VALLEY COMMUNITY COLLEGE
Kalamazoo, Michigan

Students with LD Served by Program	120	ADD/ADHD Services	✓
Staff	1 full-time, 5 part-time	Summer Preparation Program	n/a
LD Program or Service Fee	n/a	Alternative Test Arrangements	✓
LD Program Began	1989	LD Student Organization	n/a

Special Services Office began offering services in 1989. The program serves approximately 120 undergraduate students. Faculty consists of 1 full-time and 5 part-time staff members. Services are provided by academic advisers, remediation/learning specialists, and graduate assistants/students.
Special preparation or orientation Optional orientation held individually by special arrangement.
Counseling and advisement Academic advisement by a staff member affiliated with the program is available.
Auxiliary aids and services *Aids:* scan and read programs (e.g., Kurzweil), screen-enlarging programs, screen readers, speech recognition programs (e.g., Dragon), taped textbooks. *Services and accommodations:* advocates, alternative test arrangements, readers, note-takers, and scribes.
ADD/ADHD Students with ADD/ADHD are eligible for the same services available to students with LD, as well as distraction-free testing environments.
Application Upon acceptance, documentation of need for special services should be sent only to your LD program or unit.
LD program contact Lois Baldwin, Special Services Advisor, 6767 West "O" Avenue, Kalamazoo, MI 49009. *Phone:* 616-372-5384. *Fax:* 616-372-5555.

Kalamazoo Valley Community College (continued)

Application contact Kalamazoo Valley Community College, PO Box 4070, Kalamazoo, MI 49003-4070. *Web address:* http://www.kvcc.edu/.

KENT STATE UNIVERSITY, ASHTABULA CAMPUS
Ashtabula, Ohio

Students with LD Served by Program	15	ADD/ADHD Services	✓
Staff	1 full-time	Summer Preparation Program	n/a
LD Program or Service Fee	n/a	Alternative Test Arrangements	n/a
LD Program Began	1995	LD Student Organization	n/a

Student Services (Developmental Education) began offering services in 1995. The program serves approximately 15 undergraduate students. Faculty consists of 1 full-time staff member. Services are provided by regular education teachers and remediation/learning specialists.

Policies Students with LD may take up to 18 credit hours per semester; 12 credit hours per semester are required to maintain full-time status; 1 credit hour per semester is required to be eligible for financial aid.

Basic skills remediation Available in reading, learning strategies, written language, and math. Offered one-on-one and in class-size groups by regular education teachers and trained peer tutors.

Subject-area tutoring Available in some subjects. Offered one-on-one by trained peer tutors.

Special courses Available in career planning, study skills, college survival skills, reading, math, and written composition skills. Some courses are offered for credit; some enter into overall grade point average.

Counseling and advisement Career counseling and individual counseling are available.

Auxiliary aids and services *Aids:* personal computers, screen-enlarging programs, tape recorders, taped textbooks. *Services and accommodations:* readers, note-takers, and scribes.

ADD/ADHD Students with ADD/ADHD are eligible for the same services available to students with LD, as well as distraction-free testing environments.

Application *Required:* high school transcript, interview, separate application to your LD program or unit, and psychoeducational report (5 years old or less). *Recommended:* ACT or SAT I (extended-time or untimed test accepted) and documentation of high school services (e.g., Individualized Education Program [IEP] or 504 plan). Upon application, documentation of need for special services should be sent only to your LD program or unit. Upon acceptance, documentation of need for special services should be sent only to your LD program or unit. *Application deadline (institutional):* rolling/continuous for fall and rolling/continuous for spring. *Application deadline (LD program):* rolling/continuous for fall and rolling/continuous for spring.

LD program contact Chris Dalheim, Coordinator of Student Services, 3325 West 13th Street, Ashtabula, OH 44004-2299. *Phone:* 440-964-4210. *Fax:* 440-964-4269. *E-mail:* dalheim@ashtabula.kent.edu.

Application contact Kent State University, Ashtabula Campus, 3325 West 13th Street, Ashtabula, OH 44004-2299. *E-mail:* robinson@ashtabula.kent.edu. *Web address:* http://www.ashtabula.kent.edu/.

KENT STATE UNIVERSITY, TRUMBULL CAMPUS
Warren, Ohio

Students with LD Served by Program	10	ADD/ADHD Services	✓
Staff	1 full-time, 15 part-time	Summer Preparation Program	n/a
LD Program or Service Fee	n/a	Alternative Test Arrangements	✓
LD Program Began	1990	LD Student Organization	n/a

Student Disability Services began offering services in 1990. The program serves approximately 10 undergraduate students. Faculty consists of 1 full-time and 15 part-time staff members. Services are provided by remediation/learning specialists and trained peer tutors.

Policies 12 credit hours per semester are required to maintain full-time status.

Auxiliary aids and services *Services and accommodations:* advocates and alternative test arrangements.

ADD/ADHD Students with ADD/ADHD are eligible for the same services available to students with LD

Application *Required:* high school transcript. Upon application, documentation of need for special services should be sent only to your LD program or unit. Upon acceptance, documentation of need for special services should be sent only to your LD program or unit. *Application deadline (institutional):* rolling/continuous for fall and rolling/continuous for spring. *Application deadline (LD program):* rolling/continuous for fall and rolling/continuous for spring.

LD program contact Elaine Shively, Coordinator, Academic Services, 4314 Mahoning Avenue, NW, Warren, OH 44483-1998. *Phone:* 330-847-0571 Ext. 2332. *Fax:* 330-847-0363. *E-mail:* shivelye@trumbull.kent.edu.

Application contact Kerrianne Kacik, Admissions Clerk, Kent State University, Trumbull Campus, 4314 Mahoning Avenue, NW, Warren, OH 44483-1998. *Phone:* 330-847-0571 Ext. 2367. *E-mail:* info@lyceum.trumbull.kent.edu. *Web address:* http://www.trumbull.kent.edu/.

KILGORE COLLEGE
Kilgore, Texas

Students with LD Served by Program	60	ADD/ADHD Services	✓
Staff	4 full-time	Summer Preparation Program	n/a
LD Program or Service Fee	n/a	Alternative Test Arrangements	✓
LD Program Began	1991	LD Student Organization	n/a

Special Populations began offering services in 1991. The program serves approximately 60 undergraduate students. Faculty consists of 4 full-time staff members. Services are provided by regular education teachers, counselors, trained peer tutors, and professional tutors.

Policies 6 hours per term are required to be eligible for financial aid.

Basic skills remediation Available in study skills, computer skills, reading, time management, social skills, learning strategies, spelling, written language, and math. Offered in class-size groups by computer-based instruction, regular education teachers, professional tutors, and trained peer tutors.

Subject-area tutoring Available in most subjects. Offered one-on-one and in small groups by computer-based instruction, professional tutors, and trained peer tutors.

Counseling and advisement Career counseling, individual counseling, and support groups are available.

Auxiliary aids and services *Aids:* personal computers, personal spelling/word-use assistants (e.g., Franklin Speller), screen-enlarging programs, screen readers, taped textbooks. *Services and accommodations:* advocates, alternative test arrangements, readers, note-takers, and scribes.

ADD/ADHD Students with ADD/ADHD are eligible for the same services available to students with LD, as well as distraction-free study areas and distraction-free testing environments.

Application *Required:* high school transcript, psychoeducational report (5 years old or less), and documentation of high school services (e.g., Individualized Education Program [IEP] or 504 plan). Upon application, documentation of need for special services should be sent to both admissions and your LD program or unit. Upon acceptance, documentation of need for special services should be sent to both admissions and your LD program or unit. *Application deadline (institutional):* 8/30 for fall and 1/6 for spring. *Application deadline (LD program):* 8/30 for fall and 1/6 for spring.

LD program contact Pam Gatton, Special Population Counselor, 1100 Broadway, Kilgore, TX 75662-3299. *Phone:* 903-983-8682. *Fax:* 903-983-8215. *E-mail:* gattonp@killfore.cc.tx.us.

Application contact O. L. Kelly, Assistant Director of Admissions, Kilgore College, 1100 Broadway Boulevard, Kilgore, TX 75662-3299. *Phone:* 903-983-8218. *Web address:* http://www.kilgore.cc.tx.us/.

KIRKWOOD COMMUNITY COLLEGE
Cedar Rapids, Iowa

Students with LD Served by Program	250	ADD/ADHD Services	✓
Staff	5 full-time, 2 part-time	Summer Preparation Program	n/a
LD Program or Service Fee	n/a	Alternative Test Arrangements	✓
LD Program Began	1992	LD Student Organization	n/a

ADA Case Management began offering services in 1992. The program serves approximately 250 undergraduate students. Faculty consists of 5 full-time and 2 part-time staff members. Services are provided by academic advisers, counselors, trained peer tutors, and professional tutors.

Policies The college has written policies regarding course substitutions.

Basic skills remediation Available in study skills, computer skills, reading, time management, social skills, learning strategies, written language, and math. Offered one-on-one and in small groups by computer-based instruction and regular education teachers.

Subject-area tutoring Available in most subjects. Offered one-on-one and in small groups by computer-based instruction, professional tutors, and trained peer tutors.

Counseling and advisement Career counseling and individual counseling are available. Academic advisement by a staff member affiliated with the program is available.

Auxiliary aids and services *Aids:* personal computers, personal spelling/word-use assistants (e.g., Franklin Speller), scan and read programs (e.g., Kurzweil), screen-enlarging programs, screen readers, speech recognition programs (e.g., Dragon), tape recorders, taped textbooks. *Services and accommodations:* advocates, alternative test arrangements, readers, and scribes.

ADD/ADHD Students with ADD/ADHD are eligible for the same services available to students with LD, as well as distraction-free testing environments.

Application *Required:* separate application to your LD program or unit, psychoeducational report (3 years old or less), and documentation of high school services (e.g., Individualized Education Program [IEP] or 504 plan). Upon application, documen-

tation of need for special services should be sent only to your LD program or unit. Upon acceptance, documentation of need for special services should be sent only to your LD program or unit. *Application deadline (institutional):* rolling/continuous for fall and rolling/continuous for spring. *Application deadline (LD program):* rolling/continuous for fall and rolling/continuous for spring.

LD program contact Chuck Hinz, Dean, Developmental Education, 6301 Kirkwood Boulevard SW, Cedar Rapids, IA 52404. *Phone:* 319-398-5574. *Fax:* 319-398-4933. *E-mail:* chinz@kirkwood.cc.ia.us.

Application contact Kirkwood Community College, PO Box 2068, Cedar Rapids, IA 52406-2068. *E-mail:* dbannon@kirkwood.cc.ia.us. *Web address:* http://www.kirkwood.cc.ia.us/.

LABETTE COMMUNITY COLLEGE
Parsons, Kansas

Students with LD Served by Program	20	ADD/ADHD Services	✓
Staff	7 full-time	Summer Preparation Program	✓
LD Program or Service Fee	n/a	Alternative Test Arrangements	✓
LD Program Began	1985	LD Student Organization	n/a

LCC Learning Center began offering services in 1985. The program serves approximately 20 undergraduate students. Faculty consists of 7 full-time staff members. Services are provided by academic advisers, counselors, remediation/learning specialists, LD specialists, trained peer tutors, and professional tutors.

Policies Students with LD may take up to 15 credit hours per semester; 9 credit hours per semester are required to maintain full-time status and to be eligible for financial aid.

Special preparation or orientation Optional summer program offered prior to entering college.

Diagnostic testing Available for reading, written language, and math.

Basic skills remediation Available in study skills, reading, time management, handwriting, learning strategies, spelling, written language, math, and spoken language. Offered one-on-one by computer-based instruction, LD specialists, professional tutors, and trained peer tutors.

Subject-area tutoring Available in all subjects. Offered one-on-one by professional tutors, trained peer tutors, and LD specialists.

Special courses Available in study skills, test taking, reading, time management, learning strategies, vocabulary development, math, and written composition skills. Some courses are offered for credit; some enter into overall grade point average.

Counseling and advisement Academic advisement by a staff member affiliated with the program is available.

Auxiliary aids and services *Aids:* calculators, screen-enlarging programs, screen readers, tape recorders, taped textbooks. *Services and accommodations:* alternative test arrangements, readers, note-takers, and scribes.

ADD/ADHD Students with ADD/ADHD are eligible for the same services available to students with LD

Application *Recommended:* high school transcript, participation in extracurricular activities, ACT or SAT I, interview, personal statement, and documentation of high school services (e.g., Individualized Education Program [IEP] or 504 plan). Upon application, documentation of need for special services should be sent only to your LD program or unit. Upon acceptance, documentation of need for special services should be sent only to your LD program or unit. *Application deadline (institutional):* rolling/continuous for fall and rolling/continuous for spring. *Application deadline (LD program):* rolling/continuous for fall and rolling/continuous for spring.

Labette Community College (continued)

LD program contact Viv Metcalf, Director of Learning Center, LCC, 200 South 14th Street, Parsons, KS 67357. *Phone:* 316-421-6700. *Fax:* 316-421-8284. *E-mail:* vivm@labette.cc.ks.us.

Application contact Labette Community College, 200 South 14th Street, Parsons, KS 67357-4299. *Web address:* http://www.labette.cc.ks.us/.

LAKE LAND COLLEGE
Mattoon, Illinois

Students with LD Served by Program	160	ADD/ADHD Services	✓
Staff	1 full-time, 2 part-time	Summer Preparation Program	n/a
LD Program or Service Fee	n/a	Alternative Test Arrangements	✓
LD Program Began	1992	LD Student Organization	n/a

Special Needs Office began offering services in 1992. The program serves approximately 160 undergraduate students. Faculty consists of 1 full-time and 2 part-time staff members. Services are provided by academic advisers, counselors, diagnostic specialists, LD specialists, trained peer tutors, professional tutors, and teacher aides.

Policies The college has written policies regarding grade forgiveness. Students with LD may take up to 20 credit hours per semester; 12 credit hours per semester are required to maintain full-time status; 6 credit hours per semester are required to be eligible for financial aid.

Basic skills remediation Available in study skills, computer skills, reading, learning strategies, spelling, written language, and math. Offered in small groups by LD specialists, professional tutors, and trained peer tutors.

Subject-area tutoring Available in most subjects. Offered one-on-one and in small groups by computer-based instruction, professional tutors, trained peer tutors, LD specialists, and Teacher aides.

Special courses Available in study skills, college survival skills, practical computer skills, test taking, reading, time management, learning strategies, vocabulary development, math, and written composition skills. Some courses are offered for credit; some enter into overall grade point average.

Counseling and advisement Career counseling and individual counseling are available. Academic advisement by a staff member affiliated with the program is available.

Auxiliary aids and services *Aids:* calculators, scan and read programs (e.g., Kurzweil), screen-enlarging programs, screen readers, tape recorders, taped textbooks. *Services and accommodations:* alternative test arrangements, readers, note-takers, and scribes.

ADD/ADHD Students with ADD/ADHD are eligible for the same services available to students with LD, as well as distraction-free testing environments.

Application *Required:* high school transcript and separate application to your LD program or unit. *Recommended:* psychoeducational report and documentation of high school services (e.g., Individualized Education Program [IEP] or 504 plan). Upon application, documentation of need for special services should be sent only to your LD program or unit. Upon acceptance, documentation of need for special services should be sent only to your LD program or unit. *Application deadline (institutional):* rolling/continuous for fall and rolling/continuous for spring. *Application deadline (LD program):* rolling/continuous for fall and rolling/continuous for spring.

LD program contact Emily M. Hartke, Special Needs Counselor, 5001 Lake Land Boulevard, Mahoon, IL 61938. *Phone:* 217-234-5259. *Fax:* 217-234-5390. *E-mail:* ehartke@lakeland.cc.il.us.

Application contact Lake Land College, 5001 Lake Land Boulevard, Mattoon, IL 61938-9366. *Web address:* http://www.lakeland.cc.il.us/.

LAKELAND COMMUNITY COLLEGE
Kirtland, Ohio

Students with LD Served by Program	200	ADD/ADHD Services	✓
Staff	1 full-time, 15 part-time	Summer Preparation Program	✓
LD Program or Service Fee	n/a	Alternative Test Arrangements	✓
LD Program Began	1987	LD Student Organization	✓

Services for Students with Disabilities began offering services in 1987. The program serves approximately 200 undergraduate students. Faculty consists of 1 full-time and 15 part-time staff members. Services are provided by academic advisers, regular education teachers, counselors, remediation/learning specialists, and professional tutors.

Policies Students with LD may take up to 12 credit hours per quarter; 6 credit hours per quarter are required to maintain full-time status.

Special preparation or orientation Optional summer program offered prior to entering college. Required orientation held before registration, during registration, before classes begin, after classes begin, during summer prior to enrollment, and individually by special arrangement.

Basic skills remediation Available in study skills, computer skills, reading, time management, learning strategies, spelling, written language, and math. Offered one-on-one and in small groups by computer-based instruction, regular education teachers, and professional tutors.

Subject-area tutoring Available in all subjects. Offered one-on-one and in small groups by computer-based instruction and professional tutors.

Special courses Available in career planning, study skills, college survival skills, test taking, reading, time management, learning strategies, vocabulary development, math, and written composition skills. All courses are offered for credit; some enter into overall grade point average.

Counseling and advisement Career counseling, individual counseling, and support groups are available. Academic advisement by a staff member affiliated with the program is available.

Auxiliary aids and services *Aids:* personal computers, scan and read programs (e.g., Kurzweil), screen-enlarging programs, screen readers, speech recognition programs (e.g., Dragon), tape recorders, taped textbooks. *Services and accommodations:* advocates, priority registration, alternative test arrangements, readers, note-takers, and scribes.

Student organization There is a student organization for students with LD.

ADD/ADHD Students with ADD/ADHD are eligible for the same services available to students with LD, as well as distraction-free study areas, distraction-free testing environments and personal coach or mentors.

Application *Required:* interview, separate application to your LD program or unit, psychoeducational report, and documentation of high school services (e.g., Individualized Education Program [IEP] or 504 plan). *Recommended:* high school transcript. Upon application, documentation of need for special services should be sent only to your LD program or unit. Upon acceptance, documentation of need for special services should be sent only to your LD program or unit. *Application deadline (institutional):* rolling/continuous for fall and rolling/continuous for spring. *Application deadline (LD program):* rolling/continuous for fall and rolling/continuous for spring.

LD program contact Alan B. Kirsh, Counselor for Students with Disabilities, 7700 Clocktower Drive, A-1044e, Kirtland, OH 44094-5198. *Phone:* 440-953-7245. *Fax:* 440-975-4734. *E-mail:* akirsh@lakeland.cc.oh.us.

Application contact Lakeland Community College, 7700 Clocktower Drive, Kirtland, OH 44094-5198. *E-mail:* wkraus@lcc2.lakeland.cc.oh.us. *Web address:* http://www.lakeland.cc.oh.us/.

LAKE REGION STATE COLLEGE
Devils Lake, North Dakota

Students with LD Served by Program	70	ADD/ADHD Services	✓
Staff	1 full-time	Summer Preparation Program	n/a
LD Program or Service Fee	n/a	Alternative Test Arrangements	✓
LD Program Began	1977	LD Student Organization	n/a

Learning Resource Center began offering services in 1977. The program serves approximately 70 undergraduate students. Faculty consists of 1 full-time staff member. Services are provided by academic advisers, counselors, and trained peer tutors.

Policies Students with LD may take up to 16 credit hours per semester; 12 credit hours per semester are required to maintain full-time status; 6 credit hours per semester are required to be eligible for financial aid.

Special preparation or orientation Required orientation held before registration, during registration, before classes begin, after classes begin, during summer prior to enrollment, and individually by special arrangement.

Basic skills remediation Available in study skills, computer skills, reading, time management, learning strategies, spelling, written language, and math. Offered one-on-one, in small groups, and class-size groups by regular education teachers.

Subject-area tutoring Available in most subjects. Offered one-on-one and in small groups by computer-based instruction and trained peer tutors.

Special courses Available in career planning, study skills, college survival skills, practical computer skills, test taking, and written composition skills. Some courses are offered for credit; some enter into overall grade point average.

Counseling and advisement Career counseling, individual counseling, small-group counseling, and support groups are available. Academic advisement by a staff member affiliated with the program is available.

Auxiliary aids and services *Aids:* scan and read programs (e.g., Kurzweil), screen-enlarging programs, tape recorders, taped textbooks. *Services and accommodations:* alternative test arrangements, readers, note-takers, and scribes.

ADD/ADHD Students with ADD/ADHD are eligible for the same services available to students with LD, as well as distraction-free study areas and distraction-free testing environments.

Application *Required:* high school transcript, ACT (extended-time or untimed test accepted), psychoeducational report (2 years old or less), and documentation of high school services (e.g., Individualized Education Program [IEP] or 504 plan). *Recommended:* interview. Upon application, documentation of need for special services should be sent to both admissions and your LD program or unit. Upon acceptance, documentation of need for special services should be sent to both admissions and your LD program or unit. *Application deadline (institutional):* rolling/continuous for fall and rolling/continuous for spring. *Application deadline (LD program):* 8/1 for fall and 12/1 for spring.

LD program contact Theresa Leiphon, Director of Learning Resource Center, 1801 College Drive N, Devils Lake, ND 58301. *Phone:* 701-662-1529. *Fax:* 701-662-1570. *E-mail:* leiphont@lrsc.nodak.edu.

Application contact Sheri Wagner, Administrative Assistant, Lake Region State College, 1801 College Drive North, Devils Lake, ND 58301-1598. *Phone:* 701-662-1514. *E-mail:* wagners@shorelines.und-lr.nodak.edu. *Web address:* http://www.lrsc.nodak.edu/.

LAKE TAHOE COMMUNITY COLLEGE
South Lake Tahoe, California

Students with LD Served by Program	250	ADD/ADHD Services	✓
Staff	n/a	Summer Preparation Program	n/a
LD Program or Service Fee	n/a	Alternative Test Arrangements	✓
LD Program Began	1975	LD Student Organization	n/a

Disability Resource Center began offering services in 1975. The program serves approximately 250 undergraduate students. Services are provided by counselors and LD specialists.

Policies The college has written policies regarding course substitutions and grade forgiveness. Students with LD may take up to 19 units per quarter; 12 units per quarter are required to maintain full-time status.

Special preparation or orientation Optional orientation held individually by special arrangement.

Diagnostic testing Available for auditory processing, motor skills, spelling, intelligence, learning strategies, reading, learning styles, visual processing, and math.

Basic skills remediation Available in study skills, computer skills, reading, spelling, written language, and math. Offered in class-size groups.

Subject-area tutoring Available in most subjects. Offered one-on-one by graduate assistants/students.

Special courses Available in study skills, practical computer skills, reading, vocabulary development, math, and written composition skills. All courses are offered for credit; all enter into overall grade point average.

Counseling and advisement Academic is available.

Auxiliary aids and services *Aids:* calculators, personal computers, personal spelling/word-use assistants (e.g., Franklin Speller), scan and read programs (e.g., Kurzweil), screen-enlarging programs, screen readers, speech recognition programs (e.g., Dragon), tape recorders, taped textbooks. *Services and accommodations:* advocates, priority registration, alternative test arrangements, readers, note-takers, and scribes.

ADD/ADHD Students with ADD/ADHD are eligible for the same services available to students with LD, as well as distraction-free testing environments.

Application Upon acceptance, documentation of need for special services should be sent only to your LD program or unit.

LD program contact Joyce Petitt, Disability Resource Center Program Assistant, One College Drive, South Lake Tahoe, CA 96150. *Phone:* 530-541-4660 Ext. 249. *E-mail:* petitt@ltcc.cc.ca.us.

Application contact Lake Tahoe Community College, One College Drive, South Lake Tahoe, CA 96150-4524. *Web address:* http://www.ltcc.cc.ca.us/.

LAKE WASHINGTON TECHNICAL COLLEGE

Kirkland, Washington

Students with LD Served by Program	250	ADD/ADHD Services	✓
Staff	1 full-time, 1 part-time	Summer Preparation Program	n/a
LD Program or Service Fee	n/a	Alternative Test Arrangements	✓
LD Program Began	1992	LD Student Organization	n/a

Disabled Student Services began offering services in 1992. The program serves approximately 250 undergraduate students. Faculty consists of 1 full-time and 1 part-time staff member. Services are provided by academic advisers, counselors, and career specialist.

Policies Students with LD may take up to 15 credit hours per quarter; 15 credit hours per quarter are required to maintain full-time status; 8 credits per quarter are required to be eligible for financial aid.

Special preparation or orientation Optional orientation held during registration, before classes begin, and individually by special arrangement.

Basic skills remediation Available in study skills, reading, time management, handwriting, learning strategies, spelling, written language, and math. Offered one-on-one, in small groups, and class-size groups by trained peer tutors and career specialist.

Subject-area tutoring Available in some subjects. Offered by trained peer tutors.

Counseling and advisement Career counseling and individual counseling are available. Academic advisement by a staff member affiliated with the program is available.

Auxiliary aids and services *Aids:* personal spelling/word-use assistants (e.g., Franklin Speller), scan and read programs (e.g., Kurzweil), screen-enlarging programs, screen readers, speech recognition programs (e.g., Dragon), tape recorders, taped textbooks. *Services and accommodations:* priority registration, alternative test arrangements, readers, note-takers, and scribes.

ADD/ADHD Students with ADD/ADHD are eligible for the same services available to students with LD, as well as distraction-free testing environments.

Application *Required:* separate application to your LD program or unit, documentation of high school services (e.g., Individualized Education Program [IEP] or 504 plan), and adult assessment for students over 18. *Recommended:* interview. Upon application, documentation of need for special services should be sent only to your LD program or unit. Upon acceptance, documentation of need for special services should be sent only to your LD program or unit. *Application deadline (institutional):* rolling/continuous for spring and 8/1 for fall. *Application deadline (LD program):* rolling/continuous for spring and 8/1 for fall.

LD program contact Michael S. Miller, Career Specialist for Disabled Students, 11605 132nd Avenue NE, Kirkland, WA 98034. *Phone:* 425-739-8100 Ext. 500. *Fax:* 425-739-8198. *E-mail:* michael.miller@lwtc.ctc.edu.

Application contact David Minger, Director of Admissions/Registrar, Lake Washington Technical College, 11605 132nd Avenue NE, Kirkland, WA 98034-8506. *Phone:* 425-739-8100 Ext. 233.

LEE COLLEGE

Baytown, Texas

Students with LD Served by Program	40	ADD/ADHD Services	✓
Staff	1 full-time, 5 part-time	Summer Preparation Program	n/a
LD Program or Service Fee	n/a	Alternative Test Arrangements	✓
LD Program Began	1989	LD Student Organization	n/a

Office of Disability Services began offering services in 1989. The program serves approximately 40 undergraduate students. Faculty consists of 1 full-time and 5 part-time staff members. Services are provided by counselors and student assistant note-takers, tutors.

Policies Students with LD may take up to 18 credit hours per semester; 12 credit hours per semester are required to maintain full-time status; 3 credit hours per semester are required to be eligible for financial aid.

Diagnostic testing Available for spelling, intelligence, reading, written language, and math.

Basic skills remediation Available in reading, learning strategies, spelling, written language, and math. Offered in class-size groups by computer-based instruction and regular education teachers.

Subject-area tutoring Available in all subjects. Offered one-on-one by trained peer tutors.

Counseling and advisement Career counseling and individual counseling are available.

Auxiliary aids and services *Aids:* screen-enlarging programs, screen readers, speech recognition programs (e.g., Dragon), tape recorders, taped textbooks. *Services and accommodations:* priority registration, alternative test arrangements, readers, note-takers, and scribes.

ADD/ADHD Students with ADD/ADHD are eligible for the same services available to students with LD, as well as distraction-free testing environments.

Application *Required:* high school transcript, psychoeducational report (5 years old or less), and documentation of high school services (e.g., Individualized Education Program [IEP] or 504 plan). Upon application, documentation of need for special services should be sent only to your LD program or unit. Upon acceptance, documentation of need for special services should be sent only to your LD program or unit. *Application deadline (institutional):* rolling/continuous for fall and rolling/continuous for spring. *Application deadline (LD program):* rolling/continuous for fall and rolling/continuous for spring.

LD program contact Dr. Rosemary Coffman, Counselor for Students with Disabilities, PO Box 818, Baytown, TX 77522-0818. *Phone:* 281-425-6384. *Fax:* 281-425-6382. *E-mail:* rcoffman@lee.edu.

Application contact Lee College, PO Box 818, Baytown, TX 77522-0818. *Web address:* http://www.lee.edu/.

LIMA TECHNICAL COLLEGE

Lima, Ohio

Students with LD Served by Program	93	ADD/ADHD Services	✓
Staff	1 full-time	Summer Preparation Program	n/a
LD Program or Service Fee	n/a	Alternative Test Arrangements	✓
LD Program Began	n/a	LD Student Organization	✓

Learning Assistance Program serves approximately 93 undergraduate students. Faculty consists of 1 full-time staff member. Services are provided by academic advisers, LD specialists, trained peer tutors, and professional tutors.

Policies Students with LD may take up to 12 credit hours per quarter; 12 credit hours per quarter are required to maintain full-time status and to be eligible for financial aid. LD services are also available to graduate students.

Subject-area tutoring Available in some subjects. Offered one-on-one and in small groups by professional tutors and trained peer tutors.

Counseling and advisement Individual counseling and support groups are available. Academic advisement by a staff member affiliated with the program is available.

Auxiliary aids and services *Aids:* calculators, scan and read programs (e.g., Kurzweil), screen-enlarging programs, speech recognition programs (e.g., Dragon), tape recorders, taped textbooks. *Services and accommodations:* alternative test arrangements, readers, note-takers, and scribes.

Student organization There is a student organization for students with LD.

ADD/ADHD Students with ADD/ADHD are eligible for the same services available to students with LD, as well as distraction-free testing environments.

Application *Required:* high school transcript, interview, and documentation of high school services (e.g., Individualized Education Program [IEP] or 504 plan). Upon application, documentation of need for special services should be sent only to admissions. Upon acceptance, documentation of need for special services should be sent to both admissions and your LD program or unit. *Application deadline (institutional):* 9/20 for fall and 3/26 for spring. *Application deadline (LD program):* 9/20 for fall and 3/26 for spring.

LD program contact Cathy L. Kohli, Student Advising and Development Representative, 4240 Campus Drive, Lima, OH 45804. *Phone:* 419-995-8060. *Fax:* 419-995-8098. *E-mail:* kohlic@ltc.tec.oh.us.

Application contact Eric E. Davis, Assistant Director, Student Recruitment and Marketing, Lima Technical College, 4240 Campus Drive, Lima, OH 45804-3597. *Phone:* 419-995-8001. *E-mail:* peterl@ltc.tec.oh.us. *Web address:* http://www.ltc.tec.oh.us/.

LINCOLN LAND COMMUNITY COLLEGE
Springfield, Illinois

Students with LD Served by Program	250	ADD/ADHD Services	✓
Staff	101 part-time	Summer Preparation Program	✓
LD Program or Service Fee	n/a	Alternative Test Arrangements	✓
LD Program Began	1980	LD Student Organization	n/a

Special Needs Office, Learning Lab began offering services in 1980. The program serves approximately 250 undergraduate students. Faculty consists of 101 part-time staff members. Services are provided by academic advisers, counselors, remediation/learning specialists, trained peer tutors, professional tutors, and Special Needs coordinator, trained note takers and readers.

Policies The college has written policies regarding grade forgiveness and substitution and waivers of requirements for admission. 12 credit hours per semester are required to maintain full-time status; 6 credit hours per semester are required to be eligible for financial aid.

Special preparation or orientation Optional summer program offered prior to entering college. Required orientation held individually by special arrangement.

Basic skills remediation Available in study skills, reading, time management, learning strategies, written language, math, and stress management. Offered one-on-one by regular education teachers and study skills specialists.

Subject-area tutoring Available in all subjects. Offered one-on-one and in small groups by professional tutors, trained peer tutors, and college instructors.

Special courses Available in study skills, college survival skills, test taking, reading, time management, learning strategies, vocabulary development, stress management, and written composition skills. Some courses are offered for credit; some enter into overall grade point average.

Counseling and advisement Career counseling and individual counseling are available. Academic advisement by a staff member affiliated with the program is available.

Auxiliary aids and services *Aids:* calculators, scan and read programs (e.g., Kurzweil), screen-enlarging programs, screen readers, speech recognition programs (e.g., Dragon), tape recorders, taped textbooks, Alpha Smart keyboards. *Services and accommodations:* advocates, priority registration, alternative test arrangements, readers, note-takers, scribes, and tutors.

ADD/ADHD Students with ADD/ADHD are eligible for the same services available to students with LD, as well as distraction-free study areas and distraction-free testing environments.

Application *Required:* psychoeducational report (3 years old or less) and documentation of high school services (e.g., Individualized Education Program [IEP] or 504 plan). Upon application, documentation of need for special services should be sent only to your LD program or unit. Upon acceptance, documentation of need for special services should be sent only to your LD program or unit. *Application deadline (institutional):* 8/20 for fall and 1/14 for spring. *Application deadline (LD program):* rolling/continuous for fall and rolling/continuous for spring.

LD program contact Linda Chriswell, Special Needs Professional, 5250 Shepherd Road, PO Box 19256, Springfield, IL 62794-9256. *Phone:* 217-786-2828. *Fax:* 217-786-2251. *E-mail:* linda.chriswell@llcc.cc.il.us.

Application contact Lincoln Land Community College, 5250 Shepherd Road, PO Box 19256, Springfield, IL 62794-9256. *Web address:* http://www.llcc.cc.il.us/.

LINN-BENTON COMMUNITY COLLEGE
Albany, Oregon

Students with LD Served by Program	30	ADD/ADHD Services	✓
Staff	3 full-time, 4 part-time	Summer Preparation Program	n/a
LD Program or Service Fee	n/a	Alternative Test Arrangements	✓
LD Program Began	n/a	LD Student Organization	n/a

Office of Disability Services serves approximately 30 undergraduate students. Faculty consists of 3 full-time and 4 part-time staff members. Services are provided by academic advisers, regular education teachers, remediation/learning specialists, and staff tutors.

Policies 12 credit hours per term are required to maintain full-time status and to be eligible for financial aid.

Special preparation or orientation Optional orientation held before classes begin and after classes begin.

Diagnostic testing Available for written language and learning styles.

Basic skills remediation Available in study skills, reading, written language, and math. Offered in small groups and class-size groups by regular education teachers.

Linn-Benton Community College (continued)

Subject-area tutoring Available in some subjects. Offered one-on-one and in small groups by professional tutors, trained peer tutors, and faculty, instructional assistants.

Counseling and advisement Individual counseling is available. Academic advisement by a staff member affiliated with the program is available.

Auxiliary aids and services *Aids:* calculators, personal computers, personal spelling/word-use assistants (e.g., Franklin Speller), scan and read programs (e.g., Kurzweil), screen-enlarging programs, screen readers, speech recognition programs (e.g., Dragon), tape recorders, taped textbooks. *Services and accommodations:* advocates, alternative test arrangements, readers, note-takers, and scribes.

ADD/ADHD Students with ADD/ADHD are eligible for the same services available to students with LD, as well as distraction-free study areas, distraction-free testing environments and time management/organization coaching.

Application *Required:* separate application to your LD program or unit and psychoeducational report (5 years old or less). *Recommended:* documentation of high school services (e.g., Individualized Education Program [IEP] or 504 plan). Upon application, documentation of need for special services should be sent only to your LD program or unit. Upon acceptance, documentation of need for special services should be sent only to your LD program or unit. *Application deadline (LD program):* rolling/continuous for fall and rolling/continuous for spring.

LD program contact Cheryl E. Allison, Disability Services Coordinator, LRC 200, 6500 Pacific Boulevard SW, Albany, OR 97321. *Phone:* 541-917-4683. *Fax:* 541-917-4681. *E-mail:* allisoc@gw.lbcc.cc.or.us.

Application contact Linn-Benton Community College, 6500 Southwest Pacific Boulevard, Albany, OR 97321. *E-mail:* tepperg@gw.lbcc.cc.or.us.

LONGVIEW COMMUNITY COLLEGE
Lee's Summit, Missouri

Students with LD Served by Program	89	ADD/ADHD Services	✓
Staff	2 full-time, 25 part-time	Summer Preparation Program	n/a
LD Program or Service Fee	varies	Alternative Test Arrangements	✓
LD Program Began	1991	LD Student Organization	n/a

Academic Bridges to Learning Effectiveness (ABLE) began offering services in 1991. The program serves approximately 89 undergraduate students. Faculty consists of 2 full-time and 25 part-time staff members. Services are provided by academic advisers, regular education teachers, counselors, remediation/learning specialists, diagnostic specialists, special education teachers, graduate assistants/students, LD specialists, trained peer tutors, and professional tutors.

Policies Students with LD may take up to 18 credit hours per semester; 6 credit hours per semester are required to maintain full-time status and to be eligible for financial aid.

Fees *LD Program or Service Fee:* ranges from $210 to $1435 per year.

Special preparation or orientation Required orientation held orientation class taken first semester in program.

Diagnostic testing Available for spelling, intelligence, reading, written language, learning styles, and math.

Basic skills remediation Available in study skills, reading, time management, learning strategies, spelling, written language, and math. Offered one-on-one by regular education teachers, LD specialists, and professional tutors.

Subject-area tutoring Offered one-on-one, in small groups, and class-size groups by trained peer tutors and LD specialists.

Special courses Available in career planning, oral communication skills, study skills, college survival skills, practical computer skills, test taking, reading, time management, learning strategies, self-advocacy, vocabulary development, math, stress management, and written composition skills. All courses are offered for credit; all enter into overall grade point average.

Counseling and advisement Individual counseling and support groups are available. Academic advisement by a staff member affiliated with the program is available.

Auxiliary aids and services *Aids:* calculators, personal computers, personal spelling/word-use assistants (e.g., Franklin Speller), scan and read programs (e.g., Kurzweil), screen-enlarging programs, screen readers, speech recognition programs (e.g., Dragon), tape recorders, taped textbooks. *Services and accommodations:* advocates, priority registration, alternative test arrangements, readers, note-takers, and scribes.

ADD/ADHD Students with ADD/ADHD are eligible for the same services available to students with LD, as well as distraction-free testing environments.

Application *Required:* separate application to your LD program or unit and ASSET placement tests or ACT. *Recommended:* high school transcript and psychoeducational report (5 years old or less). Upon application, documentation of need for special services should be sent only to your LD program or unit. Upon acceptance, documentation of need for special services should be sent only to your LD program or unit. *Application deadline (institutional):* rolling/continuous for fall and rolling/continuous for spring. *Application deadline (LD program):* rolling/continuous for fall and rolling/continuous for spring.

LD program contact Mary Ellen Jenison, ABLE Program Director/Learning Disabilities Faculty, 500 Southwest Longview Road, Lee's Summit, MO 64081-2105. *Phone:* 816-672-2105. *Fax:* 816-672-2025. *E-mail:* jenison@longview.cc.mo.us.

Application contact Longview Community College, 500 Southwest Longview Road, Lee's Summit, MO 64081-2105. *Web address:* http://www.kcmetro.cc.mo.us/admissions/applyForm.html.

LOS ANGELES VALLEY COLLEGE
Valley Glen, California

Students with LD Served by Program	300	ADD/ADHD Services	✓
Staff	n/a	Summer Preparation Program	✓
LD Program or Service Fee	n/a	Alternative Test Arrangements	✓
LD Program Began	n/a	LD Student Organization	✓

Disabled Students Programs and Services (DSPS) serves approximately 300 undergraduate students. Services are provided by academic advisers, regular education teachers, counselors, remediation/learning specialists, diagnostic specialists, special education teachers, graduate assistants/students, LD specialists, trained peer tutors, professional tutors, and assistive technology specialists.

Policies Students with LD may take up to 19 units per semester; 12 units per semester are required to maintain full-time status and to be eligible for financial aid.

Fees *Diagnostic Testing Fee:* $11.

Special preparation or orientation Optional summer program offered prior to entering college. Held individually by special arrangement.

Diagnostic testing Available for auditory processing, motor skills, spelling, neuropsychological, spoken language, intelligence, study skills, learning strategies, reading, written language, visual processing, and math.

Basic skills remediation Available in study skills, reading, time management, learning strategies, and spelling. Offered one-on-one, in small groups, and class-size groups by computer-based instruction, special education teachers, LD specialists, and trained peer tutors.

Subject-area tutoring Available in some subjects. Offered one-on-one and in small groups by computer-based instruction, professional tutors, graduate assistants/students, trained peer tutors, and LD specialists.

Special courses Available in career planning, study skills, college survival skills, test taking, reading, time management, and learning strategies. All courses are offered for credit; none enter into overall grade point average.

Counseling and advisement Career counseling, individual counseling, and support groups are available. Academic advisement by a staff member affiliated with the program is available.

Auxiliary aids and services *Aids:* scan and read programs (e.g., Kurzweil), screen-enlarging programs, screen readers, speech recognition programs (e.g., Dragon), tape recorders. *Services and accommodations:* priority registration and alternative test arrangements.

Student organization There is a student organization for students with LD.

ADD/ADHD Students with ADD/ADHD are eligible for the same services available to students with LD, as well as distraction-free study areas, distraction-free testing environments and high tech accommodations.

Application *Required:* separate application to your LD program or unit. *Recommended:* high school transcript, psychoeducational report (3 years old or less), and documentation of high school services (e.g., Individualized Education Program [IEP] or 504 plan). Upon application, documentation of need for special services should be sent only to your LD program or unit. Upon acceptance, documentation of need for special services should be sent only to your LD program or unit.

LD program contact Dr. Kathleen Sullivan, Director, 5800 Fulton Avenue, Valley Nillege, CA 91401. *Phone:* 818-947-2681.

Application contact Billy Reed, Associate Dean of Admissions and Records, Los Angeles Valley College, 5800 Fulton Avenue, Valley Glen, CA 91401-4096. *Phone:* 818-947-2671. *Web address:* http://www.lavc.cc.ca.us/.

LOUISIANA TECHNICAL COLLEGE-SLIDELL CAMPUS
Slidell, Louisiana

Students with LD Served by Program	50	ADD/ADHD Services	✓
Staff	1 full-time	Summer Preparation Program	n/a
LD Program or Service Fee	varies	Alternative Test Arrangements	✓
LD Program Began	n/a	LD Student Organization	n/a

Basic Skills Improvement Program serves approximately 50 undergraduate students. Faculty consists of 1 full-time staff member. Services are provided by regular education teachers.

Fees *LD Program or Service Fee:* ranges from $100 to $200 per year.

Special preparation or orientation Required orientation held individually by special arrangement.

Basic skills remediation Available in study skills, computer skills, reading, learning strategies, spelling, written language, and math. Offered one-on-one, in small groups, and class-size groups by computer-based instruction, regular education teachers, and professional tutors.

Subject-area tutoring Available in some subjects. Offered one-on-one and in small groups by professional tutors.

Special courses Available in math. No courses are offered for credit; none enter into overall grade point average.

Counseling and advisement Career counseling and individual counseling are available.

Auxiliary aids and services *Aids:* personal computers, taped textbooks. *Services and accommodations:* alternative test arrangements.

ADD/ADHD Students with ADD/ADHD are eligible for the same services available to students with LD, as well as distraction-free study areas.

Application *Required:* interview and Test of Adult Basic Education . *Recommended:* high school transcript and documentation of high school services (e.g., Individualized Education Program [IEP] or 504 plan). Upon application, documentation of need for special services should be sent to both admissions and your LD program or unit. Upon acceptance, documentation of need for special services should be sent to both admissions and your LD program or unit.

LD program contact Mary K. Roy, Director, PO Box 827, Slidell, LA 70459-0827. *Phone:* 504-646-6430. *Fax:* 504-646-6442.

Application contact Louisiana Technical College-Slidell Campus, 1000 Canulette Road, Slidell, LA 70459-0827.

MADISONVILLE COMMUNITY COLLEGE
Madisonville, Kentucky

Students with LD Served by Program	12	ADD/ADHD Services	✓
Staff	n/a	Summer Preparation Program	n/a
LD Program or Service Fee	n/a	Alternative Test Arrangements	✓
LD Program Began	n/a	LD Student Organization	n/a

Disability Resources serves approximately 12 undergraduate students.

Policies Students with LD may take up to 19 credit hours per semester; 12 credit hours per semester are required to maintain full-time status; 6 credit hours per semester are required to be eligible for financial aid.

Auxiliary aids and services *Aids:* scan and read programs (e.g., Kurzweil), screen-enlarging programs, tape recorders, taped textbooks. *Services and accommodations:* advocates, priority registration, alternative test arrangements, readers, note-takers, and scribes.

ADD/ADHD Students with ADD/ADHD are eligible for the same services available to students with LD, as well as distraction-free testing environments.

Application *Required:* high school transcript and ACT (extended-time test accepted). Upon application, documentation of need for special services should be sent only to your LD program or unit. Upon acceptance, documentation of need for special services should be sent only to your LD program or unit. *Application deadline (institutional):* 8/17 for fall and 1/10 for spring.

LD program contact Valerie Wolfe, Disability Resources Coordinator, 2000 College Drive, Madisonville, KY 42431. *Phone:* 270-821-2250. *Fax:* 270-821-1555.

Application contact Madisonville Community College, 2000 College Drive, Madisonville, KY 42431-9185. *Web address:* http://www.madcc.uky.edu/.

MANATEE COMMUNITY COLLEGE
Bradenton, Florida

Students with LD Served by Program	135	ADD/ADHD Services	✓
Staff	2 full-time, 6 part-time	Summer Preparation Program	n/a
LD Program or Service Fee	n/a	Alternative Test Arrangements	✓
LD Program Began	1989	LD Student Organization	n/a

Office of Disabled Student Services (ODSS) began offering services in 1989. The program serves approximately 135 undergraduate students. Faculty consists of 2 full-time and 6 part-time staff members. Services are provided by academic advisers, counselors, and LD specialists.

Policies The college has written policies regarding course substitutions, grade forgiveness, and substitution and waivers of requirements for admission and graduation. Students with LD may take up to 18 credit hours per semester; 12 credit hours per semester are required to maintain full-time status; 3 credit hours per semester are required to be eligible for financial aid.

Special preparation or orientation Optional orientation held individually by special arrangement.

Basic skills remediation Available in study skills, computer skills, reading, learning strategies, and math. Offered in class-size groups by computer-based instruction, regular education teachers, and trained peer tutors.

Subject-area tutoring Available in some subjects. Offered by computer-based instruction and trained peer tutors.

Counseling and advisement Career counseling and individual counseling are available. Academic advisement by a staff member affiliated with the program is available.

Auxiliary aids and services *Aids:* calculators, personal computers, personal spelling/word-use assistants (e.g., Franklin Speller), scan and read programs (e.g., Kurzweil), screen-enlarging programs, screen readers, speech recognition programs (e.g., Dragon), tape recorders, taped textbooks. *Services and accommodations:* advocates, priority registration, alternative test arrangements, readers, note-takers, and scribes.

ADD/ADHD Students with ADD/ADHD are eligible for the same services available to students with LD, as well as distraction-free testing environments.

Application *Required:* high school transcript. *Recommended:* ACT or SAT I (extended-time or untimed test accepted), psycho-educational report, and documentation of high school services (e.g., Individualized Education Program [IEP] or 504 plan). Upon application, documentation of need for special services should be sent only to your LD program or unit. Upon acceptance, documentation of need for special services should be sent only to your LD program or unit. *Application deadline (institutional):* rolling/continuous for fall and rolling/continuous for spring. *Application deadline (LD program):* rolling/continuous for fall and rolling/continuous for spring.

LD program contact Angela Powell, Accommodation Specialist, PO Box 1849, Bradenton, FL 34206. *Phone:* 941-755-1511 Ext. 65298. *Fax:* 941-727-6839. *E-mail:* powella@bc.mcc.cc.fl.us.

Application contact Manatee Community College, 5840 26th Street West, PO Box 1849, Bradenton, FL 34206-7046. *Web address:* http://www.mcc.cc.fl.us/.

MARYMOUNT COLLEGE, PALOS VERDES, CALIFORNIA
Rancho Palos Verdes, California

Students with LD Served by Program	50	ADD/ADHD Services	✓
Staff	1 full-time	Summer Preparation Program	n/a
LD Program or Service Fee	n/a	Alternative Test Arrangements	✓
LD Program Began	1987	LD Student Organization	n/a

Disability Resources began offering services in 1987. The program serves approximately 50 undergraduate students. Faculty consists of 1 full-time staff member. Services are provided by LD specialists.

Policies Students with LD may take up to 16 credit hours per semester; 12 credit hours per semester are required to maintain full-time status and to be eligible for financial aid.

Special preparation or orientation Optional orientation held before registration, after classes begin, and individually by special arrangement.

Basic skills remediation Available in study skills, reading, time management, learning strategies, spelling, written language, and math. Offered one-on-one by LD specialists, trained peer tutors, and faculty tutors.

Subject-area tutoring Available in most subjects. Offered one-on-one and in small groups by trained peer tutors, LD specialists, and faculty tutors.

Auxiliary aids and services *Aids:* calculators, personal spelling/word-use assistants (e.g., Franklin Speller), scan and read programs (e.g., Kurzweil), speech recognition programs (e.g., Dragon), tape recorders, taped textbooks. *Services and accommodations:* advocates, priority registration, alternative test arrangements, and note-takers.

ADD/ADHD Students with ADD/ADHD are eligible for the same services available to students with LD, as well as distraction-free testing environments and personal coach or mentors.

Application *Required:* high school transcript. *Recommended:* SAT I (extended-time or untimed test accepted), interview, personal statement, and letter(s) of recommendation. Upon application, documentation of need for special services should be sent only to your LD program or unit. Upon acceptance, documentation of need for special services should be sent only to your LD program or unit. *Application deadline (institutional):* rolling/continuous for fall and rolling/continuous for spring. *Application deadline (LD program):* rolling/continuous for fall and rolling/continuous for spring.

LD program contact Ruth Proctor, Coordinator, Disability Resources, 30800 Palos Verdes Drive N, Rancho Palos Verdes, CA 90275. *Phone:* 310-377-5501. *Fax:* 310-377-6223. *E-mail:* rproctor@marymountpv.edu.

Application contact Marymount College, Palos Verdes, California, 30800 Palos Verdes Drive East, Rancho Palos Verdes, CA 90275-6299. *E-mail:* admission@marymountpv.edu. *Web address:* http://www.marymountpv.edu/.

MAYLAND COMMUNITY COLLEGE
Spruce Pine, North Carolina

Students with LD Served by Program	20	ADD/ADHD Services	✓
Staff	4 full-time, 2 part-time	Summer Preparation Program	n/a
LD Program or Service Fee	n/a	Alternative Test Arrangements	✓
LD Program Began	1988	LD Student Organization	n/a

Support Options for Achievement and Retention (SOAR) Program began offering services in 1988. The program serves approximately 20 undergraduate students. Faculty consists of 4 full-time and 2 part-time staff members. Services are provided by counselors.

Policies Students with LD may take up to 18 hours per semester; 12 hours per semester are required to maintain full-time status; 6 hours per semester are required to be eligible for financial aid.

Basic skills remediation Available in study skills, computer skills, reading, time management, learning strategies, spelling, written language, math, and spoken language. Offered one-on-one and in small groups by computer-based instruction, regular education teachers, and trained peer tutors.

Subject-area tutoring Available in most subjects. Offered one-on-one and in small groups by computer-based instruction, professional tutors, and trained peer tutors.

Counseling and advisement Individual counseling is available.

Auxiliary aids and services *Aids:* calculators, personal spelling/word-use assistants (e.g., Franklin Speller), scan and read programs (e.g., Kurzweil), tape recorders, taped textbooks. *Services and accommodations:* alternative test arrangements, readers, note-takers, and scribes.

ADD/ADHD Students with ADD/ADHD are eligible for the same services available to students with LD, as well as distraction-free testing environments.

Application *Required:* high school transcript, separate application to your LD program or unit, and psychoeducational report (5 years old or less). *Recommended:* documentation of high school services (e.g., Individualized Education Program [IEP] or 504 plan). Upon application, documentation of need for special services should be sent only to your LD program or unit. Upon acceptance, documentation of need for special services should be sent only to your LD program or unit. *Application deadline (institutional):* rolling/continuous for fall and rolling/continuous for spring. *Application deadline (LD program):* rolling/continuous for fall and rolling/continuous for spring.

LD program contact Nancy Godwin, Director, PO Box 547, Spruce Pine, NC 28777. *Phone:* 828-765-7351. *Fax:* 828-765-0728. *E-mail:* ngodwin@mayland.cc.nc.us.

Application contact Paula Crowder, Admissions Retention, Mayland Community College, PO Box 547, Spruce Pine, NC 28777-0547. *Phone:* 828-765-7351. *Web address:* http://www.mayland.cc.nc.us/.

MCHENRY COUNTY COLLEGE
Crystal Lake, Illinois

Students with LD Served by Program	175	ADD/ADHD Services	✓
Staff	2 full-time, 14 part-time	Summer Preparation Program	n/a
LD Program or Service Fee	n/a	Alternative Test Arrangements	✓
LD Program Began	1977	LD Student Organization	✓

Special Needs Services began offering services in 1977. The program serves approximately 175 undergraduate students. Faculty consists of 2 full-time and 14 part-time staff members. Services are provided by regular education teachers, counselors, diagnostic specialists, LD specialists, and professional tutors.

Policies Students with LD may take up to 18 credit hours per semester; 12 credit hours per semester are required to maintain full-time status; 6 credit hours per semester are required to be eligible for financial aid.

Fees *Diagnostic Testing Fee:* $200.

Special preparation or orientation Optional orientation held before classes begin.

Diagnostic testing Available for auditory processing, spelling, intelligence, reading, written language, visual processing, and math.

Basic skills remediation Available in reading, written language, and math. Offered one-on-one and in class-size groups by regular education teachers and professional tutors.

Subject-area tutoring Available in most subjects. Offered one-on-one and in small groups by computer-based instruction, professional tutors, trained peer tutors, and LD specialists.

Auxiliary aids and services *Aids:* calculators, personal computers, personal spelling/word-use assistants (e.g., Franklin Speller), scan and read programs (e.g., Kurzweil), screen-enlarging programs, screen readers, speech recognition programs (e.g., Dragon), tape recorders, taped textbooks. *Services and accommodations:* advocates, alternative test arrangements, readers, note-takers, and scribes.

Student organization There is a student organization for students with LD.

ADD/ADHD Students with ADD/ADHD are eligible for the same services available to students with LD, as well as distraction-free testing environments.

Application *Required:* high school transcript, psychoeducational report (3 years old or less), and documentation of high school services (e.g., Individualized Education Program [IEP] or 504 plan). Upon application, documentation of need for special services should be sent only to your LD program or unit. Upon acceptance, documentation of need for special services should be sent only to your LD program or unit.

LD program contact Howard Foreman, Director of Special Needs, 8900 US Highway 14, Crystal Lake, IL 60012. *Phone:* 815-455-8710. *Fax:* 815-455-3766. *E-mail:* hforeman@pobox.mchenry.cc.il.us.

Application contact Sue Grenwis, Admissions Processor, McHenry County College, 8900 US Highway 14, Crystal Lake, IL 60012-2761. *Phone:* 815-455-8530. *Web address:* http://www.mchenry.cc.il.us/.

MERCER COUNTY COMMUNITY COLLEGE
Trenton, New Jersey

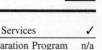

Students with LD Served by Program	120	ADD/ADHD Services	✓
Staff	3 full-time	Summer Preparation Program	n/a
LD Program or Service Fee	n/a	Alternative Test Arrangements	✓
LD Program Began	1989	LD Student Organization	n/a

Office of Special Services began offering services in 1989. The program serves approximately 120 undergraduate students. Faculty consists of 3 full-time staff members. Services are provided by academic advisers, regular education teachers, counselors, LD specialists, trained peer tutors, and professional tutors.

Policies Students with LD may take up to 15 credit hours per semester; 12 credit hours per semester are required to maintain full-time status. LD services are also available to graduate students.

Fees *Diagnostic Testing Fee:* $150.

Special preparation or orientation Optional orientation held after classes begin.

Diagnostic testing Available for auditory processing, spelling, handwriting, spoken language, reading, written language, learning styles, visual processing, and math.

Basic skills remediation Available in study skills, reading, written language, and math. Offered in class-size groups by regular education teachers.

Mercer County Community College (continued)

Subject-area tutoring Available in some subjects. Offered one-on-one and in small groups by computer-based instruction, professional tutors, and trained peer tutors.

Counseling and advisement Academic advisement by a staff member affiliated with the program is available.

Auxiliary aids and services *Aids:* calculators, scan and read programs (e.g., Kurzweil), screen-enlarging programs, screen readers, speech recognition programs (e.g., Dragon). *Services and accommodations:* alternative test arrangements.

ADD/ADHD Students with ADD/ADHD are eligible for the same services available to students with LD, as well as distraction-free study areas and distraction-free testing environments.

Application *Required:* high school transcript and psychoeducational report (3 years old or less). Upon application, documentation of need for special services should be sent only to your LD program or unit. Upon acceptance, documentation of need for special services should be sent only to your LD program or unit. *Application deadline (institutional):* rolling/continuous for fall and rolling/continuous for spring. *Application deadline (LD program):* rolling/continuous for fall and rolling/continuous for spring.

LD program contact Arlene Stinson, Coordinator of Special Services, 1200 Old Trenton Road, PO Box B, West Windsor, NJ 08690. *Phone:* 609-586-4800 Ext. 3525. *Fax:* 609-890-0471. *E-mail:* stinsona@mccc.edu.

Application contact Carlos Figueroa, Assistant Director of Admissions, Mercer County Community College, 1200 Old Trenton Road, PO Box B, Trenton, NJ 08690-1004. *Phone:* 609-586-4800 Ext. 3286. *E-mail:* figueroc@mccc.edu. *Web address:* http://www.mccc.edu/.

MERCY COLLEGE OF NORTHWEST OHIO

Toledo, Ohio

Students with LD Served by Program	15	ADD/ADHD Services	✓
Staff	1 full-time, 4 part-time	Summer Preparation Program	n/a
LD Program or Service Fee	n/a	Alternative Test Arrangements	✓
LD Program Began	1998	LD Student Organization	n/a

Office of Accessibility began offering services in 1998. The program serves approximately 15 undergraduate students. Faculty consists of 1 full-time and 4 part-time staff members. Services are provided by academic advisers, counselors, remediation/learning specialists, and trained peer tutors.

Policies Students with LD may take up to 18 credit hours per semester; 12 credit hours per semester are required to maintain full-time status; 6 credit hours per semester are required to be eligible for financial aid.

Basic skills remediation Available in study skills, computer skills, reading, time management, learning strategies, written language, and math. Offered one-on-one, in small groups, and class-size groups by computer-based instruction and LD specialists.

Subject-area tutoring Available in some subjects. Offered one-on-one and in small groups by computer-based instruction and Faculty tutors.

Counseling and advisement Career counseling, individual counseling, and small-group counseling are available. Academic advisement by a staff member affiliated with the program is available.

Auxiliary aids and services *Aids:* calculators, scan and read programs (e.g., Kurzweil), tape recorders, taped textbooks. *Services and accommodations:* alternative test arrangements, readers, note-takers, scribes, and extended testing time, isolated testing.

ADD/ADHD Students with ADD/ADHD are eligible for the same services available to students with LD, as well as distraction-free study areas and distraction-free testing environments.

Application *Required:* high school transcript, ACT or SAT I (extended-time or untimed test accepted), and psychoeducational report (5 years old or less). *Recommended:* documentation of high school services (e.g., Individualized Education Program [IEP] or 504 plan). Upon application, documentation of need for special services should be sent only to your LD program or unit. Upon acceptance, documentation of need for special services should be sent only to your LD program or unit. *Application deadline (institutional):* 7/1 for fall and 11/1 for spring.

LD program contact Marlene Szurminski, Coordinator of Student Success Center, 2221 Madison Avenue, Toledo, OH 43624-1132. *Phone:* 419-251-1710. *Fax:* 419-251-1462. *E-mail:* marlene_szurminski@mhsnr.org.

Application contact Shelly Susor, Registrar and Admissions Coordinator, Mercy College of Northwest Ohio, 2221 Madison Avenue, Toledo, OH 43624. *Phone:* 419-251-8989. *Web address:* http://www.mercycollege.edu/.

MIDLANDS TECHNICAL COLLEGE

Columbia, South Carolina

Students with LD Served by Program	90	ADD/ADHD Services	✓
Staff	1 full-time, 4 part-time	Summer Preparation Program	n/a
LD Program or Service Fee	n/a	Alternative Test Arrangements	✓
LD Program Began	1979	LD Student Organization	✓

Counseling Services/Disability Resource Center began offering services in 1979. The program serves approximately 90 undergraduate students. Faculty consists of 1 full-time and 4 part-time staff members. Services are provided by regular education teachers, counselors, and undergraduate students.

Policies 6 credit hours per semester are required to maintain full-time status.

Special preparation or orientation Optional orientation held before classes begin, after classes begin, and individually by special arrangement.

Counseling and advisement Career counseling, individual counseling, and support groups are available.

Auxiliary aids and services *Aids:* calculators, personal computers, personal spelling/word-use assistants (e.g., Franklin Speller), scan and read programs (e.g., Kurzweil), screen-enlarging programs, screen readers, speech recognition programs (e.g., Dragon), tape recorders, taped textbooks. *Services and accommodations:* advocates, alternative test arrangements, readers, note-takers, scribes, and reduced course loads.

Student organization There is a student organization for students with LD.

ADD/ADHD Students with ADD/ADHD are eligible for the same services available to students with LD, as well as distraction-free study areas.

Application *Required:* separate application to your LD program or unit and high school equivalency certificate, college placement test. *Recommended:* high school transcript. Upon application, documentation of need for special services should be sent only to your LD program or unit. Upon acceptance, documentation of need for special services should be sent only to your LD program or unit. *Application deadline (institutional):* 7/23 for fall and 11/29 for spring. *Application deadline (LD program):* 7/12 for fall and 11/16 for spring.

LD program contact Jennifer Osmer, Coordinator, Disability Resource Centers, PO Box 2408, Columbia, SC 29202. *Phone:* 803-822-3505. *Fax:* 803-822-3295. *E-mail:* osmerj@mtc.mid.tec.sc.us.

Application contact Midlands Technical College, PO Box 2408, West Cola, SC 29171. *Web address:* http://www.mid.tec.sc.us/.

MINNESOTA WEST COMMUNITY AND TECHNICAL COLLEGE-GRANITE FALLS CAMPUS
Granite Falls, Minnesota

Students with LD Served by Program	15	ADD/ADHD Services	✓
Staff	3 full-time, 2 part-time	Summer Preparation Program	n/a
LD Program or Service Fee	n/a	Alternative Test Arrangements	✓
LD Program Began	1980	LD Student Organization	n/a

The Success Center began offering services in 1980. The program serves approximately 15 undergraduate students. Faculty consists of 3 full-time and 2 part-time staff members. Services are provided by academic advisers, counselors, trained peer tutors, and professional tutors.

Policies Students with LD may take up to 18 credits per semester; 12 credits per semester are required to maintain full-time status; 6 credits per semester are required to be eligible for financial aid.

Basic skills remediation Available in study skills, computer skills, reading, time management, learning strategies, written language, and math. Offered one-on-one, in small groups, and class-size groups by professional tutors and trained peer tutors.

Subject-area tutoring Available in most subjects. Offered one-on-one and in small groups by professional tutors and trained peer tutors.

Counseling and advisement Career counseling and individual counseling are available. Academic advisement by a staff member affiliated with the program is available.

Auxiliary aids and services *Aids:* personal computers, personal spelling/word-use assistants (e.g., Franklin Speller), scan and read programs (e.g., Kurzweil), tape recorders, taped textbooks. *Services and accommodations:* advocates, alternative test arrangements, readers, note-takers, and scribes.

ADD/ADHD Students with ADD/ADHD are eligible for the same services available to students with LD, as well as distraction-free study areas and distraction-free testing environments.

Application *Required:* high school transcript, separate application to your LD program or unit, psychoeducational report (3 years old or less), and documentation of high school services (e.g., Individualized Education Program [IEP] or 504 plan). Upon application, documentation of need for special services should be sent only to your LD program or unit. Upon acceptance, documentation of need for special services should be sent only to your LD program or unit. *Application deadline (institutional):* rolling/continuous for fall and rolling/continuous for spring. *Application deadline (LD program):* rolling/continuous for fall and rolling/continuous for spring.

LD program contact John Joosten, Campus Dean/Supervisor of Special Needs, 1593 11th Avenue, Granite Falls, MN 56241. *Phone:* 320-564-4511. *Fax:* 320-564-4582. *E-mail:* jjoosten@gf.mnwest.mnscu.edu.

Application contact Alison Koering, Campus Admissions, Minnesota West Community and Technical College-Granite Falls Campus, 1593 11th Avenue, Granite Falls, MN 56241. *Phone:* 320-564-4511. *E-mail:* loria@tc/pipstone.swp.tec.mn.us. *Web address:* http://www.mnwest.mnscu.edu/.

MINNESOTA WEST COMMUNITY AND TECHNICAL COLLEGE-WORTHINGTON CAMPUS
Worthington, Minnesota

Students with LD Served by Program	50	ADD/ADHD Services	✓
Staff	3 full-time, 30 part-time	Summer Preparation Program	✓
LD Program or Service Fee	n/a	Alternative Test Arrangements	✓
LD Program Began	1990	LD Student Organization	n/a

Academic Success Center (ASC) began offering services in 1990. The program serves approximately 50 undergraduate students. Faculty consists of 3 full-time and 30 part-time staff members. Services are provided by regular education teachers, trained peer tutors, and professional tutors.

Special preparation or orientation Optional summer program offered prior to entering college.

Basic skills remediation Available in study skills, reading, time management, learning strategies, written language, and math. Offered one-on-one and in small groups by special education teachers.

Subject-area tutoring Available in most subjects. Offered one-on-one, in small groups, and class-size groups by computer-based instruction, professional tutors, and trained peer tutors.

Auxiliary aids and services *Aids:* calculators, personal computers, personal spelling/word-use assistants (e.g., Franklin Speller), scan and read programs (e.g., Kurzweil), screen-enlarging programs, screen readers, tape recorders, taped textbooks. *Services and accommodations:* advocates, alternative test arrangements, readers, note-takers, and scribes.

ADD/ADHD Students with ADD/ADHD are eligible for the same services available to students with LD, as well as distraction-free study areas and distraction-free testing environments.

Application *Required:* high school transcript, separate application to your LD program or unit, psychoeducational report (3 years old or less), and documentation of high school services (e.g., Individualized Education Program [IEP] or 504 plan). *Recommended:* interview. Upon application, documentation of need for special services should be sent only to your LD program or unit. Upon acceptance, documentation of need for special services should be sent only to your LD program or unit. *Application deadline (institutional):* rolling/continuous for fall and rolling/continuous for spring. *Application deadline (LD program):* rolling/continuous for fall and rolling/continuous for spring.

LD program contact Debra A. Carrow, Support Services Manager, 1314 North Hiawatha Avenue, Pipestone, MN 56164. *Phone:* 507-825-6800. *E-mail:* debrac@ps.mnwest.mnscu.edu.

Application contact Minnesota West Community and Technical College-Worthington Campus, 1450 College Way, Worthington, MN 56187-3024. *E-mail:* dfleming@ur.cc.mn.us.

MINOT STATE UNIVERSITY-BOTTINEAU CAMPUS
Bottineau, North Dakota

Students with LD Served by Program	10	ADD/ADHD Services	✓
Staff	1 full-time, 2 part-time	Summer Preparation Program	n/a
LD Program or Service Fee	n/a	Alternative Test Arrangements	✓
LD Program Began	1992	LD Student Organization	n/a

Learning Center began offering services in 1992. The program serves approximately 10 undergraduate students. Faculty consists of 1 full-time and 2 part-time staff members. Services are provided by LD specialists, trained peer tutors, and professional tutors.

Policies Students with LD may take up to 20 credit hours per semester; 12 credit hours per semester are required to maintain full-time status and to be eligible for financial aid.

Basic skills remediation Available in study skills, computer skills, reading, written language, and math. Offered one-on-one and in small groups by regular education teachers and LD specialists.

Subject-area tutoring Available in all subjects. Offered one-on-one and in small groups by professional tutors, trained peer tutors, and LD specialists.

Special courses Available in career planning, study skills, reading, and written composition skills. All courses are offered for credit; all enter into overall grade point average.

Counseling and advisement Career counseling and individual counseling are available.

Auxiliary aids and services *Services and accommodations:* advocates, alternative test arrangements, readers, and note-takers.

ADD/ADHD Students with ADD/ADHD are eligible for the same services available to students with LD, as well as distraction-free testing environments.

Application *Required:* high school transcript and ACT (extended-time or untimed test accepted). *Recommended:* psychoeducational report (3 years old or less) and documentation of high school services (e.g., Individualized Education Program [IEP] or 504 plan). Upon acceptance, documentation of need for special services should be sent only to your LD program or unit. *Application deadline (institutional):* rolling/continuous for fall and rolling/continuous for spring. *Application deadline (LD program):* rolling/continuous for fall and rolling/continuous for spring.

LD program contact Jan Nahiurk, Director of the Learning Center, 105 Simrall Boulevard, Bottineau, ND 58318. *Phone:* 701-228-5479. *Fax:* 701-228-5468. *E-mail:* nahinurk@misu.nodak.edu.

Application contact Thomas Berube, Admissions Counselor, Minot State University-Bottineau Campus, 105 Simrall Boulevard, Bottineau, ND 58318-1198. *Phone:* 701-228-5426 Ext. 426. *E-mail:* groszk@warp6.cs.misu.nodak.edu. *Web address:* http://www.misu-b.nodak.edu/.

MISSISSIPPI GULF COAST COMMUNITY COLLEGE
Perkinston, Mississippi

Students with LD Served by Program	100	ADD/ADHD Services	✓
Staff	n/a	Summer Preparation Program	n/a
LD Program or Service Fee	n/a	Alternative Test Arrangements	✓
LD Program Began	1993	LD Student Organization	n/a

Special Populations began offering services in 1993. The program serves approximately 100 undergraduate students. Services are provided by academic advisers, regular education teachers, counselors, remediation/learning specialists, special education teachers, trained peer tutors, and professional tutors.

Policies Students with LD may take up to 18 semester hours per semester; 12 hours per semester are required to maintain full-time status.

Basic skills remediation Available in study skills, computer skills, reading, time management, learning strategies, written language, math, and spoken language. Offered one-on-one and in small groups by computer-based instruction, regular education teachers, special education teachers, LD specialists, and professional tutors.

Subject-area tutoring Available in all subjects. Offered one-on-one, in small groups, and class-size groups by computer-based instruction, professional tutors, and LD specialists.

Special courses Available in college survival skills and learning strategies. Some courses are offered for credit; most enter into overall grade point average.

Counseling and advisement Career counseling, individual counseling, and support groups are available. Academic advisement by a staff member affiliated with the program is available.

Auxiliary aids and services *Aids:* calculators, personal computers, personal spelling/word-use assistants (e.g., Franklin Speller), scan and read programs (e.g., Kurzweil), screen-enlarging programs, screen readers, tape recorders, taped textbooks. *Services and accommodations:* alternative test arrangements, readers, note-takers, and scribes.

ADD/ADHD Students with ADD/ADHD are eligible for the same services available to students with LD

Application *Required:* high school transcript, psychoeducational report (2 years old or less), and documentation of high school services (e.g., Individualized Education Program [IEP] or 504 plan). *Recommended:* ACT. Upon application, documentation of need for special services should be sent only to admissions. Upon acceptance, documentation of need for special services should be sent to both admissions and your LD program or unit. *Application deadline (institutional):* rolling/continuous for fall and rolling/continuous for spring. *Application deadline (LD program):* rolling/continuous for fall and rolling/continuous for spring.

LD program contact Dr. Hal Higdon, Associate Vice President for Human Resources, PO Box 294, Perkinston, MS 39573. *Phone:* 601-928-6285. *Fax:* 601-928-6386. *E-mail:* hal.higdon@mgccc.cc.ms.us.

Application contact Ann Provis, Director of Admissions, Mississippi Gulf Coast Community College, PO Box 548, Perkinston, MS 39573-0548. *Phone:* 601-928-6264. *Web address:* http://www.mgccc.cc.ms.us/.

MOHAWK VALLEY COMMUNITY COLLEGE
Utica, New York

Students with LD Served by Program	200	ADD/ADHD Services	✓
Staff	1 full-time, 1 part-time	Summer Preparation Program	n/a
LD Program or Service Fee	n/a	Alternative Test Arrangements	✓
LD Program Began	1989	LD Student Organization	n/a

Office for Services to Students with Disabilities (OSSD) began offering services in 1989. The program serves approximately 200 undergraduate students. Faculty consists of 1 full-time and 1 part-time staff member. Services are provided by LD specialists.

Policies Students with LD may take up to 18 credits per semester; 12 credits per semester are required to maintain full-time status; 6 credits per semester are required to be eligible for financial aid. LD services are also available to graduate students.

Counseling and advisement Individual counseling and support groups are available.

Auxiliary aids and services *Aids:* calculators, personal computers, personal spelling/word-use assistants (e.g., Franklin Speller), scan and read programs (e.g., Kurzweil), screen-enlarging programs, tape recorders, taped textbooks. *Services and accommodations:* priority registration, alternative test arrangements, note-takers, and scribes.

ADD/ADHD Students with ADD/ADHD are eligible for the same services available to students with LD, as well as distraction-free testing environments and support groups for ADD/ADHD.

Application *Required:* documentation of high school services (e.g., Individualized Education Program [IEP] or 504 plan). *Recommended:* high school transcript and psychoeducational report (5 years old or less). Upon application, documentation of need for special services should be sent to both admissions and your LD program or unit. Upon acceptance, documentation of need for special services should be sent to both admissions and your LD program or unit. *Application deadline (institutional):* rolling/continuous for fall and rolling/continuous for spring. *Application deadline (LD program):* rolling/continuous for fall and rolling/continuous for spring.

LD program contact Veda Candeloro, Learning Disabilities Specialist, 1101 Sherman Drive, Utica, NY 13501. *Phone:* 315-731-5702. *Fax:* 315-792-5696. *E-mail:* vcandeloro@mvcc.edu.

Application contact Sandra Fiebiger, Electronic Data Processing Clerk, Admissions, Mohawk Valley Community College, 1101 Sherman Drive, Utica, NY 13501-5394. *Phone:* 315-792-5640. *E-mail:* dkennelty@mvcc.edu. *Web address:* http://www.mvcc.edu/.

MONTANA STATE UNIVERSITY COLLEGE OF TECHNOLOGY-GREAT FALLS
Great Falls, Montana

Students with LD Served by Program	14	ADD/ADHD Services	✓
Staff	3 full-time, 4 part-time	Summer Preparation Program	n/a
LD Program or Service Fee	n/a	Alternative Test Arrangements	✓
LD Program Began	1990	LD Student Organization	n/a

Disability Services began offering services in 1990. The program serves approximately 14 undergraduate students. Faculty consists of 3 full-time and 4 part-time staff members. Services are provided by academic advisers, counselors, remediation/learning specialists, trained peer tutors, and professional tutors.

Policies The college has written policies regarding course substitutions.

Special preparation or orientation Required orientation held before registration, during registration, before classes begin, after classes begin, during summer prior to enrollment, and individually by special arrangement.

Basic skills remediation Available in study skills, computer skills, reading, time management, handwriting, social skills, learning strategies, spelling, and math. Offered in class-size groups by computer-based instruction, regular education teachers, and special education teachers.

Subject-area tutoring Available in most subjects. Offered one-on-one by computer-based instruction, professional tutors, and trained peer tutors.

Special courses Available in college survival skills, health and nutrition, time management, learning strategies, self-advocacy, and stress management. No courses are offered for credit; none enter into overall grade point average.

Counseling and advisement Career counseling, individual counseling, and small-group counseling are available. Academic advisement by a staff member affiliated with the program is available.

Auxiliary aids and services *Aids:* calculators, personal computers, personal spelling/word-use assistants (e.g., Franklin Speller), scan and read programs (e.g., Kurzweil), screen-enlarging programs, screen readers, speech recognition programs (e.g., Dragon), tape recorders, taped textbooks. *Services and accommodations:* advocates, priority registration, alternative test arrangements, readers, note-takers, and scribes.

ADD/ADHD Students with ADD/ADHD are eligible for the same services available to students with LD, as well as distraction-free study areas and distraction-free testing environments.

Application *Required:* high school transcript, ACT or SAT I (extended-time or untimed test accepted), psychoeducational report (2 years old or less), and Asset test or Compass. Upon application, documentation of need for special services should be sent only to your LD program or unit. Upon acceptance, documentation of need for special services should be sent only to your LD program or unit. *Application deadline (institutional):* 8/20 for fall and 1/7 for spring. *Application deadline (LD program):* rolling/continuous for fall.

LD program contact Diana Wyatt, Coordinator of Disability Services, Box 6010, 2100 16th Avenue S, Great Falls, MT 59405. *Phone:* 406-771-4311. *Fax:* 406-771-4317. *E-mail:* dwyatt@msugf.edu.

Application contact David Farrington, Director of Admissions and Records, Montana State University College of Technology-Great Falls, 2100 16th Avenue, South, Great Falls, MT 59405. *Phone:* 406-771-4300. *E-mail:* zgf2001@maia.oscs.montana.edu. *Web address:* http://msucotgf.montana.edu/~msucotgf/.

MONTCALM COMMUNITY COLLEGE
Sidney, Michigan

Students with LD Served by Program	65	ADD/ADHD Services	✓
Staff	2 full-time, 40 part-time	Summer Preparation Program	n/a
LD Program or Service Fee	n/a	Alternative Test Arrangements	✓
LD Program Began	1985	LD Student Organization	n/a

Montcalm Community College (continued)

Learning Assistance Program began offering services in 1985. The program serves approximately 65 undergraduate students. Faculty consists of 2 full-time and 40 part-time staff members. Services are provided by counselors, trained peer tutors, and professional tutors.

Subject-area tutoring Available in most subjects. Offered one-on-one, in small groups, and class-size groups by professional tutors and trained peer tutors.

Auxiliary aids and services *Services and accommodations:* advocates, alternative test arrangements, readers, note-takers, scribes, and text on tape, instructional classroom aids.

ADD/ADHD Students with ADD/ADHD are eligible for the same services available to students with LD

Application *Required:* high school transcript, separate application to your LD program or unit, documentation of high school services (e.g., Individualized Education Program [IEP] or 504 plan), and documented disability. Upon application, documentation of need for special services should be sent only to your LD program or unit. *Application deadline (institutional):* rolling/continuous for fall and rolling/continuous for spring. *Application deadline (LD program):* rolling/continuous for fall and rolling/continuous for spring.

LD program contact Charlotte Fokens, Special Populations Counselor, 2800 College Drive, Sidney, MI 48885. *Phone:* 517-328-2111. *E-mail:* charlottef@montcalm.cc.mi.us.

Application contact Kathie Lofts, Assistant Director of Enrollment Services/Admissions, Montcalm Community College, 2800 College Drive, SW, PO Box 300, Sidney, MI 48885-0300. *Phone:* 517-328-1250. *E-mail:* admissions@montcalm.cc.mi.us. *Web address:* http://www.montcalm.cc.mi.us/.

MONTGOMERY COLLEGE
Conroe, Texas

Students with LD Served by Program	150	ADD/ADHD Services	✓
Staff	8 full-time, 37 part-time	Summer Preparation Program	n/a
LD Program or Service Fee	n/a	Alternative Test Arrangements	✓
LD Program Began	1995	LD Student Organization	n/a

Extended Learning Center began offering services in 1995. The program serves approximately 150 undergraduate students. Faculty consists of 8 full-time and 37 part-time staff members. Services are provided by academic advisers, regular education teachers, remediation/learning specialists, graduate assistants/students, LD specialists, trained peer tutors, and professional tutors.

Policies Students with LD may take up to 18 credit hours per semester; 12 credit hours per semester are required to maintain full-time status; 6 credit hours per semester are required to be eligible for financial aid.

Diagnostic testing Available for auditory processing, study skills, learning strategies, reading, written language, learning styles, visual processing, and math.

Basic skills remediation Available in auditory processing, study skills, computer skills, reading, time management, visual processing, learning strategies, written language, and math. Offered one-on-one and in small groups by LD specialists, professional tutors, and trained peer tutors.

Subject-area tutoring Available in most subjects. Offered one-on-one, in small groups, and class-size groups by computer-based instruction, professional tutors, trained peer tutors, and LD specialists.

Counseling and advisement Career counseling and individual counseling are available. Academic advisement by a staff member affiliated with the program is available.

Auxiliary aids and services *Aids:* calculators, scan and read programs (e.g., Kurzweil), screen-enlarging programs, tape recorders. *Services and accommodations:* alternative test arrangements, readers, note-takers, and scribes.

ADD/ADHD Students with ADD/ADHD are eligible for the same services available to students with LD, as well as distraction-free study areas and distraction-free testing environments.

Application *Required:* interview, psychoeducational report (5 years old or less), and Placement Testing. Upon application, documentation of need for special services should be sent only to admissions. Upon acceptance, documentation of need for special services should be sent only to admissions. *Application deadline (institutional):* rolling/continuous for fall and rolling/continuous for spring. *Application deadline (LD program):* rolling/continuous for fall and rolling/continuous for spring.

LD program contact Sharon Herrmann, Assistant Dean, 3200 College Park Drive, Conroe, TX 77384. *Phone:* 936-273-7371.

Application contact Suzy Englert, Admissions/Advising Coordinator, Montgomery College, 3200 College Park Drive, Conroe, TX 77384. *Phone:* 409-273-7236. *E-mail:* lindab@nhmccd.cc.tx.us. *Web address:* http://wwwmc.nhmccd.edu/.

MONTGOMERY COMMUNITY COLLEGE
Troy, North Carolina

Students with LD Served by Program	35	ADD/ADHD Services	✓
Staff	1 full-time	Summer Preparation Program	n/a
LD Program or Service Fee	n/a	Alternative Test Arrangements	✓
LD Program Began	n/a	LD Student Organization	n/a

Counseling Services serves approximately 35 undergraduate students. Faculty consists of 1 full-time staff member. Services are provided by counselors.

Policies The college has written policies regarding course substitutions.

Special preparation or orientation Optional orientation held before registration, before classes begin, and individually by special arrangement.

Diagnostic testing Available for learning strategies, reading, written language, learning styles, and math.

Basic skills remediation Available in auditory processing, computer skills, reading, time management, learning strategies, written language, and math. Offered one-on-one by regular education teachers and trained peer tutors.

Subject-area tutoring Available in all subjects. Offered one-on-one by trained peer tutors.

Special courses Available in math and written composition skills. Some courses are offered for credit.

Counseling and advisement Career counseling, individual counseling, small-group counseling, and support groups are available.

Auxiliary aids and services *Aids:* calculators, personal spelling/word-use assistants (e.g., Franklin Speller), scan and read programs (e.g., Kurzweil), screen-enlarging programs, tape recorders, taped textbooks. *Services and accommodations:* alternative test arrangements, readers, and note-takers.

ADD/ADHD Students with ADD/ADHD are eligible for the same services available to students with LD

Application *Required:* high school transcript, psychoeducational report, documentation of high school services (e.g., Individualized Education Program [IEP] or 504 plan), and Asset, Compass

Assessment. *Recommended:* personal statement. Upon application, documentation of need for special services should be sent only to your LD program or unit. Upon acceptance, documentation of need for special services should be sent only to your LD program or unit.

LD program contact Margo H. Gaddy, Counselor, 1011 Page Street, Troy, NC 27371. *Phone:* 910-576-6222. *Fax:* 910-576-2176. *E-mail:* gaddym@mcc.montgomery.cc.nc.us.

Application contact Stacey Hilliard, Admissions Officer, Montgomery Community College, PO Box 787, Troy, NC 27371-0787. *Phone:* 910-576-6222 Ext. 264. *E-mail:* hilliards@mcc.montgomery.cc.nc.us. *Web address:* http://www.montgomery.cc.nc.us/.

MORAINE VALLEY COMMUNITY COLLEGE
Palos Hills, Illinois

Students with LD Served by Program	150	ADD/ADHD Services	✓
Staff	2 full-time, 4 part-time	Summer Preparation Program	n/a
LD Program or Service Fee	n/a	Alternative Test Arrangements	✓
LD Program Began	1978	LD Student Organization	✓

Learning Disabilities Student Services (LDS) began offering services in 1978. The program serves approximately 150 undergraduate students. Faculty consists of 2 full-time and 4 part-time staff members. Services are provided by counselors and special education teachers.

Policies The college has written policies regarding grade forgiveness.

Fees *Diagnostic Testing Fee:* $100.

Special preparation or orientation Required orientation held before registration and during summer prior to enrollment.

Diagnostic testing Available for auditory processing, spelling, spoken language, intelligence, reading, written language, and visual processing.

Basic skills remediation Available in reading and written language. Offered in class-size groups by regular education teachers and special education teachers.

Subject-area tutoring Available in some subjects. Offered in small groups by professional tutors.

Special courses Available in math and written composition skills. No courses are offered for credit; none enter into overall grade point average.

Counseling and advisement Career counseling, individual counseling, small-group counseling, and support groups are available.

Auxiliary aids and services *Aids:* tape recorders. *Services and accommodations:* advocates, priority registration, alternative test arrangements, readers, note-takers, and scribes.

Student organization There is a student organization for students with LD.

ADD/ADHD Students with ADD/ADHD are eligible for the same services available to students with LD, as well as distraction-free testing environments and personal coach or mentors.

Application *Required:* interview, separate application to your LD program or unit, psychoeducational report, and documentation of high school services (e.g., Individualized Education Program [IEP] or 504 plan). *Recommended:* high school transcript. Upon application, documentation of need for special services should be sent only to your LD program or unit. *Application deadline (LD program):* 5/1 for fall and 11/1 for spring.

LD program contact Director, Center for Disabilities, 10900 South 88th Avenue, Palos Hills, IL 60525. *Phone:* 708-974-5711.

Application contact Moraine Valley Community College, 10900 South 88th Avenue, Palos Hills, IL 60465-0937. *Web address:* http://www.moraine.cc.il.us/.

MOTLOW STATE COMMUNITY COLLEGE
Tullahoma, Tennessee

Students with LD Served by Program	60	ADD/ADHD Services	✓
Staff	1 full-time, 1 part-time	Summer Preparation Program	n/a
LD Program or Service Fee	n/a	Alternative Test Arrangements	✓
LD Program Began	1993	LD Student Organization	n/a

Student Affairs Services for Students with Disabilities began offering services in 1993. The program serves approximately 60 undergraduate students. Faculty consists of 1 full-time and 1 part-time staff member. Services are provided by academic advisers, counselors, remediation/learning specialists, trained peer tutors, and professional tutors.

Subject-area tutoring Available in most subjects. Offered one-on-one by professional tutors and trained peer tutors.

Counseling and advisement Career counseling, individual counseling, and support groups are available. Academic advisement by a staff member affiliated with the program is available.

Auxiliary aids and services *Aids:* calculators, screen-enlarging programs, screen readers, tape recorders, taped textbooks. *Services and accommodations:* advocates, priority registration, alternative test arrangements, readers, note-takers, and scribes.

ADD/ADHD Students with ADD/ADHD are eligible for the same services available to students with LD, as well as distraction-free study areas and distraction-free testing environments.

Application *Required:* high school transcript, ACT (extended-time or untimed test accepted), interview, separate application to your LD program or unit, and psychoeducational report (2 years old or less). *Recommended:* participation in extracurricular activities, personal statement, letter(s) of recommendation, and documentation of high school services (e.g., Individualized Education Program [IEP] or 504 plan). Upon application, documentation of need for special services should be sent only to your LD program or unit. Upon acceptance, documentation of need for special services should be sent only to your LD program or unit. *Application deadline (institutional):* rolling/continuous for fall and rolling/continuous for spring. *Application deadline (LD program):* rolling/continuous for fall and rolling/continuous for spring.

LD program contact Ann Simmons, Dean of Student Development, PO Box 8500, Department 540, Lynchburg, TN 37352. *Phone:* 931-393-1765. *Fax:* 931-393-1761. *E-mail:* asimmons@mscc.cc.tn.us.

Application contact Michael Russell, Director of New Student Admissions, Motlow State Community College, PO Box 88100, Tullahoma, TN 37388-8100. *Phone:* 931-393-1764. *Web address:* http://www.mscc.cc.tn.us/.

MOUNT WACHUSETT COMMUNITY COLLEGE

Gardner, Massachusetts

Students with LD Served by Program	200	ADD/ADHD Services	✓
Staff	2 full-time, 3 part-time	Summer Preparation Program	n/a
LD Program or Service Fee	n/a	Alternative Test Arrangements	✓
LD Program Began	1982	LD Student Organization	n/a

Students with Disabilities began offering services in 1982. The program serves approximately 200 undergraduate students. Faculty consists of 2 full-time and 3 part-time staff members. Services are provided by academic advisers, counselors, remediation/learning specialists, graduate assistants/students, LD specialists, trained peer tutors, and professional tutors.
Policies The college has written policies regarding course substitutions and substitution and waivers of requirements for admission and graduation.
Special preparation or orientation Optional orientation held individually by special arrangement.
Basic skills remediation Available in study skills, reading, time management, social skills, learning strategies, written language, and math. Offered in class-size groups by regular education teachers.
Subject-area tutoring Available in most subjects. Offered one-on-one and in small groups by computer-based instruction, professional tutors, trained peer tutors, and LD specialists.
Counseling and advisement Career counseling, individual counseling, and support groups are available. Academic advisement by a staff member affiliated with the program is available.
Auxiliary aids and services *Aids:* calculators, personal computers, personal spelling/word-use assistants (e.g., Franklin Speller), scan and read programs (e.g., Kurzweil), screen-enlarging programs, screen readers, speech recognition programs (e.g., Dragon), tape recorders, taped textbooks. *Services and accommodations:* advocates, alternative test arrangements, readers, note-takers, and scribes.
ADD/ADHD Students with ADD/ADHD are eligible for the same services available to students with LD, as well as distraction-free study areas and distraction-free testing environments.
Application *Required:* high school transcript. Upon application, documentation of need for special services should be sent only to your LD program or unit. Upon acceptance, documentation of need for special services should be sent only to your LD program or unit. *Application deadline (institutional):* rolling/continuous for fall and rolling/continuous for spring. *Application deadline (LD program):* rolling/continuous for fall and rolling/continuous for spring.
LD program contact Juliette Loring, Counselor, 444 Green Street, Gardner, MA 01440. *Phone:* 978-632-6600. *Fax:* 978-632-6155. *E-mail:* j-loring@mwcc.mass.edu.
Application contact Mount Wachusett Community College, 444 Green Street, Gardner, MA 01440-1000. *E-mail:* admissions@mwcc.mass.edu. *Web address:* http://www.mwcc.mass.edu/.

MUSKEGON COMMUNITY COLLEGE

Muskegon, Michigan

Students with LD Served by Program	150	ADD/ADHD Services	✓
Staff	2 full-time	Summer Preparation Program	n/a
LD Program or Service Fee	n/a	Alternative Test Arrangements	✓
LD Program Began	n/a	LD Student Organization	n/a

Special Service Programs Office serves approximately 150 undergraduate students. Faculty consists of 2 full-time staff members. Services are provided by academic advisers, counselors, trained peer tutors, and professional tutors.
Policies LD services are also available to graduate students.
Counseling and advisement Career counseling and individual counseling are available. Academic advisement by a staff member affiliated with the program is available.
Auxiliary aids and services *Aids:* personal spelling/word-use assistants (e.g., Franklin Speller), screen readers, speech recognition programs (e.g., Dragon), tape recorders, taped textbooks. *Services and accommodations:* alternative test arrangements, readers, note-takers, and scribes.
ADD/ADHD Students with ADD/ADHD are eligible for the same services available to students with LD, as well as distraction-free testing environments.
Application *Required:* interview and psychoeducational report. *Recommended:* documentation of high school services (e.g., Individualized Education Program [IEP] or 504 plan). Upon application, documentation of need for special services should be sent only to your LD program or unit. Upon acceptance, documentation of need for special services should be sent only to your LD program or unit. *Application deadline (institutional):* rolling/continuous for fall and rolling/continuous for spring. *Application deadline (LD program):* rolling/continuous for fall and rolling/continuous for spring.
LD program contact Janice W. Alexander, Director of Special Services, 221 South Quarterline Road, Muskegon, MI 49442. *Phone:* 231-777-0309. *Fax:* 231-777-0250. *E-mail:* alexandj@muskegon.cc.mi.us.
Application contact Lynda Schwartz, Admissions Coordinator, Muskegon Community College, 221 South Quarterline Road, Muskegon, MI 49442-1493. *Phone:* 616-773-9131 Ext. 366.

NASSAU COMMUNITY COLLEGE

Garden City, New York

Students with LD Served by Program	500	ADD/ADHD Services	✓
Staff	9 full-time, 5 part-time	Summer Preparation Program	n/a
LD Program or Service Fee	n/a	Alternative Test Arrangements	✓
LD Program Began	1969	LD Student Organization	✓

Center for Students with Disabilities began offering services in 1969. The program serves approximately 500 undergraduate students. Faculty consists of 9 full-time and 5 part-time staff members. Services are provided by academic advisers, counselors, remediation/learning specialists, special education teachers, LD specialists, professional tutors, and Test Proctor.
Policies Students with LD may take up to 17 credit hours per semester; 12 credit hours per semester are required to maintain full-time status; 3 credit hours per semester are required to be eligible for financial aid.
Special preparation or orientation Optional orientation held individually by special arrangement.
Basic skills remediation Available in auditory processing, study skills, computer skills, reading, time management, handwriting, social skills, visual processing, learning strategies, written language, math, and spoken language. Offered one-on-one and in small groups by special education teachers, LD specialists, and professional tutors.
Subject-area tutoring Available in most subjects. Offered one-on-one and in small groups by professional tutors and LD specialists.

Counseling and advisement Career counseling, individual counseling, small-group counseling, and support groups are available. Academic advisement by a staff member affiliated with the program is available.

Auxiliary aids and services *Aids:* calculators, personal computers, personal spelling/word-use assistants (e.g., Franklin Speller), scan and read programs (e.g., Kurzweil), screen-enlarging programs, screen readers, speech recognition programs (e.g., Dragon), tape recorders, taped textbooks. *Services and accommodations:* advocates, priority registration, alternative test arrangements, readers, and scribes.

Student organization There is a student organization for students with LD.

ADD/ADHD Students with ADD/ADHD are eligible for the same services available to students with LD, as well as distraction-free study areas and distraction-free testing environments.

Application *Required:* high school transcript. Upon acceptance, documentation of need for special services should be sent only to your LD program or unit. *Application deadline (institutional):* rolling/continuous for fall and rolling/continuous for spring.

LD program contact Prof. Janis Schimsky, Coordinator, 1 Education Drive, Garden City, NY 11530. *Phone:* 516-572-7138. *Fax:* 516-572-9874. *E-mail:* schimsj@sunynassau.edu.

Application contact Nassau Community College, 1 Education Drive, Garden City, NY 11530-6793. *Web address:* http://www.sunynassau.edu/.

NAUGATUCK VALLEY COMMUNITY COLLEGE

Waterbury, Connecticut

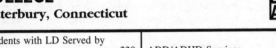

Students with LD Served by Program	220	ADD/ADHD Services	✓
Staff	2 full-time	Summer Preparation Program	n/a
LD Program or Service Fee	n/a	Alternative Test Arrangements	✓
LD Program Began	1991	LD Student Organization	✓

Learning Disabilities Office began offering services in 1991. The program serves approximately 220 undergraduate students. Faculty consists of 2 full-time staff members. Services are provided by academic advisers, regular education teachers, counselors, and professional tutors.

Basic skills remediation Available in study skills, reading, learning strategies, written language, and math. Offered in class-size groups by computer-based instruction and regular education teachers.

Subject-area tutoring Available in some subjects. Offered one-on-one and in small groups by professional tutors.

Special courses Available in career planning, study skills, college survival skills, test taking, reading, time management, math, and written composition skills. Some courses are offered for credit; some enter into overall grade point average.

Counseling and advisement Career counseling and individual counseling are available. Academic advisement by a staff member affiliated with the program is available.

Auxiliary aids and services *Aids:* calculators, tape recorders. *Services and accommodations:* advocates, priority registration, alternative test arrangements, readers, note-takers, and scribes.

Student organization There is a student organization for students with LD.

ADD/ADHD Students with ADD/ADHD are eligible for the same services available to students with LD, as well as distraction-free testing environments.

Application *Required:* high school transcript, psychoeducational report, documentation of high school services (e.g., Individualized Education Program [IEP] or 504 plan), and Placement testing. Upon application, documentation of need for special services should be sent only to your LD program or unit. Upon acceptance, documentation of need for special services should be sent only to your LD program or unit.

LD program contact Louise L. Myers, Coordinator of the LD Program, 750 Chase Parkway, E515C, Waterbury, CT 06708. *Phone:* 203-575-8161. *Fax:* 203-575-8001. *E-mail:* lmyers_@nvctc5.commnet.edu.

Application contact Naugatuck Valley Community College, 750 Chase Parkway, Waterbury, CT 06708-3000. *Web address:* http://www.nvctc.commnet.edu/.

NEW HAMPSHIRE COMMUNITY TECHNICAL COLLEGE, NASHUA/CLAREMONT

Nashua, New Hampshire

Students with LD Served by Program	n/a	ADD/ADHD Services	✓
Staff	1 full-time	Summer Preparation Program	n/a
LD Program or Service Fee	n/a	Alternative Test Arrangements	✓
LD Program Began	n/a	LD Student Organization	n/a

Services for Students with Disabilities faculty consists of 1 full-time staff member. Services are provided by academic advisers, regular education teachers, counselors, remediation/learning specialists, trained peer tutors, professional tutors, and Faculty tutors.

Policies LD services are also available to graduate students.

Special preparation or orientation Optional orientation held individually by special arrangement.

Basic skills remediation Available in study skills, computer skills, reading, learning strategies, written language, and math. Offered one-on-one and in small groups by computer-based instruction, teacher trainees, professional tutors, and trained peer tutors.

Counseling and advisement Academic advisement by a staff member affiliated with the program is available.

Auxiliary aids and services *Aids:* calculators, personal spelling/word-use assistants (e.g., Franklin Speller), screen-enlarging programs, tape recorders, taped textbooks. *Services and accommodations:* alternative test arrangements, readers, note-takers, and scribes.

ADD/ADHD Students with ADD/ADHD are eligible for the same services available to students with LD

Application *Required:* high school transcript, ACT, interview, psychoeducational report (3 years old or less), and documentation of high school services (e.g., Individualized Education Program [IEP] or 504 plan). Upon application, documentation of need for special services should be sent only to your LD program or unit.

LD program contact Mary Oswald, Disabilities Coordinator, 505 Amherst Street, Nashua, NH 03061-2052. *Phone:* 603-882-6503 Ext. 1451. *Fax:* 603-882-8690. *E-mail:* m_oswald@tec.nh.us.

Application contact New Hampshire Community Technical College, Nashua/Claremont, 505 Amherst Street, Nashua, NH 03061-2052. *E-mail:* nashua@tec.nh.us. *Web address:* http://www.nashua.tec.nh.us/.

NEW HAMPSHIRE TECHNICAL INSTITUTE

Concord, New Hampshire

Students with LD Served by Program	200	ADD/ADHD Services	✓
Staff	1 full-time, 4 part-time	Summer Preparation Program	✓
LD Program or Service Fee	n/a	Alternative Test Arrangements	✓
LD Program Began	1990	LD Student Organization	✓

Office of the Coordinator of Disabilities Services began offering services in 1990. The program serves approximately 200 undergraduate students. Faculty consists of 1 full-time and 4 part-time staff members. Services are provided by academic advisers, remediation/learning specialists, trained peer tutors, and professional tutors.

Policies 12 credit hours per term are required to maintain full-time status; 6 credit hours per term are required to be eligible for financial aid.

Special preparation or orientation Optional summer program offered prior to entering college. Optional orientation held before classes begin, during summer prior to enrollment, and individually by special arrangement.

Basic skills remediation Available in study skills, computer skills, reading, time management, social skills, learning strategies, spelling, written language, and math. Offered one-on-one and in small groups by computer-based instruction, professional tutors, and trained peer tutors.

Subject-area tutoring Available in most subjects. Offered one-on-one and in small groups by computer-based instruction, professional tutors, and trained peer tutors.

Counseling and advisement Career counseling, individual counseling, small-group counseling, support groups, and self-advocacy training are available. Academic advisement by a staff member affiliated with the program is available.

Auxiliary aids and services *Aids:* calculators, personal spelling/word-use assistants (e.g., Franklin Speller), scan and read programs (e.g., Kurzweil), screen-enlarging programs, speech recognition programs (e.g., Dragon), tape recorders, taped textbooks. *Services and accommodations:* alternative test arrangements.

Student organization There is a student organization for students with LD.

ADD/ADHD Students with ADD/ADHD are eligible for the same services available to students with LD, as well as distraction-free study areas, distraction-free testing environments and success seminar series.

Application *Required:* high school transcript. *Recommended:* participation in extracurricular activities, ACT (extended-time or untimed test accepted), SAT I (extended-time or untimed test accepted), letter(s) of recommendation, separate application to your LD program or unit, psychoeducational report (3 years old or less), and documentation of high school services (e.g., Individualized Education Program [IEP] or 504 plan). Upon application, documentation of need for special services should be sent only to your LD program or unit. Upon acceptance, documentation of need for special services should be sent only to your LD program or unit. *Application deadline (institutional):* rolling/continuous for fall and rolling/continuous for spring. *Application deadline (LD program):* rolling/continuous for fall and rolling/continuous for spring.

LD program contact Frank Meyer, Director of Admissions, 11 Institute Drive, Concord, NH 03301. *Phone:* 603-271-7131. *Fax:* 603-271-7139.

Application contact Francis P. Meyer, Director of Admissions, New Hampshire Technical Institute, 11 Institute Drive, Concord, NH 03301-7412. *Phone:* 603-271-7131. *Web address:* http://www.nhti.net/.

NEW YORK CITY TECHNICAL COLLEGE OF THE CITY UNIVERSITY OF NEW YORK

Brooklyn, New York

Students with LD Served by Program	150	ADD/ADHD Services	✓
Staff	2 full-time, 3 part-time	Summer Preparation Program	✓
LD Program or Service Fee	n/a	Alternative Test Arrangements	✓
LD Program Began	1971	LD Student Organization	✓

Student Support Services Program began offering services in 1971. The program serves approximately 150 undergraduate students. Faculty consists of 2 full-time and 3 part-time staff members. Services are provided by academic advisers, counselors, LD specialists, and professional tutors.

Policies 12 credit hours per term are required to maintain full-time status and to be eligible for financial aid.

Special preparation or orientation Optional summer program offered prior to entering college. Optional orientation held before classes begin.

Subject-area tutoring Available in most subjects. Offered one-on-one and in small groups by professional tutors.

Counseling and advisement Career counseling, individual counseling, and small-group counseling are available. Academic advisement by a staff member affiliated with the program is available.

Auxiliary aids and services *Aids:* calculators, personal computers, personal spelling/word-use assistants (e.g., Franklin Speller), scan and read programs (e.g., Kurzweil), screen-enlarging programs, screen readers, speech recognition programs (e.g., Dragon), tape recorders. *Services and accommodations:* advocates, priority registration, alternative test arrangements, readers, note-takers, and scribes.

Student organization There is a student organization for students with LD.

ADD/ADHD Students with ADD/ADHD are eligible for the same services available to students with LD, as well as distraction-free study areas and distraction-free testing environments.

Application *Required:* interview and documentation of high school services (e.g., Individualized Education Program [IEP] or 504 plan). *Recommended:* psychoeducational report (5 years old or less). Upon application, documentation of need for special services should be sent only to your LD program or unit. Upon acceptance, documentation of need for special services should be sent only to your LD program or unit. *Application deadline (institutional):* 3/15 for fall and 1/21 for spring. *Application deadline (LD program):* rolling/continuous for fall and rolling/continuous for spring.

LD program contact Faith Fogelman, Director, Student Support Services Program, 300 Jay Street, A237, Brooklyn, NY 11201. *Phone:* 718-260-5143. *Fax:* 718-254-8539. *E-mail:* ffogelman@nyctc.cuny.edu.

Application contact Joseph Lento, Director of Admissions, New York City Technical College of the City University of New York, 300 Jay Street, Brooklyn, NY 11201-2983. *Phone:* 718-260-5500. *Web address:* http://www.nyctc.cuny.edu/.

NORTH CENTRAL TEXAS COLLEGE
Gainesville, Texas

Students with LD Served by Program	100	ADD/ADHD Services	✓
Staff	2 full-time	Summer Preparation Program	n/a
LD Program or Service Fee	n/a	Alternative Test Arrangements	✓
LD Program Began	1992	LD Student Organization	n/a

Special Populations began offering services in 1992. The program serves approximately 100 undergraduate students. Faculty consists of 2 full-time staff members. Services are provided by academic advisers, remediation/learning specialists, counselors, and LD specialists.

Policies Students with LD may take up to 18 semester credit per semester; 12 semester credit per semester are required to maintain full-time status; 6 semester credit per semester are required to be eligible for financial aid.

Basic skills remediation Available in reading, written language, and math. Offered one-on-one and in class-size groups by computer-based instruction, regular education teachers, and student workers in the Learning Centers.

Subject-area tutoring Available in most subjects. Offered one-on-one and in small groups by computer-based instruction and student workers in the Learning Centers.

Counseling and advisement Career counseling, individual counseling, and support groups are available. Academic advisement by a staff member affiliated with the program is available.

Auxiliary aids and services *Aids:* calculators, personal computers, tape recorders. *Services and accommodations:* advocates, priority registration, alternative test arrangements, readers, note-takers, scribes, and peer tutors, extended time.

ADD/ADHD Students with ADD/ADHD are eligible for the same services available to students with LD, as well as distraction-free study areas and distraction-free testing environments.

Application *Required:* high school transcript. *Recommended:* psychoeducational report (3 years old or less) and documentation of high school services (e.g., Individualized Education Program [IEP] or 504 plan). Upon application, documentation of need for special services should be sent only to your LD program or unit. Upon acceptance, documentation of need for special services should be sent only to your LD program or unit. *Application deadline (institutional):* rolling/continuous for fall and rolling/continuous for spring. *Application deadline (LD program):* rolling/continuous for fall and rolling/continuous for spring.

LD program contact Bobbie Owen, Special Populations Coordinator, 1525 West California, Gainesville, TX 76240. *Phone:* 940-668-4216 Ext. 344. *Fax:* 940-668-6049. *E-mail:* rowen@nctc.cc.tx.us.

Application contact North Central Texas College, 1525 West California Street, Gainesville, TX 76240-4699. *Web address:* http://www.nctc.cc.tx.us/.

NORTH DAKOTA STATE COLLEGE OF SCIENCE
Wahpeton, North Dakota

Students with LD Served by Program	95	ADD/ADHD Services	✓
Staff	1 full-time	Summer Preparation Program	✓
LD Program or Service Fee	n/a	Alternative Test Arrangements	✓
LD Program Began	1994	LD Student Organization	n/a

Academic Services Center began offering services in 1994. The program serves approximately 95 undergraduate students. Faculty consists of 1 full-time staff member. Services are provided by academic advisers, regular education teachers, counselors, and trained peer tutors.

Policies Students with LD may take up to 23 credits per semester; 12 credits per semester are required to maintain full-time status; 6 credits per semester are required to be eligible for financial aid.

Special preparation or orientation Optional summer program offered prior to entering college.

Basic skills remediation Available in study skills, computer skills, reading, time management, learning strategies, spelling, and math. Offered in small groups and class-size groups by computer-based instruction and regular education teachers.

Subject-area tutoring Available in most subjects. Offered in small groups by trained peer tutors.

Special courses Available in study skills, practical computer skills, reading, math, and written composition skills. All courses are offered for credit; none enter into overall grade point average.

Counseling and advisement Career counseling, individual counseling, and support groups are available. Academic advisement by a staff member affiliated with the program is available.

Auxiliary aids and services *Aids:* scan and read programs (e.g., Kurzweil), screen-enlarging programs, screen readers, tape recorders, taped textbooks. *Services and accommodations:* alternative test arrangements, readers, note-takers, and scribes.

ADD/ADHD Students with ADD/ADHD are eligible for the same services available to students with LD, as well as distraction-free study areas and distraction-free testing environments.

Application *Required:* high school transcript and ACT or SAT I (extended-time or untimed test accepted). *Recommended:* interview, separate application to your LD program or unit, psychoeducational report (3 years old or less), documentation of high school services (e.g., Individualized Education Program [IEP] or 504 plan), and report of functional limitations. Upon application, documentation of need for special services should be sent to both admissions and your LD program or unit. Upon acceptance, documentation of need for special services should be sent only to your LD program or unit.

LD program contact Bunnie Johnson, Interim Director/Disability Services Coordinator, 800 North 6th Street, Wahpeton, ND 58076-0002. *Phone:* 701-671-2623. *Fax:* 701-671-2674. *E-mail:* bunjohns@badlands.nodak.edu.

Application contact North Dakota State College of Science, 800 North Sixth Street, Wahpeton, ND 58076. *E-mail:* riholm@plains.nodak.edu. *Web address:* http://www.ndscs.nodak.edu/.

NORTHEAST COMMUNITY COLLEGE
Norfolk, Nebraska

Students with LD Served by Program	100	ADD/ADHD Services	n/a
Staff	2 part-time	Summer Preparation Program	n/a
LD Program or Service Fee	n/a	Alternative Test Arrangements	✓
LD Program Began	1986	LD Student Organization	n/a

Learning Disabilities Opportunities Program began offering services in 1986. The program serves approximately 100 undergraduate students. Faculty consists of 2 part-time staff members. Services are provided by academic advisers, regular education teachers, counselors, remediation/learning specialists, LD specialists, and trained peer tutors.

Northeast Community College (continued)

Basic skills remediation Available in study skills, reading, time management, learning strategies, spelling, written language, and math. Offered one-on-one, in small groups, and class-size groups by computer-based instruction, regular education teachers, and LD specialists.

Subject-area tutoring Available in most subjects. Offered one-on-one and in small groups by trained peer tutors.

Counseling and advisement Career counseling, individual counseling, and support groups are available. Academic advisement by a staff member affiliated with the program is available.

Auxiliary aids and services *Aids:* personal spelling/word-use assistants (e.g., Franklin Speller), scan and read programs (e.g., Kurzweil), tape recorders, taped textbooks. *Services and accommodations:* alternative test arrangements and note-takers.

Application *Required:* ACT or SAT I (extended-time or untimed test accepted), psychoeducational report (3 years old or less), and ASSET in place of ACT or SAT I. *Recommended:* high school transcript and documentation of high school services (e.g., Individualized Education Program [IEP] or 504 plan). Upon application, documentation of need for special services should be sent only to your LD program or unit. Upon acceptance, documentation of need for special services should be sent only to your LD program or unit. *Application deadline (institutional):* rolling/continuous for fall and rolling/continuous for spring. *Application deadline (LD program):* rolling/continuous for fall and rolling/continuous for spring.

LD program contact Dr. Karen J. Severson, Dean of Admissions, PO Box 469, Norfolk, NE 68702-0469. *Phone:* 402-644-0435. *Fax:* 402-644-0650. *E-mail:* karens@alpha.necc.cc.ne.us.

Application contact Northeast Community College, 801 East Benjamin Ave, PO Box 469, Norfolk, NE 68702-0469. *Web address:* http://alpha.necc.cc.ne.us/.

NORTHEAST IOWA COMMUNITY COLLEGE, CALMAR CAMPUS
Calmar, Iowa

Students with LD Served by Program	60	ADD/ADHD Services	✓
Staff	3 full-time, 3 part-time	Summer Preparation Program	n/a
LD Program or Service Fee	n/a	Alternative Test Arrangements	✓
LD Program Began	1972	LD Student Organization	n/a

NICC Learning Center began offering services in 1972. The program serves approximately 60 undergraduate students. Faculty consists of 3 full-time and 3 part-time staff members. Services are provided by regular education teachers, counselors, trained peer tutors, and professional tutors.

Policies The college has written policies regarding course substitutions. Students with LD may take up to 12 credit hours per semester; 12 credit hours per semester are required to maintain full-time status and to be eligible for financial aid.

Basic skills remediation Available in study skills, computer skills, reading, time management, learning strategies, spelling, written language, math, spoken language, and Science. Offered one-on-one by computer-based instruction, graduate assistants/students, professional tutors, and trained peer tutors.

Subject-area tutoring Available in most subjects. Offered one-on-one and in small groups by computer-based instruction, professional tutors, graduate assistants/students, and trained peer tutors.

Counseling and advisement Career counseling and individual counseling are available.

Auxiliary aids and services *Aids:* calculators, personal spelling/word-use assistants (e.g., Franklin Speller), screen-enlarging programs, screen readers, speech recognition programs (e.g., Dragon), tape recorders, taped textbooks. *Services and accommodations:* advocates, alternative test arrangements, readers, note-takers, and scribes.

ADD/ADHD Students with ADD/ADHD are eligible for the same services available to students with LD, as well as distraction-free study areas and distraction-free testing environments.

Application *Required:* ASSET text from ACT, Iowa City. *Recommended:* high school transcript, psychoeducational report, and documentation of high school services (e.g., Individualized Education Program [IEP] or 504 plan). Upon application, documentation of need for special services should be sent only to your LD program or unit. Upon acceptance, documentation of need for special services should be sent only to your LD program or unit. *Application deadline (institutional):* rolling/continuous for fall and rolling/continuous for spring. *Application deadline (LD program):* rolling/continuous for fall and rolling/continuous for spring.

LD program contact Patricia Running, Learning Center Instructor, PO Box 400, Calmar, IA 52132. *Phone:* 319-562-3263 Ext. 256. *Fax:* 319-562-3719. *E-mail:* runningp@nicc.ia.us.

Application contact Northeast Iowa Community College, Calmar Campus, Box 400, Calmar, IA 52132-0480.

NORTHEAST IOWA COMMUNITY COLLEGE, PEOSTA CAMPUS
Peosta, Iowa

Students with LD Served by Program	150	ADD/ADHD Services	✓
Staff	5 full-time	Summer Preparation Program	n/a
LD Program or Service Fee	n/a	Alternative Test Arrangements	✓
LD Program Began	1990	LD Student Organization	n/a

Developmental Education Program began offering services in 1990. The program serves approximately 150 undergraduate students. Faculty consists of 5 full-time staff members. Services are provided by academic advisers, counselors, remediation/learning specialists, and trained peer tutors.

Policies The college has written policies regarding course substitutions. 12 credit hours per semester are required to maintain full-time status; 3 credits per semester are required to be eligible for financial aid.

Basic skills remediation Available in study skills, computer skills, reading, time management, social skills, learning strategies, spelling, written language, and math. Offered one-on-one and in small groups by regular education teachers and trained peer tutors.

Subject-area tutoring Available in most subjects. Offered one-on-one and in small groups by computer-based instruction and trained peer tutors.

Counseling and advisement Career counseling and individual counseling are available. Academic advisement by a staff member affiliated with the program is available.

Auxiliary aids and services *Aids:* calculators, personal computers, personal spelling/word-use assistants (e.g., Franklin Speller), scan and read programs (e.g., Kurzweil), screen-enlarging programs, screen readers, speech recognition programs (e.g., Dragon), tape recorders, taped textbooks, adapted keyboards, large track balls. *Services and accommodations:* advocates, alternative test arrangements, readers, note-takers, and scribes.

ADD/ADHD Students with ADD/ADHD are eligible for the same services available to students with LD, as well as distraction-free study areas and distraction-free testing environments.

Application *Required:* psychoeducational report and documentation of high school services (e.g., Individualized Education Program [IEP] or 504 plan). *Recommended:* high school transcript. Upon application, documentation of need for special services should be sent only to your LD program or unit. Upon acceptance, documentation of need for special services should be sent only to your LD program or unit. *Application deadline (institutional):* rolling/continuous for fall and rolling/continuous for spring. *Application deadline (LD program):* rolling/continuous for fall and rolling/continuous for spring.

LD program contact Myra Benzer, Coordinator of Developmental Education, 10250 Sundown Road, Peosta, IA 52068. *Phone:* 319-556-5110 Ext. 280. *Fax:* 319-557-0352.

Application contact Northeast Iowa Community College, Peosta Campus, 10250 Sundown Road, Peosta, IA 52068-9776. *Web address:* http://www.nicc.cc.ia.us/.

NORTHEAST WISCONSIN TECHNICAL COLLEGE
Green Bay, Wisconsin

Students with LD Served by Program	200	ADD/ADHD Services	✓
Staff	5 full-time	Summer Preparation Program	n/a
LD Program or Service Fee	n/a	Alternative Test Arrangements	✓
LD Program Began	1981	LD Student Organization	n/a

Special Needs Office began offering services in 1981. The program serves approximately 200 undergraduate students. Faculty consists of 5 full-time staff members. Services are provided by regular education teachers, counselors, special education teachers, LD specialists, and trained peer tutors.

Policies The college has written policies regarding course substitutions and substitution and waivers of requirements for admission. Students with LD may take up to 19 credit hours per semester; 12 credit hours per semester are required to maintain full-time status; 6 credit hours per semester are required to be eligible for financial aid.

Special preparation or orientation Optional orientation held before registration, before classes begin, after classes begin, during summer prior to enrollment, and individually by special arrangement.

Basic skills remediation Available in study skills, computer skills, reading, learning strategies, spelling, written language, and math. Offered one-on-one by computer-based instruction, regular education teachers, special education teachers, LD specialists, and trained peer tutors.

Subject-area tutoring Available in all subjects. Offered one-on-one by computer-based instruction, trained peer tutors, and LD specialists.

Special courses Available in study skills, test taking, reading, learning strategies, vocabulary development, and math. No courses are offered for credit; none enter into overall grade point average.

Counseling and advisement Career counseling, individual counseling, and transition counseling are available.

Auxiliary aids and services *Aids:* calculators, personal computers, scan and read programs (e.g., Kurzweil), screen-enlarging programs, speech recognition programs (e.g., Dragon), tape recorders, taped textbooks. *Services and accommodations:* alternative test arrangements, readers, note-takers, and scribes.

ADD/ADHD Students with ADD/ADHD are eligible for the same services available to students with LD, as well as distraction-free study areas and distraction-free testing environments.

Application *Required:* high school transcript, interview, documentation of high school services (e.g., Individualized Education Program [IEP] or 504 plan), and entrance skill inventory if no ACT or SAT. *Recommended:* ACT or SAT I (extended-time or untimed test accepted) and psychoeducational report (5 years old or less). Upon application, documentation of need for special services should be sent only to your LD program or unit. Upon acceptance, documentation of need for special services should be sent only to your LD program or unit. *Application deadline (institutional):* 8/17 for fall and 1/13 for spring. *Application deadline (LD program):* 8/17 for fall and 1/13 for spring.

LD program contact Jerome L. Miller, Special Needs Counselor, 2740 West Mason Street, PO Box 19042, Green Bay, WI 54307-9042. *Phone:* 920-498-5470. *Fax:* 920-498-6242. *E-mail:* jmiller@nwtc.tec.wi.us.

Application contact Susan Ellis, Operational Assistant, Services for Students, Northeast Wisconsin Technical College, 2740 W Mason Street, PO Box 19042, Green Bay, WI 54307-9042. *Phone:* 920-498-5522 Ext. 522. *Web address:* http://www.nwtc.tec.wi.us/.

NORTHLAND PIONEER COLLEGE
Holbrook, Arizona

Students with LD Served by Program	45	ADD/ADHD Services	✓
Staff	1 full-time	Summer Preparation Program	✓
LD Program or Service Fee	n/a	Alternative Test Arrangements	✓
LD Program Began	1992	LD Student Organization	n/a

Disability Resources and Access began offering services in 1992. The program serves approximately 45 undergraduate students. Faculty consists of 1 full-time staff member. Services are provided by academic advisers, regular education teachers, remediation/learning specialists, trained peer tutors, professional tutors, and Disability Resources and Access Coordinator.

Policies 12 credit hours per semester are required to maintain full-time status; 3 credit hours per semester are required to be eligible for financial aid.

Special preparation or orientation Optional summer program offered prior to entering college. Optional orientation held before registration, during registration, before classes begin, after classes begin, during summer prior to enrollment, and individually by special arrangement.

Basic skills remediation Available in study skills, computer skills, reading, time management, social skills, learning strategies, spelling, written language, and math. Offered one-on-one, in small groups, and class-size groups by computer-based instruction, regular education teachers, graduate assistants/students, professional tutors, and trained peer tutors.

Subject-area tutoring Available in all subjects. Offered one-on-one and in small groups by professional tutors, graduate assistants/students, trained peer tutors, and DRA Coordinator.

Special courses Available in career planning, study skills, college survival skills, practical computer skills, test taking, reading, time management, learning strategies, vocabulary development, math, and written composition skills. Some courses are offered for credit; some enter into overall grade point average.

Counseling and advisement Academic advisement by a staff member affiliated with the program is available.

Auxiliary aids and services *Aids:* calculators, personal spelling/word-use assistants (e.g., Franklin Speller), scan and read programs (e.g., Kurzweil), screen-enlarging programs, screen readers,

Northland Pioneer College (continued)

speech recognition programs (e.g., Dragon), tape recorders, taped textbooks. *Services and accommodations:* advocates, priority registration, alternative test arrangements, readers, note-takers, and scribes.

ADD/ADHD Students with ADD/ADHD are eligible for the same services available to students with LD, as well as distraction-free study areas, distraction-free testing environments, tutors and advocacy.

Application *Required:* interview, personal statement, separate application to your LD program or unit, and psychoeducational report (3 years old or less). *Recommended:* high school transcript, letter(s) of recommendation, and documentation of high school services (e.g., Individualized Education Program [IEP] or 504 plan). Upon application, documentation of need for special services should be sent only to your LD program or unit. Upon acceptance, documentation of need for special services should be sent only to your LD program or unit. *Application deadline (institutional):* rolling/continuous for fall and rolling/continuous for spring. *Application deadline (LD program):* rolling/continuous for fall and rolling/continuous for spring.

LD program contact Betsyann Wilson, Coordinator, Disability Resources and Access, PO Box 610-SCC, Holbrook, AZ 86025-6257. *Phone:* 520-536-6257. *Fax:* 520-536-6221. *E-mail:* stwlady@hotmail.com.

Application contact Northland Pioneer College, PO Box 610, Holbrook, AZ 86025-0610. *Web address:* http://www.northland.cc.az.us/.

NORTHWESTERN MICHIGAN COLLEGE

Traverse City, Michigan

Students with LD Served by Program	50	ADD/ADHD Services	✓
Staff	1 full-time, 2 part-time	Summer Preparation Program	n/a
LD Program or Service Fee	n/a	Alternative Test Arrangements	✓
LD Program Began	1981	LD Student Organization	n/a

Instructional Support Center began offering services in 1981. The program serves approximately 50 undergraduate students. Faculty consists of 1 full-time and 2 part-time staff members.

Policies Students with LD may take up to 12 credit hours per semester; 12 credit hours per semester are required to maintain full-time status; 6 credit hours per semester are required to be eligible for financial aid.

Basic skills remediation Available in study skills, reading, time management, learning strategies, spelling, written language, and math. Offered one-on-one and in class-size groups by computer-based instruction, regular education teachers, and trained peer tutors.

Subject-area tutoring Available in most subjects. Offered one-on-one, in small groups, and class-size groups by computer-based instruction and trained peer tutors.

Special courses Available in career planning, study skills, test taking, reading, time management, learning strategies, math, and written composition skills. No courses are offered for credit; all enter into overall grade point average.

Counseling and advisement Career counseling and individual counseling are available.

Auxiliary aids and services *Aids:* personal computers, screen-enlarging programs, screen readers, speech recognition programs (e.g., Dragon), tape recorders, taped textbooks. *Services and accommodations:* alternative test arrangements, readers, note-takers, and scribes.

ADD/ADHD Students with ADD/ADHD are eligible for the same services available to students with LD, as well as distraction-free testing environments and personal coach or mentors.

Application *Required:* high school transcript, psychoeducational report (3 years old or less), and documentation of high school services (e.g., Individualized Education Program [IEP] or 504 plan). *Recommended:* participation in extracurricular activities and interview. Upon application, documentation of need for special services should be sent only to your LD program or unit. Upon acceptance, documentation of need for special services should be sent only to your LD program or unit.

LD program contact Denny Everett, Disabilities Specialist, Instructional Support Center, 1701 East Front Street, Traverse City, MI 49686. *Phone:* 231-922-1139. *Fax:* 231-922-1056. *E-mail:* deverett@nmc.edu.

Application contact Northwestern Michigan College, 1701 East Front Street, Traverse City, MI 49686-3061. *E-mail:* wprinsen@nmc.edu cforsyth@nmc.edu. *Web address:* http://www.nmc.edu/.

NORTHWEST MISSISSIPPI COMMUNITY COLLEGE

Senatobia, Mississippi

Students with LD Served by Program	22	ADD/ADHD Services	✓
Staff	3 full-time, 1 part-time	Summer Preparation Program	n/a
LD Program or Service Fee	n/a	Alternative Test Arrangements	✓
LD Program Began	1981	LD Student Organization	✓

Disability Support Services began offering services in 1981. The program serves approximately 22 undergraduate students. Faculty consists of 3 full-time staff members and 1 part-time staff member. Services are provided by regular education teachers, counselors, and trained peer tutors.

Policies Students with LD may take up to 13 credit hours per semester; 12 credit hours per semester are required to maintain full-time status; 3 credit hours per semester are required to be eligible for financial aid.

Counseling and advisement Career counseling and individual counseling are available.

Auxiliary aids and services *Aids:* tape recorders, taped textbooks. *Services and accommodations:* advocates, priority registration, alternative test arrangements, and note-takers.

Student organization There is a student organization for students with LD.

ADD/ADHD Students with ADD/ADHD are eligible for the same services available to students with LD, as well as distraction-free study areas, distraction-free testing environments and personal coach or mentors.

Application *Required:* high school transcript, ACT (extended-time test accepted), and SAT I (extended-time test accepted). *Recommended:* psychoeducational report (3 years old or less) and documentation of high school services (e.g., Individualized Education Program [IEP] or 504 plan). Upon application, documentation of need for special services should be sent only to your LD program or unit. Upon acceptance, documentation of need for special services should be sent only to your LD program or unit. *Application deadline (institutional):* rolling/continuous for fall and rolling/continuous for spring. *Application deadline (LD program):* rolling/continuous for fall and rolling/continuous for spring.

LD program contact Mike Dottorey, Coordinator/Counselor, PO Box 5555, Senatobia, MS 38668. *Phone:* 662-562-3309. *Fax:* 662-562-3315. *E-mail:* mldottorey@nwcc.cc.ms.us.

Application contact Deanna Ferguson, Director of Admissions and Recruiting, Northwest Mississippi Community College, 4975 Highway 51 North, Senatobia, MS 38668-1701. *Phone:* 601-562-3222. *Web address:* http://www.nwcc.cc.ms.us/.

NORWALK COMMUNITY COLLEGE
Norwalk, Connecticut

Students with LD Served by Program	100	ADD/ADHD Services	✓
Staff	1 full-time	Summer Preparation Program	n/a
LD Program or Service Fee	n/a	Alternative Test Arrangements	✓
LD Program Began	n/a	LD Student Organization	n/a

Services for Students with Disabilities serves approximately 100 undergraduate students. Faculty consists of 1 full-time staff member. Services are provided by counselors.

Policies Students with LD may take up to 18 credit hours per semester; 12 credit hours per semester are required to maintain full-time status; 3 credit hours per semester are required to be eligible for financial aid. LD services are also available to graduate students.

Basic skills remediation Available in study skills, time management, and learning strategies. Offered one-on-one by developmental studies counselor.

Counseling and advisement Career counseling, individual counseling, and educational counseling, academic advisement are available.

Auxiliary aids and services *Aids:* calculators, personal computers, personal spelling/word-use assistants (e.g., Franklin Speller), scan and read programs (e.g., Kurzweil), screen-enlarging programs, screen readers, speech recognition programs (e.g., Dragon), tape recorders, taped textbooks. *Services and accommodations:* advocates, alternative test arrangements, readers, note-takers, and scribes.

ADD/ADHD Students with ADD/ADHD are eligible for the same services available to students with LD, as well as distraction-free testing environments.

Application *Required:* high school transcript. Upon application, documentation of need for special services should be sent only to your LD program or unit. Upon acceptance, documentation of need for special services should be sent only to your LD program or unit. *Application deadline (institutional):* rolling/continuous for fall and rolling/continuous for spring. *Application deadline (LD program):* rolling/continuous for fall and rolling/continuous for spring.

LD program contact Loretta Orvetti, Developmental Studies Counselor, 188 Richards Avenue, Norwalk, CT 06854. *Phone:* 203-857-7192. *Fax:* 203-857-7297.

Application contact Danita Brown, Admissions Counselor, Norwalk Community College, 188 Richards Avenue, Norwalk, CT 06854-1655. *Phone:* 203-857-7060. *Web address:* http://www.nctc.commnet.edu/.

OAKLAND COMMUNITY COLLEGE
Bloomfield Hills, Michigan

Students with LD Served by Program	250	ADD/ADHD Services	✓
Staff	1 full-time, 30 part-time	Summer Preparation Program	n/a
LD Program or Service Fee	n/a	Alternative Test Arrangements	✓
LD Program Began	1987	LD Student Organization	n/a

Programs for Academic Support Services (PASS) began offering services in 1987. The program serves approximately 250 undergraduate students. Faculty consists of 1 full-time and 30 part-time staff members. Services are provided by counselors, LD specialists, and professional tutors.

Policies Students with LD may take up to 15 credit hours per semester; 12 credit hours per semester are required to maintain full-time status; 6 credit hours per semester are required to be eligible for financial aid. LD services are also available to graduate students.

Basic skills remediation Available in study skills, computer skills, reading, time management, learning strategies, spelling, written language, math, and spoken language. Offered one-on-one and in small groups by computer-based instruction, LD specialists, professional tutors, and trained peer tutors.

Subject-area tutoring Available in all subjects. Offered one-on-one and in small groups by computer-based instruction, professional tutors, trained peer tutors, and LD specialists.

Counseling and advisement Career counseling, individual counseling, support groups, and academic planning are available.

Auxiliary aids and services *Aids:* personal computers, scan and read programs (e.g., Kurzweil), screen-enlarging programs, screen readers, speech recognition programs (e.g., Dragon), tape recorders. *Services and accommodations:* advocates, alternative test arrangements, readers, note-takers, and scribes.

ADD/ADHD Students with ADD/ADHD are eligible for the same services available to students with LD, as well as distraction-free study areas and distraction-free testing environments.

Application *Required:* psychoeducational report and documentation of high school services (e.g., Individualized Education Program [IEP] or 504 plan). *Recommended:* high school transcript. Upon application, documentation of need for special services should be sent only to your LD program or unit. Upon acceptance, documentation of need for special services should be sent only to your LD program or unit. *Application deadline (institutional):* rolling/continuous for fall and rolling/continuous for spring. *Application deadline (LD program):* rolling/continuous for fall and rolling/continuous for spring.

LD program contact Wanda Harris, Coordinator, Southfield Campus, 22322 Rutland Drive, Southfield, MI 48075. *Phone:* 248-552-2644. *Fax:* 248-552-2649. *E-mail:* wxpernel@occ.cc.mi.us.

Application contact Oakland Community College, 2480 Opdyke Road, Bloomfield Hills, MI 48304-2266. *Web address:* http://www.occ.cc.mi.us/.

OKALOOSA-WALTON COMMUNITY COLLEGE
Niceville, Florida

Students with LD Served by Program	80	ADD/ADHD Services	✓
Staff	1 full-time	Summer Preparation Program	n/a
LD Program or Service Fee	n/a	Alternative Test Arrangements	✓
LD Program Began	1980	LD Student Organization	✓

Office of Services for Students with Special Needs began offering services in 1980. The program serves approximately 80 undergraduate students. Faculty consists of 1 full-time staff member. Services are provided by regular education teachers and counselors.

Policies The college has written policies regarding course substitutions. 12 credit hours per term are required to be eligible for financial aid.

Counseling and advisement Career counseling and individual counseling are available.

Okaloosa-Walton Community College (continued)

Auxiliary aids and services *Aids:* calculators, personal spelling/word-use assistants (e.g., Franklin Speller), scan and read programs (e.g., Kurzweil), screen-enlarging programs, screen readers, speech recognition programs (e.g., Dragon), tape recorders. *Services and accommodations:* priority registration, alternative test arrangements, readers, note-takers, and scribes.

Student organization There is a student organization for students with LD.

ADD/ADHD Students with ADD/ADHD are eligible for the same services available to students with LD, as well as distraction-free study areas and distraction-free testing environments.

Application *Required:* high school transcript. Upon application, documentation of need for special services should be sent only to your LD program or unit. Upon acceptance, documentation of need for special services should be sent only to your LD program or unit. *Application deadline (institutional):* 8/30 for fall and 1/12 for spring. *Application deadline (LD program):* 8/30 for fall and 1/12 for spring.

LD program contact Jody Swenson, Counselor/Coordinator of Services to Students with Special Needs, 100 College Boulevard, Niceville, FL 32578. *Phone:* 850-729-6079. *Fax:* 850-729-5323. *E-mail:* swensonj@owcc.net.

Application contact Okaloosa-Walton Community College, 100 College Boulevard, Niceville, FL 32578-1295. *Web address:* http://www.owcc.cc.fl.us/.

OKLAHOMA STATE UNIVERSITY, OKMULGEE
Okmulgee, Oklahoma

Students with LD Served by Program	45	ADD/ADHD Services	✓
Staff	2 full-time	Summer Preparation Program	n/a
LD Program or Service Fee	n/a	Alternative Test Arrangements	✓
LD Program Began	n/a	LD Student Organization	n/a

Sponsored and Disabled Student Services serves approximately 45 undergraduate students. Faculty consists of 2 full-time staff members. Services are provided by regular education teachers.

Policies Students with LD may take up to 21 credit hours per trimester; 12 credit hours per trimester are required to maintain full-time status and to be eligible for financial aid.

Counseling and advisement Individual counseling is available.

Auxiliary aids and services *Aids:* screen-enlarging programs. *Services and accommodations:* alternative test arrangements, readers, and extended time on in-class projects.

ADD/ADHD Students with ADD/ADHD are eligible for the same services available to students with LD, as well as distraction-free testing environments.

Application *Required:* high school transcript, ACT (extended-time test accepted), interview, separate application to your LD program or unit, psychoeducational report (3 years old or less), and copy of enrollment schedule, signed "release of confidential information" form. Upon application, documentation of need for special services should be sent only to your LD program or unit. Upon acceptance, documentation of need for special services should be sent only to your LD program or unit. *Application deadline (institutional):* rolling/continuous for fall and rolling/continuous for spring. *Application deadline (LD program):* rolling/continuous for fall and rolling/continuous for spring.

LD program contact Janie Weller, Information Specialist/Sponsored and Disabled Student Services, 1801 East 4th Street, Okmulgee, OK 74447-3901. *Phone:* 918-293-4996. *Fax:* 918-293-4650. *E-mail:* bettyjweller@osu-okmulgee.edu.

Application contact Oklahoma State University, Okmulgee, 1801 East Fourth Street, Okmulgee, OK 74447-3901. *E-mail:* shill@okway.okstate.edu. *Web address:* http://www.osu-okmulgee.edu/.

OLYMPIC COLLEGE
Bremerton, Washington

Students with LD Served by Program	110	ADD/ADHD Services	✓
Staff	1 full-time, 3 part-time	Summer Preparation Program	n/a
LD Program or Service Fee	n/a	Alternative Test Arrangements	✓
LD Program Began	n/a	LD Student Organization	✓

Office of Disability Support Services serves approximately 110 undergraduate students. Faculty consists of 1 full-time and 3 part-time staff members. Services are provided by academic advisers, regular education teachers, counselors, remediation/learning specialists, and trained peer tutors.

Policies The college has written policies regarding course substitutions and grade forgiveness. 12 credit hours per quarter are required to maintain full-time status; 6 credit hours per quarter are required to be eligible for financial aid. LD services are also available to graduate students.

Special preparation or orientation Optional orientation held before registration, during registration, before classes begin, after classes begin, during summer prior to enrollment, and individually by special arrangement.

Subject-area tutoring Available in most subjects. Offered one-on-one and in small groups by computer-based instruction, professional tutors, and trained peer tutors.

Counseling and advisement Career counseling, individual counseling, small-group counseling, and support groups are available. Academic advisement by a staff member affiliated with the program is available.

Auxiliary aids and services *Aids:* calculators, scan and read programs (e.g., Kurzweil), screen-enlarging programs, screen readers, speech recognition programs (e.g., Dragon), tape recorders, taped textbooks. *Services and accommodations:* advocates, priority registration, alternative test arrangements, readers, note-takers, and scribes.

Student organization There is a student organization for students with LD.

ADD/ADHD Students with ADD/ADHD are eligible for the same services available to students with LD, as well as distraction-free testing environments and medication management.

Application *Recommended:* ACT or SAT I (extended-time or untimed test accepted). Upon application, documentation of need for special services should be sent only to your LD program or unit.

LD program contact Karen Fusco, Disability Support Services Manager, 1600 Chester Avenue, Bremerton, WA 98337-1699. *Phone:* 360-475-7542. *Fax:* 360-475-7547. *E-mail:* kfusco@oc.ctc.edu.

Application contact Olympic College, 1600 Chester Avenue, Bremerton, WA 98337-1699. *E-mail:* jramaker@ctc.edu. *Web address:* http://www.oc.ctc.edu/~oc/.

PALO VERDE COLLEGE
Blythe, California

Students with LD Served by Program	30	ADD/ADHD Services	✓
Staff	2 full-time, 4 part-time	Summer Preparation Program	n/a
LD Program or Service Fee	n/a	Alternative Test Arrangements	✓
LD Program Began	1990	LD Student Organization	✓

Disabled Student Programs and Services began offering services in 1990. The program serves approximately 30 undergraduate students. Faculty consists of 2 full-time and 4 part-time staff members. Services are provided by regular education teachers, counselors, remediation/learning specialists, LD specialists, and trained peer tutors.

Policies Students with LD may take up to 12 credits per semester; 12 credits per semester are required to maintain full-time status; 3 credits per semester are required to be eligible for financial aid.

Special preparation or orientation Optional orientation held individually by special arrangement.

Diagnostic testing Available for intelligence, reading, written language, visual processing, and math.

Basic skills remediation Available in study skills, reading, spelling, written language, and math. Offered one-on-one and in small groups by computer-based instruction and trained peer tutors.

Subject-area tutoring Available in some subjects. Offered one-on-one and in small groups by computer-based instruction and trained peer tutors.

Counseling and advisement Career counseling and individual counseling are available.

Auxiliary aids and services *Aids:* calculators, personal computers, personal spelling/word-use assistants (e.g., Franklin Speller), scan and read programs (e.g., Kurzweil), screen-enlarging programs, screen readers, speech recognition programs (e.g., Dragon), tape recorders, taped textbooks. *Services and accommodations:* priority registration, alternative test arrangements, readers, note-takers, scribes, and tutors.

Student organization There is a student organization for students with LD.

ADD/ADHD Students with ADD/ADHD are eligible for the same services available to students with LD, as well as distraction-free study areas and distraction-free testing environments.

Application *Required:* interview and psychoeducational report (5 years old or less). *Recommended:* high school transcript and personal statement. Upon application, documentation of need for special services should be sent only to your LD program or unit. Upon acceptance, documentation of need for special services should be sent only to your LD program or unit. *Application deadline (institutional):* rolling/continuous for fall and rolling/continuous for spring. *Application deadline (LD program):* rolling/continuous for fall and rolling/continuous for spring.

LD program contact Joseph Jondreau, Coordinator, 811 Chanslorway, Blythe, CA 92225. *Phone:* 760-921-5311. *Fax:* 760-921-3608. *E-mail:* jjondreau@paloverde.cc.ca.us.

Application contact Palo Verde College, 811 West Chanslorway, Blythe, CA 92225-1118.

PARKLAND COLLEGE
Champaign, Illinois

Students with LD Served by Program	300	ADD/ADHD Services	✓
Staff	2 full-time, 1 part-time	Summer Preparation Program	n/a
LD Program or Service Fee	n/a	Alternative Test Arrangements	✓
LD Program Began	1990	LD Student Organization	✓

Counseling Office began offering services in 1990. The program serves approximately 300 undergraduate students. Faculty consists of 2 full-time staff members and 1 part-time staff member. Services are provided by counselors, LD specialists, and disability accommodations specialist.

Policies Students with LD may take up to 18 credit hours per semester; 12 credit hours per semester are required to maintain full-time status; 6 credit hours per semester are required to be eligible for financial aid.

Special preparation or orientation Optional orientation held before registration and during high school year.

Basic skills remediation Available in study skills, time management, and learning strategies. Offered one-on-one and in class-size groups by regular education teachers, teacher trainees, trained peer tutors, and learning lab.

Subject-area tutoring Available in some subjects. Offered one-on-one and in small groups by trained peer tutors.

Special courses Available in college survival skills. All courses are offered for credit; all enter into overall grade point average.

Counseling and advisement Career counseling and individual counseling are available.

Auxiliary aids and services *Aids:* calculators, personal spelling/word-use assistants (e.g., Franklin Speller), scan and read programs (e.g., Kurzweil), screen-enlarging programs, screen readers, speech recognition programs (e.g., Dragon), tape recorders, taped textbooks. *Services and accommodations:* advocates, alternative test arrangements, readers, note-takers, and scribes.

Student organization There is a student organization for students with LD.

ADD/ADHD Students with ADD/ADHD are eligible for the same services available to students with LD, as well as distraction-free testing environments and personal coach or mentors.

Application *Required:* high school transcript, separate application to your LD program or unit, and psychoeducational report (3 years old or less). *Recommended:* documentation of high school services (e.g., Individualized Education Program [IEP] or 504 plan). Upon application, documentation of need for special services should be sent only to your LD program or unit. Upon acceptance, documentation of need for special services should be sent only to your LD program or unit.

LD program contact Nancy Rowley, Disability Accommodations Specialist, 2400 West Bradley Avenue, Champaign, IL 61821. *Phone:* 217-351-2588. *Fax:* 217-351-2581. *E-mail:* nrowley@parkland.cc.il.us.

Application contact Admissions Representative, Parkland College, 2400 West Bradley Avenue, Champaign, IL 61821-1899. *Phone:* 217-351-2482. *Web address:* http://www.parkland.cc.il.us/.

PASSAIC COUNTY COMMUNITY COLLEGE

Paterson, New Jersey

Students with LD Served by Program	70	ADD/ADHD Services	✓
Staff	1 full-time, 7 part-time	Summer Preparation Program	✓
LD Program or Service Fee	n/a	Alternative Test Arrangements	n/a
LD Program Began	n/a	LD Student Organization	n/a

Counseling Department serves approximately 70 undergraduate students. Faculty consists of 1 full-time and 7 part-time staff members. Services are provided by academic advisers, counselors, remediation/learning specialists, LD specialists, trained peer tutors, and professional tutors.

Policies Students with LD may take up to 12 credit hours per semester; 12 credit hours per semester are required to maintain full-time status; 6 credits per units are required to be eligible for financial aid.

Fees *Diagnostic Testing Fee:* ranges from $600 to $1000.

Special preparation or orientation Optional summer program offered prior to entering college.

Basic skills remediation Available in study skills, reading, time management, written language, math, and spoken language. Offered one-on-one and in small groups by computer-based instruction, professional tutors, and trained peer tutors.

Subject-area tutoring Available in some subjects. Offered one-on-one by computer-based instruction and trained peer tutors.

Counseling and advisement Career counseling, individual counseling, small-group counseling, and support groups are available. Academic advisement by a staff member affiliated with the program is available.

Auxiliary aids and services *Aids:* calculators, personal computers, screen-enlarging programs, tape recorders. *Services and accommodations:* note-takers.

ADD/ADHD Students with ADD/ADHD are eligible for the same services available to students with LD, as well as distraction-free testing environments and individual and small group tutoring.

Application *Required:* high school transcript, interview, psychoeducational report (3 years old or less), and documentation of high school services (e.g., Individualized Education Program [IEP] or 504 plan). Upon application, documentation of need for special services should be sent to both admissions and your LD program or unit. Upon acceptance, documentation of need for special services should be sent only to your LD program or unit. *Application deadline (institutional):* rolling/continuous for fall and rolling/continuous for spring. *Application deadline (LD program):* rolling/continuous for fall and rolling/continuous for spring.

LD program contact Diane Moscaritolo, Special Needs Counselor, One College Boulevard, Paterson, NJ 07505. *Phone:* 973-684-6395. *Fax:* 973-684-5843. *E-mail:* dmoscaritolo@pccc.cc.nj.us.

Application contact Passaic County Community College, One College Boulevard, Paterson, NJ 07505-1179.

PATRICK HENRY COMMUNITY COLLEGE

Martinsville, Virginia

Students with LD Served by Program	56	ADD/ADHD Services	✓
Staff	5 full-time, 17 part-time	Summer Preparation Program	n/a
LD Program or Service Fee	n/a	Alternative Test Arrangements	✓
LD Program Began	1988	LD Student Organization	✓

Student Support Services (SSS) began offering services in 1988. The program serves approximately 56 undergraduate students. Faculty consists of 5 full-time and 17 part-time staff members. Services are provided by counselors, LD specialists, trained peer tutors, and computer laboratory assistants.

Policies The college has written policies regarding grade forgiveness.

Subject-area tutoring Available in all subjects. Offered one-on-one and in small groups by professional tutors, trained peer tutors, and LD specialists.

Counseling and advisement Career counseling, individual counseling, and support groups are available.

Auxiliary aids and services *Aids:* calculators, personal computers, personal spelling/word-use assistants (e.g., Franklin Speller), scan and read programs (e.g., Kurzweil), screen-enlarging programs, screen readers, speech recognition programs (e.g., Dragon), tape recorders, taped textbooks, electronic keyboards (Alpha Smart Pro), word prediction software (Text Help). *Services and accommodations:* advocates, priority registration, alternative test arrangements, readers, note-takers, and scribes.

Student organization There is a student organization for students with LD.

ADD/ADHD Students with ADD/ADHD are eligible for the same services available to students with LD, as well as distraction-free testing environments and support groups for ADD/ADHD.

Application *Required:* high school transcript and GED if no high school diploma. *Recommended:* psychoeducational report and documentation of high school services (e.g., Individualized Education Program [IEP] or 504 plan). Upon acceptance, documentation of need for special services should be sent only to your LD program or unit. *Application deadline (institutional):* rolling/continuous for fall and rolling/continuous for spring. *Application deadline (LD program):* rolling/continuous for fall and rolling/continuous for spring.

LD program contact Dr. Mary McAlexander, Learning Disabilities Specialist, PO Box 5311, Martinsville, VA 24115-5311. *Phone:* 540-656-0223. *Fax:* 540-656-0327. *E-mail:* phmcalm@ph.cc.va.us.

Application contact Patrick Henry Community College, PO Box 5311, Martinsville, VA 24115-5311. *E-mail:* phvaleg%vccscent@vtbit.cc.vt.edu. *Web address:* http://www.ph.cc.va.us/.

PELLISSIPPI STATE TECHNICAL COMMUNITY COLLEGE

Knoxville, Tennessee

Students with LD Served by Program	200	ADD/ADHD Services	✓
Staff	1 part-time	Summer Preparation Program	n/a
LD Program or Service Fee	n/a	Alternative Test Arrangements	✓
LD Program Began	1990	LD Student Organization	✓

Services for Students with Disabilities began offering services in 1990. The program serves approximately 200 undergraduate students. Faculty consists of 1 part-time staff member. Services are provided by academic advisers, counselors, special education teachers, LD specialists, and professional tutors.

Policies The college has written policies regarding course substitutions. Students with LD may take up to 20 credit hours per semester; 12 credit hours per semester are required to maintain full-time status; 6 credit hours per semester are required to be eligible for financial aid.

Special preparation or orientation Optional orientation held before classes begin.

Basic skills remediation Available in study skills, computer skills, reading, written language, and math. Offered one-on-one by computer-based instruction, special education teachers, and LD specialists.

Subject-area tutoring Available in some subjects. Offered one-on-one by professional tutors.

Counseling and advisement Career counseling, individual counseling, and support groups are available. Academic advisement by a staff member affiliated with the program is available.

Auxiliary aids and services *Aids:* scan and read programs (e.g., Kurzweil), screen-enlarging programs, screen readers, speech recognition programs (e.g., Dragon), tape recorders, taped textbooks. *Services and accommodations:* advocates, priority registration, alternative test arrangements, readers, note-takers, and scribes.

Student organization There is a student organization for students with LD.

ADD/ADHD Students with ADD/ADHD are eligible for the same services available to students with LD, as well as support groups for ADD/ADHD.

Application *Required:* high school transcript, ACT or SAT I (extended-time tests accepted), and psychoeducational report (3 years old or less). *Recommended:* participation in extracurricular activities and documentation of high school services (e.g., Individualized Education Program [IEP] or 504 plan). Upon application, documentation of need for special services should be sent only to your LD program or unit. Upon acceptance, documentation of need for special services should be sent only to your LD program or unit. *Application deadline (institutional):* rolling/continuous for fall and rolling/continuous for spring. *Application deadline (LD program):* rolling/continuous for fall and rolling/continuous for spring.

LD program contact Ann Satkowiak, Assistant Coordinator, Services for Students with Disabilities, 10915 Hardin Valley Road, PO Box 22990, Knoxville, TN 37933-0990. *Phone:* 865-539-7153. *Fax:* 865-539-7218. *E-mail:* asatkowiak@pstcc.cc.tn.us.

Application contact Kim Thomas, Admissions Coordinator, Pellissippi State Technical Community College, PO Box 22990, Knoxville, TN 37933-0990. *Phone:* 423-694-6681. *E-mail:* jpuckett@pstcc.cc.tn.us.

PENNSYLVANIA STATE UNIVERSITY HAZLETON CAMPUS OF THE COMMONWEALTH COLLEGE
Hazleton, Pennsylvania   LD& ADD

Students with LD Served by Program	20	ADD/ADHD Services	✓
Staff	2 full-time	Summer Preparation Program	n/a
LD Program or Service Fee	n/a	Alternative Test Arrangements	✓
LD Program Began	n/a	LD Student Organization	n/a

Disability Services serves approximately 20 undergraduate students. Faculty consists of 2 full-time staff members. Services are provided by academic advisers, counselors, and remediation/learning specialists.

Policies The college has written policies regarding course substitutions. Students with LD may take up to 19 credit hours per semester; 12 credit hours per semester are required to maintain full-time status; 9 credit hours per semester are required to be eligible for financial aid.

Counseling and advisement Career counseling and individual counseling are available. Academic advisement by a staff member affiliated with the program is available.

Auxiliary aids and services *Aids:* scan and read programs (e.g., Kurzweil), tape recorders, taped textbooks. *Services and accommodations:* advocates, priority registration, alternative test arrangements, readers, note-takers, and scribes.

ADD/ADHD Students with ADD/ADHD are eligible for the same services available to students with LD, as well as distraction-free study areas and distraction-free testing environments.

Application *Required:* high school transcript and SAT I (extended-time test accepted). *Recommended:* interview, personal statement, and psychoeducational report (2 years old or less). Upon acceptance, documentation of need for special services should be sent only to your LD program or unit.

LD program contact Jacqueline Walters, Coordinator of Disability Services, Highacres, Hazleton, PA 18201. *Phone:* 570-450-3005. *Fax:* 570-450-3182. *E-mail:* jxw2@psu.edu.

Application contact Pennsylvania State University Hazleton Campus of the Commonwealth College, Hazleton, PA 18201-1291. *E-mail:* admissions@psu.edu. *Web address:* http://www.psu.edu/.

PENNSYLVANIA STATE UNIVERSITY NEW KENSINGTON CAMPUS OF THE COMMONWEALTH COLLEGE
New Kensington, Pennsylvania   LD& ADD

Students with LD Served by Program	12	ADD/ADHD Services	✓
Staff	4 part-time	Summer Preparation Program	n/a
LD Program or Service Fee	n/a	Alternative Test Arrangements	✓
LD Program Began	n/a	LD Student Organization	n/a

The Learning Center serves approximately 12 undergraduate students. Faculty consists of 4 part-time staff members. Services are provided by counselors, trained peer tutors, and professional tutors.

Policies Students with LD may take up to 19 credits per semester; 12 credits per semester are required to maintain full-time status and to be eligible for financial aid.

Basic skills remediation Available in study skills, reading, written language, and math. Offered in class-size groups by regular education teachers.

Subject-area tutoring Available in some subjects. Offered one-on-one, in small groups, and class-size groups by professional tutors and trained peer tutors.

Counseling and advisement Career counseling and individual counseling are available.

Auxiliary aids and services *Aids:* calculators, tape recorders. *Services and accommodations:* advocates, alternative test arrangements, readers, and note-takers.

ADD/ADHD Students with ADD/ADHD are eligible for the same services available to students with LD

Pennsylvania State University New Kensington Campus of the Commonwealth College (continued)

Application *Required:* high school transcript and SAT I (extended-time or untimed test accepted). *Recommended:* separate application to your LD program or unit, psychoeducational report, and documentation of high school services (e.g., Individualized Education Program [IEP] or 504 plan). Upon application, documentation of need for special services should be sent only to your LD program or unit. Upon acceptance, documentation of need for special services should be sent only to your LD program or unit.

LD program contact Jay Schrader, Campus Counselor, 3550 7th Street Road, Upper Burrell, PA 15068. *Phone:* 724-334-6096. *Fax:* 724-334-6111. *E-mail:* jas1@psu.edu.

Application contact Pennsylvania State University New Kensington Campus of the Commonwealth College, 3550 7th Street Road, RT 780, New Kensington, PA 15068-1798. *E-mail:* admissions@psu.edu. *Web address:* http://www.psu.edu/.

PENNSYLVANIA STATE UNIVERSITY YORK CAMPUS OF THE COMMONWEALTH COLLEGE
York, Pennsylvania

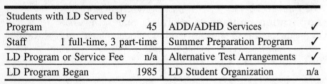

Students with LD Served by Program	45	ADD/ADHD Services	✓
Staff	1 full-time, 3 part-time	Summer Preparation Program	✓
LD Program or Service Fee	n/a	Alternative Test Arrangements	✓
LD Program Began	1985	LD Student Organization	n/a

The Learning Center began offering services in 1985. The program serves approximately 45 undergraduate students. Faculty consists of 1 full-time and 3 part-time staff members. Services are provided by academic advisers, remediation/learning specialists, LD specialists, trained peer tutors, and professional tutors.

Policies The college has written policies regarding course substitutions. Students with LD may take up to 18 credit hours per semester; 12 credit hours per semester are required to maintain full-time status. LD services are also available to graduate students.

Special preparation or orientation Optional summer program offered prior to entering college. Optional orientation held after classes begin and during summer prior to enrollment.

Basic skills remediation Available in study skills, computer skills, time management, and learning strategies. Offered one-on-one by LD specialists, professional tutors, and trained peer tutors.

Subject-area tutoring Available in most subjects. Offered one-on-one by professional tutors, trained peer tutors, and LD specialists.

Counseling and advisement Individual counseling is available. Academic advisement by a staff member affiliated with the program is available.

Auxiliary aids and services *Aids:* calculators, personal spelling/word-use assistants (e.g., Franklin Speller), scan and read programs (e.g., Kurzweil), screen-enlarging programs, screen readers, tape recorders, taped textbooks. *Services and accommodations:* advocates, alternative test arrangements, readers, note-takers, and scribes.

ADD/ADHD Students with ADD/ADHD are eligible for the same services available to students with LD, as well as distraction-free testing environments.

Application *Required:* high school transcript. *Recommended:* ACT or SAT I (extended-time or untimed test accepted), interview, letter(s) of recommendation, psychoeducational report (5 years old or less), and documentation of high school services (e.g., Individualized Education Program [IEP] or 504 plan). Upon application, documentation of need for special services should be sent only to admissions. Upon acceptance, documentation of need for special services should be sent to both admissions and your LD program or unit. *Application deadline (institutional):* rolling/continuous for fall and rolling/continuous for spring. *Application deadline (LD program):* rolling/continuous for fall and rolling/continuous for spring.

LD program contact Dr. Cora M. Dzubak, Learning Center Director, 1031 Edgecomb Avenue, York, PA 17403. *Phone:* 717-771-4013. *Fax:* 717-771-4022. *E-mail:* cmd14@psu.edu.

Application contact Pennsylvania State University York Campus of the Commonwealth College, 1031 Edgecomb Avenue, York, PA 17403-3298. *E-mail:* admissions@psu.edu. *Web address:* http://www.psu.edu/.

PENSACOLA JUNIOR COLLEGE
Pensacola, Florida

Students with LD Served by Program	200	ADD/ADHD Services	✓
Staff	3 full-time, 4 part-time	Summer Preparation Program	✓
LD Program or Service Fee	n/a	Alternative Test Arrangements	✓
LD Program Began	1985	LD Student Organization	✓

Disability Support Services began offering services in 1985. The program serves approximately 200 undergraduate students. Faculty consists of 3 full-time and 4 part-time staff members. Services are provided by academic advisers, regular education teachers, counselors, diagnostic specialists, LD specialists, and trained peer tutors.

Policies The college has written policies regarding course substitutions and substitution and waivers of requirements for admission and graduation. LD services are also available to graduate students.

Special preparation or orientation Optional summer program offered prior to entering college. Optional orientation held during registration.

Diagnostic testing Available for intelligence, learning strategies, reading, learning styles, and math.

Basic skills remediation Available in reading, learning strategies, and math. Offered one-on-one and in small groups by computer-based instruction, LD specialists, and trained peer tutors.

Subject-area tutoring Available in most subjects. Offered one-on-one and in small groups by computer-based instruction, trained peer tutors, and LD specialists.

Special courses Available in career planning and college survival skills. Some courses are offered for credit; some enter into overall grade point average.

Counseling and advisement Career counseling, individual counseling, and support groups are available. Academic advisement by a staff member affiliated with the program is available.

Auxiliary aids and services *Aids:* calculators, personal computers, personal spelling/word-use assistants (e.g., Franklin Speller), scan and read programs (e.g., Kurzweil), screen-enlarging programs, screen readers, speech recognition programs (e.g., Dragon), tape recorders, taped textbooks. *Services and accommodations:* advocates, priority registration, alternative test arrangements, readers, note-takers, and scribes.

Student organization There is a student organization for students with LD.

ADD/ADHD Students with ADD/ADHD are eligible for the same services available to students with LD, as well as distraction-free study areas, distraction-free testing environments and support groups for ADD/ADHD.

Application *Required:* high school transcript, interview, psychoeducational report (5 years old or less), and documentation of high school services (e.g., Individualized Education Program [IEP] or 504 plan). Upon application, documentation of need for special services should be sent only to your LD program or unit. Upon acceptance, documentation of need for special services should be sent only to your LD program or unit. *Application deadline (institutional):* 8/15 for fall and 12/15 for spring. *Application deadline (LD program):* 8/15 for fall and 12/15 for spring.
LD program contact Dr. Jim Nickles, Director, Disability Support Services, 1000 College Boulevard, Pensacola, FL 32504. *Phone:* 850-484-1637. *Fax:* 850-484-2049. *E-mail:* jnickles@pjc.cc.fl.us.

Application contact Martha Flood Caughey, Coordinator of Admissions and Registration, Pensacola Junior College, 1000 College Boulevard, Pensacola, FL 32504-8998. *Phone:* 850-484-1600. *Web address:* http://www.pjc.cc.fl.us/.

PIERCE COLLEGE
Lakewood, Washington

Students with LD Served by Program	250	ADD/ADHD Services	✓
Staff	2 full-time, 1 part-time	Summer Preparation Program	n/a
LD Program or Service Fee	n/a	Alternative Test Arrangements	✓
LD Program Began	1970	LD Student Organization	n/a

Disability Support Services began offering services in 1970. The program serves approximately 250 undergraduate students. Faculty consists of 2 full-time staff members and 1 part-time staff member. Services are provided by coordinators and advisor of Disability Support Services.
Policies The college has written policies regarding course substitutions. 10 credits per quarter are required to maintain full-time status.
Basic skills remediation Available in study skills, reading, written language, math, and spoken language. Offered in class-size groups by regular education teachers.
Subject-area tutoring Available in some subjects. Offered one-on-one and in small groups by trained peer tutors.
Special courses Available in career planning, study skills, college survival skills, test taking, health and nutrition, time management, and stress management. Most courses are offered for credit; all enter into overall grade point average.
Auxiliary aids and services *Aids:* personal spelling/word-use assistants (e.g., Franklin Speller), scan and read programs (e.g., Kurzweil), screen-enlarging programs, screen readers, speech recognition programs (e.g., Dragon), tape recorders, taped textbooks. *Services and accommodations:* priority registration, alternative test arrangements, readers, note-takers, and scribes.
ADD/ADHD Students with ADD/ADHD are eligible for the same services available to students with LD, as well as distraction-free testing environments.
Application *Required:* psychoeducational report (5 years old or less). *Recommended:* documentation of high school services (e.g., Individualized Education Program [IEP] or 504 plan). Upon application, documentation of need for special services should be sent only to your LD program or unit. Upon acceptance, documentation of need for special services should be sent only to your LD program or unit. *Application deadline (institutional):*

9/27 for fall and 3/31 for spring. *Application deadline (LD program):* rolling/continuous for fall and rolling/continuous for spring.
LD program contact Jackie Hjorleifsson, Coordinator, Disability Support Services, 9401 Farwest Drive SW, Lakewood, WA 98498. *Phone:* 253-964-6526. *Fax:* 253-964-6427. *E-mail:* jhjorlei@pierce.ctd.edu.
Application contact William Ponder, Director of Admissions and Registration, Pierce College, 9401 Farwest Drive, SW, Lakewood, WA 98498-1999. *Phone:* 253-964-6623. *Web address:* http://www.pierce.ctc.edu/.

PIKES PEAK COMMUNITY COLLEGE
Colorado Springs, Colorado

Students with LD Served by Program	150	ADD/ADHD Services	✓
Staff	2 full-time, 2 part-time	Summer Preparation Program	n/a
LD Program or Service Fee	n/a	Alternative Test Arrangements	✓
LD Program Began	n/a	LD Student Organization	✓

Center for Students with Disabilities serves approximately 150 undergraduate students. Faculty consists of 2 full-time and 2 part-time staff members. Services are provided by academic advisers, regular education teachers, counselors, remediation/learning specialists, LD specialists, trained peer tutors, and assistive technology specialist.
Special preparation or orientation Optional orientation held before classes begin.
Basic skills remediation Available in study skills, computer skills, time management, learning strategies, and written language. Offered one-on-one, in small groups, and class-size groups by computer-based instruction, special education teachers, LD specialists, trained peer tutors, and assistive technology specialist.
Subject-area tutoring Available in most subjects. Offered one-on-one and in small groups by professional tutors, trained peer tutors, and LD specialists.
Special courses Available in adaptive computer. All courses are offered for credit; all enter into overall grade point average.
Counseling and advisement disability strategies is available. Academic advisement by a staff member affiliated with the program is available.
Auxiliary aids and services *Aids:* calculators, personal spelling/word-use assistants (e.g., Franklin Speller), scan and read programs (e.g., Kurzweil), screen-enlarging programs, screen readers, speech recognition programs (e.g., Dragon), tape recorders, taped textbooks. *Services and accommodations:* advocates, alternative test arrangements, readers, note-takers, and scribes.
Student organization There is a student organization for students with LD.
ADD/ADHD Students with ADD/ADHD are eligible for the same services available to students with LD, as well as distraction-free testing environments, personal coach or mentors, and support groups for ADD/ADHD.
Application *Required:* interview, separate application to your LD program or unit, and psychoeducational report. *Recommended:* documentation of high school services (e.g., Individualized Education Program [IEP] or 504 plan). Upon application, documentation of need for special services should be sent only to your LD program or unit. Upon acceptance, documentation of need for special services should be sent only to your LD program or unit. *Application deadline (institutional):* rolling/continuous for fall and rolling/continuous for spring. *Application deadline (LD program):* rolling/continuous for fall and rolling/continuous for spring.

Pikes Peak Community College (continued)

LD program contact Sandra L. Johannsen, Coordinator, 5675 South Academy Boulevard, Colorado Springs, CO 80906. *Phone:* 800-456-6847. *Fax:* 719-540-7090. *E-mail:* sandra.johannsen@ppcc.cccoes.edu.

Application contact Pikes Peak Community College, 5675 South Academy Boulevard, Colorado Springs, CO 80906-5498. *E-mail:* harris@ppcc.colorado.edu. *Web address:* http://www.ppcc.cccoes.edu/.

PITT COMMUNITY COLLEGE
Greenville, North Carolina

Students with LD Served by Program	160	ADD/ADHD Services	✓
Staff	2 full-time, 1 part-time	Summer Preparation Program	n/a
LD Program or Service Fee	n/a	Alternative Test Arrangements	✓
LD Program Began	1993	LD Student Organization	n/a

Disability Services began offering services in 1993. The program serves approximately 160 undergraduate students. Faculty consists of 2 full-time staff members and 1 part-time staff member. Services are provided by counselors and LD specialists.

Policies The college has written policies regarding course substitutions and grade forgiveness. Students with LD may take up to 16 credit hours per semester; 12 credit hours per semester are required to maintain full-time status; 6 credit hours per semester are required to be eligible for financial aid.

Special preparation or orientation Optional orientation held during summer prior to enrollment.

Basic skills remediation Available in reading and math. Offered one-on-one by computer-based instruction and trained peer tutors.

Subject-area tutoring Available in most subjects. Offered one-on-one by trained peer tutors.

Counseling and advisement Career counseling, individual counseling, small-group counseling, and support groups are available.

Auxiliary aids and services *Aids:* personal computers, personal spelling/word-use assistants (e.g., Franklin Speller), scan and read programs (e.g., Kurzweil), screen-enlarging programs, tape recorders. *Services and accommodations:* advocates, priority registration, alternative test arrangements, readers, note-takers, and scribes.

ADD/ADHD Students with ADD/ADHD are eligible for the same services available to students with LD, as well as distraction-free study areas, distraction-free testing environments and support groups for ADD/ADHD.

Application *Required:* high school transcript, personal statement, psychoeducational report (3 years old or less), and documentation of high school services (e.g., Individualized Education Program [IEP] or 504 plan). *Recommended:* participation in extracurricular activities and interview. Upon application, documentation of need for special services should be sent only to your LD program or unit. Upon acceptance, documentation of need for special services should be sent only to your LD program or unit. *Application deadline (institutional):* rolling/continuous for fall and rolling/continuous for spring. *Application deadline (LD program):* rolling/continuous for fall and rolling/continuous for spring.

LD program contact Michael Bridgers, Coordinator of Disability Services, PO Drawer 7007, Greenville, NC 27835-7007. *Phone:* 252-321-4294. *Fax:* 252-321-4401. *E-mail:* mbridgers@pcc.pitt.cc.tlc.us.

Application contact Norma Barrett, Director of Counseling, Pitt Community College, Highway 11 South, PO Drawer 7007, Greenville, NC 27835-7007. *Phone:* 252-321-4245. *Web address:* http://sphynx.pitt.cc.nc.us:8080/home.htm.

PORTLAND COMMUNITY COLLEGE
Portland, Oregon

Students with LD Served by Program	220	ADD/ADHD Services	✓
Staff	4 full-time, 3 part-time	Summer Preparation Program	n/a
LD Program or Service Fee	n/a	Alternative Test Arrangements	✓
LD Program Began	1979	LD Student Organization	✓

Office for Students with Disabilities began offering services in 1979. The program serves approximately 220 undergraduate students. Faculty consists of 4 full-time and 3 part-time staff members. Services are provided by academic advisers, counselors, diagnostic specialists, and LD specialists.

Policies 12 credits per quarter are required to maintain full-time status; 3 credits per quarter are required to be eligible for financial aid.

Special preparation or orientation Optional orientation held before classes begin.

Diagnostic testing Available for auditory processing, spelling, intelligence, learning strategies, reading, written language, learning styles, visual processing, and math.

Subject-area tutoring Available in some subjects. Offered one-on-one by trained peer tutors.

Counseling and advisement Career counseling, individual counseling, and support groups are available. Academic advisement by a staff member affiliated with the program is available.

Auxiliary aids and services *Aids:* calculators, personal computers, personal spelling/word-use assistants (e.g., Franklin Speller), scan and read programs (e.g., Kurzweil), screen-enlarging programs, screen readers, speech recognition programs (e.g., Dragon), tape recorders, taped textbooks. *Services and accommodations:* advocates, priority registration, alternative test arrangements, readers, note-takers, and scribes.

Student organization There is a student organization for students with LD.

ADD/ADHD Students with ADD/ADHD are eligible for the same services available to students with LD, as well as distraction-free study areas, distraction-free testing environments and personal coach or mentors.

Application *Recommended:* high school transcript, interview, psychoeducational report, and documentation of high school services (e.g., Individualized Education Program [IEP] or 504 plan). Upon application, documentation of need for special services should be sent only to your LD program or unit. *Application deadline (institutional):* rolling/continuous for fall and rolling/continuous for spring. *Application deadline (LD program):* rolling/continuous for fall and rolling/continuous for spring.

LD program contact Clark Hochstetler, Counselor/Faculty Department Chair, PO Box 19000, Portland, OR 97280-0990. *Phone:* 503-977-4343. *Fax:* 503-977-4882. *E-mail:* chochste@pcc.edu.

Application contact Portland Community College, PO Box 19000, Portland, OR 97280-0990. *E-mail:* admissions@pcc.edu. *Web address:* http://www.pcc.edu/.

PRINCE GEORGE'S COMMUNITY COLLEGE

Largo, Maryland

Students with LD Served by Program	115	ADD/ADHD Services	✓
Staff	8 full-time, 37 part-time	Summer Preparation Program	n/a
LD Program or Service Fee	n/a	Alternative Test Arrangements	✓
LD Program Began	1985	LD Student Organization	n/a

Student Support Services began offering services in 1985. The program serves approximately 115 undergraduate students. Faculty consists of 8 full-time and 37 part-time staff members. Services are provided by academic advisers, counselors, remediation/learning specialists, trained peer tutors, and notetakers.

Policies Students with LD may take up to 18 credit hours per semester; 12 credit hours per semester are required to maintain full-time status; 3 credit hours per semester are required to be eligible for financial aid.

Diagnostic testing Available for handwriting, study skills, learning strategies, and learning styles.

Basic skills remediation Available in auditory processing, study skills, reading, time management, visual processing, learning strategies, spelling, and notetaking. Offered one-on-one and in small groups by professional tutors, trained peer tutors, and remediation/learning specialist, counselor.

Subject-area tutoring Available in some subjects. Offered one-on-one and in small groups by professional tutors, trained peer tutors, and remediation/learning specialist.

Counseling and advisement Career counseling, individual counseling, small-group counseling, and support groups are available. Academic advisement by a staff member affiliated with the program is available.

Auxiliary aids and services *Aids:* calculators, personal spelling/word-use assistants (e.g., Franklin Speller), scan and read programs (e.g., Kurzweil), screen-enlarging programs, screen readers, speech recognition programs (e.g., Dragon), tape recorders, taped textbooks. *Services and accommodations:* advocates, priority registration, alternative test arrangements, readers, note-takers, scribes, and mentoring.

ADD/ADHD Students with ADD/ADHD are eligible for the same services available to students with LD, as well as distraction-free study areas, distraction-free testing environments and medication management.

Application *Required:* separate application to your LD program or unit and psychoeducational report (3 years old or less). *Recommended:* documentation of high school services (e.g., Individualized Education Program [IEP] or 504 plan). Upon application, documentation of need for special services should be sent only to your LD program or unit. Upon acceptance, documentation of need for special services should be sent only to your LD program or unit. *Application deadline (institutional):* 9/1 for fall and 1/24 for spring. *Application deadline (LD program):* 8/7 for fall and 1/5 for spring.

LD program contact Dr. Daniel Jones, Coordinator of Disability Support Services, 301 Largo Road, Largo, MD 20774-2199. *Phone:* 301-322-0838. *Fax:* 301-336-8315. *E-mail:* jonesdf@pgcc.md.us.

Application contact Vera Bagley, Director of Admissions and Records, Prince George's Community College, 301 Largo Road, Largo, MD 20774-2199. *Phone:* 301-322-0801. *Web address:* http://PGWEB.pg.cc.md.us/.

RAINY RIVER COMMUNITY COLLEGE

International Falls, Minnesota

Students with LD Served by Program	16	ADD/ADHD Services	✓
Staff	1 part-time	Summer Preparation Program	n/a
LD Program or Service Fee	n/a	Alternative Test Arrangements	✓
LD Program Began	1986	LD Student Organization	n/a

Services to Students with Disabilities began offering services in 1986. The program serves approximately 16 undergraduate students. Faculty consists of 1 part-time staff member. Services are provided by academic advisers, trained peer tutors, and professional tutors.

Policies Students with LD may take up to 18 credits per semester; 12 credits per semester are required to be eligible for financial aid.

Diagnostic testing Available for intelligence, personality, study skills, learning strategies, reading, written language, learning styles, and math.

Basic skills remediation Available in study skills, computer skills, reading, written language, and math. Offered in class-size groups by regular education teachers, special education teachers, and professional tutors.

Subject-area tutoring Available in some subjects. Offered one-on-one, in small groups, and class-size groups by computer-based instruction, professional tutors, and trained peer tutors.

Counseling and advisement Career counseling and individual counseling are available. Academic advisement by a staff member affiliated with the program is available.

Auxiliary aids and services *Aids:* calculators, personal spelling/word-use assistants (e.g., Franklin Speller), scan and read programs (e.g., Kurzweil), screen-enlarging programs, screen readers, tape recorders, taped textbooks. *Services and accommodations:* advocates, priority registration, alternative test arrangements, readers, note-takers, and scribes.

ADD/ADHD Students with ADD/ADHD are eligible for the same services available to students with LD, as well as distraction-free testing environments.

Application *Recommended:* high school transcript. Upon application, documentation of need for special services should be sent only to your LD program or unit. Upon acceptance, documentation of need for special services should be sent only to your LD program or unit. *Application deadline (institutional):* rolling/continuous for fall and rolling/continuous for spring. *Application deadline (LD program):* rolling/continuous for fall and rolling/continuous for spring.

LD program contact Carol Grim, Director of Services to Students with Disabilities, 1501 Highway 71, International Falls, MN 56649. *Phone:* 218-285-7722. *Fax:* 218-285-2239. *E-mail:* cgrim@rrcc.mnscu.edu.

Application contact Rainy River Community College, 1501 Highway 71, International Falls, MN 56649. *E-mail:* admissions@rr.mn.us. *Web address:* http://www.rrcc.mnscu.edu/.

RENTON TECHNICAL COLLEGE

Renton, Washington

Students with LD Served by Program	150	ADD/ADHD Services	✓
Staff	1 full-time	Summer Preparation Program	n/a
LD Program or Service Fee	n/a	Alternative Test Arrangements	✓
LD Program Began	n/a	LD Student Organization	n/a

Renton Technical College (continued)

Disabled Student Services/Special Population Program serves approximately 150 undergraduate students. Faculty consists of 1 full-time staff member. Services are provided by regular education teachers, counselors, trained peer tutors, professional tutors, and special populations coordinator.

Special preparation or orientation Optional orientation held before registration, before classes begin, and individually by special arrangement.

Diagnostic testing Available for LD inventory.

Basic skills remediation Available in study skills, computer skills, reading, written language, math, and spoken language. Offered one-on-one, in small groups, and class-size groups by computer-based instruction, regular education teachers, trained peer tutors, and basic studies department.

Subject-area tutoring Available in all subjects. Offered one-on-one, in small groups, and class-size groups by computer-based instruction, trained peer tutors, and basic studies department.

Special courses Available in study skills, practical computer skills, reading, math, and written composition skills. Some courses are offered for credit; some enter into overall grade point average.

Counseling and advisement Career counseling and individual counseling are available.

Auxiliary aids and services *Aids:* calculators, personal computers, screen-enlarging programs, speech recognition programs (e.g., Dragon), tape recorders, taped textbooks. *Services and accommodations:* advocates, alternative test arrangements, readers, note-takers, scribes, and interpreters.

ADD/ADHD Students with ADD/ADHD are eligible for the same services available to students with LD, as well as distraction-free study areas, distraction-free testing environments and counseling.

Application *Required:* high school transcript, interview, separate application to your LD program or unit, and psychoeducational report (5 years old or less). *Recommended:* documentation of high school services (e.g., Individualized Education Program [IEP] or 504 plan). Upon application, documentation of need for special services should be sent only to your LD program or unit. Upon acceptance, documentation of need for special services should be sent only to your LD program or unit. *Application deadline (institutional):* rolling/continuous for fall and rolling/continuous for spring. *Application deadline (LD program):* rolling/continuous for fall and rolling/continuous for spring.

LD program contact Michael E. Dahl, Special Populations Coordinator/Counselor, 3000 Northeast 4th Street, Renton, WA 98056. *Phone:* 425-235-2352 Ext. 5544. *Fax:* 425-235-7832. *E-mail:* mdahl@rtc.ctc.edu.

Application contact Renton Technical College, 3000 Fourth Street, NE, Renton, WA 98056. *E-mail:* edaniels@ctc.ctc.edu. *Web address:* http://www.renton-tc.ctc.edu/.

RICKS COLLEGE
Rexburg, Idaho

Students with LD Served by Program	60	ADD/ADHD Services	✓
Staff	1 full-time, 5 part-time	Summer Preparation Program	n/a
LD Program or Service Fee	n/a	Alternative Test Arrangements	✓
LD Program Began	1985	LD Student Organization	n/a

Services for Students with a Disability (SSD) began offering services in 1985. The program serves approximately 60 undergraduate students. Faculty consists of 1 full-time and 5 part-time staff members. Services are provided by academic advisers, regular education teachers, counselors, remediation/learning specialists, and trained peer tutors.

Policies The college has written policies regarding course substitutions. 12 credit hours per semester are required to maintain full-time status; 12 credits per semester are required to be eligible for financial aid.

Subject-area tutoring Available in most subjects. Offered one-on-one and in small groups by trained peer tutors.

Counseling and advisement Career counseling, individual counseling, small-group counseling, and support groups are available. Academic advisement by a staff member affiliated with the program is available.

Auxiliary aids and services *Aids:* personal computers, tape recorders. *Services and accommodations:* advocates, priority registration, alternative test arrangements, readers, and note-takers.

ADD/ADHD Students with ADD/ADHD are eligible for the same services available to students with LD, as well as distraction-free study areas, distraction-free testing environments, medication management and support groups for ADD/ADHD.

Application *Required:* high school transcript, ACT (extended-time or untimed test accepted), personal statement, psychoeducational report, and documentation of high school services (e.g., Individualized Education Program [IEP] or 504 plan). Upon acceptance, documentation of need for special services should be sent only to your LD program or unit. *Application deadline (institutional):* 2/15 for fall and 10/15 for spring. *Application deadline (LD program):* 2/15 for fall and 10/15 for spring.

LD program contact Dr. Richard G. Taylor, Director, Services for Students with a Disability, Rexburg, ID 83460-4121. *Phone:* 208-356-1159. *Fax:* 208-356-2390. *E-mail:* taylorr@ricks.edu.

Application contact Steven Davis, Assistant Director of Admissions, Ricks College, Rexburg, ID 83460-4107. *Phone:* 208-356-1026. *E-mail:* birchm@ricks.edu. *Web address:* http://www.ricks.edu/.

ROANE STATE COMMUNITY COLLEGE
Harriman, Tennessee

Students with LD Served by Program	75	ADD/ADHD Services	✓
Staff	1 full-time, 3 part-time	Summer Preparation Program	n/a
LD Program or Service Fee	n/a	Alternative Test Arrangements	✓
LD Program Began	1995	LD Student Organization	n/a

Disability Services began offering services in 1995. The program serves approximately 75 undergraduate students. Faculty consists of 1 full-time and 3 part-time staff members. Services are provided by counselors, remediation/learning specialists, and diagnostic specialists.

Policies Students with LD may take up to 19 credit hours per semester; 12 credit hours per semester are required to maintain full-time status; 6 credit hours per semester are required to be eligible for financial aid.

Diagnostic testing Available for spelling, intelligence, reading, and math.

Subject-area tutoring Available in some subjects. Offered by trained peer tutors.

Counseling and advisement Career counseling and individual counseling are available.

Auxiliary aids and services *Aids:* calculators, personal computers, personal spelling/word-use assistants (e.g., Franklin Speller), screen-enlarging programs, screen readers, tape recorders, taped textbooks. *Services and accommodations:* alternative test arrangements, readers, note-takers, and scribes.

ADD/ADHD Students with ADD/ADHD are eligible for the same services available to students with LD, as well as distraction-free study areas and distraction-free testing environments.
Application *Required:* high school transcript and ACT (extended-time test accepted). *Recommended:* separate application to your LD program or unit, psychoeducational report (3 years old or less), and documentation of high school services (e.g., Individualized Education Program [IEP] or 504 plan). Upon acceptance, documentation of need for special services should be sent only to your LD program or unit. *Application deadline (institutional):* rolling/continuous for fall and rolling/continuous for spring. *Application deadline (LD program):* rolling/continuous for fall and rolling/continuous for spring.
LD program contact H. R. Anderson, Director of Counseling and Disability Services, 276 Patton Lane, Harriman, TN 37748-5011. *Phone:* 865-882-4546. *Fax:* 865-882-4547.
Application contact Marsha Bankston, Director of Records and Registration, Roane State Community College, 276 Patton Lane, Harriman, TN 37748-5011. *Phone:* 423-882-4526. *E-mail:* richardson_a@a1.rscc.cc.tn.us. *Web address:* http://www.rscc.cc.tn.us/.

ROBESON COMMUNITY COLLEGE
Lumberton, North Carolina

Students with LD Served by Program	2	ADD/ADHD Services	✓
Staff	n/a	Summer Preparation Program	n/a
LD Program or Service Fee	n/a	Alternative Test Arrangements	✓
LD Program Began	n/a	LD Student Organization	n/a

Counseling and Career Services serves approximately 2 undergraduate students. Services are provided by counselors.
Policies Students with LD may take up to 25 credit hours per semester; 12 credit hours per semester are required to maintain full-time status; 6 credit hours per semester are required to be eligible for financial aid.
Subject-area tutoring Available in most subjects. Offered one-on-one by professional tutors and trained peer tutors.
Special courses Available in career planning and college survival skills. Some courses are offered for credit; some enter into overall grade point average.
Counseling and advisement Career counseling, individual counseling, small-group counseling, and support groups are available.
Auxiliary aids and services *Aids:* calculators, personal computers, scan and read programs (e.g., Kurzweil), screen-enlarging programs, screen readers, tape recorders, taped textbooks. *Services and accommodations:* priority registration, alternative test arrangements, readers, and note-takers.
ADD/ADHD Students with ADD/ADHD are eligible for the same services available to students with LD, as well as distraction-free study areas and distraction-free testing environments.
Application *Required:* high school transcript, psychoeducational report (3 years old or less), and documentation of high school services (e.g., Individualized Education Program [IEP] or 504 plan). Upon application, documentation of need for special services should be sent only to your LD program or unit. Upon acceptance, documentation of need for special services should be sent only to your LD program or unit. *Application deadline (institutional):* rolling/continuous for fall and rolling/continuous for spring. *Application deadline (LD program):* rolling/continuous for fall and rolling/continuous for spring.
LD program contact Director of Counseling and Testing, P O Box 1420, Lumberton, NC 28358. *Phone:* 910-738-7101. *Fax:* 910-618-5686.

Application contact Judy Revels, Director of Admissions, Robeson Community College, Highway 301 North, PO Box 1420, Lumberton, NC 28359-1420. *Phone:* 910-738-7101 Ext. 251. *Web address:* http://www.robeson.cc.nc.us/.

ROCKINGHAM COMMUNITY COLLEGE
Wentworth, North Carolina

Students with LD Served by Program	30	ADD/ADHD Services	✓
Staff	1 full-time	Summer Preparation Program	n/a
LD Program or Service Fee	n/a	Alternative Test Arrangements	✓
LD Program Began	1990	LD Student Organization	n/a

Student Services began offering services in 1990. The program serves approximately 30 undergraduate students. Faculty consists of 1 full-time staff member. Services are provided by counselors.
Policies Students with LD may take up to 18 credit hours per semester; 12 credit hours per semester are required to maintain full-time status; 6 credit hours per semester are required to be eligible for financial aid.
Auxiliary aids and services *Aids:* personal spelling/word-use assistants (e.g., Franklin Speller), scan and read programs (e.g., Kurzweil), screen-enlarging programs, tape recorders. *Services and accommodations:* priority registration, alternative test arrangements, readers, note-takers, and scribes.
ADD/ADHD Students with ADD/ADHD are eligible for the same services available to students with LD, as well as distraction-free testing environments and personal coach or mentors.
Application *Required:* high school transcript and psychoeducational report. Upon acceptance, documentation of need for special services should be sent only to your LD program or unit.
LD program contact LaVonne James, Counselor/Coordinator, Center for Academic Progress, PO Box 38, Wentworth, NC 27375-0038. *Phone:* 336-342-4261 Ext. 2243. *Fax:* 336-342-1809. *E-mail:* jamesl@rcc.cc.nc.us.
Application contact Rockingham Community College, PO Box 38, Wentworth, NC 27375-0038. *Web address:* http://www.rcc.cc.nc.us/.

ST. CLAIR COUNTY COMMUNITY COLLEGE
Port Huron, Michigan

Students with LD Served by Program	40	ADD/ADHD Services	✓
Staff	6 full-time, 1 part-time	Summer Preparation Program	n/a
LD Program or Service Fee	n/a	Alternative Test Arrangements	✓
LD Program Began	1978	LD Student Organization	n/a

Student Learning Center began offering services in 1978. The program serves approximately 40 undergraduate students. Faculty consists of 6 full-time staff members and 1 part-time staff member. Services are provided by counselors, remediation/learning specialists, special education teachers, trained peer tutors, and professional tutors.
Policies Students with LD may take up to 18 credit hours per semester; 12 credit hours per semester are required to maintain full-time status; 1 credit hour per semester is required to be eligible for financial aid.

St. Clair County Community College (continued)

Basic skills remediation Available in study skills, computer skills, reading, time management, learning strategies, written language, and math. Offered in class-size groups by computer-based instruction, regular education teachers, special education teachers, professional tutors, and trained peer tutors.

Subject-area tutoring Available in all subjects. Offered one-on-one, in small groups, and class-size groups by computer-based instruction, professional tutors, and trained peer tutors.

Special courses Available in career planning, study skills, college survival skills, practical computer skills, test taking, reading, time management, learning strategies, vocabulary development, math, stress management, and written composition skills. Most courses are offered for credit; all enter into overall grade point average.

Counseling and advisement Career counseling and individual counseling are available.

Auxiliary aids and services *Aids:* calculators, personal spelling/word-use assistants (e.g., Franklin Speller), scan and read programs (e.g., Kurzweil), screen-enlarging programs, tape recorders. *Services and accommodations:* alternative test arrangements, readers, note-takers, and scribes.

ADD/ADHD Students with ADD/ADHD are eligible for the same services available to students with LD, as well as distraction-free testing environments.

Application *Required:* high school transcript and referral by external agency. Upon application, documentation of need for special services should be sent only to your LD program or unit. Upon acceptance, documentation of need for special services should be sent only to your LD program or unit. *Application deadline (LD program):* rolling/continuous for fall and rolling/continuous for spring.

LD program contact Gerri Barber, Coordinator, Student Learning Center, 323 Erie, Port Huron, MI 48061-5015. *Phone:* 810-989-5555. *Fax:* 810-984-4730. *E-mail:* gbarber@stclair.cc.mi.us.

Application contact St. Clair County Community College, 323 Erie Street, PO Box 5015, Port Huron, MI 48061-5015. *Web address:* http://www.stclair.cc.mi.us/.

ST. LOUIS COMMUNITY COLLEGE AT MERAMEC
Kirkwood, Missouri

Students with LD Served by Program	400	ADD/ADHD Services	✓
Staff	6 full-time, 1 part-time	Summer Preparation Program	n/a
LD Program or Service Fee	n/a	Alternative Test Arrangements	✓
LD Program Began	1972	LD Student Organization	n/a

ACCESS Office, Disability Support Services began offering services in 1972. The program serves approximately 400 undergraduate students. Faculty consists of 6 full-time staff members and 1 part-time staff member. Services are provided by academic advisers, regular education teachers, counselors, remediation/learning specialists, LD specialists, and trained peer tutors.

Policies The college has written policies regarding course substitutions and grade forgiveness.

Special preparation or orientation Held before classes begin and individually by special arrangement.

Counseling and advisement Career counseling, individual counseling, small-group counseling, and support groups are available. Academic advisement by a staff member affiliated with the program is available.

Auxiliary aids and services *Aids:* calculators, personal spelling/word-use assistants (e.g., Franklin Speller), scan and read programs (e.g., Kurzweil), screen-enlarging programs, screen readers,

speech recognition programs (e.g., Dragon), taped textbooks. *Services and accommodations:* advocates, alternative test arrangements, readers, note-takers, and scribes.

ADD/ADHD Students with ADD/ADHD are eligible for the same services available to students with LD, as well as distraction-free testing environments and support groups for ADD/ADHD.

Application *Required:* high school transcript and psychoeducational report. *Recommended:* ACT or SAT I (extended-time tests accepted) and documentation of high school services (e.g., Individualized Education Program [IEP] or 504 plan). Upon application, documentation of need for special services should be sent only to your LD program or unit. Upon acceptance, documentation of need for special services should be sent only to your LD program or unit. *Application deadline (institutional):* rolling/continuous for fall and rolling/continuous for spring. *Application deadline (LD program):* rolling/continuous for fall and rolling/continuous for spring.

LD program contact ACCESS Office, 11333 Big Bend Boulevard, St. Louis, MO 63122. *Phone:* 314-984-7673. *Fax:* 314-984-7123. *E-mail:* dkoenig@mcmail.stlcc.cc.mo.us.

Application contact Mike Cundiff, Coordinator of Admissions, St. Louis Community College at Meramec, 11333 Big Bend Boulevard, Kirkwood, MO 63122-5720. *Phone:* 314-984-7608. *Web address:* http://www.stlcc.cc.mo.us/mc/.

ST. PAUL TECHNICAL COLLEGE
St. Paul, Minnesota

Students with LD Served by Program	39	ADD/ADHD Services	✓
Staff	1 full-time	Summer Preparation Program	n/a
LD Program or Service Fee	n/a	Alternative Test Arrangements	n/a
LD Program Began	1990	LD Student Organization	n/a

Office of Disability Services began offering services in 1990. The program serves approximately 39 undergraduate students. Faculty consists of 1 full-time staff member. Services are provided by trained peer tutors.

Policies Students with LD may take up to 18 credits per semester; 12 credits per semester are required to maintain full-time status and to be eligible for financial aid.

Basic skills remediation Available in study skills, reading, learning strategies, written language, and math. Offered in class-size groups by regular education teachers.

Subject-area tutoring Available in all subjects. Offered one-on-one by trained peer tutors.

Auxiliary aids and services *Aids:* personal computers, personal spelling/word-use assistants (e.g., Franklin Speller), screen-enlarging programs, speech recognition programs (e.g., Dragon), tape recorders, taped textbooks. *Services and accommodations:* priority registration, readers, note-takers, and scribes.

ADD/ADHD Students with ADD/ADHD are eligible for the same services available to students with LD, as well as distraction-free study areas and distraction-free testing environments.

Application *Required:* separate application to your LD program or unit, psychoeducational report (3 years old or less), and documentation of high school services (e.g., Individualized Education Program [IEP] or 504 plan). Upon application, documentation of need for special services should be sent only to your LD program or unit. Upon acceptance, documentation of need for special services should be sent only to your LD program or unit. *Application deadline (institutional):* rolling/continuous for fall and rolling/continuous for spring. *Application deadline (LD program):* rolling/continuous for fall and rolling/continuous for spring.

LD program contact Linda Klein, Disability Coordinator, 235 Marshall Avenue, St. Paul, MN 55102. *Phone:* 651-228-4300. *Fax:* 651-221-1416. *E-mail:* lklein@stp.tec.mn.us.

Application contact Lisa Netzley, Admissions Counselor, St. Paul Technical College, 235 Marshall Avenue, St. Paul, MN 55102-1800. *Phone:* 651-221-1333. *Web address:* http://www.sptc.tec.mn.us/.

SAN DIEGO MESA COLLEGE
San Diego, California

Students with LD Served by Program	200	ADD/ADHD Services	✓
Staff	2 full-time, 3 part-time	Summer Preparation Program	n/a
LD Program or Service Fee	n/a	Alternative Test Arrangements	✓
LD Program Began	1975	LD Student Organization	n/a

Disabled Students Programs and Services (DSPS) began offering services in 1975. The program serves approximately 200 undergraduate students. Faculty consists of 2 full-time and 3 part-time staff members. Services are provided by counselors, LD specialists, and professional tutors.

Policies The college has written policies regarding grade forgiveness.

Fees *Diagnostic Testing Fee:* $5.50.

Special preparation or orientation Required orientation held every month.

Diagnostic testing Available for LD eligibility model for California colleges.

Subject-area tutoring Available in most subjects. Offered one-on-one and in small groups by LD specialists and learning accommodation lab.

Special courses Available in study skills, learning strategies, vocabulary development, and written composition skills. All courses are offered for credit; none enter into overall grade point average.

Counseling and advisement Individual counseling, small-group counseling, and support groups are available.

Auxiliary aids and services *Aids:* calculators, personal computers, personal spelling/word-use assistants (e.g., Franklin Speller), scan and read programs (e.g., Kurzweil), screen-enlarging programs, screen readers, speech recognition programs (e.g., Dragon), tape recorders, taped textbooks. *Services and accommodations:* advocates, priority registration, alternative test arrangements, readers, note-takers, and scribes.

ADD/ADHD Students with ADD/ADHD are eligible for the same services available to students with LD, as well as distraction-free testing environments.

Application *Required:* separate application to your LD program or unit. *Recommended:* high school transcript, psychoeducational report, and documentation of high school services (e.g., Individualized Education Program [IEP] or 504 plan). Upon application, documentation of need for special services should be sent only to your LD program or unit. Upon acceptance, documentation of need for special services should be sent only to your LD program or unit. *Application deadline (institutional):* rolling/continuous for fall and rolling/continuous for spring. *Application deadline (LD program):* rolling/continuous for fall and rolling/continuous for spring.

LD program contact Jill Huttenbrauck, LD Specialist/Counselor, Disabled Students Programs and Services, H202, 7250 Mesa College Drive, San Diego, CA 92111. *Phone:* 858-627-2780. *Fax:* 858-627-2460. *E-mail:* jhutten@sdccd.net.

Application contact San Diego Mesa College, 7250 Mesa College Drive, San Diego, CA 92111-4998. *Web address:* http://www.sdmesa.sdccd.cc.ca.us/.

SAN JACINTO COLLEGE-SOUTH CAMPUS
Houston, Texas

Students with LD Served by Program	60	ADD/ADHD Services	✓
Staff	1 full-time	Summer Preparation Program	n/a
LD Program or Service Fee	n/a	Alternative Test Arrangements	✓
LD Program Began	n/a	LD Student Organization	n/a

Special Populations Department serves approximately 60 undergraduate students. Faculty consists of 1 full-time staff member. Services are provided by academic advisers, regular education teachers, counselors, remediation/learning specialists, graduate assistants/students, and trained peer tutors.

Policies 12 credit hours per semester are required to maintain full-time status; 6 credit hours per semester are required to be eligible for financial aid. LD services are also available to graduate students.

Basic skills remediation Available in study skills, computer skills, reading, time management, learning strategies, spelling, written language, math, and spoken language. Offered in class-size groups by computer-based instruction and regular education teachers.

Subject-area tutoring Offered one-on-one by graduate assistants/students and trained peer tutors.

Counseling and advisement Career counseling and individual counseling are available. Academic advisement by a staff member affiliated with the program is available.

Auxiliary aids and services *Aids:* calculators, personal computers, scan and read programs (e.g., Kurzweil), screen-enlarging programs, tape recorders. priority registration, alternative test arrangements, readers, note-takers, and scribes.

ADD/ADHD Students with ADD/ADHD are eligible for the same services available to students with LD, as well as distraction-free study areas and distraction-free testing environments.

Application *Required:* high school transcript, letter(s) of recommendation, psychoeducational report, and documentation of high school services (e.g., Individualized Education Program [IEP] or 504 plan). Upon application, documentation of need for special services should be sent only to your LD program or unit. Upon acceptance, documentation of need for special services should be sent only to your LD program or unit. *Application deadline (institutional):* rolling/continuous for fall and rolling/continuous for spring.

LD program contact Constance Ginn, Special Populations Coordinator, 13735 Beamer Road, Houston, TX 77089-6099. *Phone:* 281-922-3453. *Fax:* 281-929-4626. *E-mail:* cginn@sjcd.cc.tx.us.

Application contact San Jacinto College-South Campus, 13735 Beamer Road, Houston, TX 77089-6099. *E-mail:* season@sjcd.cc.tx.us. *Web address:* http://www.sjcd.cc.tx.us/.

SANTA FE COMMUNITY COLLEGE
Gainesville, Florida

Students with LD Served by Program	400	ADD/ADHD Services	✓
Staff	6 full-time, 3 part-time	Summer Preparation Program	n/a
LD Program or Service Fee	n/a	Alternative Test Arrangements	✓
LD Program Began	1994	LD Student Organization	n/a

Santa Fe Community College (continued)

Disabilities Resource Center began offering services in 1994. The program serves approximately 400 undergraduate students. Faculty consists of 6 full-time and 3 part-time staff members. Services are provided by counselors, graduate assistants/students, and trained peer tutors.

Policies The college has written policies regarding course substitutions and substitution and waivers of requirements for admission and graduation. Students with LD may take up to 18 credit hours per term; 12 credit hours per term are required to maintain full-time status; 6 credit hours per term are required to be eligible for financial aid.

Basic skills remediation Available in reading, written language, and math. Offered in class-size groups by computer-based instruction and regular education teachers.

Subject-area tutoring Available in some subjects. Offered one-on-one by trained peer tutors.

Counseling and advisement Individual counseling is available.

Auxiliary aids and services *Aids:* calculators, personal spelling/word-use assistants (e.g., Franklin Speller), scan and read programs (e.g., Kurzweil), screen-enlarging programs, screen readers, speech recognition programs (e.g., Dragon), tape recorders, taped textbooks. *Services and accommodations:* advocates, priority registration, alternative test arrangements, readers, note-takers, and scribes.

ADD/ADHD Students with ADD/ADHD are eligible for the same services available to students with LD, as well as distraction-free testing environments.

Application *Required:* high school transcript and psychoeducational report (3 years old or less). *Recommended:* ACT or SAT I (extended-time tests accepted) and documentation of high school services (e.g., Individualized Education Program [IEP] or 504 plan). Upon application, documentation of need for special services should be sent only to your LD program or unit. Upon acceptance, documentation of need for special services should be sent only to your LD program or unit. *Application deadline (institutional):* rolling/continuous for fall and rolling/continuous for spring. *Application deadline (LD program):* rolling/continuous for fall and rolling/continuous for spring.

LD program contact Dr. L. Douglas Fols, Coordinator, 3000 Northwest 83rd Street, Gainesville, FL 32607. *Phone:* 352-395-4400. *Fax:* 352-395-4100. *E-mail:* doug.fols@santefe.cc.fl.us.

Application contact Santa Fe Community College, 3000 Northwest 83rd Street, Gainesville, FL 32606-6200. *Web address:* http://www.santafe.cc.fl.us/.

SAUK VALLEY COMMUNITY COLLEGE

Dixon, Illinois

Students with LD Served by Program	75	ADD/ADHD Services	✓
Staff	1 full-time, 6 part-time	Summer Preparation Program	n/a
LD Program or Service Fee	n/a	Alternative Test Arrangements	✓
LD Program Began	1997	LD Student Organization	n/a

Student Needs Coordinator's Office began offering services in 1997. The program serves approximately 75 undergraduate students. Faculty consists of 1 full-time and 6 part-time staff members. Services are provided by academic advisers, counselors, diagnostic specialists, special education teachers, trained peer tutors, and professional tutors.

Special preparation or orientation Required orientation held after classes begin.

Diagnostic testing Available for learning styles.

Basic skills remediation Available in reading and math. Offered one-on-one and in small groups by regular education teachers.

Subject-area tutoring Available in some subjects. Offered in small groups by professional tutors and trained peer tutors.

Counseling and advisement Individual counseling is available. Academic advisement by a staff member affiliated with the program is available.

Auxiliary aids and services *Aids:* calculators, personal spelling/word-use assistants (e.g., Franklin Speller), scan and read programs (e.g., Kurzweil), screen-enlarging programs, screen readers, speech recognition programs (e.g., Dragon), tape recorders, taped textbooks. *Services and accommodations:* priority registration, alternative test arrangements, readers, note-takers, and scribes.

ADD/ADHD Students with ADD/ADHD are eligible for the same services available to students with LD, as well as distraction-free study areas and distraction-free testing environments.

Application *Required:* high school transcript, interview, psychoeducational report (3 years old or less), and documentation of high school services (e.g., Individualized Education Program [IEP] or 504 plan). Upon application, documentation of need for special services should be sent only to admissions. Upon acceptance, documentation of need for special services should be sent only to your LD program or unit. *Application deadline (institutional):* rolling/continuous for fall and rolling/continuous for spring. *Application deadline (LD program):* rolling/continuous for fall and rolling/continuous for spring.

LD program contact Keith Bos, Student Needs Coordinator, 123 Illinois Route 2, Dixon, IL 61021. *Phone:* 815-288-5511 Ext. 246. *E-mail:* bosk@succ.edu.

Application contact Sauk Valley Community College, 173 Illinois Route 2, Dixon, IL 61021. *Web address:* http://www.svcc.edu/.

SEMINOLE COMMUNITY COLLEGE

Sanford, Florida

Students with LD Served by Program	100	ADD/ADHD Services	✓
Staff	2 full-time, 1 part-time	Summer Preparation Program	n/a
LD Program or Service Fee	n/a	Alternative Test Arrangements	✓
LD Program Began	1983	LD Student Organization	✓

Disability Support Services began offering services in 1983. The program serves approximately 100 undergraduate students. Faculty consists of 2 full-time staff members and 1 part-time staff member. Services are provided by academic advisers, counselors, remediation/learning specialists, diagnostic specialists, and trained peer tutors.

Policies The college has written policies regarding course substitutions. 6 credits per semester are required to be eligible for financial aid.

Subject-area tutoring Available in most subjects. Offered one-on-one by trained peer tutors.

Counseling and advisement Academic advisement by a staff member affiliated with the program is available.

Auxiliary aids and services *Aids:* calculators, personal spelling/word-use assistants (e.g., Franklin Speller), scan and read programs (e.g., Kurzweil), screen-enlarging programs, screen readers, speech recognition programs (e.g., Dragon), tape recorders, taped textbooks. *Services and accommodations:* alternative test arrangements, note-takers, and scribes.

Student organization There is a student organization for students with LD.

ADD/ADHD Students with ADD/ADHD are eligible for the same services available to students with LD, as well as distraction-free testing environments.

Application *Required:* high school transcript, separate application to your LD program or unit, psychoeducational report (3 years old or less), and ACT, SAT I, or CPT. *Recommended:* documentation of high school services (e.g., Individualized Education Program [IEP] or 504 plan). Upon application, documentation of need for special services should be sent only to your LD program or unit. Upon acceptance, documentation of need for special services should be sent only to your LD program or unit. *Application deadline (institutional):* rolling/continuous for fall and rolling/continuous for spring. *Application deadline (LD program):* rolling/continuous for fall and rolling/continuous for spring.

LD program contact Dottie Paishon, Coordinator, 100 Weldon Boulevard, Sanford, FL 32773-6199. *Phone:* 407-328-2109. *Fax:* 407-328-2139. *E-mail:* paishond@mail.seminole.cc.fl.us.

Application contact Seminole Community College, 100 Weldon Boulevard, Sanford, FL 32773-6199. *Web address:* http://www.seminole.cc.fl.us/.

SINCLAIR COMMUNITY COLLEGE
Dayton, Ohio

Students with LD Served by Program	250	ADD/ADHD Services	✓
Staff	2 full-time, 1 part-time	Summer Preparation Program	n/a
LD Program or Service Fee	n/a	Alternative Test Arrangements	✓
LD Program Began	1990	LD Student Organization	n/a

Office of Disability Services began offering services in 1990. The program serves approximately 250 undergraduate students. Faculty consists of 2 full-time staff members and 1 part-time staff member. Services are provided by counselors.

Policies The college has written policies regarding course substitutions and grade forgiveness.

Special preparation or orientation Optional orientation held during summer prior to enrollment.

Basic skills remediation Available in study skills, computer skills, time management, and learning strategies. Offered one-on-one by regular education teachers, trained peer tutors, and counselor, adaptive equipment technician.

Subject-area tutoring Available in most subjects. Offered one-on-one and in small groups by computer-based instruction and trained peer tutors.

Special courses Available in career planning, study skills, reading, vocabulary development, math, and written composition skills. All courses are offered for credit; some enter into overall grade point average.

Counseling and advisement Career counseling and individual counseling are available.

Auxiliary aids and services *Aids:* calculators, personal computers, personal spelling/word-use assistants (e.g., Franklin Speller), scan and read programs (e.g., Kurzweil), screen-enlarging programs, screen readers, speech recognition programs (e.g., Dragon), tape recorders. *Services and accommodations:* advocates, alternative test arrangements, readers, note-takers, and scribes.

ADD/ADHD Students with ADD/ADHD are eligible for the same services available to students with LD, as well as distraction-free study areas and distraction-free testing environments.

Application *Required:* high school transcript, separate application to your LD program or unit, psychoeducational report (3 years old or less), and intake interview. *Recommended:* documentation of high school services (e.g., Individualized Educa-

tion Program [IEP] or 504 plan). Upon application, documentation of need for special services should be sent only to your LD program or unit. Upon acceptance, documentation of need for special services should be sent only to your LD program or unit. *Application deadline (institutional):* rolling/continuous for fall and rolling/continuous for spring.

LD program contact Brenda Bruggeman, Counselor, Office of Disability Services, 444 West Third Street, Dayton, OH 45402-1460. *Phone:* 937-512-5113. *E-mail:* bbruggem@sinclair.edu.

Application contact Sinclair Community College, 444 West Third Street, Dayton, OH 45402-1460. *E-mail:* ssmith@sinclair.edu. *Web address:* http://www.sinclair.edu/.

SOUTH ARKANSAS COMMUNITY COLLEGE
El Dorado, Arkansas

Students with LD Served by Program	8	ADD/ADHD Services	✓
Staff	1 part-time	Summer Preparation Program	n/a
LD Program or Service Fee	n/a	Alternative Test Arrangements	✓
LD Program Began	1997	LD Student Organization	n/a

Student Support Services began offering services in 1997. The program serves approximately 8 undergraduate students. Faculty consists of 1 part-time staff member. Services are provided by academic advisers, regular education teachers, counselors, remediation/learning specialists, and LD specialists.

Policies Students with LD may take up to 18 credit hours per semester; 12 credit hours per semester are required to maintain full-time status; 6 credit hours per semester are required to be eligible for financial aid.

Basic skills remediation Available in study skills, reading, time management, and math. Offered one-on-one and in small groups by computer-based instruction, regular education teachers, and LD specialists.

Subject-area tutoring Available in all subjects. Offered one-on-one and in small groups by computer-based instruction, professional tutors, and LD specialists.

Counseling and advisement Career counseling, individual counseling, small-group counseling, and support groups are available. Academic advisement by a staff member affiliated with the program is available.

Auxiliary aids and services *Services and accommodations:* advocates, alternative test arrangements, readers, note-takers, and scribes.

ADD/ADHD Students with ADD/ADHD are eligible for the same services available to students with LD

Application *Required:* high school transcript, ACT or SAT I (extended-time or untimed test accepted), psychoeducational report, and documentation of high school services (e.g., Individualized Education Program [IEP] or 504 plan). *Recommended:* participation in extracurricular activities. Upon acceptance, documentation of need for special services should be sent only to your LD program or unit. *Application deadline (institutional):* rolling/continuous for fall and rolling/continuous for spring. *Application deadline (LD program):* rolling/continuous for fall and rolling/continuous for spring.

LD program contact Elizabeth Dugal, Counselor/Coordinator, PO Box 7010, El Dorado, AR 71731-7010. *Phone:* 870-862-8131. *Fax:* 870-864-7109. *E-mail:* edugal@southark.cc.ar.us.

Application contact South Arkansas Community College, PO Box 7010, El Dorado, AR 71731-7010. *E-mail:* admissions@fox.saccw.cc.ar.us. *Web address:* http://seminole.saccw.cc.ar.us/.

SOUTHEASTERN COMMUNITY COLLEGE

Whiteville, North Carolina

Students with LD Served by Program	10	ADD/ADHD Services	✓
Staff	1 part-time	Summer Preparation Program	n/a
LD Program or Service Fee	n/a	Alternative Test Arrangements	n/a
LD Program Began	1990	LD Student Organization	✓

Counseling/Admissions Department began offering services in 1990. The program serves approximately 10 undergraduate students. Faculty consists of 1 part-time staff member. Services are provided by counselors and trained peer tutors.

Policies 12 semester hours per semester are required to maintain full-time status.

Subject-area tutoring Available in some subjects. Offered one-on-one by computer-based instruction and trained peer tutors.

Auxiliary aids and services *Aids:* calculators, personal computers, screen-enlarging programs, tape recorders, taped textbooks.

Student organization There is a student organization for students with LD.

ADD/ADHD Students with ADD/ADHD are eligible for the same services available to students with LD, as well as distraction-free testing environments.

Application *Required:* high school transcript and psychoeducational report (3 years old or less). *Recommended:* documentation of high school services (e.g., Individualized Education Program [IEP] or 504 plan). Upon application, documentation of need for special services should be sent only to your LD program or unit. Upon acceptance, documentation of need for special services should be sent only to your LD program or unit. *Application deadline (institutional):* rolling/continuous for fall and rolling/continuous for spring. *Application deadline (LD program):* rolling/continuous for fall and rolling/continuous for spring.

LD program contact Sharon Jarvis, Counselor, PO Box 151, Whiteville, NC 28472. *Phone:* 910-642-7141. *Fax:* 910-642-5658. *E-mail:* s.jarvis@mail.southeast.ce.nc.us.

Application contact Linda Nelms, Coordinator of Student Records, Southeastern Community College, PO Box 151, Whiteville, NC 28472-0151. *Phone:* 910-642-7141 Ext. 264. *Web address:* http://www.southeastern.cc.nc.us/.

SOUTHERN MAINE TECHNICAL COLLEGE

South Portland, Maine

Students with LD Served by Program	60	ADD/ADHD Services	✓
Staff	3 full-time	Summer Preparation Program	n/a
LD Program or Service Fee	n/a	Alternative Test Arrangements	✓
LD Program Began	1989	LD Student Organization	n/a

Learning Assistance began offering services in 1989. The program serves approximately 60 undergraduate students. Faculty consists of 3 full-time staff members. Services are provided by professional tutors.

Policies Students with LD may take up to 18 credit hours per semester; 12 credit hours per semester are required to maintain full-time status and to be eligible for financial aid.

Basic skills remediation Available in study skills, reading, learning strategies, and written language. Offered in class-size groups by regular education teachers.

Subject-area tutoring Available in most subjects. Offered one-on-one by professional tutors.

Auxiliary aids and services *Aids:* scan and read programs (e.g., Kurzweil), screen readers, speech recognition programs (e.g., Dragon), tape recorders. *Services and accommodations:* alternative test arrangements, readers, note-takers, and scribes.

ADD/ADHD Students with ADD/ADHD are eligible for the same services available to students with LD, as well as distraction-free testing environments.

Application *Required:* high school transcript, ACT or SAT I (extended-time tests accepted), and personal statement. *Recommended:* interview, letter(s) of recommendation, and documentation of high school services (e.g., Individualized Education Program [IEP] or 504 plan). Upon application, documentation of need for special services should be sent only to your LD program or unit. Upon acceptance, documentation of need for special services should be sent only to your LD program or unit. *Application deadline (institutional):* rolling/continuous for fall and rolling/continuous for spring. *Application deadline (LD program):* rolling/continuous for fall and rolling/continuous for spring.

LD program contact Mark Krogman, ADA Coordinator, 2 Fort Road, South Portland, ME 04106. *E-mail:* mkrogman@smtc.net.

Application contact Robert A. Weimont, Director of Admissions, Southern Maine Technical College, Fort Road, South Portland, ME 04106. *Phone:* 207-767-9520. *Web address:* http://www.smtc.net/.

SOUTHERN WEST VIRGINIA COMMUNITY AND TECHNICAL COLLEGE

Mount Gay, West Virginia

Students with LD Served by Program	20	ADD/ADHD Services	✓
Staff	1 full-time	Summer Preparation Program	n/a
LD Program or Service Fee	n/a	Alternative Test Arrangements	✓
LD Program Began	1991	LD Student Organization	n/a

Horizons, Disabled Student Services began offering services in 1991. The program serves approximately 20 undergraduate students. Faculty consists of 1 full-time staff member.

Auxiliary aids and services *Aids:* calculators, scan and read programs (e.g., Kurzweil), screen-enlarging programs, speech recognition programs (e.g., Dragon), tape recorders, taped textbooks. *Services and accommodations:* advocates, alternative test arrangements, readers, note-takers, and scribes.

ADD/ADHD Students with ADD/ADHD are eligible for the same services available to students with LD, as well as distraction-free testing environments.

Application *Required:* high school transcript, ACT (extended-time or untimed test accepted), and psychoeducational report. *Recommended:* documentation of high school services (e.g., Individualized Education Program [IEP] or 504 plan). Upon acceptance, documentation of need for special services should be sent only to your LD program or unit.

LD program contact Sherry Dempsey, Program Manager, PO Box 2900, Mount Gay, WV 25637. *Phone:* 304-792-7098. *Fax:* 304-792-7113. *E-mail:* sherryd@southern.wvnet.edu.

Application contact Southern West Virginia Community and Technical College, PO Box 2900, Mount Gay, WV 25637-2900. *E-mail:* admissions@southern.wvnet.edu. *Web address:* http://www.southern.wvnet.edu/.

SOUTH PLAINS COLLEGE
Levelland, Texas

Students with LD Served by Program	70	ADD/ADHD Services	✓
Staff	2 full-time	Summer Preparation Program	n/a
LD Program or Service Fee	n/a	Alternative Test Arrangements	✓
LD Program Began	n/a	LD Student Organization	n/a

Special Services serves approximately 70 undergraduate students. Faculty consists of 2 full-time staff members. Services are provided by academic advisers, counselors, and trained peer tutors.
Policies Students with LD may take up to 18 credit hours per semester; 12 credit hours per semester are required to maintain full-time status; 6 credit hours per semester are required to be eligible for financial aid.
Diagnostic testing Available for intelligence, reading, written language, and math.
Basic skills remediation Available in reading, written language, and math. Offered in class-size groups by regular education teachers.
Subject-area tutoring Available in most subjects. Offered one-on-one and in small groups by trained peer tutors.
Special courses Available in study skills, reading, learning strategies, vocabulary development, math, and written composition skills. All courses are offered for credit; some enter into overall grade point average.
Counseling and advisement Career counseling and individual counseling are available. Academic advisement by a staff member affiliated with the program is available.
Auxiliary aids and services *Aids:* calculators, personal computers, personal spelling/word-use assistants (e.g., Franklin Speller), screen-enlarging programs, screen readers, tape recorders, taped textbooks. *Services and accommodations:* priority registration, alternative test arrangements, readers, note-takers, and scribes.
ADD/ADHD Students with ADD/ADHD are eligible for the same services available to students with LD, as well as distraction-free study areas and distraction-free testing environments.
Application *Required:* high school transcript and psychoeducational report (3 years old or less). *Recommended:* documentation of high school services (e.g., Individualized Education Program [IEP] or 504 plan). Upon application, documentation of need for special services should be sent only to your LD program or unit. Upon acceptance, documentation of need for special services should be sent only to your LD program or unit. *Application deadline (institutional):* rolling/continuous for fall and rolling/continuous for spring. *Application deadline (LD program):* rolling/continuous for fall and rolling/continuous for spring.
LD program contact Julie Towe, Special Services Coordinator, Box 171, 1401 College Avenue, Levelland, TX 79336. *Phone:* 806-894-9611 Ext. 2529. *Fax:* 806-894-5274. *E-mail:* jtowe@spc.cc.tx.us.
Application contact South Plains College, 1401 South College Avenue, Levelland, TX 79336-6595. *E-mail:* bjames@spc.cc.tx.us. *Web address:* http://www.spc.cc.tx.us/.

SOUTHWESTERN COLLEGE
Chula Vista, California

Students with LD Served by Program	300	ADD/ADHD Services	n/a
Staff	3 full-time	Summer Preparation Program	✓
LD Program or Service Fee	n/a	Alternative Test Arrangements	✓
LD Program Began	1976	LD Student Organization	✓

Disability Support Services began offering services in 1976. The program serves approximately 300 undergraduate students. Faculty consists of 3 full-time staff members. Services are provided by counselors, diagnostic specialists, and LD specialists.
Fees *Diagnostic Testing Fee:* $6.50.
Special preparation or orientation Optional summer program offered prior to entering college. Optional orientation held before registration, after classes begin, and during summer prior to enrollment.
Diagnostic testing Available for intelligence, reading, written language, and math.
Basic skills remediation Available in auditory processing, study skills, time management, learning strategies, spelling, and math. Offered in class-size groups by computer-based instruction and LD specialists.
Subject-area tutoring Available in some subjects. Offered in small groups.
Special courses Available in career planning, college survival skills, reading, learning strategies, math, and written composition skills. All courses are offered for credit; all enter into overall grade point average.
Counseling and advisement Individual counseling is available.
Auxiliary aids and services *Aids:* personal computers, personal spelling/word-use assistants (e.g., Franklin Speller), scan and read programs (e.g., Kurzweil), screen-enlarging programs, screen readers, speech recognition programs (e.g., Dragon), tape recorders, taped textbooks, Alphpro Smart. *Services and accommodations:* priority registration, alternative test arrangements, readers, note-takers, and scribes.
Student organization There is a student organization for students with LD.
Application *Required:* high school transcript, separate application to your LD program or unit, psychoeducational report (3 years old or less), and documentation of high school services (e.g., Individualized Education Program [IEP] or 504 plan). Upon application, documentation of need for special services should be sent only to your LD program or unit. Upon acceptance, documentation of need for special services should be sent only to your LD program or unit. *Application deadline (institutional):* rolling/continuous for fall and rolling/continuous for spring. *Application deadline (LD program):* rolling/continuous for fall and rolling/continuous for spring.
LD program contact Disability Support Services, 900 Otay Lakes Road, Chula Vista, CA 91910. *Phone:* 619-421-6700. *Fax:* 619-482-6512.
Application contact Georgia Copeland, Director of Admissions and Records, Southwestern College, 900 Otay Lakes Road, Chula Vista, CA 91910-7299. *Phone:* 619-482-6306. *Web address:* http://www.swc.cc.ca.us/.

SOUTHWESTERN MICHIGAN COLLEGE

Dowagiac, Michigan

Students with LD Served by Program	50	ADD/ADHD Services	✓
Staff	1 full-time, 1 part-time	Summer Preparation Program	n/a
LD Program or Service Fee	n/a	Alternative Test Arrangements	✓
LD Program Began	1984	LD Student Organization	n/a

Special Needs Office began offering services in 1984. The program serves approximately 50 undergraduate students. Faculty consists of 1 full-time and 1 part-time staff member. Services are provided by Special Needs staff.

Policies 12 credit hours per semester are required to maintain full-time status; 3 credit hours per semester are required to be eligible for financial aid.

Diagnostic testing Available for reading, written language, and math.

Basic skills remediation Available in study skills, reading, learning strategies, written language, and math. Offered in class-size groups by regular education teachers.

Subject-area tutoring Available in most subjects. Offered one-on-one and in small groups by graduate assistants/students.

Counseling and advisement Career counseling and individual counseling are available.

Auxiliary aids and services *Aids:* tape recorders, taped textbooks. *Services and accommodations:* alternative test arrangements and note-takers.

ADD/ADHD Students with ADD/ADHD are eligible for the same services available to students with LD

Application *Required:* high school transcript and evidence of learning disabilities. Upon acceptance, documentation of need for special services should be sent only to your LD program or unit. *Application deadline (institutional):* 9/1 for fall and 1/1 for spring.

LD program contact Linda Mangus, Special Needs Coordinator, 58900 Cherry Grove Road, Dowagiac, MI 49047-9793. *Phone:* 616-782-1312. *Fax:* 616-782-8414. *E-mail:* lmangus@smc.cc.mi.us.

Application contact Southwestern Michigan College, 58900 Cherry Grove Road, Dowagiac, MI 49047-9793. *E-mail:* cchurch@smc.cc.mi.us. *Web address:* http://www.smc.cc.mi.us/.

SOUTHWESTERN OREGON COMMUNITY COLLEGE

Coos Bay, Oregon

Students with LD Served by Program	140	ADD/ADHD Services	✓
Staff	1 full-time	Summer Preparation Program	n/a
LD Program or Service Fee	n/a	Alternative Test Arrangements	✓
LD Program Began	1989	LD Student Organization	n/a

Disability Student Services Office began offering services in 1989. The program serves approximately 140 undergraduate students. Faculty consists of 1 full-time staff member. Services are provided by counselors, remediation/learning specialists, trained peer tutors, and professional tutors.

Policies The college has written policies regarding substitution and waivers of requirements for admission.

Special preparation or orientation Required orientation held before registration, before classes begin, and individually by special arrangement.

Basic skills remediation Available in motor skills, study skills, computer skills, reading, time management, social skills, visual processing, learning strategies, spelling, written language, math, and spoken language. Offered one-on-one and in small groups by computer-based instruction, LD specialists, professional tutors, and trained peer tutors.

Subject-area tutoring Available in all subjects. Offered one-on-one and in small groups by computer-based instruction, professional tutors, and trained peer tutors.

Counseling and advisement Career counseling, individual counseling, small-group counseling, and support groups are available.

Auxiliary aids and services *Aids:* calculators, personal computers, scan and read programs (e.g., Kurzweil), screen-enlarging programs, screen readers, speech recognition programs (e.g., Dragon), tape recorders, taped textbooks. *Services and accommodations:* advocates, alternative test arrangements, readers, note-takers, and scribes.

ADD/ADHD Students with ADD/ADHD are eligible for the same services available to students with LD, as well as distraction-free study areas and distraction-free testing environments.

Application *Required:* interview, personal statement, psycho-educational report (3 years old or less), and documentation of high school services (e.g., Individualized Education Program [IEP] or 504 plan). *Recommended:* high school transcript, participation in extracurricular activities, ACT (extended-time test accepted), SAT I (extended-time test accepted), and letter(s) of recommendation. Upon application, documentation of need for special services should be sent only to your LD program or unit. Upon acceptance, documentation of need for special services should be sent to both admissions and your LD program or unit. *Application deadline (institutional):* rolling/continuous for fall and rolling/continuous for spring. *Application deadline (LD program):* rolling/continuous for fall and rolling/continuous for spring.

LD program contact Hunter Fales, ADA Coordinator, 1988 Newmark, Coos Bay, OR 97420. *Phone:* 541-888-7349. *Fax:* 541-888-7227. *E-mail:* hfales@southwestern.cc.or.us.

Application contact Southwestern Oregon Community College, 1988 Newmark Avenue, Coos Bay, OR 97420-2912. *Web address:* http://www.southwestern.cc.or.us/.

SOUTHWEST MISSOURI STATE UNIVERSITY-WEST PLAINS

West Plains, Missouri

Students with LD Served by Program	6	ADD/ADHD Services	✓
Staff	4 full-time	Summer Preparation Program	n/a
LD Program or Service Fee	n/a	Alternative Test Arrangements	✓
LD Program Began	n/a	LD Student Organization	n/a

Academic Support Center serves approximately 6 undergraduate students. Faculty consists of 4 full-time staff members. Services are provided by academic advisers, remediation/learning specialists, and professional tutors.

Policies Students with LD may take up to 18 credit hours per semester; 12 credit hours per semester are required to maintain full-time status; 6 credit hours per term are required to be eligible for financial aid.

Basic skills remediation Offered one-on-one by LD specialists.

Subject-area tutoring Available in most subjects. Offered one-on-one by computer-based instruction, professional tutors, and trained peer tutors.

Counseling and advisement Academic advisement by a staff member affiliated with the program is available.

Auxiliary aids and services *Aids:* scan and read programs (e.g., Kurzweil), screen-enlarging programs, screen readers, tape recorders, taped textbooks. *Services and accommodations:* priority registration, alternative test arrangements, readers, note-takers, and scribes.

ADD/ADHD Students with ADD/ADHD are eligible for the same services available to students with LD, as well as distraction-free study areas and distraction-free testing environments.

Application *Required:* high school transcript, ACT (extended-time or untimed test accepted), separate application to your LD program or unit, psychoeducational report (3 years old or less), and documentation of high school services (e.g., Individualized Education Program [IEP] or 504 plan). *Recommended:* participation in extracurricular activities, SAT I, and interview. Upon application, documentation of need for special services should be sent only to your LD program or unit. Upon acceptance, documentation of need for special services should be sent only to your LD program or unit.

LD program contact Janice Johnson, Academic Support Coordinator, 128 Garfield, West Plains, MO 65775. *Phone:* 417-257-1400. *Fax:* 417-256-2303. *E-mail:* jjohnson@wp.smsu.edu.

Application contact Melissa Jett, Admissions Assistant, Southwest Missouri State University-West Plains, 128 Garfield, West Plains, MO 65775. *Phone:* 417-255-7955. *E-mail:* ash862t@nic.smsu.edu. *Web address:* http://www.wp.smsu.edu/.

SOUTHWEST WISCONSIN TECHNICAL COLLEGE
Fennimore, Wisconsin

Students with LD Served by Program	30	ADD/ADHD Services	✓
Staff	3 full-time, 1 part-time	Summer Preparation Program	n/a
LD Program or Service Fee	n/a	Alternative Test Arrangements	✓
LD Program Began	1980	LD Student Organization	n/a

Special Populations Support Center began offering services in 1980. The program serves approximately 30 undergraduate students. Faculty consists of 3 full-time staff members and 1 part-time staff member. Services are provided by regular education teachers, remediation/learning specialists, LD specialists, and professional tutors.

Policies The college has written policies regarding course substitutions and substitution and waivers of requirements for admission and graduation. Students with LD may take up to 18 credits per semester; 12 credits per semester are required to maintain full-time status; 3 credits per semester are required to be eligible for financial aid.

Basic skills remediation Available in study skills, reading, learning strategies, spelling, written language, math, and spoken language. Offered one-on-one by computer-based instruction, regular education teachers, and special education teachers.

Subject-area tutoring Available in all subjects. Offered one-on-one and in small groups by trained peer tutors.

Special courses Available in study skills, college survival skills, and learning strategies. All courses are offered for credit; all enter into overall grade point average.

Auxiliary aids and services *Aids:* calculators, personal computers, personal spelling/word-use assistants (e.g., Franklin Speller), scan and read programs (e.g., Kurzweil), screen-enlarging programs, screen readers, speech recognition programs (e.g., Dragon), tape recorders, taped textbooks. *Services and accommodations:* advocates, alternative test arrangements, readers, note-takers, scribes, and assistance with financial aid forms.

ADD/ADHD Students with ADD/ADHD are eligible for the same services available to students with LD, as well as distraction-free study areas, distraction-free testing environments and personal coach or mentors.

Application *Required:* high school transcript, interview, personal statement, psychoeducational report, documentation of high school services (e.g., Individualized Education Program [IEP] or 504 plan), and college transition profile. Upon application, documentation of need for special services should be sent only to your LD program or unit. Upon acceptance, documentation of need for special services should be sent only to your LD program or unit. *Application deadline (institutional):* rolling/continuous for fall and rolling/continuous for spring.

LD program contact Alan Propst, Special Services Coordinator, 1800 Bronson Boulevard, Building 100, Room 108, Fennimore, WI 53809. *Phone:* 800-362-3322 Ext. 2130. *Fax:* 608-822-6019. *E-mail:* apropst@southwest.tec.wi.us.

Application contact Kathy Kreul, Admissions, Southwest Wisconsin Technical College, 1800 Bronson Boulevard, Fennimore, WI 53809-9778. *Phone:* 608-822-3262 Ext. 2355. *Web address:* http://www.southwest.tec.wi.us/.

SPOKANE COMMUNITY COLLEGE
Spokane, Washington

Students with LD Served by Program	115	ADD/ADHD Services	✓
Staff	9 full-time, 1 part-time	Summer Preparation Program	n/a
LD Program or Service Fee	n/a	Alternative Test Arrangements	✓
LD Program Began	n/a	LD Student Organization	n/a

Disabled Student Services serves approximately 115 undergraduate students. Faculty consists of 9 full-time staff members and 1 part-time staff member. Services are provided by academic advisers, regular education teachers, counselors, remediation/learning specialists, teacher trainees, and trained peer tutors.

Policies The college has written policies regarding course substitutions and substitution and waivers of requirements for admission. Students with LD may take up to 20 credits per quarter; 12 credits per quarter are required to maintain full-time status; 5 credits per quarter are required to be eligible for financial aid.

Special preparation or orientation Optional orientation held before registration, during registration, before classes begin, after classes begin, during summer prior to enrollment, and individually by special arrangement.

Diagnostic testing Available for study skills and learning strategies.

Basic skills remediation Available in study skills, computer skills, reading, time management, social skills, visual processing, learning strategies, spelling, written language, and math. Offered in class-size groups by regular education teachers and trained peer tutors.

Subject-area tutoring Available in some subjects. Offered one-on-one, in small groups, and class-size groups by trained peer tutors.

Counseling and advisement Career counseling, individual counseling, small-group counseling, and support groups are available. Academic advisement by a staff member affiliated with the program is available.

Auxiliary aids and services *Aids:* calculators, personal computers, personal spelling/word-use assistants (e.g., Franklin Speller), scan and read programs (e.g., Kurzweil), screen-enlarging programs, screen readers, speech recognition pro-

Spokane Community College (continued)

grams (e.g., Dragon), tape recorders, taped textbooks. *Services and accommodations:* advocates, alternative test arrangements, readers, and note-takers.

ADD/ADHD Students with ADD/ADHD are eligible for the same services available to students with LD, as well as distraction-free study areas and distraction-free testing environments.

Application *Required:* high school transcript, ACT (extended-time or untimed test accepted), and documentation of high school services (e.g., Individualized Education Program [IEP] or 504 plan). *Recommended:* participation in extracurricular activities and interview. Upon application, documentation of need for special services should be sent only to your LD program or unit. Upon acceptance, documentation of need for special services should be sent only to your LD program or unit. *Application deadline (institutional):* rolling/continuous for fall and rolling/continuous for spring. *Application deadline (LD program):* rolling/continuous for fall and rolling/continuous for spring.

LD program contact Richard A. Villalobos, Program Manager, 1810 North Greene Street, MS 2160, Spokane, WA 99217-5399. *Phone:* 509-533-7356. *Fax:* 509-533-8877. *E-mail:* rvillalobos@ scc.spokane.cc.wa.us.

Application contact Dan Chacon, Vice President of Student Services, Spokane Community College, 1810 North Greene Street, Spokane, WA 99217-5399. *Phone:* 509-533-7015. *Web address:* http://www.scc.spokane.cc.wa.us/.

SPRINGFIELD TECHNICAL COMMUNITY COLLEGE
Springfield, Massachusetts

Students with LD Served by Program	150	ADD/ADHD Services	✓
Staff	2 full-time	Summer Preparation Program	n/a
LD Program or Service Fee	n/a	Alternative Test Arrangements	✓
LD Program Began	1987	LD Student Organization	n/a

Office of Disability Services began offering services in 1987. The program serves approximately 150 undergraduate students. Faculty consists of 2 full-time staff members. Services are provided by LD specialists and accommodation specialists.

Policies The college has written policies regarding course substitutions. Students with LD may take up to 15 hours per semester; 6 hours per semester are required to maintain full-time status; 9 hours per semester are required to be eligible for financial aid.

Counseling and advisement Career counseling and advising are available.

Auxiliary aids and services *Aids:* calculators, personal spelling/word-use assistants (e.g., Franklin Speller), scan and read programs (e.g., Kurzweil), screen-enlarging programs, screen readers, speech recognition programs (e.g., Dragon), tape recorders, taped textbooks. *Services and accommodations:* priority registration, alternative test arrangements, readers, note-takers, and scribes.

ADD/ADHD Students with ADD/ADHD are eligible for the same services available to students with LD, as well as distraction-free testing environments.

Application *Required:* high school transcript, ACT or SAT I (extended-time or untimed test accepted), interview, and personal statement. Upon application, documentation of need for special services should be sent only to your LD program or unit. Upon acceptance, documentation of need for special services should be sent only to your LD program or unit. *Application*

deadline (institutional): rolling/continuous for fall and rolling/continuous for spring. *Application deadline (LD program):* rolling/continuous for fall and rolling/continuous for spring.

LD program contact Peter Shea, Learning Disabilities Specialist, 1 Amory Square, Springfield, MA 01101. *Phone:* 413-755-4474. *Fax:* 413-731-0978.

Application contact Springfield Technical Community College, 1 Armory Square, Springfield, MA 01105-1296. *Web address:* http://www.stcc.mass.edu/.

STARK STATE COLLEGE OF TECHNOLOGY
Canton, Ohio

Students with LD Served by Program	60	ADD/ADHD Services	✓
Staff	1 full-time	Summer Preparation Program	n/a
LD Program or Service Fee	n/a	Alternative Test Arrangements	✓
LD Program Began	1991	LD Student Organization	n/a

Disability Support Services (DSS) began offering services in 1991. The program serves approximately 60 undergraduate students. Faculty consists of 1 full-time staff member. Services are provided by DSS coordinator, faculty.

Policies 12 credit hours per semester are required to maintain full-time status.

Special preparation or orientation Held before classes begin.

Counseling and advisement Career counseling and individual counseling are available.

Auxiliary aids and services *Aids:* scan and read programs (e.g., Kurzweil), screen-enlarging programs, tape recorders, taped textbooks. *Services and accommodations:* alternative test arrangements, note-takers, and scribes.

ADD/ADHD Students with ADD/ADHD are eligible for the same services available to students with LD

Application *Required:* high school transcript, psychoeducational report (5 years old or less), and documentation of high school services (e.g., Individualized Education Program [IEP] or 504 plan). *Recommended:* ACT (extended-time test accepted) and SAT I (extended-time test accepted). Upon application, documentation of need for special services should be sent only to your LD program or unit. Upon acceptance, documentation of need for special services should be sent only to your LD program or unit. *Application deadline (institutional):* rolling/continuous for fall and rolling/continuous for spring. *Application deadline (LD program):* rolling/continuous for fall and rolling/continuous for spring.

LD program contact Karen A. Saracusa, Counselor/Coordinator, Disability Support Services, 6200 Frank Road, NW, Canton, OH 44720. *Phone:* 330-494-6170. *Fax:* 330-497-6313. *E-mail:* ksaracusa@ stark.cc.oh.us.

Application contact Wallace Hoffer, Dean of Student Services, Stark State College of Technology, 6200 Frank Avenue, NW, Canton, OH 44720-7299. *Phone:* 330-966-5450.

STATE TECHNICAL INSTITUTE AT MEMPHIS
Memphis, Tennessee

Students with LD Served by Program	200	ADD/ADHD Services	✓
Staff	5 full-time	Summer Preparation Program	n/a
LD Program or Service Fee	n/a	Alternative Test Arrangements	✓
LD Program Began	1973	LD Student Organization	n/a

Counseling Center began offering services in 1973. The program serves approximately 200 undergraduate students. Faculty consists of 5 full-time staff members. Services are provided by counselors and remediation/learning specialists.

Policies Students with LD may take up to 21 credit hours per semester; 12 credit hours per semester are required to maintain full-time status and to be eligible for financial aid.

Diagnostic testing Available for reading, written language, learning styles, math, and occupational, interests.

Basic skills remediation Available in study skills, reading, spelling, written language, and math. Offered in class-size groups by regular education teachers.

Subject-area tutoring Available in all subjects. Offered one-on-one by computer-based instruction, professional tutors, trained peer tutors, and videotapes.

Counseling and advisement Individual counseling is available.

Auxiliary aids and services *Aids:* screen-enlarging programs. *Services and accommodations:* alternative test arrangements, readers, note-takers, and scribes.

ADD/ADHD Students with ADD/ADHD are eligible for the same services available to students with LD

Application *Required:* high school transcript and ACT (extended-time or untimed test accepted). *Recommended:* psychoeducational report. Upon application, documentation of need for special services should be sent to both admissions and your LD program or unit.

LD program contact Maxine Ford5983 Macon Cove, Memphis, TN 38134. *Phone:* 901-333-4223. *Fax:* 901-333-4505. *E-mail:* mford@stim.tec.tn.us.

Application contact Vanessa Dowdy, Assistant Director of Recruiting, State Technical Institute at Memphis, 5983 Macon Cove, Memphis, TN 38134-7693. *Phone:* 901-383-4275. *E-mail:* jturner@stim.tec.tn.us. *Web address:* http://www.stim.tec.tn.us/.

STATE UNIVERSITY OF NEW YORK COLLEGE OF AGRICULTURE AND TECHNOLOGY AT MORRISVILLE
Morrisville, New York

Students with LD Served by Program	175	ADD/ADHD Services	✓
Staff	1 full-time	Summer Preparation Program	n/a
LD Program or Service Fee	n/a	Alternative Test Arrangements	✓
LD Program Began	n/a	LD Student Organization	n/a

Services for Students with Disabilities serves approximately 175 undergraduate students. Faculty consists of 1 full-time staff member. Services are provided by LD specialists and trained peer tutors.

Policies Students with LD may take up to 18 credit hours per semester; 12 credit hours per semester are required to maintain full-time status and to be eligible for financial aid.

Special preparation or orientation Held during registration, before classes begin, and individually by special arrangement.

Subject-area tutoring Available in most subjects. Offered one-on-one and in small groups by trained peer tutors and LD specialists.

Auxiliary aids and services *Aids:* personal computers, scan and read programs (e.g., Kurzweil), screen-enlarging programs, tape recorders. *Services and accommodations:* advocates, alternative test arrangements, and note-takers.

ADD/ADHD Students with ADD/ADHD are eligible for the same services available to students with LD, as well as distraction-free study areas and distraction-free testing environments.

Application *Required:* high school transcript. *Recommended:* participation in extracurricular activities, ACT or SAT I (extended-time tests accepted), interview, personal statement, and letter(s) of recommendation. Upon acceptance, documentation of need for special services should be sent only to your LD program or unit. *Application deadline (institutional):* 11/1 for fall and 11/1 for spring.

LD program contact David A. Symonds, Disability Specialist, College Skills Center, Morrisville, NY 13408. *Phone:* 315-684-6042. *Fax:* 315-684-6350.

Application contact State University of New York College of Agriculture and Technology at Morrisville, PO Box 901, Morrisville, NY 13408-0901. *E-mail:* admitor@snymorva.cs.snymor.edu. *Web address:* http://www.morrisville.edu/.

STATE UNIVERSITY OF NEW YORK COLLEGE OF TECHNOLOGY AT ALFRED
Alfred, New York

Students with LD Served by Program	350	ADD/ADHD Services	✓
Staff	2 full-time	Summer Preparation Program	n/a
LD Program or Service Fee	n/a	Alternative Test Arrangements	✓
LD Program Began	1980	LD Student Organization	n/a

Services for Students with Disabilities began offering services in 1980. The program serves approximately 350 undergraduate students. Faculty consists of 2 full-time staff members. Services are provided by academic advisers, counselors, LD specialists, and trained peer tutors.

Special preparation or orientation Optional orientation held during summer prior to enrollment and individually by special arrangement.

Subject-area tutoring Available in most subjects. Offered one-on-one and in small groups by trained peer tutors.

Counseling and advisement Career counseling, individual counseling, and small-group counseling are available. Academic advisement by a staff member affiliated with the program is available.

Auxiliary aids and services *Aids:* calculators, personal spelling/word-use assistants (e.g., Franklin Speller), scan and read programs (e.g., Kurzweil), screen-enlarging programs, tape recorders, taped textbooks. *Services and accommodations:* advocates, priority registration, alternative test arrangements, readers, note-takers, and scribes.

ADD/ADHD Students with ADD/ADHD are eligible for the same services available to students with LD, as well as distraction-free testing environments.

Application *Required:* high school transcript, psychoeducational report (5 years old or less), and documentation of high school services (e.g., Individualized Education Program [IEP] or 504 plan). *Recommended:* participation in extracurricular activities, ACT or SAT I (extended-time tests accepted), interview, and letter(s) of recommendation. Upon application, documentation

State University of New York College of Technology at Alfred (continued)
of need for special services should be sent only to your LD program or unit. Upon acceptance, documentation of need for special services should be sent only to your LD program or unit. *Application deadline (institutional):* rolling/continuous for fall and rolling/continuous for spring.

LD program contact Heather Meacham, Counselor, Services for Students with Disabilities, Student Development Center, Alfred, NY 14802. *Phone:* 607-587-4506. *Fax:* 607-587-3210. *E-mail:* meachamh@alfredtech.edu.

Application contact State University of New York College of Technology at Alfred, Alfred, NY 14802. *E-mail:* admissions@asc. alfredtech.edu. *Web address:* http://www.alfredtech.edu/.

STATE UNIVERSITY OF NEW YORK COLLEGE OF TECHNOLOGY AT DELHI
Delhi, New York

Students with LD Served by Program	175	ADD/ADHD Services	✓
Staff	1 full-time, 8 part-time	Summer Preparation Program	n/a
LD Program or Service Fee	n/a	Alternative Test Arrangements	✓
LD Program Began	1992	LD Student Organization	n/a

Services for Students with Disabilities began offering services in 1992. The program serves approximately 175 undergraduate students. Faculty consists of 1 full-time and 8 part-time staff members. Services are provided by counselors, LD specialists, trained peer tutors, and professional tutors.
Policies The college has written policies regarding course substitutions. Students with LD may take up to 18 credit hours per semester; 9 credit hours per semester are required to maintain full-time status; 12 credit hours per semester are required to be eligible for financial aid.
Special preparation or orientation Required orientation held before registration and before classes begin.
Basic skills remediation Available in study skills, computer skills, reading, time management, social skills, learning strategies, spelling, written language, and math. Offered one-on-one and in small groups by LD specialists, professional tutors, and trained peer tutors.
Subject-area tutoring Available in most subjects. Offered one-on-one and in small groups by professional tutors, trained peer tutors, and LD specialists.
Special courses Available in college survival skills, reading, learning strategies, math, and stress management. Some courses are offered for credit; most enter into overall grade point average.
Counseling and advisement Career counseling and individual counseling are available.
Auxiliary aids and services *Aids:* calculators, personal computers, personal spelling/word-use assistants (e.g., Franklin Speller), scan and read programs (e.g., Kurzweil), screen-enlarging programs, tape recorders, taped textbooks. *Services and accommodations:* advocates, alternative test arrangements, readers, note-takers, and scribes.
ADD/ADHD Students with ADD/ADHD are eligible for the same services available to students with LD, as well as distraction-free testing environments, medication management and personal coach or mentors.
Application *Required:* high school transcript, psychoeducational report (3 years old or less), and documentation of high school services (e.g., Individualized Education Program [IEP] or 504 plan). *Recommended:* interview. Upon application, documentation of need for special services should be sent only to your LD

program or unit. Upon acceptance, documentation of need for special services should be sent only to your LD program or unit. *Application deadline (institutional):* rolling/continuous for fall and rolling/continuous for spring. *Application deadline (LD program):* rolling/continuous for fall and rolling/continuous for spring.

LD program contact George E. Irwin, Coordinator, 341 Bush Hall, Delhi, NY 13753. *Phone:* 607-746-4593. *Fax:* 607-746-4368. *E-mail:* irwinge@delhi.edu.

Application contact Chris Tacea, Director of Admissions, State University of New York College of Technology at Delhi, Main Street, Delhi, NY 13753. *Phone:* 607-746-4550. *Web address:* http://www.delhi.edu/.

TACOMA COMMUNITY COLLEGE
Tacoma, Washington

Students with LD Served by Program	350	ADD/ADHD Services	✓
Staff	1 full-time, 3 part-time	Summer Preparation Program	n/a
LD Program or Service Fee	n/a	Alternative Test Arrangements	✓
LD Program Began	1993	LD Student Organization	n/a

Disability Services began offering services in 1993. The program serves approximately 350 undergraduate students. Faculty consists of 1 full-time and 3 part-time staff members. Services are provided by academic advisers, regular education teachers, counselors, graduate assistants/students, trained peer tutors, and professional tutors.
Policies Students with LD may take up to 15 credit hours per quarter; 12 credit hours per quarter are required to maintain full-time status; 6 credit hours per quarter are required to be eligible for financial aid. LD services are also available to graduate students.
Counseling and advisement Career counseling and individual counseling are available. Academic advisement by a staff member affiliated with the program is available.
Auxiliary aids and services *Aids:* scan and read programs (e.g., Kurzweil), screen-enlarging programs, screen readers, speech recognition programs (e.g., Dragon), tape recorders, taped textbooks. *Services and accommodations:* advocates, priority registration, alternative test arrangements, readers, note-takers, and scribes.
ADD/ADHD Students with ADD/ADHD are eligible for the same services available to students with LD, as well as distraction-free study areas and distraction-free testing environments.
Application Upon application, documentation of need for special services should be sent only to your LD program or unit. Upon acceptance, documentation of need for special services should be sent only to your LD program or unit. *Application deadline (institutional):* 9/25 for fall and 4/3 for spring. *Application deadline (LD program):* rolling/continuous for fall and rolling/continuous for spring.

LD program contact Kirsten Vallier, Accommodations Coordinator, 6501 South 19th Street, Building #18, Tacoma, WA 98466. *Phone:* 253-566-5338. *Fax:* 253-566-6011. *E-mail:* kvallier@tcc. tacoma.ctc.edu.

Application contact Annette Hayward, Admissions Officer, Tacoma Community College, 6501 South 19th Street, Tacoma, WA 98466. *Phone:* 253-566-5108. *E-mail:* ahayward@msmail. tacoma.ctc.edu. *Web address:* http://www.tacoma.ctc.edu/.

TALLAHASSEE COMMUNITY COLLEGE

Tallahassee, Florida

Students with LD Served by Program	460	ADD/ADHD Services	✓
Staff	2 full-time, 7 part-time	Summer Preparation Program	n/a
LD Program or Service Fee	n/a	Alternative Test Arrangements	✓
LD Program Began	1982	LD Student Organization	n/a

Disability Support Services (DSS) began offering services in 1982. The program serves approximately 460 undergraduate students. Faculty consists of 2 full-time and 7 part-time staff members. Services are provided by academic advisers, counselors, graduate assistants/students, and trained peer tutors.

Policies The college has written policies regarding course substitutions and substitution and waivers of requirements for admission and graduation. Students with LD may take up to 12 credit hours per semester; 12 credit hours per semester are required to maintain full-time status; 6 credit hours per semester are required to be eligible for financial aid.

Special courses Available in math. All courses are offered for credit; all enter into overall grade point average.

Counseling and advisement Career counseling and individual counseling are available. Academic advisement by a staff member affiliated with the program is available.

Auxiliary aids and services *Aids:* calculators, personal computers, personal spelling/word-use assistants (e.g., Franklin Speller), scan and read programs (e.g., Kurzweil), screen-enlarging programs, screen readers, speech recognition programs (e.g., Dragon), tape recorders, taped textbooks. *Services and accommodations:* priority registration, alternative test arrangements, readers, note-takers, and scribes.

ADD/ADHD Students with ADD/ADHD are eligible for the same services available to students with LD, as well as distraction-free testing environments.

Application *Required:* psychoeducational report (4 years old or less). *Recommended:* documentation of high school services (e.g., Individualized Education Program [IEP] or 504 plan). Upon application, documentation of need for special services should be sent only to your LD program or unit. Upon acceptance, documentation of need for special services should be sent only to your LD program or unit. *Application deadline (institutional):* 7/26 for fall and 11/18 for spring.

LD program contact Margaret Hardee, Counseling Specialist II, 444 Appleyard Drive, Tallahassee, FL 32304-2895. *Phone:* 850-413-0004. *Fax:* 850-921-6383. *E-mail:* dss@mail.tcc.cc.fl.us.

Application contact Sharon Jefferson, Director of Enrollment Services, Tallahassee Community College, 444 Appleyard Drive, Tallahassee, FL 32304-2895. *Phone:* 850-921-0646. *E-mail:* enroll@mail.tallahassee.cc.fl.us. *Web address:* http://www.tallahassee.cc.fl.us/.

TARRANT COUNTY COLLEGE DISTRICT

Fort Worth, Texas

Students with LD Served by Program	75	ADD/ADHD Services	✓
Staff	2 full-time, 1 part-time	Summer Preparation Program	n/a
LD Program or Service Fee	n/a	Alternative Test Arrangements	✓
LD Program Began	n/a	LD Student Organization	n/a

Disability Support Services serves approximately 75 undergraduate students. Faculty consists of 2 full-time staff members and 1 part-time staff member. Services are provided by academic advisers, counselors, and student assistants.

Policies 12 credit hours per semester are required to maintain full-time status and to be eligible for financial aid.

Subject-area tutoring Available in most subjects. Offered one-on-one by trained peer tutors.

Counseling and advisement Academic advisement by a staff member affiliated with the program is available.

Auxiliary aids and services *Aids:* calculators, personal computers, scan and read programs (e.g., Kurzweil), screen readers, speech recognition programs (e.g., Dragon), tape recorders, taped textbooks. *Services and accommodations:* alternative test arrangements, readers, note-takers, and scribes.

ADD/ADHD Students with ADD/ADHD are eligible for the same services available to students with LD, as well as distraction-free testing environments.

Application *Required:* high school transcript, interview, separate application to your LD program or unit, and documentation of high school services (e.g., Individualized Education Program [IEP] or 504 plan). *Recommended:* psychoeducational report (2 years old or less). Upon application, documentation of need for special services should be sent only to your LD program or unit. Upon acceptance, documentation of need for special services should be sent only to your LD program or unit. *Application deadline (institutional):* 8/30 for fall and 1/14 for spring. *Application deadline (LD program):* rolling/continuous for fall and rolling/continuous for spring.

LD program contact Joan L. Moyer, Coordinator, 2100 TCJC Parkway, Arlington, TX 76108. *Phone:* 817-515-3593. *Fax:* 817-515-3191. *E-mail:* joan.moyer@tccd.net.

Application contact Tarrant County College District, 1500 Houston Street, Fort Worth, TX 76102-6599. *Web address:* http://www.tcjc.cc.tx.us/.

TERRA STATE COMMUNITY COLLEGE

Fremont, Ohio

Students with LD Served by Program	40	ADD/ADHD Services	✓
Staff	1 full-time	Summer Preparation Program	n/a
LD Program or Service Fee	n/a	Alternative Test Arrangements	✓
LD Program Began	1989	LD Student Organization	n/a

Disability Support Services began offering services in 1989. The program serves approximately 40 undergraduate students. Faculty consists of 1 full-time staff member. Services are provided by regular education teachers, counselors, and coordinator of services.

Special preparation or orientation Optional orientation held before classes begin.

Basic skills remediation Available in study skills, computer skills, reading, learning strategies, written language, and math. Offered in class-size groups by computer-based instruction and regular education teachers.

Subject-area tutoring Available in most subjects. Offered one-on-one and in small groups by graduate assistants/students and trained peer tutors.

Counseling and advisement Career counseling, individual counseling, and support groups are available.

Terra State Community College (continued)

Auxiliary aids and services *Aids:* calculators, personal spelling/word-use assistants (e.g., Franklin Speller), screen-enlarging programs, screen readers, tape recorders, taped textbooks. *Services and accommodations:* alternative test arrangements, readers, note-takers, and scribes.

ADD/ADHD Students with ADD/ADHD are eligible for the same services available to students with LD

Application *Required:* psychoeducational report (3 years old or less) and Compass testing. *Recommended:* high school transcript, ACT or SAT I (extended-time tests accepted), interview, and documentation of high school services (e.g., Individualized Education Program [IEP] or 504 plan). Upon application, documentation of need for special services should be sent only to your LD program or unit. Upon acceptance, documentation of need for special services should be sent only to your LD program or unit.

LD program contact Richard Newman, Coordinator of Counseling and Disability Support Services, 2830 Napoleon Road, Fremont, OH 43420. *Phone:* 419-334-8400 Ext. 208. *Fax:* 419-334-9035.

Application contact Jadlynne Flick, Admissions Advisor, Terra State Community College, 2830 Napoleon Road, Fremont, OH 43420-9670. *Phone:* 419-334-8400 Ext. 350. *E-mail:* dkayden@terra.cc.oh.us. *Web address:* http://www.terra.cc.oh.us/.

TEXAS STATE TECHNICAL COLLEGE
Sweetwater, Texas

Students with LD Served by Program	35	ADD/ADHD Services	✓
Staff	3 full-time	Summer Preparation Program	✓
LD Program or Service Fee	n/a	Alternative Test Arrangements	✓
LD Program Began	1993	LD Student Organization	n/a

Counseling and Testing Department began offering services in 1993. The program serves approximately 35 undergraduate students. Faculty consists of 3 full-time staff members. Services are provided by academic advisers, regular education teachers, counselors, remediation/learning specialists, trained peer tutors, and professional tutors.

Special preparation or orientation Optional summer program offered prior to entering college.

Basic skills remediation Available in reading, written language, and math. Offered in class-size groups by computer-based instruction and regular education teachers.

Subject-area tutoring Available in all subjects. Offered one-on-one, in small groups, and class-size groups by computer-based instruction, professional tutors, and trained peer tutors.

Counseling and advisement Individual counseling is available. Academic advisement by a staff member affiliated with the program is available.

Auxiliary aids and services *Aids:* calculators, tape recorders, taped textbooks. *Services and accommodations:* alternative test arrangements, readers, note-takers, and scribes.

ADD/ADHD Students with ADD/ADHD are eligible for the same services available to students with LD, as well as distraction-free study areas and distraction-free testing environments.

Application *Required:* interview, personal statement, psychoeducational report, and documentation of high school services (e.g., Individualized Education Program [IEP] or 504 plan). Upon application, documentation of need for special services should be sent only to your LD program or unit. Upon acceptance, documentation of need for special services should be sent only to your LD program or unit. *Application deadline (institutional):*

rolling/continuous for fall and rolling/continuous for spring. *Application deadline (LD program):* rolling/continuous for fall and rolling/continuous for spring.

LD program contact Greta Estes, Coordinator of Counseling and Testing, 300 College Drive, Sweetwater, TX 79556. *Phone:* 915-235-7414. *Fax:* 915-235-7416. *E-mail:* greta.estes@sweetwater.tstc.edu.

Application contact Jeff Waite, Director of Marketing, Texas State Technical College, 300 College Drive, Sweetwater, TX 79556-4108. *Phone:* 915-235-7352. *E-mail:* kshipp@tstc.edu. *Web address:* http://www.sweetwater.tstc.edu/.

TEXAS STATE TECHNICAL COLLEGE-WACO/MARSHALL CAMPUS
Waco, Texas

Students with LD Served by Program	100	ADD/ADHD Services	✓
Staff	1 full-time	Summer Preparation Program	n/a
LD Program or Service Fee	n/a	Alternative Test Arrangements	✓
LD Program Began	1996	LD Student Organization	✓

Deaf/Disabled Student Services began offering services in 1996. The program serves approximately 100 undergraduate students. Faculty consists of 1 full-time staff member. Services are provided by remediation/learning specialists, trained peer tutors, and notetakers, test on tape readers.

Policies The college has written policies regarding course substitutions. 12 credit hours per quarter are required to maintain full-time status; 9 credit hours per quarter are required to be eligible for financial aid.

Basic skills remediation Available in computer skills, reading, written language, and math. Offered in small groups and class-size groups by computer-based instruction and regular education teachers.

Subject-area tutoring Available in most subjects. Offered one-on-one by computer-based instruction and trained peer tutors.

Auxiliary aids and services *Aids:* scan and read programs (e.g., Kurzweil), tape recorders, taped textbooks. *Services and accommodations:* alternative test arrangements, readers, and note-takers.

Student organization There is a student organization for students with LD.

ADD/ADHD Students with ADD/ADHD are eligible for the same services available to students with LD, as well as distraction-free testing environments.

Application *Required:* high school transcript, separate application to your LD program or unit, psychoeducational report (5 years old or less), documentation of high school services (e.g., Individualized Education Program [IEP] or 504 plan), and college placement test (Accuplacer). Upon application, documentation of need for special services should be sent only to your LD program or unit. Upon acceptance, documentation of need for special services should be sent only to your LD program or unit. *Application deadline (institutional):* 9/12 for fall and 1/17 for spring.

LD program contact Brent A. Burns, Coordinator, 3801 Campus Drive, Waco, TX 76705. *Phone:* 254-867-3600. *Fax:* 254-867-3601. *E-mail:* baburns@tstc.edu.

Application contact Texas State Technical College-Waco/Marshall Campus, 3801 Campus Drive, Waco, TX 76705-1695. *E-mail:* lrobert@tstc.edu. *Web address:* http://www.tstc.edu/.

THREE RIVERS COMMUNITY COLLEGE
Norwich, Connecticut

Students with LD Served by Program	100	ADD/ADHD Services	✓
Staff	1 full-time	Summer Preparation Program	n/a
LD Program or Service Fee	n/a	Alternative Test Arrangements	✓
LD Program Began	1963	LD Student Organization	n/a

Learning Specialist began offering services in 1963. The program serves approximately 100 undergraduate students. Faculty consists of 1 full-time staff member.

Policies The college has written policies regarding course substitutions and substitution and waivers of requirements for admission and graduation. Students with LD may take up to 18 semester hours per semester; 12 semester hours per semester are required to maintain full-time status; 3 semester hours per semester are required to be eligible for financial aid. LD services are also available to graduate students.

Basic skills remediation Available in study skills, computer skills, reading, time management, learning strategies, written language, and math. Offered in class-size groups by computer-based instruction, regular education teachers, professional tutors, and trained peer tutors.

Subject-area tutoring Available in most subjects. Offered one-on-one, in small groups, and class-size groups by computer-based instruction, professional tutors, trained peer tutors, and LD specialists.

Counseling and advisement Individual counseling is available.

Auxiliary aids and services *Aids:* tape recorders. *Services and accommodations:* priority registration, alternative test arrangements, and note-takers.

ADD/ADHD Students with ADD/ADHD are eligible for the same services available to students with LD, as well as distraction-free testing environments.

Application *Required:* high school transcript. Upon application, documentation of need for special services should be sent only to your LD program or unit. Upon acceptance, documentation of need for special services should be sent only to your LD program or unit. *Application deadline (institutional):* rolling/continuous for fall and rolling/continuous for spring. *Application deadline (LD program):* rolling/continuous for fall and rolling/continuous for spring.

LD program contact Chris Scarborough, Learning Specialist, Mahan Drive, Norwich, CT 06360. *Phone:* 860-892-5751. *Fax:* 860-886-0691.

Application contact Aida Garcia, Admissions and Recruitment Counselor, Mohegan Campus, Three Rivers Community College, Mahan Drive, Norwich, CT 06360. *E-mail:* info3rivers@sirus.commnet.edu. *Web address:* http://www.trctc.commnet.edu/.

TRIDENT TECHNICAL COLLEGE
Charleston, South Carolina

Students with LD Served by Program	300	ADD/ADHD Services	✓
Staff	2 full-time	Summer Preparation Program	n/a
LD Program or Service Fee	n/a	Alternative Test Arrangements	✓
LD Program Began	1987	LD Student Organization	n/a

Services for Students with Disabilities began offering services in 1987. The program serves approximately 300 undergraduate students. Faculty consists of 2 full-time staff members. Services are provided by counselors.

Policies 12 credit hours per semester are required to maintain full-time status.

Special preparation or orientation Held after initial intake meeting with student.

Counseling and advisement Career counseling, individual counseling, and appropriate community referrals are available.

Auxiliary aids and services *Aids:* calculators, personal spelling/word-use assistants (e.g., Franklin Speller), screen-enlarging programs, tape recorders, taped textbooks. *Services and accommodations:* alternative test arrangements and note-takers.

ADD/ADHD Students with ADD/ADHD are eligible for the same services available to students with LD, as well as distraction-free testing environments.

Application *Required:* high school transcript and college placement test or SAT/ACT. Upon application, documentation of need for special services should be sent only to your LD program or unit. Upon acceptance, documentation of need for special services should be sent only to your LD program or unit. *Application deadline (institutional):* rolling/continuous for fall and rolling/continuous for spring. *Application deadline (LD program):* rolling/continuous for fall and rolling/continuous for spring.

LD program contact Pamela Middleton, Counselor, 7000 Rivers Avenue, PO Box 118067 CD-M, Charleston, SC 29423-8067. *Phone:* 843-574-6303. *Fax:* 843-574-6342. *E-mail:* zpmiddletonp@trident.tec.sc.us.

Application contact Trident Technical College, 7000 Rivers Avenue, Charleston, SC 29423-8067. *Web address:* http://www.trident.tec.sc.us/.

TROCAIRE COLLEGE
Buffalo, New York

Students with LD Served by Program	18	ADD/ADHD Services	✓
Staff	1 full-time	Summer Preparation Program	n/a
LD Program or Service Fee	n/a	Alternative Test Arrangements	✓
LD Program Began	1988	LD Student Organization	n/a

Services for Students with Special Needs began offering services in 1988. The program serves approximately 18 undergraduate students. Faculty consists of 1 full-time staff member. Services are provided by academic advisers, regular education teachers, and LD specialists.

Policies The college has written policies regarding substitution and waivers of requirements for admission. Students with LD may take up to 12 credit hours per semester; 12 credit hours per semester are required to maintain full-time status and to be eligible for financial aid.

Special preparation or orientation Required orientation held before classes begin.

Diagnostic testing Available for auditory processing, learning strategies, and reading.

Basic skills remediation Available in study skills, reading, time management, and math. Offered in small groups by computer-based instruction, LD specialists, and trained peer tutors.

Subject-area tutoring Available in all subjects. Offered one-on-one by LD specialists.

Special courses Available in study skills, college survival skills, test taking, reading, time management, learning strategies, and math. Some courses are offered for credit; some enter into overall grade point average.

Counseling and advisement Individual counseling is available. Academic advisement by a staff member affiliated with the program is available.

Trocaire College (continued)

Auxiliary aids and services *Aids:* calculators, personal computers, screen-enlarging programs, tape recorders, taped textbooks. *Services and accommodations:* alternative test arrangements, readers, and note-takers.

ADD/ADHD Students with ADD/ADHD are eligible for the same services available to students with LD, as well as distraction-free study areas, distraction-free testing environments and personal coach or mentors.

Application *Required:* high school transcript, SAT I (extended-time test accepted), psychoeducational report (1 year old or less), and documentation of high school services (e.g., Individualized Education Program [IEP] or 504 plan). Upon application, documentation of need for special services should be sent to both admissions and your LD program or unit. Upon acceptance, documentation of need for special services should be sent to both admissions and your LD program or unit. *Application deadline (institutional):* rolling/continuous for fall and rolling/continuous for spring.

LD program contact Sr. Mary Norine Truax, RSM, Coordinator, 360 Choate Avenue, Buffalo, NY 14220. *Phone:* 716-826-1200 Ext. 1227. *Fax:* 716-828-6107. *E-mail:* truaxn@trocaire.edu.

Application contact Theresa Horner, Associate Director of Admissions, Trocaire College, 360 Choate Avenue, Buffalo, NY 14220-2094. *Phone:* 716-826-1200 Ext. 1259. *Web address:* http://www.trocaire.edu/.

TYLER JUNIOR COLLEGE
Tyler, Texas

Students with LD Served by Program	50	ADD/ADHD Services	✓
Staff	n/a	Summer Preparation Program	n/a
LD Program or Service Fee	n/a	Alternative Test Arrangements	✓
LD Program Began	1986	LD Student Organization	n/a

Support Services began offering services in 1986. The program serves approximately 50 undergraduate students. Services are provided by academic advisers, counselors, trained peer tutors, and professional tutors.

Policies Students with LD may take up to 15 credit hours per semester; 12 credit hours per semester are required to maintain full-time status and to be eligible for financial aid.

Subject-area tutoring Available in most subjects. Offered one-on-one and in small groups by computer-based instruction, professional tutors, and trained peer tutors.

Counseling and advisement Academic advisement by a staff member affiliated with the program is available.

Auxiliary aids and services *Aids:* scan and read programs (e.g., Kurzweil), screen-enlarging programs, screen readers, taped textbooks. *Services and accommodations:* advocates, priority registration, alternative test arrangements, readers, note-takers, and scribes.

ADD/ADHD Students with ADD/ADHD are eligible for the same services available to students with LD, as well as distraction-free testing environments.

Application *Required:* high school transcript, interview, separate application to your LD program or unit, psychoeducational report (3 years old or less), and documentation of high school services (e.g., Individualized Education Program [IEP] or 504 plan). Upon application, documentation of need for special services should be sent only to your LD program or unit.

LD program contact Dr. Vickie Geisel, Counselor/Director, Support Services, PO Box 9020, Tyler, TX 75711. *Phone:* 903-510-2395. *Fax:* 903-510-2894. *E-mail:* vgei@tjc.tyler.cc.tx.us.

Application contact Tyler Junior College, PO Box 9020, Tyler, TX 75711-9020. *Web address:* http://www.tyler.cc.tx.us/.

UMPQUA COMMUNITY COLLEGE
Roseburg, Oregon

Students with LD Served by Program	45	ADD/ADHD Services	✓
Staff	1 full-time, 1 part-time	Summer Preparation Program	n/a
LD Program or Service Fee	n/a	Alternative Test Arrangements	✓
LD Program Began	1985	LD Student Organization	n/a

Disability Services began offering services in 1985. The program serves approximately 45 undergraduate students. Faculty consists of 1 full-time and 1 part-time staff member. Services are provided by academic advisers, regular education teachers, counselors, remediation/learning specialists, diagnostic specialists, graduate assistants/students, LD specialists, and trained peer tutors.

Policies Students with LD may take up to 19 credit hours per term; 12 credit hours per term are required to maintain full-time status and to be eligible for financial aid.

Diagnostic testing Available for auditory processing, spelling, handwriting, intelligence, learning strategies, reading, written language, visual processing, and math.

Special courses Available in learning strategies and computer access/technology. All courses are offered for credit; none enter into overall grade point average.

Counseling and advisement Academic advisement by a staff member affiliated with the program is available.

Auxiliary aids and services *Aids:* personal spelling/word-use assistants (e.g., Franklin Speller), scan and read programs (e.g., Kurzweil), screen-enlarging programs, screen readers, speech recognition programs (e.g., Dragon), tape recorders, taped textbooks, Alpha-Smart notetaking keyboards. *Services and accommodations:* advocates, alternative test arrangements, readers, note-takers, scribes, and reserved seating in classroom.

ADD/ADHD Students with ADD/ADHD are eligible for the same services available to students with LD, as well as distraction-free testing environments.

Application *Required:* ACT (extended-time test accepted) and psychoeducational report (5 years old or less). *Recommended:* documentation of high school services (e.g., Individualized Education Program [IEP] or 504 plan) and transition materials from high school special education. Upon application, documentation of need for special services should be sent only to your LD program or unit. Upon acceptance, documentation of need for special services should be sent only to your LD program or unit. *Application deadline (institutional):* rolling/continuous for fall and rolling/continuous for spring. *Application deadline (LD program):* rolling/continuous for fall and rolling/continuous for spring.

LD program contact Barbara Stoner, Coordinator, PO Box 967, Roseburg, OR 97470. *Phone:* 541-440-4600 Ext. 741. *Fax:* 541-440-4665. *E-mail:* stonerb@umpqua.cc.or.us.

Application contact Umpqua Community College, PO Box 967, Roseburg, OR 97470-0226. *E-mail:* shiplel@ucc.ccay.us. *Web address:* http://www.umpqua.cc.or.us/.

UNIVERSITY OF ALASKA ANCHORAGE, KENAI PENINSULA COLLEGE

Soldotna, Alaska

Students with LD Served by Program	10	ADD/ADHD Services	✓
Staff	3 full-time, 3 part-time	Summer Preparation Program	n/a
LD Program or Service Fee	n/a	Alternative Test Arrangements	✓
LD Program Began	1989	LD Student Organization	n/a

The Learning Center began offering services in 1989. The program serves approximately 10 undergraduate students. Faculty consists of 3 full-time and 3 part-time staff members. Services are provided by academic advisers, counselors, trained peer tutors, and adult education instructors.

Policies 6 credit hours per semester are required to be eligible for financial aid. LD services are also available to graduate students.

Special preparation or orientation Optional orientation held individually by special arrangement.

Basic skills remediation Available in study skills, computer skills, reading, learning strategies, written language, and math. Offered one-on-one, in small groups, and class-size groups by computer-based instruction, graduate assistants/students, trained peer tutors, and adult education instructors.

Subject-area tutoring Available in most subjects. Offered one-on-one and in small groups by computer-based instruction, graduate assistants/students, and adult education instructors.

Special courses Available in college survival skills, reading, vocabulary development, and written composition skills. All courses are offered for credit; all enter into overall grade point average.

Counseling and advisement Career counseling and individual counseling are available. Academic advisement by a staff member affiliated with the program is available.

Auxiliary aids and services *Aids:* calculators, personal computers, personal spelling/word-use assistants (e.g., Franklin Speller), screen-enlarging programs, tape recorders, taped textbooks. *Services and accommodations:* alternative test arrangements, readers, note-takers, and scribes.

ADD/ADHD Students with ADD/ADHD are eligible for the same services available to students with LD, as well as distraction-free study areas and distraction-free testing environments.

Application *Required:* psychoeducational report (10 years old or less). *Recommended:* high school transcript and documentation of high school services (e.g., Individualized Education Program [IEP] or 504 plan). Upon application, documentation of need for special services should be sent only to your LD program or unit. Upon acceptance, documentation of need for special services should be sent only to your LD program or unit. *Application deadline (institutional):* rolling/continuous for fall and rolling/continuous for spring. *Application deadline (LD program):* rolling/continuous for fall and rolling/continuous for spring.

LD program contact Diane Taylor, Coordinator, 34820 College Drive, Soldotna, AK 99669. *Phone:* 907-262-0328. *Fax:* 907-262-0398. *E-mail:* ifdtt@uaa.alaska.edu.

Application contact Shelly Love, Admission and Registration Coordinator, University of Alaska Anchorage, Kenai Peninsula College, 34820 College Drive, Soldotna, AK 99669-9798. *Phone:* 907-262-0311. *Web address:* http://www.uaa.alaska.edu/kenai/.

UNIVERSITY OF ARKANSAS COMMUNITY COLLEGE AT BATESVILLE

Batesville, Arkansas

Students with LD Served by Program	10	ADD/ADHD Services	✓
Staff	1 full-time	Summer Preparation Program	n/a
LD Program or Service Fee	n/a	Alternative Test Arrangements	✓
LD Program Began	n/a	LD Student Organization	n/a

Division of Student Services serves approximately 10 undergraduate students. Faculty consists of 1 full-time staff member. Services are provided by academic advisers, counselors, and trained peer tutors.

Policies The college has written policies regarding course substitutions. Students with LD may take up to 18 credit hours per semester; 12 credit hours per semester are required to maintain full-time status; 3 credit hours per semester are required to be eligible for financial aid.

Basic skills remediation Available in study skills, reading, and learning strategies. Offered in class-size groups by regular education teachers.

Subject-area tutoring Available in most subjects. Offered one-on-one and in small groups by computer-based instruction and trained peer tutors.

Special courses Available in college survival skills and reading. All courses are offered for credit; all enter into overall grade point average.

Counseling and advisement Career counseling and individual counseling are available. Academic advisement by a staff member affiliated with the program is available.

Auxiliary aids and services *Aids:* scan and read programs (e.g., Kurzweil), screen-enlarging programs, tape recorders, taped textbooks. *Services and accommodations:* alternative test arrangements, readers, and note copy options.

ADD/ADHD Students with ADD/ADHD are eligible for the same services available to students with LD, as well as distraction-free testing environments.

Application *Required:* high school transcript, ACT (extended-time or untimed test accepted), and documentation of high school services (e.g., Individualized Education Program [IEP] or 504 plan). Upon application, documentation of need for special services should be sent only to your LD program or unit. Upon acceptance, documentation of need for special services should be sent only to your LD program or unit. *Application deadline (institutional):* rolling/continuous for fall and rolling/continuous for spring. *Application deadline (LD program):* rolling/continuous for fall and rolling/continuous for spring.

LD program contact Tammy Jolley, Counselor, PO Box 3350, Batesville, AR 72503. *Phone:* 870-793-7581. *Fax:* 870-793-4988. *E-mail:* tjolley@uaccb.cc.ar.us.

Application contact University of Arkansas Community College at Batesville, PO Box 3350, Batesville, AR 72503.

UNIVERSITY OF WISCONSIN-SHEBOYGAN

Sheboygan, Wisconsin

Students with LD Served by Program	12	ADD/ADHD Services	✓
Staff	1 part-time	Summer Preparation Program	n/a
LD Program or Service Fee	n/a	Alternative Test Arrangements	✓
LD Program Began	n/a	LD Student Organization	n/a

Student Services Office serves approximately 12 undergraduate students. Faculty consists of 1 part-time staff member. Services are provided by academic advisers, regular education teachers, and trained peer tutors.

Policies 12 credits per semester are required to maintain full-time status; 6 credits per semester are required to be eligible for financial aid.

Counseling and advisement Academic advisement by a staff member affiliated with the program is available.

Auxiliary aids and services *Aids:* personal computers, personal spelling/word-use assistants (e.g., Franklin Speller), scan and read programs (e.g., Kurzweil), screen readers, speech recognition programs (e.g., Dragon), tape recorders, taped textbooks. *Services and accommodations:* advocates, priority registration, alternative test arrangements, readers, note-takers, and scribes.

ADD/ADHD Students with ADD/ADHD are eligible for the same services available to students with LD, as well as distraction-free testing environments.

Application *Required:* psychoeducational report (2 years old or less). Upon application, documentation of need for special services should be sent only to your LD program or unit. Upon acceptance, documentation of need for special services should be sent only to your LD program or unit. *Application deadline (institutional):* rolling/continuous for fall and rolling/continuous for spring. *Application deadline (LD program):* rolling/continuous for fall and rolling/continuous for spring.

LD program contact John Landrum, Assistant Director of Student Services, One University Drive, Sheboygan, WI 53081. *Phone:* 920-459-6633. *Fax:* 920-459-6662. *E-mail:* jlandrum@uwc.edu.

Application contact University of Wisconsin-Sheboygan, 1 University Drive, Sheboygan, WI 53081-4789.

VALENCIA COMMUNITY COLLEGE

Orlando, Florida

Students with LD Served by Program	800	ADD/ADHD Services	✓
Staff	4 full-time, 3 part-time	Summer Preparation Program	n/a
LD Program or Service Fee	n/a	Alternative Test Arrangements	n/a
LD Program Began	1980	LD Student Organization	n/a

Office for Students with Disabilities began offering services in 1980. The program serves approximately 800 undergraduate students. Faculty consists of 4 full-time and 3 part-time staff members. Services are provided by academic advisers, counselors, diagnostic specialists, LD specialists, and trained peer tutors.

Policies The college has written policies regarding course substitutions and substitution and waivers of requirements for admission and graduation. Students with LD may take up to 18 credit hours per semester; 12 credit hours per semester are required to maintain full-time status.

Diagnostic testing Available for intelligence.

Basic skills remediation Available in reading, written language, and math. Offered in class-size groups by regular education teachers.

Counseling and advisement Academic advisement by a staff member affiliated with the program is available.

Auxiliary aids and services *Aids:* calculators, personal computers, screen-enlarging programs, speech recognition programs (e.g., Dragon), tape recorders, taped textbooks.

ADD/ADHD Students with ADD/ADHD are eligible for the same services available to students with LD, as well as distraction-free study areas and distraction-free testing environments.

Application *Required:* high school transcript, SAT I (extended-time test accepted), and psychoeducational report (3 years old or less). *Recommended:* participation in extracurricular activities, ACT (extended-time test accepted), and documentation of high school services (e.g., Individualized Education Program [IEP] or 504 plan). Upon application, documentation of need for special services should be sent only to your LD program or unit. Upon acceptance, documentation of need for special services should be sent only to your LD program or unit. *Application deadline (institutional):* rolling/continuous for fall and rolling/continuous for spring. *Application deadline (LD program):* rolling/continuous for fall and rolling/continuous for spring.

LD program contact Joyce Knight, Program Director, PO Box 3028, Orlando, FL 32802-3028. *Phone:* 407-299-5000 Ext. 2236. *Fax:* 407-277-0621. *E-mail:* jknight@gwmail.valencia.cc.fl.us.

Application contact Charles H. Drosin, Director of Admissions and Records, Valencia Community College, PO Box 3028, Orlando, FL 32802-3028. *Phone:* 407-299-5000 Ext. 1506. *Web address:* http://www.valencia.cc.fl.us/.

VERMONT TECHNICAL COLLEGE

Randolph Center, Vermont

Students with LD Served by Program	50	ADD/ADHD Services	✓
Staff	1 full-time	Summer Preparation Program	✓
LD Program or Service Fee	n/a	Alternative Test Arrangements	✓
LD Program Began	n/a	LD Student Organization	n/a

Disability Services serves approximately 50 undergraduate students. Faculty consists of 1 full-time staff member. Services are provided by counselors, LD specialists, and professional tutors.

Policies 12 credit hours per semester are required to maintain full-time status; 6 credit hours per semester are required to be eligible for financial aid. LD services are also available to graduate students.

Special preparation or orientation Optional summer program offered prior to entering college.

Diagnostic testing Available for auditory processing, motor skills, neuropsychological, intelligence, written language, and visual processing.

Basic skills remediation Available in computer skills, reading, time management, learning strategies, spelling, written language, and math. Offered one-on-one, in small groups, and class-size groups by regular education teachers and professional tutors.

Subject-area tutoring Available in most subjects. Offered one-on-one and in small groups by professional tutors, graduate assistants/students, and trained peer tutors.

Counseling and advisement Career counseling and individual counseling are available.

Auxiliary aids and services *Aids:* calculators, personal spelling/word-use assistants (e.g., Franklin Speller), screen-enlarging programs, screen readers, speech recognition programs (e.g.,

Dragon), tape recorders, rehab engineering technology lab. *Services and accommodations:* advocates, alternative test arrangements, readers, note-takers, and scribes.

ADD/ADHD Students with ADD/ADHD are eligible for the same services available to students with LD, as well as distraction-free study areas and distraction-free testing environments.

Application *Required:* high school transcript. *Recommended:* participation in extracurricular activities, SAT I (extended-time test accepted), and interview. Upon application, documentation of need for special services should be sent only to your LD program or unit. Upon acceptance, documentation of need for special services should be sent only to your LD program or unit. *Application deadline (institutional):* rolling/continuous for fall and rolling/continuous for spring. *Application deadline (LD program):* rolling/continuous for fall and rolling/continuous for spring.

LD program contact Barbara Bendix, Director, Randolph Center, VT 05061. *Phone:* 802-728-1278. *Fax:* 802-728-1390. *E-mail:* bbendix@vtc.vsc.edu.

Application contact Vermont Technical College, PO Box 500, Randolph Center, VT 05061-0500. *E-mail:* admissions@night.vtc.vsc.edu. *Web address:* http://www.vtc.vsc.edu/.

VIRGINIA HIGHLANDS COMMUNITY COLLEGE
Abingdon, Virginia

Students with LD Served by Program	100	ADD/ADHD Services	✓
Staff	1 full-time	Summer Preparation Program	n/a
LD Program or Service Fee	n/a	Alternative Test Arrangements	✓
LD Program Began	1976	LD Student Organization	n/a

Americans with Disabilities began offering services in 1976. The program serves approximately 100 undergraduate students. Faculty consists of 1 full-time staff member. Services are provided by academic advisers, regular education teachers, counselors, and trained peer tutors.

Policies Students with LD may take up to 15 credit hours per semester; 9 credit hours per semester are required to maintain full-time status and to be eligible for financial aid. LD services are also available to graduate students.

Diagnostic testing Available for auditory processing, handwriting, personality, study skills, learning strategies, reading, learning styles, and math.

Basic skills remediation Available in study skills, computer skills, reading, spelling, and math. Offered one-on-one and in class-size groups by computer-based instruction and regular education teachers.

Subject-area tutoring Available in most subjects. Offered one-on-one by trained peer tutors.

Counseling and advisement Career counseling, individual counseling, small-group counseling, and support groups are available. Academic advisement by a staff member affiliated with the program is available.

Auxiliary aids and services *Aids:* calculators, personal spelling/word-use assistants (e.g., Franklin Speller), screen-enlarging programs, screen readers, speech recognition programs (e.g., Dragon). *Services and accommodations:* advocates, alternative test arrangements, readers, note-takers, and scribes.

ADD/ADHD Students with ADD/ADHD are eligible for the same services available to students with LD, as well as distraction-free testing environments, medication management and personal coach or mentors.

Application *Recommended:* high school transcript and documentation of high school services (e.g., Individualized Education Program [IEP] or 504 plan). Upon application, documentation of need for special services should be sent only to admissions. Upon acceptance, documentation of need for special services should be sent only to admissions. *Application deadline (institutional):* rolling/continuous for fall and rolling/continuous for spring. *Application deadline (LD program):* rolling/continuous for fall and rolling/continuous for spring.

LD program contact Dr. Jack R. Garland, Director of College Advancement, PO Box 828, Abingdon, VA 24210. *Phone:* 540-676-5484. *Fax:* 540-676-5591. *E-mail:* jgarland@vh.cc.va.us.

Application contact Virginia Highlands Community College, PO Box 828, Abingdon, VA 24212-0828. *Web address:* http://www.vh.cc.va.us/.

VIRGINIA WESTERN COMMUNITY COLLEGE
Roanoke, Virginia

Students with LD Served by Program	120	ADD/ADHD Services	✓
Staff	5 full-time, 20 part-time	Summer Preparation Program	n/a
LD Program or Service Fee	n/a	Alternative Test Arrangements	✓
LD Program Began	1990	LD Student Organization	n/a

Student Support Services began offering services in 1990. The program serves approximately 120 undergraduate students. Faculty consists of 5 full-time and 20 part-time staff members. Services are provided by academic advisers, counselors, LD specialists, trained peer tutors, and professional tutors.

Policies Students with LD may take up to 18 credit hours per semester; 9 credit hours per semester are required to maintain full-time status; 3 credit hours per semester are required to be eligible for financial aid.

Special preparation or orientation Optional orientation held before classes begin.

Basic skills remediation Available in study skills, time management, and learning strategies. Offered by computer-based instruction, LD specialists, and workshops offered by our staff.

Subject-area tutoring Available in most subjects. Offered one-on-one and in small groups by professional tutors and trained peer tutors.

Counseling and advisement Career counseling and individual counseling are available. Academic advisement by a staff member affiliated with the program is available.

Auxiliary aids and services *Aids:* scan and read programs (e.g., Kurzweil), screen-enlarging programs, screen readers, speech recognition programs (e.g., Dragon), tape recorders, taped textbooks. *Services and accommodations:* priority registration, alternative test arrangements, and note-takers.

ADD/ADHD Students with ADD/ADHD are eligible for the same services available to students with LD, as well as distraction-free testing environments.

Application *Required:* high school transcript, separate application to your LD program or unit, and psychoeducational report. *Recommended:* documentation of high school services (e.g., Individualized Education Program [IEP] or 504 plan) and English and math placement tests. Upon acceptance, documentation of need for special services should be sent only to your LD program or unit. *Application deadline (institutional):* 8/31 for fall and 1/18 for spring. *Application deadline (LD program):* 11/1 for fall and 3/15 for spring.

LD program contact Martha Richardson, Director/ADA Coordinator, PO Box 14007, Roanoke, VA 24015. *Phone:* 540-857-7286. *Fax:* 540-857-7918. *E-mail:* mrichardson@vw.cc.va.us.

Virginia Western Community College (continued)

Application contact Admissions Office, Virginia Western Community College, PO Box 14007, Roanoke, VA 24038. *Phone:* 540-857-7231. *Web address:* http://www.vw.cc.va.us/.

VISTA COMMUNITY COLLEGE
Berkeley, California

Students with LD Served by Program	100	ADD/ADHD Services	✓
Staff	4 full-time, 1 part-time	Summer Preparation Program	n/a
LD Program or Service Fee	n/a	Alternative Test Arrangements	✓
LD Program Began	1992	LD Student Organization	n/a

Disabled Student Programs and Services (DSPS) began offering services in 1992. The program serves approximately 100 undergraduate students. Faculty consists of 4 full-time staff members and 1 part-time staff member. Services are provided by counselors and LD specialists.
Fees *Diagnostic Testing Fee:* $5.50.
Diagnostic testing Available for auditory processing, spelling, intelligence, personality, reading, written language, learning styles, visual processing, and math.
Special courses Available in study skills. Most courses are offered for credit; all enter into overall grade point average.
Counseling and advisement Individual counseling is available.
Auxiliary aids and services *Aids:* personal computers, scan and read programs (e.g., Kurzweil), screen readers, speech recognition programs (e.g., Dragon), tape recorders, taped textbooks. *Services and accommodations:* priority registration, alternative test arrangements, readers, note-takers, and scribes.
ADD/ADHD Students with ADD/ADHD are eligible for the same services available to students with LD, as well as distraction-free testing environments.
Application *Required:* psychoeducational report (3 years old or less). *Recommended:* high school transcript and documentation of high school services (e.g., Individualized Education Program [IEP] or 504 plan). Upon application, documentation of need for special services should be sent only to your LD program or unit. *Application deadline (institutional):* rolling/continuous for fall and rolling/continuous for spring. *Application deadline (LD program):* rolling/continuous for fall and rolling/continuous for spring.
LD program contact Nina C. Kindblad, Learning Disabilities Specialist, 2020 Milvia Street, Berkeley, CA 94704. *Phone:* 510-841-8431 Ext. 240. *Fax:* 510-841-7333. *E-mail:* nkindblad@peralta.cc.ca.us.
Application contact Barbara SimmonsVista Community College, 2020 Milvia Street, 3rd Floor, Berkeley, CA 94704-5102. *Phone:* 510-466-7370. *E-mail:* scoopfoggy@aol.com. *Web address:* http://www.peralta.cc.ca.us/.

WALLACE STATE COMMUNITY COLLEGE
Hanceville, Alabama

Students with LD Served by Program	75	ADD/ADHD Services	✓
Staff	1 full-time	Summer Preparation Program	n/a
LD Program or Service Fee	n/a	Alternative Test Arrangements	✓
LD Program Began	1990	LD Student Organization	n/a

ADA Coordinator's Office began offering services in 1990. The program serves approximately 75 undergraduate students. Faculty consists of 1 full-time staff member. Services are provided by academic advisers and counselors.
Policies Students with LD may take up to 18 credit hours per semester; 12 credit hours per semester are required to maintain full-time status and to be eligible for financial aid. LD services are also available to graduate students.
Basic skills remediation Available in auditory processing, study skills, computer skills, reading, handwriting, learning strategies, spelling, written language, math, and spoken language. Offered one-on-one, in small groups, and class-size groups by computer-based instruction, regular education teachers, teacher trainees, professional tutors, and trained peer tutors.
Subject-area tutoring Available in most subjects. Offered one-on-one and in small groups by computer-based instruction and trained peer tutors.
Counseling and advisement Career counseling, individual counseling, and small-group counseling are available. Academic advisement by a staff member affiliated with the program is available.
Auxiliary aids and services *Aids:* calculators, personal spelling/word-use assistants (e.g., Franklin Speller), screen-enlarging programs, tape recorders, taped textbooks. *Services and accommodations:* advocates, priority registration, alternative test arrangements, readers, note-takers, and scribes.
ADD/ADHD Students with ADD/ADHD are eligible for the same services available to students with LD, as well as distraction-free study areas and distraction-free testing environments.
Application *Required:* high school transcript, separate application to your LD program or unit, psychoeducational report, and documentation of high school services (e.g., Individualized Education Program [IEP] or 504 plan). *Recommended:* ACT (extended-time or untimed test accepted). Upon application, documentation of need for special services should be sent only to your LD program or unit. Upon acceptance, documentation of need for special services should be sent only to your LD program or unit.
LD program contact Tommy Hale, ADA Coordinator/504 Officer, PO Box 2000, Hanceville, AL 35077. *Phone:* 256-352-8222. *Fax:* 256-352-8228.
Application contact Wallace State Community College, PO Box 2000, Hanceville, AL 35077-2000. *Web address:* http://wallacestatehanceville.edu/.

WESTARK COLLEGE
Fort Smith, Arkansas

Students with LD Served by Program	90	ADD/ADHD Services	✓
Staff	1 full-time	Summer Preparation Program	n/a
LD Program or Service Fee	n/a	Alternative Test Arrangements	✓
LD Program Began	1991	LD Student Organization	✓

ADA Student Services began offering services in 1991. The program serves approximately 90 undergraduate students. Faculty consists of 1 full-time staff member. Services are provided by academic advisers, regular education teachers, remediation/learning specialists, graduate assistants/students, and trained peer tutors.
Policies Students with LD may take up to 18 credit hours per semester; 12 credit hours per semester are required to maintain full-time status; 6 credit hours per semester are required to be eligible for financial aid.
Special preparation or orientation Required orientation held individually by special arrangement.

Basic skills remediation Available in study skills, computer skills, reading, time management, handwriting, learning strategies, spelling, and math. Offered in small groups by computer-based instruction, regular education teachers, graduate assistants/students, and trained peer tutors.

Subject-area tutoring Available in most subjects. Offered one-on-one by computer-based instruction, graduate assistants/students, and trained peer tutors.

Special courses Available in career planning, study skills, college survival skills, practical computer skills, test taking, reading, time management, math, and written composition skills. Some courses are offered for credit; some enter into overall grade point average.

Counseling and advisement Career counseling is available. Academic advisement by a staff member affiliated with the program is available.

Auxiliary aids and services *Aids:* calculators, personal computers, personal spelling/word-use assistants (e.g., Franklin Speller), scan and read programs (e.g., Kurzweil), screen-enlarging programs, tape recorders, taped textbooks. *Services and accommodations:* alternative test arrangements and note-takers.

Student organization There is a student organization for students with LD.

ADD/ADHD Students with ADD/ADHD are eligible for the same services available to students with LD, as well as distraction-free testing environments.

Application *Required:* high school transcript, separate application to your LD program or unit, psychoeducational report (4 years old or less), and documentation of high school services (e.g., Individualized Education Program [IEP] or 504 plan). *Recommended:* ACT or SAT I (extended-time or untimed test accepted). Upon application, documentation of need for special services should be sent only to your LD program or unit. Upon acceptance, documentation of need for special services should be sent only to your LD program or unit. *Application deadline (institutional):* rolling/continuous for fall and rolling/continuous for spring. *Application deadline (LD program):* rolling/continuous for fall and rolling/continuous for spring.

LD program contact Roger A. Young, ADA Coordinator, PO Box 3649, Fort Smith, AR 72913. *Phone:* 501-788-7577. *Fax:* 501-788-7178. *E-mail:* ryoung@systema.westark.edu.

Application contact Westark College, PO Box 3649, Fort Smith, AR 72913-3649. *E-mail:* sjohnson@systema.westark.edu. *Web address:* http://www.westark.edu/.

WESTERN WISCONSIN TECHNICAL COLLEGE

La Crosse, Wisconsin

Students with LD Served by Program	150	ADD/ADHD Services	✓
Staff	2 full-time	Summer Preparation Program	n/a
LD Program or Service Fee	n/a	Alternative Test Arrangements	✓
LD Program Began	1991	LD Student Organization	n/a

Disability Services began offering services in 1991. The program serves approximately 150 undergraduate students. Faculty consists of 2 full-time staff members. Services are provided by remediation/learning specialists and professional tutors.

Special preparation or orientation Optional orientation held individually by special arrangement.

Basic skills remediation Available in study skills, computer skills, reading, time management, learning strategies, spelling, written language, math, and science. Offered in class-size groups by remedial instructors.

Subject-area tutoring Available in all subjects. Offered one-on-one and in small groups by professional tutors and trained peer tutors.

Counseling and advisement Career counseling and individual counseling are available.

Auxiliary aids and services *Aids:* scan and read programs (e.g., Kurzweil), screen-enlarging programs, screen readers, speech recognition programs (e.g., Dragon), tape recorders, taped textbooks. *Services and accommodations:* alternative test arrangements, readers, note-takers, and scribes.

ADD/ADHD Students with ADD/ADHD are eligible for the same services available to students with LD, as well as distraction-free study areas and distraction-free testing environments.

Application *Required:* high school transcript and ASSET, application. Upon application, documentation of need for special services should be sent only to your LD program or unit. Upon acceptance, documentation of need for special services should be sent only to your LD program or unit.

LD program contact Kristina Puent, Instructional Support Specialist, 304 North 6th Street, LaCrosse, WI 54601. *Phone:* 608-785-9875. *E-mail:* puentk@western.tec.wi.us.

Application contact Western Wisconsin Technical College, 304 6th Street North, PO Box C-908, La Crosse, WI 54602-0908. *E-mail:* milde@a1.western.tec.wi.us. *Web address:* http://www.tec.wi.us.

WESTERN WYOMING COMMUNITY COLLEGE

Rock Springs, Wyoming

Students with LD Served by Program	22	ADD/ADHD Services	✓
Staff	3 full-time, 3 part-time	Summer Preparation Program	n/a
LD Program or Service Fee	n/a	Alternative Test Arrangements	✓
LD Program Began	1994	LD Student Organization	✓

Student Development Center began offering services in 1994. The program serves approximately 22 undergraduate students. Faculty consists of 3 full-time and 3 part-time staff members. Services are provided by academic advisers, counselors, special education teachers, graduate assistants/students, LD specialists, and trained peer tutors.

Policies Students with LD may take up to 21 credit hours per semester; 12 credit hours per semester are required to maintain full-time status; 6 credit hours per semester are required to be eligible for financial aid.

Basic skills remediation Available in reading, learning strategies, written language, and math. Offered in class-size groups by regular education teachers, special education teachers, and LD specialists.

Subject-area tutoring Available in all subjects. Offered one-on-one and in small groups by trained peer tutors.

Counseling and advisement Career counseling, individual counseling, small-group counseling, and support groups are available. Academic advisement by a staff member affiliated with the program is available.

Auxiliary aids and services *Aids:* calculators, personal spelling/word-use assistants (e.g., Franklin Speller), scan and read programs (e.g., Kurzweil), screen-enlarging programs, speech recognition programs (e.g., Dragon), tape recorders, taped textbooks, FM systems. *Services and accommodations:* advocates, alternative test arrangements, readers, note-takers, and scribes.

Student organization There is a student organization for students with LD.

Western Wyoming Community College (continued)

ADD/ADHD Students with ADD/ADHD are eligible for the same services available to students with LD, as well as distraction-free testing environments and support groups for ADD/ADHD.
Application *Required:* high school transcript and GED. *Recommended:* ACT or SAT I (extended-time or untimed test accepted). Upon application, documentation of need for special services should be sent only to your LD program or unit. Upon acceptance, documentation of need for special services should be sent only to your LD program or unit. *Application deadline (institutional):* rolling/continuous for fall and rolling/continuous for spring. *Application deadline (LD program):* rolling/continuous for fall and rolling/continuous for spring.
LD program contact Sandy Baker, ADA Learning Specialist, 2500 College Drive, PO Box 428, Rock Springs, WY 82901. *Phone:* 307-382-1806. *Fax:* 307-382-7665. *E-mail:* sbaker@wwcc. cc.wy.us.
Application contact Laurie Watkins, Assistant Director of Admissions, Western Wyoming Community College, PO Box 428, Rock Springs, WY 82902-0428. *Phone:* 307-382-1647. *E-mail:* jfreeze@ wwcc.cc.wy.us. *Web address:* http://www.wwcc.cc.wy.us/.

WESTMORELAND COUNTY COMMUNITY COLLEGE
Youngwood, Pennsylvania

Students with LD Served by Program	62	ADD/ADHD Services	✓
Staff	1 full-time	Summer Preparation Program	n/a
LD Program or Service Fee	n/a	Alternative Test Arrangements	✓
LD Program Began	1987	LD Student Organization	n/a

Services for Students with Disabilities began offering services in 1987. The program serves approximately 62 undergraduate students. Faculty consists of 1 full-time staff member. Services are provided by counselors, trained peer tutors, and professional tutors.
Policies 12 credit hours per semester are required to maintain full-time status; 6 credit hours per semester are required to be eligible for financial aid.
Special preparation or orientation Required orientation held individually by special arrangement.
Subject-area tutoring Available in most subjects. Offered one-on-one and in small groups by computer-based instruction, professional tutors, and trained peer tutors.
Counseling and advisement Career counseling and individual counseling are available.
Auxiliary aids and services *Aids:* calculators, personal spelling/word-use assistants (e.g., Franklin Speller), screen-enlarging programs, tape recorders, taped textbooks. *Services and accommodations:* alternative test arrangements, readers, note-takers, and scribes.
ADD/ADHD Students with ADD/ADHD are eligible for the same services available to students with LD, as well as distraction-free testing environments.
Application *Recommended:* high school transcript, interview, personal statement, separate application to your LD program or unit, psychoeducational report (2 years old or less), and documentation of high school services (e.g., Individualized Educa-

tion Program [IEP] or 504 plan). Upon application, documentation of need for special services should be sent only to your LD program or unit. Upon acceptance, documentation of need for special services should be sent only to your LD program or unit. *Application deadline (institutional):* rolling/continuous for fall and rolling/continuous for spring. *Application deadline (LD program):* rolling/continuous for fall and rolling/continuous for spring.
LD program contact Mary Ellen Beres, Counselor, Student Support Services, Armbrust Road, Youngwood, PA 15697. *Phone:* 724-925-4189. *Fax:* 724-925-5804. *E-mail:* beresm@wccc. westmoreland.cc.pa.us.
Application contact Westmoreland County Community College, 400 Armbrust Road, Youngwood, PA 15697-1895. *E-mail:* admission@wccc.westmoreland.cc.pa.us. *Web address:* http://www.westmoreland.cc.pa.us/.

YORK COUNTY TECHNICAL COLLEGE
Wells, Maine

Students with LD Served by Program	30	ADD/ADHD Services	✓
Staff	1 part-time	Summer Preparation Program	n/a
LD Program or Service Fee	n/a	Alternative Test Arrangements	✓
LD Program Began	n/a	LD Student Organization	n/a

Student Services serves approximately 30 undergraduate students. Faculty consists of 1 part-time staff member. Services are provided by academic advisers, regular education teachers, and trained peer tutors.
Policies LD services are also available to graduate students.
Subject-area tutoring Available in most subjects. Offered one-on-one and in small groups through math lab, writing lab.
Special courses Available in math. All courses are offered for credit; none enter into overall grade point average.
Counseling and advisement Individual counseling and small-group counseling are available. Academic advisement by a staff member affiliated with the program is available.
Auxiliary aids and services *Aids:* calculators, personal computers, screen-enlarging programs, speech recognition programs (e.g., Dragon), tape recorders, taped textbooks. *Services and accommodations:* advocates, alternative test arrangements, readers, note-takers, and scribes.
ADD/ADHD Students with ADD/ADHD are eligible for the same services available to students with LD, as well as distraction-free testing environments.
Application Upon application, documentation of need for special services should be sent only to your LD program or unit. Upon acceptance, documentation of need for special services should be sent only to your LD program or unit. *Application deadline (institutional):* rolling/continuous for fall and rolling/continuous for spring. *Application deadline (LD program):* rolling/continuous for fall and rolling/continuous for spring.
LD program contact Paula S. Gagnow, Dean of Students, 112 College Drive, Wells, ME 04090. *Phone:* 207-646-9282 Ext. 302. *Fax:* 207-641-0837. *E-mail:* pgagnow@yctc.net.
Application contact York County Technical College, 112 College Drive, Wells, ME 04090. *E-mail:* admissions@yctc.net. *Web address:* http://www.yctc.net/.

► INDEX ◄

The names of colleges with **comprehensive programs** for students with LD or ADD are printed in bold-face type; those with special services for students with LD or ADD are in regular type.

A

Abilene Christian University, TX	79
Abraham Baldwin Agricultural College, GA	275
Academy of Art College, CA	29
Academy of Medical Arts and Business, PA	275
Adelphi University, NY	29
Adirondack Community College, NY	227
Adrian College, MI	79
Alaska Pacific University, AK	79
Albany State University, GA	80
Albuquerque Technical Vocational Institute, NM	276
Alexandria Technical College, MN	276
Alfred University, NY	80
Alma College, MI	81
Alverno College, WI	81
Amarillo College, TX	276
American International College, MA	29
American University, DC	30
Anderson University, IN	30
Andrew College, GA	227
Anne Arundel Community College, MD	277
Antelope Valley College, CA	228
Antioch College, OH	81
Aquinas College, MI	82
Arapahoe Community College, CO	277
Arizona State University, AZ	82
Arkansas State University, AR	31
The Art Institute of Pittsburgh, PA	277
Ashland Community College, KY	278
Athabasca University, AB, Canada	83
Atlantic Cape Community College, NJ	278
Atlantic Union College, MA	31
Auburn University, AL	83
Auburn University Montgomery, AL	84
Augsburg College, MN	32
Averett College, VA	84

B

Babson College, MA	84
Bainbridge College, GA	279
Barat College, IL	32
Barry University, FL	32
Barton County Community College, KS	279
Bates College, ME	85
Baylor University, TX	85
Bellarmine College, KY	86
Bethany College, WV	33
Big Bend Community College, WA	280
Biola University, CA	86
Blackhawk Technical College, WI	280
Blinn College, TX	281
Bluffton College, OH	87
Boston University, MA	34
Bowling Green State University, OH	87
Brenau University, GA	34
Brevard College, NC	87
Brevard Community College, FL	281
Brewton-Parker College, GA	88
Briarwood College, CT	282
Brigham Young University, UT	88
Bristol Community College, MA	282

Broome Community College, NY	282
Broward Community College, FL	283
Brown University, RI	89
Bryn Mawr College, PA	89
Bunker Hill Community College, MA	283
Butler County Community College, KS	284

C

Cabrillo College, CA	228
Caldwell College, NJ	89
Calhoun Community College, AL	284
California Polytechnic State University, San Luis Obispo, CA	90
California State University, Bakersfield, CA	90
California State University, Dominguez Hills, CA	91
California State University, Fresno, CA	91
California State University, Fullerton, CA	91
California State University, Hayward, CA	34
California State University, Long Beach, CA	92
California State University, Northridge, CA	35
California State University, Sacramento, CA	35
California State University, San Marcos, CA	92
California State University, Stanislaus, CA	93
Calvin College, MI	93
Camden County College, NJ	229
Canisius College, NY	93
Cape Cod Community College, MA	229
Cardinal Stritch University, WI	94
Carleton University, ON, Canada	94
Carnegie Mellon University, PA	95
Casper College, WY	285
Catawba College, NC	95
Catawba Valley Community College, NC	285
The Catholic University of America, DC	96
Cedar Valley College, TX	229
Centenary College, NJ	36
Center for Creative Studies—College of Art and Design, MI	96
Central College, IA	96
Central Community College-Hastings Campus, NE	286
Central Community College-Platte Campus, NE	286
Central Missouri State University, MO	97
Central Ohio Technical College, OH	287
Central Piedmont Community College, NC	230
Central State University, OH	97
Central Washington University, WA	98
Cerro Coso Community College, CA	230
Champlain College, VT	98
Charles Stewart Mott Community College, MI	287
Chattanooga State Technical Community College, TN	287
Chemeketa Community College, OR	288
Chesapeake College, MD	288
City College of the City University of New York, NY	98
City Colleges of Chicago, Harold Washington College, IL	289
City Colleges of Chicago, Richard J. Daley College, IL	289
Clayton College & State University, GA	99
Clemson University, SC	99
Cleveland Institute of Art, OH	100
Clinton Community College, NY	289
Cloud County Community College, KS	290
Cochise College, Douglas, AZ	290
Coe College, IA	100
Colby-Sawyer College, NH	100
College Misericordia, PA	36
College of Aeronautics, NY	101
College of Lake County, IL	291
College of Mount St. Joseph, OH	37
The College of New Jersey, NJ	101
College of Notre Dame of Maryland, MD	101
The College of Saint Rose, NY	102
The College of St. Scholastica, MN	102

College of San Mateo, CA   231
College of Staten Island of the City University of New York,
   NY   103
College of the Canyons, CA   231
College of the Desert, CA   232
College of the Siskiyous, CA   232
Collin County Community College District, TX   291
Colorado Christian University, CO   103
Colorado Northwestern Community College, CO   291
Colorado State University, CO   103
Columbia Basin College, WA   292
Columbia College, NY   104
Columbia College Chicago, IL   104
Columbus State Community College, OH   292
Columbus State University, GA   105
Community College of Allegheny County, PA   233
Community College of Aurora, CO   293
The Community College of Baltimore County-Catonsville
   Campus, MD   293
The Community College of Baltimore County-Essex Campus,
   MD   294
Community College of Rhode Island, RI   294
Community Hospital of Roanoke Valley-College of Health
   Sciences, VA   105
Concordia College, NY   37
Concordia University at Austin, TX   106
Connecticut College, CT   106
Copiah-Lincoln Community College, MS   233
Cornell University, NY   106
Corning Community College, NY   294
County College of Morris, NJ   233
Crafton Hills College, CA   234
Craven Community College, NC   295
Creighton University, NE   107
Cuesta College, CA   235
The Culinary Institute of America, NY   107
Cumberland County College, NJ   235
Curry College, MA   38
Cuyahoga Community College, Eastern Campus, OH   236

D

Dalhousie University, NS, Canada   108
Daniel Webster College, NH   108
Davis & Elkins College, WV   38
Dawson Community College, MT   295
Daytona Beach Community College, FL   295
De Anza College, CA   236
Delaware County Community College, PA   237
Delta College, MI   296
Denison University, OH   108
DePaul University, IL   39
Diablo Valley College, CA   237
Dickinson College, PA   109
Dickinson State University, ND   109
Dona Ana Branch Community College, NM   238
Dordt College, IA   109
Dowling College, NY   39
Drexel University, PA   110
Dyersburg State Community College, TN   296

E

Eastern Connecticut State University, CT   110
Eastern Mennonite University, VA   111
Eastern Michigan University, MI   111
Eastern New Mexico University, NM   111
Eastern New Mexico University-Roswell, NM   238
East Los Angeles College, CA   297
East Stroudsburg University of Pennsylvania, PA   112
East Tennessee State University, TN   40
Edinboro University of Pennsylvania, PA   40
Edmonds Community College, WA   297
El Centro College, TX   298
Ellsworth Community College, IA   239
Emory University, GA   112
Eugenio Maria de Hostos Community College of the City
   University of New York, NY   298
Everett Community College, WA   299

F

Fairmont State College, WV   113
Fashion Institute of Technology, NY   40
Finger Lakes Community College, NY   299
Finlandia University, MI   41
**Fiorello H. LaGuardia Community College of the City
   University of New York, NY**   239
Fitchburg State College, MA   41
Flathead Valley Community College, MT   240
Florida Agricultural and Mechanical University, FL   42
Florida Atlantic University, FL   113
Florida Community College at Jacksonville, FL   299
Florida Gulf Coast University, FL   113
Florida International University, FL   114
Fond du Lac Tribal and Community College, MN   240
Fontbonne College, MO   114
Foothill College, CA   241
Fort Valley State University, GA   115
Fox Valley Technical College, WI   300
Frederick Community College, MD   300
Fulton-Montgomery Community College, NY   241

G

Galveston College, TX   301
Gannon University, PA   42
Gardner-Webb University, NC   115
Gavilan College, CA   241
George C. Wallace Community College, AL   301
The George Washington University, DC   116
Georgia College and State University, GA   116
Georgian Court College, NJ   116
Georgia State University, GA   43
Glendale Community College, CA   242
Glen Oaks Community College, MI   301
Glenville State College, WV   43
Gloucester County College, NJ   302
Green Mountain College, VT   117
Guilford Technical Community College, NC   302
Gustavus Adolphus College, MN   117

H

Hamilton College, NY   118
Hamline University, MN   118
Hampshire College, MA   118
Hampton University, VA   119
Harcum College, PA   242
Harrisburg Area Community College, PA   303
Hawaii Community College, HI   303
Hawkeye Community College, IA   303
Hennepin Technical College, MN   304
Herkimer County Community College, NY   304
Hillsborough Community College, FL   243
Hiram G. Andrews Center, PA   243
Hocking College, OH   305
Hofstra University, NY   44
Holy Cross College, IN   244
Holyoke Community College, MA   305
Hood College, MD   119
Houghton College, NY   119
Housatonic Community College, CT   305
Howard Community College, MD   244
Humboldt State University, CA   120
Hunter College of the City University of New York, NY   120

I

Idaho State University, ID   121
Illinois Central College, IL   306
Illinois State University, IL   121
Imperial Valley College, CA   245
Indiana University of Pennsylvania, PA   122
Indiana University Southeast, IN   122
Indiana Wesleyan University, IN   122
International Académy of Merchandising & Design, Ltd., IL   123
Iona College, NY   44
Iowa Western Community College, IA   245
Ithaca College, NY   44
Ivy Tech State College-Central Indiana, IN   306
Ivy Tech State College-Columbus, IN   307

Ivy Tech State College-Northeast, IN 307
Ivy Tech State College-Southcentral, IN 308
Ivy Tech State College-Southwest, IN 308
Ivy Tech State College-Wabash Valley, IN 308

J

Jamestown Community College, NY 309
Johnson & Wales University, CO 309
Johnson & Wales University, FL 45
Johnson & Wales University, RI 123
Johnson & Wales University, SC 124
Johnson County Community College, KS 310
Johnson C. Smith University, NC 124
Johnson State College, VT 125
Johnson Technical Institute, PA 310
John Tyler Community College, VA 311
Joliet Junior College, IL 311

K

Kalamazoo Valley Community College, MI 311
Kansas State University, KS 125
Kean University, NJ 125
Kent State University, OH 126
Kent State University, Ashtabula Campus, OH 312
Kent State University, Trumbull Campus, OH 312
Kilgore College, TX 312
King's College, PA 45
Kirkwood Community College, IA 313

L

Labette Community College, KS 313
Lake City Community College, FL 246
Lake Land College, IL 314
Lakeland Community College, OH 314
Lake Region State College, ND 315
Lakeshore Technical College, WI 246
Lake Superior College, MN 247
Lake Tahoe Community College, CA 315
Lake Washington Technical College, WA 316
Laurentian University, ON, Canada 126
Lawrence University, WI 127
Lebanon Valley College, PA 127
Lee College, TX 316
Lee University, TN 46
Leeward Community College, HI 247
Lenoir-Rhyne College, NC 128
Liberty University, VA 46
Life University, GA 128
Lima Technical College, OH 316
Limestone College, SC 46
Lincoln Land Community College, IL 317
Linfield College, OR 47
Linn-Benton Community College, OR 317
Long Island University, C.W. Post Campus, NY 47
Longview Community College, MO 318
Longwood College, VA 128
Lon Morris College, TX 248
Loras College, IA 48
Los Angeles Valley College, CA 318
Louisburg College, NC 248
Louisiana College, LA 48
Louisiana State University at Eunice, LA 248
Louisiana Technical College-Slidell Campus, LA 319
Loyola University New Orleans, LA 129
Luna Vocational Technical Institute, NM 249
Luther College, IA 129
Lynn University, FL 49

M

Macalester College, MN 49
Macon State College, GA 130
Madisonville Community College, KY 319
Madonna University, MI 130
Manatee Community College, FL 320
Manhattanville College, NY 49
Maranatha Baptist Bible College, WI 130
Marian College of Fond du Lac, WI 131
Marist College, NY 50

Marshalltown Community College, IA 249
Marshall University, WV 50
Marymount College, Palos Verdes, California, CA 320
Marymount Manhattan College, NY 51
Marywood University, PA 131
Massachusetts College of Liberal Arts, MA 132
Mayland Community College, NC 320
McDowell Technical Community College, NC 250
McHenry County College, IL 321
McMaster University, ON, Canada 132
Mendocino College, CA 250
Menlo College, CA 133
Mercer County Community College, NJ 321
Mercy College, NY 51
Mercy College of Northwest Ohio, OH 322
Mercyhurst College, PA 52
Meredith College, NC 52
Merritt College, CA 251
Messiah College, PA 133
Metropolitan State College of Denver, CO 133
Middlesex County College, NJ 251
Middle Tennessee State University, TN 53
Midland Lutheran College, NE 134
Midlands Technical College, SC 322
Midwestern State University, TX 134
Millersville University of Pennsylvania, PA 135
Millikin University, IL 135
Mills College, CA 53
Milwaukee Area Technical College, WI 252
Milwaukee Institute of Art and Design, WI 135
Minnesota State University, Mankato, MN 136
Minnesota State University Moorhead, MN 136
Minnesota West Community and Technical College-Granite Falls Campus, MN 323
Minnesota West Community and Technical College-Worthington Campus, MN 323
Minot State University-Bottineau Campus, ND 324
MiraCosta College, CA 252
Mississippi Gulf Coast Community College, MS 324
Mississippi State University, MS 136
Missouri Southern State College, MO 137
Mitchell College, CT 253
Modesto Junior College, CA 253
Mohawk Valley Community College, NY 325
Molloy College, NY 137
Monmouth University, NJ 138
Montana State University College of Technology-Great Falls, MT 325
Montana Tech of The University of Montana, MT 138
Montcalm Community College, MI 325
Montgomery College, TX 326
Montgomery College-Rockville Campus, MD 254
Montgomery Community College, NC 326
Moorpark College, CA 254
Moraine Valley Community College, IL 327
Moravian College, PA 138
Motlow State Community College, TN 327
Mount Allison University, NB, Canada 54
Mount Ida College, MA 139
Mount Mercy College, IA 139
Mount Vernon Nazarene College, OH 140
Mount Wachusett Community College, MA 328
Murray State University, KY 54
Muskegon Community College, MI 328
Muskingum College, OH 55

N

Napa Valley College, CA 255
Nashville State Technical Institute, TN 255
Nassau Community College, NY 328
Naugatuck Valley Community College, CT 329
Nazareth College of Rochester, NY 140
New Hampshire Community Technical College, Nashua/Claremont, NH 329
New Hampshire Technical Institute, NH 330
New Jersey Institute of Technology, NJ 140
New Mexico Institute of Mining and Technology, NM 141
New River Community College, VA 256
Newschool of Architecture, CA 141

New York City Technical College of the City University of
New York, NY 330
New York University, NY 142
Nicholls State University, LA 55
Nipissing University, ON, Canada 142
Norfolk State University, VA 143
Normandale Community College, MN 256
Northampton County Area Community College, PA 256
North Carolina State University, NC 143
North Carolina Wesleyan College, NC 143
North Central College, IL 144
North Central Texas College, TX 331
North Dakota State College of Science, ND 331
Northeast Community College, NE 331
Northeastern Illinois University, IL 144
Northeastern State University, OK 145
Northeastern University, MA 55
Northeast Iowa Community College, Calmar Campus, IA 332
Northeast Iowa Community College, Peosta Campus, IA 332
Northeast Wisconsin Technical College, WI 333
Northern Arizona University, AZ 56
Northern State University, SD 145
North Georgia College & State University, GA 146
North Idaho College, ID 257
North Lake College, TX 257
Northland College, WI 146
Northland Pioneer College, AZ 333
Northwest College, WY 258
Northwestern College, MN 146
Northwestern Michigan College, MI 334
Northwestern State University of Louisiana, LA 147
Northwest Mississippi Community College, MS 334
Northwood University, MI 147
Norwalk Community College, CT 335
Notre Dame College of Ohio, OH 148

O

Oakland Community College, MI 335
Ocean County College, NJ 258
The Ohio State University, OH 148
The Ohio State University at Lima, OH 149
The Ohio State University at Marion, OH 149
The Ohio State University-Newark Campus, OH 149
Okaloosa-Walton Community College, FL 335
Okanagan University College, BC, Canada 150
Oklahoma City University, OK 150
Oklahoma Panhandle State University, OK 151
Oklahoma State University, Okmulgee, OK 336
Old Dominion University, VA 151
Olympic College, WA 336
Oral Roberts University, OK 151

P

Pacific Union College, CA 56
Palo Verde College, CA 337
Parkland College, IL 337
Passaic County Community College, NJ 338
Patrick Henry Community College, VA 338
Peace College, NC 152
Pellissippi State Technical Community College, TN 338
Pennsylvania State University Abington College, PA 152
**Pennsylvania State University Delaware County Campus
of the Commonwealth College, PA** 259
Pennsylvania State University Harrisburg Campus of the
Capital College, PA 153
Pennsylvania State University Hazleton Campus of the
Commonwealth College, PA 339
Pennsylvania State University New Kensington Campus of the
Commonwealth College, PA 339
Pennsylvania State University University Park Campus, PA . 153
Pennsylvania State University York Campus of the
Commonwealth College, PA 340
Pensacola Junior College, FL 340
Pepperdine University, CA 153
Phoenix College, AZ 259
Piedmont Baptist College, NC 57
Pierce College, WA 341
Pikes Peak Community College, CO 341

Pima Community College, AZ 260
Pitt Community College, NC 342
Portland Community College, OR 342
Prince George's Community College, MD 343
Providence College, RI 154
Purdue University North Central, IN 154

Q

**Queensborough Community College of the City
University of New York, NY** 260
Queens College of the City University of New York, NY .. 155

R

Rainy River Community College, MN 343
Randolph Community College, NC 261
Randolph-Macon Woman's College, VA 155
Reedley College, CA 261
Reinhardt College, GA 57
Rensselaer Polytechnic Institute, NY 155
Renton Technical College, WA 343
Rhode Island College, RI 156
The Richard Stockton College of New Jersey, NJ 156
Ricks College, ID 344
Rider University, NJ 157
Riverside Community College, CA 261
Rivier College, NH 157
Roane State Community College, TN 344
Robert Morris College, IL 157
Robeson Community College, NC 345
Rochester Institute of Technology, NY 158
Rockingham Community College, NC 345
Rockland Community College, NY 262
Roger Williams University, RI 158
Roosevelt University, IL 58

S

Sacred Heart University, CT 159
The Sage Colleges, NY 159
Saginaw Valley State University, MI 160
St. Ambrose University, IA 160
St. Andrews Presbyterian College, NC 160
St. Bonaventure University, NY 161
St. Clair County Community College, MI 345
St. Gregory's University, OK 58
St. Lawrence University, NY 161
Saint Leo University, FL 161
St. Louis Community College at Meramec, MO 346
Saint Louis University, MO 58
Saint Mary's College of California, CA 162
Saint Mary's University, NS, Canada 162
Saint Mary's University of Minnesota, MN 163
St. Norbert College, WI 163
St. Paul Technical College, MN 346
Salem State College, MA 59
San Bernardino Valley College, CA 262
San Diego City College, CA 263
San Diego Mesa College, CA 347
San Diego Miramar College, CA 263
San Francisco State University, CA 59
San Jacinto College-South Campus, TX 347
San Jose State University, CA 60
Santa Ana College, CA 264
Santa Barbara City College, CA 264
Santa Clara University, CA 163
Santa Fe Community College, FL 347
Sauk Valley Community College, IL 348
Savannah State University, GA 60
Schoolcraft College, MI 264
School of the Art Institute of Chicago, IL 164
Schreiner College, TX 61
Seattle Pacific University, WA 164
Seminole Community College, FL 348
Shawnee State University, OH 165
Shelby State Community College, TN 265
Sheldon Jackson College, AK 165
Shippensburg University of Pennsylvania, PA 166
Siena College, NY 166
Sierra Nevada College, NV 166

Simon Fraser University, BC, Canada | 61
Sinclair Community College, OH | 349
Sonoma State University, CA | 167
South Arkansas Community College, AR | 349
South Carolina State University, SC | 167
South Dakota School of Mines and Technology, SD | 168
Southeastern College of the Assemblies of God, FL | 168
Southeastern Community College, NC | 350
Southeastern Louisiana University, LA | 168
Southeastern Oklahoma State University, OK | 169
Southern Illinois University Carbondale, IL | 62
Southern Maine Technical College, ME | 350
Southern Methodist University, TX | 169
Southern Polytechnic State University, GA | 170
Southern Utah University, UT | 170
Southern Vermont College, VT | 170
Southern West Virginia Community and Technical College, WV | 350
South Plains College, TX | 351
Southwestern College, CA | 351
Southwestern Michigan College, MI | 352
Southwestern Oregon Community College, OR | 352
Southwest Missouri State University-West Plains, MO | 352
Southwest Texas State University, TX | 62
Southwest Wisconsin Technical College, WI | 353
Spokane Community College, WA | 353
Springfield College, MA | 171
Springfield Technical Community College, MA | 354
Stark State College of Technology, OH | 354
State Technical Institute at Memphis, TN | 355
State University of New York at Albany, NY | 171
State University of New York at Binghamton, NY | 172
State University of New York at Oswego, NY | 172
State University of New York at Stony Brook, NY | 173
State University of New York College at Brockport, NY | 173
State University of New York College at Buffalo, NY | 173
State University of New York College at Fredonia, NY | 174
State University of New York College at Geneseo, NY | 174
State University of New York College at Oneonta, NY | 174
State University of New York College at Potsdam, NY | 175
State University of New York College of Agriculture and Technology at Morrisville, NY | 355
State University of New York College of Environmental Science and Forestry, NY | 175
State University of New York College of Technology at Alfred, NY | 355
State University of New York College of Technology at Canton, NY | 176
State University of New York College of Technology at Delhi, NY | 356
State University of New York Institute of Technology at Utica/Rome, NY | 176
State University of West Georgia, GA | 176
Suffolk University, MA | 177
Sullivan County Community College, NY | 265

Tacoma Community College, WA | 356
Taft College, CA | 266
Tallahassee Community College, FL | 357
Tarleton State University, TX | 177
Tarrant County College District, TX | 357
Taylor University, IN | 178
Temple University, PA | 178
Tennessee State University, TN | 63
Terra State Community College, OH | 357
Texas A&M University, TX | 178
Texas A&M University-Commerce, TX | 179
Texas A&M University-Kingsville, TX | 179
Texas State Technical College, TX | 358
Texas State Technical College-Waco/Marshall Campus, TX | 358
Texas Tech University, TX | 63
Thiel College, PA | 180
Thomas More College, KY | 180
Three Rivers Community College, CT | 359
Tidewater Community College, VA | 266
Toccoa Falls College, GA | 181
Towson University, MD | 181
Trent University, ON, Canada | 181

Trident Technical College, SC | 359
Trinity College, DC | 182
Trocaire College, NY | 359
Troy State University Montgomery, AL | 182
Truckee Meadows Community College, NV | 267
Tufts University, MA | 183
Tulane University, LA | 183
Tyler Junior College, TX | 360

Umpqua Community College, OR | 360
Union College, NE | 64
United States International University, CA | 183
University College of the Cariboo, BC, Canada | 184
University College of the Fraser Valley, BC, Canada | 184
The University of Alabama, AL | 185
The University of Alabama in Huntsville, AL | 185
University of Alaska Anchorage, Kenai Peninsula College, AK | 361
University of Alaska Fairbanks, AK | 186
The University of Arizona, AZ | 64
University of Arkansas at Little Rock, AR | 186
University of Arkansas Community College at Batesville, AR | 361
University of Calgary, AB, Canada | 186
University of California, Berkeley, CA | 187
University of California, Los Angeles, CA | 187
University of California, San Diego, CA | 65
University of California, Santa Barbara, CA | 65
University of Colorado at Boulder, CO | 65
University of Colorado at Colorado Springs, CO | 188
University of Colorado at Denver, CO | 188
University of Connecticut, CT | 66
University of Dayton, OH | 188
University of Denver, CO | 66
University of Guelph, ON, Canada | 189
University of Hartford, CT | 189
University of Hawaii at Hilo, HI | 189
University of Houston, TX | 67
University of Houston-Clear Lake, TX | 190
University of Idaho, ID | 190
University of Illinois at Urbana-Champaign, IL | 191
University of Indianapolis, IN | 67
University of Louisiana at Lafayette, LA | 191
University of Louisiana at Monroe, LA | 192
University of Louisville, KY | 192
University of Maine at Machias, ME | 192
University of Mary, ND | 193
University of Maryland, Baltimore County, MD | 193
University of Maryland, College Park, MD | 193
University of Maryland Eastern Shore, MD | 194
University of Massachusetts Amherst, MA | 68
University of Massachusetts Dartmouth, MA | 194
University of Miami, FL | 195
University of Michigan-Dearborn, MI | 195
University of Michigan-Flint, MI | 196
University of Minnesota, Crookston, MN | 196
University of Minnesota, Morris, MN | 196
University of Missouri-Columbia, MO | 68
University of Missouri-Kansas City, MO | 197
The University of Montana-Missoula, MT | 197
University of Nebraska-Lincoln, NE | 198
University of New Hampshire, NH | 198
University of New Hampshire at Manchester, NH | 198
University of New Haven, CT | 199
University of New Mexico, NM | 199
University of New Orleans, LA | 200
University of North Alabama, AL | 200
The University of North Carolina at Chapel Hill, NC | 69
The University of North Carolina at Greensboro, NC | 200
The University of North Carolina at Wilmington, NC | 69
University of Northern Iowa, IA | 201
University of Notre Dame, IN | 201
University of Oregon, OR | 202
University of Ottawa, ON, Canada | 69
University of Pittsburgh, PA | 202
University of Pittsburgh at Bradford, PA | 202
University of Redlands, CA | 203
University of Regina, SK, Canada | 203
University of Rhode Island, RI | 204
University of Rochester, NY | 204

T

U

The University of Scranton, PA	204
University of South Carolina, SC	205
University of South Carolina Spartanburg, SC	205
University of Southern California, CA	205
University of Southern Indiana, IN	206
University of Southern Mississippi, MS	206
The University of Tennessee at Martin, TN	70
The University of Tennessee Knoxville, TN	207
The University of Texas at Austin, TX	207
The University of Texas at El Paso, TX	208
The University of Texas at San Antonio, TX	208
University of the District of Columbia, DC	208
University of the Incarnate Word, TX	209
University of the Ozarks, AR	70
University of Tulsa, OK	209
University of Utah, UT	210
University of Vermont, VT	71
University of Waterloo, ON, Canada	210
The University of Western Ontario, ON, Canada	211
University of West Florida, FL	211
University of Windsor, ON, Canada	71
University of Wisconsin-Eau Claire, WI	211
University of Wisconsin-La Crosse, WI	212
University of Wisconsin-Madison, WI	212
University of Wisconsin-Oshkosh, WI	72
University of Wisconsin-Parkside, WI	213
University of Wisconsin-Platteville, WI	213
University of Wisconsin-River Falls, WI	213
University of Wisconsin-Sheboygan, WI	362
University of Wisconsin-Superior, WI	214
University of Wisconsin-Whitewater, WI	72
Ursuline College, OH	73
Utah State University, UT	214
Utica College of Syracuse University, NY	73

V

Valdosta State University, GA	215
Valencia Community College, FL	362
Valparaiso University, IN	215
Vanderbilt University, TN	215
Vanguard University of Southern California, CA	216
Vassar College, NY	216
Ventura College, CA	267
Vermont Technical College, VT	362
Villanova University, PA	217
Vincennes University, IN	268
Virginia Commonwealth University, VA	217

Virginia Highlands Community College, VA	363
Virginia Intermont College, VA	217
Virginia Wesleyan College, VA	74
Virginia Western Community College, VA	363
Vista Community College, CA	364
Voorhees College, SC	218

W

Waldorf College, IA	268
Wallace State Community College, AL	364
Washington State University, WA	218
Washington University in St. Louis, MO	218
Washtenaw Community College, MI	269
Waukesha County Technical College, WI	269
Wayne State University, MI	219
Westark College, AR	364
Western Baptist College, OR	219
Western Carolina University, NC	219
Western Dakota Technical Institute, SD	269
Western Illinois University, IL	220
Western New England College, MA	220
Western Washington University, WA	221
Western Wisconsin Technical College, WI	365
Western Wyoming Community College, WY	365
West Hills Community College, CA	270
Westminster College, MO	74
Westmoreland County Community College, PA	366
West Valley College, CA	270
West Virginia State College, WV	221
West Virginia University at Parkersburg, WV	271
West Virginia Wesleyan College, WV	222
Wheelock College, MA	222
Whitman College, WA	222
Whittier College, CA	223
Widener University, PA	75
Wilfrid Laurier University, ON, Canada	75
Wilkes Community College, NC	271
William Rainey Harper College, IL	272
Wingate University, NC	223
Wright State University, OH	76

X

Xavier University, OH	223

Y

York County Technical College, ME	366

ABOUT THE AUTHORS

Charles T. Mangrum II, Ed.D.

Dr. Mangrum is Professor of Special Education and Reading at the University of Miami, Coral Gables, Florida. He attended high school in Chicago and then graduated from Northern Michigan University with a degree in education. He taught in elementary and secondary schools before entering graduate school. Dr. Mangrum earned an Ed.D. from Indiana University in 1968. He has been on the faculty at the University of Miami since 1968, where he trains teachers who teach students with reading and learning disabilities.

Stephen S. Strichart, Ph.D.

Dr. Strichart is Professor of Special Education and Learning Disabilities at Florida International University, Miami, Florida. He grew up in New York City, where he attended school from kindergarten through graduate school. He taught children with various types of disabilities before entering graduate school. Dr. Strichart earned a Ph.D. from Yeshiva University in 1972. He has been on the faculty at Florida International University since 1975, where he trains teachers to work with students with learning disabilities.

Dr. Mangrum and Dr. Strichart have evaluated and counseled several thousand students with learning disabilities. Over the past two decades, much of their work has focused on the needs of college-bound students with learning disabilities. They coauthored *College and the Learning Disabled Student*, which was first published in 1984. This book was used by personnel at colleges and universities throughout the nation to establish programs and services for students with learning disabilities. The first edition of *Peterson's Guide to Colleges with Programs for Students with Learning Disabilities* appeared in 1986 to meet the needs of students, parents, and advocates for a source of accurate and complete information about college opportunities for students with learning disabilities. The sixth edition of this guide, titled *Peterson's Colleges with Programs for Students with Learning Disabilities or Attention Deficit Disorders* reflects the inclusion of information about services for students with ADD and continues their efforts to provide the most accurate, complete, and useful guide on the subject.

Peterson's unplugged

graduate programs

distance learning

adult education

executive training

colleges and universities

private secondary schools

internships and careers

study-abroad programs

financial aid/scholarships

summer programs

Peterson's quality on every page!

For more than three decades, we've offered a complete selection of books to guide you in all of your educational endeavors. You can find our vast collection of titles at your local bookstore or online at **petersons.com**.

High school student headed for college?

Busy professional interested in distance learning?

Parent searching for the perfect private school or summer camp?

Human resource manager looking for executive education programs?

AOL Keyword: Petersons
Phone: 800-338-3282

Virtually anything is possible @ petersons.com

graduate programs
distance learning
adult education
executive training
colleges and universities
private secondary schools
internships and careers
study-abroad programs
financial aid/scholarships
summer programs

Peterson's quality with every click!

Whether you're a high school student headed for college or a busy professional interested in distance learning, you'll find all of the tools you need, literally at your fingertips!

Petersons.com is your ultimate online adviser, connecting you with "virtually any" educational or career need.

Visit us today at **petersons.com**
AOL Keyword: Petersons

Count on us to show you how to:

Apply to more than 1,200 colleges online

Finance the education of your dreams

Find a summer camp for your child

Make important career choices

Earn a degree online

Search executive education programs

Peterson's
Thomson Learning™